American Presidents

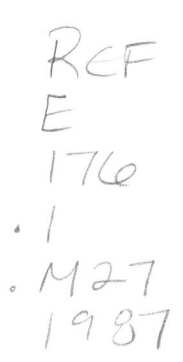

American Presidents
A Bibliography

Fenton S. Martin
Robert U. Goehlert
Indiana University

Congressional Quarterly Inc.
1414 22nd Street N.W.
Washington, D.C. 20037

Congressional Quarterly Inc.

Congressional Quarterly Inc., an editorial research service and publishing company, serves clients in the fields of news, education, business, and government. It combines Congressional Quarterly's specific coverage of Congress, government, and politics with the more general subject range of an affiliated service, Editorial Research Reports.

Congressional Quarterly publishes the *Congressional Quarterly Weekly Report* and a variety of books, including college political science textbooks under the CQ Press imprint and public affairs paperbacks designed as timely reports to keep journalists, scholars, and the public abreast of developing issues and events. CQ also publishes information directories and reference books on the federal government, national elections, and politics, including the *Guide to Congress*, the *Guide to the U.S. Supreme Court*, the *Guide to U.S. Elections*, and *Politics in America*. The *CQ Almanac*, a compendium of legislation for one session of Congress, is published each year. *Congress and the Nation*, a record of government for a presidential term, is published every four years.

CQ publishes the *Congressional Monitor*, a daily report on current and future activities of congressional committees, and several newsletters including *Congressional Insight*, a weekly analysis of congressional action, and *Campaign Practices Reports*, a semimonthly update on campaign laws.

An electronic online information system, the Washington Alert Service, provides immediate access to CQ's databases of legislative action, votes, schedules, profiles, and analyses.

Copyright © 1987 Congressional Quarterly Inc.

All rights reserved. No part of this publication may be reproduced or transmitted in any form or by any means, electronic or mechanical, including photocopy, recording, or any information storage and retrieval system, without permission in writing from the publisher.

Printed in the United States of America

Library of Congress Cataloging-in-Publication Data

Martin, Fenton S.
   American presidents.

   Includes indexes.
   1. Presidents--United States--Bibliography.
I. Goehlert, Robert, 1948-   . II. Title.
Z1249.P7M36   1987   [E176.1]   016.973'092'2   86-30938
ISBN 0-87187-416-4

Table of Contents

Introduction	xi
George Washington	1
Biographies	1
Private Life	6
General	6
Family	10
Mount Vernon	13
Religion	14
Tributes	15
Washingtoniana	18
The West	22
Youth	24
Public Career	24
General	24
Revolution	27
Presidential Years	30
Writings	34
John Adams	39
Biographies	39
Private Life	40
Public Career	42
Presidential Years	45
Writings	47
Thomas Jefferson	51
Biographies	51
Private Life	55
General	55
Agriculture	60
Architecture	61
Arts	62
Education	64
Family	66
Law	67
Literature	67
Monticello	70
Philosophy	71
Press	75
Religion	75
Science	77
Public Career	79
General	79
Declaration of Independence	84
Diplomat	86
Party Politics	88
Revolution	91
Virginia Politics	93
Presidential Years	94
General	94
Foreign Affairs	98
Human Rights	100
Judicial	102
Writings	103
James Madison	111
Biographies	111
Private Life	111
Public Career	113
Presidential Years	117
Writings	119
James Monroe	121
Biographies	121
Private Life	121
Public Career	122
Presidential Years	123
Writings	123

John Quincy Adams — 125
- Biographies — 125
- Private Life — 125
- Public Career — 126
- Presidential Years — 128
- Writings — 129

Andrew Jackson — 133
- Biographies — 133
- Private Life — 135
- Public Career — 138
- Presidential Years — 143
- Writings — 148

Martin Van Buren — 149
- Biographies — 149
- Private Life — 149
- Public Career — 150
- Presidential Years — 151
- Writings — 152

William Henry Harrison — 153
- Biographies — 153
- Private Life — 153
- Public Career — 154
- Presidential Years — 155
- Writings — 155

John Tyler — 157
- Biographies — 157
- Private Life — 157
- Public Career — 157
- Presidential Years — 158
- Writings — 158

James K. Polk — 161
- Biographies — 161
- Private Life — 161
- Public Career — 162
- Presidential Years — 162
- Writings — 164

Zachary Taylor — 167
- Biographies — 167
- Private Life — 168
- Public Career — 168
- Presidential Years — 168
- Writings — 169

Millard Fillmore — 171
- Biographies — 171
- Private Life — 171
- Public Career — 171
- Presidential Years — 171
- Writings — 172

Franklin Pierce — 173
- Biographies — 173
- Private Life — 173
- Public Career — 173
- Presidential Years — 173
- Writings — 174

James Buchanan — 175
- Biographies — 175
- Private Life — 175
- Public Career — 176
- Presidential Years — 176
- Writings — 178

Abraham Lincoln — 181
- Biographies — 181
- Private Life — 188
  - *General* — 188
  - *Chronologies* — 192
  - *Education* — 193
  - *Family* — 194
  - *Legend* — 197
  - *Lincolniana* — 199
  - *Literature* — 204
  - *Personality* — 205
  - *Philosophy* — 206
  - *Portraits and Prints* — 209
  - *Recollections* — 210
  - *Religion* — 214
  - *Travels* — 216
  - *Tributes* — 218
  - *Youth* — 220
- Public Career — 221
  - *General* — 221
  - *Congressman* — 225
  - *Lawyer* — 226
  - *Lincoln-Douglas Debates* — 228
- Presidential Years — 230
  - *General* — 230
  - *Assassination* — 236
  - *Campaigns* — 240

Table of Contents vii

Civil War	243	Private Life	304
Gettysburg Address	248	Public Career	305
Inaugurations	249	Presidential Years	305
Indians	249	Writings	308
Judicial	250		
Press	251	**Benjamin Harrison**	311
Reconstruction	253	Biographies	311
Slavery	253	Private Life	311
Writings	256	Public Career	311
		Presidential Years	312
Andrew Johnson	265	Writings	312
Biographies	265		
Private Life	265	**William McKinley**	315
Public Career	266	Biographies	315
Presidential Years	268	Private Life	316
Writings	273	Public Career	316
		Presidential Years	317
Ulysses S. Grant	275	Writings	319
Biographies	275		
Private Life	278	**Theodore Roosevelt**	321
Public Career	280	Biographies	321
Presidential Years	282	Private Life	324
Writings	283	Public Career	328
		Presidential Years	333
Rutherford B. Hayes	285	*General*	333
Biographies	285	*Foreign Affairs*	342
Private Life	285	Writings	344
Public Career	287		
Presidential Years	287	**William Howard Taft**	349
General	287	Biographies	349
Election	290	Private Life	349
Writings	291	Public Career	350
		Presidential Years	351
James A. Garfield	293	Writings	355
Biographies	293		
Private Life	294	**Woodrow Wilson**	357
Public Career	295	Biographies	357
Presidential Years	296	Private Life	359
Writings	298	Public Career	362
		Presidential Years	367
Chester A. Arthur	299	*General*	367
Biographies	299	*Campaigns*	371
Private Life	299	*Domestic Policy*	372
Public Career	300	*Foreign Affairs*	374
Presidential Years	300	*League of Nations*	378
Writings	301	*Mexican Revolution*	380
		Versailles	381
Grover Cleveland	303	*World War I*	382
Biographies	303	Writings	384

Warren G. Harding ... 389
- Biographies ... 389
- Private Life ... 390
- Public Career ... 391
- Presidential Years ... 392
- Writings ... 393

Calvin Coolidge ... 395
- Biographies ... 395
- Private Life ... 395
- Public Career ... 397
- Presidential Years ... 397
- Writings ... 399

Herbert Hoover ... 401
- Biographies ... 401
- Private Life ... 402
- Public Career ... 404
- Presidential Years ... 407
- Writings ... 411

Franklin D. Roosevelt ... 415
- Biographies ... 415
- Private Life ... 417
  - General ... 417
  - Eleanor Roosevelt ... 420
- Public Career ... 422
- Presidential Years ... 423
  - General ... 423
  - Congress ... 433
  - Domestic Policy ... 433
  - Elections ... 436
  - Foreign Affairs ... 438
  - Judicial ... 442
  - New Deal ... 444
  - World War II ... 449
- Writings ... 453

Harry S Truman ... 455
- Biographies ... 455
- Private Life ... 456
- Public Career ... 457
- Presidential Years ... 458
  - General ... 458
  - Atomic Bomb ... 464
  - Domestic Policy ... 464
  - Elections ... 468
  - Foreign Affairs ... 468
  - Korean War ... 472
  - Middle East ... 473
  - Truman Doctrine ... 474
- Writings ... 475

Dwight D. Eisenhower ... 477
- Biographies ... 477
- Private Life ... 479
- Public Career ... 479
- Presidential Years ... 480
  - General ... 480
  - Domestic Policy ... 485
  - Elections ... 487
  - Foreign Affairs ... 488
- Writings ... 492

John F. Kennedy ... 495
- Biographies ... 495
- Private Life ... 496
- Public Career ... 498
- Presidential Years ... 500
  - General ... 500
  - Assassination ... 509
  - Congress ... 514
  - Cuba ... 515
  - Domestic Affairs ... 517
  - Elections ... 519
  - Foreign Affairs ... 521
  - Press ... 525
- Writings ... 526

Lyndon B. Johnson ... 529
- Biographies ... 529
- Private Life ... 530
- Public Career ... 532
- Presidential Years ... 535
  - General ... 535
  - Domestic Policy ... 544
  - Elections ... 548
  - Foreign Affairs ... 548
  - Great Society ... 550
  - Press ... 550
  - Vietnam ... 551
- Writings ... 553

Richard Nixon ... 555
- Biographies ... 555
- Private Life ... 556

Table of Contents ix

Public Career	557	*Domestic Policy*	598
Presidential Years	558	*Elections*	602
General	558	*Foreign Affairs*	605
Domestic Policy	567	*Human Rights*	610
Elections	570	Writings	611
Foreign Affairs	573		
Watergate	577	**Ronald Reagan**	613
Writings	580	Biographies	613
		Private Life	613
Gerald R. Ford	583	Public Career	614
Biographies	583	Presidential Years	615
Private Life	583	*Budget*	624
Public Career	583	*Domestic Policy*	625
Presidential Years	584	*Elections*	629
Writings	589	*Foreign Affairs*	631
		Nuclear Weapons	636
Jimmy Carter	591	*Reaganomics*	637
Biographies	591	Writings	639
Private Life	591		
Public Career	592	**Author Index**	641
Presidential Years	593		
General	593	**Subject Index**	713

Introduction

In *American Presidents: A Bibliography* we offer the most comprehensive listing of references to works about U.S. presidents. This book focuses on the accomplishments, policies, and activities of the individual presidents, including their private lives and public careers, as chief executive and in other capacities. A companion volume, *The American Presidency: A Bibliography*, contains citations about the office of the presidency, including its history, development, powers, and relations with the other branches of the federal government. Each volume is a separate bibliography; no citation from one volume appears in the other, and the author and subject indexes for each volume index citations only for that volume. As complements to one another, the books may be used together. For example, the bibliography on the presidents includes works about the foreign policies of specific presidents, while the bibliography on the presidency has a section on the presidency and foreign affairs.

Scope

This bibliography is designed to assist librarians, reseachers, government personnel, and the general reader interested in the presidents. The citations were drawn from a variety of fields, including business, economics, political science, law, history, public administration, and the general social sciences and humanities.

The bibliography cites books, articles, dissertations, essays, and research reports. Because an overwhelming array of U.S. government documents dealing with the presidents exists, we felt that it would be best to omit them.

Since the bibliography is intended primarily for an English-speaking audience, all the citations are to English-language works. In general, the time period covered is from 1885 to 1986, although we did put in some citations to materials published earlier.

For the most part works included in the bibliography fulfill three main criteria; writings are analytical, scholarly, and not merely descriptive. Consequently, the emphasis is on research monographs, articles from major journals, and dissertations. Because the amount of descriptive material aimed at policy makers is enormous, we selectively chose to include such works in some categories, especially in areas where little scholarly work has been done. Thus, while the bibliography does contain a considerable amount of popular literature, it is not comprehensive. Excluded are the *Public Papers of the President* series. Generally, we tended to list only materials that were commercially available and that could be found in academic libraries and large public libraries.

We arranged the bibliography according to presidents in chronological order. For each president we divided the citations into five categories: Biographies, Private Life,

xii *Introduction*

Public Career, Presidential Years, and Writings. The first subsection has citations to works that are general biographies covering the complete life of the president. Materials in the Private Life section deal with the president's personal life and his activities and philosophies outside of public office. The Public Career category covers other offices that the president held, such as service as governor or as a member of Congress. The materials in the subsection on Presidential Years focus on the time the president held office. The final subsection contains the president's writings. When a subsection had an abundance of citations we divided it into smaller categories, arranged in alphabetical order by topic. In this bibliography some citations are listed more than once. For example, a book or article about two or more presidents is included under each president. We also have provided a detailed Subject Index, which identifies more specific subjects, and an Author Index. Because we arranged the citations by topic, the best way to look for materials is to use the Table of Contents and the Subject Index.

Compilation

In compiling this bibliography, we checked a variety of sources. Primarily, we searched thirty-nine indexes:

ABC POLSCI
ABS Guide to Recent Publications in Social and Behavioral Sciences
Air University Library Index to Military Periodicals
America: History and Life
American Political Science Research Guide
Art Index
Annual Legal Bibliography
British Humanities Index
Business Periodicals Index
Combined Retrospective Index to Journals in History
Combined Retrospective Index to Journals in Political Science
Criminal Justice Periodical Index
Current Contents: Social and Behavioral Sciences
Current Index to Journals in Education
Education Index
Historical Abstracts
Human Resources Abstracts
Humanities Index
Index to Legal Periodicals
Index to Periodical Articles Related to Law
Index to U.S. Government Periodicals
International Bibliography of the Social Sciences: Political Science
International Political Science Abstracts
Legal Resource Index
Library Literature
Psychological Abstracts
Public Affairs Information Service Bulletin
Quarterly Strategic Bibliography
Reader's Guide to Periodical Literature
Religion Index One
Sage Public Administration Abstracts

Sage Urban Studies Abstracts
Selected Rand Abstracts
Social Sciences Citation Index
Social Sciences Index, Sociological Abstracts
United States Political Science Documents
Urban Affairs Abstracts
Women's Studies Abstracts
Writings on American History

For dissertations, we made an exhaustive key word search of *Comprehensive Dissertation Index* and *Dissertation Abstracts*. For books and research reports, we checked *Books in Print, Cumulative Book Index, American Book Publishing Record, Public Affairs Information Service Bulletin, National Union Catalog, Biographical Books 1876-1949*, and *Biographical Books 1950-1980* as well as the holdings of the Indiana University libraries.

We also searched six databases: *AMERICA: HISTORY AND LIFE, PAIS INTERNATIONAL, PSYCINFO, SOCIAL SCISEARCH, SOCIOLOGICAL ABSTRACTS*, and *LEGAL RESOURCE INDEX*.

Many bibliographies on presidents are available. We searched completely the following seventy-six:

Angel, Paul M. *A Shelf of Lincoln Books: A Critical Selected Bibliography of Lincolnia.* New Brunswick, NJ: Rutgers University Press, 1946.

Baker, Monty R. "Abraham Lincoln in Theses and Dissertations." *Lincoln Herald* 74 (Summer 1972): 107-111.

Baker, William S. *Bibliotheca Washington: A Descriptive List of the Biographies and Biographical Sketches of George Washington.* Detroit, MI: Gale, 1967.

Barton, William E. "The Lincoln of the Biographers." *Illinois State Historical Society Transactions* 36 (1929): 58-116.

Bishop, Arthur, ed. *Rutherford B. Hayes, 1822-1893: Chronology, Documents, Bibliographical Aids.* Dobbs Ferry, NY: Oceana, 1969.

Bishop, Arthur, ed. *Thomas Jefferson, 1743-1826: Chronology, Documents, Bibliographical Aids.* Dobbs Ferry, NY: Oceana, 1971.

Black, Gilbert J., ed. *Theodore Roosevelt, 1858-1919: Chronology, Documents, Bibliographical Aids.* Dobbs Ferry, NY: Oceana, 1970.

Black, Gilbert J., ed. *William Howard Taft, 1857-1930: Chronology, Documents, Bibliographical Aids.* Dobbs Ferry, NY: Oceana, 1970.

Bohanan, Robert D., comp. *Dwight D. Eisenhower: A Selected Bibliography of Periodical and Dissertation Literature.* Abilene, KS: Dwight D. Eisenhower Library, 1981.

Bremer, Howard F., ed. *Franklin Delano Roosevelt, 1882-1945: Chronology, Documents, Bibliographical Aids.* Dobbs Ferry, NY: Oceana, 1971.

Bremer, Howard F., ed. *George Washington, 1732-1799: Chronology, Documents, Bibliographical Aids.* Dobbs Ferry, NY: Oceana, 1967.

Bremer, Howard F., ed. *Richard M. Nixon, 1913-: Chronology, Documents, Bibliographical Aids.* Dobbs Ferry, NY: Oceana, 1975.

Bremer, Howard F., ed. *John Adams, 1735-1826: Chronology, Documents, Bibliographical Aids.* Dobbs Ferry, NY: Oceana, 1967.

Burns, Richard D. *Harry S. Truman: A Bibliography of His Times and Presidency.* Wilmington, DE: Scholarly Resources, 1984.

xiv *Introduction*

Committee to Investigate Assassinations. *American Political Assassinations: A Bibliography of Works Published, 1963-1970, Related to the Assassination of John F. Kennedy, Martin Luther King, Robert F. Kennedy.* Washington, DC: Georgetown University Library, 1973.

Compton, Gail W. "Franklin Delano Roosevelt: An Annotated Bibliography of His Speaking." Ph.D. dissertation, University of Wisconsin, 1966.

Crown, James T. *The Kennedy Literature: A Bibliographical Essay on John F. Kennedy.* New York: New York University Press, 1968.

Dailey, Wallace T. "Theodore Roosevelt in Periodic Literature, 1950-1981." *Theodore Roosevelt Association Journal* 8 (Fall 1982): 4-15.

Dickinson, John N., comp. *Andrew Johnson, 1803-1875: Chronology, Documents, Bibliographical Aids.* Dobbs Ferry, NY: Oceana, 1970.

Durfee, David A. *William Henry Harrison, 1773-1841/John Tyler, 1790-1862: Chronology, Documents, Bibliographical Aids.* Dobbs Ferry, NY: Oceana, 1970.

Elliot, Ian, ed. *Abraham Lincoln, 1809-1865: Chronology, Documents, Bibliographical Aids.* Dobbs Ferry, NY: Oceana, 1969.

Elliot, Ian, ed. *James Madison, 1751-1836: Chronology, Documents, Bibliographical Aids.* Dobbs Ferry, NY: Oceana, 1969.

Elliott, Ian, ed. *James Monroe, 1758-1831: Chronology, Documents, Bibliographical Aids.* Dobbs Ferry, NY: Oceana, 1969.

Farrell, John J., ed. *Zachary Taylor, 1784-1850/Millard Fillmore, 1800-1874: Chronology, Documents, Bibliographical Aids.* Dobbs Ferry, NY: Oceana, 1971.

Farrell, John J., ed. *James K. Polk, 1795-1849: Chronology, Documents, Bibliographical Aids.* Dobbs Ferry, NY: Oceana, 1970.

Fitch, Nancy E. *The Management Style of Ronald Reagan, Chairman of the Board of the United States of America: An Annotated Bibliography.* Monticello, IL: Vance Bibliographies, 1982.

Furer, Howard B., ed. *Harry S. Truman, 1884-1972: Chronology, Documents, Bibliographical Aids.* Dobbs Ferry, NY: Oceana, 1970.

Furer, Howard B., ed. *James A. Garfield, 1831-1881/Chester A. Arthur, 1830-1886: Chronology, Documents, Bibliographical Aids.* Dobbs Ferry, NY: Oceana, 1970.

Furer, Howard B., ed. *Lyndon B. Johnson, 1908-: Chronology, Documents, Bibliographical Aids.* Dobbs Ferry, NY: Oceana, 1971.

Gunderson, Robert G. "Another Shelf of Lincoln Books." *Quarterly Journal of Speech* 48 (October 1962): 308-313.

Guth, DeLoyd J., and David R. Wrone. *The Assassination of John F. Kennedy: Comprehensive History and Legal Bibliography, 1963-1979.* Westport, CT: Greenwood Press, 1980.

Haight, David, and George H. Curtis. "Abilene, Kansas, and the History of World War II: Resources and Research Opportunities at the Dwight D. Eisenhower Library." *Military Affairs* 41 (December 1977): 195-200.

Halpern, Paul J., ed. *Why Watergate?* Pacific Palisades, CA: Palisades Publishers, 1975.

Hebblethwaite, Frank P. "John Fitzgerald Kennedy, 1917-1963." *Inter-American Review of Bibliography* 14 (July/September 1964): 257-261.

Huddleston, Eugene L. *Thomas Jefferson: A Reference Guide.* Boston: G. K. Hall, 1982.

Irwin, Thomas H., and Hazel Hale, comps. *A Bibliography of Books, Newspaper and Magazine Articles, Published Outside the United States of America, Related to the*

Assassination of John F. Kennedy. Belfast: The Authors, 1975.

Johnson, Richard H. *A Contribution to a Bibliography of Thomas Jefferson.* Washington, DC: The Author, 1905.

Jones, Kenneth V., ed. *John Q. Adams, 1767-1848: Chronology, Documents, Bibliographical Aids.* Dobbs Ferry, NY: Oceana, 1970.

Kirkendall, Richard S., ed. *The Truman Period as a Research Field, A Reappraisal, 1972.* Columbia: University of Missouri Press, 1974.

Kranz, Marvin W. *Bibliographies of the Presidents of the United States.* Washington, DC: Library of Congress, 1977.

Lankevich, George J., ed. *Gerald Ford, 1913-: Chronology, Documents, Bibliographical Aids.* Dobbs Ferry, NY: Oceana, 1977.

Lankevich, George J., ed. *James E. Carter, 1924-: Chronology, Documents, Bibliographical Aids.* Dobbs Ferry, NY: Oceana, 1981.

Leveque, Lawrence L. "General George Washington and the Revolution: A Select Bibliography." *Indiana Social Studies Quarterly* 28 (Spring 1975): 5-13.

Lyndon B. Johnson: A Bibliography. Austin: University of Texas Press, 1984.

Miles, William. *The Image Makers: A Bibliography of American Presidential Campaign Biographies.* Metuchen, NJ: Scarecrow Press, 1979.

Monaghan, Jay. *Lincoln Bibliography, 1839-1939.* 2 vols. Springfield: Illinois State Historical Library, 1945.

Moran, Philip R., ed. *Calvin Coolidge, 1872-1933: Chronology, Documents, Bibliographical Aids.* Dobbs Ferry, NY: Oceana, 1970.

Moran, Philip R., ed. *Ulysses S. Grant, 1822-1885: Chronology, Documents, Bibliographical Aids.* Dobbs Ferry, NY: Oceana, 1968.

Moran, Philip R., ed. *Warren G. Harding, 1865-1923: Chronology, Documents, Bibliographical Aids.* Dobbs Ferry, NY: Oceana, 1970.

Newcomb, Joan I. *John F. Kennedy: An Annotated Bibliography.* Metuchen, NJ: Scarecrow Press, 1977.

Oakleaf, Joseph B. *Lincoln Bibliography: A List of Books and Pamphlets Relating to Abraham Lincoln.* Cedar Rapids, IA: Torch Press, 1925.

Peden, William H. *Some Aspects of Jefferson Bibliography: A Paper Read before the Bibliographical Society of America.* Lexington, VA: Journalism Laboratory Press, Washington and Lee University, 1941.

Rice, A. S., ed. *Herbert Hoover, 1874-1964: Chronology, Documents, Bibliographical Aids.* Dobbs Ferry, NY: Oceana, 1971.

Rice, William R., comp. *John F. Kennedy-Robert F. Kennedy: Assassination Bibliography.* Orangeville, CA: Rice, 1975.

Sable, Martin H. *A Bio-Bibliography of the Kennedy Family.* Metuchen, NJ: Scarecrow Press, 1969.

Schachner, Nathan. *Thomas Jefferson: A Bibliography.* 2 vols. New York: Appleton, 1951.

Searcher, Victor. *Lincoln Today: An Introduction to Modern Lincolniana.* New York: T. Yoseloff, 1969.

Shaw, Ronald E., ed. *Andrew Jackson, 1767-1845: Chronology, Documents, Bibliographical Aids.* Dobbs Ferry, NY: Oceana, 1969.

Shuffleton, Frank. *Thomas Jefferson: A Comprehensive Annotated Bibliography of Writing about Him (1836-1980).* New York: Garland, 1983.

Sievers, Harry J., ed. *Benjamin Harrison, 1833-1901: Chronology, Documents, Biblio-*

xvi *Introduction*

graphical Aids. Dobbs Ferry, NY: Oceana, 1970.
Sievers, Harry J., ed. *William McKinley, 1804-1869: Chronology, Documents, Bibliographical Aids*. Dobbs Ferry, NY: Oceana, 1970.
Sloan, Irving J., ed. *Franklin Pierce, 1804-1869: Chronology, Documents, Bibliographical Aids*. Dobbs Ferry, NY: Oceana, 1968.
Sloan, Irving J., ed. *Martin Van Buren, 1782-1862: Chronology, Documents, Bibliographical Aids*. Dobbs Ferry, NY: Oceana, 1968.
Stapleton, Margaret L. *The Truman and Eisenhower Years, 1945-1960: A Selective Bibliography*. Metuchen, NJ: Scarecrow Press, 1973.
Stewart, William J., comp. *Era of Franklin D. Roosevelt: A Selected Bibliography of Periodical, Essay, and Dissertation Literature, 1945-1971*. 2d ed. Hyde Park, NY: Franklin D. Roosevelt Library, National Archives and Records Service, General Services Administration, 1974.
Stone, Ralph A., ed. *John F. Kennedy, 1917-1963: Chronology, Documents, Bibliographical Aids*. Dobbs Ferry, NY: Oceana, 1971.
Tompkins, Hamilton B. *Bibliotheca Jeffersoniana*. New York: Putnam, 1887.
Thompson, William C. *A Bibliography of Literature Relating to the Assassination of President John F. Kennedy*. San Antonio, TX: Copy Distributing, 1968.
U.S. Library of Congress. *John Fitzgerald Kennedy, 1917-1963: A Chronological List of References*. Washington, DC: General Reference and Bibliography Division, Reference Department, Library of Congress, 1964.
Vexler, Robert I., ed. *Grover Cleveland, 1837-1908: Chronology, Documents, Bibliographical Aids*. Dobbs Ferry, NY: Oceana, 1968.
Vexler, Robert I. *Woodrow Wilson, 1856-1924: Chronology, Documents, Bibliographical Aids*. Dobbs Ferry, NY: Oceana, 1970.
Wessen, Ernest J. "Lincoln Bibliography — Its Present Status and Needs." *Bibliographical Society of America Papers* 34 (1940): 327-348.
Wheelock, John H. *A Bibliography of Theodore Roosevelt*. New York: Scribners, 1920.
Wise, W. Harvey, Jr., and John W. Cronin. *Bibliography of Andrew Jackson and Martin Van Buren*. New York: Burt Franklin, 1970.
Wrone, David R. "The Assassination of John Fitzgerald Kennedy: An Annotated Bibliography." *Wisconsin Magazine of History* 56 (Autumn 1973): 21-36.
Wyllie, John C. "Footnote for an Andrew Jackson Bibliography." *Bibliographical Society of America Paper* 59 (October 1965): 437.

In addition, we searched twenty-seven bibliographies dealing with elections, campaigning, law, and the national government:
Agranoff, Robert. *Elections and Electoral Behavior: A Bibliography*. Dekalb: Northern Illinois University, 1971.
Agranoff, Robert. *Political Campaigns: A Bibliography*. Dekalb: Center for Governmental Studies, Northern Illinois University, 1972.
The American Electorate: A Historical Bibliography. Santa Barbara, CA: ABC-Clio, 1983.
Andrews, Joseph L. *The Law in the United States of America: A Selective Bibliographical Guide*. New York: New York University Press, 1965.
Burke, Robert E., and Richard Lowitt. *The New Era and the New Deal, 1920-1940*. Arlington Heights, IL: Harlan Davidson, 1981.
Burns, Richard D., ed. *Guide to American Foreign Relations since 1700*. Santa Barbara,

CA: ABC-Clio, 1983.
Cassare, Ernest. *History of the United States: A Guide to Information Sources.* Detroit, MI: Gale, 1977.
Chambliss, William J., and Robert B. Seidman. *Sociology of the Law: A Research Bibliography.* Berkeley: Glendessary Press, 1970.
Cronon, E. David. *The Second World War and the Atomic Age, 1940-1973.* Northbrook, IL: AHM, 1975.
De Santis, Vincent P. *The Golden Age, 1877-1896.* Northbrook, IL: AHM, 1973.
The Democratic and Republican Parties in America: A Historical Bibliography. Santa Barbara, CA: ABC-Clio, 1983.
Donald, David. *The Nation in Crisis, 1861-1877.* New York: Appleton, 1969.
Fehrenbacher, Don E. *Manifest Destiny and the Coming of the Civil War, 1840-1861.* New York: Appleton, 1970.
Ferguson, E. James. *Confederation, Constitution, and Early National Period, 1781-1815.* Northbrook, IL: AHM, 1975.
Goehlert, Robert U., and Richard Sayre. *The United States Congress: A Bibliography.* New York: Free Press, 1982.
Kaid, Lynda L., Keith R. Sanders, and Robert O. Hirsch. *Political Campaign Communication: A Bibliography and Guide to the Literature.* Metuchen, NJ: Scarecrow Press, 1974.
Leary, William M., and Arthur S. Link. *The Progressive Era and the Great War, 1896-1920.* Arlington Heights, IL: AHM, 1978.
Mason, Alpheus T., and D. Grier Stephenson. *American Constitutional Development.* Arlington Heights, IL: AHM, 1977.
Mauer, David J. *United States Politics and Elections: A Guide to Information Sources.* Detroit, MI: Gale, 1978.
McCarrick, Earlean M. *The U.S. Constitution: A Guide to Information Sources.* Detroit, MI: Gale, 1980.
Millet, Stephen M. *A Selected Bibliography of American Constitutional History.* Santa Barbara, CA: ABC-Clio, 1975.
Plishke, Elmer. *U.S. Foreign Relations: A Guide to Information Sources.* Detroit, MI: Gale Research, 1975.
Remini, Robert V., and Edwin A. Miles. *The Era of Good Feeling and the Age of Jackson, 1816-1841.* Arlington Heights, IL: AHM, 1979.
Smith, Dwight L., and Lloyd W. Garrison, eds. *The American Political Process: Selected Abstracts of Periodical Literature (1954-1971).* Santa Barbara, CA: ABC-Clio, 1972.
Tingley, Donald F. *Social History of the United States: A Guide to Information Sources.* Detroit, MI: Gale Research, 1979.
The United States Capitol: An Annotated Bibliography. Norman: University of Oklahoma Press, 1973.
Wynar, Lubomyr R., comp. *American Political Parties: A Selective Guide to Parties and Movements of the 20th Century.* Littleton, CO: Libraries Unlimited, 1969.

We hope that this bibliography will prove beneficial to researchers and students in the field of American politics and history. The book also is intended to generate more interest in research on the presidents by surveying what has been done and pointing out areas that have been neglected.

We wish to thank the Political Science Department at Indiana University for its support of our research. Special thanks go to Doris Burton (assistant to the chair), Steve Flinn (systems manager), and Fern Bennett (data archivist/word processing operator). We also wish to thank Julie England, Rae Ferrell, Barbara Hopkins, Ada Jaime, Diana Scharenberg, Roberta Scott, and Meredith Wolff for their help in preparing this manuscript for publication.

Fenton S. Martin
Robert U. Goehlert

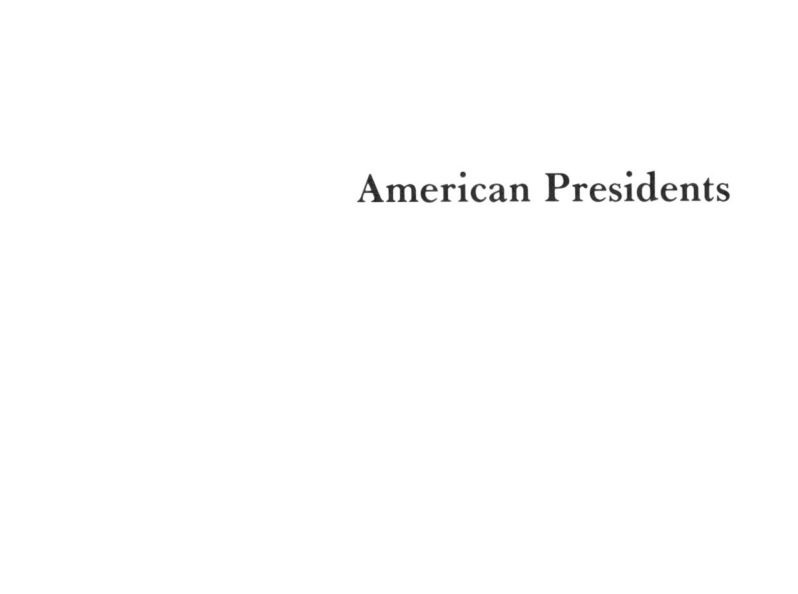

American Presidents

George Washington

Biographies

1. Abbott, John S. C. *George Washington*. New York: Dodd, Mead, 1903.

2. Abernethy, Arthur T. *Did Washington Aspire to Be King?* New York: Neale, 1906.

3. Adams, Randolph G. *The Dignity of George Washington*. Ann Arbor: G. Wahr, 1932.

4. Aikman, Lonnelle. *Washington: The Man, His City, and His Home*. Washington, DC: Tee Loftin, 1982.

5. Alden, John R. *George Washington: A Biography*. Baton Rouge: Louisiana State University Press, 1984.

6. Anderson, Patricia A. *Promoted to Glory: The Apotheosis of George Washington*. Northampton, MA: Smith College, 1980.

7. Aulaire, Ingri M. *George Washington*. Garden City, NY: Doubleday, 1957.

8. Bacheller, Irving, and Herbert Kates. *Great Moments in the Life of Washington*. New York: Grossett and Dunlap, 1932.

9. Baker, William S. *Character Portraits of Washington as Delineated by Historians, Orators, and Divines, Selected and Arranged in Chronological Order with Biographical Notes and References*. Philadelphia: R. M. Lindsay, 1887.

10. Baker, William S. *Early Sketches of George Washington*. Philadelphia: Lippincott, 1894.

11. Bancroft, Aaron. *An Essay on the Life of George Washington*. Worcester, MA: Thomas and Sturtevant, 1807.

12. Bancroft, Aaron. *Life of George Washington, Commander in Chief of the American Army through the Revolutionary War, and the First President of the United States*. London: J. Stockdale, 1808.

13. Beck, James M. "George Washington." *New Republic* 32 (October 25, 1922): 221-222.

14. Bordon, Morton, comp. *George Washington*. Englewood, NJ: Prentice-Hall, 1969.

15. Bulla, Charles D. *George Washington, The Second-Mile American*. Nashville, TN: Partheon Press, 1931.

16. Caldwell, Charles. *Character of General Washington*. Philadelphia: True American, 1801.

17. Callahan, North. *George Washington, Soldier and Man*. New York: Morrow, 1972.

18. Carrington, Henry B. *Washington the Soldier*. Boston: Lamson, Wolffe, 1898.

19. Chesterton, G. K. "George Washington." *Fortnightly Review* 131 (March 1932): 303-310.

20. Clark, Jonathan. *Life of General Washington, Late President of the United States*. Albany, NY: Packard and Van Benthuysen, 1813.

21. Clark, Philip. *Washington*. Hove, East Sussex, England: Wayland, 1981.

22. Clark, Thomas A. *George Washington, Biography and Selections from His Writings: Written Especially for School Reading*. Taylorville, IL: Parker Publishing Co., 1931.

23. Coe, Edward B. "Washington — The Man." *Magazine of History* 9 (February 1909): 92-103.

24. Condie, Thomas. *Biographical Memoirs of the Illustrious General George Washington*. Philadelphia: Charles and Ralston, 1800.

25. Condie, Thomas. *Life of George Washington*. New York: S. and D. A. Forbes, 1829.

26. Corry, John. *Biographical Memoirs of the Illustrious General George Washington*. Barnard, VT: Joseph Dix, 1813.

27. Corry, John. *The Life of George Washington, First President and Commander in Chief of the Armies of the United States of America*. New York: McCarty and White, 1809.

28. Coulcomb, Charles A. "George Washington in Recent Biographies." *Historical Outlook* 23 (February 1932): 70-80.

29. Custis, George W. *Recollections and Private Memoirs of Washington*. Washington, DC: W. H. Moore, 1859.

30. Emery, Noemi. *Washington: A Biography*. New York: Putnam, 1976.

31. Everett, Edward. *The Life of George Washington*. New York: Sheldon, 1860.

32. Farrington, Harry W. *Walls of America*. Bradley Beach, NJ: Rough and Brown Press, 1925.

33. Farriss, Charles S. *The American Soul*. Boston: Stratford, 1920.

34. Fay, Bernard. *George Washington, Republican Aristocrat*. Boston: Houghton Mifflin, 1931.

35. Fish, Carl R. "George Washington: The Man." *Illinois State Historical Society Transactions* 39 (1932): 21-40.

36. Fitzpatrick, John C. *George Washington Himself: A Common-Sense Biography Written from His Manuscripts*. Indianapolis, IN: Bobbs-Merrill, 1933.

37. Flanagan, Vincent. *George Washington, First President of the United States*. Charlotteville, NY: SamHar Press, 1973.

38. Fleming, Thomas J. *First in Their Hearts: A Biography of George Washington*. New York: Norton, 1968.

39. Flexner, James T. *George Washington and the New Nation*. Boston: Little, Brown, 1970.

40. Flexner, James T. *George Washington: Anguish and Farewell*. Boston: Little, Brown, 1969.

41. Flexner, James T. *George Washington in the American Revolution*. Boston: Little, Brown, 1968.

42. Flexner, James T. *Washington*. New York: New American Library, 1974.

43. Flexner, James T. *Washington, The Indispensable Man*. Boston: Little, Brown, 1974.

44. Ford, Paul L. *George Washington*. Philadelphia: Lippincott, 1924.

45. Ford, Paul L. *The True George Washington*. Philadelphia: Lippincott, 1896.

46. Ford, Paul L. *Washington and the Theatre*. New York: Dunlap Society, 1899.

47. Ford, Worthington C. *George Washington*. Boston: Small, Maynard and Co., 1910.

48. Foster, Genevieve. *George Washington's World.* New York: Scribner's, 1977.

49. Freeman, Douglas S. *George Washington: A Biography.* 7 vols. New York: Scribner's, 1948-1957.

50. Freeman, Douglas S. *Washington.* Edited by Richard Harwell. New York: Scribner's, 1968.

51. Frost, John. *An Illustrated History of Washington and His Times.* Norwich, CT: William Hutchison, 1868.

52. Frost, John. *Pictorial Life of George Washington.* Philadelphia: Croome and Devereux, 1847.

53. Gerwig, George W. *Washington, The Young Leader.* New York: Scribner's, 1923.

54. Habberton, John. *George Washington (1732-1799).* New York: Holt, 1884.

55. Hale, Edward E. *The Life of George Washington, Studied Anew.* New York: Putnam, 1888.

56. Hancock, Morris H., ed. *Washington's Life and Military Career.* Chicago: Thompson and Thompson, 1902.

57. Hapgood, Norman. *George Washington.* New York: Macmillan, 1901.

58. Harrison, James A. *George Washington, Patriot, Soldier, Statesman, First President of the United States.* New York: Putnam, 1906.

59. Hart, Albert B. *George Washington.* Chicago: American Library Association, 1927.

60. Hart, Albert B. "A Study of Washington Biography." *Publishers Weekly* 119 (February 14, 1931): 820-822.

61. Hart, Albert B. *Washington, The Man of Mind.* Washington, DC: George Washington Bicentennial Commission, 1931.

62. Hart, Albert B. "Washington to Order." *Massachusetts Historical Society Proceedings* 60 (December 1926): 66-81.

63. Headley, Joel T. *The Illustrated Life of Washington.* New York: G. and F. Bill, 1859.

64. Henley, Leonard. *Life of Washington.* New York: John W. Lovell Co., 1882.

65. Hill, Frederick T. *Washington, The Man of Action.* New York: Appleton, 1914.

66. Holmes, Mabel D. *George Washington, the Soul of a Nation: His Complete Life Story.* Philadelphia: Winston, 1932.

67. Hubbard, Elbert. *George Washington.* New York: Putnam, 1968.

68. Hughes, Rupert. *George Washington.* 3 vols. New York: Morrow, 1926-1930.

69. Hutchins, Frank, and Cortelle Hutchins. *Washington and the Lafayettes.* New York: Longmans, Green, 1939.

70. Hutchinson, Paul. "Washington." *Tennessee Historical Magazine* 2 (January 1932): 147-152.

71. Irving, Washington. *George Washington: A Biography.* Edited by Charles Neider. Garden City, NY: Doubleday, 1976.

72. Irving, Washington. *The Life and Times of Washington.* New York: Putnam, 1872.

73. Irving, Washington. *Life of George Washington.* 5 vols. New York: Putnam, 1855-1859.

74. Irving, Washington. *Washington and His Country: Being Irving's Life of Washington, Abridged for the Use of Schools....* Boston: Ginn, 1887.

75. Johnson, Albert W. "George Washington." *Western Pennsylvania Historical Magazine* 11 (October 1928): 203-216.

76. Johnson, Bradley T. *...General Washington.* New York: Appleton, 1894.

77. Johnston, Elizabeth B., comp. *George Washington Day by Day*. New York: Cycle Publishing Co., 1895.

78. Jones, Robert F. *George Washington*. Boston: Twayne, 1979.

79. Ketchum, Richard M. *The World of George Washington*. New York: American Heritage Publishing Co., 1974.

80. Kingery, Hugh M. "An Old Latin Life of Washington." *Magazine of History* 5 (May 1907): 285-289.

81. Kingston, John. *The Life of General George Washington*. Baltimore, MD: The Author, 1813.

82. Kinnaird, Clark. *George Washington: The Pictorial Biography*. New York: Hastings House, 1967.

83. Kirkland, Carolina M. *Memoirs of Washington*. New York: Appleton, 1857.

84. Knollenberg, Bernhard. *George Washington: The Virginia Period, 1732-1775*. Durham, NC: Duke University Press, 1964.

85. Little, Shelby M. *George Washington*. New York: Minton, Balch, 1929.

86. Lodge, Henry C. *The Life of George Washington*. 2 vols. Boston: Houghton Mifflin, 1920.

87. Lossing, Benson J. *Life of Washington: A Biography, Personal, Military, and Political*. 3 vols. New York: Virtue, 1860.

88. McCamant, Wallace S. "George Washington, the Gentleman." In *1922-1923 Year Book . . . Louisiana Society Sons of the American Revolution*, 64-67. New Orleans, LA: The Society, 1923.

89. McCamant, Wallace S. "Washington as a Man." *Oregon Law Review* 12 (December 1932): 22-36.

90. McCann, Alfred W. *Greatest of Men, Washington*. New York: Devin-Adair, 1927.

91. Madison, Lucy F. *Washington*. Philadelphia: Penn Publishing Co., 1925.

92. Meadowcroft, Enid. *The Story of George Washington*. New York: Grosset and Dunlap, 1952.

93. Meany, Edmond S. *Washington from Life*. Seattle, WA: Dogwood Press, 1931.

94. *Memory of Washington: Comprising a Sketch of His Life and Character, and the National Testimonials of Respect*. Newport, RI: Oliver Fransworth, 1800.

95. Mondadori Editore, Arnoldo. *The Life and Times of Washington*. Chicago: Rand McNally, 1967.

96. Morgan, Edmund S. *The Genius of George Washington*. New York: Norton, 1981.

97. Morgan, Edmund S. "George Washington: The Aloof American." *Virginia Quarterly Review* 52 (Summer 1976): 410-436.

98. Nelson, William. "A Latin Life of Washington: A Literary Curiosity with a History." *Americana* 8 (October 1913): 884-890.

99. Nordham, George W. *George Washington and Money*. Washington, DC: University Press of America, 1982.

100. Nordham, George W. *George Washington and the Law*. Chicago: Adams Press, 1982.

101. O'Boyle, James. *Life of George Washington, The Father of Modern Democracy*. New York: Longmans, 1915.

102. Parsons, Eugene. *George Washington, A Character Sketch*. Milwaukee, WI: H. G. Campbell Publishing Co., 1898.

103. Parsons, Eugene. *The Life of George Washington, First President of the United States, 1789-1797*. Chicago: Laird and Lee, 1913.

104. Partin, Robert. "The Changing Images of George Washington from Weems to Freeman." *Social Studies* 56 (February 1965): 52-59.

105. Paulding, James K. *Life of Washington.* New York: Harper and Brothers, 1858.

106. Phillips, Charles. "The Naked Washington." *Catholic World* 124 (February 1927): 577-586.

107. Pollard, Josephine. *The Life of George Washington.* New York: McLoughlin Brothers, 1893.

108. Ramsay, David. *The Life of George Washington....* New York: Hopkins and Seymour, 1807.

109. Reed, Anna C. *The Life of George Washington.* Philadelphia: American Sunday School Union, 1832.

110. Rideing, William H. *George Washington.* New York: Macmillan, 1916.

111. Rivoire, Mario. *The Life and Times of Washington.* Philadelphia: Curtis, 1968.

112. Roz, Firmin. *Washington.* Paris: Dunod, 1933.

113. Russell, Ada. *George Washington.* New York: Stokes, 1921.

114. Santrey, Laurence. *George Washington, Young Leader.* Mahway, NJ: Troll Associates, 1982.

115. Sawyer, Joseph D. *Washington.* 2 vols. New York: Macmillan, 1927.

116. Schafer, Joseph. "Washington and His Biographers." *Wisconsin Magazine of History* 11 (December 1927): 218-228.

117. Schmidt, Ferdinand. *...George Washington.* Translated by George P. Upton. Chicago: McClurg, 1911.

118. Schmucker, Samuel M. *The Life and Times of George Washington.* Philadelphia: Potter, 1859.

119. Schroeder, John F. *Life and Times of Washington.* 4 vols. Rev. ed. Albany, NY: Washington Press, 1903.

120. Scudder, Horace E. *George Washington, An Historical Biography.* Boston: Houghton Mifflin, 1924.

121. Sears, Louis M. *George Washington.* New York: Crowell, 1932.

122. Seelye, Elizabeth. *The Story of Washington.* New York: Appleton, 1893.

123. Smith, James M., ed. *George Washington: A Profile.* New York: Hill and Wang, 1969.

124. Smyth, Clifford. *George Washington, The Story of the First American.* New York: Funk and Wagnalls, 1931.

125. Sparks, Jared. *The Life of George Washington.* Boston: F. Andrews, 1839.

126. Stephenson, Nathaniel W. "The Romantics and George Washington." *American Historical Review* 39 (January 1934): 274-283.

127. Stephenson, Nathaniel W., and Waldo H. Dunn. *George Washington.* 2 vols. New York: Oxford University Press, 1940.

128. Stoddard, William O. *George Washington.* New York: White, Stokes and Allen, 1886.

129. Swiggett, Howard. *The Great Man: George Washington as a Human Being.* Garden City, NY: Doubleday, 1953.

130. Syle, Bertrand C. "Intimate Studies of Washington and Lincoln." *Independent* 110 (February 17, 1923): 132-133.

131. Taylor, Edward M. *George Washington, The Ideal Patriot.* New York: Eaton, 1897.

132. Thayer, William M. *... From Farm House to White House: The Life of George Washington.* Chicago: A. Whitman and Co., 1927.

133. Thayer, William R. *George Washington.* Boston: Houghton Mifflin, 1922.

134. Thorsmar, Thora. *George Washington.* Chicago: Scott, Foresman, 1931.

135. Townsend, Virginia F. *Life of Washington.* New York: Worthington, 1887.

136. Treadway, Sandra G. "Popes Creek Plantation: Birthplace of George Washington." *Virginia Cavalcade* 31 (Spring 1982): 192-205.

137. Upham, Charles W. *The Life of Washington, In the Form of an Autobiography.* Boston: Marsh, Capen, Lyon and Webb, 1840.

138. Van Dyke, Henry. *The Americanism of Washington.* New York: Harper and Row, 1906.

139. Van Dyke, Paul. *George Washington, The Son of His Country, 1732-1775.* New York: Scribner's, 1931.

140. Van Dyke, Paul. "Washington." *American Philosophical Society Proceedings* 71 (1932): 191-205.

141. Wall, Charles C. *George Washington, Citizen-Soldier.* Charlottesville: University of Virginia Press, 1980.

142. Weems, Mason L. *A History of the Life and Death, Virtues and Exploits of General George Washington.* Cleveland, OH: World Publishing, 1965.

143. Weems, Mason L. *The Life of George Washington.* Cambridge: Belknap Press, 1962.

144. Weems, Mason L. *The Life of Washington the Great.* New York: Garland, 1977.

145. Weld, Horatio H. *Pictorial Life of George Washington: Embracing Anecdotes, Illustrative of His Character.* Philadelphia: Lindsay and Blakiston, 1845.

146. Whipple, Wayne. *The Heart of Washington: An Intimate Study of the Father of His Country from the Personal, Human Side.* Philadelphia: Jacobs, 1916.

147. Whipple, Wayne, *The Story of Young George Washington.* Philadelphia: Henry Altemus, 1915.

148. Whipple, Wayne, comp. *The Story-Life of Washington: A Life-History in Five Hundred True Stories, Selected from Original Sources and Fitted Together in Order.* 2 vols. Philadelphia: Winston, 1911.

149. Wilbur, William H. *Making of George Washington.* 2d ed. De Land, FL: Patriotic, 1974.

150. Williamson, Mary L. *George Washington, Soldier and Statesman.* Chicago: Beckley-Cardy, 1951.

151. Williamson, Mary L. *Life of Washington.* Richmond, VA: B. F. Johnson Publishing Co., 1911.

152. Winthrop, Robert C. *Washington, Bowdoin, and Franklin, As Portrayed in Occasional Addresses.* Boston: Little, Brown, 1876.

153. Wister, Owen. *The Seven Ages of Washington: A Biography.* New York: Macmillan, 1907.

154. Woodward, William E. *George Washington, The Image and the Man.* New York: Boni and Liveright, 1926.

Private Life

General

155. Bellamy, Francis. *The Private Life of George Washington.* New York: Crowell, 1951.

156. Birge, William S. "Washington before the Revolution." *Americana* 5 (January 1910): 37-45.

157. Blanton, Wyndham B. "Washington's Medical Knowledge and Its Sources." *Annals of Medical History* 5 (January 1933): 52-61.

158. Bomberger, C. M. *George Washington, Mason.* Jeannette, PA: Jeannette Publishing Co., 1931.

159. Brown, William M. *George Washington, Freemason.* Richmond: Garrett and Massie, 1952.

160. Castelot, Andre. *My Friend Lafayette: "Mon Ami Washington."* Paris: Librairie Academique Perrin, 1976.

161. Chase, Enoch A. "George Washington's Heirlooms at Arlington." *Current History* 29 (March 1929): 972-980.

162. Clemens, J. R. "George Washington's Pronunciation." *American Speech* 7 (August 1932): 438-441.

163. Cloud, Archibald J., and Vierling Kersey. *Episodes in the Life of George Washington.* New York: Scribner's, 1932.

164. Coblentz, Catherine C. "George Washington's Animals." *National Historical Magazine* 73 (February 1939): 31-34.

165. Coolidge, Calvin. "George Washington and Education." *National Education Association Journal* 15 (April 1926): 99-102.

166. Coolidge, Ruth D., and Richard B. Coolidge. "Medford and George Washington." *Medford Historical Register* 34 (1931): 58-65.

167. Corning, A. Elwood. *Washington at Temple Hill.* Newburgh, NY: Lanmere Publishing Co., 1932.

168. Decatur, Stephen. *Private Affairs of George Washington, From the Records and Accounts of Tobias Lear, Esquire, His Secretary.* Boston: Houghton Mifflin, 1933.

169. Douglass, William B. "Washington as an Engineer." *Professional Engineer* 15 (January 1930): 17-23.

170. England, George A. "Washington's Old Home Farm." *Daughters of the American Revolution Magazine* 59 (December 1925): 737-744.

171. Everett, Edwin M. "Washington, The Human Being." *Georgia Historical Quarterly* 11 (March 1927): 54-59.

172. Fitzpatrick, John C. "George Washington as Santa Claus Again." *Historical Outlook* 20 (February 1929): 68-70.

173. Fitzpatrick, John C. "The George Washington Scandals." *Scribner's Magazine* 81 (April 1927): 389-395.

174. Ford, Worthington C. *Washington as an Employer and Importer of Labor.* Brooklyn, NY: Privately Printed, 1889.

175. "George Washington, Farmer and Weather Observer." *Environmental Data and Information Service* 11 (March 1980): 20-22.

176. "George Washington: 1732-1932." *Current History* 35 (February 1932): 676-689.

177. Grant, Ulysses S. *Washington as Engineer and City Builder.* Washington, DC: George Washington Bicentennial Commission, 1931.

178. Griswold, Rufus W. *... The Military and Civil Life of George Washington for the People.* New York: W. H. Graham, 1849.

179. Gross, K. Frederick. "George Washington: Justice of the Peace." *Brooklyn Barrister* 12 (February 1961): 130-131.

180. Haley, John W. *George Washington and Rhode Island.* Providence: State of Rhode Island, 1932.

181. Hays, James, Jr. "George Washington, Inventor." *Scientific American* 145 (March 1932): 140-141.

182. Hazlitt, William. "'Washington,' The Hazlitt Story." Edited by Mary A. Miller. *Picket Post* 43 (January 1953): 9-11.

8 George Washington

183. Helderman, Leonard C. *George Washington, Patron of Learning.* New York: Century, 1932.

184. Henkels, Stan V. "Washington's Social Life." *Magazine of History* 5 (June 1907): 332-335.

185. Hobby, Laura A. *Washington the Lover.* Dallas, TX: Southwest Press, 1932.

186. Hulbert, Archer B. "Washington: The Pioneer Investor." *Chautaugan* 38 (September 1903): 43-48.

187. Hulbert, Archer B. "Washington: The Promoter and Prophet." *Chautaugan* 38 (October 1903): 149-154.

188. Hutchins, Frank. "Some Bicentennial Errors." *Daughters of the American Revolution Magazine* 68 (February 1934): 86-90.

189. Hutchins, Frank, and Cortelle Hutchins. *Washington's Washington.* Washington, DC: Historical Research Service, 1925.

190. "The Inventory of Washington's Library." *Nation* 83 (August 23, 1906): 161-162.

191. Kauffman, Erie. *Trees of Washington, The Man — The City.* Washington, DC: Outdoor Press, 1932.

192. Keast, Lewis. "George Washington and Education." *Education* 54 (February 1934): 321-322.

193. Kenner, Sumner. "Some Phases of Washington's Life of Particular Interest to Lawyers." *Indiana Law Journal* 8 (April 1933): 428-438.

194. Knight, George M., and Richard Harwood-Staderman. *What You Don't Know about George Washington.* Washington, DC: American Good Government Society, 1941.

195. Knox, J. H. Mason, Jr. "The Medical History of George Washington, His Physicians, Friends, and Advisers." *Bulletin of the Institute of the History of Medicine* (Johns Hopkins University) 1 (June 1933): 174-191.

196. Laidley, W. S. "Large Land Owners: George Washington as a Land Owner: Agreement to Make Salt, Between Lawrence A. Washington and Benjamin F. Reeder." *West Virginia Historical Magazine* 3 (July 1903): 242-253.

197. Lawrence, Henry W. "The Misused Washington." *Historical Outlook* 23 (October 1932): 267-269.

198. Lewis, Fielding O. "Washington's Last Illness." *Annals of Medical History* 4 (1932): 245-248.

199. Lichtenstein, Gaston. *George Washington's Lost Birthday....* Richmond: William Byrd Press, 1924.

200. Lippincott, Horace M. "George Washington and the University of Pennsylvania." *University of Pennsylvania Alumni Register* 18 (February 1916): 356-383.

201. Lively, Bruce R. "George Washington Almost Joined the Navy." *All Hands* 714 (July 1976): 32-33.

202. Long, Charles C. "George Washington, The Engineer." *Military Engineer* 31 (May/June 1939): 172-173.

203. McCarthy, Charles H. "Washington, His Allies and His Friends." *Catholic University Bulletin* 20 (December 1914): 576-593.

204. McKeldin, Theodore. *Hats on for General Washington.* Baltimore: Maryland Historical Society, 1973.

205. Marx, Rudolph. "A Medical Profile of George Washington." *American Heritage* 6 (August 1955): 43-57, 106-107.

206. Milliken, R. C. V. "The Hunting Days of Our First President." *Daughters* *of the American Revolution Magazine* 66 (August 1932): 505-507.

207. Mitchell, Broadus. "Hamilton's Quarrel with Washington, 1781." *William and Mary Quarterly* 12 (April 1955): 199-216.

208. Moore, Charles, ed. *George Washington's Rules of Civility and Decent Behaviour in Company and Conversation*. Boston: Houghton Mifflin, 1926.

209. Moore, R. Walton. "George Washington as a Judge and His Attitude towards Courts and Lawyers." *American Bar Association Journal* 18 (March 1932): 151-154.

210. Morris, Griffith. "George Washington as a Real Estate Agent." *American History Magazine* 4 (May 1909): 272-274.

211. Mosley, James D. "George Washington: Seeds of Statesmanship, 1753-1758." Ph.D. dissertation, Claremont Graduate School, 1974.

212. Muzzey, David S. "The Vision of Washington." *Legion D'Honneur Magazine* 9 (1939): 301-318.

213. Nordham, George W. *A George Washington Treasury*. Chicago: Adams Press, 1983.

214. Norris, Walter B. "The Annual Register and Weems's Life of Washington." *Nation* 92 (June 8, 1911): 578.

215. O'Brien, Michael J. *George Washington's Associations with the Irish*. New York: P. J. Kennedy and Sons, 1937.

216. Padover, Saul K. "George Washington — Portrait of a True Conservative." *Social Research* 22 (Summer 1955): 199-222.

217. Pape, T. "The Washington and Sulgrave Manor." *William and Mary Quarterly* 19 (October 1939): 474-484.

218. Peterson, Raymond G., Jr. "George Washington, Capitalistic Farmer: A Documentary Study of Washington's Business Activities and the Sources of His Wealth." Ph.D. dissertation, Ohio University, 1970.

219. Powell, J. H. "General Washington and the Jack Ass." *South Atlantic Quarterly* 76 (Autumn 1977): 409-423.

220. Preston, John H. "The Rebirth of George Washington." *Forum* 87 (March 1932): 136-141.

221. Prussing, Eugene E. "George Washington, Captain of Industry." *Scribner's Magazine* 70 (October 1921): 412-428; (November 1921): 549-559.

222. Prussing, Eugene E. *George Washington: In Love and Otherwise*. Chicago: Covici, 1925.

223. Prussing, Eugene E. *The Estate of George Washington, Deceased*. Boston: Little, Brown, 1927.

224. Reznikoff, Phillip. "A Note on Washington." *International Journal of Psychoanalysis* 15 (April/July 1934): 301-302.

225. Ritter, Halsted L. *Washington as a Business Man*. New York: Sears Publishing Co., 1931.

226. Robbins, Jessie M. "Washington, The Founder of Washington." *National Education Association Journal* 13 (February 1924): 53-55.

227. Rudolph, Norman. *Christmas with George Washington, 1776-1779*. Philadelphia: Franklin, 1900.

228. Sabine, William. *Murder, 1776, and Washington's Policy of Silence*. New York: T. Gaus' Sons, 1973.

229. Sargent, George H. "Washington on Preparedness." *Magazine of History* 22 (January 1916): 62-65.

230. Saunders, Frances W. "Equestrian Washington from Rome to Richmond." *Virginia Cavalcade* 25 (Summer 1975): 4-13.

231. Schroeder, John F. *Maxims of Washington*. Mount Vernon, VA: Mt. Vernon Ladies' Association, 1942.

232. Shaw, Elton R. *The Love Affairs of Washington and Lincoln: The Love Affairs of Abraham Lincoln, The Boyhood and Love Affairs of Washington*. Berwyn, IL: Shaw Publishing Co., 1923.

233. Spaulding, Oliver L., Jr. "The Military Studies of George Washington." *American Historical Review* 29 (July 1924): 675-680.

234. Sterling, Adaline W. "Washington, The Man." *Patriot* 1 (February 1915): 45-51.

235. Stetson, Charles W. *Washington and His Neighbors*. Richmond, VA: Garrett and Massie, 1956.

236. Toner, Joseph M. *George Washington as an Inventor and Promoter of the Useful Arts, An Address Delivered at Mount Vernon, April 10, 1891*. Washington, DC: Gedney and Roberts, 1892.

237. U.S. George Washington Bicentennial Commission. *The Music of George Washington's Time*. Washington, DC: George Washington Bicentennial Commission, 1931.

238. Wall, Charles C. "George Washington, The Image and the Man." *Western Pennsylvania Historical Magazine* 50 (January 1967): 1-6.

239. "Washington at Yale." *Magazine of History* 20 (March 1915): 174-176.

240. "The Washingtons in Kingston." *Olde Ulster* 3 (January 1907): 6-17.

241. Wayland, John W. "Washington West of the Blue Ridge." *Virginia Magazine of History* 48 (July 1940): 193-201.

242. Weinberger, Bernhard W. "George Washington and His Dental Disturbances." *Trained Nurse and Hospital Review* (New York) 104 (1940): 115-122.

243. Welles, Edward O., Jr. "George Washington Slept Here ... And Here's How It Really Looked." *Historic Preservation* 34 (1982): 22-27.

244. Whipple, Wayne. "Washington's Sense of Humor." *Century Magazine* 81 (March 1911): 785-790.

245. Whittlesey, Walter L. "George Washington's World of Tomorrow." *Survey Graphic* 28 (May 1939): 312-315.

246. Wills, Garry. "George Washington and the Guilty, Dangerous, and Vulgar Honor." *American Heritage* 31 (February/March 1980): 4-11.

247. Wilson, Samuel M. "George Washington's Contacts with Kentucky." *Filson Club History Quarterly* 6 (July 1932): 215-260.

248. Wilson, Samuel M. "Washington's Relations to Tennessee and Kentucky." *East Tennessee Historical Society's Publications* 5 (1933): 3-21.

249. Windley, Lathan A. "Runaway Slave Advertisements of George Washington and Thomas Jefferson." *Journal of Negro History* 63 (Fall 1978): 373-374.

250. Zunder, Theodore A. "Joel Barlow and George Washington." *Modern Language Notes* 44 (April 1929): 254-256.

Family

251. Barrett, Wayne. "George and Betsy and Polly and Patsy and Sally ... and Sally ... and Sally." *Smithsonian* 4 (November 1973): 90-99.

252. Bourne, Miriam A. *First Family: George Washington and His Intimate Relations*. New York: Norton, 1982.

253. Branscombe, Arthur. "Washington's Ancestral Farm: The Manor Farm, Granted to Lawrence Washington by

Henry VIII." *World's Work* 13 (April 1907): 8722-8726.

254. Butler, Joseph G., Jr. "A Day in Washington's Country: Account of a Visit to the Places Where the Ancestors of Our First President Lived, Worshiped, Died, and Were Buried." *Journal of American History* 15 (January 1921): 41-47.

255. Caemmerer, Hans P. " 'Wakefield' — Birth Place of Washington." *Daughters of the American Revolution Magazine* 66 (July 1932): 425-429.

256. Cole, Adelaide M. "Martha Washington: The First First Lady." *Daughters of the American Revolution Magazine* 113 (February 1979): 136-140.

257. Corbin, John. "Washington and Sally Fairfax." *Scribner's Magazine* 86 (October 1929): 402-413.

258. Custis, George W. *Memoirs of Washington, By His Adopted Son, With a Memoir of the Author, By His Daughter, and Illustrative and Explanatory Notes, By Benson J. Lossing.* Philadelphia: Edgewood Publishing Co., 1859.

259. Desmond, Alice. *Martha Washington: Our First Lady.* New York: Dodd, Mead, 1942.

260. Fields, Joseph E. "The Correspondence of the First First Lady." *Manuscripts* 8 (Fall 1956): 287-290.

261. Fitzpatrick, John C. "When Mrs. Washington Went to Camp." *Daughters of the American Revolution Magazine* 59 (March 1925): 135-147.

262. Gahn, Bessie W. "Mrs. Washington's Long-Lost Message." *Daughters of the American Revolution Magazine* 65 (May 1931): 291-295.

263. Gray, Arthur. "The White House — Washington's Marriage Place." *Virginia Magazine of History* 42 (July 1934): 229-240.

264. Harris, Estelle. "The Portraits of Mary, The Mother of Washington." *Daughters of the American Revolution Magazine* 65 (March 1931): 141-144.

265. Hart, Albert B. "The English Ancestry of George Washington." *Massachusetts Historical Society Proceedings* 63 (October 1929): 3-16.

266. Holland, Corabelle A. "A Visit to Warton: The Lancashire Home of President Washington's Ancestors." *American Foreign Service Journal* 9 (November 1932): 417-419.

267. Hoppin, Charles A. "The Erroneous Published Age of Washington's Mother." *Tyler's Quarterly Historical and Genealogical Magazine* 12 (January 1931): 152-156.

268. Hoppin, Charles A. "George Washington's Birthplace." *Tyler's Quarterly Historical and Genealogical Magazine* 15 (April 1934): 270-273.

269. Hoppin, Charles A. "The House in Which George Washington Was Born." *Tyler's Quarterly Historical and Genealogical Magazine* 8 (October 1926): 73-103.

270. Hoppin, Charles A. "How the Size and Character of Washington's Birthplace Were Ascertained by the Wakefield National Memorial Association, Inc." *Tyler's Quarterly Historical and Genealogical Magazine* 11 (January 1930): 145-162.

271. Hoppin, Charles A. "The Origin of Wakefield, Washington's Birthplace." *Tyler's Quarterly Historical and Genealogical Magazine* 8 (April 1927): 217-241.

272. Hulbert, Archer B. "George Washington's Heritage: Executive Ability of His Father, An Able Business Man Who Made a Fortune in Lands, Mines, and Trading Ventures." *World's Work* 49 (February 1925): 425-447.

273. Hutchins, Frank, and Cortelle

Hutchins. "The Christening of Washington: When and Where — Why George Washington." *Daughters of the American Revolution Magazine* 61 (April 1927): 255-261.

274. Jackson, Donald. "George Washington's Beautiful Nelly." *American Heritage* 28 (February 1977): 80-85.

275. Koontz, Louis K. "George Washington as Santa Claus." *History Outlook* 19 (December 1928): 368-370.

276. Minnigerode, Meade. "Martha Washington, An Informal Biography." *Saturday Evening Post* 195 (April 4, 1922-1923): 20-21.

277. Moore, Charles. *The Family Life of George Washington.* Boston: Houghton Mifflin, 1926.

278. Moore, Charles. "George Washington's Courtship and Marriage." *Daughters of the American Revolution Magazine* 57 (February 1923): 63-68.

279. Moore, Charles. "The Step-Fatherhood of George Washington." *Daughters of the American Revolution Magazine* 58 (November 1924): 661-668; (December 1924): 745-753; 59 (February 1925): 69-76; (May 1925): 291-298; (July 1925): 425-433; (November 1925): 661-671.

280. Moore, Charles. "Washington's Family Life at Mount Vernon." *Daughters of the American Revolution Magazine* 57 (May 1923): 288-294.

281. Moore, Charles. "Washington's In-Laws." *Daughters of the American Revolution Magazine* 57 (July 1923): 399-408.

282. Niles, Blair. *Martha's Husband: An Informal Portrait of George Washington.* New York: McGraw-Hill, 1951.

283. Nordham, George W. *George Washington's Women: Mary, Martha, Sally, and 146 Others.* Philadelphia: Dorrance, 1977.

284. Palmer, Lillian R. "George and Martha: Host and Hostess." *Daughters of the American Revolution Magazine* 113 (May 1979): 528-531, 640.

285. Paullin, Charles O. "The Birthplace of George Washington." *William and Mary Quarterly* 14 (January 1934): 1-8.

286. Perry, Armstrong. "Wakefield, The Birthplace of George Washington." *Daughters of the American Revolution Magazine* 58 (March 1924): 149-154.

287. Pier, Arthur S. "George Washington and Sally Fairfax." *Massachusetts Historical Society Proceedings* 64 (January 1932): 405-415.

288. Pope, T. "New Light on George Washington's Ancestors." *Tyler's Quarterly Historical and Genealogical Magazine* 22 (July 1940): 34-37.

289. Rush, Richard. *Washington in Domestic Life.* Philadelphia: Lippincott, 1857.

290. Seitz, Don C. "Washington's Wedding." *Daughters of the American Revolution Magazine* 60 (August 1926): 453-457.

291. Smith, Harold C. *Sulgrave Manor and the Washingtons: A History and Guide to the Tudor Home of George Washington's Ancestors.* London: J. Cape, 1933.

292. Thomson, Alfred R. "Pilgrimage to Warton." *American Foreign Service Journal* 9 (September 1932): 341-342.

293. Turner, Junius T. "Facts about George Washington." *Washington Historical Quarterly* 12 (July 1921): 163-165.

294. Wagoner, Jean B. *Martha Washington, Girl of Old Virginia: Martha Washington, America's First First Lady.* Indianapolis, IN: Bobbs-Merrill, 1982.

295. Washington, S. H. Lee. "New Light on the Washington's and Sulgrave Manor." *Landmark* 19 (February 1937): 137-140.

296. Washington, S. H. Lee. "Sulgrave Manor and the Washingtons." *William and Mary Quarterly* 19 (April 1939): 214-225.

297. "Washington's Connections with Selby, England." *Magazine of History* 20 (February 1915): 77-80.

298. "Washington's English Ancestors." *Magazine of American History* 31 (April 1903): 26.

299. Waters, Henry F. G. *An Examination of the English Ancestry of George Washington.* Boston: New England Historic Genealogical Society, 1889.

300. Welles, Albert. *The Pedigree and History of the Washington Family.* New York: Society Library, 1879.

301. Wharton, Anne H. *Martha Washington.* New York: Scribner's, 1897.

302. Wilson, James G. "Washington and His English Ancestors." *Independent* 70 (February 23, 1911): 388-394.

303. Worner, William F. "Centenary of George Washington's Birth Observed in Lancaster." *Lancaster County Historical Society Papers* 36 (1932): 132-136.

304. Worner, William F. "George Washington in Lancaster." *Lancaster County Historical Society Papers* 37 (1933): 181-228.

Mount Vernon

305. "Articles of Agreement between George Washington and His Gardener." *U.S. Law Review* 68 (1934): 462-463.

306. Claudy, Carl H. *Washington's Home and Fraternal Life.* Washington, DC: George Washington Bicentennial Commission, 1931.

307. Cooney, Charles F. "George Washington Is Not Buried Here." *American History Illustrated* 15 (November 1980): 48-49.

308. Cullen, Joseph P. "Washington at Mount Vernon." *American History Illustrated* 9 (May 1974): 4-11, 45-48.

309. Eulenberg, Herbert. "The Master of Mount Vernon." *Living Age* 31 (July 28, 1923): 175-180.

310. Haworth, Paul L. *George Washington, Country Gentleman: Being an Account of His Home Life and Agricultural Activities.* Indianapolis, IN: Bobbs-Merrill, 1925.

311. Herbert, Leila. *The First American: His Homes and His Households.* New York: Harper and Brothers, 1900.

312. Johnson, Gerald W. *Mount Vernon: The Story of a Shrine.* New York: Random House, 1953.

313. King, Grace. *Mount Vernon on the Potomac: History of the Mount Vernon Ladies' Association of the Union.* New York: Macmillan, 1929.

314. Latrobe, Benjamin. "George Washington: Country Gentleman: An Account of a Visit to Mount Vernon from the Diary of Benjamin Latrobe." *Country Life* 41 (December 1921): 35-41.

315. Miller, Helen. *Christmas at Mt. Vernon with George and Martha Washington.* New York: Longmans, 1957.

316. Moore, Charles. "Last Days at Mount Vernon: Passages from Letters of Nelly Custis to Mrs. Charles Cotesworth Pinckney." *Daughters of the American Revolution Magazine* 56 (April 1922): 187-195.

317. Moses, Belle. *The Master of Mount Vernon.* New York: Appleton, 1932.

318. Page, Thomas N. *Mount Vernon and Its Preservation, 1858-1910.* New York: Knickerbocker, 1932.

319. Penniman, James H. *George Washington at Mount Vernon on the Potomac*. Mount Vernon, VA: Mount Vernon Ladies' Association of the Union, 1921.

320. Rinaldi, Nicholas. "George Washington at Home in Virginia." *Early American Life* 8 (February 1977): 11-17; (April 1977): 69-76.

321. Schlesinger, Arthur M., Sr. "G. Washington, Mt. Vernon, VA." *Harvard Graduate Magazine* 40 (October 1932): 215-224.

322. Sipe, Chester H. *Mount Vernon and the Washington Family: A Concise Handbook on the Ancestry, Youth, and Family of George Washington, and History of His Home*. 3d ed. Butler, PA: Ziegler Printing Co., 1925.

323. Spender, Harold. "Washington and Mount Vernon." *Landmark* 5 (February 1923): 111-114.

324. Wilson, Hazel. *The Years Between: Washington at Home at Mount Vernon, 1783-1789*. New York: Knopf, 1969.

325. Wilstach, Paul. *Mount Vernon, Washington's Home and the Nation's Shrine*. Indianapolis, IN: Bobbs-Merrill, 1930.

326. Wineberger, James A. *The Tomb of Washington at Mount Vernon, Embracing a Full and Accurate Description of Mount Vernon as Well as of the Birthplace, Genealogy, Character, Marriage, and Last Illness of Washington...*. Washington, DC: T. McGill, 1858.

Religion

327. Barnes, Lemuel C. "George Washington and Freedom of Conscience." *Journal of Religion* 12 (October 1932): 493-526.

328. Boller, Paul F., Jr. *George Washington and Religion*. Dallas, TX: Southern Methodist University Press, 1963.

329. Buffington, Joseph. *An Overlooked Side of George Washington, Being a Bicentennial Address Made on Washington's Birthday, 1932, at Valley Forge Washington Memorial Chapel*. Philadelphia: International Printing Co., 1932.

330. Buffington, Joseph. *The Soul of George Washington: An Overlooked Side of His Character*. Philadelphia: Dorrance, 1936.

331. Camp, Norma C. *George Washington: Man of Courage and Prayer*. Milford, MI: Mott Media, 1977.

332. Davis, Edwin S. "The Religion of George Washington: A Bicentennial Report." *Air University Review* 27 (July/August 1976): 30-34.

333. Demarest, William H. "George Washington's Religion." *Huguenot* 2 (1932): 1, 12.

334. Fairfield, Louis W. "George Washington." *Lutheran Quarterly* 48 (April 1918): 202-209.

335. Fitzpatrick, John C. "George Washington and Religion." *Catholic Historical Review* 9 (April 1929): 23-42.

336. Fortenbaugh, Robert. "George Washington: Doer of the Word." *Lutheran Church Quarterly* 5 (April 1932): 109-126.

337. Griffin, Martin I. J. "George Washington's Relation to Masonry." *American Catholic Historical Researches* 5 (January 1909): 32-38.

338. Harris, Carlton D. "Was Washington a Christian or Profane, Irreligious, and Worldly-Minded?" *Minute Man* 21 (June 1926): 83-87.

339. Hayden, Sidney. *Washington and His Masonic Compeers*. 6th ed. New York:

Masonic Publishing and Manufacturing Co., 1867.

340. Johnstone, William J. *George Washington, The Christian.* New York: Abingdon Press, 1929.

341. Johnstone, William J. *How Washington Prayed.* New York: Abingdon Press, 1932.

342. Lamberton, James M. *Washington as a Freemason.* Philadelphia: Lippincott, 1902.

343. Lanier, John J. *Washington, The Great American Mason.* New York: Macoy Publishing and Masonic Supply Co., 1922.

344. McComas, Joseph P. "Washington — The Churchman in New York." *Huguenot* 2 (1932): 4, 9, 12.

345. McGuire, Edward C. *The Religious Opinions and Character of Washington.* New York: Harper and Brothers, 1836.

346. Nash, J. V. "The Religion and Philosophy of Washington." *Open Court* 46 (February 1932): 73-92.

347. Norton, John N. *Life of General Washington.* New York: General Protestant Episcopal Seminary School Union and Church Book Society, 1860.

348. Nuesse, George C. *George Washington and Masonry.* Freemasons, WI: Grand Lodge Committee on Masonic Research, 1930.

349. Oldham, G. Ashton. "Washington, Christian Statesman." *Homiletic Review* 95 (February 1928): 144-146.

350. O'Neill, Scannell. "A Forgotten Washington." *American Catholic Historical Society of Philadelphia Record* 36 (June 1925): 202-204.

351. Roberts, Allen E. G. *Washington: Master Mason.* Richmond, VA: Macoy Publishing and Masonic Supply Co., 1976.

352. Sydnor, William. "George Washington's Connection with Christ Church, Alexandria, Virginia." *Historical Magazine of the Protestant Episcopal Church* 45 (June 1976): 110-111.

353. Tatsch, Jacob H. *The Facts about George Washington as a Freemason.* 3d ed. New York: Macoy Publishing and Masonic Supply Co., 1932.

354. Taylor, Malcolm. "Washington as a Christian." *Magazine of History* 22 (March 1916): 88-93.

355. Vernon, Merle. *Washington: The Soldier and the Christian.* Boston: American Tract Society, 1862.

356. *Washington as Religious Man.* Washington, DC: George Washington Bicentennial Commission, 1931.

357. "Washington's Religious Beliefs." *Pennsylvania Magazine of History* 52 (July 1928): 282-287.

358. Wyatt, Euphemia V. R. "The Making of George Washington." *Catholic World* 134 (February 1932): 514-520.

359. Wylie, Theodore W. J. *Washington a Christian: A Discourse Preached February 23, 1862, in the First Reformed Presbyterian Church, Philadelphia, by the Pastor.* Philadelphia: W. S. and A. Martien, 1862.

360. Yates, John H. "The Steadfastness of Washington." *American Church Monthly* 13 (February 1923): 457-465.

Tributes

361. Berens, John F. " 'Like a Prophetic Spirit': Samuel Davies, American Eulogists, and the Deification of George Washington." *Quarterly Journal of Speech* 63 (October 1977): 290-297.

362. Bowen, Clarence W., ed. *The History of the Centennial Celebration of the*

Inauguration of George Washington as First President of the United States. New York: Appleton, 1892.

363. Burke, W. J. "The Washington Centennial in New York City." *New York Public Library Bulletin* 36 (June 1932): 407-413.

364. Carroll, Bishop J. *A Discourse on General Washington.* Edited by Peter Guilday. New York: P. J. Kennedy and Sons, 1931.

365. Cavanagh, Catherine F. "Where Washington Is Immortalized." *New Age* (August 1907): 183-191.

366. Chinard, Gilbert, ed. *George Washington as the French Knew Him: A Collection of Texts.* Princeton, NJ: Princeton University Press, 1940.

367. Daniel, John W. "Washington." In his *Speeches and Orations. . . .* Compiled by Edward M. Daniel, 239-266. Lynchburg, VA: J. P. Bell Co., 1911.

368. Davidson, Bill. *President Kennedy Selects Six Brave Presidents.* New York: Harper and Row, 1962.

369. DeLaBedoyere, Michael. *George Washington: An English Judgement.* London: Harrap, 1935.

370. Doty, Margaret De F. "Glorifying George." *Forum* 87 (June 1932): 345-348.

371. *Entertaining Anecdotes of Washington: Exhibiting His Patriotism and Courage, Benevolence and Piety: With Other Excellent Traits of Character. . . .* Boston: Carter, Hendec and Co., 1833.

372. Fess, Simeon D. "The George Washington Bicentennial." *Constitutional Review* 12 (July 1928): 128-132.

373. Fess, Simeon D. "200th Anniversary Celebration of the Birth of George Washington — And Why." *Daughters of the American Revolution Magazine* 64 (January 1930): 27-29.

374. Fox, Dixon R. "The National Hero." *New York History* 14 (January 1933): 21-31.

375. Galbreath, C. B. "Bicentennial Celebration — George Washington's Voyage on the Ohio River in 1770." *Ohio Archaeological and Historical Quarterly* 42 (January 1933): 3-56.

376. Garraghan, Gilbert J. "George Washington, Man of Character." *Mid-America* 17 (January 1935): 37-59.

377. Greene, L. LeRoy. "The Spirit of Washington." *Magazine of History* 18 (February 1914): 91-98.

378. Guedalla, Philip. "General George Washington, In Tradition and in Fact." *Harper's* 150 (January 1924): 98-106.

379. Hay, Robert P. "George Washington: American Moses." *American Quarterly* 21 (Winter 1969): 780-791.

380. Hillis, Newell D. "George Washington: The Ideal Americanism." In his *All the Year Round: An Outlook upon Its Great Days,* 56-76. New York: Revell, 1912.

381. "How They Did It in 1832, At Washington's Centenary." *Magazine of History* 9 (February 1909): 115-117.

382. Hulbert, Archer B. "The Washington We Forget." *Mississippi Valley Historical Association Proceedings* 4 (1912): 199-212.

383. Knowlton, Daniel C. "The Washington Bi-centennial and the History Classroom: Historical Reconstruction through Still Pictures." *Historical Outlook* 23 (November 1932): 329-335.

384. Lamb, Martha J. R. N. "The Story of the Washington Centennial." *Magazine of American History* 22 (July 1889): 1-36.

385. Larned, Josephus N. "Washington: Impressive in Greatness." In his *A Study of Greatness in Men,* 169-220. Boston:

Houghton Mifflin, 1911.

386. Lewis, Thompson H. *George Washington from 1732 to 1939.* New York: Pyramid, 1940.

387. McGroarty, William B., ed. *Washington: First in the Hearts of His Countrymen: The Orations by Men Who Had Known Washington in Person and Who Thus Could Speak with Authority.* Richmond, VA: Garrett and Massie, 1932.

388. Matthews, Albert. "Celebrations of Washington's Birthday." *Colonial Society of Massachusetts Publications* 10 (1907): 252-258.

389. Matthews, Albert. "Celebrations of Washington's Birthday at Surinam in 1792 and 1799, and by Harvard Students in 1796, 1798, and 1799." *Colonial Society of Massachusetts Publications* 18 (1917): 62-68.

390. Matthews, Albert. "Remarks on a Celebration of Washington's Birthday in 1796 by the Students of Harvard College." *Colonial Society of Massachusetts Publications* 14 (1913): 199-201.

391. Matthews, Albert. "Remarks on an Address to Washington from the Yankee Club of Stewartstown, in the County of Tyrone, and Province of Ulster, Ireland, 1783." *Colonial Society of Massachusetts Publications* 14 (1913): 198-199.

392. Matthews, Albert. "Remarks on the Celebration of Washington's Birthday in 1779." *Colonial Society of Massachusetts Publications* 13 (1912): 96-100.

393. Matthews, Albert. "The Sobriquet Favorite Son." *Colonial Society of Massachusetts Publications* 13 (1912): 100-109.

394. Matthews, Albert. "Some Sobriquets Applied to Washington." *Colonial Society of Massachusetts Publications* 8 (1906): 275-287.

395. Morrow, William W. "Washington, The Great American." *Constitutional Review* 4 (July 1920): 142-153.

396. New York Public Library. *Washington Eulogies: A Checklist of Eulogies and Funeral Orations on the Death of George Washington, December, 1799-February, 1800.* Compiled by Margaret B. Stilwell. New York: n.p., 1916.

397. Nordham, George W. "George Washington: A Remembrance on the 250th Anniversary of His Birth." *Daughters of the American Revolution Magazine* 116 (February 1982): 84-88.

398. Phillips, Charles. "Eulogy of George Washington." *New Jersey Historical Society Proceedings* 14 (January 1929): 127-128.

399. Porter, Frank G. "Washington as Asbury Saw Him: The View of a Contemporary." *Methodist Review* 46 (July 1930): 513-521.

400. Rabinowitz, Howard. "The Washington Legend 1865-1900: The Heroic Image in Flux." *American Studies* 17 (Spring 1976): 5-24.

401. Reynolds, Beatrix, and James Gabelle. *George Washington in the Hearts of His Countrymen: An Anthology.* Ridgewood, NJ: Garen Publishing Co., 1932.

402. Smith, F. DuMont. "A Criticism of the Account of George Washington, Published by the George Washington Bicentennial Commission as Written by Albert B. Hart." *Tyler's Quarterly Historical and Genealogical Magazine* 14 (October 1932): 82-89.

403. Smith, Margaret B. *The First Forty Years of Washington Society Portrayed by the Family Letters of Mrs. Samuel Harrison Smith (Margaret Bayard) from the Collection of Her Grandson J. Henley Smith.* New York: Scribner's, 1906.

404. Thompson, Ray. *Washington at Germantown.* Fort Washington, PA: Bicentennial Press, 1971.

405. Trenton Times. *Washington in Trenton*. Trenton, NJ: Trenton Times Newspapers, 1932.

406. U.S. George Washington Bicentennial Commission. *History of the George Washington Bicentennial Celebration*. 3 vols. Washington, DC: George Washington Bicentennial Commission, 1932.

407. Varin, Rene L. "George Washington: A Tribute from the City of Versailles." *Legion D'Honneur Magazine* 10 (1939): 41-45.

408. Walker, Jenny G. "An English Admiral and an American Shrine." *Daughters of the American Revolution Magazine* 63 (February 1929): 69-76.

409. "Wansey, An English Tourist in America Visits Washington in Philadelphia." *Tennessee Historical Magazine* 2 (April 1932): 205-206.

410. Washington Benevolent Society. *The Text-book of the Washington Benevolent Society: Containing, a Biography and Character of George Washington, His Farewell Address to the People of the United States, and the Federal Constitution, With the Amendments*. Concord: George Hough, 1812.

411. "The Washington Centennial." *Critic* 14 (May 4, 1889): 225-227.

412. "Washington's Birthday, 1781: The First Public Holiday Celebration." *Daughters of the American Revolution Magazine* 55 (February 1921): 66-67.

413. Wise, John S. "Virginia Folklore about George Washington." *Magazine of History* 24 (May 1919): 209-220.

414. Woodson, C. G. "The George Washington Bicentennial." *Journal of Negro History* 17 (January 1932): 103-106.

415. Young, Rowland L. "A Legend and a Man (George Washington)." *American Bar Association Journal* 68 (February 1982): 178-181.

Washingtoniana

416. Adams, Randolph G. "Notes on Portraits of George Washington Owned in Michigan." *Michigan History Magazine* 16 (Summer 1932): 304-308.

417. Albert, Alphaeus H. *Washington Historical Buttons: Washington Inaugural Buttons, and Other Buttons Bearing the Portrait of Washington or Alluding to Him and His Administration*. Highstown, NJ: n.p., 1949.

418. Ashe, Samuel A. "The Williams Portrait of Washington." *North Carolina Historical Review* 7 (January 1930): 148-151.

419. Baird, Hiram K. *George Washington: Two Plays*. Flushing, NY: New Voices, 1977.

420. Baker, William S. *The Engraved Portraits of Washington, With Notices of the Originals and Brief Biographical Sketches of the Painters*. Philadelphia: Lindsay and Baker, 1880.

421. Baker, William S. *Medallic Portraits of Washington, With Historical and Critical Notes and a Description Catalogue of Coins, Medals, Tokens, and Cards*. Philadelphia: R. M. Lindsay, 1885.

422. Barck, Dorothy C. "Proposed Memorials to Washington in New York City, 1802-1847." *New York Historical Society Bulletin* 15 (1931): 79-90.

423. Barck, Dorothy C. "Washingtoniana of the New York Historical Society." *New York Historical Society Bulletin* 15 (1932): 111-149.

424. Barker, E. Eugene. "Washington's Birthplace — A New National Shrine." *Current History* 29 (January 1929): 544-547.

425. Beatty, Albert R. "The Personal Swords of George Washington." *Antiquarian* 16 (February 1931): 34-35, 54, 56.

426. Berkley, Henry J. "The Edris and Virginia Berkley Memorial Collection of Washington Prints." *Maryland Historical Magazine* 14 (September 1919): 205-258.

427. Blake, W. B. "A Collection of Washingtoniana." *Independent* 70 (February 23, 1911): 395-397.

428. Bolton, Theodore, and Harry L. Binsse. "The Peale Portraits of Washington: The First Classification of the Many Portraits of the First President Executed by Three Members of the Peale Family." *Antiquarian* 16 (February 1931): 24-27, 58, 60, 62, 64.

429. Bryan, William A. *George Washington in American Literature, 1775-1865.* New York: Columbia University Press, 1952.

430. Calver, William L. "Washington Inaugural Buttons." *New York Historical Quarterly Bulletin* 9 (January 1926): 124-126.

431. Cummin, Hazel E. "A Young Frenchman's Portrait of Washington." *Antiques* 14 (November 1928): 437.

432. Cunliffe, Marcus. *George Washington: Man and Monument.* 2d ed. Washington, DC: Washington National Monument, 1973.

433. Cunliffe, Marcus. "Symbols We Made of a Man Named George Washington." *Smithsonian* 12 (Feburary 1982): 74-81.

434. Detweiler, Susan. *George Washington's Chinaware.* New York: Abrams, 1982.

435. Dorsey, Marian V. "The Washington Bust in the Monument: Is It a Canova or a Ceracchi?" *Patriotic Marylander* 2 (June 1916): 39-43.

436. Eisen, Gustavus A. *Portraits of Washington by Gustavus A. Eisen.* 3 vols. New York: R. Hamilton and Associates, 1932.

437. Eisen, Gustavus A., and Wilford S. Conrow. "The Leutze-Stellwagen Mask of Washington in the Corcoran Gallery of Art and Its Connections." *Art and Archaeology* 29 (February 1930): 65-74.

438. Ellesin, Dorothy E. "George Washington in Madrid." *Antiques* 109 (February 1976): 370-371.

439. Esterow, Milton. "Who Painted the George Washington Portrait in the White House?" *Art News* 74 (February 1975): 24-28.

440. "Famous Washington Portrait: Presented to This Society, March 21, 1892, by Descendants of Martha Ann Procter Nichols." *Historical Collections of the Danvers Historical Society* 2 (1914): 36-37, 86-87.

441. Fielding, Mantle. "Edward Savage's Portraits of Washington." *Pennsylvania Magazine of History* 48 (July 1924): 193-200.

442. Fielding, Mantle. *Gilbert Stuart's Portraits of George Washington.* Philadelphia: Privately Printed, 1923.

443. FitzPatrick, Benedict. "Heirs and Heirlooms of Washington." *Americana* 6 (April 1911): 331-335.

444. Garland, Claude M. *Washington and His Portraits.* Chicago: Guilford Press, 1931.

445. Greenwood, Isaac J. "Remarks on the Portraiture of Washington." *Magazine of American History* 2 (1878): 30-38.

446. Griffin, Appleton P. C. *A Catalogue of the Washington Collection in the Boston Atheneaum.* Cambridge, MA: Boston Athenaeum, 1897.

447. Hallam, John S. "Houdon's 'Washington' in Richmond: Some New Observations." *American Art Journal* 10 (November 1978): 72-80.

448. Haraszti, Zoltan. "A Notable Be-

quest of Washingtoniana." *More Books* 6 (1931): 49-57.

449. Haraszti, Zoltan. "Washington Bicentennial Exhibit." *More Books* 7 (1932): 79-97.

450. Hart, Charles H. *Catalogue of the Engraved Portraits of Washington.* New York: Grolier Club, 1904.

451. Hart, Charles H. *An Etched Profile Portrait of Washington by Joseph Hiller, 1794.* Salem, MA: Essex Institute, 1907.

452. Hart, Charles H. "Original Portraits of Washington." *Century Magazine* 37 (April 1889): 860-865.

453. Hart, Charles H. "Stuart's Lansdowne Portrait of Washington." *Harper's New Monthly Magazine* 93 (August 1896): 378-386.

454. Hochfield, Sylvia. "White House Washington Portrait: Did Gilbert Stuart Tell a Lie?" *Art News* 81 (January 1982): 61.

455. Holzer, Harold. "Lincoln and Washington: The Printmakers Blessed Their Union." *Kentucky Historical Society Register* 75 (July 1977): 202-213.

456. Holzer, Harold. "Memorial Prints of Washington and Lincoln." *Antiques* 115 (February 1979): 352-356.

457. Howes, Raymond. "Universities Bearing Washington's Name." *Daughters of the American Revolution Magazine* 66 (November 1932): 713-720.

458. Hubard, William J. "A National Standard for the Likeness of Washington." *Magazine of American History* 4 (February 1880): 83-108.

459. Hudson, J. Paul. *George Washington Birthplace National Monument, Virginia.* Washington, DC: U.S. National Park Service, 1956.

460. Jackson, Mrs. F. Nevill. "Contemporary Silhouette Portraits of George Washington." *Connoisseur* 89 (January 1932): 27-34, 108.

461. Johnston, Elizabeth B. *Original Portraits of Washington.* Boston: J. R. Osgood and Co., 1882.

462. Jones, E. Alfred. "A Lost Bust of George Washington." *Art in America* 10 (December 1921): 38.

463. Kittredge, George L. "An Irish Song Relating to Washington." *Colonial Society of Massachusetts Publications* 13 (February 1911): 254-259.

464. Klaber, John J. "On a Certain Bust of Washington." *Art and Archaeology* 7 (March 1918): 145-147.

465. Klapthor, Margaret B., and Howard Morrison. *Washington: A Figure upon the Stage.* New York: Smithsonian, 1982.

466. Knight, Franklin, ed. *Monuments of Washington's Patriotism: Containing a Fascimile of His Public Accounts, Kept During the Revolutionary War.* Washington, DC: Trustees of Washington's Manual Labor School and Male Asylum, 1841.

467. Knox, Katherine M. *The Sharples, Their Portraits of George Washington and His Contemporaries: A Diary and an Account of the Life and Work of James Shaples and His Family in England and America.* New Haven: Yale University Press, 1930.

468. Knox, Katherine M. "Washington and His Associates: An Exhibition of Portraits." *American Magazine of Art* 24 (June 1932): 399-408.

469. Landis, C. I. "Some Oldtime Lancaster Portraits of Washington." *Lancaster County Historical Society Papers* 21 (February 1917): 29-34.

470. Lincoln, Natalie S. "Selecting an 'Official' Washington Picture." *Daughters of the American Revolution Magazine* 64 (September 1930): 556-559.

471. Lincoln, Natalie S. "Washington and Custis Heirlooms." *Daughters of the American Revolution Magazine* 52 (February 1918): 67-72.

472. McRae, Sherwin. *Washington: His Person as Represented by the Artist: The Houdon Statue, Its History and Value.* Richmond: R. F. Walker, 1873.

473. Matthews, Albert. "An Early Washington Medal, 1778." *Colonial Society of Massachusetts Publications* 12 (1911): 253-354.

474. Mead, Edwin D. "Recent Washington Literature in England." *Massachusetts Historical Society Proceedings* 61 (October 1927-June 1928): 42-55.

475. Meredith, Wyndham R. "Presentation of a Bronze Bust of George Washington by the Society of the Cincinnati of the State of Virginia, To the College of William and Mary." *William and Mary Quarterly* 12 (October 1932): 260-264.

476. Mitchell, James T. *Collection of Engraved Portraits of Washington Belonging to James T. Mitchell: Catalogue Compiled and Sale Conducted by Stan V. Henkels at the Art Auction Rooms of Davis and Harvey.* Philadelphia: Press of W. F. Fell Co., 1906.

477. Moore, R. Walton. "General Washington and Houdon." *Virginia Magazine of History* 41 (January 1933): 1-10.

478. Morgan, John H. "The Ramage Miniatures of George Washington." *New York Historical Society Bulletin* 20 (1936): 95-104.

479. Morgan, John H., and Mantle Fielding. *The Life Portraits of Washington and Their Replicas.* Lancaster, PA: Lancaster Press, 1931.

480. Morton, Jennie C. "The Washington Portrait Unveiled." *Kentucky Historical Society Register* 13 (May 1915): 7-36.

481. Mott, Francis J. "Thoughts before Washington's Tomb." *Landmark* 10 (February 1928): 78-80.

482. Munn, Charles A. "Growth of Interest in Washington Portraits." *American Magazine of Art* 10 (June 1919): 279-286.

483. Mussey, Virginia T. H. *The Exploits of George Washington.* New York: Harper, 1933.

484. Nordham, George W. *George Washington: Vignettes and Memorabilia.* Philadelphia: Dorrance, 1977.

485. Pape, T. "The Washington Coat of Arms." *Connoisseur* 89 (February 1932): 100-107.

486. Pape, T. "The Washington Family and Memorials in Yorkshire, England." *Daughters of the American Revolution Magazine* 46 (February 1915): 71-76.

487. Pape, T. "Washington's Arms and 'Old Glory.'" *Connoisseur* 89 (March 1932): 179-182.

488. Payne, Frank O. "New York's Memorials of Washington." *Munsey's* 57 (February 1916): 51-66.

489. Peale, Rembrandt. "Washington Portraits: Letters of Rembrandt Peale." *Magazine of American History* 5 (August 1980): 129-134.

490. Putnam, Tarrant. "Archibald Robertson's Portrait of Washington." *New York Genealogical and Biographical Record* 51 (October 1920): 345-346.

491. Randolph, Howard S. F. "The Portrait of George Washington by Joseph Wright." *New York Genealogical and Biographical Record* 63 (1932): 109-111.

492. Robinson, Fred N. "A Second Song by Thomas O'Meehan Relating to Washington." *Colonial Society of Massachusetts Publications* 18 (February 1916): 201-206.

493. Runk, Edward J. *Washington, A*

National Epic in Six Cantos. New York: Putnam, 1897.

494. Sawitzky, William. "An Alleged Drawing of Washington from Life." *Art in America* 22 (December 1933): 20-25.

495. Shelton, William H. "A New Portrait of Washington at Forty-four." *International Studio* 71 (September 1920): 47-48.

496. Sherman, Frederic F. "Gilbert Stuart's Portraits of George Washington." *Art in America* 18 (October 1930): 261-270.

497. Sherman, Frederic F. "The Portraits of Washington from Life." *Art in America* 18 (April 1930): 150-162.

498. Smyth, Mary W. "Contemporary Songs and Verses about Washington." *New England Quarterly* 5 (April 1932): 281-292.

499. Sognnaes, Reodar F. "America's Most Famous Teeth." *Smithsonian* 3 (February 1973): 47-51.

500. Storer, Malcolm. "The Manly Washington Medal." *Massachusetts Historical Society Proceedings* 52 (November 1918): 6-7.

501. Thistlethwaite, Mark E. "The Image of George Washington: Studies in Mid-Nineteenth-Century American History Painting." Ph.D. dissertation, University of Pennsylvania, 1977.

502. Thorpe, Russell W. "Washingtoniana." *Antiquarian* 8 (June 1927): 27-30; 9 (October 1927): 45-48; (November 1927): 50-51.

503. Tuckerman, Frederick. "Stuart's Portraits of Washington." *Nation* 108 (May 24, 1919): 836.

504. Tuckerman, Henry T. *The Character and Portraits of Washington.* New York: Putnam, 1859.

505. Walter, James. *Memorials of Washington and of Mary, His Mother, and Martha, His Wife.* New York: Scribner's, 1887.

506. Washington, W. Lanier. *Historical Relics of George Washington, Inherited and Collected by Mr. William Lanier Washington.* New York: Redfiel-Kendrick-Odell, 1917.

507. Washington, W. Lanier. *William Lanier Washington's Collection of Relics and Memorabilia of George Washington.* New York: n.p., 1920.

508. *Washingtoniana: A Collection of Papers Relative to the Death and Character of General George Washington, With a Correct Copy of His ... Last Legacy to the People of America....* Petersburg, VA: Blandford Press, 1800.

509. Whelen, Henry, Jr. *The Important Collection of Engraved Portraits of Washington.* Philadelphia: Samuel T. Freeman and Co., 1909.

510. Whittemore, Frances D. *George Washington in Sculpture.* Boston: Marshall Jones, 1933.

511. Wick, Wendy C. *George Washington, An American Icon: The Eighteenth-Century Graphic Portraits.* Charlottesville: University Press of Virginia, 1982.

512. Wolkins, George G. "Two Washington Miniatures." *Massachusetts Historical Society Proceedings* 62 (June 1929): 199-208.

513. Yoder, Edwin M. "George Washington in 19th Century Popular Art." *American History Illustrated* 15 (August 1980): 35-39.

The West

514. Ambler, Charles H. *George Washington and the West.* Chapel Hill: University of North Carolina Press, 1936.

515. Catlin, George B. "George Washington Looks Westward." *Michigan History Magazine* 16 (Spring 1932): 127-142.

516. Cleland, Hugh. *George Washington in the Ohio Valley.* Pittsburgh, PA: University of Pittsburgh Press, 1955.

517. Coleman, Christopher B. "George Washington and the West." *Indiana Magazine of History* 28 (September 1931): 151-167.

518. Colket, Meredith B., Jr. "George Washington and His Vision of the West." *Daughters of the American Revolution Magazine* 109 (May 1975): 406-411, 423.

519. Cook, Roy B. *Washington's Western Lands.* Strasburg, VA: Shenandoah Publishing House, 1930.

520. Davis, John W. "Washington and the Patowmack Company." *Daughters of the American Revolution Magazine* 63 (October 1929): 601-609.

521. Evans, Nelson W. "A Debt Repudiated, The United States' Obligation to General Washington through His Ohio Land Grants." *Ohio Magazine* 2 (February 1907): 111-117.

522. Evans, Nelson W. "The Washington Claim before Congress in the Light of the Report of the Committee on Private Land Claims of the 61st Congress." *Old Northwest Genealogical Quarterly* 14 (January 1911): 28-33.

523. Galbreath, C. B. "George Washington's Interest in the Ohio Country." *Ohio Archaeological and Historical Quarterly* 41 (January 1932): 20-27.

524. "General Washington as a Land Locator and Dealer." *Old Northwest Genealogical Quarterly* 14 (January 1911): 24-27.

525. Goode, Cecil E. "Gilbert Simpson: Washington's Partner in Settling His Western Pennsylvania Lands." *Western Pennsylvania Historical Magazine* 62 (April 1979): 149-166.

526. Haworth, Paul L. "Washington and the West." *Indiana History Bulletin* 10 (March 1933): 434-452.

527. Hixon, Ada H. "George Washington Land Speculator." *Illinois State Historical Society Journal* 11 (January 1919): 566-575.

528. Jillson, Willard R. *George Washington: Landowner.* Louisville, KY: Standard Print Co., 1932.

529. Jillson, Willard R. "George Washington's Western Kentucky Lands." *Kentucky Historical Society Register* 29 (October 1931): 379-384.

530. Jillson, Willard R. *The Land Adventures of George Washington.* Louisville, KY: Standard Print Co., 1934.

531. Phillips, P. Lee. "Washington as Surveyor and Map-Maker." *Daughters of the American Revolution Magazine* 55 (March 1921): 115-132.

532. Showalter, William J. *The Travels of George Washington: Dramatic Episodes in His Career as the First Geographer of the United States.* Washington, DC: National Geographic Society, 1932.

533. Sindlinger, Edmond S. "Washington and the Ohio in 1770, As Seen by a Voyager in 1932." *Ohio Archaeological and Historical Quarterly* 42 (January 1933): 57-71.

534. Smith, Guy-Harold. "George Washington at the Great Bend of the Ohio River." *Ohio Archaeological and Historical Quarterly* 41 (October 1932): 655-667.

535. Smith, Guy-Harold. "Washington's Camp Sites on the Ohio River." *Ohio Archaeological and Historical Quarterly* 41 (January 1932): 1-19.

536. Tebbel, John W. *George Washington's America.* New York: Dutton, 1954.

Youth

537. Barton, William E. *The Father of His Country: How the Boy Washington Grew in Stature and Spirit and Became a Great Soldier and President.* Indianapolis, IN: Bobbs-Merrill, 1928.

538. "Even George Washington Was Once a Child." *Library of Congress Information Bulletin* 35 (September 24, 1976): 583-585.

539. Freeman, Douglas S. *Young Washington: A Selection from George Washington, A Biography.* New York: Scribner's, 1966.

540. Hill, Frederick T. *On The Trail of Washington: A Narrative History of Washington's Boyhood and Manhood, Based on His Own Writings, Authentic Documents, and Other Authoritative Information.* New York: Appleton, 1923.

541. Hill, Frederick T. "On the Trail of Washington: Some New Light on the Personality of Our First President." *Metropolitan* 31 (February 1910): 635-643; (March 1910): 807-814.

542. Hodges, George. *The Apprenticeship of Washington and Other Sketches of Significant Colonial Personages.* New York: Moffat, 1909.

543. Hoppin, Charles A. "The Three Homes of Washington's Boyhood." *Tyler's Quarterly of Historical and Genealogical Magazine* 12 (January 1931): 149-152.

544. Isely, Bliss. *The Horseman of the Shenandoah: A Biographical Account of the Early Days of George Washington.* Milwaukee, WI: Bruce Publishing Co., 1962.

545. Mitchell, S. Weir. *The Youth of Washington Told in the Form of an Autobiography.* New York: Century, 1904.

546. Moore, Charles. "George Washington's Boyhood." *Daughters of the American Revolution Magazine* 56 (November 1922): 637-646.

547. Morison, Samuel E. *The Young Man Washington.* Cambridge, MA: Harvard University Press, 1932.

548. Murphy, Mable A. *When Washington Was Young.* Chicago: Laidlaw Brothers, 1931.

549. Myers, Albert C. *The Boy Washington, Aged 16: His Own Account of an Iroquois Indian Dance, 1748.* Philadelphia: A. C. Myers, 1932.

550. Pickell, John. *A New Chapter in the Early Life of Washington in Connection with the Narrative History of the Potomac Co.* New York: Franklin, 1970.

551. Picknell, John. *The Early Life of Washington.* Providence, RI: Knowles, Vose, 1838.

552. Stevenson, Augusta. *George Washington, Boy Leader.* Indianapolis, IN: Bobbs-Merrill, 1959.

553. Thompson, George L. *Young George Washington.* Boston: Beacon Press, 1932.

Public Career

General

554. Baker, William S. *Washington after the Revolution, 1784-1799.* Philadelphia: Lippincott, 1898.

555. Baldridge, H. A. "Washington's Visits to Colonial Annapolis." *U.S. Naval Institute Proceedings* 54 (February 18, 1928): 90-104.

556. Barton, George. "When Washington Refused a Crown." *America* 38 (February 1928): 456-457.

557. Beck, James M. "The Political Philosophy of George Washington." *Constitutional Review* 13 (April 1929): 61-74.

558. Beck, James M. "Washington's Supreme Achievement." *Constitutional Review* 3 (July 1919): 131-145.

559. Boucher, Jonathan. *Letters of Jonathan Boucher to George Washington.* Brooklyn, NY: Historical Printing Club, 1899.

560. Boyd, Thomas M. "Death of a Hero, Death of a Friend: George Washington's Last Hours." *Virginia Cavalcade* 33 (Winter 1984): 136-143.

561. Cammerer, H. Paul. "The Sesquicentennial of the Laying of the Cornerstone of the United States Capitol by George Washington." *Columbia Historical Society Records* 44/45 (1944): 161-189.

562. Campbell, Janet. "The First Americans' Tribute to the First President." *Chronicles of Oklahoma* 57 (Summer 1979): 190-195.

563. Christensen, Lois E. "Washington's Experience and the Creation of the Presidency." Ph.D. dissertation, University of Nebraska, 1957.

564. Dauer, Manning J. "The Two John Nicholases: Their Relationship to Washington and Jefferson." *American Historical Review* 45 (January 1940): 338-354.

565. Dutcher, George M. *George Washington and Connecticut in War and Peace.* New Haven, CT: Yale University Press, 1933.

566. Eliot, Charles W. *Four American Leaders, Franklin, Washington, Channing, Emerson.* Boston: Beacon Press, 1906.

567. Ellis, Ivan C. "A Study of the Influence of Alexander Hamilton on George Washington." Ph.D. dissertation, University of Southern California, 1957.

568. Engelman, Rose C. "Washington and Hamilton: A Study in the Development of Washington's Political Ideas." Ph.D. dissertation, Cornell University, 1947.

569. Farnell, Robert S. "Positive Valuations of Politics and Government in the Thought of Five American Founding Fathers: Thomas Jefferson, John Adams, James Madison, Alexander Hamilton, and George Washington." Ph.D. dissertation, Cornell University, 1970.

570. Farrand, Max. "George Washington in the Federal Convention." *Yale Review* 16 (November 1907): 280-287.

571. Fisher, N. "Letter Describing Washington's Visit to Salem in 1789." *Essex Institute of Historical Collections* 67 (July 1931): 299-300.

572. Flick, Alexander C. "Washington's Relations to New York State." *New York History* 13 (April 1932): 115-128.

573. Ford, Henry J. *Washington and His Colleagues.* New Haven, CT: Yale University Press, 1921.

574. Hamilton, Stanislaus M., ed. *Letters to Washington and Accompanying Papers.* 5 vols. Boston: Houghton Mifflin, 1898-1902.

575. Hemphill, W. Edwin. "Virginia to George Washington, Debtor: His Income as a Delegate to the Federal Convention." *Virginia Cavalcade* 1 (Winter 1951): 42-43.

576. Holcombe, Arthur N. "The Role of Washington in the Framing of the Constitution." *Huntington Library Quarterly* 19 (August 1956): 317-334.

577. Howard, John R., comp. . . . *Patriotic Nuggets: Franklin, Washington, Jefferson, Webster, Lincoln, Beecher.* New York: Fords, Howard, Hulbert, 1899.

578. Jackson, Joseph. "Washington in Philadelphia." *Pennsylvania Magazine of History* 56 (1932): 110-155.

579. Jenkins, Charles F. *Washington in Germantown.* Philadelphia: W. J. Campbell, 1905.

580. Jusserand, Jean A. "Washington and the French." In his *With Americans of Past and Present Days,* 199-274. New York: Scribner's, 1916.

581. Kozlowski, Wladyslaw M. . . . *Washington and Kosciuszko.* Chicago: Polish R. C. Union of America, 1942.

582. Krout, John A. "Washington's Contribution to the Constitution." *Outlook* 145 (February 9, 1927): 173-174.

583. Lear, Tobias. "President Washington in New York, 1789." *Pennsylvania Magazine of History and Biography* 32 (October 1908): 498-500.

584. Leduc, Gilbert F. *Washington and "The Murder of Jumonville."* Boston: La Societe Historique Franco-Americaine, 1943.

585. Matteson, David M. *Washington and the Constitution.* Washington, DC: George Washington Bicentennial Commission, 1931.

586. Matthews, Albert. "Paper on Harvard College and Washington, 1800." *Colonial Society of Massachusetts Publications* 13 (1912): 134-139.

587. Mayo, Bernard. *Myths and Men: Patrick Henry, George Washington, Thomas Jefferson.* Athens: University of Georgia Press, 1959.

588. Mazyck, Walter H. *George Washington and the Negro.* Washington, DC: Associated Publishers, 1932.

589. Mintz, Max M. "Horatio Gates, George Washington's Rival." *History Today* 26 (July 1976): 419-428.

590. Monroe, Sarah. "A Young Lady's Sprightly Account of Washington's Visit to Lexington in 1789." *Journal of American History* 11 (January 1917): 44-65.

591. Montaque, Mary L. *John Witherspoon, Signer of the Declaration of Independence, George Washington's Close Friend and Sponsor.* Washington, DC: H. L. and J. B. McQueen, 1932.

592. Moore, Charles. "Washington in the House of Burgesses." *Daughters of the American Revolution Magazine* 57 (March 1923): 142-149.

593. Morgan, Edmund S. *The Meaning of Independence: John Adams, George Washington, Thomas Jefferson.* Charlottesville: University Press of Virginia, 1976.

594. Morris, Richard B. "Washington and Hamilton: A Great Collaboration." *American Philosophical Society Proceedings* 102 (April 1958): 107-116.

595. Nettels, Curtis P. *George Washington and American Independence.* Boston: Little, Brown, 1951.

596. Nolan, James B. *George Washington and the Town of Reading in Pennsylvania.* Reading, PA: Chamber of Commerce of Reading, 1931.

597. Page, Elwin L. *George Washington in New Hampshire.* Boston: Houghton Mifflin, 1932.

598. Pearson, Charles W. "Washington." In his *Literary and Biographical Essays,* 225-241. Boston: Sherman, French, 1908.

599. Powell, E. P. "What Do We Want of Washington?" *Independent* 70 (March 2, 1911): 463-466.

600. Preston, Howard W. *Washington's Visits to Rhode Island, Gathered from Contemporary Accounts.* Providence, RI: Oxford Press, 1932.

601. Price, Kate H. "Washington and the Heyward House." *Stone and Webster Journal* 46 (May 1930): 651-663.

602. Radziwill, Catherine. "Washington and Lafayette: Contemporary Letters Throw Fresh Light on Two Great Men."

Century Magazine 112 (July 1926): 271-278.

603. Randall, E. O. "Washington and Ohio." *Ohio Archaeological and Historical Society Publications* 16 (October 1907): 477-501.

604. Shively, Frances C. "George Washington and Henry Lee." *Daughters of the American Revolution Magazine* 111 (May 1977): 467-471, 574.

605. Siebert, Wilbur H. *General Washington and the Loyalists*. Worcester, MA: The Society, 1934.

606. Sloane, William M. "Von Moltke's View of Washington's Strategy." *Century Magazine* 73 (February 1907): 517-524.

607. Smith, F. DuMont. *Washington and the Constitution*. Chicago: American Bar Association, 1931.

608. Sparks, Jared, ed. *Correspondence of the American Revolution: Being Letters of Eminent Men to George Washington, From the Time of His Taking Command of the Army to the End of His Presidency*. 4 vols. Boston: Little, Brown, 1853.

609. Steele, Thomas J. "The Figure of Columbia: Phillis Wheatly Plus George Washington." *New England Quarterly* 54 (June 1981): 264-266.

610. Stegeman, John, and Janet Stegeman. "President Washington at Mulberry Grove." *Georgia Historical Quarterly* 61 (Winter 1977): 342-346.

611. Stein, Nathaniel E. "George Washington, P. R. Man." *Manuscripts* 28 (Summer 1976): 225-228.

612. Stevens, Maud L. "Washington and Newport." *Newport Historical Society Bulletin* 84 (1932): 2-20.

613. Trent, William P. *Southern Statesmen of the Old Regime: Washington, Jefferson, Randolph, Calhoun, Stephens, Toombs, and Jefferson Davis*. New York: Crowell, 1897.

614. Trotter, Reginald G. "George Washington and the English-Speaking Heritage." *Queen's Quarterly* 29 (Autumn 1932): 297-306.

615. Vaught, Edgar S. "The Father of His Country." *Oklahoma State Bar Journal* 3 (1933): 276-281.

616. Washington, W. Lanier. "George Washington and a League of Nations." *Landmark* 2 (February 1920): 89-93.

617. Washington, W. Lanier. "George Washington's Ideals: Revealed in an Unpublished Letter." *Forum* 61 (February 1919): 129-141.

618. Wills, Garry. *Cincinnatus: George Washington and the Enlightenment*. Garden City, NY: Doubleday, 1984.

619. Wills, Garry. "Washington's Citizen Virtue: Greenough and Houdon." *Critical Inquiry* 10 (March 1984): 420-441.

Revolution

620. Alexander, Holmes. *Washington and Lee: A Study in the Will to Win*. Belmont, MA: Western Islands, 1966.

621. Alter, N. B. "Washington in the Mohawk Valley." *New York History* 13 (April 1932): 142-145.

622. Baker, William S. *Itinerary of General Washington from June 15, 1775, to December 23, 1783*. Philadelphia: Lippincott, 1892.

623. Beattie, Donald W., and J. Richard Collins. *Washington's New England Fleet: Beverly's Role in Its Origins, 1775-1777*. Salem, MA: Newcomb and Gauss, 1957.

624. Billias, George A., ed. *George Washington's Opponents: British Generals and Admirals of the American Revolution*. New York: Morrow, 1969.

625. Burnet, Whittier. "George Washington under Fire." *Ohio Educational Monthly* 68 (February 1919): 50-52.

626. Busch, Noel F. *Winter Quarters: George Washington and the Continental Army at Valley Forge.* New York: New American Library, 1975.

627. Canfield, Cass. *Samuel Adams's Revolution, 1765-1776: With the Assistance of George Washington, Thomas Jefferson, Benjamin Franklin, John Adams, George III, and the People of Boston.* New York: Harper and Row, 1976.

628. Childs, Catherine M. "Virginia Patriarch: George Washington and His Aides." *Daughters of the American Revolution Magazine* 114 (April 1980): 446-449.

629. Clark, William B. *George Washington's Navy.* Baton Rouge: Louisiana State University Press, 1960.

630. Davis, Burke. *George Washington and the American Revolution.* New York: Random House, 1975.

631. Fish, Hamilton. *George Washington in the Highlands, Or Some Unwritten History.* Newburgh, NY: Newburgh News, 1932.

632. Flexner, James T. "The Miraculous Care of Providence: George Washington's Narrow Escapes." *American Heritage* 33 (February 1982): 82-85.

633. Fox, Dixon R. "Washington at Temple Hill." *New York History* 13 (July 1932): 284-291.

634. Gott, Joseph W. "Washington in Orange County." *New York History* 13 (April 1932): 146-153.

635. Hadden, John. "Washington's First Commission, Victory and Defeat: How a Virginia Hunter and Trapper Saved the Life of Washington." *Pennsylvania German* 10 (February 1909): 49-53.

636. Headley, Joel T. *Washington and His Generals.* 2 vols. New York: Scribner's, 1853.

637. Hutton, Ann H. *George Washington Crossed Here, Christmas Night, 1776.* Philadelphia: Dorrance, 1948.

638. Ives, Mabel L. *Washington's Headquarters.* Upper Montclair, NJ: Lucy Fortune, 1932.

639. Jackson, Donald. *George Washington and the War of Independence.* Williamsburg, VA: Virginia Independence Bicentennial Commission, 1976.

640. Kite, Elizabeth S. "General Washington and the French Engineer: Duportail and Companions." *American Catholic Historical Society Records* 43 (March 1932): 1-33; (June 1932): 97-141; (September 1932): 193-219; (December 1932): 289-319.

641. Knollenberg, Bernhard. "John Adams, Knox, and Washington." *American Antiquarian Society Proceedings* 56 (October 1946): 207-238.

642. Knollenberg, Bernhard. *Washington and the Revolution, A Reappraisal: Gates, Conway, and the Continental Congress.* New York: Macmillan, 1940.

643. Knox, Dudley W. *The Naval Genius of George Washington.* Boston: Houghton Mifflin, 1932.

644. Knox, Dudley W. "Washington Views Naval Preparedness." *U.S. Naval Institute Proceedings* 58 (August 1932): 1103-1109.

645. Loescher, Burt G. *Washington's Eyes: The Continental Light Dragoons.* Fort Collins, CO: Old Army Press, 1977.

646. Mace, William H. *Washington, A Virginia Cavalier.* Chicago: Rand McNally, 1916.

647. McKim, Katherine J. "Washington

as a General." *Ohio Magazine* 4 (February 1908): 152-158.

648. Marshall, John. *The Life of George Washington, Commander in Chief of the American Forces, During the War Which Established the Independence of His Country, and First President of the United States.* 5 vols. Philadelphia: C. P. Wayne, 1804-1807.

649. Maurer, M. "Military Justice under George Washington." *Military Affairs* 28 (Spring 1964): 8-16.

650. Mayo, Katherine. *General Washington's Dilemma.* New York: Harcourt, Brace, 1938.

651. Miller, Randall. "The Founding of a Father: John Adams and the Appointment of George Washington as Commander in Chief of the Continental Army." *Maryland Historian* 4 (Spring 1973): 13-24.

652. Miller, William D. "General Washington at Little Rest." *Rhode Island Historical Society Collections* 25 (April 1932): 47-53.

653. Moore, Charles. "Washington and the Braddock Campaign." *Daughters of the American Revolution Magazine* 56 (December 1922): 699-709.

654. Muir, Dorothy T. *General Washington's Headquarters, 1775-1783.* Troy, AL: Troy State University Press, 1977.

655. Ney, Virgil. "Washington's Continental Army." *Daughters of the American Revolution Magazine* 110 (June 1976): 827-837.

656. O'Brien, Matthew C. "John Esten Cooke, George Washington, and the Virginia Cavaliers." *Virginia Magazine of History and Biography* 84 (July 1976): 259-265.

657. "Presents of General Washington from the King of Spain and Lafayette." *Tennessee Historical Magazine* 2 (April 1932): 202-204.

658. *Recollections of Days of 1976: What Our Forefathers Thought and Said of Gen. George Washington.* New York: Gordon and Heintzelman, 1876.

659. Richardson, William H. "George Washington and Jersey City." *New York Historical Society Proceedings* 51 (1933): 151-176.

660. Richardson, William H. "Washington and the New Jersey Campaign of 1776." *New Jersey Historical Society Proceedings* 50 (April 1931): 121-161.

661. Ridout, Edith M. "Marking the Spot Where Washington Resigned His Commission as Commander in Chief of the Continental Army." *Daughters of the American Revolution Magazine* 49 (July 1916): 7-11.

662. Shreve, L. G. *Tench Tilghman: The Life and Times of Washington's Aide-de-Camp.* Centreville, MD: Tidewater Publishers, 1982.

663. Skaggs, David C. "The Generalship of George Washington." *Military Review* 54 (July 1974): 3-10.

664. Smith, Merritt R. "George Washington and the Establishment of the Harpers Ferry Armory." *Virginia Magazine of History and Biography* 81 (October 1973): 415-436.

665. U.S. Library of Congress. Manuscript Division. *Calendar of the Correspondence of George Washington, Commander in Chief of the Continental Army with the Continental Congress.* New York: Franklin, 1970.

666. Vallandigham, E. N. "Washington as a Colonial Magnate." *Putnam's* 3 (February 1908): 517-529.

667. Vestal, Samuel C. *Washington, The Military Man.* Washington, DC: George Washington Bicentennial Commission, 1931.

668. "Washington and the Medical Affairs of the Revolution." *Annals of Medical History* 4 (1932): 306-312.

669. "Washington's Letter of Acceptance of the Freedom of the City of New York." *New York Historical Society Bulletin* 1 (July 1917): 38-45.

670. Weiss, Harry B. "A Famous First Edition: The Journal of Major George Washington." *American Book Collector* 1 (June 1932): 363-364.

671. Whiteley, Emily S. "General Washington and Colonel Hamilton." *Virginia Quarterly Review* 11 (July 1935): 397-408.

672. Whiteley, Emily S. *Washington and His Aides-de-Camp*. New York: Macmillan, 1936.

673. Woodward, Isaiah A., ed. "Events Prior to and during the Day General George Washington Resigned as Commander in Chief of the Continental Army." *West Virginia History* 38 (January 1977): 157-161.

674. Wright, Esmond. *Washington and the American Revolution*. New York: Macmillan, 1957.

675. Wrong, George M. *Washington and His Comrades in Arms: A Chronicle of the War of Independence*. New Haven, CT: Yale University Press, 1921.

676. Wyman, Charles L. "Washington as a General." *Ohio Magazine* 4 (February 1908): 143-151.

677. Young, Norwood. *George Washington, Soul of the Revolution*. New York: McBride, 1932.

Presidential Years

678. Anderson, Ray M. "George Washington and the Whiskey Insurrection." Master's thesis, American University, 1970.

679. Andrews, William L. *New York as Washington Knew It after the Revolution*. New York: Scribner's, 1905.

680. Ayres, Philip W. "The Diplomatic Relations of the United States with Great Britain during the Revolution, the Confederation, and Washington's First Administration." Ph.D. dissertation, Johns Hopkins University, 1888.

681. Bemis, Samuel F. "John Quincy Adams and George Washington." *Massachussets Historical Society Proceedings* 67 (1941-1944): 365-384.

682. Bemis, Samuel F. "Washington's Farewell Address: A Foreign Policy of Independence." *American Historical Review* 39 (January 1934): 250-268.

683. Binney, Horace. *An Enquiry into the Formation of Washington's Farewell Address*. New York: Da Capo Press, 1969.

684. Bloom, Sol. "The Inauguration of George Washington." *American Foreign Service Journal* 16 (April 1939): 198-199, 225-227.

685. Boller, Paul F., Jr. "Washington and Civilian Supremacy." *Southwestern Review* 39 (Winter 1954): 9-22.

686. Bowen, Clarence W. "The Inauguration of Washington." *Century Magazine* 37 (April 1889): 803-833.

687. Bowling, Kenneth R. "The Bank Bill, the Capitol City, and President Washington." *Capitol Studies* 1 (Spring 1972): 59-72.

688. Brown, Everett S. "The Inauguration of George Washington." *Michigan Alumnus Quarterly Review* 45 (Spring 1939): 213-221.

689. Campbell, Helen M. ... *Famous Presidents: Washington, Jefferson, Madison, Lincoln, Grant*. Boston: Educational Publishing Co., 1903.

690. Carroll, John A. "President Wash-

ington and the Challenge of Neutrality, 1793-1794." Ph.D. dissertation, Georgetown University, 1956.

691. Carroll, John A., and Mary W. Ashworth. *George Washington: First In Peace, 1793-1799.* New York: Scribner's, 1957.

692. Carson, Hampton L. "Washington in His Relation to the National Idea." *Magazine of History* 11 (May 1910): 261-272.

693. Cavanagh, John W. *Our First Two Presidents, John Janson-George Washington.* New York: John W. Cavanagh, 1932.

694. Clarfield, Gerard H. "Protecting the Frontiers: Defense Policy and the Tariff Question in the First Washington Administration." *William and Mary Quarterly* 32 (July 1975): 443-464.

695. Corbin, John. *The Unknown Washington: Biographic Origins of the Republic.* New York: Scribner's, 1930.

696. Corbin, John. "Washington and the American Union." *Scribner's Magazine* 86 (November 1929): 487-497.

697. DeConde, Alexander. *Entangling Alliance: Politics and Diplomacy under George Washington.* Durham, NC: Duke University Press, 1958.

698. DeConde, Alexander. "Washington's Farewell, the French Alliance, and the Election of 1796." *Mississippi Valley Historical Review* 43 (March 1957): 641-658.

699. Dowe, Charles E. "The Inauguration of the First President." *Cosmopolitan* 6 (April 1889): 533-543.

700. Farrell, Nancy. "George Washington: The Administrator." *Historical and Philosophical Society of Ohio Bulletin* 14 (January 1956): 21-36.

701. "The First President of the United States: Estimates of Washington by a Hundred Great Minds." *Journal of American History* 8 (May/July 1914): 241-249.

702. Fitzpatrick, John C. "Washington's Election as First President of the United States." *Daughters of the American Revolution Magazine* 58 (February 1924): 69-81.

703. Frothingham, Thomas G. *Washington, Commander in Chief.* Boston: Houghton Mifflin, 1930.

704. Fry, Joseph A. "Washington's Farewell Address and American Commerce." *West Virginia History* 37 (July 1976): 281-290.

705. George, Marian M. *Lincoln and Washington.* Chicago: Flanagan, 1899.

706. "George Washington's Inaugural Journey." *Daughters of the American Revolution Magazine* 45 (November/December 1914): 247-248, 337.

707. Gibbs, George. *Memoirs of the Administration of Washington and John Adams, Edited from the Papers of Oliver Wolcott, Secretary of the Treasury.* 2 vols. New York: Privately Printed, 1846.

708. Hancock, Harold B. "Loaves and Fishes: Applications for Office from Delawareans to George Washington." *Delaware History* 14 (October 1970): 135-158.

709. Hapgood, Norman. "Washington and Lincoln." *Dial* 68 (August 9, 1919): 92-93.

710. Hart, Albert B. *Washington as President.* Washington, DC: George Washington Bicentennial Commission, 1931.

711. Henderson, Archibald. *Washington's Southern Tour, 1791.* Boston: Houghton Mifflin, 1923.

712. Jones, Robert F. "George Washington and the Politics of the Presidency." *Presidential Studies Quarterly* 10 (Winter 1980): 28-34.

713. Kaufman, Burton I., ed. *Washington's Farewell Address: The View from the*

20th Century. Chicago: Quadrangle Books, 1969.

714. King, Irving H. *George Washington's Coast Guard*. Annapolis, MD: Naval Institute Press, 1978.

715. Kingdon, Frank. *Architects of the Republic: George Washington, Thomas Jefferson, Abraham Lincoln, Franklin D. Roosevelt*. New York: Alliance Publishing Co., 1947.

716. Klein, Rose S. "Washington's Thanksgiving Proclamation." *American Jewish Archives* 20 (November 1968): 156-162.

717. Kohn, Richard H. "The Washington Administration's Decision to Crush the Whiskey Rebellion." *Journal of American History* 59 (December 1972): 567-584.

718. Lamb, Martha J. R. N. "The Inauguration of Washington, 1789." *Magazine of American History* 20 (December 1888): 433-460.

719. Lawrence, Henry W. "Washington, Capitalism, and Nationalism." *American Scholar* 1 (May 1932): 352-359.

720. L'Enfant, Pierre C. "L'Enfant's Reports to President Washington, Bearing Dates of March 26, June 22, and August 19, 1791." *Columbia Historical Society Records* 2 (1899): 26-48.

721. Libby, Orin G. "Political Factions in Washington's Administration." *Quarterly Journal of the University of North Dakota* 3 (July 1913): 293-318.

722. Lieberman, Carl. "George Washington and the Development of American Federalism." *Social Science* 51 (Winter 1976): 3-10.

723. Lombard, M. E. "The Inauguration of George Washington." *Legion D'Honneur Magazine* 9 (April 1939): 293-300.

724. McClure, William E. "Washington and His Relation to the Constitution." *Sons of American Revolution Magazine* 27 (January 1933): 224-227.

725. McDonald, Forrest. *President of George Washington*. Lawrence, KS: University Press of Kansas, 1974.

726. McLaughlin, Robert. *Washington and Lincoln*. New York: Putnam, 1912.

727. McMaster, John B. "Washington's Inauguration." *Harper's Monthly Magazine* 78 (April 1889): 671-686.

728. Markowitz, Arthur A. "Washington's Farewell and the Historians: A Critical Review." *Pennsylvania Magazine of History and Biography* 94 (April 1970): 173-191.

729. Matthewson, Timothy M. "George Washington's Policy toward the Haitian Revolution." *Diplomatic History* 3 (Summer 1979): 321-336.

730. Mead, Edwin D. "Washington, Jefferson, and Franklin on War." *World Peace Foundation Pamphlet* 3 (May 1913): 3-15.

731. Mitchell, William D. "The Supreme Court in Washington's Time." *American Business Law Journal* 18 (May 1932): 341-342.

732. Monahon, Clifford P. "Richard Bache's Letter to His Wife Describing the Inauguration of Washington, As Depicted in the John Brown House Scenic Wall Paper." *Rhode Island History* 7 (April 1948): 57-59.

733. Palmer, John M. *Washington, Lincoln, Wilson: Three War Statesmen*. Garden City, NY: Doubleday, 1930.

734. Paltsits, Victor H., ed. *Washington's Farewell Address*. New York: New York Public Library, 1935.

735. Penniman, James H. *George Washington as Commander in Chief*. Philadelphia: Wanamaker, 1918.

736. Pennypacker, Isaac R. "Washington

and Lincoln, The Father and the Saviour of the Country." *Pennsylvania Magazine of History* 56 (1932): 97-109.

737. Pew, William A. "Washington — A Great Commander." *Essex Institute of Historical Collections* 68 (April 1932): 225-239.

738. Phelps, Glenn A. "George Washington and the Building of the Constitution: Presidential Interpretation and Constitutional Development." *Congress and the Presidency* 12 (Autumn 1985): 95-110.

739. "Presidential Inaugurations: Washington — 1789." *Ladies' Magazine and Literary Gazette* 4 (October 1831): 435-440.

740. Randall, James G. "George Washington and Entangling Alliances." *South Atlantic Quarterly* 30 (July 1931): 221-229.

741. Reuter, Frank T. *Trials and Triumphs: George Washington's Foreign Policy.* Fort Worth: Texas Christian University, 1983.

742. Schwartz, Barry. "George Washington and the Whip Conception of Heroic Leadership." *American Sociological Review* 48 (February 1983): 18-33.

743. Scott, W. "George Washington: Some Great Public Services Commonly Overlooked." *Magazine of History* 20 (February 1915): 51-56.

744. Sears, Louis M. *George Washington and the French Revolution.* Detroit, MI: Wayne State University Press, 1960.

745. Sears, Louis M. "George Washington and the French Revolution — The First Phase." In *Essays in Honor of William E. Dodd, By His Former Students at the University of Chicago*, edited by Avery Craven, 15-29. Chicago: University of Chicago Press, 1935.

746. Seasongood, Murray. "George Washington and Political Parties." *American Scholar* 1 (May 1932): 265-271.

747. Simpson, Stephen. *The Lives of George Washington and Thomas Jefferson.* Philadelphia: Young, 1833.

748. Smelser, Marshall. "George Washington and the Alien and Sedition Acts." *American Historical Review* 59 (January 1954): 322-334.

749. Smelser, Marshall. "George Washington Declines the Part of El Libertador." *William and Mary Quarterly* 11 (January 1954): 42-51.

750. Smith, Thomas E. V. *The City of New York in the Year of Washington's Inauguration, 1789.* New York: A. D. F. Randolph, 1889.

751. Smucker, Isaac. "A Great Event of a Century Ago: Washington's Inauguration and Inaugural." *Magazine of Western History* 9 (March 1889): 522-526.

752. Smylie, James H. "The President as Republican Prophet and King: Clerical Reflections on the Death of Washington." *Journal of Church and State* 18 (Spring 1976): 233-252.

753. Stearns, Clifford B. "National Defense Embodying Patriotic Education: George Washington and the Constitution." *Daughters of the American Revolution Magazine* 66 (September 1932): 577-581.

754. Stein, Nathaniel E. "Presidential Letters: Some Comments on the News Coverage and the Campaign Movements of the First Presidential Elections." *Manuscripts* 19 (Summer 1967): 32-34.

755. Tagg, James D. "Benjamin Franklin Bache's Attack on George Washington." *Pennsylvania Magazine of History and Biography* 100 (April 1976): 191-230.

756. Towner, Ausburn. "Our First President's Inauguration." *Frank Leslie's Popular Monthly* 27 (April 1889): 385-395.

757. Trescot, William H. *The Diplomatic History of the Administrations of Washington and Adams, 1789-1801.* Boston: Little, Brown, 1857.

758. U.S. Constitution Sesquicentennial Commission. *George Washington, The President, Triumphant Journey as President-Elect: First Term of the First President.* Washington, DC: U.S. Government Printing Office, 1939.

759. U.S. Department of State. *Calendar of Applications and Recommendations for Office during the Presidency of George Washington.* Prepared by Gaillard Hunt. Washington, DC: U.S. Government Printing Office, 1901.

760. *Wall and Nassau: An Account of the Inauguration of George Washington in Federal Hall at Wall and Nassau Streets, April 30, 1789.* New York: Bankers Trust Co., 1939.

761. Washburn, Mabel T. R. "Election and Inauguration of Washington as President and the Beginning of the United States Government under the Constitution: A Contemporaneous Account . . . Gathered Out of Newspapers of That Day." *Journal of American History* 8 (April/June 1914): 181-220.

762. Weinberg, Albert K. "Washington's 'Great Rule' in Its Historical Evaluation." In *Historiography and Urbanization: Essays in American History in Honor of W. Stull Holt,* edited by Eric F. Goldman, 109-138. Baltimore, MD: Johns Hopkins University Press, 1941.

763. Wills, Garry. "Washington's Farewell Address: An Eighteenth-Century 'Fireside Chat.'" *Chicago History* 10 (1981): 176-179.

764. Wriston, Henry M. "Washington and the Foundations of American Foreign Policy." *Minnesota History* 8 (March 1927): 3-26.

Writings

765. Beatty, Albert R., ed. "Letters of George Washington." *Yale Review* 21 (March 1932): 466-482.

766. Brooke, Walter E., ed. *The Agricultural Papers of George Washington.* Boston: R. G. Badger, 1919.

767. Cappon, Lester J. "Jared Sparks: The Preparation of an Editor." *Massachusetts Historical Society Proceedings* 90 (1978): 3-21.

768. Eaton, Dorothy S. "George Washington Papers." *Library of Congress Quarterly Journal* 22 (January 1965): 3-28.

769. "Expense Account of Washington, In His Own Handwriting." *New York History* 13 (April 1932): 180-181.

770. Fitzpatrick, John C. *George Washington, Colonial Traveller, 1732-1775.* Indianapolis, IN: Bobbs-Merrill, 1927.

771. Fleming, Thomas J., ed. *Affectionately Yours, George Washington: A Self-Portrait in Letters of Friendship.* New York: Norton, 1967.

772. Good, H. G. "Letters between George Washington and an Early British Rousseauist." *School and Society* 38 (October 21, 1933): 522-526.

773. Haraszti, Zoltan, ed. "A Washington Letter." *More Books* 8 (1933): 169-171.

774. Haraszti, Zoltan. "Washington Letters in This Library." *More Books* 7 (1932): 43-55.

775. Hellman, George S. "New Letters of Washington." *Harper's* 114 (January 1907): 288-293.

776. Howe, Herbert B. "Colonel George Washington and Kings College." *Columbia University Quarterly* 24 (1932): 137-157.

777. Johnson, Richard R., ed. "Patience

and Planning: A Letter from George Washington." *Pacific Northwest Quarterly* 70 (January 1970): 20-23.

778. "Letter of Washington Dated 10 March, 1787, and a Letter of Tobias Lear Dated 6 June, 1800." *Colonial Society of Massachusetts Publications* 13 (February 1910): 110-111.

779. *Letters of George Washington in the Library of the Connecticut Historical Society.* Hartford, CT: Connecticut Historical Society, 1932.

780. Lossing, Benson J. *Diary of George Washington from 1789-1791.* Richmond, VA: Press of the Historical Society, 1861.

781. Merriam, George E. *More Precious Than Fine Gold: Washington Commonplace Book.* New York: Putnam, 1931.

782. Peixotto, Irma M. "Washington's Private Account Book." *Bookman* 17 (March 1903): 66-69.

783. Prestor, Howard W., ed. *Autograph Letters and Documents of George Washington Now in Rhode Island Collections.* Providence, RI: E. L. Freeman, 1932.

784. Provine, W. A. "Washington's Old Mill-Book." *Tennessee Historical Magazine* 2 (April 1932): 187-194.

785. Sifton, Paul G. "George Washington Letter." *Library of Congress Information Bulletin* 30 (May 6, 1971): 259-260.

786. Washington, George. *The Autobiography of George Washington, 1753-1799.* Edited by Edward C. Boykin. New York: Reynal and Hitchcook, 1935.

787. Washington, George. *Basic Writings of George Washington.* Edited by Saxe Commins. New York: Random House, 1948.

788. Washington, George. *Correspondence Concerning the Society of the Cincinnati.* Edited by Edgar E. Hume. Baltimore, MD: John Hopkins University Press, 1941.

789. Washington, George. *The Diaries of George Washington.* 6 vols. Edited by Donald Jackson. Charlottesville: University of Virginia, 1976-1980.

790. Washington, George. *The Diaries of George Washington, 1748-1799.* 4 vols. Edited by John C. Fitzpatrick. New York: Houghton Mifflin, 1925.

791. Washington, George. "Diary of George Washington, August 1-October 18, 1786." *Colonial Society of Massachusetts Publications* 18 (February 1915): 28-54.

792. Washington, George. *The Diary of George Washington: From 1789 to 1791: Embracing the Opening of the First Congress, His Tours through New England, Long Island, and Southern States, Together with His Journal of a Tour in the Ohio, in 1753.* New York: C. B. Richardson, 1860.

793. Washington, George. "Diary of George Washington, May-June, 1786." *Colonial Society of Massachusetts Publications* 17 (February 1914): 162-205.

794. Washington, George. "Diary of President Washington, January 1-June 21, 1796." *Pennsylvania Magazine of History* 37 (April 1913): 230-239.

795. Washington, George. "The Discarded Inaugural Address of George Washington." *Manuscripts* 10 (Spring 1958): 2-17.

796. Washington, George. *Facsimiles of Letters from His Excellency George Washington, President of the United States of America, To Sir John Sinclair on Agricultural and Other Interesting Topics.* Philadelphia: J. T. Bowen, 1839.

797. Washington, George. *Farewell Address, In Facsimile, With Transliterations of All the Drafts of Washington, Madison, and Hamilton, Together with Their Correspondence and Other Supporting Documents.* New York: New York Public Library, 1935.

798. Washington, George. *George Washington: A Biography in His Own Words.* Edited by Ralph K. Andrist. New York: Newsweek, 1972.

799. Washington, George. *George Washington and Mount Vernon: A Collection of Washington's Unpublished Agricultural and Personal Letters.* Edited by Moncure D. Conway. Brooklyn, NY: Long Island Historical Society, 1889.

800. Washington, George. *George Washington Papers.* Washington, DC: Library of Congress, 1964.

801. Washington, George. *The George Washington Papers.* Edited by Frank Donovan. New York: Dodd, Mead, 1964.

802. Washington, George. *George Washington, Sportsman, From His Own Journals.* Cambridge, MA: Cosmos Press, 1928.

803. Washington, George. "George Washington to His Brother Charles." *Mississippi Valley Historical Review* 1 (June 1914): 98-101.

804. Washington, George. *George Washington's Accounts of Expenses While Commander in Chief of the Continental Army, 1775-1783.* Edited by John C. Fitzpatrick. Boston: Houghton Mifflin, 1917.

805. Washington, George. *The Journal of Major George Washington: An Account of His First Official Mission, Made as Emissary from the Governor of Virginia to the Commandant of the French Force on the Ohio, October 1753 — January 1754.* New York: Holt, 1959.

806. Washington, George. *Journal of My Journey over the Mountains.* Albany, NY: Munsell's Sons, 1892.

807. Washington, George. *The Journal of the Proceedings of the President, 1793-1797.* Edited by Dorothy Twohig. Charlottesville: University Press of Virginia, 1981.

808. Washington, George. *Legacies of Washington: Being a Collection of the Most Approved Writings of the Late General Washington.* Trenton, NJ: Sherman, Mershon and Thomas, 1800.

809. Washington, George. "A Letter of Washington, Dated 27 January, 1794." *Colonial Society of Massachusetts Publications* 10 (February 1906): 260.

810. Washington, George. "Letter of Washington to Mr. S. Sommers Apparently on a Boundary Line Controversy." *Magazine of History* 11 (June 1910): 354.

811. Washington, George. "Letter Written by General Washington to George Clinton, Governor of the State of New York." *New York Historical Society Bulletin* 12 (July 1928): 69-70.

812. Washington, George. "Letter Written by George Washington to James Duane Concerning the Evaluation of the City of New York in 1783." *New York Historical Society Bulletin* 12 (July 1928): 71.

813. Washington, George. *Letters and Addresses.* New York: Sun Dial Classics, 1909.

814. Washington, George. *Letters and Recollections of George Washington: Being Letters to Tobias Lear and Others between 1790 and 1799. . . .* Garden City, NY: Doubleday, 1906.

815. Washington, George. *Letters from His Excellency George Washington, President of the United States, To Sir John Sinclair, Bart. M. P., On Agricultural and Other Interesting Topics.* London: W. Bulmer, 1800.

816. Washington, George. *The Letters of George Washington in the Robert Hudson Tannahill Research Library.* Edited by Jerome I. Smith. Dearborn, MI: Greenfield Village and Henry Ford Museum, 1976.

817. Washington, George. "Letters of Washington to Fielding Lewis, His Nephew." *Magazine of History* 12 (November 1910): 277-278.

818. Washington, George. "Letters of Washington to John Gill." *Magazine of History* 13 (May 1911): 242-243.

819. Washington, George. *Maxims of George Washington.* New York: Sandstone Press, 1978.

820. Washington, George. *Maxims of Washington, Political, Social, Moral, and Religious.* Rev. ed. Edited by John F. Schroeder. Mount Vernon, VA: Mount Vernon Ladies' Association, 1942.

821. Washington, George. "New Letters of Washington." *Harper's* 114 (January 1907): 288-293.

822. Washington, George. *The Only Authenticated Copy, Full and Complete, of the Last Will and Testament of George Washington, of Mt. Vernon.* 2d ed. Wilmington, DE: James and Webb, 1876.

823. Washington, George. *Papers of George Washington.* Edited by William W. Abbot. Charlottesville: University Press of Virginia, 1982.

824. Washington, George. *President Washington's Diaries, 1791 to 1799.* Compiled by Joseph A. Hoskins. Summerfield, NC: The Compiler, 1921.

825. Washington, George. *Rules of Conduct, Diary of Adventure, Letters, and Farewell Address, by George Washington.* Boston: Houghton Mifflin, 1887.

826. Washington, George. *Selections from the Correspondence of George Washington and James Anderson.* Charlestown, MA: Samuel Etheridge, 1800.

827. Washington, George. *The Spurious Letters Attributed to Washington.* Bibliographical Note by Worthington C. Ford. Brooklyn, NY: Privately Printed, 1889.

828. Washington, George. "Three New Washington Letters at Yale." Edited by Bernhard Knollenberg. *Yale University Library Gazette* 14 (1939): 17-22.

829. Washington, George. "Three Private Letters of General Washington." *Pennsylvania Magazine of History* 41 (October 1917): 502-503.

830. Washington, George. "Three Washington Letters." Edited by Bernhard Knollenberg. *Yale University Library Gazette* 15 (1940): 5-8.

831. Washington, George. "Two Letters of Washington." *Maryland Historical Magazine* 4 (December 1909): 375-377.

832. Washington, George. *Washington and the West: Being George Washington's Diary of September, 1784, Kept during His Journey into the Ohio Basin.* . . . New York: Century, 1905.

833. Washington, George. *The Washington-Crawford Letters, Being the Correspondence between George Washington and William Crawford, From 1767 to 1781, Concerning Western Lands.* Edited by Consul W. Butterfield. Cincinnati, OH: R. Clerke Co., 1877.

834. Washington, George. *Washington-Irvine Correspondence: The Official Letters Which Passed between Washington and Brig. Gen. William Irvine and between Irvine and Others Concerning Military Affairs in the West from 1781 to 1783.* Edited by Consul W. Butterfield. Madison, WI: D. Atwood, 1882.

835. Washington, George. *The Washington Papers: Basic Selections from the Public and Private Writings of George Washington.* Edited by Saul K. Padover. New York: Harper and Row, 1955.

836. Washington, George. *Washington Speaks for Himself.* Edited by Lucretia P. Osborn. New York: Scribner's, 1927.

837. Washington, George. "Washington

to the German Lutherans." *Pennsylvania German* 10 (April 1909): 152-153.

838. Washington, George. *The Washington Year Book: Maxims and Models of "The Father of His Country."* Chicago: McClurg, 1908.

839. Washington, George. *Washington's Journal of a Tour over the Alleghany Mountains.* Boston: Jared Sparks, 1934-1937.

840. Washington, George. "Washington's Ledger, 1754-1756: Communicated by Worthington C. Ford." *Colonial Society of Massachusetts Publications* 12 (February 1908): 88-99.

841. Washington, George. *Washington's Masonic Correspondence as Found among the Washington Papers in the Library of Congress.* Edited by Julius F. Sachse. Lancaster, PA: Press of the New Era Print Co., 1915.

842. Washington, George. *Washington's Political Legacies.* Boston: John Russell and John West, 1800.

843. Washington, George. *The Words of Washington: Being Selections from the Most Celebrated of His Papers.* New York: Useful Knowledge Publishing Co., 1882.

844. Washington, George. *Writings.* Edited by Lawrence B. Evans. New York: Putnam, 1908.

845. Washington, George. *Writings.* 14 vols. Edited by Worthington C. Ford. New York: Putnam, 1889-1893.

846. Washington, George. *The Writings of George Washington.* 12 vols. Edited by Jared Sparks. Boston: American Stationer's Co., 1837.

847. Washington, George. *The Writings of George Washington from the Original Manuscript Sources, 1745-1799.* 39 vols. Edited by John C. Fitzpatrick. Washington, DC: U.S. Government Printing Office, 1931-1944.

John Adams

Biographies

848. Adams, Charles F. *The Life of John Adams.* Rev. ed. 2 vols. Philadelphia: Lippincott, 1871.

849. Adams, James T. *The Adams Family.* Boston: Little, Brown, 1930.

850. Banes, Ruth A. "The Exemplary Self: Autobiography in Eighteenth Century America." *Biography* 5 (Summer 1982): 226-239.

851. Burleigh, Anne H. *John Adams.* New Rochelle, NY: Arlington House, 1969.

852. Chinard, Gilbert. *Honest John Adams.* Boston: Little, Brown, 1933.

853. Cranch, William. *Memoir of the Life, Character, and Writings of John Adams: Read March 16, 1927, In the Capitol, In the City of Washington, At the Request of the Columbian Institute, and Published by Their Order.* Washington, DC: S. A. Eliot, 1827.

854. Dauer, Manning J. *The Adams Federalists.* Baltimore, MD: Johns Hopkins University Press, 1953.

855. East, Robert A. *John Adams.* Boston: Twayne, 1979.

856. Haraszti, Zoltan. *John Adams and the Prophets of Progress.* Cambridge, MA: Harvard University Press, 1952.

857. Iacuzzi, Alfred. *John Adams, Scholar.* New York: S. F. Vanni, 1952.

858. Kagle, Steven E. "Instrument for Ambition: The Personal and Artistic Significance of the Diary of John Adams." Ph.D. dissertation, University of Michigan, 1967.

859. McCoy, Samuel. *This Man Adams: The Man Who Never Died.* New York: Brentano's, 1928.

860. Morse, John T., Jr. *John Adams.* Boston: Houghton Mifflin, 1885.

861. Nagel, Paul. *Descent from Glory: Four Generations of the Johns Adams Family.* Oxford: Oxford University Press, 1983.

862. Oliver, Andrew. *Portraits of John and Abigail Adams.* Cambridge, MA: Harvard University Press, 1967.

863. Shaw, Peter. *The Character of John Adams.* Chapel Hill: University of North Carolina Press, 1976.

864. Shepherd, Jack. *The Adams Chronicles: Four Generations of Greatness.* Boston: Little, Brown, 1975.

865. Smith, Page. *John Adams.* 2 vols. Garden City, NY: Doubleday, 1962.

866. Smyth, Clifford. *John Adams, The Man Who Was Called "Father of American Independence."* New York: Funk and Wagnalls, 1931.

867. Stoddard, William O. *John Adams and Thomas Jefferson.* New York: White, Stokes and Allen, 1887.

868. Willard, Samuel. *John Adams, A Character Sketch, With Supplementary Essay by G. Mercer Adam.* Milwaukee, WI: Campbell, 1903.

Private Life

869. Adair, Douglass. "Gilbert Chinard's 'Honest John Adams,' An Appreciation." *Princeton University Library Chronicle* 26 (Spring 1965): 197-199.

870. Adams, Abigail S. *The Adams Family in Auteuil, 1784-1785: As Told in the Letters of Abigail Adams.* Boston: Massachusetts Historical Society, 1956.

871. Adams, Abigail S. *The Book of Abigail and John: Selected Letters of the Adams Family, 1762-1784.* Edited by Lyman H. Butterfield, Marc Friedlaender, and Mary-Jo Kline. Cambridge, MA: Harvard University Press, 1975.

872. Adams, Abigail S. *Letters of Mrs. John Adams, The Wife of John Adams.* 4th ed. Boston: Wilkins, Carter, 1848.

873. Adams, Abigail S. *New Letters of Abigail Adams, 1788-1801.* Edited by Steward Mitchell. Boston: Houghton Mifflin, 1947.

874. Adams, Charles F. "The Book-Plate of John Adams." *Massachusetts Historical Society Proceedings* 20 (1907): 84-86.

875. Adams, Henry, ed. *The Adams Mansion, The Home of John Adams and John Quincy Adams, Presidents of the United States.* Quincy, MA: Adams Memorial Society, 1935.

876. Akers, Charles W. *Abigail Adams, An American Woman.* Boston: Little, Brown, 1980.

877. Allison, John M. *Adams and Jefferson, The Story of a Friendship.* Norman: University of Oklahoma Press, 1966.

878. Aring, Charles D. "Adams and Jefferson, A Correspondence." *History Today* 21 (September 1971): 609-618.

879. Bobbe, Dorothie D. *Abigail Adams, The Second First Lady.* New York: Minton, Balch, 1929.

880. Butler, Lorine L. "Abigail Adams — Correspondent of History." *Daughters of the American Revolution Magazine* 90 (July 1956): 623-627.

881. Butterfield, Lyman H. "The Dream of Benjamin Rush: The Reconciliation of John Adams and Thomas Jefferson." *Yale Review* 40 (December 1950): 297-319.

882. Butterfield, Lyman H. "The Papers of the Adams Family: Some Account of Their History." *Massachusetts Historical Society Proceedings* 71 (1953-1957): 328-356.

883. Coit, Margaret L. "Dearest Friends: With Excerpts from Letters during Courtship and Marriage." *American Heritage* 19 (October 1968): 9-13.

884. Cole, Adelaide M. "Abigail Adams: A Vignette." *Daughters of the American Revolution Magazine* 113 (May 1979): 494-499.

885. Ford, Susan. "Thomas Jefferson and John Adams on the Classics." *Arion* 6 (Spring 1967): 116-132.

886. Garrett, Wendell D. "Bicentennial Outlook: The Monumental Friendship of Jefferson and Adams." *Historic Preservation* 28 (April 1976): 28-35.

887. Gleason, Gene. "Young John Adams Comes to Worcester." *New England Galaxy* 16 (1974): 3-10.

888. Gould, Elizabeth P. *John Adams and Daniel Webster as Schoolmasters.* Boston: Palmer, 1903.

889. Grey, Lennox. "John Adams and John Trumbull in the 'Boston Cycle.'" *New England Quarterly* 4 (July 1931): 509-514.

890. Gummere, Richard M. "The Classical Politics of John Adams." *Boston Public Library Quarterly* 9 (October 1957): 167-182.

891. Hamilton, Joseph G. de Roulhac. "Jefferson and Adams at Ease." *South Atlantic Quarterly* 26 (October 1927): 359-372.

892. Handler, Edward. "Nature Itself Is All Arcanum: The Scientific Outlook of John Adams." *American Philosophical Society Proceedings* 120 (June 1976): 216-229.

893. Hay, Robert P. "The Glorious Departure of the American Patriarchs: Contemporary Reactions to the Deaths of Jefferson and Adams." *Journal of Southern History* 35 (November 1969): 543-555.

894. "John Adams." *Bar Bulletin* 35 (September 1930): 3-16.

895. Kelly, Regina Z. *Abigail Adams: The President's Lady.* New York: Houghton Mifflin, 1962.

896. Meschutt, David. "Adams-Jefferson Portrait Exchange." *American Art Journal* 14 (Spring 1982): 47-54.

897. Miles, Edwin A. "President Adams' Billiard Table." *New England Quarterly* 45 (March 1972): 31-43.

898. Mugridge, Donald H. "The Adams Papers." *American Archivist* 25 (October 1962): 449-454.

899. Musto, David F. "Continuity Across Generations: The Adams Family Myth." In *New Directions in Psychohistory: The Adelphi Papers in Honor of Erik H. Erikson*, edited by Mel Albin, 117-129. Lexington, MA: Heath, 1980.

900. Pearson, Samuel C. "Nature's God: A Reassessment of the Religion of the Founding Fathers." *Religion in Life* 46 (Summer 1977): 152-162.

901. Pound, Ezra. "The Jefferson-Adams Correspondence." *North American Review* 244 (Winter 1937-1938): 314-324.

902. Schulz, Constance B. "The Radical Religious Ideas of Thomas Jefferson and John Adams: A Comparison." Ph.D. dissertation, University of Cincinnati, 1973.

903. *A Selection of Eulogies, Pronounced in the Several States, In Honor of Those Illustrious Patriots and Statesmen, John Adams and Thomas Jefferson.* Hartford, CT: D. F. Robinson, 1826.

904. Smith, Helen B. "The First Lady of the White House, Mrs. John Adams." *Pearson's Magazine* 21 (March 1909): 263-267.

905. Sprague, Waldo C., ed. *The President John Adams and President John Quincy Adams Birthplaces, Quincy, Mass.: Their Origin, Early History, and Changes Down to the Present Time.* Quincy, MA: Quincy Historical Society, 1959.

906. Stewart, Donald H., and George P. Clark. "Misanthrope or Humanitarian? John Adams in Retirement." *New England Quarterly* 28 (June 1955): 216-236.

907. Whitney, Janet P. *Abigail Adams.* Boston: Little, Brown, 1947.

908. Wilstach, Paul, ed. "Reconciliation: Correspondence of John Adams and Thomas Jefferson." *Atlantic Monthly* 134 (December 1924): 811-819.

909. Wirt, William. *A Discourse on the Lives and Characters of Thomas Jefferson and John Adams, Who Both Died on the Fourth of July, 1926.* Washington, DC: Gales and Seaton, 1824.

910. Withey, Lynne. *Dearest Friend: A Life of Abigail Adams.* New York: Free Press, 1981.

Public Career

911. Appleby, Joyce. "The New Republican Synthesis and the Changing Political Ideas of John Adams." *American Quarterly* 25 (December 1973): 578-595.

912. Baskin, Darryl B. "The Pluralist Vision in American Political Thought: Adams, Madison, and Calhoun on Community, Citizenship, and the Public Interest." Ph.D. dissertation, University of California, Berkeley, 1966.

913. Bezayiff, David. "Legal Oratory of John Adams: An Early Instrument of Protest." *Western Speech Communication* 40 (Winter 1976): 63-71.

914. Binder, Frederick M. "The Color Problem in Early National America as Viewed by John Adams, Jefferson, and Jackson." Ed.D. dissertation, Columbia University, 1962.

915. Bowen, Catherine D. *John Adams and the American Revolution*. Boston: Little, Brown, 1950.

916. Breen, Timothy H. "John Adams' Fight against Innovation in the New England Constitution: 1776." *New England Quarterly* 40 (December 1967): 501-520.

917. Brooks, Phillip C. *Diplomacy and the Borderlands: The Adams-Onis Treaty of 1819*. New York: Octagon, 1970.

918. Canfield, Cass. *Samuel Adams' Revolution, 1765-1776: With the Assistance of George Washington, Thomas Jefferson, Benjamin Franklin, John Adams, George III, and the People of Boston*. New York: Harper and Row, 1976.

919. Carroll, Warren H. "John Adams, Puritan Revolutionist: A Study of His Part in Making the American Revolution, 1764-1776." Ph.D. dissertation, Columbia University, 1959.

920. Charles, Joseph. "Adams and Jefferson: The Origins of the American Party System." *William and Mary Quarterly* 12 (July 1955): 410-446.

921. Cournos, Helen S. N., and John Cournos. *John Adams: Independence Forever*. New York: Holt, 1954.

922. Dauer, Manning J. "The Basis of the Support for John Adams in the Federalist Party." Ph.D. dissertation, University of Illinois, 1933.

923. Dauer, Manning J. "The Political Economy of John Adams." *Political Science Quarterly* 56 (December 1941): 545-572.

924. Devine, Francis E. "Ostracism in Popular Government: Burke and Adams." *Southern Quarterly* 14 (October 1975): 17-20.

925. Ellsworth, John W. "John Adams: The American Revolution as a Change of Heart?" *Huntington Library Quarterly* 28 (August 1965): 293-300.

926. Evans, William B. "John Adams' Opinion of Benjamin Franklin." *Pennsylvania Magazine of History and Biography* 92 (April 1968): 220-228.

927. Farnell, Robert S. "Positive Valuations of Politics and Government in the Thought of Five American Founding Fathers: Thomas Jefferson, John Adams, James Madison, Alexander Hamilton, and George Washington." Ph.D. dissertation, Cornell University, 1970.

928. Ferling, John E. " 'Oh That I Was a Soldier': John Adams and the Anguish of War." *American Quarterly* 36 (Summer 1984): 258-275.

929. Fischer, David H. "The Myth of the Essex Junto." *William and Mary Quarterly* 21 (April 1964): 191-235.

930. Gribbin, William. "Reply of John Adams on Episcopacy and the American Revolution." *Historical Magazine of the Protestant Episcopal Church* 44 (September 1975): 277-283.

931. Grinnell, Frank W. "John Winthrop and the Constitutional Thinking of John Adams." *Massachusetts Historical Society Proceedings* 63 (February 1930): 91-119.

932. Guerrero, Linda D. "John Adams' Vice-Presidency, 1789-1797: The Neglected Man in the Forgotten Office." Ph.D. dissertation, University of California, Santa Barbara, 1978.

933. Handler, Edward. *America and Europe in Political Thought of John Adams.* Cambridge, MA: Harvard University Press, 1964.

934. Howe, John R., Jr. *The Changing Political Thought of John Adams.* Princeton, NJ: Princeton University Press, 1966.

935. Howe, John R., Jr. "John Adams' View of Slavery." *Journal of Negro History* 49 (July 1964): 201-206.

936. Hutson, James H. "John Adams and the Birth of Dutch-American Friendship, 1780-1782." *Bijdragen en Mededelingen Betreffeude de Geschiedeuis der Nederlanden* 97 (July 1982): 409-422.

937. Hutson, James H. *John Adams and the Diplomacy of the American Revolution.* Lexington: University of Kentucky Press, 1980.

938. Hutson, James H. "John Adams' Title Campaign." *New England Quarterly* 41 (March 1968): 30-39.

939. Jenkins, Starr. "American Statemen as Men of Letters: Franklin, Adams, Jefferson, John Quincy Adams, Lincoln, Theodore Roosevelt, and Wilson Considered as Writers." Ph.D. dissertation, University of New Mexico, 1972.

940. Kelly, John J., Jr. "The Struggle for American Seaborne Independence as Viewed by John Adams." Ph.D. dissertation, University of Maine, 1973.

941. Ketcham, Ralph L. "John Adams, Franklin, Jefferson, and the Puritan Ethic" and "Conceptions of New Nationhood: Jefferson and Hamilton." In his *From Colony to Country, The Revolution in American Thought, 1750-1820,* 159-172, 195-212. New York: Macmillan, 1974.

942. Knollenberg, Bernhard. "John Adams, Knox, and Washington." *American Antiquarian Society Proceedings* 56 (October 1946): 207-238.

943. Knollenberg, Bernhard. "John Dickinson vs. John Adams: 1774-1776." *American Philosophical Society Proceedings* 107 (April 1963): 138-144.

944. Koch, Adrienne. "Philosopher-Statesmen of the Republic." *Sewanee Review* 55 (Summer 1974): 384-405.

945. Koch, Adrienne. *Power, Morals, and the Founding Fathers: Essays in the Interpretation of the American Enlightenment.* Ithaca, NY: Cornell University Press, 1961.

946. Kurtz, Stephen G. "The Political Science of John Adams, A Guide to His Statecraft." *William and Mary Quarterly* 25 (October 1968): 605-613.

947. Lint, Gregg L. "John Adams on the Drafting of the Treaty Plan of 1776." *Diplomatic History* 2 (Summer 1978): 313-320.

948. Little, John E. "John Adams and American Foreign Affairs, 1755-1780." Ph.D. dissertation, Princeton University, 1966.

949. Lycan, Gilbert L. *Alexander Hamilton and American Foreign Policy: A Design for Greatness.* Norman: University of Oklahoma Press, 1970.

950. Massachusetts Historical Society. *John Adams and a Sigynal Triumph: The Beginning of 200 Years of American-Dutch Friendship.* Boston: Massachusetts Historical Society, 1982.

951. Mitchell, Broadus. *Alexander Ham-*

ilton: The National Adventure, 1788-1804. 2 vols. New York: Macmillan, 1957-1962.

952. Morgan, Edmund S. *The Meaning of Independence: John Adams, George Washington, Thomas Jefferson.* Charlottesville: University Press of Virginia, 1976.

953. Murphy, William J., Jr. "John Adams: The Politics of the Additional Army." *New England Quarterly* 52 (June 1979): 234-249.

954. Peterson, Merrill D. *Adams and Jefferson: A Revolutionary Dialogue.* Athens: University of Georgia Press, 1976.

955. Peterson, Merrill D. "Adams and Jefferson: A Revolutionary Dialogue." *Wilson Quarterly* 1 (Autumn 1976): 108-125.

956. Reid, John P. "A Lawyer Acquitted: John Adams and the Boston Massacre Trials." *American Journal of Legal History* 18 (July 1974): 189-207.

957. Reyerson, Richard A. "John Adams' First Diplomatic Mission: Philadelphia, 1774." *Massachusetts Historical Society Proceedings* 95 (1983): 17-28.

958. Richards, Leonard L. "John Adams and the Moderate Federalists: The Cape Fear Valley as a Test Case." *North Carolina Historical Review* 43 (January 1966): 14-30.

959. Ripel, Barbara D. "The Political Mind of John Adams: A Study of the Continuity in His Thought." Ph.D. dissertation, State University of New York, Stony Brook, 1971.

960. Rodesch, Jerrold C. "America and the Middle Ages: A Study in the Thought of John and John Quincy Adams." Ph.D. dissertation, Rutgers University, 1971.

961. Rossiter, Clinton L. "Homage to John Adams." *Michigan Alumnus Quarterly Review* 64 (May 1958): 228-239.

962. Rossiter, Clinton L. "The Legacy of John Adams." *Yale Review* 46 (Summer 1957): 528-550.

963. Ryerson, Edward. "On John Adams." *American Quarterly* 6 (Fall 1954): 253-258.

964. Saltman, Helen S. "John Adams' Earliest Essays: The Humphrey Ploughjogger Letters." *William and Mary Quarterly* 37 (January 1980): 125-138.

965. Saltman, Helen S. "John Adams' Political Satires: The Humphrey Ploughjogger Letters." Ph.D. dissertation, University of California, Los Angeles, 1980.

966. Sanders, Frederick K. *John Adams, Speaking: Pound's Sources for the Adams' Cantos.* Orono, ME: National Poetry Foundation, 1975.

967. Schulz, Constance B. "John Adams on the Best of All Possible Worlds." *Journal of the History of Ideas* 44 (October/December 1983): 561-577.

968. Schutz, John A., and Douglass Adair, eds. *The Spur of Fame: Dialogues of John Adams and Benjamin Rush 1805 to 1813.* San Marino, CA: Huntington Library, 1980.

969. Selby, John E. "Richard Henry Lee, John Adams, and the Virginia Constitution of 1776." *Virginia Magazine of History and Biography* 84 (October 1976): 387-400.

970. Shaw, Peter. "John Adams' Crisis of Conscience." *Rutgers University Library Journal* 42 (1980): 1-25.

971. Smelser, Marshall. *The Congress Founds the Navy, 1787-1798.* South Bend, IN: University of Notre Dame Press, 1959.

972. Spengler, Joseph J. "The Political Economy of Jefferson, Madison, and Adams." In *American Studies in Honor of William Kenneth Boyd,* edited by David

K. Jackson, 3-59. Durham, NC: Duke University Press, 1940.

973. Storch, Neil T. "Adams, Franklin, and the Origin of Consular Representation." *Foreign Service Journal* 52 (October 1975): 11-13.

974. Sutter, Richard L. "A Trinity in Unity: The Principles and Origins of the Political Thought of John Adams." Ph.D. dissertation, Claremont Graduate School, 1974.

975. Taylor, Robert J. "John Adams: Legalist as Revolutionist." *Massachussetts Historical Society Proceedings* 89 (1977): 55-71.

976. Thompson, Harry C. "The Second Place in Rome: John Adams as Vice President." *Presidential Studies Quarterly* 10 (Spring 1980): 171-178.

977. Thorpe, Francis N. "Adams and Jefferson: 1826-1926." *North American Review* 223 (June/July/August 1926): 234-247.

978. Von Abele, Rudolph. "A *Mercury* Reappraisal: The World of John Adams." *American Mercury* 68 (July 1949): 66-73.

979. Waldo, Samuel P. *Biographical Sketches of Distinguished American Naval Heroes in the War of the Revolution, Between the American Republic and the Kingdom of Great Britain....* Hartford, CT: Silas Andrus, 1823.

980. Walsh, Correa M. *The Political Science of John Adams: A Study in the Theory of Mixed Government and the Bicameral System.* New York: Putnam, 1915.

981. Warren, Charles. "John Adams and American Constitutions." *Massachusetts Law Quarterly* 12 (February 1927): 66-82.

982. Webster, Daniel. *The Bunker Hill Monument, Adams, and Jefferson.* New York: Houghton Mifflin, 1893.

983. Williamson, Hugh P. "John Adams, Counsellor of Courage." *American Bar Association Journal* 54 (February 1968): 148-151.

Presidential Years

984. Anderson, William G. "John Adams and the Creation of the American Navy." Ph.D. dissertation, State University of New York, Stony Brook, 1975.

985. Anderson, William G. "John Adams, the Navy, and the Quasi-War with France." *American Neptune* 30 (April 1970): 117-132.

986. Appleby, Joyce. "The Jefferson-Adams Rupture and the First French Translation of John Adams' Defence." *American Historical Review* 73 (April 1968): 1084-1091.

987. Aronson, Sidney H. *Status and Kinship in the High Civil Service: The Administrations of John Adams, Thomas Jefferson, and Andrew Jackson.* Cambridge, MA: Harvard University Press, 1964.

988. Bergeron, Paul H. "Politics and Patronage in Tennessee during the Adams and Jackson Years." *Prologue* 2 (Spring 1970): 19-24.

989. Boles, John B. "Politics, Intrigue, and the Presidency: James McHenry to Bishop John Carroll, May 16, 1800." *Maryland Historical Magazine* 69 (Spring 1974): 64-85.

990. Brown, Ralph A. *The Presidency of John Adams.* Lawrence: Regents Press of Kansas, 1975.

991. Brown, Walter F., Jr. "John Adams and the American Press, 1797-1801: The First Full Scale Confrontation between the Executive and the Media." Ph.D. dissertation, University of Notre Dame, 1974.

992. Calkins, Carlos G. "The American Navy and the Opinions of One of Its

Founders, John Adams, 1735-1826." *U.S. Naval Institute Proceedings* 37 (June 1911): 453-483.

993. Carr, James A. "John Adams and the Barbary Problem: The Myth and the Record." *American Neptune* 26 (October 1966): 231-257.

994. Clarfield, Gerard H. "John Adams: The Marketplace and American Foreign Policy." *New England Quarterly* 52 (September 1979): 345-357.

995. Cooke, Jacob E. "Country above Party: John Adams and the 1799 Mission to France." In *Fame and the Founding Fathers*, edited by Edmund P. Wills, 53-77. Bethlehem, PA: Morovian College, 1967.

996. Cress, Larry D. "The Jonathan Robbins Incident: Extradition and the Separation of Powers in the Adams Administration." *Essex Institute of Historical Collections* 111 (April 1975): 99-121.

997. Dorfman, Joseph. "The Regal Republic of John Adams." *Political Science Quarterly* 59 (June 1944): 227-247.

998. Falkner, Leonard. *The President Who Wouldn't Retire*. New York: Coward-McCann, 1967.

999. Fredman, Lionel E., and Gerald Kurland. *John Adams, American Revolutionary Leader and President*. Charlotteville, NY: SamHar Press, 1973.

1000. Gibbs, George. *Memoirs of the Administration of Washington and John Adams, Edited from the Papers of Oliver Wolcolt, Secretary of the Treasury*. 2 vols. New York: Privately Printed, 1846.

1001. Hamilton, Alexander. *Letter from Alexander Hamilton, Concerning the Public Conduct and Character of John Adams, Esq., President of the United States*. New York: George F. Hopkins, 1800.

1002. Hayes, Frederic H. "John Adams and American Sea Power." *American Neptune* 25 (January 1965): 34-45.

1003. Holder, Jean S. "The John Adams Presidency: War Crisis Leadership in the Early Republic." Ph.D. dissertation, American University, 1983.

1004. Hunt, Gaillard. "Office-Seeking during the Administration of John Adams." *American Historical Review* 2 (January 1897): 241-261.

1005. Koch, Adrienne, ed. *Adams and Jefferson: "Posterity Must Judge."* Chicago: Rand McNally, 1963.

1006. Kramer, Eugene. "John Adams, Elbridge Gerry, and the Origins of XYZ Affair." *Essex Institute of Historical Collections* 94 (January 1958): 57-68.

1007. Kurtz, Stephen G. "The French Mission of 1799-1800: Concluding Chapter in the Statecraft of John Adams." *Political Science Quarterly* 80 (December 1965): 543-557.

1008. Kurtz, Stephen G. *The Presidency of John Adams: The Collapse of Federalism, 1795-1800*. Philadelphia: University of Pennsylvania Press, 1957.

1009. Lape, Fred. "For John Adams: His Winter and His Second Spring." *Virginia Quarterly Review* 39 (Spring 1963): 202-205.

1010. Miroff, Bruce. "John Adams: Merit, Fame, and Political Leadership." *Journal of Politics* 48 (February 1986): 116-133.

1011. Morgan, William G. "The 'Corrupt Bargain' Charge against Clay and Adams: An Historiographical Analysis." *Filson Club Historical Quarterly* 42 (April 1968): 132-149.

1012. Morse, Anson D. "The Politics of John Adams." *American Historical Review* 4 (January 1899): 292-312.

1013. Porter, J. M., and Stewart Farnell.

"John Adams and American Constitutionalism." *American Journal of Jurisprudence* 21 (1976): 20-23.

1014. Powell, E. P. "New England's First President." *Arena* 24 (July 1900): 31-46.

1015. Sisson, Daniel. *The American Revolution of 1800.* New York: Knopf, 1974.

1016. Smith, James M. "John Adams Pardons William Darrell: A Note on Sedition Proceedings, 1789-1800." *New York Historical Society Quarterly* 40 (April 1956): 176-181.

1017. Smith, James M. "President John Adams, Thomas Cooper, and Sedition: A Case Study in Suppression." *Mississippi Valley Historical Review* 42 (December 1955): 438-465.

1018. Smith, William L. *The Pretentions of Thomas Jefferson to the Presidency Examined: And the Charges against John Adams Refuted.* Philadelphia: s.n., 1976.

1019. Stinchcombe, William C. *The XYZ Affair.* Westport, CT: Greenwood Press, 1980.

1020. Taggert, Hugh T. "The Presidential Journey, In 1800, From the Old to the New Seat of Government." *Columbia Historical Society Records* 3 (1900): 180-209.

1021. Trescot, William H. *The Diplomatic History of the Administrations of Washington and Adams, 1789-1801.* Boston: Little, Brown, 1857.

1022. Turner, Kathryn. "The Appointment of John Marshall." *William and Mary Quarterly* 17 (April 1960): 143-163.

1023. Vaughan, Harold C. *The XYZ Affair, 1797-98: The Diplomacy of the Adams Administration and an Undeclared War with France.* New York: Franklin Watts, 1972.

1024. Warren, Charles. "John Adams and American Constitutions — A Discussion of Government by Executive Regulations." In *Kentucky State Bar Association, Proceedings of the Twenty-seventh Annual Meeting,* 124-145. Louisville: Press of Westerfield-Bonte Co., 1928.

1025. Wood, John. *The History of the Administration of John Adams, Esq., Late President of the United States.* New York: n.s., 1802.

Writings

1026. Adams, Charles F., ed. *Letters of John Adams Addressed to His Wife.* 2 vols. Boston: Little, Brown, 1841.

1027. Adams, John. *The Adams-Jefferson Letters: The Complete Correspondence between Thomas Jefferson and Abigail and John Adams.* Edited by Lester J. Cappon. Chapel Hill: University of North Carolina Press, 1959.

1028. Adams, John. *Adams to Jefferson and Jefferson to Adams: A Dialogue from Their Correspondence, 1812-1826.* Edited by Richard K. Arnold. San Francisco: Jerico Press, 1975.

1029. Adams, John. *A Collection of State-Papers, Relative to the First Acknowledgement of the Sovereignity [sic] of the United States of America, and the Reception of Their Minister Plenipotentiary, By Their High Mightinesses the States-General of the United Netherlands.* London: J. Fielding, 1982.

1030. Adams, John. *Correspondence between the Hon. John Adams and the Late William Cunningham, Esq., Beginning in 1803, and Ending in 1812.* Boston: E. M. Cunningham, 1823.

1031. Adams, John. *Correspondence of the Late President Adams, Originally Published in the Boston Patriot: In a Series of Letters.* Boston: Everett and Munroe, 1809-1810.

1032. Adams, John. *Deeds and Other*

John Adams

Documents Relating to the Several Pieces of Land, and to the Library Presented to the Town of Quincy, By President Adams, Together with a Catalogue of the Books. Cambridge, MA: Hilliard and Metcalf, 1823.

1033. Adams, John. *A Defense of the Constitutions of Government of the United States of America.* 3 vols. London: C. Dilly, 1787-1788.

1034. Adams, John. *Diary and Autobiography of John Adams.* 4 vols. Edited by Lyman H. Butterfield, et al. Cambridge, MA: Harvard University Press, 1961.

1035. Adams, John. *Discourses on Davila, A Series of Papers, On Political History: Written in the Year 1790, and Then Published in the Gazette of the United States.* Boston: Russell and Cutler, 1805.

1036. Adams, John. *The Earliest Diary of John Adams: June 1753-April 1754, September 1758-January 1759.* Edited by Lyman H. Butterfield, et al. Cambridge, MA: Harvard University Press, 1966.

1037. Adams, John. *Familiar Letters of John Adams and His Wife Abigail Adams, During the Revolution.* New York: Hurd and Houghton, 1876.

1038. Adams, John. *The Founding Fathers: John Adams: A Biography in His Own Words.* Edited by James B. Peabody. New York: Harper and Row, n.d.

1039. Adams, John. *The John Adams Papers.* Edited by Frank Donovan. New York: Dodd, Mead, 1965.

1040. Adams, John. "Letter of John Adams to Charles Cushing, 1756." *Massachusetts Historical Society Proceedings* 46 (1913): 410-412.

1041. Adams, John. *Letters from a Distinguished American: Twelve Essays by John Adams on American Foreign Policy, 1780.* Washington, DC: U.S. Government Printing Office, 1978.

1042. Adams, John. *Message of the President of the U.S. to Both Houses of Congress, April 3, 1798: Letters of Credence and Full Powers to the Envoys from the U.S. to the French Republic.* Philadelphia: Dobson and Ormrod, 1798.

1043. Adams, John. *Novanglus, and Massachusettensis: Or, Political Essays Published in the Years 1774 and 1775, On the Principal Points of Controversy, Between Great Britain and Her Colonies: The Former by John Adams, The Latter by Jonathan Sewall; To Which Are Added, A Number of Letters, Lately Written by President Adams to the Honourable William Tudor: Some of Which Were Never before Published.* Boston: Hews and Goss, 1819.

1044. Adams, John. *Old Family Letters: Copied from the Originals for Alexander Biddle.* Philadelphia: Lippincott, 1892.

1045. Adams, John. *The Papers of John Adams 1755-1775.* 6 vols. Edited by Robert J. Taylor. Cambridge, MA: Harvard University Press, 1977.

1046. Adams, John. *The Political Writings of John Adams: Representative Selections.* Edited by George A. Peek, Jr. New York: Liberal Arts Press, 1954.

1047. Adams, John. *The Selected Writings of John and John Quincy Adams.* Edited by Adrienne Koch and William Peden. New York: Knopf, 1946.

1048. Adams, John. *Statesman and Friend: Correspondence of John Adams with Benjamin Waterhouse, 1784-1822.* Edited by Worthington C. Ford. Boston: Little, Brown, 1927.

1049. Adams, John. *Thoughts on Government Applicable to the Present State of the American Colonies.* Philadelphia: Dunlap, 1776.

1050. Adams, John. *A Treatise on the Principles and Practice of the Action of*

Ejectment with Copious Notes and References to the American and English Decision. Edited by John L. Tillinghast, et al. New York: Banks, Gould, 1854.

1051. Adams, John. *Twenty-six Letters, Upon Interesting Subjects, Respecting the Revolution of America.* New York: John Fenno, 1789.

1052. Adams, John. *Warren-Adams Letters, Being Chiefly a Correspondence among John Adams, Samuel Adams, and James Warren, 1743-1814.* Boston: Massachusetts Historical Society, 1917-1925.

1053. Adams, John. *The Works of John Adams, Second President of the United States: With a Life of the Author.* 10 vols. Boston: Little, Brown, 1850-1856.

1054. Butterfield, Lyman H. "The Jefferson-Adams Correspondence in the Adams Manuscript Trust (1777-1826)." *Library of Congress Quarterly Journal* 5 (February 1948): 3-6.

1055. Butterfield, Lyman H. "John Adams' Correspondence with Hezekiah Niles." *Maryland Historical Magazine* 57 (June 1962): 150-154.

1056. Laska, Vera. "The Many-Splendored Correspondence of Abigail and John Adams." *New England Social Studies Bulletin* 34 (1976-1977): 11-13.

1057. Peek, George A., Jr. *Political Writings of John Adams: Representative Selections.* New York: Liberal Arts Press, 1954.

1058. Wilstach, Paul, ed. *Correspondence of John Adams and Thomas Jefferson (1812-1816).* Indianapolis, IN: Bobbs-Merill, 1925.

1059. Wright, Esmond. "The Papers of Great Men: John Adams." *History Today* 12 (March 1962): 197-198, 213.

1060. Wroth, L. Kinvin, and Hiller B. Zobel, eds. *Legal Papers of John Adams.* 3 vols. Cambridge, MA: Harvard University Press, 1965.

Thomas Jefferson

Biographies

1061. Abbott, Lawrence F. "Thomas Jefferson." *Outlook* 143 (May 26, 1926): 131-133.

1062. Adams, James T. *The Living Jefferson*. New York: Scribner's, 1936.

1063. Adams, Randolph G. "Thomas Jefferson, Librarian." In his *Three Americanists*, 69-96. Philadelphia: University of Pennsylvania Press, 1939.

1064. Alderman, Edwin A. "Thomas Jefferson." *University of Virginia Alumni Bulletin* 17 (July 1924): 270-272.

1065. Baldwin, Joseph G. *Party Leaders: Sketches of Thomas Jefferson, Alexander Hamilton, Andrew Jackson, Henry Clay, John Randolph of Roanoke: Including Notices of Many Other Distinguished American Statesmen*. New York: Appleton, 1855.

1066. Banes, Ruth A. "The Exemplary Self: Autobiography in Eighteenth Century America." *Biography* 5 (Summer 1982): 226-239.

1067. Barrett, Marvin. *Meet Thomas Jefferson*. New York: Random House, 1967.

1068. Baugh, Albert C. "Thomas Jefferson: Linguistic Liberal." In *Studies for William A. Read, A Miscellany Presented by Some of His Colleagues and Friends*, edited by Nathaniel M. Caffee and Thomas A. Kirby, 88-108. Baton Rouge: Louisiana State University Press, 1940.

1069. Beard, Charles A. "Thomas Jefferson: A Civilized Man." *Mississippi Valley Historical Review* 30 (September 1943): 159-170.

1070. Bemis, Samuel F. "Thomas Jefferson." In *The American Secretaries of State and Their Diplomacy*. Vol. 2, edited by Samuel F. Bemis, 3-93. New York: Knopf, 1927.

1071. Binger, Carl. "Conflicts in the Life of Thomas Jefferson." *American Journal of Psychiatry* 125 (February 1969): 1098-1107.

1072. Binger, Carl. *Thomas Jefferson: A Well-Tempered Mind*. New York: Norton, 1970.

1073. Blinderman, Charles S. "Thomas Jefferson: Humanist." *Humanist* 20 (July/August 1960): 203-211.

1074. Boorstin, Daniel J. *The Lost World of Thomas Jefferson*. New York: Holt, 1948.

1075. Bottorff, William K. "Introduction: The Age of Jefferson." *Midcontinent American Studies Journal* 9 (Spring 1966): 5-7.

1076. Bottorff, William K. *Thomas Jefferson*. Boston: Twayne, 1979.

1077. Bowers, Claude G. *The Young Jefferson, 1743-1789.* Boston: Houghton Mifflin, 1945.

1078. Bridges, David L. "A Historical Study of Thomas Jefferson." Master's thesis, North Texas State University, 1958.

1079. Brodie, Fawn M. "Jefferson Biographers and the Psychology of Canonization." *Journal of Interdisciplinary History* 2 (Summer 1971): 155-172.

1080. Brodie, Fawn M. "Political Hero in America: His Fate and His Future." *Virginia Quarterly Review* 46 (Winter 1970): 46-60.

1081. Brodie, Fawn M. *Thomas Jefferson: An Intimate History.* New York: Norton, 1974.

1082. Brown, Stuart G. *Thomas Jefferson.* New York: Washington Square Press, 1966.

1083. Carlton, Mabel M. *Thomas Jefferson: An Outline of His Life and Service with the Story of Monticello, The Home He Reared and Loved.* New York: Thomas Jefferson Memorial Foundation, 1924.

1084. Cavanagh, Catherine F. "The Youth of Jefferson." *New Age* 6 (July 1907): 29-32.

1085. Chinard, Gilbert. *Thomas Jefferson, The Apostle of Americanism.* 2d ed. Ann Arbor: University of Michigan Press, 1957.

1086. Clark, Graves. G. *Thomas Jefferson.* Richmond, VA: Johnson, 1947.

1087. Cobb, Joseph B. "Thomas Jefferson." In his *Leisure Labors: Or, Miscellanies Historical, Literary, and Political,* 5-130. New York: Appleton, 1858.

1088. Cooke, John E. "Thomas Jefferson." *Southern Literary Messenger* 30 (May 1860): 321-341.

1089. Cox, James M. "Jefferson's Autobiography: Recovering Literature's Lost Ground." *Southern Review* 14 (Autumn 1978): 633-652.

1090. Curtis, Thomas E. *The True Thomas Jefferson.* Philadelphia: Lippincott, 1901.

1091. Davis, Thomas J. *A Sketch of the Life, Character, and Public Services of Thomas Jefferson, With Some Account of the Aid He Rendered in Establishing Our Independence and Government.* Philadelphia: Claxton, Remson and Haffelfinger, 1876.

1092. Donaldson, Thomas. *The House in Which Thomas Jefferson Wrote the Declaration of Independence.* Philadelphia: Avil Printing Co., 1898.

1093. Dos Passos, John R. *The Head and Heart of Thomas Jefferson.* Garden City, NY: Doubleday, 1954.

1094. Dwight, Theodore. *The Character of Thomas Jefferson.* Boston: Weeks, Jordan, 1839.

1095. Eastman, Fred. "Thomas Jefferson." In his *Men of Power: Sixty Minute Biographies,* Vol. 1, 9-50. Nashville, TN: Cokesbury Press, 1938.

1096. Egan, Clifford. "How Not to Write a Biography: A Critical Look at Fawn Brodie's Thomas Jefferson." *Social Science* 14 (April 1977): 128-136.

1097. Ellis, Edward S. *The Life of Thomas Jefferson, Third President of the U.S.* Chicago: Laird and Lee, 1913.

1098. Farber, Joseph C. *The Worlds of Thomas Jefferson.* New York: Weathervane Books, 1971.

1099. Fishwick, Marshall W. "Thomas Jefferson." In his *Gentlemen of Virginia,* 125-143. New York: Dodd, Mead, 1961.

1100. Fleming, Thomas J. *The Man from Monticello: An Intimate Life of Thomas Jefferson.* New York: Morrow, 1969.

1101. Ford, Paul L. *The Autobiography of Thomas Jefferson.* New York: Putnam, 1914.

1102. Ford, Worthington C. *Thomas Jefferson and James Thomson Callender, 1798-1802.* Brooklyn, NY: Historical Printers Club, 1897.

1103. Fritchman, Stephen H. "Thomas Jefferson." In his *Men of Liberty: Ten Unitarian Pioneers,* 83-104. Port Washington, NY: Kennikat Press, 1944.

1104. Garrett, Wendell D., and Joseph C. Farber. *Thomas Jefferson Redivivus.* Barre, MA: Barre Publishers, 1971.

1105. Georgiady, Nicholas P., and Louis G. Romano. *Events in the Life of Thomas Jefferson.* Milwaukee, WI: Independents Publishing Co., 1966.

1106. Gilpin, Henry D. *A Biographical Sketch of Thomas Jefferson.* Philadelphia: n.p., 1828.

1107. Goodman, Nathan G. "Thomas Jefferson, A Really Wonderful, All-Round Man, 1743-1826." *Historical Outlook* 17 (December 1926): 365-366.

1108. Graff, Henry F., ed. *Thomas Jefferson.* Morristown, NJ: Silver Burdett, 1968.

1109. Hale, Edward E. "Memories of a Hundred Years: Thomas Jefferson." *Outlook* 70 (February 1, 1902): 320-323.

1110. Hart, Charles H. "Life Portraits of Thomas Jefferson." *McClure's Magazine* 11 (May 1898): 47-55.

1111. Hollis, Christopher. "Thomas Jefferson." In his *The American Heresy,* 6-81. New York: Minton, Balch, 1930.

1112. Howell, Wilbur S. "Thomas Jefferson." *Commentary* 67 (January 1979): 8-9.

1113. Hutchins, Frank. *Thomas Jefferson.* New York: Longmans, Green, 1946.

1114. Kimball, Marie G. *Jefferson, The Road to Glory, 1743 to 1776.* New York: Coward-McCann, 1943.

1115. Kimball, Marie G. *Jefferson, The Scene of Europe, 1784-1789.* New York: Coward-McCann, 1950.

1116. Kimball, Marie G. *Jefferson, War, and Peace, 1776 to 1784.* New York: Coward-McCann, 1947.

1117. Koch, Adrienne, ed. *Jefferson.* Englewood Cliffs, NJ: Prentice-Hall, 1971.

1118. Kuper, Theodore F. *Thomas Jefferson the Giant.* New York: Thomas Jefferson Memorial Foundation, 1927.

1119. Larson, Martin A. *Thomas Jefferson: Magnificent Populist.* Greenwich, CT: Devin-Adair, 1981.

1120. Lehmann-Hartleben, Karl. *Thomas Jefferson, American Humanist.* New York: Macmillan, 1947.

1121. Linn, William. *The Life of Thomas Jefferson.* Ithaca, NY: Mack and Andrus, 1834.

1122. Lisitzky, Genevieve H. *Thomas Jefferson.* New York: Viking Press, 1933.

1123. Lyman, T. P. H. *The Life of Thomas Jefferson, Esq., LL.D., Late Ex-President of the U.S.* Philadelphia: D. and S. Neall, 1826.

1124. Malone, Dumas. *Jefferson and the Ordeal of Liberty.* Boston: Little, Brown, 1962.

1125. Malone, Dumas. *The Jeffersonian Heritage.* Boston: Beacon Press, 1953.

1126. Malone, Dumas. *Jefferson the Virginian.* Boston: Little, Brown, 1948.

1127. Malone, Dumas. "Thomas Jefferson." In *Dictionary of American Biography,* Vol. 10, 17-35. New York: Scribner's, 1928-1936.

1128. Malone, Dumas. *Thomas Jefferson*

as a Political Leader. Berkeley: University of California Press, 1963.

1129. Malone, Dumas. *The Sage of Monticello.* Boston: Little, Brown, 1981.

1130. Mansfield, Harvey C. "Thomas Jefferson." In *American Political Thought,* edited by Morton Frisch and Richard Stevens, 23-50. New York: Scribner's, 1971.

1131. Matthews, Richard K. *The Radical Politics of Thomas Jefferson.* Lawrence: University Press of Kansas, 1984.

1132. Merwin, Henry C. *Thomas Jefferson.* Boston: Houghton Mifflin, 1901.

1133. Morse, John T., Jr. *Thomas Jefferson.* Boston: Houghton Mifflin, 1883.

1134. Moscow, Henry. *Thomas Jefferson and His World.* New York: American Heritage Publishing Co., 1960.

1135. Murphy, Dan. *Thomas Jefferson.* St. Louis, MO: Jefferson National, 1978.

1136. Muzzey, David S. *Thomas Jefferson.* New York: Scribner's, 1918.

1137. Nash, Roderick. "Thomas Jefferson." In his *From These Beginnings: A Biographical Approach to American History,* Vol. 1, 101-148. New York: Harper and Row, 1978.

1138. Nock, Albert J. *Jefferson.* New York: Harcourt, Brace, 1926.

1139. Padover, Saul K. *Jefferson.* New York: Harcourt, Brace, 1942.

1140. Parker, Theodore. "Thomas Jefferson." In his *Historic Americans,* 233-295. Boston: Horace B. Fuller, 1871.

1141. Parton, James. *Life of Thomas Jefferson, Third President of the United States.* Boston: J. R. Osgood, 1874.

1142. Petersen, Arnold. "Thomas Jefferson." In his *Reviling of the Great,* 9-18. New York: New York Labor News Co., 1949.

1143. Peterson, Merrill D. *The Jefferson Image in the American Mind.* New York: Oxford University Press, 1960.

1144. Peterson, Merrill D. *Thomas Jefferson and the New Nation: A Biography.* New York: Oxford University Press, 1970.

1145. Peterson, Merrill D., and Aida D. Donald, comps. *Thomas Jefferson: A Profile.* New York: Hill and Wang, 1967.

1146. Pettengill, Samuel B. *Jefferson, The Forgotten Man.* New York: America's Future, 1938.

1147. Randall, Henry S. *The Life of Thomas Jefferson.* 3 vols. New York: Derby and Jackson, 1858.

1148. Richardson, James D. "Thomas Jefferson." *New Age* 6 (July 1907): 18-24; (August 1907): 114-122; (September 1907): 224-230.

1149. Royner, B. L. *Life of Thomas Jefferson with Selections from the Most Valuable Portions of His Voluminous and Unrivalled Private Correspondence.* Boston: Lilly, Wait, Colman and Holden, 1834.

1150. Santrey, Laurence. *Thomas Jefferson.* Mahwah, NJ: Troll Associates, 1984.

1151. Schmucker, Samuel M. *The Life of Thomas Jefferson, With Notes by Henry Ketcham....* New York: Burt, 1903.

1152. Schouler, James. *Thomas Jefferson.* New York: Dodd, Mead, 1893.

1153. Simpson, Stephen. *The Lives of George Washington and Thomas Jefferson.* Philadelphia: Young, 1833.

1154. Smith, Page. *Jefferson: A Revealing Biography.* New York: McGraw-Hill, 1976.

1155. Stone, Gene. *The Story of Thomas Jefferson.* New York: Barse and Hopkins, 1922.

1156. Tauber, Gisela. "Reconstruction in Psychoanalytic Biography: Understanding

Thomas Jefferson." *Journal of Psychohistory* 7 (Fall 1979): 189-207.

1157. Taylor, Cornelia J. "Gleanings from the Life of Thomas Jefferson." *American Monthly Magazine* 2 (January 1893): 29-34.

1158. Thomas, Elbert D. *Thomas Jefferson, World Citizen*. New York: Modern Age Books, 1942.

1159. Thornton, William W. *Who Was Thomas Jefferson?* Richmond, VA: Richmond Press, 1909.

1160. Thornton, William W. "Who Was Thomas Jefferson?" *Tennessee Bar Association Proceedings* 32 (1913): 122-147.

1161. Trent, William P. "Thomas Jefferson." *Columbia University Quarterly* 16 (September 1914): 392-398.

1162. "The True Thomas Jefferson." *Outlook* 70 (January 25, 1902): 239-241.

1163. Tucker, George. *The Life of Thomas Jefferson, Third President of the United States, With Parts of His Correspondence Never before Published, and Notices of His Opinions on Questions of Civil Government, National Policy, and Constitutional Law*. Philadelphia: Carey, Lea and Blanchard, 1837.

1164. Van Loon, Hendrik W. *Thomas Jefferson*. New York: Dodd, Mead, 1943.

1165. Van Loon, Hendrik W. "Thomas Jefferson." In his *Fighters for Freedom: Jefferson and Bolivar*, 3-101. New York: Dodd, Mead, 1962.

1166. Watson, Thomas E. *The Life and Times of Thomas Jefferson*. New York: Appleton, 1903.

1167. Weymouth, Lally, ed. *Thomas Jefferson: The Man ... His World ... His Influence*. London: Weidenfeld and Nicolson, 1973.

1168. Wibberly, Leonard P. O. *Man of Liberty: A Life of Thomas Jefferson*. New York: Farrar, Straus and Giroux, 1968.

1169. Wilbur, Marguerite K. *Thomas Jefferson: Apostle of Liberty*. New York: Liveright, 1962.

Private Life

General

1170. Abrams, Rochonne. "Meriwether Lewis: Two Years with Jefferson, The Mentor." *Missouri Historical Society Bulletin* 36 (October 1979): 3-18.

1171. Adair, Douglass. "The New Thomas Jefferson." *William and Mary Quarterly* 3 (January 1946): 123-133.

1172. Adams, W. Howard. *The Eye of Thomas Jefferson*. Charlottesville: University Press of Virginia, 1981.

1173. Alexander, Edward P. "Jefferson and Kosciuszko: Friends of Liberty and Man." *Pennsylvania Magazine of History and Biography* 92 (January 1968): 87-103.

1174. Allison, Andrew M., K. DeLynn Cook, M. Richard Maxfield, and W. Cleon Skousen. *The Real Thomas Jefferson*. 2d ed. Washington, DC: National Center for Constitutional Studies, 1983.

1175. Allison, John M. *Adams and Jefferson, the Story of a Friendship*. Norman: University of Oklahoma Press, 1966.

1176. Beard, Charles A. "Jefferson in America Now." *Yale Review* 25 (Winter 1935): 241-257.

1177. Benson, C. Randolph. *Thomas Jefferson as Social Scientist*. Rutherford, NJ: Fairleigh Dickinson University Press, 1971.

1178. Bigelow, John. "Jefferson's Financial Diary." *Harper's New Monthly Magazine* 70 (March 1885): 534-542.

1179. Bliven, Bruce. "Our Legacy from Mr. Jefferson." *Reader's Digest* 82 (March 1963): 160-168.

1180. Boller, Paul F., Jr. "Jefferson Dreams of the Future." *Southwest Review* 44 (Spring 1959): 109-114.

1181. Booth, Edward T. "Thomas Jefferson's Piedmont Villa." In his *Country Life in America: As Lived by Ten Presidents of the United States*, 76-103. New York: Knopf, 1947.

1182. Bowers, Claude G. "Jefferson and the American Way of Life." In *The Heritage of Jefferson*, edited by Alexander Trachtenberg, 11-27. New York: Worker's School, 1945.

1183. Bowers, Claude G., and Earl Browder. *The Heritage of Jefferson*. New York: Worker's School, 1943.

1184. Bowling, Kenneth R. "Dinner at Jefferson's: A Note on Jacob E. Cooke's 'The Compromise of 1790.'" *William and Mary Quarterly* 28 (October 1971): 629-648.

1185. Boyd, Julian P. "Jefferson's French Baggage Crated and Uncrated." *Massachusetts Historical Society Proceedings* 83 (1971): 16-27.

1186. Boyd, Julian P. "Thomas Jefferson Survives." *American Scholar* 20 (Spring 1951): 163-173.

1187. Brent, Robert A. "Puncturing Some Jeffersonian Mythology." *Southern Quarterly* 6 (January 1966): 175-190.

1188. Brogan, Denis W. "The Ghost of Jefferson." *Fortnightly* 140 (July 1936): 88-92.

1189. Broun, Heywood. "Shades of Thomas Jefferson." *New Republic* 95 (July 20, 1938): 305.

1190. Browne, Edythe H. "The Great Simplicity of Jefferson." *Commonweal* 4 (July 14, 1926): 261-262.

1191. Bulfinch, Thomas. "Jefferson's Private Character." *North American Review* 91 (July 1860): 107-118.

1192. Bullock, Helen C. D. *My Head and My Heart, A Little History of Thomas Jefferson and Maria Cosway*. New York: Putnam, 1945.

1193. Bumstead, Samuel A. "A Description of Jefferson." *Virginia Magazine of History and Biography* 24 (June 1916): 309-310.

1194. Bush, Alfred L. *The Life Portraits of Thomas Jefferson: Catalogue of an Exhibition at the University Museum of Fine Arts (April 12 through 26)*. Charlottesville, VA: Thomas Jefferson Memorial Foundation, 1962.

1195. Butterfield, Lyman H., and Howard C. Rice, Jr. "Jefferson's Earliest Note to Maria Cosway with Some New Facts and Conjectures on His Broken Wrist." *William and Mary Quarterly* 5 (January 1948): 26-33; (October 1948): 620-621.

1196. "Cerrachi's Bust of Jefferson." *Tyler's Quarterly Historical and Genealogical Magazine* 8 (April 1927): 243-246.

1197. Chiang, C. Y. Jesse. "Understanding Thomas Jefferson." *International Review of History and Political Science* 14 (August 1977): 51-61.

1198. Chuinard, E. G. "Thomas Jefferson and the Corps of Discovery: Could He Have Done More?" *American West* 12 (November 1975): 4-13.

1199. Colbourn, H. Trevor. "The Saxon Heritage: Thomas Jefferson Looks at English History." Ph.D. dissertation, Johns Hopkins University, 1953.

1200. Cometti, Elizabeth. "Maria Cosway's Rediscovered Miniature of Jefferson." *William and Mary Quarterly* 9 (April 1952): 152-155.

1201. Commager, Henry S. "Thomas Jefferson Still Survives." *Publishers Weekly* 143 (April 10, 1943): 1504-1506.

1202. Comstock, Helen. "A Portrait of Jefferson in His Old Age." *International Studio* 96 (June 1930): 17-18.

1203. Cooke, John E. "Jefferson as a Lover." *Appleton's Journal of Literature, Science and Art* 12 (August 1874): 23-32.

1204. Coolidge, Harold J. *Thoughts on Thomas Jefferson, Or, What Jefferson Was Not.* Edited by Lawrence Coolidge. Boston: Club of Old Volumes, 1936.

1205. "The Cult of Jefferson." *Commonweal* 32 (April 9, 1943): 604.

1206. Daniel, Frederick S. "Virginian Reminiscences of Jefferson." *Harper's Weekly* 48 (November 1904): 1766-1768.

1207. Davis, Richard B. "Jefferson as a Collector of Virginiana." In *Studies in Bibliography: Papers of the Bibliographical Society of the University of Virginia*, Vol. 14, 117-144. Charlottesville: Bibliographical Society of the University of Virginia, 1961.

1208. Davis, Richard B. "John Holt Rice vs. Thomas Jefferson on the Great Deluge." *Virginia Magazine of History and Biography* 74 (January 1966): 108-109.

1209. Davis, Robert R., Jr. "Pell-Mell: Jeffersonian Etiquette and Protocol." *Historian* 43 (August 1981): 509-529.

1210. Dewey, Frank L. "Thomas Jefferson's Notes on Divorce." *William and Mary Quarterly* 39 (January 1982): 212-223.

1211. Dorsey, John M., ed. "Jefferson, His Own Physician." In his *The Jefferson-Dunglison Letters*, 83-106. Charlottesville: University of Virginia Press, 1960.

1212. Duke, Richard T. W., Jr. "The Private Life of Thomas Jefferson." *University of Virginia Alumni Bulletin* 14 (July 1921): 47-52.

1213. Dumbauld, Edward. *Thomas Jefferson, American Tourist, Being an Account of His Journeys in the United States of America, England, France, Italy, and Low Countries, and Germany.* Norman: University of Oklahoma Press, 1946.

1214. Dumbauld, Edward. "Where Did Jefferson Live in Paris?" *William and Mary Quarterly* 23 (January 1943): 64-68.

1215. Dwight, H. G. "Jefferson Simplicity." *Harper's Magazine* 169 (June 1934): 91-99.

1216. Early, Ruth H. "Thomas Jefferson, Citizen of 'Poplar Forest.'" *University of Virginia Alumni Bulletin* 15 (October 1922): 374-380.

1217. Ellis, Edward S. *Thomas Jefferson, A Character Sketch....* Milwaukee, WI: Campbell, 1903.

1218. "Exhibit on Jefferson's Library to Open at LC." *Library of Congress Information Bulletin* 35 (February 27, 1976): 124-125.

1219. Fesperman, Francis I. "Jefferson's Bible." *Ohio Journal of Religious Studies* 4 (October 1976): 78-88.

1220. Foley, John P. "Outdoor Life of the Presidents: No. 2, Thomas Jefferson." *Outing: An Illustrated Monthly Magazine of Recreation* 13 (December 1899): 250-259.

1221. Foley, John P., ed. *The Jeffersonian Cyclopedia: A Comprehensive Collection of the Views of Thomas Jefferson Classified and Arranged in Alphabetical Order under Nine Thousand Titles Relating to Government, Politics, Law, Education, Political Economy, Finance, Science, Art, Literature, Religious Freedom, Morals, etc.* New York: Funk and Wagnalls, 1900.

1222. Garrett, Wendell D. "Bicentennial Outlook: The Monumental Friendship of Jefferson and Adams." *Historic Preservation* 28 (April 1976): 28-35.

1223. Goff, Frederick R. "Jefferson the Book Collector." *Library of Congress Quarterly Journal* 29 (January 1972): 32-47.

1224. Golladay, V. Dennis. "Jefferson's 'Malignant Neighbor,' John Nicholas, Jr." *Virginia Magazine of History and Biography* 86 (July 1978): 306-319.

1225. Gray, Francis C. *Thomas Jefferson in 1814, Being an Account of a Visit to Monticello, Virginia*. Boston: Club of Odd Volumes, 1924.

1226. Hamilton, Joseph G. de Roulhac. "Jefferson and Adams at Ease." *South Atlantic Quarterly* 26 (October 1927): 359-372.

1227. Hamilton, Joseph G. de Roulhac. "Jefferson's Americanism." *Virginia Quarterly Review* 6 (January 1930): 117-122.

1228. Hamilton, Joseph G. de Roulhac. "Ripened Years: Thomas Jefferson: Time Treated Him Kindly." *Century Magazine* 114 (August 1927): 476-485.

1229. Harris, Ramon. "Thomas Jefferson: Female Identification." *American Imago* 25 (Winter 1968): 371-383.

1230. Harrison, Mary L. "The Sage of Monticello." *Daughters of the American Revolution Magazine* 52 (January 1918): 32-36.

1231. Hendrickson, Walter B. "Thomas Jefferson — Up from Slander." *Social Education* 18 (October 1954): 244-248.

1232. Henkels, Stan V. "Jefferson to William Short on Mr. and Mrs. Merry, 1804." *American Historical Review* 33 (July 1928): 832-835.

1233. Hitchcock, Margaret R. "The Mastodon of Thomas Jefferson." *Washington Academy of Sciences Journal* 21 (March 4, 1931): 80-86.

1234. Holland, Corabelle A. "The Jefferson Memorial in Wales." *American Foreign Service Journal* 10 (November 1933): 396-397.

1235. Hubbard, Elbert, and John J. Lentz. *Thomas Jefferson, Being Two Attempts to Help Perpetuate the Memory and Pass along the Influence of the Great American*. East Aurora, NY: Roycrofters, 1906.

1236. "In Honor of Jefferson." *Missouri Historical Review* 37 (January 1943): 193-196.

1237. Jackson, Donald. *Thomas Jefferson and the Stony Mountains: Exploring the West from Monticello*. Champaign: University of Illinois Press, 1981.

1238. Jacobs, Victor. "Was Thomas Jefferson Really Very Bright?" *Manuscripts* 34 (Winter 1982): 21-24.

1239. "Jefferson and His Landlord." *Researcher* 1 (October 1926): 5-8.

1240. Kimball, Marie G. "Jefferson in Paris." *North American Review* 248 (Autumn 1939): 73-86.

1241. Kimball, Marie G. "A Playmate of Thomas Jefferson." *North American Review* 213 (February 1921): 145-156.

1242. Kimball, Marie G. *Thomas Jefferson's Cook Book*. Richmond, VA: Garrett and Massie, 1938.

1243. Kimball, Marie G. "Thomas Jefferson's Rhine Journey." *American German Review* 13 (October 1946): 4-9; (December 1946): 11-15; (February 1947): 4-8.

1244. Kimball, Marie G. "Three Friends of Jefferson." *Virginia Quarterly Review* 4 (October 1928): 624-628.

1245. Kimball, S. Fiske. "In Search of

Thomas Jefferson's Birthplace." *Virginia Magazine of History and Biography* 51 (October 1943): 313-325.

1246. Kimball, S. Fiske. "The Life Portraits of Jefferson and Their Replicas." *American Philosophical Society Proceedings* 88 (December 1944): 497-534.

1247. Kuenzli, Esther W. *The Last Years of Thomas Jefferson, 1809-1826.* Hicksville, NY: Exposition Press, 1975.

1248. Kuper, Theodore F. "Jefferson and Italy: The Vital Contacts between Two Great Peoples." *Atlantica* 15 (December 1933): 8-10, 37.

1249. Larson, Martin A. *The Essence of Jefferson.* Bridgeport, CT: J. J. Binns, 1977.

1250. Lehmann-Hartleben, Karl. "Thomas Jefferson, Archaeologist." *American Journal of Archaeology* 47 (April/June 1943): 161-163.

1251. Lerman, Louis. "Mr. Jefferson's Plow." *New Masses* 13 (April 1943): 14-15.

1252. McAdie, Alexander. "Thomas Jefferson at Home." *American Antiquarian Society Proceedings* 40 (April 1930): 27-46.

1253. MacLeish, Archibald. "The Ghost of Thomas Jefferson." In his *Riders on the Earth: Essays and Recollections,* 57-65. Boston: Houghton Mifflin, 1978.

1254. Malone, Dumas. "Mr. Jefferson's Private Life." *American Antiquarian Society Proceedings* 84 (April 1974): 65-72.

1255. Mayo, Barbara. "Twilight at Monticello." *Virginia Quarterly Review* 17 (Autumn 1941): 502-516.

1256. Mehlinger, Howard D. "When I See Mr. Jefferson, I'm Going to Tell Him...." *Social Education* 42 (January 1978): 54-60.

1257. Meschutt, David. "Gilbert Stuart's Portraits of Thomas Jefferson." *American Art Journal* 13 (Winter 1981): 2-16.

1258. Minnigerode, Meade. *Jefferson, Friend of France, 1793: The Career of Edmund Charles Genet, 1763-1834.* New York: Putnam, 1928.

1259. Noland, Nancy. "Jefferson and Palladio." *Vassar Journal of Undergraduate Studies* 16 (May 1943): 1-15.

1260. Parton, James. "Thomas Jefferson as a Sore-Head." *Atlantic Monthly* 30 (September 1872): 273-288.

1261. Peden, William H. "Some Notes Concerning Thomas Jefferson's Libraries." *William and Mary Quarterly* 1 (July 1944): 265-272.

1262. Peterson, Merrill D. "The Jefferson Image, 1829." *American Quarterly* 3 (Fall 1951): 204-220.

1263. Philips, Edward H. "Timothy Pickering's 'Portrait' of Thomas Jefferson." *Essex Institute of Historical Collections* 94 (October 1958): 309-327.

1264. Powell, E. P. "A Study of Thomas Jefferson." *Arena* 3 (May 1891): 712-713.

1265. Pulley, Judith. "The Bittersweet Friendship of Thomas Jefferson and Abigail Adams." *Essex Institute of Historical Collections* 108 (July 1972): 193-216.

1266. Reid, Whitelaw. "Thomas Jefferson." In his *American and English Studies,* Vol. 2, 37-70. New York: Scribner's, 1913.

1267. Reps, John W. "Thomas Jefferson's Checkerboard Towns." *Society of Architectural Historians Journal* 20 (October 1961): 108-114.

1268. Rice, Howard C., Jr. "Saint-Memin's Portrait of Jefferson." *Princeton University Library Chronicle* 20 (Summer 1959): 182-192.

1269. Rice, Howard C., Jr., ed. *Thomas Jefferson's Paris.* Princeton, NJ: Princeton University Press, 1976.

1270. Richardson, E. P. "Life Drawing of Jefferson by John Trumbull." *American Art Journal* 7 (November 1975): 4-9.

1271. Richardson, E. P. "A Life Drawing of Jefferson by John Trumbull." *Maryland Historical Magazine* 70 (Winter 1975): 363-371.

1272. Robins, Elizabeth. "The Old Jefferson House, Philadelphia." *Harper's Weekly* 27 (April 14, 1883): 228.

1273. Schachner, Nathan. "Jefferson: The Man and the Myth." *American Mercury* 65 (July 1947): 46-52.

1274. Sherman, E. David. "Geriatric Profile of Thomas Jefferson." *Journal of the American Geriatrics Society* 25 (March 1977): 112-117.

1275. Sowerby, E. Millicent. "Thomas Jefferson and His Library." *Bibliographical Society of America Papers* 50 (1956): 213-228.

1276. Sowerby, E. Millicent, comp. *Catalogue of the Library of Thomas Jefferson*. 5 vols. Charlottesville: University Press of Virginia, 1983.

1277. Spivey, Herman E. "William Cullen Bryant Changes His Mind: An Unpublished Letter about Thomas Jefferson." *New England Quarterly* 22 (December 1949): 528-529.

1278. Sternberg, Richard R. "The Jefferson Birthday Dinner, 1830." *Journal of Southern History* 4 (August 1938): 334-345.

1279. Thompson, D. P. "A Talk with Jefferson." *Harper's New Monthly Magazine* 26 (May 1863): 833-835.

1280. Thorpe, Russell W. "A Portrait of Thomas Jefferson, A Lost Picture since 1897 — Painted by Robert Field." *Antiquarian* 4 (March 1925): 17-18.

1281. Thorup, Oscar A. "Jefferson's Admonition." *Mayo Clinic Proceedings* 47 (March 1972): 199-201.

1282. True, Katharine M. "The Romantic Voyage of Thomas Jefferson." *Harper's Magazine* 129 (September 1914): 489-497.

1283. Watson, Ross. "Thomas Jefferson's Visit to England, 1786." *History Today* 27 (January 1977): 3-13.

1284. Weaver, Bettie W. "Mary Jefferson and Eppington." *Virginia Cavalcade* 19 (Autumn 1969): 30-35.

1285. Wertenbaker, Thomas J. "Glimpses of Thomas Jefferson." *Emory University Quarterly* 9 (March 1953): 48-55.

1286. Whitty, J. H. "Thomas Jefferson's Bull Moose." *Nation* 95 (September 5, 1912): 211.

1287. Wilson, Douglas L. "Sowerby Revisited: The Unfinished Catalogue of Thomas Jefferson's Library." *William and Mary Quarterly* 41 (October 1984): 615-628.

1288. Wilstach, Paul. "Jefferson Out of Harness." *American Mercury* 4 (January 1925): 63-68.

1289. Wilstach, Paul. "Thomas Jefferson's Secret Home." *Country Life* 53 (April 1928): 41-43.

1290. Winston, Alexander. "Mr. Jefferson in Paris." *American Society Legion of Honor Magazine* 35 (1964): 139-150.

1291. Wyman, William I. "Thomas Jefferson and the Patent System." *Journal of the Patent Office Society* 1 (September 1918): 5-8.

Agriculture

1292. Bennett, Hugh H. *Thomas Jefferson: Soil Conservationist*. Washington,

DC: U.S. Government Printing Office, 1944.

1293. Bridgman, Richard. "Jefferson's Farmer before Jefferson." *American Quarterly* 14 (Winter 1962): 567-577.

1294. Browne, Charles A. "Thomas Jefferson and Agricultural Chemistry." *Scientific Monthly* 60 (January 1945): 55-62.

1295. Cragan, Thomas M. "Thomas Jefferson's Early Attitudes toward Manufacturing, Agriculture, and Commerce." Ph.D. dissertation, University of Tennessee, 1965.

1296. Edwards, Everett E. "The National Agricultural Jefferson Bicentenary Committee: Its Activities and Recommendations." *Agricultural History* 19 (July 1945): 167-178.

1297. Edwards, Everett E., comp. *Jefferson and Agriculture: A Sourcebook.* Washington, DC: U.S. Bureau of Agricultural Economics, 1943.

1298. Griswold, A. Whitney. "The Jeffersonian Ideal." In his *Farming and Democracy*, 18-46. New Haven, CT: Yale University Press, 1948.

1299. Luther, Frederic N. "Jefferson as a Naturalist." *Magazine of American History* 13 (April 1885): 379-390.

1300. Miller, August C., Jr. "Jefferson as an Agriculturist." *Agricultural History* 16 (April 1942): 65-78.

1301. Mitchell, Henry. "Thomas Jefferson, The Young Gardener." *Horticulture* 54 (June 1976): 38-51.

1302. Peterson, Martin S., and Marvin P. Grim. "The Farmer Who Founded Democracy: Thomas Jefferson Rotated Crops and Went through Farm Depressions at Monticello." *Wallaces Farmer* 54 (July 26, 1929): 6, 29.

1303. Quinn, Patrick F. "Agrarianism and the Jeffersonian Philosophy." *Review of Politics* 2 (January 1940): 87-104.

1304. Roberson, Samuel A. "Thomas Jefferson and the Eighteenth-Century Landscape Garden Movement in England." Ph.D. dissertation, Yale University, 1974.

1305. Ward, James E. "Monticello: An Experimental Farm." *Agricultural History* 19 (July 1945): 183-185.

1306. Weaver, Neal. "Thomas Jefferson: Statesman, Artist, Scientist, and One-Man Horticultural Exchange." *Garden Journal* 26 (October 1976): 147-150.

1307. Wickard, Claude R. "Thomas Jefferson — Founder of American Agriculture." *Agricultural History* 19 (July 1945): 179-180.

1308. Williams, Morley J. "The Gardens at Monticello." *Landscape Architecture* 24 (January 1934): 64-71.

1309. Wilson, Douglas L. "The American Agricola: Jefferson's Agrarianism and the Classical Tradition." *South Atlantic Quarterly* 80 (Summer 1981): 339-354.

1310. Wilson, Milburn L. "Jefferson and His Moldboard Plow." *Land* 3 (Summer 1943): 59-64.

1311. Wilson, Milburn L. "Jefferson, Father of Agricultural Science." *Extension Service Review* 14 (May 1943): 74.

1312. Wilson, Milburn L. "Thomas Jefferson — Farmer." *American Philosophical Society Proceedings* 87 (July 1943): 216-222.

Architecture

1313. Beiswanger, William. "Jefferson's Designs for Garden Structures at Monticello." *Society of Architectural Historians Journal* 35 (December 1976): 310-312.

1314. Crenshaw, Frank S. "Minor Architectural Designs of Thomas Jefferson: The

Executed and Non-executed Residential Designs and Executed Non-residential Designs." Master's thesis, University of Virginia, 1961.

1315. Donnelly, Marian C. "Jefferson Observatory Design." *Society of Architectural Historians Journal* 36 (March 1977): 33-35.

1316. Frary, Ihna T. *Thomas Jefferson, Architect and Builder.* 3d ed. Richmond, VA: Garrett and Massie, 1950.

1317. Guinness, Desmond. "Thomas Jefferson: Visionary Architect." *Horizon* 22 (April 1979): 51-59.

1318. Guinness, Desmond, and Julius T. Sadler, Jr. *Mr. Jefferson: Architect.* New York: Viking Press, 1977.

1319. Heatwole, C. J. "Thomas Jefferson as an Architect." *Virginia Journal of Education* 19 (May 1926): 361-363.

1320. Isham, Norman M. "Jefferson's Place in Our Architectural History." *Journal of the American Institute of Architects* 2 (May 1914): 230-235.

1321. Kimball, S. Fiske. "A Church Designed by Jefferson." *Architectural Record* 53 (February 1923): 184-186.

1322. Kimball, S. Fiske. "Form and Function in the Architecture of Jefferson." *Magazine of Art* 40 (April 1947): 150-153.

1323. Kimball, S. Fiske. "Jefferson as Architect." *Nation* 98 (January 8, 1914): 33.

1324. Kimball, S. Fiske. "Jefferson the Architect." *Forum* 75 (June 1926): 926-931.

1325. Kimball, S. Fiske. "Thomas Jefferson as Architect: Monticello and Shadwell." *Architectural Quarterly of Harvard University* 2 (June 1914): 89-137.

1326. Kimball, S. Fiske, ed. *Thomas Jefferson, Architect: Original Designs in the Collection of Thomas Jefferson Coolidge, Jr.* Boston: Riverside Press, 1915.

1327. Lambeth, William A., and Warren H. Manning. *Thomas Jefferson as an Architect and a Designer of Landscapes.* Boston: Houghton Mifflin, 1913.

1328. Nichols, Frederick D., ed. *Thomas Jefferson's Architectural Drawings.* 2d ed. Charlottesville: University Press of Virginia, 1961.

1329. Nichols, Frederick D., and Ralph E. Griswald. *Thomas Jefferson, Landscape Architect.* Charlottesville: University Press of Virginia, 1981.

1330. O'Neal, William B. *Jefferson's Fine Arts Library for the University of Virginia, With Additional Notes on Architectural Volumes Known to Have Been Owned by Jefferson.* Charlottesville: University of Virginia Press, 1956.

1331. Pickens, Buford. "Mr. Jefferson as Revolutionary Architect." *Society of Architectural Historians Journal* 34 (December 1975): 257-279.

1332. Ruck, William S. "Jefferson the Architect." *Virginia Quarterly Review* 8 (January 1932): 139-143.

1333. Stapley, Mildred. "Thomas Jefferson, The Architect: A Tribute." *Architectural Record* 29 (February 1911): 178-185.

1334. Suro, Dario. "Jefferson, The Architect." *Americas* 25 (November/December 1973): 29-35.

Arts

1335. Adams, W. Howard, ed. *Jefferson and the Arts: An Extended View.* Charlottesville: University Press of Virginia, 1976.

1336. Allan, Alfred K. "The Music Lover of Monticello." *Music Journal* 13 (September 1955): 39, 58.

1337. Berman, Eleanor D. *Thomas Jeffer-*

son among the Arts: An Essay in Early American Esthetics. New York: Philosophical Library, 1947.

1338. Biancolli, Louis. "Thomas Jefferson, Fiddler." *Life* 22 (April 7, 1947): 13-20.

1339. Bullock, Helen C. D. "Mr. Jefferson, Musician." *Etude* 61 (October 1943): 633-634, 688.

1340. Cripe, Helen L. "Music: Thomas Jefferson's 'Delightful Recreation.'" *Antiques* 102 (July 1972): 124-128.

1341. Cripe, Helen L. "Thomas Jefferson and Music." Ph.D. dissertation, University of Notre Dame, 1972.

1342. Ford, Susan. "Thomas Jefferson and John Adams on the Classics." *Arion* 6 (Spring 1967): 116-132.

1343. Garbett, Arthur S. "Thomas Jefferson's Life-Long Love of Music." *Etude* 59 (August 1941): 510, 568.

1344. Gauss, Charles E. "Thomas Jefferson's Musical Interests." *Etude* 51 (June 1933): 367-368, 419.

1345. Gelders, Ruth B. "The World of Music — For Thomas Jefferson and Other Presidents." *Daughters of the American Revolution Magazine* 105 (April 1971): 403-407, 475.

1346. Harbrecht, Rosemary. "Thomas Jefferson: Man of Culture." *Social Studies* 41 (October 1950): 258-260.

1347. Howard, Seymour. "Thomas Jefferson Art Gallery for Monticello." *Art Bulletin* 59 (December 1977): 583-600.

1348. Kallen, Horace M. "The Arts and Thomas Jefferson." *Ethics* 53 (July 1943): 279-283.

1349. Kimball, Marie G. "Thomas Jefferson, Patron of the Arts." *Antiques* 43 (April 1943): 164-167.

1350. Kimball, S. Fiske. "Jefferson and the Arts." *American Philosophical Society Proceedings* 87 (July 1943): 238-245.

1351. Kimball, S. Fiske. "Thomas Jefferson and the Origins of the Classical Revival in America." *Art and Archaeology* 1 (May 1915): 219-227.

1352. Krancik, John. "Thomas Jefferson's Interest in Italian Life, Language, and Art." *Kentucky Foreign Language Quarterly* 13 (1966): 130-137.

1353. Ladenson, Alex. "'I Cannot Live without Books': Thomas Jefferson Bibliophile." *Wilson Library Bulletin* 52 (April 1978): 624-631.

1354. Long, Orie W. *Thomas Jefferson and George Ticknor, A Chapter in American Scholarship.* Williamstown, MA: McClelland Press, 1933.

1355. Mayor, A. Hyatt. "Jefferson's Enjoyment of the Arts." *Metropolitan Museum of Art Bulletin* 2 (December 1943): 140-146.

1356. Nolan, Carolyn G. "Thomas Jefferson: Gentleman Musician." Master's thesis, University of Virginia, 1967.

1357. Ostrander, Gilman M. "Jefferson and Scottish Culture." *Historical Reflections* 5 (Winter 1978): 233-248.

1358. Parks, Edd W. "Jefferson as a Man of Letters." *Georgia Review* 6 (Winter 1952): 450-459.

1359. Peden, William H. "Thomas Jefferson: Book Collector." Ph.D. dissertation, University of Virginia, 1942.

1360. Sanford, Charles L. "The Art of Virtue: Franklin and Jefferson." In his *The Quest for Paradise: Europe and the American Moral Imagination*, 114-134. Urbana: University of Illinois Press, 1961.

1361. Shackelford, George G. "Thomas Jefferson and the Fine Arts of Northern Italy: 'A Peep into Elysium.'" In *America, the Middle Period: Essays in Honor of*

Bernard Mayo, edited by John B. Boles, 14-35. Charlottesville: University Press of Virginia, 1973.

1362. Stolba, K. Marie. "Music in the Life of Thomas Jefferson." *Daughters of the American Revolution Magazine* 108 (March 1974): 196-202.

1363. *Thomas Jefferson and the World of Books: A Symposium Held at the Library of Congress, September 21, 1976.* Washington, DC: Library of Congress, 1977.

1364. Thompson, Wilma. "Thomas Jefferson: Lifelong Musician." Master's thesis, Southern Illinois University, 1973.

1365. Wright, Louis B. "Thomas Jefferson and the Classics." *American Philosophical Society Proceedings* 87 (July 1943): 222-233.

Education

1366. Adams, Herbert B. *Thomas Jefferson and the University of Virginia.* Washington, DC: U.S. Government Printing Office, 1888.

1367. Arrowood, Charles F., ed. *Thomas Jefferson and Education in a Republic.* New York: McGraw-Hill, 1930.

1368. Carey, Alma P. "Thomas Jefferson's Ideal University: Dream and Actuality." Master's thesis, University of Texas, 1937.

1369. Carey, John P. "Influences on Thomas Jefferson's Theory and Practice of Higher Education." Ph.D. dissertation, University of Michigan, 1969.

1370. Cauthen, Irby B., Jr. " 'A Complete and Generous Education': Milton and Jefferson." *Virginia Quarterly Review* 55 (Spring 1979): 222-233.

1371. Chandler, Julian A. C. "Jefferson and the College of William and Mary." *Virginia Journal of Education* 19 (May 1926): 349-352.

1372. Chandler, Julian A. C. "Jefferson and William and Mary." *William and Mary Quarterly* 19 (October 1934): 304-307.

1373. Conant, James B. "Education for a Classless Society: The Jeffersonian Tradition." *Atlantic Monthly* 165 (May 1940): 593-602.

1374. Conant, James B. *Thomas Jefferson and the Development of American Public Education.* Berkeley: University of California Press, 1962.

1375. Dabney, Virginius. *Mr. Jefferson's University: A History.* Charlottesville: University Press of Virginia, 1981.

1376. Dalton, David C., and Thomas C. Hunt. "Thomas Jefferson's Theories on Education as Revealed through a Textual Reading of Several of His Letters." *Journal of Thought* 14 (November 1979): 263-271.

1377. Davis, Richard. "A Postscript on Thomas Jefferson and His University Professors." *Journal of Southern History* 12 (August 1946): 422-432.

1378. Densford, John P. "The Educational Philosophy of Thomas Jefferson." Ed.D. dissertation, Oklahoma State University, 1961.

1379. Ganter, Herbert L. "William Small, Jefferson's Beloved Teacher." *William and Mary Quarterly* 4 (October 1947): 505-511.

1380. Hart, Andrew D. "Thomas Jefferson's Influence on the Foundation of Medical Instruction at the University of Virginia." *Annals of Medical History* 10 (January 1938): 47-60.

1381. Hellenbrand, Harold L. "The Unfinished Revolution: Education and Community in the Thought of Thomas Jefferson." Ph.D. dissertation, Stanford University, 1980.

1382. Henderson, John C. *Thomas Jefferson's Views on Public Education.* New York: Putnam, 1890.

1383. Heslep, Robert D. *Thomas Jefferson and Education Studies in the Western Educational Tradition.* New York: Random House, 1969.

1384. Heslep, Robert D. "The Views of Jefferson and Dewey as Bases for Clarifying the Role of Education in an American Democratic State." Ph.D. dissertation, University of Chicago, 1963.

1385. Honeywell, Roy J. *The Educational Work of Thomas Jefferson.* Cambridge, MA: Harvard University Press, 1931.

1386. Honeywell, Roy J. "A Note on the Educational Work of Thomas Jefferson." *History of Education Quarterly* 9 (Spring 1969): 64-72.

1387. Lancaster, Dabney S. "Thomas Jefferson and Public Education." *Virginia Journal of Education* 19 (May 1926): 363-364.

1388. Lee, Gordon C., ed. "Learning and Liberty: The Jeffersonian Tradition in Education." In his *Crusade against Ignorance: Thomas Jefferson on Education*, 1-26. New York: Bureau of Publications, Columbia University, 1961.

1389. Lokensgard, Hjalmar O. "Aristocratic Elements in Jefferson's Education Plan." Master's thesis, University of Iowa, 1932.

1390. Malone, Dumas. "Jefferson Goes to School in Williamsburg." *Virginia Quarterly Review* 33 (Autumn 1957): 481-496.

1391. Malone, Dumas. "Thomas Jefferson, Educational Pioneer." *Virginia Journal of Education* 19 (May 1926): 352-354.

1392. Morison, Samuel E. "Is Liberal Education Democratic: What Jefferson Advocated." *Hispania* 27 (February 1944): 78-79.

1393. Morrow, L. C., and J. M. Davis. "Thomas Jefferson's Philosophy of Education." *Virginia Journal of Education* 15 (December 1921): 141-142.

1394. Patton, John S. *Jefferson, Cabell, and the University of Virginia.* New York: Neale, 1906.

1395. Pleasants, Samuel A. "Thomas Jefferson: Educational Philosopher." *American Philosophical Society Proceedings* 111 (February 17, 1966): 1-4.

1396. Purcell, Richard J. "Thomas Jefferson's Educational Views." *Catholic Educational Review* 30 (September 1932): 401-410.

1397. Sand, Norbert. "The Classics in Jefferson's Theory of Education." *Classical Journal* 40 (November 1944): 92-98.

1398. Shawen, Neil M. "The Casting of a Lengthened Shadow: Thomas Jefferson's Role in Determining the Site for a State University in Virginia." Ed.D. dissertation, George Washington University, 1980.

1399. Smith, Doris N. "Thomas Jefferson's Proposals Concerning Public Education of an Educated Electorate." Master's thesis, Bowling Green State University, 1962.

1400. Spencer, Thomas E. "Education and American Liberalism: A Comparison of the Views of Thomas Jefferson, Ralph Waldo Emerson, and John Dewey." Ph.D. dissertation, University of Illinois, 1963.

1401. "Thomas Jefferson and the University of Virginia." *Tyler's Quarterly Historical and Genealogical Magazine* 9 (July 1927): 42-45.

1402. Todd, Terry E. "Thomas Jefferson and the Founding of the University of

Virginia." Master's thesis, University of California, Riverside, 1965.

1403. Wagoner, Jennings, Jr. *Thomas Jefferson and the Education of a New Nation.* Bloomington, IN: Phi Delta Kappa Educational Foundation, 1976.

1404. Woodburn, Robert O. "An Historical Investigation of the Opposition to Jefferson's Educational Proposals in the Commonwealth of Virginia." Ph.D. dissertation, American University, 1974.

Family

1405. Adair, Douglass. "The Jefferson Scandals." In *Fame and the Founding Fathers: Essays by Douglas Adair,* edited by Trevor Colbourn, 160-191. New York: Norton, 1973.

1406. Beloff, Max. "The Sally Hemings Affair: A 'Founding Father.'" *Encounter* 43 (September 1974): 52-56.

1407. Bennett, Lerone. "Thomas Jefferson's Negro Grandchildren." *Ebony* 10 (November 1953): 78-80.

1408. Brodie, Fawn M. "Great Jefferson Taboo: Sally Hemings and Her Seven Children." *American Heritage* 23 (June 1972): 48-57, 97-100.

1409. Brodie, Fawn M. "Thomas Jefferson's Unknown Grandchildren." *American Heritage* 27 (October 1976): 28-33, 94-99.

1410. Dabney, Virginius. *The Jefferson Scandals: A Rebuttal.* New York: Dodd, Mead, 1981.

1411. Farrison, W. Edward. "Clotel, Thomas Jefferson, and Sally Hemings." *College Language Association Journal* 17 (December 1973): 147-174.

1412. Graham, Pearl M. "Thomas Jefferson and Sally Hemings." *Journal of Negro History* 46 (April 1961): 89-103.

1413. Guernsey, A. H. "Thomas Jefferson and His Family." *Harper's New Monthly Magazine* 43 (August 1871): 366-380.

1414. Hall, Gordon L. *Mr. Jefferson's Ladies.* Boston: Beacon Press, 1966.

1415. Haworth, Paul L. "Jefferson Family." *Tyler's Quarterly Historical and Genealogical Magazine* 6 (January 1925): 199-201; 6 (April 1925): 264-269.

1416. Kimball, Marie G. "Jefferson's Farewell to Romance." *Virginia Quarterly Review* 4 (July 1928): 402-419.

1417. Kimball, Marie G. "William Short, Jefferson's Only 'Son.'" *North American Review* 223 (September/October/November 1926): 471-486.

1418. Knudson, Jerry W. "Jefferson the Father of Slave Children? One View of the Book Reviewers." *Journalism History* 3 (Summer 1976): 56-58.

1419. Krock, Arthur. "Jefferson's Stepchildren." *American Mercury* 7 (February 1926): 129-135.

1420. Kukla, Jon. "Flirtation and Feux d'Artifices: Mr. Jefferson, Mrs. Cosway, and Fireworks." *Virginia Cavalcade* 26 (Autumn 1976): 52-63.

1421. Malone, Dumas. "Polly Jefferson and Her Father." *Virginia Quarterly Review* 7 (January 1931): 81-95.

1422. Mayo, Bernard, ed. *Thomas Jefferson and His Unknown Brother Randolph, Twenty-eight Letters.* Charlottesville: University Press of Virginia, 1942.

1423. Merrill, Boynton. *Jefferson's Nephews: A Frontier Tragedy.* Princeton, NJ: Princeton University Press, 1976.

1424. Randolph, Sarah N. *The Domestic Life of Thomas Jefferson, Compiled from Family Letters and Reminiscences by His Great-Granddaughter.* New York: Harper, 1871.

1425. Shackelford, George G. "William Short, Jefferson's Adopted Son, 1758-1849." Ph.D. dissertation, University of Virginia, 1955.

1426. "Thomas Jefferson and James Callender: The Myth of Black Sally." *Negro History Bulletin* 32 (November 1969): 15-22.

1427. Van Pelt, Charles E. "Thomas Jefferson and Maria Cosway." *American Heritage* 22 (August 1971): 24-29, 102-103.

Law

1428. Brown, Elizabeth G. "A Jeffersonian's Recommendations for a Lawyer's Education." *American Journal of Legal History* 13 (April 1969): 139-144.

1429. Caldwell, Lynton K. "The Jurisprudence of Thomas Jefferson." *Indiana Law Journal* 18 (April 1943): 193-213.

1430. Cohen, Morris L. "Thomas Jefferson Recommends a Course of Law Study." *University of Pennsylvania Law Review* 119 (April 1971): 823-844.

1431. Davis, John W. "Thomas Jefferson: Attorney at Law." *American Bar Association Journal* 13 (February 1927): 63-68.

1432. Dewey, Frank L. "Thomas Jefferson's Law Practice: The Norfolk Anti-inoculation Riots." *Virginia Magazine of History and Biography* 91 (January 1983): 39-53.

1433. Dewey, Frank L. "The Waterson-Madison Episode: An Incident in Thomas Jefferson's Law Practice." *Virginia Magazine of History and Biography* 90 (April 1982): 165-176.

1434. Didier, Eugene L. "Thomas Jefferson as a Lawyer." *Green Bag* 15 (April 1903): 153-159.

1435. Eaton, Clement. "A Mirror of the Southern Colonial Lawyer: The Fee Books of Patrick Henry, Thomas Jefferson, and Waightstill Avery." *William and Mary Quarterly* 8 (October 1951): 520-534.

1436. Finkelnburg, G. A. "Thomas Jefferson as a Lawyer." *American Law Review* 39 (May/June 1905): 321-329.

1437. Morris, Roland S. "Jefferson as a Lawyer." *American Philosophical Society Proceedings* 87 (July 1943): 211-215.

1438. Patterson, C. Perry. "Jefferson, The Lawyer." *University of Pittsburgh Law Review* 11 (Spring 1950): 369-396.

1439. Price, William J. "'The Characteristic Bent of a Lawyer' in Jefferson." *Georgetown Law Journal* 16 (November 1927): 41-54.

Literature

1440. Abbott, Lawrence F. "Thomas Jefferson, The Aristocrat." In *Twelve Great Modernists*, 95-124. Garden City, NY: Doubleday, 1927.

1441. Andrews, Stuart. "Thomas Jefferson, American Encyclopaedist." *History Today* 17 (August 1966): 501-509.

1442. Arnold, Malcolm H. "Thomas Jefferson: A Pioneer in Anglo-Saxon." Ph.D. dissertation, University of Virginia, 1915.

1443. Berman, Eleanor D., and E. C. McClintock. "Thomas Jefferson and Rhetoric." *Quarterly Journal of Speech* 33 (February 1947): 1-8.

1444. Boutell, Lewis H. *Thomas Jefferson, The Man of Letters*. Chicago: Thompson, 1891.

1445. Boyd, Julian P. "Jefferson's Expression of the American Mind." *Virginia Quarterly Review* 50 (Autumn 1974): 538-562.

1446. Chinard, Gilbert. "Jefferson and Ossian." *Modern Language Notes* 38 (April 23, 1923): 201-205.

1447. Clark, Kenneth B. "Thomas Jefferson and the Italian Renaissance." *Virginia Quarterly Review* 48 (Autumn 1972): 519-531.

1448. Cox, Stephen D. "The Literary Aesthetic of Thomas Jefferson." In *Essays in Early Virginia Literature Honoring Richard Beale Davis*, edited by J. A. Leo Lemay, 235-256. New York: Franklin, 1977.

1449. Davis, Richard B. "Thomas Jefferson as Collector of Virginiana." In his *Literature and Society in Early Virginia, 1608-1840*, 192-232. Baton Rouge: Louisiana State University Press, 1973.

1450. Eubanks, Seaford W. "A Vocabulary Study of Thomas Jefferson's *Notes on Virginia*." Master's thesis, University of Missouri, 1940.

1451. Ford, Paul L. "Jefferson's Notes on Virginia." *Nation* 8 (February 1, 1894): 80-81, 98-99.

1452. Hauer, Stanley R. "Thomas Jefferson and the Anglo-Saxon Language." *PMLA* 98 (October 1983): 879-898.

1453. Haworth, Paul L. "Thomas Jefferson — Poet." *Bookman* 31 (August 1910): 647-650.

1454. Hellenbrand, Harold. "Roads to Happiness: Rhetorical and Philosophical Design in Jefferson's Notes on the State of Virginia." *Early American Literature* 70 (Spring 1985): 3-23.

1455. Hench, Atcheson L. "Jefferson and Ossian." *Modern Language Notes* 43 (December 1928): 537.

1456. Henline, Ruth. "A Study of *Notes on the State of Virginia* as Evidence of Jefferson's Reaction against the Theories of the French Naturalists." *Virginia Magazine of History and Biography* 55 (July 1947): 233-246.

1457. Henneman, John B. "Two Pioneers in the Historical Study of English: Thomas Jefferson and Louis F. Klipstein." *PMLA* 8 (1983): 43-49.

1458. Herzberg, Max J. "Thomas Jefferson as a Man of Letters." *South Atlantic Quarterly* 13 (October 1914): 310-327.

1459. Hubbell, Jay B. "Thomas Jefferson." In his *The South in American Literature, 1607-1900*, 122-134. Durham, NC: Duke University Press, 1954.

1460. Jenkins, Starr. "American Statesmen as Men of Letters: Franklin, Adams, Jefferson, John Quincy Adams, Lincoln, Theodore Roosevelt, and Wilson Considered as Writers." Ph.D. dissertation, University of New Mexico, 1972.

1461. Jones, Howard M. "Jeffersonianism." In his *Jeffersonianism and the American Novel*, 16-24. New York: Teachers College Press, 1966.

1462. Levitsky, Ihor. "The Tolstoy Gospel in the Light of the Jefferson Bible." *Canadian Slavonic Papers* 21 (September 1979): 347-355.

1463. Martin, John S. "Rhetoric, Society, and Literature in the Age of Jefferson." *Midcontinent American Studies Journal* 9 (Spring 1968): 77-90.

1464. Medlin, Dorothy. "Thomas Jefferson, Andre Morellet, and the French Version of Notes on the State of Virginia." *William and Mary Quarterly* 35 (January 1978): 85-99.

1465. Moffat, Alexander D. "A Defense of the New World: Jefferson's *Notes on Virginia* and Some 18th Century Theories of American Degeneracy." Master's thesis, Southern Methodist University, 1966.

1466. Montgomery, Henry C. "Thomas Jefferson and the Classical Tradition."

Ph.D. dissertation, University of Illinois, 1946.

1467. Montgomery, Henry C. "Thomas Jefferson as a Philologist." *American Journal of Philology* 65 (October 1944): 367-371.

1468. Ogburn, Floyd, Jr. "Structure and Meaning in Thomas Jefferson's 'Notes on Virginia.'" *Early American Literature* 15 (Fall 1980): 141-150.

1469. Peterson, Merrill D. "Thomas Jefferson and the Enlightenment: Reflections on Literary Influence." *Lex et Scientia* 11 (January/April 1975): 89-127.

1470. Peterson, Merrill D. "Thomas Jefferson's Notes on the State of Virginia." In *Studies in Eighteenth-Century Culture*, edited by Roseann Runte, Vol. 7, 49-72. Madison: University of Wisconsin Press, 1978.

1471. Philbrick, Thomas. "Thomas Jefferson." In *American Literature, 1764-1789: The Revolutionary Years*, edited by Everett Emerson, 145-169. Madison: University of Wisconsin Press, 1977.

1472. Prescott, F. C. "Jefferson and Bishop Burnet." *American Literature* 7 (March 1935): 87.

1473. Sanford, Charles B. *Thomas Jefferson and His Library: A Study of His Literary Interests and of the Religious Attitudes Revealed by Relevant Titles in His Library*. Hamden, CT: Archon Books, 1977.

1474. Scheick, William J. "Chaos and Imaginative Order in Thomas Jefferson's Notes on the State of Virginia." In *Essays in Early Virginia Literature Honoring Richard Beale Davis*, edited by J. A. Leo Lemay, 221-234. New York: Burt Franklin, 1977.

1475. Schick, Joseph S. "Poe and Jefferson." *Virginia Magazine of History and Biography* 54 (October 1946): 316-320.

1476. Shepherd, Henry E. "Thomas Jefferson as a Philologist." *American Journal of Philology* 3 (October 1882): 211-214.

1477. Shonting, Donald A. "Romantic Aspects in the Works of Thomas Jefferson." Ph.D. dissertation, Ohio University, 1977.

1478. Skallerup, Harry R. "'For His Excellency Thomas Jefferson, Esq.': The Tale of a Wandering Book." *Library of Congress Quarterly Journal* 31 (April 1974): 116-121.

1479. Tucker, David. "Jefferson's 'Notes on the State of Virginia.'" Ph.D. dissertation, Claremont Graduate School, 1981.

1480. Verner, Coolie. *A Further Checklist of the Separate Editions of Jefferson's Notes on the State of Virginia*. Charlottesville: Bibliographical Society of the University of Virginia, 1950.

1481. Verner, Coolie. "The Maps and Plates Appearing with the Several Editions of Mr. Jefferson's 'Notes on the State of Virginia.'" *Virginia Magazine of History and Biography* 59 (January 1951): 21-23.

1482. Verner, Coolie. "Some Observations on the Philadelphia 1794 Edition of Jefferson's *Notes*." In *Studies in Bibliography: Papers of the Bibliographical Society of the University of Virginia*, Vol. 2, edited by Fredson Bowers, 201-204. Charlottesville: Bibliographical Society of the University of Virginia, 1950.

1483. Verner, Coolie, and P. J. Conkwright. "The Printing of Jefferson's 'Notes,' 1793-1794." In *Studies in Bibliography: Papers of the Bibliographical Society of the University of Virginia*, Vol. 5, edited by Fredson Bowers, 201-203. Charlottesville: Bibliographical Society of the University of Virginia, 1952.

1484. Wayland, John W. "The Poetical Tastes of Thomas Jefferson." *Sewanee Review* 18 (July 1910): 283-299.

1485. Williams, Edward K. "Jefferson's Theories of Language." Master's thesis, University of Wyoming, 1948.

1486. Wolff, Philippe. "Jefferson on Provence and Languedoc." *Proceeding of the Third Annual Meeting of the Western Society for French History* 3 (December 1975): 191-205.

1487. Woodfin, Maude H. "Thomas Jefferson and William Byrd's Manuscript Histories of the Dividing Line." *William and Mary Quarterly* 1 (October 1944): 363-373.

Monticello

1488. Bear, James A., Jr. "The Furniture and Furnishings of Monticello." *Antiques* 102 (July 1972): 113-123.

1489. Bear, James A., Jr. *Report of the Curator to the Board of Trustees of the Thomas Jefferson Memorial Foundation for the Year 1977*. Monticello, VA: Thomas Jefferson Memorial Foundation, 1977.

1490. Bear, James A., Jr., comp. *Jefferson at Monticello*. Charlottesville: University Press of Virginia, 1967.

1491. Betts, Edwin M. "Jefferson's Garden at Monticello." *Agricultural History* 19 (July 1945): 180-182.

1492. Betts, Edwin M., and Hazlehurst B. Perkins. *Thomas Jefferson's Flower Garden at Monticello*. Richmond, VA: Dietz Press, 1941.

1493. Brown, B. Bolton. "Thomas Jefferson at Monticello." *Mentor* 13 (October 1925): 37-43.

1494. Cable, Mary, and Annabelle Prager. "The Levys of Monticello." *American Heritage* 29 (March 1978): 30-39.

1495. Cheatham, Edgar, and Patricia Cheatham. "Reunion at Monticello." *Early American Life* 8 (December 1977): 40-43.

1496. Dabney, Virginius, and Jon Kukla. "The Monticello Scandals: History and Fiction." *Virginia Cavalcade* 29 (Autumn 1979): 52-61.

1497. Davis, Betty E. *Monticello Scrapbook*. Charlottesville, VA: Michie Co., 1939.

1498. Ferguson, Henry N. "The Man Who Saved Monticello." *American History Illustrated* 14 (February 1980): 20-27.

1499. Fleming, Thomas J. "Monticello's Long Career — From Riches to Rags to Riches." *Smithsonian* 4 (June 1973): 62-69.

1500. Haskins, Caryl P. "Mr. Jefferson's Sacred Gardens." *Virginia Quarterly Review* 43 (Autumn 1966): 529-544.

1501. Judge, Joseph. "Mr. Jefferson's Monticello." *National Geographic Magazine* 130 (September 1966): 426-444.

1502. Kallen, Horace M. "Jefferson's Garden Wall." *American Bookman* 1 (Winter 1944): 78-82.

1503. Kimball, Marie G. *The Furnishings of Monticello*. Charlottesville, VA: Thomas Jefferson Memorial Foundation, 1949.

1504. Kimball, Marie G. "Jefferson's Furniture Comes Home to Monticello." *House Beautiful* 66 (August 1929): 164-165, 186, 188, 190.

1505. Kimball, Marie G. "The Original Furnishings of the White House." *Antiques* 15 (June 1929): 481-489; 16 (July 1929): 33-37.

1506. Kimball, Marie G. "Thomas Jefferson's French Furniture." *Antiques* 14 (February 1929): 123-128.

1507. Kimball, S. Fiske. "Monticello, The Home of Jefferson." *AIA Journal* 12 (April 1924): 174-181.

1508. Llewellyn, Robert. *Mr. Jefferson's*

Monticello. Charlottesville, VA: Thomasson-Grant, 1983.

1509. Miller, Sue F. "Mr. Jefferson's Passion: His Grove at Monticello." *Historic Preservation* 32 (1980): 32-35.

1510. Montgomery, Henry C. "Epicurus at Monticello." In *Classical Studies Presented to Ben Edwin Perry by His Students and Colleagues at the University of Illinois, 1924-1960,* 80-87. Urbana: University of Illinois Press, 1969.

1511. Nicolay, J. G. "Thomas Jefferson's Home." *Century Magazine* 34 (September 1887): 643-653.

1512. Patton, John S., and Sallie J. Doswell. *Monticello and Its Master.* Charlottesville, VA: Michie Co., 1925.

1513. Pierson, Hamilton W. *Jefferson at Monticello: The Private Life of Thomas Jefferson, From Entirely New Materials.* New York: Scribner's, 1862.

1514. Rhodes, Thomas L. *The Story of Monticello.* Washington, DC: American Publishing, 1928.

1515. Sadler, Elizabeth H. *The Bloom of Monticello.* Richmond, VA: Whittet and Shepperson, 1925.

1516. Stockton, Frank R. "The Later Years of Monticello." *Century Magazine* 34 (September 1887): 654-658.

1517. Storey, Helen A. "Jefferson's Furniture at Monticello." *Antiquarian* 15 (July 1930): 38-40, 68-70.

1518. Wallace, M. G. "Monticello." *American Monthly Magazine* 22 (January 1903): 106-107.

1519. Williams, T. Harry. "On the Couch at Monticello." *Reviews in American History* 2 (December 1974): 523-529.

1520. Wilstach, Paul. *Jefferson and Monticello.* 5th ed. Garden City, NY: Doubleday, 1935.

1521. Wilstach, Paul. "Jefferson's Little Mountain: Romance Enfolds Monticello, The Restored Home of the Author of the Declaration of Independence." *National Geographic Magazine* 55 (April 1929): 481-503.

Philosophy

1522. Appleby, Joyce. "What Is Still American in the Political Philosophy of Thomas Jefferson?" *William and Mary Quarterly* 39 (April 1982): 287-309.

1523. Atwell, Priscilla A. "Freedom and Diversity: Continuity in the Political Tradition of Thomas Jefferson and John C. Calhoun." Ph.D. dissertation, University of California, Los Angeles, 1967.

1524. Becker, Carl. "What Is Still Living in the Political Philosophy of Thomas Jefferson?" *American Historical Review* 48 (July 1943): 691-706.

1525. Bromfield, Louis. "Thomas Jefferson vs. Karl Marx." In his *A Few Brass Tacks,* 171-222. New York: Harper and Row, 1946.

1526. Bryan, William J. "Jeffersonian Principles." *North American Review* 168 (June 1899): 670-678.

1527. Chamberlain, Alexander F. "Thomas Jefferson's Ethnological Opinions and Activities." *American Anthropologist* 9 (July/September 1907): 499-509.

1528. Chaudhuri, Joyotpaul. "Jefferson's Unheavenly City: A Bicentennial Look." *American Journal of Economics and Sociology* 34 (October 1975): 397-410.

1529. Chaudhuri, Joyotpaul. "Jefferson's Unheavenly City: An Interpretation." In his *Non-Lockean Roots of American Democratic Thought,* 17-29. Tucson: University of Arizona Press, 1977.

1530. Chianese, Mary L. "Thomas Jefferson: Enlightened American." *Daughters of the American Revolution Magazine* 109 (May 1975): 417-423.

1531. Chinard, Gilbert. "Jefferson among the Philosophers." *Ethics* 53 (July 1943): 255-268.

1532. Chinard, Gilbert. "Jefferson and the American Philosophical Society." *American Philosophical Society Proceedings* 87 (July 1943): 263-276.

1533. Chinard, Gilbert. "Thomas Jefferson as a Classical Scholar." *American Scholar* 1 (March 1932): 133-143.

1534. Chinard, Gilbert. "Thomas Jefferson as a Classical Scholar." *Johns Hopkins Alumni Magazine* 18 (June 1929): 291-303.

1535. Colbourn, H. Trevor. "Thomas Jefferson's Use of the Past." *William and Mary Quarterly* 15 (January 1977): 56-70.

1536. Commager, Henry S. *Jefferson, Nationalism, and the Enlightenment: Spread of Enlightenment from Old World to New.* New York: Braziller, 1975.

1537. Davis, Richard B. *Intellectual Life in Jefferson's Virginia, 1790-1830.* Chapel Hill: University of North Carolina, 1964.

1538. Defalco, Anthony A. "A Comparison of John Dewey's and Thomas Jefferson's Concept of Human Nature." Ed.D. dissertation, Rutgers University, 1976.

1539. DeLeon, Daniel. "Jefferson on Revolution." In his *Americanism: Our Revolutionary Fathers and the Voice of Madison,* 24-26. New York: Industrial Union Party, 1935.

1540. D'Elia, Donald J. "Jefferson, Rush, and the Limits of Philosophical Friendship." *American Philosophical Society Proceedings* 117 (October 1973): 333-343.

1541. DeTerra, Helmut. "Alexander von Humboldt's Correspondence with Jefferson, Madison, and Gallatin." *American Philosophical Society Proceedings* 103 (December 1959): 783-806.

1542. Dorfman, Joseph. "The Economic Philosophy of Thomas Jefferson." *Political Science Quarterly* 55 (March 1940): 98-121.

1543. Fabian, Bernhard. "Jefferson's *Notes on Virginia*: The Genesis of Query XVII." *William and Mary Quarterly* 12 (January 1955): 124-138.

1544. Farnell, Robert S. "Positive Valuations of Politics and Government in the Thought of Five American Founding Fathers: Thomas Jefferson, John Adams, James Madison, Alexander Hamilton, and George Washington." Ph.D. dissertation, Cornell University, 1970.

1545. Ferguson, Robert A. " 'Mysterious Obligation': Jefferson's Notes on the State of Virginia." *American Literature* 52 (November 1980): 381-406.

1546. Fisher, George P. "Jefferson and the Social Compact Theory." *Yale Review* 2 (February 1894): 403-417.

1547. Fisher, Marvin. "An Answer to Jefferson on Manufactures." *South Atlantic Quarterly* 61 (Summer 1962): 345-353.

1548. Fowler, Samuel. "The Political Opinions of Jefferson." *North American Review* 101 (October 1865): 313-335.

1549. Gabriel, Ralph H. "Thomas Jefferson and Twentieth-Century Rationalism." *Virginia Quarterly Review* 26 (Summer 1950): 321-335.

1550. Ganter, Herbert L. "Jefferson's 'Pursuit of Happiness' and Some Forgotten Men." *William and Mary Quarterly* 16 (July 1936): 422-434; (October 1936): 558-585.

1551. Garrison, Frank W. "Jefferson and the Physiocrats." *Freeman* 8 (October 31, 1923): 180-182.

1552. Grampp, William D. "Re-examination of Jeffersonian Economics." *Southern Economic Journal* 12 (January 1946): 263-282.

1553. Hall, Richard. "Jefferson and the Physiocrats." Master's thesis, University of Virginia, 1950.

1554. Hamilton, Joseph G. de Roulhac. "The Pacificism of Thomas Jefferson." *Virginia Quarterly Review* 31 (Autumn 1955): 607-620.

1555. Harrold, Frances L. "The Upper House in Jeffersonian Political Theory." *Virginia Magazine of History and Biography* 78 (July 1970): 281-294.

1556. Hartman, Daniel W. "Thomas Jefferson's Theory of Ward Republics: Its Impact on the Practice of American Local Government Today." Master's thesis, Mankato State University, 1971.

1557. Heslep, Robert D. "Thomas Jefferson's Major Philosophical Principles." *Educational Theory* 16 (April 1966): 151-162.

1558. Hill, C. William. "Contrasting Themes in the Political Theories of Jefferson, Calhoun, and John Taylor of Caroline." *Publius* 6 (Summer 1976): 73-92.

1559. Hines, Mary E. "Dissent in the Political Philosophy of Thomas Jefferson." Ph.D. dissertation, Catholic University of America, 1981.

1560. Hoeveler, J. David, Jr. "Thomas Jefferson and the American 'Provincial' Mind." *Modern Age* 25 (Summer 1981): 271-280.

1561. Hofstadter, Richard. "Parrington and the Jeffersonian Tradition." *Journal of the History of Ideas* 2 (October 1941): 391-400.

1562. Israel, John. "An Introduction to Liu Tho-Ch'ang's 'The Democratic Thought of Thomas Jefferson.'" *Chinese Studies in History* 14 (Spring 1981): 3-6.

1563. Israel, John, and Steven H. Hochman. "Discovering Jefferson in the People's Republic of China." *Virginia Quarterly Review* 57 (Summer 1981): 401-419.

1564. Jones, James F., Jr. "Montesquieu and Jefferson Revisited: Aspects of a Legacy." *French Review* 51 (March 1978): 577-585.

1565. Ketcham, Ralph L. "The Transatlantic Background of Thomas Jefferson's Ideas of Executive Power." *Studies in Eighteenth-Century Culture* 11 (1982): 163-180.

1566. Klenner, Hermann. "Jefferson and Ho Chi Minh: Shingo Shibata's Conception of Human Rights." *Social Praxis* 6 (1979): 94-98.

1567. Koch, Adrienne. "Jefferson and the Pursuit of Happiness." In his *Power, Morals, and the Founding Fathers: Essays in the Interpretation of the American Enlightenment*, 23-49. Ithaca, NY: Cornell University Press, 1961.

1568. Koch, Adrienne. "Philosopher — Statesmen of the Republic." *Sewanee Review* 55 (Summer 1947): 384-405.

1569. Koch, Adrienne. *The Philosophy of Thomas Jefferson*. New York: Columbia University Press, 1943.

1570. Lamers, Claude C. "Jefferson's Aristocracy of Talent Proposal." *Social Studies* 60 (October 1969): 195-201.

1571. Lane, Lawrence. "An Enlightened Controversy — Jefferson and Buffon." *Enlightenment Essays* 3 (Spring 1972): 37-40.

1572. Lewis, Jan. *The Purist of Happiness: Family and Values in Jefferson's Virginia*. New York: Cambridge University Press, 1983.

1573. Lindley, Thomas F., Jr. "The Philosophical Presuppositions of Thomas

Jefferson's Social Theories." Ph.D. dissertation, Boston University, 1952.

1574. Little, David. "The Origins of Perplexity: Civil Religion and Moral Belief: In the Thought of Thomas Jefferson." In *American Civil Religion,* edited by Russell E. Richey and Donald G. Jones, 185-210. New York: Harper and Row, 1974.

1575. Liu, Zuochang. "The Democratic Thought of Thomas Jefferson." *Chinese Studies in History* 14 (Spring 1981): 7-37.

1576. Lukonic, Joseph L. "Thomas Jefferson's Concepts of Human Nature." Master's thesis, West Texas State University, 1969.

1577. Luttrell, Clifton B. "Thomas Jefferson on Money and Banking: Disciple of David Hume and Forerunner of Some Modern Monetary Views." *History of Political Economy* 7 (Summer 1975): 156-173.

1578. Lynch, William O. "Jefferson, The Liberal." *Indiana Magazine of History* 40 (March 1944): 41-47.

1579. McCorvey, Thomas C. "Thomas Jefferson and His Political Philosophy." In his *Alabama Historical Sketches,* 185-207. Charlottesville: University of Virginia Press, 1960.

1580. McCoy, Drew R. "Jefferson and Madison on Malthus: Population Growth in Jeffersonian Political Economy." *Virginia Magazine of History and Biography* 88 (July 1980): 259-275.

1581. Martin, Edwin T. "Thomas Jefferson and the Idea of Progress." Ph.D. dissertation, University of Wisconsin, 1941.

1582. Merriam, Charles E. "The Political Theory of Jefferson." *Political Science Quarterly* 17 (March 1902): 24-25.

1583. Muzzey, David S. "Thomas Jefferson, Humanitarian." *American Review* 4 (January 1926): 36-44.

1584. Parks, Edd W. "Jefferson's Attitude toward History." *Georgia Historical Quarterly* 36 (December 1952): 336-341.

1585. Parks, William. "The Influence of Scottish Sentimentalist Ethical Theory of Thomas Jefferson's Philosophy of Human Nature." Ph.D. dissertation, College of William and Mary in Virginia, 1975.

1586. Patterson, C. Perry. *The Constitutional Principles of Thomas Jefferson.* Austin: University of Texas Press, 1953.

1587. Reinhardt, John F. "Political Philosophy from John Locke to Thomas Jefferson." *University of Kansas City Law Review* 13 (1944): 13-47; 13 (1945): 128-159.

1588. Russell, Phillips. *Jefferson, Champion of the Free Mind.* New York: Dodd, Mead, 1956.

1589. Schneider, Herbert W. "The Enlightenment in Thomas Jefferson." *Ethics* 53 (July 1943): 246-254.

1590. Shapley, Harlow. "Notes on Thomas Jefferson as a Natural Philosopher." *American Philosophical Society Proceedings* 87 (July 1943): 234-237.

1591. Sheehan, Bernard W. "Paradise and the Noble Savage in Jeffersonian Thought." *William and Mary Quarterly* 26 (July 1969): 327-359.

1592. Smith, Thomas V. "Thomas Jefferson and the Perfectibility of Mankind." *Ethics* 53 (July 1943): 293-310.

1593. Spengler, Joseph J. "The Political Economy of Jefferson, Madison, and Adams." In *American Studies in Honor of William Kenneth Boyd,* edited by David K. Jackson, 3-59. Durham, NC: Duke University Press, 1940.

1594. Walton, Craig. "Hume and Jefferson on the Uses of History." In *Philosophy and the Civilizing Arts: Essays Presented to Herbert W. Schneider,* edited by Craig

1595. Wayland, John W. *The Political Opinions of Thomas Jefferson.* New York: Neale, 1907.

1596. Weiss, Harry B. "Thomas Jefferson and Economic Entomology." *Journal of Economic Entomology* 37 (December 1944): 836-841.

1597. Weyant, Robert G. "Helvetius and Jefferson: Studies of Human Nature and Government in the Eighteenth Century." *Journal of the History of the Behavioral Sciences* 9 (January 1973): 29-41.

1598. White, Morton G., and Lucia White. "The Irenic Age: Franklin, Crevecoeur, and Jefferson." In their *The Intellectual vs. the City: From Thomas Jefferson to Frank Lloyd Wright*, 6-20. Cambridge, MA: Harvard University Press, 1962.

1599. Williams, Kenneth R. "The Ethics of Thomas Jefferson." Ph.D. dissertation, Boston University, 1962.

1600. Wiltse, Charles M. "Thomas Jefferson: A Study in the Philosophy of the State." Ph.D. dissertation, Cornell University, 1932.

1601. Yoder, Edwin M. "Political Thought of Thomas Jefferson." *Chinese Studies in History* 14 (Spring 1981): 3-37.

Press

1602. Ford, Worthington C. "Jefferson and the Newspaper." *Columbia Historical Society Records* 8 (1905): 78-111.

1603. Granato, Leonard A. "Freneau, Jefferson, and Genet: Independent Journalism in the Partisan Press." In *Newsletters to Newspapers: Eighteenth Century Journalism*, edited by Donovan H. Bond and W. Reynolds McLeod, 291-301. Morgantown: West Virginia University School of Journalism, 1976.

1604. Jones, Paul W. "Jefferson and the *National Gazette.*" Master's thesis, Bowling Green State University, 1961.

1605. Marsh, Philip M. "Freneau and Jefferson: The Post-Editor Speaks for Himself about the *National Gazette* Episode." *American Literature* 8 (May 1936): 180-189.

1606. Marsh, Philip M. "The Griswold Story of Frenau and Jefferson." *American Historical Review* 51 (October 1945): 68-73.

1607. Marsh, Philip M. "Jefferson and Freneau." *American Scholar* 16 (Spring 1947): 201-210.

1608. Marsh, Philip M. "Jefferson and Journalism." *Huntington Library Quarterly* 9 (February 1946): 209-212.

1609. Marsh, Philip M. "Jefferson's Conduct of the *National Gazette.*" *New Jersey Historical Society Proceedings* 63 (April 1945): 69-78.

1610. Mott, Frank L. *Jefferson and the Press.* Baton Rouge: Louisiana State University Press, 1943.

1611. Mutersbaugh, Bert M. "Jeffersonian Journalist: Thomas Ritchie and the Richmond 'Enquirer,' 1804-1820." Ph.D. dissertation, University of Missouri, 1973.

1612. Robbins, Jan C. "Jefferson and the Press: The Resolution of an Antinomy." *Journalism Quarterly* 48 (Autumn 1971): 421-430, 465.

Religion

1613. Adams, Dickinson W. "Jefferson's Politics of Morality: The Purpose and Meaning of His Extracts from the Evangelists, 'The Philosophy of Jesus of Nazareth' and 'The Life and Morals of Jesus of Nazareth.'" Ph.D. dissertation, Brown University, 1970.

1614. Bennett, H. Omer. "The Religion of Thomas Jefferson." *Social Science* 5 (August 1930): 460-465.

1615. Brent, Robert A. "The Jefferson Outlook on Religion." *Southern Quarterly* 5 (July 1966): 517-532.

1616. Brigham, Johnson. "Jefferson on Christianity and the Common Law: A Forgotten Chapter in the Life of Jefferson." *Green Bag* 12 (August 1900): 441-449.

1617. Costanzo, Joseph F. "Thomas Jefferson, Religious Education, and Public Law." *Journal of Public Law* 8 (Spring 1959): 81-108.

1618. Crawford, Nelson A. "Thomas Jefferson and Religious Freedom." *American Collector* 2 (May 1926): 292-295.

1619. Drouin, Edmond G. "Madison and Jefferson on Clergy in the Legislature." *America* 138 (January 28, 1978): 58-59.

1620. Foote, Henry W. *The Religion of Thomas Jefferson.* Boston: Beacon Press, 1947.

1621. Foote, Henry W. *Thomas Jefferson, Champion of Religious Freedom, Advocate of Christian Morals.* Boston: Beacon Press, 1947.

1622. Forrest, W. M. "Thomas Jefferson and Religious Freedom." *Virginia Journal of Education* 19 (May 1926): 355-357.

1623. Goodspeed, Edgar J. "Thomas Jefferson and the Bible." *Harvard Theological Review* 40 (January 1947): 71-76.

1624. Gould, William D. "The Religious Opinions of Thomas Jefferson." *Mississippi Valley Historical Review* 20 (September 1933): 191-208.

1625. Gurley, James L. "Thomas Jefferson's Philosophy and Theology: As Related to His Political Principles, Including Separation of Church and State." Ph.D. dissertation, University of Michigan, 1975.

1626. Hall, J. Leslie. "The Religious Opinions of Thomas Jefferson." *Sewanee Review* 21 (April 1913): 164-176.

1627. Hamilton, Joseph G. de Roulhac. "Jefferson and Religion." *Reviewer* 5 (October 1925): 5-15.

1628. Haraszti, Zoltan. "Jefferson's Bill of Religious Freedom." *Boston Public Library Quarterly* 7 (October 1955): 221-223.

1629. Healey, Robert M. *Jefferson on Religion in Public Education.* New Haven, CT: Yale University Press, 1962.

1630. Hedges, Brown. "Jefferson on Religion." *America* 69 (May 8, 1943): 126.

1631. Huntley, William B. "Jefferson's Public and Private Religion." *South Atlantic Quarterly* 79 (Summer 1980): 286-301.

1632. Kessler, Sanford. "Locke's Influence on Jefferson's Bill for Establishing Religious Freedom." *Journal of Church and State* 25 (Spring 1983): 231-252.

1633. Johnson, Peggy A. "Diamonds in a Dunghill: The Gospel According to Thomas Jefferson." Master's thesis, University of California, Riverside, 1967.

1634. Jones, Edgar D. "Thomas Jefferson and Religion." *Christian Century* 43 (June 17, 1926): 774-775.

1635. Kinsolving, Arthur B. "The Religious Opinions of Thomas Jefferson." *Historical Magazine of the Protestant Episcopal Church* 20 (September 1951): 325-327.

1636. Kirk, Russell A. "Jefferson and the Faithless." *South Atlantic Quarterly* 40 (July 1941): 220-227.

1637. Knoles, George H. "The Religious Ideas of Thomas Jefferson." *Mississippi Valley Historical Review* 30 (September 1943): 187-204.

1638. Luebke, Frederick C. "The Origins

of Thomas Jefferson's Anticlericalism." *Church History* 32 (September 1963): 344-356.

1639. Lydon, James G. "Thomas Jefferson and the Mathurins." *Catholic Historical Review* 49 (April 1963): 192-202.

1640. Mabee, Charles. "Thomas Jefferson's Anti-Clerical Bible." *Historical Magazine of the Protestant Episcopal Church* 48 (December 1979): 473-481.

1641. Magnuson, Roger P. "Thomas Jefferson and the Separation of Church and State." *Educational Forum* 27 (May 1963): 417-421.

1642. Mehta, M. J. "The Religion of Thomas Jefferson." *Indo-Asian Culture* 16 (April 1966): 95-103.

1643. Mott, Royden J. "Sources of Jefferson's Ecclesiastical Views." *Church History* 3 (December 1934): 267-284.

1644. Newton, Joseph F. "Thomas Jefferson and the Religion of America." *Forum* 78 (December 1927): 890-896.

1645. Pearson, Samuel C. "Nature's God: A Reassessment of the Religion of the Founding Fathers." *Religion in Life* 46 (Summer 1977): 152-165.

1646. Powell, E. P. "Jefferson and Religion." *Open Court* 10 (June 11, 1896): 4943-4945.

1647. Price, John W. "Thomas Jefferson's Statute of Religious Freedom." *Virginia State Bar Association Proceedings* 42 (1931): 245-257.

1648. Sandler, S. Gerald. "Lockean Ideas in Thomas Jefferson's Bill Establishing Religious Freedom." *Journal of the History of Ideas* 21 (January/March 1960): 110-116.

1649. Schulz, Constance B. "Of Bigotry in Politics and Religion: Jefferson's Religion, the Federalist Press, and the Syllabus." *Virginia Magazine of History and Biography* 91 (January 1983): 73-91.

1650. Schulz, Constance B. "The Radical Religious Ideas of Thomas Jefferson and John Adams: A Comparison." Ph.D. dissertation, University of Cincinnati, 1973.

1651. Sensabaugh, George F. "Jefferson's Use of Milton in the Ecclesiastical Controversies of 1776." *American Literature* 26 (January 1955): 552-559.

1652. Smithline, Arnold. "Thomas Jefferson." In his *Natural Religion in American Literature*, 56-64. New Haven, CT: College and University Press Services, 1966.

1653. Swancara, Frank. *Thomas Jefferson versus Religious Oppression*. New York: University Books, 1969.

1654. Wicks, Elliot K. "Thomas Jefferson — A Religious Man with a Passion for Religious Freedom." *Historical Magazine of the Protestant Episcopal Church* 36 (September 1967): 271-284.

Science

1655. Adcock, Louis H. "Thomas Jefferson, Scientist." *Chemistry* 48 (September 1975): 14-15.

1656. Baron, Sherry. "Thomas Jefferson: Scientist as Politician." *Synthesis* 3 (Spring 1975): 6-21.

1657. Bedini, Silvio A. *Thomas Jefferson and His Copying Machines*. Charlottesville: University Press of Virginia, 1984.

1658. Brasch, Frederick E. "Thomas Jefferson, The Scientist." *Science* 97 (April 2, 1943): 300-301.

1659. Brown, Roland W. "Jefferson's Contributions of Paleontology." *Washington Academy of Sciences Journal* 33 (September 15, 1943): 257-259.

1660. Browne, Charles A. *Thomas Jeffer-*

son and the Scientific Trends of His Time. Waltham, MA: Chronica Botanica Co., 1943.

1661. Browne, Charles A. "Thomas Jefferson's Relation to Chemistry." *Journal of Chemical Education* 20 (December 1943): 574.

1662. Ciolli, Antoinette. "Thomas Jefferson as a Man of Science." Master's thesis, Brooklyn College, 1940.

1663. Clark, Austin H. "Thomas Jefferson and Science." *Washington Academy of Sciences Journal* 33 (July 15, 1943): 193-203.

1664. Cohen, I. Bernard, ed. *Thomas Jefferson and the Sciences.* New York: Arno, 1980.

1665. Edward, C. "Jefferson, Sullivan, and the Moose." *American History Illustrated* 9 (November 1974): 18-19.

1666. Greely, Arthur W. "Jefferson as a Geographer." *National Geographic Magazine* 7 (August 1896): 269-271.

1667. Greene, John C. *American Science in the Age of Jefferson.* Ames: Iowa State University Press, 1984.

1668. Greene, John C. "Science and the Public in the Age of Jefferson." *Isis* 49 (March 1958): 13-25.

1669. Lucas, Frederic A. "Thomas Jefferson — Palaeontologist." *Natural History* 26 (May 1926): 328-330.

1670. Martin, Edwin T. "Thomas Jefferson: A Scientist in the White House." *Emory University Quarterly* 8 (March 1952): 38-49.

1671. Martin, Edwin T. *Thomas Jefferson: Scientist.* New York: Schuman, 1952.

1672. Martin, Edwin T. "Thomas Jefferson's Interest in Science and the Useful Arts." *Emory University Quarterly* 2 (June 1946): 65-73.

1673. Meier, Hugo A. "Thomas Jefferson and the Growth of American Technology." *Intellect* 106 (November 1977): 192.

1674. Northrop, F. S. C. "Jefferson's Conception of the Role of Science in World History." *Cahiers d'Histoire Mondiale* 9 (April 1966): 891-911.

1675. Oliver, John W. "Thomas Jefferson — Scientist." *Scientific Monthly* 56 (May 1943): 460-467.

1676. Osborn, Henry F. "Thomas Jefferson as a Palaeontologist." *Science* 82 (December 6, 1935): 533-538.

1677. Osborn, Henry F. "Thomas Jefferson, The Pioneer of American Palaeontology." *Science* 69 (April 19, 1929): 410-413.

1678. Patton, John S. "Thomas Jefferson's Contributions to Natural History." *Natural History* 19 (April 1919): 405-410.

1679. Rice, Howard C., Jr. "Jefferson's Gift of Fossils to the Museum of Natural History in Paris." *American Philosophical Society Proceedings* 95 (December 1951): 597-627.

1680. Smith, David E. "Thomas Jefferson and Mathematics." In his *The Poetry of Mathematics,* 49-70. New York: Scripta Mathematica, Yeshiva College, 1934.

1681. Spratt, John S. "Thomas Jefferson: The Scholarly Politician and His Influence on Medicine." *Southern Medical Journal* 69 (March 1976): 360-366.

1682. Surface, George T. "Thomas Jefferson: A Pioneer Student of American Geography." *American Geographical Society Bulletin* 41 (December 1909): 743-750.

1683. True, Rodney H. "Thomas Jefferson in Relation to Botany." *Scientific Monthly* 3 (October 1915): 345-360.

1684. Wayland, John W. "Jefferson as a Scientist." *Virginia Journal of Education* 19 (May 1926): 358-359.

1685. Whiting, Margaret A. "The Father of Gadgets." *Stone and Webster Journal* 49 (May 1931): 302-315.

Public Career

General

1686. Adams, Hewitt D. "A Note on Jefferson's Knowledge of Economics." *Virginia Magazine of History and Biography* 75 (January 1966): 69-74.

1687. Anderson, Judith L. "Thomas Jefferson's Case for an Arcadian America." Ph.D. dissertation, Indiana University, 1970.

1688. Bailyn, Bernard. "Boyd's Jefferson: Notes for a Sketch." *New England Quarterly* 13 (September 1960): 380-401.

1689. Bellot, Hugh H. "Thomas Jefferson in American Historiography." *Royal Historical Society Transactions* 4 (1954): 135-155.

1690. Berkhofer, Robert F. "Jefferson, the Ordinance of 1784, and the Origins of the American Territorial System." *William and Mary Quarterly* 29 (April 1972): 231-262.

1691. Boehm, Dwight, and Edward Schwartz. "Jefferson and the Theory of Degeneracy." *American Quarterly* 9 (Winter 1957): 448-453.

1692. Bowers, Claude G. "Architect of the All-American System." *Virginia Quarterly Review* 19 (Spring 1943): 178-188.

1693. Bowers, Claude G. "Jefferson, Master Politician." *Virginia Quarterly Review* 2 (July 1926): 321-333.

1694. Bowman, Isaiah. "Jeffersonian 'Freedom of Speech' from the Standpoint of Science." *Science* 82 (December 1935): 529-532.

1695. Boyd, Julian P. "The Megalonyx, The Megatherium, and Thomas Jefferson's Lapse of Memory." *American Philosophical Society Proceedings* 102 (October 1958): 420-435.

1696. Boyd, Julian P. "The Relevance of Thomas Jefferson for the Twentieth Century." *American Scholar* 22 (Winter 1952-1953): 61-76.

1697. Brown, Sharon. "Creating the Dream: Jefferson National Expansion Memorial 1933-1935." *Missouri Historical Review* 76 (April 1982): 302-326.

1698. Brown, Sharon. "Jefferson National Expansion Memorial: The 1947-1948 Competition." *Gateway Heritage* 1 (Winter 1980): 40-48.

1699. Bryan, Mina R. "Thomas Jefferson through the Eyes of His Contemporaries." *Princeton University Library Chronicle* 9 (June 1948): 219-224.

1700. Coles, Harry L. "Some Recent Interpretations of Jeffersonian America." In *Indiana Historical Society Lectures*, 62-88. Indianapolis: Indiana Historical Society, 1970.

1701. Cometti, Elizabeth, ed. "Mr. Jefferson Prepares an Itinerary." *Journal of Southern History* 12 (February 1946): 89-106.

1702. Commager, H. Steele. "Jefferson and the Book-Burners." *American Heritage* 9 (August 1958): 65-68.

1703. Coolidge, Archibald C. "Jefferson and the Problems of Today." *University of Virginia Alumni Bulletin* 14 (July 1921): 53-58.

1704. Cox, R. Merritt. "Thomas Jefferson and Spanish: 'To Every Inhabitant Who Means to Look Beyond the Limits of His Farm.'" *Romance Notes* 14 (Autumn 1972): 116-121.

1705. Crane, Fergus. "Thomas Jefferson

and Tomorrow." *Eclectic Magazine of Foreign Literature, Science and Art* 148 (June 1907): 485-491.

1706. Cunliffe, Marcus. "Thomas Jefferson and the Danger of the Past." *Wilson Quarterly* 6 (Winter 1982): 96-107.

1707. Daiker, Virginia. "The Capitol of Jefferson and Latrobe." *Library of Congress Quarterly Journal* 32 (January 1975): 25-32.

1708. Dauer, Manning J. "The Two John Nicholases: Their Relation to Washington and Jefferson." *American Historical Review* 45 (January 1940): 338-354.

1709. Dewey, Frank L. "Thomas Jefferson and a Williamsburg Scandal: The Case of *Blair v. Blair*." *Virginia Magazine of History and Biography* 89 (January 1981): 44-63.

1710. Dodd, William E. "Thomas Jefferson." In his *Statesmen of the Old South, Or From Radicalism to Conservative Revolt*, 1-88. New York: Macmillan, 1911.

1711. Dumbauld, Edward. "Jefferson and Local Government." *County Officer* 15 (April 1950): 8-10, 28-29.

1712. Dumbauld, Edward. "Thomas Jefferson and American Constitutional Law (1776-1801)." *Journal of Public Law* 2 (Fall 1953): 370-389.

1713. Dumbauld, Edward. "Thomas Jefferson and Pennsylvania." *Pennsylvania History* 5 (July 1938): 157-165.

1714. Edwards, Mike W., and Linda Bartlett. "Architect of Freedom: Thomas Jefferson." *National Geographic Magazine* 149 (February 1976): 231-260.

1715. Evans, Edith R. "Thomas Jefferson in Annapolis." *Maryland Historical Magazine* 41 (June 1946): 115-124.

1716. Fleming, Thomas. "Verdicts of History." *American Heritage* 19 (December 1967): 22-27.

1717. Ford, Worthington C., ed. "Thomas Jefferson and James Thomas Callender." *New England Historical and Genealogical Register* 50 (July 1896): 321-333; (October 1896): 445-458; 51 (January 1897): 19-25; (April 1897): 153-158; (July 1897): 323-328.

1718. Gooch, Robert K. "Reconciling Jeffersonian Principles with the New Deal." *Southwestern Social Science Quarterly* 16 (June 1935): 1-13.

1719. Gray, Giles W. "Thomas Jefferson's Interest in Parliamentary Practice." *Speech Monographs* 27 (November 1960): 315-322.

1720. Griswold, A. Whitney. "Thomas Jefferson: Anti-Totalitarian." In *Understanding the American Past*, edited by Edward N. Saveth, 178-189. Boston: Little, Brown, 1954.

1721. Guzzetta, Charles. "Jefferson, Rumford, and the Problem of Poverty." *Midwest Quarterly* 26 (Spring 1985): 343-356.

1722. Hamilton, Joseph G. de Roulhac. "Mr. Jefferson Visits the Sesquicentennial." *Virginia Quarterly Review* 3 (January 1927): 38-47.

1723. Hay, Robert P. "The Glorious Departure of the American Patriarchs: Contemporary Reactions to the Deaths of Jefferson and Adams." *Journal of Southern History* 35 (November 1969): 543-555.

1724. Houghton, William M. "An Open Letter to Mr. Jefferson." *American Mercury* 37 (March 1936): 273-276.

1725. Johnson, Cary, Jr. "New Priests of Jefferson." *Virginia Quarterly Review* 12 (July 1936): 457-460.

1726. Jones, Anna C. "Antlers for Jefferson." *New England Quarterly* 12 (June 1939): 333-348.

1727. Judson, Clara I. *Thomas Jefferson:*

Champion of the People. Chicago: Wilcox and Follett, 1952.

1728. Keller, William F. "Jefferson Refutes a Tory Argument." *Americana* 34 (July 1940): 447-457.

1729. Ketcham, Ralph L., ed. "Jefferson and Madison and the Doctrines of Interposition and Nullification: A Letter of John Quincy Adams." *Virginia Magazine of History and Biography* 66 (April 1958): 178-182.

1730. Kimball, Marie G. "Jefferson's Four Freedoms." *Virginia Quarterly Review* 19 (Spring 1943): 204-221.

1731. Knoles, George H. "Thomas Jefferson: Crusader for Freedom." *Social Studies* 33 (November 1942): 297-304.

1732. Kuper, Theodore F. *Thomas Jefferson Still Lives: An Outline of the Life of the Architect of Our American Heritage.* New York: Patriotic Publishing Co., 1973.

1733. Laing, Alexander. "Jefferson's Usufruct Principle." *Nation* 223 (July 3-10, 1976): 7-16.

1734. Lathrop, Mary F. "Jefferson's Contribution to the Law of the West." In *Pennsylvania Bar Association Reports of the Thirty-third Annual Meeting,* 297-307. Philadelphia: Pennsylvania Bar Association, 1927.

1735. "Library of Congress Publishes Pamphlets on Thomas Jefferson." *Library of Congress Information Bulletin* 37 (June 30, 1978): 381-382.

1736. Lingelbach, Anna L. "Jefferson Today." *Current History* 5 (November 1943): 225-228.

1737. Lokke, Carl L. "Jefferson and the Leclerc Expedition." *American Historical Review* 33 (January 1928): 322-328.

1738. Lotts, Velma C. "Jefferson's Pre-presidential Criticism of the Federal Judiciary." *Marshall Review* 3 (June 1940): 27-33.

1739. McCoy, Drew R. *The Elusive Republic: Political Economy in Jeffersonian America.* Chapel Hill: University of North Carolina Press, 1980.

1740. McKenna, George. "The Roots of Populism: Thomas Jefferson." In his *American Populism,* 7-30. New York: Putnam, 1974.

1741. Malone, Dumas. "Jefferson and the New Deal." *Scribner's Magazine* 93 (June 1933): 356-359.

1742. Malone, Dumas. "Mr. Jefferson and the Living Generation." *American Scholar* 41 (Autumn 1972): 587-598.

1743. Malone, Dumas. "The Relevance of Mr. Jefferson." *Virginia Quarterly Review* 37 (Summer 1961): 332-349.

1744. Malone, Dumas. "The Return of a Virginian." *Virginia Quarterly Review* 27 (August 1951): 528-543.

1745. Marsh, Philip M. "The Jefferson-Madison Vacation." *Pennsylvania Magazine of History and Biography* 71 (October 1947): 70-72.

1746. Marsh, Philip M. "The Vindication of Mr. Jefferson." *South Atlantic Quarterly* 45 (January 1946): 61-67.

1747. Mayo, Bernard. "A Peppercorn for Mr. Jefferson." *Virginia Quarterly Review* 19 (Spring 1943): 222-235.

1748. Mearns, David C. "Mr. Jefferson to His Namesakes." *Library of Congress Quarterly Journal of Current Acquisitions* 14 (November 1956): 1-5.

1749. Merriam, Charles E., and Frank P. Bourgin. "Jefferson as a Planner of Natural Resources." *Ethics* 53 (July 1943): 284-292.

1750. Meschutt, David. "Adams-Jefferson Portrait Exchange." *American Art Journal* 14 (Spring 1982): 47-54.

1751. Midgley, Louis. "The Brodie Connection: Thomas Jefferson and Joseph Smith." *Brigham Young University Studies* 19 (Fall 1979): 59-67.

1752. "Mr. Jefferson and His Detractors." *Tyler's Quarterly Historical and Genealogical Magazine* 2 (January 1921): 151-153.

1753. "Mr. Jefferson's 'Dig.'" *American History Illustrated* 6 (November 1971): 38-41.

1754. Moore, John H. "That 'Commodious' Annex to Jefferson's Rotunda: Was It Really a National Mausoleum?" *Virginia Cavalcade* 29 (Winter 1980): 114-123.

1755. Mumford, Lewis. "The Universalism of Thomas Jefferson." In his *The South in Architecture*, 43-78. New York: Harcourt, Brace, 1941.

1756. Norton, Paul F. *Latrobe, Jefferson, and the National Capitol.* New York: Garland, 1977.

1757. Osgood, Ernest S. "A Prairie Dog for Mr. Jefferson." *Montana: The Magazine of Western History* 19 (April 1969): 54-56.

1758. Padover, Saul K., ed. *Thomas Jefferson and the National Capitol: Containing Notes and Correspondence Exchanged between Jefferson, Washington, L'Enfant, Ellicott, Hallett, Thornton, Latrobe, the Commissioners, and Others, Relating to the Founding, Surveying, Planning, Designing, Constructing, and Administering the City of Washington, 1783-1818.* Washington, DC: U.S. Government Printing Office, 1946.

1759. Peden, William H. "The Jefferson Monument at the University of Missouri." *Missouri Historical Review* 72 (October 1977): 67-77.

1760. Peden, William H. "Thomas Jefferson and Charles Brockden Brown." *Maryland Quarterly* 2 (1944): 65-68.

1761. Peterson, Merrill D. "Bowers, Roosevelt, and the New Jefferson." *Virginia Quarterly Review* 34 (Autumn 1958): 530-543.

1762. Peterson, Merrill D. "Dumas Malone: The Completion of a Monument." *Virginia Quarterly Review* 58 (Winter 1982): 26-31.

1763. Peterson, Merrill D. "Mr. Jefferson's Sovereignty of the Living Generation." *Virginia Quarterly Review* 52 (Summer 1976): 437-447.

1764. Peterson, Merrill D. "Thomas Jefferson and Commercial Policy, 1783-1793." *William and Mary Quarterly* 22 (October 1965): 584-610.

1765. Phau, Donald. "The Treachery of Thomas Jefferson." *Campaigner* 13 (March 1980): 5-32.

1766. Philips, Edith. *Louis Hue Girardin and Nicholas Gouin Dufief and Their Relations with Thomas Jefferson: An Unknown Episode of the French Emigration in America.* Baltimore, MD: Johns Hopkins University Press, 1926.

1767. Plumer, William. "Thomas Jefferson and Company." *Historical New Hampshire* 23 (Summer 1968): 29-31.

1768. Randall, James G. "When Jefferson's Home Was Bequeathed to the United States." *South Atlantic Quarterly* 23 (January 1924): 35-39.

1769. Rice, Howard C., Jr. "Jefferson in Europe a Century and a Half Later: Notes of a Roving Researcher." *Princeton University Library Chronicle* 12 (Autumn 1951): 19-35.

1770. Ross, Michael. "Homogeneity and Heterogeneity in Jefferson and Madison." *International Review of History and Political Science* 13 (November 1976): 47-50.

1771. Rossiter, Clinton L. "Which Jefferson Do You Quote?" *Reporter* 13 (December 15, 1955): 33-36.

1772. Rothschild, Richard. *Three Gods Give an Evening to Politics: Jefferson, Lenin, Socrates.* New York: Random House, 1936.

1773. Schachner, Nathan. "Jefferson: A Slippery Politician." *American Mercury* 46 (January 1939): 49-55.

1774. *A Selection of Eulogies, Pronounced in the Several States, In Honor of Those Illustrious Patriots and Statesmen, John Adams and Thomas Jefferson.* Hartford, CT: D. F. Robinson, 1826.

1775. Sheehan, Bernard W. "Jefferson and the West." *Virginia Quarterly Review* 58 (Spring 1982): 345-352.

1776. Sherman, Stewart P. "Thomas Jefferson: An English Interpretation." In his *The Main Stream*, 17-27. New York: Scribner's, 1927.

1777. Simpson, Lloyd D. *Notes on Thomas Jefferson.* Philadelphia: Sherman, 1885.

1778. Skeen, C. Edward. "Jefferson and the West, 1798-1808." Master's thesis, Ohio State University, 1960.

1779. Skeen, C. Edward. *Jefferson and the West, 1798-1808.* Columbus: Anthony Wayne Parkway Board, Ohio State Museum, 1960.

1780. Sterling, Peter R. "Society in Jefferson's Day." *National Republic* 17 (October 1929): 28.

1781. Stevenson, Adlai E. "Jefferson and Our National Leadership." *Virginia Quarterly Review* 36 (Summer 1960): 337-349.

1782. Stewart, Robert A. "Jefferson and His Landlord." *Researcher* 1 (October 1926): 5-8.

1783. Sullivan, Mark. "Seeing America with Jefferson's Eyes: An Article on Political Progress." *World's Work* 52 (July 1926): 328-332.

1784. Summy, Ralph. "Comparative Political Biography: Jayaprakash Narayan and Thomas Jefferson." *Biography* 6 (Summer 1983): 220-237.

1785. Szasz, Paul C. "Thomas Jefferson Conceives an International Organization." *American Journal of International Law* 75 (January 1981): 138-140.

1786. Trachtenberg, Alexander, ed. *The Heritage of Jefferson.* New York: Workers School, 1945.

1787. Trainor, M. Rosaleen. "Thomas Jefferson on Freedom of Conscience." Ph.D. dissertation, St. Johns University, 1966.

1788. Trent, William P. *Southern Statesmen of the Old Regime: Washington, Jefferson, Randolph, Calhoun, Stephens, Toombs, and Jefferson Davis.* New York: Crowell, 1897.

1789. Turner, Lynn W. "Thomas Jefferson through the Eyes of a New Hampshire Politician." *Mississippi Valley Historical Review* 30 (September 1943): 205-214.

1790. Tyler, Lyon G. "What Jefferson Stood For." *Tyler's Quarterly Historical and Genealogical Magazine* 7 (January 1926): 154-163.

1791. Verner, Coolie. "Mr. Jefferson Makes a Map." *Imago Mvndi: A Review of Early Cartography* 14 (1957): 97-108.

1792. Waite, Edward F. "Jefferson's 'Wall of Separation': What and Where?" *Minnesota Law Review* 33 (April 1949): 495-516.

1793. Warde, William F. "Jefferson, Lincoln, and Dewey." *Marxist Essays in American History*, edited by Robert Himmel, 124-128. New York: Merit, 1966.

1794. Warren, Charles. "How Jefferson's Death Was Reported in the Campaign of 1800." In his *Odd Byways in American History*, 127-135. Cambridge, MA: Harvard University Press, 1942.

1795. Watson, Francis J. B. "America's First Universal Man Had a Very Acute Eye." *Smithsonian* 7 (June 1976): 88-95.

1796. Webster, Daniel. ... *The Bunker Hill Monument, Adams and Jefferson.* New York: Houghton Mifflin, 1893.

1797. Wecter, Dixon. "Thomas Jefferson, The Gentle Radical." In his *The Hero in America: A Chronicle of Hero-Worship,* 148-180. New York: Scribner's, 1941.

1798. Whealon, John F. "The Great 'Preamble': Did Bellarmine Influence Jefferson? A Look at the Record." *Commonweal* 42 (July 6, 1946): 284-285.

1799. Williams, John S. *Thomas Jefferson: His Permanent Influence on American Institutions.* New York: Columbia University Press, 1913.

1800. Wilson, Francis G. "On Jeffersonian Tradition." *Review of Politics* 5 (July 1943): 302-321.

1801. Wilstach, Paul. "Thomas Jefferson." In his *Patriots Off Their Pedestals,* 145-181. Indianapolis, IN: Bobbs-Merrill, 1927.

1802. Wirt, William. *A Discourse on the Lives and Characters of Thomas Jefferson and John Adams, Who Both Died on the Fourth of July, 1826.* Washington, DC: Gales and Seaton, 1826.

1803. Wise, James W., ed. *Thomas Jefferson, Then and Now: 1743-1943.* New York: Bill of Rights Sesquicentennial Committee, 1943.

1804. Wittke, Carl F. *Jefferson Lives On: A Lecture Delivered at the Ohio State University October 26, 1942.* Columbus: Ohio State University, 1942.

1805. Wood, G. S. "Problem of Jefferson." *Virginia Quarterly Review* 47 (Winter 1971): 137-141.

1806. Wright, Esmond. "Thomas Jefferson and the Jeffersonian Idea." In *British Essays in American History,* edited by Harry C. Allen and Charles P. Hill, 61-82. New York: St. Martin's Press, 1957.

1807. Yoder, Edwin M. "The Sage at Sunset." *Virginia Quarterly Review* 1 (Winter 1982): 32-37.

Declaration of Independence

1808. Alvord, Clarence W. "Thomas Jefferson, Apostle of Democracy." *Contemporary Review* 130 (July 1926): 39-45.

1809. Beard, Charles A. "Jefferson and the New Freedom." *New Republic* 1 (November 14, 1914): 18-19.

1810. Beard, Charles A. *Jefferson, Corporations, and the Constitution.* Washington, DC: National Home Library Foundation, 1936.

1811. Beloff, Max. *Thomas Jefferson and American Democracy.* New York: Macmillan, 1949.

1812. Boyd, Julian P. *The Declaration of Independence: The Evolution of the Text as Shown in Facsimiles of Various Drafts by Its Author, Thomas Jefferson.* Princeton, NJ: Princeton University Press, 1945.

1813. Brown, William H. *Constitution, Jefferson's Manual, and Rules of the House of Representatives of the United States.* Washington, DC: U.S. Government Printing Office, 1975.

1814. Cooke, John E. "The Writer of the Declaration: A Familiar Sketch." *Harper's New Monthly Magazine* 53 (July 1876): 211-216.

1815. Detweiler, Philip F. "The Declaration of Independence in Jefferson's Lifetime." Ph.D. dissertation, Tulane University, 1955.

1816. Donovan, Frank. *Mr. Jefferson's Declaration: The Story Behind the Decla-*

ration of Independence. New York: Dodd, Mead, 1966.

1817. Dumbauld, Edward. *The Declaration of Independence and What It Means Today.* Norman: University of Oklahoma Press, 1950.

1818. Gittleman, Edwin. "Jefferson's 'Slave Narrative': The Declaration of Independence as a Literary Text." *Early American Literature* 8 (Fall 1974): 239-256.

1819. Graff, Polly A. C. *Thomas Jefferson, Author of Independence.* Champaign, IL: Garrard, 1963.

1820. Hamowy, Ronald. "Jefferson and the Scottish Enlightenment: A Critique of Garry Wills's *Inventing America: Jefferson's Declaration of Independence.*" *William and Mary Quarterly* 36 (October 1979): 503-523.

1821. Harvey, Alexander M. *Jefferson and the American Constitution.* Topeka, KS: Capper Printing Co., 1926.

1822. Holliday, Carl. "The Man Who Wrote the Declaration." *Methodist Quarterly Review* 73 (July 1924): 453-468.

1823. Kingdon, Frank. *Architects of the Republic: George Washington, Thomas Jefferson, Abraham Lincoln, Franklin D. Roosevelt.* New York: Alliance Publishing Co., 1947.

1824. Klapthor, Margaret B. "The Story of the Declaration of Independence Desk and How It Came to the National Museum." In *Smithsonian Institution Annual Report, 1953,* 455-462. Washington, DC: The Institution, 1954.

1825. Levin, David. "Cotton Mather's Declaration of Gentlemen and Thomas Jefferson's Declaration of Independence." *New England Quarterly* 50 (September 1977): 509-514.

1826. Lewis, Alfred H. "Jefferson's Great Day: A Pregnant Scene from the Drama of American Independence." *Everybody's Magazine* 7 (December 1902): 561-570.

1827. Lynn, Kenneth S. "Falsifying Jefferson." *Commentary* 66 (October 1978): 66-71.

1828. Malone, Dumas. "Jefferson, Hamilton, and the Constitution." In *Theory and Practice in American Politics,* edited by William H. Nelson and Francis L. Loewenheim, 13-23. Chicago: University of Chicago Press, 1964.

1829. Malone, Thomas J. "The Man Who Wrote the Declaration." *Independent* 116 (July 3, 1926): 11-12.

1830. Mintz, Max M. "A Conversation between Thomas Jefferson and Gouverieur Morris: The Author of the Declaration of Independence and Penman of the Constitution." *Connecticut Review 1975-1976* 9 (November): 21-26.

1831. Morgan, Edmund S. *The Meaning of Independence: John Adams, George Washington, Thomas Jefferson.* Charlottesville: University Press of Virginia, 1976.

1832. Morgan, Edmund S., ed. "Thomas Jefferson." In his *The Meaning of Independence: John Adams, George Washington, Thomas Jefferson,* 59-81. Charlottesville: University Press of Virginia, 1976.

1833. Mullen, Arthur F. "The Father of the Constitution." In *Report of the Third Annual Meeting of the State Bar of South Dakota, Held at Aberdeen, South Dakota, August 24th and 25th, 1933,* 169-180. Pierre: South Dakota State Bar Association, 1933.

1834. Munves, James. *Thomas Jefferson and the Declaration of Independence: The Writing and Editing of the Document That Marked the Birth of the United States of America.* New York: Scribner's, 1978.

1835. Padover, Saul K. "Jefferson's

Prose-Poem: The Declaration of Independence." *American Mercury* 54 (February 1942): 165-171.

1836. Page, Rosewell. "Thomas Jefferson and the Declaration of Independence." *Virginia Journal of Education* 19 (May 1926): 343-345.

1837. Patterson, C. Perry. "Thomas Jefferson and the Constitution." *Minnesota Law Review* 29 (March 1945): 265-279.

1838. Randall, David A. "Dukedom Large Enough: Thomas Jefferson and the Declaration of Independence." *Bibliographical Society of America Papers* 56 (1962): 472-480.

1839. Schaff, David S. "The Bellarmine — Jefferson Legend and the Declaration of Independence." *American Society of Church History Papers* 8 (1928): 239-276.

1840. Tyler, Moses C. "Thomas Jefferson and the Great Declaration." In his *The Literary History of the American Revolution, 1763-1783*, 494-521. New York: Putnam, 1897.

1841. Wham, Benjamin. "Jefferson Wins over Hamilton: Historical Explanation of Constitutional Changes." *American Bar Association Journal* 35 (January 1949): 23-26, 86-87.

1842. Wills, Garry. *Inventing America: Jefferson's Declaration of Independence*. Garden City, NY: Doubleday, 1978.

1843. Zwierlein, Frederick J. "Jefferson, Jesuits, and the Declaration." *America* 49 (July 8, 1958): 321-323.

Diplomat

1844. Andrews, Stuart. "Jefferson and the French Revolution." *History Today* 18 (May 1968): 299-306, 368.

1845. Banning, Lance. "Jeffersonian Ideology and the French Revolution: A Question of Liberticide at Home." *Studies in Burke and His Times* 17 (Winter 1976): 5-26.

1846. Bernstein, Samuel. "Jefferson and the French Revolution." *Science and Society* 7 (Spring 1943): 115-140.

1847. Bowman, Albert H. "Jefferson, Hamilton, and American Foreign Policy." *Political Science Quarterly* 71 (March 1956): 18-41.

1848. Boyd, Julian P. "Two Diplomats between Revolutions: John Jay and Thomas Jefferson." *Virginia Magazine of History and Biography* 66 (April 1958): 131-146.

1849. Carriere, Joseph M. "Mr. Jefferson Sponsors a New French Method." *French Review* 19 (May 1946): 394-405.

1850. DeConde, Alexander. "Foreclosure of a Peacemaker's Career: A Criticism of Thomas Jefferson's Isolation." *Huntington Library Quarterly* 15 (May 1952): 297-304.

1851. Devol, Edward. "From Thomas Jefferson to Cyrus Vance." *Foreign Service Journal* 54 (November 1977): 6-10.

1852. Dodd, William E. "Napoleon Breaks Thomas Jefferson." *American Mercury* 5 (July 1925): 303-313.

1853. Ford, Paul L. "The French Revolution and Jefferson." *Nation* 61 (July 25, 1895): 61.

1854. Goldberg, Stephen H. "Thomas Jefferson and American Foreign Policy, 1783-1798: Prelude to Power." Master's thesis, City University of New York, 1970.

1855. Hazen, Charles D. "Thomas Jefferson in France." In *Contemporary American Opinion of the French Revolution*, Vol. 16, 1-53. Baltimore, MD: Johns Hopkins University Press, 1897.

1856. Kaplan, Lawrence S. "The Consensus of 1789: Jefferson and Hamilton on

American Foreign Policy." *South Atlantic Quarterly* 71 (Winter 1972): 91-105.

1857. Kaplan, Lawrence S. *Jefferson and France: An Essay on Politics and Political Ideas.* New Haven, CT: Yale University Press, 1967.

1858. Kaplan, Lawrence S. "Jefferson, the Napoleonic Wars, and the Balance of Power." *William and Mary Quarterly* 14 (April 1957): 196-217.

1859. Kaplan, Lawrence S. "Jefferson's Foreign Policy and Napoleon's Ideologies." *William and Mary Quarterly* 19 (July 1962): 344-359.

1860. Kaplan, Lawrence S. "Reflections on Jefferson as a Francophile." *South Atlantic Quarterly* 79 (Winter 1980): 38-50.

1861. Landin, Harold W. "Thomas Jefferson and the French Revolution." Ph.D. dissertation, Cornell University, 1928.

1862. McGrath, Paul C. "Secretary Jefferson and Revolutionary France, 1790-1793." Ph.D. dissertation, Boston University, 1950.

1863. Marsh, Philip M. "Jefferson's Retirement as Secretary of State." *Pennsylvania Magazine of History and Biography* 69 (July 1945): 220-224.

1864. Mead, Edwin D. "Washington, Jefferson, and Franklin on War." *World Peace Foundation Pamphlet* 3 (May 1913): 3-15.

1865. Powell, Burt E. "Jefferson and the Consular Service." *Political Science Quarterly* 21 (December 1906): 626-638.

1866. Pulley, Judith. "Thomas Jefferson at the Court of Versailles: An American 'Philosophe' and the Coming of the French Revolution." Ph.D. dissertation, University of Virginia, 1966.

1867. Putnam, Samuel. "Jefferson and the Young Brazilians in France." *Science and Society* 10 (Winter 1946): 185-192.

1868. Randall, E. O. "Jefferson's Ordinance of 1784." *Ohio Archaeological and Historical Society Publications* 20 (January 1911): 118-123.

1869. Rice, Howard C., Jr. "A French Source of Jefferson's Plan for the Prison at Richmond." *Society of Architectural Historians Journal* 12 (December 1953): 28-30.

1870. Rice, Philip A., II. "Thomas Jefferson and the Balance of Power Principle, 1783-1793." Master's thesis, California State University, Fullerton, 1969.

1871. Ritcheson, Charles R. "The Fragile Memory: Thomas Jefferson at the Court of George III." *Eighteenth Century Life* 6 (January/May 1981): 1-16.

1872. Ritcheson, Charles R. "The Fragile Memory: What Really Happened When Thomas Jefferson Met George III." *American Heritage* 33 (December 1981): 72-77.

1873. Sears, Louis M. "Jefferson and the Law of Nations." *American Political Science Review* 13 (August 1919): 379-399.

1874. Serpell, Jean K. "Thomas Jefferson: His Relationship with France." Master's thesis, Stetson University, 1957.

1875. Sestanovich, Stephen. "Thomas Jefferson, PAO." *Foreign Service Journal* 43 (July 1966): 23-25.

1876. Shulim, Joseph I. "Thomas Jefferson Views Napoleon." *Virginia Magazine of History and Biography* 60 (April 1952): 288-304.

1877. Shurr, Georgia H. "Thomas Jefferson and the French Revolution." *American Society Legion of Honor Magazine* 50 (Winter 1979-1980): 161-182.

1878. Spiro, Jeffery H. "Thomas Jefferson and the Origins of American Neutrality." Master's thesis, City University of New York, 1975.

1879. Wiltse, Charles M. "Thomas Jefferson on the Law of Nations." *American Journal of International Law* 29 (January 1935): 66-81.

1880. Woolery, William K. *The Relation of Thomas Jefferson to American Foreign Policy, 1783-1793.* Baltimore, MD: Johns Hopkins University Press, 1927.

Party Politics

1881. Adair, Douglass. "The Intellectual Origins of Jeffersonian Democracy: Republicanism, Class Struggle, and the Virtuous Farmer." Ph.D. dissertation, Yale University, 1943.

1882. Adams, James T. "Jefferson and Hamilton Today: The Dichotomy in American Thought." *Atlantic Monthly* 141 (April 1928): 443-450.

1883. Alvord, Clarence W. "Thomas Jefferson versus Alexander Hamilton." *Landmark* 8 (March 1926): 194-196.

1884. Ashworth, John. "The Jeffersonians: Classical Republicans or Liberal Capitalists?" *Journal of American Studies* 18 (December 1984): 425-435.

1885. Banning, Lance. *The Jeffersonian Persuasion: Evolution of a Party Ideology.* Ithaca, NY: Cornell University Press, 1978.

1886. Baumann, Roland M. "Philadelphia's Manufacturers and the Exise Taxes of 1794: The Forging of the Jeffersonian Coalition." *Pennsylvania Magazine of History and Biography* 106 (January 1982): 3-40.

1887. Bias, Randolph. "Jefferson and Hamilton." *West Virginia Law Quarterly and the Bar* 33 (December 1926): 1-28.

1888. Blair, Albert L. "Was Jefferson a Democrat?" *Arena* 21 (May 1899): 633-645.

1889. Bonn, Franklyn G., Jr. "The Idea of Political Party in the Thought of Thomas Jefferson and James Madison." Ph.D. dissertation, University of Minnesota, 1964.

1890. Bowers, Claude G. *Jefferson and Hamilton: The Struggle for Democracy in America.* Boston: Houghton Mifflin, 1925.

1891. Bowers, Claude G. *Jefferson in Power: The Death Struggle of the Federalists.* Boston: Houghton Mifflin, 1936.

1892. Bowers, Claude G. *Making Democracy a Reality: Jefferson, Jackson, and Polk.* Memphis, TN: Memphis State College Press, 1954.

1893. Bowers, Claude G. "Thomas Jefferson: His Final and Decisive Struggle for American Democracy." In his *Making Democracy a Reality: Jefferson, Jackson, and Polk*, 1-39. Memphis, TN: Memphis State College Press, 1954.

1894. Brown, Stuart G. *The First Republicans: Political Philosophy and Public Policy in the Party of Jefferson and Madison.* Syracuse, NY: Syracuse University Press, 1954.

1895. Caldwell, Lynton K. *The Administrative Theories of Hamilton and Jefferson: Their Contribution to Thought on Public Administration.* Chicago: University of Chicago Press, 1944.

1896. Charles, Joseph. "Adams and Jefferson: The Origins of the American Party System." *William and Mary Quarterly* 12 (July 1955): 410-446.

1897. Chidsey, Donald B. *Mr. Hamilton and Mr. Jefferson.* Nashville, TN: Thomas Nelson, 1975.

1898. Cunningham, Noble E., Jr. *The Jeffersonian Republicans in Power: Party Operations, 1801-1809.* Chapel Hill: University of North Carolina Press, 1963.

1899. Cunningham, Noble E., Jr. *The*

Jeffersonian Republicans: The Formation of Party Organization, 1789-1801. Chapel Hill: University of North Carolina Press, 1957.

1900. Daniels, Jonathan. *Ordeal of Ambition: Jefferson, Hamilton, Burr.* Garden City, NY: Doubleday, 1970.

1901. Dethloff, Henry C., ed. *Thomas Jefferson and American Democracy.* Lexington, MA: Heath, 1971.

1902. Dewey, John. "Thomas Jefferson and the Democratic Faith." *Virginia Quarterly Review* 16 (Winter 1940): 1-13.

1903. DeWitt, Cornelius H. *Jefferson and the American Democracy.* Translated by R. S. H. Church. London: Longman, Green, 1862.

1904. Dix, John P. "Thomas Jefferson, Father of American Democracy." *Social Studies* 38 (December 1947): 357-366.

1905. Dorfman, Joseph. "Thomas Jefferson: Commercial Agrarian Democrat." In his *The Economic Mind in American Civilization, 1606-1865,* Vol. 1, 433-447. New York: Viking Press, 1946.

1906. Douglass, Elisha P. "Thomas Jefferson and Revolutionary Democracy." In her *Rebels and Democrats,* 287-316. Chapel Hill: University of North Carolina Press, 1955.

1907. Dunlap, John R. *Jeffersonian Democracy, Which Means the Democracy of Thomas Jefferson, Andrew Jackson, and Abraham Lincoln.* New York: Jeffersonian Society, 1903.

1908. Eaton, Clement. "The Jeffersonian Tradition of Liberalism in America." *South Atlantic Quarterly* 43 (January 1944): 1-10.

1909. Fischer, David H. *The Revolution of American Conservatism: The Federalist Party in the Era of Jeffersonian Democracy.* New York: Harper and Row, 1965.

1910. Foster, Franklin P. *The World War, Jefferson, and Democracy.* Anderson, IN: History Club, 1917.

1911. Franklin, Francis. "The Democratic Philosophy of Thomas Jefferson." In *The Heritage of Jefferson,* edited by Alexander Trachtenberg, 38-46. New York: Workers School, 1945.

1912. Fried, Albert. *The Jeffersonian and Hamiltonian Traditions in American Politics.* Garden City, NY: Doubleday, 1966.

1913. Fuller, Melville W. "Jefferson and Hamilton." *Dial* 4 (May 1883): 4-6.

1914. Govan, Thomas P. "Jefferson and Hamilton: A Christian Evaluation." *Christian Scholar* 40 (March 1957): 6-12.

1915. Griswold, A. Whitney. "The Agrarian Democracy of Thomas Jefferson." *American Political Science Review* 40 (August 1946): 657-681.

1916. Griswold, A. Whitney. "Jefferson's Republic: The Rediscovery of Democratic Philosophy." *Fortune* 41 (April 1950): 111-112, 126-130, 134-136.

1917. Haines, Charles G. "The Views of Thomas Jefferson and of Leading Democrat-Republicans." In his *The American Doctrine of Judicial Supremacy,* 2d ed., 241-253. New York: Russell and Russell, 1959.

1918. Harvey, Alexander M. "Hamilton, Jefferson, and the American Constitution." *Kansas State Historical Society Collections* 17 (1928): 744-787.

1919. Hofstadter, Richard. *The Idea of a Party System, 1780-1840.* Berkeley: University of California Press, 1969.

1920. Hofstadter, Richard. "Thomas Jefferson: The Aristocrat as Democrat." In his *The American Political Tradition and the Men Who Made It,* 18-48. New York: Vintage Press, 1948.

1921. Huegli, Jon M. "Jeffersonian

Rhetoric: Persistent Witness to Democratic Republicanism." Master's thesis, Indiana University, 1967.

1922. Johnson, Luciana. "Thomas Jefferson and the Beginning of the Republican Party (1790-92)." Master's thesis, University of California, Riverside, 1956.

1923. McColley, Robert. "Jefferson's Rivals: The Shifting Character of the Federalists." *Midcontinent American Studies Journal* 9 (Spring 1968): 23-33.

1924. Marsh, Philip M., ed. *Monroe's Defense of Jefferson and Frenaeu against Hamilton.* Oxford, OH: The Author, 1948.

1925. Mayer, Frederick. "The Historical Significance of the Struggle between Hamilton and Jefferson." *Social Studies* 40 (April 1949): 165-167.

1926. Merriam, Charles E. "Jeffersonian Democracy." In his *A History of American Political Theories,* 143-175. New York: Macmillan, 1903.

1927. Meyer, Donald H. "Thomas Jefferson and the Rhetoric of Republicanism." In *The Democratic Enlightenment,* 109-128. New York: Putnam, 1976.

1928. Mitchell, Broadus. "Jefferson and Hamilton Today." *Virginia Quarterly Review* 10 (July 1934): 394-407.

1929. Palmer, Robert R. "Dubious Democrat: Thomas Jefferson in Bourbon, France." *Political Science Quarterly* 72 (September 1957): 388-404.

1930. Pancake, John S. *Thomas Jefferson and Alexander Hamilton.* Woodbury, NJ: Barron's, 1974.

1931. Parkes, Henry B. "Jeffersonian Democracy." *Symposium* 4 (July 1933): 302-323.

1932. Parrington, Vernon L. "Thomas Jefferson — Agrarian Democrat." In his *Main Currents in American Thought: Vol. 1, 1620-1800, The Colonial Mind,* 342-362. New York: Harcourt, Brace, 1927.

1933. Parton, James. "Meeting of Jefferson and Hamilton." *Atlantic Monthly* 30 (December 1872): 704-719.

1934. Pole, Jack R. "Personifications of the American Future: Hamilton and Jefferson." In *Foundations of American Independence, 1763-1815,* edited by Jack P. Greene, 201-211. Indianapolis, IN: Bobbs-Merrill, 1972.

1935. Powell, E. P. "Jefferson and Hamilton in Our Education." *New England Magazine* 14 (August 1896): 699-706.

1936. Prescott, Frederick. *Alexander Hamilton and Thomas Jefferson: Representative Selections, With Introduction, Bibliography, and Notes.* New York: American Book Co., 1934.

1937. Rogers, Robert, Jr. "Thomas Jefferson's Leadership of the Republican Party, January, 1797 to June, 1798." Master's thesis, University of California, Berkeley, 1953.

1938. Russell, William E. "Jefferson and His Party Today." *Forum* 21 (July 1896): 513-524.

1939. Rutland, Robert A. "The Jeffersonian Genesis." In his *The Democrats: From Jefferson to Carter,* 1-28. Baton Rouge: Louisiana State University Press, 1979.

1940. Saint, Percy. "Thomas Jefferson and Government by Party." *Louisiana Historical Quarterly* 8 (January 1925): 41-51.

1941. Schapsmeier, Edward L., and Frederick H. Schapsmeier. "The Hamilton-Jefferson Confrontation: Origins of the American Political System." *Social Science* 46 (June 1971): 138-147.

1942. Scruggs, J. H., Jr. "Thomas Jefferson's Views of Democracy and the Negro." *Alabama Historical Quarterly* 8 (Spring 1946): 95-102.

1943. Sears, Louis M. "Democracy as Understood by Thomas Jefferson." *Mid-America* 24 (April 1942): 85-95.

1944. Shalhope, Robert E. "Thomas Jefferson's Republicanism and Antebellum Southern Thought." *Journal of Southern History* 42 (November 1976): 529-556.

1945. Sheehan, Vincent. *Thomas Jefferson: Father of Democracy.* New York: Random House, 1953.

1946. Smyth, Clifford. *Thomas Jefferson, The Father of American Democracy.* New York: Funk and Wagnalls, 1931.

1947. Stead, John P. "The Roots of Democracy in Thomas Jefferson and Mao Tse-Tung." Ph.D. dissertation, University of Southern California, 1976.

1948. Sutton, Robert P. "Sectionalism and Social Structure: A Case Study of Jeffersonian Democracy." *Virginia Magazine of History and Biography* 80 (January 1972): 70-84.

1949. White, Leonard D. "The Hamilton-Jefferson Feud." In *The Gaspard G. Bacon Lectures on the Constitution of the United States, 1940-1950,* 213-231. Boston: Boston University Press, 1953.

1950. Wiltse, Charles M. "Jeffersonian Democracy: A Dual Tradition." *American Political Science Review* 28 (October 1934): 838-851.

1951. Wiltse, Charles M. *The Jeffersonian Tradition in American Democracy.* Chapel Hill: University of North Carolina Press, 1935.

Revolution

1952. Browder, Earl. "Jefferson and the People's Revolution." In *The Heritage of Jefferson,* edited by Alexander Trachtenberg, 28-37. New York: Workers School, 1945.

1953. Butterfield, Lyman H. "The Dream of Benjamin Rush: The Reconciliation of John Adams and Thomas Jefferson." *Yale Review* 40 (December 1950): 297-319.

1954. Butterfield, Lyman H. "Psychological Warfare in 1776: The Jefferson and Franklin Plan to Cause Hessian Desertions." *American Philosophical Society Proceedings* 94 (June 1950): 233-241.

1955. Canfield, Cass. *Samuel Adams' Revolution, 1765-1776: With the Assistance of George Washington, Thomas Jefferson, Benjamin Franklin, John Adams, George III, and the People of Boston.* New York: Harper and Row, 1976.

1956. Flower, B. O. "Jefferson's Service to Civilization during the Founding of the Republic." *Arena* 29 (May 1903): 500-518.

1957. Hans, Nicholas. "Franklin, Jefferson, and the English Radicals at the End of the Eighteenth Century." *American Philosophical Society Proceedings* 98 (December 1954): 406-426.

1958. Howard, John R., comp. *... Patriotic Nuggets: Franklin, Washington, Jefferson, Webster, Lincoln, Beecher.* New York: Fords, Howard and Hulbert, 1899.

1959. James, Marquis. *They Had Their Hour: Benjamin Franklin, Thomas Jefferson.* Darby, PA: Arden Library, 1982.

1960. Katz, Stanley N. "Thomas Jefferson and the Right to Property in Revolutionary America." *Journal of Law and Economics* 19 (October 1976): 467-488.

1961. Kelley, Darwin. "Jefferson and the Separation of Powers in the States, 1776-1787." *Indiana Magazine of History* 54 (March 1958): 25-40.

1962. Ketcham, Ralph L. "John Adams, Franklin, Jefferson, and the Puritan Ethic" and "Conceptions of New Nationhood: Jefferson and Hamilton." In his *From*

Colony to Country, The Revolution in American Thought, 1750-1820, 159-172, 195-212. New York: Macmillan, 1974.

1963. Kirkland, Frederic R. "Jefferson and Franklin." *Pennsylvania Magazine of History and Biography* 71 (July 1947): 218-222.

1964. Kloman, William. "The Jefferson Theory of Revolution." *Cybernetica* 21 (1978): 193-204.

1965. Koch, Adrienne. *Jefferson and Madison: The Great Collaboration.* New York: Oxford University Press, 1964.

1966. Koch, Adrienne. "Power and Morals and the Founding Fathers: Jefferson." *Review of Politics* 15 (October 1953): 470-490.

1967. Koch, Adrienne. *Power, Morals, and the Founding Fathers: Essays in the Interpretation of the American Enlightenment.* Ithaca, NY: Cornell University Press, 1961.

1968. Koch, Adrienne, ed. *Adams and Jefferson: "Posterity Must Judge."* Chicago: Rand McNally, 1963.

1969. Lewis, Anthony M. "Jefferson and the American Union, 1769-1781." Ph.D. dissertation, University of Michigan, 1946.

1970. Lewis, Anthony M. "Jefferson's *Summary View* as a Chart of Political Union." *William and Mary Quarterly* 5 (January 1948): 34-51.

1971. Lichtenstein, Gaston. *Thomas Jefferson as War Governor, Also Three Travel Articles and Some North Carolina History.* Richmond, VA: William Byrd Press, 1925.

1972. Lynd, Staughton. "Beard, Jefferson, and the Tree of Liberty." *American Studies* 9 (Spring 1968): 8-22.

1973. Mayo, Bernard. "Lecture Three: The Strange Case of Thomas Jefferson." In his *Myths and Men: Patrick Henry, George Washington, Thomas Jefferson,* 49-71. Athens: University of Georgia Press, 1959.

1974. Mayo, Bernard. *Myths and Men: Patrick Henry, George Washington, Thomas Jefferson.* Athens: University of Georgia Press, 1959.

1975. Mirkin, Harris G. "Rebellion, Revolution, and the Constitution: Thomas Jefferson's Theory of Civil Disobedience." *American Studies* 13 (Fall 1972): 61-74.

1976. Morgan, Robert J. " 'Time Hath Found Us': The Jeffersonian Revolutionary Vision." *Journal of Politics* 38 (August 1976): 20-36.

1977. Nelson, Virginia A. "Thomas Jefferson and the Sureties of Magna Carta." *Southern Literary Messenger* 2 (April 1940): 255-258.

1978. Osborn, Robert W. "Portrait of a Revolutionary: Thomas Jefferson and the Coming of the American Revolution." Master's thesis, Fort Hays Kansas State College, 1969.

1979. Palmer, Robert R. "A Neglected Work: Otto Vossler on Jefferson and the Revolutionary Era." *William and Mary Quarterly* 12 (July 1955): 462-471.

1980. Peterson, Merrill D. *Adams and Jefferson: A Revolutionary Dialogue.* Athens: University of Georgia Press, 1976.

1981. Peterson, Merrill D. "Adams and Jefferson: A Revolutionary Dialogue." *Wilson Quarterly* 1 (Autumn 1976): 108-125.

1982. Pierard, Richard V. "Faith of Our Fathers: Some Post-bicentennial Reflections." *Covenant Quarterly* 35 (November 1977): 15-25.

1983. Stoddard, William O. *John Adams and Thomas Jefferson.* New York: White, Stokes and Allen, 1887.

1984. Thorpe, Francis N. "Adams and Jefferson: 1826-1926." *North American*

Review 223 (June/July/August 1926): 234-247.

1985. Vossler, Otto. *Jefferson and the American Revolutionary Ideal.* Lanham, MD: University Press of America, 1980.

1986. Waldo, Samuel P. *Biographical Sketches of Distinguished American Naval Heroes in the War of the Revolution, Between the American Republic and the Kingdom of Great Britain....* Hartford, CT: Silas Andrus, 1823.

1987. Wish, Harvey. "The Revolutionary Era of Hancock and Jefferson." In his *Society and Thought in America,* 184-222. New York: Longmans, Green, 1950.

Virginia Politics

1988. Ammon, Harry. "The Jeffersonian Republicans in Virginia: An Interpretation." *Virginia Magazine of History and Biography* 71 (April 1963): 153-167.

1989. Anderson, Dice R. "Jefferson and the Virginia Constitution." *American Historical Review* 21 (July 1916): 750-754.

1990. Dabney, William M. "Jefferson's Albemarle: History of Albemarle County, Virginia, 1727-1819." Ph.D. dissertation, University of Virginia, 1951.

1991. Ford, Worthington C. "Jefferson's Constitution for Virginia." *Nation* 51 (August 7, 1890): 107-109.

1992. Harrold, Frances L. "Thomas Jefferson and the Commonwealth of Virginia: A Study in Constitutional Thought." Ph.D. dissertation, Bryn Mawr College, 1960.

1993. "How the 'Common Man' Voted in Jefferson's Virginia." In *America, The Middle Period: Essays in Honor of Bernard Mayo,* edited by John B. Boles, 36-64. Charlottesville: University Press of Virginia, 1973.

1994. Johnson, Allen. *Jefferson and His Colleagues: A Chronicle of the Virginia Dynasty,* New Haven, CT: Yale University Press, 1921.

1995. Jordan, Daniel P. *Political Leadership in Jefferson's Virginia.* Charlottesville: University Press of Virginia, 1982.

1996. Kean, Robert G. H. "Thomas Jefferson as a Legislator." *Virginia Law Journal* 11 (December 1887): 705-724.

1997. Koch, Adrienne, and Harry Ammon. "The Virginia and Kentucky Resolutions: An Episode in Jefferson's and Madison's Defense of Civil Liberties." *William and Mary Quarterly* 5 (April 1948): 145-176.

1998. Lewellyn, Robert. *Mr. Jefferson's Upland Virginia.* Charlottesville, VA: Thomasson-Grant, 1983.

1999. Lewis, Anthony M. "Jefferson and Virginia's Pioneers, 1774-1781." *Mississippi Valley Historical Review* 34 (March 1948): 551-588.

2000. Malone, Dumas. "Mr. Jefferson and the Traditions of Virginia." *Virginia Magazine of History and Biography* 75 (April 1967): 131-142.

2001. Meisen, Adolf F. "Thomas Jefferson, War Governor of Virginia." Ph.D. dissertation, University of North Carolina, 1943.

2002. Parton, James. "Jefferson, A Reformer of Old Virginia." *Atlantic Monthly* 30 (July 1872): 32-49.

2003. Prufer, Julius F. "The Franchise in Virginia from Jefferson through the Convention of 1829." *William and Mary Quarterly* 7 (October 1927): 255-270.

2004. Pryor, John C. "Thomas Jefferson and the Golden Age of the Old Dominion." *Virginia Law Register* 13 (January 1928): 513-525.

2005. Riley, I. Woodbridge. "Virginia

and Jefferson." In his *American Philosophy, The Early Schools,* 266-295. New York: Russell and Russell, 1907.

2006. Royster, Charles. "A Battle of Memoirs: Light-Horse Harry Lee and Thomas Jefferson." *Virginia Cavalcade* 31 (Autumn 1981): 112-127.

2007. Woodfin, Maude H. "Contemporary Opinion in Virginia of Thomas Jefferson." In *Essays in Honor of William E. Dodd,* edited by Avery Craven, 30-85. Chicago: University of Chicago Press, 1935.

Presidential Years

General

2008. Abernethy, Thomas P. *The Burr Conspiracy.* New York: Oxford University Press, 1954.

2009. Adams, Henry. *History of the United States of America during the Administrations of Jefferson and Madison.* 9 vols. New York: Scribner's, 1891-1898, 1909-1911.

2010. Adams, Henry. *History of the United States of America during the First Administration of Thomas Jefferson.* 2 vols. New York: Scribner's, 1889.

2011. Adams, Henry. *History of the United States of America during the Second Administration of Thomas Jefferson.* Cambridge, MA: John Wilson and Son, 1885.

2012. Adams, Mary P. "Jefferson's Military Policy with Special Reference to the Frontier, 1805-1809." Ph.D. dissertation, University of Virginia, 1958.

2013. American Philosophical Society. "Thomas Jefferson: Papers Read before the American Philosophical Society in Celebration of the Bicentennial of Thomas Jefferson, Third President of the Society." *American Philosophical Society Proceedings* 86 (July 14, 1943): 199-389.

2014. Aronson, Sidney H. *Status and Kinship in the Higher Civil Service: The Administrations of John Adams, Thomas Jefferson, and Andrew Jackson.* Cambridge, MA: Harvard University Press, 1964.

2015. Bernard, John. "Recollections of President Jefferson." In *Retrospections of America, 1797-1811,* edited by Mrs. B. Bernard, 232-243. New York: Harper and Row, 1887.

2016. Boyd, Julian P. "Thomas Jefferson's 'Empire of Liberty.'" *Virginia Quarterly Review* 24 (Autumn 1948): 538-554.

2017. Bradley, Bert B. "Jefferson and Reagan: The Rhetoric of Two Inaugurals." *Southern Speech Communication Journal* 48 (Winter 1983): 119-136.

2018. Brent, Robert A. "Nicholas Philip Trist — A Link between Jefferson and Jackson?" *Southern Quarterly* 1 (October 1962): 87-97.

2019. Brewer, Paul W. "Jefferson's Administration of the Patronage: New York, 1801-1804." Master's thesis, University of Virginia, 1968.

2020. Brown, Edward A. "An Investigation of the Attitudes Expressed by Richmond's Press toward Thomas Jefferson in the Presidential Elections of 1800, 1804, and 1808." Master's thesis, University of Richmond, 1964.

2021. Bruce, Philip A. "President Thomas Jefferson." In his *The Virginia Plutarch,* Vol. 2, 19-37. Chapel Hill: University of North Carolina Press, 1929.

2022. Bryce, James. "Thomas Jefferson: Third President of the United States and Founder of the University of Virginia." In his *University and Historical Addresses, Delivered during a Residence in the Unit-*

ed States as Ambassador of Great Britain, 109-124. New York: Macmillan, 1913.

2023. Busey, Samuel C. "The Centennial of the First Inauguration of a President at the Permanent Seat of the Government." *Columbia Historical Society Records* 5 (1902): 96-111.

2024. Campbell, Helen M. ... *Famous Presidents: Washington, Jefferson, Madison, Lincoln, Grant.* Boston: Educational Publishing Co., 1903.

2025. Channing, Edward. *Jeffersonian System: Eighteen Hundred and One to Eighteen Hundred and Eleven.* Totawa, NJ: Cooper Square, 1968.

2026. Cole, Charles C. "Brockden Brown and the Jefferson Administration." *Pennsylvania Magazine of History* 72 (July 1948): 253-263.

2027. Cooke, Jacob E. "Assistant to Jefferson." In *Tench Coxe and the Early Republic*, edited by Harold Hutcheson, 468-490. Chapel Hill: University of North Carolina Press, 1978.

2028. Cooke, Jacob E. "The Collaboration of Tench Coxe and Thomas Jefferson." *Pennsylvania Magazine of History and Biography* 100 (October 1976): 468-490.

2029. Cooper, Joseph. "Jeffersonian Attitudes toward Executive Leadership and Committee Development in the House of Representatives, 1789-1829." *World Politics* 18 (March 1965): 45-63.

2030. Crackel, Theodore J. "The Founding of West Point: Jefferson and the Politics of Security." *Armed Forces and Society* 7 (Summer 1981): 529-543.

2031. Crackel, Theodore J. "Jefferson, Politics, and the Army: An Examination of the Military Peace Establishment Act of 1802." *Journal of the Early Republic* 2 (Spring 1982): 21-38.

2032. Cunningham, Noble E., Jr. *The Image of Thomas Jefferson in the Public Eye: Portraits of the People, 1800-1809.* Charlottesville: University Press of Virginia, 1981.

2033. Cunningham, Noble E., Jr. *The Process of Government under Jefferson.* Princeton, NJ: Princeton University Press, 1978.

2034. Cunningham, Noble E., Jr. "The Virginia Jeffersonians' Victory Celebration in 1801." *Virginia Cavalcade* 8 (Summer 1958): 4-9.

2035. Cutright, Paul R. "Jefferson's Instructions to Lewis and Clark." *Missouri Historical Society Bulletin* 22 (April 1966): 302-320.

2036. Dargo, George. *Jefferson's Louisiana: Politics and the Clash of Legal Traditions.* Cambridge, MA: Harvard University Press, 1975.

2037. Dos Passos, John. *The Shackles of Power: Three Jeffersonian Decades.* Garden City, NY: Doubleday, 1966.

2038. Douty, Esther. *Mr. Jefferson's Washington.* Champaign, IL: Garrard, 1970.

2039. Downes, Randolph C. "Thomas Jefferson and the Removal of Governor St. Clair in 1802." *Ohio Archaeological and Historical Society Publications* 36 (January 1927): 62-77.

2040. Duyckinck, Evert A. "Jefferson and Coleridge." *Historical Magazine* 9 (January 1865): 24-25.

2041. "Farewell Address to Thomas Jefferson, President of the United States, and Resolution Relative Thereto." *William and Mary Quarterly* 11 (January 1931): 59-60.

2042. Ferguson, Eugene S. "Mr. Jefferson's Dry Docks." *American Neptune* 11 (April 1951): 108-114.

2043. Forman, Sidney. "Thomas Jefferson on Universal Military Training." *Military Affairs* 11 (Fall 1947): 177-178.

2044. Freidel, Frank B. "Thomas Jefferson, Third President." *National Geographic Magazine* 126 (November 1964): 664-671.

2045. Gooch, Robert K. "Jeffersonianism and the Third Term Issue: A Retrospect." *Southern Review* 6 (Spring 1941): 735-749.

2046. Halsey, Robert H. *How the President, Thomas Jefferson, and Doctor Benjamin Waterhouse Established Vaccination as a Public Health Procedure.* New York: The Author, 1936.

2047. Harrison, Lowell H. "John Breckinridge and the Jefferson Administration." *Rocky Mountain Social Science Journal* 4 (October 1967): 83-91.

2048. Hart, James. "Some Notes on Public Administration and Administrative Law by Thomas Jefferson." *Journal of Politics* 9 (February 1947): 1-9.

2049. Hellman, C. Doris. "Jefferson's Efforts towards the Decimalization of United States Weights and Measures." *Isis* 16 (November 1931): 266-313.

2050. Helms, Dorcas K. "An Uneasy Alliance: The Relationship between Jefferson and Burr: 1791-1807." Master's thesis, North Texas State University, 1979.

2051. Hendrix, Jerry A. "Presidential Addresses to Congress: Woodrow Wilson and the Jeffersonian Tradition." *Southern Speech Journal* 31 (Summer 1966): 285-294.

2052. Henrich, Joseph G. "The Triumph of Ideology: The Jeffersonians and the Navy, 1779-1807." Ph.D. dissertation, Duke University, 1971.

2053. Hickey, Donald R. "Timothy Pickering and the Haitian Slave Revolt: A Letter to Thomas Jefferson in 1806." *Essex Institute of Historical Collections* 120 (July 1984): 149-163.

2054. Higginson, Thomas W. "The Early American Presidents: Thomas Jefferson." *Harper's New Monthly Magazine* 68 (March 1884): 548-560.

2055. Honeywell, Roy J. "President Jefferson and His Successor." *American Historical Review* 46 (October 1940): 64-75.

2056. Hunt, Gaillard. "Office-Seeking during Jefferson's Administration." *American Historical Review* 3 (January 1898): 270-291.

2057. Jackson, Donald. "Jefferson, Meriwether Lewis, and the Reduction of the United States Army." *American Philosophical Society Proceedings* 124 (April 29, 1980): 91-96.

2058. Jahoda, Gloria. "John Beckley: Jefferson's Campaign Manager." *New York Public Library Bulletin* 64 (May 1960): 247-260.

2059. Jenkinson, Isaac. *Aaron Burr, His Personal and Political Relations with Thomas Jefferson and Alexander Hamilton.* Richmond, IN: M. Cullaton, 1902.

2060. Johnstone, Robert M., Jr. *Jefferson and the Presidency, Leadership in the Young Republic.* Ithaca, NY: Cornell University Press, 1978.

2061. Kimball, Marie G. "The Epicure of the White House: Thomas Jefferson." *Virginia Quarterly Review* 9 (January 1933): 71-81.

2062. Kimball, S. Fiske. "The Genesis of the White House." *Century Magazine* 95 (February 1918): 523-528.

2063. Knudson, Jerry W. "The Case of Albert Gallatin and Jeffersonian Patronage." *Western Pennsylvania Historical Magazine* 52 (July 1969): 241-250.

2064. Knudson, Jerry W. "The Jefferson

Years: Response by the Press, 1801-1809." Ph.D. dissertation, University of Virginia, 1962.

2065. Koenig, Louis W. "Consensus Politics, 1800-1805." *American Heritage* 18 (February 1967): 4-7.

2066. Kundson, Jerry W. "The Case of Albert Gallatin and Jeffersonian Patronage." *Western Pennsylvania Historical Magazine* 52 (July 1969): 241-250.

2067. Lacy, Alexander B. "Jefferson and Congress: Congressional Method and Politics: 1801-1809." Ph.D. dissertation, University of Virginia, 1964.

2068. Lerche, Charles O., Jr. "Jefferson and the Election of 1800: A Case Study in the Political Smear." *William and Mary Quarterly* 5 (October 1948): 467-491.

2069. Levy, Richard. "The First Inaugural Address of Thomas Jefferson: The Founding of the American Republic." Master's thesis, University of Chicago, 1966.

2070. Long, Everett L. "Jefferson and Congress: A Study of the Jeffersonian Legislative System, 1801-1809." Ph.D. dissertation, University of Missouri, 1966.

2071. Lorant, Stefan. "Thomas Jefferson: The Fourth and Fifth Elections." In his *The Glorious Burden: The American Presidency*, 53-79. New York: Harper and Row, 1968.

2072. McBrien, D. D. "Thomas Jefferson and the Question of Presidential Tenure." *Historian* 6 (Autumn 1943): 5-14.

2073. McDonald, Forrest. *The Presidency of Thomas Jefferson*. Lawrence: Regents Press of Kansas, 1976.

2074. MacLeod, Julia H. "Jefferson and the Navy: A Defense." *Huntington Library Quarterly* 8 (February 1945): 153-184.

2075. Malone, Dumas. "Jefferson and Lincoln." *Abraham Lincoln Quarterly* 5 (June 1949): 327-347.

2076. Malone, Dumas. *Jefferson the President: First Term, 1801-1805*. Boston: Little, Brown, 1970.

2077. Malone, Dumas. *Jefferson the President: Second Term, 1805-1809*. Boston: Little, Brown, 1974.

2078. Malone, Dumas. "Mr. Jefferson to Mr. Roosevelt: An Imaginary Letter." *Virginia Quarterly Review* 19 (Spring 1943): 161-177.

2079. Malone, Dumas. "Presidential Leadership and National Unity: The Jeffersonian Example." *Journal of Southern History* 35 (February 1969): 3-17.

2080. Morgan, James M. "How President Jefferson Was Informed of Burr's Conspiracy." *Pennsylvania Magazine of History and Biography* 27 (1903): 56-59.

2081. Mumper, James A. "The Jefferson Image in the Federalist Mind, 1801-1809: Jefferson's Administration from the Federalist Point of View." Ph.D. dissertation, University of Virginia, 1966.

2082. Munson, Lyman E. "Comparative Study of Jefferson and Lincoln." *Connecticut Magazine* 8 (April/June 1903): 49-56.

2083. Norton, Paul F. "Jefferson's Plan for Mothballing the Frigates." *U.S. Naval Institute Proceedings* 82 (July 1956): 737-743.

2084. Parton, James. "The Art of Being President, Gathered from the Experience of Thomas Jefferson." *Atlantic Monthly* 30 (August 1873): 129-148.

2085. Peterson, Merrill D. "Henry Adams on Jefferson the President." *Virginia Quarterly Review* 39 (Spring 1963): 187-201.

2086. "Presidential Inaugurations: Jefferson — 1801." *Ladies' Magazine and Lit-*

erary Gazette 4 (November 1831): 481-485.

2087. Prince, Carl E. "The Passing of the Aristocracy: Jefferson's Removal of the Federalists, 1801-1805." *Journal of American History* 57 (December 1970): 563-575.

2088. Rosenberger, Francis C., ed. *Jefferson Reader, A Treasury of Writings about Thomas Jefferson.* New York: Dutton, 1953.

2089. Shippen, Rebecca L. "Inauguration of President Thomas Jefferson, 1801." *Pennsylvania Magazine of History and Biography* 25 (April 1901): 71-76.

2090. Showalter, William J. "Jefferson as President." *Virginia Journal of Education* 19 (May 1926): 345-349.

2091. Smith, Robert H. "Albert Gallatin and American Fiscal Policy during Jefferson's First Administration." Ph.D. dissertation, Syracuse University, 1954.

2092. Smith, William L. *The Pretensions of Thomas Jefferson to the Presidency Examined: And the Charges against John Adams Refuted.* Philadelphia: n.p., 1796.

2093. Sprague, Stuart S. "Jefferson, Kentucky and the Closing the Port of New Orleans, 1802-1803." *Register of the Kentucky Historical Society* 70 (October 1972): 312-317.

2094. Van der Linden, Frank. *The Turning Point: Jefferson's Battle for the Presidency.* Washington, DC: Robert B. Luce, 1962.

2095. Warren, Charles. "Why Jefferson Abandoned the Presidential Speech to Congress." *Massachusetts Historical Society Proceedings* 57 (November 1923): 123-172.

2096. White, Leonard D. *The Jeffersonians: A Study in Administrative History, 1801-1829.* New York: Macmillan, 1951.

Foreign Affairs

2097. Adams, Mary P. "Jefferson's Reaction to the Treaty of San Ildefonso." *Journal of Southern History* 21 (May 1955): 173-188.

2098. Allen, Milford E. "Thomas Jefferson and the Louisiana — Arkansas Frontier." *Arkansas Historical Quarterly* 20 (Spring 1961): 39-64.

2099. Barnes, Howard A. "The Idea That Caused a War: Horace Bushnell versus Thomas Jefferson." *Journal of Church and State* 16 (Winter 1974): 73-83.

2100. Bowers, Claude G. "Thomas Jefferson and South America." *Pan American Union Bulletin* 77 (April 1943): 183-191.

2101. Bradley, Jared W. "W. C. C. Claiborne and Spain: Foreign Affairs under Jefferson and Madison, 1801-1811." *Louisiana History* 12 (Fall 1971): 297-314; 13 (Winter 1972): 5-28.

2102. Briceland, Alan V. "Ephraim Kirby: Mr. Jefferson's Emissary on the Tombigbee-Mobile Frontier in 1804." *Alabama Review* 24 (April 1971): 83-113.

2103. Brooks, Joan L. "Jefferson and Bryant: The Embargoes." Master's thesis, University of Virginia, 1966.

2104. Bruce, H. Addington. "Thomas Jefferson and the Louisiana Purchase." *Outlook* 88 (February 22, 1908): 443-446.

2105. Chinard, Gilbert. "Jefferson's Influence Abroad." *Mississippi Valley Historical Review* 30 (September 1943): 171-186.

2106. Cook, Theodore A. "The Original Intention of the Monroe Doctrine as Shown by the Correspondence of Monroe with Jefferson and Madison." *Fortnightly Review* 64 (September 1898): 357-368.

2107. Corbin, John. "From Jefferson to Wilson." *North American Review* 210 (August 1919): 172-185.

2108. Cox, Isaac J. "Pan American Policy of Jefferson and Wilkinson." *Mississippi Valley Historical Review* 1 (September 1914): 212-239.

2109. Floyd, Mildred D. "Thomas Jefferson and the Louisiana Purchase." Master's thesis, Atlanta University, 1951.

2110. Franklin, Mitchell. "The Place of Thomas Jefferson in the Expulsion of Spanish Medieval Law from Louisiana." *Tulane Law Review* 16 (April 1942): 319-338.

2111. Franklin, Mitchell. "War-Time Powers of the American Presidency as Conceived by Thomas Jefferson." *Law Guild Review* 2 (September 1942): 13-20.

2112. Hemphill, W. Edwin. "The Jeffersonian Background of the Louisiana Purchase." *Mississippi Valley Historical Review* 22 (September 1935): 177-190.

2113. Hoskins, Janina W. "'A Lesson Which All Our Countrymen Should Study': Jefferson Views Poland." *Library of Congress Quarterly Journal* 33 (January 1976): 29-46.

2114. Hoslett, Schuyler D. "Jefferson and England: The Embargo as a Measure of Coercion." *Americana* 34 (January 1940): 39-54.

2115. McCarthy, Richard J. "Some Philosophical Foundations of Thomas Jefferson's Foreign Policy." Ph.D. dissertation, St. John's University, 1958.

2116. McLemore, R. A. "Jeffersonian Diplomacy in the Purchase of Louisiana, 1803." *Louisiana Historical Quarterly* 18 (April 1935): 346-353.

2117. Mannix, Richard. "Gallatin, Jefferson, and the Embargo of 1808." *Diplomatic History* 3 (Spring 1979): 151-172.

2118. Muller, H. N. "Smuggling into Canada: How the Champlain Valley Defied Jefferson's Embargo." *Vermont History* 38 (Winter 1970): 5-21.

2119. Risjord, Norman K. "Jefferson's Empire for Liberty." In his *Forging the American Republic, 1760-1815*, 300-341. Reading, MA: Addison-Wesley, 1973.

2120. Scanlon, James E. "A Sudden Conceit: Jefferson and the Louisiana Government Bill of 1804." *Louisiana History* 9 (Spring 1968): 139-162.

2121. Sears, Louis M. *Jefferson and the Embargo*. Durham, NC: Duke University Press, 1927.

2122. Spivak, Burton. "Jefferson, England, and the Embargo: Trading Wealth and Republican Value in the Shaping of American Diplomacy, 1804-1809." Ph.D. dissertation, University of Virginia, 1975.

2123. Spivak, Burton. *Jefferson's English Crisis: Commerce, Embargo, and the Republican Revolution*. Charlottesville: University Press of Virginia, 1979.

2124. Spivak, Burton. "Republican Dreams and National Interest: The Jeffersonians and American Foreign Policy." *Society for Historians of American Foreign Relations Newsletter* 12 (1981): 1-21.

2125. Stuart, Reginald C. "Encounter with Mars: Thomas Jefferson's View of War." Ph.D. dissertation, University of Florida, 1974.

2126. Stuart, Reginald C. *The Half-Way Pacifist: Thomas Jefferson's View of War*. Toronto: University of Toronto Press, 1978.

2127. Stuart, Reginald C. "Thomas Jefferson and the Function of War: Policy or Principle?" *Canadian Journal of History* 11 (August 1976): 155-171.

2128. Stuart, Reginald C. "Thomas Jefferson and the Origins of War." *Peace and Change* 4 (Spring 1977): 22-27.

2129. Tanner, Douglas W. "Thomas Jefferson, Impressment, and the Rejection of the Monroe-Pinkney Treaty." *Essays in History* 13 (Winter 1968): 7-26.

2130. Wallace, D. D. "Jefferson's Part in the Purchase of Louisiana." *Sewanee Review* 19 (July 1911): 328-338.

Human Rights

2131. Beatty, James P. "Thomas Jefferson and Slavery." Master's thesis, North Texas State University, 1973.

2132. Binder, Frederick M. "The Color Problem in Early National America as Viewed by John Adams, Jefferson, and Jackson." Ed.D. dissertation, Columbia University, 1962.

2133. Binder, Frederick M. "Thomas Jefferson and the Indian." In his *The Color Problem in Early National America as Viewed by John Adams, Jefferson, and Jackson*, 82-119. The Hague: Mouton, 1968.

2134. Binder, Frederick M. "Thomas Jefferson and the Negro." In his *The Color Problem in Early National America as Viewed by John Adams, Jefferson, and Jackson*, 48-81. The Hague: Mouton, 1968.

2135. Bowers, Claude G. "Jefferson and Civil Liberties: Tyranny in America." *Atlantic Monthly* 191 (January 1953): 52-58.

2136. Bowers, Claude G. "Jefferson and the Bill of Rights." *Virginia Law Review* 41 (October 1955): 709-729.

2137. Bowers, Claude G. "Jefferson and the Freedom of the Human Spirit." *Ethics* 53 (July 1943): 237-245.

2138. Burke, Edmund J. *Thomas Jefferson, Apostle of Freedom and Equality of Opportunity: The Solution of Our Economic and Social Ills.* Cambridge, MA: Jefferson Club of Cambridge, 1934.

2139. Cardwell, Guy A. "Jefferson Renounced: Natural Rights in the Old South." *Yale Review* 58 (March 1969): 388-407.

2140. Carey, Paul M. "Jefferson and Slavery." Master's thesis, University of Virginia, 1952.

2141. Carsley, Mark K. "Jeffersonian Indian Policy in Practice: William Hull and the Treaty of Detroit, 1807." *Detroit Perspective* 5 (Fall 1980): 20-39.

2142. Cohen, William. "Thomas Jefferson and the Problem of Slavery." *Journal of American History* 56 (December 1969): 503-526.

2143. Coleman, John. "The Concept of Equality as Held by Thomas Jefferson." Ph.D. dissertation, University of Pittsburgh, 1934.

2144. Daugherty, James. *Thomas Jefferson: Fighter for Freedom and Human Rights.* New York: Frederick Ungar, 1961.

2145. Davis, David. B. "Jefferson's Uncertain Commitment." In his *The Problem of Slavery in the Age of Revolution, 1770-1823*, 169-183. Ithaca, NY: Cornell University Press, 1975.

2146. Davis, David B. *Was Thomas Jefferson an Authentic Enemy of Slavery? An Inaugural Lecture Delivered before the University of Oxford on 18 February 1970.* Oxford: Clarendon Press, 1970.

2147. Dawidoff, Robert. "The Fox in the Henhouse: Jefferson and Slavery." *Reviews in American History* 6 (December 1978): 503-511.

2148. Diggins, John P. "Slavery, Race, and Equality: Jefferson and the Pathos of the Enlightenment." *American Quarterly* 28 (Summer 1976): 206-228.

2149. Foley, William E., and Charles D. Rice. "Visiting the President: An Exercise in Jeffersonian Indian Diplomacy." *American West* 26 (November/December 1979): 4-15, 56.

2150. Galbreath, C. B. "Thomas Jefferson's Views on Slavery." *Ohio Archaeological and Historical Society Publications* 34 (April 1925): 184-202.

2151. Hash, Ronald J. "Slavery on Thomas Jefferson's Plantations." Master's thesis, Millersville State College, 1969.

2152. Horsman, Reginald. "The Ambivalence of Thomas Jefferson." In his *Expansion and American Indian Policy, 1783-1812*, 104-114. East Lansing: Michigan State University Press, 1966.

2153. Jefferson, Isaac. *Memoirs of a Monticello Slave, As Dictated to Charles Campbell in the 1840's by Isaac, One of Thomas Jefferson's Slaves*. Edited by Rayford W. Logan. Charlottesville: University of Virginia Press, 1951.

2154. Johansen, Bruce E. "Franklin, Jefferson, and American Indians: A Study in the Cross-Cultural Communication of Ideas." Ph.D. dissertation, University of Washington, 1979.

2155. Jordan, Winthrop D. "Thomas Jefferson: Self and Society." In his *The White Man's Burden: Historical Origins of Racism in the United States*, 165-193. New York: Oxford University Press, 1974.

2156. Kingdon, Frank. "Thomas Jefferson: Individual Liberty." In his *Architects of the Republic: George Washington, Thomas Jefferson, Abraham Lincoln, Franklin D. Roosevelt*, 87-153. New York: Alliance Publishing Co., 1947.

2157. Lane, Ann M. "The Classical Frontier: Republican Theory and the Jefferson-Cherokee Encounter." Ph.D. dissertation, University of California, 1979.

2158. Levy, Leonard W. *Jefferson and Civil Liberties: The Darker Side*. Cambridge, MA: Belknap Press, 1963.

2159. Lyman, Jane L. "Jefferson and Negro Slavery." *Journal of Negro Education* 16 (Winter 1947): 10-27.

2160. McLoughlin, William G. "Thomas Jefferson and the Beginning of Cherokee Nationalism, 1806 to 1809." *William and Mary Quarterly* 32 (October 1975): 547-580.

2161. McNaul, Willard C. *The Jefferson-Lemen Compact: The Relations of Thomas Jefferson and James Lemen in the Exclusion of Slavery from Illinois and the Northwest Territory, With Related Documents, 1781-1818*. Chicago: University of Chicago Press, 1915.

2162. Malone, Dumas. *Jefferson and the Rights of Man*. Boston: Little, Brown, 1951.

2163. Mayer, Frederick. "Jefferson and Freedom." *Social Education* 18 (March 1954): 107-109.

2164. Miller, John C. *The Wolf by the Ears: Thomas Jefferson and Slavery*. New York: Free Press, 1977.

2165. Morris, Mabel. "Jefferson and the Language of the American Indian." *Modern Language Quarterly* 6 (March 1945): 31-34.

2166. Richardson, William D. "The Possibility of Harmony between the Races: An Inquiry into the Thought of Jefferson, Tocqueville, Lincoln, and Melville." Ph.D. dissertation, State University of New York, Buffalo, 1979.

2167. Shannon, Joseph B. *Thomas Jefferson, The Advocate of Truth, Freedom, and Equality: Public Speeches of Joseph B. Shannon Touching upon Unfamiliar Phases of the Life and Teachings of the Great American Statesman*. Kansas City, MO: C. S. Demaree Stationery Co., 1930.

2168. Sheehan, Bernard W. "The Quest for Indian Origins in the Thought of the Jeffersonian Era." *Midcontinent Ameri-*

can *Studies Journal* 9 (Spring 1968): 34-51.

2169. Sheehan, Bernard W. *Seeds of Extinction: Jeffersonian Philanthropy and the American Indian.* Chapel Hill: University of North Carolina Press, 1973.

2170. Shimakawa, Masashi. "Thomas Jefferson and the Indian Problem." *American Review* 12 (1978): 214-215.

2171. Stevens, Michael E. "Thomas Jefferson, Indians, and Missing Privy Council Journals." *South Carolina Historical Magazine* 82 (April 1981): 177-185.

2172. Stowe, William M. "The Influence of Thomas Jefferson's Democratic Principles upon Abraham Lincoln's Thinking on the Question of Slavery." Ph.D. dissertation, Boston University, 1938.

2173. White, Andrew D. "Jefferson and Slavery." *Atlantic Monthly* 9 (January 1862): 29-40.

2174. Wiltshire, Susan F. "Jefferson, Calhoun, and the Slavery Debate: The Classics and the Two Minds of the South." *Southern Humanities Review* 11 (1977): 33-40.

2175. Windley, Lathan A. "Runaway Slave Advertisements of George Washington and Thomas Jefferson." *Journal of Negro History* 63 (Fall 1978): 373-374.

2176. Zaitseva, N. D. "Thomas Jefferson's Advice to the Cherokees." *Journal of Cherokee Studies* 4 (1979): 64-66.

Judicial

2177. Berger, Raoul. "Jefferson v. Marshall in the Burr Case." *American Bar Association Journal* 60 (June 1974): 702-706.

2178. Bowers, Claude G. "Thomas Jefferson and the Courts." *North Carolina Bar Association Proceedings* 29 (1927): 26-45.

2179. Boyd, Julian P. "The Chasm that Separated Thomas Jefferson from John Marshall." In *Essays on the American Constitution*, edited by Gottfried Dietze, 3-20. Englewood Cliffs, NJ: Prentice-Hall, 1966.

2180. Boyd, Julian P. "Thomas Jefferson and the Police State." *North Carolina Historical Review* 25 (April 1948): 233-253.

2181. Burger, Warren E. "The Doctrine of Judicial Review: Mr. Marshall, Mr. Jefferson, and Mr. Marbury." In *The Constitution and Chief Justice Marshall*, edited by William F. Swindler, 383-394. New York: Dodd, Mead, 1978.

2182. Dearmonst, Nelson S. "Federalist Attitudes toward Governmental Secrecy in the Age of Jefferson." *Historian* 37 (February 1975): 222-240.

2183. Dixon, Lawrence W. "Attitude of Thomas Jefferson toward the Judiciary." *Southwestern Social Science Quarterly* 28 (June 1947): 13-19.

2184. Dumbauld, Edward. *Thomas Jefferson and the Law.* Norman: University of Oklahoma Press, 1978.

2185. Dumbauld, Edward. "Thomas Jefferson and the Pennsylvania Courts." *Pennsylvania Bar Association Quarterly* 37 (March 1966): 236-247.

2186. Ellis, Richard E. *The Jeffersonian Crisis: Courts and Politics in the Young Republic.* NY: Oxford University Press, 1971.

2187. Hanchett, William. "Politics and the Judiciary under Jefferson." Master's thesis, University of California, Berkeley, 1949.

2188. Ireton, Robert E. "Jefferson and the Supreme Court." *Boston University Law Review* 17 (January 1937): 81-89.

2189. Johnson, Allen, and Edward S. Corwin. *The Age of Jefferson and Marshall.* New Haven, CT: Yale University Press, 1921.

2190. Knudson, Jerry W. "The Jeffersonian Assault on the Federalist Judiciary: 1802-1805, Political Forces and Press Reaction." *American Journal of Legal History* 14 (January 1970): 55-75.

2191. Krislov, Samuel. "Jefferson and Judicial Review: Refereeing Cahn, Commager, and Mendelson." *Journal of Public Law* 9 (Fall 1960): 374-381.

2192. Little, David. "Thomas Jefferson's Religious Views and Their Influence on the Supreme Court's Interpretation of the First Amendment." *Catholic University Law Review* 26 (Fall 1976): 57-72.

2193. MacCorkle, Stuart A. "Alas, Poor Jefferson! The Executive, Congress, and the Courts." *Sewanee Review* 44 (April 1936): 135-144.

2194. Malone, Dumas. "Executive Privilege: Jefferson and Burr and Nixon and Ehrlichman." *New York Review of Books* 21 (July 18, 1974): 36-40.

2195. Marshall, John. "John Marshall Renders His Opinion of Mr. Jefferson." *Magazine of Albemarle County History* 30 (1972): 15-18.

2196. Mendelson, Wallace. "Jefferson on Judicial Review: Consistency through Change." *University of Chicago Law Review* 29 (Winter 1962): 327-337.

2197. Noonan, John T., Jr. *Persons and Masks of the Law: Cardozo, Holmes, Jefferson, and Wythe as Makers of the Masks.* New York: Farrar, Straus and Giroux, 1976.

2198. Patterson, C. Perry. "Jefferson and Judicial Review." *American Bar Association Journal* 30 (August 1944): 443-451.

2199. Thomas, Charles S. "Jefferson and the Judiciary." *Constitutional Review* 10 (April 1926): 67-75.

2200. "Thomas Jefferson's Opinions of John Marshall and His Court." *American Law Review* 35 (January/February 1901): 63-77.

2201. Warren, Charles. "Marshall, Jefferson, and the Judiciary." In his *The Supreme Court in United States History, 1789-1835*, Vol. 1, 169-230. Boston: Little, Brown, 1927.

2202. Waterman, Julian S. "Thomas Jefferson and Blackstone's Commentaries." *Illinois Law Review* 27 (February 1933): 629-659.

Writings

2203. Adair, Douglass. "Rumbold's Dying Speech, 1685 and Jefferson's Last Words on Democracy, 1826." *William and Mary Quarterly* 9 (July 1952): 521-531.

2204. Adams, James T., ed. *Jeffersonian Principles and Hamiltonian Principles: Extracts from the Writings of Thomas Jefferson and Alexander Hamilton.* Boston: Little, Brown, 1928.

2205. Adams, John. *The Adams-Jefferson Letters: The Complete Correspondence between Thomas Jefferson and Abigail and John Adams.* Edited by Lester J. Cappon. Chapel Hill: University of North Carolina Press, 1959.

2206. Adams, John. *Adams to Jefferson and Jefferson to Adams: A Dialogue from Their Correspondence, 1812-26.* Edited by Richard K. Arnold. San Francisco: Jerico Press, 1975.

2207. Aring, Charles D. "Adams and Jefferson, A Correspondence." *History Today* 21 (September 1971): 609-618.

2208. Bailey, Thomas A. "Jeffersonian and Madisonian Democracy." In *Voices of*

America: The Nation's Story in Slogans, Sayings, and Songs, 39-50. New York: Macmillan, 1976.

2209. Baker, Gordon E. "Thomas Jefferson on Academic Freedom." *American Association of University Professors Bulletin* 39 (Autumn 1953): 377-387.

2210. Benson, C. Randolph. "Sociological Elements in Selected Writings and Works of Thomas Jefferson." Ph.D. dissertation, Louisiana State University, Agricultural and Mechanical College, 1966.

2211. Bestor, Arthur E., David C. Mearns, and Jonathan Daniels. *Three Presidents and Their Books: The Readings of Jefferson, Lincoln, and Franklin D. Roosevelt.* Champaign: University of Illinois Press, 1955.

2212. Betts, Edwin M. "The Correspondence between Constantine Samuel Rafinesque and Thomas Jefferson." *American Philosophical Society Proceedings* 87 (May 1944): 368-380.

2213. Betts, Edwin M., ed. *Thomas Jefferson's Farm Book: With Commentary and Relevant Extracts from Other Writings.* Charlottesville, VA: University Press of Virginia, 1976.

2214. Betts, Edwin M., ed. *Thomas Jefferson's Garden Book, 1766-1824, With Relevant Extracts from His Other Writings.* Philadelphia: American Philosophy Society, 1944.

2215. Boyd, Julian P. "Mr. Jefferson to Dr. Rush, With Affection." *Library of Congress Quarterly Journal of Current Acquisitions* 1 (October/December 1943): 3-6.

2216. Boykin, Edward, ed. *The Wisdom of Thomas Jefferson.* Garden City, NY: Doubleday, 1941.

2217. Brown, Glenn. "Letters from Thomas Jefferson and William Thornton, Architect, Relating to the University of Virginia." *Journal of the American Institute of Architects* 1 (January 1913): 21-27.

2218. Brown, Ralph H. "Jefferson's Notes on Virginia." *Geographical Review* 33 (July 1943): 467-473.

2219. Bullock, Helen C. D. "The Papers of Thomas Jefferson." *American Archivist* 4 (October 1941): 238-249.

2220. Butterfield, Lyman H. "The Jefferson-Adams Correspondence in the Adams Manuscript Trust." *Library of Congress Quarterly Journal* 5 (February 1948): 3-6.

2221. Butterfield, Lyman H. "The Papers of Thomas Jefferson." *American Archivist* 12 (April 1949): 131-147.

2222. Cabell, Nathaniel F., ed. *Early History of the University of Virginia, As Contained in the Letters of Thomas Jefferson and Joseph C. Cabell, Hitherto Unpublished.* Richmond, VA: J. W. Randolph, 1856.

2223. Carriere, Joseph M. "The Manuscript of Jefferson's Unpublished Errata List for Abbe Morellet's Translation of the *Notes on Virginia.*" In *Studies in Bibliography: Papers of the Bibliographical Society of the University of Virginia,* Vol. 1, edited by Fredson Bowers, 5-24. Charlottesville: Bibliographical Society of the University of Virginia, 1948.

2224. Catchings, Benjamin S., ed. *Master Thoughts of Thomas Jefferson.* New York: Nation Press, 1907.

2225. Chinard, Gilbert. *The Commonplace Book of Thomas Jefferson, A Repertory of His Ideas on Government.* Baltimore, MD: Johns Hopkins University Press, 1926.

2226. Chinard, Gilbert. *The Correspondence of Jefferson and Du Pont de Nemours, With an Introduction on Jefferson and the Physiocrats.* Baltimore, MD: Johns Hopkins University Press, 1931.

2227. Chinard, Gilbert, ed. *Houdon in America: A Collection of Documents in the Jefferson Papers in the Library of Congress.* Baltimore, MD: Johns Hopkins University Press, 1930.

2228. Cooke, J. W. "Jefferson on Liberty." *Journal of the History of Ideas* 34 (October/December 1973): 563-576.

2229. Cullen, Charles T. "20th-Century Technology and the Jefferson Papers." *Scholarly Publishing* 13 (October 1981): 45-53.

2230. Daniel, John W. "Jefferson." In his *Speeches and Orations.* Compiled by Edward M. Daniel, 637-648. Lynchburg, VA: J. P. Bell Co., 1911.

2231. DeAlba, Pedro. "Jefferson's Correspondence with DuPont de Nemours." *Pan American Union Bulletin* 77 (April 1943): 192-196.

2232. Diamond, Sigmund. "Some Jefferson Letters." *Mississippi Valley Historical Review* 28 (September 1941): 225-242.

2233. Dumbauld, Edward. "A Manuscript from Monticello: Jefferson's Library in Legal History." *American Bar Association Journal* 38 (May 1952): 389-392, 446-447.

2234. Ford, Paul L., ed. *The Works of Thomas Jefferson.* 12 vols. New York: Putnam, 1904-1905.

2235. Forman, Samuel E. *The Life and Writings of Thomas Jefferson: Including All of His Important Utterances on Public Questions, Compiled from State Papers and from His Private Correspondence.* Indianapolis, IN: Bobbs-Merrill, 1900.

2236. Gardner, Joseph L., ed. *Thomas Jefferson: A Biography in His Own Words.* New York: Harper and Row, 1974.

2437. Hamilton, Joseph G. de Roulhac, ed. *The Best Letters of Thomas Jefferson.* Boston: Houghton Mifflin, 1926.

2238. Harrison, Lowell H. "Some Thomas Jefferson-John Breckinridge Correspondence." *Filson Club History Quarterly* 42 (July 1966): 253-277.

2239. Henkels, Stan V. "Jefferson's Recollections of Patrick Henry." *Pennsylvania Magazine of History and Biography* 34 (October 1910): 385-418.

2240. Hirst, Francis W. *Life and Letters of Thomas Jefferson.* New York: Macmillan, 1926.

2241. Hoffman, John. "Queries Regarding the Western Rivers: An Unpublished Letter from Thomas Jefferson to the Geographer of the United States." *Illinois State Historical Society Journal* 75 (Spring 1982): 15-28.

2242. Irwin, Frank. *Letters of Thomas Jefferson.* Franklin, NH: Sant Bani Ash, 1975.

2243. Jefferson, Thomas. *Autobiography of Thomas Jefferson, 1743-1790, Together with a Summary of the Chief Events in Jefferson's Life.* New York: Putnam, 1914.

2244. Jefferson, Thomas. *Basic Writing of Thomas Jefferson.* Edited by Philip S. Foner. Garden City, NY: Halcyon House, 1944.

2245. Jefferson, Thomas. *Calendar of the Correspondence of Thomas Jefferson.* New York: Burt Franklin, 1970.

2246. Jefferson, Thomas. *The Complete Anas of Thomas Jefferson.* Edited by Franklin B. Sawvel. New York: Round Table Press, 1903.

2247. Jefferson, Thomas. *The Complete Jefferson, Containing His Major Writings, Published and Unpublished, Except His Letters, With Illustrations and Analytic Index.* Edited by Saul K. Padover. New York: Duell, Sloan and Pearce, 1943.

2248. Jefferson, Thomas. *Correspondence of Thomas Jefferson and Francis Walker*

Gilmer, 1814-1826. Edited by Richard B. Davis. Columbia: University of South Carolina Press, 1946.

2249. Jefferson, Thomas. *Crusade against Ignorance: Thomas Jefferson on Education.* Edited by Gordon Lee. New York: Bureau of Publications, Teachers College, Columbia University, 1961.

2250. Jefferson, Thomas. *Democracy.* Edited by Saul K. Padover. New York: Appleton, 1939.

2251. Jefferson, Thomas. *An Essay towards Facilitating Instruction in the Anglo-Saxon and Modern Dialects of the English Language.* New York: J. F. Trow, 1851.

2252. Jefferson, Thomas. *The Family Letters of Thomas Jefferson.* Edited by Edwin M. Betts and James A. Bear, Jr. Columbia: University of Missouri Press, 1966.

2253. Jefferson, Thomas. *The Jefferson-Dunglison Letters.* Edited by John M. Dorsey. Charlottesville: University of Virginia Press, 1960.

2254. Jefferson, Thomas. *Jefferson Himself, The Personal Narrative of a Many-Sided American.* Edited by Bernard Mayo. Boston: Houghton Mifflin, 1942.

2255. Jefferson, Thomas. *A Jefferson Profile as Revealed in His Letters.* Edited by Saul K. Padover. New York: J. Day, 1956.

2256. Jefferson, Thomas. *Jefferson's Germantown Letters, Together with Other Papers Relating to His Stay in Germantown during the Month of November, 1793.* Philadelphia: W. J. Campbell, 1906.

2257. Jefferson, Thomas. *Jefferson's Ideas on a University Library: Letters from the Founder of the University of Virginia to a Boston Bookseller.* Edited by Elizabeth Cometti. Charlottesville: Tracy W. McGregor Library, University of Virginia, 1950.

2258. Jefferson, Thomas. "Letters of Thomas Jefferson." *Magazine of History* 21 (November 1915): 246-256.

2259. Jefferson, Thomas. "The Letters of Thomas Jefferson to William Short." *William and Mary Quarterly* 11 (July 1931): 242-250; 12 (1932): 145-156, 287-304; 13 (January 1933): 98-116.

2260. Jefferson, Thomas. *The Life and Morals of Jesus of Nazareth, Extracted Textually from the Gospels in Greek, Latin, French, and English.* Washington, DC: U.S. Government Printing Office, 1904.

2261. Jefferson, Thomas. *The Life and Selected Writings of Thomas Jefferson.* Edited by Adrienne Koch and William Peden. New York: Modern Library, 1944.

2262. Jefferson, Thomas. *The Literary Bible of Thomas Jefferson, His Commonplace Book of Philosophers and Poets.* Baltimore, MD: Johns Hopkins University Press, 1928.

2263. Jefferson, Thomas. *The Living Thoughts of Thomas Jefferson, Presented by John Dewey.* New York: Longmans, Green, 1940.

2264. Jefferson, Thomas. *A Manual of Parliamentary Practice, For the Use of the United States.* Washington, DC: S. H. Smith, 1801.

2265. Jefferson, Thomas. *Master Thoughts of Thomas Jefferson.* New York: Nation Press, 1907.

2266. Jefferson, Thomas. *Memoir, Correspondence, and Miscellanies, From the Papers of Thomas Jefferson.* 4 vols. Edited by Thomas J. Randolph. Charlottesville, VA: F. Carr, 1829.

2267. Jefferson, Thomas. *Notes on the State of Virginia.* London: J. Stockdale, 1787.

2268. Jefferson, Thomas. *Notes on the State of Virginia.* Edited by William Peden. Chapel Hill: University of North Carolina Press, 1955.

2269. Jefferson, Thomas. "On the Question of Re-election: Excerpts from Correspondence." *Current History* 7 (September 1944): 178-180.

2270. Jefferson, Thomas. *The Papers of Thomas Jefferson.* 20 vols. Edited by Julian P. Boyd. Princeton, NJ: Princeton University Press, 1950-1974.

2271. Jefferson, Thomas. *Political Writings: Representative Selections.* Edited by Edward Dumbauld. New York: Liberal Arts Press, 1955.

2272. Jefferson, Thomas. *The Portable Thomas Jefferson.* Edited by Merrill D. Peterson. New York: Viking Press, 1975.

2273. Jefferson, Thomas. *The Proceedings of the Government of the United States, In Maintaining the Public Right to the Beach of the Mississippi, Adjacent to New Orleans, Against the Intrusion of Edward Livingston.* New York: Ezra Sergeant, 1812.

2274. Jefferson, Thomas. *Reports of Cases Determined in the General Court of Virginia, From 1730 to 1740, and from 1768 to 1770.* Charlottesville, VA: F. Carr, 1829.

2275. Jefferson, Thomas. *A Summary View of the Rights of British America, Set Forth in Some Resolutions Intended for the Inspection of the Present Delegates of the People of Virginia, Now in Convention.* Williamsburg, VA: Clementian Rind, 1774.

2276. Jefferson, Thomas. *Thomas Jefferson and His Unknown Brother Randolph: Twenty-eight Letters Exchanged between Thomas and Randolph Jefferson . . . During the Years 1807 to 1815.* Charlottesville: Tracy W. McGregor Library, University of Virginia, 1942.

2277. Jefferson, Thomas. *Thomas Jefferson and the National Capital: Containing Notes and Correspondence Exchanged between Jefferson, Washington, L'Enfant, Ellicott, Hallet, Thornton, Latrobe, the Commissioners, and Others, Relating to the Founding, Surveying, Planning, Designing, Constructing, and Administering of the City of Washington, 1783-1818.* Edited by Saul K. Padover. Washington, DC: U.S. Government Printing Office, 1946.

2278. Jefferson, Thomas. *Thomas Jefferson, Architect: Original Designs in the Collection of Thomas Jefferson Coolidge, Junior.* Boston: Riverside Press, 1916.

2279. Jefferson, Thomas. *Thomas Jefferson Correspondence, Printed from the Originals in the Collections of William K. Bixby.* Boston: n.p., 1916.

2280. Jefferson, Thomas. *Thomas Jefferson Papers.* New York: Dodd, Mead, 1963.

2281. Jefferson, Thomas. *Thomas Jefferson: Revolutionary Philosopher, A Selection of Writings.* Woodbury, NY: Barron's, 1976.

2282. Jefferson, Thomas. "Two Unpublished Letters of Thomas Jefferson." *William and Mary Quarterly* 17 (July 1908): 18-20.

2283. Jefferson, Thomas. *The Writings.* Edited by Saul K. Padover. Luneburg, VT: Stinehour Press, 1967.

2284. Jefferson, Thomas. *Writings: Containing His Autobiography, Notes on Virginia, Parliamentary Manual, Official Papers, Messages and Addresses, and Other Writings, Official and Private, Now Collected in Their Entirety for the First Time.* 20 vols. Edited by Andrew A. Lipscomb. Washington, DC: Thomas Jefferson Memorial Association of the United States, 1903-1904.

2285. Jefferson, Thomas. *The Writings of Thomas Jefferson.* 10 vols. Edited by Paul L. Ford. New York: Putnam, 1892-1900.

2286. Jefferson, Thomas, and Dickinson W. Adams. *Jefferson's Extracts from the Gospels: "The Philosophy of Jesus" and "The Life and Morals of Jesus."* Princeton, NJ: Princeton University Press, 1983.

2287. "Jefferson Papers." *William and Mary Quarterly* 6 (October 1926): 334-338.

2288. Kimball, Marie G. "Unpublished Correspondence of Mme. de Stael with Thomas Jefferson." *North American Review* 208 (July 1918): 63-71.

2289. Kohler, Max J. "Unpublished Correspondence between Thomas Jefferson and Some American Jews." *American Jewish Historical Society Publications* 20 (1911): 11-30.

2290. Lafayette, Marquis. *The Letters of Lafayette and Jefferson.* Baltimore, MD: Johns Hopkins University Press, 1929.

2291. Lafayette, Marquis. "Thomas Jefferson." *Independent* 55 (January 1, 1903): 26-27.

2292. "Letters to Jefferson from Archibald Cary and Robert Gamble." *William and Mary Quarterly* 6 (April 1926): 122-130.

2293. Lucke, Jessie. "Some Correspondence with Thomas Jefferson Concerning the Public Printers." In *Studies in Bibliography: Papers of the Bibliographical Society of the University of Virginia*, Vol. 1, edited by Fredson Bowers, 25-38. Charlottesville: Bibliographical Society of the University of Virginia, 1948.

2294. McIlwaine, Henry R., ed. *The Letters of Thomas Jefferson.* Lawrence: University Press of Kansas, 1976.

2295. Malone, Dumas, ed. *Correspondence between Thomas Jefferson and Pierre Samuel du Pont de Nemours, 1798-1817.* Translated by Linwood Lehman. Boston: Houghton Mifflin, 1930.

2296. Mansfield, Harvey C., ed. *Thomas Jefferson: Selected Writings.* Arlington Heights, IL: Harlan Davidson, 1979.

2297. Marraro, Howard R. "The Four Versions of Jefferson's Letter to Mazzei." *William and Mary Quarterly* 22 (January 1942): 18-29.

2298. Marraro, Howard R. "Jefferson Letters Concerning the Settlement of Mazzei's Virginia Estate." *Mississippi Valley Historical Review* 30 (September 1943): 235-242.

2299. Marraro, Howard R. "Unpublished Correspondence of Jefferson and Adams to Mazzei." *Virginia Magazine of History and Biography* 51 (April 1943): 111-133.

2300. Marraro, Howard R. "An Unpublished Jefferson Letter to Mazzei." *Italica* 35 (June 1958): 83-87.

2301. "New Jefferson Letters Acquired by Library of Congress." *Library of Congress Information Bulletin* 35 (September 17, 1976): 563-565.

2302. Parker, William, and Jonas Viles, eds. *Letters and Addresses of Thomas Jefferson.* New York: Wessels, 1907.

2303. Pound, Ezra. "The Jefferson-Adams Correspondence." *North American Review* 244 (Winter 1937-1938): 314-324.

2304. Roberts, John G. "An Exchange of Letters between Jefferson and Quesnay de Beaurepaire." *Virginia Magazine of History and Biography* 50 (April 1942): 134-142.

2305. Schwartz, Bernard. "Jefferson-Madison Correspondence." In his *The Great Rights of Mankind: A History of the American Bill of Rights*, 115-118. New York: Oxford University Press, 1977.

2306. Sellers, Horace W. "Letters of Thomas Jefferson to Charles Willson Peale, 1796-1825." *Pennsylvania Magazine of History and Biography* 28 (1904): 136-154, 295-319, 403-420.

2307. Sifton, Paul G. "The Provenance of the Thomas Jefferson Papers." *American Archivist* 40 (January 1977): 17-30.

2308. Thomas, Charles M. "Date Inaccuracies in Thomas Jefferson's Writings." *Mississippi Valley Historical Review* 19 (June 1932): 87-90.

2309. Thorpe, Francis N., ed. "A Letter of Jefferson on the Political Parties, 1798." *American Historical Review* 2 (April 1898): 488-489.

2310. Virginia. Governor. *Official Letters of the Governors of the State of Virginia: Vol. 2. The Letters of Thomas Jefferson.* Richmond: Virginia State Library, 1928.

2311. Virginia. University. Library. *Guide to the Microfilm Edition of the Jefferson Papers of the University of Virginia, 1732-1828.* Charlottesville: The Library, 1977.

2312. Virginia. University. *The Jefferson Papers of the University of Virginia.* Charlottesville: University Press of Virginia, 1973.

2313. Voorhees, Daniel W. "Thomas Jefferson." In *Forty Years of Oratory ... Lectures, Addresses, and Speeches,* Vol. 1, 43-77. Indianapolis, IN: Bobbs-Merrill, 1898.

2314. Wettstein, A. Arnold. "Religionless Religion: In the Letters and Papers from Monticello." *Religion in Life* 45 (Summer 1976): 152-160.

2315. Wilstach, Paul, ed. *Correspondence of John Adams and Thomas Jefferson (1812-1826).* Indianapolis, IN: Bobbs-Merrill, 1925.

2316. Wilstach, Paul, ed. "Reconciliation: Correspondence of John Adams and Thomas Jefferson." *Atlantic Monthly* 134 (December 1924): 811-819.

2317. Wyllie, John C. "The Second Mrs. Wayland: An Unpublished Jefferson Opinion on a Case in Equity." *American Journal of Legal History* 9 (January 1965): 64-68.

James Madison

Biographies

2318. Adair, Douglass, ed. "James Madison's Autobiography." *William and Mary Quarterly* 2 (April 1945): 191-209.

2319. Banning, Lance. "Moderate as Revolutionary: An Introduction to Madison's Life." *Library of Congress Quarterly Journal* 37 (Spring 1980): 162-175.

2320. Beloff, Max. "James Madison." *History Today* 1 (February 1957): 68-73.

2321. Brant, Irving. *The Fourth President: A Life of James Madison*. Indianapolis, IN: Bobbs-Merrill, 1970.

2322. Brant, Irving. *James Madison*. 6 vols. Indianapolis, IN: Bobbs-Merrill, 1941-1961.

2323. Brant, Irving. *James Madison and American Nationalism*. Princeton, NJ: Van Nostrand, 1968.

2324. Brant, Irving. "James Madison and His Times." *American Historical Review* 57 (July 1952): 853-870.

2325. Burns, Edward M. *James Madison, Philosopher of the Constitution*. New York: Octagon, 1968.

2326. Dos Passos, John. *The Men Who Made the Nation*. Garden City, NY: Doubleday, 1957.

2327. Gay, Sydney H. *James Madison*. Boston: Houghton Mifflin, 1899.

2328. Hunt, Gaillard. *The Life of James Madison*. Garden City, NY: Doubleday, 1902.

2329. Ketcham, Ralph L. *James Madison: A Biography*. New York: Macmillan, 1971.

2330. Ketcham, Ralph L. "The Mind of James Madison, D.S.S." Ph.D. dissertation, Syracuse University, 1956.

2331. Moore, Virginia. *The Madisons: A Biography*. New York: McGraw-Hill, 1979.

2332. Riemer, Neal. *James Madison*. New York: Washington Square Press, 1968.

2333. Rives, William C. *History of the Life and Times of James Madison*. 3 vols. Boston: Little, Brown, 1859-1868.

2334. Schultz, Harold S. *James Madison*. New York: Twayne, 1970.

2335. Smith, Abbot. *James Madison: Builder, A New Estimate of a Memorable Career*. New York: Wilson-Erickson, 1937.

Private Life

2336. Alderman, Edwin A. "A Madison Letter and Some Digressions." *North*

American Review 217 (June 1923): 785-796.

2337. Anthony, Katharine S. *Dolly Madison, Her Life and Times.* Garden City, NY: Doubleday, 1949.

2338. Armstrong, Walter P. "James Madison: Virginia Revolutionist and Ardent Nationalist." *American Bar Association Journal* 34 (May 1948): 356-359.

2339. Arnett, Ethel S. *Mrs. James Madison: The Incomparable Dolley.* Greensboro, NC: Piedmont Press, 1972.

2340. Brant, Irving. *The Books of James Madison, With Some Comments on the Readings of FDR and JFK: An Address Delivered during the Celebration of the 25th Anniversary of the Tracy W. McGregor Library, 1929-1964.* Charlottesville: University of Virginia, 1965.

2341. Cahn, Edmond N. "Madison and the Pursuit of Happiness." *New York University Law Quarterly Review* 27 (April 1952): 265-275.

2342. Clark, Allen C. *Life and Letters of Dolly Madison.* Washington, DC: W. F. Roberts Co., 1914.

2343. Corwin, Edward S. "James Madison: Layman, Publicist, and Exegete." *New York University Law Review* 27 (April 1952): 277-298.

2344. Corwin, Edward S. "The Posthumous Career of James Madison (1751-1836) as Lawyer." *American Bar Association Journal* 25 (October 1939): 821-824.

2345. Dean, Elizabeth L. *Dolly Madison, The Nation's Hostess.* Boston: Lothrop, Lee and Shepard, 1928.

2346. DeTerra, Helmut. "Alexander von Humboldt's Correspondence with Jefferson, Madison, and Gallatin." *American Philosophical Society Proceedings* 103 (December 1959): 783-806.

2347. Dewey, Donald O. "James Madison Helps Clio Interpret the Constitution." *American Journal of Legal History* 15 (January 1971): 38-55.

2348. Farrand, Max. "If James Madison Had Had a Sense of Humor." *Pennsylvania Magazine of History* 62 (April 1938): 130-139.

2349. Gerson, Noel B. *The Velvet Glove: A Life of Dolly Madison.* New York: Nelson, 1975.

2350. Goodwin, Maud W. *Dolly Madison.* New York: Scribner's, 1896.

2351. "Hancock Sculpture of Madison Readied for New Building." *Library of Congress Information Bulletin* 54 (April 4, 1975): 125-126.

2352. Hughes, Charles E. "James Madison." *American Bar Association Journal* 18 (January 1932): 854-858.

2353. Hunt, Katharine C. "The White House Furnishings of the Madison Administration, 1809-1817." Master's thesis, University of Delaware, 1971.

2354. Hunt-Jones, Conover. *Dolley and the "Great Little Madison."* Washington, DC: American Institute of Architects Foundation, 1977.

2355. Ketcham, Ralph L. "James Madison and the Nature of Man." *Journal of the History of Ideas* 16 (January 1958): 62-76.

2356. Ketcham, Ralph L., ed. "James Madison and Religion: A New Hypothesis." *Journal of the Presbyterian Historical Society* 38 (June 1960): 65-91.

2357. Klapthor, Margaret B. "Benjamin Latrobe and Dolley Madison Decorate the White House, 1809-1811." *United States National Museum Bulletin* 241 (1965): 153-164.

2358. Madison, Dolley. *Memoirs and Letters of Dolley Madison, Wife of James Madison, President of the United States.*

Edited by Lucia Cutts. Boston: Houghton Mifflin, 1886.

2359. "Major Exhibition, Publication Honor James Madison." *Library of Congress Information Bulletin* 40 (December 1981): 425-427.

2360. Moore, Virginia. "Dolley Madison: Queen of Society, Debt-Ridden Widow." *Smithsonian* 10 (November 1979): 173-185.

2361. Paulding, James K. "An Unpublished Sketch of James Madison." Edited by Ralph L. Ketcham. *Virginia Magazine of History and Biography* 67 (October 1955): 432-437.

2362. Rutland, Robert A. "Madison's Bookish Habits." *Library of Congress Quarterly Journal* 37 (Spring 1980): 176-191.

2363. Schaedler, Louis C. "James Madison, Literary Craftman." *William and Mary Quarterly* 3 (October 1946): 515-533.

2364. Sifton, Paul G. "'What a Dread Prospect...': Dolley Madison's Plague Year." *Pennsylvania Magazine of History and Biography* 87 (April 1963): 182-188.

2365. Thane, Elswyth. *Dolley Madison, Her Life and Times.* New York: Crowell-Collier Press, 1970.

2366. Thomas, Katherine E. "Two Famous White House Recipes." *Good Housekeeping* 53 (July 1911): 109-112.

2367. Whitridge, Arnold. "Dolley Madison." *History Today* 8 (January 1958): 3-9.

2368. Wright, Esmond. "The Political Education of James Madison." *History Today* 31 (December 1981): 17-23.

Public Career

2369. Adair, Douglass. "'That Politics May Be Reduced to a Science': David Hume, James Madison, and the Tenth Federalist." *Huntington Library Quarterly* 20 (August 1957): 343-360.

2370. Agresto, John. "A System without a President — James Madison and the Revolution in Republican Liberty." *South Atlantic Quarterly* 82 (Spring 1983): 129-144.

2371. Banning, Lance. "The Hamiltonian Madison: A Reconsideration." *Virginia Magazine of History and Biography* 92 (January 1984): 3-28.

2372. Banning, Lance. "James Madison and the Nationalists, 1780-1783." *William and Mary Quarterly* 40 (April 1983): 227-255.

2373. Baskin, Darryl B. "The Pluralist Vision in American Political Thought: Adams, Madison, and Calhoun on Community, Citizenship, and the Public Interest." Ph.D. dissertation, University of California, Berkeley, 1966.

2374. Bonn, Franklyn G., Jr. "The Ideas of Political Party in the Thought of Thomas Jefferson and James Madison." Ph.D. dissertation, University of Minnesota, 1964.

2375. Bourke, Paul F. "The Pluralist Reading of James Madison's Tenth Federalist." *Perspectives in American History* 9 (1975): 271-295.

2376. Branson, Roy. "Madison and the Scottish Enlightenment." *Journal of the History of Ideas* 40 (April/June 1979): 235-250.

2377. Brant, Irving. "James Madison as Founder of the Constitution." *New York University Law Review* 27 (April 1952): 248-264.

2378. Brant, Irving. *James Madison: Father of the Constitution, 1787-1800.* Indianapolis, IN: Bobbs-Merrill, 1950.

2379. Brant, Irving. "James Madison:

His Greatness Emerges after Two Centuries." *American Bar Association Journal* 37 (August 1951): 563-566.

2380. Brant, Irving. "James Madison, Nationalist." *American Mercury* 66 (May 1948): 606-612.

2381. Brant, Irving. *James Madison: Secretary of State, 1801-1809*. Indianapolis, IN: Bobbs-Merrill, 1953.

2382. Brant, Irving. *James Madison: The Nationalist, 1780-1787*. Indianapolis, IN: Bobbs-Merrill, 1948.

2383. Brant, Irving. *James Madison: The Virginia Revolutionist*. Indianapolis, IN: Bobbs-Merrill, 1941.

2384. Brant, Irving. "The Madison Heritage." *New York University Law Review* 35 (April 1960): 882-902.

2385. Brant, Irving. "Madison on the Separation of Church and State." *William and Mary Quarterly* 8 (January 1951): 3-24.

2386. Burns, Edward M. "The Political Philosophy of James Madison." Ph.D. dissertation, University of Pittsburgh, 1935.

2387. Carey, George W. "Majority Tyranny and the Extended Republic Theory of James Madison." *Modern Age* 20 (Winter 1976): 40-54.

2388. Colbourn, H. Trevor. "Madison Eulogized." *William and Mary Quarterly* 8 (January 1951): 108-119.

2389. Conniff, James. "The Enlightenment and American Political Thought: A Study of the Origins of Madison's *Federalist Number 10*." *Political Theory* 8 (August 1980): 381-402.

2390. Conniff, James. "On the Obsolescence of the General Will: Rousseau, Madison, and the Evolution of Republican Political Thought." *Western Political Quarterly* 28 (March 1975): 32-58.

2391. Crosskey, William W. "The Ex-Post Facto and the Contracts Clauses in the Federal Convention: A Note on the Editorial Ingenuity of James Madison." *University of Chicago Law Review* 35 (1968): 248-254.

2392. DeLeon, Daniel. *James Madison and Karl Marx, A Contrast and a Similarity*. New York: New York Labor News Co., 1932.

2393. Dewey, Donald O. "Madison's Response to Jackson's Foes." *Tennessee Historical Quarterly* 20 (June 1961): 167-176.

2394. Dewey, Donald O. "Madison's Views of Electoral Reform." *Western Political Quarterly* 15 (March 1962): 140-145.

2395. Dewey, Donald O. "The Sage of Montpelier: James Madison's Constitutional and Political Thought, 1817-1836." Ph.D. dissertation, University of Chicago, 1960.

2396. Dietze, Gottfried. "Madison's Federalist: A Treatise for Free Government." *Georgetown Law Journal* 46 (Fall 1957): 21-51.

2397. Donovan, Frank. *Mr. Madison's Constitution*. New York: Dodd, Mead, 1965.

2398. Draper, Theodore. "Hume and Madison: The Secrets of *Federalist Paper No. 10*." *Encounter* 58 (February 1982): 34-47.

2399. Drouin, Edmond G. "Madison and Jefferson on Clergy in the Legislature." *America* 138 (January 28, 1978): 58-59.

2400. Einhorn, Lois J. "Basic Assumptions in the Virginia-Ratification Debates: Patrick Henry vs. James Madison on the Nature of Man and Reason." *Southern Speech Communication Journal* 46 (Summer 1981): 327-340.

2401. Farnell, Robert S. "Positive Valuations of Politics and Government in the

Thought of Five American Founding Fathers: Thomas Jefferson, John Adams, James Madison, Alexander Hamilton, and George Washington." Ph.D. dissertation, Cornell University, 1970.

2402. Fornoff, Charles W. "Madison on the Nature of Politics." Ph.D. dissertation, University of Illinois, 1926.

2403. Hagan, Horace H. "James Madison: Constructive Political Philosopher." *American Bar Association Journal* 16 (January 1930): 51-56.

2404. Hobson, Charles F. "The Negative on State Laws: James Madison, the Constitution, and the Crisis of Republican Government." *William and Mary Quarterly* 36 (April 1979): 215-235.

2405. Hunt, Gaillard. "Madison and Religious Liberty." *American Historical Association Annual Report* 1 (1902): 163-171.

2406. Ingersoll, David E. "Machiavelli and Madison: Perspectives on Political Stability." *Political Science Quarterly* 85 (June 1970): 259-280.

2407. Jillson, Calvin C. "The Representation Question in the Federal Convention of 1787: Madison's Virginia Plan and Its Opponents." *Congressional Studies* 8 (1981): 21-41.

2408. Kennedy, Patrick J. "The Profound Politician and Scholar: An Examination of the Charges of Inconsistency within the Political Theory of President James Madison." Ph.D. dissertation, Fordham University, 1970.

2409. Ketcham, Ralph L. "Jefferson and Madison and the Doctrines of Interposition and Nullification: A Letter of John Quincy Adams." *Virginia Magazine of History and Biography* 66 (April 1958): 178-182.

2410. Ketcham, Ralph L. "Notes on James Madison's Sources for the Tenth Federalist Papers." *Midwest Journal of Political Science* 1 (May 1957): 20-25.

2411. Koch, Adrienne. "James Madison and the Library of Congress." *Library of Congress Quarterly Journal* 37 (Spring 1980): 158-161.

2412. Koch, Adrienne. "James Madison and the Politics of Republicanism." In *The Federalists vs. the Jefferson Republicans*, edited by Paul Goodman, 66-76. New York: Holt, Reinhart and Winston, 1967.

2413. Koch, Adrienne. *Jefferson and Madison: The Great Collaboration.* New York: Oxford University Press, 1964.

2414. Koch, Adrienne. *Madison's "Advice to My Country."* Princeton, NJ: Princeton University Press, 1966.

2415. Koch, Adrienne. "Philosopher-Statesmen of the Republic." *Sewanee Review* 55 (Summer 1947): 384-405.

2416. Koch, Adrienne. *Power, Morals, and the Founding Fathers: Essays in the Interpretation of the American Enlightenment.* Ithaca, NY: Cornell University Press, 1961.

2417. Koch, Adrienne, and Harry Ammon. "The Virginia and Kentucky Resolutions: An Episode in Jefferson's and Madison's Defense of Civil Liberties." *William and Mary Quarterly* 5 (April 1948): 145-176.

2418. Landi, Alexander R. *The Politics of James Madison.* Dallas, TX: University of Dallas, 1973.

2419. Lecky, William. *Historical and Political Essays.* Salem, NY: Ayer, 1908.

2420. Lodge, Henry C. *Historical and Political Essays.* Boston: Houghton Mifflin, 1892.

2421. Lutz, Donald S. "James Madison as a Conflict Theorist: The Madisonian Model Extended." Ph.D. dissertation, Indiana University, 1969.

2422. McCoy, Drew R. "Jefferson and Madison on Malthus: Population Growth in Jeffersonian Political Economy." *Virginia Magazine of History and Biography* 88 (July 1980): 259-275.

2423. McCoy, Drew R. "Madison's America: Polity, Economy, and Society." *Library of Congress Quarterly Journal* 37 (Spring 1980): 259-264.

2424. McCoy, Drew R. "Republicanism and American Foreign Policy: James Madison and the Political Economy of Commercial Discrimination, 1789 to 1794." *William and Mary Quarterly* 31 (October 1974): 633-646.

2425. McGrath, Dennis R. "James Madison and Social Choice Theory: The Possibility of Republicanism." Ph.D. dissertation, University of Maryland, 1983.

2426. Mead, Sidney E. "Neither Church nor State: Reflections on James Madison's Line of Separation." *Journal of Church and State* 10 (Autumn 1968): 349-364.

2427. Meyers, Marvin. "Revolution and Founding: On Publius-Madison and the American Genesis." *Library of Congress Quarterly Journal* 37 (Spring 1980): 192-200.

2428. Meyers, Marvin, ed. *Mind of the Founder: Sources of the Political Thought of James Madison*. Rev. ed. Hanover, NH: University Press of New England, 1981.

2429. Morgan, Robert J. "Madison's Analysis of the Sources of Political Authority." *American Political Science Review* 75 (September 1981): 613-625.

2430. Morgan, Robert J. "Madison's Theory of Representation in the Tenth Federalist." *Journal of Politics* 36 (November 1974): 852-885.

2431. Rachal, William M. E. "James Madison, Father of the Constitution." *Virginia Cavalcade* 1 (Winter 1951): 26-31.

2432. Riemer, Neal. *James Madison: Creating the American Constitution*. Washington, DC: Congressional Quarterly, 1986.

2433. Riemer, Neal. "James Madison's Theory of the Self-Destructive Features of Republican Government." *Ethics* 65 (October 1954): 34-43.

2434. Riemer, Neal. "The Republicanism of James Madison." *Political Science Quarterly* 69 (March 1954): 45-64.

2435. Rogow, Arnold A. "The Federal Convention: Madison and Yates." *American Historical Review* 60 (January 1955): 323-335.

2436. Ross, Michael. "Homogeneity and Heterogeneity in Jefferson and Madison." *International Review of History and Political Science* 13 (November 1976): 47-50.

2437. Rossiter, Clinton L. *1787, The Grand Convention*. New York: Macmillan, 1966.

2438. Rutland, Robert A. *James Madison and the Search for Nationhood*. Washington, DC: Library of Congress, 1981.

2439. Schultz, Harold S. "James Madison: Father of the Constitution?" *Library of Congress Quarterly Journal* 37 (Spring 1980): 215-222.

2440. Scott, James B. *James Madison's Notes of Debates in the Federal Convention of 1787 and Their Relation to a More Perfect Society of Nations*. New York: Oxford University Press, 1918.

2441. Singleton, Marvin K. "Colonial Virginia as First Amendment Matrix: Henry, Madison, and the Establishment Clause." *Journal of Church and State* 8 (Autumn 1966): 344-364.

2442. Skeen, C. Edward. "Mr. Madison's Secretary of War." *Pennsylvania Magazine of History and Biography* 100 (July 1976): 336-355.

2443. Smith, Loren E. "The Library List of 1783: Being a Catalogue of Books, Composed and Arranged by James Madison and Others, and Recommended for the Use of Congress on January 24, 1783, With Notes and an Introduction." Ph.D. dissertation, Claremont Graduate School, 1968.

2444. Spengler, Joseph J. "The Political Economy of Jefferson, Madison, and Adams." In *American Studies in Honor of William Kenneth Boyd*, edited by David K. Jackson, 3-59. Durham, NC: Duke University Press, 1940.

2445. Ulmer, S. Sidney. "James Madison and the Pinckney Plan." *South Carolina Law Quarterly* 9 (Spring 1957): 415-444.

2446. Vanderoef, John S. "The Political Thought of James Madison." Ph.D. dissertation, Princeton University, 1968.

2447. Walker, Mary M. "Problems of Majority Rule in the Political Thought of James Madison and John C. Calhoun." Ph.D. dissertation, Indiana University, 1971.

2448. Weber, Paul J. "James Madison and Religious Equality: The Perfect Separation." *Review of Politics* 44 (April 1982): 163-186.

2449. Woodburn, James A. *The Making of the Constitution, A Syllabus of "Madison's Journal of the Constitutional Convention," Together with a Few Outlines Based on "The Federalist."* Chicago: Scott, Foresman, 1908.

2450. Wright, Elliot. "Goldwater, Madison, and the 'Free Exercise of Religion.'" *Christian Century* 98 (November 25, 1981): 1228-1230.

2451. Young, John W. "Madison's Answer to Machiavelli: Concerning the Legal Relation of Organized Religion to Government in a Republic." *Freeman* 27 (July 1977): 421-431.

2452. Zvesper, John. "The Madisonian Systems." *Western Political Quarterly* 37 (June 1984): 236-256.

Presidential Years

2453. Adams, Henry. *History of the United States of America during the Administrations of Jefferson and Madison.* 9 vols. New York: Scribner's, 1909-1911.

2454. Adams, Henry. *History of the United States of America during the Administration of Jefferson and Madison.* Edited by Ernest Samuels. Chicago: University of Chicago Press, 1979.

2455. Asberry, Robert L. "James Madison and the Patronage Problem, 1809-1817." Master's thesis, North Texas State University, 1973.

2456. Bell, Rudolph M. "Mr. Madison's War and Long-Term Congressional Voting Behavior." *William and Mary Quarterly* 36 (July 1979): 373-395.

2457. Bradley, Jared W. "W. C. C. Claiborne and Spain: Foreign Affairs under Jefferson and Madison, 1801-1811." *Louisiana History* 12 (Fall 1971): 297-314; 13 (Winter 1972): 5-28.

2458. Brant, Irving. *James Madison: Commander in Chief, 1812-1836.* Indianapolis, IN: Bobbs-Merrill, 1961.

2459. Brant, Irving. "Madison and the War of 1812." *Virginia Magazine of History and Biography* 74 (January 1966): 51-67.

2460. Brant, Irving. *Madison the President, 1809-1812.* Indianapolis, IN: Bobbs-Merrill, 1956.

2461. Brant, Irving. "Timid President? Futile War?" *American Heritage* 10 (October 1959): 46-47, 85-89.

2462. Brown, Roger L. *The Republic in*

Peril: 1812. New York: Columbia University Press, 1964.

2463. Burns, Edward M. "Madison's Theory of Judicial Review." *Kentucky Law Journal* 24 (May 1936): 412-423.

2464. Burton, Harold H. "The Cornerstone of Constitutional Law: The Extraordinary Case of *Marbury vs. Madison.*" *American Bar Association Journal* 36 (October 1950): 805-808, 881-883.

2465. Campbell, Helen M. . . . *Famous Presidents: Washington, Jefferson, Madison, Lincoln, Grant.* Boston: Educational Publishing Co., 1903.

2466. Cook, Theodore A. "The Original Intention of the Monroe Doctrine as Shown by the Correspondence of Monroe with Jefferson and Madison." *Fortnightly Review* 64 (September 1898): 357-368.

2467. Costello, Frank B. "James Madison and the Hamilton Funding Plan: A Change of Inconsistency Investigated." *History Bulletin* 32 (November 1953): 12-26.

2468. Cunliffe, Marcus. "Madison (1812-1815)." In *The Ultimate Decision: The President as Commander in Chief,* edited by Ernest R. May, 21-54. New York: Braziller, 1960.

2469. Curry, Patricia E. "James Madison and the Berger Court: Converging Views of Church-State Separation." *Indiana Law Journal* 56 (Summer 1981): 615-616.

2470. Dangerfield, George B. "If Only Mr. Madison Had Waited." *American Heritage* 7 (April 1956): 8-10, 92-94.

2471. Drakeman, Donald L. "Religion and the Republic: James Madison and the First Amendment." *Journal of Church and State* 25 (Autumn 1983): 427-445.

2472. Dunbar, Leslie W. "James Madison and the Ninth Amendment." *Virginia Law Review* 42 (June 1956): 627-643.

2473. Fredman, Lionel E. *James Madison, American President and Constitutional Author.* Charlottesville, NY: SamHar Press, 1974.

2474. Glover, Richard. "The French Fleet, 1807-1814: Britain's Problem and Madison's Opportunity." *Journal of Modern History* 39 (September 1967): 233-252.

2475. Hunt, Gaillard. "Madison, The Statesman." *Constitutional Review* 5 (January 1921): 14-17.

2476. Kaplan, Lawrence S. "France and Madison's Decision for War, 1812." *Mississippi Valley Historical Review* 50 (March 1964): 652-671.

2477. Ketcham, Ralph L. "James Madison and Judicial Review: 1787-1834." *Syracuse Law Review* 8 (Spring 1957): 158-165.

2478. Ketcham, Ralph L. "James Madison: The Unimperial President." *Virginia Quarterly Review* 54 (Winter 1978): 116-136.

2479. Ketcham, Ralph L. "Party and Leadership in Madison's Conception of the Presidency." *Library of Congress Quarterly Journal* 37 (Spring 1980): 242-258.

2480. McLaughlin, Andrew C. "*Marbury vs. Madison* Again." *American Bar Association Journal* 14 (March 1928): 155-159.

2481. Pancake, John S. "The 'Invisibles': A Chapter in the Opposition to President Madison." *Journal of Southern History* 21 (February 1955): 17-37.

2482. Patterson, C. Perry. "James Madison and Judicial Review." *California Law Review* 28 (November 1939): 22-33.

2483. Pennoyer, Sylvester. "The Case of *Marbury vs. Madison.*" *American Law Review* 30 (March/April 1896): 188-202.

2484. Pinchbeck, Raymond. "James

Madison: Fourth President of the United States." *Northern Neck Historical Magazine* 1 (December 1951): 42-55.

2485. "Presidential Inaugurations: Madison — 1806." *Ladies' Magazine and Literary Gazette* 4 (December 1831): 529-537.

2486. Rutland, Robert A. *Madison's Alternatives: The Jeffersonian Republicans and the Coming of War, 1805-1812.* Philadelphia: Lippincott, 1975.

2487. Smith, Abbot. "Mr. Madison's War: An Unsuccessful Experiment in the Conduct of National Policy." *Political Science Quarterly* 57 (June 1942): 229-246.

2488. Stagg, John C. "The Coming of the War of 1812: The View from the Presidency." *Library of Congress Quarterly Journal* 37 (Spring 1980): 223-241.

2489. Stagg, John C. "James Madison and the 'Malcontents': The Political Origins of the War of 1812." *William and Mary Quarterly* 33 (October 1976): 557-585.

2490. Stagg, John C. *Mr. Madison's War: Politics, Diplomacy, and Warfare in the Early American Republic, 1783-1830.* Princeton, NJ: Princeton University Press, 1983.

2491. Stoddard, William O. *... James Madison, James Monroe, and John Quincy Adams.* New York: Stokes, 1887.

2492. Stuart, Reginald C. "James Madison and the Militants: Republican Disunity and Replacing the Embargo." *Diplomatic History* 6 (Spring 1982): 145-167.

2493. Swancara, Frank. *Separation of Religion and Government: The First Amendment, Madison's Intent, and the McCollum Decision — A Study of Separationism in America.* New York: Truth Seeker Co., 1950.

2494. Tully, Andrew. *When They Burned the White House.* New York: Popular Library, 1963.

Writings

2495. Ketcham, Ralph L., ed. "The Madison Family Papers: Case Study in a Search for Historical Manuscripts." *Manuscripts* 11 (Summer 1959): 49-55.

2496. Madison, James. *An Address Delivered before the Agricultural Society of Albemarle, On Tuesday, May 12, 1818.* Richmond, VA: Shepherd and Pollard, 1818.

2497. Madison, James. *Calendar of the Correspondence of James Madison.* New York: Franklin, 1970.

2498. Madison, James. *The Complete Madison: His Basic Writings.* Edited by Saul K. Padover. New York: Harper and Row, 1953.

2499. Madison, James. *Drafting the Federal Constitution: A Rearrangement of Madison's Notes Giving Consecutive Developments of Provisions in the Constitution of the United States, Supplemented by Documents Pertaining to the Philadelphia Convention and to Ratification Processes, and Including Insertions by the Compiler.* Compiled by Arthur Prescott. Baton Rouge: Louisiana State University Press, 1941.

2500. Madison, James. *An Examination of the British Doctrine, Which Subjects to Capture a Neutral Trade, Not Open in Time of Peace.* Philadelphia: n.p., 1806.

2501. Madison, James. *The Federalist: A Collection of Essays, Written in Favour of the New Constitution, As Agreed upon by the Federal Convention, September 17, 1787.* 2 vols. New York: J. and A. McLean, 1788.

2502. Madison, James. *The Federalist Papers of James Madison, Alexander*

Hamilton, and John Jay. New Rochelle, NY: Arlington House, 1966.

2503. Madison, James. *James Madison, A Biography in His Own Words.* Edited By Merrill D. Peterson. New York: Harper and Row, 1974.

2504. Madison, James. "James Madison's Attitude toward the Negro." *Journal of Negro History* 6 (January 1921): 74-102.

2505. Madison, James. "James Madison's Autobiography." Edited by Douglass Adair. *William and Mary Quarterly* 2 (April 1945): 191-209.

2506. Madison, James. *Journal of the Federal Convention, Kept by James Madison.* Edited by E. H. Scott. Freeport, NY: Books for Libraries Press, 1970.

2507. Madison, James. *Letters and Other Writings.* Philadelphia: Lippincott, 1865.

2508. Madison, James. *Letters and Other Writings of James Madison.* 4 vols. New York: Worthington, 1884.

2509. Madison, James. *Letters of Helvidius: Written in Reply to Pacificus, On the President's Proclamation of Neutrality.* Philadelphia: S. H. Smith, 1796.

2510. Madison, James. *Notes of Debates in the Federal Convention of 1787, Reported by James Madison.* Athens: Ohio University Press, 1966.

2511. Madison, James. *The Papers of James Madison.* 13 vols. Edited by William T. Hutchinson, et al. Chicago: University of Chicago Press, 1962-1981.

2512. Madison, James. *The Papers of James Madison.* 14 vols. Edited by Robert A. Rutland and Thomas A. Mason. Charlottesville: University Press Virginia, 1962.

2513. Madison, James. *The Papers of James Madison, Purchased by Order of Congress: Being His Correspondence and Reports of Debates during the Congress of the Confederation, and His Reports of Debates in the Federal Convention.* 3 vols. Washington, DC: Langtree and O'Sullivan, 1840.

2514. Madison, James. *The Writings of James Madison Comprising His Public Papers and His Private Correspondence, Including Numerous Letters and Documents Now for the First Time Printed.* 9 vols. Edited by Gaillard Hunt. New York: Putnam, 1900-1910.

2515. "Madison Miniature Presented to Library of Congress." *Library of Congress Information Bulletin* 35 (September 24, 1976): 586-587.

2516. Schwartz, Bernard. "Jefferson-Madison Correspondence." In his *The Great Rights of Mankind: A History of the American Bill of Rights,* 115-118. New York: Oxford University Press, 1977.

2517. Sifton, Paul G. "Recent Additions to the James Madison Papers at the Library of Congress." *Library of Congress Quarterly Journal* 37 (Spring 1980): 265-273.

James Monroe

Biographies

2518. Cresson, William P. *James Monroe.* Chapel Hill: University of North Carolina Press, 1946.

2519. Dangerfield, George. *The Era of Good Feelings.* New York: Harcourt, Brace, 1952.

2520. Dickson, Charles E. "Politics in a New Nation: The Early Career of James Monroe." Ph.D. dissertation, Ohio State University, 1971.

2521. Gilman, Daniel C. *James Monroe.* Edited by John T. Morse. Boston: Houghton Mifflin, 1896.

2522. Gilman, Daniel C. *James Monroe in His Relations to the Public Service during Half a Century, 1776 to 1826.* Boston: Houghton Mifflin, 1883.

2523. Morgan, George. *The Life of James Monroe.* Boston: Small, Maynard, 1921.

2524. Styron, Arthur. *Last of the Cocked Hats: James Monroe of the Virginia Dynasty.* Norman: University of Oklahoma Press, 1945.

Private Life

2525. Alderman, Edwin A. "James Monroe." *University of Virginia Alumni Bulletin* 17 (July 1924): 323-325.

2526. Ammon, Harry. "James Monroe and the Era of Good Feelings." *Virginia Magazine of History and Biography* 66 (October 1958): 387-398.

2527. Hall, Edward H. "The Monroe House, A Landmark History of the House in New York City in Which President James Monroe Died on July 4, 1831, With Biographical Notes Concerning Some of the Owners." In *American Scenic and Historic Preservation Society Annual Report, Appendix C* 28 (1922-1923): 251-266.

2528. Hay, Robert P. "The Meaning of Monroe's Death: The Contemporary Response." *West Virginia History* 30 (January 1969): 427-435.

2529. Hoes, Ingrid W. "James Monroe — Neglected Son of Virginia." *Virginia and the Virginia Record* 76 (December 1954): 18-19.

2530. Hooes, Rose G. "James Monroe, Soldier: His Part in the War of the American Revolution." *Daughters of the American Revolution Magazine* 57 (December 1923): 721-727.

2531. Johnson, Monroe. "James Monroe, Soldier." *William and Mary Quarterly* 9 (April 1928): 110-117.

2532. Johnson, Monroe. "The Maryland Ancestry of James Monroe." *Maryland Historical Magazine* 23 (June 1928): 193-195.

2533. Nadler, Solomon. "The Green Bag: James Monroe and the Fall of DeWitt Clinton." *New York Historical Society Quarterly* 59 (July 1975): 202-225.

2534. *A Narrative of a Tour of Observation, Made during the Summer of 1817, By James Monroe, President of the United States, Through the North-Eastern and North-Western Departments of the Union: With a View to the Examination of Their Several Military Defenses.* Philadelphia: S. A. Mitchell and H. Ames, 1818.

2535. Rachal, William M. E. "President Monroe's Return to Virginia." *Virginia Cavalcade* 3 (Summer 1953): 43-47.

2536. Wilmerding, Lucius, Jr. "James Monroe and the Furniture Fund." *New York Historical Society Quarterly* 44 (April 1960): 132-149.

2537. Wolfe, Maxine G. "Where Monroe Practiced Law." *American Bar Association Journal* 59 (November 1973): 1282-1284.

2538. Wolfe, Udolpho. *Grand Civic and Military Demonstration in Honor of the Removal of the Remains of James Monroe, Fifth President of the United States, From New York to Virginia.* New York: Wolfe, 1858.

Public Career

2539. Ammon, Harry. "James Monroe and the Election of 1808 in Virginia." *William and Mary Quarterly* 20 (January 1963): 33-56.

2540. Ammon, Harry. *James Monroe: The Quest for National Identity.* New York: McGraw-Hill, 1971.

2541. Angel, Edward. "James Monroe's Mission to Paris, 1794-1796." Ph.D. dissertation, George Washington University, 1979.

2542. Berkeley, Dorothy S., and Edmund Berkeley. "The Piece Left Behind: Monroe's Authorship of a Political Pamphlet Revealed." *Virginia Magazine of History and Biography* 75 (April 1967): 174-180.

2543. Bond, Beverly W., Jr. *The Monroe Mission to France 1794-1796.* Baltimore, MD: Johns Hopkins University Press, 1907.

2544. Cox, Isaac J. "Monroe and the Early Mexican Revolutionary Agents." *American Historical Association Annual Report* 1 (1911): 199-215.

2545. Dickson, Charles E. "James Monroe's Defense of Kentucky's Interests in the Confederation Congress: An Example of Early North/South Party Alignment." *Kentucky Historical Society Register* 74 (October 1976): 261-280.

2546. Marsh, Philip M., ed. *Monroe's Defense of Jefferson and Freneau against Hamilton.* Oxford, OH: The Author, 1948.

2547. Pratt, Julius W. "James Monroe, Secretary of State, November 25, 1811, to March 3, 1817 (ad interim, April 3 to November 25, 1811)." In *The American Secretaries of State and Their Diplomacy,* Vol. 3, edited by Samuel F. Bemis, 201-277. New York: Knopf, 1927.

2548. Risjord, Norman K. *The Old Republicans: Southern Conservatism in the Age of Jefferson.* New York: Columbia University Press, 1965.

2549. Skeen, C. Edward. "Monroe and Armstrong: A Study in Political Rivalry." *New York Historical Society Quarterly* 57 (April 1973): 121-147.

2550. Smith, Carlton B. "Congressional Attitudes toward Military Preparedness during the Monroe Administration." *Military Affairs* 40 (Feburary 1976): 22-25.

2551. Steel, Anthony. "Impressment in the Monroe-Pinckney Negotiation, 1806-1807." *American Historical Review* 57 (January 1952): 352-369.

2552. Waldo, Samuel P. *Biographical Sketches of Distinguished American Naval Heroes in the War of the Revolution, Between the American Republic and the Kingdom of Great Britain....* Hartford, CT: Silas Andrus, 1823.

2553. Waldo, Samuel P. *The Tour of James Monroe.* 2d ed. Hartford, CT: Silas Andrus, 1820.

2554. Waldo, Samuel P. *The Tour of James Monroe, President of the United States through the Northern and Eastern States in 1817: His Tour in the Year 1818, Together with a Sketch of His Life....* Hartford, CT: Silas Andrus, 1819.

2555. Wilmerding, Lucius, Jr. *James Monroe, Public Claimant.* New Brunswick, NJ: Rutgers University Press, 1960.

Presidential Years

2556. Brown, Everett S., ed. *Missouri Compromises and Presidential Politics, 1820-1825: From the Letters of William Plumer, Jr.* St. Louis: Missouri Historical Society, 1926.

2557. Dangerfield, George. *The Awakening of American Nationalism: 1815-1818.* New York: Harper and Row, 1965.

2558. Gronet, Richard W. "Early Latin American-United States Contracts: An Analysis of Jeremy Robinson's Communications to the Monroe Administration, 1817-1823." Ph.D. dissertation, Catholic University of America, 1970.

2559. Gustafson, Milton O. "The Monroe Doctrine." *Manuscripts* 27 (1975): 12-17.

2560. Guthrie, Blaine A., Jr. "A Visit by That Confidential Character — President Monroe." *Filson Club Historical Quarterly* 51 (January 1977): 44-48.

2561. Lathrop, Barnes F., comp. "Monroe on the Adams-Clay 'Bargain.'" *American Historical Review* 42 (January 1937): 273-276.

2562. Lovat-Fraser, J. A. "President James Monroe and His Doctrine." *London Quarterly Review* 6 (1935): 372-381.

2563. May, Ernest R. *The Making of the Monroe Doctrine.* Cambridge, MA: Harvard University Press, 1979.

2564. Moore, Glover. *The Missouri Controversy, 1819-1821.* Lexington: University of Kentucky Press, 1953.

2565. Moore, Glover. "Monroe's Re-election in 1820." *Mississippi Quarterly* 11 (Summer 1958): 131-140.

2566. Noonan, John T., Jr. *The Antelope: The Ordeal of the Recaptured Africans in the Administrations of James Monroe and John Quincy Adams.* Berkeley: University of California Press, 1977.

2567. Perkins, Dexter. *The Monroe Doctrine, 1823-1826.* Cambridge, MA: Harvard University Press, 1927.

2568. Radcliffe, Richard. *The President's Tour.* New Ipswich, NH: S. Wilder, 1822.

2569. Rappaport, Armin, ed. *The Monroe Doctrine.* New York: Holt, Rinehart and Winston, 1966.

2570. Stathis, Stephen W. "Dr. Barton's Case and the Monroe Precedent of 1818." *William and Mary Quarterly* 32 (July 1975): 465-474.

2571. Stoddard, William O. *...James Madison, James Monroe, and John Quincy Adams.* New York: Stokes, 1887.

2572. Turner, Lynn W. "Electoral Vote against Monroe in 1820 — An American Legend." *Mississippi Valley Historical Review* 42 (September 1955): 250-273.

Writings

2573. Monroe, James. *Autobiography.*

Edited by Stuart G. Brown. Syracuse, NY: Syracuse University Press, 1959.

2574. Monroe, James. "Letters of James Monroe." *Tyler's Quarterly Historical and Genealogical Magazine* 4 (October 1922): 96-108.

2575. Monroe, James. *The Memoir of James Monroe, Esq., Relating to His Unsettled Claims upon the People and Government of the United States.* Charlottesville, VA: Gilmer, Davis, 1828.

2576. Monroe, James. *The People of the Sovereigns: Being a Comparison of the Government of the United States with Those of the Republics Which Have Existed before, With the Causes of Their Decadence and Fall.* Edited by Samuel L. Gouvernour. Philadelphia: Lippincott, 1867.

2577. Monroe, James. *A View of the Conduct of the Executive, In the Foreign Affairs of the United States, Connected with the Mission to the French Republic, During the Years 1794, 1795, and 1796.* Philadelphia: B. F. Bache, 1797.

2578. Monroe, James. *The Writings of James Monroe, Including a Collection of His Public and Private Papers and Correspondence Now for the First Time Printed.* 7 vols. Edited by Stanislaus M. Hamilton. New York: Putnam, 1898-1903.

2579. Sifton, Paul G. "Library Acquires Late Monroe Letter." *Library of Congress Information Bulletin* 29 (January 8, 1970): 1-3.

John Quincy Adams

Biographies

2580. Bemis, Samuel F. "John Quincy Adams and George Washington." *Massachusetts Historical Society Proceedings* 67 (1941-1944): 365-384.

2581. Bobbe, Dorothie D. *Mr. and Mrs. John Quincy Adams, An Adventure in Patriotism.* New York: Minton Balch, 1930.

2582. Clark, Bennett C. *John Quincy Adams, "Old Man Eloquent."* Boston: Little, Brown, 1932.

2583. East, Robert A. *John Quincy Adams: The Critical Years: 1785-1794.* New York: Bookman Associates, 1962.

2584. Good, H. G. "To the Future Biographers of John Quincy Adams." *Science Monthly* 39 (1934): 247-251.

2585. Hecht, Marie B. *John Quincy Adams: A Personal History of an Independent Man.* New York: Macmillan, 1972.

2586. Morse, John T., Jr. *John Quincy Adams.* Boston: Houghton Mifflin, 1882.

2587. Nagel, Paul. *Descent from Glory: Four Generations of the John Adams Family.* Oxford: Oxford University Press, 1983.

2588. Oliver, Andrew. *Portraits of John Quincy Adams and His Wife.* Cambridge, MA: Harvard University Press, 1970.

2589. Quincy, Josiah. *Memoir of the Life of John Quincy Adams.* Boston: Phillips, Sampson, 1858.

2590. Seward, William H. *Life and Public Services of John Quincy Adams, Sixth President of the United States.* Auburn, NY: Derby, Miller, 1849.

2591. Shepherd, Jack. *Cannibals of the Heart: A Personal Biography of Louisa Catherine and John Quincy Adams.* New York: McGraw-Hill, 1981.

2592. Stewart, Gideon T. *Framed in American History: The Lives of John Adams and John Quincy Adams, Father and Son, Each a Former President of the United States.* Norwalk, OH: n.p., 1906.

Private Life

2593. Branton, Harriet K. "Another Album Leaf by John Quincy Adams." *Western Pennsylvania Historical Magazine* 60 (October 1977): 415-418.

2594. Butterfield, Lyman H. "Tending a Dragon-Killer: Notes for the Biographer of Mrs. John Quincy Adams." *American Philosophical Society Proceedings* 118 (April 1974): 165-178.

2595. Collins, Herbert R., and David B. Weaver. "Wills of the U.S. Presidents: John Quincy Adams." *Trusts and Estates* 115 (January 1976): 18-24.

2596. Eriksson, Erik M. "John Quincy Adams: Anti-Masonic Letter Writer." *Grand Lodge Bulletin* 27 (March 1926): 87-94.

2597. Everett, Edward. *A Eulogy of the Life and Character of John Quincy Adams, Delivered at the Request of the Legislature of Massachusetts, In Faneuil Hall, April 15, 1848.* . . . Boston: Dutton and Wentworth, 1848.

2598. Faust, A. B. "John Quincy Adams and Wieland." *American German Review* 5 (April 1939): 8-11.

2599. Goodfellow, Donald M. "Your Old Friend, J. Q. Adams." *New England Quarterly* 21 (June 1948): 217-231.

2600. Illick, Joseph E. "John Quincy Adams: The Maternal Influence." *Journal of Psychohistory* 4 (Fall 1976): 185-195.

2601. Jones, Maldwyn A. "John Quincy Adams." *History Today* 30 (November 1980): 5-8.

2602. Kerr, Laura. *Louisa: The Life of Mrs. John Quincy Adams.* New York: Wilfred Funk, 1964.

2603. Kline, Sherman J. "John Quincy Adams — 'The Old Man Eloquent.'" *Americana* 21 (October 1927): 479-497.

2604. Klingelhofer, Herbert E. "John Quincy Adams, Literary Editor." *Manuscripts* 35 (Fall 1983): 265-272.

2605. Morris, Walter J. "John Quincy Adams: Germanophile." Ph.D. dissertation, Pennsylvania State University, 1963.

2606. Morris, Walter J. "John Quincy Adams's German Library with a Catalog of His German Books." *American Philosophical Society Proceedings* 118 (September 1974): 321-333.

2607. Morrison, Katherine L. "A Reexamination of Brooks and Henry on John Quincy Adams." *New England Quarterly* 54 (June 1981): 163-179.

2608. Musto, David F. "The Youth of John Quincy Adams." *American Philosophical Society Proceedings* 113 (August 15, 1969): 269-282.

2609. Newhall, Beaumont. "Daguerreotype of John Quincy Adams by Philip Haas." *Metropolitan Museum Journal* 12 (1977): 151-154.

2610. Parsons, Lynn H. "The 'Splendid Pageant': Observations on the Death of John Quincy Adams." *New England Quarterly* 53 (December 1980): 464-482.

2611. Smoot, Joseph G. "A Presbyterian Minister Calls on President John Quincy Adams." *New England Quarterly* 34 (September 1961): 379-382.

2612. Sprague, Waldo C., ed. *The President John Adams and President John Quincy Adams Birthplaces, Quincy, Mass.: Their Origin, Early History, and Changes Down to the Present Time.* Quincy, MA: Quincy Historical Society, 1959.

2613. Stirk, S. D. "John Quincy Adams's Letters on Silesia." *New England Quarterly* 9 (September 1936): 485-499.

Public Career

2614. Adams, Charles F., ed. "John Quincy Adams and Speaker Andrew Stevenson, Of Virginia: An Episode of the Twenty-second Congress (1832)." *Massachusetts Historical Society Proceedings* 39 (1906): 504-553.

2615. Banninga, Jerald L. "John Quincy Adams: A Critic in the Golden Age of American Oratory." Ph.D. dissertation, Indiana University, 1963.

2616. Banninga, Jerald L. "John Quincy Adams' Address of July 4, 1821." *Quarterly Journal of Speech* 53 (February 1967): 44-49.

2617. Banninga, Jerald L. "John Quincy

Adams on the Right of a Slave to Petition Congress." *Southern Speech Communication Journal* 38 (Winter 1972): 151-163.

2618. Baron, Stephan M. "John Quincy Adams and the American Party System." Ph.D. dissertation, Northern Illinois University, 1978.

2619. Bates, Jack W. "John Quincy Adams and the Antislavery Movement." Ph.D. dissertation, University of Southern California, 1953.

2620. Bemis, Samuel F. "John Quincy Adams and Russia." *Virginia Quarterly Review* 21 (October 1945): 553-568.

2621. Bergquist, Harold E., Jr. "John Quincy Adams and the Promulgation of the Monroe Doctrine, October-December, 1823." *Essex Institute of Historical Collections* 3 (January 1975): 37-52.

2622. Callanan, Harold J. "The Political Economy of John Quincy Adams." Ph.D. dissertation, Boston University, 1975.

2623. Crapol, Edward P. "John Quincy Adams and the Monroe Doctrine: Some New Evidence." *Pacific Historical Review* 48 (August 1979): 413-419.

2624. Davidson, Bill. *President Kennedy Selects Six Brave Presidents*. New York: Harper and Row, 1962.

2625. Downey, William G., Jr. "John Quincy Adams' Monroe Doctrine." *Thought* 14 (December 1939): 620-632.

2626. Farnum, George R. "Historic New England Shrines of the Law: Otis, Adams, and Hancock." *American Bar Association Journal* 22 (June 1936): 383-388.

2627. Farnum, George R. "Historical New England Shrines of the Law: Quincy and the Adamses." *American Bar Association Journal* 22 (May 1936): 309-312.

2628. Ford, Worthington C. "John Quincy Adams and the Monroe Doctrine." *American Historical Review* 7 (July 1902): 676-696.

2629. Ford, Worthington C. *John Quincy Adams, His Connection with the Monroe Doctrine (1823-1842) by W. C. Ford, and with Emancipation under Martial Law (1819-1842) by Charles Francis Adams*. Cambridge, MA: J. Wilson, 1902.

2630. Ford, Worthington C. "The Recall of John Quincy Adams in 1808." *Massachusetts Historical Society Proceedings* 45 (1912): 354-373.

2631. Glick, Wendell. "The Best Possible World of John Quincy Adams." *New England Quarterly* 37 (March 1964): 3-17.

2632. Jenkins, Starr. "American Statesmen as Men of Letters: Franklin, Adams, Jefferson, John Quincy Adams, Lincoln, Theodore Roosevelt, and Wilson Considered as Writers." Ph.D. dissertation, University of New Mexico, 1972.

2633. Johannesen, Richard L. "John Quincy Adams' Speaking on Territorial Expansion, 1836-1848." Ph.D. dissertation, University of Kansas, 1964.

2634. Johnson, Willis F. "John Quincy Adams and Secession, 1842." *Magazine of History* 25 (September 1917): 96-99.

2635. Kaye, Jacqueline. "John Quincy Adams and the Conquest of Ireland." *Eire-Ireland* 16 (1981): 34-54.

2636. Ketcham, Ralph L., ed. "Jefferson and Madison and the Doctrine of Interposition and Nullification: A Letter of John Quincy Adams." *Virginia Magazine of History and Biography* 66 (April 1958): 178-182.

2637. Knapp, Frank A., Jr. "John Quincy Adams: Defensor de Mexico?" *Historia Mexicana* 7 (September 1957): 116-123.

2638. Lewis, Mary E. "An Annotated Reference to John Quincy Adams' 'Letters on Rhetoric and Oratory' Based on the

Requirements of the Boyeston Chair Committee." Master's thesis, California State University, 1972.

2639. Lipsky, George A. *John Quincy Adams: His Theory and Ideas.* New York: Crowell, 1950.

2640. MacLean, William J. "John Quincy Adams and Reform." Ph.D. dissertation, University of North Carolina, 1971.

2641. MacLean, William J. "Othello Scorned: The Racial Thought of John Quincy Adams." *Journal of the Early Republic* 4 (Summer 1984): 143-160.

2642. Macoll, John D. "Congressman John Quincy Adams, 1831-1833." Ph.D. dissertation, Indiana University, 1973.

2643. Macoll, John D. "Representative John Quincy Adams's Compromise Tariff of 1832." *Capitol Studies* 1 (Fall 1972): 41-58.

2644. Martin, Dan M. "John Quincy Adams and the Whig Ideology." Ph.D. dissertation, Princeton University, 1968.

2645. Mayo, Lawrence S. "Jeremy Belknap and J. Q. Adams, 1787." *Massachusetts Historical Society Proceedings* 59 (February 1926): 203-209.

2646. Morgan, H. Wayne. "John Quincy Adams as Minister to Russia, 1809-1956." *Western Humanities Review* 10 (Autumn 1956): 375-382.

2647. Morgan, William G. "John Quincy Adams versus Andrew Jackson: Their Biographers and the 'Corrupt Bargain' Charge." *Tennessee Historical Quarterly* 26 (Spring 1967): 43-58.

2648. Noonan, John T., Jr. *The Antelope: The Ordeal of the Recaptured Africans in the Administrations of James Monroe and John Quincy Adams.* Berkeley: University of California Press, 1977.

2649. Owens, Patrick J. "John Quincy Adams and American Utilitarianism." Ph.D. dissertation, University of Notre Dame, 1976.

2650. Parsons, Lynn H. "Censoring Old Man Eloquent: Foreign Policy and Disunion, 1842." *Capitol Studies* 3 (Fall 1975): 89-106.

2651. Parsons, Lynn H. "A Perpetual Harrow upon My Feeling: John Quincy Adams and the American Indian." *New England Quarterly* 46 (September 1973): 339-379.

2652. Rahskopf, Horace G. "John Quincy Adams' Theory and Practice of Public Speaking." *Archives of Speech* 1 (September 1936): 7-98.

2653. Reingold, Nathan. "The Scientific Mixed with the Political: John Quincy, Brooks, and Henry Adams." Ph.D. dissertation, University of Pennsylvania, 1951.

2654. Rodesch, Jerrold C. "America and the Middle Ages: A Study in the Thought of John and John Quincy Adams." Ph.D. dissertation, Rutgers University, 1971.

2655. Stenberg, Richard R. "J. Q. Adams: Imperialist and Apostate." *Southwestern Social Science Quarterly* 16 (March 1936): 37-49.

2656. Wiltse, Charles M. "John Quincy Adams and the Party System: A Review Article." *Journal of Politics* 4 (August 1942): 407-414.

Presidential Years

2657. Adams, Charles F. "John Quincy Adams and Martial Law." *Massachusetts Historical Society Proceedings* 15 (1901-1902): 436-478.

2658. Bemis, Samuel F. *John Quincy Adams and the Foundations of American Foreign Policy.* New York: Knopf, 1949.

2659. Bemis, Samuel F. *John Quincy Ad-

ams and the Union. New York: Knopf, 1956.

2660. Bemis, Samuel F. "The Scuffle in the Rotunda: A Footnote to the Presidency of John Quincy Adams and to the History of Dueling." *Massachusetts Historical Society Proceedings* 71 (1953-1957): 156-166.

2661. Carroll, Eber M. "Politics during the Administration of John Quincy Adams." *South Atlantic Quarterly* 23 (April 1924): 141-154.

2662. Hackett, Charles W. "The Development of John Quincy Adams' Policy with Respect to an American Confederation and the Panama Congress, 1822-1825." *Hispanic American Historical Review* 8 (November 1928): 496-525.

2663. Hoehling, Mary D. *Yankee in the White House: John Quincy Adams.* New York: Messner, 1963.

2664. Paullin, Charles O. "The Electoral Vote for John Quincy Adams in 1820." *American Historical Review* 21 (January 1916): 318-319.

2665. Perkins, Dexter. "John Quincy Adams." In *American Secretaries of State*, Vol. 4, edited by Samuel F. Bemis, 1-111. New York: Knopf, 1928.

2666. Stoddard, William O. . . . *James Madison, James Monroe, and John Quincy Adams.* New York: Stokes, 1887.

Writings

2667. Adams, Henry, ed. *Documents Relating to New England Federalism, 1800-1815.* Boston: Little, Brown, 1877.

2668. Adams, John Q. *Address to His Constituents of the Twelfth Congressional District at Braintree, September 17th, 1842.* Boston: J. H. Eastburn, 1842.

2669. Adams, John Q. "Address to the Massachusetts Historical Society, November 22, 1841, On the Opium War between Great Britain and China." Edited by Charles F. Adams. *Massachusetts Historical Society Proceedings* 43 (1910): 295-325.

2670. Adams, John Q. *American Principles: A Review of the Works of Fisher Ames.* Boston: Everett and Munroe, 1809.

2671. Adams, John Q. *An Answer to Paine's Rights of Man.* London: J. Stockdale, 1793.

2672. Adams, John Q. *Argument, Before the Supreme Court of the United States, In the Case of the United States, Appellants, vs. Cinique, and Others, Africans, Captured in the Schooner Amistad, by Lieut. Gedney, Delivered on the 24th of February and 1st of March, 1841.* New York: S. W. Benedict, 1841.

2673. Adams, John Q. *A Catalogue of the Books of John Quincy Adams Deposited in the Boston Athenaeum, With Notes on Books, Adams Seals, and Book-Plates by Henry Adams.* Boston: Boston Athenaeum, 1938.

2674. Adams, John Q. *Correspondence between John Quincy Adams, Esquire, President of the United States, and Several Citizens of Massachusetts Concerning the Change of a Design to Dissolve the Union Alleged to Have Existed in That State.* Boston: Boston Daily Advertiser, 1829.

2675. Adams, John Q. "Correspondence of John Quincy Adams, 1811-1814." Edited by Charles F. Adams. *American Antiquarian Society Proceedings* 23 (April 1913): 110-169.

2676. Adams, John Q. *Dermot MacMorrogh, Or The Conquest of Ireland: An Historical Tale of the Twelfth Century, In Four Cantos.* Boston: Carter, Hendee, 1832.

2677. Adams, John Q. *Diary of John Quincy Adams.* 2 vols. Edited by David G.

Allen. Cambridge, MA: Harvard University Press, 1981-1982.

2678. Adams, John Q. *Diary of John Quincy Adams, 1794-1845: American Diplomacy and Political, Social, and Intellectual Life from Washington to Polk.* Edited by Allan Nevins. New York: Scribner's, 1951.

2679. Adams, John Q. *A Discourse on Education, Delivered at Braintree, Thursday, Oct. 24, 1839.* Boston: Perkins and Marvin, 1840.

2680. Adams, John Q. *The Duplicate Letters, the Fisheries, and the Mississippi, Documents Relating to the Transactions at the Negotiation of Ghent.* Washington, DC: Davis and Force, 1822.

2681. Adams, John Q. *An Eulogy: On the Life and Character of James Monroe, Fifth President of the United States.* Boston: J. H. Eastburn, 1831.

2682. Adams, John Q. *An Inaugural Oration, Delivered at the Author's Installation, As Boylston's Professor of Rhetorick and Oratory, At Harvard University, In Cambridge, Massachusetts, On Thursday, 12 June, 1806.* Boston: Monroe and Francis, 1806.

2683. Adams, John Q. *The Jubilee of the Constitution, A Discourse Delivered at the Request of the New York Historical Society.* New York: S. Colman, 1839.

2684. Adams, John Q. *Lectures on Rhetoric and Oratory, Delivered to the Classes of Senior and Junior Sophisters in Harvard University.* 2 vols. Cambridge, MA: Hilliard and Metcalf, 1810.

2685. Adams, John Q. *A Letter to the Hon. Harrison Gray Otis, A Member of the Senate of Massachusetts, On the Present State of Our National Affairs: With Remarks on Mr. Pickering's Letter to the Governor of the Commonwealth.* Boston: Oliver and Munroe, 1808.

2686. Adams, John Q. *Letters and Address on Freemasonry.* Dayton, OH: United Brethren Publishing House, 1875.

2687. Adams, John Q. *Letters from John Quincy Adams to His Constituents of the Twelfth Congressional District in Massachusetts, To Which Is Added His Speech in Congress Delivered February 9, 1837.* Boston: J. Knapp, 1837.

2688. Adams, John Q. "Letters of John Quincy Adams to Alexander Everett, 1811-1837." *American Historical Review* 11 (October 1905): 88-116; (January 1906): 332-354.

2689. Adams, John Q. *Letters of John Quincy Adams to His Son, On the Bible and Its Teachings.* Auburn, MA: J. M. Alden, 1850.

2690. Adams, John Q. *Letters on Silesia: Written during a Tour through That Country in the Years 1800-1801.* London: J. Budd, 1804.

2691. Adams, John Q. *Letters on the Masonic Institution.* Boston: T. R. Marvin, 1847.

2692. Adams, John Q. *Life in a New England Town: 1787, 1788, Diary of John Quincy Adams While a Student in the Office of Theophilus Parsons at Newburyport.* Boston: Little, Brown, 1903.

2693. Adams, John Q. *Lives of Celebrated Statesmen.* New York: W. H. Graham, 1846.

2694. Adams, John Q. *The Lives of James Madison and James Monroe.* Buffalo, NY: G. H. Derby, 1850.

2695. Adams, John Q. *Memoirs of John Quincy Adams, Comprising Portions of His Diary from 1795-1848.* 12 vols. Edited by Charles F. Adams. Philadelphia: Lippincott, 1847-1877.

2696. Adams, John Q. *The New England Confederacy of MDCXLIII: A Discourse*

Delivered before the Massachusetts Historical Society, At Boston, On the 29th of May, 1843: In Celebration of the Second Centennial Anniversary of That Event. Boston: Little, Brown, 1843.

2697. Adams, John Q. *An Oration Delivered before the Cincinnati Astronomical Society, On the Occasion of Laying the Corner Stone of an Astronomical Observatory, On the 10th of November, 1843.* Cincinnati, OH: Shepard, 1843.

2698. Adams, John Q. *An Oration Delivered before the Inhabitants of the Town of Newburyport, At Their Request, On the Sixty-first Anniversary of the Declaration of Independence, July 4th, 1837.* Newburyport, MA: Morse and Brewster, 1837.

2699. Adams, John Q. *Oration on the Life and Character of Gibert Motier de Lafayette: Delivered at the Request of Both Houses of the Congress of the United States . . . on the 31th of December, 1834.* Washington, DC: Green, 1835.

2700. Adams, John Q. *Parties in the United States.* New York: Greenberg, 1941.

2701. Adams, John Q. *Poems of Religion and Society, With Notices of His Life and Character by John Davis and T. H. Benton.* New York: W. H. Graham, 1850.

2702. Adams, John Q. *Report upon Weights and Measures.* Washington, DC: Gales and Seaton, 1821.

2703. Adams, John Q. *The Selected Writings of John and John Quincy Adams.* Edited by Adrienne Koch and William Peden. New York: Knopf, 1946.

2704. Adams, John Q. *The Social Compact, Exemplified in the Constitution of the Commonwealth of Massachusetts: With Remarks on the Theories of Divine Right of Hobbes and of Filmer, and the Counter Theories of Sidney, Lock, Montesquieu, and Rousseau. . .: A Lecture, Delivered before the Franklin Lyceum, At Providence, R. I., November 25, 1842.* Providence, RI: Knowles and Vose, 1842.

2705. Adams, John Q. "Ten Unpublished Letters of John Quincy Adams, 1796-1837." Edited by Edward H. Tatum, Jr. *Huntington Library Quarterly* 4 (April 1941): 369-388.

2706. Adams, John Q. *Upon the Right of the People, Men, and Women, to Petition.* Salem, NY: Ayer, 1969.

2707. Adams, John Q. *Writings of John Quincy Adams.* 7 vols. Edited by Worthington C. Ford. New York: Macmillan, 1913-1917.

2708. Adams, John Q., and Lewis Condict. *Report of the Minority of the Committee on Manufactures, Submitted to the House of Representatives of the United States, February 28, 1833.* Boston: J. H. Eastburn, 1833.

2709. Allen, David G., et al., eds. *Diary of John Quincy Adams: November 1779-December 1788.* 2 vols. Cambridge, MA: Harvard University Press, 1981.

2710. LaFeber, Walter F., ed. *John Quincy Adams and American Continental Empire: Letters, Papers, and Speeches.* Chicago: Quadrangle Books, 1965.

2711. McLaughlin, Andrew C., ed. "Letters of John Quincy Adams to Alexander Hamilton Everett, 1811-1837, I." *American Historical Review* 11 (October 1905): 88-116.

Andrew Jackson

Biographies

2712. Bassett, John S. *The Life of Andrew Jackson*. Rev. ed. New York: Macmillan, 1928.

2713. Brady, Cyrus T. *The True Andrew Jackson*. Philadelphia: Lippincott, 1906.

2714. Brown, William G. *Andrew Jackson*. Boston: Houghton Mifflin, 1900.

2715. Buell, Augustus C. *History of Andrew Jackson: Pioneer, Patriot, Soldier, Politician, President*. 2 vols. New York: Scribner's, 1904.

2716. Chidsey, Donald B. *Andrew Jackson: Hero*. Nashville TN: T. Nelson, 1976.

2717. Cobbett, William. *The Life of Andrew Jackson, President of the USA*. Baltimore, MD: J. Robinson, 1834.

2718. Coit, Margaret L. *Andrew Jackson*. Boston: Houghton Mifflin, 1965.

2719. Colyar, Arthur S. *Life and Times of Andrew Jackson, Soldier, Statesman, President*. Nashville, TN: Marshall and Bruce, 1904.

2720. Craven, Bruce. "The Life and Times of Andrew Jackson." *Watson's Jeffersonian Magazine* 4 (January 1906): 23-24; (February 1906): 113-123; (March 1906): 207-213; (April 1906): 287-300; (May 1906): 376-382.

2721. Davis, Burke. *Old Hickory: A Life of Andrew Jackson*. New York: Dial, 1977.

2722. Downing, Jack. *The Life of Andrew Jackson*. Philadephia: T. K. Greenbank, 1834.

2723. Dyer, Oliver. *General Andrew Jackson*. New York: R. Bonner's Sons, 1891.

2724. Eaton, John H. *The Complete Memoirs of Andrew Jackson*. New York: n.p., 1878.

2725. Eaton, John H. *The Life of Andrew Jackson, Major General in the Service of the United States*. Philadelphia: Samuel F. Bradford, 1824.

2726. Eaton, John H. *The Life of Major General Andrew Jackson: Comprising a History of the War in the South.... Addenda: Containing a Brief History of the Seminole War and Cession and Government of Florida*. 3d ed. Philadelphia: McCarty and Davis, 1828.

2727. Eaton, John H. *Memoirs of Andrew Jackson, Late Major-General and Commander in Chief of the Southern Division of the Army of the United States*. Boston: Charles Ever, 1828.

2728. Frost, John. *Old Hickory*. New York: C T. Dillingham, 1887.

2729. Frost, John. *Pictorial Life of Andrew Jackson*. Philadelphia: M. Bomberger, 1847.

2730. Goodwin, Philo A. *Biography of Andrew Jackson, President of the United States, Formerly Major General in the Army of the United States.* Hartford, CT: Clapp and Benton, 1832.

2731. Headley, Joel T. *The Lives of Winfield Scott and Andrew Jackson.* New York: Scribner's, 1852.

2732. Heiskell, Samuel G. *Andrew Jackson and Early Tennessee History.* 2d ed. 3 vols. Nashville, TN: Ambrose Printing Co., 1920-1921.

2733. Herd, Elmer D., Jr. *Andrew Jackson, South Carolinian: A Study of the Enigma of His Birth.* Lancaster, SC: Lancaster County Historical Commission, 1963.

2734. Hill, Isaac. *Brief Sketch of the Life, Character, and Services of Major General Andrew Jackson.* Concord, MA: Manahan, Hoag, 1828.

2735. James, Marquis. *Andrew Jackson, Portrait of a President.* Indianapolis, IN: Bobbs-Merrill, 1937.

2736. James, Marquis. *Andrew Jackson: The Border Captain.* Indianapolis, IN: Bobbs-Merrill, 1933.

2737. James, Marquis. *The Life of Andrew Jackson, Complete in One Volume.* Indianapolis, IN: Bobbs-Merrill, 1938.

2738. Jenkins, John S. *Jackson and the Generals of the War of 1812.* Philadelphia: J. B. Smith, 1856.

2739. Jenkins, John S. *Life and Public Services of Gen. Andrew Jackson.* Buffalo, NY: G. H. Derby, 1852.

2740. Jenkins, John S. *The Life of Gen. Andrew Jackson.* Buffalo, NY: Derby and Hewson, 1847.

2741. Johnson, Gerald W. *Andrew Jackson: An Epic in Homespun.* New York: Minton, Balch, 1927.

2742. Judson, Clara I. *Andrew Jackson, Frontier Statesman.* Chicago: Follett, 1954.

2743. Karsner, David. *Andrew Jackson, The Gentle Savage.* New York: Brentano's, 1929.

2744. Lewis, Alfred H. "The Story of Andrew Jackson." *Cosmopolitan* 41 (June 1906): 143-150; (July 1906): 290-296; (August 1906): 415-422; (September 1906): 488-495; (October 1906): 655-662; 42 (November 1906): 61-68; (December 1906): 208-213; (January 1907): 340-346; (February 1907): 441-447; (March 1907): 551-557; (April 1907): 661-666; 43 (May 1907): 84-88.

2745. Lewis, Alfred H. *When Men Grew Tall: Or, The Story of Andrew Jackson.* New York: Appleton, 1907.

2746. Lindsey, David. *Andrew Jackson and John C. Calhoun.* Woodbury, NY: Barron's Educational Series, 1973.

2747. Myers, Elisabeth P. *Andrew Jackson.* Chicago: Reilly and Lee, 1970.

2748. Nolan, Jeannette C. *Andrew Jackson.* New York: Messner, 1961.

2749. Parton, James. *General Jackson.* New York: Appleton, 1893.

2750. Parton, James. *Life of Andrew Jackson.* 3 vols. New York: Mason Brothers, 1860.

2751. *Reflections on the Character and Public Services of Andrew Jackson . . . by a Native American.* New York: George F. Hopkins, 1828.

2752. Reid, John, and John H. Eaton. *The Life of Andrew Jackson.* Edited by Frank L. Owsley, Jr. University: University of Alabama Press, 1974.

2753. Remini, Robert V. *Andrew Jackson.* New York: Harper and Row, 1969.

2754. Remini, Robert V. *Andrew Jackson*

and the Course of American Democracy, 1833-1845. New York: Harper and Row, 1984.

2755. Remini, Robert V. *Andrew Jackson and the Course of American Empire, 1767-1821*. New York: Harper and Row, 1977.

2756. Remini, Robert V. *Andrew Jackson and the Course of American Freedom: 1822-1832*. New York: Harper and Row, 1981.

2757. Schlesinger, Arthur M., Jr. *The Age of Jackson*. Boston: Little, Brown, 1945.

2758. Sellers, Charles G., Jr., comp. *Andrew Jackson, A Profile*. New York: Hill and Wang, 1971.

2759. Smyth, Clifford. *Andrew Jackson, The Man Who Preserved Union and Democracy*. New York: Funk and Wagnalls, 1931.

2760. Snelling, William J. *A Brief and Impartial History of the Life and Actions of Andrew Jackson, President of the United States . . . by a Free Man*. Boston: Stimpson and Clapp, 1831.

2761. Stevenson, Augusta. *Andy Jackson, Boy Soldier*. Indianapolis, IN: Bobbs-Merrill, 1962.

2762. Sumner, William G. *Andrew Jackson*. Rev. ed. Boston: Houghton Mifflin, 1900.

2763. Waldo, Samuel P. *Civil and Military History of Andrew Jackson, Late Major-General in the Army of the United States, Commander in Chief of the Southern Division*. New York: P. M. Davis, 1825.

2764. Waldo, Samuel P. *Memoirs of Andrew Jackson*. Hartford, CT: Silas Andrus, 1819.

2765. Walsh, Robert. *Biographical Sketch of the Life of Andrew Jackson, Major-General of the Armies of the United States, the Hero of New Orleans. . . .* Hudson: William E. Norman, 1828.

2766. Watson, Thomas E. "The Life and Times of Andrew Jackson." *Watson's Jeffersonian Magazine* 3 (April 1906): 278-285; (May 1906): 357-367; (June 1906): 460-467; (July 1906): 548-558; (September 1906): 630-635; (October 1906): 721-724; (November 1906): 801-806, 887-893.

2767. Watson, Thomas E. *The Life and Times of Andrew Jackson*. Thomson, GA: Press of the Jeffersonian Publishing Co., 1912.

2768. Wright, Frances F. *Andrew Jackson Fighting Frontiersman*. New York: Abingdon Press, 1958.

2769. Yarbrough, Edward. *Old Hickory, A Biography of Andrew Jackson*. Tyler, TX: n.p., 1953.

Private Life

2770. Brent, Robert A. "Nicholas Philip Trist — A Link between Jefferson and Jackson?" *Southern Quarterly* 1 (October 1962): 87-97.

2771. Burke, Pauline W. *Emily Donelson of Tennessee*. 2 vols. Richmond, VA: Garrett and Massie, 1941.

2772. Cabral, Peter C. "United States vs. Major General Andrew Jackson." *Loyola University of Los Angeles Law Review* 7 (July 1926): 133-144.

2773. Caldwell, Joshua W. "Last Days of Andrew Jackson." In *Joshua William Caldwell: A Memorial Volume, Containing His Biography, Writings, and Addresses*, 153-162. Nashville, TN: Brandon Printing Co., 1909.

2774. Caldwell, Mary F. *Andrew Jackson's Hermitage*. Nashville, TN: Ladies' Hermitage Association, 1933.

2775. Caldwell, Mary F. *General Jack-*

son's Lady: A Story of the Life and Times of Rachel Donelson Jackson, Beloved Wife of General Andrew Jackson, Seventh President of the United States.* Nashville, TN: Kingsport Press, 1936.

2776. Campbell, Mrs. A. A. "Andrew Jackson." *Confederate Veteran* 28 (May 1920): 166-167.

2777. Canfield, Frederick A. "The Figurehead of Jackson." *Tennessee Historical Magazine* 8 (July 1924): 144-145.

2778. Clark, Thomas D. "The Jackson Purchase: A Dramatic Chapter in Southern Indiana Policy and Relations." *Filson Club Historical Quarterly* 50 (July 1976): 302-320.

2779. Cohalan, Daniel F. "Andrew Jackson." *American Irish Historical Society* 28 (1930): 173-187.

2780. Craven, Bruce. "The Life and Times of Andrew Jackson." *Watson's Jeffersonian Magazine* 4 (January 1908): 23-24; (February 1908): 113-123; (March 1908): 207-213; (April 1908): 287-300; (May 1908): 376-382.

2781. Craven, Bruce. "The Truth about Jackson's Birthplace." *North Carolina Booklet* 9 (April 1910): 232-235.

2782. Cubberly, Frederick. "Andrew Jackson, Judge." *American Law Review* 56 (September/October 1922): 686-701.

2783. Davis, Andrew M. "Jackson's LL.D. — A Tempest in a Teapot." *Massachusetts Historical Society Proceedings* 20 (December 1906): 490-512.

2784. Davis, Andrew M. "A Tempest in a Teapot: Jackson's 'LL.D.'" *Tennessee Historical Magazine* 8 (October 1924): 191-210.

2785. Delzell, Earl B. "Andrew Jackson." *Grand Lodge Bulletin* 31 (October 1930): 694-703.

2786. Deutsch, Eberhard P. "The United States versus Major General Andrew Jackson." *American Bar Association Journal* 46 (September 1960): 966-972.

2787. DeWitt, John H., Jr. "Andrew Jackson and His Ward, Andrew Jackson Hutchings: A History Hitherto Unpublished." *Tennessee Historical Magazine* 1 (January 1931): 83-106.

2788. Didier, Eugene L. "Andrew Jackson as a Lawyer." *Green Bag* 15 (August 1903): 349-356.

2789. Dodd, William E. "Andrew Jackson and His Enemies, and the Great Noise They Made in the World." *Century Magazine* 111 (April 1926): 734-745.

2790. Dodd, William E. "The Making of Andrew Jackson: All Things Worked Together for Good to Old Hickory." *Century Magazine* 111 (March 1926): 531-538.

2791. Dorris, Mary C. *The Hermitage, Home of General Andrew Jackson.* Nashville TN: Brandon Printing Co., 1913.

2792. Doughty, Francis W. "Medallic History of Andrew Jackson." *Numismatist* 73 (October 1960): 1459-1460.

2793. Ely, James W., Jr. "Andrew Jackson as Tennessee State Court Judge, 1798-1804." *Tennessee Historical Quarterly* 40 (Summer 1981): 144-157.

2794. Ely, James W., Jr. "The Legal Practice of Andrew Jackson." *Tennessee Historical Quarterly* 38 (Winter 1979): 421-435.

2795. Eriksson, Erik M. "Andrew Jackson, The Man and Mason." *Builder* 11 (June 1925): 164-165; (July 1925): 206-207.

2796. Farrell, Brian. "Bellona and the General: Andrew Jackson and the Affair of Mrs. Eaton." *History Today* 7 (July 1958): 474-484.

2797. Faust, Richard H. "Another Look at General Jackson and the Indians of the

Mississippi Territory." *Alabama Review* 28 (July 1975): 202-217.

2798. Fox-Genovese, Elizabeth. "Psychohistory vs. Psychodeterminism: The Case of Rogin's Jackson." *Reviews in American History* 3 (December 1975): 407-418.

2799. Galloway, Linda B. "Andrew Jackson, Junior." *Tennessee Historical Quarterly* 9 (September 1950): 195-216; (December 1950): 306-343.

2800. Gerry, Margarita S. "The Real Andrew Jackson." *Century Magazine* 115 (November 1927): 54-64; (December 1927): 218-230.

2801. Goff, Reda C. "A Physical Profile of Andrew Jackson." *Tennessee Historical Quarterly* 28 (Fall 1969): 297-309.

2802. Green, John W. "Judges Overton, Jackson, and White." *Tennessee Law Review* 18 (1944): 413-427.

2803. Hay, Robert P. "The Case for Andrew Jackson in 1824: Eaton's 'Wyoming Letters.'" *Tennessee Historical Quarterly* 29 (Summer 1970): 139-157.

2804. Hay, Robert P. "And Ten Dollars Extra, For Every Hundred Lashes Any Person Will Give Him, To the Amount of Three Hundred: A Note on Andrew Jackson's Runaway Slave Ad of 1804 and on the Historian's Use of Evidence." *Tennessee Historical Quarterly* 36 (Winter 1977): 468-478.

2805. Hickey, Donald R. "Andrew Jackson and the Army Haircut: Individual Rights vs. Military Discipline." *Tennessee Historical Quarterly* 35 (Winter 1976): 365-375.

2806. Hoogenboom, Ari, and Olive Hoogenboom. "Francis Preston Blair and the Image of Andrew Jackson." *Reviews in American History* 9 (March 1981): 76-81.

2807. Horn, Stanley F. *The Hermitage, Home of Old Hickory*. Richmond, VA: Garret and Massie, 1938.

2808. Ladies' Hermitage Association. *The Historic Hermitage Properties*. Hermitage, TN: The Association, 1972.

2809. Lionberger, I. H. "Andrew Jackson, Lawyer." *St. Louis Law Review* 5 (1920): 72-79.

2810. Mellen, George F. "Sidelights on Andrew Jackson." *Methodist Quarterly Review* 67 (July 1918): 494-505.

2811. Mott, David C. "Iowa Territory and General Jackson's Fire." *Annals of Iowa* 16 (July 1927): 58-64.

2812. "Presidential Lawyers: Judge Andrew Jackson." *American Law Review* 31 (July/August 1897): 601-607.

2813. Prucha, Francis P. "General Jackson, Expansionist." *Reviews in American History* 6 (September 1978): 331-336.

2814. Purdy, Virginia C. "Your Zealous Friend, Andrew Jackson." *Prologue* 1 (Winter 1969): 36-37.

2815. Quinn, Yancey M., Jr. "Jackson's Military Road." *Journal of Mississippi History* 41 (1979): 335-350.

2816. Quitt, Martin H. "Jackson, Indians, and Psychohistory: Review Essay." *History of Childhood Quarterly* 3 (Spring 1976): 543-551.

2817. Read, Allen W. "Could Andrew Jackson Spell?" *American Speech* 38 (October 1963): 188-195.

2818. Remini, Robert V. "The Final Days and Hours in the Life of General Andrew Jackson." *Tennessee Historical Quarterly* 39 (Summer 1980): 167-177.

2819. Revill, Janie. *President Andrew Jackson's Birthplace, As Found by Janie Revill*. Columbia, SC: n.p., 1966.

2820. Robbins, Peggy. "Andrew and Rachel Jackson." *American History Illustrated* 12 (August 1977): 22-28.

2821. Sellers, Charles G., Jr. "Andrew

Jackson versus the Historians." *Mississippi Valley Historical Review* 44 (March 1958): 615-634.

2822. Sellers, Charles G., Jr. "Jackson Men with Feet of Clay." *American Historical Review* 62 (April 1957): 537-551.

2823. Smith, Graeme M. "Fearless Fighters and Learning People: Andrew Jackson and Rachel Donelson Jackson as Revealed by Their Ancestors." *National Historical Magazine* 73 (September 1939): 60-61.

2824. Sprague, Lynn T. " 'Old Hickory' and His Indian Campaigns." *Outing: An Illustrative Monthly Magazine of Recreation* 49 (November 1906): 223-231.

2825. Stickley, Julia W. "Catholic Ceremonies in the White House, 1832-1833: Andrew Jackson's Forgotten Ward, Mary Lewis." *Catholic Historical Review* 51 (July 1965): 192-198.

2826. Walker, Arda S. "Andrew Jackson: Planter." *East Tennessee Historical Society's Publications* 18 (1946): 59-86.

2827. Walker, Arda S. "The Educational Training and Views of Andrew Jackson." *East Tennessee Historical Society's Publications* 16 (1944): 22-29.

2828. Walker, Arda S. "The Religious Views of Andrew Jackson." *East Tennessee Historical Society's Publications* 17 (1945): 61-70.

Public Career

2829. Abernethy, Thomas P. "Andrew Jackson and the Rise of Southwestern Democracy." *American Historical Review* 33 (October 1927): 64-77.

2830. "Andrew Jackson and Edward Livingston." *American Law Review* 31 (September/October 1897): 767-773.

2831. Ashford, Gerald. "Jacksonian Liberalism and Spanish Law in Early Texas." *Southwestern Historical Quarterly* 57 (July 1953): 1-37.

2832. Bassett, John S. "Major Lewis on the Nomination of Andrew Jackson." *American Antiquarian Society Proceedings* 33 (April 1923): 12-33.

2833. Benson, Lee. *Concept of Jacksonian Democracy*. New York: Atheneum, 1964.

2834. Binder, Frederick M. "The Color Problem in Early National America as Viewed by John Adams, Jefferson, and Jackson." Ed.D. dissertation, Columbia University, 1962.

2835. Blau, Joseph L., ed. *Social Theories of Jacksonian Democracy, 1825-1850: Representative Writings of the Period, 1825-1850*. Indianapolis, IN: Bobbs-Merrill, 1954.

2836. Bowers, Claude G. *The Party Battles of the Jackson Period*. Boston: Houghton Mifflin, 1922.

2837. Bonner, James C., ed. "Andrew Jackson Comments on Polk's Cabinet." *Tennessee Historical Quarterly* 27 (Fall 1968): 287-288.

2838. Brasington, George F., Jr. "Representative Government in Jacksonian Political Thought." Ph.D. dissertation, University of Illinois, 1958.

2839. Brent, Robert A. "The Triumph of Jacksonian Democracy in the United States." *Southern Quarterly* 7 (October 1968): 43-57.

2840. Brown, Richard H. *The Hero and the People: The Meaning of Jacksonian Democracy*. New York: Macmillan, 1964.

2841. Brown, Richard H. "The Missouri Crisis, Slavery, and the Politics of Jacksonianism." *South Atlantic Quarterly* 65 (Winter 1966): 55-72.

2842. Bugg, James L., Jr., and Peter C. Stewart, eds. *Jacksonian Democracy: Myth* or *Reality?* 2d ed. New York: Praeger, 1976.

2843. Burke, John E. "Andrew Jackson as Seen by Foreigners." *Tennessee Historical Quarterly* 10 (March 1951): 25-45.

2844. Cain, Marvin R. "William Wirt against Andrew Jackson: Reflection on an Era." *Mid-America* 47 (April 1965): 113-138.

2845. Cave, Alfred A. *Jacksonian Democracy and the Historians*. Gainesville: University of Florida Press, 1964.

2846. Chase, James S. "Jacksonian Democracy and the Rise of the Nominating Convention." *Mid-America* 45 (October 1963): 229-249.

2847. Curtis, James C. *Andrew Jackson and the Search for Vindication*. Boston: Little, Brown, 1976.

2848. Doherty, Herbert J., Jr. "The Governorship of Andrew Jackson." *Florida Historical Quarterly* 33 (July 1954): 3-31.

2849. Doherty, Herbert J., Jr., ed. "Andrew Jackson and Manhood Suffrage." *Tennessee Historical Quarterly* 15 (March 1956): 57-60.

2850. Dunlap, John R. *Jeffersonian Democracy, Which Means the Democracy of Thomas Jefferson, Andrew Jackson, and Abraham Lincoln*. New York: Jeffersonian Society, 1903.

2851. Eaton, Clement, ed. *The Leaven of Democracy: The Growth of the Democratic Spirit in the Time of Jackson*. New York: Braziller, 1963.

2852. Fellman, Michael. "The Earthbound Eagle: Andrew Jackson and the American Pantheon." *American Studies* 12 (Fall 1971): 67-76.

2853. Forsythe, Robert S. "Andrew Jackson Signed a Testimonial." *University of North Dakota Journal* 20 (March 1930): 104-106.

2854. Hay, Robert P. "John Fitzgerald: Presidential Image-Maker for Andrew Jackson in 1823." *Tennessee Historical Quarterly* 42 (Summer 1983): 138-150.

2855. Hellegers, John F. "Some Bases of Early Pro-Jackson Sentiment in Western Pennsylvania." *Western Pennsylvania Historical Magazine* 45 (March 1962): 31-46.

2856. Hoffman, William S. *Andrew Jackson and North Carolina Politics*. Chapel Hill: University of North Carolina Press, 1958.

2857. Hofstadter, Richard. "Andrew Jackson and the Rise of Liberal Capitalism." In his *The American Political Tradition and the Men Who Made It*, 44-66. New York: Knopf, 1948.

2858. Jackson, Carlton L. "The Internal Improvement Vetoes of Andrew Jackson." *Tennessee Historical Quarterly* 25 (Fall 1966): 261-180.

2859. Klingberg, Frank J. "The Americanism of Andrew Jackson." *South Atlantic Quarterly* 21 (April 1922): 127-143.

2860. Latner, Richard B. "The Nullification Crisis and Republican Subversion." *Journal of Southern History* 43 (February 1977): 19-38.

2861. Lebowitz, Michael A. "The Jacksonians: Paradox Lost?" In *Towards a New Past: Dissenting Essays in American History*, edited by Barton J. Bernstein, 565-589. New York: Pantheon Books, 1968.

2862. Lowe, Gabriel L. "John H. Eaton, Jackson's Campaign Manager." *Tennessee Historical Quarterly* 11 (June 1952): 99-147.

2863. McCormick, Richard P. *The Second American Party System: Party Formation in the Jacksonian Era*. Chapel Hill: University of North Carolina Press, 1966.

2864. MacDonald, William. *Jacksonian*

Democracy. New York: Harper and Row, 1906.

2865. McFaul, John M. *The Politics of Jacksonian Finance.* Ithaca, NY: Cornell University Press, 1972.

2866. McMahon, Edward J. "Was Jackson a Political Opportunist?" *Social Studies* 46 (February 1955): 49-54.

2867. Malcolm, James. "Jackson Campaign of 1824 Recalled." *State Service* 7 (May 1923): 154-156.

2868. Mayo, Edward L. "Republicanism, Antipartyism, and Jacksonian Party Politics: A View from the Nation's Capital." *American Quarterly* 31 (Spring 1979): 3-20.

2869. Meyers, Marvin. "The Jacksonian Persuasion." *American Quarterly* 5 (Spring 1953): 3-15.

2870. Meyers, Marvin. *The Jacksonian Persuasion: Politics and Belief.* Stanford, CA: Stanford University Press, 1957.

2871. Miles, Edwin A. "Andrew Jackson and Senator George Poindexter." *Journal of Southern History* 24 (February 1958): 51-66.

2872. Miles, Edwin A. *Jacksonian Democracy in Mississippi.* New York: Da Capo Press, 1970.

2873. Miller, Douglas T. *Jacksonian Aristocracy: Class and Democracy in New York, 1830-1860.* New York: Oxford University Press, 1967.

2874. Moody, Robert E. "The Influence of Martin Van Buren on the Career and Acts of Andrew Jackson." *Michigan Academy of Science, Arts and Letters Papers* 7 (1927): 225-240.

2875. Morgan, William G. "John Quincy Adams versus Andrew Jackson: Their Biographers and the 'Corrupt Bargain' Charge." *Tennessee Historical Quarterly* 26 (Spring 1967): 43-58.

2876. Munro, William B. "Jackson and Smith: Two Battling Democrats a Century Apart." *Century Magazine* 66 (October 1928): 641-645.

2877. Neufeld, Maurice F. "The Size of the Jacksonian Labor Movement: A Cautionary Account." *Labor History* 23 (Fall 1982): 599-607.

2878. Parks, Warren B. "United States v. Major General Andrew Jackson." *Case and Comment* 24 (October 1917): 363-366.

2879. Pessen, Edward. "Did Labor Support Jackson? The Boston Story." *Political Science Quarterly* 64 (June 1949): 262-274.

2880. Pessen, Edward. *Jacksonian America: Society, Personality, and Politics.* Rev. ed. Homewood, IL: Dorsey Press, 1978.

2881. Pessen, Edward. *Most Uncommon Jacksonians: The Radical Leaders of the Early Labor Movement.* Albany: State University of New York Press, 1967.

2882. Pessen, Edward. *New Perspectives on Jacksonian Parties and Politics.* Boston: Allyn and Bacon, 1969.

2883. Pessen, Edward. "Should Labor Have Supported Jackson? Or Questions the Quantitative Studies Do Not Answer." *Labor History* 13 (Summer 1972): 427-437.

2884. Pessen, Edward. "Society and Politics in the Jacksonian Era." *Kentucky Historical Society Register* 82 (Winter 1984): 1-27.

2885. Pessen, Edward. "The Working Men's Movement of the Jacksonian Era." *Mississippi Valley Historical Review* 43 (December 1956): 428-443.

2886. Pessen, Edward, ed. *The Many-Faceted Jacksonian Era: New Interpretations.* Westport, CT: Greenwood Press, 1977.

2887. Phillips, Kim T. "The Pennsylvania Origins of the Jackson Movement." *Political Science Quarterly* 91 (Fall 1976): 489-508.

2888. Prucha, Francis P. "Andrew Jackson's Indian Policy: A Reassessment." *Journal of American History* 56 (December 1969): 529-539.

2889. Remini, Robert V. *The Age of Jackson.* Columbia: University of South Carolina Press, 1972.

2890. Richards, Leonard L. "The Jacksonians and Slavery." In *Antislavery Reconsidered: New Perspectives on the Abolitionists,* edited by Lewis Perry and Michael Fellman, 99-118. Baton Rouge: Louisiana State University Press, 1979.

2891. Rowland, Eron O. *Andrew Jackson's Campaign against the British, Or The Mississippi Territory in the War of 1812, Concerning the Military Operations of the Americans, Creek Indians, British, and Spanish, 1813-1815.* New York: Macmillan, 1926.

2892. Rozwenc, Edwin C., ed. *Ideology and Power in the Age of Jackson.* New York: New York University Press, 1964.

2893. Rozwenc, Edwin C., ed. *The Meaning of Jacksonian Democracy.* Boston: Heath, 1963.

2894. Satz, Ronald N. *American Indian Policy in the Jacksonian Era.* Lincoln: University of Nebraska Press, 1974.

2895. Satz, Ronald N. "Remini's Andrew Jackson (1767-1821): Jackson and the Indians." *Tennessee Historical Quarterly* 38 (Summer 1979): 158-166.

2896. Sellers, Charles G., Jr. *Jacksonian Democracy.* Washington, DC: American Historical Association, 1958.

2897. Shalhope, Robert E. "Republicanism and Early American Historiography." *William and Mary Quarterly* 39 (April 1982): 334-356.

2898. Singletary, Michael W. "The New Editorial Voice for Andrew Jackson: Happenstance or Plan?" *Journalism Quarterly* 53 (Winters 1976): 672-678.

2899. Smith, Culver H. "Propaganda Technique in the Jackson Campaign of 1828." *East Tennessee Historical Society's Publications* 6 (1934): 44-66.

2900. Smith, Elbert B. "Francis P. Blair and the GLOBE: Nerve Center of the Jacksonian Democracy." *Kentucky Historical Society Register* 57 (October 1957): 340-353.

2901. Somit, Albert. "Andrew Jackson as Political Theorist." *Tennessee Historical Quarterly* 8 (June 1949): 99-126.

2902. Somit, Albert. "Andrew Jackson: Legend and Reality." *Tennessee Historical Quarterly* 7 (December 1948): 291-313.

2903. Somit, Albert. "The Political and Administrative Ideas of Andrew Jackson." Ph.D. dissertation, University of Chicago, 1947.

2904. Stark, Cruce. "The Historical Irrelevance of Heroes: Henry Adam's Andrew Jackson." *American Literature* 46 (May 1974): 170-181.

2905. Steiner, Bernard C. "Jackson and the Missionaries." *American Historical Review* 29 (July 1924): 722-723.

2906. Stenberg, Richard R. "Jackson, Anthony Butler, and Texas." *Southwestern Social Science Quarterly* 13 (December 1932): 264-287.

2907. Stenberg, Richard R. "Jackson, Buchanan, and the 'Corrupt Bargain' Calumny." *Pennsylvania Magazine of History and Biography* 58 (1934): 61-85.

2908. Stenberg, Richard R. "Jackson's 'Rhea Letter' Hoax." *Journal of Southern History* 2 (November 1936): 480-496.

2909. Stenberg, Richard R. "The Texas Schemes of Jackson and Houston." *South-*

western *Social Science Quarterly* 15 (December 1934): 229-250.

2910. Stevens, Harry R. *The Early Jackson Party in Ohio*. Durham, NC: Duke University Press, 1957.

2911. Sullivan, John L. "The Case of 'A Late Student': Pictorial Satire in Jacksonian America." *American Antiquarian Society Proceedings* 83 (October 1973): 277-286.

2912. Sullivan, John L. "Jackson Caricatured: Two Historical Errors." *Tennessee Historical Quarterly* 31 (Spring 1972): 39-34.

2913. Sullivan, John L. "Politics and Personality: The Development of the Counter-Image of Andrew Jackson." Ph.D. dissertation, Indiana University, 1970.

2914. Sullivan, William A. "Did Labor Support Andrew Jackson?" *Political Science Quarterly* 62 (December 1947): 579-580.

2915. Syrett, Harold C., ed. *Andrew Jackson: His Contribution to the American Tradition*. Indianapolis, IN: Bobbs-Merrill, 1953.

2916. Temin, Peter, *Jacksonian Economy*. New York: Norton, 1969.

2917. Thompson, Arthur W. *Jacksonian Democracy on the Florida Frontier*. Gainesville: University Press of Florida, 1961.

2918. Tilly, Bette B. "The Jackson-Dinsmoor Feud: A Paradox in a Minor Key." *Journal of Mississippi History* 39 (May 1977): 117-131.

2919. Tregle, Joseph G. "Andrew Jackson and the Continuing Battle of New Orleans." *Journal of the Early Republic* 1 (Winter 1981): 373-393.

2920. "The Triumph of Jacksonian Democracy in the United States." *Southern Quarterly* 7 (October 1966): 43-57.

2921. Van Deusen, Glyndon G. *The Rise and Decline of Jacksonian Democracy*. Melbourne, FL: Krieger, 1979.

2922. Van Deusen, Glyndon G. "Some Aspects of Whig Thought and Theory in the Jacksonian Period." *American Historical Review* 63 (January 1958): 305-322.

2923. Walker, Alexander. *Jackson and New Orleans, An Authentic Narrative of the Memorable Achievements of the American Army, Under Andrew Jackson, Before New Orleans, In the Winter of 1814, 1815*. New York: J. C. Derby, 1856.

2924. Walker, Arda S. "Andrew Jackson: Frontier Democrat." *East Tennessee Historical Society's Publications* 18 (1946): 59-86.

2925. Ward, John W. *Andrew Jackson, Symbol for an Age*. New York: Oxford University Press, 1962.

2926. Wason, James R. "Labor and Politics in Washington in the Early Jacksonian Era." Ph.D. dissertation, American University, 1964.

2927. Watson, Harry L. *Jacksonian Politics and Community Conflict: The Emergence of the Second American Party System in Cumberland County, North Carolina*. Baton Rouge: Louisiana State University Press, 1981.

2928. Wert, Jeffry D. "Old Hickory and the Seminoles." *American History Illustrated* 15 (October 1980): 28-35.

2929. Wilson, Major L. "Andrew Jackson: The Great Compromiser." *Tennessee Historical Quarterly* 26 (Spring 1967): 64-78.

2930. Worner, William F. "Andrew Jackson in Lancaster." *Lancaster County Historical Society Papers* 33 (1929): 83-84.

Presidential Years

2931. Ahl, Frances N. *Andrew Jackson and the Constitution.* Boston: Christopher Publishing House, 1939.

2932. Albjerg, Victor L. "Jackson's Influence on Internal Improvements." *Tennessee Historical Magazine* 2 (July 1932): 259-269.

2933. Aronson, Sidney H. *Status and Kinship in the Higher Civil Service: The Administrations of John Adams, Thomas Jefferson, and Andrew Jackson.* Cambridge, MA: Harvard University Press, 1964.

2934. Baldwin, Joseph G. *Party Leaders: Sketches of Thomas Jefferson, Alexander Hamilton, Andrew Jackson, Henry Clay, John Randolph of Roanoke: Including Notices of Many Other Distinguished American Statesmen.* New York: Appleton, 1855.

2935. Barbee, David R. "Andrew Jackson and Peggy O'Neale." *Tennessee Historical Quarterly* 15 (March 1956): 37-52.

2936. Barker, Eugene C. "President Jackson and the Texas Revolution." *American Historical Review* 12 (July 1907): 788-809.

2937. Bassett, John S. "Notes on Jackson's Visit to New England, June, 1833." *Massachusetts Historical Society Proceedings* 56 (July 1923): 244-260.

2938. Belohlavek, John M. "Andrew Jackson and the Malaysian Pirates: A Question of Diplomacy and Politics." *Tennessee Historical Quarterly* 36 (Spring 1977): 19-29.

2939. Belohlavek, John M. "Assault on the President: The Jackson-Randolph Affair of 1833." *Presidential Studies Quarterly* 12 (Summer 1982): 361-368.

2940. Belohlavek, John M. "Let the Eagle Soar!: Democratic Constraints on the Foreign Policy of Andrew Jackson." *Presidential Studies Quarterly* 10 (Winter 1980): 36-50.

2941. Bergeron, Paul H. "The Jacksonian Party on Trial: Presidential Politics in Tennessee, 1836-1856." Ph.D. dissertation, Vanderbilt University, 1965.

2942. Bergeron, Paul H. "Politics and Patronage in Tennessee during the Adams and Jackson Years." *Prologue* 2 (Spring 1970): 19-24.

2943. Bowers, Claude G. *Making Democracy a Reality: Jefferson, Jackson, and Polk.* Memphis, TN: Memphis State College Press, 1954.

2944. Brasington, George F., Jr. "Jackson, Calhoun, and State Rights." *Emory University Quarterly* 15 (October 1959): 168-175.

2945. Brown, Norman D. "Webster-Jackson Movement for a Constitution and Union Party in 1833." *Mid-America* 46 (July 1964): 147-171.

2946. Bruns, Roger. "Assassination Attempt on President Andrew Jackson." *West Tennessee Historical Society Papers* 31 (1977): 33-43.

2947. Chambers, William N. "Andrew Jackson." In *America's Ten Greatest Presidents,* edited by Morton Borden, 81-112. Chicago: Rand McNally, 1961.

2948. Chroust, Anton-Hermann. "Did President Jackson Actually Threaten the Supreme Court of the United States with the Nonenforcement of Its Injunction against the State of Georgia?" *American Journal of Legal History* 4 (January 1960): 76-78.

2949. Clark, Anna. "Jackson's Administration of Florida." *Florida Historical Society Quarterly* 5 (July 1926): 44-49.

2950. Cook, Richard A. "Andrew Jackson and American Indian Policy." *Denver*

Westerners Roundup 40 (July/August 1984): 3-16.

2951. Cullen, Joseph P. "The People's Day." *American History Illustrated* 14 (May 1979): 30-33.

2952. Curtis, James C. "Andrew Jackson and His Cabinet — Some New Evidence." *Tennessee Historical Quarterly* 27 (Summer 1968): 157-164.

2953. Dahl, Curtis. "The Clergyman, the Hussy, and Old Hickory: Ezra Stiles Ely and the Peggy Eaton Affair." *Journal of the Presbyterian Historical Society* 52 (Summer 1974): 137-155.

2954. DeRosier, Arthur H., Jr. "Andrew Jackson and Negotiations for the Removal of the Choctaw Indians." *History* 29 (May 1967): 343-362.

2955. Downes, Randolph C., ed. "How Andrew Jackson Settled the Ohio-Michigan Boundary Dispute of 1835." *Northwestern Ohio Quarterly* 23 (Autumn 1951): 186-190.

2956. Eriksson, Erik M. "The Federal Civil Service under President Jackson." *Mississippi Valley Historical Review* 13 (March 1927): 517-540.

2957. Eriksson, Erik M. "Official Newspaper Organs and Jackson's Reelection, 1832." *Tennessee Historical Magazine* 9 (April 1925): 37-58.

2958. Eriksson, Erik M. "President Jackson's Propaganda Agencies." *Pacific Historical Review* 6 (1937): 47-57.

2959. Faircloth, Ronald W. "The Impact of Andrew Jackson on Georgia Politics, 1828-1840." Ph.D. dissertation, University of Georgia, 1971.

2960. Feldberg, Michael. *The Turbulent Era: Riot and Disorder in Jacksonian America*. London: Oxford University Press, 1980.

2961. Feller, Daniel. *The Public Lands in Jacksonian Politics*. Madison: University of Wisconsin Press, 1984.

2962. Fish, Carl R. *The Rise of the Common Man, 1830-1850*. New York: Macmillan, 1927.

2963. Fraser, Hugh R. *Democracy in the Making: The Jackson-Tyler Era*. Indianapolis, IN: Bobbs-Merrill, 1938.

2964. Freidel, Frank. "Jackson's Political Removals as Seen by Historians." *Historian* 2 (Winter 1939): 41-52.

2965. Goldberg, M. Hirsh. "Jackson: The Presidential Image Grows Larger." *Times of Israel* 1 (August 1974): 20-25.

2966. Govan, Thomas P. "Fundamental Issues of the Bank War." *Pennsylvania Magazine of History and Biography* 82 (July 1958): 305-315.

2967. Govan, Thomas P. "John M. Berrien and the Administration of Andrew Jackson." *Journal of Southern History* 6 (November 1939): 447-467.

2968. Gragg, Larry. "The Reign of King Mob, 1829." *History Today* 28 (April 1978): 236-241.

2969. Green, Fletcher M. "On Tour with President Andrew Jackson." *New England Quarterly* 36 (June 1963): 209-228.

2970. Hall, Kermit L. "Andrew Jackson and the Judiciary: The Michigan Territorial Judiciary as a Test Case, 1828-1832." *Michigan History* 59 (Fall 1975): 131-151.

2971. Hammond, Bray. "Jackson, Biddle, and the Bank of the United States." *Journal of Economic History* 7 (May 1947): 1-23.

2972. Hammond, Bray. "Jackson's Fight with the 'Money Power': Old Hickory's Attack on Biddle's Bank Had Some Unexpected Consequences." *American Heritage* 7 (June 1956): 8-11, 100-103.

2973. Herbert, William C. "Jackson, the

Bank, and the Press." Ph.D. dissertation, University of Missouri, 1975.

2974. Hoffman, William S. "Andrew Jackson, State Rightist: The Case of the Georgia Indians." *Tennessee Historical Quarterly* 11 (December 1952): 329-345.

2975. Hoogenboom, Ari, and Herbert Ershkowitz. "Levi Woodbury's 'Intimate Memoranda' of the Jackson Administration." *Pennsylvania Magazine of History and Biography* 92 (October 1968): 507-515.

2976. Hugins, Walter E. *Jacksonian Democracy and the Working Class: A Study of the New York Workingmen's Movement, 1829-1937*. Stanford, CA: Stanford University Press, 1960.

2977. Hummel, Jeffrey R. "The Jacksonians, Banking, and Economic Theory: A Reinterpretation." *Journal of Libertarian Studies* 2 (Summer 1978): 151-165.

2978. Jackson, Carlton L. "Another Time, Another Place: The Attempted Assassination of Andrew Jackson." *Tennessee Historical Quarterly* 26 (Summer 1967): 184-190.

2979. Kielbowicz, Richard B. "Party Press Cohesiveness: Jacksonian Newspapers, 1832." *Journalism Quarterly* 60 (Autumn 1983): 518-521.

2980. Kindig, Everett W., II. "Western Opposition to Jackson's 'Democracy': The Ohio Valley as a Case Study, 1827-1836." Ph.D. dissertation, Stanford University, 1975.

2981. Klingberg, Frank J. "Personal Traits of President Andrew Jackson." *Historical Outlook* 14 (January 1923): 10-14.

2982. Kupfer, Barbara S. "A Presidential Patron of the Sport of Kings: Andrew Jackson." *Tennessee Historical Quarterly* 29 (Fall 1970): 243-255.

2983. Latner, Richard B. "Andrew Jackson and His Advisors: White House Politics, 1829-1837." Ph.D. dissertation, University of Wisconsin, 972.

2984. Latner, Richard B. "The Kitchen Cabinet and Andrew Jackson's Advisory System." *Journal of American History* 65 (September 1978): 367-388.

2985. Latner, Richard B. "A New Look at Jacksonian Politics." *Journal of American History* 61 (March 1975): 943-969.

2986. Latner, Richard B. *The Presidency of Andrew Jackson: White House Politics, 1829-1837*. Athens: University of Georgia Press, 1979.

2987. Lee, Henry. *A Vindication of the Character and Public Services of Andrew Jackson*. Boston: True and Green, 1828.

2988. Lewis, Alfred H. "Great Days in Great Careers, Andrew Jackson, 1832." *Everybody's Magazine* 8 (January 1903): 73-82.

2989. Longaker, Richard P. "Andrew Jackson and the Judiciary." *Political Science Quarterly* 71 (September 1956): 341-364.

2990. Longaker, Richard P. "Andrew Jackson and the Presidency." Ph.D. dissertation, Cornell University, 1954.

2991. Longaker, Richard P. "Was Jackson's Kitchen Cabinet a Cabinet?" *Mississippi Valley Historical Review* 44 (June 1957): 94-108.

2992. Lovat-Fraser, J. A. "Andrew Jackson: First People's President of the United States." *London Quarterly Review* 76 (October 1929): 185-197.

2993. McBride, Robert M. "Andrew Jackson and the Bank of the United States: A Footnote." *Tennessee Historical Quarterly* 21 (December 1962): 377-378.

2994. McCormick, Richard P. "New Perspectives on Jacksonian Politics." *Ameri-

can Historical Review 65 (January 1960): 288-301.

2995. McCrary, Royce C., Jr. "'The Long Agony Is Nearly Over': Samuel D. Ingham Reports on the Dissolution of Andrew Jackson's First Cabinet." *Pennsylvania Magazine of History and Biography* 100 (April 1976): 231-242.

2996. McNeill, Sarah B. "Andrew Jackson and Texas Affairs, 1819-1836." *East Tennessee Historical Society's Publications* 28 (1956): 86-101.

2997. Marshall, Lynn L. "The Authorship of Jackson's Bank Veto Message." *Mississippi Valley Historical Review* 50 (December 1963): 466-477.

2998. Martin, David A. "Mettallism, Small Notes, and Jackson's War with the B.U.S." *Explorations in Economic History* 11 (Spring 1974): 227-247.

2999. Miller, Richard G. "The Tariff of 1832: The Issue That Failed." *Filson Club Historical Quarterly* 49 (July 1975): 221-230.

3000. Morris, Richard B. "Andrew Jackson, Strikerbreaker." *American Historical Review* 55 (October 1949): 54-68.

3001. Mugleston, William F. "Andrew Jackson and the Spoils System: An Historiographical Survey." *Mid-America* 59 (April/July 1977): 117-125.

3002. Nicolay, Helen. *Andrew Jackson, The Fighting President.* New York: Century, 1929.

3003. Nye, Russell B. *Fettered Freedom: Civil Liberties and the Slavery Controversy, 1830-1860.* East Lansing: Michigan State University Press, 1949.

3004. Ogg, Frederic A. *The Reign of Andrew Jackson: A Chronicle of the Frontier in Politics.* New Haven, CT: Yale University Press, 1921.

3005. Parsons, R. C. "History of the Impeachment Trial of Andrew Jackson, President of the United States." *Western Reserve Law Journal* 2 (February 1896): 1-7; (March 1896): 35-49.

3006. Perry, Lewis "Fathers and Children: Andrew Jackson and the Subjugation of the American Indian." *History and Theory* 16 (May 1977): 174-195.

3007. Plous, Harold J. "Jackson, the Bank War, and Liberalism." *Southwestern Social Science Quarterly* 38 (September 1957): 99-110.

3008. "Presidential Inaugurations: Jackson — 1829." *Ladies' Magazine and Literary Gazette* 5 (March 1832): 112-117.

3009. Remini, Robert V. *Andrew Jackson and the Bank War: A Study in the Growth of Presidential Power.* New York: Norton, 1967.

3010. Remini, Robert V. *The Election of Andrew Jackson.* Philadelphia: Lippincott, 1963.

3011. Remini, Robert V. *The Revolutionary Age of Andrew Jackson.* New York: Harper and Row, 1976.

3012. Republican Party. New Hampshire. Convention. 1828. *Proceedings, and Address of the New Hampshire Republican State Convention of Delegates Friendly to the Election of Andrew Jackson to the Next Presidency of the United States, Assembled at Concord, June 11 and 12, 1828.* Concord, NH: Patriot Office, 1828.

3013. Rogin, Michael. *Fathers and Children: Andrew Jackson and the Subjugation of the American Indian.* New York: Knopf, 1975.

3014. Rohrs, Richard C. "Partisan Politics and the Attempted Assassination of Andrew Jackson." *Journal of the Early Republic* 1 (Summer 1981): 149-163.

3015. Rozett, John M. "The Social Bases of Party Conflict in the Age of Jackson:

Individual Voting Behavior in Green County, Illinois, 1838-1848." Ph.D. dissertation, University of Michigan, 1974.

3016. Russo, David J. "The Major Political Issues of the Jacksonian Period and the Development of Party Loyalty in Congress, 1830-1840." *American Philosophical Society Transactions* 61 (1972): 1-51.

3017. Scheiber, Harry N. "Some Documents on Jackson's Bank War." *Pennsylvania History* 30 (January 1963): 46-55.

3018. Sellers, Charles G., Jr. *Andrew Jackson, Nullification, and the State-Rights Tradition.* Chicago: Rand McNally, 1963.

3019. Sharp, James R. "Andrew Jackson and the Limits of Presidential Power." *Congressional Studies* 7 (Winter 1980): 63-80.

3020. Silbey, Joel H., ed. *Political Ideology and Voting Behavior in the Age of Jackson.* Englewood Cliffs, NJ: Prentice-Hall, 1973.

3021. Smith, William E. "Pen-Executive of Andrew Jackson." *Mississippi Valley Historical Review* 17 (March 1931): 543-556.

3022. Somit, Albert. "Andrew Jackson as Administrator." *Public Administration Review* 8 (Summer 1948): 188-196.

3023. Somit, Albert. "Andrew Jackson as an Administrative Reformer." *Tennessee Historical Quarterly* 13 (September 1954): 204-223.

3024. Somit, Albert. "New Papers: Some Sidelights upon Jackson in Administration." *Mississippi Valley Historical Review* 35 (June 1948): 91-98.

3025. Souryal, Safwat S. "Andrew Jackson and Gamal Abdul-Nasser: A Behavioral Study in Comparative Political Leadership." Ph.D. dissertation, University of Utah, 1971.

3026. Stenberg, Richard R. "Jacksons's Quarrel with the Alleged 'Calhounite' Cabinet Members in 1830-31." *Tyler's Quarterly Historical and Genealogical Magazine* 22 (April 1941): 208-228.

3027. Stenberg, Richard R. "A Note on the Jackson-Calhoun Breach of 1830-1831." *Tyler's Quarterly Historical and Genealogical Magazine* 21 (October 1939): 65-69.

3028. Stoddard, William O. . . . *Andrew Jackson and Martin Van Buren.* New York: Stokes, 1887.

3029. Sumner, William G. *Andrew Jackson as a Public Man: What He Was, What Chances He Had, and What He Did with Them.* Boston: Houghton Mifflin, 1893.

3030. Taylor, George R., ed. *Jackson versus Biddle's Bank: Struggle over the Second Bank of the U.S.* Lexington, MA: Heath, 1972.

3031. Thomas, Robert C. "Andrew Jackson versus France: American Policy toward France, 1834-1836." *Tennessee Historical Quarterly* 35 (Spring 1976): 51-64.

3032. Thompson, Seymour D. "Andrew Jackson and His Collusions with Judges and Lawyers." *American Law Review* 31 (November/December 1897): 801-826.

3033. Tucker, Edward L., ed. "The Attempted Assassination of President Jackson: A Letter by Richard Henry Wilde." *Georgia Historical Quarterly* 58 (1974): 193-199.

3034. Valliere, Kenneth L. "Benjamin Currey, Tennessean among the Cherokees: A Study of the Removal Policy of Andrew Jackson." *Tennessee Historical Quarterly* 41 (Summer 1982): 140-158; (Fall 1982): 239-256.

3035. Van Deusen, Glyndon G. *The Jacksonian Era, 1828-1848.* New York: Harper and Row, 1959.

3036. Wallace, Sarah A., ed. "Opening Days of Jackson's Presidency as Seen in Private Letters." *Tennessee Historical Quarterly* 9 (December 1950): 367-371.

3037. Whatley, George C. "Jackson's Justice and the Federal System, 1830-1856." Ph.D. dissertation, University of Alabama, 1969.

3038. White, Leonard D. *The Jacksonians: A Study in Administrative History, 1829-1861.* New York: Macmillan, 1954.

3039. Young, Mary E. "Indian Removal and Land Allotment: The Civilized Tribes and Jacksonian Justice." *American Historical Review* 64 (October 1958): 31-45.

3040. Zaitseva, N. D. "Andrew Jackson's Advice to the Cherokees." *Journal of Cherokee Studies* 4 (1979): 96-97.

Writings

3041. Craven, Avery O., ed. "Letters of Andrew Jackson." *Huntington Library Bulletin* 3 (February 1933): 109-134.

3042. DePuy, Henry F., ed. "Some Letters of Andrew Jackson." *American Antiquarian Society Proceedings* 31 (April 13, 1921): 70-88.

3043. Horn, Stanley, F., ed. "Some Jackson-Overton Correspondence." *Tennessee Historical Quarterly* 6 (June 1947): 161-175.

3044. Jackson, Andrew. "Andrew Jackson's Correspondence with James W. Breedlove." Edited by John S. Kendall. *Louisiana Historical Quarterly* 6 (April 1923): 179-188.

3045. Jackson, Andrew. *Correspondence of Andrew Jackson.* 7 vols. Edited by John S. Bassett. Washington, DC: Carnegie Institution of Washington, 1926-1935.

3046. Jackson, Andrew. "A Jackson Letter." Edited by Dorsey D. Jones. *Journal of Southern History* 20 (February 1954): 91-92.

3047. Jackson, Andrew. "Letter to Richard K. Call." *Gulf State Historical Magazine* 1 (May 1903): 438-439.

3048. Jackson, Andrew. "Letters of Andrew Jackson." Edited by Avery O. Craven. *Huntington Library Bulletin* 3 (February 1933): 109-134.

3049. Jackson, Andrew. *Messages to the United States Congress: With a Biographical Sketch of His Life.* Cincinnati, OH: Day, 1837.

3050. Jackson, Andrew. *The Papers of Andrew Jackson.* Vol. 1. Edited by Sam B. Smith and Harriet C. Owsley. Knoxville: University of Tennessee Press, 1980.

3051. Jackson, Andrew. *The Statesmanship of Andrew Jackson as Told in His Writings and Speeches.* Edited by Francis N. Thorpe. New York: Tandy-Thomas, 1909.

3052. Owsley, Harriet C. "Discoveries Made in Editing the Papers of Andrew Jackson." *Manuscripts* 27 (Fall 1975): 275-279.

3053. "The Papers of Andrew Jackson." *Georgia Historical Quarterly* 56 (Winter 1972): 587-588.

3054. Whealen, John J., ed. "The Jackson-Dawson Correspondence." *Bulletin of the Business Historical Society of Ohio* 16 (January 1958): 3-30.

Martin Van Buren

Biographies

3055. Alexander, Holmes. *The American Talleyrand: The Career and Contemporaries of Martin Van Buren, Eighth President.* New York: Harper and Row, 1935.

3056. Butler, William A. *Martin Van Buren: Lawyer, Statesman, and Man.* New York: Appleton, 1862.

3057. Crockett, David. *The Life of Martin Van Buren, Heir-Apparent to the "Government," and the Appointed Successor of General Andrew Jackson, Containing Every Authentic Particular by Which His Extraordinary Character Has Been Formed....* Philadelphia: Robert Wright, 1835.

3058. Dawson, Moses. *Sketches of the Life of Martin Van Buren, President of the United States.* Cincinnati, OH: J. W. Ely, 1840.

3059. Emmons, William. *Biography of Martin Van Buren, President of the United States, With an Appendix....* Washington, DC: Jacob Gideon, 1835.

3060. Holland, William M. *The Life and Political Opinions of Martin Van Buren, Vice President of the United States.* 2d ed. Hartford, CT: Belknap and Hamersley, 1835.

3061. Irelan, John R. *History of the Life, Administration, and Times of Martin Van Buren.* Chicago: Fairbanks and Palmer, 1887.

3062. Lynch, Denis T. *An Epoch and a Man, Martin Van Buren and His Times.* 2 vols. New York: Liveright, 1929.

3063. McElhiney, Thomas. *Life of Martin Van Buren.* Pittsburgh: J. T. Shryock, 1853.

3064. Mackenzie, William L. *The Life and Times of Martin Van Buren: The Correspondence of His Friends, Family, and Pupils....* Boston: Cooke, 1846.

3065. Rayback, Joseph G. *Martin Van Buren.* New York: Eastern Acorn Press, 1982.

3066. Shepard, Edward M. *Martin Van Buren.* Rev. ed. Boston: Houghton Mifflin, 1899.

Private Life

3067. Joline, Adrian H. "Martin Van Buren, The Lawyer." *Law Student's Helper* 18 (November 1910): 328-335.

3068. Koenig, Louis W. "Rise of the Little Magician." *American Heritage* 13 (June 1962): 29-31.

3069. McCracken, George E. "The Ancestry of President Martin Van Buren." *American Genealogist* 35 (April 1956): 73-75.

Public Career

3070. Ashby, John H. "The Political Ideas of Martin Van Buren." Master's thesis, American University, 1966.

3071. Bassett, John S. "Martin Van Buren." In *American Secretaries of State*. Vol. 4, edited by Samuel F. Bemis, 161-204. New York: Knopf, 1928.

3072. Blair, Montgomery. "Martin Van Buren, Diplomat." *Harper's* 119 (July 1909): 274-281.

3073. Brown, Richard H. "'Southern Planters and Plain Republicans of the North': Martin Van Buren's Formula for National Politics." Ph.D. dissertation, Yale University, 1955.

3074. Carleton, William G. "Political Aspects of the Van Buren Era." *South Atlantic Quarterly* 50 (April 1951): 167-185.

3075. Cone, Leon W., Jr. "Martin Van Buren: The Architect of the Democratic Party, 1837-1840." Ph.D. dissertation, University of Chicago, 1950.

3076. Donovan, Herbert D. A. *The Barnburners: A Study of the Internal Movements in the Political History of New York State, 1830-1852*. New York: Porcupine Press, 1952.

3077. Gatell, Frank O. "Sober Second Thoughts on Van Buren, the Albany Regency, and the Wall Street Conspiracy." *Journal of American History* 53 (June 1966): 19-40.

3078. Hamilton, James A. *Martin Van Buren's Calumnies Repudiated*. New York: Scribner's, 1870.

3079. Harrison, Joseph H., Jr. "Martin Van Buren and His Southern Supporters." *Journal of Southern History* 22 (November 1956): 438-458.

3080. McPherson, Elizabeth G., ed. "Unpublished Letters from North Carolinians to Van Buren." *North Carolina Historical Review* 15 (January 1938): 53-81.

3081. Mintz, Max M. "The Political Ideas of Martin Van Buren." *New York History* 30 (October 1949): 422-448.

3082. Moody, Robert E. "The Influence of Martin Van Buren on the Career and Acts of Andrew Jackson." *Michigan Academy of Science, Arts and Letters Papers* 7 (1927): 225-240.

3083. Nigro, Felix A. "Van Buren Confirmation before the Senate." *Western Political Quarterly* 14 (March 1961): 148-159.

3084. Parks, Gordon E. "Martin Van Buren and the Re-organization of the Democratic Party, 1841-1844." Ph.D. dissertation, University of Wisconsin, 1965.

3085. Rank, Vernon E. "Martin Van Buren's Political Speaking in His Rise to Political Power." Ph.D. dissertation, Pennsylvania State University, 1961.

3086. Rayback, Joseph G. "Martin Van Buren: His Place in the History of New York and the United States." *New York History* 64 (April 1983): 120-135.

3087. Rayback, Joseph G. "Martin Van Buren's Break with James K. Polk: The Record." *New York History* 36 (January 1955): 51-62.

3088. Rayback, Joseph G. "A Myth Reexamined: Martin Van Buren's Role in the Presidential Election of 1816." *American Philosophical Society Proceedings* 124 (April 29, 1980): 106-118.

3089. Rayback, Joseph G., ed. "Martin Van Buren's Desire for Revenge in the Campaign of 1848." *Mississippi Valley Historical Review* 40 (March 1954): 707-716.

3090. Remini, Robert V. "The Albany Regency." *New York History* 39 (October 1958): 341-355.

3091. Remini, Robert V. "The Early Political Career of Martin Van Buren, 1782-1828." Ph.D. dissertation, Columbia University, 1951.

3092. Remini, Robert V. *Martin Van Buren and the Making of the Democratic Party*. New York: Columbia University Press, 1959.

3093. Roper, Donald M. "Martin Van Buren as Tocqueville's Lawyer: The Jurisprudency of Politics." *Journal of the Early Republic* 2 (Summer 1982): 169-189.

3094. Smith, Richard W. "The Career of Martin Van Buren in Connection with the Slavery Controversy through the Election of 1840." Ph.D. dissertation, Ohio State University, 1959.

3095. Sullivan, Wilson. "Martin Van Buren: Old Kinderhood the Politician." *Mankind* 3 (June 1972): 34-40.

3096. Whitehurst, Alto L. "Martin Van Buren and the Free Soil Movement." Ph.D. dissertation, University of Chicago, 1932.

Presidential Years

3097. Bancroft, George. *Martin Van Buren to the End of His Political Career*. New York: Harper and Brothers, 1889.

3098. Blake, May B. "Martin Van Buren: First American to Be Chosen from New York State." *Daughters of the American Revolution Magazine* 109 (May 1975): 450-452.

3099. Cole, Donald B. *Martin Van Buren and the American Political System*. Princeton, NJ: Princeton University Press, 1984.

3100. Curtis, James C. *The Fox at Bay: Martin Van Buren and the Presidency, 1837-1841*. Lexington: University of Kentucky Press, 1970.

3101. Curtis, James C. "The Heritage Imperiled: Martin Van Buren and the Presidency, 1837-1841." Ph.D. dissertation, Northwestern University, 1967.

3102. Curtis, James C. "In the Shadow of Old Hickory: The Political Travail of Martin Van Buren." *Journal of the Early Republic* 1 (Fall 1981): 249-267.

3103. Dubovitskii, G. A. "The Democratic Party and the Political Struggle in the United States during the Presidency of M. Van Buren (1836-1840)." *Soviet Studies in History* 19 (Summer 1980): 61-86.

3104. Jones, Howard. "Anglophobia and the Aroostook War." *New England Quarterly* 48 (December 1975): 519-539.

3105. McGrane, Reginald C. *The Panic of 1837*. Chicago: University of Chicago Press, 1924.

3106. Miley, Cora. "A Forgotten President — The Enigmatical 'Little Magician,' Martin Van Buren." *Americana* 23 (April 1929): 169-181.

3107. Murray, Anne W. "Van Buren versus Harrison: The Campaign of 1840." *American Collector* 17 (October 1948): 24-25.

3108. Nance, Joseph H. *After San Jacinto: The Texas-American Frontier, 1836-1841*. Austin: University of Texas Press, 1963.

3109. Niven, John. *Martin Van Buren: The Romantic Age of American Politics*. New York: Oxford University Press, 1983.

3110. Remini, Robert V. "Martin Van Buren and the Tariff of Abominations." *American Historical Review* 63 (July 1958): 903-917.

3111. Rezneck, Samuel. "The Social History of an American Depression, 1837-1843." *American Historical Review* 40 (July 1937): 662-687.

3112. Stoddard, William O. ... *Andrew Jackson and Martin Van Buren*. New York: Stokes, 1887.

3113. Wilson, Major L. "Lincoln and Van Buren in the Steps of the Fathers: Another Look at the Lyceum Address." *Civil War History* 29 (September 1983): 197-211.

3114. Wilson, Major L. *The Presidency of Martin Van Buren*. Lawrence: University Press of Kansas, 1984.

Writings

3115. Hale, Edward E. "Anecdotes of Martin Van Buren." *Outlook* 70 (April 5, 1902): 849-852.

3116. Van Buren, Martin. *The Autobiography of Martin Van Buren*. Edited by John C. Fitzpatrick. Washington, DC: U.S. Government Printing Office, 1920.

3117. Van Buren, Martin. "A Father's Advice on How to Become President." Edited by Nathaniel E. Stein. *Manuscripts* 9 (Fall 1957): 261-264.

3118. Van Buren, Martin. "How to Become President — Martin Van Buren Grooms His Son." *Collector* 65 (March 1952): 49-53.

3119. Van Buren, Martin. *Inquiry into the Origin and Course of Political Parties in the United States*. New York: Hurd and Houghton, 1867.

3120. West, Elisabeth, H., ed. *The Calendar of the Papers of Martin Van Buren*. Washington, DC: U.S. Government Printing Office, 1910.

William Henry Harrison

Biographies

3121. Burr, Samuel J. *The Life and Times of William Henry Harrison.* New York: L. W. Ransom, 1840.

3122. Cleaves, Freeman. *Old Tippecanoe: William Henry Harrison and His Time.* New York: Scribner's, 1939.

3123. Cushing, Caleb. *Brief Sketch of the Life and Public Services, Civil and Military, Of William Henry Harrison, Of Ohio....* Augusta, ME: Severance and Dorr, 1840.

3124. Cushing, Caleb. *Outlines of the Life and Public Services, Civil and Military, Of William Henry Harrison.* Boston: Weeks, Jordan and Co., 1840.

3125. Goebel, Dorothy B. *William Henry Harrison: A Political Biography.* Indianapolis: Indiana Library and Historical Board, 1926.

3126. Green, James A. *William Henry Harrison, His Life and Times.* Richmond, VA: Garrett and Massie, 1941.

3127. Hall, James. *A Memoir of the Public Services of William Henry Harrison, Of Ohio.* Philadelphia: Edward C. Biddle, 1836.

3128. *"Hero of Tippecanoe": Or The Story of the Life of William Henry Harrison.* New York: J. P. Giffing, 1840.

3129. Jackson, Isaac R. *General William Henry Harrison....* Philadelphia: Jesper Harding, 1840.

3130. Jackson, Isaac R. *The Life of William Henry Harrison, (of Ohio), The People's Candidate for the Presidency, With a History of the Wars with the British and Indians on Our Northwestern Frontier.* 4th ed. Philadelphia: Marshall, Williams and Butler, 1840.

3131. Jackson, Isaac R. *A Sketch of the Life and Public Services of William Henry Harrison.* Columbus, OH: Scott and Wright, 1836.

3132. Montgomery, Henry. *The Life of Major-General William H. Harrison, Ninth President of the United States.* Philadelphia: Porter and Coates, 1852.

3133. Peckham, Howard H. *William Henry Harrison: Young Tippecanoe.* Indianapolis, IN: Bobbs-Merrill, 1951.

3134. Stoddard, William O. *... William Henry Harrison, John Tyler, and James Knox Polk.* New York: Stokes, 1888.

Private Life

3135. Bishop, H. O. "Benjamin Harrison, The Signer." *Tyler's Quarterly Historical and Genealogical Magazine* 17 (July 1935): 82-84.

3136. Bond, Beverly W., Jr. "William Henry Harrison and the Old Northwest." *Bulletin of the Historical and Philosophical Society of Ohio* 7 (January 1949): 10-17.

3137. Booth, Edward T. "William Henry Harrison: Ohio Alluvial." In his *Country Life in America as Lived by Ten Presidents of the U.S.*, 148-168. New York: Knopf, 1947.

3138. Daughters of the American Revolution. Indiana. Francis Vigo Chapter, Vincennes. *Grouseland, The Home of William Henry Harrison*. Compiled by Benjamin F. Sager. Vincennes, IN: n.p., 1942.

3139. Dawson, Moses. *A Historical Narrative of the Civil and Military Services of Major-General William H. Harrison, and a Vindication of His Character and Conduct as a Statesman, a Citizen, and a Soldier*. Cincinnati, OH: M. Dawson, 1824.

3140. Fabian, Monroe H. "A Portrait of William Henry Harrison." *Prologue* 1 (Winter 1969): 29-32.

3141. Gay, James T. "Harrison, Blaine, and Cronyism." *Alaska Journal* 3 (Winter 1973): 12-19.

3142. Lewis, Edward S. "The Death and Funeral of President William Henry Harrison." *Ohio Archaeological and Historical Quarterly* 37 (October 1928): 605-612.

3143. *The Life of Major-General William Henry Harrison: Comprising a Brief Account of His Important Civil and Military Services, and an Accurate Description of the Council at Vincennes with Tecumseh, as well as the Victories of Tippecanoe, Fort Meigs, and the Thames*. Philadelphia: Grigg and Elliot, 1840.

3144. Peckham, Howard H. "Tears for Old Tippecanoe: Religious Interpretations of President Harrison's Death." *American Antiquarian Society Proceedings* 69 (April 1959): 17-36.

3145. Symmes, John C. *The Intimate Letters of John Cleves Symmes and His Family, Including Those of His Daughter, Mrs. William Henry Harrison, Wife of the Ninth President of the United States*. Edited by Beverly W. Bond, Jr. Cincinnati: Historical and Philosophical Society of Ohio, 1956.

3146. Todd, Charles S. *Sketches of the Civil and Military Services of William Henry Harrison*. Cincinnati, OH: U. P. James, 1840.

3147. Walker, Kenneth R. "The Death of a President." *Northwestern Ohio Quarterly* 28 (Summer 1956): 157-162.

3148. Wood, Clarence A. "Riverhead Boasts First Lady, Too." *Long Island Forum* 13 (August 1950): 149-151.

3149. Yzenbaard, John H. "The Harrison Bandwagon." *American Heritage* 26 (October 1975): 18-27.

Public Career

3150. Bond, Beverly W., Jr. "William Henry Harrison in the War of 1812." *Mississippi Valley Historical Review* 13 (March 1967): 499-516.

3151. Carter, Clarence E., ed. "William Henry Harrison and the Mexican Appointment, 1823-1824." *Mississippi Valley Historical Review* 25 (September 1938): 251-262.

3152. Garrard, Daniel. *Address to the Young Men of Kentucky, Comprising a Brief Review of the Military Services of General William Henry Harrison, During the Late War between Great Britain and the United States*. Frankfort, KY: Robinson and Adams, 1840.

3153. Murray, Anne W. "Van Buren versus Harrison: The Campaign of 1840." *American Collector* 17 (October 1948): 24-25.

3154. Webster, Homer J. *William Henry Harrison's Administration of Indiana Territory.* Indianapolis, IN: Sentinel Printing Co., 1907.

3155. "William Henry Harrison: First Governor of Indiana Territory." *Indiana History Bulletin* 50 (February 1973): 15-19.

3156. Wilson, Robert E. "Old Tippecanoe in Bogota." *Foreign Service Journal* 55 (January 1978): 12-13, 30.

Presidential Years

3157. Carwardine, Richard. "Evangelicals, Whigs, and the Election of William Henry Harrison." *Journal of American Studies* 17 (April 1983): 47-75.

3158. Halford, E. W. "General Harrison's Attitude toward the Presidency." *Century Magazine* 84 (June 1912): 305-310.

3159. "Harrison's Great Speech at the 'Log Cabin' Campaign Meeting at Ft. Meigs in 1840." *Ohio Archaeological and Historical Society Publications* 17 (April 1908): 197-207.

3160. Norton, Anthony B. *The Great Revolution of 1840, Reminiscences of the Log Cabin and Hard Cider Campaign.* Mount Vernon, OH: A. B. Norton, 1888.

3161. "Washington Twenty Years Ago: Inauguration of President Harrison." *Leisure Hour* 10 (April 4, 1861): 215-216, 218.

Writings

3162. Barnhart, John D. "Letters of William H. Harrison to Thomas Worthington, 1799-1813." *Indiana Magazine of History* 47 (March 1951): 53-84.

3163. Harrison, William H. *A Discourse on the Aborigines of the Valley of the Ohio.* Cincinnati, OH: Cincinnati Express, 1838.

3164. Harrison, William H. *Governor's Messages and Letters: Messages and Letters of William Henry Harrison.* 2 vols. Edited by Logan Esarey. Indianapolis: Indiana Historical Commission, 1922.

3165. Harrison, William H. *Messages and Letters of William Henry Harrison.* 2 vols. Edited by Logan Esarey. Indianapolis: Indiana Historical Commission, 1922.

3166. Harrison, William H. *Remarks of General Harrison, Late Envoy Extraordinary and Minister Plenipotentiary of the United States to the Republic of Columbia, On Certain Charges Made against Him by That Government.* Washington, DC: Gales and Seaton, 1830.

3167. "Letter from William Henry Harrison to Harmar Denny of Pittsburgh, Accepting the Nomination to the Office of President of the United States, By the Convention of the Anti-Masonic Party, Held at Philadelphia, In the Fall of 1838." *Western Pennsylvania Historical Magazine* 1 (July 1918): 144-151.

John Tyler

Biographies

3168. Chidsey, Donald B. *And Tyler Too.* Nashville, TN: T. Nelson, 1978.

3169. Ellett, Katherine T. *Young John Tyler.* Richmond, VA: Diety Printing Co., 1957.

3170. Gordon, Armistead C. *Virginian Portraits: Essays in Biography.* Staunton, VA: McClure, 1924.

3171. Hoyt, Edwin P. *John Tyler.* London: Abelard-Schuman, 1969.

3172. *Life of John Tyler, President of the United States, Up to the Class of the Second Session of the Twenty-Seventh Congress....* New York: Harper and Brothers, 1843.

3173. Seager, Robert. *And Tyler Too: A Biography of John and Julia Gardiner Tyler.* New York: McGraw-Hill, 1963.

3174. Young, Stanley P. *Tippecanoe and Tyler, Too!* New York: Random House, 1957.

Private Life

3175. Bradshaw, Herbert C. "A President's Bride at 'Sherwood Forest.'" *Virginia Cavalcade* 7 (Spring 1958): 30-39.

3176. Coleman, Elizabeth T. *Priscilla Cooper Tyler and the American Scene, 1816-1889.* University: University of Alabama Press, 1955.

3177. Perling, Joseph J. *A President Takes a Wife.* Middleburg, VA: Denlinger's, 1959.

3178. Wallace, Sarah A. "Letters of the Presidentess, Julia Gardiner Tyler, 1844-1845." *Daughters of the American Revolution Magazine* 87 (April 1953): 641-646.

Public Career

3179. Barbee, David R., ed. "Tyler's Intentions Become Achievements." *Tyler's Quarterly Historical and Genealogical Magazine* 31 (April 1950): 219-221.

3180. Chitwood, Oliver P. *John Tyler: Champion of the Old South.* New York: Appleton, 1939.

3181. Tyler, Lyon G. "John Tyler and the Vice-Presidency." *Tyler's Quarterly Historical and Genealogical Magazine* 9 (October 1927): 89-95.

3182. Wise, Henry A. *Seven Decades of the Union: The Humanities and Materialism, Illustrated by a Memoire of John Tyler, With Reminiscences of Some of His Great Contemporaries.* Philadelphia: Lippincott, 1872.

Presidential Years

3183. Cain, Marvin R. "Return to Republicanism: A Reappraisal of Hugh Swinton Legare and the Tyler Presidency." *South Carolina Historical Magazine* 79 (October 1978): 264-280.

3184. Dinnerstein, Leonard. "The Accession of John Tyler to the Presidency." *Virginia Magazine of History and Biography* 70 (October 1962): 447-458.

3185. Ewing, Thomas. "Diary, August and September, 1841." *American Historical Review* 18 (October 1912): 97-112.

3186. Fraser, Hugh R. *Democracy in the Making: The Jackson-Tyler Era.* Indianapolis, IN: Bobbs-Merrill, 1938.

3187. Gotlieb, Howard B., and Gail Grimes. "President Tyler and the Gardiners: A New Portrait." *Yale University Library Gazette* 34 (July 1955): 2-12.

3188. Harrison, Lowell H. "The President without a Party." *American History Illustrated* 16 (April 1981): 12-21.

3189. "John Tyler and the Ladies of Brazoria." *Tyler's Quarterly Historical and Genealogical Magazine* 11 (July 1929): 1-4.

3190. Kesilman, Sylvan H. "John Tyler and the Presidency: Old School Republicanism, Partisan Realignment, and Support for His Administration." Ph.D. dissertation, Ohio State University, 1973.

3191. Kleber, Louis C. "John Tyler: Tenth President." *History Today* 25 (October 1975): 697-703.

3192. Krueger, David W. "The Clay-Tyler Feud, 1841-1842." *Filson Club History Quarterly* 42 (April 1968): 162-175.

3193. Lambert, Oscar D. *Presidential Politics in the United States, 1841-1844.* Durham, NC: Duke University Press, 1936.

3194. Merk, Frederick. *Fruits of Propaganda in the Tyler Administration.* Cambridge, MA: Harvard University Press, 1971.

3195. Miley, Cora. "John Tyler, The President without a Party." *Americana* 23 (October 1929): 411-420.

3196. Morgan, Robert J. "The Presidency under John Tyler: A Study in Constitutional History." Ph.D. dissertation, University of Virginia, 1951.

3197. Morgan, Robert J. *A Whig Embattled: The Presidency under John Tyler.* Lincoln: University of Nebraska Press, 1954.

3198. Reeves, Jesse S. *American Diplomacy under Tyler and Polk.* Baltimore, MD: Johns Hopkins University Press, 1907.

3199. Shelley, Fred. "The Vice President Receives Bad News in Williamsburg: A Letter of James Lyons to John Tyler." *Virginia Magazine of History and Biography* 76 (July 1968): 337-339.

3200. Siebeneck, Henry K. "John Tyler: Our First Accidental President." *Western Pennsylvania Historical Magazine* 34 (March 1951): 35-50; (June 1951): 119-133.

3201. Stathis, Stephen W. "John Tyler's Presidential Succession: A Reappraisal." *Prologue* 8 (Winter 1976): 223-236.

3202. Stoddard, William O. ... *William Henry Harrison, John Tyler, and James Knox Polk.* New York: Stokes, 1888.

3203. Swindler, William F. "John Tyler's Nominations: 'Robin Hood,' Congress, and the Court." *Supreme Court Historical Society Yearbook* (1977): 39-43.

Writings

3204. Tyler, John. *An Address before the*

Two Literary Societies of Randolph-Macon College, June 19, 1838. Richmond, VA: J. C. Walker, 1838.

3205. Tyler, John. *An Address, Delivered before the Literary Societies of the University of Virginia, On the Anniversary of the Declaration of Independence by the State of Virginia, June 29th, 1850*. Charlottesville, VA: J. Alexander, 1850.

3206. Tyler, John. *Lecture Delivered before the Maryland Institute for the Promotion of the Mechanic Arts, March 20, 1855*. Baltimore, MD: J. Murphy, 1855.

3207. Tyler, John. *A Lecture Prepared at the Request of the Library Association of Petersburg, and Delivered on the 4th of May, 1854*. Petersburg, VA: Banks and Lewellen, 1854.

3208. Tyler, Lyon G. *The Letters and Times of the Tylers*. 3 vols. Richmond, VA: Whittel and Shepperson, 1884-1896.

James K. Polk

Biographies

3209. Bassett, John S., ed. *The Southern Plantation Overseer as Revealed in His Letters.* Northampton, MA: Smith College, 1925.

3210. Billington, Ray A. *The Far Western Frontier.* New York: Harper and Row, 1956.

3211. Burt, Jesse. "Editor Eastman Writes James K. Polk." *East Tennessee Historical Society's Publications* 39 (1967): 103-117.

3212. Goodpasture, Albert V. "The Boyhood of President Polk." *Tennessee Historical Magazine* 7 (April 1921): 36-50.

3213. Hickman, George H. *The Life and Public Services of the Hon. James Knox Polk, With a Compendium of His Speeches on Various Public Measures.* Baltimore, MD: N. Hickman, 1844.

3214. Jenkins, John S. *James Knox Polk.* Auburn, NY: J. M. Alden, 1851.

3215. McCormac, Eugene I. *James K. Polk, A Political Biography.* Berkeley: University of California Press, 1922.

3216. McCoy, Charles A. *Polk and the Presidency.* Austin: University of Texas Press, 1960.

3217. Morrel, Martha M. "*Young Hickory*," *The Life and Times of President James K. Polk.* New York: Dutton, 1949.

3218. Sellers, Charles G., Jr. *James K. Polk, Jacksonian: 1795-1843.* Princeton, NJ: Princeton University Press, 1957.

3219. Severn, William. *Frontier President: James K. Polk.* New York: I. Washburn, 1965.

3220. Stoddard, William O. . . . *William Henry Harrison, John Tyler, and James Knox Polk.* New York: Stokes, 1888.

Private Life

3221. Ikard, Robert W. "Surgical Operations on James K. Polk by Ephraim McDowell or the Search for Polk's Gallstone." *Tennessee Historical Quarterly* 43 (Summer 1984): 121-131.

3222. Nelson, Anson, and Fanny Nelson. *Memorials of Sarah Childress Polk, Wife of the Eleventh President of the United States.* New York: A. D. F. Randolph, 1892.

3223. Polk, Sarah C. "Letters of Mrs. James K. Polk to Her Husband, 1839-1843." *Tennessee Historical Quarterly* 11 (June 1952): 180-191; (September 1952): 282-288.

3224. Trickey, Katharine S. "Young Hickory and Sarah." *Daughters of the*

American Revolution Magazine 108 (May 1974): 430-434.

Public Career

3225. Abernethy, Thomas P. "The Origin of the Whig Party in Tennessee." *Mississippi Valley Historical Review* 12 (March 1926): 504-522.

3226. Bassett, John S. "James K. Polk and His Constituents, 1831-1832." *American Historical Review* 28 (October 1922): 68-77.

3227. Moore, Powell. "James K. Polk and Tennessee Politics, 1839-1841." *East Tennessee Historical Society's Publications* 9 (1937): 31-52.

3228. Moore, Powell. "James K. Polk and the 'Immortal Thirteen.'" *East Tennessee Historical Society's Publications* 11 (1939): 20-33.

3229. Moore, Powell. "James K. Polk: Tennessee Politician." *Journal of Southern History* 17 (November 1951): 493-516.

3230. Pukl, Joseph M., Jr. "James K. Polk's Congressional Campaigns." *Tennessee Historical Quarterly* 40 (Winter 1981): 348-365.

3231. Pukl, Joseph M., Jr. "James K. Polk's Congressional Campaigns of 1835 and 1837." *Tennessee Historical Quarterly* 41 (Summer 1982): 105-123.

3232. Pukl, Joseph M., Jr. "James K. Polk's Early Congressional Campaigns of 1825 and 1827." *Tennessee Historical Quarterly* 39 (Winter 1980): 440-458.

3233. Schlup, Leonard. "Polk and Clay: The Politics of Texas in 1844." *Quarterly Review of Historical Studies* (India) 18 (1979): 211-217.

3234. Sellers, Charles G., Jr. "The Early Career of James K. Polk, 1795-1839." Ph.D. dissertation, University of North Carolina, 1950.

3235. Sellers, Charles G., Jr. "James K. Polk's Political Apprenticeship." *East Tennessee Historical Society's Publications* 25 (1953): 37-53.

Presidential Years

3236. Bauer, K. Jack. *The Mexican War, 1846-1848*. New York: Naval Institute Press, 1974.

3237. Benjamin, Thomas. "Recent Historiography of the Origins of the Mexican War." *New Mexico Historical Review* 54 (July 1979): 169-181.

3238. Bergeron, Paul H. "James K. Polk and the Jacksonian Press in Tennessee." *Tennessee Historical Quarterly* 41 (Fall 1982): 257-277.

3239. Bill, Alfred H. *Rehearsal for Conflict*. New York: History Book Club, 1947.

3240. Bowers, Claude G. *Making Democracy a Reality: Jefferson, Jackson, and Polk*. Memphis, TN: Memphis State College Press, 1954.

3241. Callcott, Wilfred H. *Santa Anna: The Story of an Enigma Who Once Was Mexico*. Norman: University of Oklahoma Press, 1936.

3242. Chandler, Walter. "Centenary of James K. Polk and His Administration." *West Tennessee Historical Society Papers* 3 (1949): 27-38.

3243. Chase, Lucien B. *History of the Polk Administration*. New York: Putnam, 1850.

3244. DeVoto, Bernard. *1846, Year of Decision*. Boston: Little, Brown, 1943.

3245. Everett, Robert B. "James K. Polk and the Election of 1844 in Tennessee." *West Tennessee Historical Society Papers* 16 (1962): 5-28.

3246. Fujita, Fumiko. "Foreign Policy in a Democracy: Polk, Buchanan, and Oregon." *American Review* 7 (1973): 107-144.

3247. Fuller, John D. P. *The Movement for the Acquisition of All Mexico, 1846-1848.* Baltimore, MD: Johns Hopkins University Press, 1936.

3248. Gilley, B. H. " 'Polk's War' and the Louisiana Press." *Louisiana History* 20 (Winter 1979): 5-24.

3249. Graebner, Norman A. "James K. Polk, A Study in Federal Patronage." *Mississippi Valley Historical Review* 38 (March 1952): 613-652.

3250. Graebner, Norman A. "Lessons of the Mexican War." *Pacific Historical Review* 47 (August 1978): 325-342.

3251. Graebner, Norman A. "Polk, Politics, and Oregon." *East Tennessee Historical Society's Publications* 24 (1952): 11-25.

3252. Hellerman, Leon. "An Analysis of President Polk's Mexican Policy in Selected American History Textbooks for Secondary Schools." Ed.D. dissertation, New York University, 1972.

3253. Horn, James J. "Trends in Historical Interpretation: James K. Polk." *North Carolina Historical Review* 42 (October 1965): 454-464.

3254. Irwin, Ramon L. "Congressional Debates of James K. Polk's Administration — A Study in Factionalism." Ph.D. dissertation, University of Minnesota, 1948.

3255. Johnson, Allen. "Presidential Initiative in Determining Foreign Policy: President Polk's War Message." In his *Readings in American Constitutional History*, 393-404. Boston: Houghton Mifflin, 1912.

3256. Largent, Robert J. "Legal and Constitutional Aspects of President Polk's Mexican Policy." *Marshall Review* 1 (June 1937): 3-12.

3257. Learned, Henry B. "Cabinet Meetings under President Polk." *American Historical Association Annual Report* 1 (1914): 231-242.

3258. McCoy, Charles A. "James K. Polk and the American Presidency." Ph.D. dissertation, Boston University, 1958.

3259. Marsh, Richard D. "James K. Polk and Slavery." Master's thesis, North Texas State University, 1977.

3260. Merk, Frederick, and Lois B. Merk. *The Monroe Doctrine and American Expansionism, 1848-1849.* New York: Knopf, 1966.

3261. Miles, Edwin A. "Fifty-four Forty or Fight — An American Political Legend." *Mississippi Valley Historical Review* 44 (September 1957): 291-309.

3262. Miley, Cora. "James K. Polk, The First 'Dark Horse' Elected to the Presidency." *Americana* 24 (July 1930): 343-369.

3263. Nelson, Anna K. "Secret Agents and Security Leaks: President Polk and the Mexican War." *Journalism Quarterly* 52 (Spring 1975): 9-14.

3264. Nelson, Anna K. "The Secret Diplomacy of James K. Polk during the Mexican War, 1846-1847." Ph.D. dissertation, George Washington University, 1972.

3265. Parkman, Francis. *The Oregon Trail.* Boston: Little, Brown, 1872.

3266. Pletcher, David M. *The Diplomacy of Annexation: Texas, Oregon, and the Mexican War.* Columbia: University of Missouri Press, 1973.

3267. Polk, John F. "Vera Cruz, 1847: A Lesson in Command." *Marine Corps Gazette* 63 (September 1979): 61-66.

3268. Pratt, Julius W. "James K. Polk and John Bull." *Canadian Historical Review* 24 (December 1943): 341-349.

3269. *Presidents North Carolina Gave the Nation.* Raleigh: Commission for a Memorial to the Three North Carolina Presidents, 1949.

3270. Price, Glenn W. "The Origins of the War with Mexico: The Polk-Stockton Intrigue." Ph.D. dissertation, University of Southern California, 1966.

3271. Rayback, Joseph G. "Presidential Politics, 1845-1848." Ph.D. dissertation, Case Western Reserve University, 1939.

3272. Reeves, Jesse S. *American Diplomacy under Tyler and Polk.* Baltimore, MD: Johns Hopkins University Press, 1907.

3273. Schroeder, John H. "Congress and Opposition to the Mexican War." *Capitol Studies* 3 (Fall 1975): 15-30.

3274. Schroeder, John H. *Mr. Polk's War: American Opposition and Dissent, 1846-1848.* Madison: University of Wisconsin Press, 1973.

3275. Schuyler, Robert L. "Polk and the Oregon Compromise of 1846." *Political Science Quarterly* 26 (September 1911): 443-461.

3276. Sellers, Charles G., Jr. *James K. Polk, Continentalist: 1843-1846.* Princeton, NJ: Princeton University Press, 1966.

3277. Silbey, Joel H. *The Shrine of Party: Congressional Voting Behavior, 1841-1852.* Pittsburgh, PA: University of Pittsburgh Press, 1967.

3278. Singletary, Otis A. *The Mexican War.* Chicago: University of Chicago Press, 1960.

3279. Smith, Justin H. *The War with Mexico.* New York: Macmillan, 1919.

3280. Stenberg, Richard R. "The Failure of Polk's Mexican War Intrigue of 1845." *Pacific Historical Review* 4 (1935): 39-68.

3281. Stephenson, Nathaniel W. *Texas and the Mexican War.* New York: U.S. Publishers Association, 1921.

3282. Tays, George. "Fremont Had No Special Instructions." *Pacific Historical Review* 9 (June 1940): 157-171.

3283. Theisen, Lee S. "James K. Polk, Not So Dark a Horse." *Tennessee Historical Quarterly* 30 (Winter 1971): 383-401.

3284. Thurber, James. "Something about Polk." *Wisconsin Magazine of History* 50 (Winter 1967): 145-146.

3285. Van Horn, James. "Trends in Historical Interpretation: James K. Polk." *North Carolina Historical Review* 42 (October 1965): 454-464.

3286. Walton, Brian G. "James K. Polk and the Democratic Party in the Aftermath of the Wilmot Proviso." Ph.D. dissertation, Vanderbilt University, 1968.

Writings

3287. Nevins, Allan, ed. *Polk: The Diary of a President, 1845-1849, Covering the Mexican War, the Acquisition of Oregon, and the Conquest of California and the Southwest.* New York: Longmans, 1929.

3288. Polk, James K. *Correspondence of James K. Polk.* 5 vols. Edited by Herbert Weaver, et al. Nashville, TN: Vanderbilt University Press, 1969-1983.

3289. Polk, James K. *The Diary of James K. Polk during His Presidency, 1845 to 1849: Now First Printed from the Original Manuscript in the Collections of the Chicago Historical Society.* 4 vols. Edited by Milo M. Quaife. Chicago: McClurg, 1910.

3290. Polk, James K. "Letters of James

K. Polk to Andrew J. Donelson, 1843-1848." *Tennessee Historical Magazine* 3 (March 1917): 51-73.

3291. Polk, James K. "Letters of James K. Polk to Cave Johnson, 1833-1848." *Tennessee Historical Magazine* 1 (September 1915): 209-256.

3292. Polk, James K. "Polk and His Constituents, 1831-1832: Contributed by John Spencer Bassett." *American Historical Review* 27 (October 1922): 68-77.

3293. Thweatt, John H. "The James K. Polk Papers." *Tennessee Historical Quarterly* 33 (Spring 1974): 93-98.

Zachary Taylor

Biographies

3294. Dyer, Brainerd. *Zachary Taylor.* Baton Rouge: Louisiana State University Press, 1946.

3295. Frost, John. *Life of Major General Zachary Taylor: With Notices of the War in New Mexico: And Biographical Sketches of Officers Who Have Distinguished Themselves in the War with Mexico.* New York: Appleton, 1847.

3296. Frost, John. *The People's Life of General Zachary Taylor, The Hero of Palo Alto, Monterey, and Buena Vista: With Numerous Illustrative Anecdotes, Also, a Biography of Millard Fillmore.* Philadelphia: Lindsay and Blakiston, 1848.

3297. Fry, Joseph R. *A Life of Gen. Zachary Taylor: Compromising a Narrative of Events Connected with His Professional Career, Derived from Public Documents and Private Correspondence ... and Authentic Incidents of His Early Years, From Materials Collected by Robert T. Conrad ....* Philadelphia: Grigg, Elliot and Co., 1848.

3298. Hamilton, Holman. *Zachary Taylor.* 2 vols. Indianapolis, IN: Bobbs-Merrill, 1941-1951.

3299. Hoyt, Edwin P. *Zachary Taylor.* Chicago: Reilly and Lee Co., 1966.

3300. McKinley, Silas B., and Silas Bent. *Old Rough and Ready, The Life and Time of Zachary Taylor.* New York: Vanguard Press, 1946.

3301. Montgomery, Henry. *The Life of Major General Zachary Taylor, Twelfth President of the United States.* 2d ed. Auburn, NY: Derby, Miller, 1851.

3302. Powell, C. Frank. *Life of Major-General Zachary Taylor: With an Account of His Brilliant Achievements on the Rio Grande, and Elsewhere ... With Sketches ....* New York: Appleton, 1846.

3303. Stearns, Charles. *Facts in the Life of General Taylor: The Cuba Blood-Hound Importer, the Extensive Slave-Holder, and the Mexican War.* Boston: The Author, 1848.

3304. Sumpter, Arthur. *The Life of Major-General Zachary Taylor, The Whig Nominee for President of the United States, With a Brief Biographical Sketch of the Hon. Millard Fillmore....* New York: Ensign and Thayer, 1848.

3305. Sumpter, Arthur. *The Lives of General Zachary Taylor and General Winfield Scott: To Which Is Appealed an Outline History of Mexico, Aboriginal, Colonial, and Republican: And a Brief History of the Mexican War....* New York: H. Phelps and Co., 1848.

3306. *Taylor and His Generals: A Biogra-*

phy of Major-General Zachary Taylor: And Sketches of the Lives of Generals Worth, Wool, and Twiggs: With a Full Account of the Various Actions of Their Divisions in a History of the Bombardment of Vera Cruz, and a Sketch of the Life of Major-General Winfield Scott. Philadelphia: E. H. Butler and Co., 1847.

Private Life

3307. Currie, Stephen, ed. "Zachary Taylor, Plantation Owner." *Civil War History* 30 (June 1984): 144-156.

3308. Hamilton, Holman. "A Youth of Good Morals: Zachary Taylor Sends His Only Son to School." *Filson Club Historical Quarterly* 27 (October 1953): 303-307.

3309. Mansfield, Luther S. "Melville's Comic Articles on Zachary Taylor." *American Literature* 9 (January 1938): 411-418.

Public Career

3310. *Compromising Memoirs of Generals Taylor, Worth, Wool, and Bulter: Colonels May, Cross, Clay, Hardin, Yell, Hays, and Other Distinguished Officers....* Philadelphia: Grigg, Elliot and Co., 1848.

3311. Hamilton, Holman. "Zachary Taylor and Minnesota." *Minnesota History* 30 (June 1949): 97-110.

3312. Hamilton, Holman. "Zachary Taylor: Resident or Fighter in 15 States." *American Heritage* 4 (Summer 1953): 10-13.

3313. Howard, Oliver O. *General Taylor*. New York: Appleton, 1892.

3314. *Life and Public Services of Gen. Z. Taylor: Including a Minute Account of His Defense of Fort Harrison, in 1812: The Battle of Okee-chobee, in 1837: And the Battles of Palo Alto and Resaca de la Palma, in 1846... To Which Is Added, Sketches of the Officers Who Have Fallen in the Late Contest.* New York: H. Long and Brother, 1846.

3315. Nichols, Edward J. *Zachary Taylor's Little Army.* Garden City, NY: Doubleday, 1963.

3316. Spurlin, Charles. "With Taylor and McCulloch through the Battle of Monterey." *Texas Military History* 6 (Fall 1967): 111-127.

3317. Viola, Herman J. "Zachary Taylor and the Indiana Volunteers." *Southwestern Historical Quarterly* 72 (January 1969): 335-346.

Presidential Years

3318. Dyer, Brainerd. "Zachary Taylor and the Election of 1848." *Pacific Historical Review* 9 (June 1940): 173-182.

3319. Foster, Herbert D. "Webster's Seventh of March Speech and the Secession Movement, 1850." *American Historical Review* 27 (January 1922): 245-270.

3320. Hamilton, Holman. "Democratic Senate Leadership and the Compromise of 1850." *Mississippi Valley Historical Review* 41 (December 1954): 403-418.

3321. Hamilton, Holman. *The Three Kentucky Presidents: Lincoln, Taylor, Davis.* Lexington: University Press of Kentucky, 1978.

3322. Hodder, Frank H. "The Authorship of the Compromise of 1850." *Mississippi Valley Historical Review* 22 (March 1936): 525-536.

3323. Lavender, David. "How to Make It to the White House without Really Trying." *American Heritage* 16 (June 1967): 26-27, 80-86.

3324. Louisiana State Museum, New Orleans. *General Zachary Taylor, The Louisiana President of the United States of America: Louisiana's Part in the War with Mexico.* New Orleans, LA: The Museum, 1937.

3325. Lynch, William O. "Zachary Taylor as President." *Journal of Southern History* 4 (August 1938): 279-294.

3326. Murray, Anne W. "Zachary Taylor for President: The Campaign of 1848." *American Collector* 17 (November 1948): 15-17.

3327. Stoddard, William O. . . . *Zachary Taylor, Millard Fillmore, Franklin Pierce, and James Buchanan.* New York: Stokes, 1888.

3328. Walton, Brian G. "The Elections for the Thirtieth Congress and the Presidential Candidacy of Zachary Taylor." *Journal of Southern History* 35 (May 1969): 186-202.

Writings

3329. Taylor, Zachary. *Letters of Zachary Taylor, From the Battle-Field of the Mexican War.* Rochester, NY: Genesee Press, 1908.

3330. Taylor, Zachary. "Zachary Taylor and Old Fort Snelling: A Letter." *Minnesota History* 28 (March 1947): 15-19.

3331. Taylor, Zachary. "Zachary Taylor on Jackson and the Military Establishment, 1835." Edited by W. D. Hoyt. *American Historical Review* 51 (April 1946): 480-484.

Millard Fillmore

Biographies

3332. Barre, W. L. *The Life and Public Services of Millard Fillmore.* Buffalo, NY: Wanzer, McKim and Co., 1856.

3333. Chamberlain, Ivory. *Biography of Millard Fillmore.* Buffalo, NY: Thomas and Lathrops, 1856.

3334. Griffis, William E. *Millard Fillmore, Constructive Statesman, Defender of the Constitution, President of the United States.* Ithaca, NY: Andrus and Church, 1915.

3335. Rayback, Robert J. "Biography of Millard Fillmore, 13th President of the United States." Ph.D. dissertation, University of Wisconsin, 1948.

3336. Rayback, Robert J. *Millard Fillmore: Biography of a President.* Buffalo, NY: Henry Stewart, 1959.

3337. Scarry, Robert J. *Millard Fillmore, 13th President.* Moravia, NY: The Author, 1970.

Private Life

3338. Eriksson, Erik M. "Millard Fillmore: Anti-Mason." *Grand Lodge Bulletin* 27 (January 1926): 5-9.

Public Career

3339. Weed, Thurlow. *Life of Thurlow Weed Including His Autobiography and Memoir.* 2 vols. Edited by Harriet A. Weed. Boston: Houghton Miffin, 1883-1884.

Presidential Years

3340. Bailey, Howard. "Millard Fillmore: The Forgotten President." *American History Illustrated* 6 (June 1971): 26-35.

3341. Billington, Ray A. *The Protestant Crusade, 1800-1860.* New York: Macmillan, 1938.

3342. Carmon, Harry J., and Reinhard H. Luthin. "The Seward-Fillmore Feud and the Crisis of 1850: The Seward-Fillmore Feud and the Disruption of the Whig Party." *New York History* 24 (April 1943): 163-184; (July 1943): 335-357.

3343. Degler, Carl N. "There Was Another South." *American Heritage* 11 (August 1960): 53-55, 100-103.

3344. Grayson, Benson L. *The Unknown President: The Administration of President Millard Fillmore.* Lanham, MD: University Press of America, 1981.

3345. Hinton, Wayne K. "Millard Fillmore, Utah's Friend in the White House." *Utah Historical Quarterly* 48 (Spring 1980): 112-128.

3346. O'Brian, John. "A Forgotten President." *Niagara Frontier* 1 (Winter 1953): 1-10.

3347. Park, Julian. "Fillmore's Inaugural: Comments on Fillmore's Inaugural." *Niagara Frontier* 9 (Summer/Autumn 1962): 29-33.

3348. Russel, Robert R. "What Was the Compromise of 1850?" *Journal of Southern History* 22 (August 1956): 292-309.

3349. Schelin, Robert C. "Millard Fillmore: Anti-Mason to Know-Nothing: A Moderate in New York Politics, 1828-1856." Ph.D. dissertation, State University of New York, Binghamton, 1975.

3350. Stoddard, William O. . . . *Zachary Taylor, Millard Fillmore, Franklin Pierce, and James Buchanan*. New York: Stokes, 1888.

3351. Van Alstyne, Richard W. "British Diplomacy and the Clayton-Bulwer Treaty, 1850-1856." *Journal of Modern History* 11 (June 1939): 149-183.

Writings

3352. Fillmore, Millard. *The Early Life of Millard Fillmore: A Personal Reminiscence*. Buffalo, NY: Salisbury Club, 1958.

3353. Fillmore, Millard. *An Examination of the Question, "Is It Right to Require Any Religious Test as a Qualification to be a Witness in a Court of Justice?"* Buffalo, NY: C. Faxon, 1832.

3354. Fillmore, Millard. "Ex-President Fillmore Opposes Lincoln." *Illinois State Historical Society Journal* 46 (Autumn 1953): 302.

3355. Fillmore, Millard. *Millard Fillmore Papers*. 2 vols. Edited by Frank H. Severance. Buffalo, NY: Buffalo Historical Society, 1907.

3356. Snyder, Charles M. "Forgotten Fillmore Papers Examined: Sources of Reinterpretation of a Little-Known President." *American Archivist* 32 (January 1969): 11-14.

3357. Snyder, Charles M., ed. *The Lady and the President: The Letters of Dorothea Dix and Millard Fillmore*. Lexington: University Press of Kentucky, 1975.

Franklin Pierce

Biographies

3358. Bartlett, David V. G. *The Life of General Franklin Pierce, Of New Hampshire, The Democratic Candidate for President of the United States.* Buffalo, NY: G. H. Derby, 1852.

3359. Bell, Carl I. *They Knew Franklin Pierce.* Springfield, VT: April Hill, 1980.

3360. Hawthorne, Nathaniel. *Life of Franklin Pierce.* Boston: Ticknor, Reed and Fields, 1852.

3361. Hoyt, Edwin P. *Franklin Pierce: The Fourteenth President of the United States.* New York: Harper and Row, 1972.

Private Life

3362. Anderson, Louise K. "Franklin Pierce and the Pierce Mansion." *Daughters of the American Revolution Magazine* 94 (May 1960): 373-375.

3363. Boas, Norman F. *Jane M. Pierce (1806-1863).* Stonington, CT: Seaport Autographs, 1983.

3364. Nichols, Roy F. *Franklin Pierce: Young Hickory of the Granite Hills.* 2d ed. Philadelphia: University of Pennsylvania Press, 1958.

3365. Taylor, Lloyd C., Jr. "A Wife for Mr. Pierce." *New England Quarterly* 28 (September 1955): 339-348.

Public Career

3366. Klement, Frank. "Franklin Pierce and the Treason Charges of 1861-1862." *Historian* 23 (August 1961): 436-448.

Presidential Years

3367. Brown, Wenzell. "Franklin Pierce: The Reluctant President." *American Mercury* 71 (November 1950): 598-607.

3368. Donovan, Theresa A. "President Pierce's Ministers at the Court of St. James." *Pennsylvania Magazine of History and Biography* 91 (October 1967): 457-470.

3369. Manning, Seaton W. "Tragedy of the Ten-Million Acre Bill." *Social Service Review* 36 (March 1962): 44-50.

3370. Metcalf, Henry H. "Franklin Pierce and Edmund Burke: A President and a President Maker." *Granite Monthly* 59 (October 1927): 289-295.

3371. Nichols, Roy F. *The Stakes of Power, 1845-1877.* New York: Hill and Wang, 1961.

3372. Page, Elwin L. "Franklin Pierce and Abraham Lincoln — Parallels and

Contrasts." *Abraham Lincoln Quarterly* 5 (December 1949): 455-472.

3373. Purcell, Richard J. "Franklin Pierce: A Forgotten President." *Catholic Educational Review* 31 (August 1933): 134-141.

3374. Russel, Robert R. "Issues in the Congressional Struggle over the Kansas-Nebraska Bill, 1854." *Journal of Southern History* 29 (May 1963): 187-210.

3375. Stoddard, William O. ... *Zachary Taylor, Millard Fillmore, Franklin Pierce, and James Buchanan.* New York: Stokes, 1888.

3376. Upton, Richard F. "Franklin Pierce and the Shakers — A Subchapter in the Struggle for Religious Liberty." *Historical New Hampshire* 23 (Summer 1968): 3-11.

3377. Wallace, Edward S. *Destiny and Glory.* New York: Coward-McCann, 1957.

3378. Warner, Lee H. "Nathaniel Hawthorne and the Making of the President — 1852." *Historical New Hampshire* 28 (Spring 1973): 21-36.

3379. Warner, Lee H. "With Pierce and Hawthorne, In Mexico." *Essex Institute of Historical Collections* 111 (July 1975): 213-220.

3380. Webster, Sidney. *Franklin Pierce and His Administration.* New York: Appleton, 1892.

Writings

3381. Ray, P. Orman, ed. "Some Papers of Franklin Pierce, 1852-1862." *American Historical Review* 10 (October 1904): 110-127; (January 1905): 350-370.

James Buchanan

Biographies

3382. Auchampaugh, Philip G. *James Buchanan: A Political Portrait 1856, According To His Friends and Enemies.* Reno, NV: n.p., 1946.

3383. Curtis, George T. *Life of James Buchanan, Fifteenth President of the United States.* 2 vols. New York: Harper, 1883.

3384. Hoyt, Edwin P. *James Buchanan.* Chicago: Reilly and Lee, 1966.

3385. Jerome, C. *Life of James Buchanan.* Claremont, NH: Tracy Kenney and Co., 1856.

3386. Klein, Philip S. *President James Buchanan: A Biography.* University Park: Pennsylvania State University Press, 1962.

3387. McFarlane, Ian D. *Buchanan.* London: Duckworth, 1981.

3388. Mowry, George E. "James Buchanan." In *Collier's Encyclopedia*, Vol. 4, 646-648. New York: Collier, 1983.

3389. Worner, William F. "James Buchanan." *Lancaster County Historical Society Papers* 36 (1932): 59-83.

3390. Worner, William F. "James Buchanan." *Lancaster County Historical Society Papers* 38 (1934): 103-144.

Private Life

3391. Auchampaugh, Philip G. "James Buchanan, The Bachelor of the White House: An Inquiry on the Subject of Feminine Influence in the Life of Our Fifteenth President." *Tyler's Quarterly Historical and Geneological Magazine* 20 (January 1939): 154-166, 218-234.

3392. Auchampaugh, Philip G. "James Buchanan, The Squire from Lancaster." *Pennsylvania Magazine of History and Biography* 56 (1932): 15-32.

3393. Auchampaugh, Philip G. "James Buchanan, The Squire of Lancaster." *Pennsylvania Magazine of History and Biography* 55 (1931): 289-300.

3394. Hensel, William U. *The Attitude of James Buchanan, A Citizen of Lancaster County, Toward the Institution of Slavery in the United States.* Lancaster, PA: New Era Printing Co., 1911.

3395. Hensel, William U. "James Buchanan as a Lawyer." *University of Pennsylvania Law Review* 60 (May 1912): 546-573.

3396. Hensel, William U. "A Pennsylvania Presbyterian President: An Inquiry into the Religious Sentiments of James Buchanan, Fifteenth President of the United States." *Presbyterian Historical Society Journal* 4 (March 1908): 203-216.

3397. Hensel, William U. *The Religious Convictions and Character of James Buchanan, Fifteenth President of the United States — A Citizen of Lancaster County — A Member of the Presbyterian Church.* Lancaster, PA: Intelligencer Print, 1912.

3398. Hutton, Amy. "Buchanan Family Reminiscences." *Maryland Historical Magazine* 35 (September 1940): 262-269.

3399. Klein, Philip S. "Bachelor Father: James Buchanan as a Family Man." *Western Pennsylvania Historical Magazine* 50 (July 1967): 199-214.

3400. Klein, Philip S. "James Buchanan and Ann Coleman." *Pennsylvania History* 21 (January 1954): 1-20.

3401. Klein, Frederic S. "Wheatland: Home of James Buchanan." *American Heritage* 5 (Spring 1954): 44-49.

3402. Klein, Philip S. *The Story of Wheatland.* Lancaster, PA: Junior League of Lancaster, 1936.

3403. McMurtry, R. Gerald. "James Buchanan in Kentucky, 1813." *Filson Club History Quarterly* 8 (April 1934): 73-87.

3404. Pendleton, Lawson A. "James Buchanan's Attitude toward Slavery." Ph.D. dissertation, University of North Carolina, 1964.

3405. Ranck, James B. "The Attitude of James Buchanan towards Slavery (A Personal Study Based upon the Works of James Buchanan Himself)." *Pennsylvania Magazine of History* 51 (April 1927): 126-142.

3406. Taylor, Lloyd C. "Harriet Lane — Mirror of an Age." *Pennsylvania History* 30 (April 1963): 213-225.

Public Career

3407. Baylen, Joseph O. "James Buchanan's 'Calm of Despotism.'" *Pennsylvania Magazine of History and Biography* 77 (July 1953): 294-310.

3408. Bobr-Tylingo, Stanislaw. "James Buchanan and Poland in 1854." *Antemurale* 23 (1979): 75-93.

3409. Claussen, E. Neal. "Hendrick B. Wright and the 'Nocturnal Committee.'" *Pennsylvania Magazine of History and Biography* 89 (April 1965): 199-206.

3410. Hillman, Franklin P. "The Diplomatic Career of James Buchanan." Ph.D. dissertation, George Washington University, 1953.

3411. Hostetter, Ida L. K. "Harriet Lane." *Lancaster County Historical Society Journal* 33 (1929): 97-112.

3412. Meerse, David E. "Origins of the Buchanan-Douglas Feud Reconsidered." *Illinois State Historical Society Journal* 67 (April 1974): 154-174.

3413. Miller, C. L. "The Importance of the Adoption of Buchanan's Minority Report on the Repeal of the Twenty-fifth Section of the Judiciary Act of 1789." *University of Pennsylvania Law Review* 60 (May 1912): 574-581.

3414. Sioussat, St. George L. "James Buchanan, Secretary of State, March 5, 1845, to March 6, 1849." In *The American Secretaries of State and Their Diplomacy*, edited by Samuel F. Bemis, Vol. 5, 237-336, 391-416. New York: Knopf, 1928.

3415. Stenberg, Richard R. "Jackson, Buchanan, and the 'Corrupt Bargain' Calumny." *Pennsylvania Magazine of History and Biography* 58 (1934): 61-85.

Presidential Years

3416. Auchampaugh, Philip G. *James Buchanan and His Cabinet on the Eve of Secession.* Lancaster, PA: Privately Printed, 1926.

3417. Auchampaugh, Philip G. "James Buchanan, the Court, and the Dred Scott Case." *Tennessee Historical Magazine* 9 (January 1928): 231-240.

3418. Auchampaugh, Philip G. "James Buchanan, The Squire in the White House." *Pennsylvania Magazine of History and Biography* 58 (1934): 270-285.

3419. Auchampaugh, Philip G. "John B. Floyd and James Buchanan." *Tyler's Quarterly Historical and Geneological Magazine* 4 (April 1923): 381-388.

3420. Barondess, Benjamin. "Buchanan and the Dred Scott Justices." *Manuscripts* 10 (Winter 1958): 2-9.

3421. Barondess, Benjamin. "Buchanan and the Supreme Court Justices." *Manuscripts* 10 (Winter 1958): 2-9.

3422. Brown, J. Hay. "President Buchanan — Misunderstood — Wrongly Judged." *Lancaster County Historical Society Papers* 32 (June 1928): 88-92.

3423. Campbell, John A., Jr. "James Buchanan: Advocate in Congress, Cabinet, and Presidency." Ph.D. dissertation, University of Florida, 1968.

3424. Carlson, Robert E. "James Buchanan and Public Office." *Pennsylvania Magazine of History and Biography* 91 (July 1961): 255-279.

3425. Davis, Robert R., Jr. "James Buchanan and the Suppression of the Slave Trade, 1859-1861." *Pennsylvania History* 33 (October 1966): 446-459.

3426. Davis, Robert R., Jr., ed. "Buchanan Espionage: A Report on Illegal Slave Trading in the South in 1859." *Journal of Southern History* 37 (May 1971): 271-278.

3427. Dumond, Dwight L. *The Secession Movement, 1860-1861.* New York: Macmillan, 1931.

3428. Farley, Foster M. "William B. Reed: President Buchanan's Minister to China 1857-1858." *Pennsylvania History* 37 (July 1970): 269-280.

3429. Fujita, Fumiko. "Foreign Policy in a Democracy: Polk, Buchanan, and Oregon." *American Review* 7 (1973): 107-144.

3430. Halstead, Murat. *Trimmers, Trucklers, and Temporizers: Notes of Murat Halstead from the Political Conventions of 1856.* Edited by William B. Hesseltine and Rex G. Fisher. Madison: State Historical Society of Wisconsin, 1961.

3431. Hubbell, John T. "Jeremiah Sullivan Black and the Great Secession Winter." *Western Pennsylvania Historical Magazine* 57 (1974): 255-274.

3432. Johnson, Kenneth R., ed. "A Southern Student Describes the Inauguration of President James Buchanan." *Alabama Historical Quarterly* 31 (Fall/Winter 1969): 237-240.

3433. Kettell, Thomas P. *Southern Wealth and Northern Profits.* New York: G. W. and J. A. Wood, 1860.

3434. King, Horatio C. *Turning on the Light: A Dispassionate Survey of President Buchanan's Administration, From 1860 to Its Close.* Philadelphia: Lippincott, 1895.

3435. Klein, Philip S. "The Inauguration of President James Buchanan." *Lancaster County Historical Society Journal* 61 (October 1957): 145-168.

3436. Klein, Frederic S. "James Buchanan — Man on a Tightrope." *American History Illustrated* 1 (May 1966): 13-20, 24.

3437. Klein, Philip S. "James Buchanan — Selfish Politician or Christian Statesman?" *Journal of Presbyterian History* 42 (March 1964): 1-18.

3438. Klein, Philip S. "Patriotic Myths and Political Realities: Buchanan and the

Origins of the Civil War." *Lock Haven Review* 15 (1974): 65-78.

3439. Klingberg, Frank W. "James Buchanan and the Crisis of the Union." *Journal of Southern History* 9 (November 1943): 455-474.

3440. Mackinnon, William P. "The Buchanan Spoils System and the Utah Expedition: Careers of W. M. F. Magraw and John M. Hockaday." *Utah Historical Quarterly* 31 (Spring 1963): 127-150.

3441. Mackinnon, William P. "The Gap in the Buchanan Revival: The Utah Expedition of 1857-1858." *Utah Historical Quarterly* 45 (Winter 1977): 36-46.

3442. Meerse, David E. "Buchanan, Corruption, and the Election of 1860." *Civil War History* 12 (June 1966): 116-131.

3443. Meerse, David E. "Buchanan's Patronage Policy: An Attempt to Achieve Political Strength." *Pennsylvania History* 40 (January 1973): 37-57.

3444. Meerse, David E. "James Buchanan, the Patronage, and the Northern Democratic Party, 1857-1858." Ph.D. dissertation, University of Illinois, 1969.

3445. Nevins, Allan. "The Needless Conflict: If Buchanan Had Met the Kansas Problem Firmly We Might Have Avoided Civil War." *American Heritage* 7 (August 1955): 4-9, 88-90.

3446. Nichols, Alice. *Bleeding Kansas.* New York: Oxford University Press, 1954.

3447. Nichols, Roy F. "James Buchanan: Lessons in Leadership in Trying Times." In *Bulwark of Liberty: Early Years at Dickinson*, 165-174. New York: Revell, 1950.

3448. Owens, Robert L. "James Buchanan — Diplomat, International Statesman, President." *Lancaster County Historical Society Papers* 32 (June 1928): 93-97.

3449. Pressly, Thomas J. *Americans Interpret Their Civil War.* Princeton, NJ: Princeton University Press, 1954.

3450. Russ, William A., Jr. "Time Lag and Political Change as Seen in the Administration of Buchanan and Hoover." *South Atlantic Quarterly* 46 (July 1947): 336-343.

3451. Scheips, Paul J. "Buchanan and the Chiriqui Naval Station Sites." *Military Affairs* 18 (Summer 1954): 64-80.

3452. Scott, Winfield. *Memoirs of Lieut. General Scott, LLD.* New York: Sheldon and Co., 1864.

3453. Sellers, Charles G., Jr., ed. *The Southerner as American.* Chapel Hill: University of North Carolina Press, 1960.

3454. Smith, Elbert B. *The Presidency of James Buchanan.* Lawrence: University Press of Kansas, 1975.

3455. Stoddard, William O. . . . *Zachary Taylor, Millard Fillmore, Franklin Pierce, and James Buchanan.* New York: Stokes, 1888.

3456. Woodward, Isaiah A. "John Brown's Raid at Harper's Ferry and Governor Henry Alexander Wise's Letter to President James Buchanan Concerning the Invasion." *West Virginia History* 42 (Spring/Summer 1981): 307-313.

Writings

3457. Buchanan, James. "James Buchanan to Thomas W. Gilmer." *William and Mary Quarterly* 20 (October 1911): 118-119.

3458. Buchanan, James. *Mr. Buchanan's Administration on the Eve of the Rebellion.* New York: Appleton, 1866.

3459. Buchanan, James. "Unpublished Letters of James Buchanan." *Lancaster County Historical Society Papers* 32 (May 1928): 67-72; (October 1928): 118-121.

3460. Buchanan, James. *The Works of James Buchanan: Comprising His Speeches, State Papers, and Private Correspondence.* 12 vols. Edited by John B. Moore. Philadelphia: Lippincott, 1908-1911.

3461. Horton, Rushmore G. *The Life and Public Services of James Buchanan.... Including the Most Important of His State Papers, With an Accurate Portrait on Steel.* New York: Derby and Jackson, 1856.

3462. Worner, William F. "Tablet Unveiled to James Buchanan." *Lancaster County Historical Society Papers* 39 (1935): 69-71.

3463. Worner, William F., ed. "Letters of James Buchanan." *Lancaster County Historical Society Papers* 35 (1931): 189-192.

Abraham Lincoln

Biographies

3464. Abbott, Abbott A. *The Life of Abraham Lincoln.* New York: T. R. Dawley, 1864.

3465. Abbott, John S. C. *Life of Abraham Lincoln.* Chicago: Illustrated Book Co., 1900.

3466. Agar, Herbert. *Abraham Lincoln.* New York: Macmillan, 1952.

3467. Anderson, David D. *Abraham Lincoln.* New York: Twayne, 1970.

3468. Anderson, Dwight G. *Abraham Lincoln: The Quest for Immortality.* New York: Knopf, 1982.

3469. Arnold, Isaac N. *The Life of Abraham Lincoln.* 3d ed. Chicago: McClurg, 1885.

3470. Arnold, Issac N. *Sketch of the Life of Abraham Lincoln.* New York: J. B. Bachelder, 1869.

3471. Bailey, Bernadine F. *The Story of Abraham Lincoln.* Chicago: Rand McNally, 1942.

3472. Bains, Rae. *Abraham Lincoln.* Mahwah, NJ: Troll Associates, 1984.

3473. Baldwin, James. *Abraham Lincoln.* New York: American Book Co., 1904.

3474. Barnard, George G. *Barnard's Lincoln.* Cincinnati, OH: Stewart and Kidd, 1917.

3475. Barnwell, Robert W. *The Lines and Nature of Lincoln's Greatness.* Columbia, SC: State Co., 1931.

3476. Bartlett, David V. *Life of Abraham Lincoln.* Philadelphia: Bradley, 1860.

3477. Barton, William E. *The Life of Abraham Lincoln.* 2 vols. Indianapolis, IN: Bobbs-Merrill, 1925.

3478. Basler, Roy P. *Lincoln.* New York: Grove Press, 1962.

3479. Beveridge, Albert J. *Abraham Lincoln, 1809-1858.* 2 vols. Boston: Houghton Mifflin, 1828.

3480. "The Beveridge 'Lincoln.'" *Abraham Lincoln Association Bulletin* 13 (December 1, 1928): 1-8.

3481. Binns, Henry B. *Abraham Lincoln.* New York: Dutton, 1907.

3482. Binns, Henry B. *The Life of Abraham Lincoln.* New York: Dutton, 1927.

3483. Bissett, Clark P. *Abraham Lincoln, A Universal Man.* San Francisco: J. Howell, 1923.

3484. Bowers, John H. *Life of Abraham Lincoln.* Girard, KS: Haldeman-Julius, 1922.

3485. Brogan, Denis W. *Abraham Lincoln.* New York: Schocken, 1963.

3486. Brooks, Noah. *Washington in Lincoln's Time.* New York: Century, 1895.

3487. Brown, Charles R. *Lincoln, The Greatest Man of the Nineteenth Century.* New York: Macmillan, 1922.

3488. Browne, Francis F., comp. *The Everyday Life of Abraham Lincoln: Lincoln's Life and Character Portrayed by Those Who Knew Him.* Rev. ed. New York: N. D. Thompson, 1913.

3489. Bullock, Alonzo M. *Lincoln.* Appleton, WS: n.p., 1913.

3490. Carnegie, Dale B. *Lincoln, The Unknown.* New York: Century, 1932.

3491. Cary, Barbara. *Meet Abraham Lincoln.* New York: Random House, 1965.

3492. Charnwood, Godfrey R. B. *Abraham Lincoln.* New York: Holt, 1917.

3493. Choate, Joseph H. *Abraham Lincoln.* New York: Crowell, 1901.

3494. Clark, Philip. *Abraham Lincoln.* Hove, East Sussex, England: Wayland, 1981.

3495. Coffin, Charles C. *Abraham Lincoln.* New York: Harper and Brothers, 1893.

3496. Colver, Anne. *Abraham Lincoln: For the People.* New York: Dell, 1960.

3497. Courtenay, Calista. *Abraham Lincoln.* New York: M. A. Donohue, 1917.

3498. Cravens, Francis. *The Story of Lincoln.* Bloomington, IL: Public School Publishing Co., 1898.

3499. Crew, C. C. *Life and Times of Abraham Lincoln, 1809-1865.* Exeter, England: A. Wheaton, 1935.

3500. Croll, P. C. "Abraham Lincoln: A Summer Study." *Pennsylvania German* 11 (February 1910): 87-93.

3501. Crosby, Franklin. *Life of Abraham Lincoln.* New York: International Book Co., 1865.

3502. Current, Richard N. *The Lincoln Nobody Knows.* New York: McGraw-Hill, 1958.

3503. Curtis, William E. *Abraham Lincoln.* Philadelphia: Lippincott, 1902.

3504. Daugherty, James. *Abraham Lincoln.* New York: Viking Press, 1943.

3505. D'Aulaire, Ingri M. *Abraham Lincoln.* Garden City, NY: Doubleday, 1957.

3506. Delahay, Mark W. *Abraham Lincoln.* New York: P. H. Newhall, 1939.

3507. Diamond, Martin. "An Excerpt from 'Lincoln's Greatness.'" *Interpretation* 8 (May 1980): 22-25.

3508. Dodge, Daniel K. *Abraham Lincoln, Master of Words.* New York: Appleton, 1924.

3509. Donald, David H. *Lincoln Herndon.* New York: Knopf, 1948.

3510. Draper, Andrew S. *What Makes Lincoln Great?* Edited by Harlan H. Horner. Cedar Rapids, IA: Torch Press, 1940.

3511. Elias, Edith. *Abraham Lincoln.* New York: Stokes, 1920.

3512. Foster, Genevieve. *Abraham Lincoln.* New York: Scribner's, 1950.

3513. French, Charles W. *Abraham Lincoln.* New York: Funk and Wagnalls, 1891.

3514. George, Marian M. *Lincoln and Washington.* Chicago: Flanagan, 1899.

3515. Gordy, Wilbur F. *Abraham Lincoln.* New York: Scribner's, 1917.

3516. Gray, William C. *Life of Abraham Lincoln.* Cincinnati, OH: Western Tract and Book Society, 1867.

3517. Gridley, Eleanor. *The Story of*

Abraham Lincoln. New York: M. A. Donohue and Co., 1900.

3518. Gruber, Michael. *Abraham Lincoln.* New York: American R. D. M. Corp., 1965.

3519. Hamilton, Mary A. *The Story of Abraham Lincoln.* New York: Dutton, 1906.

3520. Hanaford, Phebe A. *Abraham Lincoln.* New York: Werner, 1895.

3521. Handlin, Oscar, and Lilian Handlin. *Abraham Lincoln and the Union.* Boston: Little, Brown, 1980.

3522. Hapgood, Norman. *Abraham Lincoln, The Man of the People.* New York: Macmillan, 1899.

3523. Hart, Hugh. *Lincoln ... The Man of the Ages.* Monmouth, IL: F. L. Seybald and Co., 1945.

3524. Hein, David. "The Significance for Lincoln Studies of Lewis Saum's Work on Ante-Bellum Culture." *Lincoln Herald* 85 (Winter 1983): 280-281.

3525. Herndon, William H., and Jesse W. Weik. *Abraham Lincoln: The True Story of a Great Life.* 2 vols. New York: Appleton, 1916.

3526. Herndon, William H., and J. William Weik. *Herndon's Lincoln: The True Story of a Great Life, The History and Personal Recollections of Abraham Lincoln.* 3 vols. Chicago: Belford, Clarke, 1889.

3527. Hertz, Emanuel. *Abraham Lincoln: A New Portrait.* 2 vols. New York: Liveright, 1931.

3528. Hill, John W. *If Lincoln Were Here.* New York: Putnam, 1925.

3529. Holland, Josiah G. *Life of Abraham Lincoln.* Springfield, MA: G. Bill, 1865.

3530. Hope, Eva. *New World Heros, Lincoln and Garfield: The Life Story of Two Self-Made Men, Whom the People Made Presidents.* London: W. Scott, 1884.

3531. Horgan, Paul. *Abraham Lincoln: Citizen of New Salem.* New York: Macmillan, 1961.

3532. Horgan, Paul. *Citizen of New Salem.* New York: Farrar, 1961.

3533. Horner, Harlan H. *Lincoln and Greeley.* Urbana: University of Illinois Press, 1953.

3534. House, Albert V., Jr. "The Trials of a Ghost-Writer of Lincoln Biography — Chauncey F. Black's Authorship of Lamon's Lincoln." *Illinois State Historical Society Journal* 31 (September 1938): 262-296.

3535. Howells, William D. *Life of Abraham Lincoln.* Bloomington: Indiana University Press, 1960.

3536. Ingersoll, Robert G. *Abraham Lincoln.* New York: Lane, 1894.

3537. Jayne, William. *Abraham Lincoln.* Chicago: Grand Army Hall and Memorial Association, 1908.

3538. Jennings, Janet. *Abraham Lincoln, The Greatest American.* Madison, WI: Cantwell Print Co., 1909.

3539. Judson, Clara I. *Abraham Lincoln, Friend of the People.* Chicago: Wilcox and Follett, 1950.

3540. Jusserand, Jean A. "Abraham Lincoln." In his *With Americans of Past and Present Days,* 277-306. New York: Scribner's, 1916.

3541. Kelley, William D. *Lincoln and Stanton.* New York: Putnam, 1885.

3542. Ketcham, Henry. *The Life of Abraham Lincoln.* New York: A. L. Burt, 1901.

3543. Kharas, Theodore. *Lincoln, A Master of Efficiency.* Wilkes-Barre, PA: T. L. Printery, 1921.

3544. Kingdon, Frank. *Architects of the Republic: George Washington, Thomas Jefferson, Abraham Lincoln, Franklin D. Roosevelt*. New York: Alliance Publishing Co., 1947.

3545. Kolpas, Norman. *Abraham Lincoln*. New York: McGraw-Hill, 1981.

3546. Komroff, Manuel. *Abraham Lincoln*. New York: Putnam, 1959.

3547. Kunhardt, Dorothy M. *Twenty Days*. New York: Harper and Row, 1965.

3548. Kunkel, Mable. *Abraham Lincoln, Unforgettable American*. Charlotte, NC: Delmar, 1976.

3549. Lawson, McEwan. *Here Greatness Stands: The Story of Abraham Lincoln*. London: Butterworth, 1948.

3550. Levy, T. Aaron. *Lincoln, The Politician*. Boston: R. G. Badger, 1918.

3551. Lewis, Lloyd. *Myths after Lincoln*. New York: Harcourt, Brace, 1929.

3552. *The Lincoln Album: Life of the Preserver of the Union, the Liberator of a People, and the First American, Told by Authentic Pictures....* St. Louis, MO: Hawkins Publishing Co., 1907.

3553. Lockridge, Ross F. *A. Lincoln*. New York: World Books, 1930.

3554. Long, John D. *The Life Story of Abraham Lincoln*. Chicago: Revell, 1930.

3555. Longford, Frank. *Abraham Lincoln*. New York: Putnam, 1975.

3556. Lorant, Stefan. *The Life of Abraham Lincoln: A Short Illustrated Biography*. New York: McGraw-Hill, 1954.

3557. Lowitz, Sadyebeth. *Barefoot Abe: A Really Truly Story by Sadyebeth and Anson Lowitz, With Illustrations by the Latter*. Minneapolis, MN: Lerner Publications Co., 1967.

3558. Ludwig, Emil. *Abraham Lincoln: The Full Life Story of Our Martyred President*. New York: Liveright, 1949.

3559. Luthin, Reinhard H. *The Real Abraham Lincoln: A Complete One Volume History of His Life and Times*. Englewood Cliffs, NJ: Prentice-Hall, 1960.

3560. MacChesney, Nathan W., ed. *Abraham Lincoln: The Tribute of a Century, 1809-1909, Commemorative of the Lincoln Centenary and Containing the Principal Speeches Made in Connection Therewith*. Chicago: McClurg, 1910.

3561. McClure, Alexander K. *Portrait for Posterity: Lincoln and His Biographers*. New Brunswick, NJ: Rutgers University Press, 1947.

3562. Mace, William H. *Lincoln, The Man of the People*. New York: Rand McNally, 1912.

3563. McLaughlin, Robert. *Washington and Lincoln*. New York: Putnam, 1912.

3564. Madison, Lucy F. *Lincoln*. Philadelphia: Penn Publishing Co., 1928.

3565. "The Making of Lincoln." *Outlook* 91 (February 13, 1909): 327-330.

3566. Maltby, Charles. *The Life and Public Services of Abraham Lincoln*. Stockton, CA: Daily Independent Steam Power Plant, 1884.

3567. Martin, Patricia M. *Abraham Lincoln*. New York: Putnam, 1964.

3568. Masters, Edgar L. *Lincoln the Man*. New York: Dodd, Mead, 1931.

3569. Meadowcroft, Enid. *Abraham Lincoln*. New York: Crowell, 1942.

3570. Mearns, David C. *Largely Lincoln*. New York: St. Martin's Press, 1961.

3571. Merriam, Charles E. *Four American Party Leaders*. New York: Macmillan, 1926.

3572. Miller, Francis T. *Portrait Life of*

Lincoln: Life of Abraham Lincoln, The Greatest American.... Springfield, MA: Patriot Publishing Co., 1910.

3573. Minor, Charles L. *The Real Lincoln.* Richmond, VA: Everett Waddey, 1901.

3574. Mitgang, Herbert. *The Fiery Trail: A Life of Lincoln.* New York: Viking Press, 1974.

3575. Moores, Charles W. *Abraham Lincoln.* Greenfield, IN: William Mitchell, 1922.

3576. Morse, John T., Jr. *Abraham Lincoln.* 2 vols. Boston: Houghton Mifflin, 1893.

3577. Moses, Elbert R. *Abraham Lincoln: From Cabin to Capitol.* Daytona Beach, FL: College Publishing Co., 1955.

3578. Mumford, Mary E. *A Sketch of the Life and Times of Abraham Lincoln.* Philadelphia: Bradley, 1865.

3579. Nevins, Allan. *The Emergence of Lincoln.* 2 vols. New York: Scribner's, 1950.

3580. Nevins, Allan, and Irving Stone, eds. *Lincoln: A Contemporary Portrait.* Garden City, NY: Doubleday, 1962.

3581. Newton, Joseph F. *Abraham Lincoln: An Essay.* Cedar Rapids, IA: Torch Press, 1910.

3582. Newton, Joseph F. *Lincoln and Herndon.* Cedar Rapids, IA: Torch Press, 1910.

3583. Nicolay, John G. *A Short Life of Abraham Lincoln, Condensed from Nicolay and Hay's Abraham Lincoln: A History.* New York: Century, 1902.

3584. Nicolay, John G., and John Hay. *Abraham Lincoln: A History.* 10 vols. New York: Century, 1890.

3585. Nolan, Jeannette C. *Abraham Lincoln.* New York: Messner, 1965.

3586. North, Sterling. *Abe Lincoln, Log Cabin to White House.* New York: Random House, 1956.

3587. Oates, Stephen B. *Abraham Lincoln: The Man behind the Myths.* New York: Harper and Row, 1984.

3588. Oates, Stephen B. *With Malice toward None: The Life of Abraham Lincoln.* New York: Harper and Row, 1977.

3589. Oberholtzer, Ellis P. *Abraham Lincoln.* Philadelphia: G. W. Jacobs and Co., 1904.

3590. Packard, Roy D. *A. Lincoln.* Cleveland, OH: Carpenter Print, 1948.

3591. Paradise, Frank I. *Abraham Lincoln, Democrat.* London: Mills and Boon, 1921.

3592. Paul, Eden, and Cedar Paul. *Abraham Lincoln and the Times That Tried His Soul.* New York: Fawcett, 1956.

3593. Phillips, Isaac N. *Abraham Lincoln.* Bloomington, IL: n.p., 1901.

3594. Phillips, Isaac N. *Lincoln.* Chicago: McClurg, 1910.

3595. Power, John C. *Abraham Lincoln.* Springfield, IL: E. A. Wilson, 1875.

3596. Pratt, Harry E. *Lincoln, 1840-1846.* Springfield, IL: Abraham Lincoln Association, 1939.

3597. Pratt, Harry E. *Lincoln, 1809-1839.* Springfield, IL: Abraham Lincoln Association, 1941.

3598. Putnam, George H. *Abraham Lincoln: The People's Leader in the Struggle for National Existence.* New York: Putnam, 1909.

3599. Randall, James G. *Lincoln and the South.* Baton Rouge: Louisiana State University Press, 1946.

3600. Randall, James G. *Lincoln, The Liberal Statesman.* New York: Dodd, Mead, 1947.

3601. Randall, James G. *Lincoln, The President.* 4 vols. New York: Dodd, Mead, 1945-1955.

3602. Randall, James G. *Mr. Lincoln.* Edited by Richard N. Current. New York: Dodd, Mead, 1957.

3603. Rankin, Henry B. "The First American — Abraham Lincoln." *Illinois State Historical Society Journal* 8 (July 1915): 260-267.

3604. Rasmussen, Della M. *The Power of Trying Again: The Story of Abe Lincoln.* Antioch, CA: Power Tales, Eagle Systems International, 1981.

3605. Raymond, Henry J., and John Savage. *The Life of Abraham Lincoln, and of Andrew Johnson.* New York: National Union Executive Committee, 1864.

3606. Reid, Whitelaw. *Abraham Lincoln.* London: Harrison and Sons, 1910.

3607. Richards, John T. *Abraham Lincoln, The Lawyer-Statesman.* Boston: Houghton Mifflin, 1916.

3608. Ridley, Maurice R. *Abraham Lincoln.* London: Blackie and Son, 1945.

3609. Rogers, Agnes. *Abraham Lincoln, A Biography in Pictures with Accompanying Text.* Boston: Little, Brown, 1939.

3610. Rothschild, Alonzo. *Lincoln, Master of Men: A Study in Character.* Boston: Houghton Mifflin, 1906.

3611. Russell, G. Darrell, Jr. *Lincoln and Kennedy: Looked at Kindly Together.* New York: Carlton, 1973.

3612. Sanchez-Torrento, Eugenio. *A Modern Biography of Abraham Lincoln.* Miami: Impresso Editorial A. I. P., 1970.

3613. Sandburg, Carl. *Abraham Lincoln, The Prairie Years.* 2 vols. New York: Harcourt, Brace, 1926.

3614. Schurz, Carl. *Abraham Lincoln, An Essay.* Boston: Houghton Mifflin, 1891.

3615. Scripps, John L. *Life of Abraham Lincoln.* New York: Greenwood Press, 1961.

3616. Sharp, Alfred. *Abraham Lincoln.* London: Epworth Press, 1919.

3617. Shaw, Albert. *Abraham Lincoln: Profusely Illustrated with Contemporary Cartoons, Portraits, and Scenes.* 2 vols. New York: Review of Reviews, 1929.

3618. Shirley, Ralph. *A Short Life of Abraham Lincoln.* New York: Funk and Wagnalls, 1919.

3619. Shuster, George N. "Mr. Beveridge's Lincoln." *Commonweal* 8 (October 1931): 658-659.

3620. Shutes, Milton H. *Lincoln and the Doctors: A Medical Narrative of the Life of Abraham Lincoln.* New York: Pioneer Press, 1933.

3621. Smith, Dwight L., ed. "Robert Livingston Stanton's Lincoln." *Lincoln Herald* 76 (Winter 1974): 172-180.

3622. Smith, John D. "Contributions of Louis A. Warren to Lincoln Scholarship." *Lincoln Herald* 80 (Summer 1978): 95-101.

3623. Snider, Denton J. *Abraham Lincoln, An Interpretation in Biography.* St. Louis, MO: Sigma Publishing Co., 1908.

3624. Starr, John W. *Lincoln and the Railroads: A Biographical Study.* New York: Dodd, Mead, 1927.

3625. Stoddard, William O. *Abraham Lincoln.* New York: Fords, Howard, and Hulbert, 1888.

3626. Stoddard, William O. *Abraham Lincoln and Andrew Johnson.* New York: Stokes, 1888.

3627. Stoddard, William O. *Lincoln at Work, Sketches from Life.* Boston: United Society of Christian Endeavor, 1900.

3628. Strozier, Charles B. *Lincoln's Quest*

for Union: Public and Private Meanings. New York: Basic Books, 1982.

3629. Strunsky, Rose. *Abraham Lincoln.* London: Methuen, 1914.

3630. Sumner, Guy L. *Meet Abraham Lincoln.* New York: Harper and Row, 1946.

3631. Suppiger, Joseph E. *The Intimate Lincoln.* Lanham, MD: University Press of America, 1985.

3632. Suppiger, Joseph E. "The Intimate Lincoln." *Lincoln Herald* 83 (Spring 1981): 604-614; (Summer 1981): 668-676; (Fall 1981): 737-746; (Winter 1981): 774-785; 84 (Spring 1982): 26-37; (Summer 1982): 114-125; (Fall 1982): 149-154; (Winter 1982): 222-236; 85 (Spring 1983): 7-20; (Summer 1983): 80-94; (Fall 1983): 152-166; (Winter 1983): 242-253.

3633. Tarbell, Ida M. *In the Footsteps of the Lincolns.* New York: Harper and Row, 1924.

3634. Thayer, William M. *From Pioneer Home to White House: Life of Abraham Lincoln.* Rev. ed. Norwich, CT: Henry Bill Publishing Co., 1882.

3635. Thayer, William M. *Life and Character of Abraham Lincoln.* Boston: Walker, Wise, 1864.

3636. Thomas, Benjamin P. *Abraham Lincoln, A Biography.* New York: Knopf, 1952.

3637. Thomas, Benjamin P. *Lincoln.* Springfield, IL: Abraham Lincoln Association, 1936.

3638. Thomas, Benjamin P. *Portrait for Posterity: Lincoln and His Biographers.* New Brunswick, NJ: Rutgers University Press, 1947.

3639. Thompson, David D. *Abraham Lincoln.* New York: Hunt and Eaton, 1894.

3640. Tilley, John S. *Lincoln Takes Command.* Chapel Hill: University of North Carolina Press, 1941.

3641. Trueblood, David E. *Abraham Lincoln: Theologian of American Anguish.* New York: Harper and Row, 1973.

3642. Victor, Orville J. *The Private and Public Life of Abraham Lincoln.* New York: Beadle, 1864.

3643. Wade, Mary H. *Abraham Lincoln.* Boston: R. G. Badger, 1914.

3644. Wanamaker, Reuben M. *The Voice of Lincoln.* New York: Scribner's, 1920.

3645. Warren, Louis A. *Abraham Lincoln, A Concise Biography.* Fort Wayne, IN: Lincoln National Life Insurance Co., 1934.

3646. Weik, Jesse W. *The Real Lincoln: A Portrait.* Boston: Houghton Mifflin, 1922.

3647. Wheare, Kenneth C. *Abraham Lincoln and the United States.* New York: Macmillan, 1949.

3648. Wheeler, Daniel E. *Abraham Lincoln.* New York: Macmillan, 1916.

3649. Whitlock, Brand. *Abraham Lincoln.* New York: Appleton, 1930.

3650. Whitney, Henry C. *Life of Abraham Lincoln.* 2 vols. New York: Baker and Taylor, 1908.

3651. Wiley, Bell I. "Lincoln, Plain Man of the People." *Emory University Quarterly* 14 (December 1958): 195-206.

3652. Wiley, Earl W. *Abraham Lincoln: Portrait of a Speaker.* New York: Vantage Press, 1970.

3653. Williams, Francis H. *The Burden Bearer: An Epic of Lincoln.* Philadelphia: Jacobs, 1908.

3654. Williams, Wayne C. *A Rail Splitter for President.* Denver, CO: University of Denver Press, 1951.

3655. Wood, Leonora W. *Abraham Lincoln.* Piedmont, WV: Herald Printing House, 1942.

3656. Woody, Robert H. "Inexhaustible Lincoln." *South Atlantic Quarterly* 52 (October 1953): 587-610.

Private Life

General

3657. "Abraham Lincoln." *Spectator* 102 (February 13, 1909): 254-255.

3658. "Abraham Lincoln." *Spectator* 106 (February 11, 1911): 213-214.

3659. *Abraham Lincoln Fact Book and Teacher's Guide.* Philadelphia: Eastern Acorn Press, 1983.

3660. Anderson, Levere. "The Forgotten Lincoln." *Mankind* 1 (February 1969): 84-94.

3661. Angle, Paul M. "The Changing Lincoln." In *The John H. Hauberg Historical Essays,* edited by O. Fritiof Ander, 1-17. Rock Island, IL: Augustana Book Concern, 1954.

3662. Angle, Paul M. "Masters' 'Lincoln the Man': A Factual Criticism." *Abraham Lincoln Association Bulletin* 23 (June 1931): 6-9.

3663. Atkinson, Eleanor. "Lincoln's Alma Mater." *Harper's* 126 (May 1913): 942-947.

3664. Atkinson, Eleanor. *Lincoln's Love Story.* Garden City, NY: Doubleday, 1909.

3665. Babcock, Bernie. "Unforgotten Ann Rutledge." *Daughters of the American Revolution Magazine* 62 (February 1928): 80-83.

3666. Bachelder, Louise, ed. *Abraham Lincoln: Wisdom and Wit.* Mount Vernon, NY: Peter Pauper Press, 1965.

3667. Bartlett, Truman H. "The Physiognomy of Lincoln." *McClure's* 29 (August 1907): 391-407.

3668. Barton, Robert. *Lincoln, The Grocer.* Foxboro, MA: Brochure Publishing Co., 1937.

3669. Barton, William E. *A Beautiful Blunder: The True Story of Lincoln's Letter to Mrs. Lydia A. Bixby.* Indianapolis, IN: Bobbs-Merrill, 1926.

3670. Barton, William E. "The Enduring Lincoln." *Illinois State Historical Society Journal* 20 (July 1927): 243-254.

3671. Barton, William E. "A Noble Fragment: Beveridge's Life of Lincoln." *Mississippi Valley Historical Review* 15 (March 1929): 497-510.

3672. Barton, William E. *The Women Lincoln Loved.* Indianapolis, IN: Bobbs-Merrill, 1927.

3673. Basler, Roy P. "Abraham Lincoln — Artist." *North American Review* 245 (Spring 1938): 144-153.

3674. Bauer, Charles J. "Lincoln and Sam Musick's Bridge." *Lincoln Herald* 76 (Summer 1974): 94-96.

3675. Blair, Harry C., and Rebecca Tarshis. *The Life of Colonel Edward S. Baker, Lincoln's Constant Ally.* Portland: Oregon Historical Society, 1960.

3676. Borglum, Gutzon. "The Beauty of Lincoln." *Everybody's Magazine* 22 (February 1910): 217-220.

3677. Bullard, F. Lauriston. *Abraham Lincoln and the Widow Bixby.* New Brunswick, NJ: Rutgers University Press, 1946.

3678. Bullard, F. Lauriston. *Was "Abe" Lincoln a Gentleman?* Boston: Boston University Press, 1952.

3679. Carruthers, Olive, and R. Gerald McMurtry. *Lincoln's Other Mary.* New York: Ziff-Davis, 1946.

3680. Chafin, Eugene W. *Lincoln, The Man of Sorrow.* Chicago: Lincoln Temperance Press, 1908.

3681. Charnwood, Godfrey R. B. "Concerning Abraham Lincoln." *Anglo-French Review* 3 (February 1920): 46-52; (March 1920): 155-161; (April 1920): 359-366; (May 1920): 486-491; (June 1920): 594-598; 4 (August 1920): 75-80.

3682. Chipperfield, Burnett M. "Abraham Lincoln." *American Law Review* 57 (March/April 1923): 292-302.

3683. Crady, Wilson. "Incident of Destiny." *Lincoln Herald* 83 (Fall 1981): 730-733.

3684. Cromer, Lord. "Abraham Lincoln." *Spectator* 117 (August 10, 1915): 212-213.

3685. Cunningham, J. O. "Abraham Lincoln." *Firelands Pioneer* 17 (December 1909): 1456-1473.

3686. Cunningham, John L. "Lincoln at Brady's Gallery." Edited by Carl Haverlin. *Illinois State Historical Society Journal* 48 (Spring 1955): 52-58.

3687. Davis, Cullum, Charles B. Strozier, Rebecca M. Veach, and Geoffrey C. Ward, eds. *The Public and the Private Lincoln: Contemporary Perspectives.* Carbondale: Southern Illinois University Press, 1979.

3688. Davis, Harvey O. "Lincoln." *Lincoln Herald* 67 (Fall 1965): 109-110.

3689. Dondero, George A. "Why Lincoln Wore a Beard." *Illinois State Historical Society Journal* 24 (July 1931): 321-332.

3690. Dowding, Nancy E. "Sandburg the Biographer." *Lincoln Herald* 81 (Fall 1979): 159-162.

3691. Dunne, Edward F. "Abraham Lincoln." *Illinois State Historical Society Journal* 9 (April 1915): 8-22.

3692. "Edward Dickinson Baker — Lincoln's Forgotten Friend." *Lincoln Herald* 53 (Summer 1951): 33-36.

3693. Ehrmann, Bess V. *The Missing Chapter in the Life of Abraham Lincoln.* Chicago: W. M. Hill, 1938.

3694. Fairbanks, Avard T. "The Face of Abraham Lincoln." In *Lincoln for the Ages,* edited by Ralph G. Newman, 160-165. Garden City, NY: Doubleday, 1960.

3695. Flagg, Norman G. "Abraham Lincoln." *Illinois State Historical Society Journal* 10 (April 1917): 123-126.

3696. Foster, Bertram G. *Abraham Lincoln, Inventor.* Federalsburg, MD: n.p., 1928.

3697. Friend, Henry C. *Abraham Lincoln's Commercial Practice: A Series of Articles by Henry C. Friend.* Chicago: Commercial Law Foundation, 1970.

3698. Garner, Wayne L. "Abraham Lincoln and the Uses of Humor." Ph.D. dissertation, University of Iowa, 1963.

3699. Gates, Arnold F. *Amberglow of Abraham Lincoln and Ann Rutledge.* West Leisinring, PA: Griglak Printer, 1939.

3700. "The Genius of Lincoln." *Nation* 4 (February 1909): 705-706.

3701. Grant, Ulysses S. "Abe and Little Alec." *Collector* 62 (December 1949): 257-258.

3702. Greene, Peter. "Lincoln." *Lincoln Herald* 68 (Spring 1966): 1-2.

3703. Griffith, Albert H. *The Heart of Abraham Lincoln.* Madison: Lincoln Fellowship of Wisconsin Historical Bulletin, 1950.

3704. Gunderson, Robert G. "Reading Lincoln's Mail." *Indiana Magazine of History* 55 (December 1959): 379-392.

3705. Haerdter, Robert. "Abraham Lincoln." *Monat* 17 (April 1965): 29-36.

3706. Hambrecht, George P. "Abraham Lincoln." *Wisconsin Magazine* 2 (January 1924): 8-9.

3707. Harlan, Edgar R. "Lincoln's Iowa Lands." *Annals of Iowa* 15 (April 1927): 621-623.

3708. Holliday, Carl. "Lincoln's First Levee." *Illinois State Historical Society Journal* 11 (October 1918): 386-390.

3709. Holzer, Harold. "The Bearding of the President, 1860: The Portraitists Put on Hairs." *Lincoln Herald* 78 (Fall 1976): 95-101.

3710. Holzer, Harold. "If I Had Another Face, Do You Think I'd Wear This One?" *American Heritage* 34 (February/March 1983): 56-63.

3711. Howard, James Q. *The Life of Abraham Lincoln: With Extracts from His Speeches*. Columbus: Follett, Foster, 1860.

3712. Hubbard, Elbert. *Abe Lincoln and Nancy Hanks, Being One of Elbert Hubbard's Famous Little Journeys to Which Is Added for Full Measure a Tribute to the Mother of Lincoln*. East Aurora, NY: Roycrofters, 1920.

3713. Jackson, H. LeRoy. "Concerning the Financial Affairs of Abraham Lincoln, Esquire." *Connecticut Bar Journal* 34 (September 1960): 240-248.

3714. Jennison, Keith W. *Humorous Mr. Lincoln*. New York: Bonaza, 1965.

3715. Larned, Josephus N. "Abraham Lincoln." *Buffalo Historical Society Publications* 19 (1915): 49-54.

3716. Learned, Marion D. *Abraham Lincoln: An American Migration*. Philadelphia: W. J. Campbell, 1909.

3717. Lewis, Joseph. *Lincoln the Freethinker*. New York: Lincoln Publishing Co., 1924.

3718. Lilienthal, David E. "Lincoln, The Man." *Outlook* 136 (February 27, 1924): 358-359.

3719. "Lincoln's Land Holdings and Investments." *Abraham Lincoln Association Bulletin* 16 (September 1, 1929): 1-8.

3720. Ludwig, Emil. *Lincoln*. Translated by Eden and Cedar Paul. Boston: Little, Brown, 1930.

3721. McPike, H. G. "The Lincoln-Shields Duel." *Magazine of History* 4 (September 1906): 145-147.

3722. Mantripp, J. C. "Abraham Lincoln." *Holborn Review* 12 (April 1921): 172-188.

3723. Meese, William A. *Abraham Lincoln: Incidents in His Life Relating to Waterways*. Moline, IL: Desaulniers and Co., 1908.

3724. Miller, Marion M., ed. *Life and Works of Abraham Lincoln*. 9 vols. New York: Current Literature Publishing Co., 1907.

3725. Milner, Duncan C. *Lincoln and Liquor*. New York: Neale, 1920.

3726. Minor, Wilma F. "Lincoln, The Lover." *Atlantic Monthly* 142 (December 1928): 838-856; 143 (January 1929): 1-14; (February 1929): 215-225.

3727. Mitchell, Wilmot B. *Abraham Lincoln: The Man and the Crisis*. Portland, ME: Smith and Sale, 1910.

3728. Morse, John T., Jr. "Lord Charnwood's 'Life of Abraham Lincoln.'" *Massachusetts Historical Society Proceedings* 51 (1918): 90-105.

3729. Mowry, Duane. "Abraham Lincoln." *Green Bag* 15 (February 1903): 53-61.

3730. Murphy, James P. "Abraham Lincoln, Doughboy." *Infantry Journal* 34 (February 1929): 121-123.

3731. "New Light on the Women Whom Lincoln Loved." *Current Opinion* 74 (February 1923): 166-168.

3732. Norton, Eliot. *Abraham Lincoln: A Lover of Mankind: An Essay*. New York: Moffat, Yard, 1911.

3733. Oakleaf, Joseph B. *Abraham Lincoln, His Friendship for Humanity, and Sacrifice for Others*. Moline, IL: Desaulniers and Co., 1910.

3734. Parry, Judge. "Abraham Lincoln, Advocate." *Cornhill Magazine* 42 (June 1917): 631-642.

3735. "Patent Records Reveal Abraham Lincoln as an Inventor." *Popular Mechanics Magazine* 41 (March 1924): 360-363.

3736. Phillips, Charles. "Abraham Lincoln." *Catholic World* 128 (February 1929): 513-522; (April 1929): 513-522; 129 (April 1930): 48-59.

3737. Pratt, Harry E. " 'Judge' Abraham Lincoln." *Illinois State Historical Society Journal* 48 (Spring 1955): 28-39.

3738. Pratt, Harry E. *The Personal Finances of Abraham Lincoln*. Springfield, IL: Abraham Lincoln Association, 1943.

3739. Pratt, Harry E. "The Sandburg 'Lincoln.' " *Abraham Lincoln Association Bulletin* 58 (December 1939): 3-6.

3740. Pratt, Harry E., ed. *Concerning Mr. Lincoln, In Which Abraham Lincoln Is Pictured as He Appeared to Letter Writers of His Time*. Springfield, IL: Abraham Lincoln Association, 1944.

3741. Quarles, Joseph V. "Abraham Lincoln." *Putnam's* 2 (April 1907): 57-64.

3742. Rennick, Percival G. *Abraham Lincoln and Ann Rutledge: An Old Salem Romance*. Peoria, IL: E. J. Jacob, 1932.

3743. Schurz, Carl. *Abraham Lincoln, A Biographical Essay: With an Essay on the Portraits of Lincoln by Truman H. Bartlett*. Boston: Houghton Mifflin, 1907.

3744. Scoville, Samuel, Jr. *Abraham Lincoln: His Story*. Philadelphia: American Sunday-School Union, 1918.

3745. Shaw, Elton R. *The Love Affairs of Washington and Lincoln: The Love Affairs of Abraham Lincoln, The Boyhood and Love Affairs of Washington*. Berwyn, IL: Shaw Publishing Co., 1923.

3746. Shaw, James. "A Neglected Episode in the Life of Abraham Lincoln." *Illinois Historical Society Transactions* (1922): 51-58.

3747. Sheppard, Robert D. *The Life of Abraham Lincoln, Sixteenth President of the United States, 1861-1865: Famous Gettysburg and Springfield Addresses, Pathetic Letter to the Mother of Five Sons Slain in Battle: Sayings, Characteristics, and Chronology*. Chicago: Laird and Lee, 1913.

3748. Shook, Chester R. *The Lincoln Story*. Cincinnati, OH: n.p., 1950.

3749. Shutes, Milton H. *Abraham Lincoln and the New Almaden Mine*. San Francisco: L. Kennedy, 1936.

3750. Smith, Samuel G. "Abraham Lincoln." *Methodist Review* 41 (January 1925): 81-90.

3751. Spears, Zarel C., and Robert S. Barton. *Berry and Lincoln, Frontier Merchants: The Store That "Winked Out."* New York: Stratford House, 1947.

3752. Starr, John W. *Lincoln's Last Day*. New York: Stokes, 1922.

3753. Stephenson, Nathaniel W. *Lincoln: An Account of His Personal Life, Especially of Its Springs of Action as Revealed and Deepened by the Ordeals of War*. Indianapolis, IN: Bobbs-Merrill, 1922.

3754. Stoddard, William O. "Face to Face with Lincoln, By His Secretary William O. Stoddard." Edited by William O. Stoddard, Jr. *Atlantic Monthly* 135 (March): 332-339.

3755. Tarbell, Ida M. "Abraham Lincoln's Money Sense." *American Magazine* 96 (September 1923): 13-15.

3756. Tarbell, Ida M. *The Life of Abraham Lincoln, Drawn from Original Sources and Containing Many Speeches, Letters, and Telegrams Hitherto Unpublished.* 2 vols. Rev. ed. New York: Macmillan, 1917.

3757. Temple, Wayne C. *Lincoln and Bennett: The Story of a Store Account.* Harrogate, TN: Lincoln Memorial University, 1967.

3758. Temple, Wayne C. "Lincoln and W. H. W. Cushman." *Lincoln Herald* 68 (Summer 1966): 81-87.

3759. Temple, Wayne C. *Lincoln the Railsplitter.* La Crosse, WI: Willow Press, 1961.

3760. Thomas, Benjamin P., and Harold M. Hyman. *Stanton: The Life and Times of Lincoln's Secretary of War.* New York: Knopf, 1962.

3761. Townsend, William H. *Lincoln and Liquor.* New York: Press of the Pioneers, 1934.

3762. Treadway, William E. "The Estate of Abraham Lincoln." *Lincoln Herald* 76 (Spring 1974): 7-11.

3763. Tyler, Lyon G. "How Lincoln Got Rich." *Tyler's Quarterly Historical and Genealogical Magazine* 17 (July 1935): 3-9.

3764. Wakefield, Sherman D. "Abraham Lincoln and the Bixby Letter." *Amateur Book Collector* 6 (October 1955): 1-8.

3765. Wanamaker, John. *Wanamaker Primer on Abraham Lincoln.* Philadelphia: Times Printing House, 1909.

3766. Warren, Raymond. *The Prairie President.* Chicago: Reilly and Lee, 1930.

3769. Whipple, Wayne. "Abraham Lincoln, The Greatest American Humorist." *Hampton Magazine* 28 (February 1912): 28-30, 66-68.

3768. Weisenburger, Francis P. "Lincoln and His Ohio Friends." *Ohio Historical Quarterly* 68 (July 1955): 223-256.

3769. Whipple, Wayne. "Abraham Lincoln, the Greatest American Humorist." *Hampton Magazine* 28 (February 1912): 28-30, 66-68.

3770. Whipple, Wayne, comp. *Abraham Lincoln Don'ts.* Philadelphia: Henry Altemus, 1918.

3771. Wright, Anna M. R. *The Dramatic Life of Abraham Lincoln ... Illustrated with Scenes from the Photoplay, A First National Picture.* New York: Grosset and Dunlap, 1925.

3772. Wright, Carrie D. *Lincoln's First Love.* Chicago: McClurg, 1901.

3773. Zilversmit, Arthur. *Lincoln on Black and White: A Documentary History.* Melbourne, FL: Krieger, 1983.

Chronologies

3774. Allen, James S. "Abraham Lincoln in 1848." *National Magazine* 31 (February 1910): 523-525.

3775. Angle, Paul M. *Lincoln, 1854-1861: Being the Day-by-Day Activities of Abraham Lincoln from January 1, 1854 to March 4, 1861.* Springfield, IL: Abraham Lincoln Association, 1933.

3776. Angle, Paul M. *Lincoln in the Year 1854: Being the Day-by-Day Activities of Abraham Lincoln during That Year.* Springfield, IL: Lincoln Centennial Association, 1928.

3777. Angle, Paul M. *Lincoln in the Year 1855: Being the Day-by-Day Activities of Abraham Lincoln during That Year.* Springfield, IL: Abraham Lincoln Association, 1929.

3778. Angle, Paul M. *Lincoln in the Year 1856: Being the Day-by-Day Activities of Abraham Lincoln during That Year.* Springfield, IL: Abraham Lincoln Association, 1930.

3779. Angle, Paul M. *Lincoln in the Year 1857: Being the Day-by-day Activities of Abraham Lincoln during That Year.* Springfield, IL: Abraham Lincoln Association, 1930.

3780. Angle, Paul M. *Lincoln in the Year 1858: Being the Day-by-Day Activities of Abraham Lincoln during That Year.* Springfield, IL: Lincoln Centennial Association, 1926.

3781. Angle, Paul M. *Lincoln in the Year 1859: Being the Day-by-Day Activities of Abraham Lincoln during That Year.* Springfield, IL: Lincoln Centennial Association, 1927.

3782. Angle, Paul M. *Lincoln in the Year 1860: And as President-Elect: Being the Day-by-Day Activities of Abraham Lincoln from January 1, 1860 to March 5, 1861.* Springfield, IL: Lincoln Centennial Association, 1927.

3783. Caverno, Charles. "A Day with Lincoln." *Magazine of History* 22 (March 1915): 94-99.

3784. Eisendrath, Joseph L., Jr. "Lincoln's First Appearance on the National Scene, July 1847." *Lincoln Herald* 76 (Summer 1974): 59-62.

3785. Hughes, Paul F. "Lincoln at Exeter: A Forgotten Contemporary Account." *Historical New Hampshire* 37 (Spring 1982): 63-78.

3786. Lathrop, Stanley E. "Lincoln at Beliot in 1859." *Wisconsin Magazine* 2 (January 1924): 3-4.

3787. Lufkin, Richard F. "Mr. Lincoln's Light from under a Bushel — 1854." *Lincoln Herald* 56 (Winter 1954): 3-24.

3788. Lufkin, Richard F. "Mr. Lincoln's Light from under a Bushel — 1851-1852." *Lincoln Herald* 53 (Winter 1951): 2-25; 54 (Winter 1952): 2-26, 60.

3789. Miers, Earl S., ed. *Lincoln Day by Day: A Chronology, 1809-1865.* 3 vols. Washington, DC: U.S. Lincoln Sesquicentennial Commission, 1960.

3790. Miles, Mary L. "The Fatal First of January, 1841." *Illinois State Historical Society Journal* 20 (April 1927): 13-48.

3791. Pratt, Harry E. *Abraham Lincoln Chronology, 1809-1865.* Springfield: Illinois State Historical Library, 1953.

3792. Schouler, James. "Abraham Lincoln at Tremont Temple in 1848." *Massachusetts Historical Society Proceedings* 42 (January 1909): 70-83.

3793. Seaver, William J. "Some Impressions of Abraham Lincoln in 1856." *Magazine of History* 14 (December 1911): 242-247.

3794. Temple, Wayne C. "Two More Days in the Life of A. Lincoln." *Lincoln Herald* 80 (Winter 1978): 159-161.

3795. Villard, Henry. *Lincoln on the Eve of '61: A Journalist's Story.* New York: Knopf, 1941.

3796. Wall, Bernhardt. *Following Abraham Lincoln, 1809-1865.* New York: Wise-Parslow, 1943.

3797. White, Horace. "Abraham Lincoln in 1854." *Illinois State Historical Society Transactions* (1909): 25-47.

3798. Zinsmeister, Robert, Jr. "The Pigeon Creek Baptist Church." *Lincoln Herald* 80 (Winter 1978): 161-163.

Education

3799. Armstrong, William H. *The Education of Abraham Lincoln.* New York: Coward, McCann and Geoghegan, 1974.

3800. Herrick, Cheesman A. "How Abraham Lincoln Was Educated." *Educational Review* 71 (February 1926): 78-86.

3801. Houser, Martin L. *The Education of Abraham Lincoln*. Peoria, IL: L. O. Schriver, 1938.

3802. Houser, Martin L. *Lincoln's Education and Other Essays*. New York: Bookman Associates, 1957.

3803. Jones, Henry C. "Abraham Lincoln's Attitude towards Education." *Iowa Law Review* 12 (June 1927): 336-392.

3804. Kincaid, Robert L. "The Self-Education of Abraham Lincoln." In *Lincoln for the Ages*, edited by Ralph G. Newman, 150-154. Garden City, NY: Doubleday, 1960.

3805. McFadden, L. E. "Abraham Lincoln: His Education and Moral Courage." *Education* 40 (December 1919): 238-246.

3806. Wham, George D. "The Education of Abraham Lincoln." *Chicago Schools Journal* 12 (February 1930): 225-231.

Family

3807. Ames, Marilyn C. "Lincoln's Stepbrother: John D. Johnston." *Lincoln Herald* 82 (Spring 1980): 302-311.

3808. Appleman, Roy E. "Lincoln's Birthplace: American Shrine." *Regional Review* 2 (1939): 21-24.

3809. Barton, William E. "Abraham Lincoln's Ancestry." *Indiana Historical Bulletin* 2 (January 1925): 55-74.

3810. Barton, William E. "The Ancestry of Abraham Lincoln." *Illinois State Historical Society Transactions* 31 (1924): 123-138.

3811. Barton, William E. "The Hankses." *Illinois State Historical Society Journal* 20 (January 1928): 499-522.

3812. Barton, William E. "Is Lincoln among the Aristocrats?" *Illinois State Historical Society Journal* 22 (April 1929): 65-78.

3813. Barton, William E. *The Lineage of Lincoln*. Indianapolis, IN: Bobbs-Merrill, 1929.

3814. Barton, William E. *The Paternity of Abraham Lincoln*. New York: Doran, 1920.

3815. Bassett, Margaret B. *Abraham and Mary Todd Lincoln*. New York: Crowell, 1973.

3816. Bauer, Charles J. *Tad's Scrapbook — Lincoln's Boy: 200 Cartoons of His Father's Day, Comments and Poems, Including Alice in Wonderland!* Silver Spring, MD: Silver Spring Press, 1978.

3817. Bayne, Julia T. *Tad Lincoln's Father*. Boston: Little, Brown, 1931.

3818. Bradford, Gamaliel. "The Wife of Abraham Lincoln." *Harper's Magazine* 151 (September 1925): 489-498.

3819. Bullard, F. Lauriston. "The New England Ancestry of Abraham Lincoln." *New England Magazine* 39 (February 1909): 685-691.

3820. Bullard, F. Lauriston. *Tad and His Father*. Boston: Little, Brown, 1915.

3821. Cannon, Jouett T. "Abraham Lincoln, Senior, and His Land on Green River." *Kentucky Historical Society Register* 27 (January 1929): 406-410.

3822. "Ceremonies at the Grave of Thomas Lincoln." *Illinois State Historical Society Journal* 28 (April 1935): 92-94.

3823. Coggins, James C. *Abraham Lincoln a North Carolinian: With Proof*. 2d ed. Gastonia, NC: Advocate Publishing Co., 1927.

3824. Current, Richard N. "Lincoln, Husband and Father." In *Abraham Lin-*

coln: A New Portrait, edited by Henry B. Kranz, 134-139. New York: Putnam, 1959.

3825. Donald, David H. *Herndon and Mrs. Lincoln*. Providence, RI: Friends of the Library of Brown University, 1950.

3826. Durham, Harriet F. "Lincoln's Sons and the Marfan Syndrome." *Lincoln Herald* 79 (Summer 1977): 67-71.

3827. Evans, Sam T. *Lincolns*. Gallatin, MS: The Author, 1981.

3828. Evans, William A. *Mrs. Abraham Lincoln, A Study of Her Personality and Her Influence on Lincoln*. New York: Knopf, 1932.

3829. Fisher, Aileen L. *My Cousin Abe*. New York: Nelson, 1962.

3830. Gallardo, Florence. "'Til Death Do Us Part': The Marriage of Abraham Lincoln and Mary Todd." *Lincoln Herald* 84 (Spring 1982): 3-10.

3831. Gernon, Blaine B. "The Lincolns in Chicago." *Illinois State Historical Society Journal* 27 (October 1934): 243-284.

3832. Grimsley, Elizabeth T. "Six Months in the White House." *Illinois State Historical Society Journal* 19 (October/January 1926-1927): 43-73.

3833. Hackensmith, C. W. "Family Background and Education of Mary Todd." *Kentucky Historical Society Register* 69 (July 1971): 187-196.

3834. Helm, Katherine. *The True Story of Mary, Wife of Lincoln: Containing the Recollections of Mary Lincoln's Sister Emilie (Mrs. Ben Hardin Helm), Extracts from Her Wartime Diary, Numerous Letters, and Other Documents Now First Published by Her Niece*. New York: Harper and Row, 1928.

3835. Hennighausen, Louis P. "Is It Lincoln or Linkhorn?" *Pennsylvania German* 11 (April 1910): 229-231.

3836. Hickey, James T. "'Own the House Till It Ruins Me': Robert Todd Lincoln and His Parents' Home in Springfield." *Illinois State Historical Society Journal* 74 (Winter 1981): 279-296.

3837. Hickey, James T. "Robert S. Todd Seeks a Job for His Son-in-Law, Abraham Lincoln." *Illinois State Historical Society Journal* 72 (November 1979): 273-276.

3838. Hickey, James T. "Robert Todd Lincoln and the 'Purely Private' Letters of the Lincoln Family." *Illinois State Historical Society Journal* 74 (Spring 1981): 58-79.

3839. Hickey, James T. "Some Robert Lincoln Letters on the 'Dreadful Statue' by George Grey Barnard." *Illinois State Historical Society Journal* 73 (Summer 1980): 132-139.

3840. Higgins, Lucy P. "A Sketch of Abraham Lincoln's Mother." *Americana* 13 (April 1919): 156-166.

3841. James, Jeannie H., and Wayne C. Temple. "Mrs. Lincoln's Clothing." *Lincoln Herald* 62 (Summer 1960): 54-65.

3842. Keiser, David S. "Lincoln's Ancestors Came from Ireland!" *Lincoln Herald* 79 (Winter 1977): 146-150.

3843. Kinnaird, Virginia. "Mrs. Lincoln as a White House Hostess." *Illinois State Historical Society Papers* (1938): 64-87.

3844. Lea, James H., and J. R. Hutchinson. *The Ancestry of Abraham Lincoln*. Boston: Houghton Mifflin, 1909.

3845. Lincoln, Mary T. "The Mary Lincoln Letters to Mrs. Felician Slataper (1868-74)." Edited by Justin G. Turner. *Illinois State Historical Society Journal* 49 (Spring 1956): 7-33.

3846. Lincoln, Mary T. "Mary Lincoln Writes to Noah Brooks." Edited by Francis W. Hatch. *Illinois State Historical Society Journal* 48 (Spring 1955): 45-51.

3847. Lincoln, Mary T. *Mary Todd Lincoln: Her Life and Letters.* Edited by Justin G. Turner and Linda L. Turner. New York: Knopf, 1972.

3848. Lincoln, Robert T. *A Portrait of Abraham Lincoln in Letters by His Oldest Son.* Edited by Paul M. Angle. Chicago: Chicago Historical Society, 1968.

3849. Lincoln, Waldo. *History of the Lincoln Family.* Worchester, MA: Commonwealth Press, 1923.

3850. McGregor, Thomas B. "Some New Facts about Abraham Lincoln's Parents." *Kentucky Historical Society Register* 20 (May 1922): 213-218.

3851. Martin, James M. *A Defence of Lincoln's Mother, Conversion and Creed.* Minneapolis, MN: Privately Printed, 1921.

3852. Massey, Mary E. "Mary Todd Lincoln." *American History Illustrated* 10 (May 1975): 4-9, 44-48.

3853. Morrow, Honore M. W. *Mary Todd Lincoln: An Appreciation of the Wife of Abraham Lincoln.* New York: Morrow, 1928.

3854. Newman, Ralph G. *Robert Todd Lincoln.* Madison: Lincoln Fellowship of Wisconsin, 1982.

3855. Ostendorf, Lloyd. "The Photographs of Mary Todd Lincoln." *Illinois State Historical Society Journal* 61 (Autumn 1968): 269-332.

3856. Randall, Ruth P. *The Courtship of Mr. Lincoln.* Boston: Little, Brown, 1957.

3857. Randall, Ruth P. *Lincoln's Sons.* Boston: Little, Brown, 1955.

3858. Randall, Ruth P. *Mary Lincoln: Biography of a Marriage.* Boston: Little, Brown, 1953.

3859. Randall, Ruth P. "Mary Lincoln: Judgement Appealed." *Abraham Lincoln Quarterly* 5 (September 1949): 379-404.

3860. Rhodes, James A. *The Trial of Mary Todd Lincoln.* Indianapolis, IN: Bobbs-Merrill, 1959.

3861. Ritze, C. C. "In Defense of Mrs. Lincoln." *Illinois State Historical Society Journal* 30 (January 1937): 5-69.

3862. Ross, Ishbel. *The President's Wife: Mary Todd Lincoln, A Biography.* New York: Putnam, 1973.

3863. Ross, Rodney A. "Mary Todd Lincoln, Patient at Bellevue Place, Batavia." *Illinois State Historical Society Journal* 63 (Spring 1970): 5-34.

3864. Sandburg, Carl, and Paul M. Angle. *Mary Lincoln, Wife and Widow.* New York: Harcourt, Brace, 1932.

3865. Sklar, Kathryn K. "Victorian Women and Domestic Life: Mary Todd Lincoln, Elizabeth Cady Stanton, and Harriet Beecher Stowe." In *The Public and the Private Lincoln: Contemporary Perspectives,* edited by Cullom Davis, Charles B. Strozier, Rebecca M. Veach, and Geoffrey C. Ward, 20-37. Carbondale: Southern Illinois University Press, 1979.

3866. Smith, Harvey G. *Lincoln and the Lincolns.* New York: Pioneer Publications, 1931.

3867. Smyser, George H. "The Lincoln Family in 1861: A History of the Painting and Engraving by Mr. J. C. Buttre." *Illinois State Historical Society Journal* 22 (July 1929): 357-361.

3868. Sprague, Ver Lynn. "Mary Lincoln — Accessory to Murder." *Lincoln Herald* 81 (Winter 1981): 238-242.

3869. Squires, J. Duane. "Mrs. Abraham Lincoln's Visit to Mount Washington in 1863." *Appalachia* 33 (December 15, 1961): 452-457.

3870. Stevens, H. Beresford. "The English Home of the 'Lincolns.'" *Landmark* 7 (March 1925): 175-178.

3871. Stone, Irving. *Mary Todd Lincoln, A Final Judgement?* Springfield, IL: Abraham Lincoln Association, 1973.

3872. Temple, Wayne C. "Mary Todd Lincoln as a Sailor." *Lincoln Herald* 61 (Fall 1959): 101-110.

3873. Temple, Wayne C. "Mary Todd Lincoln's Travels." *Illinois State Historical Society Journal* 52 (Spring 1959): 180-194.

3874. Townsend, William H. *Lincoln and His Wife's Home Town.* Indianapolis, IN: Bobbs-Merrill, 1929.

3875. Trump, Fred. *Lincoln's Little Girl.* Salina, KS: Heritage Books, 1977.

3876. Turner, Justin G. *Mary Todd Lincoln: Her Life and Letters.* New York: Knopf, 1972.

3877. Tyler, Lyon G. *Barton and the Lineage of Lincoln.* Holdcroft, VA: n.p., 1930.

3878. Warren, Louis A. "Abraham Lincoln, Senior, Grandfather of the President." *Filson Club History Quarterly* 5 (July 1931): 136-152.

3879. Warren, Louis A. "Lincoln Lands and Lineage, 'A Typical American Migration.'" *Illinois State Historical Society Transactions* 34 (1927): 144-153.

3880. Warren, Louis A. "Lincoln's Honorable Parentage, His Family Skeletons Turn Out to be Apparitions." *Century Magazine* 112 (September 1926): 532-539.

3881. Warren, Louis A. *Lincoln's Parentage and Childhood: A History of the Kentucky Lincolns Supported by Documentary Evidence.* New York: Century, 1926.

3882. Warren, Louis A. "Lincoln's Pioneer Father." *New England Historical and Genealogical Register* 84 (October 1930): 389-400.

3883. Warren, Louis A. "Sarah Bush Lincoln, The Stepmother of Abraham Lincoln." *Illinois State Historical Society Transactions* 33 (1926): 80-88.

3884. Warren, Louis A. "Three Generations of Kentucky Lincolns." *Filson Club History Quarterly* 12 (April 1938): 65-78.

Legend

3885. Ander, Oscar F. *Lincoln Images: Augustana College Centennial Essays.* Rock Island, IL: Augustana College Library, 1960.

3886. Anderson, Marcus. "Father Abraham, Analysis of a Myth." *Tyler's Quarterly Historical and Genealogical Magazine* 20 (July 1938): 77-98.

3887. Barton, William E. *The Greatness of Abraham Lincoln.* Chicago: Munsell Publishing Co., 1922.

3888. Basler, Roy P. *The Lincoln Legend: A Study in Changing Conceptions.* Boston: Houghton Mifflin, 1935.

3889. Blegen, Theodore C. "Lincoln's Imagery." In *Abraham Lincoln: A New Portrait,* edited by Henry B. Kranz, 123-128. New York: Putnam, 1959.

3890. Bloom, Robert L. "The Lincoln Image — Then and Now." *Lincoln Herald* 85 (Fall 1983): 175-187.

3891. Blue, Merle D. "Sleuthing Lincoln Myths." *Indiana Social Studies Quarterly* 29 (Spring 1976): 43-51.

3892. Blum, Herman. "The Mystery of the Dying President's Attendants." *Lincoln Herald* 69 (Spring 1967): 22-25.

3893. Bradford, M. E. "The Lincoln Legacy: A Long View." *Modern Age* 24 (Fall 1980): 355-363.

3894. Bramantip, Bocardo. *The Abraham Lincoln Myth.* New York: Mascot Publishing Co., 1894.

3895. Bryan, George S. *The Great Ameri-*

can Myth. New York: Carrick and Evans, 1940.

3896. Carleton, William G. "Sources of the Lincoln Legend." *Prairie Schooner* 25 (Summer 1951): 184-190.

3897. Cash, Kenneth P. "A Real Look at the Real Lincoln." *Lincoln Herald* 83 (Winter 1981): 801-803.

3898. Coleman, Christopher B. "The Lincoln Legend." *Indiana Magazine of History* 29 (December 1933): 277-286.

3899. Dowdey, Clifford. "The Myth of Lincoln . . . The South's Friend." *Virginia Record* 80 (September 1958): 7, 29; (October 1958): 5, 24.

3900. Gates, Arnold F. "Abraham Lincoln: Great Image of America." In *Abraham Lincoln: A New Portrait*, edited by Henry B. Kranz, 166-174. New York: Putnam, 1959.

3901. Grob, Gerald N. "The Lincoln Legend." *Social Studies* 52 (January 1961): 3-8.

3902. Herrick, Cheesman A. "The Americanism of Lincoln." *North American Review* 215 (February 1922): 179-187.

3903. Hill, Frederick T. *Lincoln's Legacy of Inspiration*. New York: Stokes, 1909.

3904. Hurt, James. "All the Living and the Dead: Lincoln's Imagery." *American Literature* 52 (November 1980): 351-380.

3905. Johannsen, Robert W. "In Search of the Real Lincoln, Or Lincoln at the Crossroads." *Illinois State Historical Society Journal* 61 (Autumn 1968): 229-247.

3906. Knowles, Robert E. "The Mystery of Lincoln." *Canadian Magazine* 32 (February 1909): 345-351.

3907. Lawrence, Henry W. "Abraham Lincoln Still Unknown." *Social Studies* 29 (March 1938): 108-110.

3908. Lewis, Montgomery. *Legends That Libel Lincoln*. New York: Rinehart, 1946.

3909. Lykes, Richard W. "Teaching the Lincoln Legend." *Social Education* 23 (February 1959): 75-78.

3910. McMurtry, R. Gerald. *Let's Talk of Lincoln, Of His Life, Of His Career, Of His Deeds, Of His Immortality*. Harrogate, TN: Department of Lincolniana, Lincoln Memorial University, 1939.

3911. Mearns, David C. "Our Reluctant Contemporary: Abraham Lincoln." *Abraham Lincoln Quarterly* 6 (June 1950): 73-102.

3912. Neely, Mark E., Jr. "The Lincoln Theme since Randall's Call: The Promise and Perils of Professionalism." *Abraham Lincoln Association Papers* 1 (1979): 10-70.

3913. Oates, Stephen B. "Lincoln: The Man, The Myth." *Civil War Times Illustrated* 22 (February 1984): 10-19.

3914. "Old and New Lincoln Literature." *Review of Reviews* 39 (February 1909): 249-250.

3915. Pennypacker, Isaac R. "The Lincoln Legend." *American Mercury* 1 (January 1924): 1-7.

3916. Potter, David M. *The Lincoln Theme and American National Historiography, An Inaugural Lecture Delivered before the University of Oxford on 19 November 1947*. Oxford: Clarendon Press, 1948.

3917. Pressly, Thomas J. "Writings about Abraham Lincoln in the 1970's: A Review Article." *Pacific Northwest Quarterly* 72 (April 1981): 72-75.

3918. Purvis, Thomas L. "The Making of a Myth: Abraham Lincoln's Family Background in the Perspective of Jacksonian Politics." *Illinois State Historical Society Journal* 75 (Summer 1982): 149-160.

3919. Sherwood, John. "Alfred Whital

Stern: In Pursuit of the Lincoln Legend." *Library of Congress Quarterly Journal* 38 (Spring 1981): 108-116.

3920. Smith, Thomas V. *Lincoln, Living Legend.* Chicago: University of Chicago Press, 1940.

3921. Stevens, Sylvester K. "Lincoln as the Uncommon Common Man." *Civil War Times Illustrated* 1 (February 1963): 21-27.

3922. Suppiger, Joseph E. "Lincoln Legends." *Lincoln Herald* 81 (Spring 1979): 33-38.

3923. Swift, Lester L. "A Different Lincoln." *Lincoln Herald* 67 (Fall 1965): 134-140.

3924. Tarbell, Ida M. "He Cut His Way Up with an Ax: Lincoln Knew the Dignity of Labor." *Collier's* 72 (February 9, 1924): 7-11.

3925. Taylor, Rhea A. "Abraham Lincoln, The Man." *Filson Club History Quarterly* 33 (April 1955): 109-116.

3926. Teillard, Dorothy L. "Lincoln in Myth and in Fact." *World's Work* 21 (February 1911): 14040-14044.

3927. Temple, Wayne C. "Lincoln's Fence Rails." *Illinois State Historical Society Journal* 32 (Spring 1954): 20-34.

3928. Tyler, Lyon G. "Was Lincoln an Ideal?" *Tyler's Quarterly Historical and Genealogical Magazine* 8 (January 1927): 145-155.

3929. Woldman, Albert A. "Lincoln Never Said That." *Harper's* 200 (May 1950): 70-74.

3930. Zornow, William F. "The Unwanted Mr. Lincoln." *Illinois State Historical Society Journal* 45 (Summer 1952): 146-163.

Lincolniana

3931. Ashton, J. Hubley. "Lincolniana: A Glimpse of Lincoln in 1864." *Illinois State Historical Society Journal* 69 (February 1976): 67-69.

3932. Bailey, Louis J. "A Library of Lincolniana." *Library Journal* 56 (May 1931): 397, 405.

3933. Boosel, Harry X. "Abraham Lincoln and 1873." *Numismatic Scrapbook* 26 (November 1960): 3457-3460.

3934. Browne, Ray B., ed. *Lincoln-Lore: Lincoln in the Popular Mind.* Bowling Green, OH: Popular Press, 1975.

3935. Bullard, F. Lauriston. *Lincoln in Marble and Bronze.* New Brunswick, NJ: Rutgers University Press, 1952.

3936. Cadman, S. Parkes. "Abraham Lincoln." *Homiletic Review* 95 (February 1928): 147-150.

3937. "Cartoons of the 'Beardless Lincoln.' " *Old Print Shop Portfolio* 9 (January 1950): 124-127.

3938. Chandler, Albert. "Lincoln and the Telegrapher." *American Heritage* 12 (April 1961): 32-34.

3939. Charnwood, Godfrey R. B. "Abraham Lincoln." *Illinois Historical Society Journal* 12 (January 1920): 498-502.

3940. Charnwood, Godfrey R. B. "The Illinois Centennial and Abraham Lincoln." *Landmark* 1 (February 1919): 92-93.

3941. Chicago Historical Society. "Lincoln's Drive through Richmond." *Chicago History* 4 (Fall 1955): 129-134.

3942. Conwell, Russell H. *Why Lincoln Laughed.* New York: Harper and Row, 1922.

3943. Croy, Homer. "Discovered — An Authentic Lincoln Fingerprint." *Illinois*

State Historical Society Journal 49 (Autumn 1956): 262-270.

3944. Croy, Homer. "A Lincoln Fingerprint." *Manuscripts* 10 (Winter 1958): 54-58, 73.

3945. Dodge, Daniel K. "The Lincoln Illinois Country." *Independent* 66 (February 11, 1909): 309-314.

3946. Eaton, Vincent L. "Abraham Lincoln: His Hand and Pen." *Manuscripts* 11 (Winter 1955): 5-12.

3947. Ensor, Allison R. "Lincoln, Mark Twain, and Lincoln Memorial University." *Lincoln Herald* 78 (Summer 1976): 43-51.

3948. Fleming, Thomas J. *The Living Land of Lincoln.* New York: Reader's Digest Press, 1980.

3949. *Freeport's Lincoln: Exercises Attendant upon the Unveiling of a Statue of Abraham Lincoln: Freeport, Illinois, August 27, 1929, The Seventy-first Anniversary of the Freeport Lincoln-Douglas Debate....* Freeport, IL: W. T. Rawleigh, 1930.

3950. Gammans, Harold W. *Lincoln Names and Epithets.* Boston: Bruce Humphries, 1955.

3951. Griffith, Albert H. "Lincoln Literature, Lincoln Collections, and Lincoln Collectors." *Wisconsin Magazine of History* 15 (December 1931): 148-167.

3952. Gutman, Richard J. S. "A Roster of Early Lincoln Impersonators: Lincoln's Image in the Cinema, 1900-1930." *Lincoln Herald* 78 (Winter 1976): 139-146.

3953. Hamilton, Holman. "Lincoln Memorial University and the Lincoln Collection." *Lincoln Herald* 75 (Summer 1973): 53-54.

3954. Hickey, James T. "The Lincoln Account at the Corneau and Diller Drug Store, 1849-1861, A Springfield Tradition." *Illinois State Historical Society Journal* 77 (Spring 1984): 60-66.

3955. Hickey, James T. "Lincolniana: A Family Divided." *Illinois State Historical Society Journal* 70 (February 1977): 22-26.

3956. Hickey, James T. "Lincolniana: A Small Receipt Reveals a Large Story." *Illinois State Historical Society Journal* 75 (February 1982): 73-80.

3957. Hobson, Jonathan T. *Footprints of Abraham Lincoln: Presenting Many Interesting Facts, Reminiscences, and Illustrations, Never before Published.* Dayton, OH: Otterbein Press, 1909.

3958. Holzer, Harold, and Lloyd Ostendorf. "Sculptures of Abraham Lincoln from Life." *Antiques* 113 (February 1978): 382-393.

3959. Horgan, Paul. *Songs after Lincoln.* New York: Farrar, 1965.

3960. Howe, Beverly W. *Abraham Lincoln in Great Britain.* Chicago: Winslow Publishing Co., 1940.

3961. Illinois State Historical Society. *Lincoln's Inner Circle: Thirty-one Pictures of Abraham Lincoln and His Family, Cabinet, Home, Statues, and Tomb.* Springfield, IL: The Society, 1955.

3962. Kerwood, John R. "The Plot to Rob Lincoln's Tomb." *American History Illustrated* 5 (January 1971): 12-17.

3963. Kimmel, Stanley P. *Mr. Lincoln's Washington.* New York: Coward-McCann, 1957.

3964. King, Robert P. *Lincoln in Numismatics.* Waynesboro, VA: Token and Medal Society, 1966.

3965. Klement, Frank. "Jane Grey Swesshelm and Lincoln: A Feminist Fusses and Frets." *Abraham Lincoln Quarterly* 6 (December 1950): 227-238.

3966. Kubicek, Earl C. "The Case of the Mad Hatter." *Lincoln Herald* 83 (Fall 1981): 708-719.

3967. "The Lincoln Memorial Tablet." *New England Historical and Genealogical Register* 76 (July 1922): 163-170.

3968. Lincoln Memorial University. Abraham Lincoln Library and Museum. *Dedication Ceremonies, June 4, 1977.* Harrowgate, TN: Lincoln Memorial University, 1977.

3969. Lindsey, Richard A. "Lincoln and Shields." *Lincoln Herald* 80 (Summer 1978): 65-69.

3970. "Lorado Taft's Statue of Lincoln Unveiled at Urbana, Illinois, July 3, 1927." *Illinois State Historical Society Journal* 20 (July 1927): 240-242.

3971. Louthan, Henry T. "A Proposed Abduction of Lincoln." *Confederate Veteran* 11 (April 1903): 157-158.

3972. Loux, Martha D. "The Last Lincoln Singer." *Frontier* 10 (March 1930): 192-194.

3973. McClary, Ben H. "Sut Lovingood Views 'Abe Linkhorn.'" *Lincoln Herald* 56 (Fall 1954): 44-45.

3974. McClelland, Stewart W. "The Urgency of Preserving and Using the Vast Lincoln Era Collection at the Lincoln Memorial University." *Lincoln Herald* 75 (Summer 1973): 58.

3975. McClure, Stanley W. *The Lincoln Museum and the House Where Lincoln Died, Washington, DC.* Rev. ed. Washington, DC: U.S. National Park Service, 1960.

3976. McCorison, J. L., Jr. "The Great Lincoln Collections and What Became of Them." *Lincoln Herald* 50 (December 1948): 2-16; 51 (February 1949): 36.

3977. McMurtry, R. Gerald. "A Brief History of a Great Lincoln Collection." *Lincoln Herald* 75 (Summer 1973): 45-46.

3978. McMurtry, R. Gerald. "In the Lincoln Memorial University Collection . . . Presentation Copy of James Russell Lowell's 'Commemoration Ode.'" *Lincoln Herald* 76 (Spring 1974): 36-39.

3979. McMurtry, R. Gerald. "The Kentucky Delegation That Attended Lincoln's Funeral, May 3-4, 1865." *Lincoln Herald* 53 (Summer 1951): 38-40.

3980. Malone, Thomas J. "How Lincoln Dressed." *Commonweal* 9 (February 6, 1929): 395-396.

3981. Mead, Franklin B. *Heroic Statues in Bronze of Abraham Lincoln, Introducing the Hoosier Youth of Paul Manship.* Fort Wayne, IN: Lincoln National Life Foundation, 1932.

3982. Meany, Edmond S., ed. *Lincoln Esteemed Washington.* Seattle, WA: F. McCaffrey, 1933.

3983. Mearns, David C. "Exquisite Collector, Or The Scalping of Abraham Lincoln." *Illinois State Historical Society Journal* 52 (Spring 1955): 45-51.

3984. Mecklenburg, George. "The Soul of Lincoln's America." *Methodist Review* 44 (July 1928): 561-568.

3985. Merriam, Arthur L. "Final Internment of President Abraham Lincoln's Remains at the Lincoln Monument in Oak Ridge Cemetery, Springfield, Illinois." *Illinois State Historical Society Journal* 23 (April 1930): 171-174.

3986. "A Mistake in Bronze." *Art World* 2 (June 1917): 211-220.

3987. Mutch, Verna E. "Abraham Lincoln in Statuary." *National Historical Magazine* 74 (February 1940): 4-9.

3988. Neely, Mark E., Jr. *The Abraham Lincoln Encyclopedia.* New York: DaCapo Press, 1984.

3989. Neely, Mark E., Jr. "American Nationalism in the Image of Henry Clay: Abraham Lincoln's Eulogy on Henry Clay in Context." *Kentucky Historical Society Register* 73 (January 1975): 31-60.

3990. Newkirk, Garrett. *Lincoln Lessons for Today*. New York: Duffield and Co., 1921.

3991. Newman, Ralph G. "The Importance to All Americans of a Center for Lincoln Studies." *Lincoln Herald* 75 (Summer 1973): 47-48.

3992. O'Connell, Margaret J. *Lincoln Lives*. New York: Vantage Press, 1957.

3993. Oldroyd, Osborn H. *The Lincoln Memorial: Album Immortelles*. New York: Carlton, 1882.

3994. Ostendorf, Lloyd. "History of a Lincoln Bed." *Lincoln Herald* 83 (Fall 1981): 733-736.

3995. Ostendorf, Lloyd. "Lincoln and the Hoblits." *Lincoln Herald* 77 (Spring 1975): 49-52.

3996. Ostendorf, Lloyd. "A Relic from His Last Birthday: The Mills Life-Mask of Lincoln." *Lincoln Herald* 75 (Fall 1973): 79-85.

3997. Ostendorf, Lloyd, and Harold Holzer. "The John Henry Brown Miniature of Lincoln: A Critical Re-Assessment (and a Controversy over Primacy Explained)." *Lincoln Herald* 78 (Summer 1976): 78-81.

3998. Payne, Frank O. "Abraham Lincoln as a Theme for Sculptural Art." *Art and Archaeology* 13 (June 1922): 261-268.

3999. Payne, Frank O. "Lincoln in Bronze." *Munsey's* 54 (April 1915): 497-509.

4000. Peterson, Gloria. *An Administrative History of Abraham Lincoln Birthplace National Historic Site*. Washington, DC: Division of History, Office of Archaeology and Historic Preservation, 1968.

4001. "The Poetical Cult of Lincoln." *Nation* 108 (May 17, 1919): 777.

4002. Pratt, Silas G. *Lincoln in Story*. New York: Appleton, 1901.

4003. Randall, James G. "Has the Lincoln Theme Been Exhausted?" *American Historical Review* 41 (January 1936): 270-294.

4004. Rankin, Frank C. "The Lincoln Collection: A Hallowed Wellspring of History." *Lincoln Herald* 75 (Summer 1973): 59.

4005. Rankin, Henry B. "Comments and Corrections on 'The Lincoln Life-Mask and How It Was Made.'" *Illinois State Historical Society Journal* 8 (July 1915): 249-259.

4006. Redway, Maurine W., and Dorothy K. Bracken. *Marks of Lincoln on Our Land*. New York: Hastings House, 1957.

4007. Richman, Michael. "The Long Labor of Making Nation's Favorite Statue." *Smithsonian* 7 (July 1977): 54-61.

4008. Robertson, James O. "Horatio Alger, Andrew Carnegie, Abraham Lincoln, and the Cowboy." *Midwest Quarterly* 20 (Spring 1979): 241-257.

4009. Rogers, Kate B. "The Name of Lincoln." *Illinois State Historical Society Journal* 7 (July 1914): 60-69.

4010. Root, Elihu. "Mr. Root's Speech at the Unveiling of the Lincoln Statue." *Spectator* 125 (August 7, 1920): 168-169.

4011. Sandburg, Carl. *Lincoln Collector: The Story of Oliver R. Barrett's Great Private Collection*. New York: Harcourt, Brace, 1949.

4012. Sandburg, Carl. "Lincoln's Genius of Places." *Abraham Lincoln Association Bulletin* 22 (1931): 1-9.

4013. Schuyler, Montgomery. "A Medallic History of Lincoln." *Putnam's* 5 (March 1909): 676-681.

4014. Scovel, James M. "Side-Lights on Lincoln." *National Magazine* 18 (July 1903): 458-459.

4015. Searcher, Victor. *Lincoln Today: An Introduction to Modern Lincolniana.* New York: T. Yoseloff, 1969.

4016. Seitz, Don C. "Lincoln and Liquor." *Churchman* 140 (July 6, 1929): 10-11.

4017. Shea, John D. G. *The Lincoln Memorial.* New York: Bunce and Huntington, 1865.

4018. "Side-Lights on Lincoln." *Century Magazine* 81 (February 1911): 589-598.

4019. Smith, Grace P. "More Lincoln Lore." *Midwest Folklore* 4 (Fall 1954): 169-170.

4020. Stathis, Stephen W., and Lee Roderick. "Mallet, Chisel, and Curls." *American Heritage* 27 (February 1976): 44-47, 94-96.

4021. Stern, Philip V. D. *Abraham Lincoln: A Biography in Pictures.* New York: Birk, 1960.

4022. Stewart, Thomas D. "An Anthropologist Looks at Lincoln." *Smithsonian Institute Annual Report* (1952): 419-437.

4023. Suppiger, Joseph E. "The Official Opening of the Abraham Lincoln Library and Museum." *Lincoln Herald* 79 (Summer 1977): 47-52.

4024. Suppiger, Joseph E. "Some New and Exciting Uses for the Lincoln Collection of the Lincoln Memorial University." *Lincoln Herald* 75 (Summer 1973): 60-61.

4025. Temple, Wayne C. "The Importance of the Lincoln Collection at Lincoln Memorial University." *Lincoln Herald* 75 (Summer 1973): 55, 76.

4026. Thompson, Charles M. "The 'Lincoln Way' Investigation in Illinois." *Magazine of History* 19 (August 1914): 101-105.

4027. Turner, Justin G. "Lincoln and the Cannibals." *Lincoln Herald* 77 (Winter 1975): 212-218.

4028. Van Doren, Mark A. "A Playwright Looks at Lincoln." In *Lincoln for the Ages,* edited by Ralph G. Newman, 395-399. Garden City, NY: Doubleday, 1960.

4029. Volk, Leanard W. "The Lincoln Life-Mask and How It Was Made." *Illinois State Historical Society Journal* 8 (July 1915): 238-248.

4030. Warren, Louis A. *Lincoln Log Cabin, Hodgenville, Kentucky.* Morganfield, KY: Munford Publishing Co., 1927.

4031. White, Charles T. *Lincoln and Prohibition.* New York: Abingdon Press, 1921.

4032. Wolfe, J. W. "Lincoln Medals." *American Collector* 5 (February 1928): 202-203.

4033. Wolfe, Richard J. "A Visit with the Lincoln Collection of the Lincoln Memorial University." *Lincoln Herald* 75 (June 1973): 62.

4034. Wood, Harry. "How Both Abraham Lincolns Helped Found Arizona." *Lincoln Herald* 78 (Fall 1976): 109-116.

4035. Workman, Charles H. "Tablet to Abraham Lincoln at Mansfield: Speech by Honorable Charles H. Workman." *Ohio Archaeological and Historical Quarterly* 34 (October 1925): 505-521.

4036. Zinsmeister, Robert, Jr. "A Lincoln Presidential Library Issue: Colonel Harland Sanders Center for Lincoln Studies." *Lincoln Herald* 75 (Summer 1973): 43, 44-48, 50-67, 75-76.

Literature

4037. Abbatt, William, comp. *The Lincoln Centenary in Literature, Selections from the Principal Magazines of February and March 1909, With a Few from 1907-08.* New York: n.p., 1909.

4038. "Abraham Lincoln, the Democratic Spirit, and the Poets of the People." *Arena* 41 (July 1909): 480-483.

4039. Angle, Paul M. "Some Thoughts on Lincoln Literature." *Abraham Lincoln Association Bulletin* 24 (September 1931): 3-6.

4040. Barton, William E. *Abraham Lincoln and His Books.* Chicago: M. Field and Co., 1920.

4041. Barton, William E. *Abraham Lincoln and Walt Whitman.* Indianapolis, IN: Bobbs-Merrill, 1928.

4042. Barzun, Jacques. *Lincoln: The Literary Genius.* Evanston, IL: Schori Private Press, 1960.

4043. Basler, Roy P. "The Evolution of Abraham Lincoln's Handwriting." *Manuscripts* 25 (October 1973): 2-11.

4044. Basler, Roy P. "Lincoln in Literature." *Illinois State Historical Society Journal* 52 (Spring 1955): 33-44.

4045. Bestor, Arthur E., David C. Mearns, and Jonathan Daniels. *Three Presidents and Their Books: The Readings of Jefferson, Lincoln, and Franklin D. Roosevelt.* Champaign: University of Illinois Press, 1955.

4046. Boller, Paul F., Jr. "The Laughing and the Literary Lincoln." *Social Science* 55 (Spring 1980): 71-76.

4047. Brown, Clarence A. "Walt Whitman and Lincoln." *Illinois State Historical Society Journal* 47 (Summer 1954): 176-184.

4048. Burt, Silas W. "Lincoln on His Own Story-Telling, Including an Incident of Secret History Concerning the Relations of the Governor of New York and the President of the United States." *Century Magazine* 73 (February 1907): 499-502.

4049. Chapman, John J. "Lincoln and Hamlet." *North American Review* 209 (March 1919): 371-379.

4050. Edwards, Herbert J., and John E. Hankins. *Lincoln the Writer, The Development of His Literary Style.* Orono: University of Maine, 1962.

4051. Grover, Leonard. "Lincoln's Interest in the Theater." *Century Magazine* 77 (April 1909): 943-950.

4052. Harkness, David J. "Lincoln as a Subject for Drama." *Lincoln Herald* 55 (Spring 1953): 35-37.

4053. Harkness, David J. "Lincoln's Taste in Fiction." *Lincoln Herald* 55 (Winter 1953): 42-45.

4054. Harkness, David J., and R. Gerald McMurtry. *Lincoln's Favorite Poets.* Knoxville: University of Tennessee Press, 1959.

4055. Jenkins, Starr. "American Statesmen as Men of Letters: Franklin, Adams, Jefferson, John Quincy Adams, Lincoln, Theodore Roosevelt, and Wilson Considered as Writers." Ph.D. dissertation, University of New Mexico, 1972.

4056. Lang, H. Jack. *Lincoln's Fireside Reading: The Books That Made the Man: The Story of Five Basic Books Which Served as the Foundation for Abraham Lincoln's Remarkable Self-Education.* Cleveland, OH: World Publishing, 1965.

4057. Lewis, Mort R. "Abraham Lincoln: Storyteller." In *Lincoln for the Ages*, edited by Ralph G. Newman, 130-134. Garden City, NY: Doubleday, 1960.

4058. McClure, Alexander K. *Lincoln's Yarns and Stories.* Chicago: J. C. Winston, 1900.

4059. McMurtry, R. Gerald. "Lincoln Knew Shakespeare." *Indiana Magazine of History* 31 (December 1935): 265-277.

4060. Miller, Marion M. "The Literary Genius of Abraham Lincoln." *National Magazine* 43 (February 1916): 787-793.

4061. Monaghan, Jay. "The Growth of Abraham Lincoln's Influence in Literature since His Death." *Lincoln Herald* 51 (October 1949): 2-11.

4062. Moore, Charles. "Lincoln, The Story Teller." *American Foreign Service Journal* 14 (February 1937): 78-80, 102-104.

4063. Paullin, Charles O. "Hawthorne and Lincoln." *Americana* 4 (November 1909): 889-895.

4064. Perry, James R. "The Poetry of Lincoln." *North American Review* 193 (February 1911): 213-220.

4065. Phillips, Charles. "The Poets' Lincoln." *Catholic World* 107 (May 1918): 145-160.

4066. Robinson, Luther E. *Abraham Lincoln as a Man of Letters*. Chicago: Reilly and Britton, 1918.

4067. Sandburg, Carl. *A Lincoln and Whitman Miscellany*. Chicago: Holiday Press, 1938.

4068. Schuyler, Montgomery. "Lincoln's English." *Forum* 41 (February 1909): 120-128.

4069. Sumner, Guy L. *Lincoln and His Books*. New York: Charles Francis Press, 1934.

4070. Thomas, Benjamin P. "Recent Lincoln Literature." *Abraham Lincoln Association Bulletin* 30 (1933): 8-9.

4071. Wagenknecht, Edward C., ed. *Abraham Lincoln: His Life, Work, and Character: An Anthology of History and Biography, Fiction, Poetry, Drama, and Belles-Lettres*. New York: Creative Age Press, 1947.

4072. Whitford, Kathryn. *Abraham Lincoln: An Assessment of His Place in American Literature*. Madison: State Historical Society of Wisconsin, 1973.

4073. Williams, Talcott. "Lincoln the Reader." *Review of Reviews* 61 (February 1920): 193-196.

Personality

4074. Barton, William E. *The Soul of Abraham Lincoln*. New York: Doran, 1920.

4075. Beardslee, Clark S. *Abraham Lincoln's Cardinal Traits: A Study in Ethics, With an Epilogue Addressed to Theologies*. Boston: R. G. Badger, 1914.

4076. Beckner, Lucien. "Abraham Lincoln: Influences That Produced Him." *Filson Club History Quarterly* 33 (April 1955): 125-138.

4077. Campbell, Willard S. "Estimates of Lincoln — A Son of American Democracy." *National Educational Association Proceedings* 77 (July 1939): 72-76.

4078. Capps, Donald. "The Myth of Father Abraham: Psychosocial Influences in the Formation of Lincoln Biography." In his *Encounter with Erikson*, 253-280. Missoula, MT: n.p., 1977.

4079. Cardiff, Ira D. *The Deification of Lincoln*. Boston: Christopher Publishing House, 1943.

4080. "Character of Abraham Lincoln." *Homiletic Review* 69 (February 1915): 160-162.

4081. Clark, Leon P. *Lincoln: A Psycho-Biography*. New York: Scribner's, 1933.

4082. Clark, Leon P. "Unconscious Motives Underlying the Personalities of Great

Statesmen and Their Relating to Epoch-Making Events: A Psychoanalytic Study of Abraham Lincoln." *Psychoanalytic Review* 8 (January 1921): 1-21.

4083. Creelman, James. *Why We Love Lincoln*. New York: Outing Publishing Co., 1909.

4084. Creelman, James. "Why We Love Lincoln." *Pearson's Magazine* 20 (October 1908): 356-379; (November 1908): 461-482.

4085. Edwards, Elisha J. *The Solitude of Abraham Lincoln: Typical Reminiscences Illustrating a Life Whose Deepest Moments Were Lived Alone*. Putnam, CT: Privately Printed, 1916.

4086. Foner, Eric. "A New Abraham Lincoln?" *Reviews in American History* 7 (September 1979): 375-379.

4087. Forgie, George B. *Patricide in the House Divided: A Psychological Interpretation of Lincoln and His Age*. New York: Norton, 1979.

4088. Funk, A. B. *Abraham Lincoln: A Character Study*. Des Moines, IA: Prairie Club, 1925.

4089. Kempf, Edward J. "Abraham Lincoln's Organic and Emotional Neurosis." *Archives of Neurology and Psychiatry* 67 (April 1952): 419-433.

4090. Larned, Josephus N. "Lincoln: Simplest in Greatness." In his *A Study of Greatness in Men*, 221-303. Boston: Houghton Mifflin, 1911.

4091. Nicolay, Helen. *Personal Traits of Abraham Lincoln*. New York: Century, 1912.

4092. Phillips, Daniel T. *A Prize Treatise on the Character of Abraham Lincoln*. New York: John M. Davis, 1884.

4093. Plummer, Mark A. "The Herndon-Oglesby Exchange on the Character of Lincoln." *Lincoln Herald* 79 (Winter 1977): 169-173.

4094. Randall, Robert L. "Lincoln's Crises: A Psycho-Historical Interpretation." *Lincoln Herald* 79 (1977): 116-121.

4095. Rankin, Henry B. *Intimate Character Sketches of Abraham Lincoln*. Philadelphia: Lippincott, 1924.

4096. Sheppard, Robert D. *Abraham Lincoln, A Character Sketch*. Milwaukee, WI: H. G. Campbell, 1899.

4097. Shutes, Milton H. *Lincoln's Emotional Life*. Philadelphia: Dorrance, 1957.

4098. Syle, Bertrand C. "Intimate Studies of Washington and Lincoln." *Independent* 110 (February 17, 1923): 132-133.

4099. Sweeney, Martin A. "The Personality of Lincoln the War President." *Social Studies* 65 (April 1974): 164-167.

4100. Thompson, Charles M. "An Early Character Sketch of Mr. Lincoln." *Illinois State Historical Society Journal* 7 (April 1914): 59-61.

4101. Warren, Louis A. "The Mystery of Lincoln's Melancholy." In *Proceedings of the Southwestern Indiana Historical Society during Its Sixth Year*, 53-60. Indianapolis: Historical Bureau of the Indiana Library and Historical Department, 1925.

4102. "Was Lincoln a Typical American?" *Nation* 116 (February 14, 1923): 164-165.

4103. Whitehead, John M. "The Personality of Lincoln." *Wisconsin Magazine of History* 18 (December 1934): 188-191.

Philosophy

4104. Auble, John L. "Abraham Lincoln and the American Liberal Tradition." Ph.D. dissertation, Northwestern University, 1960.

4105. Bradford, M. E. "Dividing the House: The Gnosticism of Lincoln's Political Rhetoric." *Modern Age* 23 (Winter 1979): 10-24.

4106. Bullard, F. Lauriston. "Lincoln as a Jeffersonian." *More Books* 23 (October 1948): 283-300.

4107. Cathey, James H. *The Genesis of Lincoln*. Atlanta, GA: Franklin, 1904.

4108. Corlett, William S., Jr., and Glen E. Thurow. "The Availability of Lincoln's Political Religion." *Political Theory* 10 (November 1982): 520-546.

4109. Corson, Oscar T. "Lincoln's Views of the Electoral College and of Amendments to the Constitution." *Ohio Educational Monthly* 70 (January 1921): 23-25.

4110. Corson, Oscar T. "Loyalty as Exemplified in Abraham Lincoln." *Ohio Educational Monthly* 68 (January 1919): 7-15.

4111. Current, Richard N. *The Political Thought of Abraham Lincoln*. Indianapolis, IN: Bobbs-Merrill, 1967.

4112. Davis, Burnet V. "President Abraham Lincoln and the Perpetuation of a Republican Regime." Ph.D. dissertation, University of Chicago, 1973.

4113. Dowd, Morgan D. "Abraham Lincoln, the Rule of Law and Crisis Government: A Study of His Constitutional Law Theories." *University of Detroit Law Journal* 39 (June 1962): 633-649.

4114. Dunlap, John R. *Jeffersonian Democracy, Which Means the Democracy of Thomas Jefferson, Andrew Jackson, and Abraham Lincoln*. New York: Jeffersonian Society, 1903.

4115. Elazar, Daniel J. "The Constitution, the Union, and the Liberties of the People: Abraham Lincoln's Teaching about the American Political System as Articulated on His Tour from Springfield to Washington in February, 1861." *Publius* 8 (Summer 1978): 141-176.

4116. Fehrenbacher, Don E. "The Anti-Lincoln Tradition." *Abraham Lincoln Association Papers* 4 (1982): 7-28.

4117. Fox, Edward J. "Influence of Law on the Life of Abraham Lincoln." *Case and Comment* 33 (March 1927): 1-6.

4118. Franklin, John H. "Lincoln and Public Morality." *Topic* 9 (Spring 1965): 27-43.

4119. Franklin, John H. *Lincoln and Public Morality: An Address Delivered at the Chicago Historical Society on February 12, 1959*. Chicago: Chicago Historical Society, 1959.

4120. Frisch, Morton J. "The Principles of Lincoln's Statecraft." Ph.D. dissertation, Pennsylvania State University, 1953.

4121. Ghent, W. J. "Lincoln and Labor." *Independent* 66 (February 11, 1909): 301-305.

4122. Graebner, Norman A. "The Apostle of Progress." In *The Public and the Private Lincoln: Contemporary Perspectives*, edited by Cullom Davis, Charles B. Strozier, Rebecca M. Veach, and Geoffrey C. Ward, 71-85. Carbondale: Southern Illinois University Press, 1979.

4123. Graebner, Norman A. "Lincoln's Humility." In *Lincoln for the Ages*, edited by Ralph G. Newman, 384-389. Garden City, NY: Doubleday, 1960.

4124. Hein, David. "Lincoln and Political Decision-Making." *Lincoln Herald* 85 (Spring 1983): 3-6.

4125. Jones, Edgar D. *The Influence of Henry Clay upon Abraham Lincoln*. Lexington, KY: Henry Clay Memorial Foundation, 1952.

4126. Jordau, Philip D. "Lincoln's Views on Mob Action." *Lincoln Herald* 70 (Summer 1968): 73-75.

4127. Kempf, Edward J. *Abraham Lincoln's Philosophy of Common Sense: An*

Analytical Biography of a Great Mind. 3 vols. New York: New York Academy of Sciences, 1965.

4128. Kooker, Arthur R. "Abraham Lincoln: Spokesman for Democracy." *Journal of the West* 4 (April 1965): 260-271.

4129. Lodge, Henry C. "The Democracy of Abraham Lincoln." In his *The Democracy of the Constitution, and Other Addresses and Essays,* 122-159. New York: Scribner's, 1915.

4130. Lonergan, Thomas S. "Abraham Lincoln: An Example of Patriotism and Self Education." *Americana* 7 (February 1912): 123-129.

4131. McClure, Alexander K. *The Lincoln Ideals, His Personality and Principles as Reflected in His Own Words.* Washington, DC: Lincoln Sesquicentennial Commission, 1959.

4132. Minger, Ralph E. "Abraham Lincoln: His Philosophy of Politics and His Leadership Qualities." *Journal of the West* 4 (April 1965): 272-276.

4133. Mulder, Gerhard E. "Abraham Lincoln and the Doctrine of Necessity." *Lincoln Herald* 66 (Summer 1964): 59-66.

4134. Neely, Mark E., Jr. "Abraham Lincoln's Nationalism Reconsidered." *Lincoln Herald* 76 (Spring 1974): 12-28.

4135. Nevins, Allan. "Lincoln's Ideals of Democracy." *Topic* (Spring 1965): 11-26.

4136. Pargellis, Stanley. "Lincoln's Political Philosophy." *Abraham Lincoln Quarterly* 3 (June 1945): 275-290.

4137. Phelps, William L. "Political Ideas of Daniel Webster and Abraham Lincoln." *Ladies' Home Journal* 40 (February 1923): 18-19.

4138. Pressly, Thomas J. "Bullets and Ballots: Lincoln and the 'Right of Revolution.'" *American Historical Review* 67 (April 1962): 647-662.

4139. Randall, James G. "Lincoln and the Governance of Men." *Abraham Lincoln Quarterly* 6 (June 1951): 327-352.

4140. Rawley, James A. "The Nationalism of Abraham Lincoln." *Civil War History* 9 (September 1963): 283-298.

4141. Schultz, Harold S. "Lincoln: Partisan or Patriot?" *Social Studies* 54 (February 1963): 63-68.

4142. Sherlock, Richard K. "Liberalism, Public Policy, and the Life Not Worth Living: Abraham Lincoln on Beneficent Euthanasia." *American Journal of Jurisprudence* 26 (1981): 47-65.

4143. Smith, Thomas V. "Lincoln and Democracy." In *Abraham Lincoln: A New Portrait,* edited by Henry B. Kranz, 69-74. New York: Putnam, 1959.

4144. Strunsky, Rose. "Abraham Lincoln's Social Ideals." *Century Magazine* 87 (February 1914): 588-592.

4145. Sumner, Charles. "Promises of the Declaration of Independence, and Abraham Lincoln." In his *The Works of Charles Sumner,* Vol. 9, 367-428. Boston: Lee and Shepard, 1875.

4146. Thomas, Benjamin P. "The Individuality of Lincoln as Revealed in His Writings." *Abraham Lincoln Association Bulletin* 32 (1933): 3-9, 10.

4147. Warde, William F. "Jefferson, Lincoln, and Dewey." *Marxist Essays in American History,* edited by Robert Himmel, 124-128. New York: Merit Publishers, 1966.

4148. Whitcomb, Paul S. "Lincoln and Democracy." *Tyler's Quarterly Historical and Genealogical Magazine* 9 (July 1927): 5-33.

4149. Wiest, Walter E. "Lincoln's Political Ethic: An Alternative to American Millennialism." *American Journal of Theology and Philosophy* 4 (September 1983): 116-126.

4150. Wrone, David R. "Abraham Lincoln's Idea of Property." *Science and Society* 33 (Winter 1969): 54-70.

4151. Wrone, David R. "Lincoln: Democracy's Touchstone." *Abraham Lincoln Association Papers* 1 (1979): 71-83.

Portraits and Prints

4152. Eaton, Edward B. "Gallery of Famous Lincoln Portraits." *Journal of American History* 5 (May/July 1911): 201-214.

4153. Hamilton, Charles, and Lloyd Ostendorf. *Lincoln in Photographs: An Album of Every Known Pose*. Norman: University of Oklahoma Press, 1963.

4154. Harvey, Cordelia A. P. "A Wisconsin Woman's Picture of President Lincoln." *Wisconsin Magazine of History* 1 (March 1918): 233-255.

4155. Holzer, Harold. "Hohenstein: Lincoln's 'Print Doctor.'" *Lincoln Herald* 76 (Winter 1974): 181-186.

4156. Holzer, Harold. "How the Printmakers Saw Lincoln: Not-So-Honest Portraits of 'Honest Abe.'" *Winterthur Portfolio* 14 (Summer 1979): 143-170.

4157. Holzer, Harold. "Lincoln and His Prints: 'A Very Indifferent Judge.'" *Lincoln Herald* 77 (Winter 1975): 203-211.

4158. Holzer, Harold. "Lincoln and the Ohio Printmakers." *Ohio History* 89 (Autumn 1980): 400-419.

4159. Holzer, Harold. "Lincoln and Washington: The Printmakers Blessed Their Union." *Kentucky Historical Society Register* 75 (July 1977): 202-213.

4160. Holzer, Harold. "Lincolniana: Lincoln and the Printmakers." *Illinois State Historical Society Journal* 68 (February 1975): 74-84.

4161. Holzer, Harold. "Making of a President? Engravings and Lithographs of Abraham Lincoln." *Connoisseur* 203 (February 1980): 77-91.

4162. Holzer, Harold. "Memorial Prints of Washington and Lincoln." *Antiques* 115 (February 1979): 352-356.

4163. Holzer, Harold. "Out from the Wilderness: Little Known Contemporary Paintings of Abraham Lincoln." *Connoisseur* 199 (October 1978): 124-131.

4164. Holzer, Harold. "Presidential Proximity: 'Musical Chairs' in Lincoln Emancipation Prints." *Lincoln Herald* 80 (Fall 1978): 148-153.

4165. Holzer, Harold. "Some Contemporary Paintings of Abraham Lincoln." *Antiques* 107 (February 1975): 314-322.

4166. Holzer, Harold. "White House Lincolniana: The First Family's Print of the Lincolns." *Lincoln Herald* 76 (Fall 1974): 132-138.

4167. Holzer, Harold, and Lloyd Ostendorf. "The Long Lost Lincolns." *Civil War Times Illustrated* 18 (May 1979): 32-41.

4168. Holzer, Harold, Gabor S. Borit, and Mark E. Neely, Jr. *The Lincoln Image: Abraham Lincoln and the Popular Print*. New York: Scribner's, 1984.

4169. Jillson, Willard R. "Abraham Lincoln: The Story of a New Portrait." *Kentucky Historical Society Register* 30 (July 1932): 205-210.

4170. Lorant, Stefan. *Lincoln, A Picture Story of His Life*. Rev. ed. New York: Harper and Row, 1957.

4171. Lorant, Stefan. *Lincoln, His Life in Photographs*. New York: Grosset and Dunlap, 1941.

4172. Mellon, James. *The Face of Lincoln*. New York: Viking Press, 1979.

4173. Meredith, Roy. *Mr. Lincoln's Contemporaries: An Album of Portraits by Mathew B. Brady.* New York: Scribner's, 1951.

4174. Meredith, Roy. "The Photogenic Mr. Lincoln." In *Lincoln for the Ages,* edited by Ralph G. Newman, 319-324. Garden City, NY: Doubleday, 1960.

4175. Meserve, Frederick H., and Carl Sandburg. *The Photographs of Abraham Lincoln.* New York: Harcourt, Brace, 1944.

4176. "A New Portrait of Lincoln." *Art World* 2 (August 1917): 421-422.

4177. Ostendorf, Lloyd. "Faces Lincoln Knew — Photographs from the Past." *Lincoln Herald* 79 (Spring 1977): 29-32.

4178. Ostendorf, Lloyd. *Lincoln and His Photographers: Address at Annual Meeting.* Madison: Lincoln Fellowship of Wisconsin, 1971.

4179. Ostendorf, Lloyd. "Lincoln's Elusive Photograph." *Hobbies* 61 (February 1961): 56-57, 67.

4180. Pratt, Harry E. "Only Known Photograph of Lincoln in His Coffin." *Illinois State Historical Society Journal* 45 (Autumn 1952): 252-256.

4181. Truesdell, Winfred P. *Engraved and Lithographed Portraits of Abraham Lincoln.* Champlain, NY: Troutsdale Press, 1933.

4182. Vanderbilt, Paul. "Two Photographs of Abraham Lincoln." *Library of Congress Quarterly Journal* 10 (August 1953): 185-189.

4183. Vaughan, Olive. *The Life of Abraham Lincoln, As Told in Pictures.* Johnstown, PA: Statler Press, 1925.

4184. Warren, Louis A. "The Early Portraits of Lincoln." *Kentucky Historical Society Register* 30 (July 1932): 211-220.

4185. Wetmore, Alexander. *Two Original Photographic Negatives of Abraham Lincoln.* Washington, DC: Smithsonian Institution Press, 1936.

4186. Wilmerding, Lucius, Jr. "Images of Lincoln in Peto's Late Paintings." *Archives of American Art Journal* 22 (1982): 2-12.

4187. Wilson, Rufus R. *Lincoln in Caricature: 165 Poster Cartoons and Drawings for the Press.* Elmira, NY: Primavera Press, 1945.

4188. Wilson, Rufus R. *Lincoln in Portraiture: Sixty-two Portraits.* New York: Press of the Pioneers, 1935.

Recollections

4189. *Abraham Lincoln by Some Men Who Knew Him: Being Personal Recollections of Judge Owen T. Reeves, Hon. James S. Ewing, Col. Richard P. Morgan, Judge Franklin Blades, and John W. Burn.* Bloomington, IL: Pantagraph Printing and Stationery Co., 1910.

4190. "Abraham Lincoln Was a Hero to His Valet-Coachman." *Current Opinion* 76 (February 1924): 204-205.

4191. Angle, Paul M. *Abraham Lincoln, By Some Men Who Knew Him.* Salem, NH: Ayer, 1950.

4192. Aubere, Jewell H. "A Reminiscence of Abraham Lincoln: A Conversation with Speaker Cannon." *World's Work* 13 (February 1907): 8528-8530.

4193. Ayres, Philip W. "Lincoln as a Neighbor." *Review of Reviews* 57 (February 1918): 183-185.

4194. Bancroft, T. B. "An Audience with Abraham Lincoln." *McClure's* 32 (March 1909): 447-450.

4195. Barton, William E. "Abraham Lincoln as We Know Him Now." *Homiletic*

Review 97 (February 1929): 90-93.

4196. Benson, Godfrey R. *Abraham Lincoln.* New York: Pocket Books, 1917.

4197. Beveridge, Albert J. "Lincoln as His Partner Knew Him." *Literary Digest International Book Review* 1 (September 1923): 33-35, 51.

4198. Bowen, Henry C. "Recollections of Abraham Lincoln." *Independent* 64 (February 11, 1909): 292-296.

4199. Brooks, Noah. "Lincoln Reminiscences." *Magazine of History* 9 (February 1909): 107-108.

4200. Brooks, Noah. "Personal Recollections of Lincoln." *Harper's Magazine* 31 (July 1865): 222-230.

4201. Charnwood, Godfrey R. B. "Abraham Lincoln as Now Known to Us." *Discovery* 1 (July/August 1920): 209-211, 245-247.

4202. Chrisman, Herring. *Memoirs of Lincoln.* Mapleton, IA: W. H. Chrisman, 1930.

4203. Colburn, Harvey. "A Family Letter with Views on Lincoln, 1862." *Maryland Historical Magazine* 53 (March 1958): 75-78.

4204. Cole, Cornelius C. "The Lincoln I Knew." *Collier's* 71 (February 10, 1923): 29.

4205. Conant, Alban J. "A Portrait Painter's Reminiscences of Lincoln." *McClure's* 32 (March 1909): 512-516.

4206. Cowen, Benjamin R. *Abraham Lincoln: An Appreciation by One Who Knew Him.* Cincinnati, OH: R. Clark Co., 1909.

4207. Crook, William H. "Lincoln as I Knew Him." Compiled by Margarita S. Gerry. *Harper's Magazine* 115 (June 1907): 41-48.

4208. Davis, John M. "The Image of Lincoln in the South: From Secession to Lincoln Centennial Year (1860-1909)." Ph.D. dissertation, Rice University, 1967.

4209. Dent, Thomas. "A Note to Abraham Lincoln." *Chicago Legal News* 49 (April 12, 19, 26, May 10, 31, 1917): 293, 301, 308, 325, 349.

4210. Dodge, Grenville M. *Personal Recollections of President Abraham Lincoln, Gen. Ulysses S. Grant, and Gen. William T. Sherman.* Council Bluffs, IA: Monarch Printing Co., 1914.

4211. Eaton, John. *Grant, Lincoln, and the Freedmen: Reminiscences of the Civil War with Special Reference to the Work for the Contrabands and Freedmen of the Mississippi Valley.* New York: Longmans, Green, 1907.

4212. Fischer, Leroy H. "Samuel C. Parks's Reminiscences of Abraham Lincoln." *Lincoln Herald* 68 (Spring 1966): 11-18.

4213. Gerry, Margarita S., ed. *Through Five Administrations: Reminiscences of Colonel William H. Crook, Body-Guard to President Lincoln.* New York: Harper and Brothers, 1910.

4214. Gould, Levi S. "Personal Recollections of Abraham Lincoln." *Magazine of History* 16 (January 1913): 9-15.

4215. Greeley, Horace. *Greely on Lincoln.* New York: Baker and Taylor, 1893.

4216. Hannon, Stuart L. "Portrait of Lincoln." *Foreign Service Journal* 31 (February 1954): 20-23, 40-48.

4217. Harris, Mary M. *Lincoln Memoirs.* Springfield, IL: Phillips Brothers, 1908.

4218. Hertz, Emanuel, ed. *Lincoln Talks: A Biography in Anecdote.* New York: Viking Press, 1939.

4219. Howard, Oliver O. "Personal Recollections of Abraham Lincoln." *Century Magazine* 75 (April 1908): 873-877.

4220. Howard, Oliver O. "Some Reminiscences of Abraham Lincoln." *Lincoln Herald* 55 (Fall 1953): 20-22.

4221. Hunt, Eugenia. *My Personal Recollections of Abraham and Mary Todd Lincoln.* Peoria, IL: H. A. Moser, 1966.

4222. Johns, Jane M. *Personal Recollections of Early Decatur, Abraham Lincoln, Richard J. Oglesby, and the Civil War.* Decatur, IL: Decatur Chapter Daughters of the American Revolution, 1912.

4223. Johnson, Byron B. *Abraham Lincoln and Boston Corbett, With Personal Recollections of Each.* Waltham, MA: B. B. Johnson, 1914.

4224. Keckley, Elizabeth H. *Behind the Scenes: Or Thirty Years a Slave and Four Years in the White House.* New York: Carleton, 1868.

4225. Lamon, Ward H. *Recollections of Abraham Lincoln, 1847-1865.* Edited by Dorothy L. Teilland. Washington: The Editor, 1911.

4226. Lansden, John M. "Abraham Lincoln, Judge David Davis and Judge Edward Bates." *Illinois State Historical Society Journal* 7 (April 1914): 56-58.

4227. Laugel, Antoine A. "A Glimpse of President Lincoln." *Legion D'Honneur Magazine* 7 (1936): 57-59.

4228. Lincoln Group of Chicago. *Lincoln Group Papers: The Ten Addresses Delivered before the Lincoln Group of Chicago, 1934-1935, On Varied Aspects of Abraham Lincoln's Life and Interests.* Edited by Douglas C. McMurtrie. Chicago: Black Cat Press, 1936.

4229. McBride, Robert W. *Personal Recollections of Abraham Lincoln.* Indianapolis, IN: Bobbs-Merrill, 1926.

4230. Masonic Trowel, Springfield, IL. "Lincoln and the Masons." *Illinois State Historical Society Journal* 48 (Summer 1955): 191-198.

4231. Nadal, Ehrman S. "Abraham Lincoln: Some Recollections and Comparisons." *Outlook* 112 (February 9, 1916): 335-340.

4232. Nadal, Ehrman S. "Some Impressions of Lincoln." *Scribner's Magazine* 39 (March 1906): 368-377.

4233. Nicolay, Helen. "Characteristic Anecdotes of Lincoln: From Unpublished Notes of His Private Secretary, John. G. Nicolay." *Century Magazine* 84 (September 1912): 697-703.

4234. Nicolay, Helen. *Lincoln's Secretary, A Biography of John G. Nicolay.* New York: Longmans, Green, 1949.

4235. Paton, William A. "A Schoolboy's Interview with Abraham Lincoln." *Scribner's Magazine* 54 (December 1913): 709-710.

4236. Phillips, Isaac N. *Abraham Lincoln by Some Men Who Knew Him.* Bloomington, IL: Pantagraph Printing and Stationery Co., 1910.

4237. Pickett, Mrs. George. "President Lincoln, Intimate Personal Recollections." *Lippincott's* 77 (May 1906): 555-560.

4238. Planck, Gary R. "Lincoln and Bailey: A Forgotten Friendship." *Lincoln Herald* 76 (Fall 1974): 143-147.

4239. Raney, McKendree L. *If Lincoln Had Lived.* Chicago: University of Chicago Press, 1935.

4240. Rankin, Henry B. *Personal Recollections of Abraham Lincoln.* New York: Putnam, 1916.

4241. Rantoul, Robert S. "Reminiscences of Lincoln." *Massachusetts Historical Society Proceedings* 2 (January 1909): 84-87.

4242. "Recollections of Lincoln: Three Letters of Intimate Friends." *Abraham Lincoln Association Bulletin* 25 (December 1931): 3-9.

4243. Rice, Allen T., ed. *Reminiscences of*

Abraham Lincoln by Distinguished Men of His Time. Rev. ed. New York: Harper and Row, 1909.

4244. Rindlaub, M. "More Recollections of Abraham Lincoln." *Wisconsin Magazine of History* 5 (March 1922): 292-296.

4245. Rindlaub, M. "Personal Recollections of Abraham Lincoln." *National Magazine* 43 (February 1916): 839-846.

4246. Scovel, James M. "Personal Recollections of Lincoln and Statesmen of His Time." *National Magazine* 17 (March 1903): 693-702.

4247. Scoville, Samuel, Jr. "When Lincoln and Beecher Met: A Revealing Episode in Lincoln's Life." *Independent* 116 (February 13, 1926): 180-182.

4248. Seward, William H. "Reminiscences of Lincoln." *Magazine of History* 9 (February 1909): 104-107.

4249. Shaw, George W. *Personal Reminiscences of Abraham Lincoln.* Moline, IL: Carlson Printing Co., 1924.

4250. Snow, Marshall S. "Abraham Lincoln, A Personal Reminiscence." *Magazine of History* 11 (February 1910): 63-66.

4251. Stanton, Robert B. "Abraham Lincoln: Personal Memories of the Man." *Scribner's Magazine* 68 (July 1920): 32-41.

4252. Stevens, Walter B. *A Reporter's Lincoln.* Saint Louis: Missouri Historical Society, 1916.

4253. Stimmel, Smith. *Personal Reminiscences of Abraham Lincoln.* Minneapolis, MN: W. H. M. Adams, 1928.

4254. Stoddard, William O. *Lincoln's Third Secretary: The Memoirs of William O. Stoddard.* New York: Exposition Press, 1955.

4255. Tarbell, Ida M. *He Knew Lincoln.* New York: McClure, 1907.

4256. Tarbell, Ida M. *A Reporter for Lincoln: Story of Henry E. Wing, Soldier and Newspaperman.* New York: Macmillan, 1927.

4257. Temple, Wayne C. "Tinsmith to the Late Mr. Lincoln: Samuel S. Elder." *Illinois State Historical Society Journal* 71 (August 1978): 176-184.

4258. Tucker, Glenn. "Lincoln's Jesse W. Weik." *Lincoln Herald* 77 (Spring 1975): 3-15; (Summer 1975): 72-86.

4259. Turner, Arlin. "Elizabeth Peabody Visits Lincoln, February 1865." *New England Quarterly* 48 (March 1975): 116-124.

4260. Tyler, Moses C. "One of Mr. Lincoln's Old Friends." *Illinois State Historical Society Journal* 28 (January 1936): 247-257.

4261. Vinson, John W. "Personal Reminiscences of Mr. Lincoln." *Illinois State Historical Society Journal* 8 (January 1916): 572-580.

4262. Washington, John E. *They Knew Lincoln.* New York: Dutton, 1942.

4263. Weik, Jesse W. "Abraham Lincoln: Personal Recollections." *Outlook* 91 (February 13, 1909): 345-348.

4264. Weik, Jesse W. "A Law Student's Recollection of Abraham Lincoln." *Outlook* 97 (February 11, 1911): 311-314.

4265. Whipple, Wayne. *The Heart of Lincoln: The Soul of the Man as Revealed in Story and Anecdote.* Philadelphia: G. W. Jacobs, 1915.

4266. Whipple, Wayne. *The Story-Life of Lincoln: A Biography Composed of Five Hundred True Stories Told by Abraham Lincoln and His Friends, Selected from All Authentic Sources, and Fitted Together in Order, Forming His Complete Life History.* Philadelphia: Winston, 1908.

4267. Wilson, James G. "Recollections of

Lincoln." *Putnam's* 5 (February 1909): 515-529; (March 1909): 670-675.

4268. Wilson, James G. "Reminiscences of Abraham Lincoln." *Independent* 74 (February 20, 1913): 395-397.

4269. Wilson, Rufus R., ed. *Intimate Memories of Lincoln*. Elmira, NY: Primavera Press, 1945.

4270. Wilson, Rufus R., ed. *Lincoln among His Friends: A Sheaf of Intimate Memories*. Caldwell, ID: Caxton, 1942.

4271. Zane, Charles S. "Lincoln as I Knew Him." *Illinois State Historical Society Journal* 14 (April/July 1921): 74-84.

Religion

4272. Abbott, Lyman. "Abraham Lincoln's Religion." *Outlook* 113 (June 7, 1915): 330-331.

4273. Abbott, Lyman. "The Agnosticism of Abraham Lincoln." *Outlook* 84 (November 17, 1906): 654-655.

4274. Abbott, Lyman. "The Religion of Abraham Lincoln." *Outlook* 124 (April 14, 1920): 656-657.

4275. Barton, William E. "Abraham Lincoln and the Eucharistic Congress." *Outlook* 143 (July 14, 1926): 375-377.

4276. Endy, Melvin B., Jr. "Abraham Lincoln and American Civil Religion: A Reinterpretation." *Church History* 44 (June 1975): 229-241.

4277. Erickson, Gary L. "Lincoln's Civil Religion and the Lutheran Heritage." *Lincoln Herald* 75 (Winter 1973): 158-171.

4278. Fish, Carl R. "Lincoln and Catholicism." *American Historical Review* 29 (July 1924): 723-724.

4279. Fitzgerrell, James J. *Lincoln Was a Spiritualist*. Los Angeles: Austin Publishing Co., 1924.

4280. Fleckles, Elliot. *Willie Speaks Out: The Psychic World of Abraham Lincoln*. St. Paul, MN: Llewellyn Publications, 1974.

4281. Goodman, James F. *Lincoln at Heart: Or His Moral and Religious Life*. Albion, MI: Art Craft Press, 1931.

4282. Grierson, Francis. *Abraham Lincoln, The Practical Mystic*. New York: Lane, 1918.

4283. Hein, David. "The Calvinistic Tenor of Abraham Lincoln's Religious Thought." *Lincoln Herald* 85 (Winter 1983): 212-220.

4284. Hein, David. "Research on Lincoln's Religious Beliefs and Practices: A Bibliographical Essay." *Lincoln Herald* 86 (Spring 1984): 2-5.

4285. Hertz, Emanuel. *Abraham Lincoln, The Tribute of the Synagogue*. New York: Bloch Publishing Co., 1927.

4286. Hill, John W. "Abraham Lincoln — A Prophet of God." *National Magazine* 43 (March 1916): 975-978.

4287. Hill, John W. *Abraham Lincoln: Man of God*. 2d ed. New York: Putnam, 1922.

4288. Hillis, Newell D. "Abraham Lincoln: His Religious Attitude." In his *All the Year Round: An Outlook upon Its Great Days*, 36-55. New York: Revell, 1912.

4289. Holliday, Carl. "Lincoln's God." *South Atlantic Quarterly* 18 (January 1919): 15-23.

4290. Horner, Harlan H. *The Growth of Lincoln's Faith*. New York: Abingdon Press, 1939.

4291. House, Albert V., Jr. "The Genesis of the Lincoln Religious Controversy."

Association of History Teachers of the Middle States and Maryland 36 (1938): 44-54.

4292. Hubbard, George U. "Abraham Lincoln as Seen by the Mormons." *Utah Historical Quarterly* 31 (Spring 1963): 91-108.

4293. Jackson, Samuel T. *Lincoln's Use of the Bible.* New York: Jennings, 1909.

4294. Johnson, George B. "The Quakerism of Abraham Lincoln." *Friend's Historical Association Bulletin* 38 (Spring 1939): 63-67.

4295. Johnstone, William J. *Abraham Lincoln, The Christian.* Rev. ed. New York: Abingdon Press, 1928.

4296. Johnstone, William J. *How Lincoln Prayed.* New York: Abingdon Press, 1931.

4297. Jones, Edgar D. *Lincoln and the Preachers.* New York: Harper and Row, 1948.

4298. Jones, Jenkin L. "Abraham Lincoln, 1809-1909." *Methodist Quarterly Review* 58 (July 1909): 534-547.

4299. Kubicek, Earl C. "Abraham Lincoln's Faith." *Lincoln Herald* 85 (Fall 1983): 188-194.

4300. Lemmon, Walter M. "The Bible on the Tongue of Lincoln." *Methodist Review* 89 (January 1907): 93-108.

4301. Lindstrom, Ralph G. *Lincoln Finds God.* New York: Longmans, Green, 1958.

4302. Locke, Charles E. "Lincoln Not an Unbeliever." *Methodist Review* 89 (September 1907): 737-744.

4303. Macartney, Clarence E. *Lincoln and the Bible.* New York: Abingdon Press, 1949.

4304. McMurtrie, Douglas C., ed. *Lincoln's Religion, the Text of Addresses Delivered by William H. Herndon and Rev. James A. Reed, and a Letter by C. F. B.* Chicago: Black Cat Press, 1936.

4305. Markens, Isaac. "Lincoln and the Jews." *American Jewish Historical Society Publications* 17 (1909): 109-165.

4306. Maynard, Nettie C. *Was Abraham Lincoln a Spiritualist?* Philadelphia: R. C. Hartrant, 1891.

4307. Myers, James E. "Lincoln and the Jews." *Midstream* 27 (February 1981): 26-29.

4308. "New Light on Abraham Lincoln's Religion." *Current Opinion* 48 (April 1920): 515-518.

4309. Owen, G. Frederick. *Abraham Lincoln: The Man and His Faith.* Wheaton, IL: Tyndale, 1981.

4310. Owen, G. Frederick. *A Heart That Yearned for God: Abraham Lincoln, His Life and Faith.* Washington, DC: Third Century Publishers, 1976.

4311. Pennel, Orrin H. *The Religious Views of Abraham Lincoln.* Alliance, OH: H. H. Timby, 1904.

4312. Penniman, Josiah H. "Abraham Lincoln and Christian Education." *Pennsylvania Gazette* 23 (March 6, 1925): 465-468.

4313. Peters, Madison C. *Abraham Lincoln's Religion.* Boston: R. G. Badger, 1909.

4314. Robbins, Peggy. "The Lincolns and Spiritualism." *Civil War Times Illustrated* 15 (August 1976): 4-10, 46-47.

4315. Robinson, Luther E. "Lincoln's Religion Restated." *Bookman* 51 (July 1920): 547-552.

4316. Roper, R. C. "The Religious Beliefs of Abraham Lincoln." *Open Court* 17 (February 1903): 76-85.

4317. Rubinger, Naphtali J. *Abraham Lincoln and the Jews.* New York: J. David, 1962.

4318. Short, Isaac M. "The Manner of

Mr. Lincoln's Religion: Illustrated by the Song He Liked." *Methodist Review* 113 (January/February 1930): 89-98.

4319. Smith, Thomas V. *Abraham Lincoln and the Spiritual Life*. Boston: Beacon Press, 1951.

4320. Speakman, Frederick B. "Can the Church Join Abraham Lincoln?" *Princeton Seminary Bulletin* 1 (Winter 1976): 24-27.

4321. Starr, John W. "What Was Abraham Lincoln's Religion?" *Magazine of History* 15 (January 1912): 18-31.

4322. Suppiger, Joseph E. "Lincoln and Pope." *Lincoln Herald* 77 (Winter 1975): 218-222.

4323. Thurow, Glen E. *Abraham Lincoln and American Political Religion*. Albany: State University of New York Press, 1976.

4324. Tucker, Glenn. "Was Lincoln a Converted Christian?" *Lincoln Herald* 78 (Fall 1976): 102-108.

4325. Warren, Louis A. "The Religious Background of the Lincoln Family." *Filson Club History Quarterly* 6 (January 1932): 72-88.

4326. Warren, Raymond. *Abraham Lincoln as a Spiritual Influence*. Chicago: Progressive Century Co., 1933.

4327. Wettstein, Carl T., comp. *Was Abraham Lincoln an Infidel?* Boston: C. M. Clark Publishing Co., 1910.

4328. White, Charles T. "Lincoln and Three Methodists." *Methodist Review* 47 (1931): 38-45.

4329. Wolf, William J. *Lincoln's Religion*. New York: Pilgrim Press, 1970.

4330. Wolf, William J. *The Religion of Abraham Lincoln*. Rev. ed. New York: Seabury, 1963.

4331. Woodall, Charles L. "Lincoln's Religion and the Denominations." *Lincoln Herald* 84 (Fall 1982): 168-172.

4332. Wright, James C. "Lincoln and the Beatitudes: The Abuse He Suffered Would Have Made an Ordinary Man Strike Back." *Christianity Today* 27 (February 4, 1983): 21.

Travels

4333. Anderson, Richard D. "Abraham Lincoln at Niagara." *Niagara Frontier* 8 (Winter 1962): 117-120.

4334. Angle, Paul M. *"Here I Have Lived": A History of Lincoln's Springfield, 1821-1865*. Springfield, IL: Abraham Lincoln Association, 1935.

4335. Blunk, S. M. "The Lincoln Way." *Abraham Lincoln Association Bulletin* 11 (June 1, 1928): 1-8.

4336. Bryner, Byron L. *Abraham Lincoln in Peoria, Ill*. Peoria, IL: Lincoln Historical Publishing Co., 1926.

4337. Buck, Solon J. "Lincoln and Minnesota." *Minnesota History* 6 (December 1925): 355-361.

4338. Carpenter, C. C. "Lincoln at Petersburg." *Magazine of History* 11 (February 1910): 95-98.

4339. Coleman, Charles H. *Abraham Lincoln and Coles County, Illinois*. New Brunswick, NJ: Scarecrow Press, 1955.

4340. Cottman, George S. "Lincoln in Indianapolis." *Indiana Magazine of History* 24 (March 1928): 1-14.

4341. Currey, J. Seymour. "Abraham Lincoln's Early Visits to Chicago." *Illinois State Historical Society Journal* 12 (October 1919): 412-416.

4342. Davis, Edwin. "Lincoln and Macon County, Illinois, 1830-1831." *Illinois State Historical Society Journal* 25 (April/July 1932): 63-107.

4343. Ehrmann, Max. "Lincoln's Visit to Terre Haute." *Indiana Magazine of History* 32 (March 1936): 59-61.

4344. Evans, Joseph F. "Lincoln at Galesburg — A Sketch Written on the One Hundred and Seventh Anniversary of the Birthday of Abraham Lincoln." *Illinois Historical Society Journal* 8 (January 1916): 559-568.

4345. Fiore, Jordan D. *Abraham Lincoln Visits the Old Colony.* Taunton, MA: Old Colony Historical Society, 1978.

4346. Frazier, Carl. *The Lincoln Country in Pictures.* New York: Hastings House, 1964.

4347. Freeman, Andrew A. *Abraham Lincoln Goes to New York.* New York: Coward-McCann, 1960.

4348. Gernon, Blaine B. "Lincoln's Visits to Chicago." *Chicago Historical Society Bulletin* 1 (February 1935): 33-41.

4349. Hanna, William F., III. "Abraham Lincoln's 1860 Visit to Rhode Island." *Lincoln Herald* 81 (Fall 1979): 197-201.

4350. Hanna, William F., III. "This Side of the Mountains: Abraham Lincoln's 1848 Visit to Massachusetts." *Lincoln Herald* 80 (Summer 1978): 56-65.

4351. Holmes, Frederick L. *Abraham Lincoln Traveled This Way: The Log Book of a Pilgrim to the Lincoln Country.* Boston: Page, 1930.

4352. Jefferson, Henry. "Lincoln in Massachusetts." *Magazine of History* 9 (February 1909): 109-110.

4353. Kaiser, P. H. "Lincoln at Fort Stevens." *National Magazine* 31 (February 1910): 525-526.

4354. Kyle, Otto R. *Abraham Lincoln in Decatur.* New York: Vantage Press, 1957.

4355. Lewis, Theodore B., ed. "Enoch Lewis's Account of Lincoln's Secret Journey from Harrisburg to Philadelphia, February 22, 1861." *Lincoln Herald* 76 (Fall 1974): 148-149.

4356. Lloyd, John A. *Snowbound with Mr. Lincoln.* New York: Vantage Press, 1979.

4357. Longacre, Edward G. "With Lincoln on His Last Journey." *Lincoln Herald* 84 (Winter 1982): 239-241.

4358. McMurtry, R. Gerald. *A Series of Monographs Concerning the Lincolns and Hardin County, Kentucky.* Elizabethtown, KY: Enterprise Press, 1938.

4359. Murr, J. Edward. "Lincoln in Indiana." *Indiana Magazine of History* 13 (December 1917): 307-348; 14 (March 1918): 13-75; 14 (June 1918): 148-182.

4360. Olson, Julius E. "Lincoln in Wisconsin." *Wisconsin Magazine of History* 4 (September 1920): 44-54.

4361. Page, Elwin L. *Abraham Lincoln in New Hampshire.* Boston: Houghton Mifflin, 1929.

4362. Pratt, Harry E. "Abraham Lincoln in Bloomington, Illinois." *Illinois State Historical Society Journal* 29 (April 1936): 42-69.

4363. Reep, Thomas P. *Lincoln at New Salem.* Chicago: n.p., 1927.

4364. Renne, Louis O. *Lincoln and the Land of the Sangamon.* Boston: Chapman and Grimes, 1945.

4365. Roberts, Octavia. *Lincoln in Illinois.* Boston: Houghton Mifflin, 1918.

4366. Ryan, Daniel J. *Lincoln and Ohio.* Columbus: Ohio State Archaeological and Historical Society, 1923.

4367. Smith, George W. *When Lincoln Came to Egypt.* Herrin, IL: Trouillion Private Press, 1940.

4368. Stern, Philip V. D. "Lincoln's Journey to Greatness." In *Abraham Lincoln: A New Portrait*, edited by Henry B.

Kranz, 158-165. New York: Putnam, 1959.

4369. Thomas, Benjamin P. "Lincoln and New Salem, A Study in Environment." *Illinois State Historical Society Transactions* 41 (1934): 61-75.

4370. Turner, James W. *On Abraham Lincoln's Trail from Hodgenville to Springfield, Containing Narratives Written with a Special View to Historical Accuracy.* Evansville, IN: Turner Publishing Co., 1930.

4371. Viele, Egbert L. "A Trip with Lincoln, Chase, and Stanton." *Scribner's Monthly* 16 (October 1878): 813-822.

4372. Warren, Louis A. "Lincoln Stumps Kentucky." *Kentucky Historical Society Register* 27 (May 1929): 545-547.

4373. Wiley, Earl W. "Lincoln Spoke in Rockville, Maryland, 1848." *Illinois State Historical Society Journal* 29 (July 1936): 178-180.

Tributes

4374. "Abraham Lincoln: A Tribute." *Western Pennsylvania Historical Magazine* 3 (October 1920): 178-192.

4375. *Abraham Lincoln: Tributes from His Associates: Reminiscences of Soldiers, Statesmen, and Citizens.* New York: Crowell, 1895.

4376. Arthur, Samuel J. *Lincoln's Legacy: A Tribute to the World's Great Commoner.* Boston: R. G. Badger, 1923.

4377. Bancroft, George. *Abraham Lincoln: A Tribute.* New York: A. Wessels Co., 1908.

4378. Barton, William E. *Abraham Lincoln and the Hooker Letter: An Address . . . Delivered before the Pennell Club of Philadelphia at a Dinner Given in the Union League Club.* New York: Bowling Green Press, 1928.

4379. Basler, Roy P. *A Touchstone for Greatness: Essays, Addresses, and Occasional Pieces about Abraham Lincoln.* Westport, CT: Greenwood Press, 1973.

4380. Bernard, Kenneth A., comp. *The Lincoln Group of Boston: Forty Years of Its History, 1938-1978.* Boston: The Group, 1978.

4381. Chapin, Benjamin. "Lincoln in the Hearts of the People." *Independent* 66 (February 11, 1909): 305-308.

4382. Choate, Joseph H. *Abraham Lincoln, and Other Addresses in England.* New York: Century, 1910.

4383. Cortada, James W. "Spanish Views on Abraham Lincoln, 1861-1865." *Lincoln Herald* 76 (Summer 1974): 80-85.

4384. Cox, Henry C. *Abraham Lincoln: An Appreciation.* Chicago: Abbey, 1911.

4385. Davidson, Bill. *President Kennedy Selects Six Brave Presidents.* New York: Harper and Row, 1962.

4386. "An English Interpretation of Lincoln." *Nation* 104 (January 4, 1917): 20-21.

4387. "A French Tribute to Lincoln, The Gold Medal Presented to His Widow in 1866." *Putnam's* 7 (March 1910): 669-671.

4388. Goldsmith, Marcus A. *Abraham Lincoln, His Life: A True Story of One of the World's Best Men.* Cleveland, OH: Goldsmith Publishing Co., 1918.

4389. Greeley, Horace. *Greeley's Estimate of Lincoln: An Unpublished Address.* Hancock, NY: Herald Printery, 1932.

4390. Grout, Josiah. *A Lincoln Book, A Soldier's Tribute to His Chief.* Rutland, VT: Tuttle, 1925.

4391. Hambrecht, George P. *Abraham*

Lincoln, His Spirit Lives: An Appreciation. Stoughton, WI: Vocational School, 1926.

4392. Humphrey, Grace. "Lincoln and the Immigrant." *Outlook* 115 (February 7, 1917): 234-235.

4393. Jennings, A. H. "A View of Rutledge's 'Lincoln: A Southern View.'" *Confederate Veteran* 33 (April 1925): 129-130.

4394. Keys, Thomas B. "Lincoln's Voice from the Grave: A Spiritualistic Conversation with Carl Schurz." *Lincoln Herald* 77 (Summer 1975): 121-123.

4395. Kim, Donggill. "Abraham Lincoln: An Oriental Interpretation." Ph.D. dissertation, Boston University, 1971.

4396. Kincaid, Robert L. *The Lincoln Heritage in the Cumberlands.* Los Angeles: Lincoln Fellowship of Southern California, 1951.

4397. Kincaid, Robert L. *Lincoln, Martyred Friend of the South.* Washington, DC: U.S. Government Printing Office, 1949.

4398. Krans, Horatio S., ed. *The Lincoln Tribute Book: Appreciations by Statesmen, Men of Letters, and Poets at Home and Abroad, Together with a Lincoln Centenary Medal from the Second Design Made for the Occasion by Roine.* New York: Putnam, 1909.

4399. Lamon, Ward H. "Lincoln's Last Laugh." *Americana* 6 (October 1911): 977-922.

4400. "The Lincoln Centennial Celebration." *Review of Reviews* 39 (February 1909): 172-175.

4401. Linder, Usher F. "Linder's Tribute to Lincoln." *Illinois State Historical Society Journal* 51 (Spring 1958): 99-104.

4402. McGlynn, Frank. *Sidelights on Lincoln.* Los Angeles: Wetzel Publishing Co., 1947.

4403. Mearns, David C. *Lincoln and the Image of America.* Hamilton, Ont: Lincoln Fellowship of Hamilton, 1953.

4404. Mitgang, Herbert, ed. *Lincoln as They Saw Him.* New York: Rinehart, 1956.

4405. Newton, Joseph F. *We Here Highly Resolve Three Tributes to Abraham Lincoln.* New York: Harper and Row, 1939.

4406. Patterson, Robert F. "A Confederate Veteran's Tribute to Abraham Lincoln." Edited by Robert L. Kincaid. *Lincoln Herald* 57 (Fall 1955): 20-24.

4407. Phillips, Josephine. "A Personal Tribute to Lincoln." Edited by Philip Goodman. *American Jewish Historical Society Publications* 41 (December 1951): 204-207.

4408. Randall, Robert L. "Healthy Idealization of Abraham Lincoln." *Lincoln Herald* 80 (Summer 1978): 188-191.

4409. Reid, Whitelaw. "Abraham Lincoln." In his *American and English Studies*, Vol. 2, 3-33. New York: Scribner's, 1913.

4410. Rose, Uriah M. "Abraham Lincoln Address on the One Hundredth Anniversary of President Lincoln's Birth." In the *Addresses of U. M. Rose*, 133-167. Chicago: G. I. Jones, 1914.

4411. Ross, Riley R. "Lincoln: A World Light." *National Magazine* 39 (February 1914): 777-794.

4412. Rutledge, Archibald. "A Southerner Views Lincoln." *Scribner's Magazine* 83 (February 1928): 204-213.

4413. Schambra, William. "Martin Diamond on 'Lincoln's Greatness.'" *Interpretation* 8 (May 1980): 26-28.

4414. Scott, James B. "Honorable Elihu Root's London Addresses on Abraham Lincoln." *American Journal of Interna-*

tional Law 14 (October 1920): 590-595.

4415. Scott, Milton R. *Essay on Lincoln: Was He an Inspired Prophet?* Newark, OH: n.p., 1906.

4416. Searcher, Victor. *The Farewell to Lincoln.* New York: Abingdon Press, 1965.

4417. Sherwood, A. "Lincoln and Darwin, Extraordinary Contrasts in the Careers of the Two Great Personalities of the Last Century Who Were Born on the Same Day." *World's Work* 17 (January 1909): 11128-11132.

4418. Stern, Philip V. D. *Abraham Lincoln Seventy-five Years After.* New Brunswick, NJ: Rutgers University Press, 1940.

4419. Sumner, Guy L. *Abraham Lincoln as a Man among Men.* New York: Harper and Row, 1922.

4420. Swift, Clarence F. "Abraham Lincoln, Master." *Magazine of History* 11 (February 1910): 67-79.

4421. Thomas, Benjamin P. "A Russian Estimate of Lincoln." *Abraham Lincoln Association Bulletin* 23 (1931): 3-6.

4422. Thomas, W. G. M. "Lincoln after Forty-four Years." *Methodist Quarterly Review* 58 (July 1909): 548-561.

4423. Tokuda, Sumiko. "Abraham Lincoln: A Japanese Interpretation." *Abraham Lincoln Association Bulletin* 15 (June 1, 1929): 1-4, 7-8.

4424. Utley, Francis L. *Lincoln Wasn't There: Or Lord Raglan's Hero.* Washington, DC: College English Association, 1965.

4425. Walters, Helen B. *No Luck for Lincoln.* Nashville, TN: Abingdon, 1981.

4426. Warren, Louis A., comp. *A Man for the Ages: Tributes to Abraham Lincoln.* Fort Wayne, IN: Louis A. Warren Lincoln Library and Museum, 1978.

4427. Wiley, Bell I. *Abraham Lincoln: A Southerner's Estimate after 110 Years.* New Orleans, LA: Graduate School, Tulane University, 1976.

Youth

4428. Alger, Horatio, Jr. *Abraham Lincoln, The Backwoods Boy.* New York: American Publishers, 1883.

4429. Angle, Paul M. "Young Mr. Lincoln." *Abraham Lincoln Association Bulletin* 56 (June 1939): 8-10.

4430. Atkinson, Eleanor. *The Boyhood of Lincoln.* New York: McClure, 1908.

4431. Bacheller, Irving. *A Boy for the Ages.* New York: Farrar and Rinehart, 1937.

4432. Baringer, William E. *Lincoln's Vandalia, A Pioneer Portrait.* New Brunswick, NJ: Rutgers University Press, 1949.

4433. Barker, Harry E. *Abraham Lincoln, His Life in Illinois.* New York: Barrows, 1940.

4434. Barton, William E. "Abraham Lincoln and New Salem." *Illinois State Historical Society Journal* 19 (October/January 1926-1927): 74-101.

4435. Barton, William E. *The Great Good Man: How the Boy Lincoln Grew to Manhood and Achieved Immortality.* Indianapolis, IN: Bobbs-Merrill, 1927.

4436. Brandt, Keith. *Abe Lincoln: The Young Years.* Mahwah, NJ: Troll Associates, 1982.

4437. Brooks, Noah. *Abraham Lincoln, His Youth and Early Manhood, With a Brief Account of His Later Life.* New York: Putnam, 1901.

4438. Cavanah, Frances E. "Abe Lincoln and His Books." *Wilson Library Bulletin* 28 (February 1928): 485-487.

4439. Chandler, Josephine C. *New Salem: Early Chapters in Lincoln's Life.* Springfield, IL: Journal Print Co., 1930.

4440. Gore, John R. *The Boyhood of Abraham Lincoln: From the Spoken Narratives of Austin Gollaher.* Louisville, KY: Standard Print Co., 1935.

4441. Kaine, John L. "Lincoln as a Boy Knew Him." *Century Magazine* 85 (February 1913): 555-559.

4442. Morgan, Arthur E. "New Light on Lincoln's Boyhood." *Atlantic Monthly* 125 (February 1920): 208-218.

4443. Morgan, James. *Abraham Lincoln, The Boy and the Man.* New York: Macmillan, 1908.

4444. Oates, Stephen B. "Wilderness Fugue: Lincoln's Journey to Manhood on the Kentucky and Indiana Frontier." *American West* 13 (March/April 1976): 4-13.

4445. Rothschild, Alonzo. *"Honest Abe": A Study in Integrity Based on the Early Life of Abraham Lincoln.* Boston: Houghton Mifflin, 1917.

4446. Sandburg, Carl. *Abe Lincoln Grows Up.* New York: Harcourt, Brace, 1928.

4447. Short, Isaac M. *Abraham Lincoln: Early Days in Illinois, Reminiscences of Different Persons Who Became Eminent in American History.* Kansas City, MO: Simpson Publishing Co., 1927.

4448. Stevens, Charles M. *The Wonderful Story of Lincoln, and the Meaning of His Life for the Youth and Patriotism of America.* New York: Cupples and Leon, 1917.

4449. Tarbell, Ida M. *The Early Life of Abraham Lincoln.* New York: McClure, 1896.

4450. Thomas, Benjamin P. *Lincoln's New Salem.* Rev. ed. New York: Knopf, 1954.

4451. Van Natter, Francis M. *Lincoln's Boyhood: A Chronicle of His Indiana Years.* Washington, DC: Public Affairs Press, 1964.

4452. Vannest, Charles G. *Lincoln the Hoosier: Abraham Lincoln's Life in Indiana.* St. Louis, MO: Edin Publishing House, 1928.

4453. Warren, Louis A. "Lincoln's Hoosier Schoolmasters." *Indiana Magazine of History* 27 (June 1931): 104-118.

4454. Warren, Louis A. *Lincoln's Youth: Indiana Years, Seven to Twenty-One, 1816-1830.* New York: Appleton, 1959.

4455. Warren, Raymond. *Abe Lincoln, Kentucky Boy.* Chicago: Reilly and Lee, 1931.

4456. Watson, Stuart L. "Lincoln Lives in Appalachia." *Lincoln Herald* 75 (Summer 1973): 56-57.

4457. Whipple, Wayne. *The Story of Young Abraham Lincoln.* Philadelphia: Henry Altemus, 1915.

4458. White, Charles T. *Lincoln the Athlete, and Other Stories.* New York: Terry Press, 1930.

Public Career

General

4459. Abbott, Lyman. "Lincoln as a Labor Leader." *Outlook* 91 (February 27, 1909): 499-505.

4460. "Abraham Lincoln's Mastery of Men." *Outlook* 83 (July 14, 1906): 623-625.

4461. Allen, Eric R. "Abraham Lincoln: An Interpretation." *Hartford Seminary Record* 19 (April 1909): 103-112.

4462. Ambrose, Stephen E. "An Appraisal of Lincoln: The Savior of His Country." *Civil War Times Illustrated* 6 (February 1968): 27-34.

4463. Angle, Paul M. "Dirty Politics." *Chicago History* 8 (1967): 58-60.

4464. Ashe, Samuel A. "Abraham Lincoln, The Citizen." *Tyler's Quarterly Historical and Genealogical Magazine* 16 (October 1934): 150-156.

4465. Auer, John J. "Cooper Institute: Tom Corwin and Abraham Lincoln." *New York History* 32 (October 1951): 399-413.

4466. Barbee, David R. "Lincoln, Chase, and the Rev. Dr. Richard Fuller." *Maryland Historical Magazine* 46 (June 1951): 108-123.

4467. Baringer, William E. "Lincoln as President Elect: Springfield Phase." Ph.D. dissertation, University of Illinois, 1940.

4468. Bartlett, David W. *Life and Public Services of Hon. Abraham Lincoln.* Boston: Thayer and Eldridge, 1860.

4469. Barton, William E. "The Influence of Illinois in the Development of Abraham Lincoln." *Illinois Historical Society Transactions* 28 (1921): 32-53.

4470. Basler, Roy P. "As One Southerner to Another, Concerning Lincoln and the Declaration of Independence." *South Atlantic Quarterly* 42 (January 1943): 45-53.

4471. Blacknall, Oscar W. *Lincoln as the South Should Know Him.* Raleigh, NC: Edwards and Broughton, 1915.

4472. Borit, Gabor S. "Lincoln and Taxation during His Illinois Legislative Years." *Illinois State Historical Society Journal* 61 (Autumn 1968): 365-373.

4473. Borit, Gabor S. "Lincoln and the Economics of the American Dream: The Whig Years, 1832-1854." Ph.D. dissertation, Boston University, 1968.

4474. Borit, Gabor S. "Lincoln's Opposition to the Mexican War." *Illinois State Historical Society Journal* 67 (February 1974): 79-100.

4475. Borit, Gabor S. "The Right to Rise." In *The Public and the Private Lincoln: Contemporary Perspectives*, edited by Cullom Davis, Charles B. Strozier, Rebecca M. Veach, and Geoffrey C. Ward, 57-70. Carbondale: Southern Illinois University Press, 1979.

4476. Borst, William A. "Lincoln's Historical Perspective." *Lincoln Herald* 76 (Winter 1974): 195-203.

4477. Braden, Waldo W. "Lincoln's Delivery." *Lincoln Herald* 85 (Fall 1983): 167-174.

4478. Browne, Robert H. *Abraham Lincoln and the Men of His Time.* New York: Eaton and Mains, 1901.

4479. Burnham, J. H. "When Lincoln Failed to Draw a Crowd." *Illinois State Historical Society Journal* 28 (April 1935): 95-97.

4480. Burr, Nelson R. "Abraham Lincoln: Western Star over Connecticut." *Lincoln Herald* 85 (Spring 1983): 21-36; (Fall 1983): 133-151; 86 (Spring 1984): 6-18; (Summer 1984): 77-92.

4481. Carson, Steven L. "Lincoln and the Mayor of New York." *Lincoln Herald* 67 (Winter 1965): 184-191.

4482. Chu, James C. Y. "Horace White: His Association with Abraham Lincoln, 1854-1860." *Journalism Quarterly* 49 (Spring 1972): 51-60.

4483. Cooper, Homer H. "The Lincoln-Thornton Debate of 1856 at Shelbyville, Illinois." *Illinois Historical Society Journal* 10 (April 1917): 101-122.

4484. Cunliffe, Marcus. "Humour as an American Political Style: The Case of Abraham Lincoln." *Jahrbuch fur Ameri* *kastudien* (West Germany) 11 (1966): 29-40.

4485. Current, Richard N. "Lincoln and Daniel Webster." *Illinois State Historical Society Journal* 48 (Autumn 1955): 307-321.

4486. David, Michael. *The Image of Lincoln in the South*. Knoxville: University of Tennessee Press, 1971.

4487. Dickson, Edward A. "Lincoln and Baker: The Story of a Great Friendship." *Historical Society of Southern California Quarterly* 34 (September 1952): 229-242.

4488. Dodd, William E. "The Rise of Abraham Lincoln." *Century Magazine* 113 (March 1927): 569-584.

4489. Drinkwater, John. *The World's Lincoln*. New York: Bowling Green Press, 1928.

4490. Ellsworth, Edward W. "Lincoln and the Education Convention: Education in Illinois — A Jeffersonian Heritage." *Lincoln Herald* 80 (Summer 1978): 69-78.

4491. Farrington, Harry W. *Walls of America*. Bradley Beach, NJ: Rough and Brown Press, 1925.

4492. Farriss, Charles S. *The American Soul*. Boston: Stratford, 1920.

4493. Fehrenbacher, Don E. *The Changing Image of Lincoln in American Historiography: An Inaugural Lecture Delivered before the University of Oxford on 21 May 1968*. Oxford: Clarendon Press, 1968.

4494. Fehrenbacher, Don E. "Lincoln and the Mayor of Chicago." *Wisconsin Magazine of History* 40 (Summer 1961): 237-244.

4495. Fehrenbacher, Don E. "The Origins and Purpose of Lincoln's 'House-Divided' Speech." *Mississippi Valley Historical Review* 46 (March 1960): 615-643.

4496. Fehrenbacher, Don E. *Prelude to Greatness: Lincoln in the 1850's*. Stanford, CA: Stanford University Press, 1962.

4497. Fillmore, Millard. "Ex-President Fillmore Opposes Lincoln." *Illinois State Historical Society Journal* 46 (Autumn 1953): 302.

4498. Fredrickson, George M. "The Search for Order and Community." In *The Public and the Private Lincoln: Contemporary Perspectives*, edited by Cullom Davis, Charles B. Strozier, Rebecca M. Veach, and Geoffrey C. Ward, 86-98. Carbondale: Southern Illinois University Press, 1979.

4499. Genung, John F. "Lincoln as a Master of Expression." *Magazine of History* 11 (February 1910): 80-84.

4500. Grierson, Francis. *The Valley of Shadows*. New York: History Book Club, 1948.

4501. Hamilton, Holman. "Abraham Lincoln and Zachary Taylor." *Lincoln Herald* 53 (Fall 1951): 14-19.

4502. Hamilton, Joseph G. de Roulhac. "Lincoln and the South." *Sewanee Review* 17 (April 1909): 129-138.

4503. Hamilton, Joseph G. de Roulhac. "The Many-Sired Lincoln." *American Mercury* 5 (June 1925): 129-135.

4504. Hapgood, Norman. "Washington and Lincoln." *Dial* 68 (August 9, 1919): 92-93.

4505. Harwell, Richard B. "Lincoln and the South." In *Lincoln for the Ages*, edited by Ralph G. Newman, 203-207. Garden City, NY: Doubleday, 1960.

4506. Havlik, Robert J. "Abraham Lincoln and the Technology of 'Young America.'" *Lincoln Herald* 79 (Spring 1977): 3-11.

4507. Hill, John W. "Lincoln's 'House Divided against Itself.'" *National Magazine* 45 (February 1917): 668-670.

4508. Horner, Harlan H. "Lincoln Replies to William Henry Seward." *Lincoln Herald* 54 (Spring 1952): 3-11, 54; (Summer 1952): 33-40.

4509. Hostick, King V. "Lincoln Seeks Patronage for Illinois Whigs: A New Letter." *Lincoln Herald* 71 (Winter 1969): 142-143.

4510. Leibiger, Stuart. "Lincoln's 'White Elephants': The Trent Affair." *Lincoln Herald* 84 (Summer 1982): 84-92.

4511. Levy, Aaron. "Abraham Lincoln as Politician." Ph.D. dissertation, Syracuse University, 1909.

4512. "Lincoln as Leader." *New Republic* 33 (February 14, 1923): 306-308.

4513. Mallam, William D. "Lincoln and the Conservatives." *Journal of Southern History* 28 (February 1962): 31-45.

4514. Malone, Dumas. "Jefferson and Lincoln." *Abraham Lincoln Quarterly* 5 (June 1949): 327-347.

4515. Mohrmann, Gerald P., and Michael C. Leff. "Lincoln at Cooper Union: A Rationale for Neo-Classical Criticism." *Quarterly Journal of Speech* 60 (December 1974): 459-467.

4516. Neely, Mark E., Jr. "Lincoln and the Mexican War: An Argument by Analogy." *Civil War History* 24 (March 1978): 5-24.

4517. Nevins, Allan. "Lincoln Takes Charge." *American Heritage* 11 (October 1960): 42-47.

4518. Nichols, Roy F. "Abraham Lincoln: Master Politician." In *Lincoln for the Ages*, edited by Ralph G. Newman, 236-241. Garden City, NY: Doubleday, 1960.

4519. Northrup, Jack. "Governor Richard Yates and President Lincoln." *Lincoln Herald* 70 (Winter 1968): 193-205.

4520. Northrup, Jack. "Lincoln and Yates: The Climb to Power." *Lincoln Herald* 73 (Winter 1971): 242-253.

4521. Page, Elwin L. "Franklin Pierce and Abraham Lincoln — Parallels and Contrasts." *Abraham Lincoln Quarterly* 5 (December 1949): 455-472.

4522. Paludan, Phillip S. "Lincoln, the Rule of Law, and the American Revolution." *Illinois State Historical Society Journal* 70 (February 1977): 10-17.

4523. Rawley, James A. "Lincoln and Governor Morgan." *Abraham Lincoln Quarterly* 6 (March 1951): 272-300.

4524. Ross, Earle D. "Lincoln and Agriculture." *Agricultural History* 3 (April 1929): 51-66.

4525. Ruiz, Ramon E. "A Commentary on Morality: Lincoln, Justin H. Smith, and the Mexican War." *Illinois State Historical Society Journal* 69 (February 1976): 26-34.

4526. Samuels, Ernest. "Abraham Lincoln: Strategist of Conciliation." *Lincoln Herald* 64 (Summer 1962): 70-79.

4527. Seitz, Don C. *Lincoln the Politician: How the Railsplitter and Flatboat man Played the Great American Game.* New York: Coward-McCann, 1931.

4528. Sewell, Richard H. "Lincoln and the 'Postheroic' Generation." *Reviews in American History* 8 (March 1980): 52-56.

4529. Simon, Paul. *Lincoln's Preparation for Greatness: The Illinois Legislature Years.* Norman: University of Oklahoma Press, 1965.

4530. Smiley, David L. "Abraham Lincoln Deals with Cassius M. Clay — Portrait of a Patient Politician." *Lincoln Herald* 55 (Winter 1953): 15-23.

4531. Smith, D. C. "The Lincoln-Thornton Debate at Shelbyville, Illinois, June 15, 1856." *Illinois State Historical Society Journal* 10 (April 1917): 97-100.

4532. Stutler, Boyd B. "Abraham Lincoln and John Brown — A Parallel." *Civil War History* 8 (September 1962): 290-299.

4533. Temple, Wayne C. "Lincoln in the Census." *Lincoln Herald* 68 (Fall 1966): 135-139.

4534. Temple, Wayne C. "Lincoln in the Governor's Chambers of the Illinois State House." *Lincoln Herald* 84 (Winter 1982): 201-204.

4535. Thomas, Benjamin P. "Lincoln the Postmaster." *Abraham Lincoln Association Bulletin* 31 (1933): 3-9.

4536. Van Hoesen, Henry B. "Lincoln and John Hay." *Books at Brown* 18 (October 1960): 141-180.

4537. Walton, Clyde C. "Abraham Lincoln: Illinois Legislator." In *Lincoln for the Ages*, edited by Ralph G. Newman, 74-78. Garden City, NY: Doubleday, 1960.

4538. Warren, Louis A. "Lincoln's Early Political Background." *Illinois State Historical Society Journal* 23 (May 1931): 618-629.

4539. Weik, Jesse W. "Lincoln's Vote for Vice-President in the Philadelphia Convention of 1856." *Century Magazine* 76 (June 1908): 186-189.

4540. Wiley, Earl W. "Lincoln in the Campaign of 1856." *Illinois State Historical Society Journal* 22 (January 1930): 582-592.

4541. Wiley, Earl W. "Lincoln the Speaker." *Quarterly Journal of Speech* 21 (June 1935): 305-322.

4542. Wiley, Earl W. "Lincoln the Speaker — 1816-1830." *Quarterly Journal of Speech* 20 (February 1934): 1-15.

4543. Wiley, Earl W. "Motivation as a Factor in Lincoln's Rhetoric." *Quarterly Journal of Speech* 24 (December 1938): 615-621.

4544. Williams, Gary L. "Lincoln's Neutral Allies: The Case of the Kentucky Unionists." *South Atlantic Quarterly* 73 (Winter 1974): 70-84.

4545. Williams, T. Harry. *Lincoln and the Radicals*. Madison: University of Wisconsin Press, 1941.

4546. Wilson, Major L. "Lincoln and Van Buren in the Steps of the Fathers: Another Look at the Lyceum Address." *Civil War History* 29 (September 1983): 197-211.

4547. Wolf, George D. "Lincoln, The Master Politician." *Lincoln Herald* 81 (Fall 1979): 163-168.

4548. Yarborough, Ralph W. "Lincoln as a Liberal Statesman." In *Lincoln for the Ages*, edited by Ralph G. Newman, 279-283. Garden City, NY: Doubleday, 1960.

4549. Yzenbaard, John H. "Praise for the 'Most Available Candidate.'" *Illinois State Historical Society Journal* 71 (February 1978): 71-72.

Congressman

4550. Barringer, William E. *Lincoln's Rise to Power*. Boston. Little, Brown, 1937.

4551. Findley, Paul. *A. Lincoln, The Crucible of Congress*. New York: Crown, 1979.

4552. Packard, Roy D. *The Lincoln of the Thirtieth Congress*. Boston: Christopher Publishing House, 1950.

4553. Paullin, Charles O. "Abraham Lincoln in Congress, 1847-1849." *Illinois State Historical Society Journal* 14 (April/July 1921): 85-89.

4554. Riddle, Donald W. *Congressman*

Abraham Lincoln. Urbana: University of Illinois Press, 1957.

4555. Riddle, Donald W. "Congressman Abraham Lincoln from Illinois, 1846-48." In *Lincoln for the Ages*, edited by Ralph G. Newman, 96-100. Garden City, NY: Doubleday, 1960.

4556. Riddle, Donald W. *Lincoln Runs for Congress: A Publication of the Abraham Lincoln Association, Springfield, Ill.* New Brunswick, NJ: Rutgers University Press, 1948.

4557. Temple, Wayne C. "Lincoln's Joint Resolutions." *Lincoln Herald* 84 (Summer 1981): 641-645.

Lawyer

4558. *A. Lincoln, The Circuit Lawyer, 1839-1859, McLean County, Illinois*. Bloomington, IL: McLean County Historical Society, 1977.

4559. Abbott, Lawrence F. "Was He an Oafish Country Lawyer?" *Outlook* 144 (November 27, 1926): 363-365.

4560. Ashe, Samuel A. "Lincoln the Lawyer." *Tyler's Quarterly Historical and Geneological Magazine* 16 (July 1934): 15-20.

4561. Benjamin, R. M. "Lincoln the Lawyer." *Central Law Journal* 68 (March 19, 1909): 217-218.

4562. Bergen, A. "Abraham Lincoln as a Lawyer." *American Bar Association Journal* 12 (June 1926): 390-394.

4563. Chapman, Francis. "Lincoln, The Lawyer." *Temple Law Quarterly* 9 (April 1935): 277-291.

4564. Charbonneau, Louis H. "Lincoln the Lawyer." *Detroit Lawyer* 16 (February 1948): 27-32, 36.

4565. Donald, David H. "Herndon: Lincoln's Law Partner." Ph.D. dissertation, University of Illinois, 1946.

4566. Donder, George A. "Lincoln the Lawyer." *Michigan State Bar Journal* 38 (February 1959): 22-30.

4567. Duff, John J. *A. Lincoln: Prairie Lawyer*. New York: Rinehart, 1960.

4568. Ericson, Eston E. "An Eighteenth Century 'Lincoln Story.'" *Illinois State Historical Society Journal* 31 (March 1938): 105-106.

4569. Ferguson, Duncan. "True Story of the Almanac Used by Abraham Lincoln in the Famous Trial of Duff Armstrong." *Illinois State Historical Society Journal* 15 (October 1922/January 1923): 688-691.

4570. Frank, John P. *Lincoln as a Lawyer*. Urbana: University of Illinois Press, 1961.

4571. Goodhart, Arthur L. "Lincoln and the Law." *American Bar Association Journal* 50 (May 1964): 433-441.

4572. Gunderson, Robert G. "'Stoutly Argufy': Lincoln's Legal Speaking." *Wisconsin Magazine of History* 46 (Winter 1962): 109-117.

4573. Harper, Ellahue A. "Lincoln, The Lawyer." *Dickinson Law Review* 28 (January 1924): 95-112.

4574. Herndon, William H. *The Hidden Lincoln, From the Letters and Papers of William H. Herndon*. Edited by Emanuel Hertz. New York: Viking Press, 1938.

4575. Herriott, Frank I. "Abraham Lincoln and His Clients." *Annals of Iowa* 9 (April 1910): 388-391.

4576. Hertz, Emanuel. *Abraham Lincoln, More Than a Country Lawyer*. New York: Bronx County Bar Association, 1928.

4577. Hertz, Emanuel. "'Lawyer Lincoln,' A Review." *St. John's Law Review* 11 (April 1937): 354-359.

4578. Hertz, Emanuel. "Lincoln, The Lawyer." *United States Law Review* 71 (February 1937): 79-102.

4579. Hill, Frederick T. *Lincoln the Lawyer.* New York: Century, 1906.

4580. King, Willard L. "The Case That Made Lincoln." *Lincoln Herald* 83 (Winter 1981): 786-790.

4581. Landis, Frederick. "Lincoln the Lawyer." *Lawyer and Banker* 19 (July 1926): 246-257.

4582. "Lincoln as a Lawyer." *Law Notes* 17 (February 1914): 204-205.

4583. "'Lincoln, the Lawyer': Proposed Statue by Hermon A. McNeil." *Art World* 3 (February 1918): 366-368.

4584. Montgomery, Harry E. "Abraham Lincoln, The Lawyer." *American Law Review* 37 (May 1903): 358-362.

4585. Moores, Charles W. "Abraham Lincoln, Lawyer." *Indiana Historical Society Publications* 7 (1922): 483-535.

4586. Moores, Charles W. "The Career of a Country Lawyer — Abraham Lincoln." *American Bar Association Report* 35 (August/September 1910): 440-477.

4587. Ogden, James M. "Lincoln's Early Impressions of the Law in Indiana." *Notre Dame Lawyer* 7 (March 1932): 325-329.

4588. Pratt, Harry E. "Abraham Lincoln's First Murder Trial." *Illinois State Historical Society Journal* 37 (September 1944): 242-249.

4589. Quinn, James H. "Lincoln, The Lawyer." *Case and Comment* 21 (February 1915): 705-709.

4590. Ransom, William L. "Abraham Lincoln . . . Profession a Lawyer." *American Bar Association Journal* 22 (March 1936): 155-159.

4591. Richards, John T. "Abraham Lincoln: His Standing as a Lawyer." *Case and Comment* 23 (July 1916): 106-108.

4592. Roske, Ralph J. "Lincoln and Lyman Trumbull." In *Lincoln Images: Augustana College Centennial Essays*, edited by O. Fritiof Ander, 61-81. Rock Island, IL: Augustan College Library, 1960.

4593. Shaw, Lord. "Lincoln as a Lawyer." *Forum* 77 (February 1927): 220-229.

4594. Spencer, Omar C. "Abraham Lincoln, The Lawyer." *Oregon Law Review* 4 (April 1925): 177-187.

4595. Stewart, Judd. "Law Partnerships of Abraham Lincoln." *Illinois Historical Society Journal* 9 (July 1916): 209-210.

4596. Stubbs, Roy S. "Lawyer Lincoln — A Canadian Estimate." *Connecticut Bar Journal* 27 (September 1953): 335-358.

4597. Temple, Wayne C. "Lincoln's First Step to Becoming a Lawyer." *Lincoln Herald* 70 (Winter 1968): 207-208.

4598. Townsend, William H. *Abraham Lincoln, Defendant: Lincoln's Most Interesting Lawsuit.* Boston: Houghton Mifflin, 1924.

4599. Townsend, William H. "Commonwealth of Kentucky vs. Abraham Lincoln." *American Bar Association Journal* 14 (February 1928): 80-82.

4600. Townsend, William H. "Lincoln on the Circuit." *American Bar Association Journal* 12 (January 1926): 91-95.

4601. Townsend, William H. "Lincoln, The Lawyer." In *Abraham Lincoln: A New Portrait*, edited by Henry B. Kranz, 42-47. New York: Putnam, 1959.

4602. Townsend, William H. "Lincoln, The Litigant." *American Bar Association Journal* 10 (February 1924): 83-88.

4603. Townsend, William H. *Lincoln the Litigant.* Boston: Houghton Mifflin, 1925.

4604. Townsend, William H. "Lincoln's

Defense of Duff Armstrong." *American Bar Association Journal* 11 (February 1925): 81-83.

4605. Townsend, William H. "Lincoln's Law Books." *American Bar Association Journal* 15 (March 1929): 125-126.

4606. Townsend, William H. "Logan and Lincoln." *American Bar Association Journal* 19 (February 1933): 87-90.

4607. Townsend, William H. "Stuart and Lincoln." *American Bar Association Journal* 17 (February 1931): 82-85.

4608. Whitney, Henry C. *Life on the Circuit with Lincoln.* Caldwell, ID: Caxton, 1940.

4609. Woldman, Albert A. "The Centennial of Lincoln's Admission to the Bar — An Historic Event." *American Bar Association Journal* 23 (March 1937): 167-171.

4610. Woldman, Albert A. *Lawyer Lincoln.* Boston: Houghton Mifflin, 1936.

4611. Wright, Allen H., ed. "A New Light on Lincoln as an Advocate." *Green Bag* 20 (February 1908): 78-80.

4612. Zane, John M. *Lincoln, The Constitutional Lawyer.* Chicago: Caxton Club, 1932.

Lincoln-Douglas Debates

4613. Anderson, James W. "The Real Issue: An Analysis of the Final Lincoln-Douglas Debate." *Lincoln Herald* 69 (Spring 1967): 27-38.

4614. Angle, Paul M. *Created Equal? The Complete Lincoln-Douglas Debate of 1858.* Chicago: University of Chicago Press, 1958.

4615. Angle, Paul M. "The Peoria Truce (October 16, 1854)." *Illinois State Historical Society Journal* 22 (January 1929): 500-505.

4616. Bauer, Charles J. *The Lincoln-Douglas Triangle — With Naughty Mary Lincoln, Seduced by Latest Paris Fashions.* Silver Spring, MD: Silver Spring Press, 1980.

4617. Bezanson, Walter E. "Lincoln and Douglas and the Naughty Nursery Rhyme." *Rutgers University Library Journal* 14 (December 1950): 9-13.

4618. Breiseth, Christopher N. "Lincoln and Frederick Douglass: Another Debate." *Illinois State Historical Society Journal* 68 (February 1975): 9-26.

4619. Breiseth, Christopher N. "Lincoln, Douglas, and Springfield in the 1858 Campaign." In *The Public and the Private Lincoln: Contemporary Perspectives,* edited by Cullom Davis, Charles B. Strozier, Rebecca M. Veach, and Geoffrey C. Ward, 101-120. Carbondale: Southern Illinois University Press, 1979.

4620. Carter, Orrin N. "Lincoln and Douglas as Lawyers." *Mississippi Valley Historical Association Proceedings* 4 (1910-1911): 213-240.

4621. Crocker, Lionel. *An Analysis of Lincoln and Douglas as Public Speakers and Debaters.* Springfield, IL: Thomas, 1968.

4622. Dennis, Frank L. *The Lincoln-Douglas Debates.* New York: Mason and Lipscomb, 1974.

4623. Douglas, Paul H. "Lincoln and Douglas." In *Lincoln for the Ages,* edited by Ralph G. Newman, 124-129. Garden City, NY: Doubleday, 1960.

4624. Fehrenbacher, Don E. "The Historical Significance of the Lincoln-Douglas Debates." *Wisconsin Magazine of History* 42 (Spring 1959): 193-199.

4625. Fehrenbacher, Don E. "Lincoln, Douglas, and the 'Freeport Question.'" *American Historical Review* 66 (April 1961): 599-617.

4626. Fish, Daniel. *Legal Phases of the Lincoln and Douglas Debates: Annual Address before the State Bar Association of Minnesota at Minneapolis, July 14, 1909.* Minneapolis, MN: n.p., 1909.

4627. Heckman, Richard A. "The Douglas-Lincoln Campaign of 1858." Ph.D. dissertation, Indiana University, 1960.

4628. Heckman, Richard A. "The Lincoln-Douglas Debates: A Case Study in 'Stump Speaking.'" *Civil War History* 12 (March 1966): 54-66.

4629. Heckman, Richard A. *Lincoln vs. Douglas: The Great Debates Campaign.* Washington, DC: Public Affairs Press, 1967.

4630. Heckman, Richard A. "Out-of-State Influences and the Lincoln-Douglas Campaign of 1858." *Illinois State Historical Society Journal* 59 (Spring 1966): 30-47.

4631. Heckman, Richard A. "Political Fortunes of Lincoln and Douglas in 1858-1859." *Lincoln Herald* 67 (Winter 1965): 161-170.

4632. Heckman, Richard A. "Some Impressions of Lincoln and Douglas during the Campaign of 1958." *Lincoln Herald* 66 (Fall 1964): 135-139.

4633. Hill, Frederick T. "The Lincoln-Douglas Debates, Fifty Years After." *Century Magazine* 77 (November 1908): 3-19.

4634. Jaffa, Harry V. *Crisis of the House Divided: An Interpretation of the Issues in the Lincoln-Douglas Debates.* Garden City, NY: Doubleday, 1959.

4635. Jaffa, Harry V. "Value Consensus in Democracy: The Issue in the Lincoln-Douglas Debates." *American Political Science Review* 52 (September 1958): 745-753.

4636. James, D. D. "Lincoln-Douglas Debate — Charleston." *Illinois State Historical Society Journal* 8 (January 1916): 569-571.

4637. Johannsen, Robert W. "The Lincoln-Douglas Campaign of 1858: Background and Perspective." *Illinois State Historical Society Journal* 73 (Winter 1980): 242-262.

4638. Johannsen, Robert W. *Lincoln-Douglas Debates of 1858.* New York: Oxford University Press, 1965.

4639. Jordan, Harriet P. "The Lincoln-Douglas Debates of 1858: A Presentation of the Rhetorical Scene and Setting with a Plot Film Script of the Ottowa Debate." Ph.D. dissertation, University of Illinois, 1958.

4640. Krug, Mark M. "Lyman Trumbull and the Real Issues in the Lincoln-Douglas Debates." *Illinois State Historical Society Journal* 57 (Winter 1964): 380-396.

4641. Lake, Harry F. "The Influence of Douglas on the Life of Lincoln." *Granite Monthly* 60 (March 1928): 149-157.

4642. Lincoln-Douglas Society, Freeport, Ill. *The Freeport Debate and Its Centennial Commemoration: Abraham Lincoln-Stephen A. Douglas, 1858-August 27-1958.* Freeport, IL: The Society, 1959.

4643. "The Lincoln They Saw." *Outlook* 127 (February 9, 1921): 216-219.

4644. Lynch, William O. "The Convergence of Lincoln and Douglas." *Illinois State Historical Society Transactions* (1925): 155-173.

4645. Monaghan, Jay. "When Were the Debates First Published?" *Illinois State Historical Society Journal* 42 (September 1949): 344-347.

4646. Nevins, Allan. "He Did Hold Lincoln's Hat." *American Heritage* 10 (February 1959): 98-99.

4647. Petersen, William F. *Lincoln-*

Douglas: The Weather as Destiny. Springfield, IL: Thomas, 1943.

4648. Peterson, Gary L. "A Critical Edition of the Lincoln-Douglas Debates of 1858." Ph.D. dissertation, Ohio University, 1965.

4649. Plummer, Mark A. "Lincoln's First Direct Reply to Douglas on Squatter Sovereignty Recalled." *Lincoln Herald* 71 (Spring 1969): 27-31.

4650. Reilly, Tom. "Lincoln-Douglas Debates of 1858 Forced New Role on the Press." *Journalism Quarterly* 56 (Winter 1979): 734-743, 752.

4651. Schapsmeier, Edward L., and Frederick H. Schapsmeier. "Lincoln and Douglas: Their Versions of the West." *Journal of the West* 7 (October 1968): 542-552.

4652. Sigelschiffer, Saul. *The American Conscience: The Drama of the Lincoln-Douglas Debate.* New York: Horizon, 1973.

4653. Sparks, Edwin E. *The Lincoln-Douglas Debates of 1858.* Springfield, IL: Trustees of the Illinois State Historical Library, 1908.

4654. Stewart, Charles J. "The People and the Lincoln-Douglas Campaign of 1858." *Kentucky Historical Society Register* 65 (October 1967): 284-293.

4655. Taylor, Hannis. "The Lincoln-Douglas Debates and Their Application to Present Problems." *North American Review* 189 (February 1909): 161-173.

4656. Thompson, Seymour D. "Lincoln and Douglas: The Great Freeport Debate." *American Law Review* 39 (March/April 1905): 161-177.

4657. Townsend, William H. " 'Old Abe' and the 'Little Giant'?" *American Bar Association Journal* 13 (February 1927): 99-104.

Presidential Years

General

4658. "Abraham Lincoln: The Democratic Dictator." *Saturday Review* 71 (February 5, 1915): 131-132.

4659. Baringer, William E. "The Epic Historical Significance of President Lincoln." *Illinois State Historical Society Journal* 42 (1935): 111-124.

4660. Baringer, William E. *A House Dividing: Lincoln as President Elect.* Springfield, IL: Abraham Lincoln Association, 1945.

4661. Barton, William E. *President Lincoln.* 2 vols. Indianapolis, IN: Bobbs-Merrill, 1933.

4662. Baumgardner, James L. "Abraham Lincoln, Andrew Jackson, and the Federal Patronage: An Attempt to Save Tennessee for the Union?" *East Tennessee Historical Society's Publications* 45 (1973): 51-60.

4663. Baxter, Maurice G. "Orville H. Browning: Lincoln's Colleague and the Critic." *Illinois State Historical Society Journal* 48 (Winter 1955): 431-455.

4664. Bollinger, James W. *Lincoln, Statesman and Logician.* Muscatine, IA: Prairie Press, 1944.

4665. Borit, Gabor S. "Old Wine into New Bottles: Abraham Lincoln and the Tariff Reconsidered." *Historian* 28 (February 1966): 289-317.

4666. Brandt, Keith. *President.* Mahwah, NJ: Troll Associates, 1985.

4667. Brooks, Noah. *Lincoln, By Friend and Foe, Noah Brooks: Democratic Manual of 1864.* Edited by Robert A. Cole. London: Gold Medal Library, 1922.

4668. Brooks, Noah. "Lincoln, Chase, and Grant." *Century Magazine* 49 (February 1895): 607-619.

4669. Bryson, Lyman. "Lincoln in Power." *Political Science Quarterly* 61 (June 1946): 161-174.

4670. Buice, David. "Lincoln's Unissued Proclamation." *Prologue* 10 (Fall 1978): 153-169.

4671. Bullard, F. Lauriston. "Abraham Lincoln and the Statehood of Nevada." *American Bar Association Journal* 26 (March 1940): 210-213, 236; 26 (April 1940): 313-317.

4672. Bullard, F. Lauriston. "Lincoln Pardons Conspirator on Plea of an English Statesman." *American Bar Association Journal* 25 (March 1939): 215-220.

4673. Bullard, F. Lauriston. "When Lincoln 'Ruled' Alone." *Massachussetts Historical Society Proceedings* 68 (1952): 301-349.

4674. Burt, Jesse. "East Tennessee, Lincoln, and Sherman." *East Tennessee Historical Society's Publications* 34 (1962): 3-25; 35 (1963): 54-75.

4675. Campbell, Helen M. . . . *Famous Presidents: Washington, Jefferson, Madison, Lincoln, Grant.* Boston: Educational Publishing Co., 1903.

4676. Carabelli, Angelina J. *Abraham Lincoln: His Legacy to American Agriculture.* Beltsville, MD: Associates of the National Agricultural Library, 1972.

4677. Cardinale, Gary W. "An Analysis of the Conflict Management Style of Abraham Lincoln." Ed.D. dissertation, University of LaVerne, 1980.

4678. Carman, Harry J., and Reinhard H. Luthin. *Lincoln and the Patronage.* New York: Columbia University Press, 1943.

4679. Carpenter, Francis B. *Six Months at the White House with Abraham Lincoln: The Story of a Picture.* New York: Hurd and Houghton, 1866.

4680. Catton, Bruce. "Lincoln's Difficult Decisions." *Civil War History* 23 (June 1956): 5-12.

4681. Chandler, Robert J. "Crushing Dissent: The Pacific Coast Tests Lincoln's Policy of Suppression, 1862." *Civil War History* 30 (September 1984): 235-254.

4682. Chandler, Robert J. "The Release of the Chapman Pirates: A California Sidelight on Lincoln's Amnesty Policy." *Civil War History* 23 (July 1977): 129-143.

4683. Chittenden, Lucius E. *Lincoln and the Sleeping Sentinel: The True Story.* New York: Harper and Row, 1909.

4684. Chittenden, Lucius E. *Recollections of President Lincoln and His Administration.* New York: Harper and Row, 1891.

4685. Clark, Allen C. *Abraham Lincoln in the National Capital.* Washington, DC: W. F. Roberts, 1925.

4686. Clark, Allen C. *Abraham Lincoln, The Merciful President, The Pardon of the Sleeping Sentinel.* Washington, DC: W. F. Roberts Co., 1927.

4687. Cole, Arthur C. "President Lincoln and the Illinois Radical Republicans." *Mississippi Valley Historical Review* 4 (March 1918): 417-426.

4688. Coulter, John. *Our Martyr Presidents: Lincoln, Garfield, McKinley, Their Illustrious Lives, Public and Private, and Their Glorious Deeds. . . .* Chicago: Memorial Publishing House, 1901.

4689. Count, Susan J. "Salmon P. Chase and Abraham Lincoln." *Cincinnati Historical Society Bulletin* 39 (Winter 1981): 250-260.

4690. Crissey, Elwell. "Afar Off, Lincoln Glimpses the White House." *Lincoln Herald* 69 (Winter 1967): 151-157.

4691. Croce, Lewis H. "The Lincoln Administration." Ph.D. dissertation, University of Maryland, 1968.

4692. Croce, Lewis H. "Was Lincoln Prepared for the Presidency?" *Lincoln Herald* 78 (Fall 1976): 160-164.

4693. Crofts, Daniel W. "A Reluctant Unionist: John A. Gilmore and Lincoln's Cabinet." *Civil War History* 24 (September 1978): 225-249.

4694. Current, Richard N. "The Lincoln Presidents." *Presidential Studies Quarterly* 9 (Winter 1979): 25-34.

4695. Current, Richard N. *Speaking of Abraham Lincoln: The Man and His Meaning for Our Times.* Urbana: University of Illinois Press, 1983.

4696. Cuthbert, Norma B., ed. *Lincoln and the Baltimore Plot, 1861: From Pinkerton Records and Related Papers.* San Marino, CA: Huntington Library, 1949.

4697. Dahl, Curtis. "Lincoln Saves a Reformer." *American Heritage* 23 (October 1972): 74-78.

4698. Dana, Charles A. *Lincoln and His Cabinet: A Lecture Delivered on Tuesday, March 10, 1986.* Cleveland, OH: DeVinne Press, 1896.

4699. Dell, Christopher. *Lincoln and the War Democrats: The Grand Erosion of Conservative Tradition.* Rutherford, NJ: Fairleigh Dickinson University Press, 1975.

4700. Dodd, William E. "Lincoln's Last Struggle and the End of His Long Career." *Century Magazine* 114 (May 1927): 46-61.

4701. Donald, David H. *Lincoln Reconsidered: Essays on the Civil War Era.* New York: Knopf, 1956.

4702. Dorris, Jonathan T. *Pardon and Amnesty under Lincoln and Johnson: The Restoration of the Confederates to Their Rights and Privileges, 1861-1898.* Chapel Hill: University of North Carolina Press, 1953.

4703. Dorris, Jonathan T. "President Lincoln's Clemency." *Illinois State Historical Society Journal* 20 (January 1928): 547-568.

4704. Ehrmann, Bess V. "The Lincoln Inquiry." *Indiana Magazine of History* 21 (March 1925): 3-17.

4705. Elmore, Harry. "A Parallel in Statesmanship: Lincoln and Asquith." *Contemporary Review* 111 (January 1917): 11-18.

4706. Fehrenbacher, Don E. *The Leadership of Abraham Lincoln.* New York: Wiley, 1970.

4707. Fehrenbacher, Don E. "Lincoln and the Weight of Responsibility." *Illinois State Historical Society Journal* 68 (February 1975): 45-56.

4708. Fischer, Leroy H. "Lincoln's First Congress." *Illinois History* 15 (February 1962): 101-102.

4709. Fish, Carl R. "Lincoln and the Patronage." *American Historical Review* 8 (October 1902): 53-69.

4710. Fries, Sylvia D. "Abraham Lincoln and the Language of Sectional Crisis." *Lincoln Herald* 79 (Summer 1977): 61-66; (Fall 1977): 104-109.

4711. Gernon, Blaine B. *Lincoln in the Political Circus: Being a Study in Summary and Outline of Abraham Lincoln's Political Relationships with His Constituency, Including the Background of Slavery, Men, Factions, and Parties, Together with Hitherto Unpublished State Election, Tables, and a Classified Bibliography.* Chicago: Black Cat Press, 1936.

4712. Gilder, Richard W. "Lincoln the Leader." *Century Magazine* 77 (February 1909): 479-507.

4713. Gilder, Richard W. *Lincoln, The*

Leader and Lincoln's Genius for Expression. Boston: Houghton Mifflin, 1909.

4714. Glover, Waldo F. *Abraham Lincoln and the Sleeping Sentinel of Vermont.* Montpelier: Vermont Historical Society, 1936.

4715. Good, Douglas. "Abraham Lincoln: Paradigm of Forgiveness." *Fides et Historia* 15 (Spring/Summer 1983): 28-43.

4716. Gordon, Leonard. "Lincoln and Juarez: A Brief Reassessment of That Relationship." *Hispanic American Historical Review* 48 (February 1968): 75-80.

4717. Goss, Dwight. *Lincoln, The Man and the Statesman.* Chicago: Row, Peterson, 1914.

4718. Graebner, Norman A., ed. *The Enduring Lincoln: Lincoln Sequicentennial Lectures at the University of Illinois.* Urbana: University of Illinois Press, 1959.

4719. Gunderson, Robert G. "Lincoln and the Policy of Eloquent Silence: November 1860 to March 1861." *Quarterly Journal of Speech* 47 (February 1961): 1-9.

4720. Hamilton, Holman. *The Three Kentucky Presidents: Lincoln, Taylor, Davis.* Lexington: University Press of Kentucky, 1978.

4721. Hanby, Alice L. H. "The Lincoln Inquiry — John Pitcher." *Southwestern Indiana Historical Society Proceedings* 16 (January 31, 1922): 50-60.

4722. Harbison, Winfred A. "The Opposition to President Lincoln within the Republican Party." Ph.D. dissertation, University of Illinois, 1930.

4723. Hesseltine, William B. "Abraham Lincoln and the Politicians." *Civil War History* 6 (March 1960): 43-55.

4724. Hesseltine, William B. "Lincoln's Problems in Wisconsin." *Wisconsin Magazine of History* 48 (Spring 1965): 187-195.

4725. Hesseltine, William B., and Hazel C. Wolf. "Lincoln, the Governors, and States' Rights." *Social Studies* 39 (December 1948): 350-355.

4726. Hesseltine, William B., and Hazel C. Wolf. "The New England Governors vs. Lincoln: The Providence Conference." *Rhode Island History* 5 (October 1946): 105-112.

4727. Hirschfield, Robert S. "Lincoln and the Crisis Presidency." *Lincoln Herald* 64 (Spring 1962): 15-25.

4728. Holden, Raymond. *Abraham Lincoln: The Politician and the Man.* New York: Minton, Balch, 1929.

4729. Holzer, Harold. " 'Tokens of Respect' and 'Heart-Felt Thanks': How Abraham Lincoln Coped with Presidential Gifts." *Illinois State Historical Society Journal* 77 (Autumn 1984): 177-192.

4730. Howland, Glenn C. "Organize! Organize! The Lincoln Wide-Awakes in Vermont." *Vermont History* 48 (Winter 1980): 28-32.

4731. Hyman, Harold M. "Lincoln and Congress: Why Not Congress and Lincoln?" *Illinois State Historical Society Journal* 68 (February 1975): 57-73.

4732. Jones, Evan R. *Lincoln, Stanton, and Grant.* New York: Scribner's, 1875.

4733. King, Willard L. "Lincoln and the Illinois Copperheads." *Lincoln Herald* 80 (Fall 1978): 132-137.

4734. Linkugel, Wil A. "Lincoln, Kansas, and Cooper Union." *Speech Monographs* 37 (August 1970): 172-179.

4735. Longacre, Edward G. "Mr. Lincoln's Policeman." *Civil War Times Illustrated* 9 (November 1970): 22-31.

4736. McDonough, John. "Lincoln, Welles, and the Public Service." *Library of Congress Quarterly Journal* 26 (October 1969): 213-215.

4737. McFeely, William S. "The Jacksonian Naval Person in Lincoln's Cabinet." *Reviews in American History* 2 (June 1974): 394-401.

4738. McKay, Ernest A. "Lincoln and Henry Wilson." *Lincoln Herald* 65 (Winter 1963): 187-189.

4739. Markens, Isaac. *President Lincoln and the Case of John Y. Beall*. New York: The Author, 1911.

4740. Markens, Isaac. *Why President Lincoln Spared Three Lives*. New York: The Author, 1911.

4741. Marszalek, John F., Jr. "Lincoln's Special Session." *Civil War Times Illustrated* 10 (June 1971): 22-27.

4742. Maxwell, William Q. *Lincoln's Fifth Wheel: The Political History of the United States Sanitary Commission*. New York: Longmans, Green, 1956.

4743. Monaghan, Jay. *Diplomat in Carpet Slippers: Abraham Lincoln Deals with Foreign Affairs*. Indianapolis, IN: Bobbs-Merrill, 1945.

4744. Monaghan, Jay. "Lincoln, The Diplomat and Statesman." In *Abraham Lincoln: A New Portrait*, edited by Henry B. Kranz, 75-82. New York: Putnam, 1959.

4745. Munson, Lyman E. "Comparative Study of Jefferson and Lincoln." *Connecticut Magazine* 8 (April/June 1903): 49-56.

4746. Musmanno, Michael A. *The Glory and the Dream: Abraham Lincoln before and after Gettysburg*. New Canaan, CT: Long House, 1967.

4747. Neely, Mark E. "The Lincoln Administration and Arbitrary Arrests: A Reconsideration." *Abraham Lincoln Association Papers* 5 (1983): 39-47.

4748. Neill, Edward D. *Abraham Lincoln and His Mailbag: Two Documents by Edward D. Neill*. St. Paul, MN: Minnesota Historical Society, 1964.

4749. Newman, Francis W. *The Good Cause of President Lincoln*. London: Emancipation Society, 1863.

4750. Nicolay, Helen. "Lincoln's Cabinet." *Abraham Lincoln Quarterly* 5 (March 1949): 255-292.

4751. Oates, Stephen B. "Lincoln and Stanton: An Uncommon Friendship." *Timeline* 1 (October 1984): 2-8.

4752. Oliver, David L. "The Contribution of Kentucky to Lincoln's Fourth of July Session of Congress, 1861." *Kentucky Historical Society Register* 60 (April 1962): 134-142.

4753. Paullin, Charles O. "President Lincoln and the Navy." *American Historical Review* 14 (January 1909): 284-303.

4754. Pease, Theodore C. *The Diary of Orville H. Browning, A New Source for Lincoln's Presidency*. Chicago: University of Chicago Press, 1924.

4755. Perkins, Frederic B. *The Picture and the Men*. New York: A. J. Johnson, 1867.

4756. Potter, John M. *Thirteen Desperate Days*. New York: Obolensky, 1964.

4757. Pratt, Fletcher. *Stanton: Lincoln's Secretary of War*. Westport, CT: Greenwood Press, 1970.

4758. Randall, James G. "Lincoln in the Role of a Dictator." *South Atlantic Quarterly* 28 (July 1929): 236-252.

4759. Randall, James G. "The 'Rule of Law' under the Lincoln Administration." *Historical Outlook* 17 (October 1926): 272-278.

4760. Raymond, Henry J. *History of the Administration of President Lincoln: Including His Speeches, Letters, Addresses, Proclamations, and Messages, With a Pre-*

liminary Sketch of His Life. New York: Derby and Miller, 1864.

4761. Raymond, Henry J. *The Life and Public Services of Abraham Lincoln: To Which Are Added Anecdotes and Personal Reminiscences of President Lincoln.* New York: Derby and Miller, 1865.

4762. Riches, William T. M. "The Commoners: Andrew Johnson and Abraham Lincoln to 1861." Ph.D. dissertation, University of Texas, 1976.

4763. Robertson, John B. "Lincoln and Congress." Ph.D. dissertation, University of Wisconsin, 1966.

4764. Rogin, Michael. "The King's Two Bodies: Abraham Lincoln, Richard Nixon, and Presidential Self-Sacrifice." *Massachusetts Review* 20 (Autumn 1979): 553-573.

4765. Ryan, Joseph F. "Abraham Lincoln and New York City, 1861-1865: War and Politics." Ph.D. dissertation, St. John's University, 1969.

4766. Sanders, Neill F. "Lincoln's Consuls in the British Isles, 1861-1865." Ph.D. dissertation, University of Missouri, 1971.

4767. Sanders, Neill F. " 'Unfit for Consul'? The English Consulates and Lincoln's Patronage Policy." *Lincoln Herald* 82 (Fall 1980): 464-474.

4768. Sanders, Neill F. " 'When a House Is on Fire': The English Consulates and Lincoln's Patronage Policy." *Lincoln Herald* 83 (Spring 1981): 579-591.

4769. Shaffer, Dallas S. "Lincoln and the Vast Question of West Virginia." *West Virginia History* 32 (January 1971): 86-100.

4770. Squires, J. Duane. "Lincoln and West Virginia Statehood." *West Virginia History* 24 (July 1963): 325-331.

4771. Squires, J. Duane. "Some Enduring Achievements of the Lincoln Administration, 1861-1865." *Abraham Lincoln Quarterly* 5 (December 1948): 191-211.

4772. Stebbins, Phillip. "Lincoln's Dictatorship." *American History Illustrated* 6 (November 1971): 32-37.

4773. Stephenson, Nathaniel W. *Abraham Lincoln and the Union.* New Haven, CT: Yale University Press, 1918.

4774. Stevenson, Charles S. "Abraham Lincoln and the Russian Fleet Myth." *Military Review* 50 (August 1970): 35-37.

4775. Street, Charles M. "Lincoln as a Statesman." *Dial* 50 (January 1911): 8-9.

4776. Tegeder, Vincent G. "Lincoln and the Territorial Patronage: The Ascendancy of the Radicals in West." *Mississippi Valley Historical Review* 35 (June 1948): 77-90.

4777. Thayer, William M. *The Character and Public Services of Abraham Lincoln, President of the United States. . . .* Boston: Walker, Wise, 1864.

4778. Thomas, Benjamin P. "The President Reads His Mail." *Lincoln Herald* 55 (Spring 1953): 30-34.

4779. Van Dalen, D. B. "Body Image and the Presidency — A. Lincoln." *Research Quarterly* 46 (December 1975): 489-497.

4780. Welles, Gideon. "Administration of Abraham Lincoln." In *Selected Essays by Gideon Welles: Lincoln's Administration,* edited by Albert Mordell, 47-177. New York: Twayne, 1960.

4781. Welles, Gideon. *Lincoln and Seward: Remarks upon the Memorial Address of Chas. Francis Adams, On the Late William H. Seward.* New York: Sheldon, 1874.

4782. Westwood, Howard C. "President Lincoln's Overture to Sam Houston." *Southwestern Historical Quarterly* 88 (October 1984): 125-144.

4783. Woldman, Albert A. *Lincoln and the Russians.* Cleveland, OH: World Publishing, 1952.

4784. Woodward, Isaiah A. "Lincoln and the Crittenden Compromise." *Negro History Bulletin* 22 (April 1955): 153-155.

4785. Zornow, William F. "Lincoln, Man of Peace." In *Abraham Lincoln: A New Portrait,* edited by Henry B. Kranz, 91-97. New York: Putnam, 1959.

Assassination

4786. Abbott, Martin. "Southern Reaction to Lincoln's Assassination." *Abraham Lincoln Quarterly* 7 (September 1952): 111-127.

4787. Aldridge, Derek A. "George Alfred Townsend and the Lincoln Assassins." Master's thesis, Michigan State University, 1978.

4788. Armour, Rollin S. "Sidelights on Florida Baptist History: The Winter Assembly at Umatilla and a Connection with the Assassination of President Lincoln." *Baptist History and Heritage* 8 (October 1973): 225-231.

4789. Arnold, Samuel B. *Defiance and Prison Experiences of a Lincoln Conspirator.* Hattiesburg, MS: Book Farm, 1943.

4790. Barrett, Frank W. Z. *Mourning for Lincoln.* Philadelphia: Winston, 1909.

4791. Barton, William E. "The American Pulpit on the Death of Lincoln." *Open Court* 37 (September 1923): 513-528; (October 1923): 622-640; (November 1923): 682-704.

4792. Bates, Finis L. *The Escape and Suicide of John Wilkes Booth: The First True Account of Lincoln's Assassination, Containing a Complete Confession by Booth Many Years after His Crime.* Memphis, TN: Historical Publishing Co., 1907.

4793. Beall, John N. "Why Booth Killed Lincoln." *Columbia Historical Society Records* 48-49 (1949): 127-141.

4794. Becker, J. W. "The Lincoln Funeral Train." *Illinois State Historical Society Journal* 9 (October 1915): 315-319.

4795. Bishop, James A. *The Day Lincoln Was Shot.* New York: Harper and Row, 1955.

4796. Bone, Beverly. "Edwin Stanton in the Wake of the Lincoln Assassination." *Lincoln Herald* 82 (Winter 1980): 508-521.

4797. Brenner, Walter C. *The Ford Theatre Lincoln Assassination Play-Bills.* Philadelphia: Privately Printed, 1937.

4798. Buckingham, John E. *Reminiscences and Souvenirs of the Assassination of Abraham Lincoln.* Washington, DC: R. H. Darby, 1894.

4799. Clark, Bayard S. "A Sermon by Phillips Brooks on the Death of Abraham Lincoln." *Historical Magazine of the Protestant Episcopal Church* 48 (March 1980): 37-49.

4800. Clarke, Asia. *Unlocked Book: A Memoir of John Wilkes Booth by His Sister.* Salem, NH: Ayer, 1938.

4801. Coggeshall, E. W. *The Assassination of Lincoln.* Chicago: W. M. Hill, 1920.

4802. Cooney, Charles F., ed. "At the Trial of the Lincoln Conspirators: The Reminiscences of a General August V. Kautz." *Civil War Times Illustrated* 12 (August 1973): 22-31.

4803. Crook, William H. "Lincoln's Last Day." Compiled by Margarita S. Gerry. *Harper's* 115 (September 1907): 519-530.

4804. Culyer, John Y. "The Assassination of Abraham Lincoln." *Magazine of History* 22 (March 1915): 58-60.

4805. Curran, John W. "Lincoln Conspiracy Trial and Military Jurisdiction over Civilians." *Notre Dame Lawyer* 9 (November 1933): 26-49.

4806. Curran, John W. "Lincoln Conspiracy Trial — Mysterious Phases." *American Book Collector* 7 (February 1957): 4-20.

4807. Curran, John W. "Lincoln Conspiracy Trial — Mysterious Phases." *Notre Dame Lawyer* 10 (March 1935): 259-276.

4808. Currie, George E. "The Assassination of Abraham Lincoln." *Magazine of History* 11 (February 1910): 87-94.

4809. DeMotte, William H. "The Assassination of Abraham Lincoln." *Illinois State Historical Society Journal* 20 (October 1927): 422-428.

4810. DeWitt, David M. *The Assassination of Abraham Lincoln and Its Expiation*. New York: Macmillan, 1909.

4811. Eisenschiml, Otto. "Addenda to Lincoln's Assassination." *Illinois State Historical Society Journal* 43 (Summer 1950): 91-99; (Autumn 1950): 204-209.

4812. Eisenschiml, Otto. *In the Shadow of Lincoln's Death*. New York: Wilfred Funk, 1940.

4813. Eisenschiml, Otto. *Why Was Lincoln Murdered?* Boston: Little, Brown, 1937.

4814. Engel, Bernard F. "Lincoln's Death as Seen in Verse." *Lincoln Herald* 83 (Winter 1981): 804-807.

4815. Ferguson, William J. *I Saw Booth Shoot Lincoln*. Boston: Houghton Mifflin, 1930.

4816. Ferguson, William J. "Lincoln's Death." *Saturday Evening Post* 199 (February 12, 1927): 37-40.

4817. Fiske, Daniel W. *On the Death of Abraham Lincoln*. Florence: Landi Press, 1903.

4818. Gates, Arnold F. "The Nation Mourns." In *Lincoln for the Ages*, edited by Ralph G. Newman, 405-409. Garden City, NY: Doubleday, 1960.

4819. Giddens, Paul H., ed. "Benn Pitman and the Trial of Lincoln's Assassin." *Tyler's Quarterly Historical and Genealogical Magazine* 22 (July 1940): 6-21.

4820. Gleason, D. H. L. "The Conspiracy against Lincoln." *Magazine of History* 13 (February 1911): 59-65.

4821. Gurley, Phineas D. "The Funeral Sermon of Abraham Lincoln." *Journal of the Presbyterian Historical Society* 39 (June 1961): 65-75.

4822. Hanchett, William. "Booth's Diary." *Illinois State Historical Society Journal* 72 (February 1979): 39-56.

4823. Hanchett, William. *The Lincoln Murder Conspiracies Campaign*. Urbana: University of Illinois Press, 1983.

4824. Hanchett, William. "The War Department and Booth's Abduction Plot." *Lincoln Herald* 82 (Winter 1980): 499-508.

4825. Harrison, Lowell H. "An Australian Reaction to Lincoln's Death." *Lincoln Herald* 78 (Spring 1976): 12-17.

4826. Hemminger, Art. "Mr. Lincoln Goes to the Theatre." *Illinois State Historical Society Journal* 33 (December 1940): 469-477.

4827. Herold, David E. *The Assassination of President Lincoln and the Trial of the Conspirators: The Courtroom Testimony as Originally Compiled by Benn Pitman*. New York: Funk and Wagnalls, 1954.

4828. Hurwitz, Michael R. "The Lincoln Conspiracy Re-examined." *Manuscripts* 30 (Spring 1978): 108-111.

4829. Hyman, Harold M. *With Malice toward Some: Scholarship (Or Something Less) on the Lincoln Murder*. Springfield,

IL: Abraham Lincoln Association, 1979.

4830. Kauffman, Mike. "Fort Lesley McNair and the Lincoln Conspirators." *Lincoln Herald* 80 (Winter 1978): 176-188.

4831. Keys, Thomas B. "Were the Lincoln Conspirators Dealt Justice?" *Lincoln Herald* 80 (Spring 1978): 38-46.

4832. Kichorowsky, Theodosia. "Library Catalogs Playbills from Night of Lincoln's Assassination." *Library of Congress Information Bulletin* 40 (November 6, 1981): 390-392.

4833. Kunhardt, Dorothy M., and Philip B. Kunhardt, Jr. "Assassination!" *American Heritage* 16 (April 1965): 4-35.

4834. Lanis, Edward S. "Allen Pinkerton and the Baltimore 'Assassination' Plot against Lincoln." *Maryland Historical Magazine* 45 (March 1950): 1-13.

4835. Lattimer, John K. *Lincoln and Kennedy: Medical Ballistic Comparisons of Their Assassinations.* New York: Harcourt Brace, 1980.

4836. Laughlin, Clara E. *The Death of Lincoln: The Story of Booth's Plot, His Deed, and the Penalty.* Garden City, NY: Doubleday, 1909.

4837. McCarty, Burke. *The Suppressed Truth about the Assassination of Abraham Lincoln.* Washington: The Author, 1922.

4838. Markowitz, Arthur M., ed. "Tragedy of an Age: An Eyewitness Account of Lincoln's Assassination." *Illinois State Historical Society Journal* 66 (Summer 1973): 205-211.

4839. Missouri Historical Society. "Unexplored Lincoln Material: The Pursuit and Capture of John Wilkes Booth." *Missouri Historical Society Bulletin* 7 (January 1951): 167-181.

4840. Moore, Guy W. *The Case of Mrs. Surratt: Her Controversial Trial and Execution for Conspiracy in the Lincoln Assassination.* Norman: University of Oklahoma Press, 1954.

4841. Morris, James R. "Assassination of Abraham Lincoln." *Ohio State Archaeological and Historical Quarterly Publications* 30 (January 1921): 1-5.

4842. Mudd, Richard. "President Lincoln and His Assassination." *Columbia Historical Society Records* 50 (1952): 341-378.

4843. Newman, Ralph G. " 'In This Sad World of Ours, Sorrow Comes to All': A Timetable for the Lincoln Funeral Train." *Illinois State Historical Society Journal* 58 (Spring 1965): 5-20.

4844. Oldroyd, Osborn H. *The Assasination of Abraham Lincoln.* Washington, DC: O. H. Oldroyd, 1901.

4845. Ostendorf, Lloyd. "Lincoln's Assassination: More 'Forgotten' Litigation: *Ex Parte Mudd* (1868)." *Lincoln Herald* 76 (Summer 1974): 86-90.

4846. Parsons, Lewis B. "General Parsons Writes of Lincoln's Death." *Illinois State Historical Society Journal* 44 (Winter 1951): 355-357.

4847. Parsons, R. C. "The Trial of the Assassins of Abraham Lincoln." *Western Reserve Law Journal* 2 (October 1896): 153-164.

4848. Peirce, William F. "Lincoln's Death — Some Personal Consequences." *Antiques Journal* 5 (April 1950): 12-17, 31.

4849. Peterson, Fred. "The Death of President Lincoln: Being an Interview of Fred Peterson, From a Photostatic Copy of the *New York Times*, February 9, 1913." *Chicago Historical Society Bulletin* 3 (February 1926): 63-65.

4850. Planck, Gary R. "Lincoln Assassination: The 'Forgotten' Investigation, A. C. Richards, Superintendent of the Metropolitan Police." *Lincoln Herald* 82 (Winter 1980): 521-539.

4851. Planck, Gary R. "Lincoln's Assassination: More 'Forgotten' Litigation-*Ex Parte Mudd*." *Lincoln Herald* 76 (Summer 1974): 86-90.

4852. Potter, John M. "Abraham Lincoln: Marked for Murder." *Mankind* 1 (February 1968): 11-19.

4853. Rankin, Mrs. Mckee. "The News of Lincoln's Death, Including Two Stories of John Wilkes Booth." *American Magazine* 67 (January 1909): 259-262.

4854. Read, Harry. " 'A Hand to Hold While Dying': Dr. Charles A. Leale at Lincoln's Side." *Lincoln Herald* 79 (Spring 1977): 21-26.

4855. Rietveld, Ronald D., ed. "An Eyewitness Account of Abraham Lincoln's Assassination." *Civil War History* 22 (March 1976): 60-69.

4856. Robertson, Deane, and Peggy Robertson. "The Plot to Steal Lincoln's Body." *American Heritage* 33 (April/May 1982): 76-83.

4857. Roscoe, Theodore. *The Well of Conspiracy: The Complete Story of the Men Who Murdered Abraham Lincoln*. Englewood Cliffs, NJ: Prentice-Hall, 1959.

4858. Sedgwick, Paul J. "Some Legal Aspects of the Trial of the Lincoln Conspirators." *Lincoln Herald* 68 (Spring 1966): 3-10.

4859. Shaw, E. R. "The Assassination of Lincoln, The Hitherto Unpublished Account of an Eye-Witness." *McClure's* 32 (December 1908): 181-185.

4860. Starkey, Larry. *Wilkes Booth Came to Washington*. New York: Random House, 1976.

4861. Steers, Edward, Jr. "Inter Arma Silent Leges: The Military Trial of the Lincoln Conspirators." *Lincoln Herald* 83 (Fall 1981): 719-730.

4862. Stern, Philip V. D. *The Man Who Killed Lincoln*. New York: Random House, 1939.

4863. Stewart, Charles J. "A Rhetorical Study of the Reaction of the Protestant Pulpit in the North to Lincoln's Assassination." Ph.D. dissertation, University of Illinois, 1963.

4864. Storey, Moorfield. "Dickens, Stanton, Sumner, and Storey." *Atlantic Monthly* 145 (April 1930): 463-465.

4865. Sweet, W. W. "Bishop Matthew Simpson and the Funeral of Abraham Lincoln." *Illinois State Historical Society Journal* 7 (April 1914): 62-71.

4866. *Trial of the Assassins and Conspirators for the Murder of Abraham Lincoln, and the Attempted Assassination of Vice-President Johnson and the Whole Cabinet*. Port Tobacco, MD: J. L. Barbour, 1981.

4867. Truett, Randle B. "Mr. Lincoln Goes to the Theatre." In *Lincoln for the Ages*, edited by Ralph G. Newman, 400-404. Garden City, NY: Doubleday, 1960.

4868. Turner, Thomas R. *Beware the People Weeping: Public Opinion and the Assassination of Abraham Lincoln*. Baton Rouge: Louisiana State University Press, 1982.

4869. Turner, Thomas R. "Did Weichmann Turn State's Evidence to Save Himself? A Critique of a True History of the Assassination of Abraham Lincoln." *Lincoln Herald* 81 (Winter 1979): 265-267.

4870. Turner, Thomas R. "Public Opinion and the Assassination of Abraham Lincoln." *Lincoln Herald* 78 (Spring 1976): 17-24; (Summer 1976): 66-76.

4871. Turner, Thomas R. "Public Opinion: The Assassination of Abraham Lincoln, the Trial of the Conspirators, and the

Trial of John H. Surratt." Ph.D. dissertation, Boston University, 1971.

4872. Vickers, James E. *Controversial Documents Connected to the Lincoln Assassination and Its Aftermath.* New York: Irvington, 1983.

4873. Watts, R. A. "The Trial and Execution of the Lincoln Conspirators." *Michigan History Magazine* 5 (1922): 81-110.

4874. Weichmann, Louis J. *A True History of the Assassination of Abraham Lincoln and of the Conspiracy of 1865.* New York: Random House, 1977.

4875. Weik, Jesse W. "A New Story of Lincoln's Assassination: An Unpublished Record of an Eye-Witness." *Century Magazine* 85 (February 1913): 559-562.

4876. Weissman, Philip. "Why Booth Killed Lincoln: A Psychoanalytic Study of an Historical Tragedy." *Psychoanalysis and the Social Sciences* 5 (1959): 99-118.

4877. *While Lincoln Lay Dying: A Facsimile Reproduction of the First Testimony Taken of President Abraham Lincoln.* Philadelphia: Union League of Philadelphia, 1968.

4878. Wright, Annie F. F. "The Assassination of Abraham Lincoln." *Magazine of History* 9 (February 1909): 113-114.

Campaigns

4879. Bennett, Hiram R. "Financing Mr. Lincoln's First Campaign." *Lincoln Herald* 50 (October 1948): 11-22.

4880. Borit, Gabor S. "Was Lincoln a Vulnerable Candidate in 1860?" *Civil War History* 27 (March 1981): 32-48.

4881. Brumgardt, John R. "Overwhelmingly for 'Old Abe': Sherman's Soldiers and the Election of 1864." *Lincoln Herald* 78 (Winter 1976): 153-159.

4882. Carr, Clark E. "Why Lincoln Was Not Renominated by Acclamation." *Century Magazine* 73 (February 1907): 503-506.

4883. Clark, Mary K. "Lincoln's Nomination as Seen by a Young Girl from New York." *Putnam's* 5 (February 1909): 536-538.

4884. Cole, Arthur C. "Lincoln and the Presidential Election of 1864." *Illinois State Historical Society Transactions* 23 (1917): 130-138.

4885. Coleman, Charles H. "Was Lincoln Eligible for Election to the United States Senate in 1855?" *Lincoln Herald* 60 (Fall 1958): 91-93.

4886. Conkling, Clinton L. "How Mr. Lincoln Received the News of His First Nomination." *Illinois State Historical Society Transactions* 14 (1909): 63-66.

4887. Crofts, Daniel W., ed. "Re-electing Lincoln: The Struggle in Newark." *Civil War History* 30 (March 1984): 34-79.

4888. Dahlinger, Charles W. "Abraham Lincoln in Pittsburgh and the Birth of the Republican Party." *Western Pennsylvania Historical Magazine* 3 (October 1920): 145-177.

4889. Davis, John M. *How Abraham Lincoln Became President.* Springfield, IL: Illinois Co., 1909.

4890. Dittenhoefer, Abram J. *How We Elected Lincoln: Personal Recollections of Lincoln and Men of His Time.* New York: Harper and Row, 1915.

4891. Fischer, Leroy H. "Adam Gurowski Views Lincoln's Re-election." *Lincoln Herald* 66 (Summer 1964): 83-86.

4892. Fischer, Leroy H. "Lincoln's Gadfly — Adam Gurowski!" *Mississippi Valley Historical Review* 36 (December 1949): 415-434.

4893. Gloneck, James F. "Lincoln, Johnson, and the Baltimore Ticket." *Lincoln Quarterly* 6 (March 1951): 255-271.

4894. Green, Fletcher M. "Lincoln: The Taste Is in My Mouth a Little." *South Atlantic Quarterly* 59 (Autumn 1960): 510-520.

4895. Halstead, Murat. *Three against Lincoln: Murat Halstead and the Caucuses of 1860.* Edited by William B. Hesseltine. Baton Rouge: Louisiana State University Press, 1960.

4896. Hamilton, Charles G. *Lincoln and the Know Nothing Movement.* Washington, DC: Public Affairs Press, 1954.

4897. Harbison, Winfred A. "The Elections of 1862 as a Vote of Want of Confidence in President Lincoln." *Michigan Academy of Science, Arts and Letters Papers* 14 (1931): 499-513.

4898. Harris, Sheldon H. "Abraham Lincoln Stumps a Yankee Audience." *New England Quarterly* 38 (June 1965): 227-233.

4899. Hayes, Melvin L. *Mr. Lincoln Runs for President.* New York: Citadel Press, 1960.

4900. Hazelton, Gerry W. "Lincoln and the Convention of 1860." *Granite Monthly* 48 (October 1916): 300-306.

4901. Herriott, Frank I. "Iowa and the First Nomination of Abraham Lincoln." *Annals of Iowa* 9 (April 1909): 45-64; (October 1909): 186-228.

4902. Hesseltine, William B., ed. *Three against Lincoln: Murat Halstead Reports the Caucuses of 1860.* Baton Rouge: Louisiana State University Press, 1960.

4903. Holzer, Harold. "An All-Purpose Campaign Poster." *Lincoln Herald* 84 (Spring 1982): 42-45.

4904. Holzer, Harold. "How America Met Mr. Lincoln: Engravings and Lithographs from the First-Lincoln Campaign." *Nineteenth Century* 6 (Spring 1980): 52-57.

4905. Holzer, Harold. "The Imagemakers: Portraits of Lincoln in the 1860 Campaign." *Chicago History* 7 (Winter 1978-1979): 198-207.

4906. Horowitz, Murray M. "Benjamin F. Butler: Seventeenth President?" *Lincoln Herald* 77 (Winter 1975): 191-203.

4907. Hubbard, Paul G., Jr. "The Lincoln-McClellan Presidential Election in Illinois." Ph.D. dissertation, University of Illinois, 1949.

4908. Johns, Jane M. "The Nomination of Abraham Lincoln to the Presidency, An Unsolved Psychological Problem." *Illinois Historical Society Journal* 10 (January 1918): 561-567.

4909. Kidd, T. W. S. "How Abraham Lincoln Received the News of His Nomination for President." *Illinois State Historical Society Journal* 15 (April 1922): 507-509.

4910. King, Willard L. *Lincoln's Manager, David Davis.* Cambridge, MA: Harvard University Press, 1960.

4911. Kleppner, Paul. "Lincoln and the Immigrant Vote: A Case of Religious Polarization." *Mid-America* 48 (July 1966): 176-195.

4912. Kremm, Thomas W. "Cleveland and the First Lincoln Election: The Ethnic Response to Nativism." *Journal of Interdisciplinary History* 8 (Summer 1977): 69-86.

4913. Lawson, Elizabeth. *Lincoln's Third Party.* New York: International Publishers, 1948.

4914. Lorenz, Alfred L., Jr. "Lincoln, Medill, and Republican Nomination of 1860." *Lincoln Herald* 68 (Winter 1966): 199-204.

4915. Lowden, Lucy. "The Granite State

for Lincoln: New Hamphire's Role in the Nomination of Abraham Lincoln at the Republican National Convention, 1860." *Historical New Hampshire* 25 (Spring 1970): 3-23.

4916. Luebke, Frederick C. *Ethnic Voters and the Election of Lincoln.* Lincoln: University of Nebraska Press, 1971.

4917. Luthin, Reinhard H. *The First Lincoln Campaign.* Cambridge, MA: Harvard University Press, 1944.

4918. McClelland, Clarence P. "An Illinois Colonel's Visit to Jeff Davis in 1864: His Contribution to Lincoln's Re-election." *Illinois State Historical Society Journal* 55 (Spring 1962): 31-44.

4919. Maynard, Douglas. "Dudley of New Jersey and the Nomination of Lincoln." *Pennsylvania Magazine of History and Biography* 82 (January 1958): 100-108.

4920. Monaghan, Jay. *The Man Who Elected Lincoln.* Indianapolis, IN: Bobbs-Merrill, 1956.

4921. Newman, Leonard. "Opposition to Lincoln in the Elections of 1864." *Science and Society* 8 (Fall 1944): 305-327.

4922. Oakleaf, Joseph B. *National Union Convention of 1864 and Why Lincoln Was Not Nominated by Acclamation.* Moline, IL: Carlson, 1924.

4923. Oldroyd, Osborn H. *Lincoln's Campaign: Or the Political Revolution of 1860.* Chicago: Laird and Lee, 1896.

4924. Potter, David M. *Lincoln and His Party in the Secession Crisis.* New Haven, CT: Yale University Press, 1942.

4925. Putnam, George H. "The Speech That Won the East for Lincoln." *Outlook* 130 (February 8, 1922): 220-223.

4926. Rankin, David C., ed. "Political Parades and American Democracy: Jean-Charles Houzeau on Lincoln's 1864 Re-election Campaign." *Civil War History* 30 (December 1984): 324-329.

4927. Raringer, William E. "Lincoln as President-Elect: Springfield Phase." Ph.D. dissertation, University of Illinois, 1941.

4928. Reilly, Tom. "Early Coverage of a President-Elect: Lincoln at Springfield 1860." *Journalism Quarterly* 49 (Autumn 1972): 469-479.

4929. Roll, Charles. "Indiana's Part in the Nomination of Lincoln in 1860." *Indiana Magazine of History* 25 (March 1929): 1-13.

4930. Scripps, John L. *John Locke Scripps' 1860 Campaign Life of Abraham Lincoln, Annotated.* Peoria, IL: E. J. Jacob, 1931.

4931. Segal, Charles M. "Abraham Jonas' Role in Lincoln's First Presidential Nomination." *American Jewish Historical Society Publications* 44 (December 1954): 98-105.

4932. Simon, Donald E. "Brooklyn in the Election of 1860." *New York Historical Society Quarterly* 51 (July 1967): 249-262.

4933. Spencer, Ivor D. "Chicago Helps to Reelect Lincoln." *Illinois State Historical Society Journal* 63 (Summer 1970): 167-179.

4934. Wakefield, Sherman D. *How Lincoln Became President: The Part Played by Bloomington, Illinois, and Certain of Its Citizens in Preparing Him for the Presidency and Securing His Nomination and Election.* New York: Wilson-Erickson, 1936.

4935. Wynne, Patricia H. "Lincoln's Western Image in the 1860 Campaign." *Maryland Historical Magazine* 59 (June 1964): 165-181.

4936. Zornow, William F. "Lincoln and Chase: Presidential Rivals." *Lincoln Herald* 52 (February 1950): 17-28; 52 (June 1950): 6-12, 21.

4937. Zornow, William F. *Lincoln and the Party Divided*. Norman: University of Oklahoma Press, 1954.

4938. Zornow, William F. "Lincoln's Influence in the Election of 1864." *Lincoln Herald* 51 (June 1949): 22-32.

4939. Zornow, William F. "Treason as a Campaign Issue in the Re-election of Lincoln." *Abraham Lincoln Quarterly* 5 (June 1949): 348-363.

4940. Zornow, William F. "Words and Money to Re-elect Lincoln." *Lincoln Herald* 54 (Spring 1952): 22-30.

Civil War

4941. Anderson, Ken. "The Role of Abraham Lincoln and Members of His Family in the Charleston Riot during the Civil War." *Lincoln Herald* 79 (Summer 1977): 53-60.

4942. Bakeless, John. "Lincoln's Private Eye." *Civil War Times Illustrated* 14 (October 1975): 22-30.

4943. Ballard, Colin R. *The Military Genius of Abraham Lincoln: An Essay*. Rev. ed. Cleveland, OH: World Publishing, 1952.

4944. Bates, David H. *Lincoln in the Telegraph Office: Recollections of the U.S. Military Telegraph Corp during the Civil War*. New York: Century, 1907.

4945. Bates, David H. *Lincoln Stories, Told by Him in the Military Office in the War Department during the Civil War, Recorded by One of the Listeners*. New York: Rudge, 1926.

4946. Bernard, Kenneth A. "Lincoln and the Civil War as Viewed by a Dissenting Yankee of Connecticut." *Lincoln Herald* 76 (Winter 1974): 208-214.

4947. Bernard, Kenneth A. "Lincoln and the Music of the Civil War: Hail to the Chief." *Lincoln Herald* 63 (Spring 1961): 29-35.

4948. Bridges, Roger D. "Lincoln Reacts to the Civil War." *Lincoln Herald* 81 (Summer 1979): 63-77.

4949. Brooks, Noah. *Abraham Lincoln, The Nation's Leader in the Great Struggle through Which Was Maintained the Existence of the United States*. New York: Putnam, 1909.

4950. Brooks, Noah. *Mr. Lincoln's Washington: Selections from the Writings of Noah Brooks, Civil War Correspondent*. Edited by P. J. Standenraus. South Brunswick, NJ: Thomas Yoseloff, 1967.

4951. Bruce, Robert V. *Lincoln and the Tools of War*. Indianapolis, IN: Bobbs-Merrill, 1956.

4952. Brumgardt, John R. "Presidential Duel at Midsummer: The 'Peace' Missions to Canada and Richmond, 1864." *Lincoln Herald* 77 (Summer 1975): 96-102.

4953. Cain, Marvin R. "Lincoln as Soldier of the Union: A Reappraisal." *Lincoln Herald* 83 (Spring 1981): 592-603.

4954. Canby, Courtlandt, ed. *Lincoln and the Civil War: A Profile and a History*. New York: Braziller, 1960.

4955. Catton, Bruce. *Mr. Lincoln's Army*. Garden City, NY: Doubleday, 1962.

4956. Catton, Bruce. *Terrible Swift Sword*. Garden City, NY: Doubleday, 1963.

4957. Catton, William, and Bruce Catton. *Two Roads to Sumter*. New York: McGraw-Hill, 1963.

4958. Chambrum, Charles Adolphe de Pineton. *Impressions of Lincoln and the Civil War, A Foreigner's Account*. Translated by Aldebert de Chambrum. New York: Random House, 1952.

4959. Chapman, Ervin S. *Latest Light on Abraham Lincoln, and War-Time Memories Including Many Heretofore Unpublished Incidents and Historical Facts Concerning His Ancestry, Boyhood, Family, Religion, Public Life, Trials, and Triumphs.* New York: Revell, 1917.

4960. Chase, Salmon P. *Inside Lincoln's Cabinet: The Civil War Diaries of Salmon P. Chase.* Edited by David Donald. New York: Longmans, Green, 1954.

4961. Conger, Arthur L. "President Lincoln as War Statesman." *Wisconsin Historical Society Proceedings* 44 (1917): 106-140.

4962. Cope, Frank D. "The Military Role of Lincoln in the War of Secession." *Lincoln Herald* 72 (Spring 1970): 20-26.

4963. Cramer, John H. *Lincoln under Enemy Fire, The Complete Account of His Experiences during Early's Attack on Washington.* Baton Rouge: Louisiana State University Press, 1948.

4964. Current, Richard N. *Lincoln and the First Shot.* Philadelphia: Lippincott, 1964.

4965. Current, Richard N. "Lincoln, the Civil War, and the American Mission." In *The Public and the Private Lincoln: Contemporary Perspectives,* edited by Cullom Davis, Charles B. Strozier, Rebecca M. Veach, and Geoffrey C. Ward, 137-146. Carbondale: Southern Illinois University Press, 1979.

4966. Dodd, William E. *Lincoln or Lee.* New York: Century, 1928.

4967. Dodd, William E. "Lincoln or Lee: No Peace without Victory in a War-Mad World." *Century Magazine* 113 (April 1927): 661-673.

4968. Dorris, Jonathan T. "President Lincoln's Treatment of Confederates." *Filson Club Historical Quarterly* 33 (April 1959): 139-160.

4969. Doster, William E. *Lincoln and Episodes of the Civil War.* New York: Putnam, 1915.

4970. Dupuy, Trevor N. *The Military Life of Abraham Lincoln, Commander in Chief.* New York: Franklin Watts, 1969.

4971. Durishin, John F. "The War Powers of Lincoln." *Picket Post* 30 (October 1950): 9-19.

4972. Gilbert, C. E. *Two Presidents: Abraham Lincoln and Jefferson Davis.* San Antonio, TX: Naylor Co., 1973.

4973. Gilmore, James R. *Personal Recollections of Abraham Lincoln and the Civil War.* London: J. Macqueen, 1899.

4974. Greene, Francis V. "Lincoln as Commander in Chief." *Scribner's Magazine* 46 (July 1909): 104-115.

4975. Hanna, William F., III. *Abraham among the Yankees: Abraham Lincoln's 1848 Visit to Massachusetts.* Taunton, MA: Old Colony Historical Society, 1983.

4976. Harper, Robert S. "The Unpopular Mr. Lincoln." In *Lincoln for the Ages,* edited by Ralph G. Newman, 307-311. Garden City, NY: Doubleday, 1960.

4977. Harrison, Lowell H., ed. "John C. Underwood, Reminiscences of Interviews with Senator Charles Sumner, President Abraham Lincoln, and Judge Thomas Corwin." *Lincoln Herald* 76 (Spring 1974): 29-34.

4978. Hattaway, Herman, and Archer Jones. "Lincoln as Military Strategist." *Civil War History* 26 (December 1980): 293-303.

4979. Haverlin, Carl. "Lincoln and His Hope for a Just and Lasting Peace." In *Lincoln for the Ages,* edited by Ralph G. Newman, 325-331. Garden City, NY: Doubleday, 1960.

4980. Hay, John. *Lincoln and the Civil War in the Diaries and Letters of John*

Hay. New York: Dodd, Mead, 1939.

4981. Hay, Thomas R. "President Lincoln and the Army of the Potomac." *Georgia Historical Quarterly* 10 (December 1926): 277-301.

4982. Hendrick, Burton J. *Lincoln's War Conduct.* Boston: Little, Brown, 1946.

4983. Henry, Milton L., Jr. "Pre-Civil War Compromise Efforts: A Re-evaluation." *Louisiana Studies* 12 (Spring 1973): 376-382.

4984. Hertz, Emanuel. "Abraham Lincoln — The Jurist of the Civil War." *New York University Law Quarterly Review* 14 (May 1937): 473-501.

4985. Hess, Earl. "Alvin P. Hovey and Abraham Lincoln's 'Broken Promises': The Politics of Promotion." *Indiana Magazine of History* 80 (March 1984): 35-50.

4986. Hesseltine, William B. *Lincoln and the War Governors.* New York: Knopf, 1948.

4987. Heysinger, I. W. "Lincoln, Commander in Chief of the Army and Navy of All the Armed Forces of the United States." *Journal of Military Services Institute* 53 (September 1913): 165-180.

4988. Horowitz, Murray M. "That Presidential Grub: Lincoln versus His Generals." *Lincoln Herald* 79 (Winter 1977): 157-168.

4989. Johnson, Ludwell H. "Jefferson Davis and Abraham Lincoln as War Presidents: Nothing Succeeds Like Success." *Civil War History* 27 (March 1981): 49-63.

4990. Johnson, Ludwell H. "Lincoln's Solution to the Problem of Peace Terms, 1864-1865." *Journal of Southern History* 34 (November 1968): 576-586.

4991. Joshi, Manoj K. "Lincoln, Labour, and the Civil War." *Indian Journal of American Studies* 9 (January 1979): 44-53.

4992. Joynt, Robert H. "Abraham Lincoln and the Capture of Norfolk." *Lincoln Herald* 76 (Summer 1974): 69-79.

4993. Kelley, Darwin. *Milligan's Fight against Lincoln.* New York: Exposition Press, 1973.

4994. Kincaid, Robert L. "Joshua Fry Speed: Lincoln's Confidential Agent." *Lincoln Herald* 55 (Fall 1953): 2-10, 19.

4995. Langdon, William C. *Abraham Lincoln Today: A War-Time Tribute, Being the Lincoln Day Convocation of the University of Illinois, 1918.* Urbana: University of Illinois Press, 1918.

4996. Lewis, Lloyd. "Lincoln and the Pinkerton." *Illinois State Historical Society Journal* 41 (December 1948): 367-382.

4997. "Lincoln and Lee." *South Atlantic Quarterly* 26 (January 1927): 4-21.

4998. Lindsey, David. *A. Lincoln/Jefferson Davis: The House Divided.* Cleveland, OH: H. Allen, 1960.

4999. Macartney, Clarence E. *Lincoln and His Generals.* Philadelphia: Dorrance, 1925.

5000. McClure, Alexander K. *Lincoln and Men of War Times.* Philadelphia: Rolley and Reynolds, 1962.

5001. McMurray, Richard. "The Presidents' Tenth and the Battle of Olustee." *Civil War Times Illustrated* 16 (January 1978): 12-24.

5002. Maurice, Frederick. "Lincoln as a Strategist." *Forum* 75 (February 1926): 161-169.

5003. Meade, Robert D. "Lincoln and the Statesmen of Rebellion." In *Lincoln for the Ages,* edited by Ralph G. Newman, 295-300. Garden City, NY: Doubleday, 1960.

5004. Milton, George F. *Abraham Lincoln and the Fifth Column.* New York: Vanguard Press, 1942.

5005. Moore, J. Preston. "Lincoln and the Escape of the Confederate Commissioner." *Illinois State Historical Society Journal* 57 (Spring 1964): 23-29.

5006. Neely, Mark E., Jr. "War and Partisanship: What Lincoln Learned from James K. Polk." *Illinois State Historical Society Journal* 76 (Autumn 1981): 199-216.

5007. Oates, Stephen B. *Our Fiery Trial: Abraham Lincoln, John Brown, and the Civil War Era.* Amherst: University of Massachusetts Press, 1979.

5008. Oedel, Howard T. "Lincoln Takes the Pulse of the Confederacy at Charleston in March, 1861." *Lincoln Herald* 73 (Fall 1971): 156-161.

5009. Olsen, Otto H. "Abraham Lincoln as Revolutionary." *Civil War History* 24 (September 1978): 213-214.

5010. Ostendorf, Lloyd. "Lincoln in Stereo." *Civil War Times Illustrated* 14 (February 1976): 4-9.

5011. Palmer, John M. "President Lincoln's War Problem." *Illinois State Historical Society Journal* 21 (July 1927): 41-53.

5012. Palmer, John M. *Washington, Lincoln, Wilson: Three War Statesmen.* Garden City, NY: Doubleday, 1930.

5013. Parish, P. J. "Lincoln and Fort Sumter." *History Today* 11 (April 1961): 262-270.

5014. Petz, Weldon. "Some Views on the Lincoln and Civil War Collection of the Lincoln Memorial University." *Lincoln Herald* 75 (Summer 1973): 50-52.

5015. Pullar, Walter S. "Abe Lincoln's Brown Water Navy." *Naval War College Review* 21 (April 1969): 71-88.

5016. Putnam, George H. *Abraham Lincoln, The Great Captain: Personal Reminiscences by a Veteran of the Civil War, A Lecture Delivered at Oxford.* Oxford: Clarendon Press, 1928.

5017. Randall, James G. "Civil and Military Relationships under Lincoln." *Pennsylvania Magazine of History and Biography* 69 (July 1945): 199-206.

5018. Randall, James G. "Lincoln's Peace and Wilson's." *South Atlantic Quarterly* 42 (July 1943): 225-242.

5019. Randall, James G. "Lincoln's Task and Wilson's." *South Atlantic Quarterly* 29 (October 1930): 349-368.

5020. Rawley, James A., comp. *Lincoln and Civil War Politics.* New York: Holt, Rinehart and Winston, 1969.

5021. Roth, Lawrence V. *Abraham Lincoln on War and Peace, 1860-1864.* Boston: Old South Association, 1918.

5022. Russ, William A., Jr. "The Struggle between President Lincoln and Congress over Disfranchisement of Rebels." *Susquehanna University Studies* 3 (March 1948): 241-243.

5023. Rutledge, Archibald. "Abraham Lincoln Fights the Battle of Fort Sumter." *South Atlantic Quarterly* 34 (October 1935): 368-383.

5024. Rutledge, Archibald. "Lincoln and the Theory of Secession." *South Atlantic Quarterly* 41 (October 1942): 370-383.

5025. Sandburg, Carl. *Abraham Lincoln: The War Years.* 4 vols. New York: Harcourt, Brace, 1939.

5026. Sandburg, Carl. "Lincoln and Conscription." *Illinois State Historical Society Journal* 32 (March 1939): 5-19.

5027. Schlesinger, Arthur M., Sr. "Lincoln and Lee." *American Heritage* 4 (Winter 1953): 18-19.

5028. Schwengel, Frederic D. "The War Powers of President Lincoln." In *Lincoln for the Ages,* edited by Ralph G. Newman,

273-278. Garden City, NY: Doubleday, 1960.

5029. Sowle, Patrick. "A Reappraisal of Seward's Memorandum of April 1, 1861, to Lincoln." *Journal of Southern History* 33 (May 1967): 234-239.

5030. Speer, Emory. *Lincoln, Lee, Grant, and Other Biographical Addresses.* New York: Neale, 1909.

5031. Stampp, Kenneth M. "Lincoln and the Strategy of Defense in the Crisis of 1861." *Journal of Southern History* 11 (August 1945): 297-323.

5032. Stoddard, William O. *Inside the White House in War Times.* New York: C. L. Webster, 1890.

5033. Stradling, James M. "The Tail of the Army Calls on Lincoln: An Unpublished Letter of a Quaker Sergeant." *Outlook* 130 (February 15, 1922): 256-258.

5034. Symonds, Craig L. "Lincoln and the Strategy of Union." *Naval War College Review* 27 (March/April 1975): 63-70.

5035. Taylor, John M. "Representative Recruit for Abraham Lincoln." *Civil War Times Illustrated* 17 (June 1978): 34-35.

5036. Tenney, Craig D. "To Suppress or Not to Suppress: Abraham Lincoln and the Chicago *Times.*" *Civil War History* 27 (September 1981): 248-259.

5037. Theodore, Terry C. "The Civil War on the New York Stage from 1861-1900." *Lincoln Herald* 74 (Spring 1972): 34-40.

5038. Theodore, Terry C. "President Lincoln on the Confederate Stage." *Lincoln Herald* 78 (Winter 1976): 147-153.

5039. Tilton, Clint C. "Lincoln and Lamon: Partners and Friends." *Illinois State Historical Society Transactions* (1931): 175-228.

5040. Trefousse, Hans L. "Zachariah Chandler and the Withdrawal of Fremont in 1864: New Answers to an Old Riddle." *Lincoln Herald* 70 (Winter 1968): 181-188.

5041. True, Marshall. "A Reluctant Warrior Advises the President: Ethan Allen Hitchcock, Abraham Lincoln, and the Union Army, Spring, 1862." *Vermont History* 50 (Summer 1982): 143-150.

5042. Tyrner-Tyrnauer, A. R. *Lincoln and the Emperors.* New York: Harcourt, Brace and World, 1962.

5043. Vandiver, Frank E. "Abraham Lincoln and Jefferson Davis." In *Lincoln for the Ages,* edited by Ralph G. Newman, 284-288. Garden City, NY: Doubleday, 1960.

5044. Waldron, Webb. "If Lincoln Had Yielded and Withdrawn Major Anderson from Fort Sumter in 1861." *Century Magazine* 112 (June 1926): 151-156.

5045. Werstein, Irving. *Abraham Lincoln versus Jefferson Davis.* New York: Crowell, 1959.

5046. West, Richard S., Jr. "Lincoln's Hand in Naval Matters." *Civil War History* 4 (June 1958): 175-183.

5047. West, Richard S., Jr. *Mr. Lincoln's Navy.* New York: Longmans, Green, 1957.

5048. Westwood, Howard C. "The Joint Committee on the Conduct of the War — A Look at the Record." *Lincoln Herald* 80 (Spring 1978): 3-15.

5049. Westwood, Howard C. "Lincoln and the Hampton Roads Peace Conference." *Lincoln Herald* 81 (Winter 1979): 243-256.

5050. Williams, Kenneth P. *Lincoln Finds a General.* 5 vols. New York: Macmillan, 1949-1956.

5051. Williams, T. Harry. *Lincoln and His Generals.* New York: Knopf, 1952.

5052. Williams, T. Harry. *Two War Leaders: Lincoln and Davis.* Springfield, IL: Abraham Lincoln Association, 1972.

5053. Young, James H. "Anna Elizabeth Dickinson and the Civil War: For and against Lincoln." *Mississippi Valley Historical Review* 31 (June 1944): 59-80.

Gettysburg Address

5054. Andrews, Mary R. S. "The Perfect Tribute." *Scribner's Magazine* 40 (January 1906): 17-24.

5055. Barton, William E. *Lincoln at Gettysburg: What He Intended to Say, What He Said, What He Reported to Have Said, What He Wished He Had Said.* Indianapolis, IN: Bobbs-Merrill, 1930.

5056. Bloom, Robert L. "The Gettysburg Address." *Lincoln Herald* 83 (Winter 1981): 765-774.

5057. Carmichael, Orton H. *Lincoln's Gettysburg Address.* New York: Abingdon Press, 1917.

5058. Carr, Clark E. "Lincoln at Gettysburg." *Illinois State Historical Society Transactions* 11 (1906): 138-152.

5059. Carr, Clark E. *Lincoln at Gettysburg.* Chicago: McClurg, 1906.

5060. Carson, Herbert L. "Nor Long Remember: Lincoln at Gettysburg." *Pennsylvania History* 28 (October 1961): 365-371.

5061. DeAlvarez, Leo P., ed. *Abraham Lincoln: The Gettysburg Address and American Constitutionalism.* Dallas, TX: University of Dallas Press, 1976.

5062. Dozer, Donald M. "Lincoln's Rival at Gettysburg 1863." *Filson Club Historical Quarterly* 45 (January 1971): 77-81.

5063. Eisendrath, Joseph L., Jr. "Suggestions That Inspired Immortal Words." *Abraham Lincoln Quarterly* 5 (December 1948): 212-215.

5064. Emsley, Bert. "Phonetic Structure in Lincoln's Gettysburg Address." *Quarterly Journal of Speech* 24 (April 1938): 281-287.

5065. Goodman, Florence J. "Pericles at Gettysburg." *Midwest Quarterly* 6 (April 1965): 317-336.

5066. Heathcote, Charles W. "President Lincoln and John Burns at Gettysburg." *Lincoln Herald* 53 (Spring 1951): 31-33.

5067. Jacobs, Henry. *Lincoln's Gettysburg World-Message.* Philadelphia: United Lutheran Publication House, 1919.

5068. Kunhardt, Philip B., Jr. *A New Birth of Freedom: Lincoln at Gettysburg.* Boston: Little, Brown, 1983.

5069. "Lincoln at Gettysburg." *Nation* 97 (July 10, 1913): 26-27.

5070. Michel, Dorothy. "That This Nation Shall Not Perish from This Earth." *Lincoln Herald* 80 (Fall 1978): 141-143.

5071. Moore, Charles, comp. *Lincoln's Gettysburg Address and Second Inaugural, Texts and Illustrations.* Boston: Houghton Mifflin, 1927.

5072. Nevins, Allan. *Lincoln and the Gettysburg Address: Commemorative Papers by John Dos Passos and Others.* Urbana: University of Illinois Press, 1964.

5073. Owsley, Clifford D. "Genesis of the World's Greatest Speech." *Lincoln Herald* 64 (Fall 1963): 136-139.

5074. Reid, Ronald F. "Newspaper Responses to the Gettysburg Address." *Quarterly Journal of Speech* 53 (February 1967): 50-60.

5075. Robinson, A. H. "On the Field of Gettysburg." *Contemporary Review* 221 (October 1972): 204-206.

5076. Roelofs, H. Mark. "The Gettysburg Address: An Exercise in Presidential Legitimation." *Presidential Studies Quarterly* 8 (Summer 1978): 226-236.

5077. Stevens, Sylvester K. "Lincoln at Gettysburg." *American Heritage* 5 (Winter 1954): 38-39, 63.

5078. Tausek, Joseph. *The True Story of the Gettysburg Address.* New York: Dial, 1933.

5079. Tilberg, Frederick. "The Location of the Platform from Which Lincoln Delivered the Gettysburg Address." *Pennsylvania History* 40 (April 1973): 179-191.

5080. Warren, Louis A., and Frederick Tilberg. "Have We Done Lincoln Justice at Gettysburg?" *Civil War Times Illustrated* 15 (July 1976): 10-17.

5081. Weik, Jesse W. "Lincoln's Gettysburg Address." *Outlook* 104 (July 12, 1913): 572-574.

5082. Whitcomb, Paul S. "Lincoln's 'Gettysburg Address.'" *Tyler's Quarterly Historical and Genealogical Magazine* 12 (April 1931): 221-235.

5083. Wilson, James G. "Lincoln's Gettysburg Address." *Independent* 74 (April 24, 1913): 910-912.

Inaugurations

5084. Adams, Charles F. "Lincoln's First Inauguration." *Massachusetts Historical Society Proceedings* 42 (1908-1909): 145-151.

5085. Aldrich, Charles. "At Lincoln's First Inauguration." *Annals of Iowa* 8 (April 1907): 43-50.

5086. Andrews, Helen R. "President-Elect Abraham Lincoln's Inaugural Train Stop at Erie, Pa., Sat. Feb. 16, 1861." *Journal of Erie Studies* 6 (Spring 1977): 41-43.

5087. Gunderson, Robert G. "Lincoln and Governor Morgan: A Financial Footnote." *Abraham Lincoln Quarterly* 6 (December 1951): 431-437.

5088. Hahn, Dan F., and Anne Morlando. "A Burkean Analysis of Lincoln's Second Inaugural Address." *Presidential Studies Quarterly* 9 (Fall 1979): 376-379.

5089. Hall, Abraham O. "The Great Lincoln Inauguration." *Frank Leslie's Popular Monthly* 43 (March 1897): 254-260.

5090. Hubbell, Jay B. "Lincoln's First Inaugural Address." *American Historical Review* 36 (April 1931): 550-552.

5091. Janny, W. A. "Lincoln's Inauguration: A Letter from W. A. Janny to His Friend Will Thomson." *Lincoln Herald* 54 (Winter 1952): 44-46.

5092. Miller, William L. "Lincoln's Second Inaugural: The Zenith of Statecraft." *Center Magazine* 13 (July/August 1980): 53-64.

5093. Phelan, Mary K. *Mr. Lincoln's Inaugural Journey.* New York: Crowell, 1972.

5094. Searcher, Victor. *Lincoln's Journey to Greatness: A Factual Account of the Twelve-Day Inaugural Trip.* Philadelphia: Winston, 1960.

5095. Somkin, Fred. "Scripture Notes to Lincoln's Second Inaugural." *Civil War History* 27 (June 1981): 172-173.

5096. "A Vermonter Describes the Mood at Lincoln's First Inaugural." *Vermont History* 36 (Spring 1968): 61-63.

5097. Wallis, G. B. "Honest Abe and the Little Grant: A Reminiscence of Lincoln's First Inauguration." *Outlook* 127 (February 9, 1921): 217-219.

5098. Wessen, Ernest J. "Lincoln's First Inaugural Address." *Abraham Lincoln Quarterly* 3 (March 1944): 34-37.

Indians

5099. Holman, Tom. "William G. Coffin, Lincoln's Superintendent of Indian Affairs for the Southern Superintendency." *Kansas Historical Quarterly* 39 (Winter 1973): 491-514.

5100. Kelsey, Harry. "Abraham Lincoln and American Indian Policy." *Lincoln Herald* 77 (Fall 1975): 139-148.

5101. King, Jeffrey S. "A Memorable Spectacle: Lincoln's Meeting with Plains Indians on March 27, 1863." *Lincoln Herald* 81 (Spring 1979): 20-27.

5102. King, Jeffrey S. "President Lincoln as the Great White Father: Lincoln and the Indians." *Lincoln Herald* 84 (Fall 1982): 141-146.

5103. Moulton, Gary E. "John Ross and W. P. Dole: A Case Study of Lincoln's Indian Policy." *Journal of the West* 12 (July 1973): 414-423.

5104. Nichols, David A. *Lincoln and the Indians: Civil War Policy and Politics.* Columbia: University of Missouri Press, 1978.

5105. Nichols, David A. "The Other Civil War: Lincoln and the Indians." *Minnesota History* 44 (1974): 2-15.

5106. Nichols, David A. "The Other Civil War: Lincoln and the Indians." Ph.D. dissertation, College of William and Mary in Virginia, 1975.

5107. Suppiger, Joseph E. "Private Lincoln and the Spy Battalion." *Lincoln Herald* 80 (Spring 1978): 46-49.

5108. Viola, Herman J. *Lincoln and the Indians: Address at Annual Meeting, Lincoln Fellowship of Wisconsin, Madison, 1975.* Madison: The Fellowship, 1976.

Judicial

5109. Atwood, Harry. "Lincoln and the Constitution." *Constitutional Review* 13 (July 1929): 126-134.

5110. Bernard, Kenneth A. "Lincoln and Civil Liberties." *Abraham Lincoln Quarterly* 6 (September 1951): 375-399.

5111. Bullard, F. Lauriston. "Lincoln and the Courts of the District of Columbia." *American Bar Association Journal* 24 (February 1938): 117-120.

5112. Cain, Marvin R. *Lincoln's Attorney General: Edward Bates of Missouri.* Columbia: University of Missouri Press, 1965.

5113. Carpenter, Richard V. "Lincoln's First Supreme Court Case." *Illinois State Historical Society Journal* 4 (October 1911): 317-323.

5114. Cole, Arthur C. "Lincoln and the American Tradition of Civil Liberty." *Illinois State Historical Society Journal* 19 (October 1926/January 1927): 102-114.

5115. Delaplaine, Edward S. "Lincoln after Taney's Death." *Lincoln Herald* 79 (Winter 1977): 151-157.

5116. Dilliard, Irving. "Lincoln Remakes the Supreme Court." In *Lincoln for the Ages,* edited by Ralph G. Newman, 301-306. Garden City, NY: Doubleday, 1960.

5117. Fehrenbacher, Don E. "Lincoln and Judicial Supremacy: A Note on the Galena Speech of July 23, 1856." *Civil War History* 16 (September 1970): 197-204.

5118. Fehrenbacher, Don E. "Lincoln and the Constitution." In *The Public and Private Lincoln: Contemporary Perspectives,* edited by Cullom Davis, 137-146. Carbondale: Southern Illinois University Press, 1979.

5119. Frank, John P. "Edward Bates, Lincoln's Attorney General." *American Journal of Legal History* 10 (January 1966): 34-50.

5120. Halbert, Sherrill. "Lincoln and the Fourteenth Amendment." In *Lincoln for* *the Ages,* edited by Ralph G. Newman, 24-43. Garden City, NY: Doubleday, 1960.

5121. Halbert, Sherrill. "The Suspension of the Writ of Habeas Corpus by President Lincoln." *American Journal of Legal History* 2 (April 1958): 95-116.

5122. Hay, Logan. "Lincoln's Attitude toward the Supreme Court and the *Dred Scott* Decision." In the *Annual Report of the Illinois State Bar Association,* 90-100. Springfield, IL: Schnapp and Barnes, 1937.

5123. Hyman, Harold M. "Mars and the Constitution." *Civil War Times Illustrated* 12 (June 1973): 36-42.

5124. Johnson, Monroe. "Taney and Lincoln." *American Bar Association Journal* 16 (August 1930): 499-502.

5125. Kubicek, Earl C. "The Lincoln Corpus Caper." *Lincoln Herald* 82 (Fall 1980): 474-480.

5126. Lightner, David. "Abraham Lincoln and the Idea of Equality." *Illinois State Historical Society Journal* 75 (Winter 1982): 289-307.

5127. Long, Joseph C. "*Ex Parte Merryman:* The Showdown between Two Great Antagonists: Lincoln and Taney." *South Dakota Law Review* 14 (Spring 1969): 207-249.

5128. Luthin, Reinhard H. "Lincoln and the American Tradition." *Midwest Journal* 3 (Winter 1951): 1-10.

5129. McLaughlin, Andrew C. "Lincoln, the Constitution, and Democracy." *International Journal of Ethics* 47 (October 1936): 1-24.

5130. McMahon, Edward. "Lincoln and Civil Liberty." *Pacific Review* 1 (June 1920): 6-23.

5131. McNeil, Floyd A. "Lincoln's Attorney General: Edward Bates." Ph.D. dissertation, University of Iowa, 1934.

5132. Martin, David L. "When Lincoln Suspended Habeas Corpus." *American Bar Association Journal* 60 (January 1974): 99-102.

5133. Miller, Justin. "Lincoln and the Thirteenth Amendment." In *Lincoln for the Ages,* edited by Ralph G. Newman, 332-337. Garden City, NY: Doubleday, 1960.

5134. Poland, Charles P., Jr. "Abraham Lincoln and Civil Liberties: A Reappraisal." *Lincoln Herald* 76 (Fall 1974): 119-132.

5135. Pomeroy, Earl S. "Lincoln, the Thirteenth Amendment, and the Admission of Nevada." *Pacific Historical Review* 12 (December 1943): 362-368.

5136. Randall, James G. *Constitutional Problems under Lincoln.* Rev. ed. Urbana: University of Illinois Press, 1951.

5137. Silver, David M. *Lincoln's Supreme Court.* Urbana: University of Illinois Press, 1956.

5138. Spector, Robert M. "Lincoln and Taney: A Study in Constitutional Polarization." *American Journal of Legal History* 15 (July 1971): 199-214.

5139. Ulrich, Bartow A. *Abraham Lincoln and Constitutional Government.* Chicago: Chicago Legal News, 1916-1921.

5140. Wilson, Rufus R. "Mr. Lincoln's First Appointment to the Supreme Court." *Lincoln Herald* 50 (December 1948): 26-27; 51 (February 1949): 39.

Press

5141. Bardolph, Richard. "Malice toward One: Lincoln in the North Carolina Press." *Lincoln Herald* 53 (Winter 1951): 34-45.

5142. Basler, Roy P. "Lincoln in Politics, 1948." *Abraham Lincoln Quarterly* 5 (December 1948): 216-233.

5143. Bloom, Robert L. "As the British Press Saw Lincoln." *Topic* 9 (Spring 1965): 44-62.

5144. Dunlap, Lloyd A. "President Lincoln and Editor Greeley." *Abraham Lincoln Quarterly* 5 (June 1948): 94-110.

5145. George, Joseph, Jr. " 'Abraham Africanus 1': President Lincoln through the Eyes of a Copperhead Editor." *Civil War History* 14 (September 1968): 226-235.

5146. George, Joseph, Jr. " 'A Catholic Family Newspaper' Views the Lincoln Administration: John Mullaly's Copperhead Weekly." *Civil War History* 24 (June 1978): 112-132.

5147. George, Joseph, Jr. "Philadelphia's Catholic Herald Evaluates President Lincoln." *Lincoln Herald* 82 (Fall 1980): 447-453.

5148. Hanna, William F., III. "Abraham Lincoln and the New England Press, 1858-1860." Ph.D. dissertation, Boston College, 1980.

5149. Harper, Robert S. *Lincoln and the Press*. New York: McGraw-Hill, 1951.

5150. Heathcote, Charles W. "Three Pennsylvanians and Lincoln's Nomination — 1860." *Lincoln Herald* 51 (June 1949): 38-41.

5151. Heckman, Richard A. "The British Press Reacts to Lincoln's Election." *Illinois State Historical Society Journal* 63 (Autumn 1970): 257-269.

5152. Heuring, A. J. "Lincoln's First View of a Press: Saw Washington Hand Press at Vincennes." *National Printer Journalist* 52 (February 1934): 26-27.

5153. Horner, Harlan H. "Lincoln Replies to Horace Greeley." *Lincoln Herald* 53 (Spring 1951): 2-10, 27; (Summer 1951): 14-25.

5154. Jillson, Willard R. *Lincoln Back Home, Two Episodes in the Career of the Great Civil War President Mirrored in the Daily Kentucky Press, 1860-1865*. Lexington, KY: Transylvania Press, 1932.

5155. Johnson, Ellis A. "Greeley, Lincoln, and a Note on White Elephants." *Social Education* 26 (January 1962): 23-24.

5156. McGinty, Brian. " 'Castine' and Mr. Lincoln: A Reporter at the White House." *Civil War Times Illustrated* 16 (November 1977): 26-35.

5157. Mitgang, Herbert. *Abraham Lincoln, A Press Portrait: His Life and Times from the Original Newspaper Documents of the Union, the Confederacy, and Europe*. Chicago: Quadrangle Books, 1971.

5158. Park, Joseph H. "Lincoln and Contemporary English Periodicals." *Dalhousie Review* 6 (October 1926): 297-311.

5159. Schimpf, Sheila O. "The 'Lansing State Republican's' Coverage of Abraham Lincoln from 1860 to 1865." Master's thesis, Michigan State University, 1981.

5160. Stevens, Lucia A. "Growth of Public Opinion in the East in Regard to Lincoln Prior to November, 1860." *Illinois State Historical Library Publications* 11 (January 1907): 284-301.

5161. Stoddard, William O. "A Journalist Sees Lincoln by William Stoddard." *Atlantic Monthly* 135 (February 1925): 171-177.

5162. Taylor, Maurice P. "President Lincoln and the Press." *Lincoln Herald* 84 (Winter 1982): 205-209.

5163. Turner, John J., Jr., and Michael D'Innocenzo. "The President and the Press: Lincoln, James Gordon Bennett, and the Election 1864." *Lincoln Herald* 76 (Summer 1974): 63-69.

5164. Walsh, William S. *Abraham Lincoln and the London Punch.* New York: Moffat, Yard, 1909.

5165. Wilgus, A. Curtis. "Some Views of President Lincoln Held by the London *Times*, 1861 to 1865." *Illinois State Historical Society Journal* 17 (April 1924): 157-164.

Reconstruction

5166. Dell, Christopher. "Reconstruction, Had Lincoln Lived." *Lincoln Herald* 81 (Winter 1979): 257-265.

5167. DuBois, William E. B. *Black Reconstruction in America, 1860-1880.* New York: Harcourt, Brace, 1935.

5168. Fehrenbacher, Don E. "Lincoln and Reconstruction." *Illinois History* 16 (February 1963): 99-100.

5169. Hesseltine, William B. *Lincoln's Plan of Reconstruction.* Tuscaloosa: Confederate Publishing Co., 1960.

5170. Lewis, Lloyd. "Lincoln's Legacy to Grant." *Abraham Lincoln Quarterly* 5 (June 1948): 75-93.

5171. McCarthy, Charles H. *Lincoln's Plan of Reconstruction.* New York: McClure, Phillips, 1901.

5172. McCarthy, Charles H. "Reconstruction under President Lincoln." Ph.D. dissertation, University of Pennsylvania, 1898.

5173. McCrary, J. Peyton. *Abraham Lincoln and Reconstruction: The Louisiana Experiment.* Princeton, NJ: Princeton University Press, 1979.

5174. McCrary, J. Peyton. "Moderation in a Revolutionary World: Lincoln and the Failure of Reconstruction in Louisiana." Ph.D. dissertation, Princeton University, 1972.

5175. Maslowski, Peter. "From Reconciliation to Reconstruction: Lincoln, Johnson, and Tennessee." *Tennessee Historical Quarterly* 42 (Fall 1983): 281-298; (Winter 1983): 343-361.

5176. Morris, Robert L. "The Lincoln-Johnson Plan for Reconstruction and the Republican Convention of 1864." *Lincoln Herald* 71 (Spring 1969): 33-39.

5177. Schlegel, Marvin W. "Lincoln versus Johnson: The Tragedy of Reconstruction." *Virginia Social Science Journal* 2 (November 1967): 119-127.

5178. Trefousse, Hans L. "Lincoln and Johnson." *Topic* 9 (Spring 1965): 63-75.

5179. Trefousse, Hans L. *The Radical Republicans: Lincoln's Vanguard for Racial Justice.* New York: Knopf, 1969.

Slavery

5180. Arnold, Isaac N. *History of Abraham Lincoln and Overthrow of Slavery.* Chicago: Clarke, 1866.

5181. Basler, Roy P. "Lincoln, Blacks, and Women." In *The Public and the Private Lincoln: Contemporary Perspectives,* edited by Cullom Davis, Charles B. Strozier, Rebecca M. Veach, and Geoffrey C. Ward, 38-53. Carbondale: Southern Illinois University Press, 1979.

5182. Bernard, Kenneth A. "Lincoln, The Emancipator." In *Abraham Lincoln: A New Portrait,* edited by Henry B. Kranz, 36-41. New York: Putnam, 1959.

5183. Beveridge, John W. "Lincoln's View on Slavery and Blacks as Expressed in the Debates with Stephen A. Douglas." *Lincoln Herald* 84 (Winter 1981): 791-800.

5184. Brooks, Noah. *Abraham Lincoln and the Downfall of American Slavery.* New York: Putnam, 1894.

5185. Cain, Marvin R. "Lincoln's Views on Slavery and the Negro: A Suggestion." *Historian* 26 (August 1964): 502-520.

5186. Cardoso, J. J. "Lincoln, Abolitionism, and Patronage: The Case of Hinton Rowan Helper." *Journal of Negro History* 53 (April 1968): 144-160.

5187. Chroust, Anton-Hermann. "Abraham Lincoln Argues a Pro-Slavery Case." *American Journal of Legal History* 5 (October 1961): 299-308.

5188. Cox, Earnest S. *Lincoln's Negro Policy*. Richmond, VA: William Byrd Press, 1938.

5189. Cox, LaWanda C. *Lincoln and Black Freedom: A Study in Presidential Leadership*. Urbana: University of Illinois Press, 1985.

5190. Donovan, Frank. *Mr. Lincoln's Proclamation: The Story of the Emancipation Proclamation*. New York: Dodd, Mead, 1964.

5191. Douglas, William O. *Mr. Lincoln and the Negroes: The Long Road to Equality*. New York: Atheneum, 1963.

5192. Dreher, Ernest O. "Lincoln's Plan for a Free America: Dream vs. Reality." *Illinois History* 16 (February 1963): 101-102.

5193. Drinkwater, John. *Lincoln, The World Emancipator*. Boston: Houghton Mifflin, 1920.

5194. Dunlap, Lloyd A. "Lincoln's Emancipation Proclamation." *Lincoln Herald* 64 (Fall 1962): 107-121.

5195. Eliot, Christopher R. "The Lincoln Emancipation Statute." *Journal of Negro History* 29 (October 1944): 471-475.

5196. Fehrenbacher, Don E. "Only His Stepchildren: Lincoln and the Negro." *Civil War History* 20 (December 1974): 293-310.

5197. Fleischman, Richard K. "The Devil's Advocate: A Defense of Lincoln's Attitude toward the Negro, 1837-1863." *Lincoln Herald* 81 (Fall 1979): 172-186.

5198. Franklin, John H. *The Emancipation Proclamation*. Garden City, NY: Doubleday, 1963.

5199. Fredrickson, George M. "A Man But Not a Brother: Abraham Lincoln and Racial Equality." *Journal of Southern History* 44 (Spring 1975): 175-184.

5200. Hamlett, J. Arthur. "Abraham Lincoln and Race Relations." *Methodist Review* 40 (July 1924): 611-616.

5201. Harris, Alfred G. "Lincoln and the Question of Slavery in the District of Columbia." *Lincoln Herald* 51 (June 1949): 17-21, 48.

5202. Harris, Alfred G. "Lincoln and the Question of Slavery in the District of Columbia: The District Emancipation Law." *Lincoln Herald* 53 (Spring 1951): 11-18.

5203. Harris, Alfred G. "Lincoln and the Question of Slavery in the District of Columbia: The Enforcement of the District Emancipation Act." *Lincoln Herald* 54 (Spring 1952): 12-21.

5204. Harris, Alfred G. "Lincoln and the Question of Slavery in the District of Columbia: The Enforcement of the Fugitive Slave Laws, 1861-1864." *Lincoln Herald* 52 (February 1950): 2-16, 43.

5205. Harrison, Lowell H. "Lincoln and Compensated Emancipation in Kentucky." *Lincoln Herald* 84 (Spring 1982): 11-17.

5206. Hart, Franklin W. *Abraham Lincoln, The Great Commoner, The Sublime Emancipator*. Pasadena, CA: Press of Pasadena Star-News, 1927.

5207. Hill, Frederick T. *Lincoln, Emancipator of the Nation*. New York: Appleton, 1928.

5208. Holzer, Harold. "When Lincoln Purchased an Emancipation Engraving." *Lincoln Herald* 83 (Spring 1981): 617-620.

5209. Howard, Victor B. "Lincoln Slave Policy in Kentucky: A Study of Pragmatic Strategy." *Kentucky Historical Society Record* 80 (Summer 1982): 281-308.

5210. Hubert, James H. *The Life of Abraham Lincoln, Its Significance to Negroes and Jews.* New York: W. Malliet and Co., 1939.

5211. Hyman, Harold M. "Lincoln and Equal Rights for Negroes: The Irrelevancy of the 'Wadsworth Letter.'" *Civil War History* 12 (September 1966): 258-266.

5212. Johnson, Ludwell H. "Lincoln and Equal Rights: A Reply." *Civil War History* 13 (March 1967): 66-73.

5213. Johnson, Ludwell H. "Lincoln and Equal Rights: The Authenticity of the Wadsworth Letter." *Journal of Southern History* 32 (February 1966): 83-87.

5214. Krug, Mark M. "Lincoln, the Republican Party, and the Emancipation Proclamation." *History Teacher* 7 (November 1973): 48-61.

5215. Leacock, Stephen B. *Lincoln Frees the Slaves.* New York: Putnam, 1934.

5216. Leland, Charles G. *Abraham Lincoln and the Abolition of Slavery in the U.S.* New York: Putnam, 1879.

5217. Lewis, Joseph. *Lincoln's Kalamazoo Address against Extending Slavery, Also His Life by Joseph J. Lewis, Both Annotated by Thomas I. Starr.* Detroit, MI: Detroit Fine Book Circle, 1941.

5218. Lindsey, David. "'The Only Substantial Difference': Lincoln and the Negro." *Lincoln Herald* 68 (Summer 1966): 95-96.

5219. Lockwood, Theodore D. "Garrison and Lincoln the Abolitionist." *Abraham Lincoln Quarterly* 6 (December 1950): 199-226.

5220. McIntyre, Duncan T. "Lincoln and the Matson Slave Case." *Illinois Law Review* 1 (January 1907): 386-391.

5221. Marr, William L. "On the Economics of Lincoln's Proposal for Compensated Emancipation." *American Journal of Economics and Sociology* 35 (January 1976): 105-107.

5222. Neely, Mark E., Jr. "Abraham Lincoln and Black Colonization: Benjamin Butler's Spurious Testimony." *Civil War History* 25 (March 1979): 77-83.

5223. Nelson, Paul D. "From Intolerance to Moderation: The Evolution of Abraham Lincoln's Racial Views." *Kentucky Historical Society Register* 72 (January 1974): 1-9.

5224. Newbold, Catherine. "The Antislavery Background of the Principal State Department Appointees in the Lincoln Administration." Ph.D. dissertation, University of Michigan, 1962.

5225. Oates, Stephen B. "The Man of Our Redemption: Abraham Lincoln and the Emancipation of the Slaves." *Presidential Studies Quarterly* 9 (Winter 1979): 15-24.

5226. Oates, Stephen B. "Toward a New Birth of Freedom: Abraham Lincoln and Reconstruction, 1854-1865." *Lincoln Herald* 82 (Spring 1980): 287-296.

5227. Pennypacker, Isaac R. "Washington and Lincoln, The Father and the Saviour of the Country." *Pennsylvania Magazine of History* 56 (1932): 97-109.

5228. Pickett, William P. *Negro Problem: Abraham Lincoln's Solution.* New York: Putnam, 1909.

5229. Pillsbury, Albert E. *Lincoln and Slavery.* Boston: Houghton Mifflin, 1913.

5230. Planck, Gary R. "'Deep Pool of

Black Silence': Abraham Lincoln, Tragic Hero." *Lincoln Herald* 78 (Summer 1976): 62-65.

5231. Quarles, Benjamin. *Lincoln and the Negro.* New York: Oxford University Press, 1962.

5232. Rice, H. LaMarr. "Lincoln and Freedom: And How Free Is Freedom?" *Lincoln Herald* 69 (Spring 1967): 6-8.

5233. Rietveld, Ronald D. "Lincoln and the Politics of Morality." *Illinois State Historical Society Journal* 68 (February 1975): 27-43.

5234. Schluter, Herman. *Lincoln, Labor, and Slavery.* New York: Russell and Russell, 1965.

5235. Schweikart, Larry. "The Mormon Connection: Lincoln, the Saints, and the Crisis of Equality." *Western Humanities Review* 34 (Winter 1980): 1-22.

5236. Silverman, Jason H. " 'In Isles Beyond the Main': Abraham Lincoln's Philosophy on Black Colonization." *Lincoln Herald* 80 (Fall 1978): 115-122.

5237. Sisson, Edward O. "Lincoln's Lost Cause." *Open Court* 48 (January 1934): 1-15.

5238. Smyth, Clifford. *Abraham Lincoln, The Great Emancipator, Who Preserved the Union.* New York: Funk and Wagnalls, 1931.

5239. Sprague, Dean. *Freedom under Lincoln.* Boston: Houghton Mifflin, 1965.

5240. Townsend, William H. *Lincoln and the Bluegrass: Slavery and Civil War in Kentucky.* Lexington: University of Kentucky Press, 1955.

5241. Warren, Louis A. *The Slavery Atmosphere of Lincoln's Youth.* Fort Wayne, IN: Lincolniana Publishers, 1933.

5242. White, Elliott. "The Humility Complex in American Politics: Was Lincoln Created Equal?" *Publius* 1 (1971): 89-114.

5243. Wilbur, Henry W. *President Lincoln's Attitude towards Slavery and Emancipation, With a Review of Events before and since the Civil War.* Philadelphia: W. H. Jenkins, 1914.

5244. Wilson, Rufus R. "President Lincoln and Emancipation." *Lincoln Herald* 51 (June 1949): 43-46.

5245. Withers, Henry. *Abraham Lincoln, A Champion of Freedom.* London: Religious Tract Society, 1927.

5246. Wright, John S. *Lincoln and the Politics of Slavery.* Reno: University of Nevada Press, 1970.

5247. Zoellner, Robert H. "Negro Colonization: The Climate of Opinion Surrounding Lincoln, 1860-1865." *Mid-America* 42 (July 1960): 131-150.

Writings

5248. Adam, G. Mercer, ed. *Speeches of Abraham Lincoln, Including Inaugurals and Proclamations.* New York: Burt, 1906.

5249. "Americana." *Manuscripts* 10 (Spring 1958): 32-34.

5250. Angle, Paul M. "The Record of a Friendship: A Series of Letters from Lincoln to Henry E. Dummer." *Illinois State Historical Society Journal* 31 (June 1938): 125-137.

5251. Angle, Paul M., ed. *The Lincoln Reader.* New Brunswick, NJ: Rutgers University Press, 1947.

5252. Angle, Paul M., comp. *New Letters and Papers of Lincoln.* Boston: Houghton Mifflin, 1930.

5253. Appleman, Roy E., ed. *Abraham Lincoln, From His Own Words and Contemporary Accounts.* Rev. ed. Washington,

DC: U.S. Government Printing Office, 1956.

5254. Avary, Myrta L. "A Lincoln Souvenir in the South: A Letter from Abraham Lincoln to Alexander H. Stephens, Which Hangs on the Wall of a Southern Home." *Century Magazine* 73 (February 1907): 506-508.

5255. Baber, Adin. *Abraham Lincoln with Compass and Chain: Surveying Career as Seen in His Notes and Maps, and with an Account of the Hanks Family Cousins, Makers of Fine Surveying and Mathematical Instruments.* Kansas, IL: The Author, 1968.

5256. Baer, Emily A. "Words and Deeds: Lincoln as Literary Artist, A Historiographical Survey." *Lincoln Herald* 83 (Fall 1981): 695-704.

5257. Barondess, Benjamin. *Three Lincoln Masterpieces: Cooper Institute Speech, Gettysburg Address, Second Inaugural.* Charleston: Education Foundation of West Virginia, 1954.

5258. Barrett, Joseph H. *Life of Abraham Lincoln (of Illinois), With a Condensed View of His Most Important Speeches, Also a Sketch of the Life of Hannibal Hamlin (of Maine).* Cincinnati, OH: Moore, Wilstach, Keys, 1860.

5259. Barrett, Joseph H. *Life of Abraham Lincoln, Presenting His Early History, Political Career, and Speeches in and out of Congress, Also a General View of His Policy as President of the United States, With His Messages, Proclamations, Letters, etc., and a Concise History of the War.* Cincinnati, OH: Moore, Walstach and Baldwin, 1864.

5260. Basler, Roy P., ed. *Abraham Lincoln: His Speeches and Writings.* Cleveland, OH: World Publishing, 1946.

5261. Basler, Roy P. "Abraham Lincoln's Rhetoric." *American Literature* 11 (January 1939-1940): 167-182.

5262. Berry, Mildred F. "Abraham Lincoln: His Development in the Skills of the Platform." In Speech Association of America, *A History and Criticism of American Public Address*, 2d ed., edited by William N. Brigance, 828-858. New York: Russell and Russell, 1960.

5263. Berry, Mildred F. "Lincoln — The Speaker." *Quarterly Journal of Speech* 17 (February 1931): 25-40; (April 1931): 177-190.

5264. Blair, Francis G. "An Address at the Patriotic Pilgrimage Made to the Lincoln Memorial, July 4, 1924." *National Educational Association Proceedings* 62 (June/July 1924): 225-232.

5265. Borit, Gabor S. "Another New Lincoln Text? Some Thoughts Concerning an Outrageous Suggestion about Abraham Lincoln, Corporation Lawyer." *Lincoln Herald* 77 (Spring 1975): 27-32.

5266. Borit, Gabor S. "A New Lincoln Text: An Opinion on an Illinois Tax." *Lincoln Herald* 75 (Winter 1973): 152-157.

5267. Bridges, Roger D., ed. "Lincolniana: Three Letters from a Lincoln Law Student." *Illinois State Historical Society Journal* 66 (Spring 1973): 79-87.

5268. Brockett, Linus P. *The Life and Times of Abraham Lincoln, Sixteenth President of the United States, Including His Speeches, Messages, Inaugurals, Proclamations, etc.* Philadelphia: Bradley, 1865.

5269. Collier, Bonnie B. "A New Lincoln Letter." *Yale University Library Gazette* 48 (January 1974): 192-194.

5270. Condict, Alden S., and Rhea Barzilay. "A Rare Lincoln Letter." *Autograph Collector's Journal* 1 (January 1949): 14-15.

5271. Corson, Oscar T. *Abraham Lincoln: His Words and Deeds.* Dansville, NY: F. A. Owen Publishing Co., 1927.

5272. Cushman, Esther C. "The McLellan Lincoln Collection at Brown University." *American Collector* 4 (September 1927): 199-205.

5273. "The Discovery: A New Storehouse of Lincoln Material." *Atlantic Monthly* 142 (December 1928): 834-837.

5274. Draper, Andrew S. "Lincoln in His Writings." In his *Addresses and Papers, 1911-1912,* 39-46. Albany: State of New York Education Department, 1912.

5275. East, Ernest E., ed. "A Newly Discovered Speech of Lincoln, Delivered at Bloomington, September 26, 1854." *Illinois State Historical Society Journal* 28 (April 1935): 65-77.

5276. Eisendrath, Joseph L., Jr. "A Lincoln Letter Riddle." *Manuscripts* 10 (Spring 1958): 53-57, 68.

5277. Fehrenbacher, Don E., ed. *Abraham Lincoln: A Documentary Portrait through His Speeches and Writings.* Palo Alto, CA: Stanford University Press, 1964.

5278. Fehrenbacher, Don E. "Lincoln's Lost Love Letters." *American Heritage* 32 (February 1981): 70-80.

5279. Findley, Paul. "A Lincoln Speech to Illinois General Assembly." *Lincoln Herald* 69 (Summer 1967): 51-52.

5280. Ford, Worthington C. "Forged Lincoln Letters." *Massachusetts Historical Society Proceedings* 61 (May 1928): 183-195.

5281. Fried, Albert, and Gerald E. Stern, eds. *The Essential Lincoln, Selected Writings.* New York: Collier Books, 1962.

5282. Geary, James W. "Another Lost Lincoln Letter: The President as Pragmatist or Humanitarian?" *Lincoln Herald* 76 (Fall 1974): 149-151.

5283. George, Joseph, Jr. "The Lincoln Writings of Charles P. T. Chiniquy." *Illinois State Historical Society Journal* 69 (February 1976): 17-25.

5284. Gienapp, William E. "Lincolniana: The 1856 Election: An Unpublished Lincoln Letter." *Illinois State Historical Society Journal* 70 (February 1977): 18-21.

5285. Gross, Anthony, ed. *Lincoln's Own Stories.* New York: Harper and Row, 1912.

5286. Gunn, John W. *The Humor and Wisdom of Abraham Lincoln.* Girard, KS: Haldeman-Julius, 1923.

5287. Hannah, Mary E. "A Comparative Study of the Uses of Humor in Selected Political Speeches of Abraham Lincoln and Adlai E. Stevenson II." Ph.D. dissertation, University of Illinois, 1967.

5288. Harlan, Edgar R. "The Lincoln Mass of American People." *Annals of Iowa* 17 (April 1931): 563-577.

5289. Henry, Anne H. "A. Lincoln: Notes on Small Cards." *Manuscripts* 36 (Winter 1984): 5-16.

5290. Herriott, Frank I. "The Premises and Significance of Abraham Lincoln's Letter to Theodore Canisius." *Deutsch-Amerikanische Geschichtsblatter* 15 (1915): 181-254.

5291. Howard, John R., comp. . . . *Patriotic Nuggets: Franklin, Washington, Jefferson, Webster, Lincoln, Beecher.* New York: Fords, Howard and Hulbert, 1899.

5292. Howells, William D., and John L. Hayes. *Lives and Speeches of Abraham Lincoln and Hannibal Hamlin.* Columbus, OH: Follett, Foster, 1860.

5293. Hunt, Samuel F. "Abraham Lincoln." In his *Orations and Historical Addresses,* 370-387. Cincinnati, OH: R. Clarke Co., 1908.

5294. Iglehart, John E. "Correspondence between Lincoln Historians and This Society." *Southwestern Indiana Historical So-*

ciety *Proceedings* 18 (February 28, 1923): 63-88.

5295. Kansas State Historical Society. "When Abraham Lincoln Spoke in Leavenworth in 1859." *Kansas Historical Quarterly* 20 (August 1953): 530-536.

5296. Kincaid, Robert L. "Abraham Lincoln: The Speaker." *Southern Speech Journal* 16 (May 1951): 241-250.

5297. Kranz, Henry B., ed. *Abraham Lincoln: A New Portrait*. New York: Putnam, 1959.

5298. Lapsley, Arthur B., ed. *The Writings of Abraham Lincoln*. 8 vols. New York: Putnam, 1905-1906.

5299. Leff, Michael C., and Gerald P. Mohrmann. "Lincoln at Cooper Union: A Rhetorical Analysis of the Text." *Quarterly Journal of Speech* 60 (October 1974): 346-358.

5300. Lewis, Gene D., ed. "Lincoln's Cincinnati Speech of 1854." *Cincinnati Historical Society Bulletin* 23 (July 1965): 147-178.

5301. Lincoln, Abraham. *Abraham Lincoln: An Autobiographical Narrative*. Edited by Ralph G. Newman. Lincoln, IL: Lincoln College, 1971.

5302. Lincoln, Abraham. *Abraham Lincoln, His Autobiographical Writings Now Brought Together for the First Time*. New Brunswick, NJ: Rutgers University Press, 1948.

5303. Lincoln, Abraham. *Abraham Lincoln: His Story in His Own Words*. Edited by Ralph G. Newman. Garden City, NY: Doubleday, 1975.

5304. Lincoln, Abraham. *Abraham Lincoln: Selected Speeches, Messages, and Letters*. Edited by Harry Williams. New York: Rinehart, 1957.

5305. Lincoln, Abraham. *Abraham Lincoln's Speech at Peoria, Illinois in Reply to Senator Douglas: Seven Numbers of the Illinois Daily Journal, Springfield, October 21, 23-28, 1854*. Peoria, IL: E. J. Jacob, 1952.

5306. Lincoln, Abraham. *Abraham Lincoln's Speeches*. Compiled by L. E. Chittenden. New York: Dodd, Mead, 1923.

5307. Lincoln, Abraham. *Abraham Lincoln's Speeches and Letters, 1832-1865*. Rev. ed. Edited by Paul M. Angle. New York: Dutton, 1957.

5308. Lincoln, Abraham. *Abraham Lincoln's Stories and Speeches*. Chicago: Rhodes and McClure, 1898.

5309. Lincoln, Abraham. *Anecdotes of Abraham Lincoln*. Edited by J. B. McClure. Chicago: Rhodes and McClure, 1889.

5310. Lincoln, Abraham. *An Autobiography of Abraham Lincoln, Consisting of the Personal Portions of His Letters, Speeches, and Conversations*. Compiled by Nathaniel W. Stephenson. Indianapolis, IN: Bobbs-Merrill, 1926.

5311. Lincoln, Abraham. *Collected Works*. 9 vols. Edited by Ray P. Basler. New Brunswick, NJ: Rutgers University Press, 1953-1955.

5312. Lincoln, Abraham. *Complete Works*. 2 vols. Rev. ed. Edited by John G. Nicolay and John Hay. New York: Tandy-Thomas, 1905.

5313. Lincoln, Abraham. *Conversations with Lincoln*. Edited by Charles M. Segal. New York: Putnam, 1961.

5314. Lincoln, Abraham. *An Evening with Lincoln*. Rochester, NY: Sherwin Cody School of English, 1907.

5315. Lincoln, Abraham. *The Illinois Political Campaign of 1858: A Facsimile of the Printer's Copy and His Debates with Senator Stephen Arnold Douglas*. Washington, DC: Library of Congress, 1958.

5316. Lincoln, Abraham. *In the Name of the People: Speeches and Writings of Lincoln and Douglas in the Ohio Campaign of 1859.* Edited by Harry Jaffa and Robert W. Johannsen. Columbus: Ohio State University Press, 1959.

5317. Lincoln, Abraham. "Letter of Abraham Lincoln to Charles R. Welles." *Illinois State Historical Society Journal* 7 (October 1914): 218-221.

5318. Lincoln, Abraham. "Letter Written by Abraham Lincoln in 1841." *Albany Law Journal* 70 (May 1908): 149-150.

5319. Lincoln, Abraham. *Letters and Addresses of Abraham Lincoln.* New York: Unit, 1907.

5320. Lincoln, Abraham. *Letters and Addresses of Abraham Lincoln.* New York: H. W. Bell, 1903.

5321. Lincoln, Abraham. *The Life and Public Service of General Zachary Taylor, An Address by Abraham Lincoln.* Boston: Houghton Mifflin, 1922.

5322. Lincoln, Abraham. *The Life and Writings of Abraham Lincoln.* Edited by Philip V. D. Stern. New York: Modern Library, 1942.

5323. Lincoln, Abraham. *Lincoln and the New York Herald: Unpublished Letters of Abraham Lincoln from the Collection of Judd Stewart.* Plainfield, NJ: Privately Printed, 1907.

5324. Lincoln, Abraham. "A Lincoln Anthology in Brief." Collected by Jacques Barzun. *American Scholar* 28 (Spring 1955): 166-182.

5325. Lincoln, Abraham. *Lincoln, His Works and His World.* Fort Atkinson, WI: Home Library Publishing Co., 1976.

5326. Lincoln, Abraham. *Lincoln Ideals, His Personality and Principles Reflected in His Own Words.* Washington, DC: Lincoln Sesquicentennial Commission, 1959.

5327. Lincoln, Abraham. *Lincoln Letters.* Norwood, MA: Plimpton Press, 1913.

5328. Lincoln, Abraham. *Lincoln Letters Hitherto Unpublished in the Library of Brown University and Other Providence Libraries.* Providence, RI: Brown University Press, 1927.

5329. Lincoln, Abraham. "A Lincoln Manuscript in Medford." Edited by Gladys N. Hoover. *Medford Historical Register* 41 (1938): 24-27.

5330. Lincoln, Abraham. *Lincoln Papers.* 2 vols. Garden City, NY: Doubleday, 1948.

5331. Lincoln, Abraham. *Lincoln Speaks.* Chicago: Regnery, 1963.

5332. Lincoln, Abraham. *The Lincoln Treasury.* Compiled by Caroline T. Harnsberger. Chicago: Wilcox and Follett, 1950.

5333. Lincoln, Abraham. *Lincoln's Last Speech in Springfield.* Chicago: University of Chicago Press, 1925.

5334. Lincoln, Abraham. *The Literary Works of Abraham Lincoln.* Edited by David D. Anderson. Columbus, OH: Merrill, 1970.

5335. Lincoln, Abraham. *The Literary Works of Abraham Lincoln.* Edited by Carl Van Doren. New York: Heritage Press, 1942.

5336. Lincoln, Abraham. *The Living Lincoln: The Man, His Mind, His Times, and the War He Fought, Reconstructed from His Own Writings.* Edited by Paul M. Angle and Earl S. Miers. New Brunswick, NJ: Rutgers University Press, 1955.

5337. Lincoln, Abraham. *The Living Words of Abraham Lincoln: Selected Writings of a Great President.* Edited by Edward Lewis and Jack Belck. Kansas City, MO: Hallmark, 1967.

5338. Lincoln, Abraham. *The Martyr's*

Monument. New York: Amnews Co., 1865.

5339. Lincoln, Abraham. *Mister Lincoln's Funny Bone*. New York: Howell, Soskin, 1942.

5340. Lincoln, Abraham. "New Letters Bare Lincoln Politics." *Manuscripts* 7 (Spring 1955): 184-186.

5341. Lincoln, Abraham. *Note Speeches of Abraham Lincoln*. New York: Moffat, Yard, 1911.

5342. Lincoln, Abraham. *The Philosophy of Abraham Lincoln in His Own Words*. Compiled by William E. Baringer. Indian Hills, CO: Falcon's Wing Press, 1959.

5343. Lincoln, Abraham. *Political Debates between Abraham Lincoln and Stephen A. Douglas*. Cleveland, OH: Burrows Brothers, 1894.

5344. Lincoln, Abraham. *The President's Words*. Boston: Walker, Fuller, 1865.

5345. Lincoln, Abraham. *Quotations from Abraham Lincoln*. Edited by Ralph Y. McGinnis. Chicago: Nelson-Hall, 1977.

5346. Lincoln, Abraham. *Readings from Lincoln*. New York: Holt, 1927.

5347. Lincoln, Abraham. *Selections from Abraham Lincoln*. New York: American Book Co., 1911.

5348. Lincoln, Abraham. *Selections from Lincoln*. New York: Scribner's, 1927.

5349. Lincoln, Abraham. *The Speeches of Abraham Lincoln*. New York: Chesterfield Society, 1908.

5350. Lincoln, Abraham. *A Strange Affair*. Edited by Roger W. Barrett. Peoria, IL: E. J. Jacob, 1933.

5351. Lincoln, Abraham. *The Table Talk of Abraham Lincoln*. Edited by William Stoddard. New York: Stokes, 1894.

5352. Lincoln, Abraham. *Treasury of Lincoln Quotations*. Edited by F. Kerner. Garden City, NY: Doubleday, 1965.

5353. Lincoln, Abraham. *Uncollected Works of Abraham Lincoln*. Compiled by R. Rockwell Wilson. New York: Primavera Press, 1947.

5354. Lincoln, Abraham. "Unpublished Letters: Contributed by Major William H. Lambert." *Pennsylvania Magazine of History* 27 (1903): 60-62.

5355. Lincoln, Abraham. *Wisdom and Wit*. Mt. Vernon, NY: Peter Pauper Press, 1967.

5356. Lincoln, Abraham. *Wit and Wisdom of Abraham Lincoln*. Edited by H. J. Lang. Cleveland, OH: World Publishing, 1965.

5357. Lincoln, Abraham. *Words of Lincoln*. Compiled by Osborn H. Oldroyd. Washington, DC: O. H. Oldroyd, 1895.

5358. Lincoln, Abraham. *The Works of Abraham Lincoln*. . . . 8 vols. Edited by John H. Clifford and Marion M. Miller. New York: University Society, 1908.

5359. Lincoln, Abraham. *The Writings of Abraham Lincoln*. 8 vols. Edited by A. B. Lapsley. New York: Putnam, 1905-1906.

5360. "Lincoln's 1859 Address at Milwaukee." *Wisconsin Magazine of History* 10 (March 1927): 243-258.

5361. Mearns, David C. *The Lincoln Papers: The Story of the Collection, With Selections to July 4, 1861*. 2 vols. Garden City, NY: Doubleday, 1948.

5362. "Memorable Words of Abraham Lincoln." *Independent* 66 (February 11, 1909): 315-318.

5363. "Misdated Lincoln Letters and Speeches." *Abraham Lincoln Association Bulletin* 24 (September 1931): 7-9.

5364. Nevins, Allan. "Hiram Barney and Lincoln: Three Unpublished Documents."

Huntington Library Quarterly 26 (November 1962): 1-10.

5365. Newman, Ralph G., ed. *Lincoln for the Ages*. New York: Pyramid, 1964.

5366. Nicolay, Helen. "The Writing of Abraham Lincoln: A History." *Illinois State Historical Society Journal* 42 (September 1949): 259-271.

5367. Norris, O. O. "Some Lincoln Anecdotes." *American Schoolmaster* 14 (January 1921): 19-27.

5368. Notaro, Carmen A. "Lincoln to Kasson: A New Letter." *Lincoln Herald* 69 (Summer 1967): 3-4.

5369. Oldys, Henry. "An Unpublished Lincoln Letter." *Independent* 66 (February 11, 1909): 296-300.

5370. Onstott, R. J. "Lincoln and Ann Rutledge: Letter of R. J. Onstott." *Indiana Magazine of History* 32 (March 1936): 66-67.

5371. Parsons, Frank. "Lincoln's Message to Young Men." *Arena* 39 (May 1908): 569-572.

5372. Paulmier, Hilah, ed. *Abe Lincoln: An Anthology*. New York: Knopf, 1953.

5373. Pearson, Charles W. "Lincoln." In his *Literary and Biographical Essays*, 245-260. Boston: Sherman, French, 1908.

5374. Phifer, Gregg. "Lincoln and Johnson as Speakers." *Lincoln Herald* 53 (Fall 1951): 28-34.

5375. Procter, Addison G. *Lincoln and the Convention of 1860: An Address before the Chicago Historical Society, April 4, 1918*. Chicago: Chicago Historical Society, 1918.

5376. Richards, John T. "Abraham Lincoln at the Bar of Illinois: An Address Delivered before the Chicago Bar Association, February 11, 1909." *Chicago Legal News* 41 (February 20, 1909): 237-238.

5377. Richardson, Guy. *My Abraham Lincoln, Radio and Other Addresses*. Boston: Baker and Taylor, 1937.

5378. Schauffler, Robert H. *Lincoln's Yarns and Sayings*. Grand Rapids, MI: Bengal Press, 1980.

5379. Schauffler, Robert H., ed. *Lincoln's Birthday: A Comprehensive View of Lincoln as Given in the Most Noteworthy Essays, Orations, and Poems, In Fiction and in Lincoln's Own Writings*. New York: Moffat, 1909.

5380. Scott, Milton R. *Supposed Diary of President Lincoln from the Repeal of the Missouri Compromise in 1854 until April 14, 1865*. Newark, OH: Heer Printing Co., 1913.

5381. Selby, Paul. *Anecdotal Lincoln*. Chicago: Thompson and Thomas, 1900.

5382. Selby, Paul. *The Life, Stories, and Speeches of Abraham Lincoln*. Chicago: G. M. Hill Co., 1900.

5383. Shaw, Archer H., ed. *The Lincoln Encyclopedia: The Spoken and Written Words of A. Lincoln, Arranged for Ready Reference*. New York: Macmillan, 1950.

5384. Stein, Max. *Abe Lincoln's Jokes: Wit and Humor, History, Chronology*. Chicago: Stein Publishing House, 1943.

5385. Strickler, Joe. *Abraham Lincoln Speaks: An Appreciation*. DuQuoin, IL: Bierman Printing Service, 1931.

5386. Strozier, Charles B. "Lincoln's Life Preserver." *American Heritage* 33 (February/March 1982): 106-108.

5387. Taussig, Frank W. "The Lincoln Tariff Myth Finally Disposed Of." *Quarterly Journal of Economics* 35 (May 1921): 500.

5388. Tracy, Gilbert A., comp. *Uncollected Letters of Abraham Lincoln, Now First Brought Together by Gilbert A. Tracy*. Boston: Houghton Mifflin, 1917.

5389. Vose, Reuben. *The Life and*

Speeches of Abraham Lincoln, and Hannibal Hamlin. Fort Wayne, IN: Lincoln National Life Foundation, 1938.

5390. Williams, Henry L., comp. *Lincolnics: Familiar Sayings of Abraham Lincoln.* New York: Putnam, 1906.

5391. Wills, John W. "Abraham Lincoln's Speech Textbooks." *Southern Speech Communication Journal* 27 (Spring 1962): 220-225.

5392. Winn, Ralph B., ed. *A Concise Lincoln Dictionary: Thoughts and Statements.* New York: Philosophical Library, 1959.

5393. Wright, Marcia. "The Growth of the Abraham Lincoln Papers." *Library of Congress Quarterly Journal of Current Acquisitions* 18 (November 1960): 5-9.

5394. Wright-Davis, Mary, comp. *The Book of Lincoln.* New York: Doran, 1919.

5395. Yzenbaard, John H. "An Apology to Edward Mendel: The Original of Lincoln's Letter Found in Chicago." *Chicago History* 8 (1979): 78-79.

5396. Zall, Paul M. *Abe Lincoln Laughing: Humorous Anecdotes from Original Sources by and about Abraham Lincoln.* Berkeley: University of California Press, 1982.

5397. Zinsmeister, Robert, Jr. " 'The Coming Rude Storms' of Lincoln Writings: William H. Herndon and the Lincoln Legend." *Illinois State Historical Society Journal* 71 (February 1978): 66-70.

5398. Zinsmeister, Robert, Jr. " 'Everybody Likes to Shake Hands with Him': Letters of Elbridge Atwood." *Illinois State Historical Society Journal* 72 (May 1979): 139-142.

Andrew Johnson

Biographies

5399. Bowers, Claude G. *The Tragic Era: Revolution after Lincoln.* Boston: Houghton Mifflin, 1929.

5400. Brabson, Fay W. *Andrew Johnson: A Life in Pursuit of the Right Course, 1808-1875.* Durham, NC: Seeman Printery, 1972.

5401. Crane, William D. *Andrew Johnson, Tailor from Tennessee.* New York: Dodd, Mead, 1968.

5402. Foster, Lillian. *Andrew Johnson, President of the United States: His Life and Speeches....* New York: Richardson, 1866.

5403. Jones, James S. *Life of Andrew Johnson, Seventeenth President of the United States.* Greenville, TN: East Tennessee Publishing Co., 1902.

5404. McKitrick, Eric L., comp. *Andrew Johnson: A Profile.* New York: Hill and Wang, 1969.

5405. Milton, George F. *The Age of Hate: Andrew Johnson and the Radicals.* New York: Coward-McCann, 1930.

5406. Notaro, Carmen A. "History of the Biographic Treatment of Andrew Johnson in the Twentieth Century." *Tennessee Historical Quarterly* 24 (Summer 1965): 143-156.

5407. Rayner, Kenneth. *Life and Times of Andrew Johnson, Seventeenth President of the United States.* New York: Appleton, 1866.

5408. Reece, Brazilla C. *The Courageous Commoner: A Biography of Andrew Johnson.* Charleston, WV: Education Foundation, 1962.

5409. Savage, John. *The Life and Public Services of Andrew Johnson, Seventeenth President of the United States ... With an Accurate Portrait on Steel by Ritchie and Other Illustrations.* New York: Derby, Miller, 1866.

5410. Severn, William. *In Lincoln's Footsteps: The Life of Andrew Johnson.* New York: I. Washburn, 1966.

5411. Steele, Robert V. P. *The First President Johnson: The Three Lives of the Seventeenth President of the United States of America.* New York: Morrow, 1968.

5412. Stryker, Lloyd P. *Andrew Johnson, A Study in Courage.* New York: Macmillan, 1930.

5413. Winston, Robert W. *Andrew Johnson, Plebeian and Patriot.* New York: Holt, 1928.

Private Life

5414. Abernethy, Thomas P. *From Frontier to Plantation in Tennessee.* Chapel

Hill: University of North Carolina Press, 1932.

5415. Bentley, Hubert B. "Andrew Johnson and the Tennessee State Penitentiary, 1853-1857." *East Tennessee Historical Society's Publications* 47 (1975): 28-45.

5416. Castel, Albert. "Andrew Johnson — A Profile." *American History Illustrated* 4 (October 1969): 4-11, 47.

5417. Castel, Albert. "Andrew Johnson: His Historiographical Rise and Fall." *Mid-America* 45 (July 1963): 175-184.

5418. Clark, Blanche H. *The Tennessee Yeoman, 1840-1860.* Nashville, TN: Vanderbilt University Press, 1942.

5419. Connally, Ernest A. "The Andrew Johnson Homestead at Greenville, Tennessee." *East Tennessee Historical Society's Publications* 29 (1957): 118-140.

5420. Cox, John H., and LaWanda C. Cox. "Andrew Johnson and His Ghost Writers." *Mississippi Valley Historical Review* 48 (December 1961): 460-479.

5421. DeWitt, John H., Jr. "Andrew Johnson and the Hermit." *Tennessee Historical Quarterly* 27 (Spring 1968): 50-61.

5422. Dunning, William A. "A Little More Light on Andrew Johnson." *Massachusetts Historical Society Proceedings* 19 (November 1906): 395-405.

5423. Dunning, William A. "More Light on Andrew Johnson." *American Historical Review* 11 (April 1906): 574-594.

5424. Freshly, Dwight L. "Vacillation and Venom: Andrew Johnson vs. William L. Yancey." *Southern Speech Communication Journal* 28 (Winter 1962): 98-108.

5425. Hager, Paul A. "Andrew Johnson of East Tennessee." Ph.D. dissertation, Johns Hopkins University, 1975.

5426. Harrison, James T. "A Mississippian's Appraisal of Andrew Johnson: Letters of James T. Harrison, December 1865." *Journal of Mississippi History* 17 (January 1955): 43-48.

5427. Haskins, Ralph W. "Internecine Strife in Tennessee: Andrew Johnson versus Parson Brownlow." *Tennessee Historical Quarterly* 24 (Winter 1965): 321-340.

5428. Hays, Willard. "Andrew Johnson's Reputation." *East Tennessee Historical Society's Publications* 31 (1959): 1-21; 32 (1960): 18-50.

5429. Lawing, Hugh A. "Andrew Johnson National Monument." *Tennessee Historical Quarterly* 20 (June 1961): 103-119.

5430. Milton, George F. "Andrew Johnson — Man of Courage." *East Tennessee Historical Society's Publications* 3 (1931): 23-34.

5431. Scovel, James M. "Personal Recollections of President Andrew Johnson." *National Magazine* 18 (April 1903): 111-119.

5432. Turner, Harriot S. "Recollections of Andrew Johnson." *Harper's* 120 (January 1910): 168-176.

5433. U.S. National Park Service. *Andrew Johnson National Monument.* Washington, DC: U.S. Government Printing Office, 1946.

5434. Wagstaff, Thomas. "Andrew Johnson and the National Union Movement, 1865-1866." Ph.D. dissertation, University of Wisconsin, 1967.

Public Career

5435. "Andrew Johnson 'Swings' through Michigan." *Old Northwest* 3 (September 1977): 251-273.

5436. Berwanger, Eugene R. "Three against Johnson: Colorado Republican Editors React to Reconstruction." *Social*

Science Journal 12 (October 1975-January 1976): 149-158.

5437. Bowen, David W. "Andrew Johnson and the Negro." *East Tennessee Historical Society's Publications* 40 (1968): 28-49.

5438. Bowen, David W. "Andrew Johnson and the Negro." Ph.D. dissertation, University of Tennessee, 1977.

5439. Brownlow, Paul C. "The Northern Protestant Pulpit and Andrew Johnson." *Southern Speech Communication Journal* 39 (Spring 1974): 248-259.

5440. Bumgardner, Edward. *The Life of Edmund G. Ross, The Man Whose Vote Saved the President.* Kansas City, MO: Fielding-Turner Press, 1949.

5441. Caskey, W. M. "First Administration of Governor Andrew Johnson." *East Tennessee Historical Society's Publications* 1 (1929): 43-59.

5442. Caskey, W. M. "The Second Administration of Governor Andrew Johnson." *East Tennessee Historical Society's Publications* 2 (1930): 34-54.

5443. Cimprich, John. "Military Governor Johnson and Tennessee Blacks, 1862-1865." *Tennessee Historical Quarterly* 39 (Winter 1980): 459-470.

5444. Gloneck, James F. "Lincoln, Johnson, and the Baltimore Ticket." *Lincoln Quarterly* 6 (March 1951): 255-271.

5445. Graf, LeRoy P. "Andrew Johnson and the Coming of the War." *Tennessee Historical Quarterly* 19 (September 1960): 208-221.

5446. Hall, Clifton R. *Andrew Johnson, Military Governor of Tennessee.* Princeton, NJ: Princeton University Press, 1916.

5447. Hardison, Edwin T. "In the Toils of War: Andrew Johnson and the Federal Occupation of Tennessee, 1862-1865." Ph.D. dissertation, University of Tennessee, 1981.

5448. Haskins, Ralph W. "Andrew Johnson and the Preservation of the Union." *East Tennessee Historical Society's Publications* 33 (December 1961): 43-60.

5449. Haws, Willard. "Andrew Johnson's Reputation." *East Tennessee Historical Society's Publications* 31 (1959): 1-31.

5450. Locke, David R. *Andy's Trip to the West Together with a Life of Its Hero.* New York: J. C. Haney, 1866.

5451. Marshall, Lynn L. "The Genesis of Grass-Roots Democracy in Kentucky." *Mid-America* 47 (October 1965): 269-287.

5452. Miscamble, William G. "Andrew Johnson and the Election of William G. ('Parson') Brownlow as Governor of Tennessee." *Tennessee Historical Quarterly* 37 (Fall 1978): 308-320.

5453. Mooney, Chase C. *Slavery in Tennessee.* Bloomington: Indiana University Press, 1957.

5454. Nettels, Curtis P. "Andrew Johnson and the South." *South Atlantic Quarterly* 25 (January 1926): 55-64.

5455. Parks, Joseph H. "Memphis under Military Rule." *East Tennessee Historical Society's Publications* 14 (1942): 31-58.

5456. Rable, George C. "Anatomy of a Unionist: Andrew Johnson in the Secession Crisis." *Tennessee Historical Quarterly* 32 (Winter 1973): 332-354.

5457. Riches, William T. M. "The Commoners: Andrew Johnson and Abraham Lincoln to 1861." Ph.D. dissertation, University of Tennessee, 1976.

5458. Robinson, Dan M. "Andrew Johnson on the Dignity of Labor." *Tennessee Historical Quarterly* 23 (March 1964): 80-85.

5459. Russell, Robert. "Andrew Johnson

and the Charleston Convention of 1860." *East Tennessee Historical Society's Publications* 47 (1975): 46-75.

5460. Sharkey, Robert P. *Money, Class, and Party: An Economic Study of the Civil War and Reconstruction.* Baltimore, MD: Johns Hopkins University Press, 1959.

5461. Temple, Oliver P. *East Tennessee and the Civil War.* Cincinnati, OH: R. Clarke Co., 1899.

5462. Wells, Ruth M. "Andrew Johnson: Senator from Tennessee, 1857-1862." Master's thesis, University of Pennsylvania, 1933.

5463. Williams, Harry. "Andrew Johnson as a Member of the Committee on the Conduct of the War." *East Tennessee Historical Society's Publications* 2 (1940): 70-83.

Presidential Years

5464. Albjerg, Marguerite H. "The New York Press and Andrew Johnson." *South Atlantic Quarterly* 26 (October 1927): 404-416.

5465. Andrews, Rena M. "Johnson's Plan of Restoration in Relation to That of Lincoln." *Tennessee Historical Quarterly* 1 (April 1931): 165-181.

5466. "Authors of Presidential Messages." *Nation* 82 (February 1, 1906): 91-92.

5467. Barber, James D. "Adult Identity and Presidential Style: The Rhetorical Emphasis." *Daedalus* 97 (Summer 1968): 938-968.

5468. Baumgardner, James L. "Andrew Johnson and the Patronage." Ph.D. dissertation, University of Tennessee, 1968.

5469. Bayless, R. W. "Peter G. Van Winkle and Waitman T. Willey in the Impeachment Trial of Andrew Johnson." *West Virginia History* 13 (January 1952): 75-89.

5470. Beale, Howard K. *The Critical Year: A Study of Andrew Johnson and the Reconstruction.* New York: Harcourt, Brace, 1930.

5471. Bell, John L., Jr. "Andrew Johnson, National Politics, and Presidential Reconstruction in South Carolina." *South Carolina Historical Magazine* 82 (October 1981): 354-366.

5472. Benedict, Michael L. *The Impeachment and Trial of Andrew Johnson.* New York: Norton, 1973.

5473. Benedict, Michael L. "A New Look at the Impeachment of Andrew Johnson." *Political Science Quarterly* 88 (September 1973): 349-367.

5474. Bentley, Hubert B. *Andrew Johnson, Governor of Tennessee, 1853-1857.* Knoxville: University of Tennessee Press, 1972.

5475. Bridges, Roger D. "John Sherman and the Impeachment of Andrew Johnson." *Ohio History* 82 (Summer/Autumn 1973): 176-191.

5476. Cashdollar, Charles D. "Andrew Johnson and the Philadelphia Election of 1866." *Pennsylvania Magazine of Historical Biography* 92 (July 1968): 365-383.

5477. Castel, Albert. *The Presidency of Andrew Johnson.* Lawrence: Regents Press of Kansas, 1979.

5478. Chadsey, Charles E. "The Struggle between President Johnson and Congress over Reconstruction." Ph.D. dissertation, Columbia University, 1896.

5479. Chapin, Walter T. "Presidential Reconstruction in Texas, 1865-1867." Master's thesis, North Texas State University, 1979.

5480. Cox, LaWanda C., and John H. Cox. *Politics, Principle, and Prejudice,*

1865-1866: Dilemma of Reconstruction America. New York: Harper and Row, 1963.

5481. Davidson, Bill. *President Kennedy Selects Six Brave Presidents.* New York: Harper and Row, 1962.

5482. Dearing, Mary R. "The Role of the G.A.R. in the Constitutional Crisis of 1867-1868." In *The Military in America: From the Colonial Era to the Present,* edited by Peter Karsten, 173-183. New York: Free Press, 1980.

5483. DeWitt, David M. *The Impeachment and Trial of Andrew Johnson, Seventeenth President of the United States: A History.* New York: Macmillan, 1903.

5484. DeWitt, David M. "Vice-President Andrew Johnson." *Southern History Association Papers* 8 (November 1904): 437-442; 9 (January 1905): 1-23; (March 1905): 71-86; (May 1905): 151-159; (July 1905): 213-225.

5485. Dobson, Wayne W. "Some Phases of the Congressional Career of Andrew Johnson." Master's thesis, East Tennessee State University, 1952.

5486. Domer, Thomas. "The Role of George S. Boutwell in the Impeachment and Trial of Andrew Johnson." *New England Quarterly* 49 (December 1976): 596-617.

5487. Donald, David H. *The Politics of Reconstruction, 1863-1867.* Baton Rouge: Louisiana State University Press, 1965.

5488. Donald, David H. "Why They Impeached Andrew Johnson." *American Heritage* 8 (December 1956): 20-25, 102-103.

5489. Dorris, Jonathan T. *Pardon and Amnesty under Lincoln and Johnson: The Restoration of the Confederates to Their Rights and Privileges, 1861-1898.* Chapel Hill: University of North Carolina Press, 1953.

5490. DuBois, William E. B. *Black Reconstruction in America, 1860-1880.* New York: Harcourt, Brace, 1935.

5491. Dunning, William A. *Reconstruction, Political and Economic, 1865-1877.* New York: Harper and Row, 1907.

5492. Foner, Eric, ed. "Andrew Johnson and Reconstruction: A British View." *Journal of Social History* 41 (August 1975): 381-390.

5493. Foster, G. Allen. *Impeached: The President Who Almost Lost His Job.* New York: Criterion Books, 1964.

5494. Frierson, William L. "The Impeachment and Trial of Andrew Johnson." In *Proceedings of the Bar Association of Tennessee . . . 1922,* 125-138. Memphis: Tennessee State Bar Association, 1922.

5495. Gerry, Margarita S., ed. "Andrew Johnson in the White House: Being the Reminiscences of William H. Crook." *Century* 76 (September 1908): 653-669; (October 1908): 863-877.

5496. Gerson, Noel B. *The Trial of Andrew Johnson.* New York, NY: Lodestar Books, 1977.

5497. Gipson, Lawrence H. "The Statesmanship of President Johnson: A Study in the Presidential Reconstruction Policy." *Mississippi Valley Historical Review* 2 (December 1915): 363-383.

5498. Halperin, Bernard S. "Andrew Johnson, the Radicals, and the Negro, 1865-1866." Ph.D. dissertation, Florida State University, 1966.

5499. Hayes, Merwyn A. "The Andrew Johnson Impeachment Trial: A Case Study in Argumentation." Ph.D. dissertation, University of Illinois, 1966.

5500. Howard, Thomas W. "Peter G. Van Winkle's Vote in the Impeachment of President Andrew Johnson: A West Virginian as a Profile in Courage." *West Virginia History* 35 (July 1974): 290-295.

5501. Hughes, David F. "Chief Justice Chase at the Impeachment Trial of Andrew Johnson." *New York State Bar Journal* 41 (April 1969): 218-233.

5502. Hunt, Gaillard, and Benjamin C. Truman. "The Impeachment of Andrew Johnson." *Century Magazine* 85 (January 1913): 421-440.

5503. Hyman, Harold M. "Johnson, Stanton, and Grant: A Reconsideration of the Army's Role in the Events Leading to Impeachment." *American Historical Review* 66 (October 1960): 85-100.

5504. Jones, James S. "Why Judge Black Withdrew from the Trial of President Johnson." *American Historical Magazine and Tennessee Historical Society Quarterly* 7 (July 1902): 244-248.

5505. Kilar, Jeremy W. "Andrew Johnson 'Swings' through Michigan: Community Response to a Presidential Crusade." *Old Northwest Genealogical Quarterly* 3 (September 1977): 251-273.

5506. Kilar, Jeremy W. " 'The Blood-Rugged Issue Is Impeachment or Anarchy': Michigan and the Impeachment and Trial of Andrew Johnson." *Old Northwest Genealogical Quarterly* 6 (Fall 1980): 245-269.

5507. Kurtz, Henry I. "The Impeachment of Andrew Johnson." *History Today* 24 (May 1974): 299-305; (June 1974): 396-405.

5508. Lewis, H. H. Walker. "The Impeachment of Andrew Johnson: A Political Tragedy." *American Bar Association Journal* 40 (January 1954): 15-18, 80-87.

5509. Lomask, Milton. *Andrew Johnson: President on Trial*. New York: Farrar, Straus, 1960.

5510. McDonough, James L., and William T. Alderson, eds. "Republican Politics and the Impeachment of Andrew Johnson." *Tennessee Historical Quarterly* 26 (Summer 1967): 177-183.

5511. McKitrick, Eric L. *Andrew Johnson and Reconstruction*. Chicago: University of Chicago Press, 1960.

5512. Majeske, Penelope K. "Johnson, Stanton, and Grant: A Reconsideration of the Events Leading to the First Reconstruction Act." *Southern Studies* 22 (Winter 1983): 340-350.

5513. Malone, James H. "The Supreme Court Vindicates Andrew Johnson." *Current History* 26 (April 1927): 7-12.

5514. Mantell, Martin E. *Johnson, Grant, and the Politics of Reconstruction*. New York: Columbia University Press, 1973.

5515. Maslowski, Peter. "From Reconciliation to Reconstruction: Lincoln, Johnson, and Tennessee." *Tennessee Historical Quarterly* 42 (Fall 1983): 281-298; (Winter 1983): 343-361.

5516. Middleton, Thomas J. "Andrew Johnson and the Homestead Law." *Sewanee Review* 15 (July 1907): 316-320.

5517. Milton, George F. "Canonization of a Maligned President." *Independent* 121 (September 1, 1928): 200-202.

5518. Moore, William G. "Notes of Colonel W. G. Moore, Private Secretary to President Johnson, 1866-1868." Edited by St. George L. Sioussat. *American Historical Review* 19 (October 1913): 98-132.

5519. Morris, Robert L. "The Lincoln-Johnson Plan for Reconstruction and the Republican Convention of 1864." *Lincoln Herald* 71 (Spring 1969): 33-39.

5520. Mushkat, Jerome. "The Impeachment of Andrew Johnson: A Contemporary View." *New York History* 48 (July 1967): 275-286.

5521. Nash, Howard P., Jr. *Andrew Johnson: Congress and Reconstruction*.

East Brunswick, NJ: Fairleigh Dickinson University Press, 1972.

5522. Nieman, Donald G. "Andrew Johnson, the Freedmen's Bureau, and the Problem of Equal Rights, 1865-1866." *Journal of Southern History* 44 (August 1978): 399-420.

5523. Oder, Broeck N. "Andrew Johnson and the 1866 Illinois Election." *Illinois State Historical Society Journal* 73 (Autumn 1980): 189-200.

5524. Ortiz-Garcia, Angel L. "Andrew Johnson's Veto of the First Reconstruction Act." D.A. dissertation, Carnegie-Mellon University, 1970.

5525. Patton, James W. "Tennessee's Attitude toward the Impeachment and Trial of Andrew Johnson." *East Tennessee Historical Society's Publications* 9 (1937): 65-76.

5526. Perdue, M. Kathleen. "Salmon P. Chase and the Impeachment Trial of Andrew Johnson." *Historian* 27 (November 1964): 75-92.

5527. Perman, Michael. "A President and His Impeachment." *Reviews in American History* 3 (December 1975): 462-466.

5528. Phifer, Gregg. "Andrew Johnson Argues a Case." *Tennessee Historical Quarterly* 11 (June 1952): 148-170.

5529. Phifer, Gregg. "Andrew Johnson Delivers His Argument." *Tennessee Historical Quarterly* 11 (September 1952): 212-234.

5530. Phifer, Gregg. "Andrew Johnson Loses His Battle." *Tennessee Historical Quarterly* 11 (December 1951): 291-328.

5531. Phifer, Gregg. "Andrew Johnson Takes a Trip." *Tennessee Historical Quarterly* 11 (March 1952): 2-23.

5532. Phifer, Gregg. "Andrew Johnson versus the Press in 1866." *East Tennessee Historical Society's Publications* 25 (1953): 3-23.

5533. Phifer, Gregg. "The Last Stand of Presidential Reconstruction: A Rhetorical Study of Andrew Johnson's Swing around the Circle in 1866." Ph.D. dissertation, State University of Louisiana, 1954.

5534. Phifer, Gregg. "Lincoln and Johnson as Speakers." *Lincoln Herald* 53 (Fall 1951): 28-34.

5535. Pierce, Michael D. "Andrew Johnson and the South 1865-1867." Ph.D. dissertation, North Texas State University, 1970.

5536. Rable, George C. "Forces of Darkness, Forces of Light: The Impeachment of Andrew Johnson and the Paranoid Style." *Social Studies* 17 (Summer 1978): 151-173.

5537. Ramage, Burr J. "Andrew Johnson's Administration." *South Atlantic Quarterly* 1 (April 1902): 171-181; (July 1902): 256-264.

5538. Reese, Lee F. "Andrew Johnson: 17th President of the United States." *Daughters of the American Revolution Magazine* 108 (January 1974): 18-20.

5539. Riddleberger, Patrick W. "The 'Radicals' Abandonment of the Negro during Reconstruction." *Journal of Negro History* 45 (April 1960): 88-102.

5540. Roske, Ralph J. "Republican Newspaper Support for the Acquittal of President Johnson." *Tennessee Historical Quarterly* 11 (September 1952): 263-273.

5541. Roske, Ralph J. "The Seven Martyrs?" *American Historical Review* 64 (January 1959): 323-330.

5542. Ross, Edmund G. *History of the Impeachment of Andrew Johnson.* Santa Fe, NM: New Mexican Printing Co., 1896.

5543. Royall, Margaret S. *Andrew John-*

son — *Presidential Scapegoat: A Biographical Re-evaluation*. New York: Exposition Press, 1958.

5544. Russell, J. F. S. "Lincoln's Successor: President Andrew Johnson." *History Today* 4 (September 1954): 618-626.

5545. Russell, Robert G. "Prelude to the Presidency: The Election of Andrew Johnson to the Senate." *Tennessee Historical Quarterly* 26 (Summer 1967): 148-176.

5546. Schoonover, Thomas. "Mexican Affairs and the Impeachment of President Andrew Johnson." *East Tennessee Historical Society's Publications* 46 (1974): 76-93.

5547. Schoonover, Thomas. "The Mexican Minister Describes Andrew Johnson's 'Swing around the Circle.'" *Civil War History* 19 (June 1973): 149-161.

5548. Schouler, James. "President Johnson and Negro Suffrage." *Outlook* 82 (January 13, 1906): 69-73.

5549. Schouler, James. "President Johnson and Posterity." *Bookman* 34 (January 1912): 498-504.

5550. Sefton, James E. *Andrew Johnson and the Uses of Constitutional Power*. Boston: Little, Brown, 1980.

5551. Sefton, James E. "The Impeachment of Andrew Johnson: A Century of Writing." *Civil War History* 14 (June 1968): 120-147.

5552. Shofner, Jerrell H. "Andrew Johnson and the Fernandina Unionists." *Prologue* 10 (Winter 1978): 211-223.

5553. Simon, John Y., and Felix James. "Andrew Johnson and the Freedmen." *Lincoln Herald* 79 (Summer 1977): 71-75.

5554. Sioussat, St. George L. "Andrew Johnson and the Early Phases of the Homestead Bill." *Tennessee Historical Magazine* 6 (July 1920): 14-45.

5555. Smith, Gene. *High Crimes and Misdemeanors: The Impeachment and Trial of Andrew Johnson*. New York: Morrow, 1977.

5556. Sproat, John G. "Blueprint for Radical Reconstruction." *Journal of Southern History* 23 (February 1957): 25-44.

5557. Stampp, Kenneth M. *Andrew Johnson and the Failure of the Agrarian Dream*. Oxford: Clarendon Press, 1962.

5558. Stampp, Kenneth M. *The Era of Reconstruction, 1865-1877*. New York: Vintage Books, 1965.

5559. Stoddard, William O. *Abraham Lincoln and Andrew Johnson*. New York: Stokes, 1888.

5560. Tappan, George L. *Andrew Johnson — Not Guilty*. New York: Comet Press, 1954.

5561. Tracy, John E. "The Impeachment and Trial of Andrew Johnson." *Michigan Alumnus Quarterly Review* 60 (December 1953): 1-11.

5562. Trefousse, Hans L. "The Acquittal of Andrew Johnson and the Decline of the Radicals." *Civil War History* 14 (June 1968): 148-161.

5563. Trefousse, Hans L. "Ben Wade and the Failure of the Impeachment of Johnson." *Bulletin of the Historical and Philosophical Society of Ohio* 18 (October 1960): 240-252.

5564. Trefousse, Hans L. *Impeachment of a President: Andrew Johnson, the Blacks, and Reconstruction*. Knoxville: University of Tennessee Press, 1975.

5565. Trefousse, Hans L. "Impeachment of Andrew Johnson: Presidential Bargains and Acquittal." *Intellect* 103 (October 1974): 61-64.

5566. Trefousse, Hans L. "Lincoln and Johnson." *Topic* 9 (Spring 1965): 63-75.

5567. Weaver, Bill L. "That Brief but Pleasant Kentucky Interlude: Andrew

Johnson's 'Swing around the Circle,' 1866." *Filson Club History Quarterly* 53 (July 1979): 239-249.

5568. Woodward, C. Vann. "That Other Impeachment." *New York Times Magazine* 123 (August 11, 1974): 9, 26-30, 32.

Writings

5569. Graf, LeRoy P. "Editing the Andrew Johnson Papers." *Mississippi Quarterly* 15 (Summer 1962): 113-119.

5570. Johnson, Andrew. *The Impeachment and Trial of Andrew Johnson, President of the United States.* New York: Dover Publications, 1974.

5571. Johnson, Andrew. *Papers of Andrew Johnson.* 5 vols. Edited by LeRoy P. Graf and Ralph W. Haskins. Knoxville: University of Tennessee Press, 1967.

5572. Johnson, Andrew. *Speeches of Andrew Johnson, President of the United States.* Edited by Frank Moore. Boston: Little, Brown, 1865.

5573. Johnson, Andrew. *Trial of Andrew Johnson, President of the United States, Before the Senate of the United States, On Impeachment by the House of Representatives for High Crimes and Misdemeanors.* 3 vols. Washington, DC: U.S. Government Printing Office, 1868.

5574. Schouler, James. "President Johnson's Papers." *Massachusetts Historical Society Proceedings* 20 (October 1906): 427-437.

5575. Smith, Russell M. "The Andrew Johnson Papers." *Library of Congress Quarterly Journal of Current Acquisitions* 17 (November 1959): 13-16.

Ulysses S. Grant

Biographies

5576. Abbott, John S. C. *The Life of General Ulysses S. Grant: Containing a Brief But Faithful Narrative of Those Military and Diplomatic Achievements Which Have Entitled Him to the Confidence and Gratitude of His Countrymen....* Boston: B. B. Russell, 1868.

5577. Allen, Walter. *Ulysses S. Grant.* Boston: Houghton Mifflin, 1901.

5578. Arnold, Matthew. *General Grant, With a Rejoinder by Mark Twain.* Edited by John Y. Simon. Carbondale: Southern Illinois University Press, 1966.

5579. Badeau, Adam. *Grant in Peace, from Appomattox to Mount McGregor: A Personal Memoir.* Hartford, CT: S. S. Scranton, 1887.

5580. Balch, William R. *Life and Public Services of General Grant.* Philadelphia: Etna Publishing Co., 1885.

5581. Barnes, William H. *Lives of General Ulysses S. Grant and Hon. Henry Wilson.* New York: W. H. Barnes, 1872.

5582. Boyd, James P. *Military and Civil Life of Gen. Ulysses S. Grant.* Chicago: P. W. Ziegler, 1885.

5583. Brockett, Linus P. *Grant and Colfax: Their Lives and Services.* New York: Richardson, 1868.

5584. Brooks, Elbridge S. *The True Story of U. S. Grant.* Boston: Lothrop, 1897.

5585. Brooks, William E. *Grant of Appomattox, A Study of the Man.* Indianapolis, IN: Bobbs-Merrill, 1942.

5586. Brown, Emma E. *Life of Ulysses Simpson Grant.* Boston: Lothrop, 1885.

5587. Burr, Frank A. *A New, Original, and Authentic Record of the Life and Deeds of General U. S. Grant.* St. Paul, MN: Empyreal, 1885.

5588. Burton, Alma H. *The Story of Ulysses S. Grant.* New York: Werner School Book Co., 1898.

5589. Carpenter, John A. *Ulysses S. Grant.* New York: Twayne, 1970.

5590. Carpenter, John A. "Ulysses S. Grant: Tarnished Hero." *Topic* 5 (Spring 1965): 76-82.

5591. Chetlain, Augustus L. "Reminiscences of General Grant." *Magazine of History* 5 (March 1907): 155-165; (April 1907): 198-205.

5592. Childs, George W. *Recollections of General Grant.* Philadelphia: Lippincott, 1889.

5593. Conger, Arthur L. *The Rise of U. S. Grant.* New York: Century, 1931.

5594. Cookinham, Henry J. "Ulysses Simpson Grant." *Oneida Historical Society Year Book* 13 (1914): 35-56.

5595. Coolidge, Louis A. *Ulysses S. Grant.* Boston: Houghton Mifflin, 1917.

5596. Coombs, Lovell. *U. S. Grant.* New York: Macmillan, 1915.

5597. Corckell, William. *The Eventful History of Grant and His Wonderful Donkey....* Algonquin, IL: Peoples Publishing Co., 1972.

5598. Crafts, William A. *Life of Ulysses S. Grant: His Boyhood, Campaigns, and Services, Military and Civil.* Boston: Samuel Walker and Co., 1868.

5599. Cross, Nelson. *Life of General Grant, His Political Record, etc.* New York: J. S. Redfield, 1872.

5600. Dana, Charles A. *The Life of Ulysses S. Grant, General of the Armies of the United States.* Springfield, MA: Gurdon Bill and Co., 1868.

5601. Deming, Henry C. *The Life of Ulysses S. Grant, General, United States Army.* Hartford, CT: S. S. Scranton, 1868.

5602. Denison, Charles W. *The Tanner-Boy and How He Became Lieutenant-General.* Boston: Roberts Brothers, 1864.

5603. Dye, John S. *Life and Public Services of Gen. U. S. Grant, The Nation's Choice for President in 1868.* Philadelphia: Samuel Loag, 1868.

5604. Edmonds, Franklin S. *Ulysses S. Grant.* Philadelphia: G. W. Jacobs and Co., 1915.

5605. Frost, Lawrence A. *U. S. Grant Album: A Pictorial Biography of Ulysses S. Grant, From Leather Clerk to the White House.* Seattle: Superior Publishing Co., 1966.

5606. Garland, Hamlin. "General Grant." *Mentor* 8 (July 1, 1920): 1-11.

5607. Garland, Hamlin. *Ulysses S. Grant: His Life and Character.* New York: Macmillan, 1898.

5608. Goldhurst, Richard. *Many Are the Hearts: The Agony and the Triumph of Ulysses S. Grant.* New York: Reader's Digest Press, 1975.

5609. Grant, Jesse R. *In the Days of My Father, General Grant.* New York: Harper and Row, 1925.

5610. Grant, Ulysses S., III. *Ulysses S. Grant: Warrior and Statesman.* New York: Morrow, 1969.

5611. Green, Horace. *General Grant's Last Stand: A Biography.* New York: Scribner's, 1936.

5612. Headley, Joel T. *The Life and Travels of General Grant....* Philadelphia: Hubbard Brothers, 1879.

5613. Headley, Joel T. *The Life of Ulysses S. Grant....* New York: E. B. Treat and Co., 1868.

5614. Headley, Phineas C. *The Hero Boy: Or, The Life and Deeds of Lieut.-Gen. Grant.* New York: Appleton, 1864.

5615. Headley, Phineas C. *The Life and Campaigns of Lieut.-Gen. U. S. Grant, From His Boyhood to the Surrender of Lee.... With Portraits on Steel of Stanton, Grant, and His Generals, and Other Illustrations....* New York: Derby and Miller, 1866.

5616. Headley, Phineas C. *The Life and Deeds of General Ulysses S. Grant.* Boston: B. B. Russell, 1885.

5617. Hill, Frederick T. *On the Trail of Grant and Lee: A Narrative History of the Boyhood and Manhood of Two Great Americans.* New York: Appleton, 1911.

5618. Hobbs, Richard G. *Ulysses Simpson Grant, Man, Soldier, Statesman: A Galena Appreciation.* Galena, IL: Gazette Print, 1940.

5619. Howard, Oliver O. "Ulysses S. Grant." *Century Magazine* 72 (October 1907): 956-960.

5620. Howland, Edward. *Grant as a Soldier and Statesman: Being a Succinct History of His Military and Civil Career.* Hartford, CT: J. B. Bun and Co., 1868.

5621. King, Charles. *The True Ulysses S. Grant.* Philadelphia: Lippincott, 1914.

5622. Larke, Julian K. *General U. S. Grant: His Early Life and Military Career, With a Brief Account of His Presidential Administration and Tour around the World.* New York: W. J. Johnson, 1879.

5623. Lewis, Lloyd. *Captain Sam Grant.* Boston: Little, Brown, 1950.

5624. McClure, James B. *Stories, Sketches, and Speeches of General Grant at Home and Abroad, In Peace and in War.* Chicago: Rhodes and McClure, 1880.

5625. McFeely, William S. *Grant, A Biography.* New York: Norton, 1981.

5626. McMaster, John B. *The Life, Memoirs, Military Career, and Death of General U. S. Grant.* Philadelphia: Barday, 1885.

5627. Mansfield, Edward D. *A Popular and Authentic Life of Ulysses S. Grant.* Cincinnati, OH: R. W. Carroll and Co., 1868.

5628. Marshall, Edward C. *The Ancestry of General Grant and Their Contemporaries.* New York: Sheldon, 1869.

5629. Meyer, Howard N. *Let Us Have Peace: The Story of Ulysses S. Grant.* New York: Collier Books, 1966.

5630. Ogg, Frederic A. "When Grant Came Home: A Remarkable Historical Parallel to the Reception of Ex-President Roosevelt on His Return to America." *Munsey's Magazine* 43 (July 1910): 537-541.

5631. Palmer, Loomis T. *The Life of General U. S. Grant, His Early Life, Military Achievements, and History of His Civil Administration, His Sickness and Death, Together with His Tour around the World.* Chicago: Fairbanks and Palmer, 1885.

5632. Park, Clyde W. *That Grant Boy.* Cincinnati, OH: C. J. Krehbiel Co., 1957.

5633. Phelps, Charles A. *Life and Public Services of Ulysses S. Grant, From His Birth to the Present Time, and a Biographical Sketch of Hon. Henry Wilson, Embellished with a Steel Portrait, and Tour Illustrations From Designs by Hammatt Billings.* Boston: Lee and Shepard, 1872.

5634. Pollard, Josephine. *Our Hero, General U. S. Grant.* New York: McLoughlin, 1885.

5635. Poore, Benjamin P., and Otis H. Tiffany. *Life of U. S. Grant.* Philadelphia: Hubbard Brothers, 1885.

5636. Republican Party. National Committee. *Life and Services of General U. S. Grant.* Washington, DC: Philip and Solomons, 1868.

5637. Richardson, Albert D. *A Personal History of Ulysses S. Grant, Illustrated by Twenty-six Engravings: Eight Facsimiles . . . and Six Maps with a Portrait and Sketch of Schuyler Colfax. . . .* Hartford, CT: American Publishing Co., 1868.

5638. Ringwalt, John L. *Anecdotes of General Ulysses S. Grant.* Philadelphia: Lippincott, 1886.

5639. Sinclair, Robert. *Life of Ulysses S. Grant, President of the U.S. and Commander in Chief of the United States Army.* New York: Norman L. Munro, 1872.

5640. Smith, Nicholas. *Grant, The Man of Mystery.* Milwaukee, WI: Young Churchman Co., 1909.

5641. Smyth, Clifford. *Ulysses S. Grant, Whose Motto Was "Let Us Have Peace."* New York: Funk and Wagnalls, 1931.

5642. Speer, Emory. *Lincoln, Lee, Grant,*

and *Other Biographical Addresses.* New York: Neale, 1909.

5643. Stansfield, F. W. H. *The Life of General U. S. Grant, The General in Chief of the United States Army.* New York: T. R. Dawley, 1864.

5644. Stoddard, William O. *Ulysses S. Grant.* New York: White, Stokes and Allen, 1886.

5645. Swift, John L. *About Grant.* Boston: Lee and Shepard, 1880.

5646. Thayer, William M. *From the Tannery to the White House.* New York: T. Nelson and Sons, 1887.

5647. Todd, Helen. *A Man Named Grant.* Boston: Houghton Mifflin, 1940.

5648. Van Orden, William H. *Life and Military Services of General U. S. Grant.* New York: Street and Smith, 1896.

5649. Wilkin, Jacob W. "Personal Reminiscences of General U. S. Grant." *Illinois State Historical Library Publications* 12 (1908): 131-140.

5650. Willett, Edward. *The Life of Ulysses S. Grant, General, U.S.A. . . .* New York: Beadle and Co., 1885.

5651. Wilson, James G. *General Grant.* New York: Appleton, 1897.

5652. Wilson, James G. *The Life and Public Services of Ulysses Simpson Grant, General of the United States Army, and Twice President of the United States.* New York: Dewitt, 1885.

5653. Wilson, James H. *The Life of Ulysses S. Grant, General of the Armies of the United States.* Springfield, MA: Gurdon Bill, 1868.

5654. Wister, Owen. *Ulysses S. Grant.* Boston: Small, Maynard, 1900.

5655. Woodward, William E. *Meet General Grant.* New York: Liveright, 1928.

5656. Wright, Marcus J. "Personal Recollections of General Grant." *Confederate Veteran* 17 (August 1909): 400-403.

5657. Yates, Richard. "Ulysses S. Grant." *Illinois State Historical Society Journal* 20 (July 1927): 216-236.

Private Life

5658. Bale, Florence G. "Galena's Memories of General Ulysses S. Grant." *Illinois State Historical Society Journal* 21 (October 1928): 409-418.

5659. Bryson, Thomas A. "Walter George Smith and General Grant's Memoirs." *Pennsylvania Magazine of History and Biography* 94 (April 1970): 233-244.

5660. Chang, Richard T. "General Grant's 1879 Visit to Japan." *Monumenta Nipponica* 24 (1969): 373-392.

5661. Chapple, Joseph M. "U. S. Grant —His Life Struggles." *National Magazine* 46 (May 1917): 253-263.

5662. Corbett, Elizabeth. "Ulysses S. Grant and the Stuff of Which He Was Made." *Century Magazine* 116 (June 1928): 188-197.

5663. Corson, Oscar T. "Birth, Boyhood, and Education of General Grant." *Ohio Educational Monthly* 71 (January 1922): 2-9.

5664. Corson, Oscar T. "Grant after the War." *Ohio Educational Monthly* 71 (March 1922): 73-78; (April 1922): 107-111.

5665. Corson, Oscar T. "The Grant Centennial." *Ohio Educational Monthly* 70 (December 1921): 331-334.

5666. Crane, James L. "Grant from Galena." *Civil War Times Illustrated* 18 (July 1979): 26-29.

5667. Day, Berry. "Grant's Father Didn't Want Him Elected President." *Illinois*

State Historical Society Journal 43 (Winter 1949): 296-298.

5668. "Dedication of Memorial Building over the Grant Cottage at State Fair Grounds." *Ohio Archaeological and Historical Publications* 31 (July 1922): 289-294.

5669. Dodge, Grenville M. "Some Characteristics of Gen. U. S. Grant." *Annals of Iowa* 10 (January 1913): 570-589.

5670. Draper, Andrew S. "Inborn Qualities in the Character of Grant: Grant's Birthday Exercises, State Normal College, Albany, NY." In his *Addresses by Andrew S. Draper*, 60-75. Albany, NY: State Education Department, 1906.

5671. Galbreath, C. B. "Centennial Anniversary of the Birth of Ulysses S. Grant." *Ohio Archaeological and Historical Society Publications* 31 (July 1922): 221-288.

5672. Grant, Frederick D. "Memories of General Grant." *National Magazine* 31 (January 1910): 375-377.

5673. Grant, Frederick D. "Reminiscences of Gen. U. S. Grant, Read before the Illinois Commandery, Loyal Legion of the United States, January 27, 1910." *Illinois State Historical Society Journal* 7 (April 1914): 72-76.

5674. Grant, Jesse R. "A Boy in the White House: Recollections of My Father, General Grant." *Harper's* 150 (January 1925): 129-140; (February 1925): 333-341; (March 1925): 465-474.

5675. Grant, Jesse R. "General Grant and the Queen: Unnarrated Incidents of Grant's Trip around the World." *Harper's* 151 (August 1925): 304-310.

5676. Jones, Frank H. "Grant's Boyhood and Early Manhood." *Chicago Historical Society Bulletin* 1 (November 1922): 30-32.

5677. Kahn, David M. "The Grant Monument." *Architectural Historians Journal* 41 (October 1982): 212-231.

5678. McCabe, James D. *A Tour around the World by General Grant. . . .* Philadelphia: National Publishing Co., 1879.

5679. Nichols, Hugh L. "Character Sketch of General Ulysses S. Grant." *Ohio Archaeological and Historical Quarterly* 31 (April 1922): 163-171.

5680. Packard, J. F. *Grant's Tour around the World . . . Carefully Edited and Arranged from the Correspondence of the New York Herald. . . .* Philadelphia: William Flent, 1880.

5681. Ross, Ishbel. *The General's Wife: The Life of Mrs. Ulysses S. Grant.* New York: Dodd, Mead, 1959.

5682. Shrady, George F. "General Grant's Last Days." *Century Magazine* 76 (May 1908): 102-113; (June 1908): 275-285; (July 1908): 411-429.

5683. Shrady, George F. *General Grant's Last Days, By One of His Consulting Surgeons.* New York: De Vinne Press, 1908.

5684. Simon, John Y., ed. *The Personal Memoirs of Julia Dent Grant.* New York: Putnam, 1975.

5685. Stevens, Alice B. "General Grant's Love of Horses and His Stage-Coach Ride in the White Mountains." *Granite Monthly* 34 (February 1903): 95-113.

5686. Stevens, Walter B. *Grant in St. Louis: From Letters in the Manuscript Collection of William K. Bixby.* St. Louis, MO: Franklin Club of St. Louis, 1916.

5687. Stevenson, Augusta. *U. S. Grant, Young Horseman.* Indianapolis, IN: Bobbs-Merrill, 1947.

5688. Vernon, A. W. "The Figure of Grant." *New Republic* 30 (April 26, 1922): 252-254.

5689. Young, John R. *Around the World*

with General Grant: A Narrative of the Visit of General U. S. Grant, Ex-President of the United States, To Various Countries in Europe, Asia, and Africa, In 1877, 1878, and 1879. 2 vols. New York: American News Co., 1879.

Public Career

5690. Badeau, Adam. *Military History of Ulysses S. Grant from April 1861 to April 1865.* 3 vols. New York: Appleton, 1868-1881.

5691. Boutwell, George S. *The Lawyer, the Statesman, and the Soldier.* New York: Appleton, 1887.

5692. Brown, Lytle. "U. S. Grant — An Example of Leadership." *Military Engineer* 20 (November 1928): 502-511.

5693. Buckmaster, Henrietta. *Freedom Bound.* New York: Macmillan, 1965.

5694. Cadwallader, Sylvanus. *Three Years with Grant, As Recalled by War Correspondent, Sylvanus Caldwallader.* Edited by Benjamin P. Thomas. New York: Knopf, 1955.

5695. Catton, Bruce. *Grant Moves South.* Boston: Little, Brown, 1960.

5696. Catton, Bruce. *Grant Takes Command.* Boston: Little, Brown, 1979.

5697. Catton, Bruce. *U. S. Grant and the American Military Tradition.* Boston: Little, Brown, 1954.

5698. Catton, Bruce. "U. S. Grant: Man of Letters." *American Heritage* 19 (June 1968): 97-100.

5699. Conger, Arthur L. "The Military Education of Grant as General." *Wisconsin Magazine History* 4 (March 1921): 239-262.

5700. Coppee, Henry. *Grant and His Companies: A Military Biography.* New York: Richardson, 1866.

5701. Corson, Oscar T. "Grant, The Soldier." *Ohio Educational Monthly* 71 (February 1922): 37-45.

5702. Eckert, Edward K. "The McClellans and the Grants: Generalship and Strategy in the Civil War." *Military Review* 55 (June 1975): 58-67.

5703. Farnen, Russell F., Jr. "Ulysses S. Grant: The Soldier as Politician (1861 to 1868)." D.S.S. dissertation, Syracuse University, 1963.

5704. Farnum, George R. "John A. Rawlins: Country Lawyer and Grant's Lieutenant." *American Bar Association Journal* 29 (November 1943): 650-651, 675.

5705. Frassanito, William A. *Grant and Lee: The Virginia Campaigns, 1864-1865.* New York: Scribner's, 1983.

5706. Fuller, John F. C. *The Generalship of Ulysses S. Grant.* New York: Dodd, Mead, 1929.

5707. Fuller, John F. C. *Grant and Lee, A Study in Personality and Generalship.* London: Eyre and Spottiswoode, 1933.

5708. "Grant and Vicksburg." *Chicago Historical Society Bulletin* 1 (May 1922): 2-8.

5709. Hardy, O. "Ulysses S. Grant, President of the Mexican Southern Railroad." *Pacific Historical Review* 24 (May 1955): 111-120.

5710. Headley, Joel T. *Grant and Sherman: Their Campaigns and Generals.* New York: E. B. Freat, 1866.

5711. Hyman, Harold M. "Johson, Stanton, and Grant: A Reconsideration of the Army's Role in the Events Leading to Impeachment." *American Historical Review* 66 (October 1966): 85-100.

5712. Isaacs, A. Joakim. "Candidate Grant and the Jews." *American Jewish Archives* 17 (April 1965): 3-16.

5713. Jones, Evan R. *Lincoln, Stanton,*

and Grant. New York: Scribner, Welford and Armstrong, 1875.

5714. Jones, Terry L. "Grant's Canals in Northeast Louisiana." *North Louisiana Historical Association Journal* 10 (1979): 7-17.

5715. Kohlsaat, Herman H. "General Grant at Galena, 1861." *Saturday Evening Post* 95 (March 17, 1923): 19-23.

5716. Larke, Julian K. *General Grant and His Campaigns.* New York: Derby and Miller, 1864.

5717. Lebowich, Joseph. "General Ulysses Grant and the Jews." *American Jewish Historical Society Publications* 17 (1909): 71-79.

5718. Leiter, B. Kelly. "A Study of the Relationship between General Ulysses S. Grant and Various Illinois Newspapers Covering the Period March, 1864, to November, 1868." Ph.D. dissertation, Southern Illinois University, 1970.

5719. Leitman, Spencer L. "The Revival of an Image: Grant and the 1880 Republican Nominating Campaign." *Missouri Historical Society Bulletin* 30 (April 1974): 196-204.

5720. Macartney, Clarence E. *Grant and His Generals.* New York: McBride, 1953.

5721. McCormick, Robert R. *Ulysses S. Grant, The Great Soldier of America.* New York: Appleton, 1934.

5722. McGhee, James E. "The Neophyte General: U. S. Grant and the Belmont Campaign." *Missouri Historical Review* 67 (July 1973): 463-483.

5723. Mallam, William D. "The Grant-Butler Relationship." *Mississippi Valley Historical Review* 41 (September 1954): 259-276.

5724. Miers, Earl S. *Grant's Civil War.* New York: Collier, 1962.

5725. Miers, Earl S. *The Web of Victory: Grant at Vicksburg.* New York: Knopf, 1955.

5726. Mosby, John S. "Personal Recollections of General Grant." *Munsey's Magazine* 44 (March 1911): 761-766.

5727. Nickell, Franklin D. "Grant's Lieutenants in the West, 1861-1863." Ph.D. dissertation, University of New Mexico, 1972.

5728. Odell, Samuel W. *The Lives and Campaigns of Grant and Lee.* Chicago: Star Publishing Co., 1895.

5729. Okie, Howard S. *General U. S. Grant: A Defense.* New York: Vantage Press, 1970.

5730. "Personal Recollections of General Grant's Life in the Field." *National Magazine* 18 (June 1903): 318-320.

5731. Pitkin, Thomas M. *Grant, The Soldier.* Washington, DC: Acropolis Books, 1966.

5732. Randall, James G., and David Donald. *The Civil War and Reconstruction.* 2d ed. Boston: Heath, 1961.

5733. Seifert, Shirley. *Captain Grant.* Philadelphia: Lippincott, 1946.

5734. Simon, John Y. "Grant at Belmont." *Military Affairs* 45 (December 1981): 161-166.

5735. Smith, Gene. *Lee and Grant.* New York: McGraw-Hill, 1984.

5736. Temple, Wayne C. "U. S. Grant in Military Service for the State of Illinois." *Lincoln Herald* 83 (Fall 1981): 705-708.

5737. Theodore, Terry C. "The Civil War on the New York Stage from 1861-1900." *Lincoln Herald* 74 (Spring 1972): 34-40.

5738. Utley, Robert M. "The Celebrated Policy of General Grant." *North Dakota History* 20 (July 1953): 121-142.

5739. Westwood, Howard C. "The Singing Wire Conspiracy: Manipulation of Men and Messages for Peace." *Civil War Time Illustrated* 19 (December 1980): 30-35.

5740. Williams, T. Harry. *McClellan, Sherman, and Grant*. New Brunswick, NJ: Rutgers University Press, 1962.

Presidential Years

5741. Barton, George. "General Grant and the Third Term." *America* 39 (June 9, 1928): 201-203.

5742. Boutwell, George S. "General Grant and a Third Term." *North American Review* 130 (April 1880): 370-388.

5743. Brisbin, James S. *The Campaign Lives of Ulysses S. Grant and Schuyler Colfax*. Cincinnati, OH: C. F. Vent and Co., 1868.

5744. Campbell, Helen M. ... *Famous Presidents: Washington, Jefferson, Madison, Lincoln, Grant*. Boston: Educational Publishing Co., 1903.

5745. Carter, Hodding. *The Angry Scar: The Story of Reconstruction*. Garden City, NY: Doubleday, 1959.

5746. Catton, Bruce. "Grant and the Politicians." *American Heritage* 19 (June 1968): 97-100.

5747. Chamberlin, Everett. *The Struggle of '72*. Chicago: Union Publishing Co., 1872.

5748. Church, William C. *Ulysses S. Grant and the Period of National Preservation and Reconstruction*. New York: Putnam, 1877.

5749. Coulter, E. Merton. "Presidential Visits to Georgia during Ante-Bellum Times." *Georgia Historical Quarterly* 55 (Fall 1971): 329-364.

5750. Cox, LaWanda C., and John H. Cox. *Politics, Principle, and Prejudice, 1865-1866: Dilemma of Reconstruction America*. New York: Harper and Row, 1963.

5751. Creel, George. "Scandals of 1876." *Collier's* 80 (September 17, 1927): 19-20.

5752. Crume, John B. "President Grant and His Santo Domingo Annexation Project — A Study of Ill Judgement." Master's thesis, Florida Atlantic University, 1972.

5753. Dodge, Grenville M. *Personal Recollections of President Abraham Lincoln, Gen. Ulysses S. Grant, and Gen. William T. Sherman*. Council Bluffs, IA: Monarch Printing Co., 1914.

5754. DuBois, William E. B. *Black Reconstruction in America, 1860-1880*. New York: Harcourt, Brace, 1935.

5755. Dunne, Gerald T. "President Grant and Chief Justice Chase, A Footnote to the Legal Tender Case." *St. Louis University Law Journal* 5 (Fall 1959): 539-553.

5756. Dunning, William A. *Reconstruction: Political and Economic, 1865-1877*. New York: Harper and Row, 1907.

5757. Eaton, John. *Grant, Lincoln, and the Freedmen: Reminiscences of the Civil War with Special Reference to the Work for the Contrabands and Freedmen of the Mississippi Valley*. New York: Longman, Green, 1907.

5758. Gillett, William. *Retreat from Reconstruction: A Political History, 1867-1878*. Baton Rouge: Louisiana State University Press, 1979.

5759. *The Great American Empire: Or Gen. Ulysses S. Grant, Emperor of North America*. St. Louis, MO.: W. S. Bryan, 1879.

5760. Hall, William. "Grant and the Third Term." *Americana* 7 (September 1912): 848-850.

5761. Hartje, Robert. "Grant and the Centennial of 1876." *Occasional Review* 5 (Autumn 1976): 67-84.

5762. Hesseltine, William B. *Ulysses S. Grant, Politician.* New York: Dodd, Mead, 1935.

5763. Kerwood, John. "Inauguration Day — 1869." *Capitol Dome* 4 (January 1969): 2-4.

5764. Leiter, B. Kelly. "A President and One Hour-Paper: U. S. Grant and the *Chicago Tribune.*" *Journalism Quarterly* 47 (Spring 1970): 71-80.

5765. McCabe, James D. *The New Administrator.* New York: G. S. Wilcox, 1869.

5766. McPherson, James M. "Grant or Greely? The Abolitionist Dilemma in the Election of 1872." *American Historical Review* 71 (October 1965): 43-61.

5767. Mantell, Martin E. *Johnson, Grant, and the Politics of Reconstruction.* New York: Columbia University Press, 1973.

5768. Nason, Elias. *The Life and Public Services of Henry Wilson, Late Vice-President of the United States.* Boston: B. B. Russell, 1876.

5769. Nevins, Allan. *Hamilton Fish: The Inner History of the Grant Administration.* New York: Dodd, Mead, 1946.

5770. Porter, Horace. *Campaigning with Grant.* New York: Century, 1897.

5771. "President Grant's Second Inauguration." *Frank Leslie's Illustrated Newspaper* 36 (March 15, 1873): 5-6.

5772. Ratner, Sidney. "Was the Supreme Court Packed by President Grant?" *Political Science Quarterly* 50 (September 1935): 343-358.

5773. Stern, Norton B. "Los Angeles Jewish Voters during Grant's First Presidential Race." *Western States Jewish Historical Quarterly* 13 (January 1981): 179-185.

5774. Swisher, J. A. "Grant's Des Moines Speech." *Palimpsest* 6 (December 1925): 409-421.

5775. Tatum, Lawrie. *Our Red Brothers and the Peace Policy of President Ulysses S. Grant.* Lincoln: University of Nebraska Press, 1970.

5776. Waltmann, Henry G. "Circumstantial Reformer: President Grant and the Indian Problem." *Arizona and the West* 13 (Winter 1971): 323-342.

5777. Whitner, Robert L. "Grant's Indian Peace Policy on the Yakima Reservation, 1870-1882." *Pacific Northwest Quarterly* 5 (October 1959): 135-143.

Writings

5778. Grant, Ulysses S. *General Grant's Letters to a Friend, 1861-1880.* New York: Crowell, 1897.

5779. Grant, Ulysses S. "General Grant's Letters to General Beale." *Scribner's Magazine* 50 (October 1911): 472-479.

5780. Grant, Ulysses S. *Letters of Ulysses S. Grant to His Father and His Youngest Sister, 1857-1878.* Edited by Jesse G. Cramer. New York: Putnam, 1912.

5781. Grant, Ulysses S. *Mr. Lincoln's General: U. S. Grant, An Illustrated Autobiography.* Edited by Roy Meredith. New York: Dutton, 1959.

5782. Grant, Ulysses S. *The Papers of Ulysses S. Grant.* 12 vols. Edited by John Y. Simon. Carbondale: Southern Illinois University Press, 1967-1977.

5783. Grant, Ulysses S. *Personal Memoirs of U. S. Grant.* Edited by Everette B. Long. New York: World Publishing, 1952.

5784. Grant, Ulysses S. *Personal Memoirs of U. S. Grant.* New York: G. L. Webster, 1885-1886.

5785. Grant, Ulysses S. *Ulysses S. Grant: Conversations and Unpublished Letters.* Edited by Michael J. Cramer. New York: Eaton and Mains, 1897.

5786. Grant, Ulysses S. *Ulysses S. Grant Papers.* Washington, DC: Library of Congress, 1965.

5787. Grant, Ulysses S. *Washington as Engineer and City Builder.* Washington, DC: United States George Washington Bicentennial Commission, 1931.

5788. Kull, Irving S. "Two Letters of U. S. Grant." *Rutgers University Library Journal* 2 (December 1938): 1-5.

5789. Simmons, William K. "The Unpublished Letters of Grant." *Americana* 7 (November 1912): 1025-1036.

5790. Wilson, David L., and John Y. Simon, ed. *Ulysses S. Grant: Essays and Documents.* Carbondale: Southern Illinois University Press, 1981.

Rutherford B. Hayes

Biographies

5791. Barnard, Harry. "Biographical Memories, *in re* RBH." *Hayes Historical Journal* 2 (Fall 1978): 89-96.

5792. Barnard, Harry. *Rutherford B. Hayes and His America.* Indianapolis, IN: Bobbs-Merrill, 1954.

5793. Conwell, Russell H. *Life and Public Services of Gov. Rutherford B. Hayes.* Boston: B. B. Russell, 1876.

5794. Eckenrode, Hamilton J., and Pocahontas W. Wight. *Rutherford B. Hayes, Statesman of Reunion.* New York: Dodd, Mead, 1930.

5795. Farnum, George R. "Rutherford B. Hayes in War and in Peace." *American Bar Association Journal* 29 (August 1943): 435-436, 474.

5796. Howard, James Q. *The Life, Public Services, and Select Speeches of Rutherford B. Hayes.* Cincinnati, OH: Robert Clarke and Co., 1876.

5797. Howells, William D. *Sketch of the Life and Character of Rutherford B. Hayes, Also a Biographical Sketch of William A. Wheeler, With Portraits of Both Candidates.* New York: Hurd and Houghton, 1876.

5798. Johnson, Judge. *Speech of . . . on the Life and Character of R. B. Hayes, Delivered at Avondale, Ohio, July 21, 1876.* Cincinnati, OH: Robert Clark and Co., 1876.

5799. Marchman, Watt P. *The Hayes Memorial.* Columbus: Ohio State Archaeological and Historical Society, 1950.

5800. Myers, Elisabeth P. *Rutherford B. Hayes.* Chicago: Reilly and Lee, 1969.

5801. Payne, Alma J. "William Dean Howells and Other Early Biographers of Rutherford B. Hayes." *Hayes Historical Journal* 2 (Fall 1978): 78-88.

5802. Smyth, William H. "Conversations with Hayes: A Biographer's Notes." Edited by Curtis W. Garrison. *Mississippi Valley Historical Review* 25 (December 1938): 369-380.

5803. Williams, Charles R. *The Life of Rutherford Birchard Hayes: Nineteenth President of the United States.* 2 vols. Boston: Houghton Mifflin, 1914.

Private Life

5804. Cochrane, Elizabeth. "Nellie Bly Visits Spiegel Grove." Edited by Watt P. Marchman. *Hayes Historical Journal* 1 (Fall 1976): 133-144.

5805. David, Beverly R. "Selling the Subscription Book." *Hayes Historical Journal* 1 (1977): 192-200.

5806. "The Dedication of the Hayes Memorial at Spiegel Grove, Fremont, Ohio, Tuesday, May 30, 1916." *Ohio Archaeological and Historical Publications* 25 (October 1915): 401-484.

5807. Geer, Emily A. "Lucy Webb Hayes: An Unexceptional Woman." Ph.D. dissertation, Western Reserve University, 1962.

5808. Geer, Emily A. "Lucy Webb Hayes and Her Family." *Ohio History* 77 (Winter/Spring/Summer 1968): 33-57.

5809. Geer, Emily A. "Lucy Webb Hayes and Her Influence upon Her Era." *Hayes Historical Journal* 1 (Spring 1976): 22-35.

5810. Geer, Emily A. "Lucy Webb Hayes and the New Woman of the 1880's." *Hayes Historical Journal* 3 (Spring/Fall 1980): 18-26.

5811. Geer, Emily A. "The Rutherford B. Hayes Family." *Hayes Historical Journal* 2 (Spring 1978): 46-51.

5812. Gholson, Sam C. "The Artist as Biographer." *Hayes Historical Journal* 2 (Fall 1978): 119-131.

5813. Hayes, Walter S., Jr. "Rutherford B. Hayes and the Ohio State University." *Ohio History* 77 (Winter/Spring/Summer 1968): 168-183.

5814. Hendricks, Gordon. "Eakins Portrait of Rutherford B. Hayes." *American Art Journal* 1 (Spring 1969): 104-114.

5815. Hickerson, Frank R. "The Educational Contribution of Rutherford B. Hayes." *Northwest Ohio Quarterly* 33 (Winter 1960-1961): 46-53.

5816. Keeler, Lucy E. *The Centenary Celebration of the Birth of Rutherford Birchard Hayes at Spiegel Grove, Freemont, Ohio, October 4, 1922.* Columbus, OH: F. J. Heer Print Co., 1923.

5817. Keeler, Lucy E. "Excursion to Baltimore, Md., and Washington, D.C., January 18-February 15, 1881." Edited by Watt P. Marchman. *Hayes Historical Journal* 1 (Spring 1976): 6-21.

5818. Keeler, Lucy E. *Illustrated Catalogue, the Spiegel Grove State Park, the Hayes Memorial Library and Museum, and the Hayes Homestead, Fremont, Ohio.* Columbus: Ohio State Archaeological and Historical Society, 1926.

5819. *Lucy Webb Hayes.* Cincinnati, OH: Woman's Home Missionary Society, 1890.

5820. Marchman, Watt P. "Collections of the Rutherford B. Hayes State Memorial." *Ohio History* 71 (July 1962): 151-157.

5821. Marchman, Watt P., comp. "College Costs: What Rutherford B. Hayes Spent as a Student at Kenyon, 1838-1841." *Hayes Historical Journal* 2 (Spring 1978): 14-20.

5822. Marchman, Watt P., ed. "Hayes Album: Fourteen Panels Depicting Scenes from the Life of President Hayes." *Hayes Historical Journal* 1 (Spring 1976): 45-59.

5823. Marchman, Watt P., comp. "Rutherford B. Hayes as Painted by William Merritt Chase: The Documentary Story." *Hayes Historical Journal* 1 (Spring 1976): 36-44.

5824. Pad, Dennis N. "The Educational Contributions and Activities of Rutherford B. Hayes." Ph.D. dissertation, Ohio State University, 1970.

5825. Parker, Wyman W. "The College Reading of a President." *Library Quarterly* 21 (April 1951): 107-112.

5826. Scott, George T. *Illinois' Testimonial to Mrs. Rutherford B. Hayes (1880-81).* Springfield: Illinois State Historical Society, 1953.

5827. Swint, Henry L. "Rutherford B. Hayes, Educator." *Mississippi Valley Historical Review* 39 (June 1952): 45-60.

5828. Townsend, Samuel C. *Spiegel*

Grove: Home of Rutherford Birchard Hayes. Fremont, OH: Lesher Printers, 1965.

5829. Van Sickle, Clifton E., and James T. May. "The Birthplace of President Hayes: A Study in Oral Tradition." *Ohio State Archaeological and Historical Quarterly* 61 (April 1952): 167-172.

5830. West, Richard S., Jr. "The Kenyon Experience of R. B. Hayes." *Hayes Historical Journal* 2 (Spring 1978): 6-13.

Public Career

5831. Marchman, Watt P. "Rutherford B. Hayes: Attorney at Law." *Ohio History* 77 (Winter/Spring/Summer 1968): 5-32.

5832. Marchman, Watt P. "Rutherford B. Hayes in Lower Sandusky, 1845-1849." *Hayes Historical Journal* 1 (Fall 1976): 123-132.

5833. Porter, Daniel R. "Governor Rutherford B. Hayes." *Ohio History* 77 (Winter/Spring/Summer 1968): 58-75.

5834. Ransom, Frederick D. "The Great Unknown: Governor Rutherford B. Hayes of Ohio." Ph.D. dissertation, West Virginia University, 1978.

5835. Smith, Thomas A. "Governor Hayes Visits the Centennial." *Hayes Historical Journal* 1 (Spring 1977): 159-164.

5836. Williams, T. Harry. *Hayes of the Twenty-third: The Civil War Volunteer Officer*. New York: Knopf, 1965.

Presidential Years

General

5837. "Age of Innocence in the White House." *Literary Digest* 92 (February 5, 1927): 41-42.

5838. Bassett, John S. "The Significance of the Administration of Rutherford B. Hayes." *Southern Atlantic Quarterly* 17 (July 1918): 198-206.

5839. Baur, John E. "A President Visits Los Angeles: Rutherford B. Hayes' Tour of 1880." *Historical Society of Southern California Quarterly* 37 (March 1955): 33-47.

5840. Beatty, Bess. "A Revolution Gone Backward: The Black Response to the Hayes Administration." *Hayes Historical Journal* 4 (Spring 1983): 5-25.

5841. Beeton, Beverly. "The Hayes Administration and the Woman Question." *Hayes Historical Journal* 2 (Spring 1978): 52-56.

5842. Blynn, William C. "An Unusual Indian Peace Medal of the Hayes Era." *Hayes Historical Journal* 2 (Spring 1978): 33-37.

5843. Brown, Wenzell. "Hayes, The Forgotten President." *American Mercury* 68 (February 1949): 169-177.

5844. Burgess, John W. *The Administration of President Hayes: The Larwill Lectures, 1915, Delivered at Kenyon College*. New York: Scribner's, 1916.

5845. Clendenen, Clarence C. "President Hayes' 'Withdrawal' of the Troops — An Enduring Myth." *South Carolina Historical Magazine* 70 (October 1969): 240-250.

5846. Cole, Terrence. "The Strange Saga of the President's Desk." *American Heritage* 32 (October 1981): 62-64.

5847. Crook, William H. "Rutherford B. Hayes in the White House: Being the Reminiscences of William H. Crook: Written by Margarita Spalding Gerry." *Century Magazine* 77 (March 1909): 643-665.

5848. Davison, Kenneth E. "The Hayes Great Western Tour of 1880." *Hayes Historical Journal* 3 (Spring/Fall 1980): 95-104.

5849. Davison, Kenneth E. *The Presidency of Rutherford B. Hayes.* Westport, CT: Greenwood Press, 1972.

5850. Davison, Kenneth E. "President Hayes and the Reform of American Indian Policy." *Ohio History* 82 (Summer/Autumn 1973): 205-214.

5851. Davison, Kenneth E. "The Search for the Hayes Administration." *Hayes Historical Journal* 2 (Spring 1978): 107-118.

5852. Davison, Kenneth E. "Travels of President Rutherford B. Hayes." *Ohio History* 80 (Winter 1971): 60-72.

5853. Davison, Kenneth E., comp. "Political Cartoons of the Hayes Presidency." *Hayes Historical Journal* 2 (Spring 1978): 38-45.

5854. Davison, Kenneth E., comp. "White House during the Hayes Era." *Hayes Historical Journal* 1 (Fall 1977): 263-270.

5855. DeSantis, Vincent P. "President Hayes's Southern Policy." *Journal of Southern History* 21 (November 1955): 476-494.

5856. DeSantis, Vincent P. *Republicans Face the Southern Question, The New Departure Years, 1877-1897.* Baltimore, MD: Johns Hopkins University Press, 1959.

5857. DuBois, William E. B. *Black Reconstruction in America, 1860-1880.* New York: Harcourt, Brace, 1935.

5858. Eaton, Dorman. *The Spoils Systems and Civil Service Reform in the Custom-House and Post-Office at New York.* New York: Putnam, 1881.

5859. Franck, Timothy D. "An Historical-Descriptive Study of Rutherford Birchard Hayes and the Chautauqua." Ph.D. dissertation, Bowling Green State University, 1975.

5860. Fry, Norman E. "Representative Men: The Ohio Presidents of the Gilded Age, 1822-1896." Ph.D. dissertation, University of Waterloo, 1979.

5861. Garrison, Curtis W. "President Hayes: The Opponent of Prohibition." *Northwest Ohio Quarterly* 16 (July/October 1944): 164-177.

5862. Gibbs, William E. "Spadework Diplomacy: United States — Mexican Relations during the Hayes Administration, 1877-1881." Ph.D. dissertation, Kent State University, 1973.

5863. Gonya, Gary J. "Hayes and Unity (with a Travelogue of the Presidential Tour of 1880)." Bachelor's thesis, St. Meinrad Seminary, 1965.

5864. Harris, William C. "A Mississippi Whig and the Ascension of Rutherford B. Hayes to the Presidency." *Journal of Mississippi History* 30 (August 1968): 202-205.

5865. Hayes, Webb C., and Watt P. Marchman, comps. "The First Days of the Hayes Administration: Inauguration to Easter Sunday, 1877." *Hayes Historical Journal* 1 (Fall 1977): 230-262.

5866. Houdek, John T. "James A. Garfield and Rutherford B. Hayes: A Study in State and National Politics." Ph.D. dissertation, Michigan State University, 1970.

5867. House, Albert V., Jr. "President Hayes' Selection of David M. Key for Postmaster General." *Journal of Southern History* 4 (February 1938): 87-93.

5868. Huth, Richard A. "President Rutherford B. Hayes: Civil Service Reformer." Ph.D. dissertation, Case Western Reserve University, 1943.

5869. Krebs, Frank J. "Hayes and the South." Ph.D. dissertation, Ohio State University, 1950.

5870. McPherson, James M. "Coercion

or Conciliation? Abolitionists Debate President Hayes's Southern Policy." *New England Quarterly* 39 (December 1966): 474-497.

5871. Marchman, Watt P., ed. "The 'Memoirs' of Thomas Donaldson." *Hayes Historical Journal* 2 (Spring/Fall 1979): 157-265.

5872. Marchman, Watt P. "The Washington Visits of Jenny Halstead, 1879-1881." *Historical and Philosophical Society of Ohio Bulletin* 12 (July 1954): 179-193.

5873. Morgan, H. Wayne. *From Hayes to McKinley: National Party Politics, 1877-1896.* Syracuse, NY: Syracuse University Press, 1969.

5874. Nichols, Jeannette P. "Rutherford B. Hayes and John Sherman." *Ohio History* 77 (Winter/Spring/Summer 1968): 125-138.

5875. Palmer, Upton S. "An Historical and Critical Study of the Speeches of Rutherford B. Hayes with an Appended Edition of His Addresses." Ph.D. dissertation, University of Michigan, 1950.

5876. Plesur, Milton. "American Looking Outward: Hayes to Harrison." *Historian* 22 (May 1960): 280-295.

5877. Price, Ruth P. "The Reform Activities of Rutherford B. Hayes." Master's thesis, University of Toledo, 1948.

5878. Rhodes, James F. "A Review of President Hayes's Administration." In his *Historical Essays,* 245-264. New York: Macmillan, 1909.

5879. Richardson, Lyon N. "Men of Letters and the Hayes Administration, With Text of the Letters." *New England Quarterly* 15 (March 1942): 110-142.

5880. Richardson, Lyon N., and Curtis W. Garrison. "Curtis, Hayes, and Civil Service Reform." *Mississippi Valley Historical Review* 32 (September 1945): 235-250.

5881. Shores, Venila L. *The Hayes-Conkling Controversy, 1877-1879.* Northampton, MA: Department of History, Smith College, 1919.

5882. Sinkler, George. "Race: Principles and Policy of Rutherford B. Hayes." *Ohio History* 77 (Winter/Spring/Summer 1968): 149-167.

5883. Sproat, John G. *The Best Men.* New York: Oxford University Press, 1968.

5884. Stilwell, Lewis D. *The Hayes Administration, 1877-1881.* Hanover, NH: n.p., 1954.

5885. Stoddard, William O. ... *Rutherford Birchard Hayes, James Abram Garfield, and Chester Alan Arthur.* New York: Stokes, 1889.

5886. Swift, Donald C. "Ohio Republicans and the Hayes Administration Reforms: Part I. The Assault on the Spoils System." *Northwest Ohio Quarterly* 42 (Fall 1970): 99-106.

5887. Swift, Donald C. "Ohio Republicans and the Hayes Administration Reforms: Part II. The Policy of Reunion." *Northwest Ohio Quarterly* 43 (Winter 1971): 11-22.

5888. Thelen, David P. "Rutherford B. Hayes and the Reform Tradition in the Gilded Age." *American Quarterly* 22 (Summer 1970): 150-165.

5889. Vazzano, Frank P. "Hayes, Congress, and the Resurrection of Presidential Authority." Ph.D. dissertation, Kent State University, 1972.

5890. Weaver, Bill L. "President Hayes' Visit to Kentucky, 1877." *Filson Club History Quarterly* 46 (January 1972): 37-48.

5891. Webb, Ross A. "The Bristow Presidential Boom of 1876." *Hayes Historical Journal* 1 (Fall 1976): 79-88.

5892. Wills, Garry. "Contemporary Estimates of President Hayes." *Hayes Historical Journal* 2 (Fall 1978): 132-138.

5893. Wittke, Carl F. "Carl Schurz and Rutherford B. Hayes." *Ohio Historical Quarterly* 65 (October 1956): 337-355.

5894. Woodward, C. Vann. "Yes, There Was a Compromise of 1877." *Journal of American History* 60 (June 1973): 215-223.

Election

5895. Baetzhold, Howard G. "Mark Twain Stumps for Hayes." *Hayes Historical Journal* 1 (Fall 1976): 111-114.

5896. Campbell, John T. "The Hayes-Tilden Contest." *Illinois State Historical Society Transactions* 14 (1909): 184-189.

5897. Davison, Kenneth E. "The Nomination of Rutherford Hayes for the Presidency." *Ohio History* 77 (Fall 1968): 95-110.

5898. Davison, Kenneth E. "The Presidential Election of 1876." *Hayes Historical Journal* 1 (Fall 1976): 115-122.

5899. Edmunds, George F. "Another View of 'The Hayes-Tilden Contest': A Reply to Colonel Watterson in the May *Century*." *Century Magazine* 86 (June 1913): 193-201.

5900. Ewing, Elbert W. R. *History and Law of the Hayes-Tilden Contest before the Electoral Commission, The Florida Case, 1876-1877*. Washington, DC: Cobden Publishing Co., 1910.

5901. Haworth, Paul L. *Hayes-Tilden Disputed Presidential Election of 1876*. Cleveland, OH: Burrows Brothers, 1906.

5902. Haworth, Paul L. *The Hayes-Tilden Election*. Indianapolis, IN: Bobbs-Merrill, 1927.

5903. Hill, Frederick T. "Decisive Battle of the Law: Hayes-Tilden Contest." *Harper's* 114 (March 1907): 557-567.

5904. Lewis, Walker. "The Hayes-Tilden Election Contest." *American Bar Association Journal* 47 (January 1961): 36-40; 47 (February 1961): 163-167.

5905. Moore, Dorothy L. "William A. Howard and the Nomination of Rutherford B. Hayes for the Presidency." *Vermont History* 38 (Autumn 1970): 316-319.

5906. Robinson, Lloyd. *The Stolen Election: Hayes versus Tilden, 1876*. Garden City, NY: Doubleday, 1968.

5907. Rogers, Joseph M. "How Hayes Became President." *McClure's* 23 (May 1904): 76-88.

5908. Rosewater, Victor. "The Oregon Muddle: A Curious Phase of the Hayes-Tilden Controversy." *Century Magazine* 86 (September 1913): 764-766.

5909. Sternstein, Jerome L., ed. "The Sickles Memorandum: Another Look at the Hayes-Tilden Election-Night Conspiracy." *Journal of Southern History* 32 (August 1966): 343-357.

5910. Vaughan, Harold C. *The Hayes-Tilden Election of 1876: A Disputed Presidential Election in the Gilded Age*. New York: Franklin Watts, 1972.

5911. Watterson, Henry. "The Hayes-Tilden Contest for the Presidency: Inside History of a Great Political Crisis." *Century Magazine* 86 (May 1913): 3-20.

5912. Wyatt, Joseph R., III. "The Lessons of the Hayes-Tilden Election Controversy: Some Suggestions for Electoral College Reform." *Rutgers-Camden Law Journal* 8 (Summer 1977): 617-671.

Writings

5913. Hayes, Rutherford B. "Conversations with Hayes: A Biographer's Notes." Edited by Curtis W. Garrison. *Mississippi Valley Historical Review* 25 (December 1938): 369-380.

5914. Hayes, Rutherford B. *Diary and Letters of Rutherford Birchard Hayes, Nineteenth President of the United States.* 5 vols. Edited by Charles R. Williams. Columbus: Ohio State Archaeological and Historical Society, 1922-1926.

5915. Hayes, Rutherford B. *Hayes: The Diary of a President, 1875-1881.* Edited by T. Harry Williams, New York: McKay, 1964.

5916. Hayes, Rutherford B. *Teach the Freeman: The Correspondence of Rutherford B. Hayes and the Slater Fund for Negro Education, 1881-1887.* 2 vols. Edited by Louis D. Rubin. Baton Rouge: Louisiana State University Press, 1959.

5917. Howells, William D., and Rutherford B. Hayes. "Howell's Campaign Biography of Rutherford B. Hays: A Series of Letters." Edited by Leo P. Coyle. *Ohio Historical Quarterly* 66 (October 1957): 391-406.

5918. Parker, Wyman W. "President Hayes' Graduation Speeches." *Ohio State Archaeological and Historical Quarterly* 63 (April 1954): 134-145.

5919. Winkler, E. T., ed. "The Hayes-Bryan Correspondence." *Southwestern Historical Quarterly* 25 (October 1921): 98-120; 25 (January 1922): 198-221; 25 (April 1922): 274-295; 26 (October 1922): 149-162; 26 (January 1923): 52-73; 27 (October 1923): 164-167; 27 (January 1924): 242-250; 27 (April 1924): 305-328; 28 (July 1924): 75-80; 28 (October 1924): 164-172; 28 (January 1925): 235-242; 28 (April 1925): 323-330; 29 (July 1925): 66-76; 29 (October 1925): 151-156; 29 (January 1926): 232-238; 29 (April 1926): 301-316; 30 (July 1926): 68-74.

James A. Garfield

Biographies

5920. Bates, Richard O. *The Gentleman from Ohio: An Introduction to Garfield.* Durham, NC: Moore Publishing Co., 1973.

5921. Blaine, James. *Memorial Address Pronounced in the Hall of Representatives, February 17, 1882....* Washington, DC: U.S. Government Printing Office, 1882.

5922. Brisbin, James S. *The Early Life and Public Career of James A. Garfield, Major General, U.S.A.: The Record of a Wonderful Career....* Philadelphia: J. C. McCurdy, 1880.

5923. Brisbin, James S. *From the Tow Path to the White House.... Including also a Sketch of the Life of the Hon. Chester A. Arthur.* Philadelphia: Hubbard, 1880.

5924. Brisbin, James S., and Susan A. Edson. *Life of President Garfield: The Complete Record of a Wonderful Career, Which, by Native Energy and Untiring Industry, Led Its Hero from Obscurity to the Foremost Position of the American Nation.* Philadelphia: Hubbard, 1881.

5925. Brown, Emma E. *The Life and Public Services of James A. Garfield.... Including Full and Accurate Details of His Eventual Administration, Assassination, Last Hours, Death, etc., Together with Notable Extracts from His Speeches and Letters.* Boston: D. L. Guernsey, 1881.

5926. Bundy, Jonas M. *The Life of Gen. James A. Garfield.* New York: Barnes, 1880.

5927. Caldwell, Robert G. *James A. Garfield, Party Chieftain.* New York: Dodd, Mead, 1931.

5928. Coffin, Charles C. *The Life of James A. Garfield.... With a Sketch of the Life of Chester A. Arthur....* Boston: J. H. Earle, 1880.

5929. Converse, Julius O. *Garfield, The Ideal Man: An Address Delivered before the Genuga County Teachers' Institute, At Burton, Ohio ... August 9, 1882, and the Portage County Teachers' Institute, At Ravenna, Ohio ... August 17, 1882.* Cleveland, OH: W. W. Williams, 1882.

5930. Conwell, Russell H. *The Life, Speeches, and Public Services of Gen. James A. Garfield of Ohio....* Indianapolis, IN: Fred L. Horton, 1880.

5931. Conwell, Russell H. *The Life, Speeches, and Public Services of James A. Garfield.* Boston: B. B. Russel, 1881.

5932. Conwell, Russell H. *The Life, Speeches, and Public Services of James A. Garfield, Twentieth President of the United States, Including an Account of His Assassination, Lingering Pain, Death, and Burial.* Portland, ME: George Stinson Co., 1881.

5933. Cookinham, Henry J., comp. *In Memoriam — James A. Garfield, Twentieth President of the United States.* Utica, NY: Curtiss and Childs, 1881.

5934. Davis, Harold E., ed. *Garfield of Hiram, A Memorial to the Life and Services of James Abram Garfield, Published on the Occasion of the Centennial of His Birth, November 19, 1931.* Hiram, OH: Hiram Historical Society Publication, 1931.

5935. Doyle, Burton T., and Homer H. Swaney. *Lives of James A. Garfield and Chester A. Arthur, With a Brief Sketch of the Assassin.* Washington, DC: R. H. Darby, 1881.

5936. Gilmore, James R. *The Life of James A. Garfield, Republican Candidate for the Presidency.* New York: Harper and Brothers, 1880.

5937. Green, Francis M. *A Royal Life, Or The Eventful History of James A. Garfield.* Chicago: Central Book Concern, 1882.

5938. Hosterman, Arthur D. *Life and Times of James Abram Garfield....* Springfield, OH: Farm and Fireside Publishing Co., 1882.

5939. Lossing, Benson J. *A Biography of James A. Garfield.* New York: H. S. Goodspeed, 1882.

5940. McCabe, James D. *From the Farm to the Presidential Chair, Being an Accurate and Comprehensive Account of the Life and Public Services of Gen. James A. Garfield.... To Which Is Added the Life of Gen. Chester A. Arthur.* Philadelphia: National Publishing Co., 1880.

5941. McCabe, James D. *The Life and Public Service of Gen. James A. Garfield.* Chicago: G. W. Borland and Co., 1881.

5942. McClure, James B., ed. *General Garfield from the Log Cabin to the White House, Including His Early History, War Record, Public Speeches, Nomination, Inauguration, Assassination, Death, and Burial.* Chicago: Rhodes and McClure, 1881.

5943. Nevin, David J. *Biographical Sketches of General James A. Garfield and General Chester A. Arthur, Republican Nominees for the Presidency and Vice-Presidency of the United States.* Philadelphia: Pres. Printing and Publishing Co., 1880.

5944. Ogilvie, John S. *The Life and Death of James A. Garfield, From the Tow Path to the White House.* Cincinnati, OH: Cincinnati Publishing Co., 1881.

5945. Peskin, Allan. "From Log Cabin to Oblivion." *American History Illustrated* 11 (May 1976): 25-34.

5946. Peskin, Allan. *Garfield: A Biography.* Kent, OH: Kent State University Press, 1978.

5947. Peskin, Allan. "James A. Garfield: 1831-1863." Ph.D. dissertation, Case Western Reserve University, 1965.

5948. Ridpath, John C. *The Life and Work of James A. Garfield, Twentieth President of the United States.* Cincinnati, OH: Jones Brothers, 1881.

5949. Shaw, John. "A Shooting Star: The Life and Achievements of James A. Garfield: A Recital Drama for Five Voices." *Hayes Historical Journal* 3 (Spring 1982): 21-46.

5950. Taylor, John M. *Garfield of Ohio: The Available Man.* New York: Norton, 1970.

5951. Thayer, William M. *From Log-Cabin to the White House: Life of James A. Garfield.* Rev. ed. Norwich, CT: H. Bill Publishing Co., 1882.

Private Life

5952. Hinsdale, Burke A. *President Gar-*

field and Education: Hiram College Memorial. Boston: J. R. Osgood, 1882.

5953. Ketchen, John C. "Hale and Strong and Utterly Wholesome of Soul: James A. Garfield as Preacher." Master's thesis, Indiana University Press, 1978.

5954. Leech, Margaret, and Harry J. Brown. *The Garfield Orbit.* New York: Harper and Row, 1978.

5955. McKinstry, Levi C. *Garfield: A Poem.* Boston: The Author, 1882.

5956. Ringenberg, William C. "The Religious Thought and Practice of James A. Garfield." *Old Northwest Genealogical Quarterly* 8 (Winter 1982-1983): 365-382.

5957. Rushford, Jerry B. "Political Disciple: The Relationship between James A. Garfield and the Disciples of Christ." Ph.D. dissertation, University of California, Santa Barbara, 1977.

5958. Sawyer, Robert W. "James A. Garfield and the Classics." *Hayes Historical Journal* 3 (Fall 1981): 47-56.

5959. Short, Howard E. "President Garfield's Religious Heritage and What He Did with It." *Hayes Historical Journal* 4 (Fall 1983): 5-19.

5960. Smalley, E. V. "Characteristics of President Garfield." *Century Illustrated Monthly Magazine* 23 (1881-1882): 168-176.

5961. Smith, Thomas A. "A Pictorial Album: Garfield in Pen and Ink." *Hayes Historical Journal* 3 (Fall 1981): 31-46.

5962. Stanley-Brown, Joseph. "My Friend Garfield." *American Heritage* 22 (August 1971): 49-53, 100-101.

5963. Stern, Madeleine B. "Book from Garfield's Library: The Preface to a Preface." *Library of Congress Quarterly Journal* 30 (July 1973): 205-209.

5964. Wasson, Woodrow W. *James A. Garfield: His Religion and Education: A Study in the Religious and Educational Thought and Activity of an American Statesman.* Nashville, TN: Tennessee Book Co., 1952.

Public Career

5965. Bullard, F. Lauriston. "Garfield and Chase — Their Ideas of Lincoln." *Lincoln Herald* 51 (December 1949): 2-5, 36.

5966. Cottom, Robert I., Jr. "To Be among the First: The Early Career of James A. Garfield, 1831-1868." Ph.D. dissertation, Johns Hopkins University, 1975.

5967. Feis, Ruth S. *Mollie Garfield in the White House.* Chicago: Rand McNally, 1963.

5968. Harmon, Joseph. *Garfield, The Lawyer.* Yonkers, NY: Riverview Press, 1929.

5969. Hawkins, Seth C. "Garfield at the Bar: An Architectonic Rhetorical Criticism of Selected Speeches by James A. Garfield before the U.S. Supreme Court." Ph.D. dissertation, Bowling Green State University, 1975.

5970. Holm, James N. "A Rhetorical Study of the Public Speaking of James A. Garfield, 1851-1859." Ph.D. dissertation, Western Reserve University, 1958.

5971. North, Ira L. "A Rhetorical Criticism of the Speaking of James Abram Garfield, 1876-1880." Ph.D. dissertation, Louisiana State University, 1954.

5972. Peskin, Allan. "Blaine, Garfield, and Latin America." *Americas* 36 (July 1979): 79-89.

5973. Peskin, Allan. "James A. Garfield, Historian." *Historian* 43 (August 1981): 483-492.

5974. Smith, Theodore C. "General Garfield at Chickamauga." *Massachusetts Historical Society Proceedings* 48 (June 1915): 268-280.

5975. Starr, Michael E. "The Hiram College Garfield Commemoration Lectures." *Hayes Historical Journal* 3 (Fall 1981): 5-7.

5976. Swing, David. "James A. Garfield." In his *The Message of David Swing to His Generation: Addresses and Papers.* . . . 72-87. New York: Revell, 1913.

5977. Taylor, John M. "With More Sorrow Than I Can Tell: A Future President Turned On His Commander." *Civil War Times Illustrated* 20 (April 1981): 20-29.

5978. Thompson, Jack M. "James R. Garfield: The Making of a Progressive." *Ohio History* 74 (Spring 1965): 79-89.

5979. Wyatt-Brown, Bertram. "Reform and Anti-Reform in Garfield's Ohio." *Hayes Historical Journal* 3 (Spring 1982): 63-78.

Presidential Years

5980. Barker, Wharton. "The Secret History of Garfield's Nomination." *Pearson's Magazine* 35 (May 1916): 435-443.

5981. Blaine, James G. *Foreign Policy of the Garfield Administration, Peace Congress of the Two Americas.* Chicago: n.p., 1882.

5982. Brown, Harry J. "Garfield's Congress." *Hayes Historical Journal* 3 (Fall 1981): 57-77.

5983. Burnette, Ollen L. "The Senate Foreign Relations Committee and the Diplomacy of Garfield, Arthur, and Cleveland." Ph.D. dissertation, University of Virginia, 1952.

5984. Connery, Thomas B. "Secret History of the Garfield-Conkling Tragedy." *Cosmopolitan* 23 (June 1897): 145-162.

5985. Coulter, John. *Our Martyr Presidents: Lincoln, Garfield, McKinley, Their Illustrious Lives, Public and Private, and Their Glorious Deeds.* . . . Chicago: Memorial Publishing House, 1901.

5986. Dawes, Charles G. "Young Charles Dawes Goes to the Garfield Inauguration: A Diary." Edited by Robert H. Ferrell. *Ohio History Quarterly* 70 (October 1961): 332-342.

5987. Dawes, Henry L. "Garfield and Conkling." *Century Magazine* 47 (December 1893): 341-344.

5988. DeSantis, Vincent P. "President Garfield and the Solid South." *North Carolina Historical Review* 36 (October 1959): 442-465.

5989. Doenecke, Justus D. *The Presidencies of James A. Garfield and Chester A. Arthur.* Lawrence: Regents Press of Kansas, 1981.

5990. Fisher, Everett. "The Garfield Centennial." *Manuscripts* 33 (Spring 1981): 138-143.

5991. Hatfield, Mark O. "James A. Garfield: A Man Called, A People Served." *Hayes Historical Journal* 3 (Fall 1981): 21-30.

5992. Hinckley, Ted C. "The Politics of Sinophobia: Garfield and the Morey Letter, and the Presidential Election of 1880." *Ohio History* 89 (Fall 1980): 381-399.

5993. Hope, Eva. *New World Heros, Lincoln and Garfield: The Life-Story of Two Self-Made Men, Whom the People Made Presidents.* London: W. Scott, 1884.

5994. Houdek, John T. "James A. Garfield and Rutherford B. Hayes: A Study in State and National Politics." Ph.D. dissertation, Michigan State University, 1970.

5995. Kerwood, John R. "Assassination of President Garfield." *American History Illustrated* 5 (January 1969): 12-25.

5996. Lindsey, David. "Rehabilitating the Presidents: Garfield, Arthur, McKinley." *Reviews in American History* 10 (March 1982): 72-77.

5997. Literary Society of Washington, Washington, DC. *A Tribute of Respect from the Literary Society of Washington, To Its Late President, James Abram Garfield: Proceedings of a Meeting of the Society Held November 19, 1881.* Washington, DC: n.p., 1882.

5998. Miller, Joseph M. "The Death of James Abram Garfield." *Surgery, Gynecology, and Obstetrics* 107 (July 1958): 113-118.

5999. Mitchell, Stewart. "The Man Who Murdered Garfield." *Massachusetts Historical Society Proceedings* 67 (October/May 1941-1944): 452-489.

6000. Parker, Owen W. "The Assassination and Gunshot Wound of President James A. Garfield." *Minnesota Medicine* 34 (March 1951): 227-233, 258.

6001. Peskin, Allan. "A Century of Garfield." *Hayes Historical Journal* 3 (Fall 1981): 9-20.

6002. Peskin, Allan. "Charles Guiteau of Illinois, President Garfield's Assassin." *Illinois State Historical Society Journal* 70 (May 1977): 130-139.

6003. Peskin, Allan. "Garfield and Hayes: Political Leaders of the Gilded Age." *Ohio History* 77 (Winter/Spring/Summer 1968): 111-124.

6004. Peskin, Allan. "The 'Little Man on Horseback' and the 'Literary Fellow': Garfield's Opinions of Grant." *Mid-America* 55 (October 1973): 271-282.

6005. Peskin, Allan. "President Garfield and the Rating Game: An Evaluation of a Brief Administration." *South Atlantic Quarterly* 76 (Winter 1977): 93-102.

6006. Peskin, Allan. "President Garfield and the Southern Question: The Making of a Policy That Never Was." *South Atlantic Quarterly* 16 (July 1978): 375-386.

6007. Peskin, Allan. "President Garfield Reconsidered Hayes." *Hayes Historical Journal* 2 (Spring/Fall 1980): 35-40.

6008. Pletcher, David M. *The Awkward Years: American Foreign Policy under Garfield and Arthur.* Columbia: University of Missouri Press, 1962.

6009. "President Garfield's Inauguration: A Vast Crowd and Unusually Brilliant Spectacle." *Frank Leslie's Illustrated Newspaper* 52 (March 19, 1881): 38-39.

6010. Reid, J. A., and R. A. Reid.... *Garfield's Career: From the Tow-Path to the White House: His Seventy-nine Days Struggle for Life, and the Public Obsequies.* Providence, RI: J. A. and R. A. Reid, 1881.

6011. Rose, Galen L. "Garfield's Unfulfilled Promise: Is the Nation Still Paying for a President's Assassination?" *Christian Century* 92 (April 16, 1975): 387-388.

6012. Rosenberry, Cecil R. "The Letters of Garfield's Assassin." *Manuscripts* 7 (Winter 1955): 86-91.

6013. Stoddard, William O. . . . *Rutherford Birchard Hayes, James Abram Garfield, and Chester Alan Arthur.* New York: Stokes, 1889.

6014. Temkin, Owsei and Janet Koudelka. "Simon Newcomb and the Location of President Garfield's Bullet." *Bulletin of the History of Medicine* 24 (July/August 1950): 393-397.

6015. Tindall, William. "Echoes of a Surgical Tragedy." *Columbia Historical Society Records* 23 (1920): 147-166.

6016. Trumble, Alfred. *Guiteau's Crime: The Full History of the Murder of President James A. Garfield.* 3d ed. New York: R. K. Fox, 1881.

6017. Wimer, Charles A., comp. *Complete Medical Record of President Garfield's Case, Containing All of the Official Bulletins, From the Date of the Shooting to the Day of His Death, Together with the Official Autopsy, Made September 20, 1881, and a Diagram Showing the Course Taken by the Ball.* Washington, DC: C. A. Wimer, 1881.

Writings

6018. Fuller, Corydon E. *Reminiscences of James A. Garfield, With Notes Preliminary and Collateral.* Cincinnati, OH: Standard Publishing Co., 1887.

6019. Garfield, James A. "A Century of Congress." *Atlantic Monthly* 40 (July 1877): 49-64.

6020. Garfield, James A. *The Diary of James A. Garfield.* 4 vols. Edited by Harry J. Brown and Frederick D. Williams. East Lansing: Michigan State University Press, 1967-1981.

6021. Garfield, James A. *Discovery and Ownership of the Northwestern Territory.* Cleveland: Western Reserve and Northern Ohio Historical Society, 1881.

6022. Garfield, James A. *Garfield-Hinsdale Letters: Correspondence between James Abram Garfield and Burke Aaron Hinsdale.* Edited by Mary L. Hinsdale. Ann Arbor: University of Michigan Press, 1949.

6023. Garfield, James A. *James A. Garfield Papers.* Washington, DC: Library of Congress, 1970.

6024. Garfield, James A. "My Campaign in East Kentucky." *North American Review* 143 (December 1886): 525-535.

6025. Garfield, James A. "My Public Life." *North American Review* 144 (May 1887): 451-461.

6026. Garfield, James A. "National Appropriations and Misappropriations." *North American Review* 128 (May 1879): 572-586.

6027. Garfield, James A. "Ought the Negro to be Disfranchised? Ought He to Have Been Enfranchised?" *North American Review* 128 (March 1879): 244-250.

6028. Garfield, James A. *Review of the Transactions of the Credit Mobilier Company.* Washington, DC: Capitol News Stand, 1880.

6029. Garfield, James A. "Symposium on Negro Suffrage." *North American Review* 128 (March 1879): 244-250.

6030. Garfield, James A. *Wild Life of the Army: Civil War Letters of James A. Garfield.* Edited by Frederick D. Williams. East Lansing: Michigan State University Press, 1964.

6031. Garfield, James A. *Works of James Abram Garfield.* 2 vols. Edited by Burke A. Hinsdale. Boston: J. R. Osgood, 1882-1883.

6032. Garfield, James A., and Charles E. Henry. *Politics and Patronage in the Guilded Age: The Correspondence of James A. Garfield and Charles E. Henry.* Edited by James D. Norris and Arthur H. Shaffer. Madison: State Historical Society of Wisconsin, 1970.

6033. Smith, Theodore C. *The Life and Letters of James Abram Garfield.* 2 vols. New Haven, CT: Yale University Press, 1925.

Chester A. Arthur

Biographies

6034. Brisbin, James S. *From the Tow Path to the White House.... Including Also a Sketch of the Life of the Hon. Chester A. Arthur.* Philadelphia: Hubbard, 1880.

6035. Coffin, Charles C. *The Life of James A. Garfield ... With a Sketch of the Life of Chester A. Arthur....* Boston: J. H. Earle, 1880.

6036. Doyle, Burton T., and Homer H. Swaney. *Lives of James A. Garfield and Chester A. Arthur: With a Brief Sketch of the Assassin.* Washington, DC: R. H. Darby, 1881.

6037. McCabe, James D. *From the Farm to the Presidential Chair, Being an Accurate and Comprehensive Account of the Life and Public Services of Gen. James A. Garfield ... To Which Is Added the Life of Gen. Chester A. Arthur.* Philadelphia: National Publishing Co., 1880.

6038. Nevin, David J. *Biographical Sketches of General James A. Garfield and General Chester A. Arthur, Republican Nominees for the Presidency and Vice-Presidency of the United States.* Philadelphia: Pres. Printing and Publishing Co., 1880.

6039. Reeves, Thomas C. *Gentleman Boss: The Life of Chester Alan Arthur.* New York: Knopf, 1975.

6040. Riddle, Albert G. *The Life, Character, and Public Services of James A. Garfield.* Philadelphia: Flint, 1880.

6041. Stoddard, William O. *... Rutherford Birchard Hayes, James Abram Garfield, and Chester Alan Arthur.* New York: Stokes, 1889.

6042. Union College. *Chester Alan Arthur.* Schenectady, NY: Union College, 1948.

Private Life

6043. Bailey, Consuelo N. "Our Horses and Chester A. Arthur." *Vermont Life* 11 (Summer 1956): 10-11.

6044. Chandler, William E. *President Chester A. Arthur: Address, At Fairfield, Vermont, On August 19, 1903: On the Occasion of the Completion by the State of Vermont and Tablet to Mark the Birthplace of President Chester A. Arthur.* Concord, NH: Rumford Printing Co., 1903.

6045. Doane, Gilbert H. "The Birthplace of Chester A. Arthur." *Vermont Historical Society Proceedings* 9 (March 1941): 3-13.

6046. Reeves, Thomas C. "The Diaries of Malvina Arthur: Windows into the Past of Our 21st President." *Vermont History* 38 (Summer 1970): 177-188.

6047. Reeves, Thomas C. "The Mystery

of Chester Alan Arthur's Birthplace." *Vermont History* 38 (Autumn 1973): 291-304.

Public Career

6048. Davidson, Bill. *President Kennedy Selects Six Brave Presidents.* New York: Harper and Row, 1962.

6049. Reeves, Thomas C. "Chester A. Arthur, Vermont Schoolmaster." *Vermont History* 40 (Winter 1972): 43-46.

6050. Burnette, Ollen L. "The Senate Foreign Relations Committee and the Diplomacy of Garfield, Arthur, and Cleveland." Ph.D. dissertation, University of Virginia, 1952.

6051. DeSantis, Vincent P. "President Arthur and the Independent Movements in the South, In 1882." *Journal of Southern History* 19 (August 1953): 346-363.

6052. Doenecke, Justus D. *The Presidencies of James A. Garfield and Chester A. Arthur.* Lawrence: Regents Press of Kansas, 1981.

6053. Goff, John S. "President Arthur's Domestic Legislative Program." *New York Historical Society Quarterly* 44 (April 1960): 166-177.

6054. Howe, George F. *Chester A. Arthur: A Quarter Century of Machine Politics.* New York: Dodd, Mead, 1934.

6055. Howe, George F. "The Public Life and Presidential Administration of Chester Alan Arthur." Ph.D. dissertation, Harvard University, 1930.

6056. Kocher, Douglas J. "Temporary Vilification: The Chicago Press and Chester Arthur, 1881." *Journalism History* 9 (Summer 1982): 53-55, 60.

6057. Lindsey, David. "Rehabilitating the Presidents: Garfield, Arthur, McKinley." *Reviews in American History* 10 (March 1982): 72-77.

6058. MacLaury, Judson. "The Selection of the First U.S. Commissioner of Labor." *Monthly Labor Review* 98 (April 1975): 16-19.

6059. Pletcher, David M. *The Awkward Years: American Foreign Policy under Garfield and Arthur.* Columbia: University of Missouri Press, 1962.

6060. Poole, Susan D. *Chester A. Arthur: The President Who Reformed.* Reseda, CA: Mojave Books, 1977.

6061. Rakosnik, Eugene. "The West of Chester Alan Arthur." *Denver Westerners Roundup* 34 (September/October 1978): 3-12.

6062. Reeves, Thomas C. "Chester A. Arthur and Campaign, Assessment in the Election of 1880." *Historian* 31 (August 1969): 578-582.

6063. Reeves, Thomas C. "Chester A. Arthur and the Campaign of 1880." *Political Science Quarterly* 84 (December 1969): 628-637.

6064. Reeves, Thomas C. "President Arthur in Yellowstone National Park." *Montana: The Magazine of Western History* 19 (July 1969): 18-29.

6065. Reeves, Thomas C. "The Search for the Chester Alan Arthur Papers." *Wisconsin Magazine of History* 55 (Summer 1972): 310-329.

Presidential Years

6066. Reeves, Thomas C. "Silas Burt and Chester Arthur: A Reformer's View of the Twenty-first President." *New York Historical Society Quarterly* 54 (October 1970): 319-337.

6067. Richardson, Joe M. "The Florida Excursion of President Chester A. Arthur." *Tequesta: The Journal of the Historical Association of Southern Florida* 24 (1964): 41-47.

6068. Unck, Dunkam, pseud. *The Rajah, Or The Great Presidential Sporting Excursion of 1883: A Burlesque, In Four Cantos.* n.l.: n.p., 1884.

Writings

6069. Shelley, Fred. "The Chester A. Arthur Papers." *Library of Congress Quarterly Journal of Current Acquisitions* 16 (May 1959): 115-122.

6070. U.S. Library of Congress. Manuscript Division. *Index to the Chester A. Arthur Papers.* Washington, DC: U.S. Government Printing Office, 1961.

Grover Cleveland

Biographies

6071. Abbott, Lyman. "Grover Cleveland." *New York Genealogical and Biographical Record* 39 (October 1908): 237-241.

6072. Barnum, Augustine. *The Lives of Grover Cleveland.* Boston: George M. Smith and Co., 1884.

6073. Boyd, James P. *Biographies of Pres. Grover Cleveland and Hon. Allen G. Thurman....* Philadelphia: Franklin News Co., 1888.

6074. Bradford, Gamaliel. "Grover Cleveland." *Atlantic Monthly* 126 (November 1920): 654-664.

6075. Campbell-Copeland, Thomas. *Cleveland and Stevenson, Their Lives and Record ... The Democratic Campaign Book for 1982 ... Over Sixty Illustrations and Maps.* 3 vols. New York: Charles L. Webster and Co., 1892.

6076. Dieck, Herman. *The Life and Public Services of Our Great Reform President, Grover Cleveland ... To Which Is Added the Life and Public Services of Allen G. Thurman, The Grand Old Statesman....* Philadelphia: John C. Winston, 1888.

6077. Ferris, George T. *The Biography and Public Service of Hon. Grover Cleveland.* New York: H. S. Goodspeed, 1884.

6078. Gilder, Richard W. "Grover Cleveland." *Century Magazine* 78 (August 1909): 483-503; (September 1909): 687-705; (October 1909): 846-860; 79 (November 1909): 24-31.

6079. Gilder, Richard W. *Grover Cleveland: A Record of Friendship.* New York: Century, 1910.

6080. "Grover Cleveland as Seen by Three Friends." *Scribner's Magazine* 81 (April 1927): 339-348.

6081. Harvey, George. "Grover Cleveland." *North American Review* 188 (July 1908): 131-136.

6082. Hensel, William U., and Charles Morris. *Life and Public Services of Grover Cleveland, Twenty-second President of the United States and Democratic Nominee for Reelection in 1892 ... Also, A Sketch of the Life and Services of Hon. Adlai E. Stevenson, Vice President Nominee.* Philadelphia: Edgewood Publishing Co., 1892.

6083. LaFevre, Benjamin. *Biographies of S. Grover Cleveland, The Democratic Candidate for President, and Thomas A. Hendricks, The Democratic Candidate for Vice-President....* Chicago: Baird and Dillon, 1884.

6084. Lynch, Denis T. *Grover Cleveland, A Man Four-Square.* New York: Liveright, 1932.

6085. McClellan, George B. "Grover

Cleveland." *Outlook* 89 (August 22, 1908): 913-919.

6086. McElroy, Robert M. *Grover Cleveland, The Man and the Statesman: An Authorized Biography.* 2 vols. New York: Harper and Row, 1923.

6087. Masters, Edgar L. "Grover Cleveland." *American Mercury* 8 (August 1926): 385-397.

6088. Milburn, John G. "Grover Cleveland." *Buffalo Historical Society Publications* 17 (1913): 121-126.

6089. Mott, Frank H. "Grover Cleveland: An Appreciation." *American Bar Association Journal* 13 (October 1927): 587-590.

6090. Nelson, Henry L. "Grover Cleveland." *North American Review* 188 (August 1908): 161-187.

6091. Nevins, Allan. *Grover Cleveland: A Study in Courage.* New York: Dodd, Mead, 1932.

6092. Parker, George F. *A Life of Grover Cleveland with a Sketch of Adlai E. Stevenson.* New York: Cassell, 1892.

6093. Parker, George F. *Recollections of Grover Cleveland.* New York: Century, 1909.

6094. Peck, Harry T. "Grover Cleveland — Some Comments and Conclusions." *Forum* 40 (August 1908): 187-191.

6095. Stoddard, William O. *... Grover Cleveland.* New York: Stokes, 1888.

6096. Triplett, Frank. *The Authorized Pictorial Lives of Stephen Grover Cleveland and Thomas Andrews Hendricks ... New Steel Plate Portraits and Fine Engravings from Original Photographs, etc.* New York: N. C. Thompson and Co., 1884.

6097. Tugwell, Rexford G. *Grover Cleveland.* New York: Macmillan, 1968.

6098. Wheeler, Everett P. "Grover Cleveland." *Independent* 65 (July 2, 1909): 11-18.

6099. Williams, Jesse L. *Mr. Cleveland, A Personal Impression.* New York: Dodd, Mead, 1909.

Private Life

6100. "Cleveland's Birthplace." *Americana* 7 (February 1912): 150-153.

6101. Nevins, Allan. "Grover Cleveland: An Ill-Appreciated Personality." *American Scholar* 3 (Spring 1934): 133-143.

6102. O'Brien, Robert L. "The Personality of a Presidential Candidate." *Massachusetts Historical Society Proceedings* 57 (March 1924): 282-291.

6103. Parker, George F. "Cleveland, The Man." *McClure's* 32 (February 1909): 337-346; (March 1909): 457-472; (April 1909): 569-581.

6104. Parker, George F. "Grover Cleveland's Life in Princeton, 1897-1908." *Saturday Evening Post* 196 (November 10, 1923): 40-48.

6105. West, Andrew F. "Grover Cleveland: A Princeton Memory." *Century Magazine* 77 (January 1909): 323-337.

6106. Wickser, Philip J. "Grover Cleveland: His Character, Background, and Legal Career." *American Bar Association Journal* 33 (April 1947): 327-330, 408-409.

6107. Williams, Jesse L. "Grover Cleveland, Stories by Him, Stories about Him." *American Magazine* 67 (April 1909): 533-541.

6108. Workmaster, Wallace F. "Grover Cleveland: American Victorian." *Historian* 22 (February 1960): 185-196.

Public Career

6109. Adams, Charles F. "What Mr. Cleveland Stands For." *Forum* 13 (July 1892): 662-672.

6110. Armitage, Charles H., Jr. *Grover Cleveland as Buffalo Knew Him*. Buffalo, NY: Buffalo Evening News, 1926.

6111. Bissell, Wilson S. "Cleveland as a Lawyer: By His Law Partner." *McClure's* 32 (April 1909): 583-585.

6112. Black, Chauncey F., ed. *The Lives of Grover Cleveland and Thomas A. Hendricks, Together with a Complete History of the Democratic Party....* Philadelphia: Standard Publishing Co., 1884.

6113. Chamberlain, Eugene T. *Early Life and Public Services of Hon. Grover Cleveland, The Fearless and Independent Governor of the Empire State and Candidate for President of the United States, Reciting the Annals of His Successful Career from Obscurity to the Eminent Position Which He Now Holds in the Administration of the People: Also, The Life of Hon. Thomas A. Hendricks, Candidate for the Vice-President*. Chicago: Belford, Clark, 1884.

6114. Dorsheimer, William. *Life and Public Services of Hon. Grover Cleveland....* New York: Standard Publishing Co., 1884.

6115. Goodrich, Frederick E. *The Life and Public Services of Grover Cleveland, With Incidents of His Early Life and an Account of His Rise to Eminence in His Profession....* Wilkes Barre, PA: James A. Crogan, 1884.

6116. Handford, Thomas. *Early Life and Public Services of Hon. Grover Cleveland, The Fearless and Independent Governor of the Empire State ... Also, The Life of Hon. Thomas A. Hendricks....* Mansfield, OH: Home Publishing Co., 1884.

6117. King, Pendleton. *Life and Public Services of Grover Cleveland*. New York: Putnam, 1884.

6118. Parker, George F. "Grover Cleveland." *Outlook* 89 (July 4, 1908): 503-505.

6119. Parker, George F. "Grover Cleveland." *Outlook* 93 (December 11, 1909): 804-807.

6120. Parker, George F. "Grover Cleveland's Career in Buffalo, 1855-1882." *Saturday Evening Post* 193 (August 28, 1920): 6-7, 76, 81-82, 85-86, 89-90.

Presidential Years

6121. Ambrose, Stephen E. "The Blaine-Cleveland Election." *American History Illustrated* 1 (October 1966): 32-40.

6122. Bain, George C. "The Inauguration of President Cleveland." *Frank Leslie's Illustrated Weekly* 76 (March 9, 1893): 154-155.

6123. Baum, Dale. "'Noisy But Not Numerous': The Revolt of the Massachusetts Mugwumps." *Historian* 41 (February 1979): 241-256.

6124. Benton, Joel. "Retrospective Glimpses of Cleveland." *Forum* 40 (August 1908): 191-196.

6125. Binney, Charles C. "The White House under Cleveland." *Nation* 96 (February 27, 1913): 201-202.

6126. Blake, Nelson M. "Background of Cleveland's Venezuelan Policy." *American Historical Review* 47 (January 1942): 259-277.

6127. Blodgett, Geoffrey. "The Political Leadership of Grover Cleveland." *South Atlantic Quarterly* 82 (Summer 1983): 288-299.

6128. Bolt, Robert. "Donald M. Dickinson and the Second Election of Grover Cleveland, 1892." *Michigan History* 49 (March 1965): 28-39.

6129. Burnette, Ollen L. "The Senate Foreign Relations Committee and the Diplomacy of Garfield, Arthur, and Cleveland." Ph.D. dissertation, University of Virginia, 1952.

6130. Coletta, Paolo E. "Bryan, Cleveland, and the Disrupted Democracy, 1890-1896." *Nebraska History* 41 (March 1960): 1-27.

6131. Cross, Wilbur, and John Moses. "My God, Sir, I Think the President Is Doomed!" *American History Illustrated* 17 (November 1982): 40-45.

6132. DeSantis, Vincent P. "Grover Cleveland — Another Look." *Hayes Historical Journal* 3 (Spring/Fall 1980): 41-50.

6133. Downey, Matthew T. "Grover Cleveland and Abram S. Hewitt: The Limits of Factional Consensus." *New York Historical Society Quarterly* 54 (July 1970): 223-230.

6134. Dulebohn, George R. "Principles of Foreign Policy under the Cleveland Administrations." Ph.D. dissertation, University of Pennsylvania, 1940.

6135. Durden, Robert F. "Grover Cleveland and the Bourbon Democracy." *South Atlantic Quarterly* 57 (Summer 1958): 333-338.

6136. Faulkner, Harold U. *Politics, Reform, and Expansion, 1890-1900.* New York: Harper and Row, 1959.

6137. Fisher, Louis. "Grover Cleveland against the Senate." *Congressional Studies* 7 (Spring 1979): 11-25.

6138. Ford, Henry J. *The Cleveland Era: A Chronicle of the New Order of Politics.* New Haven, CT: Yale University Press, 1919.

6139. Gillis, James A. *The Hawaiian Incident: An Examination of Mr. Cleveland's Attitude toward the Revolution of 1893.* Boston: Lee and Shepard, 1897.

6140. Hammett, Hugh B. "The Cleveland Administration and Anglo-American Naval Friction in Hawaii, 1893-1894." *Military Affairs* 40 (February 1976): 27-31.

6141. Herbert, Hilary A. "Grover Cleveland and His Cabinet at Work." *Century Magazine* 85 (March 1913): 740-744.

6142. Hollingsworth, J. Rogers. *The Whirligig of Politics: The Democracy of Cleveland and Bryan.* Chicago: University of Chicago Press, 1963.

6143. Hugins, Roland. *Grover Cleveland: A Study in Political Courage.* Washington, DC: Anchor-Lee Publishing Co., 1922.

6144. Jager, Ronald. "The Democracy's Demise: Grover Cleveland's Rejected Supreme Court Nominations." Ph.D. dissertation, University of Texas, 1972.

6145. Josephson, Matthew. *The Politicos, 1865-1896.* New York: Harcourt, Brace, 1938.

6146. Keen, William W. *The Surgical Operations on President Cleveland in 1893.* Philadelphia: G. W. Jacobs, 1917.

6147. Kelley, Robert. "Presbyterianism, Jacksonianism, and Grover Cleveland." *American Quarterly* 18 (Winter 1966): 615-636.

6148. Keppler, Joseph. "Cleveland's Entry into Washington, March 4th, 1885." *Puck* 17 (March 4, 1885): 8-9.

6149. Kless, Margaret E. "The Second Grover Cleveland Administration and Cuba: A Study of Policy and Motivation, 1895-1897." Master's thesis, American University, 1970.

6150. Knoles, George H., ed. "Grover Cleveland on Imperialism." *Mississippi Valley Historical Review* 37 (September 1950): 303-304.

6151. Kremm, Thomas W. "Cleveland and the First Lincoln Election: The Ethnic

Response to Nativism." *Journal of Interdisciplinary History* 8 (Summer 1977): 69-86.

6152. LaFeber, Walter F. "The American Business Community and Cleveland's Venezuela Message." *Business History Review* 34 (Winter 1969): 393-402.

6153. LaFeber, Walter F. "The Background of Cleveland's Venezuelan Policy: A Reinterpretation." *American Historical Review* 66 (July 1961): 947-967.

6154. LaFeber, Walter F. "The Latin American Policy of the Second Cleveland Administration." Ph.D. dissertation, University of Wisconsin, 1959.

6155. Lingley, Charles R. "Official Characteristics of President Cleveland." *Political Science Quarterly* 33 (June 1918): 255-265.

6156. McCarthy, G. Michael. "The Forest Reserve Controversy: Colorado under Cleveland and McKinley." *Journal of Forest History* 20 (April 1976): 80-90.

6157. McSeveney, Samuel T. *The Politics of Depression: Political Behavior in the North East, 1893-1896.* New York: Oxford University Press, 1972.

6158. Marszalek, John F., Jr. "Grover Cleveland and the Tenure of Office Act." *Duquesne Review* 15 (Spring 1970): 206-219.

6159. Merrill, Horace S. *Bourbon Leader: Grover Cleveland and the Democratic Party.* Boston: Little, Brown, 1957.

6160. Neeley, Mary A. "Montgomery, 1885-1887: The Years of Jubilee." *Alabama Review* 32 (April 1979): 108-118.

6161. Norton, Charles B. *The President and His Cabinet Indicating the Progress of the Government of the United States under the Administration of Grover Cleveland and ... Illustrated with Portrait and Views.* Boston: Cupples and Hurd, 1888.

6162. O'Brien, Robert L. "Grover Cleveland as Seen by His Stenographer, July 1892-November 1895." *Massachusetts Historical Society Proceedings* 70 (1957): 128-143.

6163. Osborne, Thomas J. "What Was the Main Reason for Cleveland's Election Victory in 1884?" *Northwest Ohio Quarterly* 45 (Spring 1973): 67-71.

6164. Parker, George F. "Cleveland and the Insurance Crisis." *McClure's* 30 (June 1909): 184-191.

6165. Parker, George F. "Cleveland's Estimate of His Contemporaries." *McClure's* 30 (May 1909): 24-34.

6166. Parker, George F. "Cleveland's Second Administration as President." *Saturday Evening Post* 195 (June 9, 1918): 40-50.

6167. Parker, George F. "Cleveland's Venezuela Message." *McClure's* 30 (July 1909): 314-323.

6168. Parker, George F. "Grover Cleveland: Estimate of His Character and Work." *Saturday Evening Post* 197 (October 25, 1924): 112-122.

6169. Parker, George F. "Grover Cleveland's First Administration as President." *Saturday Evening Post* 195 (April 7, 1923): 46-56.

6170. Parker, George F. "Grover Cleveland's One Business Venture." *Saturday Evening Post* 196 (March 29, 1924): 36-39.

6171. Parker, George F. "How Grover Cleveland Was Nominated and Elected President." *Saturday Evening Post* 192 (April 24, 1920): 22-23, 168, 170, 173-174, 177-178, 181-182.

6172. Payne, Thomas. "The Administration Theory and Practice of Grover Cleveland." Ph.D. dissertation, University of Chicago, 1951.

6173. Perkins, Norman C. *A Man of Destiny.* Chicago: Belford, Clarke, 1885.

6174. "President Cleveland: Scenes and Incidents of a Brilliant Inauguration." *Frank Leslie's Illustrated Newspaper* 60 (March 14, 1885): 54-55.

6175. Rice, William G. "Cleveland's First Election." *Century Magazine* 84 (June 1912): 299-304.

6176. Robertson, Pearl L. "Cleveland's Constructive Use of the Pension Vetoes." *Mid-America* 44 (January 1962): 33-45.

6177. Robertson, Pearl L. "Cleveland's Personality as a Political Leader." *Psychoanalytic Review* 51 (Summer 1964): 130-154.

6178. Robertson, Pearl L. "Grover Cleveland as Political Leader." Ph.D. dissertation, University of Chicago, 1937.

6179. Ross, Earle D. "Grover Cleveland and the Beginning of an Era of Reform." *South Atlantic Quarterly* 18 (April 1919): 156-166.

6180. Schlup, Leonard. "Augustus Hill Garland: Gilded Age Democrat." *Arkansas Historical Quarterly* 40 (Winter 1981): 338-346.

6181. Schlup, Leonard. "Grover Cleveland and His 1892 Running Mate." *Studies in History and Society* 2 (November 1977): 60-74.

6182. Schlup, Leonard. "Presidential Disability: The Case of Cleveland and Stevenson." *Presidential Studies Quarterly* 9 (Summer 1979): 303-310.

6183. Smyth, Clifford. *Grover Cleveland, Who Put Independent Thinking into Party Politics.* New York: Funk and Wagnalls, 1931.

6184. Stevenson, Adlai E. *Something of Men I Have Known, With Some Papers of a General Nature, Political, Historical, and Retrospective.* Chicago: McClurg, 1909.

6185. Straus, Oscar S. *Under Four Administrations: From Cleveland to Taft.* Boston: Houghton Mifflin, 1922.

6186. Thomas, Harrison C. *The Return of the Democratic Party to Power in 1884.* New York: Columbia University Press, 1919.

6187. Young, George B. "The Influence of Politics on American Diplomacy during Cleveland's Administrations, 1885-1889, 1893-1897." Ph.D. dissertation, Yale University, 1939.

6188. Zornow, William F. "The Cleveland Convention, 1864, and Radical Democrats." *Mid-America* 36 (January 1954): 39-53.

Writings

6189. Cleveland, Grover. *Addresses, State Papers, and Letters.* Edited by Albert E. Bergh. New York: Sundial Classics, 1909.

6190. Cleveland, Grover. "Cleveland and the Civil Service Reformers: His Attitude as Shown in Letters to a Friend." *Century Magazine* 84 (August 1912): 625-630.

6191. Cleveland, Grover. *Fishing and Shooting Sketches.* New York: Outing Publishing Co., 1906.

6192. Cleveland, Grover. *Good Citizenship.* Philadelphia: Henry Altemus, 1908.

6193. Cleveland, Grover. *Grover Cleveland Papers.* Washington, DC: Library of Congress, 1958.

6194. Cleveland, Grover. "Independence of the Executive." *Atlantic Monthly* 85 (June 1900): 721-732; 86 (July 1900): 1-14.

6195. Cleveland, Grover. *Independence of the Executive.* Princeton, NJ: Princeton University Press, 1913.

6196. Cleveland, Grover. *Letters of Gro-*

ver Cleveland, 1850-1908.* Edited by Allan Nevins. Boston: Houghton Mifflin, 1933.

6197. Cleveland, Grover. "Letters to a Friend: Letters to H. M. Robbins of Buffalo, 1876-1890." *Niagara Frontier* 2 (Summer 1955): 49-52.

6198. Cleveland, Grover. *Presidential Problems.* New York: Century, 1904.

6199. Cleveland, Grover. *Principles and Purposes of Our Form of Government as Set Forth in Public Papers of Grover Cleveland.* Compiled by Francis Gottsberger. New York: G. G. Peck, 1892.

6200. Cleveland, Grover. *Public Papers of Grover Cleveland, Governor, 1883.* 2 vols. Albany, NY: Argus Co., 1883-1884.

6201. Cleveland, Grover. *The Self-Made Man in American Life.* New York: Crowell, 1897.

6202. Cleveland, Grover. *Writings and Speeches of Grover Cleveland.* Edited by George F. Parker. New York: Cassell, 1892.

Benjamin Harrison

Biographies

6203. Morrison, J. E., and W. B. Lane. *Life of Our President, Benjamin Harrison, Together with That of His Grandfather, William Henry Harrison.* Cincinnati, OH: Economy Printing Co., 1889.

6204. Northrop, Henry D. *The Life and Public Services of Benjamin Harrison, The Great American Statesman ... To Which Is Added the Life and Public Services of Hon. Whitelaw Reid ... Embellished with Numerous Fine Engravings and Portraits.* Cincinnati, OH: Forshee and McMakin, 1892.

6205. Sievers, Harry J. *Benjamin Harrison: Hoosier President: The White House and After.* New York: University Publishers, 1968.

6206. Sievers, Harry J. *Benjamin Harrison: Hoosier Statesman from the Civil War to the White House: 1865-1888.* New York: University Publishers, 1959.

6207. Sievers, Harry J. *Benjamin Harrison: Hoosier Warrior: 1833-1865, Through the Civil War Years.* 2d ed. New York: University Publishers, 1960.

6208. Sievers, Harry J. "The Early Life and Career of Benjamin Harrison, Twenty-third President of the United States." Ph.D. dissertation, Georgetown University, 1950.

6209. Wallace, Lew. *Life of Gen. Ben Harrison.* Philadelphia: Hubbard, 1888.

Private Life

6210. Keith, Charles P. *The Ancestry of Benjamin Harrison, President of the United States of America, 1889-1893, In Chart Form Showing Also the Descendants of William Henry Harrison, President of the United States of America in 1841, and Notes on Families Related.* Philadelphia: Lippincott, 1893.

6211. Lockridge, Ross F. "The Harrisons." In *Benjamin Harrison Memorial ... Report of the Commission.* Washington, DC: U.S. Government Printing Office, 1941.

Public Career

6212. Campbell-Copeland, Thomas. *Harrison and Reid: Their Lives and Record ... The Republican Campaign Book for 1892 ... Over Sixty Illustrations and Maps. ...* 3 vols. New York: Charles L. Webster and Co., 1892.

6213. Dozer, Donald M. "Benjamin Harrison and the Presidential Campaign of 1892." *American Historical Review* 54 (October 1948): 49-77.

6214. Farnum, George R. "Benjamin

Harrison: Man of the Law, Soldier of the Republic, and Gentleman in Politics." *American Bar Association Journal* 29 (September 1943): 514-515, 527.

6215. Harney, Gilbert. *The Lives of Benjamin Harrison and Levi P. Morton: With a History of the Republican Party, and a Statement of Its Position on the Great Issues . . . by Edwin C. Pierce.* Providence, RI: J. A. and R. A. Reid, 1888.

6216. Hirshson, Stanley P. "James S. Clarkson versus Benjamin Harrison, 1891-1893: A Political Saga." *Iowa Journal of History* 58 (July 1960): 219-227.

6217. Knox, Thomas W. *The Republican Party and Its Leaders . . . Lives of Harrison and Reid . . . Profusely Illustrated with Elegant Wood Engravings.* New York: P. F. Collier, 1892.

Presidential Years

6218. Baker, George W., Jr. "Benjamin Harrison and Hawaiian Annexation: A Reinterpretation." *Pacific Historical Review* 33 (August 1964): 295-309.

6219. DeSantis, Vincent P. "Benjamin Harrison and the Republican Party in the South, 1889-1893." *Indiana Magazine of History* 51 (December 1955): 279-302.

6220. Hinckley, Ted C. "Sheldon Jackson and Benjamin Harrison: Presbyterians and the Administration of Alaska." *Pacific Northwest Quarterly* 54 (April 1963): 66-74.

6221. Kehl, James A. "The Unmaking of a President 1889-1892." *Pennsylvania History* 39 (October 1972): 469-484.

6222. McMurry, Donald L. "The Bureau of Pension during the Administration of President Harrison." *Mississippi Valley Historical Review* 13 (December 1926): 343-364.

6223. Sinkler, George. "Benjamin Harrison and the Matter of Race." *Indiana Magazine of History* 65 (September 1969): 197-214.

6224. Spetter, Allen B. "Harrison and Blaine: Foreign Policy, 1889-1893." Ph.D. dissertation, Rutgers University, 1967.

6225. Volwiler, Albert T. "The Early Empire Days of the United States." *West Virginia History* 18 (January 1957): 116-127.

6226. Williams, John A. "Stephen B. Elkins and the Benjamin Harrison Campaign and Cabinet, 1887-1891." *Indiana Magazine of History* 68 (March 1972): 1-23.

Writings

6227. Harrison, Benjamin. "Letters of Benjamin Harrison." Edited by William B. Miller. *Presbyterian Historical Society Journal* 37 (September 1959): 143-154.

6228. Harrison, Benjamin. *Public Papers and Addresses of Benjamin Harrison, Twenty-third President of the United States, March 4, 1889 to March 4, 1893.* Washington, DC: U.S. Government Printing Office, 1893.

6229. Harrison, Benjamin. *Speeches of Benjamin Harrison, Twenty-third President of the United States: A Complete Collection of His Public Addresses from February, 1888, to February, 1892.* Compiled by Charles Hedge. New York: United States Book Co., 1892.

6230. Harrison, Benjamin. *This Country of Ours.* New York: Scribner's, 1897.

6231. Harrison, Benjamin. *Views of an Ex-President: Being His Addresses and Writings on Subjects of Public Interest since the Close of His Administration as President of the United States.* Compiled by Mary L. Harrison. Indianapolis, IN: Bowen-Merrill, 1901.

6232. Harrison, Benjamin, and James G. Blaine. *The Correspondence between Benjamin Harrison and James G. Blain, 1882-1893.* Edited by Albert T. Volwiler. Philadelphia: American Philosophical Society, 1940.

6233. Wright, Marcia. "The Benjamin Harrison Papers." *Library of Congress Quarterly Journal of Current Acquisitions* 18 (May 1961): 121-125.

William McKinley

Biographies

6234. Corning, A. Elwood. *William McKinley, A Biographical Study, With Introductory Address by President Roosevelt.* New York: Broadway Publishing Co., 1907.

6235. Davis, Oscar K. *The Life of William McKinley, Including a Genealogical Record of the McKinley Family and Copious Extracts from the Late President's Public Speeches, Messages to Congress, Proclamations, and Other State Papers.* New York: P. F. Collier, 1901.

6236. Ellis, Edward S. *The Life of William McKinley, The Twenty-fourth President of the United States.* New York: Street and Smith, 1901.

6237. Fallows, Samuel, ed. *Life of William McKinley, Our Martyred President, With Short Biographies of Lincoln and Garfield, and a Comprehensive Life of President Roosevelt, Containing the Masterpieces of McKinley Eloquence, and History of Anarchy, Its Purpose and Results.* Chicago: Regan Printing House, 1901.

6238. Grosvenor, Charles H. *William McKinley, His Life and Work.* Washington, DC: Continental Assembly, 1901.

6239. Halstead, Murat. *The Illustrious Life of William McKinley.* Chicago: Donohue, 1901.

6240. Heald, Edward T. *The William McKinley Story.* Canton, OH: Stark County Historical Society, 1964.

6241. Hoyt, Edwin P. *William McKinley.* Chicago: Reilly and Lee, 1967.

6242. McClure, Alexander K., and Charles Morris. *The Authentic Life of William McKinley ... Together with a Life Sketch of Theodore Roosevelt.* Philadelphia: n.p., 1901.

6243. Morgan, H. Wayne. *William McKinley and His America.* Syracuse, NY: Syracuse University Press, 1963.

6244. Neil, Henry. *Complete Life of William McKinley and Story of His Assassination.* Chicago: Historical Press, 1908.

6245. Ogilvie, John S., ed. *Life and Speeches of William McKinley Containing a Sketch of His Eventual Life ... Sketch of the Candidate for Vice-President ... With Introduction by Hon. Stewart L. Woodford.* New York: J. S. Ogilvie Publishing Co., 1896.

6246. Olcott, Charles S. *The Life of William McKinley.* 2 vols. Boston: Houghton Mifflin, 1916.

6247. Porter, Robert P. *Life of William McKinley Soldier, Lawyer, Statesman.* Cleveland, OH: N. G. Hamilton Publishing Co., 1896.

6248. Roe, Edward T. *The Life of Wil-*

liam McKinley, Twenty-fifth President of the United States, 1897-1901: With a Complete Chronology of His Life and Public Services. Chicago: Laird and Lee, 1913.

6249. Russell, Henry B. *The Lives of William McKinley and Garret A. Hobart, Republican Candidates of 1896: An Authorized, Impartial, Authentic, and Complete History ... Illustrated with Portraits and Full Page Engravings*. Hartford, CT: Worthington, 1896.

6250. Snow, Jane E. *The Life of William McKinley, Twenty-fifth President of the United States*. Cleveland, OH: Gardner Printing Co., 1908.

6251. Spielman, William C. *William McKinley, Stalwart Republican: A Biographical Study*. New York: Exposition Press, 1954.

6252. Townsend, George W. *Our Martyred President ... Memorial Life of William McKinley*. Philadelphia: National Publishing Co., 1901.

6253. Tyler, John. *The Life of William McKinley, Soldier, Statesman, and President....* Philadelphia: P. W. Ziegler and Co., 1901.

Private Life

6254. Bristol, F. M. "William McKinley, The Ideal American." *Methodist Review* 85 (November 1903): 849-863.

6255. Brush, Edward H. "In Remembrance of William McKinley: The Birthplace Memorial at Niles, Ohio, and Other Tributes." *National Magazine* 46 (June 1917): 386-390.

6256. Chapple, Joseph M. "The Real McKinley." *National Magazine* 44 (July 1916): 569-584.

6257. Gordon, Charles U. *William McKinley, Commemorative Tributes*. Waterloo, WI: Courier Printing Co., 1942.

6258. King, Horatio C. "How McKinley Became a Mason." *Grand Lodge Bulletin* 30 (January 1929): 7-8.

6259. Kuhns, William T. *Memories of Old Canton and My Personal Recollections of William McKinley*. Canton, OH: Privately Printed, 1937.

6260. Latcham, John S. "President McKinley's Active Positive Character: A Comparative Revision with Barber's Typology." *Presidential Studies Quarterly* 12 (Fall 1982): 491-521.

Public Career

6261. Ellis, Edward S. *From Tent to White House, Or How a Poor Boy Became President*. New York: Street and Smith, 1899.

6262. Jensen, Richard J. *The Winning of the Midwest: Social and Political Conflict, 1888-1896*. Chicago: University of Chicago Press, 1971.

6263. Miller, Charles R. "William McKinley, The Lawyer." *Ohio Law Reporter* 14 (May 29, 1916): 195-202.

6264. Morgan, H. Wayne. "The Congressional Career of McKinley." Ph.D. dissertation, University of California, Los Angeles, 1960.

6265. Morgan, H. Wayne. *From Hayes to McKinley: National Party Politics, 1877-1896*. Syracuse, NY: Syracuse University Press, 1969.

6266. Morgan, H. Wayne. "Governor McKinley's Misfortune: The Walker-McKinley Fund of 1893." *Ohio Historical Quarterly* 69 (April 1960): 103-120.

6267. Morgan, H. Wayne. "William McKinley as a Political Leader." *Review of Politics* 28 (October 1966): 417-432.

6268. Peckham, Charles A. "The Ohio National Guard and Its Police Duties, 1894." *Ohio History* 83 (Winter 1974): 51-67.

6269. Waksmudski, John. "Governor McKinley and the Workingman." *Historian* 38 (August 1976): 629-647.

6270. Weisenburger, Francis P. "The Time of Mark Hanna's First Acquaintance with McKinley." *Mississippi Valley Historical Review* 21 (June 1934): 78-80.

Presidential Years

6271. Adler, Selig. "The Operation on President McKinley." In *An American Historian: Essays to Honor Selig Adler*, edited by Milton Plesur, 37-49. Buffalo: State University of New York, 1980.

6272. Bacote, Clarence A. "Negro Officeholders in Georgia under President McKinley." *Journal of Negro History* 44 (July 1959): 217-239.

6273. Bailey, John W., Jr. "The Presidential Election of 1900 in Nebraska: McKinley over Bryan." *Nebraska History* 54 (Winter 1973): 561-584.

6274. Bristow, Joseph L. *Fraud and Politics at the Turn of the Century: McKinley and His Administration as Seen by His Principal Patronage Dispenser and Investigator*. New York: Exposition Press, 1952.

6275. Coletta, Paolo E. "Bryan, McKinley, and the Treaty of Paris." *Pacific Historical Review* 26 (May 1957): 131-146.

6276. Coletta, Paolo E. "McKinley, the Peace Negotiations, and the Acquisition of the Philippines." *Pacific Historical Review* 30 (November 1961): 341-340.

6277. Coletta, Paolo E., ed. *Threshold to American Internationalism: Essays on the Foreign Policy of William McKinley*. New York: Exposition Press, 1970.

6278. Coulter, John. *Our Martyr Presidents: Lincoln, Garfield, McKinley, Their Illustrious Lives, Public and Private, and Their Glorious Deeds....* Chicago: Memorial Publishing House, 1901.

6279. Coursey, W. S. "William McKinley as Commander in Chief of the U.S." *National Magazine* 16 (February 1902): 149-152.

6280. Damiani, Brian P. "Advocates of Empire: William McKinley, the Senate, and American Expansion, 1898-1899." Ph.D. dissertation, University of Delaware, 1978.

6281. Daniel, John W. "William McKinley." In his *Speeches and Orations...*, compiled by Edward M. Daniel, 757-784. Lynchburg, VA: J. P. Bell Co., 1911.

6282. Dawes, Charles G. *A Journal of the McKinley Years*. Edited by Bascom N. Timmons. Chicago: Lakeside Press, 1950.

6283. DuBois, William E. B. "From McKinley to Wallace: My Fifty Years as a Political Independent." *Masses and Mainstream* 1 (August 1948): 3-13.

6284. Ellis, Paul S., et al. *Great Leaders and National Issues of 1896*. Philadelphia: Monarch Publishing Co., 1896.

6285. Fine, Sidney. "Anarchism and the Assassination of McKinley." *American Historical Review* 60 (July 1955): 777-799.

6286. Freidel, Frank B. "The American Giant Comes of Age." *National Geographic Magazine* (May 1965): 708-711.

6287. Freidel, Frank B. *The Splendid Little War*. Boston: Little, Brown, 1958.

6288. Fry, Joseph A. "William McKinley and the Coming of the Spanish-American War: A Study of the Besmirching and Redemption of an Historical Image." *Diplomatic History* 3 (Winter 1979): 77-98.

6289. Gillam, Victor. "The Triumphal Entry of McKinley, March 4th, 1897."

Judge 32 (March 13, 1897): 172-173.

6290. Glad, Paul W. *McKinley, Bryan, and the People*. Philadelphia: Lippincott, 1964.

6291. Goldman, Emma. "The Assassination of McKinley." *American Mercury* 24 (September 1931): 53-67.

6292. Gould, Lewis L. *The Presidency of William McKinley*. Lawrence: Regents Press of Kansas, 1981.

6293. Gould, Lewis L. "William McKinley and the Expansion of Presidential Power." *Ohio History* 87 (Winter 1978): 5-20.

6294. Holbo, Paul W. "Presidential Leadership in Foreign Affairs: William McKinley and the Turpie-Foraker Amendment." *American Historical Review* 72 (July 1967): 1321-1335.

6295. Jeffreys-Jones, Rhodri. "The Montreal Spy Ring of 1898 and the Origins of 'Domestic' Surveillance in the United States." *Canadian Review of American Studies* 5 (Fall 1974): 119-134.

6296. Kendrick, Benjamin B. "McKinley and Foraker." *Political Science Quarterly* 31 (December 1916): 590-604.

6297. Leech, Margaret. *In the Days of McKinley*. New York: Harper and Row, 1959.

6298. Lindsey, David. "Rehabilitating the Presidents: Garfield, Arthur, McKinley." *Reviews in American History* 10 (March 10, 1982): 72-77.

6299. McCarthy, G. Michael. "The Forest Reserve Controversy: Colorado under Cleveland and McKinley." *Journal of Forest History* 20 (April 1976): 80-90.

6300. McCormick, Thomas J. " 'A Fair Field and No Favor' American China Policy during the McKinley Administrations, 1897-1902." Ph.D. dissertation, University of Wisconsin, 1960.

6301. MacDonald, Carlos F., and Edward A. Spitzka. *The Trial, Execution, Autopsy, and Mental Status of Leon F. Czolgosz, Alias Fred. Nieman, The Assassin of President McKinley, With a Report of the Post-Mortem Examination*. Philadelphia: n.p., 1902.

6302. McDonald, Timothy G. "McKinley and the Coming of War with Spain." *Midwest Quarterly* 7 (Spring 1966): 225-239.

6303. McWilliams, Tennant S. "Petition for Expansion: Mobile Businessmen and the Cuban Crisis, 1898." *Alabama Review* 28 (January 1975): 58-63.

6304. Millis, Walter. *The Martial Spirit*. New York: Literary Guild of America, 1931.

6305. Morgan, H. Wayne. "William McKinley and the Tariff." *Ohio History* 74 (Autumn 1965): 215-231.

6306. Nichols, Jeannette P. "The Monetary Problems of William McKinley." *Ohio History* 72 (October 1963): 263-292.

6307. Offner, John L. "President McKinley and the Origins of the Spanish-American War." Ph.D. dissertation, Pennsylvania State University, 1957.

6308. Oldroyd, Osborn H. *The March to Victory . . . with Platform, Portraits, Biographies, and Sketches of McKinley and Hobart*. Chicago: Laird and Lee, 1896.

6309. Perry, Frances M., and Henry W. Elson. *. . . Four Great American Presidents: No. 2. Garfield, McKinley, Cleveland, Roosevelt: A Book for American Readers*. New York: J. M. Stradling and Co., 1903.

6310. Pixton, John E., Jr. "Charles G. Dawes and the McKinley Campaign." *Illinois State Historical Society Journal* 48 (Autumn 1955): 283-306.

6311. Price, W. W. "President McKinley's Tours." *Cosmopolitan* 34 (February 1903): 383-392.

6312. Pritchett, Henry S. "Some Recollections of President McKinley and the Cuban Intervention." *North American Review* 189 (March 1909): 397-403.

6313. Rhodes, James F. *The McKinley and Roosevelt Administrations, 1897-1909.* New York: Macmillan, 1922.

6314. Sherman, Richard B. "Presidential Protection during the Progressive Era: The Aftermath of the McKinley Assassination." *Historian* 46 (November 1983): 1-20.

6315. Skinner, Charles R. "Story of McKinley's Assassination." *State Service* 3 (April 1919): 20-24.

6316. Stern, Clarence A. *Protectionist Republicanism: Republican Tariff Policy in the McKinley Period.* Oshkosh, WI: Stern, 1971.

6317. Stern, Clarence A. *Republican Heyday, Republicanism through the McKinley Years.* Ann Arbor: University of Michigan Press, 1962.

6318. Stevenson, Adlai E., et al. "Bryan or McKinley?" *North American Review* 171 (October 1900): 433-516.

6319. Straus, Oscar S. *Under Four Administrations: From Cleveland to Taft.* Boston: Houghton Mifflin, 1922.

6320. Tarbell, Ida M. "President McKinley in War Time." *McClure's Magazine* 11 (July 1898): 209-224.

6321. Throne, Mildred. "McKinley in Iowa." *Palimpsest* 45 (August 1964): 273-279.

6322. Van Alstyne, Richard W. *The Rising American Empire.* Chicago: Quadrangle Books, 1965.

6323. Waksmudski, John. "McKinley Politics and the Changing Attitudes toward American Labor, 1870-1900." Ph.D. dissertation, Ohio State University, 1972.

6324. Waksmudski, John. "William McKinley and the Railway Workers: Insight into Political Strategy." *West Virginia History* 36 (October 1974): 37-39.

6325. Weinberg, Albert K. *Manifest Destiny: A Study of Nationalist Expansion in American History.* Chicago: Quadrangle Books, 1963.

6326. West, Henry L. "The President's Recent Tour." *Forum* 31 (August 1901): 661-669.

6327. West, Henry L. "William McKinley." *Forum* 32 (October 1901): 131-137.

6328. Williams, William A. *The Roots of the Modern American Empire: A Study of the Growth and Shaping of Social Consciousness in a Marketplace Society.* New York: Random House, 1969.

Writings

6329. Andrews, Byron. *One of the People: Life and Speeches of William McKinley ... to Which Is Added a Brief Sketch of Garret A. Hobart, Candidate for Vice-President.* Chicago: F. Tennyson Neely, 1896.

6330. McKinley, William. "A Civil War Diary of William McKinley." Edited by H. Wayne Morgan. *Ohio Historical Quarterly* 69 (July 1960): 272-290.

6331. McKinley, William. *Speeches and Addresses of William McKinley, From His Election to Congress to the Present Time.* New York: Appleton, 1893.

6332. McKinley, William. *Speeches and Addresses of William McKinley, From March 1, 1897 to May 30, 1900.* New York: Doubleday and McClure, 1900.

6333. McKinley, William. *The Tariff in*

the Days of Henry Clay, and Since: An Exhaustive Review of Our Tariff Legislation from 1812 to 1896. New York: Henry Clay Publishing Co., 1896.

6334. Paget, R. L. *McKinley's Masterpieces: Selections from the Public Addresses in and out of Congress of William McKinley.* Boston: Joseph Knight, 1896.

Theodore Roosevelt

Biographies

6335. Abbott, Lawrence F. *Impressions of Theodore Roosevelt.* Garden City, NY: Doubleday, 1919.

6336. Abernathy, John R. *"Catch 'Em Alive Jack": The Life and Adventures of an American Pioneer.* New York: Associated Press, 1936.

6337. Amos, James. *Theodore Roosevelt: Hero to His Valet.* New York: John Day, 1927.

6338. Anderson, Robert G. *Leader of Men.* New York: Putnam, 1920.

6339. Banks, Charles E. *Theodore Roosevelt.* Chicago: Dominion, 1901.

6340. Beach, James C. *Theodore Roosevelt, Man of Action.* Champaign, IL: Garrard, 1960.

6341. Blackburn, Joyce. *Theodore Roosevelt, Naturalist, Statesman.* Grand Rapids, MI: Zondervan, 1967.

6342. Brown, Harriet G. *Roosevelt, A Knight of the Nineteenth Century.* Richmond, VA: Johnson Publishing Co., 1926.

6343. Brumbaugh, Martin G. *The Story of Theodore Roosevelt.* Dansville, NY: F. A. Owen Publishing Co., 1922.

6344. Burton, David H. *Theodore Roosevelt.* Boston: G. K. Hall, 1973.

6345. Busch, Noel F. *T. R., The Story of Theodore Roosevelt and His Influence on Our Times.* New York: Reynal, 1963.

6346. Cadenhead, Ivie. *A Life of Theodore Roosevelt.* Woodbury, NY: Barron's, 1974.

6347. Charnwood, Godfrey R. B. *Theodore Roosevelt.* Boston: Atlantic Monthly, 1923.

6348. Clarke, Charles F. *The Story of an American, Dedicated to the Memory of Theodore Roosevelt.* Des Moines, IA: Globe Publishing Co., 1920.

6349. Clemens, William M. *Theodore Roosevelt, The American.* New York: F. T. Neely, 1899.

6350. Colquhoun, Archibald R. "Theodore Roosevelt." *Fortnightly Review* 86 (May 1910): 832-845.

6351. "Concerning Biography and Certain Biographies of Roosevelt: By a Friend of Theodore Roosevelt." *Outlook* 126 (October 13, 1920): 291-292.

6352. Cotton, Edward H. *The Ideals of Theodore Roosevelt.* New York: Appleton, 1923.

6353. Cotton, Edward H. *Theodore Roosevelt, The American.* Boston: Beacon Press, 1926.

6354. Cushing, Otho. *The Teddyssey.* New York: Life Publishing Co., 1907.

6355. Cutright, Paul R. *Theodore Roosevelt, The Making of a Conservationist.* Urbana: University of Illinois Press, 1985.

6356. Cutright, Paul R. *Theodore Roosevelt, The Naturalist.* New York: Harper and Row, 1956.

6357. Depew, Chauncey M. "Theodore Roosevelt." *New York Genealogical and Biographical Record* 50 (April 1919): 97-107.

6358. Dewey, John. "Theodore Roosevelt." *Dial* 66 (February 8, 1919): 115-117.

6359. Douglas, George W. *The Many-Sided Roosevelt, An Anecdotal Biography.* New York: Dodd, Mead, 1907.

6360. Egloff, Franklin R. *Theodore Roosevelt, An American Portrait.* New York: Vantage Press, 1980.

6361. Einstein, Lewis. *Roosevelt, His Mind in Action.* Boston: Houghton Mifflin, 1930.

6362. Ellis, Edward S. *From the Ranch to the White House: Life of Theodore Roosevelt.* Chicago: A. Whitman and Co., 1927.

6363. Feuerlicht, Roberta. *Theodore Roosevelt: A Concise Biography.* New York: American R. D. M., 1966.

6364. Finger, Charles J. *Life of Theodore Roosevelt.* Girard, KS: Haldeman-Julius, 1924.

6365. Foster, Genevieve. *Theodore Roosevelt, An Initial Biography.* New York: Scribner's, 1954.

6366. Garraty, John A. *Theodore Roosevelt: The Strenuous Life.* New York: American Heritage Publishing Co., 1967.

6367. Grantham, Dewey W., Jr. *Theodore Roosevelt.* Englewood Cliffs, NJ: Prentice-Hall, 1971.

6368. Hagedorn, Hermann. *Roosevelt: Prophet of Unity.* New York: Scribner's, 1924.

6369. Hagedorn, Hermann. *Theodore Roosevelt: A Biographical Sketch.* New York: Roosevelt Memorial Exhibition Committee, Columbia University, 1919.

6370. Hale, Annie R. *Rooseveltian Fact and Fable.* New York: Broadway Publishing Co., 1908.

6371. Halstead, Murat. *The Life of Theodore Roosevelt....* Chicago: Saalfield Publishing Co., 1902.

6372. Hancock, Sibyl. *Theodore Roosevelt.* New York: Putnam, 1978.

6373. Handford, Thomas. *The Life and Sayings of Theodore Roosevelt....* Chicago: Donohue, 1903.

6374. Harbaugh, William H. *The Life and Times of Theodore Roosevelt.* Rev. ed. New York: Oxford University Press, 1975.

6375. Harlow, Alvin F. *Theodore Roosevelt: Strenuous American.* New York: Messner, 1943.

6376. Henderson, Daniel M. *'Great-Heart,' The Life Story of Theodore Roosevelt.* 4th ed. New York: Knopf, 1919.

6377. House, Roy T. "The Story of Theodore Roosevelt." *Normal Instructor* 28 (October 1919): 39-40.

6378. Ickes, Harold L. *The Autobiography of a Curmudgeon.* New York: Reynal and Hitchcock, 1943.

6379. Iglehart, Ferdinand C. *Theodore Roosevelt: The Man as I Knew Him.* New York: Christian Herald, 1919.

6380. Johnston, William D. *T. R., Champion of the Strenuous Life: A Photographic Biography of Theodore Roosevelt.* New York: Farrar, Straus and Cudahy, 1958.

6381. Judson, Clara I. *Theodore Roosevelt, Fighting Patriot.* Chicago: Wilcox and Follett, 1953.

6382. Keller, Morton, ed. *Theodore Roosevelt: A Profile.* New York: Hill and Wang, 1967.

6383. Leupp, Francis E. *The Man Roosevelt: A Portrait Sketch*. New York: Appleton, 1904.

6384. Lewis, William D. *The Life of Theodore Roosevelt*. New York: United Publishers, 1919.

6385. Lodge, Henry C. *Theodore Roosevelt*. Boston: Houghton Mifflin, 1919.

6386. Looker, Earle. *This Man Roosevelt*. New York: Brewer, Warren and Putnam, 1932.

6387. Lorant, Stefan. *The Life and Times of Theodore Roosevelt*. Garden City, NY: Doubleday, 1959.

6388. McCaleb, Walter F. *Theodore Roosevelt*. New York: A. and C. Boni, 1931.

6389. McSpadden, J. Walker. *The Story of Theodore Roosevelt*. New York: Barse and Hopkins, 1923.

6390. Markam, Lois. *Teddy Roosevelt*. New York: Chelsea House, 1984.

6391. Meyers, Robert C. V. *Theodore Roosevelt, Patriot and Statesman: A True Story of an Ideal American*. Philadelphia: P. W. Ziegler, 1902.

6392. Michael, Charles D. *President Roosevelt*. London: Dalton, 1908.

6393. Miller, James M., ed. *The Triumphant Life of Theodore Roosevelt*. Philadelphia: n.p., 1904.

6394. Morgan, James. *Theodore Roosevelt, The Boy and the Man*. New York: Macmillan, 1919.

6395. Morris, Charles. *The Marvelous Career of Theodore Roosevelt*. Philadelphia: John C. Winston Co., 1910.

6396. Morris, Charles. *Theodore Roosevelt and the Presidents of the U.S.* Philadelphia: World Bible House, 1905.

6397. Musso, Louis, III. *Theodore Roosevelt, Soldier, Statesman, and President.* Edited by Siguid C. Rahmas. Charlotteville, NY: SamHar Press, 1982.

6398. Norton, Aloysius A. *Theodore Roosevelt*. Boston: Twayne, 1980.

6399. Pearson, Edmund L. *Theodore Roosevelt*. New York: Macmillan, 1920.

6400. Perry, Frances M. *A Life of Theodore Roosevelt. . . .* New York: J. M. Stradling and Co., 1903.

6401. Pringle, Henry F. *Theodore Roosevelt: A Biography*. Rev. ed. New York: Harcourt, Brace, 1956.

6402. Putnam, Carleton. *Theodore Roosevelt, A Biography*. New York: Scribner's, 1958.

6403. Putnam, Charles. *Theodore Roosevelt: The Formative Years*. New York: Scribner's, 1958.

6404. Ricard, Serge. "The French Historiography of Theodore Roosevelt." *Theodore Roosevelt Association Journal* 10 (Summer 1984): 21-23.

6405. Robinson, Corinne R. *My Brother, Theodore Roosevelt*. New York: Scribner's, 1921.

6406. Roosevelt, Nicholas. *A Front Row Seat*. Norman: University of Oklahoma Press, 1953.

6407. Roosevelt, Nicholas. *Theodore Roosevelt: The Man as I Knew Him*. New York: Dodd, Mead, 1967.

6408. Root, Elihu. "Theodore Roosevelt." *North American Review* 210 (December 1919): 754-758.

6409. Russell, Thomas H. *Life and Work of Theodore Roosevelt, Typical American, Patriot, Orator, Historian, Sportsman, Soldier, Statesman, and President*. Chicago: Homewood Press, 1919.

6410. Sewall, William W. "As I Knew Roosevelt." *Forum* 61 (May 1919): 537-550.

6411. Sewall, William W. *Bill Sewall's Story of T. R.* New York: Harper and Row, 1919.

6412. Shaw, Albert. *A Cartoon History of Roosevelt's Career, Illustrated by 630 Contemporary Cartoons.* New York: Review of Reviews, 1910.

6413. Smith, Edward G. *The Real Roosevelt....* New York: National Weekly Publishing Co., 1904.

6414. Street, Julian L. *The Most Interesting American.* New York: Century, 1915.

6415. Thayer, William R. *Theodore Roosevelt, An Intimate Biography.* Boston: Houghton Mifflin, 1919.

6416. Theodore Roosevelt Centennial Commission. *A Compilation on the Life and Career of Theodore Roosevelt Relating to the Celebration in 1958 of the Hundredth Anniversary of His Birth.* Senate Document no. 84, 85th Cong., 2d sess., Washington, DC: U.S. Government Printing Office, 1958.

6417. Thwing, Eugene. *The Life and Meaning of Theodore Roosevelt.* New York: Current Literature Publishing Co., 1919.

6418. Towne, Charles H., ed. *Roosevelt as the Poets Saw Him: Tributes from the Singers of America and England to Theodore Roosevelt.* New York: Scribner's, 1923.

6419. Viereck, George S. *Roosevelt.* New York: Jackson Press, 1919.

6420. Vrooman, Frank B. *Theodore Roosevelt.* New York: H. Frowde, 1909.

6421. Wagenknecht, Edward C. *The Seven Worlds of Theodore Roosevelt.* New York: Longmans, Green, 1958.

6422. Whipple, Wayne. *The Heart of Roosevelt: An Intimate Life-Story of Theodore Roosevelt.* Philadelphia: Winston, 1923.

6423. Wister, Owen. *Roosevelt, The Story of a Friendship, 1880-1919.* New York: Macmillan, 1930.

6424. Wood, Frederick S. *Roosevelt as We Knew Him: The Personal Recollections of One Hundred and Fifty of His Friends and Associates.* Philadelphia: Winston, 1927.

Private Life

6425. Abbott, Lawrence F. "An English Portrait of Roosevelt." *Outlook* 135 (October 31, 1923): 348-349.

6426. Abbott, Lawrence F. "Theodore Roosevelt and His Four Sons: How They Trained Themselves for National Defense." *Munsey's* 42 (December 1917): 385-391.

6427. Abernathy, John R. *In Camp with Theodore Roosevelt.* Oklahoma City: Times-Journal Publishing Co., 1933.

6428. Akeley, Carl E. "Theodore Roosevelt and Africa." *National History* 19 (January 1919): 12-14.

6429. Altherr, Thomas L. "The American Hunter-Naturalist and the Development of the Code of Sportsmanship." *Journal of Sport History* 5 (Spring 1978): 7-22.

6430. Arnold, Thurman. "Roosevelt's Contribution to the American Competitive Ideal." *Centennial Review* 9 (Spring 1965): 192-208.

6431. Beale, Howard K. "Theodore Roosevelt's Ancestry, A Study in Heredity." *New York Genealogical and Biographical Record* 85 (October 1984): 196-205.

6432. Bissell, Richard. "Carefree Harvard Days of Three Presidents." *McCall's* 90 (October 1962): 89-91.

6433. Bradford, Gamaliel. "The Fury of Living: Theodore Roosevelt." *Harper's Magazine* 162 (February 1931): 353-364.

6434. Brooks, Chester L., and Ray H. Mattison. *Theodore Roosevelt and the Dakota Badlands.* Washington, DC: National Park Service, 1958.

6435. Brown, Glenn. "Roosevelt and the Fine Arts: Restoration of the White House." *American Architect* 116 (December 17, 1919): 739-752.

6436. Brown, William G. "The Personality of Theodore Roosevelt." *Independent* 55 (July 2, 1903): 1547-1551.

6437. Burroughs, John. *Camping and Tramping with Roosevelt.* Boston: Houghton Mifflin, 1907.

6438. Burroughs, John. "Theodore Roosevelt: His Americanism Reached into the Marrow of His Bones." *Natural History* 19 (January 1919): 5-7.

6439. Burroughs, John. "With Roosevelt at Pine Knot." *Outlook* 128 (May 25, 1921): 170-171.

6440. Burton, David H. *Theodore Roosevelt and His English Correspondents: A Special Relationship of Friends.* Philadelphia: American Philosophical Society, 1973.

6441. Case, Carleton B. *Good Stories about Roosevelt, The Humorous Side of a Great American.* Chicago: Shrewesbury Publishing Co., 1920.

6442. Chapin, Henry D. "A Little Journal with Theodore Roosevelt." *Outlook* 138 (October 22, 1924): 286-288.

6443. Cobb, William T. *The Strenuous Life: The "Oyster Bay" Roosevelts in Business and Finance.* New York: Rudge, 1946.

6444. Curtis, Natalie. "Mr. Roosevelt and Indian Music: A Personal Reminiscence." *Outlook* 121 (March 15, 1919): 399-400.

6445. Curtis, Natalie. "Theodore Roosevelt in Hopi-Land: Another Personal Reminiscence." *Outlook* 123 (September 17, 1919): 87-88, 92-93.

6446. Cutright, Paul R. "Theodore Roosevelt Disposes of His Boyhood Bird Specimens." *Theodore Roosevelt Association Journal* 9 (Fall 1983): 2-8.

6447. Dalton, Kathleen M. "The Early Life of Theodore Roosevelt." Ph.D. dissertation, Johns Hopkins University, 1979.

6448. Dalton, Kathleen M. "Why America Loved Theodore Roosevelt: Or Charisma Is in the Eyes of the Beholders." *Psychohistory Review* 8 (Winter 1979): 16-26.

6449. Davis, Glenn. "The Early Years of Theodore Roosevelt: A Study in Character Formation." *History of Childhood Quarterly* 2 (Spring 1975): 461-492.

6450. Donovan, Michael J. *The Roosevelt That I Know: Ten Years of Boxing with the President — And Other Memories of Famous Fighting Men.* New York: B. W. Dodge, 1909.

6451. Drinker, Frederick E., and Jay H. Mowbray. *Theodore Roosevelt, His Life and Work.* Philadelphia: National Publishing Co., 1919.

6452. Eberle, Louise. "The Fraser Bust of Roosevelt." *Scribner's Magazine* 68 (October 1920): 427-433.

6453. Farrar, Broadus F. "John Burroughs, Theodore Roosevelt, and the Nature Fakers." *Tennessee Studies in Literature* 4 (1959): 121-130.

6454. Franks, Kenny A., ed. "Roosevelt: Ranching Adventures in the Dakotas." *Great Plains Journal* 14 (Fall 1974): 87-103.

6455. Gardner, Joseph L. *Departing Glory: Theodore Roosevelt as Ex-President.* New York: Scribner's, 1973.

6456. Garland, Hamlin. "My Neighbor,

Theodore Roosevelt." *Everybody's Magazine* 41 (October 1919): 9-16.

6457. Garland, Hamlin. "Roosevelt House." *Landmark* 7 (May 1925): 273-277.

6458. Garraty, John A., ed. "Theodore Roosevelt on the Telephone." *American Heritage* 9 (December 1957): 99-108.

6459. Goldsmith, B. H. "Theodore Roosevelt, Jr." *Americana* 21 (January 1927): 93-100.

6460. Graff, Steward. *Theodore Roosevelt's Boys: Accounts of Several Times at Sagamore Hill and in the White House When the Roosevelt Children Were Entertained by Their Father, Theodore, or Got into Mischief by Themselves.* Champaign, IL: Gerrard, 1967.

6461. Grantham, Dewey W., Jr. "Theodore Roosevelt in American Historical Writing, 1945-1960." *Mid-America* 43 (January 1961): 3-35.

6462. Hagedorn, Hermann. *A Guide to Sagamore Hill: The Place, The People, The Life, The Meaning.* New York: Theodore Roosevelt Association, 1953.

6463. Hagedorn, Hermann. *The Roosevelt Family of Sagamore Hill.* New York: MacMillan, 1954.

6464. Hagedorn, Hermann. *Roosevelt in the Bad Lands.* Boston: Houghton Mifflin, 1921.

6465. Hagedorn, Hermann, comp. *The Americanism of Theodore Roosevelt.* Boston: Houghton Mifflin, 1923.

6466. Hagen, Olaf T., and Ray H. Mattison. "Pyramid Park — Where Roosevelt Came to Hunt." *Dakota History* 19 (October 1952): 215-239.

6467. Hayden, Jay G. "Was Theodore Roosevelt a Drunk?" *American Heritage* 15 (October 1964): 82-83.

6468. Hedges, Job E. "The Personality and the Philosophy of Theodore Roosevelt." *Journal of American History* 13 (July 1919): 326-334.

6469. Helicher, Karl. "The Brahmin Scholar: The Formative Years of Theodore Roosevelt." *Presidential Studies Quarterly* 15 (Summer 1985): 541-548.

6470. Henderson, Daniel M. *Jungle Roads and Other Trials of Roosevelt, A Book for Boys.* New York: Dutton, 1920.

6471. "Historic Medora, North Dakota." *Theodore Roosevelt Association Journal* 9 (Spring 1983): 2-9.

6472. Howard, Eleanor V. "This Week's Wedding at the White House." *Harper's Weekly* 50 (February 17, 1906): 222-227.

6473. Howell, Edward B. "Roosevelt in Montana: Recollections of Two Visits." *Review of Reviews* 58 (October 1923): 339-400.

6474. Hoyt, Edwin P. *Teddy Roosevelt in Africa.* New York: Duell, Sloan and Pearce, 1967.

6475. Jordan, David S. "Personal Glimpses of Theodore Roosevelt." *National History* 19 (January 1919): 15-16.

6476. Jusserand, Jean A. "Personal Memories of Theodore Roosevelt." *Journal of American History* 13 (July 1919): 320-325.

6477. Kiell, Norman. "Effects of Asthma on the Character of Theodore Roosevelt." In *The Asthmatic Child: Psychosomatic Approach to Problems and Treatment,* edited by Henry Schneer, 84-102. New York: Hoeber Medical Division, 1963.

6478. Lang, Lincoln A. *Ranching with Roosevelt, By a Comparison Rancher.* Philadelphia: Lippincott, 1926.

6479. Laughlin, J. Laurence. "Roosevelt at Harvard." *Review of Reviews* 70 (October 1924): 391-398.

6480. Leary, John J., Jr. *Talks with T. R.* Boston: Houghton Mifflin, 1920.

6481. Longworth, Alice R. *Crowded Hours: Reminiscences.* New York: Scribner's, 1933.

6482. Longworth, Alice R., and Michael Teague. *Mrs. L.: Conversations with Alice Roosevelt Longworth.* Garden City, NY: Doubleday, 1981.

6483. Looker, Earle. *The White House Gang.* New York: Revell, 1929.

6484. McCullough, David. *Mornings on Horseback.* New York: Simon and Schuster, 1981.

6485. Mattison, Ray H. "Ranching in the Dakota Badlands: A Study of Roosevelt's Contemporaries." *Dakota History* 19 (April 1952): 93-128.

6486. Merriam, C. Hart. "Roosevelt, The Naturalist." *Science* 75 (February 12, 1932): 181-183.

6487. Miller, Nathan. *The Roosevelt Chronicles.* Garden City, NY: Doubleday, 1979.

6488. Morris, Sylvia J. *Edith Kermit Roosevelt: Portrait of a First Lady.* New York: Coward, McCann and Geoghegan, 1980.

6489. Needham, Henry B. "Theodore Roosevelt — An Outdoor Man." *McClure's* 26 (January 1906): 231-252.

6490. Nelson, Gerry. "Roosevelt Ranch Life in the Badlands." *North Dakota History* 24 (October 1957): 171-174.

6491. New York State. *A Memorial to Theodore Roosevelt.* Albany, NY: J. B. Lyon Co., 1919.

6492. O'Brien, Michael J. "The Irish Ancestry of Theodore Roosevelt." *American Irish Historical Society Journal* 17 (1918): 144-145.

6493. Ogg, Frederic A. "When Grant Came Home: A Remarkable Historical Parallel to the Reception of Ex-President Roosevelt on His Return to America." *Munsey's Magazine* 43 (July 1910): 537-541.

6494. Osborn, Henry F. "Theodore Roosevelt, Naturalist." *Natural History* 19 (January 1919): 9-10.

6495. Osborne, Duffield. "Roosevelt: A Feminine Type." *Forum* 43 (February 1910): 198-200.

6496. Payne, Frank O. "More Roosevelt Sculptures." *Art and Archaeology* 8 (July 1919): 197-202.

6497. Payne, Frank O. "Theodore Roosevelt in Sculpture." *Art and Archaeology* 8 (April 1919): 109-113.

6498. Pinchot, Gifford. "Roosevelt, The Man of Abundant Life." *Natural History* 19 (January 1919): 17-18.

6499. Pollin, Burton R. "Theodore Roosevelt to the Rescue of the Poe Cottage." *Mississippi Quarterly* 34 (Winter 1980-1981): 51-59.

6500. Pratt, Lowell C. "Theodore Roosevelt 'Discovers' California." *Journal of the West* 3 (January 1964): 40-46.

6501. Putnam, Carleton. "Theodore Roosevelt: The Early Pattern." *New York Historical Society Quarterly* 42 (April 1958): 117-141.

6502. Ranlett, F. J. "Theodore Roosevelt's College Rank and Studies." *Harvard Graduates Magazine* 15 (June 1907): 578-583.

6503. Reisner, Christian F. *Roosevelt's Religion.* New York: Abingdon Press, 1922.

6504. Riis, Jacob A. *Theodore Roosevelt the Citizen ... Illustrated.* New York: Outlook Co., 1904.

6505. Roberts, Gerald F. "The Strenuous

Life: The Cult of Manliness in the Era of Theodore Roosevelt." Ph.D. dissertation, Michigan State University, 1970.

6506. "Roosevelt as Revealed in His Letters to His Children." *Current Opinion* 68 (January 1920): 41-44.

6507. "Roosevelt as the Spiritual Opposite of Henry Adams." *Current Opinion* 68 (February 1920): 215-217.

6508. "Roosevelt Memorial." *Columbia Historical Society Records* 23 (1920): 206-213.

6509. "Roosevelt the Man of Rare Courage." *State Service* 3 (January 1919): 35-38.

6510. Smith, Ronald A. "Sport, Politics, and Harvard: A Little Lesson in Honor for Theodore Roosevelt." *New England Quarterly* 54 (September 1981): 412-416.

6511. Stewart, Kate M. "Theodore Roosevelt: Hunter-Naturalist on Safari." *Library of Congress Quarterly Journal* 27 (July 1970): 242-256.

6512. Syracuse, New York Public Library. *Roosevelt, Lover of Books*. Syracuse, NY: Syracuse Public Library, 1920.

6513. Tarter, Brent. "Pine Knot: Theodore Roosevelt's Virginia Retreat." *Virginia Cavalcade* 33 (Spring 1984): 184-191.

6514. Teichmann, Howard. *Alice, The Life and Times of Alice Roosevelt Longworth*. Englewood Cliffs, NJ: Prentice-Hall, 1979.

6515. "Theodore Roosevelt's Religion." *Current Opinion* 72 (January 1922): 82-83.

6516. Unger, Frederic W. *Roosevelt's African Trip*. Philadelphia: American Book and Bible House, 1909.

6517. Volwiler, Albert T. "Roosevelt's Ranch Life in North Dakota." *University of North Dakota Quarterly Journal* 9 (October 1918): 31-49.

6518. Walker, Don D. "Wister, Roosevelt, and James: A Note on the Western." *American Quarterly* 12 (Fall 1960): 358-366.

6519. Welling, Richard. "Theodore Roosevelt at Harvard: Some Personal Reminiscences." *Outlook* 126 (October 27, 1920): 366-369.

6520. Wheelan, Fairfax H. "Something of the Class of '80: Roosevelt at Harvard, and Our Political Duty." *University of California Chronicle* 5 (January 1903): 332-341.

6521. White, William A. "Roosevelt: A Force for Righteousness." *McClure's* 28 (February 1907): 386-394.

6522. Wilhelm, Donald G. *Theodore Roosevelt as an Undergraduate*. Boston: Luce, 1910.

6523. Wilson, Robert L. *Theodore Roosevelt: Outdoorsman*. New York: Winchester Press, 1971.

6524. Zahm, J. A. "Theodore Roosevelt as a Hunter-Naturalist." *Outlook* 121 (March 12, 1919): 434-441.

Public Career

6525. Abbott, Lyman. "Theodore Roosevelt." *Outlook* 121 (January 15, 1919): 91-92.

6526. Andrews, Avery D. "Theodore Roosevelt as Police Commissioner." *New York Historical Society Quarterly* 42 (April 1958): 116-141.

6527. Barsness, John A. "Theodore Roosevelt as Cowboy: The Virginian as Jacksonian Man." *American Quarterly* 21 (Fall 1969): 609-619.

6528. Beers, Henry A. "Roosevelt as Man of Letters." *Yale Review* 8 (July 1919): 694-709.

6529. Blakey, George T. "Calling a Boss a Boss: Did Roosevelt Libel Barnes in 1915?" *New York History* 60 (April 1979): 195-216.

6530. Blum, John M. *The Republican Roosevelt*. 2d ed. Cambridge, MA: Harvard University Press, 1977.

6531. Brooks, Sydney. "Theodore Roosevelt." *Living Age* 47 (May 28, 1910): 525-532.

6532. Buchanan, Russell. "Theodore Roosevelt and American Neutrality, 1914-1917." *American Historical Review* 43 (July 1938): 775-790.

6533. Burgin, William G. "The Political Theory of Theodore Roosevelt." *South Atlantic Quarterly* 22 (April 1923): 97-114.

6534. Burkett, Elmer J. "Theodore Roosevelt." *Fortnightly Review* 87 (May 1910): 832-845.

6535. Casdorph, Paul D. "Governor William E. Glasscoch and Theodore Roosevelt's 1912 Bull Moose Candidacy." *West Virginia History* 28 (October 1966): 8-15.

6536. Chessman, G. Wallace. *Governor Theodore Roosevelt: The Albany Apprenticeship, 1898-1900*. Cambridge, MA: Harvard University Press, 1965.

6537. Chessman, G. Wallace. *Theodore Roosevelt and the Politics of Power*. Boston: Little, Brown, 1969.

6538. Chessman, G. Wallace. "Theodore Roosevelt, Governor." Ph.D. dissertation, Harvard University, 1951.

6539. Chessman, G. Wallace. "Theodore Roosevelt's Campaign against the Vice-Presidency." *Historian* 14 (Spring 1952): 173-190.

6540. Clarke, John P. "Random Recollections of Campaigning with Colonel Roosevelt." *Courier* (Syracuse) 8 (January 1971): 43-51.

6541. Davenport, Frederick M. "Roosevelt, The Greatest Democrat in the World." *Munsey's Magazine* 62 (October 1917): 17-21.

6542. Davenport, Frederick M. "Roosevelt's Influence in Politics." *State Service* 5 (May 1921): 245-248.

6543. Davis, Allen F. " 'Theodore Roosevelt — Social Worker': A Note." *Mid-America* 48 (January 1966): 58-62.

6544. Davis, Glenn. "The Maturation of Theodore Roosevelt: The Rise of an 'Affective Leader.' " *History of Childhood Quarterly* 3 (Summer 1975): 43-74.

6545. "The Dedication of Mount Theodore Roosevelt: Staff Correspondence from Travers D. Carman, Containing a Tribute by Major-General Leonard Wood." *Outlook* 122 (July 16, 1919): 428-432.

6546. Dyer, Thomas G. "Aaron's Rod: Theodore Roosevelt, Tom Watson, and Anti-Catholicism." *Research Studies* 44 (1976): 60-68.

6547. Dyer, Thomas G. *Theodore Roosevelt and the Idea of Race*. Baton Rouge: Louisiana State University Press, 1980.

6548. Egan, Maurice F. "Theodore Roosevelt in Retrospect." *Atlantic Monthly* 123 (May 1919): 676-685.

6549. Fenton, Charles. "Theodore Roosevelt as an American Man of Letters." *Western Humanities Review* 13 (Autumn 1959): 369-374.

6550. Ferguson, Charles W. "Roosevelt — Man of Letters." *Bookman* 64 (February 1927): 726-729.

6551. Ford, John. "Theodore Roosevelt's Feet of Clay." *Current History* 34 (August 1931): 678-685.

6552. Gable, John A. *The Bull Moose Years: Theodore Roosevelt and the Progressive Party*. Port Washington, NY: Kennikat Press, 1978.

6553. Gable, John A. "Theodore Roosevelt's Nobel Peace Prize." *Theodore Roosevelt Association Journal* 9 (Winter 1983): 31-37.

6554. Gibson, Scott L. "A Study of Theodore Roosevelt's Views on Criminal Justice and His Career as President of the New York City Board of Police Commissioners." Master's thesis, Michigan State University, 1976.

6555. Gibson, William M. *Theodore Roosevelt among the Humorists: W. D. Howells, Mark Twain, and Mr. Dooley.* Knoxville: University of Tennessee Press, 1980.

6556. Gilder, Joseph B. "Mr. Roosevelt as a Letterwriter." *Bellman* 26 (January 25, 1919): 103-104.

6557. Gillespie, Veronica M. "T. R. on Film." *Library of Congress Quarterly Journal* 34 (January 1977): 39-61.

6558. Gilman, Bradley. *Roosevelt, The Happy Warrior.* Boston: Little, Brown, 1921.

6559. Goetsch, Charles C. "Simon E. Baldwin, Theodore Roosevelt, and Their (1910-1911) Controversy over the Federal Employer's Liabilities Act." *Theodore Roosevelt Association Journal* 6 (Fall 1980): 2-28.

6560. Gores, Stan. "The Attempted Assassination of Teddy Roosevelt." *Wisconsin Magazine of History* 53 (Summer 1970): 269-277.

6561. Gosnell, Harold F. *Boss Platt and His New York Machine — A Study of the Political Leadership of Thomas C. Platt, Theodore Roosevelt, and Others.* Chicago: University of Chicago Press, 1924.

6562. Gould, Lewis L. "Theodore Roosevelt, William Howard Taft, and the Disputed Delegates in 1912: Texas as a Test Case." *Southwestern Historical Quarterly* 80 (July 1976): 33-56.

6563. Hagan, William T. "Civil Service Commissioner Theodore Roosevelt and the Indian Rights Association." *Pacific Historical Review* 44 (May 1975): 187-200.

6564. Harbord, James G. "Theodore Roosevelt and the Army." *Review of Reviews* 69 (January 1924): 65-75.

6565. "Has Roosevelt a Right to Accept Renomination?" *Harper's Weekly* 50 (September 15, 1906): 1307.

6566. Hauptman, Laurence M. "Governor Theodore Roosevelt and the Indians of New York State." *Academy of Political Science Proceedings* 119 (February 1975): 1-7.

6567. Haygood, William C., and Joan Severa. "Theodore Roosevelt and the State Historical Society of Wisconsin." *Wisconsin Magazine of History* 54 (Summer 1971): 273-284.

6568. Hooker, Helene M., ed. *History of the Progressive Party, 1912-1916.* New York: Washington Square Press, 1958.

6569. Howland, Harold J. *Theodore Roosevelt and His Times: A Chronicle of the Progressive Movement.* New Haven, CT: Yale University Press, 1921.

6570. Hurwitz, Howard L. *Theodore Roosevelt and Labor in New York, 1880-1900.* New York: Columbia University Press, 1943.

6571. Jensen, Richard. "Commissioner Theodore Roosevelt Visits Indian Reservations, 1892." *Nebraska History* 62 (Spring 1981): 85-106.

6572. Kitchens, Joseph. "Theodore Roosevelt and the Politics of War, 1914-1918." *International Review of History and Political Science* 13 (May 1976): 1-16.

6573. Kraft, Barbara S., and Donald Smythe. "How T. R. Tried in Vain to Fight in World War I." *Smithsonian* 4 (October 1973): 54-61.

6574. Kullnick, Max. *From Rough Rider*

to President. . . . Translated by Frederick von Reithdorf. Chicago: McClurg, 1911.

6575. Leupp, Francis E. "Roosevelt the Politician." *Atlantic Monthly* 109 (June 1912): 843-852.

6576. Lincoln, A. "Theodore Roosevelt, Hiram Johnson, and the Vice-Presidential Nomination of 1912." *Pacific Historical Review* 28 (August 1959): 267-283.

6577. Looker, Earle. *Colonel Roosevelt, Private Citizen*. New York: Revell, 1932.

6578. Lucas, Stephen E. "Theodore Roosevelt's 'The Man with the Muck-Rake': A Reinterpretation." *Quarterly Journal of Speech* 59 (December 1973): 452-462.

6579. Lucey, Lawrence. "Theodore Roosevelt and Social Justice." *Catholic World* 143 (December 1936): 301-306.

6580. McCutcheon, John T. *T. R. in Cartoons*. Chicago: McClurg, 1910.

6581. Maddox, Robert J. "Teddy Roosevelt and the Rough Riders." *American History Illustrated* 12 (November 1977): 8-19.

6582. Malin, James C. "Roosevelt and the Elections of 1884 and 1888." *Mississippi Valley Historical Review* 14 (June 1927): 25-38.

6583. Mallan, John P. "Roosevelt, Brooks Adams, and Lea: The Warrior Critique of the Business Civilization." *American Quarterly* 8 (Fall 1956): 216-230.

6584. Manners, William. *T. R. and Will: A Friendship That Split the Republican Party*. New York: Harcourt, Brace and World, 1969.

6585. Margulies, Herbert F. "La Follette, Roosevelt, and the Republican Presidential Nomination of 1912." *Mid-America* 58 (January 1976): 54-76.

6586. Matthews, Brander. "Roosevelt as a Practical Politician." *Outlook* 122 (July 16, 1919): 433-435.

6587. Matthews, Brander. "Theodore Roosevelt as a Man of Letters." *Munsey's Magazine* 66 (March 1919): 252-257.

6588. Mattison, Ray H. "Roosevelt and the Stockmen's Association." *North Dakota History* 17 (April 1950): 73-95.

6589. Mattson, Robert L. "Politics Is Up! Grigsby's Cowboys and Roosevelt's Rough Riders, 1898." *South Dakota History* 9 (Fall 1979): 303-315.

6590. Miller, Raymond C. "Theodore Roosevelt, Historian." In *Medieval and Historiographical Essays in Honor of James Westfall Thompson*, edited by James L. Cate and Eugene N. Anderson, 423-438. Chicago: University of Chicago Press, 1938.

6591. Moore, Joseph H. *Roosevelt and the Old Guard*. Philadelphia: Macrae Smith, 1925.

6592. Morris, Edmund. "The Cyclone Assemblyman." *American Heritage* 30 (February/March 1979): 34-43.

6593. Morris, Edmund. *The Rise of Theodore Roosevelt*. New York: Coward, McCann and Geoghegan, 1979.

6594. Mowbray, Jay H. *The Intellectual Giant: Roosevelt the People's Champion for Human Rights . . . Including Biographies of Roosevelt and Johnson, Candidates for President and Vice-President. . . .* Philadelphia: National Publishing Co., 1912.

6595. Mowry, George E. "Theodore Roosevelt and the Election of 1910." *Mississippi Valley Historical Review* 25 (March 1939): 523-534.

6596. Mowry, George E. *Theodore Roosevelt and the Progressive Movement*. Madison: University of Wisconsin Press, 1946.

6597. Murakata, Akiko. "Theodore Roosevelt and William Sturgis Bigelow: The Story of a Friendship." *Harvard Library Bulletin* 23 (January 1975): 90-108.

6598. Murphy, Eloise C. *Theodore Roosevelt's Night Ride to the Presidency.* Blue Mountain Lake, NY: Adirondack Museum, 1977.

6599. Nathan, Meyer J. "Theodore Roosevelt and the 1916 Election." *Rocky Mountain Social Science Journal* 5 (October 1968): 64-75.

6600. Parker, Alton B. "Roosevelt's Americanism." *Journal of American History* 13 (July 1919): 314-316.

6601. Pitkin, William A. "Issues in the Roosevelt-Taft Contest of 1912." *Mid-America* 34 (October 1952): 219-232.

6602. Prentice, Royal A. "The Rough Riders." *New Mexico Historical Review* 27 (October 1951): 261-276.

6603. Pringle, Henry F. "Theodore Roosevelt and the South." *Virginia Quarterly Review* 9 (January 1933): 14-25.

6604. Ranck, Edwin C. "What Roosevelt Did for Art in America." *Art and Archaeology* 8 (October 1919): 291-293.

6605. Reed, Marvin E., Jr. "Theodore Roosevelt: The Search for Community in the Urban Age." Ph.D. dissertation, Tulane University, 1971.

6606. Remey, Oliver E. *The Attempted Assassination of Ex-President Theodore Roosevelt.* Milwaukee, WI: Progressive Publishing Co., 1912.

6607. Ricard, Serge. "Theodore Roosevelt before the Presidency: Analysis of One Political Thought." *Canadian Review of American Studies* 12 (Fall 1981): 157-172.

6608. Robertson, Archie. "From Bully! to Vigah!" *Horizon* 5 (November 1963): 68-71.

6609. Robinson, Elwyn B. "Theodore Roosevelt: Amateur Historian." *North Dakota History* 25 (January 1959): 4-13.

6610. "Roosevelt and the Third Term." *American Review of Reviews* 45 (June 1912): 699-704.

6611. "Roosevelt as Candidate for President." *Review of Reviews* 59 (February 1919): 162-164.

6612. Rosenthal, Herbert H. "The Cruise of the Tarpon." *New York History* 39 (October 1958): 303-320.

6613. Schapsmeier, Edward L., and Frederick H. Schapsmeier. "Theodore Roosevelt's Cowboy Years." *Journal of the West* 5 (July 1966): 398-408.

6614. Schmidt, Patricia B. "New Letters on Progressive Politics: Teddy Roosevelt to Governor McGovern." *Milwaukee History* 7 (Summer 1984): 30-45.

6615. Sellen, Robert W. "Opposition Leaders in Wartime: The Case of Theodore Roosevelt and World War I." *Midwest Quarterly* 9 (April 1968): 225-242.

6616. Sellen, Robert W. "Theodore Roosevelt: Historian with a Moral." *Mid-America* 41 (October 1959): 223-240.

6617. Sherman, Stuart P. "Roosevelt and the National Psychology." *Nation* 109 (November 8, 1919): 599-605.

6618. Shore, Miles F. "On Action and Affect: The Rise of Theodore Roosevelt by Edmund Morris." *Journal of Interdisciplinary History* 11 (Autumn 1980): 287-294.

6619. Skinner, R. P. "Theodore Roosevelt — A Personal Tribute." *Landmark* 1 (February 1919): 75-77.

6620. Smeno, Kenneth. "Judge Charles Amidon's Influence on Theodore Roosevelt's Presidential Campaign of 1912." *North Dakota History* 37 (Winter 1970): 5-19.

6621. Stefansson, Vilhjalmur. "Colonel Roosevelt as Explorer." *Review of Reviews* 59 (February 1919): 165-166.

6622. Strunsky, Simeon. "Theodore Roosevelt and the Prelude to 1914." *Foreign Affairs* 4 (October 1925): 144-153.

6623. "T. R. as Revealed by Archie Butt, His Military Aide." *Current Opinion* 76 (March 1924): 336-337.

6624. "Theodore Roosevelt." *Journal of Education* 89 (April 3, 1919): 367-372.

6625. "Theodore Roosevelt." *Spectator* 122 (January 11, 1919): 29-30.

6626. Thompson, Charles W. "Roosevelt Ten Years After." *Commonweal* 9 (January 16, 1929): 308-310.

6627. Trattner, Walter I. "Theodore Roosevelt, Social Workers, and the Election of 1912: A Note." *Mid-America* 50 (January 1968): 64-69.

6628. Tuchman, Barbara W. "Perdicaris Alive or Raisuli Dead." *American Heritage* 10 (August 1959): 18-21.

6629. Tupper, Frederick. "Raleigh and Roosevelt." *Nation* 108 (March 8, 1919): 344-346.

6630. Warner, Robert M. "Chase S. Osborn and the Presidential Campaign of 1912." *Mississippi Valley Historical Review* 46 (June 1959): 19-45.

6631. Washburn, Charles G. "Roosevelt and the 1912 Campaign." *Massachusetts Historical Society Proceedings* 59 (May 1926): 303-312.

6632. Washburn, Charles G. "Theodore Roosevelt." *Harvard Graduate Magazine* 27 (June 1919): 451-481.

6633. Washburn, Charles G. *Theodore Roosevelt: The Logic of His Career*. Boston: Houghton Mifflin, 1916.

6634. Watson, Richard L., Jr. "Theodore Roosevelt: The Years of Preparation, 1868-1900." *South Atlantic Quarterly* 51 (April 1952): 301-315.

6635. Went, G. Stanley V. "Theodore Roosevelt: An Appreciation." *Landmark* 1 (February 1919): 78-81.

6636. Westermeier, Clifford P. "Teddy's Terrors: The New Mexican Volunteers of 1898." *New Mexico Historical Review* 27 (April 1952): 107-136.

6637. Whelpley, James D. "Theodore Roosevelt." *Fortnightly Review* 616 (April 1918): 602-610.

6638. White, George E. "The Eastern Establishment and the Western Experience: The West of Frederic Remington, Theodore Roosevelt, and Owen Wister." Ph.D. dissertation, Yale University, 1967.

6639. *Who Rush to Glory, The Cowboy Volunteers of 1898: Grigsby's Cowboys, Roosevelt's Rough Riders, Torrey's Rocky Mountain Riders*. Caldwell, ID: Caxton, 1958.

6640. Wiegand, Wayne A. "Ambassador in Absentia: George Meyer, William II, and Theodore Roosevelt." *Mid-America* 56 (January 1974): 3-15.

6641. Wilkins, Robert P. "Theodore Roosevelt and 'Dacotah': A Mutual Disillusionment." *North Dakota Quarterly* 26 (Spring 1958): 53-64.

6642. Williams, Jack K. "Roosevelt, Wilson, and the Progressive Movement." *South Atlantic Quarterly* 54 (April 1955): 207-211.

6643. Willis, John. *Roosevelt in the Rough*. New York: I. Washburn, 1931.

6644. Wister, Owen. "Roosevelt and the 1912 Disaster." *Harper's* 160 (May 1930): 661-676.

Presidential Years

General

6645. Aaron, Daniel, and Arthur A.

Ekirch, Jr. "Theodore Roosevelt and Brooks Adams: Pseudo-Progressives." In *Men of Good Hope: A Story of American Progressives*, edited by Daniel Aaron, 245-280. New York: Oxford University Press, 1951.

6646. Abbott, Lawrence F. "New Facts about Theodore Roosevelt." *World's Work* 38 (July 1919): 264-273; (August 1919): 400-414.

6647. Abbott, Lyman. "A Review of President Roosevelt's Administration: Its Influence on Patriotism and Public Service." *Outlook* 91 (February 27, 1909): 430-434.

6648. Abrams, Richard M. *The Burdens of Progress: 1900-1929*. Glenview, IL: Scott, Foreman, 1978.

6649. Adams, Francis A. *Roosevelt: His Policies, His Enemies, His Friends*. New York: Wintemute-Sawyer Publishing Co., 1909.

6650. Alfonso, Oscar M. "The Presidential Leadership of Theodore Roosevelt in Philippine Policy." Ph.D. dissertation, University of Chicago, 1966.

6651. Auerbach, Joseph S. *Theodore Roosevelt: An Appreciation*. New York: Longmans, 1923.

6652. Bailey, Thomas A. "Theodore Roosevelt and the Alaska Boundary Settlement." *Canadian Historical Review* 18 (June 1937): 123-135.

6653. Baker, Richard C. *The Tariff under Roosevelt and Taft*. Hastings, NB: Democrat Printing Co., 1941.

6654. Bayard, Charles J. "Theodore Roosevelt and Colorado Politics: The Roosevelt-Stewart Alliance." *Colorado Magazine* 42 (Fall 1965): 311-326.

6655. Behl, William A. "The Rhetoric of Theodore Roosevelt." Ph.D. dissertation, Northwestern University, 1942.

6656. Behl, William A. "Theodore Roosevelt's Principles of Speech Preparation and Delivery." *Speech Monographs* 12 (1945): 112-122.

6657. Bell, Samuel R. "Roosevelt as a Conservative: A Study in Historical Interpretation." *Social Education* 47 (October 1983): 374-376.

6658. Bennett, John W. *Roosevelt and the Republic*. New York: Broadway Publishing Co., 1908.

6659. Berge, William H. "The Impulse for Expansion: John W. Burgess, Alfred Thayer Mahan, Theodore Roosevelt, Josiah Strong, and the Development of a Rationale." Ph.D. dissertation, Vanderbilt University, 1969.

6660. Beringause, Arthur F. *Brooks Adams: A Biography*. New York: Knopf, 1955.

6661. Blackorby, Edward C. "Theodore Roosevelt's Conservation Policies and Their Impact upon America and the American West." *North Dakota History* 25 (October 1958): 107-117.

6662. Blum, John M. *The Progressive Presidents: Roosevelt, Wilson, Roosevelt, Johnson*. New York: Norton, 1980.

6663. Bonaparte, Charles J. "Experiences of a Cabinet Officer under Roosevelt." *Century Magazine* 79 (March 1910): 752-758.

6664. Bradford, Gamaliel. *The Quick and the Dead*. Boston: Houghton Mifflin, 1931.

6665. Burton, David H. "The Learned Presidency: Roosevelt, Taft, Wilson." *Presidential Studies Quarterly* 15 (Summer 1985): 486-497.

6666. Burton, David H. "Theodore Roosevelt's Harrisburg Speech, A Progressive Appeal to James Wilson." *Pennsylvania Magazine of History and Biography* 93 (October 1969): 527-542.

6667. Butt, Archibald W. *The Letters of Archie Butt, Personal Aide to President Roosevelt*. Edited by Lawrence F. Abbott. Garden City, NY: Doubleday, 1925.

6668. Butt, Archibald W. *Taft and Roosevelt: The Intimate Letters of Archie Butt*. 2 vols. Garden City, NY: Doubleday, Doran, 1930.

6669. Cadenhead, Ivie. *Theodore Roosevelt: The Paradox of Progressivism*. Edited by Kenneth Colegrove. Woodburg, NY: Barron's, 1974.

6670. Campbell, John P. "Taft, Roosevelt, and the Arbitration Treaties of 1911." *Journal of American History* 53 (September 1966): 279-298.

6671. Cane, Guy. "Sea Power — Teddy's 'Big Stick.'" *U.S. Naval Institute Proceedings* 102 (August 1976): 40-48.

6672. Carman, Travers D. "Campaign with Theodore Roosevelt." *Outlook* 121 (January 29, 1919): 181-182.

6673. Chalmers, David M. *Neither Socialism nor Monopoly: Theodore Roosevelt and the Decision to Regulate the Railroads*. Philadelphia: Lippincott, 1976.

6674. Cohen, Julius H. *They Builded Better Than They Knew*. New York: Messner, 1946.

6675. Coletta, Paolo E. "Will the Real Progressive Stand Up? William Jennings Bryan and Theodore Roosevelt to 1909." *Nebraska History* 65 (Spring 1984): 15-57.

6676. Collin, Richard H. "Henry Pringle's Theodore Roosevelt: A Study in Historical Revisionism." *New York History* 52 (April 1971): 151-168.

6677. Collin, Richard H. "The Image of Theodore Roosevelt in American History and Thought, 1885-1965." Ph.D. dissertation, New York University, 1966.

6678. Collin, Richard H., ed. *Theodore Roosevelt and Reform Politics*. Lexington, MA: Heath, 1972.

6679. Conrad, David E. "Creating the Nation's Largest Forest Reserve: Roosevelt, Emmons, and the Tongass National Forest." *Pacific Historical Review* 46 (February 1977): 65-83.

6680. Cooper, John M., Jr. *The Warrior and the Priest: Theodore Roosevelt and Woodrow Wilson*. Cambridge, MA: Harvard University Press, 1983.

6681. Cooper, John M., Jr. "The Warrior and the Priest: Toward a Comparative Perspective on Theodore Roosevelt and Woodrow Wilson." *South Atlantic Quarterly* 80 (Autumn 1981): 419-428.

6682. Corgan, Michael T. "Mahan and Theodore Roosevelt: The Assessment of Influence." *Naval War College Review* 33 (November/December 1980): 89-97.

6683. Corson, Oscar T. "Theodore Roosevelt, The Loyal American." *Ohio Educational Monthly* 68 (March 1919): 86-93.

6684. Coyle, David C. *Conservation: An American Story of Conflict and Accomplishment*. New Brunswick, NJ: Rutgers University Press, 1957.

6685. Creelman, James. "Mr. Roosevelt's Renunciation." *Pearson's Magazine* 19 (May 1908): 457-471.

6686. Cross, Whitney R. "Ideas in Policies: The Conservation Policies of the Two Roosevelts." *Journal of the History of Ideas* 14 (June 1953): 421-438.

6687. Crosson, David. "James S. Clarkson and Theodore Roosevelt, 1901-1904: A Study in Contrasting Political Traditions." *Annals of Iowa* 42 (Summer 1974): 344-360.

6688. Cunliffe, Marcus. "Theodore Roosevelt, President of the United States, 1901-1908." *History Today* 5 (September 1955): 592-601.

6689. Davenport, Frederick M. "President Roosevelt in the Yellowstone." *Outlook* 142 (January 6, 1926): 27-30.

6690. Davidson, Bill. *President Kennedy Selects Six Brave Presidents.* New York: Harper and Row, 1962.

6691. Davis, Oscar K. *Released for Publication: Some Inside Political History of Theodore Roosevelt and His Times, 1898-1918.* Boston: Houghton Mifflin, 1925.

6692. Dawbarn, Charles. "Theodore Roosevelt: The Man and President." *Pall Mall Magazine* 43 (January 1909): 67-70.

6693. DeVries, George, Jr. "Theodore Roosevelt: An American Synthesis." *American Studies* 9 (Fall 1968): 70-80.

6694. Eitler, Anita T. *Philosopher Chase Knox, First Attorney-General of Theodore Roosevelt, 1901-1904.* Washington, DC: Catholic University Press, 1959.

6695. Ellsworth, Clayton S. "Theodore Roosevelt's County Life Commission." *Agricultural History* 34 (October 1960): 155-172.

6696. "The English View of Roosevelt." *Review of Reviews* 39 (April 1909): 475-476.

6697. Farrington, Harry W. *Walls of America.* Bradley Beach, NJ: Rough and Brown Press, 1925.

6698. Farriss, Charles S. *The American Soul.* Boston: Stratford, 1920.

6699. Fawcett, Waldon. "The First Inauguration of the New Century." *Leslie's Weekly* 92 (March 12, 1901): 210-211.

6700. Fawcett, Waldon. "President's Business Office." *World's Work* 4 (July 1902): 2310-2316.

6701. Fawcett, Waldon. "War Room at the White House." *World's Work* 3 (March 1902): 1841-1843.

6702. Feller, John Q., Jr. "Theodore Roosevelt, the Department of Justice, and the Trust Problem: A Study in Presidential Policy." Ph.D. dissertation, Catholic University of America, 1968.

6703. Fischer, Robert, and James T. Gay. "A Post-Mortem of Theodore Roosevelt in Historical Writings, 1919-1929." *Mid-America* 56 (July 1974): 139-159.

6704. Flemings, Corinne K. "A Rhetorical Evaluation of Theodore Roosevelt's Leadership Qualities, 1911-1912." Ph.D. dissertation, University of California, 1970.

6705. Foulke, William D. *Roosevelt and the Spoilsmen.* New York: National City Service Reform League, 1925.

6706. Gable, John A. "President Theodore Roosevelt's Record on Conservation." *Theodore Roosevelt Association Journal* 10 (Fall 1984): 2-11.

6707. Garfield, James R. "A Review of President Roosevelt's Administration: Economic and Industrial Influences." *Outlook* 91 (February 20, 1909): 389-393.

6708. Garrison, Elisha E. *The Roosevelt Doctrine Being the Personal Utterance of the President....* New York: Robert Grier Cooke, 1904.

6709. Garrison, Elisha E. *Roosevelt, Wilson, and the Federal Reserve Law: A Story of the Author's Relations with Theodore Roosevelt, Woodrow Wilson, and Other Public Men, Principally as Related to the Development and Writing of the Federal Reserve Law.* Boston: Christopher Publishing House, 1931.

6710. Gatewood, Willard B., Jr. "Theodore Roosevelt and Arkansas, 1901-1912." *Arkansas Historical Quarterly* 32 (Spring 1973): 3-24.

6711. Gatewood, Willard B., Jr. "Theodore Roosevelt and Southern Republicans: The Case of South Carolina, 1901-1904."

South Carolina Historical Magazine 70 (October 1969): 251-266.

6712. Gatewood, Willard B., Jr. *Theodore Roosevelt and the Art of Controversy.* Baton Rouge: University of Louisiana, 1970.

6713. Gatewood, Willard B., Jr. "Theodore Roosevelt and the Case of Mrs. Morris." *Mid-America* 48 (January 1966): 3-18.

6714. Gatewood, Willard B., Jr. "Theodore Roosevelt and the Coinage Controversy." *American Quarterly* 18 (Spring 1966): 35-51.

6715. Gatewood, Willard B., Jr. "Theodore Roosevelt and the Indianola Affair." *Journal of Negro History* 53 (January 1968): 48-49.

6716. Gatewood, Willard B., Jr. "Theodore Roosevelt and the 'Kinetoscope Fakes': An Incident in the Campaign of 1904." *Mid-American* 49 (July 1967): 190-199.

6717. Gatewood, Willard B., Jr. "Theodore Roosevelt: Champion of Governmental Aesthetics." *Georgia Review* 21 (Summer 1967): 172-183.

6718. German, James C., Jr. "Taft, Roosevelt, and United States Steel." *Historian* 34 (August 1972): 598-613.

6719. Goodwin, Paul G. "Theodore Roosevelt: The Politics of His Candidacy, 1904, 1912." D.S.S. dissertation, Syracuse University, 1961.

6720. Gordon, Donald C. "Roosevelt's 'Smart Yankee Trick.'" *Pacific Historical Review* 30 (November 1981): 351-358.

6721. Grantham, Dewey W., Jr. "Dinner at the White House: Theodore Roosevelt, Booker T. Washington, and the South." *Tennessee Historical Quarterly* 17 (June 1958): 112-130.

6722. Griffith, William, ed. *The Roosevelt Policy: Speeches, Letters, and State Papers, Relating to Corporate Wealth and Closely Allied Topics.* 3 vols. New York: Current Literature Publishing Co., 1919.

6723. Habibuddin, Syed M. *Civil Liberties and Democracy: Attitude of a President.* Calcutta: Scientific Book Agency, 1977.

6724. Habibuddin, Syed M. "Theodore Roosevelt's Attitude toward the Judiciary." *Indian Journal of Politics* 9 (1975): 20-32.

6725. Hagedorn, Hermann. *The Bugle That Woke America: The Saga of Theodore Roosevelt's Last Battle for His Country.* New York: John Day, 1940.

6726. Hale, William B. *A Week in the White House with Theodore Roosevelt: A Study of the President at the Nation's Business.* New York: Putnam, 1908.

6727. Halstead, Albert. "President at Work." *Independent* 53 (September 1901): 2080-2086.

6728. Haney, James E. "Theodore Roosevelt and Afro-Americans, 1901-1912." Ph.D. dissertation, Kent State University, 1971.

6729. Hargrove, Erwin C. "The Tragic Hero in Politics: Theodore Roosevelt, David Lloyd George, and Fiorello La Guardia." Ph.D. dissertation, Yale University, 1963.

6730. Havig, Alan. "Presidential Images, History, and Homage: Memorializing Theodore Roosevelt, 1919-1967." *American Quarterly* 30 (Fall 1978): 514-522.

6731. Healy, Laurin H., and Luis Kutner. *The Admiral.* New York: Ziff-Davis, 1944.

6732. Heffron, Paul T. "Theodore Roosevelt and the Appointment of Mr. Justice Moody." *Vanderbilt Law Review* 18 (March 1965): 545-568.

6733. Hofstadter, Richard. "Idealists, Professors, Soreheads." *Columbia University Forum* 5 (Spring 1962): 4-11.

6734. Hofstadter, Richard, ed. *The Progressive Movement, 1900-1915.* Englewood Cliffs, NJ: Prentice-Hall, 1964.

6735. Hourihan, William J. "Roosevelt and the Sultans: The United States Navy in the Mediterranean, 1904." Ph.D. dissertation, University of Massachusetts, 1975.

6736. Hughes, Arthur J. "Amazin' Jimmy and a Mighty Fortress Was Our Teddy: Theodore Roosevelt and Jimmy Carter." *Presidential Studies Quarterly* 9 (Winter 1979): 80-82.

6737. Johnson, Arthur M. "Theodore Roosevelt and the Bureau of Corporations." *Mississippi Valley Historical Review* 45 (March 1959): 571-590.

6738. Johnson, Arthur M. "Theodore Roosevelt and the Navy." *U.S. Naval Institute Proceedings* 84 (October 1958): 76-86.

6739. Josephson, Matthew. *The President Makers: The Culture of Politics and Leadership in an Age of Enlightment, 1896-1919.* New York: Harcourt, Brace, 1940.

6740. Juergens, George. "Theodore Roosevelt and the Press." *Daedalus* 111 (Fall 1982): 113-133.

6741. King, Judson. *The Conservation Fight: From Theodore Roosevelt to the Tennessee Valley Authority.* Washington, DC: Public Affairs Press, 1959.

6742. Knee, Stuart E. "Roosevelt and Turner: Awakening in the West." *Journal of the West* 17 (April 1978): 105-112.

6743. Larson, Robert W. "Taft, Roosevelt, and New Mexico Statehood." *Mid-America* 45 (April 1963): 99-114.

6744. Leupp, Francis E. "The Inauguration." *Harper's Weekly* 9 (March 1901): 246.

6745. Leupp, Francis E. "A Review of President Roosevelt's Administration: Its Human and Social Conditions." *Outlook* 91 (February 6, 1909): 298-307.

6746. Levine, Carol. "The First Ban: How Teddy Roosevelt Saved Saccharin." *Hastings Center Report* 7 (December 1977): 6-7.

6747. Lodge, Henry C. "Theodore Roosevelt." In his *The Senate of the United States, and Other Essays and Addresses Historical and Literary,* 113-158. New York: Scribner's, 1921.

6748. Lodge, Henry C. "Why Roosevelt Should Be Elected." *North American Review* 179 (September 1904): 321-330.

6749. Loos, Rita E. "President Theodore Roosevelt and Eastern Businessmen: A Divergence of Views." Ph.D. dissertation, St. John's University, 1971.

6750. Lowry, Edward G. "The White House Now." *Harper's Weekly* 53 (May 15, 1909): 7-8.

6751. McComb, Walter J. "The Insurgent Movement in the Republican Party during the Roosevelt and Taft Administrations." Ph.D. dissertation, University of Minnesota, 1939.

6752. Merriam, Charles E. *Four American Party Leaders.* New York: Macmillan, 1926.

6753. Merrill, Milton R. "Theodore Roosevelt and Reed Smoot." *Western Political Quarterly* 4 (September 1951): 440-453.

6754. "Mr. Roosevelt's Moral Right to Become a Candidate for Reelection." *North American Review* 183 (September 7, 1906): 331-337.

6755. Morison, Elting E. "Theodore Roosevelt Appoints a Judge." *Massachusetts*

Historical Society Proceedings 72 (October/December 1957-1960): 309-322.

6756. Morris, Edmund. "Theodore Roosevelt, President." *American Heritage* 32 (June 1981): 4-15.

6757. Mowry, George E. *The Era of Theodore Roosevelt, 1900-1912.* New York: Harper and Row, 1958.

6758. Nelson, Henry L. "The Hampered Executive." *Century Magazine* 66 (May 1903): 140-151.

6759. Norwood, Irving C. "Exit — Roosevelt the Dominant." *Outing: An Illustrated Monthly Magazine of Recreation* 55 (March 1909): 718-730.

6760. O'Gara, Gordon C. *Theodore Roosevelt and the Rise of the Modern Navy.* Princeton, NJ: Princeton University Press, 1943.

6761. Peary, Robert E. "Roosevelt — The Friend of Man." *National History* 19 (January 1919): 11.

6762. Peck, Harry T. "President Roosevelt." *Bookman* 29 (March 1909): 25-31.

6763. Peffer, E. Louise. *The Closing of the Public Domain: Disposal and Reservation Policies, 1900-1950.* Stanford, CA: Stanford University Press, 1951.

6764. Phillips, David G. "How Roosevelt Became President." *Everybody's Magazine* 8 (January 1903): 90-95.

6765. Phillips, Edward H. "Teddy Roosevelt in Texas, 1905." *West Texas Historical Association Yearbook* 56 (1980): 58-67.

6766. Pinkett, Harold T. "The Keep Commission, 1905-1909: A Rooseveltian Effort for Administrative Reform." *Journal of American History* 52 (September 1965): 297-312.

6767. Post, Regis H. "How Theodore Roosevelt Made the Government Efficient." *World's Work* 41 (April 1921): 579-586.

6768. Post, Regis H. "Theodore Roosevelt's Practice of Government: Examples of His Methods in Making Government Work Effective." *World's Work* 42 (May 1921): 65-68.

6769. "Proposed Additions to the White House Offices." *Journal of the American Institute of Architects* 5 (February 1946): 73-78; (March 1946): 151-153.

6770. Quinlan, John. "Theodore Roosevelt: A Centenary Tribute." *Contemporary Review* 195 (February 1959): 108-110.

6771. Quinn, Thomas B. "Theodore Roosevelt Foresaw Felix Frankfurter." *American Mercury* 86 (February 1958): 115-116.

6772. Rakestraw, Lawrence. "Uncle Sam's Forest Reserves." *Pacific Northwest Quarterly* 44 (October 1953): 145-151.

6773. Rees, George L. "Roosevelt as a Reactionist." *Arena* 39 (March 1908): 289-299.

6774. Reter, Ronald F. "President Theodore Roosevelt and the Senate's Advice and Consent to Treaties." *Historian* 44 (August 1982): 483-504.

6775. Rhodes, James F. *The McKinley and Roosevelt Administrations, 1897-1909.* New York: Macmillan, 1922.

6776. Rochefort, David A. "The Western Moratorium of Theodore Roosevelt." *North Dakota Quarterly* 49 (Summer 1981): 42-56.

6777. "Roosevelt's Conception of the Presidency." *Harper's Weekly* 47 (June 13, 1902): 994-995.

6778. Rosmond, James A. "Nelson Aldrich, Theodore Roosevelt, and the Tariff: A Study of 1905." Ph.D. dissertation, University of North Carolina, 1974.

6779. Rowland, John A. *Triumphs of the Roosevelt Administration . . . with Introductions by Charles Dick . . . and Chauncey M. Depew.* . . . New York: Republican Publishing Co., 1904.

6780. Sadler, David F. "Theodore Roosevelt: A Symbol to Americans, 1898-1912." Ph.D. dissertation, University of Minnesota, 1954.

6781. Scheinberg, Stephen J. "The Haywood Trial: Theodore Roosevelt's Undesirable Citizens." *Idaho Yesterdays* 4 (Fall 1960): 10-15.

6782. Scheinberg, Stephen J. "Theodore Roosevelt and the A. F. of L.'s Entry into Politics, 1906-1908." *Labor History* 3 (Spring 1962): 131-148.

6783. Scheiner, Seth N. "President Theodore Roosevelt and the Negro, 1901-1908." *Journal of Negro History* 47 (July 1962): 169-182.

6784. Schoch, Henry A. *Theodore Roosevelt: The Story behind the Scenery.* Edited by Giveneth R. DenDoovan. Las Vegas, NV: K. C. Publishers, 1974.

6785. Schullery, Paul. "A Partnership in Conservation: Theodore Roosevelt and Yellowstone." *Montana* 28 (Summer 1978): 2-15.

6786. Severn, John K., and William W. Rogers. "Theodore Roosevelt Entertains Booker T. Washington: Florida's Reaction to the White House Dinner." *Florida Historical Quarterly* 54 (January 1976): 306-318.

6787. Shulimson, Jack, and Graham A. Cosmas. "Teddy Roosevelt and the Corps' Sea-Going Mission." *Marine Corps Gazette* 65 (November 1981): 54-61.

6788. Silverman, Eliane L. "Reform as a Means of Social Control: Theodore Roosevelt and Women's Suffrage." *Atlantis* (Canada) 2 (1976): 22-36.

6789. Silverman, Eliane L. "Theodore Roosevelt and Women: The Inner Conflict of a President and Its Impact on His Ideology." Ph.D. dissertation, University of California, Los Angeles, 1973.

6790. Smith, Brian L. "Theodore Roosevelt Visits Oklahoma." *Chronicles of Oklahoma* 51 (Fall 1973): 263-279.

6791. Smith, Frederic C. "Teddy Roosevelt in Iowa." *Palimpsest* 29 (October 1948): 296-302.

6792. Smith, William H. *The Life and Speeches of Hon. Charles Warren Fairbanks, Republican Candidate for Vice President.* Indianapolis, IN: W. B. Burford, 1904.

6793. Smyth, Clifford. *Theodore Roosevelt, Who Fought for the Square Deal and a New Nationalism.* New York: Funk and Wagnalls, 1931.

6794. Spring, Agnes W. "Theodore Roosevelt in Colorado." *Colorado Magazine* 35 (October 1958): 241-265.

6795. Stagner, Stephen. "The Recall of Judicial Decisions and the Due Process Debate." *American Journal of Legal History* 24 (July 1980): 257-272.

6796. Steffens, Lincoln. "Overworked President." *McClure's* 18 (April 1902): 483-492.

6797. Stein, Harry H. "Theodore Roosevelt and the Press: Lincoln Steffens." *Mid-America* 54 (April 1972): 94-107.

6798. Stillson, Albert C. "Military Policy without Political Guidance: Theodore Roosevelt's Navy." *Military Affairs* 25 (Spring 1961): 18-31.

6799. Stout, Ralph. *Roosevelt in the Kansas City Star.* Boston: Houghton Mifflin, 1921.

6800. Straus, Oscar S. *Under Four Administrations: From Cleveland to Taft.* Boston: Houghton Mifflin, 1922.

6801. Stults, Taylor. "Roosevelt, Russian

Persecution of Jews, and American Public Opinion." *Jewish Social Studies* 33 (January 1971): 13-22.

6802. Tarr, Joel A. "President Theodore Roosevelt and Illinois Politics, 1901-1904." *Illinois State Historical Society Journal* 58 (Autumn 1965): 245-264.

6803. Teplin, Joseph. "Theodore Roosevelt: A Study in Administrative Thought and Behavior." Ph.D. dissertation, University of Chicago, 1949.

6804. Thomas, Addison C. *Roosevelt among the People: Being an Account of the Fourteen Thousand Mile Journey from Ocean to Ocean of Theodore Roosevelt, Together with the Public Speeches Made by Him during the Journey.* Chicago: L. W. Walter, 1910.

6805. Thompson, William B. "Theodore Roosevelt and the Square Deal." *Journal of American History* 13 (July 1919): 304-309.

6806. Thornton, Harrison J. "Theodore Roosevelt." In *The Marcus W. Jernegan Essays in American Historiography*, edited by William T. Hutchinson, 227-251. Chicago: University of Chicago Press, 1937.

6807. Thornton, Harrison J. "The Two Roosevelts at Chautauqua." *New York History* 28 (January 1947): 33-65.

6808. Tinsley, James A. "Roosevelt, Foraker, and the Brownsville Affair." *Journal of Negro History* 41 (January 1956): 43-65.

6809. Tugwell, Rexford G. "The Two Great Roosevelts." *Western Political Quarterly* 5 (March 1952): 84-93.

6810. Tuchman, Barbara, David McCullough, and Edmund Morris. "Harvard Theodore Roosevelt Centennial Symposium." *Theodore Roosevelt Association Journal* 6 (Summer 1980): 10-17.

6811. Tweton, D. Jerome. "The Attitude and Policies of the Theodore Roosevelt Administration toward American Agriculture." Ph.D. dissertation, University of Oklahoma, 1964.

6812. Tweton, D. Jerome. "Theodore Roosevelt and Land Law Reform." *Mid-America* 49 (January 1967): 44-54.

6813. Tweton, D. Jerome. "Theodore Roosevelt and the Agrarian Myth." *North Dakota History* 34 (Spring 1967): 170-181.

6814. Venkataramani, M. S. "The Roosevelt Administration and the Great Indian Famine." *International Studies* (India) 4 (January 1963): 241-264.

6815. Wade, Mary H. *Real Americans.* Boston: Little, Brown, 1922.

6816. Watson, Richard L., Jr. "Theodore Roosevelt and Herbert Hoover." *South Atlantic Quarterly* 53 (January 1954): 109-129.

6817. Watterson, Henry. "Strange Prophecy about Roosevelt." *Cosmopolitan* 44 (January 1908): 302-308.

6818. Wert, Jeffry. "Theodore Roosevelt, Patron Saint of Dry Sundays." *American History Illustrated* 17 (April 1982): 30-35.

6819. Wessel, Thomas R. "Republican Justice: The Department of Justice under Roosevelt and Taft, 1902-1913." Ph.D. dissertation, University of Maryland, 1972.

6820. Wesser, Robert F. "Theodore Roosevelt: Reform and Reorganization of the Republican Party in New York: 1901-1906." *New York History* 46 (July 1965): 230-252.

6821. White, Leonard D. "Public Life of T. R." *Public Administration Review* 14 (Autumn 1954): 278-282.

6822. Wiebe, Robert H. "The House of Morgan and the Executive, 1905-1913." *American Historical Review* 65 (October 1959): 49-60.

6823. Woods, Randall B. "Terrorism in the Age of Roosevelt: The Miss Stone Affair, 1901-1902." *American Quarterly* 31 (Fall 1979): 478-495.

6824. Works, John D. "A Glance at President Roosevelt's Administration and His Personality." *Arena* 39 (February 1908): 156-159.

6825. Ziglar, William L. "Negro Opinion of Theodore Roosevelt." Ph.D. dissertation, University of Maine, 1972.

6826. Zwierlein, Frederick J. *Theodore Roosevelt and Catholics, 1882-1919*. St. Louis, MO: V. T. Suren, 1956.

Foreign Affairs

6827. Alfonso, Oscar M. *Theodore Roosevelt and the Philippines, 1897-1909*. Quezon City: University of the Philippines Press, 1970.

6828. Bailey, Thomas A. *Theodore Roosevelt and the Japanese-American Crisis: An Account of the International Complications Arising from the Race Problem on the Pacific Coast*. Stanford, CA: Stanford University Press, 1934.

6829. Beale, Howard K. *Theodore Roosevelt and the Rise of America to World Power*. Baltimore, MD: Johns Hopkins University Press, 1956.

6830. Blake, Nelson M. "Ambassadors at the Court of Theodore Roosevelt." *Mississippi Valley Historical Review* 42 (September 1955): 179-206.

6831. Blazsik, Gloria E. "Theodore Roosevelt's Far Eastern Policy and the Tang Shao-Yi Mission." Ph.D. dissertation, Georgetown University, 1969.

6832. Burton, David H. "Theodore Roosevelt and Egyptian Nationalism." *Mid-America* 41 (April 1959): 88-103.

6833. Burton, David H. "Theodore Roosevelt and the 'Special Relationship' with Britain." *History Today* 23 (August 1973): 527-535.

6834. Burton, David H. *Theodore Roosevelt: Confident Imperialist*. Philadelphia: University of Pennsylvania Press, 1968.

6835. Burton, David H. "Theodore Roosevelt's Social Darwinism and Views on Imperialism." *Journal of the History of Ideas* 26 (January 1965): 103-118.

6836. Campbell, Charles S., Jr. *Anglo-American Understanding, 1898-1903*. Baltimore, MD: Johns Hopkins University Press, 1957.

6837. Coletta, Paolo E. "The Diplomacy of Theodore Roosevelt and William Howard Taft." In *American Foreign Relations: A Historiographical Review*, edited by Gerald K. Haines and J. Samuel Walker, 91-113. Westport, CT: Greenwood Press, 1981.

6838. Collin, Richard H. *Theodore Roosevelt, Culture, Diplomacy, and Expansion: A New View of American Imperialism*. Baton Rouge: Louisiana State University Press, 1985.

6839. Decker, Joe F. "Theodore Roosevelt's Proposed World War I Division." *Theodore Roosevelt Association Journal* 10 (Summer 1984): 2-14.

6840. Dennett, Tyler. "President Roosevelt's Secret Pact with Japan." *Current History* 21 (October 1924): 15-21.

6841. Dennett, Tyler. *Roosevelt and the Russo-Japanese War: A Critical Study of American Policy in Eastern Asia in 1902-1905, Based Primarily upon the Private Papers of Theodore Roosevelt*. Garden City, NY: Doubleday, 1925.

6842. DuVal, Miles P., Jr. *And the Mountains Move: The Story of the Building of the Panama Canal*. Stanford, CA: Stanford University Press, 1947.

6843. Esthus, Raymond A. *Theodore Roosevelt and International Rivalries.* Waltham, MA: Ginn-Blaisdell, 1970.

6844. Esthus, Raymond A. *Theodore Roosevelt and Japan.* Seattle: University of Washington Press, 1966.

6845. Fendall, Lonny W. "Theodore Roosevelt and Africa: Deliberate Non-Involvement in the Scramble for Territory and Influence." Ph.D. dissertation, University of Oregon, 1972.

6846. Friedlander, Robert A. "A Reassessment of Roosevelt's Role in the Panamanian Revolution of 1903." *Western Political Quarterly* 14 (April 1961): 535-543.

6847. Fry, Richard T. "Community through War: A Study of Theodore Roosevelt's Rise and Fall as a Prophet and Hero in Modern America." Ph.D. dissertation, University of Minnesota, 1969.

6848. Gow, Douglas P. "How Did the Roosevelt Corollary Become Linked to the Dominican Republic?" *Mid-America* 58 (October 1976): 159-165.

6849. Hendrickson, Embert J. "Roosevelt's Second Venezuelan Controversy." *Hispanic American Historical Review* 50 (August 1970): 482-498.

6850. Hill, Howard C. *Roosevelt and the Caribbean.* Chicago: University of Chicago Press, 1927.

6851. Hussey, Lyman A., Jr. "Anglo-Canadian Relations during the Roosevelt Era, 1901-1908." Ph.D. dissertation, University of Georgia, 1969.

6852. Kim, Won M. "Theodore Roosevelt's Korean Policy in the Far East, 1901-1905." *Journal of Social Sciences and Humanities* 43 (1976): 99-116.

6853. Larsen, Peter. "Theodore Roosevelt and the Moroccan Crises, 1905-1906." Ph.D. dissertation, Princeton University, 1984.

6854. Leiner, Frederick C. "The Unknown Effort: Theodore Roosevelt's Battleship Plan and International Arms Limitation Talks, 1906-1907." *Military Affairs* 48 (October 1984): 174-179.

6855. McKee, Delber L. *Chinese Exclusion versus the Open Door Policy, 1900-1906: Clashes over China Policy in the Roosevelt Era.* Detroit, MI: Wayne State University Press, 1977.

6856. Marks, Frederick W. "Morality as a Drive Wheel in the Diplomacy of Theodore Roosevelt." *Diplomatic History* 2 (Winter 1978): 43-62.

6857. Marks, Frederick W. *Velvet on Iron: The Diplomacy of Theodore Roosevelt.* Lincoln: University of Nebraska Press, 1979.

6858. Moore, A. Georgory. "Theodore Roosevelt and China, 1901-1909." Ph.D. dissertation, Kent State University, 1979.

6859. Neu, Charles E. "Theodore Roosevelt and American Involvement in the Far East, 1901-1909." *Pacific Historical Review* 35 (November 1966): 433-449.

6860. Neu, Charles E. *An Uncertain Friendship: Theodore Roosevelt and Japan, 1906-1909.* Cambridge, MA: Harvard University Press, 1967.

6861. Nikol, John, and Francis X. Holbrook. "Naval Operations in the Panama Revolution 1903." *American Neptune* 37 (October 1977): 253-261.

6862. Olson, William C. "Theodore Roosevelt's Conception of an International League." *World Affairs Quarterly* 29 (1959): 329-353.

6863. Parsons, Edward B. "Roosevelt's Containment of the Russo-Japanese War." *Pacific Historical Review* 38 (February 1969): 21-44.

6864. Peirce, Clyde R. *The Roosevelt Panama Libel Cases.* New York: Greenwich Book Publishers, 1959.

6865. Pollock, Fred E. "Roosevelt, the Ogdensburg Agreement, and the British Fleet: All Done with Mirrors." *Diplomatic History* 5 (Summer 1981): 203-220.

6866. Radziwill, Catherine. "A Russian Appreciation of Theodore Roosevelt: A Hitherto Unpublished Document of the Portsmouth Peace Conference." *Outlook* 124 (January 7, 1920): 18-19.

6867. Reter, Ronald F. "The Real versus the Rhetorical Theodore Roosevelt in Foreign Policy Making." Ph.D. dissertation, University of Georgia, 1973.

6868. Rippy, J. Fred. "Antecedents of the Roosevelt Corollary of the Monroe Doctrine." *Pacific Historical Review* 9 (September 1940): 267-279.

6869. Ro, Kwang H., and Robert T. Smith. "Theodore Roosevelt and the Korean Intervention Question: An Analysis of a President's Defense." *Korean Quarterly* 11 (Autumn 1969): 84-92.

6870. Roosevelt, Thomas A. *Theodore Roosevelt and the Japanese-American Crises.* Gloucester, MA: P. Smith, 1964.

6871. Scott, James B. "A Review of President Roosevelt's Administration: International Relations." *Outlook* 91 (February 13, 1909): 350-357.

6872. Shepardson, Donald E. "Theodore Roosevelt and William II: The New Struggle for Atlantic Supremacy." In *Problems in European History,* edited by Harold T. Parker, 165-176. Durham, NC: Moore Publishers, 1979.

6873. Stapleton, Joseph G. "Theodore Roosevelt: Theologian of America's New Israel Concept." Ph.D. dissertation, Temple University, 1973.

6874. Varg, Paul A. "Open Door Diplomat: The Life of W. W. Rockhill." *Illinois Studies in the Social Sciences* 33 (1952): 1-137.

6875. Vevier, Charles. "The Open Door: An Idea in Action, 1906-1913." *Pacific Historical Review* 24 (February 1955): 49-62.

6876. Vevier, Charles. *The United States and China, 1906-1913: A Study of Finance and Diplomacy.* New Brunswick, NJ: Rutgers University Press, 1955.

6877. Wister, Owen. "Roosevelt and the War." *Harper's Magazine* 161 (June 1930): 34-49.

Writings

6878. Bishop, Joseph B. *Theodore Roosevelt and His Time Shown in His Own Letters.* 2 vols. New York: Scribner's, 1920.

6879. Blum, John M. "Editor's Camera: 'The Letters of Theodore Roosevelt.'" *American Documentation* 1 (October 1950): 181-184.

6880. Cordingley, Nora E. "Extreme Rarities in the Published Works of Theodore Roosevelt." *Bibliographical Society of America Papers* 38 (1945): 20-50.

6881. Crowley, John W. "'Dear Bay': Theodore Roosevelt's Letters to George Cabot Lodge." *New York History* 53 (April 1972): 177-194.

6882. Dailey, Wallace F. "The Theodore Roosevelt Collection at Harvard." *Manuscripts* 29 (Summer 1977): 146-154.

6883. Hart, Albert B., and Herbert R. Ferleger, eds. *Theodore Roosevelt Cyclopedia.* New York: Roosevelt Memorial Association, 1941.

6884. Harvard University Library. *Theodore Roosevelt Collection: Dictionary Catalogue and Shelflist.* Cambridge, MA: Harvard University Press, 1970.

6885. LaForte, Robert S. "Theodore Roosevelt's Osawatomie Speech." *Kansas His-*

torical Quarterly 32 (Summer 1966): 187-200.

6886. Lincoln, A. "My Dear Friend and Champion: Letters between Theodore Roosevelt and Hiram Johnson in 1918." *California History Quarterly* 48 (March 1969): 19-36.

6887. Lincoln, A. "My Dear Senator: Letters between Theodore Roosevelt and Hiram Johnson in 1917." *California History Quarterly* 42 (September 1963): 225-239.

6888. Little, Thomas. "The Theodore Roosevelt Collection at Harvard." *Harvard Library Bulletin* 5 (Autumn 1951): 376-378.

6889. Lodge, Henry C., and Theodore Roosevelt. *Hero Tales from American History.* New York: Century, 1895.

6890. Morison, Elting E. "The Letters of Theodore Roosevelt." *Harvard Library Bulletin* 5 (Autumn 1951): 378-381.

6891. Morison, Elting E. "Some Thoughts on the Roosevelt Papers." *Library of Congress Quarterly Journal* 15 (May 1958): 101-105.

6892. Morison, Elting E. "The Uneasy Chair: Selecting and Editing the Letters of Theodore Roosevelt." *Harvard Alumni Bulletin* 60 (May 3, 1958): 598-601.

6893. Murphy, Richard. "Theodore Roosevelt, Speech Association of America." In *A History and Criticism of American Public Address,* Vol. 3, 2d ed., edited by Marie K. Hochmuth, 313-364. New York: Longmans, 1955.

6894. Roosevelt, Theodore. *Addresses and Presidential Messages of Theodore Roosevelt, 1902-1904.* New York: Putnam, 1922.

6895. Roosevelt, Theodore. *African and European Addresses, With an Introduction Presenting a Description of the Conditions under Which the Addresses Were Given during Mr. Roosevelt's Journey in 1910 from Khartum through Europe to New York.* New York: Putnam, 1910.

6896. Roosevelt, Theodore. *African Game Trails, An Account of the American Wanderings of an American Hunter-Naturalist.* New York: Scribner's, 1910.

6897. Roosevelt, Theodore. *America and the World War.* New York: Scribner's, 1915.

6898. Roosevelt, Theodore. *American Bears: Selections from the Writings of Theodore Roosevelt.* Edited by Paul Schullery. Boulder: Colorado Associated University Press, 1983.

6899. Roosevelt, Theodore. *American Ideals and Other Essays, Social and Political.* New York: Putnam, 1897.

6900. Roosevelt, Theodore. *An Autobiography.* New York: Scribner's, 1926.

6901. Roosevelt, Theodore. *The Autobiography of Theodore Roosevelt: Condensed from the Original Version, Supplemented by Letters, Speeches, and Writings.* New York: Octagon, 1958.

6902. Roosevelt, Theodore. *Average Americans.* New York: Putnam, 1920.

6903. Roosevelt, Theodore. *A Book-Lover's Holidays in the Open.* New York: Scribner's, 1916.

6904. Roosevelt, Theodore. *Chapters of a Possible Autobiography.* New York: Outlook Co., 1913.

6905. Roosevelt, Theodore. *A Compilation of the Messages and Speeches of Theodore Roosevelt, 1901-1905.* 2 vols. Edited by Alfred H. Lewis. Washington, DC: Bureau of National Literature and Art, 1906.

6906. Roosevelt, Theodore. *Conservation of Womanhood and Childhood.* New York: Funk and Wagnalls, 1912.

6907. Roosevelt, Theodore. *Cowboys and Kings: Three Great Letters*. Cambridge, MA: Harvard University Press, 1954.

6908. Roosevelt, Theodore. *The Deer Family*. New York: Macmillan, 1903.

6909. Roosevelt, Theodore. *Fear God and Take Your Own Part*. New York: Doran, 1916.

6910. Roosevelt, Theodore. *The Foes of Our Own Household*. New York: Doran, 1917.

6911. Roosevelt, Theodore. *The Free Citizen: A Summons to Service of the Democratic Ideal: Selections from His Writings and Stories from His Record*. Edited by Hermann Hagedorn. New York: Macmillan, 1956.

6912. Roosevelt, Theodore. *Good Hunting: In Pursuit of Big Game in the West*. New York: Harper and Row, 1907.

6913. Roosevelt, Theodore. *Gouverneur Morris*. Boston: Houghton Mifflin, 1888.

6914. Roosevelt, Theodore. *The Great Adventure: Present-Day Studies in American Nationalism*. New York: Scribner's, 1918.

6915. Roosevelt, Theodore. *History as Literature, and Other Essays*. New York: Scribner's, 1913.

6916. Roosevelt, Theodore. "How the United States Acquired the Right to Dig the Panama Canal." *Outlook* 99 (October 7, 1911): 314-318.

6917. Roosevelt, Theodore. *The Hunting and Exploring Adventures of Theodore Roosevelt*. Edited by Donald Day. New York: Dial, 1955.

6918. Roosevelt, Theodore. *Hunting Trips of a Ranchman: Sketches of Sport on the Northern Cattle Plains*. New York: Putnam, 1885.

6919. Roosevelt, Theodore. *Hunting Trips on the Prairies and in the Mountains*. New York: Putnam, 1900.

6920. Roosevelt, Theodore. *Letters from Theodore Roosevelt to Anna Roosevelt Cowles, 1870-1918*. New York: Scribner's, 1924.

6921. Roosevelt, Theodore. *The Letters of Theodore Roosevelt*. 8 vols. Edited by Elting E. Morison. Cambridge, MA: Harvard University Press, 1951-1954.

6922. Roosevelt, Theodore. "Letters of Theodore Roosevelt and Charles Dwight Willard." *American Scholar* 3 (Autumn 1934): 465-486.

6923. Roosevelt, Theodore. *Letters of Theodore Roosevelt, Civil Service Commissioner, 1889-1895*. Washington, DC: U.S. Civil Service Commission, 1958.

6924. Roosevelt, Theodore. "Letters of Theodore Roosevelt to Army Friends." *Review of Reviews* 69 (January 1924): 75-78.

6925. Roosevelt, Theodore. *Letters to Kermit from Theodore Roosevelt, 1902-1908*. Edited by William H. Irwin. New York: Scribner's, 1946.

6926. Roosevelt, Theodore. *Life of Thomas Hart Benton*. Boston: Houghton Mifflin, 1887.

6927. Roosevelt, Theodore. *National Strength and International Duty*. Princeton, NJ: Princeton University Press, 1917.

6928. Roosevelt, Theodore. *The Naval Operations of the War between Great Britain and the United States, 1812-1815*. Boston: Little, Brown, 1901.

6929. Roosevelt, Theodore. *The Naval War of 1812: Or, The History of the United States Navy during the Last War with Great Britain: To Which Is Appended an Account of the Battle of New Orleans*. 4th ed. New York: Putnam, 1889.

6930. Roosevelt, Theodore. *The New Na-

tionalism. New York: Outlook Co., 1910.

6931. Roosevelt, Theodore. *New York.* New ed. New York: Longmans, Green, 1895.

6932. Roosevelt, Theodore. *Oliver Cromwell.* New York: Scribner's, 1900.

6933. Roosevelt, Theodore. *Outdoor Pastimes of an American Hunter.* Rev. ed. New York: Scribner's, 1908.

6934. Roosevelt, Theodore. "President Roosevelt's Tribute to Lincoln." *Review of Reviews* 39 (February 1909): 171.

6935. Roosevelt, Theodore. *Presidential Addresses and State Papers.* 4 vols. New York: Collier, 1905.

6936. Roosevelt, Theodore. *Public Papers of Theodore Roosevelt, Governor, 1899-1900.* 2 vols. Albany, NY: Brandow Print Co., 1899-1900.

6937. Roosevelt, Theodore. *Ranch Life and the Hunting-Trail.* New York: Century, 1888.

6938. Roosevelt, Theodore. *The Real Roosevelt, His Forceful and Fearless Utterances on Various Subjects.* Edited by Alan Warner. New York: Putnam, 1910.

6939. Roosevelt, Theodore. *Realizable Ideals (The Earl Lectures).* San Francisco: Whittaker and Ray-Wiggin Co., 1912.

6940. Roosevelt, Theodore. *Roosevelt in the Kansas City Star.* New York: Houghton Mifflin, 1921.

6941. Roosevelt, Theodore. *Roosevelt's Writings.* Edited by M. G. Fulton. New York: Macmillan, 1920.

6942. Roosevelt, Theodore. *The Rough Riders.* New York: Scribner's, 1899.

6943. Roosevelt, Theodore. "The Steel Corporation and the Panic of 1907." *Outlook* 98 (August 19, 1911): 865-868.

6944. Roosevelt, Theodore. *The Strenuous Life: Essays and Addresses.* New York: Century, 1902.

6945. Roosevelt, Theodore. *Theodore Roosevelt.* New York: Macmillan, 1913.

6946. Roosevelt, Theodore. "Theodore Roosevelt — By Himself." *Cosmopolitan* 44 (November 1907): 38-46.

6947. Roosevelt, Theodore. *Theodore Roosevelt on Race, Riots, Reds, Crime.* Compiled by Archibald B. Roosevelt. New York: Putnam, 1957.

6948. Roosevelt, Theodore. *The Theodore Roosevelt Treasure: A Self-Portrait from His Writings.* Compiled by Hermann Hagerdorn. New York: Putnam, 1957.

6949. Roosevelt, Theodore. *Theodore Roosevelt's America: Selections from the Writings of the Oysters Bay Nationalist.* Edited by Farida A. Wiley. New York: Devin-Adair, 1955.

6950. Roosevelt, Theodore. *Theodore Roosevelt's Diaries of Boyhood and Youth.* New York: Scribner's, 1928.

6951. Roosevelt, Theodore. *Theodore Roosevelt's Letters to His Children.* Edited by Joseph B. Bishop. New York: Scribner's, 1919.

6952. Roosevelt, Theodore. *Thomas H. Benton.* Boston: Houghton Mifflin, 1899.

6953. Roosevelt, Theodore. "The Three Vice-Presidential Candidates and What They Represent." *Review of Reviews* 14 (September 1896): 289.

6954. Roosevelt, Theodore. *Through the Brazilian Wilderness.* New York: Scribner's, 1914.

6955. Roosevelt, Theodore. "The Trusts, the People, and the Square Deal." *Outlook* 98 (November 1911): 649-656.

6956. Roosevelt, Theodore. "Washington and Lincoln: Let Us Do as They Did and Practice What They Preached." In his *The*

Foes of Our Own Household, 86-107. New York: Doran, 1917.

6957. Roosevelt, Theodore. *The Wilderness Hunter: An Accident of the Big Game of the United States and Its Chase with Horse, Hound, and Rifle.* New York: Putnam, 1893.

6958. Roosevelt, Theodore. *The Winning of the West.* 4 vols. New York: Putnam, 1889-1896.

6959. Roosevelt, Theodore. *Works of Theodore Roosevelt.* 20 vols. New York: Scribner's, 1926.

6960. Roosevelt, Theodore. *Writings of Theodore Roosevelt.* Edited by W. H. Harbough. Indianapolis, IN: Bobbs-Merrill, 1966.

6961. Roosevelt, Theodore, and Edmund Heller. *Life-Histories of African Game Animals.* 2 vols. New York: Scribner's, 1914.

6962. Roosevelt, Theodore, and Henry C. Lodge. *Selection from the Correspondence of Theodore Roosevelt and Henry Cabot Lodge, 1884-1918.* 2 vols. New York: Scribner's, 1925.

6963. "Roosevelt and Our Coin Designs: Letters between Theodore Roosevelt and Augustus Saint-Gaudens." Collected by Homer Saint Gaudens. *Century Magazine* 99 (April 1, 1920): 721-732.

6964. Semonche, John E. "Theodore Roosevelt's 'Muck Rake Speech': A Reassessment." *Mid-America* 46 (April 1964): 114-125.

6965. Utley, George B. "Theodore Roosevelt's The Winning of the West: Some Unpublished Letters." *Mississippi Valley Historical Review* 30 (March 1944): 495-506.

William Howard Taft

Biographies

6966. Anderson, Judith I. *William Howard Taft: An Intimate History.* New York: Norton, 1981.

6967. Davis, Oscar K. *William Howard Taft: The Man of the Hour, His Biography and His Views on the Great Questions of Today . . . and a Sketch of the Nominee for Vice President. . . .* Philadelphia: P. W. Ziegler, 1908.

6968. Duffy, Herbert S. *William Howard Taft.* New York: Minton, Balch, 1930.

6969. Dunn, Robert L. *William Howard Taft, American.* Boston: Chapple, 1908.

6970. McHale, Francis. *President and Chief Justice: The Life and Public Services of William Howard Taft.* Philadelphia: Dorrance, 1931.

6971. Myers, Elisabeth P. *William Howard Taft.* Chicago: Reilly and Lee, 1970.

6972. Pringle, Henry F. *The Life and Times of William Howard Taft: A Biography.* 2 vols. New York: Farrar, Straus, 1939.

Private Life

6973. Cotton, Edward H. *William Howard Taft, A Character Study.* Boston: Beacon Press, 1932.

6974. Greve, Charles T. "Personal Reminiscences of Chief Justice Taft." *Commercial Law Review* 35 (June 1930): 282-285.

6975. Jeffries, Ana G. "Four Years of Strife: William Howard Taft and Helen Taft." In her *In and Out of the White House.* New York: Wilfred Funk, 1966.

6976. Mackoy, Harry B. "Mr. Taft's Early Life in Cincinnati." *Independent* 70 (February 2, 1911): 227-229.

6977. North, Gene. "The Tafts Went to Texas." *Bulletin of the Historical and Philosophical Society of Ohio* 15 (October 1957): 290-301.

6978. "The Personality of the New President." *Century Magazine* 77 (March 1909): 680-684.

6979. Ross, Ishbel. *An American Family: The Tafts, 1678 to 1964.* Cleveland, OH: World Publishing, 1964.

6980. Taft, Charles P. "William Howard Taft: My Father the Chief Justice." *Supreme Court Historical Society Yearbook* (1977): 5-10.

6981. Taft, Helen H. *Recollections of Full Years.* New York: Dodd, Mead, 1914.

6982. Taft, Robert, Jr. "Will and Mabel." *Presidential Studies Quarterly* 15 (Summer 1985): 549-554.

6983. Washburn, Mabel T. R. *Ancestry*

of *William Howard Taft.* New York: Frank Allaben Genealogical Co., 1908.

Public Career

6984. Burton, David H. *William Howard Taft, In the Public Service.* Malabar, FL: Krieger, 1985.

6985. Danelski, David J. "Supreme Court Justice Steps Down." *Yale Review* 54 (March 1965): 411-425.

6986. Fish, Peter G. "William Howard Taft and Charles Evans Hughes: Conservative Politicians as Chief Judicial Reformers." *Supreme Court Review* (1975): 123-145.

6987. Hicks, Frederick C. *William Howard Taft, Yale Professor of Law and New Haven Citizen: An Academic Interlude in the Life of the Twenty-seventh President of the United States and the Tenth Chief Justice of the Supreme Court.* New Haven, CT: Yale University Press, 1945.

6988. Hollister, Howard C. "William H. Taft at the Bar and on the Bench." *Green Bag* 20 (July 1908): 337-345.

6989. Kutler, Stanley I. "Chief Justice Taft and the Delusion of Judicial Exactness — A Study in Jurisprudence." *Virginia Law Review* 48 (December 1962): 1407-1426.

6990. Kutler, Stanley I. "Chief Justice Taft, Judicial Unanimity, and Labor: The Coronado Case." *Historian* 24 (November 1961): 68-83.

6991. Kutler, Stanley I. "Chief Justice Taft, National Regulation, and the Commerce Power." *Journal of American History* 51 (March 1965): 56-68.

6992. Kutler, Stanley I. "The Judicial Philosophy of Chief Justice Taft and Organized Labor, 1921-1930." Ph.D. dissertation, Ohio State University, 1960.

6993. Manners, William. *T R and Will: A Friendship That Split the Republican Party.* New York: Harcourt, Brace and World, 1969.

6994. Mason, Alpheus T. "Chief Justice Taft at the Helm." *Vanderbilt Law Review* 18 (March 1965): 367-404.

6995. Mason, Alpheus T. "The Labor Decision of Chief Justice Taft." *University of Pennsylvania Law Review* 78 (March 1930): 585-625.

6996. Mason, Alpheus T. "President by Chance, Chief Justice by Choice." *American Bar Association Journal* 55 (January 1919): 35-39.

6997. Mason, Alpheus T. *The Supreme Court from Taft to Warren.* Rev. ed. Baton Rouge: Louisiana State University Press, 1968.

6998. Mason, Alpheus T. *William Howard Taft: Chief Justice.* New York: Simon and Schuster, 1965.

6999. Murphy, Walter F. "Chief Justice Taft and the Lower Court Bureaucracy." *Journal of Politics* 24 (August 1962): 453-476.

7000. Murphy, Walter F. "In His Own Image: Mr. Chief Justice Taft and Supreme Court Appointments." *Supreme Court Review* (1961): 159-193.

7001. Ragan, Allen E. *Chief Justice Taft.* Columbus: Ohio State Archaeological and Historical Society, 1938.

7002. Ragan, Allen E. "Free Chief Justice Taft." Ph.D. dissertation, Ohio State University, 1932.

7003. Schlup, Leonard, comp. "Selected Letters of Senator McCumber to Former President Taft Concerning the League of Nations." *North Dakota History* 46 (Summer 1979): 15-23.

7004. Slotnick, Elliot E. "Who Speaks for the Court? Majority Opinion Assignment from Taft to Burger." *American Journal of Political Science* 23 (February 1979): 60-77.

7005. Solvick, Stanley D. "The Pre-Presidential Political and Economic Thought of William Howard Taft." *Northwest Ohio Quarterly* 43 (Fall 1971): 87-97.

7006. Solvick, Stanley D. "William Howard Taft and Cannonism." *Wisconsin Magazine of History* 48 (Autumn 1964): 48-58.

7007. Spring, Samuel. "Two Chief Justices: Edward Douglass White and William Howard Taft." *Review of Reviews* 64 (August 1921): 161-170.

7008. Umbreit, Kenneth B. "William Howard Taft." In his *Our Eleven Chief Justices: A History of the Supreme Court in Terms of Their Personalities*, 393-450. New York: Harper and Row, 1938.

7009. Walker, Kenneth R. "Ohio's Three Chief Justices: Puritans on the Bench." *Northwest Ohio Quarterly* 38 (Spring 1966): 66-73.

7010. Warner, Hoyt L. *Progressivism in Ohio, 1897-1917.* Columbus: Ohio State University Press, 1965.

7011. Warren, Earl. "Chief Justice William Howard Taft." *Yale Law Journal* 67 (January 1958): 353-362.

Presidential Years

7012. Abbott, Lyman. "William H. Taft." *Outlook* 88 (April 4, 1908): 773-777.

7013. Abrams, Richard M. *The Burdens of Progress: 1900-1929.* Glenview, IL: Scott, Foreman, 1978.

7014. Abrams, Richard M. *Issues of the Populist and Progressive Period.* New York: Harper and Row, 1969.

7015. Allison, Hildreth M. "Dublin Greets a President." *Historical New Hampshire* 35 (Summer 1980): 202-206.

7016. Anderson, Donald F. "The Legacy of William Howard Taft." *Presidential Studies Quarterly* 12 (Winter 1982): 26-33.

7017. Anderson, Donald F. "William Howard Taft: A Conservative's Conception of Presidency." Ph.D. dissertation, Cornell University, 1968.

7018. Baker, Ray S. "The Negro in the Democracy." *Independent* 67 (September 1909): 584-592.

7019. Ballard, Rene N. "The Administrative Theory of William Howard Taft." *Western Political Quarterly* 7 (March 1954): 65-74.

7020. Barker, Charles E. *With President Taft in the White House: Memories of William Howard Taft.* Chicago: A. Kroch, 1947.

7021. Baylen, Joseph O. "American Intervention in Nicaragua, 1909-1933: An Appraisal of Objectives and Results." *Southwestern Social Science Quarterly* 35 (September 1954): 128-154.

7022. Bickel, Alexander M. "Mr. Taft Rehabilitates the Court." *Yale Law Journal* 79 (November 1969): 1-45.

7023. Bolt, Robert. "William Howard Taft: A Frustrated and Fretful Unitarian in the White House." *Queen City Heritage* 42 (Spring 1984): 39-48.

7024. Burton, David H. "The Learned Presidency: Roosevelt, Taft, Wilson." *Presidential Studies Quarterly* 15 (Summer 1985): 468-497.

7025. Butt, Archibald W. *Taft and Roosevelt: The Intimate Letters of Archie Butt.* 2 vols. Garden City, NY: Doubleday, 1930.

7026. Bryan, Martin. "A Study of the Speaking of William Howard Taft in the

1908 Presidential Campaign." Ph.D. dissertation, Northwestern University, 1953.

7027. Campbell, John P. "Taft, Roosevelt, and the Arbitration Treaties of 1911." *Journal of American History* 53 (September 1966): 279-298.

7028. Chay, Jongsuk. "The Taft-Katsura Memorandum Reconsidered." *Pacific Historical Review* 37 (August 1968): 321-326.

7029. Clark, Charles H. "William Howard Taft." *Independent* 64 (April 9, 1908): 780-785.

7030. Clark, Truman R. "President Taft and the Puerto Rican Appropriation Crisis of 1909." *Americas* 26 (October 1969): 152-170.

7031. Coletta, Paolo E. "The Diplomacy of Theodore Roosevelt and William Howard Taft." In *American Foreign Relations: A Historiographical Review,* edited by J. Samuel Walker, 91-113. Westport, CT: Greenwood Press, 1981.

7032. Coletta, Paolo E. *The Presidency of William Howard Taft.* Lawrence: University Press of Kansas, 1973.

7033. Coulter, E. Merton. "William Howard Taft's Visit to Athens." *Georgia Historical Quarterly* 52 (December 1968): 388-397.

7034. Crawford, Charlotte. "The Border Meeting of Presidents Taft and Diaz." *Password* 3 (July 1958): 86-96.

7035. Dolliver, Jonathan. "The Downward Revision Hoax." *Independent* 69 (September 8, 1910): 512-517.

7036. Dorroh, David L. "President Taft and the Solid South." *Nineteenth Century* 72 (November 1912): 1006-1029.

7037. Esthus, Raymond A. "The Taft-Katsura Agreement — Reality or Myth?" *Journal of Modern History* 31 (March 1959): 46-51.

7038. Fischer, Robert. "Henry Cabot Lodge and the Taft Arbitration Treaties." *South Atlantic Quarterly* 78 (Spring 1979): 244-258.

7039. German, James C., Jr. "The Taft Administration and the Sherman Antitrust Act." *Mid-America* 54 (July 1972): 172-186.

7040. Gould, Lewis L. "Theodore Roosevelt, William Howard Taft, and the Disputed Delegates in 1912: Texas as a Test Case." *Southwestern Historical Quarterly* 80 (July 1976): 33-56.

7041. Hahn, Harlan. "President Taft and the Discipline of Patronage." *Journal of Politics* 28 (May 1966): 368-390.

7042. Haley, P. Edward. *Revolution and Intervention: The Diplomacy of Taft and Wilson with Mexico, 1910-1917.* Cambridge, MA: MIT Press, 1970.

7043. Hechler, Kenneth W. *Insurgency: Personalities and Politics of the Taft Era.* New York: Columbia University Press, 1940.

7044. Hess, Stephen. "Big Bill Taft." *American Heritage* 17 (October 1966): 32-37.

7045. Hindman, E. James. "The General Arbitration Treaties of William Howard Taft." *Historian* 36 (November 1973): 52-65.

7046. Hornig, Edgar A. "Cleveland's Ghost in the Taft-Bryan Duel, 1908." *Mid-America* 51 (July 1969): 205-216.

7047. Kornhauser, Samuel J. "President Taft and the Extra-Constitutional Function of the Presidency." *North American Review* 192 (November 1910): 577-594.

7048. Larson, Robert W. "Taft, Roosevelt, and New Mexico Statehood." *Mid-America* 45 (April 1963): 99-114.

7049. Lease, Martin H., Jr. "William Howard Taft and the Power of the President." Ph.D. dissertation, Indiana University, 1961.

7050. Lefroy, A. H. F. "Ex-President Taft at the University of the United States." *Canadian Law Times* 35 (March 1915): 216-222.

7051. LeRoy, James A. "Taft as Administrator: Traits and Methods as Revealed by His Work in the Philippines." *Century Magazine* 77 (March 1909): 691-698.

7052. Lowry, Edward G. "The White House Now." *Harper's Weekly* 53 (May 15, 1909): 7-8.

7053. McBee, Silas. "The South and Mr. Taft, 1908." *Sewanee Review* 16 (October 1908): 486-494.

7054. McComb, Walter J. "The Insurgent Movement in the Republican Party during the Roosevelt and Taft Administration." Ph.D. dissertation, University of Minnesota, 1939.

7055. McHargue, Daniel S. "President Taft's Appointments to the Supreme Court." *Journal of Politics* 12 (August 1950): 478-510.

7056. McMains, Howard F. "The Road to George Ade's Farm: Origins of Taft's First Campaign Rally, September, 1908." *Indiana Magazine of History* 67 (December 1971): 317-334.

7057. Minger, Ralph E. "Panama, the Canal Zone, and Titular Sovereignty." *Western Political Quarterly* 14 (June 1961): 544-564.

7058. Minger, Ralph E. "Taft, MacArthur, and the Establishment of Civil Government in the Philippines." *Ohio History Quarterly* 70 (October 1961): 308-331.

7059. Minger, Ralph E. "Taft's Mission to Japan: A Study in Personal Diplomacy." *Pacific Historical Review* 30 (August 1961): 279-294.

7060. Minger, Ralph E. "William H. Taft and the U.S. Intervention in Cuba 1906." *Hispanic American Historical Review* 41 (February 1961): 75-89.

7061. Minger, Ralph E. *William Howard Taft and United States Foreign Policy: The Apprenticeship Years, 1900-1908*. Urbana: University of Illinois Press, 1975.

7062. Minger, Ralph E. "William Howard Taft's Forgotten Visit to Russia." *Russia Review* 22 (April 1963): 149-156.

7063. Morris, Jeffrey B. "Chief Justice Edward Douglass White and President Taft's Court." *Supreme Court Society Year Book* (1982): 27-45.

7064. Needham, David C. "William Howard Taft, the Negro, and the White South, 1908-1912." Ph.D. dissertation, University of Georgia, 1970.

7065. Ness, Gary C. "Proving Ground for a President: William Howard Taft and the Philippines 1900-1905." *Cincinnati Historical Society Bulletin* 34 (Fall 1976): 205-223.

7066. Ness, Gary C. "William Howard Taft and the Great War." *Cincinnati Historical Society Bulletin* 34 (Spring 1976): 7-24.

7067. Nye, Russell B. *Midwestern Progressive Politics*. East Lansing: Michigan State University Press, 1951.

7068. Parsons, Elsie W. "Congressional Junket in Japan: The Taft Party of 1905 Meets the Mikado." Edited by John E. Parsons. *New York Historical Society Quarterly* 41 (October 1957): 382-406.

7069. Patterson, Raymond A. *Taft's Training for the Presidency*. Boston: Chapple, 1908.

7070. Pinchot, Gifford. *Breaking New Ground*. New York: Harcourt, Brace, 1947.

7071. Pitkin, William A. "Issues in the Roosevelt-Taft Contest of 1912." *Mid-America* 34 (October 1952): 219-232.

7072. "President Taft." *Atlantic Monthly* 109 (February 1912): 164-171.

7073. Randall, Ronald. "Presidents Taft and Harding: More Than Ohio in Common." *Northwest Ohio Quarterly* 56 (Autumn 1984): 147-151.

7074. Reuter, Frank T. "William Howard Taft and the Separation of Church and State in the Philippines." *Journal of Church and State* 24 (Winter 1982): 105-117.

7075. Richardson, Elmo R. *The Politics of Conservation: Crusades and Controversies, 1897-1913*. Berkeley: University of California Press, 1962.

7076. Roebuck, James R., Jr. "The United States and East Asia 1909-1913: A Study of the Far Eastern Diplomacy of William Howard Taft." Ph.D. dissertation, University of Virginia, 1977.

7077. Rowe, Joseph M., Jr. "William Howard Taft: Diplomatic Trouble-Shooter." Ph.D. dissertation, Texas Agricultural and Mechanical University, 1977.

7078. Scholes, Walter V., and Marie V. Scholes. *The Foreign Politics of the Taft Administration*. Columbia: University of Missouri Press, 1970.

7079. Schultz, Louis P. "William Howard Taft: A Constitutionalist's View of the Presidency." *Presidential Studies Quarterly* 9 (Fall 1979): 402-414.

7080. Schultz, Louis P. "William Howard Taft: A Constitutionalist's View of the Presidency." Ph.D. dissertation, Northern Illinois University, 1979.

7081. Seltzer, Louis B. "Episode in a Railroad Station." *Collier's* 137 (September 14, 1956): 56-57.

7082. Solvick, Stanley D. "The Conservative as Progressive: William Howard Taft and the Politics of the Square Deal." *Northwest Ohio Quarterly* 39 (Summer 1967): 38-48.

7083. Solvick, Stanley D. "William Howard Taft and the Payne-Aldrich Tariff." *Mississippi Valley Historical Review* 50 (December 1963): 424-442.

7084. Solvick, Stanley D. "William Howard Taft and the Progressive Movement: A Study in Conservative Thought and Politics." Ph.D. dissertation, University of Michigan, 1963.

7085. Stahl, Rose M. "The Ballinger-Pinchot Controversy." *Smith College Studies in History* 11 (January 1926): 65-138.

7086. Straus, Oscar S. *Under Four Administrations: From Cleveland to Taft*. Boston: Houghton Mifflin, 1922.

7087. Travis, Paul D. "Gore, Bristow, and Taft: Reflections of Canadian Reciprocity, 1911." *Chronicles of Oklahoma* 53 (Summer 1975): 212-224.

7088. Vivian, James F. "Not a Patriotic American Party: William Howard Taft's Campaign against the Nonpartisan League, 1920-1921." *North Dakota History* 50 (Fall 1983): 4-10.

7089. Walker, Albert H. *The Administration of William H. Taft: A Historical Sketch*. New York: n.p., 1912.

7090. Walker, Don D. "The Taft Victory in Utah in 1912." *Utah Historical Quarterly* 32 (Winter 1964): 44-56.

7091. Weigand, Wayne A. "The Lauchheimer Controversy: A Case of Group Political Pressure during the Taft Administration." *Military Affairs* 40 (April 1976): 54-59.

7092. Wessel, Thomas R. "Republican Justice: The Department of Justice under Roosevelt and Taft, 1901-1913." Ph.D. dissertation, University of Maryland, 1972.

7093. Whytlaw, Mary G. "O, Mr. President." *Parents' Magazine* 23 (November 1948): 68.

7094. Wilensky, Norman M. *Conservatives in the Progressive Era: The Taft*

Republicans of 1912. Gainesville: University of Florida Press, 1965.

7095. "William Howard Taft." *American Judicature Society Journal* 14 (June 1930): 4-5.

Writings

7096. Gatewood, Willard B., Jr., ed. "The President and the 'Deacon' in the Campaign of 1912: The Correspondence of William Howard Taft and James Calvin Hemphill, 1911-1912." *Ohio History* 74 (Winter 1965): 35-54.

7097. Schlup, Leonard. "A Senator of Principle: Some Correspondence between LeBaron Bradford Colt and William Howard Taft." *Rhode Island History* 42 (February 1983): 2-16.

7098. Shriver, Phillip R., ed. "William Howard Taft and Myron T. Herrick: Selected Letters, 1912-1916." *Bulletin of the Historical and Philosophical Society of Ohio* 14 (October 1956): 221-231.

7099. Stewart, Kate M. "The William Howard Taft Papers." *Library of Congress Quarterly Journal of Current Acquisitions* 15 (November 1957): 1-11.

7100. Taft, William H. *Address at Dedication of Alphonso Taft Hall*. Cincinnati, OH: University of Cincinnati, 1925.

7101. Taft, William H. *The Anti-Trust Act and the Supreme Court*. New York: Harper and Row, 1914.

7102. Taft, William H. "The Boundaries between the Executive, the Legislative, and the Judicial Branches of the Government." *Yale Law Journal* 25 (June 1916): 599-616.

7103. Taft, William H. "Criticism of the Federal Judiciary." *American Law Review* 29 (September/October 1895): 641-674.

7104. Taft, William H. *Ethics in Service: Addresses Delivered in the Page Lecture Series, 1914, Before the Senior Class of the Sheffield Scientific School, Yale University*. New Haven, CT: Yale University Press, 1915.

7105. Taft, William H. *Four Aspects of Civic Duty*. New York: Scribner's, 1906.

7106. Taft, William H. "The Jurisdiction of the Supreme Court under the Act of February 13, 1925." *Yale Law Journal* 35 (November 1925): 1-12.

7107. Taft, William H. *Liberty under Law, An Interpretation of the Principles of Our Constitutional Government*. New Haven, CT: Yale University Press, 1922.

7108. Taft, William H. "My Conception of the Presidency." *Collier's Weekly* 41 (June 27, 1908): 7.

7109. Taft, William H. *Our Chief Magistrate and His Powers*. New York: Columbia University Press, 1916.

7110. Taft, William H. *Political Issues and Outlooks: Speeches Delivered between August, 1908, and February, 1909*. New York: Doubleday, 1909.

7111. Taft, William H. *Popular Government: Its Essence, Its Permanence, and Its Perils*. New Haven, CT: Yale University Press, 1913.

7112. Taft, William H. "Possible and Needed Reforms in the Administration of Civil Justice in the Federal Courts." *American Law Review* 57 (January 1923): 1-23.

7113. Taft, William H. "Power of the President." *Yale Review* 4 (October 1914): 25-42.

7114. Taft, William H. *Present Day Problems: A Collection of Addresses Delivered on Various Occasions*. New York: Dodd, Mead, 1908.

7115. Taft, William H. "Presidency." *In-*

dependent 73 (November 21, 1912): 1196-1200.

7116. Taft, William H. *The Presidency, Its Duties, Its Powers, Its Opportunities, and Its Limitations: Three Lectures.* New York: Scribner's, 1916.

7117. Taft, William H. *The President and His Powers.* New York: Columbia University Press, 1916.

7118. Taft, William H. *Presidential Addresses and State Papers of William Howard Taft.* 2 vols. Garden City, NY: Doubleday, 1910.

7119. Taft, William H. *Representative Government in the United States: Being the Opening Lecture of the James Stokes Lectureship on Politics, At New York University.* New York: New York University Press, 1921.

7120. Taft, William H. "The Right of Private Property." *Michigan Law Journal* 3 (1894): 215-233.

7121. Taft, William H. "Supreme Court of the United States and Popular Self-Government." *Harvard Graduates' Magazine* 23 (September 1914): 1-14.

7122. Taft, William H. *Taft Papers on League of Nations.* Edited by Theodore Marburg and Horace E. Flack. New York: Macmillan, 1920.

7123. Taft, William H. *The United States and Peace.* New York: Scribner's, 1914.

7124. Taft, William H. *United States Supreme Court: The Prototype of a World Court.* Baltimore, MD: American Society for Judicial Settlement of International Disputes, 1915.

7125. Taft, William H., and William J. Bryan. *World Peace: A Writer Debate between William Howard Taft and William Jennings Bryan.* New York: Doran, 1917.

7126. Taft, William H., and George B. Edwards. "Letters of Roommates: William B. Taft and George B. Edwards." Edited by Walter P. Armstrong. *American Bar Association Journal* 34 (May 1948): 383-385.

7127. "Turning Points in Mr. Taft's Career and His Attitude as Revealed in Hitherto Unpublished Letters from His Pen." *Century Magazine* 77 (March 1909): 684-689.

7128. U.S. War Department. *Special Report of William H. Taft, Secretary of War, To the President, On the Philippines.* Washington, DC: U.S. Government Printing Office, 1908.

Woodrow Wilson

Biographies

7129. Alderman, Edwin A. "Woodrow Wilson." *Outlook* 136 (February 13, 1924): 254.

7130. Alderman, Edwin A. *Woodrow Wilson.* Garden City, NY: Doubleday, 1925.

7131. Alson, E. Bowles, ed. *The Greatness of Woodrow Wilson, 1856-1956.* New York: Rinehart, 1956.

7132. Anderson, David D. *Woodrow Wilson.* Boston: Twayne, 1978.

7133. Annin, Robert E. *Woodrow Wilson: A Character Study.* New York: Dodd, Mead, 1924.

7134. Archer, Jules. *World Citizen: Woodrow Wilson.* New York: Messner, 1967.

7135. Baker, Ray S. *Woodrow Wilson: Life and Letters.* 8 vols. Garden City, NY: Doubleday, 1927-1939.

7136. Barnes, Harry E. "Woodrow Wilson." *American Mercury* 1 (April 1924): 479-490.

7137. Bellot, Hugh H. *Woodrow Wilson.* London: Athlone Press, 1955.

7138. Braeman, John. *Wilson.* Englewood Cliffs, NJ: Prentice-Hall, 1972.

7139. Brodie, Bernard. "A Psychoanalytic Interpretation of Woodrow Wilson." *World Politics* 9 (April 1957): 413-422.

7140. Bullitt, William C., and Sigmund Freud. *Thomas Woodrow Wilson, Twenty-eighth President of the U.S.: A Psychological Study.* Boston: Houghton Mifflin, 1967.

7141. Cranston, Ruth. *The Story of Woodrow Wilson.* New York: Simon and Schuster, 1945.

7142. Cronon, E. David. "Woodrow Wilson." In *America's Eleven Greatest Presidents*, 2d ed., edited by Morton Borden, 202-225. Chicago: Rand McNally, 1971.

7143. Daniels, Jonathan, et al. "Woodrow Wilson 1856-1924." *Virginia Quarterly* 32 (Autumn 1956): 481-540, 546-610.

7144. Daniels, Josephus. *The Life of Woodrow Wilson, 1856-1924.* Philadelphia: John C. Winston, 1924.

7145. Daniels, Winthrop M. *Recollections of Woodrow Wilson.* New Haven, CT: Yale University Press, 1944.

7146. De Jouvenel, Bertrand. "Woodrow Wilson." *Confluence* 5 (1957): 320-331.

7147. Durden, Robert F. "Woodrow Wilson and His New Biographers." *South Atlantic Quarterly* 56 (Autumn 1957): 500-505.

7148. Eliot, Charles W. "Woodrow Wilson." *Atlantic Monthly* 133 (June 1924): 815-823.

7149. Ford, Henry J. *Woodrow Wilson, The Man and His Work: A Biographical Study.* . . . New York: Appleton, 1916.

7150. Freud, Sigmund, and William C. Bullitt. "Woodrow Wilson." *Encounter* 28 (January 1967): 3-24; (February 1967): 3-24; (April 1967): 84-89; (July 1967): 86-89.

7151. Garraty, John A. *Woodrow Wilson: A Great Life in Brief.* New York: Knopf, 1956.

7152. George, Alexander L., and Juliette L. George. *Woodrow Wilson and Colonel House: A Personality Study.* New York: Day, 1956.

7153. Hale, William B. *The Story of a Style.* New York: B. W. Huebsch, 1920.

7154. Hale, William B. "Woodrow Wilson — A Biography." *World's Work* 22 (October 1911): 40-53; 23 (November 1911): 64-77; (January 1912): 297-310; (February 1912): 406-472; (March 1912): 522-534.

7155. Hale, William M. *Woodrow Wilson: The Story of His Life.* Garden City, NY: Doubleday, 1912.

7156. Halevy, Daniel. *President Wilson.* Translated by Hugh Stokes. New York: John Lane Co., 1919.

7157. Harris, H. Wilson. "Woodrow Wilson." *Contemporary Review* 125 (March 1924): 282-289.

7158. Harvey, A. R. "Woodrow Wilson." *Queen's Quarterly* 34 (January 1927): 241-262.

7159. Hoffs, Joshua A. "Comments on Psychoanalytic Biography, With Special Reference to Freud's Interest in Woodrow Wilson." *Psychoanalytic Review* 56 (1969): 402-414.

7160. Hosford, Hester E. "Woodrow Wilson." *Independent* 73 (July 11, 1912): 68-79.

7161. Johnson, Gerald W. "Wilson the Man." *Virginia Quarterly Review* 32 (Autumn 1948): 494-507.

7162. Lawrence, David. *The True Story of Woodrow Wilson.* New York: Doran, 1924.

7163. Link, Arthur S. "The Case for Woodrow Wilson." *Harper's* 234 (April 1967): 85-93.

7164. Link, Arthur S. *Woodrow Wilson.* 5 vols. Princeton, NJ: Princeton University Press, 1947-1965.

7165. Link, Arthur S. *Woodrow Wilson: A Brief Biography.* Cleveland, OH: World Publishing, 1963.

7166. Link, Arthur S., ed. *Woodrow Wilson: A Profile.* New York: Hill and Wang, 1968.

7167. Link, Arthur S. "Woodrow Wilson: The American as Southerner." *Journal of Southern History* 36 (February 1970): 3-17.

7168. Loth, David G. *The Story of Woodrow Wilson.* New York: Woodrow Wilson Foundation, 1955.

7169. Low, A. Maurice. *Woodrow Wilson, An Interpretation.* Boston: Little, Brown, 1918.

7170. McAdoo, Eleanor R., and Margaret Y. Gaffey. *The Woodrow Wilsons.* New York: Macmillan, 1937.

7171. McKinley, Silas B. *Woodrow Wilson, A Biography.* New York: Praeger, 1957.

7172. Mooney, Booth. *Woodrow Wilson.* Chicago: Follett, 1968.

7173. Nevins, Allan. "Woodrow Wilson Relives in a Great Biography." *Current History* 35 (January 1932): 501-506.

7174. Reid, Edith G. *Woodrow Wilson the Caricature, the Myth, and the Man.* New York: Oxford University Press, 1934.

7175. Seymour, Charles. *Woodrow Wilson in Perspective.* Stanford, CT: Overbrook Press, 1956.

7176. Shachtman, Tom. *Edith and Woodrow: A Presidential Romance.* New York: Putnam, 1981.

7177. Shorey, Paul. "Wilson — The Man and the Statesman." *Weekly Review* 4 (April 30, 1921): 414-415.

7178. Steinberg, Alfred. *Woodrow Wilson.* New York: Putnam, 1961.

7179. Walworth, Arthur C. *Woodrow Wilson.* 3d ed. New York: Norton, 1978.

7180. White, William A. *Woodrow Wilson, The Man, His Times, and His Task.* Boston: Houghton Mifflin, 1924.

7181. Williams, John H. H. "Woodrow Wilson." In his *Men of Stress: Three Dynamic Interpretations*, 25-174. London: J. Cape, 1948.

7182. Winkler, John K. *Woodrow Wilson: The Man Who Lives On.* New York: Vanguard Press, 1933.

7183. "Woodrow Wilson." *Weekly Review* 4 (March 9, 1921): 214-216.

Private Life

7184. Archer, William. "President Wilson as a Man of Letters." *Fortnightly Review* 103 (February 1918): 230-237.

7185. Athearn, Clarence R. "Woodrow Wilson's Philosophy." *Methodist Review* 45 (September 1929): 683-688.

7186. Bailey, Kenneth M. "Woodrow Wilson: The Educator Speaking." Ph.D. dissertation, University of Iowa, 1970.

7187. Baker, Ray S. *Woodrow Wilson and World Settlement: Written from His Unpublished and Personal Material.* 3 vols. Garden City, NY: Doubleday, 1922.

7188. Barnes, Harry E. "The Personality and Career of Woodrow Wilson." *American Review* 2 (September 1924): 529-552.

7189. Barton, George. "Woodrow Wilson: His Human Side." *Current History* 22 (April 1925): 1-9.

7190. Blum, John M. "Woodrow Wilson: A Study in Intellect." *Confluence* 5 (Winter 1957): 367-376.

7191. Bober, Robert A. "Young Woodrow Wilson: The Search for Immortality." Ph.D. dissertation, Case Western Reserve University, 1980.

7192. Bragdon, Henry W. *Woodrow Wilson: The Academic Years.* Cambridge, MA: Harvard University Press, 1967.

7193. Brand, Katherine E. "Woodrow Wilson in His Own Time." *Library of Congress Quarterly Journal* 13 (February 1956): 61-72.

7194. Brooks, William E. "Woodrow Wilson: A Study in Personality." *Century Magazine* 96 (August 1929): 410-420.

7195. Carleton, William G. "A New Look at Woodrow Wilson." *Virginia Quarterly Review* 38 (Autumn 1962): 545-566.

7196. Cooper, John M., Jr. "Woodrow Wilson: The Academic Man." *Virginia Quarterly Review* 58 (Winter 1982): 38-53.

7197. Craig, Hardin. *Woodrow Wilson at Princeton.* Norman: University of Oklahoma Press, 1960.

7198. Dabney, Virginius. "The Human Side of Woodrow Wilson." *Virginia Quarterly Review* 32 (Autumn 1948): 508-523.

7199. Daniel, Marjorie L. "Woodrow Wilson — Historian." *Mississippi Valley Historical Review* 21 (December 1934): 361-374.

7200. Daniel, Robert L. "The Friendship of Woodrow Wilson and Cleveland Dodge." *Mid-America* 43 (July 1961): 182-196.

7201. Dickson, Thomas H. "Bernard Shaw and Woodrow Wilson." *Virginia Quarterly Review* 7 (January 1931): 1-17.

7202. Dodd, William E. "The Social and Economic Background of Woodrow Wilson." *Journal of Political Economy* 25 (March 1917): 261-285.

7203. Elliott, Margaret R. A. *My Aunt Louisa and Woodrow Wilson*. Chapel Hill: University of North Carolina Press, 1944.

7204. Fosdick, Raymond B. "Personal Recollections of Woodrow Wilson." In *The Philosophy and Policies of Woodrow Wilson*, edited by Earl Latham, 28-45. Chicago: University of Chicago Press, 1958.

7205. Gaines, William H., Jr. "A House on 'Gospel Hill': Woodrow Wilson's Birthplace Becomes a Shrine." *Virginia Cavalcade* 6 (Winter 1956): 12-19.

7206. Gaines, William H., Jr. "A House on 'Gospel Hill': Woodrow Wilson's Homecoming to the Manse, 1912." *Virginia Cavalcade* 6 (Autumn 1956): 42-47.

7207. Garfield, Harry A. "One of History's Great Souls: Some Personal Recollections of Woodrow Wilson '79." *Princeton Alumni Weekly* 30 (January 10, 1930): 355-357.

7208. Garraty, John A. "The Training of Woodrow Wilson: His Career at Princeton Prepared Him for a Larger Role, But Also Showed His Strange Blend of Strength and Weakness." *American Heritage* 7 (August 1956): 24-27, 94.

7209. Garraty, John A. "Woodrow Wilson: A Study in Personality." *South Atlantic Quarterly* 56 (April 1957): 176-185.

7210. George, Alexander L., and Juliette L. George. "Dr. Weinstein's Interpretation of Woodrow Wilson: Some Preliminary Observations." *Psychohistory Review* 8 (Summer/Autumn 1979): 72.

7211. George, Juliette L. "Issues in Wilson Scholarship: References to Early 'Strokes' in the 'Papers of Woodrow Wilson.'" *Journal of American History* 70 (March 1984): 845-853.

7212. George, Juliette L., and Alexander L. George. "'Woodrow Wilson and Colonel House': A Reply to Weinstein, Anderson, and Link." *Political Science Quarterly* 96 (Winter 1981-1982): 641-665.

7213. Gilmore, William J. "Caught with Your Pants Down: The Limitations of Psychobiography without Physical Health in the Case of Woodrow Wilson." *Psychohistory Review* 8 (Spring 1980): 46-47.

7214. Gottlieb, Kevin C. "The Political Philosophy of Woodrow Wilson as President of Princeton, 1902-1910." Ph.D. dissertation, Syracuse University, 1970.

7215. Grayson, Cary T. *Woodrow Wilson, An Intimate Memoir*. New York: Holt, Rinehart and Winston, 1960.

7216. Griffin, Solomon B. "The Political Evolution of a College President." *Atlantic Monthly* 109 (January 1912): 43-51.

7217. Hatch, Alden. *Edith Bolling Wilson, First Lady Extraordinary*. New York: Dodd, Mead, 1961.

7218. Heusser, Albert H. *In the Footsteps of Washington: Pope's Creek to Princeton*. Paterson, NJ: Privately Printed, 1921.

7219. House, Edward M. *The Intimate Papers of Colonel House Arranged as a Narrative by Charles Seymour*. 4 vols. Boston: Houghton Mifflin, 1926-1928.

7220. Hulbert, Mary A. *The Story of Mrs. Peck*. New York: Minton, Balch, 1933.

7221. James, Edith. "Edith Bolling Wilson: A Documentary View." In *Clio Was a Woman: Studies in the History of American Women*, edited by Mabel E. Deutrich and Virginia C. Purdy, 234-240. Washington, DC: Howard University Press, 1980.

7222. Kerney, James. "Last Talks with Woodrow Wilson." *Saturday Evening Post* 196 (March 29, 1924): 3-4.

7223. Kirk, Harris E. "In Memoriam: Woodrow Wilson." *Johns Hopkins University Alumni Magazine* 12 (March 1924): 202-208.

7224. Latane, John H. "Woodrow Wilson as Student and Lecturer." *Johns Hopkins University Alumni Magazine* 12 (March 1924): 189-193.

7225. Latane, John H. "Woodrow Wilson: Memorial Address." *Johns Hopkins University Alumni Magazine* 12 (March 1924): 194-200.

7226. Lewis, McMillan. *Woodrow Wilson of Princeton*. Narberth, PA: Livingston, 1952.

7227. Link, Arthur S. "A Portrait of Wilson." *Virginia Quarterly Review* 32 (Autumn 1948): 524-540.

7228. McAdoo, William G. "The Kind of Man Woodrow Wilson Is." *Century Magazine* 85 (March 1913): 744-753.

7229. Mosher, O. W., Jr. "Woodrow Wilson's Methods in the Classroom." *Current History* 32 (June 1930): 502-505.

7230. Mulder, John M. "The Gospel of Order: Woodrow Wilson and the Development of His Religious, Political, and Educational Thought, 1856-1910." Ph.D. dissertation, Princeton University, 1974.

7231. Mulder, John M. "Wilson the Preacher: The 1905 Baccalaureate Sermon." *Journal of Presbyterian History* 51 (Autumn 1973): 267-284.

7232. Mulder, John M. *Woodrow Wilson: The Years of Preparation*. Princeton, NJ: Princeton University Press, 1977.

7233. Myers, William S., ed. *Woodrow Wilson, Some Princeton Memories by George McLean Harper, Robert K. Root, Edward S. Corwin, and Others*. Princeton, NJ: Princeton University Press, 1946.

7234. Osborn, George C. "The Influence of Joseph Ruggles Wilson on His Son Woodrow Wilson." *North Carolina Historical Review* 32 (October 1955): 519-543.

7235. Osborn, George C. "Woodrow Wilson as a Young Lawyer, 1882-1883." *Georgia Historical Quarterly* 41 (June 1957): 126-142.

7236. Osborn, George C. *Woodrow Wilson: The Early Years*. Baton Rouge: Louisiana State University Press, 1968.

7237. Osborn, George C. "Woodrow Wilson: The Evolution of a Name." *North Carolina Historical Review* 34 (October 1961): 507-516.

7238. Osborn, George C. "Woodrow Wilson's First Romance." *Ohio Historical Quarterly* 67 (January 1958): 1-20.

7239. Patterson, Archibald W. *Personal Recollections of Woodrow Wilson and Some Reflections upon His Life and Character*. Whittet and Shepperson, 1929.

7240. Perry, Bliss. "Woodrow Wilson as a Man of Letters." *Century Magazine* 85 (March 1913): 753-757.

7241. Ross, Dorothy. "Woodrow Wilson and the Case for Psychohistory." *Journal of American History* 69 (December 1982): 659-668.

7242. Ross, Ishbel. *Power with Grace: The Life Story of Mrs. Woodrow Wilson*. New York: Putnam, 1975.

7243. Saunders, Frances W. *Ellen Axson Wilson*. Chapel Hill: University of North Carolina Press, 1985.

7244. Saunders, Frances W. "Love and Guilt: Woodrow Wilson and Mary Hulbert." *American Heritage* 30 (April/May 1979): 68-77.

7245. Scott, Henry E. "Hon. Woodrow Wilson, LL.D., Litt. D." *New England Historical and Genealogical Register* 81 (April 1927): 115-119.

7246. Sears, Louis M. "Woodrow Wilson." In *The Marcus W. Jernegan Essays in American Historigraphy*, edited by William T. Hutchinson, 102-121. Chicago: University of Chicago Press, 1937.

7247. Shannon, David A. "The Making of a Princeton President, 1896-1902: An Essay Review." *Pacific Northwest Quarterly* 65 (October 1974): 184-186.

7248. Shannon, David A. "Woodrow Wilson's Youth and Personality: An Essay Review." *Pacific Northwest Quarterly* 58 (October 1967): 205-207.

7249. Shannon, Frederick F. "Woodrow Wilson: Martyr." *Methodist Quarterly Review* 74 (April 1925): 295-308.

7250. Taggart, Robert J. "Woodrow Wilson and Curriculum Reform." *New Jersey History* 93 (Autumn/Winter 1975): 99-114.

7251. Taylor, James H. *Woodrow Wilson in Church, His Membership in the Congregation of the Central Presbyterian Church, Washington, DC: 1913-1924.* Charleston, SC: n.p., 1952.

7252. Tribble, Edwin, ed. *A President in Love: The Courtship Letters of Woodrow Wilson and Edith Bolling Galt.* Boston: Houghton Mifflin, 1981.

7253. Tuchman, Barbara W. "Can History Use Freud? The Case of Woodrow Wilson." *Atlantic Monthly* 219 (February 1967): 505-520.

7254. Tumulty, Joseph P. *Woodrow Wilson as I Know Him.* Garden City, NY: Doubleday, 1921.

7255. Veysey, Laurence R. "The Academic Mind of Woodrow Wilson." *Journal of American History* 49 (March 1963): 613-634.

7256. Viereck, George S. *The Strangest Friendship in History: Woodrow Wilson and Colonel House.* New York: Liveright, 1932.

7257. Weinstein, Edwin A. *Woodrow Wilson: A Medical and Psychological Biography.* Princeton, NJ: Princeton University Press, 1981.

7258. Weinstein, Edwin A. "Woodrow Wilson's Neurological Illness." *Journal of American History* 57 (September 1970): 324-351.

7259. Wells, Wells, pseud. *Wilson the Unknown: An Explanation of an Engima of History.* New York: Scribner's, 1931.

7260. William, C. L. "Woodrow Wilson as an Undergraduate." *Current History* 31 (January 1930): 698-702.

7261. Wilson, Edith B. G. *My Memoir.* Indianapolis, IN: Bobbs-Merrill, 1939.

7262. Wilson, Theodore R. "The Birth of Greatness: A Psychological and Sociological Study of the Influences upon Woodrow Wilson during His Formative Years." Ph.D. dissertation, University of Pennsylvania, 1960.

Public Career

7263. Abrams, Richard M. *The Burdens of Progress: 1900-1929.* Glenview, IL: Scott, Foresman, 1978.

7264. Ambrosious, Lloyd E. "The Orthodoxy of Revisionism: Woodrow Wilson and the New Left." *Diplomatic History* 1 (Summer 1977): 199-214.

7265. Archer, Mary U. "Woodrow Wilson: The Post Presidential Years." Ph.D. dissertation, St. Louis University, 1963.

7266. Avery, Sheldon B. "A Private Civil War: The Controversy between George E. Chamberlain and Woodrow Wilson." Master's thesis, University of Oregon, 1967.

7267. Axson, Stockton. "Woodrow Wilson as Man of Letters — Three Public Lectures Delivered at the Rice Institute on February 18, 25, and March 4, 1934...." *Rice Institute Pamphlet* 22 (October 1935): 195-270.

7268. Bailey, Thomas A. "Woodrow Wilson Wouldn't Yield." *American Heritage* 8 (June 1957): 20-25, 105-106.

7269. Beard, Charles A. "Woodrow Wilson and Science." *New Republic* 46 (April 14, 1926): 226-227.

7270. Bell, Herbert C. F. *Woodrow Wilson and the People*. Garden City, NY: Doubleday, 1945.

7271. Bishirjian, Richard J. "Croly, Wilson, and the American Civil Religion." *Modern Age* 23 (Winter 1979): 33-38.

7272. Blum, John M. *Woodrow Wilson and the Politics of Morality*. Boston: Little, Brown, 1956.

7273. Bowers, Claude G. "Woodrow Wilson: A Reappraisal." *Current History* 34 (April 1931): 1-6.

7274. Bradford, Gamaliel. "Brains Win and Lose: Woodrow Wilson." *Atlantic Monthly* 147 (February 1931): 152-164.

7275. Bradford, Gamaliel. *The Quick and the Dead*. Boston: Houghton Mifflin, 1931.

7276. Brewster, Eugene V., comp. *The Passing of Woodrow Wilson, Being Excerpts from Various Newspapers and Magazines Gathered ... at the Time of the Death of Woodrow Wilson*. Brooklyn, NY: Brewster Publications, 1924.

7277. Carleton, William G. "The Ungenerous Approach to Woodrow Wilson." *Virginia Quarterly Review* 44 (Spring 1968): 161-181.

7278. Corbin, John. "From Jefferson to Wilson." *North American Review* 210 (August 1919): 172-185.

7279. Creel, George. *Wilson and the Issues*. New York: Century, 1916.

7280. Cronon, E. David, ed. *Political Thought of Woodrow Wilson*. Indianapolis, IN: Bobbs-Merrill, 1965.

7281. Cuff, Robert D. "Wilson and Weber: Bourgeois Critics in an Organized Age." *Public Administration Review* 38 (May/June 1978): 240-244.

7282. Curti, Merle. "Woodrow Wilson's Concept of Human Nature." *Midwest Journal of Political Science* 1 (May 1957): 1-19.

7283. Daniels, Jonathan. "The Long Shadow of Woodrow Wilson." *Virginia Quarterly Review* 32 (Autumn 1956): 481-493.

7284. Dodd, William E. "Wilsonism." *Political Science Quarterly* 38 (March 1923): 115-132.

7285. Dodd, William E. *Woodrow Wilson and His Work*. 4th ed. Garden City, NY: Doubleday, 1921.

7286. Dodd, William E. "Woodrow Wilson — Ten Years After." *Contemporary Review* 135 (January 1929): 26-38.

7287. Dudden, Arthur P., ed. *Woodrow Wilson and the World of Today*. Philadelphia: University of Pennsylvania Press, 1957.

7288. Dumond, Dwight L. "Woodrow Wilson: A Century View." *Michigan Alumnus Quarterly Review* 63 (December 1956): 67-74.

7289. Eaton, William D., and Harry D. Read. *Woodrow Wilson, His Life and Work: A Complete Story of the Life of*

Woodrow Wilson, Teacher, Historian, Philosopher, and Statesman, Including His Great Speeches, Letters, and Messages, Also a Complete Account of the World Peace Conference. Chicago: Peterson, 1919.

7290. Erikkson, Erik H. "The Strange Case of Freud, Bullitt, and Woodrow Wilson: I." *New York Review of Books* 8 (February 9, 1967): 3-6.

7291. Ezell, John S. "Woodrow Wilson as Southerner, 1856-1885: A Review Essay." *Civil War History* 15 (June 1969): 160-167.

7292. Gatewood, Willard B., Jr. "Woodrow Wilson: The Formative Years, 1856-1880." *Georgia Review* 21 (Spring 1967): 3-13.

7293. Gatewood, Willard B., Jr. "Woodrow Wilson: Years of Trial and Decision, 1881-1885." *Georgia Review* 22 (Fall 1968): 306-15.

7294. George, Alexander L. "Some Uses of Dynamic Psychology in Political Biography: Case Materials on Woodrow Wilson." In *A Sourcebook for the Study of Personality and Politics*, edited by Fred I. Greenstein and Michael Lerner, 78-98. Chicago: Markham, 1971.

7295. Glazier, Kenneth M. "W. E. B. DuBois' Impressions of Woodrow Wilson." *Journal of Negro History* 58 (October 1973): 452-459.

7296. Heckscher, August. "Woodrow Wilson: An Appraisal and Recapitulation." In *The Philosophy and Policies of Woodrow Wilson*, edited by Earl Latham, 244-259. Chicago: University of Chicago Press, 1958.

7297. Henriot, Peter J. "Woodrow Wilson: A Disciple of Edmund Burke?" *Studies in Burke and His Time* 10 (Spring 1969): 1201-1208.

7298. Herring, Pendleton. "Woodrow Wilson: A President's Reading." *Historic Preservation* 27 (July/September 1975): 38-42.

7299. Herring, Pendleton. "Woodrow Wilson — Then and Now." *PS* 7 (Summer 1974): 256-259.

7300. Hirst, David. *Woodrow Wilson Reform Governor.* New York: Van Nostrand, 1965.

7301. Hosford, Hester E. *Woodrow Wilson and New Jersey Made Over.* New York: Putnam, 1912.

7302. Hruska, Thomas J., Jr. "Woodrow Wilson: The Organic State and His Political Theory." Ph.D. dissertation, Claremont Graduate School, 1978.

7303. Hugh-Jones, Edward M. *Woodrow Wilson and American Liberalism.* New York: Macmillan, 1949.

7304. Johnson, Gerald W. "Woodrow Wilson: A Challenge to the Fighting South." *Journal of Social Forces* 3 (January 1925): 231-236.

7305. Johnson, Gerald W. *Woodrow Wilson, The Unforgettable Figure Who Has Returned to Haunt Us.* New York: Harper and Row, 1944.

7306. Johnson, Theodore R. "The Memorialization of Woodrow Wilson." Ph.D. dissertation, George Washington University, 1979.

7307. Katz, Milton. "Woodrow Wilson and the Twentieth Century." *Confluence* 5 (Autumn 1956): 229-238.

7308. Kaufman, Burton I. "Virginia Politics and the Wilson Movement, 1910-1914." *Virginia Magazine of History and Biography* 77 (January 1969): 3-21.

7309. Kelly, Florence F. "Political Coming-of-Age: The West and Wilson." *Bookman* 44 (February 1917): 557-561.

7310. Kerney, James. *The Political Edu-*

cation of *Woodrow Wilson.* New York: Century, 1924.

7311. Kerney, James. "Wilson as a Politician." *Saturday Evening Post* 196 (April 26, 1924): 16-17.

7312. Kerney, James. "Woodrow Wilson, Governor." *Independent* 70 (May 1911): 986-989.

7313. Kirwan, Kent A. "The Crisis of Identity in the Study of Public Administration: Woodrow Wilson." *Polity* 9 (Spring 1977): 321-343.

7314. Knock, Thomas J. "History with Lightning: The Forgotten Film *Wilson.*" *American Quarterly* 28 (Winter 1976): 523-543.

7315. Langer, William L. "Woodrow Wilson: His Education in World Affairs." *Confluence* 5 (Autumn 1956): 183-194.

7316. Laski, Harold J. "Woodrow Wilson after Ten Years." *Forum* 85 (March 1931): 129-133.

7317. Latham, Earl, ed. *The Philosophy and Policies of Woodrow Wilson.* Chicago: University of Chicago Press, 1958.

7318. Link, Arthur S. "The Higher Realism of Woodrow Wilson." *Journal of Presbyterian History* 41 (March 1963): 1-13.

7319. Link, Arthur S. *The Higher Realism of Woodrow Wilson and Other Essays.* Nashville, TN: Vanderbilt University Press, 1971.

7320. Link, Arthur S. *President Wilson and His English Critics: An Inaugural Lecture Delivered before the University of Oxford on 13 May 1959.* Oxford: Clarendon Press, 1959.

7321. Link, Arthur S. "Woodrow Wilson and the Progressive Movement and New Jersey." *Princeton History* 1 (1971): 25-38.

7322. Link, Arthur S. "Woodrow Wilson and the Study of Administration." *American Philosophical Association Proceedings* 112 (December 9, 1968): 431-433.

7323. Lippmann, Walter. "Woodrow Wilson's Approach to Politics." *New Republic* 133 (December 5, 1955): 15-18.

7324. McCormick, Thomas "Wilson-McCook Scheme of 1896-1897." *Pacific Historical Review* 36 (February 1967): 47-58.

7325. MacRae, D. A. "An Appreciation of Woodrow Wilson." *Dalhousie Review* 4 (April 1924): 86-97.

7326. Marion, David E. "Alexander Hamilton and Woodrow Wilson on the Spirit and Form of a Responsible Republican Government." *Review of Politics* 42 (July 1980): 309-328.

7327. Martin, Lawrence. "Necessity and Principle: Woodrow Wilson's Views." *Review of Politics* 22 (January 1960): 96-114.

7328. Meaney, Neville K. "Arthur S. Link and Thomas Woodrow Wilson." *Journal of American Studies* 1 (April 1967): 119-126.

7329. Merriam, Charles E. *Four American Party Leaders.* New York: Macmillan, 1926.

7330. Moss, Frank. *America's Mission to Serve Humanity.* Boston: Stratford, 1919.

7331. Motter, Thomas H. V. "Woodrow Wilson and the Power of Words." *Princeton University Library Chronicle* 17 (Spring 1956): 163-172.

7332. Neu, Charles E. "The Search for Woodrow Wilson." *Reviews in American History* 10 (June 1982): 223-228.

7333. Nicholas, Herbert G. *Wilsonianism at Mid-Century.* Geneva: Centenaire Woodrow Wilson, 1956.

7334. Nobel, Charles. "Wilson's Choice: The Political Origins of the Modern

American State." *Comparative Politics* 17 (April 1985): 313-336.

7335. Noble, Ransom E., Jr. *New Jersey Progressivism before Wilson.* Princeton, NJ: Princeton University Press, 1935.

7336. Noble, Ransom E., Jr. "Woodrow Wilson: Centennial Interpretations." *New Jersey Historical Society Proceedings* 75 (April 1961): 79-95.

7337. Pisney, Raymond F., ed. *Virginians Remember Woodrow Wilson.* s.l.: Mouseion Press, 1978.

7338. Pisney, Raymond F., ed. *Woodrow Wilson in Retrospect.* Verona, VA: McClure, 1978.

7339. Pomeroy, Earl S. "Woodrow Wilson: The End of His First Century." *Oregon Historical Quarterly* 57 (December 1956): 315-332.

7340. Post, Jerrold M., Juliette L. George, Alexander L. George, Edwin A. Weinstein, and Michael Marmor. "Woodrow Wilson Re-examined: The Mind-Body Controversy Redux and Other Disputations." *Political Psychology* 4 (June 1983): 289-331.

7341. Preu, James A. *Woodrow Wilson Centennial Issue.* Gainesville: University Press of Florida, 1956.

7342. Pruessen, Ronald W. "Woodrow Wilson to John Foster Dulles: A Legacy." *Princeton University Library Chronicle* 34 (Winter 1973): 109-130.

7343. Reid, Ronald F. "The Young Woodrow Wilson's Political Laboratory." *Southern Speech Communication Journal* 28 (Spring 1963): 227-235.

7344. Roberts, Derrell. "Mobile and the Visit by Woodrow Wilson." *Alabama Historical Quarterly* 27 (Spring/Summer 1965): 81-90.

7345. Rogin, Michael. "Max Weber and Woodrow Wilson: The Iron Cage in Germany and America." *Polity* 3 (Summer 1971): 557-575.

7346. Saunders, Frances W. " 'No Pale, Cold Scholar': John Singer Sargent's Portrait of Woodrow Wilson." *Virginia Cavalcade* 30 (Autumn 1980): 52-59.

7347. Seltzer, Alan L. "Woodrow Wilson as 'Corporate Liberal': Toward a Reconsideration of Left Revisionist Historiography." *Western Political Quarterly* 30 (June 1977): 183-212.

7348. Seymour, Charles. "Woodrow Wilson: A Political Balance Sheet." *American Philosophical Society Proceedings* 101 (April 1961): 135-141.

7349. Shotwell, James T. "The Leadership of Wilson." *Current History* 21 (November 1951): 263-268.

7350. Showerman, Grant. "Woodrow Wilson: An Appreciation." *Sewanee Review* 32 (April 1924): 139-145.

7351. Stillman, Richard J., II. "Woodrow Wilson and the Study of Administration: A New Look at an Old Essay." *American Political Science Review* 67 (June 1973): 582-588.

7352. Tucker, Frank H. "East Meets West: Woodrow Wilson in 1894." *Colorado Magazine* 49 (Spring 1972): 109-115.

7353. Turner, Henry A. "Woodrow Wilson and the New Jersey Legislature." *New Jersey Historical Society Proceedings* 74 (January 1956): 21-49.

7354. Turner, Henry A. "Woodrow Wilson as Administrator." *Public Administration Review* 16 (Autumn 1956): 249-257.

7355. Turner, Henry A. "Woodrow Wilson: Exponent of Executive Leadership." *Western Political Quarterly* 4 (March 1951): 97-115.

7356. Watson, Richard L., Jr. "Woodrow Wilson and His Interpreters, 1947-1957."

Mississippi Valley Historical Review 44 (September 1961): 207-236.

7357. Weisenburger, Francis P. "The Middle Western Antecedents of Woodrow Wilson." *Mississippi Valley Historical Review* 23 (December 1936): 375-390.

7358. "Wilson Centennial Number." *Virginia Quarterly Review* 32 (Fall 1956): 481-540.

7359. Wise, Jennings C. *Woodrow Wilson, Disciple of Revolution*. New York: Paisley Press, 1938.

7360. Woodhouse, Edward S. "The Place of Woodrow Wilson in American Politics — An Estimate." *South Atlantic Quarterly* 21 (January 1922): 1-13.

7361. Woodrow Wilson Centennial Celebration Commission. *Final Report of the Woodrow Wilson Centennial Celebration Commission*. Washington, DC: The Commission, 1958.

7362. Younger, Edward. "Woodrow Wilson: The Making of a Leader." *Virginia Magazine of History and Biography* 64 (October 1956): 387-401.

Presidential Years

General

7363. Abrams, Richard M. "Woodrow Wilson and the Southern Congressmen, 1913-1916." *Journal of Southern History* 22 (November 1956): 417-437.

7364. Adams, Franklin P. "An Ode in Time of Inauguration." *Collier's* 50 (March 8, 1913): 23-24.

7365. Anderson, Adrian. "President Wilson's Politician: Albert Sidney Burleson of Texas." *Southwestern Historical Quarterly* 77 (January 1974): 339-354.

7366. Auerbach, Jerold S. "Woodrow Wilson's 'Prediction' to Frank Cobb: Words Historians Should Doubt Ever Got Spoken." *Journal of American History* 54 (December 1967): 608-617.

7367. Avery, Laurence G. "Maxwell Anderson's Report on Frank Cobb's Interview with Woodrow Wilson: Documentary Source." *North Dakota Quarterly* 45 (Summer 1977): 5-14.

7368. Balch, Stephen H. "Do Strong Presidents Really Want Strong Legislative Parties? The Case of Woodrow Wilson and the House Democrats." *Presidential Studies Quarterly* 7 (Autumn 1977): 231-238.

7369. Baldwin, Elbert F. "Exit Wilson: Enter Harding." *Outlook* 127 (March 16, 1921): 414-415.

7370. Bender, Robert J. *'W. W.': Scattered Impressions of a Reporter Who for Eight Years Covered the Activities of Woodrow Wilson*. New York: United Press Association, 1924.

7371. Blum, John M. *Joe Tumulty and the Wilson Era*. Boston: Houghton Mifflin, 1951.

7372. Blum, John M. *The Progressive Presidents: Roosevelt, Wilson, Roosevelt, Johnson*. New York: Norton, 1980.

7373. Box, Pelham H. "Woodrow Wilson." In his *Three Master Builders and Another: Studies in Revolutionary and Liberal Statesmanship*, 1-33. Philadelphia: Lippincott, 1925.

7374. Brooks, Eugene C. *Woodrow Wilson as President*. Chicago: Row, Peterson, 1916.

7375. Brown, John E. "Woodrow Wilson's Vice President: Thomas R. Marshall and the Wilson Administration, 1913-1921." Ph.D. dissertation, Ball State University, 1970.

7376. Burton, David H. "The Learned Presidency: Roosevelt, Taft, Wilson."

Presidential Studies Quarterly 15 (Summer 1985): 486-497.

7377. Canfield, Leon H. *The Presidency of Woodrow Wilson: Prelude to a World in Crisis.* Rutherford, NJ: Fairleigh Dickinson University Press, 1966.

7378. Chapple, Joseph M. "The Inauguration of President Wilson." *National Magazine* 38 (April 1913): 17-28.

7379. Colby, Bainbridge. *The Close of Woodrow Wilson's Administration and the Final Years.* New York: M. Kennerley, 1930.

7380. Cornwell, Elmer E., Jr. "The Press Conferences of Woodrow Wilson." *Journalism Quarterly* 39 (Summer 1962): 292-300.

7381. Corwin, Edward S. "Woodrow Wilson and the Presidency." *Virginia Law Review* 42 (October 1956): 761-783.

7382. Curran, George A. "Woodrow Wilson's Theory and Practice Regarding Relations of President and Congress." Ph.D. dissertation, Fordham University, 1949.

7383. Dalton, Brian J. "Wilson's Prediction to Cobb: Notes on the Auerbach-Link Debate." *Historian* 32 (August 1970): 545-563.

7384. Daniels, Josephus. *The Wilson Era: Years of Peace, 1910-1917.* Chapel Hill: University of North Carolina Press, 1944.

7385. Davidson, John W. "The Response of the South to Woodrow Wilson's New Freedom, 1912-1914." Ph.D. dissertation, Yale University, 1954.

7386. Davidson, John W. "Wilson as Presidential Leader." *Current History* 39 (October 1960): 198-202.

7387. Dimock, Marshall E. "Woodrow Wilson as Legislative Leader." *Journal of Politics* 19 (February 1957): 3-19.

7388. Elletson, D. H. *Roosevelt and Wilson.* New York: International Publications Service, 1965.

7389. Ferrell, Robert H. "Woodrow Wilson: Man and Statesman." *Review of Politics* 18 (April 1956): 131-145.

7390. Folliard, Edward T. "When the Cheering Stopped the Last Years of Woodrow Wilson." *Historic Preservation* 16 (July/September 1964): 87-91.

7391. Gaines, William H., Jr. "From Staunton to the White House: Virginia, Virginians, and Woodrow Wilson." *Virginia Cavalcade* 2 (Winter 1952): 7-10.

7392. Garner, James W. "Woodrow Wilson's Ideas of the Presidency." *Review of Reviews* 47 (January 1913): 47-51.

7393. Hale, William B. "Watching President Wilson at Work." *World's Work* 26 (May 1913): 69-77.

7394. Harris, H. Wilson. *President Wilson, His Problems and His Policy.* London: Headley Brothers, 1917.

7395. Heckscher, August. "Wilson — Style in Leadership." *Confluence* 5 (Winter 1957): 332-340.

7396. Hemphill, James C. "Mr. Wilson's Cabinet." *North American Review* 202 (July 1915): 112-121.

7397. Hendrix, Jerry A. "Presidential Addresses to Congress: Woodrow Wilson and the Jeffersonian Tradition." *Southern Speech Journal* 31 (Summer 1966): 285-294.

7398. Hohner, Robert A. "Woodrow Wilson and the Presidency." *American Studies* 13 (Autumn 1982): 213-221.

7399. Holt, William S. "What Wilson Sent and What House Received: Or Scholars Need to Check Carefully." *American Historical Review* 65 (April 1960): 569-571.

7400. Hosford, Hester E. *Woodrow Wil-*

son: *His Career, His Statesmanship, and His Public Policies*. 2d ed. New York: Putnam, 1912.

7401. Houston, David F. *Eight Years with Wilson's Cabinet, 1913 to 1920: With a Personal Estimate of the President*. 2 vols. Garden City, NY: Doubleday, 1926.

7402. Houston, Michael. "The McAdoo-Wilson Relationship." Master's thesis, American University, 1971.

7403. Howard, Vincent W. "Woodrow Wilson, the Press, and Presidential Leadership: Another Look at the Passage of the Underwood Tariff, 1913." *Centennial Review* 24 (Spring 1980): 167-184.

7404. Kendrick, Jack E. "Alabama Congressmen in the Wilson Administration." *Alabama Review* 24 (October 1971): 243-260.

7405. "The Late President's Record of Achievement." *Current History* 19 (March 1924): 899-941.

7406. Laukhuff, Perry. "The Price of Woodrow Wilson's Illness." *Virginia Quarterly Review* 32 (Autumn 1956): 598-610.

7407. Lawrence, David. "The President and His Day's Work." *Century Magazine* 93 (March 1917): 641-652.

7408. Link, Arthur S. "President Wilson's Plan to Resign in 1916." *Princeton University Library Chronicle* 23 (Summer 1962): 167-172.

7409. Link, Arthur S. *Wilson: Confusions and Crises: 1915-1916*. Princeton, NJ: Princeton University Press, 1964.

7410. Link, Arthur S. *Wilson: The Road to the White House*. Princeton, NJ: Princeton University Press, 1947.

7411. Link, Arthur S. *Woodrow Wilson and a Revolutionary World, 1913-1921*. Chapel Hill: University of North Carolina Press, 1982.

7412. Link, Arthur S. *Woodrow Wilson and the Progressive Era, 1910-1917*. New York: Harper and Row, 1954.

7413. Link, Arthur S. "Woodrow Wilson: The Philosophy, Methods, and Impact of Leadership." In *Woodrow Wilson and the World of Today*, edited by Arthur P. Dudden, 1-21. Philadelphia: University of Pennsylvania Press, 1957.

7414. Lodge, Henry C. "Lodge and Wilson." Edited by Harold B. Raymond. *Colby Library Quarterly* 4 (November 1956): 141-143.

7415. Longaker, Richard P. "Woodrow Wilson and the Presidency." In *The Philosophy and Policies of Woodrow Wilson*, edited by Earl Latham, 67-81. Chicago: University of Chicago Press, 1958.

7416. Lord, Frank B. "The Inauguration." *National Monthly* 4 (March 1913): 237-238, 248-250.

7417. Lord, Frank B. *Woodrow Wilson's Administration and Achievements*. Washington, DC: J. W. Bryan Press, 1921.

7418. MacMahon, Arthur W. "Woodrow Wilson as Legislative Leader and Administrator." *American Political Science Review* 50 (September 1956): 641-675.

7419. MacMahon, Arthur W. "Woodrow Wilson: Political Leader and Administrator." In *The Philosophy and Policies of Woodrow Wilson*, edited by Earl Latham, 100-122. Chicago: University Chicago Press, 1958.

7420. Mahoney, Joseph F. "Backsliding Convert: Woodrow Wilson and the 'Seven Sisters.'" *American Quarterly* 18 (Spring 1966): 71-80.

7421. Mervin, David. "Woodrow Wilson and Presidential Myths." *Presidential Studies Quarterly* 11 (Autumn 1981): 559-564.

7422. Mims, Edwin. "Woodrow Wilson:

The Happy Warrior." *Methodist Quarterly Review* 73 (April 1924): 195-214.

7423. Olson, Keith W. "Woodrow Wilson, Franklin K. Lane, and the Wilson Cabinet Meetings." *Historian* 32 (February 1970): 270-275.

7424. "Political Virtues President Wilson Will Need." *Century Magazine* 85 (February 1913): 629-630.

7425. "The Presidency of Woodrow Wilson — A Symposium." *Pacific Review* 1 (March 1921): 562-595.

7426. "President Wilson Alone." *New Republic* 20 (October 8, 1919): 277-279.

7427. "President Wilson and Congress." *Law Times* 142 (April 14, 1917): 413-414.

7428. *President Wilson's Policy.* London: H.M.S. Office, 1920.

7429. Redfield, William C. *With Congress and Cabinet.* Garden City, NY: Doubleday, 1924.

7430. Rogers, Lindsay. "President Wilson's Theory of His Office." *Forum* 51 (February 1914): 174-186.

7431. Ryerson, Edward. "The Leadership of Woodrow Wilson." *American Scholar* 21 (Summer 1952): 301-308.

7432. Scheiber, Harry N. "What Wilson Said to Colds in 1917: Another View of Plausibility." *Wisconsin Magazine of History* 52 (Summer 1969): 344-347.

7433. Shanks, Alexander G. "Sam Rayburn in the Wilson Administration, 1913-1921." *East Texas Historical Journal* 6 (March 1968): 63-76.

7434. Skau, George H. "Woodrow Wilson and the American Presidency: Theory and Practice." Ph.D. dissertation, St. John's University, 1969.

7435. Smith, Daniel M. "Robert Lansing and the Wilson Interregnum, 1919-1920." *Historian* 21 (February 1955): 135-161.

7436. Smith, Gene. *When the Cheering Stopped: The Last Years of Woodrow Wilson.* New York: Morrow, 1964.

7437. Stratton, David H. "President Wilson's Smelling Committee." *Colorado Quarterly* 5 (Summer 1956): 164-184.

7438. Thompson, Bram. "President Wilson, The Autocrat." *Canadian Law Times* 40 (March 1920): 234-238.

7439. Turner, Henry A. "Woodrow Wilson and Public Opinion." *Public Opinion Quarterly* 21 (Winter 1958): 505-520.

7440. Wann, Andrew J. "The Development of Woodrow Wilson's Theory of the Presidency: Continuity and Change." In *The Philosophy and Policies of Woodrow Wilson,* edited by Earl Latham, 46-66. Chicago: University of Chicago Press, 1958.

7441. Weinstein, Edwin A. "Denial of Presidential Disability: A Case Study of Woodrow Wilson." *Psychiatry* 30 (November 1967): 376-391.

7442. Weinstein, Edwin A., James W. Anderson, and Arthur S. Link. "Woodrow Wilson's Political Personality: A Reappraisal." *Political Science Quarterly* 93 (Winter 1978-1979): 585-598.

7443. Williams, Jack K. "Roosevelt, Wilson, and the Progressive Movement." *South Atlantic Quarterly* 54 (April 1955): 207-211.

7444. Wimer, Kurt. "Woodrow Wilson's Plan for a Vote of Confidence." *Pennsylvania History* 28 (July 1961): 279-293.

7445. Wolff, Christopher. "Woodrow Wilson: Interpreting the Constitution." *Review of Politics* 41 (January 1979): 121-142.

7446. Zimmern, Alfred E. "A European View of President Wilson." *Pacific Review* 1 (March 1921): 443-451.

Campaigns

7447. "Aftermath of the Elections." *Outlook* 114 (December 13, 1916): 797-800.

7448. Bacon, Charles R. *A People Awakened: The Story of Woodrow Wilson's First Campaign....* Garden City, NY: Doubleday, 1912.

7449. Bagby, Wesley M. "Woodrow Wilson, a Third Term, and the Solemn Referendum." *American Historical Review* 60 (April 1955): 567-575.

7450. Billington, Monroe. "Thomas P. Gore and the Election of Woodrow Wilson." *Mid-America* 39 (July 1957): 180-191.

7451. Bradley, Vernon S. *The Wilson Ballot in Maryland Politics.* Baltimore, MD: Lowenthal-Wolf, 1911.

7452. Bryan, William J. *A Tale of Two Conventions.* New York: Funk and Wagnalls, 1912.

7453. Burner, David. "The Breakup of the Wilson Coalition of 1916." *Mid-America* 45 (January 1963): 18-35.

7454. Coletta, Paolo E. "Bryan at Baltimore, 1912: Wilson's Warwick?" *Nebraska History* 57 (Summer 1976): 201-225.

7455. Crews, Kenneth D. "Woodrow Wilson, Wisconsin, and the Election of 1912." *Presidential Studies Quarterly* 12 (Summer 1982): 369-376.

7456. Davenport, Frederick M. "Did Hughes Snub Johnson? An Inside Story — How and Why Charles E. Hughes Lost California and the Presidency in 1916." *American Political Science Review* 43 (April 1949): 321-322.

7457. Eiselen, Malcolm R. "The Day That California Changed World History." *Pacific Historian* 10 (1966): 49-57.

7458. Harvey, George. "The Political Predestination of Woodrow Wilson." *North American Review* 193 (March 1911): 321-330.

7459. Harvey, George. "Political Situation: Wilson against the Field." *North American Review* 196 (September 1912): 289-304.

7460. Harvey, George. "Wilson and a Second Term." *North American Review* 203 (February 1916): 161-170.

7461. Kelly, Frank K. *The Fight for the White House: The Story of 1912.* New York: Crowell, 1961.

7462. Kern, Jean B. "Wilson in Iowa." *Palimpsest* 45 (August 1964): 293-299.

7463. Lawrence, David. "One Term for Wilson?" *Collier's Weekly* 56 (November 6, 1915): 7-8.

7464. Leary, William J., Jr. "Woodrow Wilson, Irish Americans, and the Election of 1916." *Journal of American History* 54 (June 1967): 57-72.

7465. Link, Arthur S. *Wilson: Campaigns for Progressivism and Peace, 1916-1917.* Princeton, NJ: Princeton University Press, 1965.

7466. Link, Arthur S. "Woodrow Wilson and the Democratic Party." *Review of Politics* 18 (February 1956): 146-156.

7467. McCombs, William F. *Making Woodrow Wilson President.* Edited by Louis J. Lang. New York: Fairview, 1921.

7468. Merritt, Richard L. "Woodrow Wilson and the 'Great and Solemn Referendum,' 1920." *Review of Politics* 27 (January 1965): 78-104.

7469. Piccard, Paul J. "The Electoral Colleges of President Woodrow Wilson." *Florida State University Studies* 23 (1956): 20-64.

7470. "President Wilson and the Presidential Primaries: Poll of Congress and the Press." *Outlook* 105 (December 13, 1913): 792-795.

7471. Roady, Elston. "Woodrow Wilson's Role as Party Leader: Trust Legislation." *Florida State University Studies* 23 (1956): 1-27.

7472. Roberts, George C. "Woodrow Wilson, John W. Kern, and the 1916 Indiana Election: Defeat of a Senate Majority Leader." *Presidential Studies Quarterly* 10 (Winter 1980): 63-73.

7473. Shane, M. "How Woodrow Wilson Was Nominated and Elected." *Law Magazine* (January 1913): 19-22.

7474. Stockbridge, Frank P. "How Woodrow Wilson Won His Nomination." *Current History* 20 (July 1924): 561-572.

7475. Wilkins, Robert P. "The Peace Issue in the General Election of 1914." *North Dakota History* 30 (April/July 1963): 97-100.

7476. "Wilson in New Jersey, A New Precedent." *Nation* 96 (May 8, 1913): 459-460.

7477. Wimer, Kurt. "Woodrow Wilson and a Third Nomination." *Pennsylvania History* 29 (April 1962): 193-211.

Domestic Policy

7478. Best, Gary D. "President Wilson's Second Industrial Conference, 1919-1920." *Labor History* 16 (Fall 1975): 505-520.

7479. Blumenthal, Henry. "Woodrow Wilson and the Race Question." *Journal of Negro History* 48 (January 1963): 1-21.

7480. Boemeke, Manfred F. "The Wilson Administration, Organized Labor, and the Colorado Coal Strike, 1913-1914." Ph.D. dissertation, Princeton University, 1983.

7481. Brownlow, Louis. "Woodrow Wilson and Public Administration." *Public Administration Review* 16 (Spring 1956): 77-81.

7482. Chandler, Lester V. "Wilson's Monetary Reform." In *The Philosophy and Policies of Woodrow Wilson,* edited by Earl Latham, 112-130. Chicago: University of Chicago Press, 1958.

7483. Crosby, Earl W. "Progressive Segregation in the Wilson Administration." *Potomac Review* 6 (Summer 1973): 41-57.

7484. Cuff, Robert D. "Woodrow Wilson and Business — Government Relations during World War I." *Review of Politics* 31 (July 1969): 385-407.

7485. Cuff, Robert D. "Woodrow Wilson's Missionary to American Business, 1914-1915." *Business Historical Review* 43 (Winter 1969): 545-551.

7486. Diamond, William. *The Economic Thought of Woodrow Wilson.* Baltimore, MD: Johns Hopkins University Press, 1943.

7487. Dimock, Marshall E. "Wilson the Domestic Reformer." *Virginia Quarterly Review* 32 (Autumn 1956): 546-565.

7488. Eaton, Doris A. "Black Attitudes toward Woodrow Wilson, 1911-1914." Master's thesis, University of Miami, 1973.

7489. Frankie, Richard J. "An Analysis of Selected Administrative Theories and Practices of Woodrow Wilson in the Field of Higher Education." Ed.D. dissertation, Wayne State University, 1966.

7490. Garrison, Elisha E. *Roosevelt, Wilson, and the Federal Reserve Law: A Story of the Author's Relations with Theodore Roosevelt, Woodrow Wilson, and Other Public Men, Principally as Related to the Development and Writing of the Federal Reserve Law.* Boston: Christopher Publishing House, 1931.

7491. Gatewood, Willard B., Jr. "Progressivism: From the Old Style to the New." *Journal of Interdisciplinary History* 10 (Summer 1979): 147-153.

7492. Gawthrop, Louis C. "Administrative Responsibility: Public Policy and the Wilsonian Legacy." *Policy Studies Journal* 5 (Autumn 1976): 108-113.

7493. Graham, Sally H. "Woodrow Wilson, Alice Paul, and the Woman Suffrage Movement." *Political Science Quarterly* 98 (Winter 1983-1984): 665-679.

7494. Green, Cleveland M. "Prejudices and Empty Promises: Woodrow Wilson's Betrayal of the Negro, 1910-1919." *Crisis* 87 (November 1980): 380-388.

7495. Hall, Tom G., Jr. "Cheap Bread from Dear Wheat: Herbert Hoover, the Wilson Administration, and the Management of Wheat Prices, 1916-1920." Ph.D. dissertation, University of California, Davis, 1970.

7496. Hall, Tom G., Jr. "Wilson and the Food Crisis: Agricultural Price Control during World War I." *Agricultural History* 47 (January 1973): 25-46.

7497. Handy, Edward S. C. *Woodrow Wilson's Heritage and Environment: Ethnic and Cyclic Patterns in Time, Place, and Circumstance.* Philadelphia: Dorance, 1969.

7498. Hurvitz, Haggai. "Ideology and Industrial Conflict: President Wilson's First Industrial Conference of October 1919." *Labor History* 18 (Autumn 1977): 509-524.

7499. Jensen, Billie B. "Woodrow Wilson's Intervention in the Coal Strike of 1914." *Labor History* 15 (Winter 1974): 63-77.

7500. Johnson, James P. "The Wilsonians as War Managers: Coal and the 1917-1918 Winter Crisis." *Prologue* 9 (Winter 1977): 193-208.

7501. Jones, Dallas L. "The Wilson Administration and Organized Labor." Ph.D. dissertation, Cornell University, 1954.

7502. Kerr, K. Austin. "Decision for Federal Control: Wilson, McAdoo, and the Railroad, 1917." *Journal of American History* 54 (December 1967): 550-560.

7503. Knock, Thomas J., and Christine Lunardini. "Woodrow Wilson and Woman Suffrage: A New Look." *Political Science Quarterly* 95 (Winter 1980-1981): 655-667.

7504. Lang, Jane, and Harry N. Scheiber. "The Wilson Administration and the Wartime Mobilization of Black Americans." *Labor History* 10 (Summer 1969): 433-458.

7505. Lepore, Herbert P. "Prelude to Prejudice: Hiram Johnson, Woodrow Wilson, and the California Alien Land Law Controversy of 1913." *Southern California Quarterly* 61 (Spring 1979): 99-110.

7506. Lunardini, Christine A. "Standing Firm: William Monroe Trotter's Meetings with Woodrow Wilson, 1913-1914." *Journal of Negro History* 64 (Summer 1979): 244-264.

7507. McFarland, Charles K., and Nevin E. Neal. "The Reluctant Reformer: Woodrow Wilson and Woman Suffrage, 1913-1920." *Rocky Mountain Social Science Journal* 11 (April 1974): 33-43.

7508. McKown, Paul. "Certain Important Domestic Policies of Woodrow Wilson." Ph.D. dissertation, University of Pennsylvania, 1932.

7509. Miller, M. Sammy. "Woodrow Wilson and the Black Judge." *Crisis* 84 (February 1977): 81-86.

7510. Moynihan, Daniel P. "Was Woodrow Wilson Right?" *Commentary* 57 (May 1974): 25-31.

7511. Murray, Robert K. *Red Scare: A Study of National Hysteria, 1919-1920.* Minneapolis: University of Minnesota Press, 1955.

7512. Osborn, George C. "Woodrow Wilson Appoints a Negro Judge." *Journal of Southern History* 24 (November 1958): 481-493.

7513. Pyne, John M. "Woodrow Wilson's Abdication of Domestic and Party Leadership: Autumn 1918 to Autumn 1919." Ph.D. dissertation, University of Notre Dame, 1979.

7514. Rozwenc, Edwin C. *Roosevelt, Wilson, and the Trusts.* Boston: Heath, 1950.

7515. Scheiber, Harry N. "The Wilson Administration and Civil Liberties, 1917-1921." Ithaca, NY: Cornell University Press, 1960.

7516. Schwartz, Donald R. "From Rapprochement to Appeasement: Domestic Determinants of Anglo-American Relations under Lloyd George and Wilson." Ph.D. dissertation, New York University, 1977.

7517. Smith, John S. "Organized Labor and Government in the Wilson Era, 1913-1921: Some Conclusions." *Labor History* 3 (March 1962): 265-286.

7518. Thorsen, Niels A. "The Political and Economic Thought of Woodrow Wilson, 1875-1902." Ph.D. dissertation, Princeton University, 1981.

7519. Urofsky, Melvin I. *Big Steel and the Wilson Administration: A Study in Business-Government Relations.* Columbus: Ohio State University Press, 1969.

7520. Urofsky, Melvin I. "Wilson, Brandeis, and the Trust Issue, 1912-1914." *Mid-America* 49 (January 1967): 3-28.

7521. Wolgemuth, Kathleen L. "Woodrow Wilson and Federal Segregation." *Journal of Negro History* 44 (April 1959): 158-173.

7522. Wolgemuth, Kathleen L. "Woodrow Wilson's Appointment Policy and the Negro." *Journal of Southern History* 24 (November 1958): 457-471.

Foreign Affairs

7523. Accinelli, Robert D. "Link's Case for Wilson the Diplomatist." *Reviews in American History* 9 (September 1981): 285-294.

7524. Adler, Selig. "The Palestine Question in the Wilson Era." *Jewish Social Studies* 10 (1948): 303-334.

7525. Baker, George W., Jr. "The Caribbean Policy of Woodrow Wilson, 1913-1917." Ph.D. dissertation, University of Colorado, 1961.

7526. Baker, George W., Jr. "Ideas and Realities in the Wilson Administration's Relations with Honduras." *Americas* 21 (July 1964): 3-19.

7527. Baker, George W., Jr. "The Wilson Administration and Cuba, 1913-1921." *Mid-America* 46 (January 1964): 48-63.

7528. Baker, George W., Jr. "The Wilson Administration and Panama, 1913-1921." *Journal of Inter-American Studies* 8 (April 1966): 279-293.

7529. Baker, George W., Jr. "The Wilson Administration and Nicaragua, 1913-1921." *Americas* 22 (April 1966): 339-376.

7530. Baker, George W., Jr. "The Woodrow Wilson Administration and El Salvadoran Relations, 1913-1921." *Social Studies* 56 (March 1965): 97-102.

7531. Baker, George W., Jr. "The Woodrow Wilson Administration and Guatemalan Relations." *Historian* 27 (February 1965): 155-169.

7532. Baker, George W., Jr. "Woodrow Wilson's Use of the Non-Recognition Policy in Costa Rica." *Americas* 22 (July 1965): 3-21.

7533. Barany, George. "Wilsonian Central Europe: Lansing's Contribution." *Historian* 28 (February 1966): 224-251.

7534. Bell, Sidney. *Righteous Conquest: Woodrow Wilson and the Evolution of the*

New Diplomacy. Port Washington, NY: Kennikat Press, 1972.

7535. Bell, Sidney. "Woodrow Wilson and the Evolution of the New Diplomacy." Ph.D. dissertation, University of Wisconsin, 1969.

7536. Block, Robert H. "Southern Congressmen and Wilson's Call for Repeal of the Panama Canal Tolls Exemption." *Southern Studies* 17 (Spring 1978): 91-100.

7537. Block, Robert H. "Southern Opinion of Woodrow Wilson's Foreign Policies, 1913-1917." Ph.D. dissertation, Duke University, 1968.

7538. Bryson, Thomas A. "Woodrow Wilson, the Senate, Public Opinion, and the Armenian Mandate, 1919-1920." Ph.D. dissertation, University of Georgia, 1965.

7539. Buehrig, Edward H., ed. *Wilson's Foreign Policy in Perspective*. Bloomington: Indiana University Press, 1957.

7540. Buehrig, Edward H. "Wilson's Neutrality Re-examined." *World Politics* 3 (October 1950): 1-19.

7541. Burdick, Frank. "Woodrow Wilson and the Underwood Tariff." *Mid-America* 50 (October 1968): 272-290.

7542. Calhoun, Frederick S. *Power and Principle: Armed Intervention in Wilsonian Foreign Policy*. Kent, OH: Kent State University Press, 1986.

7543. Carter, Purvis M. "Congressional and Public Reaction to Wilson's Caribbean Policy, 1913-1917." Ph.D. dissertation, University of Colorado, 1970.

7544. Cook, Blanche W. "Woodrow Wilson and the Antimilitarists, 1914-1917." Ph.D. dissertation, Johns Hopkins University, 1970.

7545. Cooper, John M., Jr. "An 'Irony of Fate': Woodrow Wilson's Pre-World War I Diplomacy." *Diplomatic History* 3 (Fall 1979): 425-438.

7546. Cooper, John M., Jr. *The Warrior and the Priest: Theodore Roosevelt and Woodrow Wilson*. Cambridge, MA: Belknap Press, 1983.

7547. Cooper, John M., Jr. "The Warrior and the Priest: Toward a Comparative Perspective on Theodore Roosevelt and Woodrow Wilson." *South Atlantic Quarterly* 80 (Autumn 1981): 419-428.

7548. Curry, Roy W. *Woodrow Wilson and Far Eastern Policy, 1913-1921*. New York: Bookman Associates, 1957.

7549. Curry, Roy W. "Woodrow Wilson and Philippine Policy." *Mississippi Valley Historical Review* 41 (December 1954): 435-452.

7550. Curtis, George H. "The Wilson Administration, Elihu Root, and the Founding of the World Court, 1918-1921." Ph.D. dissertation, Georgetown University, 1972.

7551. Devlin, L. Patrick. *Too Proud to Fight: Woodrow Wilson's Neutrality*. New York: Oxford University Press, 1975.

7552. DeWitt, Howard A. "Hiram Johnson and Economic Opposition to Wilsonian Diplomacy: A Note." *Pacific Historian* 19 (Spring 1975): 15-23.

7553. Fifield, Russell H. *Woodrow Wilson and the Far East: The Diplomacy of the Shantung Question*. New York: Crowell, 1952.

7554. Fowler, Wilton B. *British-American Relations, 1917-1918*. Princeton, NJ: Princeton University Press, 1969.

7555. Gaines, Anne-Rosewell J. "Political Reward and Recognition: Woodrow Wilson Appoints Thomas Nelson Page Ambassador to Italy." *Virginia Magazine* *of History and Biography* 89 (July 1981): 328-340.

7556. Gelfand, Lawrence E. "The Mystique of Wilsonian Statecraft." *Diplomatic History* 7 (Spring 1983): 87-101.

7557. Gerard, James W. "The Statesmanship of Woodrow Wilson." *Current History* 19 (March 1924): 895-898.

7558. Gerson, Louis L. *Woodrow Wilson and the Rebirth of Poland, 1914-1920: A Study in the Influence on American Policy of Minority Groups of Foreign Origin.* New Haven, CT: Yale University Press, 1953.

7559. Gilderhus, Mark T. "Pan-American Initiatives: The Wilson Presidency and Regional Integration, 1914-1917." *Diplomatic History* 4 (Fall 1980): 409-423.

7560. Goodell, Stephen. "Woodrow Wilson in Latin America: Interpretations." *Historian* 28 (November 1965): 96-127.

7561. Grabill, Joseph L. "Cleveland H. Dodge, Woodrow Wilson, and the Near East." *Journal of Presbyterian History* 48 (Winter 1970): 249-264.

7562. Harrison, Benjamin T. "Chandler Anderson and Business Interests in Mexico: 1913-1920: When Economic Interests Failed to Alter U.S. Foreign Policy." *Inter-American Economic Affairs* 33 (Winter 1979): 3-24.

7563. Healy, David. *Gunboat Diplomacy in the Wilson Era: The U.S. Navy in Haiti, 1915-1916.* Madison: University of Wisconsin Press, 1976.

7564. Huthmacher, J. Joseph, and Warren I. Susman, eds. *Wilson's Diplomacy: An International Symposium.* Cambridge, MA: Schenkman, 1973.

7565. Jenkins, Starr. "American Statesmen as Men of Letters: Franklin, Adams, Jefferson, John Quincy Adams, Lincoln, Theodore Roosevelt, and Wilson Considered as Writers." Ph.D. dissertation, University of New Mexico, 1972.

7566. Jensen, Billie B. "House, Wilson, and American Neutrality, 1914-1917." Ph.D. dissertation, University of Colorado, 1962.

7567. Kaufman, Burton I. *Efficiency and Expansion: Foreign Trade Organization in the Wilson Administration, 1913-1921.* Westport, CT: Greenwood Press, 1974.

7568. Kernek, Sterling J. "Woodrow Wilson and National Self-Determination along Italy's Frontier: A Study of the Manipulation of Principles in the Pursuit of Political Interests." *American Philosophical Society Proceedings* 126 (August 1982): 243-300.

7569. Killen, Linda R. "Search for a Democratic Russia: The Wilson Administration's Russian Policy, 1917-1921." Ph.D. dissertation, University of North Carolina, 1975.

7570. Knott, Alexander W. "The Pan-American Policy of Woodrow Wilson, 1913-1921." Ph.D. dissertation, University of Colorado, 1968.

7571. Lael, Richard L. "Struggle for Ratification: Wilson, Lodge, and the Thomson-Urrutia Treaty." *Diplomatic History* 2 (Winter 1978): 81-102.

7572. Lebow, Richard N. "Woodrow Wilson and the Balfour Declaration." *Journal of Modern History* 40 (December 1968): 501-523.

7573. Li, Tien-yi. *Woodrow Wilson's China Policy, 1913-1917.* Kansas City: University of Kansas City Press, 1952.

7574. Link, Arthur S. *Wilson the Diplomatist: A Look at His Major Foreign Policies.* Baltimore, MD: Johns Hopkins University Press, 1957.

7575. Link, Arthur S. *Wilson: The Struggle for Neutrality, 1914-1915.* Princeton, NJ: Princeton University Press, 1960.

7576. Link, Arthur S., Jean-Baptiste Duroselle, Ernest Fraenkel, and H. G. Nicholas. *Wilson's Diplomacy: An International Symposium.* Cambridge, MA: Schenkman Publishing Co., 1973.

7577. Livermore, Seward W. " 'Deserving Democrats': The Foreign Service under Woodrow Wilson." *South Atlantic Quarterly* 69 (Winter 1970): 144-160.

7578. Matsuda, Takeshi. "Woodrow Wilson's Dollar Diplomacy in the Far East: The New Chinese Consortium, 1917-1921." Ph.D. dissertation, University of Wisconsin, 1979.

7579. Mayer, Arno J. *Political Origins of the New Diplomacy, 1917-1918.* New Haven, CT: Yale University Press, 1959.

7580. Moynihan, Daniel P. "Morality and American Foreign Policy: Was Woodrow Wilson Right?" *Foreign Service Journal* 51 (September 1974): 8-12, 24-25.

7581. Murillo-Jimenez, Hugo. "Wilson and Tinoco: The United States and the Policy of Non-Recognition in Costa Rica, 1917-1919." Ph.D. dissertation, University of California, San Diego, 1978.

7582. Nigro, Louis J. "Propaganda, Politics, and the New Diplomacy: The Impact of Wilsonian Propaganda on Politics and Public Opinion in Italy, 1917-1919." Ph.D. dissertation, Vanderbilt University, 1979.

7583. Notter, Harley. *The Origins of the Foreign Policy of Woodrow Wilson.* Baltimore, MD: Johns Hopkins University Press, 1937.

7584. O'Brien, Dennis J. "The Oil Crisis and the Foreign Policy of the Wilson Administration, 1917-1921." Ph.D. dissertation, University of Missouri, 1975.

7585. Patterson, David S. "Woodrow Wilson and the Mediation Movement, 1914-1917." *Historian* 33 (August 1971): 535-556.

7586. Quirk, Robert E. *An Affair of Honor: Woodrow Wilson and the Occupation of Veracruz.* Lexington: University of Kentucky Press, 1964.

7587. Radosh, Ronald. "John Spargo and Wilson's Russian Policy, 1920." *Journal of American History* 52 (December 1965): 548-565.

7588. Randall, James G. "Lincoln's Task and Wilson's." *Southern Atlantic Quarterly* 29 (October 1930): 349-368.

7589. Reinertson, John. "Colonel House, Woodrow Wilson, and European Socialism, 1917-1919." Ph.D. dissertation, University of Wisconsin, 1971.

7590. Rosenberg, Emily S. "Dollar Diplomacy under Wilson: An Ecuadorian Case." *Inter-American Economic Affairs* 25 (Autumn 1971): 47-53.

7591. Safford, Jeffrey J. "Edward Hurley and American Shipping Policy: An Elaboration on Wilsonian Diplomacy, 1918-1919." *Historian* 35 (August 1973): 568-586.

7592. Sellen, Robert W. "Why Presidents Fail in Foreign Policy: The Case of Woodrow Wilson." *Social Studies* 64 (February 1973): 64-77.

7593. Sutton, Walter A. "The Wilson Administration and a Scandal in Santo Domingo." *Presidential Studies Quarterly* 12 (Fall 1982): 552-560.

7594. Sweet, Rachel A. "Wilson: Calvinism and American Foreign Policy in China, 1913-1918." Master's thesis, California State University, Fullerton, 1968.

7595. Torodash, Martin. "Woodrow Wilson and the Tariff Question: The Importance of the Underwood Act in His Reform Program." Ph.D. dissertation, New York University, 1966.

7596. Torodash, Martin. "Woodrow Wilson's Views on the Tariff." *New Jersey History* 88 (Autumn 1970): 133-152.

7597. Trani, Eugene P. "Woodrow Wilson, China, and the Missionaries, 1913-1921." *Journal of Presbyterian History* 49 (Winter 1971): 328-351.

7598. Trask, David F. "Remarks for the Bicentennial Lecture Series, U.S. Department of State, May 1, 1981: Woodrow Wilson and the Coordination of Force and Diplomacy." *Society for the History of American Foreign Relations Newsletter* 12 (1981): 12-19.

7599. Vivian, James F. "Wilson, Bryan, and the American Delegation to the Abortive Fifth Pan American Conference, 1914." *Nebraska History* 59 (Spring 1978): 56-69.

7600. Wells, Samuel F., Jr. "New Perspectives of Wilsonian Diplomacy: The Secular Evangelism of American Political Economy." *Perspectives in American History* 6 (1972): 389-419.

7601. Woods, Randall B. "Hull and Argentina: Wilsonian Diplomacy in the Age of Roosevelt." *Journal of Interamerican Studies and World Affairs* 16 (August 1974): 350-371.

7602. Wright, Esmond. "The Foreign Policy of Woodrow Wilson: A Re-assessment." *History Today* 10 (March 1960): 149-157; (April 1960): 223-231.

League of Nations

7603. Black, Harold G. *The True Woodrow Wilson, Crusader for Democracy.* New York: Revell, 1946.

7604. Bolling, John R., comp. *Chronology of Woodrow Wilson, Together with His Most Notable Addresses, A Brief Description of the League of Nations, and the League of Nations Convenant.* New York: Stokes, 1927.

7605. Boothe, Leon E. "Anglo-American Pro-League Groups Lead Wilson, 1915-1918." *Mid-America* 51 (April 1969): 92-107.

7606. Boothe, Leon E. "Woodrow Wilson's Cold War: The President, the Public, and the League Fight, 1919-1920." Ph.D. dissertation, University of Illinois, 1966.

7607. Buehrig, Edward H. *Woodrow Wilson and the Balance of Power.* Bloomington: Indiana University Press, 1955.

7608. Burkman, Thomas W. "Japanese Christians and the Wilsonian World Order." *Japanese Christian Quarterly* 49 (Winter 1983): 38-46.

7609. Burns, Richard D., and Donald Urquidi. "Woodrow Wilson and Disarmament: Ideas versus Realities." *Aerospace Historian* 18 (Winter 1971): 186-194.

7610. Chan, Loren B. "Fighting for the League: President Wilson in Nevada: 1919." *Nevada Historical Society Quarterly* 22 (Summer 1979): 115-127.

7611. Davis, Norman H. *Woodrow Wilson's Foreign Policy and Its Effect on World Peace.* Philadelphia: n.p., 1930.

7612. Fleming, Denna F. *The United States and the League of Nations, 1918-1920.* New York: Putnam, 1932.

7613. Foley, Hamilton, comp. *Woodrow Wilson's Case for the League of Nations.* Princeton, NJ: Princeton University Press, 1923.

7614. Hudson, Manley O. *Woodrow Wilson's Fourteen Points after Eight Years.* New York: Woodrow Wilson Foundation, 1926.

7615. Jacobs, David. *An American Conscience: Woodrow Wilson's Search for World Peace.* New York: Harper and Row, 1973.

7616. Jennings, David H. "President Wilson's Tour in September 1919: A Study of Forces Operating during the League of Nations Fight." Ph.D. dissertation, Ohio State University, 1958.

7617. Knight, Lucian L. *Woodrow Wilson, The Dreamer and the Dream*. Atlanta, GA: Johnson-Dallis, 1924.

7618. Knock, Thomas J. "Woodrow Wilson and the Origins of the League of Nations." Ph.D. dissertation, Princeton University, 1982.

7619. Levin, N. Gordon, Jr. *Woodrow Wilson and the World Politics: America's Response to War and Revolution*. New York: Oxford University Press, 1968.

7620. Lindsey, Edward. "Wilson versus the 'Wilson Doctrine.'" *American Law Review* 44 (September 1910): 641-662.

7621. Link, Arthur S. *Wilson, The New Freedom*. Princeton, NJ: Princeton University Press, 1956.

7622. Loth, David G. *Woodrow Wilson, The Fifteenth Point*. Philadelphia: Lippincott, 1941.

7623. Madison, Charles A. "Woodrow Wilson: Crusade for Democracy." *Chicago Jewish Forum* 14 (Spring 1956): 167-173.

7624. Mitchell, David. "Woodrow Wilson as 'World Saviour.'" *History Today* 26 (January 1976): 3-14.

7625. Mothner, Ira. *Woodrow Wilson, Champion of Peace*. New York: Franklin Watts, 1968.

7626. O'Grady, Joseph P., ed. *The Immigrants' Influence on Wilson's Peace Policies*. Lexington: University of Kentucky Press, 1967.

7627. Osgood, Robert E. "Woodrow Wilson, Collective Security, and the Lessons of History." In *The Philosophy and Policies of Woodrow Wilson*, edited by Earl Latham, 187-198. Chicago: University of Chicago Press, 1958.

7628. Padover, Saul K., comp. *Wilson's Ideals*. Washington, DC: American Council on Public Affairs, 1943.

7629. Phifer, Gregg. "Woodrow Wilson's Swing around the Circle in Defense of His League, September 3-28, 1919." *Florida State University Studies* 23 (1956): 65-102.

7630. Pisney, Raymond F., ed. *Woodrow Wilson: Idealism and Reality*. Verona, VA: McClure, 1977.

7631. Powell, Lyman P., and Fred B. Hodgins, eds. *America and the League of Nations*. New York: Rand McNally, 1919.

7632. Raffo, Peter. "The Anglo-American Preliminary Negotiations for a League of Nations." *Journal of Contemporary History* 9 (October 1974): 153-176.

7633. Schmickle, William E. "For the Proper Use of Victory: Diplomacy and the Imperatives of Vision in the Foreign Policy of Woodrow Wilson, 1916-1919." Ph.D. dissertation, Duke University, 1979.

7634. Schwabe, Klaus. "Woodrow Wilson and Germany's Membership in the League of Nations, 1918-1919." *Central European History* 8 (March 1975): 3-22.

7635. Smith, Daniel M. *The Aftermath of War: Bainbridge Colby and Wilsonian Diplomacy, 1920-1921*. Philadelphia: American Philosophical Society, 1970.

7636. Smyth, Clifford. *Woodrow Wilson, Who Strove to Make the World Safe for Democracy*. New York: Funk and Wagnalls, 1931.

7637. Stone, Ralph A. *The Irreconcilables: The Fight against the League of Nations*. Lexington: University Press of Kentucky, 1970.

7638. Stone, Ralph A. *Wilson and the League of Nations: Why America's Rejection?* Melbourne, FL: Krieger, 1978.

7639. Trask, David F. "Woodrow Wilson and International Statecraft." *Naval War College Review* 36 (March/April 1983): 57-68.

7640. Trask, David F. "Woodrow Wilson

and the Reconciliation of Force and Diplomacy: 1917-1918." *Naval War College Review* 27 (January/February 1975): 23-31.

7641. Trow, Clifford W. " 'Something Desperate in His Face': Woodrow Wilson in Portland at the 'Very Crisis of His Career.' " *Oregon Historical Quarterly* 82 (Spring 1981): 40-64.

7642. Williams, Talcott. "President's Power to Act with a Peace League." *Review of Reviews* 55 (February 1917): 148-151.

7643. Wimer, Kurt. "Woodrow Wilson Tries Conciliation: An Effort That Failed." *Historian* 25 (August 1963): 419-438.

7644. Wimer, Kurt. "Woodrow Wilson's Plans to Enter the League of Nations through an Executive Agreement." *Western Political Quarterly* 11 (December 1958): 800-812.

Mexican Revolution

7645. Clements, Kendrick A. "Emissary from a Revolution: Luis Cabrera and Woodrow Wilson." *Americas* 35 (January 1979): 353-371.

7646. Clements, Kendrick A. "Woodrow Wilson's Mexican Policy, 1913-1915." *Diplomatic History* 4 (Spring 1980): 113-136.

7647. Gilderhus, Mark T. *Diplomacy and Revolution: U.S.-Mexican Relations under Wilson and Carranza.* Tucson: University of Arizona Press, 1977.

7648. Gilderhus, Mark T. "Wilson, Carranza, and the Monroe Doctrine: A Question of Regional Organization." *Diplomatic History* 7 (Spring 1983): 103-115.

7649. Glaser, David P. "Pacific Northwest Press Reaction to Wilson's Mexican Diplomacy, 1913-1916." Ph.D. dissertation, University of Idaho, 1965.

7650. Haley, P. Edward. *Revolution and Intervention: The Diplomacy of Taft and Wilson with Mexico, 1910-1917.* Cambridge, MA: MIT Press, 1970.

7651. Henderson, Paul V. N. "Woodrow Wilson, Victoriano Huerta, and the Recognition Issue in Mexico." *Americas* 41 (October 1984): 151-176.

7652. Hill, Larry D. *Emmissaries to a Revolution: Woodrow Wilson's Executive Agents in Mexico.* Baton Rouge: Louisiana State University Press, 1973.

7653. Hill, Larry D. "Woodrow Wilson's Executive Agents in Mexico: From the Beginning of His Administration to the Recognition of Venustiano Carranza." Ph.D. dissertation, Louisiana State University Press, 1971.

7654. Hinckley, Ted C. "Wilson, Huerta, and the Twenty-one Gun Salute." *Historian* 22 (February 1960): 197-206.

7655. Parris, Troy C. "The Wilson Mission to Mexico — 1909-1913." Master's thesis, American University, 1962.

7656. Sandos, James A. "Pancho Villa and American Security: Woodrow Wilson's Mexican Diplomacy Reconsidered." *Journal of Latin American Studies* 13 (November 1981): 293-311.

7657. Scholes, Walter V., and Marie V. Scholes. "Wilson, Grey, and Huerta." *Pacific Historical Review* 37 (May 1968): 151-158.

7658. Sessions, Tommie G. "American Reformers and the Mexican Revolution: Progressives and Woodrow Wilson's Policy in Mexico, 1913-1917." Ph.D. dissertation, American University, 1974.

7659. Sweetman, Jack. *The Landing at Veracruz....* Annapolis, MD: Naval Institute Press, 1968.

7660. Teitelbaum, Louis M. *Woodrow Wilson and the Mexican Revolution (1913-1916): A History of United States-Mexican Relations from the Murder of Madero until Villa's Provocation across the Border.* New York: Exposition Press, 1967.

7661. Trow, Clifford W. " 'Tired of Waiting': Senator Albert B. Fall's Alternative to Woodrow Wilson's Mexican Policies, 1920-1921." *New Mexico Historical Review* 57 (April 1982): 159-182.

7662. Trow, Clifford W. "Woodrow Wilson and the Mexican Interventionist Movement of 1919." *Journal of American History* 58 (June 1971): 46-72.

Versailles

7663. Ambrosious, Lloyd E. "Wilson, Clemenceau, and the German Problem at the Paris Peace Conference of 1919." *Rocky Mountain Social Science Journal* 12 (April 1975): 69-79.

7664. Ambrosious, Lloyd E. "Wilson, the Republicans, and French Security after World War I." *Journal of American History* 59 (September 1972): 341-352.

7665. Bailey, Thomas A. *Woodrow Wilson and the Great Betrayal.* New York: Macmillan, 1945.

7666. Bailey, Thomas A. *Woodrow Wilson and the Lost Peace.* New York: Macmillan, 1944.

7667. Civitello, Maryann. "The State Department and Peacemaking, 1917-1920: Attitudes of State Department Officials toward Wilson's Peacemaking Efforts." Ph.D. dissertation, Fordham University, 1981.

7668. Curry, George W. "Woodrow Wilson, Jan Smuts, and the Versailles Settlement." *American Historical Review* 66 (July 1961): 968-986.

7669. Duff, John B. "The Politics of Revenge: The Ethnic Opposition to the Peace Policies of Woodrow Wilson." Ph.D. dissertation, Columbia University, 1964.

7670. Floto, Igwa. *Colonel House in Paris: A Study of American Policy at the Peace Conference of 1919.* Princeton, NJ: Princeton University Press, 1980.

7671. Grattan, C. Hartley. "The 'Failure' of Woodrow Wilson." *North American Review* 237 (March 1934): 263-269.

7672. House, Edward M., and Charles Seymour, eds. *What Really Happened at Paris: The Story of the Peace Conference, 1918-1919, By American Delegates.* New York: Scribner's, 1921.

7673. Lansing, Robert. *The Big Four and Others of the Peace Conference.* Boston: Houghton Mifflin, 1921.

7674. Lansing, Robert. *The Peace Negotiations: A Personal Narrative.* Boston: Houghton Mifflin, 1921.

7675. Lentin, Antony. *Lloyd George, Woodrow Wilson, and the Guilt of Germany: An Essay in the Prehistory of Appeasement.* Baton Rouge: Louisiana State University Press, 1985.

7676. Manijak, William. "Polish American Pressure Groups, Woodrow Wilson, and the Thirteenth Point: The Significance of Polish Food Relief, the Polish Vote in the 1916 Presidential Election, and European Events in the Eventual Self-Determination for Poland." Ph.D. dissertation, Ball State University, 1975.

7677. Martin, Laurence W. *Peace without Victory: Woodrow Wilson and the British Liberals.* New Haven, CT: Yale University Press, 1958.

7678. Miller, David H. "Some Legal Aspects of the Visit of President Wilson to Paris." *Harvard Law Review* 36 (November 1922): 51-78.

7679. Moore, James R. "Woodrow Wilson and Post-Armistice Diplomacy: Some French Views." *Reviews in American History* 2 (June 1974): 207-213.

7680. Noble, George B. *Policies and Opinions at Paris, 1919: Wilsonian Diplomacy, the Versailles Peace, and French Public Opinion.* New York: Macmillan, 1935.

7681. O'Brien, Francis W., ed. *Two Peacemakers in Paris: The Hoover-Wilson Post-Armistice Letters, 1918-1920.* College Station: Texas Agricultural and Mechanical University Press, 1978.

7682. O'Grady, Joseph P. "Irish-Americans, Woodrow Wilson, and Self-Determination." *American Catholic Historical Society of Philadelphia Records* 74 (September 1963): 159-173.

7683. Parker, Malcolm E. "Woodrow Wilson, Austria-Hungary, and the Evolution of the Policy of Self-Determination, 1914-1918 — A Study in Presidential Diplomacy." Master's thesis, California State University, Fullerton, 1967.

7684. Randall, James G. "Lincoln's Peace and Wilson's." *South Atlantic Quarterly* 42 (July 1943): 225-242.

7685. Reiff, Philip. "Fourteen Points on Wilson." *Encounter* 28 (April 1967): 84-89.

7686. Sabki, Hisham. "Woodrow Wilson and Self-Determination in the Arab Middle East." *Journal of Social and Political Studies* 4 (Winter 1979): 381-399.

7687. Seymour, Charles. "The Paris Education of Woodrow Wilson." *Virginia Quarterly Review* 32 (Autumn 1956): 578-593.

7688. Startt, James D. "American Editorial Opinion of Woodrow Wilson and the Main Problems of Peacemaking in 1919." Ph.D. dissertation, University of Maryland, 1965.

7689. Startt, James D. "The Uneasy Partnership: Wilson and the Press at Paris." *Mid-America* 52 (January 1970): 55-69.

7690. Startt, James D. "Wilson's Mission to Paris: The Making of a Decision." *Historian* 30 (August 1968): 599-616.

7691. Zivojinovic, Dragan R. "The Vatican, Woodrow Wilson, and the Dissolution of the Hapsburg Monarchy, 1914-1918." *East European Quarterly* 3 (March 1969): 31-70.

World War I

7692. Arnett, Alex M. *Claude Kitchin and the Wilson War Policies.* Boston: Little, Brown, 1937.

7693. Coletta, Paolo E. "A Question of Alternatives: Wilson, Bryan, Lansing, and America's Intervention in World War I." *Nebraska History* 63 (Spring 1982): 33-57.

7694. Cooper, John M., Jr. *The Vanity of Power: American Isolationism and the First World War.* Westport, CT: Greenwood Press, 1969.

7695. Creel, George. *The War, the World, and Wilson.* New York: Harper and Row, 1920.

7696. Cuff, Robert D. "We Band of Brothers — Woodrow Wilson's War Managers." *Canadian Review of American Studies* 5 (Fall 1974): 135-148.

7697. Daniels, Josephus. *The Wilson Era: Years of War and After, 1917-1923.* Chapel Hill: University of North Carolina Press, 1946.

7698. Dayer, Roberta A. "Strange Bedfellows: J. P. Morgan and Co., Whitehall, and the Wilson Administration during World War I." *Business History* 18 (July 1976): 127-151.

7699. DeWeerd, Harvey A. *President*

Wilson Fights His War: World War I and the American Intervention. New York: Macmillan, 1968.

7700. Ferrell, Robert H. *Woodrow Wilson and World War I, 1917-1921.* New York: Harper and Row, 1985.

7701. Goldman, Eric F. "Woodrow Wilson: The Test of War." In *Woodrow Wilson and the World of Today*, edited by Arthur P. Dudden, 47-66. Philadelphia: University of Pennsylvania Press, 1957.

7702. Grant, Philip A., Jr. "World War I: Wilson and Southern Leadership." *Presidential Studies Quarterly* 6 (Winter/Spring 1976): 44-49.

7703. Harbaugh, William H. "Wilson, Roosevelt, and Interventionism, 1914-1917: A Study of Domestic Influences on the Formulation of American Foreign Policy." Ph.D. dissertation, Northwestern University, 1954.

7704. James, Edith. "Wilsonian Wartime Diplomacy: The Sense of the Seventies." In *American Foreign Relations: A Historiographical Review*, edited by Gerald K. Haines and J. Samuel Walker, 115-131. Westport, CT: Greenwood Press, 1981.

7705. Johnson, Donald. "Wilson, Burleson, and Censorship in the First World War." *Journal of Southern History* 28 (February 1962): 46-48.

7706. Kaufman, Burton I. "Wilson's 'War Bureaucracy' and Foreign Trade Expansion, 1917-1921." *Prologue* 6 (Spring 1974): 19-31.

7707. Kennan, George F. *The Decision to Intervene.* Princeton, NJ: Princeton University Press, 1958.

7708. Link, Arthur S. *Woodrow Wilson: Revolution, War, and Peace.* Arlington Heights, IL: AHM, 1979.

7709. Livermore, Seward W. *Politics Is Adjourned: Woodrow Wilson and the War Congress, 1916-1918.* Middletown, CT: Wesleyan University Press, 1966.

7710. Livermore, Seward W. *Woodrow Wilson and the War Congress, 1916-1918.* Seattle: University of Washington Press, 1968.

7711. McDonald, Timothy G. "The Gore-McLemore Resolution: Democratic Revolt against Wilson's Submarine Policy." *Historian* 26 (November 1963): 50-74.

7712. Maddox, Robert J. *The Unknown War with Russia: Wilson's Siberian Intervention.* San Rafael, CA: Presidio Press, 1977.

7713. Maddox, Robert J. "Woodrow Wilson, the Russian Embassy, and Siberian Intervention." *Pacific Historical Review* 36 (November 1967): 435-448.

7714. Mamatey, Victor S. *The United States and East Central Europe, 1914-1918: A Study in Wilsonian Diplomacy and Propaganda.* Princeton, NJ: Princeton University Press, 1957.

7715. Martin, William. "President Wilson." In his *Statesmen of the War in Retrospect, 1918-1928*, 217-233. New York: Minton, Balch, 1928.

7716. Mason, Julian. "Owen Wister and World War I: Appeal for Pentecost." *Pennsylvania Magazine of History and Biography* 101 (January 1977): 89-102.

7717. Mooney, Christopher F. "Moral Consensus and Law." *Thought* 51 (September 1976): 231-254.

7718. Palmer, John M. *Washington, Lincoln, Wilson: Three War Statesmen.* Garden City, NY: Doubleday, 1930.

7719. Parsons, Edward B. *Wilsonian Diplomacy: Allied-American Rivalries in War and Peace.* St. Louis, MO: Forum, 1978.

7720. "President Wilson's War Message

to Congress." *National Corporation Reporter* 55 (December 13, 1917): 735-737.

7721. Safford, Jeffrey J. *Wilsonian Maritime Diplomacy, 1913-1921.* New Brunswick, NJ: Rutgers University Press, 1978.

7722. Scheiber, Jane L., and Harry N. Scheiber. "The Wilson Administration and the Wartime Mobilization of Black Americans, 1917-1918." *Labor History* 10 (Summer 1969): 433-458.

7723. Seymour, Charles. *Woodrow Wilson and the World War: A Chronicle of Our Times.* New Haven, CT: Yale University Press, 1921.

7724. Sondermann, Fred A. "The Wilson Administration's Image of Germany." Ph.D. dissertation, Yale University, 1953.

7725. Trani, Eugene P. "Woodrow Wilson and the Decision to Intervene in Russia: A Reconsideration." *Journal of Modern History* 48 (September 1976): 440-461.

7726. Trask, David F. "Woodrow Wilson and World War I." In *American Diplomacy in the Twentieth Century*, edited by Warren F. Kimball, 1-16. St. Louis, MO: Forum, 1980.

Writings

7727. Brand, Katherine E. "The Woodrow Wilson Collection." *Library of Congress Quarterly Journal* 2 (February 1945): 3-10.

7728. Craig, Hardin. "Woodrow Wilson as an Orator." *Quarterly Journal of Speech* 38 (April 1952): 145-148.

7729. Day, Donald, ed. *Woodrow Wilson's Own Story.* Boston: Little, Brown, 1952.

7730. DeYoung, Harry R. "A Study of the Religious Speaking of Woodrow Wilson." Ph.D. dissertation, Wayne State University, 1965.

7731. Farmer, Frances, ed. *The Wilson Reader.* New York: Oceana, 1956.

7732. Francesconi, Robert A. "A Burkean Analysis of Selected Speeches of Woodrow Wilson and Henry Cabot Lodge on the League of Nations." Ph.D. dissertation, Bowling Green State University, 1975.

7733. Harper, George M., ed. *President Wilson's Addresses.* New York: Holt, 1918.

7734. Heckscher, August, ed. *The Politics of Woodrow Wilson, Selections from His Speeches and Writings.* New York: Harper and Row, 1956.

7735. Herold, Charles J., comp. *The Wisdom of Woodrow Wilson: Being Selections from His Thoughts and Comments on Political, Social, and Moral Questions.* New York: Brentano's, 1919.

7736. Linthicum, Richard, comp. *Wit and Wisdom of Woodrow Wilson: Extracts from the Public Speeches of the Leader and Interpreter of American Democracy, With Masterpieces of Eloquence.* Garden City, NY: Doubleday, 1916.

7737. Noggle, Burl. "A Note on Historical Editing: The Wilson Papers in Perspective." *Louisiana History* 8 (Summer 1967): 281-297.

7738. Osborn, George C. "Woodrow Wilson as a Speaker." *Southern Speech Journal* 22 (Winter 1956): 61-72.

7739. Tourtellot, Arthur B., ed. *Woodrow Wilson, Selections for Today.* New York: Duel, Sloan and Pearce, 1945.

7740. Wescott, John W. *Woodrow Wilson's Eloquence.* Camden, NJ: I. F. Huntzinger, 1922.

7741. Wilson, Woodrow. *Addresses Delivered by President Wilson on His Western*

Tour, September 4 to September 25, 1919, On the League of Nations, Treaty of Peace with Germany, Industrial Conditions, High Cost of Living, Race Riots, etc. Washington, DC: U.S. Government Printing Office, 1919.

7742. Wilson, Woodrow. *Addresses of President Wilson: Boston, Mass., February 24, 1919: New York, March 4, 1919.* Washington, DC: U.S. Government Printing Office, 1919.

7743. Wilson, Woodrow. *Addresses of President Wilson, On National Defense, January 27-February 3, 1916.* Washington, DC: U.S. Government Printing Office, 1916.

7744. Wilson, Woodrow. *Addresses of President Wilson on the First Trip to Europe, December 3, 1918 to February 24, 1919.* Washington, DC: U.S. Government Printing Office, 1919.

7745. Wilson, Woodrow. *America and Freedom: Being the Statements of President Wilson on the War.* London: Allen and Unwin, 1917.

7746. Wilson, Woodrow. *America Joins the World.* New York: Association Press, 1919.

7747. Wilson, Woodrow. *Americanism, Woodrow Wilson's Speeches on the War.* Edited by Oliver M. Gale. Chicago: Baldwin Syndicate, 1919.

7748. Wilson, Woodrow. *The Bases of Durable Peace as Voiced by President Wilson.* Chicago: Union League Club, 1918.

7749. Wilson, Woodrow. "Bryce's 'American Commonwealth.'" *Political Science Quarterly* 4 (March 1889): 153-169.

7750. Wilson, Woodrow. *Cabinet Government in the United States.* Stamford, CT: Overbrook Press, 1947.

7751. Wilson, Woodrow. "A Calendar of Great Americans: An Historical Essay." *Forum* 16 (February 1894): 715-727.

7752. Wilson, Woodrow. "The Centenary of Abraham Lincoln." *Princeton Alumni Weekly* 9 (February 17, 1909): 296-298.

7753. Wilson, Woodrow. "Committee or Cabinet Government." *Overland Monthly* 3 (January 1884): 17-33.

7754. Wilson, Woodrow. *Congressional Government: A Study in American Politics.* Boston: Houghton Mifflin, 1885.

7755. Wilson, Woodrow. *Constitutional Government in the United States.* New York: Columbia University Press, 1908.

7756. Wilson, Woodrow. *A Crossroads of Freedom, The 1912 Campaign Speeches.* Edited by John W. Davidson. New Haven, CT: Yale University Press, 1956.

7757. Wilson, Woodrow. *Day of Dedication: The Essential Writings and Speeches of Woodrow Wilson.* Edited by A. Fried. New York: Macmillan, 1965.

7758. Wilson, Woodrow. *Division and Reunion, 1829-1889.* New York: Longmans, Green, 1893.

7759. Wilson, Woodrow. *George Washington.* New York: Harper and Row, 1896.

7760. Wilson, Woodrow. *Guarantees of Peace: Messages and Addresses to the Congress and the People, January 31, 1918 to December 2, 1918, Together with the Peace Notes to Germany and Austria.* New York: Harper and Row, 1919.

7761. Wilson, Woodrow. *A History of the American People.* 5 vols. New York: Harper and Row, 1902.

7762. Wilson, Woodrow. *Hope of the World: Messages and Addresses Delivered by the President between July 10, 1919 and December 9, 1919, Including Selections from His Country-Wide Speeches in Behalf of the Treaty and Covenant.* New York: Harper and Row, 1920.

7763. Wilson, Woodrow. "How Governor

Wilson Feels." *Harper's Weekly* 55 (October 26, 1912): 7-8.

7764. Wilson, Woodrow. *In Our First Year of the War: Messages and Addresses to Congress and the People, March 5, 1917 to April 6, 1918.* New York: Harper and Row, 1918.

7765. Wilson, Woodrow. *International Ideals: Speeches and Addresses Made during the President's European Visit, December 14, 1918 to February 14, 1919.* New York: Harper and Row, 1919.

7766. Wilson, Woodrow. "Is the Roman Catholic Element in the United States a Menace to American Institutions?" *University of Virginia Magazine* 19 (April 1880): 448-450.

7767. Wilson, Woodrow. "Jefferson Day Address." *Princeton Alumni Weekly* 6 (April 1906): 551-554.

7768. Wilson, Woodrow. "Jefferson — Wilson: A Record and a Forecast." *North American Review* 197 (March 1913): 289-294.

7769. Wilson, Woodrow. "John Bright." *University of Virginia Magazine* 19 (March 1880): 354-370.

7770. Wilson, Woodrow. *John Wesley's Place in History.* New York: Abingdon Press, 1915.

7771. Wilson, Woodrow. *Leaders of Men.* Edited by T. H. Vail Motter. Princeton, NJ: Princeton University Press, 1952.

7772. Wilson, Woodrow. *Mere Literature, and Other Essays.* Boston: Houghton Mifflin, 1896.

7773. Wilson, Woodrow. *The Messages and Papers of Woodrow Wilson.* 2 vols. Edited by Albert Shaw. New York: Review of Reviews, 1924.

7774. Wilson, Woodrow. "Mr. Cleveland as President." *Atlantic Monthly* 79 (March 1897): 289-300.

7775. Wilson, Woodrow. "Mr. Cleveland's Cabinet." *Review of Reviews* 7 (April 1893): 286-297.

7776. Wilson, Woodrow. "Mr. Gladstone: A Character Sketch." *University of Virginia Magazine* 19 (April 1880): 401-426.

7777. Wilson, Woodrow. *The New Freedom: A Call for the Emancipation of the Generous Energies of a People.* Edited by William B. Hale. Garden City, NY: Doubleday, 1913.

7778. Wilson, Woodrow. "Of the Study of Politics." *New Princeton Review* 3 (March 1887): 188-199.

7779. Wilson, Woodrow. *An Old Master, and Other Political Essays.* New York: Scribner's, 1893.

7780. Wilson, Woodrow. *The Papers of Woodrow Wilson.* Edited by Arthur S. Link. 51 vols. Princeton, NJ: Princeton University Press, 1966-1982.

7781. Wilson, Woodrow. *The Political Thought of Woodrow Wilson.* Edited by E. David Cronin. Indianapolis, IN: Bobbs-Merrill, 1965.

7782. Wilson, Woodrow. *The Politics of Woodrow Wilson: Selections from His Speeches and Writings.* Edited by August Heckscher. New York: Harper and Row, 1956.

7783. Wilson, Woodrow. *A President in Love: The Courtship Letters of Woodrow Wilson and Edith Bolling Galt.* Edited by Edwin Tribble. Boston: Houghton Mifflin, 1981.

7784. Wilson, Woodrow. "The President of the United States." In *The World's Best Essays...*, edited by Francis H. Pritchard, 926-943. New York: Harper and Row, 1929.

7785. Wilson, Woodrow. "President Wilson on His Foreign Policy." *World's Work* 28 (October 1914): 485-494.

7786. Wilson, Woodrow. *President Wilson's Foreign Policy: Messages, Addresses, Papers.* Edited by James B. Scott. New York: Oxford University Press, 1918.

7787. Wilson, Woodrow. *President Wilson's Great Speeches and Other History-Making Documents.* Chicago: Stanton and Van Vliet, 1920.

7788. Wilson, Woodrow. *President Wilson's State Papers and Addresses.* Edited by Albert Shaw. New York: Doran, 1918.

7789. Wilson, Woodrow. "President's Forward to the Selective Service Regulations." *Massachusetts Law Quarterly* 2 (August 1917): 564-565.

7790. Wilson, Woodrow. *The Priceless Gift: The Love Letters of Woodrow Wilson and Ellen Axson Wilson.* Edited by Eleanor W. McAdoo. New York: McGraw-Hill, 1962.

7791. Wilson, Woodrow. *Proclamations by the President of the United States.* Washington, DC: U.S. Government Printing Office, 1915-1923.

7792. Wilson, Woodrow. *The Public Papers of Woodrow Wilson.* Edited by Ray S. Baker and William E. Dodd. 6 vols. New York: Harper and Row, 1925-1927.

7793. Wilson, Woodrow. "Responsible Government under the Constitution." *Atlantic Monthly* 57 (April 1886): 542-553.

7794. Wilson, Woodrow. *The Road Away from Revolution.* Boston: Atlantic Monthly Press, 1923.

7795. Wilson, Woodrow. *Robert E. Lee, An Interpretation.* Chapel Hill: University of North Carolina Press, 1924.

7796. Wilson, Woodrow. *Selected Addresses and Public Papers of Woodrow Wilson.* Edited by A. B. Hart. New York: Liveright, 1918.

7797. Wilson, Woodrow. *Selected Literary and Political Papers and Addresses of Woodrow Wilson.* 3 vols. New York: Grosset and Dunlap, 1926.

7798. Wilson, Woodrow. *Speeches on Liberty, Peace, and Justice.* Boston: Houghton Mifflin, 1918.

7799. Wilson, Woodrow. "The Spirit of Jefferson." *Princeton Alumni Weekly* 6 (April 28, 1906): 551-554.

7800. Wilson, Woodrow. *The State: Elements of Historical and Practical Politics.* Rev. ed. Boston: Heath, 1898.

7801. Wilson, Woodrow. "The Study of Administration." *Political Science Quarterly* 2 (June 1887): 197-222.

7802. Wilson, Woodrow. *The Study of Public Administration.* Washington, DC: Public Affairs Press, 1955.

7803. Wilson, Woodrow. "Taxation and Appropriation." In *The National Revenues: A Collection of Papers by American Economists*, edited by Albert Shaw, 106-111. Chicago: McClurg, 1888.

7804. Wilson, Woodrow. *The Triumph of Ideals: Speeches, Messages, and Addresses Made by the President between February 24, 1919 and July 8, 1919, Covering the Active Period of the Peace Conference at Paris.* New York: Harper and Row, 1919.

7805. Wilson, Woodrow. *War Addresses of Woodrow Wilson.* Boston: Ginn, 1918.

7806. Wilson, Woodrow. *When a Man Comes to Himself.* New York: Harper and Row, 1901.

7807. Wilson, Woodrow. "When Woodrow Wilson Came to Hopkins." *Johns Hopkins University Alumni Magazine* 28 (1940): 78-81.

7808. Wilson, Woodrow. *Why We Are at War: Messages to the Congress, January to April, 1917.* New York: Harper and Row, 1917.

7809. Wilson, Woodrow. "William Earl

Chatham." *Nassau Literary Magazine* 34 (October 1978): 99-105.

7810. Wilson, Woodrow. "Wilson on One Term." *Protectionist* 27 (February 1916): 687-689.

7811. Wilson, Woodrow. "A Young Professor in Search of a Job." In *The Status and Prospects of Political Science as a Discipline,* edited by Lionel H. Laing, 50-54. Ann Arbor: Department of Political Science, University of Michigan, 1960.

7812. Wilson, Woodrow. "Woodrow Wilson's Message to the American People." *Literary Digest* 45 (October 26, 1912): 729.

Warren G. Harding

Biographies

7813. Adams, Samuel H. *Incredible Era: The Life and Times of Warren Gamaliel Harding.* Boston: Houghton Mifflin, 1939.

7814. Alderfer, Harold F. "The Personality and Politics of Warren G. Harding." Ph.D. dissertation, Syracuse University, 1929.

7815. Asher, Cash, comp. *He Was "Just Folks": The Life and Character of Warren Gamaliel Harding, As Mirrored in the Tributes of the American Press.* Chicago: Laird and Lee, 1923.

7816. Boatmon, Ellis G. "Evolution of a President: The Political Apprenticeship of Warren G. Harding." Ph.D. dissertation, University of South Carolina, 1966.

7817. Chapple, Joseph M. *Life and Times of Warren G. Harding, Our After-War President.* Boston: Chapple, 1924.

7818. Chapple, Joseph M. *Warren G. Harding the Man.* Boston: Chapple, 1920.

7819. Cottrill, Dale E. *The Conciliator.* Philadelphia: Dorrance, 1969.

7820. Cuneo, Sherman A. *From Printer to President.* Philadelphia: Dorrance, 1922.

7821. Daugherty, Harry M., and Thomas Dixon. *The Inside Story of the Harding Tragedy.* New York: Churchill, 1932.

7822. Downes, Randolph C. *The Rise of Warren Gamaliel Harding: 1865-1920.* Columbus: Ohio State University Press, 1970.

7823. Galbreath, C. B. *The Story of Warren G. Harding.* Dansville, NY: F. A. Owen Publishing Co., 1922.

7824. Glenn, James A. *Smearing the Presidents: Harding No Exception.* Columbus, OH: n.p., 1935.

7825. Hartwell, Alena. *Hardings: History of the Harding Family.* Boston: Chapple, 1936.

7826. Johnson, Willis F. *The Life of Warren G. Harding from the Simple Life of the Farm to the Glamor and Power of the White House.* Chicago: John C. Winston, 1923.

7827. Kurland, Gerald. *Warren Harding: President Betrayed by Friends.* Charlotteville, NY: SamHar Press, 1971.

7828. Mee, Charles L., Jr. *The Ohio Gang: The World of Warren G. Harding.* New York: Evans, 1981.

7829. Russell, Francis. *The Shadow of Blooming Grove: Warren G. Harding in His Times.* New York: McGraw-Hill, 1968.

7830. Russell, Thomas H. *The Illustrious Life and Work of Warren G. Harding, Twenty-ninth President of the United States.* Chicago: n.p., 1923.

7831. Sinclair, Andrew. *The Available Man: The Life behind the Masks of Warren Gamaliel Harding.* New York: Macmillan, 1965.

7832. Trani, Eugene P., and David L. Wilson. *The Presidency of Warren G. Harding.* Lawrence: Regents Press of Kansas, 1977.

7833. Wood, Clement. *Warren Gamaliel Harding: An American Comedy.* New York: Faro, 1932.

Private Life

7834. Blanchard, Sherman. "President Harding: A Reappraisal." *Current History* 35 (October 1931): 41-47.

7835. Brainerd, Lawrence. "President Warren Gamaliel Harding." *New England Historical and Genealogical Register* 77 (October 1923): 243-249.

7836. Britton, Nan. *The President's Daughter.* New York: Elizabeth Ann Guild, 1927.

7837. Coren, Robert W. "Samuel Hopkins Adams, His Novel, and the Reputation of Warren G. Harding." *Courier* (Syracuse) 11 (Spring 1974): 3-10.

7838. DeBarthe, Joseph. *The Answer, To Deny and Refute the Scandals and Untruths, Particularly Those in the Recently Issued Volume, "The President's Daughter, by Nan Britton," Attacking the Character and Impugning the Moral Rectitude of the Late Warren Gamaliel Harding.* Marion, OH: Answer Publishers, 1928.

7839. Downes, Randolph C. "The Harding Muckfest: Warren G. Harding — Chief Victim of the Muck-for-Muck's-Sake Writers and Readers." *Northwest Ohio Quarterly* 39 (Summer 1967): 5-37.

7840. Downes, Randolph C. "A Newspaper's Childhood — The Marion Star from Hume to Harding." *Northwest Ohio Quarterly* 36 (Summer 1964): 134-145.

7841. Downes, Randolph C. "Wanted: A Scholarly Appraisal of Warren G. Harding." *Ohioana Quarterly* 2 (1959): 18-22.

7842. Duckett, Kenneth W. "The Harding Papers: How Some Were Burned." *American Heritage* 16 (February 1965): 24-31, 102-110.

7843. Frank, Glenn. "President Harding as a Salesman." *Century Magazine* 101 (February 1921): 533-536.

7844. Galbreath, C. B. "Warren Gamaliel Harding." *Ohio Archaeological and Historical Society Publications* 32 (October 1923): 555-570.

7845. Gross, Edwin K. *Vindication for Mr. Normalcy: A 100th Birthday Memorial.* Buffalo, NY: American Society for the Faithful Recording of History, 1965.

7846. Harris, Ray B. "Background and Youth of the Seventh Ohio President." *Ohio State Archaeological and Historical Quarterly* 52 (July 1943): 260-275.

7847. Harris, Ray B. *Warren G. Harding, An Account of His Nomination for the Presidency by the Republican Convention of 1920.* Washington: n.p., 1957.

7848. Jenks, Anton S. *A Dead President Makes Answer to the President's Daughter.* New York: Golden Hind Press, 1929.

7849. Jennings, David H. "Historiography and Warren G. Harding." *Ohio History* 78 (Winter 1969): 46-49.

7850. Johnson, Evans C. "Underwood and Harding: A Bi-Partisan Friendship." *Alabama Historical Quarterly* 30 (Spring 1968): 65-78.

7851. Martin, Dorothy V. "An Impression of Harding in 1916." *Ohio State Archaeological and Historical Quarterly* 62 (September 1953): 179-180.

7852. Means, Gaston B. *The Strange Death of President Harding*. New York: Guild, 1930.

7853. Miller, Clara G. *The Ancestry of President Harding and Its Relation to the Hardings of Wyoming Valley and Clifford, Pennsylvania*. Wilkes-Barre, PA: n.p., 1928.

7854. Moran, Philip R., ed. *Warren G. Harding, 1865-1923: Chronology, Documents, Biographical Aids*. Dobbs Ferry, NY: Oceana, 1970.

7855. Murray, Robert K. "Harding on History." *Journal of American History* 53 (March 1967): 781-785.

7856. Nevins, Allan. "Warren G. Harding." In *Dictionary of American Biography*, edited by Dumas Malone, 252-257. Vol. 8. New York: Scribner's, 1932.

7857. Potts, Louis W. "Who Was Warren G. Harding?" *Historian* 36 (August 1974): 621-645.

7858. Russell, Francis. "The Four Mysteries of Warren Harding." *American Heritage* 14 (April 1963): 5-9, 81-86.

7859. Russell, Francis. *President Harding: His Life and Times, 1865-1923*. London: Eyre and Spottiswoode, 1969.

7860. Russell, Francis. "The Shadow of Warren Harding." *Antioch Review* 36 (Winter 1978): 57-76.

7861. Schruben, Francis W. "An Even Stranger Death of President Harding." *Southern California Quarterly* 48 (Spring 1966): 57-78.

7862. Slosson, Preston W. "Warren G. Harding: A Revised Estimate." *Current History* 33 (November 1930): 174-179.

7863. Sullivan, Mark. *Our Times, The United States, 1900-1925*. New York: Scribner's, 1935.

7864. Thacker, May. *The Strange Death of President Harding*. New York: Guild, 1930.

7865. Timmons, Clarence P. *Pictorial Memorial of Warren Gamaliel Harding, 1865-1923, The Twenty-ninth President of the United States of America*. Washington, DC: National Service Bureau, 1923.

7866. Walker, Kenneth R., and Randolph C. Downes. "The Death of Warren G. Harding." *Northwest Ohio Quarterly* 35 (Winter 1962-1963): 7-17.

7867. Werner, Morris R., and John Starr. *Teapot Dome*. New York: Viking Press, 1959.

7868. Williams, J. R. "Hoover, Harding, and the Harding Image." *Northwest Ohio Quarterly* 45 (Winter 1972-1973): 4-20.

Public Career

7869. Anderson, Fenwick. "Hail to the Editor-in-Chief: Cox vs. Harding, 1920." *Journalism History* 1 (Summer 1974): 46-49.

7870. Bagby, Wesley M. "The 'Smoke Filled Room' and the Nomination of Warren G. Harding." *Mississippi Valley Historical Review* 41 (June 1955): 657-674.

7871. Downes, Randolph C., ed. "President Making: The Influence of Newton H. Fairbanks and Harry M. Daugherty on the Nomination of Warren G. Harding for the Presidency." *Northwest Ohio Quarterly* 31 (Fall 1959): 170-178.

7872. Downes, Randolph C. "Some Correspondence between Warren G. Harding and William Allen White during the Presidential Campaign of 1920." *Northwest Ohio Quarterly* 37 (Autumn 1965): 121-132.

7873. Margulies, Herbert F. "Irvine L. Lenroot and the Republican Vice-Presidential Nomination of 1920." *Wisconsin Magazine of History* 61 (Autumn 1977): 21-31.

7874. Norris, James D., and Arthur H. Shaffer, eds. *Politics and Patronage in the Gilded Age: The Correspondence of James A. Garfield and Charles H. Henry.* Madison: State Historical Society of Wisconsin, 1970.

7875. Sheffer, Martin S. " 'Maintenance of Peace in Armenia': A Senatorial Subcommittee Debates SJR 106, 'The Williams Resolution,' 1919." *Armenian Review* 34 (June 1981): 199-217.

7876. Warren, Sidney. "Harding's Abdication from Leadership." *Current History* 39 (October 1960): 203-207.

7877. Whitaker, W. Richard. "The Working Press and the Harding Myth." *Journalism History* 2 (Autumn 1975): 90-97.

Presidential Years

7878. Accinelli, Robert D. "Was There a 'New' Harding? Warren G. Harding and the World Court Issue, 1920-1923." *Ohio History* 84 (Autumn 1975): 168-181.

7879. Beelen, George D. "The Harding Administration and Mexico: Diplomacy by Economic Persuasion." *Americas* 41 (October 1984): 177-189.

7880. Beelen, George D. "Harding and Mexico: Diplomacy by Economic Persuasion." Ph.D. dissertation, Kent State University, 1971.

7881. Cottrill, Dale E. "The Public Speaking of Warren Gamaliel Harding." Ph.D. dissertation, Wayne State University, 1967.

7882. DeWitt, Howard A. "The 'New' Harding and American Foreign Policy: Warren G. Harding, Hiram W. Johnson, and Pragmatic Diplomacy." *Ohio History* 86 (Spring 1977): 96-114.

7883. Ficken, Robert E. "President Harding Visits Seattle." *Pacific Northwest Quarterly* 66 (July 1975): 105-114.

7884. Grieb, Kenneth J. *The Latin American Policy of Warren G. Harding.* Fort Worth: Texas Christian University Press, 1977.

7885. Grieb, Kenneth J. "Warren G. Harding and the Dominican Republic: U.S. Withdrawal, 1921-1923." *Journal of Inter-American Studies* 11 (July 1969): 425-440.

7886. Hauser, Robert E. "The Georgia Experiment: President Warren G. Harding's Attempt to Reorganize the Republican Party in Georgia." *Georgia Historical Quarterly* 62 (Winter 1978): 288-303.

7887. Hauser, Robert E. "Warren G. Harding and His Attempts to Reorganize the Republican Party in the South, 1920-1923." Ph.D. dissertation, Pennsylvania State University, 1973.

7888. Ignasias, C. Dennis. "Propaganda and Public Opinion in Harding's Foreign Affairs: The Case for Mexican Recognition." *Journalism Quarterly* 48 (Spring 1971): 41-52.

7889. Jennings, David H. "President Harding and International Organization." *Ohio History* 75 (Spring/Summer 1966): 149-165.

7890. Kane, Richard D. "The Federal Segregation of the Blacks during the Presidential Administrations of Warren G. Harding and Calvin Coolidge." *Pan-African Journal* 7 (Summer 1974): 153-171.

7891. Lowerre, Nan K. J. "Warren G. Harding and American Foreign Affairs, 1915-1923." Ph.D. dissertation, Stanford University, 1968.

7892. Mencken, Henry L. "Mr. Harding's Second Term." *Outlook* 51 (April 28, 1923): 344-345.

7893. Murray, Richard K. "The President under Fire." *American History Illustrated* 9 (August 1974): 32-40.

7894. Murray, Robert K. *The Harding Era: Warren G. Harding and His Administration.* Minneapolis: University of Minnesota Press, 1969.

7895. Murray, Robert K. "How Harding Saved the Versailles Treaty." *American Heritage* 20 (December 1968): 66-67, 111.

7896. Murray, Robert K. *The Politics of Normalcy: Governmental Theory and Practice in the Harding-Coolidge Era.* New York: Norton, 1973.

7897. Murray, Robert K. "President Harding and His Cabinet." *Ohio History* 75 (Spring/Summer 1966): 108-125.

7898. Noggle, Burl. *Teapot Dome: Oil and Politics in the 1920's.* Baton Rouge: Louisiana State University Press, 1962.

7899. Owens, John W. "Irony of the Harding Cabinet." *New Republic* 38 (March 12, 1924): 64-66.

7900. Phayre, Ignatius. "The White House and Its Occupants." *Quarterly Review* 250 (April 1928): 258-275.

7901. "President Harding's Inauguration." *Current History* 14 (April 1921): 39-44.

7902. Reichard, Gary W. "The Aberration of 1920: An Analysis of Harding's Victory in Tennessee." *Journal of Southern History* 36 (February 1970): 33-49.

7903. Rofinot, Henry L. "Normalcy and the Farmer: Agricultural Policy under Harding and Coolidge, 1920-1928." Ph.D. dissertation, Columbia University, 1958.

7904. Schapsmeier, Edward L., and Frederick H. Schapsmeier. "Disharmony in the Harding Cabinet: Hoover-Wallace Conflict." *Ohio History* 75 (Spring/Summer 1966): 126-136.

7905. Scott, James B. "President Harding's Foreign Policy." *American Journal of International Law* 15 (July 1921): 409-411.

7906. Sherman, Richard B. "The Harding Administration and the Negro: An Opportunity Lost." *Journal of Negro History* 49 (July 1964): 151-168.

7907. Stewart, David M. "Supreme Court Appointments during the Harding and Coolidge Administrations: Influence, Critics, and Voting." Ph.D. dissertation, Wayne State University, 1974.

7908. Trani, Eugene P. "Harding Administration and Recognition of Mexico." *Ohio History* 75 (Spring/Summer 1966): 137-148.

7909. Whitaker, W. Richard. "Harding: First Radio President." *Northwest Ohio Quarterly* 45 (Summer 1973): 75-86.

7910. Whitaker, W. Richard. "Warren G. Harding and the Press." Ph.D. dissertation, Ohio University, 1972.

7911. Wilson, John F. "Harding's Rhetoric of Normalcy, 1920-1923." *Quarterly Journal of Speech* 48 (December 1962): 406-411.

7912. Wimer, Kurt, and Sarah Wimer. "The Harding Administration, the League of Nations, and the Separate Peace Treaty." *Review of Politics* 29 (January 1967): 13-24.

Writings

7913. Harding, Warren G. *Our Common Country: Mutual Good Will in America.* Edited by Frederick E. Schortemeier. Indianapolis, IN: Bobbs-Merrill, 1921.

7914. Harding, Warren G. *Warren G.*

Harding Papers: A Microfilm Edition. Columbus: Manuscripts Department, Ohio Historical Society, 1969.

7915. Harding, Warren G. *The Warren G. Harding Papers: An Inventory to the Microfilm Edition.* Edited by Andrea D. Lentz. Columbus: Ohio Historical Society, 1970.

7916. Murphy, James W., comp. *Speeches and Addresses of Warren G. Harding, President of the United States, Delivered during the Course of His Tour from Washington, D.C., to Alaska and Return to San Francisco, June 20 to August 2, 1923.* Washington, DC: n.p., 1923.

7917. Pitzer, Donald E. "An Introduction to the Harding Papers." *Ohio History* 75 (Spring/Summer 1966): 76-84.

7918. Russell, Francis. "The Harding Papers . . . and Some Were Saved." *American Heritage* 16 (February 1965): 24-31, 102-110.

7919. Schortemeier, Frederick E. *Rededicating America, Life and Recent Speeches of Warren G. Harding.* Indianapolis, IN: Bobbs-Merrill, 1920.

Calvin Coolidge

Biographies

7920. Bryant, Blanche B. *Calvin Coolidge as I Knew Him.* Edited by Beatrice S. Crooker. DeLeon Springs, FL: E. O. Painter Print Co., 1971.

7921. Carpenter, Ernest C. *The Boyhood Days of President Calvin Coolidge: Or From the Green Mountains to the White House.* Rutland, VT: Tuttle, 1925.

7922. Fuess, Claude M. "Calvin Coolidge." *Vermont Life* 3 (Autumn 1948): 3, 54.

7923. Fuess, Claude M. *Calvin Coolidge, The Man from Vermont.* Boston: Little, Brown, 1938.

7924. Gilfond, Duff. *The Rise of Saint Calvin: Merry Sidelights on the Career of Mr. Coolidge.* New York: Vanguard Press, 1932.

7925. Green, Horace. *The Life of Calvin Coolidge.* New York: Duffield and Co., 1924.

7926. Hennessy, Michael E. *Calvin Coolidge from a Green Mountain Farm to the White House.* New York: Putnam, 1924.

7927. Johnston, Thomas T. *Have Faith in Calvin Coolidge: Or From a Farm House to the White House.* Cedar Falls, IA: Woolverton, 1923.

7928. Lathem, Edward C., ed. *Meet Calvin Coolidge: The Man Behind the Myth.* Brattleboro, VT: Stephen Greene Press, 1960.

7929. Phillips, Harry I. *Calvin Coolidge, 1872-1933.* New York: Sully, 1933.

7930. Rogers, Cameron. *The Legend of Calvin Coolidge.* Garden City, NY: Doubleday, 1928.

7931. Sawyer, Roland D. *Cal Coolidge, President.* Boston: Four Seas, 1924.

7932. Washburn, Robert M. *Calvin Coolidge, His First Biography: From Cornerstone to Capstone to the Accession.* Boston: Small, Maynard, 1923.

7933. White, William A. *Calvin Coolidge, The Man Who Is President.* New York: Macmillan, 1925.

7934. White, William A. *A Puritan in Babylon: The Story of Calvin Coolidge.* New York: Macmillan, 1938.

7935. Whiting, Edward E. *President Coolidge, A Contemporary Estimate.* Boston: Atlantic Monthly Press, 1923.

Private Life

7936. Adams, Charles J. "An Early Memory of Calvin Coolidge." *Vermont History* 22 (October 1954): 280, 285-286.

7937. Barton, Bruce. "Calvin Coolidge,

As Seen through the Eyes of His Friends." *Review of Reviews* 58 (September 1923): 273-278.

7938. Brigham, Clarence S. *Calvin Coolidge, President of the American Antiquarian Society.* Worcester, MA: American Antiquarian Society, 1934.

7939. Brown, Claude T. "Memories of Calvin Coolidge." *Vermont Quarterly* 21 (October 1953): 311-313.

7940. Brown, L. H. "An Ex-President Passes." *Vermonter* 40 (1935): 5-6.

7941. Coolidge, Grace A. "How I Spent My Days at the White House." *American Magazine* 108 (October 1929): 16-17, 138, 140, 142.

7942. Coolidge, Grace A. "Making Ourselves at Home in the White House." *American Magazine* 108 (November 1929): 20-21, 159, 160, 163-164.

7943. Coolidge, Grace A. "When I Became the First Lady." *American Magazine* 108 (September 1929): 11-13, 104, 106, 108.

7944. Dawes, Charles G. *Notes as Vice President, 1928-1929.* Boston: Little, Brown, 1935.

7945. Fuess, Claude M. "Calvin Coolidge — Twenty Years After." *American Antiquarian Society Proceedings* 63 (October 21, 1953): 351-369.

7946. Gladstone, Kerana. "The Man from the People: Calvin Coolidge." *Vermont History* 30 (January 1962): 43-49.

7947. Green, Horace. "Coolidge as a Student." *Forum* 71 (January 1924): 35-40.

7948. Green, Horace. "Coolidge on Beacon Hill." *Forum* 71 (February 1924): 214-219.

7949. Harvey, George. "Calvin Coolidge." *North American Review* 219 (June 1924): 721-741.

7950. Kilmartin, Thomas W. "The Last Shall Be First: The Amherst College Days of Calvin Coolidge." *Historical Journal of Western Massachusetts* 5 (1977): 1-12.

7951. McKee, John H., comp. *Coolidge Wit and Wisdom: 125 Short Stories about "Cal."* New York: Stokes, 1933.

7952. Meredith, H. L. "Beyond Humor: Will Rogers and Calvin Coolidge." *Vermont History* 40 (Summer 1972): 178-184.

7953. Reichley, Nancy. "'Silent Cal' Coolidge's 100th Birthday Commemorated in Showcase Exhibit." *Library of Congress Information Bulletin* 31 (June 30, 1972): 292-293.

7954. Roberts, Kenneth L. *Concentrated New England: A Sketch of Calvin Coolidge.* Indianapolis, IN: Bobbs-Merrill, 1924.

7955. Ross, Ishbel. *Grace Coolidge and Her Era: The Story of a President's Wife.* New York: Dodd, Mead, 1962.

7956. Scandrett, Richard M., and Richard Pollenberg. "Remembering Calvin Coolidge: An Oral History Memoir." *Vermont History* 40 (Summer 1972): 190-215.

7957. See, Anna P. "President Calvin Coolidge, Product of the Pioneers." *Daughters of the American Revolution Magazine* 57 (November 1923): 637-644.

7958. Silver, Thomas B. "Coolidge and the Historians." *American Scholar* 50 (Autumn 1981): 501-517.

7959. Silver, Thomas B. *Coolidge and the Historians.* Durham, NC: Carolina Academic, 1983.

7960. Silver, Thomas B. "Prelude to an Interpretation: Coolidge and the Historians." Ph.D. dissertation, Claremont Graduate School, 1980.

7961. Slosson, Preston W. "Calvin Coolidge: His Place in History." *Current History* 33 (October 1930): 1-6.

7962. Soule, Harris W. "The White House Calling: A Reminiscence of Calvin Coolidge at Plymouth, Vermont." *Vermont History* 37 (Winter 1969): 49-51.

7963. Teagle, Rhoda. "An Ex-Vermonter Recalls Calvin Coolidge: An Unpublished Letter Written in 1924." *Vermont History* 38 (Summer 1970): 204-206.

7964. Totten, John R. "Calvin Coolidge." *New York Genealogical and Biographical Record* 64 (1936): 101-105.

7965. Weeks, Eugene M. *Have Faith in Coolidge!* Boston: Seaver-Howland Press, 1923.

7966. Whiting, William F. *Hon. Calvin Coolidge, LL.D., An Appreciation and Interpretation.* Boston: New England Historic Genealogical Society, 1933.

7967. Woods, Robert A. *The Preparation of Calvin Coolidge: An Interpretation.* Boston: Houghton Mifflin, 1924.

Public Career

7968. Abels, Jules. *In the Time of Silent Cal.* New York: Putnam, 1969.

7969. Asbury, Herbert. *The Great Illusion: An Informal History of Prohibition.* Garden City, NY: Doubleday, 1950.

7970. Barton, Bruce. "A Governor Who Stays on the Job: A Sketch of Calvin Coolidge of Massachusetts." *Outlook* 124 (April 28, 1920): 756-757.

7971. Blair, John L., ed. "The Clark-Coolidge Correspondence and the Election of 1932." *Vermont History* 34 (April 1966): 83-114.

7972. Bradford, Gamaliel. "The Genius of the Average: Calvin Coolidge." *Atlantic Monthly* 145 (January 1930): 1-13.

7973. Chalmers, David M. *Hooded Americanism.* Garden City, NY: Doubleday, 1965.

7974. Fenno, Richard F., Jr. "Coolidge: Representative of the People." *Current History* 39 (October 1960): 208-212.

7975. Fleser, Arthur F. "Coolidge's Delivery: Everybody Liked It." *Southern Speech Journal* 32 (Winter 1966): 98-104.

7976. Fleser, Arthur F. "Coolidge's Delivery: Everybody Liked It." *Vermont History* 38 (Autumn 1970): 320-325.

7977. Fleser, Arthur F. "A New England Education: The Early Career and Rhetorical Training of Calvin Coolidge." *Vermont History* 35 (July 1967): 151-159.

7978. Glad, Paul W. "Progressives and the Business Culture of the 1920s." *Journal of American History* 53 (June 1966): 75-89.

7979. Hoffman, Frederick J. "The Temper of the Twenties." *Minnesota Review* 1 (Fall 1960): 36-41.

7980. Leighton, Isabel. *The Aspirin Age.* New York: Simon and Schuster, 1949.

7981. Link, Arthur S. "What Happened to the Progressive Movement in the 1920's." *American Historical Review* 64 (July 1959): 849-863.

7982. Mackay, Kenneth C. *The Progressive Movement of 1924.* New York: Columbia University Press, 1947.

7983. Maddox, Robert J. "Keeping Cool with Coolidge." *Journal of American History* 53 (March 1967): 772-780.

7984. Moos, Malcolm, ed. *A Carnival of Buncombe.* Baltimore, MD: Johns Hopkins University Press, 1956.

7985. Welliver, Judson C. "Calvin Coolidge — Unique Political Figure." *Review of Reviews* 70 (July 1924): 51-62.

Presidential Years

7986. Abbott, Lawrence F. "Rating the

President." *Outlook* 150 (September 26, 1928): 849-851.

7987. Abrams, Richard M. *The Burdens of Progress: 1900-1929*. Glenview, IL: Scott, Foresman, 1978.

7988. Barber, James D. "Classifying and Predicting Presidential Styles: Two 'Weak' Presidents." *Journal of Social Issues* 24 (July 1968): 51-80.

7989. Blair, John L. "Calvin Coolidge and the Advent of Radio Politics." *Vermont History* 44 (Winter 1976): 28-37.

7990. Blair, John L. "Coolidge the Image-Maker: The President and the Press, 1923-1929." *New England Quarterly* 46 (December 1973): 499-522.

7991. Brown, Wilson. "Aide to Four Presidents." *American Heritage* 6 (February 1955): 66-96.

7992. Carter, John. "Third Term: An Open Letter to President Coolidge." *Forum* 77 (June 1927): 943-946; 78 (July 1927): 139-143; 79 (August 1927): 310.

7993. Clemens, Cyril, and Athern P. Daggett. "Coolidge's 'I Do Not Choose to Run': Granite or Putty?" *New England Quarterly* 18 (June 1945): 147-163.

7994. "Coolidge's Renunciation." *Outlook* 146 (August 17, 1927): 495-497.

7995. Cornwell, Elmer E., Jr. "Coolidge and Presidential Leadership." *Public Opinion Quarterly* 21 (Summer 1957): 265-278.

7996. Falk, Gerhard. "Old Calvin Never Died: Puritanical Rhetoric by Four American Presidents Concerning Public Welfare." In *An American Historian: Essays to Honor Selig Alder,* edited by Milton Plesur, 183-190. Buffalo: State University of New York, 1980.

7997. Ferrell, Robert H., and Howard H. Quint. *The Talkative President: The Off-the-Record Press Conferences of Calvin Coolidge*. New York: Garland, 1979.

7998. Fess, Simeon D. "Shall Mr. Coolidge Have a Second Elective Term?" *American Review of Reviews* 75 (June 1927): 601-608.

7999. Gilbert, Clinton W. "President Coolidge." *Century Magazine* 107 (March 1924): 643-651.

8000. Goodfellow, Guy F. "Calvin Coolidge: A Study of Presidential Inaction." Ph.D. dissertation, University of Maryland, 1969.

8001. Green, Horace. "Coolidge and the Police Strike." *Forum* 71 (April 1924): 479-487.

8002. Harvey, George. "Paramount Issue, Coolidge or Chaos." *North American Review* 220 (September 1924): 1-9.

8003. Johnson, Roger T. "Part-Time Leader: Senator Charles L. McNary and the McNary-Haugen Bill." *Agricultural History* 54 (January 1980): 527-541.

8004. Kane, Richard D. "The Federal Segregation of the Blacks during the Presidential Administrations of Warren G. Harding and Calvin Coolidge." *Pan-African Journal* 7 (Summer 1974): 153-171.

8005. Lang, Louis J. "How Coolidge Got the News." *Outlook* 135 (September 5, 1923): 22-25.

8006. Lockwood, Charles. "President Calvin Coolidge, b. July 4, 1872: A Centennial at Plymouth Notch, Vt." *Antiques* 102 (July 1972): 108-112.

8007. Lyons, Louis M. "Calvin Coolidge and the Press." *Nieman Reports* 18 (September 1964): 6-9.

8008. McCoy, Donald R. *Calvin Coolidge, The Quiet President*. New York: Macmillan, 1967.

8009. McCoy, Samuel. "Trials of the White House Spokesman." *Independent* 115 (September 19, 1925): 317-319.

8010. Margulies, Herbert F. "The Senate and the World Court." *Capitol Studies* 4 (Fall 1976): 37-52.

8011. Merritt, Dixon. "Calvin Coolidge and His Job." *Outlook* 140 (May 20, 1925): 103-107.

8012. Murray, Robert K. *The Politics of Normalcy: Governmental Theory and Practice in the Harding-Coolidge Era.* New York: Norton, 1973.

8013. O'Connor, Richard. "Mr. Coolidge's Jungle War in Nicaragua, 1927-1933." *American Heritage* 19 (December 1967): 36-39, 89-93.

8014. Orton, Vrest. *Calvin Coolidge's Unique Vermont Inauguration: The Facts Winnowed from the Chaff: The Authentic Account of the Swearing in of Calvin Coolidge as 30th President of the United States by His Father at the Coolidge Homestead, Plymouth Notch, Vermont in 1923.* Rutland, VT: Tuttle, 1960.

8015. "President Coolidge and the Court." *Canadian Bar Review* 3 (April 1925): 221.

8016. "Reflections of a Retiring President." *Review of Reviews* 79 (January 1929): 88-89.

8017. Rofinot, Henry L. "Normalcy and the Farmer: Agricultural Policy under Harding and Coolidge, 1920-1928." Ph.D. dissertation, Columbia University, 1958.

8018. Russell, Francis. "Coolidge and the Boston Police Strike." *Antioch Review* 16 (December 1956): 403-415.

8019. Smith, Beverly. "To Cuba with Cal." *Saturday Evening Post* 1 (February 1958): 16, 17, 76, 78-79.

8020. Snyder, J. Richard. "Coolidge, Costigan, and the Tariff Commission." *Mid-America* 50 (April 1968): 131-148.

8021. Stewart, David M. "Supreme Court Appointments during the Harding and Coolidge Administrations: Influence, Critics, and Voting." Ph.D. dissertation, Wayne State University, 1974.

8022. Sullivan, Mark. "A Third Term for Coolidge?" *World Today* 45 (March 1925): 284-289.

8023. Tyson, Carl N. "I'm Off to Coolidge's Follies: Will Rogers and the Presidential Nominations, 1924-1932." *Chronicles of Oklahoma* 54 (Summer 1976): 192-198.

8024. "Use of an Electoral Deadlock." *New Republic* 40 (October 29, 1924): 216-217.

8025. Whelpley, James D. "President Coolidge Chooses." *Fortnightly Review* 128 (September 1927): 298-306.

8026. Whiting, Edward E. "The President." *Atlantic Monthly* 132 (November 1923): 577-585.

8027. "Will Coolidge Shatter the Third-Term Tradition?" *Literary Digest* 93 (May 14, 1927): 5-7.

8028. Zieger, Robert H. "Pinchot and Coolidge: The Politics of the 1923 Anthracite Crisis." *Journal of American History* 52 (December 1965): 566-581.

Writings

8029. Coolidge, Calvin. *America's Need for Education, and Other Educational Addresses.* Boston: Houghton Mifflin, 1925.

8030. Coolidge, Calvin. *The Autobiography of Calvin Coolidge.* New York: Cosmopolitan Book Corporation, 1929.

8031. Coolidge, Calvin. *Calvin Coolidge, His Ideas of Citizenship as Revealed through His Speeches and Writings*, edited by Edward E. Whiting. Boston: W. A. Wilde, 1924.

8032. Coolidge, Calvin. *Foundations of the*

Republic: Speeches and Addresses. New York: Scribner's, 1926.

8033. Coolidge, Calvin. *Have Faith in Massachusetts: A Collection of Speeches and Messages.* Boston: Houghton Mifflin, 1919.

8034. Coolidge, Calvin. "The President Lives under a Multitude of Eyes." *American Magazine* 108 (August 1, 1929): 19-21.

8035. Coolidge, Calvin. *The Price of Freedom: Speeches and Addresses.* New York: Scribner's, 1924.

8036. Coolidge, Calvin. "What It Means to Be President." *American Magazine* 108 (July 1929): 15-17.

8037. Coolidge, Calvin. *Your Son, Calvin Coolidge: A Selection of Letters from Calvin Coolidge to His Father,* edited by Edward C. Latham. Hanover, NH: University Press of New England, 1968.

8038. Slemp, Campbell B. *The Mind of the President, As Revealed by Himself in His Own Words: President Coolidge's Views on Public Questions.* Garden City, NY: Doubleday, 1926.

Herbert Hoover

Biographies

8039. Burner, David. *Herbert Hoover: A Public Life.* New York: Knopf, 1979.

8040. Corey, Herbert. *The Truth about Hoover.* Boston: Houghton Mifflin, 1932.

8041. Cook, Claude R. "Herbert Hoover's Notable Career." *Annals of Iowa* 32 (October 1954): 460-469.

8042. Darling, Jay N. *As Ding Saw Hoover,* edited by John M. Henry. Ames: Iowa State College Press, 1954.

8043. Davis, Joseph. "Herbert Hoover 1874-1964: Another Appraisal." *South Atlantic Quarterly* 68 (Summer 1969): 295-318.

8044. Degler, Carl N. "The Ordeal of Herbert Hoover." *Yale Review* 52 (June 1963): 563-583.

8045. Doane, Franklin C. *The Master Organizer: Herbert Hoover.* New York: Riverside Press, 1928.

8046. Eckley, Wilton. *Herbert Hoover.* Boston: G. K. Hall, 1980.

8047. Emerson, Edwin. *Hoover and His Times: Looking Back through the Years.* Garden City, NY: Garden City Publishing Co., 1932.

8048. Gelfand, Lawrence E., ed. *Herbert Hoover: The Great War and Its Aftermath, 1914-1923.* Iowa City: University of Iowa Press, 1979.

8049. Guerrant, Edward O. *Herbert Hoover: Franklin Roosevelt: Comparisons and Contrasts.* Cleveland, OH: H. Allen, 1960.

8050. Hamill, John. *The Strange Career of Mr. Hoover under Two Flags.* New York: Faro, 1931.

8051. Hard, William. *Who's Hoover?* New York: Dodd, Mead, 1928.

8052. Hinshaw, David. *Herbert Hoover, American Quaker.* New York: Farrar, Straus, 1950.

8053. Hoff-Wilson, Joan. *Herbert Hoover, Forgotten Progressive.* Boston: Little, Brown, 1975.

8054. Irwin, William H. *Herbert Hoover, A Reminiscent Biography.* New York: Grosset and Dunlap, 1928.

8055. Joslin, Theodore G. *Hoover Off the Record.* Garden City, NY: Doubleday, 1934.

8056. Kellogg, Vernon. *Herbert Hoover, The Man and His Work.* New York: Appleton, 1920.

8057. Knox, John. *The Great Mistake.* Washington, DC: National Foundation Press, 1930.

8058. Lane, Rose W. *The Making of Herbert Hoover.* New York: Century, 1920.

8059. Liggett, Walter W. *The Rise of Herbert Hoover.* New York: H. K. Fly, 1932.

8060. Lyons, Eugene. *Herbert Hoover, A Biography.* Garden City, NY: Doubleday, 1964.

8061. Lyons, Eugene. *The Herbert Hoover Story.* Washington, DC: Human Events, 1959.

8062. Lyons, Eugene. *Our Unknown Ex-President: A Portrait of Herbert Hoover.* Garden City, NY: Doubleday, 1948.

8063. McGee, Dorothy H. *Herbert Hoover: Engineer, Humanitarian, Statesman.* New York: Dodd, Mead, 1959.

8064. Miller, Walter L. *The Life and Accomplishments of Herbert Hoover.* Durham, NC: Moore Publishing Co., 1970.

8065. Nash, George H. *The Life of Herbert Hoover: The Engineer, 1874-1914.* New York: Norton, 1983.

8066. Reeves, Earl. *This Man Hoover.* New York: A. I. Burt Co., 1928.

8067. Robinson, Edgar E., and Vaughn D. Bornet. *Herbert Hoover: President of the United States.* Stanford, CA: Hoover Institute Press, 1975.

8068. Silva, Ruth C. *Rum, Religion, and Votes: 1928 Re-Examined.* University Park: Pennsylvania State University Press, 1962.

8069. Smith, Gene. *The Shattered Dream: Herbert Hoover and the Great Depression.* New York: Morrow, 1970.

8070. Smith, Richard N. *An Uncommon Man: The Triumph of Herbert Hoover.* New York: Simon and Schuster, 1984.

8071. Steinberg, Alfred. *Herbert Hoover.* New York: Putnam, 1967.

8072. Train, Arthur C. *The Strange Attacks on Herbert Hoover, A Current Example of What We Do to Our Presidents.* New York: John Day, 1932.

8073. Warren, Harris G. *Herbert Hoover and the Great Depression.* New York: Oxford University Press, 1959.

8074. Watson, Richard L., Jr. "Theodore Roosevelt and Herbert Hoover." *South Atlantic Quarterly* 53 (January 1954): 109-129.

8075. Wilbur, Ray L., and Arthur M. Hyde. *The Hoover Policies.* New York: Scribner's, 1937.

8076. Wolfe, Harold. *Herbert Hoover: Public Servant and Leader of the Loyal Opposition — A Study of His Life and Career.* New York: Exposition Press, 1956.

8077. Wood, Clement. *Herbert Clark Hoover: An American Tragedy.* New York: Michael Swain, 1932.

8078. Zieger, Robert H. "Herbert Hoover: A Reinterpretation." *American Historical Review* 81 (October 1976): 800-810.

Private Life

8079. Bearss, Edwin C. *Historical Base Map and Ground Study: Herbert Hoover National Historic Site, West Branch, Iowa.* Washington, DC: Division of History, Office of Archeology and Historic Preservation, 1968.

8080. Best, Gary D. *Herbert Hoover: The Postpresidential Years, 1933-1964.* 2 vols. Stanford, CA: Hoover Institution Press, 1983.

8081. Dexter, Walter F. *Herbert Hoover and American Individualism: A Modern Interpretation of a National Ideal.* New York: Macmillan, 1932.

8082. Dibner, Bern. "Hoover and Agricola." *Technology and Culture* 13 (July 1972): 417-425.

8083. Gibson, Hugh. "Herbert C. Hoover." *Century Magazine* 94 (August 1917): 508-517.

8084. Hampton, Vernon B. *Breasting World Frontiers: Herbert Hoover's Achievements.* Stapleton, NY: John Willig Press, 1933.

8085. Hart, James. "Mr. Hoover's Eligibility for the Presidency." *Virginia Law Review* 15 (March 1929): 476-478.

8086. Herbert Hoover Presidential Library. *Bibliographical Guide to the Life and Interests of Herbert Clark Hoover.* West Branch, IA: Hoover Presidential Library, n.d.

8087. Hoxie, R. Gordon. "Herbert Hoover: Multi-National Man." *Presidential Studies Quarterly* 7 (Winter 1977): 49-52.

8088. Johnson, James P. "Herbert Hoover and David Copperfield: A Tale of Two Childhoods." *Journal of Psychohistory* 7 (Spring 1980): 467-475.

8089. Kellogg, Vernon. "The Story of Hoover." *Everybody's Magazine* 42 (February 1920): 18-22; (March 1920): 33-37; (April 1920): 33-38; (May 1920): 18-22; (June 1920): 32-36.

8090. McLean, Hulda H. *The Genealogy of the Herbert Hoover Family.* Stanford, CA: Hoover Institution Press, 1967.

8091. Nash, George H. "The Social Philosophy of Herbert Hoover." *Annals of Iowa* 45 (Fall 1980): 478-496.

8092. Nelsen, Clair E. "The Image of Herbert Hoover as Reflected in the American Press." Ph.D. dissertation, Stanford University, 1956.

8093. O'Brien, James J. *Hoover's Millions and How He Made Them.* New York: James J. O'Brien Publishing Co., 1932.

8094. Olson, James S. "The Philosophy of Herbert Hoover: A Contemporary Perspective." *Annals of Iowa* 43 (Winter 1976): 181-191.

8095. Polley, Robert L., ed. *Herbert Hoover's Challenge to America: His Life and Words by the Editors of Country Beautiful.* Waukesha, WI: Country Beautiful Foundation, 1965.

8096. Pryor, Helen B. "Lou Henry Hoover." *Palimpsest* 52 (July 1971): 353-400.

8097. Pryor, Helen B. *Lou Henry Hoover: Gallant First Lady.* New York: Dodd, Mead, 1969.

8098. Schacht, John N. "The Depression and After." *Palimpsest* 63 (January/February 1982): 12-29.

8099. Schacht, John N. "The Providers." *Palimpsest* 63 (January/February 1982): 2-32.

8100. Shriver, Phillip R. "A Hoover Vignette." *Ohio History* 91 (1982): 74-82.

8101. Stratton, Maud. *Herbert Hoover's Home Town: Early History and Environment of the First President Born West of the Mississippi River.* West Branch, IA: West Branch Times, 1938.

8102. Swisher, Jacob A. *Herbert Hoover's Boyhood.* Iowa City: Armstrong, 1928.

8103. Throne, Mildred. "Herbert Hoover." *Palimpsest* 43 (September 1962): 345-360.

8104. Wade, Mary H. *Real Americans.* Boston: Little, Brown, 1922.

8105. Wagner, Bill. "My Friend Herbert Hoover." *Annals of Iowa* 37 (Winter 1965): 536-541.

8106. Wagner, William J. "A Philatec History of Herbert Hoover." *Annals of Iowa* 38 (Winter 1966): 161-181.

Public Career

8107. Adams, David K. "Hoover and Roosevelt." *British Association for American Studies Bulletin* 1 (September 1960): 72-78.

8108. Arnold, Peri E. "The 'Great Engineer' as Administrator: Herbert Hoover and Modern Bureaucracy." *Review of Politics* 42 (July 1980): 329-348.

8109. Arnold, Peri E. "Herbert Hoover and the Continuity of American Public Policy." *Public Policy* 20 (Fall 1972): 525-544.

8110. Batman, Richard D. "The Road to the Presidency: Hoover, Johnson, and the California Republican Party, 1920-1924." Ph.D. dissertation, University of Southern California, 1965.

8111. Best, Gary D. "An Evangelist among Skeptics: Hoover's Bid for the Leadership of the GOP, 1937-1938." *American Philosophical Society Proceedings* 123 (February 1979): 1-14.

8112. Best, Gary D. "Herbert Hoover as Titular Leader of the GOP, 1933-35." *Mid-America* 61 (April/July 1979): 81-97.

8113. Best, Gary D. "Herbert Hoover's Technical Mission to Yugoslavia, 1919-20." *Annals of Iowa* 42 (Fall 1974): 443-459.

8114. Best, Gary D. "The Hoover-for-President Boom of 1920." *Mid-America* 53 (October 1971): 227-244.

8115. Best, Gary D. *The Politics of American Individualism: Herbert Hoover in Transition, 1918-1921.* Westport, CT: Greenwood Press, 1975.

8116. Best, Gary D. "Totalitarianism or Peace: Herbert Hoover and the Road to War, 1939-1941." *Annals of Iowa* 44 (Winter 1979): 516-529.

8117. Brandes, Joseph. *Herbert Hoover and Economic Diplomacy: Department of Commerce Policy, 1921-1928.* Pittsburgh, PA: University of Pittsburgh Press, 1962.

8118. Brandes, Joseph. "Herbert Hoover as Secretary of Commerce: Economic Foreign Policy, 1921-1928." Ph.D. dissertation, New York University, 1958.

8119. Carleton, William G. "The Popish Plot of 1928: Smith-Hoover Presidential Campaign." *Forum* 112 (September 1949): 141-147.

8120. Chavez, Leo E. "Herbert Hoover and Food Relief: An Application of American Ideology." Ph.D. dissertation, University of Michigan, 1976.

8121. Clements, Kendrick A. "Herbert Hoover and Conservation, 1921-33." *American Historical Review* 89 (February 1984): 67-88.

8122. Clements, Kendrick A. "Herbert Hoover and the Fish." *Journal of Psychohistory* 10 (Winter 1983): 333-348.

8123. Cuff, Robert D. "The Dilemmas of Voluntarism: Hoover and the Pork-Packing Agreement of 1917-1919." *Agricultural History* 53 (October 1979): 727-747.

8124. Cuff, Robert D. "Herbert Hoover, The Ideology of Voluntarism and War Organization during the Great War." *Journal of American History* 64 (September 1977): 358-372.

8125. Deane, Hugh. "Herbert Hoover and the Kailan Mines Swindle." *Eastern Horizon* 20 (May 1981): 34-38.

8126. DeConde, Alexander. "Herbert Hoover's Good Will Tour." *Historian* 12 (Spring 1950): 167-183.

8127. Drake, Douglas C. "Herbert Hoover, Ecologist: The Politics of Oil Pollution Control, 1921-1926." *Mid-America* 55 (July 1973): 207-228.

8128. Everman, Henry E. "Herbert Hoover and the New Deal, 1933-1940." Ph.D.

dissertation, Louisiana State University, Agricultural and Mechanical College, 1971.

8129. Fesler, James W. "Administrative Literature and the Second Hoover Commission Reports." *American Political Science Review* 51 (March 1957): 135-157.

8130. Garcia, George F. "Herbert Hoover and the Issue of Race." *Annals of Iowa* 44 (Winter 1979): 507-515.

8131. Garvey, Daniel E. "Secretary Hoover and the Quest for Broadcast Regulations." *Journalism History* 3 (Autumn 1976): 66-70.

8132. Gervasi, Frank. *Big Government: The Meaning and Purpose of the Hoover Commission Report.* New York: McGraw-Hill, 1949.

8133. Giglio, James N. "Voluntarism and Public Policy between World War I and the New Deal: Herbert Hoover and the American Child Health Association." *Presidential Studies Quarterly* 13 (Summer 1983): 430-452.

8134. Guth, James L. "Herbert Hoover, the U.S. Food Administration, and the Dairy Industry, 1917-1918." *Business History Review* 55 (Summer 1981): 170-187.

8135. Hall, Tom G., Jr. "Cheap Bread from Dear Wheat: Herbert Hoover, the Wilson Administration, and the Management of Wheat Prices, 1916-1920." Ph.D. dissertation, University of California, Davis, 1970.

8136. Hawley, Ellis W., ed. *Herbert Hoover as Secretary of Commerce, 1921-1928: Studies in New Era Thought and Practice.* Iowa City: University of Iowa Press, 1981.

8137. Hawley, Ellis W. "Herbert Hoover, the Commerce Secretariat, and the Vision of an 'Associative State,' 1921-1928." *Journal of American History* 61 (June 1974): 116-140.

8138. Hawley, Ellis W. "Secretary Hoover and the Bituminous Coal Problem, 1921-1928." *Business History Review* 42 (Autumn 1968): 247-270.

8139. Hill, Harry W., ed. *President-Elect Herbert Hoover's Goodwill Cruise to Central and South America, This Being a Log of the Trip Aboard the U.S.S. Maryland.* San Francisco: Book Press, 1929.

8140. Hoff-Wilson, Joan. "Herbert Hoover's Plan for Ending the Second World War." *International Historical Review* 1 (January 1979): 84-102.

8141. Hoff-Wilson, Joan. "Hoover's Agricultural Policies, 1921-1929." *Agricultural History* 51 (April 1977): 335-361.

8142. Hurvitz, Haggai. "The Meaning of Industrial Conflict in Some Ideologies of the Early 1920's: The AFL, Organized Employers, and Herbert Hoover." Ph.D. dissertation, Columbia University, 1971.

8143. Jansky, Cyril M., Jr. "The Contribution of Herbert Hoover to Broadcasting." *Journal of Broadcasting* 1 (Summer 1957): 241-249.

8144. Johnson, Glenn A. "Secretary of Commerce Herbert C. Hoover: The First Regulator of American Broadcasting, 1921-1928." Ph.D. dissertation, University of Iowa, 1970.

8145. Johnson, William R. "Herbert Hoover and the Regulation of Grain Futures." *Mid-America* 51 (July 1969): 155-174.

8146. Karlsrud, Robert A. "The Hoover Labor Department: A Study in Bureaucratic Divisiveness." Ph.D. dissertation, University of California, 1972.

8147. Koerselman, Gary H. "Herbert Hoover and the Farm Crisis of the Twenties: A Study of the Commerce Department's Efforts to Solve the Agricultural Depression, 1921-1928." Ph.D. dissertation, Northern Illinois University, 1971.

8148. Koerselman, Gary H. "Secretary Hoover and National Farm Policy: Problems of Leadership." *Agricultural History* 51 (April 1977): 378-395.

8149. Krog, Carl E. "Organizing the Production of Leisure: Herbert Hoover and the Conservation Movement in the 1920s." *Wisconsin Magazine of History* 67 (Spring 1984): 199-218.

8150. Lee, David D. "Herbert Hoover and the Development of Commercial Aviation, 1921-26." *Business History Review* 58 (Spring 1984): 78-102.

8151. Lerski, George J., comp. *Herbert Hoover and Poland: Documentary History of a Friendship.* Stanford, CA: Hoover Institution Press, 1977.

8152. Lochner, Louis P. *Herbert Hoover and Germany.* New York: Macmillan, 1960.

8153. Lohof, Bruce A. "Herbert Hoover, Spokesman of Humane Efficiency: The Mississippi Flood of 1927." *American Quarterly* 22 (Fall 1970): 690-700.

8154. Lohof, Bruce A. "Hoover and the Mississippi Valley Flood of 1927: A Case Study of the Political Thought of Herbert Hoover." D.S.S. dissertation, Syracuse University, 1968.

8155. Lowitt, Richard. "Progressive Farm Leaders and Hoover's Moratorium." *Mid-America* 50 (July 1968): 236-239.

8156. McCarthy, G. Michael. "The Brown Derby Campaign in West Tennessee: Smith, Hoover, and the Politics of Race." *West Tennessee Historical Society Papers* 27 (1973): 81-98.

8157. McCarthy, G. Michael. "Smith vs. Hoover — The Politics of Race in West Tennessee." *Phylon* 39 (June 1978): 154-168.

8158. Margulies, Herbert F. "The Collaboration of Herbert Hoover and Irvine Lenroot, 1921-1928." *North Dakota Quarterly* 45 (Summer 1977): 30-46.

8159. Metcalf, Evan B. "Secretary Hoover and the Emergency of Macroeconomics Management." *Business History Review* 49 (Spring 1975): 60-80.

8160. Moe, Ronald C. *The Hoover Commissions Revisited.* Boulder, CO: Westview Press, 1982.

8161. Moe, Ronald C. *The Two Hoover Commissions in Retrospect.* Washington, DC: Congressional Research Service, 1982.

8162. Mrozek, Donald J. "Progressive Dissenter: Herbert Hoover's Opposition to Truman's Overseas Military Policy." *Annals of Iowa* 43 (Spring 1976): 275-291.

8163. Muessig, Raymond H. "Herbert Hoover and Education." Ed.D. dissertation, Stanford University, 1959.

8164. Nash, Gerald D. "Herbert Hoover and the Origins of the Reconstruction Finance Corporation." *Mississippi Valley Historical Review* 46 (December 1959): 455-468.

8165. Nelsen, Clair E. "Herbert Hoover, Republican." *Centennial Review* 17 (Winter 1973): 41-63.

8166. Olson, James S. "The End of Voluntarism: Herbert Hoover and the National Credit Corporation." *Annals of Iowa* 41 (Fall 1972): 104-113.

8167. Olson, James S. *Herbert Hoover and the Reconstruction Finance Corporation.* Ames: Iowa State University Press, 1977.

8168. Orfield, Lester B. "Hoover Commission and Federal Executive Reorganization." *Temple Law Quarterly* 24 (October 1950): 162-217.

8169. Prestage, Jewel L. "The Status of the First Hoover Commission Report: An Analysis of the Roles of the President and

Congress." Ph.D. dissertation, University of Iowa, 1954.

8170. Runfola, Ross T. "Herbert Hoover as Secretary of Commerce, 1921-1923: Domestic Economic Planning in the Harding Cabinet." Ph.D. dissertation, State University of New York, Buffalo, 1973.

8171. Savage, Hugh. "Political Independents of the Hoover Era: The Progressive Insurgents of the Senate." Ph.D. dissertation, University of Illinois, 1961.

8172. Schofield, Kent M. "The Figure of Herbert Hoover in the 1928 Campaign." Ph.D. dissertation, University of California, 1966.

8173. Schofield, Kent M. "The Public Image of Herbert Hoover in the 1928 Campaign." *Mid-America* 51 (October 1969): 278-293.

8174. Shideler, James H. "Herbert Hoover and the Federal Farm Board Project, 1921-1925." *Mississippi Valley Historical Review* 42 (March 1956): 710-729.

8175. Stratton, David H. "Two Western Senators and Teapot Dome: Thomas J. Walsh and Albert B. Fall." *Pacific Northwest Quarterly* 65 (April 1974): 57-65.

8176. Surface, Frank M., and Raymond L. Bland. *American Food in the World War and Reconstruction Period: Operations of the Organizations under the Direction of Herbert Hoover, 1914 to 1924.* Stanford, CA: Stanford University Press, 1931.

8177. "Task Force Report to Hoover Commission on 'Regulatory Commissions.'" *ICC Practitioners' Journal* 16 (April 1949): 651-660.

8178. U.S. Commission on Organization of the Executive Branch of the Government. *The Hoover Commission Report on Organization of the Executive Branch of the Government.* New York: McGraw-Hill, 1949.

8179. Van Meter, Robert H., Jr. "The Washington Conference of 1921-1922: A New Look." *Pacific Historical Review* 46 (November 1977): 603-624.

8180. Weissman, Benjamin M. "Herbert Hoover's 'Treaty' with Soviet Russia: August 10, 1921." *Slavic Review* 28 (June 1969): 276-288.

8181. Willis, Edward F. *Herbert Hoover and the Russian Prisoners of World War I: A Study in Diplomacy and Relief, 1918-1919.* Stanford, CA: Stanford University Press, 1951.

8182. Winters, Donald L. "The Hoover-Wallace Controversy during World War I." *Annals of Iowa* 39 (Spring 1969): 586-597.

8183. Zieger, Robert H. "Herbert Hoover, the Wage Earner, and the 'New Economic System,' 1919-1929." *Business History Review* 51 (Spring 1977): 161-189.

8184. Zieger, Robert H. "Labor, Progressivism, and Herbert Hoover in the 1920's." *Wisconsin Magazine of History* 58 (Spring 1975): 196-208.

Presidential Years

8185. Accinelli, Robert D. "The Hoover Administration and the World Court." *Peace and Change* 4 (Fall 1977): 28-36.

8186. Albjerg, Victor L. "Hoover: The Presidency in Transition." *Current History* 39 (October 1960): 213-219.

8187. Barber, James D. "Classifying and Predicting Presidential Styles: Two 'Weak' Presidents." *Journal of Social Issues* 24 (July 1968): 51-80.

8188. Barber, William J. *From New Era to New Deal: Herbert Hoover, the Economists, and American Economic Policy, 1921-1933.* New York: Cambridge University Press, 1985.

8189. Berkowitz, Edward D., and Kim McQuaid. "Bureaucrats as 'Social Engineers': Federal Welfare Programs in Herbert Hoover's America." *American Journal of Economics and Sociology* 39 (October 1980): 321-335.

8190. Brown, Wilson. "Aide to Four Presidents." *American Heritage* 6 (February 1955): 66-96.

8191. Carmen, Ira H. "The President, Politics, and the Power of Appointment: Hoover's Nomination of Mr. Justice Cardozo." *Virginia Law Review* 55 (May 1969): 616-660.

8192. Cowley, Robert. "The Drought and the Dole: Herbert Hoover's Dismal Dilemma." *American Heritage* 23 (February 1972): 16-19, 92-99.

8193. Crowther, Samuel. *The Presidency vs. Hoover*. Garden City, NY: Doubleday, 1928.

8194. Current, Richard N. "The Stimson Doctrine and the Hoover Doctrine." *American Historical Review* 59 (April 1954): 513-542.

8195. Curry, Earl R. *Hoover's Dominican Diplomacy and the Origins of the Good Neighbor Policy*. New York: Garland, 1979.

8196. Davidson, Robert H. "Inaugurating the President." *Transmitter* 17 (April 1929): 3-8.

8197. Day, David S. "Herbert Hoover and Racial Politics: The DePriest Incident." *Journal of Negro History* 65 (Winter 1980): 6-17.

8198. DeConde, Alexander. *Herbert Hoover's Latin-American Policy*. Stanford, CA: Stanford University Press, 1951.

8199. DelPapa, Eugene M. "Herbert Hoover and the Struggle for Relief, 1930-1933." Ph.D. dissertation, Miami University, 1974.

8200. Dressler, Thomas H. B. "The Foreign Policies of American Individualism: Herbert Hoover, Reluctant Internationalist." Ph.D. dissertation, Brown University, 1973.

8201. Edwards, John C. "Herbert Hoover's Public Lands Policy: A Struggle for Control of the Western Domain." *Pacific Historian* 20 (Spring 1976): 34-45.

8202. Edwards, Richard E. "Herbert Hoover and the Public Relations Approach to Economic Recovery, 1929-1932." Ph.D. dissertation, University of Iowa, 1976.

8203. Fausold, Martin L. *The Presidency of Herbert Hoover*. Lawrence: University Press of Kansas, 1984.

8204. Fausold, Martin L. "President Hoover's Farm Policies, 1929-1933." *Agricultural History* 51 (April 1977): 362-377.

8205. Fausold, Martin L., and George Mazuzan, eds. *The Hoover Presidency: A Reappraisal*. Albany: State University of New York Press, 1974.

8206. Ferrell, Robert H. *American Diplomacy in the Great Depression: Hoover-Stimson Foreign Policy, 1929-1933*. New Haven, CT: Yale University Press, 1957.

8207. Garcia, George F. "Black Disaffection from the Republican Party during the Presidency of Herbert Hoover, 1928-1932." *Annals of Iowa* 45 (Fall 1980): 462-477.

8208. Gaus, John M. "The Hoover Commission: III. The Presidency." *American Political Science Review* 43 (October 1949): 952-958.

8209. Ginzl, David J. "Herbert Hoover and Republican Patronage Politics in the South, 1928-1932." Ph.D. dissertation, Syracuse University, 1977.

8210. Ginzl, David J. "Lily-Whites versus Blacks and Tans: Mississippi Republicans during the Hoover Administration." *Journal of Mississippi History* 42 (August 1980): 194-211.

8211. Ginzl, David J. "Patronage, Race, and Georgia Republicans during the Hoover Administration." *Georgia Historical Quarterly* 64 (Fall 1980): 280-293.

8212. Ginzl, David J. "The Politics of Patronage: Florida Republicans during the Hoover Administration." *Florida Historical Quarterly* 61 (July 1982): 1-19.

8213. Gustafson, Merlin. "President Hoover and the National Religion." *Journal of Church and State* 16 (Winter 1974): 85-100.

8214. Hamilton, David E. "Herbert Hoover and the Great Drought of 1930." *Journal of American History* 68 (March 1982): 850-875.

8215. Hard, William. "Hoover the President." *World's Work* 58 (September 1929): 85-89.

8216. "How Hoover Plays at His Summer White House." *Literary Digest* 102 (September 7, 1929): 30-34.

8217. Hoxie, R. Gordon. "Hoover and the Banking Crisis." *Presidential Studies Quarterly* 4 (Summer/Fall 1974): 25-28.

8218. Huthmacher, J. Joseph, and Warren I. Susman, eds. *Herbert Hoover and the Crisis of American Capitalism.* Cambridge, MA: Schenkman, 1973.

8219. Johnson, James P. "Herbert Hoover: Orphan as President." *USA Today* 108 (September 1979): 61-62.

8220. Johnson, James P. "Herbert Hoover: The Orphan as Children's Friend." *Prologue* 12 (Winter 1980): 192-206.

8221. Karl, Barry D. "Presidential Planning and Social Science Research: Mr. Hoover's Experts." *Perspectives in American History* 3 (1969): 347-412.

8222. Kehoe, Loretta. "The Relations of Herbert Hoover to Congress, 1929-1933." Master's thesis, Loyola University, 1949.

8223. Kottman, Richard N. "Herbert Hoover and the St. Lawrence Seaway Treaty of 1932." *New York History* 56 (July 1975): 314-346.

8224. Kottman, Richard N. "Herbert Hoover and the Smoot-Hawley Tariff: Canada, A Case Study." *Journal of American History* 62 (December 1975): 609-635.

8225. Kottman, Richard N. "Hoover and Canada: Diplomatic Appointments." *Canadian Historical Review* 51 (September 1970): 292-309.

8226. Kottman, Richard N. "The Hoover-Bennett Meeting of 1931: Mismanaged Summitry." *Annals of Iowa* 42 (Winter 1974): 205-221.

8227. Lambert, C. Roger. "Hoover and the Red Cross in the Arkansas Drought in 1930." *Arkansas Historical Quarterly* 29 (Spring 1970): 3-19.

8228. Lambert, C. Roger. "Hoover, the Red Cross, and Food for the Hungry." *Annals of Iowa* 44 (Winter 1978-1979): 530-540.

8229. Lee, David D. "The Politics of Less: The Trials of Herbert Hoover and Jimmy Carter." *Presidential Studies Quarterly* 13 (Spring 1983): 305-312.

8230. Lisio, Donald J. "A Blunder Becomes a Catastrophe: Hoover, the Legion, and the Bonus Army." *Wisconsin Magazine of History* 51 (Autumn 1967): 37-50.

8231. Lisio, Donald J. *The Presidency and Protest: Hoover, Conspiracy, and the Bonus Riot.* Columbia: University of Missouri Press, 1974.

8232. Lloyd, Craig. "Aggressive Introvert: A Study of Herbert Hoover and Public Relations Management, 1912-1932." Ph.D. dissertation, University of Iowa, 1970.

8233. Lowry, Edward G. "Preface to Hoover: What Must a President Have to Be Saved?" *Century Magazine* 119 (October 1929): 130-137.

8234. McCoy, Donald R. "Trends in Viewing Herbert Hoover, Franklin D. Roosevelt, Harry S. Truman, and Dwight D. Eisenhower." *Midwest Quarterly* 20 (Winter 1979): 117-136.

8235. Marsh, William J., Jr. *Our President Herbert Hoover.* New Milford, CT: William J. and Charles Marsh, 1930.

8236. Martin, William. "Hoover." In his *Statesmen of the War in Retrospect, 1918-1928,* 234-248. New York: Minton, Balch, 1928.

8237. Meredith, John R. "Herbert Hoover and the Armed Forces: A Study of Presidential Attitudes and Policy." Ph.D. dissertation, Northwestern University, 1971.

8238. Mullins, William H. "Self-Help in Seattle, 1931-32: Herbert Hoover's Concept of Cooperative Individualism and the Unemployed Citizens' League." *Pacific Northwest Quarterly* 72 (January 1981): 11-19.

8239. Myers, William S. *The Foreign Policies of Herbert Hoover, 1929-1933.* New York: Scribner's, 1940.

8240. Myers, William S., and Walter H. Newton. *The Hoover Administration: A Documented Narrative.* New York: Scribner's, 1936.

8241. O'Brien, Francis W. "Bicentennial Reflections on Herbert Hoover and the Supreme Court." *Iowa Law Review* 61 (December 1975): 397-419.

8242. O'Brien, Patrick G., and Philip T. Rosen. "Hoover and the Historians: The Resurrection of a President." *Annals of Iowa* 46 (Summer 1981): 25-42; (Fall 1981): 83-99.

8243. Olson, James S. "Herbert Hoover and 'War' on the Depression." *Palimpsest* 54 (July/August 1973): 26-31.

8244. Olson, James S. "Rehearsal for Disaster: Hoover, the R.F.C., and the Banking Crisis in Nevada, 1932-1933." *Western Historical Quarterly* 6 (April 1975): 149-161.

8245. O'Reilly, Kenneth. "Herbert Hoover and the FBI." *Annals of Iowa* 47 (Summer 1983): 46-63.

8246. Ortquist, Richard T. "Unemployment and Relief: Michigan's Response to the Depression during the Hoover Years." *Michigan History* 57 (Fall 1973): 209-236.

8247. Philip, Kenneth. "Herbert Hoover's New Era: A False Dawn for the American Indian, 1929-1932." *Rocky Mountain Social Science Journal* 9 (April 1972): 53-60.

8248. "President Hoover's New Policy." *American Bar Association Journal* 15 (June 1929): 323-325.

8249. Rankin, Robert S. "President Hoover and the Supreme Court." *South Atlantic Quarterly* 30 (October 1931): 427-438.

8250. Rhodes, Benjamin D. "Herbert Hoover and the War Debts, 1919-33." *Prologue* 6 (Summer 1974): 130-144.

8251. Rinn, Fauneil J. "President Hoover's Bad Press." *San Jose Studies* 1 (1975): 32-44.

8252. Robbins, William G. "Herbert Hoover's Indian Reformers under Attack: The Failures of Administrative Reform." *Mid-America* 63 (October 1981): 157-170.

8253. Rogers, Benjamin. "Dear Mr. President: The Hoover-Truman Correspondence." *Palimpsest* 55 (September/October 1974): 152-158.

8254. Romasco, Albert U. *The Poverty of Abundance: Hoover, the Nation, the De-*

pression. New York: Oxford University Press, 1968.

8255. Rosen, Elliot A. *Hoover, Roosevelt, and the Brains Trust: From Depression to New Deal.* New York: Columbia University Press, 1977.

8256. Russ, William A., Jr. "Time Lag and Political Change as Seen in the Administrations of Buchanan and Hoover." *South Atlantic Quarterly* 46 (July 1947): 336-343.

8257. Schwarz, Jordan A. *The Interregnum of Despair: Hoover, Congress, and the Depression.* Urbana: University of Illinois Press, 1970.

8258. Schwarz, Jordan A. "The Politics of Fear: Congress and the Depression during the Hoover Administration." Ph.D. dissertation, Columbia University, 1967.

8259. Showan, Daniel P. "The Hoover-Roosevelt Relationship during the Interregnum." *Lock Haven Bulletin* 1 (1961): 24-50.

8260. Sizer, Rosanne. "Herbert Hoover and the Smear Books, 1930-1932." *Annals of Iowa* 47 (Spring 1984): 343-361.

8261. Snyder, J. Richard. "Hoover and the Hawley-Smoot Tariff: A View of Executive Leadership." *Annals of Iowa* 38 (Winter 1973): 1173-1189.

8262. Sobel, Robert. *Herbert Hoover at the Onset of the Great Depression, 1929-1930.* Philadelphia: Lippincott, 1975.

8263. Tarter, Brent. "All Men Are Equal before Fishes: Herbert Hoover's Camp on the Rapidan." *Virginia Cavalcade* 30 (Spring 1981): 156-165.

8264. "Third Selection of Books for White House Library." *Publishers Weekly* 132 (December 11, 1937): 2216-2220.

8265. Tucker, Ray T. "Mr. Hoover Lays a Ghost: White House Press Relations." *North American Review* 227 (June 1929): 661-669.

8266. Tugwell, Rexford G. *Mr. Hoover's Economic Policy.* New York: John Day, 1932.

8267. Tugwell, Rexford G. "The Protagonists: Roosevelt and Hoover." *Antioch Review* 13 (December 1953): 419-442.

8268. Tugwell, Rexford G. "Transition: Hoover to Roosevelt 1932-1933." *Centennial Review* 9 (Spring 1965): 160-191.

8269. Vlaun, Joan G. "Herbert Hoover's Economic Foreign Policies for Dealing with the Great Depression: 1929-1933." Ph.D. dissertation, New York University, 1977.

8270. Vogt, Daniel C. "Hoover's RFC in Action: Mississippi, Bank Loans, and Work Relief, 1932-1933." *Journal of Mississippi History* 47 (February 1985): 35-53.

8271. Weissman, Benjamin M. *Herbert Hoover and Famine Relief to Soviet Russia, 1921-1923.* Stanford, CA: Hoover Institution Press, 1974.

8272. Williams, J. R. "Hoover, Harding, and the Harding Image." *Northwest Ohio Quarterly* 45 (Winter 1972-1973): 4-20.

8273. Wilson, John R. M. "Herbert Hoover and the Armed Forces: A Study of Presidential Attitudes and Policy." Ph.D. dissertation, Northwestern University, 1971.

8274. Wilson, John R. M. "The Quaker and the Sword: Herbert Hoover's Relations with the Military." *Military Affairs* 38 (April 1974): 41-47.

Writings

8275. Danielson, Elena S., and Charles G. Palm. *Herbert Hoover: A Register of His Papers in the Hoover Institution Ar-*

chives. Stanford, CA: Hoover Institution Press, 1982.

8276. Hendrickson, John P. "Legislative Record of Republicans in the Seventy-third Congress in Relation to the Republican Platform of 1932 and the Campaign Speeches of Mr. Hoover." Ph.D. dissertation, University of Iowa, 1952.

8277. Herbert Hoover Presidential Library. *Historical Materials in the Herbert Hoover Presidential Library*. West Branch, IA: Herbert Hoover Presidential Library, National Archives and Records Service, General Services Administration, 1977.

8278. Hoover, Herbert. *Addresses upon the American Road, 1933-1938*. New York: Scribner's, 1938.

8279. Hoover, Herbert. *Addresses upon the American Road, 1940-1941*. New York: Scribner's, 1941.

8280. Hoover, Herbert. *Addresses upon the American Road, World War II, 1941-1945*. New York: Van Nostrand, 1946.

8281. Hoover, Herbert. *Addresses upon the American Road, 1945-1948*. New York: Van Nostrand, 1949.

8282. Hoover, Herbert. *Addresses upon the American Road, 1948-1950*. Stanford, CA: Stanford University Press, 1951.

8283. Hoover, Herbert. *Addresses upon the American Road, 1950-1955*. Stanford, CA: Stanford University Press, 1955.

8284. Hoover, Herbert. *Addresses upon the American Road, 1955-1960*. Caldwell, ID: Caxton, 1968.

8285. Hoover, Herbert. *An American Epic*. 4 vols. Chicago: Regnery, 1959-1964.

8286. Hoover, Herbert. *American Ideals versus the New Deal*. New York: Scribner's, 1936.

8287. Hoover, Herbert. *American Individualism*. Garden City, NY: Doubleday, 1922.

8288. Hoover, Herbert. *America's First Crusade*. New York: Scribner's, 1943.

8289. Hoover, Herbert. *America's Way Forward*. New York: Scribner's, 1939.

8290. Hoover, Herbert. *A Boyhood in Iowa*. New York: Aventine Press, 1931.

8291. Hoover, Herbert. *Campaign Speeches of 1932, By President Hoover and Ex-President Coolidge*. Garden City, NY: Doubleday, 1933.

8292. Hoover, Herbert. *A Case to Win: Five Speeches by Herbert Hoover on American Foreign Policy in Relation to Soviet Russia*. Concord, NH: Rumford Press, 1951.

8293. Hoover, Herbert. *The Challenge to Liberty*. New York: Scribner's, 1934.

8294. Hoover, Herbert. *Fishing for Fun — And Wash Your Soul*. New York: Random House, 1963.

8295. Hoover, Herbert. *Forty Key Questions about Our Foreign Policy*. New York: Updegraff Press, 1952.

8296. Hoover, Herbert. *Further Addresses upon the American Road, 1938-1940*. New York: Scribner's, 1940.

8297. Hoover, Herbert. *Herbert Hoover: Proclamations and Executive Orders, March 4, 1929 to March 4, 1933*. 2 vols. Washington, DC: U.S. Government Printing Office, 1974.

8298. Hoover, Herbert. *Herbert Hoover's Challenge to America: His Life and Words*. Waukesha, WI: Country Beautiful Foundation, 1965.

8299. Hoover, Herbert. *Hoover after Dinner: Addresses Delivered before the Gridiron Club of Washington, D.C., With Other Informal Speeches*. New York: Scribner's, 1933.

8300. Hoover, Herbert. *The Hoover-Wilson Wartime Correspondence, September 24, 1914 to November 11, 1918.* Edited by Francis W. O'Brien. Ames: Iowa State University Press, 1974.

8301. Hoover, Herbert. *The Memoirs of Herbert Hoover.* 3 vols. New York: Macmillan, 1951-1952.

8302. Hoover, Herbert. *The New Day: Campaign Speeches of Herbert Hoover, 1928.* Stanford, CA: Stanford University Press, 1928.

8303. Hoover, Herbert. *On Growing Up: Letters to American Boys and Girls Including the Uncommon Man, and Other Selections.* Edited by William Nichols. New York: Morrow, 1962.

8304. Hoover, Herbert. *The Ordeal of Woodrow Wilson.* New York: McGraw-Hill, 1958.

8305. Hoover, Herbert. "The Ordeal of Woodrow Wilson." *American Heritage* 9 (June 1958): 65-85.

8306. Hoover, Herbert. *Principles of Mining: Valuation, Organization, and Administration: Copper, Gold, Lead, Silver, Tin, and Zinc.* New York: Hill, 1909.

8307. Hoover, Herbert. "Roosevelt and the Public Conscience." *Journal of American History* 13 (July 1919): 309-311.

8308. Hoover, Herbert. *Shall We Send Our Youth to War?* New York: Coward-McCann, 1939.

8309. Hoover, Herbert. *The State Papers and Other Public Writings, 1929-33.* 2 vols. Edited by William S. Myers. Garden City, NY: Doubleday, 1934.

8310. Hoover, Herbert. *Two Peacemakers in Paris: The Hoover-Wilson Post-Armistice Letters, 1918-1920.* Edited by Francis W. O'Brien. College Station: Texas Agricultural and Mechanical University Press, 1978.

8311. Hoover, Herbert, and Hugh Gibson. *The Basis for Lasting Peace.* New York: Van Nostrand, 1945.

8312. Hoover, Herbert, and Hugh Gibson. *The Problems of Lasting Peace.* Garden City, NY: Doubleday, 1943.

8313. Hoover, Herbert, and Lou H. Hoover. *Georgius Argicola de re Metallica.* London: Mining Magazine, 1912.

8314. "Hoover Library Dedicated." *Library Journal* 87 (September 1962): 3013.

8315. Hoover Presidential Library Association. *Herbert Hoover, The Uncommon Man.* West Branch, IA: Hoover Presidential Library Association, 1974.

8316. Lohof, Bruce A., ed. "Herbert Hoover's Mississippi Valley Land Reform Memorandum: A Document." *Arkansas Historical Quarterly* 29 (Summer 1970): 112-118.

8317. Palm, Charles G., and Dale Reed, comps. *Guide to the Hoover Institution Archives.* Stanford, CA: Hoover Institution Press, 1980.

8318. Rae, John B. "The Herbert Hoover Collection of Mining and Metallurgy." *Technology and Culture* 21 (October 1980): 614-616.

8319. Rothwell, C. F. "Resources and Records in Hoover Institute and Library." *American Archivist* 18 (April 1955): 141-150.

8320. Tracey, Kathleen H., comp. *Herbert Hoover — A Bibliography: His Writings and Addresses.* Stanford, CA: Hoover Institution Press, 1977.

8321. Wilson, Carol, and Herbert Hoover. *A Challenge for Today.* New York: Evans, 1968.

Franklin D. Roosevelt

Biographies

8322. Alington, Argentine F. *Franklin Delano Roosevelt*. London: SCM Press, 1950.

8323. Alsop, Joseph. *FDR, 1882-1945: A Centenary Remembrance*. New York: Viking Press, 1981.

8324. Alsop, Joseph. "Roosevelt Remembered." *Smithsonian* 12 (January 1982): 38-49.

8325. Asbell, Bernard. *The FDR Memoirs*. Garden City, NY: Doubleday, 1973.

8326. Asbell, Bernard. *When FDR Died*. New York: Holt, Rinehart and Winston, 1961.

8327. Basso, Hamilton. "The Roosevelt Legend." *Life* 23 (November 3, 1947): 126-148.

8328. Brandeis, Erich. *Franklin D. Roosevelt the Man*. New York: New York Publishing Division, American Offset Corporation, 1936.

8329. Burns, James M. *Roosevelt: The Lion and the Fox*. New York: Harcourt, Brace, 1956.

8330. Burns, James M. *Roosevelt: The Soldier of Freedom*. New York: Harcourt, Brace, 1973.

8331. Butterfield, Roger. *FDR*. New York: Harper and Row, 1963.

8332. Dall, Curtos B. *FDR: My Exploited Father-in-Law*. Torrance, CA: Institute for Historical Review, 1983.

8333. Davis, Kenneth S. "FDR as a Biographer's Problem." *American Scholar* 53 (Winter 1983-1984): 100-108.

8334. Davis, Kenneth S. *FDR: The Beckoning of Destiny, 1882-1928, A History*. New York: Putnam, 1972.

8335. Fay, Bernard. *Roosevelt and His America*. Boston: Little, Brown, 1933.

8336. Feinberg, Barbara S. *Franklin D. Roosevelt, Gallant President*. New York: Lothrop, Lee and Shepard, 1981.

8337. Fish, Hamilton. *FDR: The Other Side of the Coin*. Torrance, CA: Noontide, 1976.

8338. Freidel, Frank B. *Franklin D. Roosevelt*. 4 vols. Boston: Little, Brown, 1952-1973.

8339. Geddes, Donald, ed. *Franklin Delano Roosevelt: A Memorial*. New York: Dial, 1945.

8340. Gies, Joseph. *Franklin D. Roosevelt: A Portrait of a President*. Garden City, NY: Doubleday, 1971.

8341. Graham, Otis L., and Meghan R. Wander, eds. *Franklin D. Roosevelt: His Life and Times, An Encyclopedic View*. Boston: G. K. Hall, 1985.

8342. Gunther, John. *Roosevelt in Retrospect: *A Profile in History.* New York: Harper and Row, 1950.

8343. Hacker, Jeffrey H. *Franklin D. Roosevelt.* New York: Franklin Watts, 1983.

8344. Halasz, Nicholas. *Roosevelt through Foreign Eyes.* Princeton, NJ: Van Nostrand, 1961.

8345. Harrity, Richard, and Ralph G. Martin. *The Human Side of FDR.* New York: Duel, Sloan and Pearce, 1960.

8346. Hatch, Alden. *Franklin D. Roosevelt: An Informal Biography.* New York: Holt, 1948.

8347. Hiebert, Roselyn, and Ray E. Hiebert. *Franklin Delano Roosevelt: President for the People.* New York: Franklin Watts, 1968.

8348. Hill, Charles P. *Franklin Roosevelt.* Fair Saxon, NJ: Oxford University Press, 1966.

8349. Kinnaird, Clark, ed. *The Real FDR.* New York: Harper and Row, 1942.

8350. Lash, Joseph P. *Eleanor and Franklin: The Story of Their Relationship Based on Eleanor Roosevelt's Private Papers.* New York: New American Library, 1971.

8351. Lasky, Joseph. *Our President, Franklin Delano Roosevelt, A Biography.* New York: Walters and Mahon, 1933.

8352. Leuchtenburg, William E., ed. *Franklin D. Roosevelt: A Profile.* New York: Hill and Wang, 1967.

8353. Lindley, Ernest K. *Half Way with Roosevelt.* Rev. ed. New York: Viking Press, 1937.

8354. Lorant, Stefan. *FDR: A Pictorial Biography.* New York: Simon and Schuster, 1950.

8355. Ludwig, Emil. *Roosevelt, A Study in Fortune and Power.* New York: Viking Press, 1933.

8356. Mackenzie, Compton. *Mr. Roosevelt.* New York: Dutton, 1944.

8357. Merriam, Eve. *The Real Book about Franklin D. Roosevelt.* Garden City, NY: Garden City Books, 1952.

8358. Miller, Nathan. *FDR: An Intimate History.* Garden City, NY: Doubleday, 1983.

8359. Montgomery, Mabel. *A Courageous Conquest: The Life Story of Franklin Delano Roosevelt.* New York: Globe Book Co., 1951.

8360. Morgan, Ted. *FDR.* New York: Simon and Schuster, 1985.

8361. Moses, Belle. *Franklin Delano Roosevelt: The Minute Man of 1933.* New York: Appleton, 1933.

8362. Nash, Gerald D., ed. *Franklin Delano Roosevelt.* Englewood Cliffs, NJ: Prentice-Hall, 1967.

8363. Nisenson, Samuel. *From Boyhood to President with Franklin Delano Roosevelt.* Cleveland, OH: World Publishing, 1934.

8364. O'Connor, Edmund. *Roosevelt.* St. Paul, MN: Greenhaven, 1980.

8365. Perkins, Frances. *The Roosevelt I Knew.* New York: Viking Press, 1946.

8366. Roosevelt, Eleanor R. *Franklin D. Roosevelt and Hyde Park: Personal Recollections.* Washington, DC: U.S. Government Printing Office, 1949.

8367. Roosevelt, Elliott. *As He Saw It.* New York: Duell Sloan, 1945.

8368. Roosevelt, Elliott, and James Brough. *A Rendezvous with Destiny: The Roosevelts of the White House.* New York: Putnam, 1975,

8369. Roosevelt, James, and Sidney Shalett. *Affectionately, FDR: A Son's Story of a*

Lonely Man. New York: Harcourt, Brace, 1959.

8370. Roosevelt, Sara D. *My Boy Franklin, As Told by Mrs. James Roosevelt to Isabelle Leighton and Gabrielle Forbush.* New York: R. Long and R. R. Smith, 1933.

8371. Roz, Firmin. *Roosevelt.* Paris: Dunod, 1948.

8372. Rosenblum, Marcus. *The Story of Franklin D. Roosevelt.* New York: Simon and Schuster, 1949.

8373. Schlesinger, Arthur M., Jr. *The Age of Roosevelt.* 3 vols. Boston: Houghton Mifflin, 1957-1960.

8374. Schlesinger, Arthur M., Jr. "His Rendezvous with History." *New Republic* 114 (April 15, 1946): 550-554.

8375. Schoor, Gene. *The Picture Story of Franklin Delano Roosevelt.* New York: Fell, 1950.

8376. Spackman, S. G. F. "Roosevelt." *History Today* 30 (June 1980): 38-43.

8377. Sullivan, Wilson, ed. *Franklin Delano Roosevelt.* New York: American Heritage Publishing Co., 1970.

8378. Thayer, William R. "Chapters of Roosevelt's Life." *North American Review* 210 (July 1985): 48-57; (August 1985): 222-234; (September 1985): 329-355; (October 1985): 512-521; (November 1985): 663-677.

8379. Thomas, Henry. *Franklin Delano Roosevelt.* New York: Putnam, 1962.

8380. Tugwell, Rexford G. *The Democratic Roosevelt: A Biography of Franklin D. Roosevelt.* Garden City, NY: Doubleday, 1957.

8381. Tugwell, Rexford G. *F. D. R.: The Architect of an Era.* New York: Macmillan, 1967.

8382. Tugwell, Rexford G. *In Search of Roosevelt.* Cambridge, MA: Harvard University Press, 1972.

8383. Tully, Grace G. *FDR, My Boss.* New York: Scribner's, 1949.

8384. Venkataramani, M. S. *The Sunny Side of FDR.* Athens: Ohio University Press, 1973.

8385. Vogt, Per. *Franklin D. Roosevelt.* Oslo: J. G. Tanum, 1948.

8386. Voss, Frederick. *FDR: The Early Years.* Washington, DC: Smithsonian Institution Press, 1982.

8387. Walker, Turnley. *Roosevelt and the Warm Springs Story.* New York: A. A. Wyn, 1953.

8388. Ward, Geoffrey C. *Before the Trumpet: Young Franklin Roosevelt 1882-1905.* New York: Harper and Row, 1985.

8389. Weingast, David E. *Franklin D. Roosevelt: Man of Destiny.* New York: Messner, 1952.

8390. Whipple, Wayne. *The Story of Young Franklin Roosevelt.* Chicago: Goldsmith Publishing Co., 1934.

8391. Wold, Ann M. *The Long Shadow of Franklin D. Roosevelt.* Philadelphia: Dorrance, 1974.

Private Life

General

8392. Asbell, Bernard. "F. D. R.'s Extra Burden: What Poliomyelitis Meant to a Political Career." *American Heritage* 24 (June 1973): 21-25.

8393. Bateman, Herman E. "Observations on President Roosevelt's Health during World War II." *Mississippi Valley Historical Review* 43 (June 1956): 82-102.

8394. Bissell, Richard. "Carefree Harvard Days of Three Presidents." *McCall's* 90 (October 1962): 89-91.

8395. Brandenburg, Earnest, and Waldo W. Braden. "Franklin D. Roosevelt's Voice and Pronunciation." *Quarterly Journal of Speech* 38 (February 1952): 23-30.

8396. Brandt, Harvey. "FDR as a Shooter." *Guns Magazine* 2 (April 1956): 20-23, 54-56.

8397. Brant, Irving. *The Books of James Madison with Some Comments on the Readings of FDR and JFK, An Address Delivered during the Celebration of the 25th Anniversary of the Tracy W. McGregor Library, 1929-1964.* Charlottesville: University of Virginia, 1965.

8398. Bruenn, Howard G. "Clinical Notes on the Illness and Death of President Franklin D. Roosevelt." *Annals of Internal Medicine* 72 (April 1970): 579-591.

8399. Bush-Brown, Albert. "A Monument for FDR." *Reporter* 22 (May 12, 1960): 32-37.

8400. Carmichael, Donald S. "An Introduction to the Log of the *Larooco*." *FDR Collector* 1 (November 1948): 1-37.

8401. Churchill, Allen. *The Roosevelts.* London: Muller, 1966.

8402. Condict, Alden S. "A Presidential Collecting Incident." *FDR Collector* 4 (November 1951): 31-35.

8403. Corey, Albert B. "Franklin D. Roosevelt — Local Historian." *New York History* 28 (October 1947): 506-511.

8404. Cowperthwaite, L. LeRoy. "Franklin D. Roosevelt at Harvard." *Quarterly Journal of Speech* 38 (February 1952): 37-41.

8405. Crowell, Laura. "Roosevelt the Grotonian." *Quarterly Journal of Speech* 38 (February 1952): 31-36.

8406. Daniels, Jonathan. "Franklin Delano Roosevelt and Books." In *Three Presidents and Their Books,* by David C. Mearns, Arthur E. Bestor, and Jonathan Daniels, 89-105. Urbana: University of Illinois Press, 1955.

8407. Davis, Kenneth S. *Invincible Summer: An Intimate Portrait of the Roosevelts, Based on the Recollections of Marion Dickerman.* New York: Atheneum, 1974.

8408. Eliasberg, W. G. "How Long Was Roosevelt Ill before His Death?" *Diseases of the Nervous System* 14 (November 1953): 323-328.

8409. Fabricant, Noah D. "Franklin D. Roosevelt, the Common Cold, and American History." *Eye, Ear, Nose, & Throat Monthly* 37 (March 1958): 179-185.

8410. Fabricant, Noah D. "Franklin D. Roosevelt's Nose and Throat Ailments." *Eye, Ear, Nose, & Throat Monthly* 36 (February 1957): 103-109.

8411. Fabricant, Noah D. "Franklin D. Roosevelt's Tonsillectomy and Poliomyelitis." *Eye, Ear, Nose, & Throat Monthly* 36 (June 1957): 348-349.

8412. Fancher, Betsy. "The Warm Springs of FDR." *Saturday Review of Literature* 52 (March 8, 1969): 42.

8413. Ferdon, Nona S. "Franklin D. Roosevelt: A Psychological Interpretation of His Childhood and Youth." Ph.D. dissertation, University of Hawaii, 1971.

8414. Freidel, Frank B. "The Education of Franklin D. Roosevelt." *Harvard Educational Review* 31 (Spring 1961): 158-167.

8415. Freidel, Frank B. "Franklin D. Roosevelt at Harvard." *New England Social Studies Bulletin* 35 (1977-1978): 35-48.

8416. Freidel, Frank B. "Roosevelt's Father." *FDR Collector* 5 (November 1952): 3-10.

8417. Gallagher, Hugh G. "FDR: Handicapped American." *Public Welfare* 42 (Spring 1984): 6-18.

8418. Gallagher, Hugh G. "FDR: An Unusual Look at a Hero." *Disabled USA* 6 (Spring 1982): 22-26.

8419. Goldberg, Richard T. *The Making of Franklin D. Roosevelt: Triumph over Disability*. Cambridge, MA: Abt Books, 1981.

8420. Gould, Jean. *A Good Fight: The Story of FDR's Conquest of Polio*. New York: Dodd, Mead, 1960.

8421. Gunther, John. "Inside FDR — What Killed Him." *Look* 14 (May 9, 1950): 89-98.

8422. Gurney, Gene, and Clare Gurney. *FDR and Hyde Park*. New York: Franklin Watts, 1970.

8423. Haber, Paul. *The House of Roosevelt*. New York: The Author, 1936.

8424. Halsted, James A. "F. D. R.'s 'Little Strokes': A Medical Myth." *Today's Health* 40 (December 1962): 53, 74-75.

8425. Hazlet, Raymond L. "Will There Be an FDR Legend?" *FDR Collector* 5 (May 1953): 3-17.

8426. Helicher, Karl. "The Education of Franklin D. Roosevelt." *Presidential Studies Quarterly* 12 (Winter 1982): 50-53.

8427. Henderson, F. P. "FDR at Warm Springs." *Marine Corps Gazette* 66 (July 1982): 54-58.

8428. Johnson, Alvin P. *Franklin D. Roosevelt's Colonial Ancestors: Their Part in the Making of American History*. Boston: Lothrop, Lee and Shepard, 1933.

8429. Josephson, Emanuel M. *The Strange Death of Franklin D. Roosevelt: History of the Roosevelt-Delano Dynasty, America's Royal Family*. New York: Chedney Press, 1948.

8430. Katterjohn, Monte. "F. D. R. Folklore." *Hoosier Folklore* 7 (March 1948): 22-23.

8431. Kearney, James R. *Anna Eleanor Roosevelt: The Evolution of a Reformer*. Boston: Houghton Mifflin, 1968.

8432. Kleeman, Rita. *Gracious Lady: The Life of Sara Delano Roosevelt*. New York: Appleton, 1935.

8433. Lippman, Theo. *The Squire of Warm Springs: F. D. R. in Georgia, 1924-1945*. New York: Playboy Press, 1977.

8434. Lorentz, Pare, ed. *The Roosevelt Year: A Photographic Record*. New York: Funk and Wagnalls, 1934.

8435. McAfee, Hoyt. "The Spiritual Side of F. D. R." *Frontier* 3 (April 1952): 4, 25.

8436. McCusker, John J. "The Roosevelt Drawing of the Continental Ship *Alfred*." *American Neptune* 28 (January 1968): 49-52.

8437. Mahoney, Tom. "FDR — America's Most Famous Stamp Collector." *Minkus Stamp Journal* 5 (November 2, 1970): 10-16.

8438. Marx, Rudolf. "FDR: A Medical History." *Today's Health* 39 (April 1961): 54-57.

8439. Miller, Nathan. *The Roosevelt Chronicles*. Garden City, NY: Doubleday, 1979.

8440. Moody, Frank K. "F. D. R. and His Neighbors: A Study of the Relationship between Franklin D. Roosevelt and the Residents of Dutchess County." Ph.D. dissertation, State University of New York, Albany, 1981.

8441. Muskie, Stephen O. *Campobello: Roosevelt's "Beloved Island."* Camden, ME: Down East, 1982.

8442. O'Sullivan, John. "To F. D. R. —

Dear Buddy." *American Speech* 43 (February 1968): 79-80.

8443. Partridge, Bellamy. *An Imperial Saga: The Roosevelt Family in America.* New York: Hillman-Curl, 1936.

8444. Potter, David M. "Sketches for the Roosevelt Portrait." *Yale Review* 39 (Autumn 1949): 39-53.

8445. Potter, Jeffrey. "This Thing about Frank." *New Yorker* 39 (August 10, 1963): 70-74.

8446. Rhoads, William B. "The Artistic Patronage of Franklin D. Roosevelt: Art as Historical Record." *Prologue* 15 (Spring 1983): 4-21.

8447. Rhoads, William B. "Franklin D. Roosevelt and Dutch Colonial Architecture." *New York History* 59 (October 1978): 430-464.

8448. Rhoads, William B. "Franklin D. Roosevelt and the Architecture of Warm Springs." *Georgia Historical Quarterly* 67 (Spring 1983): 70-87.

8449. Rollins, Alfred B., Jr. "Franklin Roosevelt's Introduction to Labor." *Labor History* 3 (Winter 1962): 3-18.

8450. Roosevelt, Elliott, and James Brough. *An Untold Story: The Roosevelts of Hyde Park.* New York: Putnam, 1973.

8451. Roosevelt, Hall. *Odyssey of an American Family.* New York: Harper and Row, 1939.

8452. Roosevelt, James. "My Father F. D. R." *Saturday Evening Post* 232 (October 10, 17, 24, 31, November 7, 1959): 15-17, 30-31, 32-33, 36, 32-33.

8453. Roosevelt, James. *My Parents: A Differing View.* Chicago: Playboy Press, 1976.

8454. Schlesinger, Arthur M., Jr. "F. D. R.'s Secret Romance." *Ladies' Home Journal* 83 (November 1966): 66-71.

8455. Shawen, Lena B. *A President's Hobby.* New York: H. L. Lindquist, 1949.

8456. Sill, Leonora. "Bird Lover of Hyde Park." *Audubon Magazine* 57 (June 1955): 116-119.

8457. Stewart, William J., and Cheryl C. Pollard. "Franklin D. Roosevelt, Collector." *Prologue* 1 (Winter 1969): 13-28.

8458. Stidger, William L. *These Amazing Roosevelts.* New York: Macfadden, 1938.

8459. Valentine, John. "FDR, Book Collector." *FDR Collector* 1 (May 1949): 13-21.

Eleanor Roosevelt

8460. Abramowitz, Mildred W. "Eleanor Roosevelt and the National Youth Administration, 1935-1943: An Extension of the Presidency." *Presidential Studies Quarterly* 14 (Autumn 1984): 569-580.

8461. Beasley, Maurine. "Eleanor Roosevelt's Press Conferences: Symbolic Importance of a Pseudo-event." *Journalism Quarterly* 61 (Summer 1984): 274-279.

8462. Beasley, Maurine, ed. *The White House Press Conferences of Eleanor Roosevelt.* New York: Garland, 1983.

8463. Berger, Jason. *A New Deal for the World: Eleanor Roosevelt and American Foreign Policy.* New York: Social Science Monographs, 1981.

8464. Black, Ruby A. *Eleanor Roosevelt, A Biography.* New York: Duell, Sloan and Pearce, 1940.

8465. Butturff, Dorothy D. *Eleanor Roosevelt, An Eager Spirit.* New York: Norton, 1984.

8466. Davis, Kenneth S. "Miss Eleanor Roosevelt." *American Heritage* 22 (October 1971): 48-59.

8467. Faber, Doris. *Eleanor Roosevelt,*

First Lady of the World. New York: Viking, 1985.

8468. Hareven, Tamara K. *Eleanor Roosevelt: An American Conscience.* Chicago: Quadrangle Books, 1968.

8469. Harrity, Richard, and Ralph G. Martin. *Eleanor Roosevelt: Her Life in Pictures.* New York: Duell, Sloan and Pearce, 1958.

8470. Hickok, Lorena A. *Eleanor Roosevelt, Reluctant First Lady.* New York: Dodd, Mead, 1980.

8471. Hoff-Wilson, Joan, and Marjorie Lightman, eds. *Without Precedent: The Life and Career of Eleanor Roosevelt.* Bloomington: Indiana University Press, 1984.

8472. Jacobs, William J. *Eleanor Roosevelt.* New York: Coward-McCann, 1983.

8473. Knapp, Sally E. *Eleanor Roosevelt, A Biography.* New York: Crowell, 1949.

8474. Lash, Joseph P. *Eleanor: The Years Alone.* New York: Norton, 1972.

8475. Lash, Joseph P. "Eleanor Roosevelt's Role in Women's History." In *Clio Was a Woman: Studies in the History of American Women,* edited by Mabel E. Deutrich and Virginia C. Purdy, 243-253. Washington, DC: Howard University Press, 1980.

8476. Lash, Joseph P. *Love, Eleanor: Eleanor Roosevelt and Her Friends.* Garden City, NY: Doubleday, 1982.

8477. Roosevelt, Eleanor R. *The Autobiography of Eleanor Roosevelt.* New York: Harper and Row, 1961.

8478. Roosevelt, Eleanor R. *Day before Yesterday.* Garden City, NY: Doubleday, 1959.

8479. Roosevelt, Eleanor R. *India and the Awakening East.* New York: Harper and Row, 1953.

8480. Roosevelt, Eleanor R. *Mother and Daughter: The Letters of Eleanor and Anna Roosevelt.* Edited by Bernard Asbell. New York: Coward, McCann and Geoghegan, 1982.

8481. Roosevelt, Eleanor R. *My Days.* New York: Dodge, 1938.

8482. Roosevelt, Eleanor R. *On My Own.* New York: Harper and Row, 1958.

8483. Roosevelt, Eleanor R. "On My Own, Conclusion: Of Stevenson, Truman, and Kennedy." *Saturday Evening Post* 230 (March 8, 1958): 32-33, 72-74.

8484. Roosevelt, Eleanor R. *This I Remember.* New York: Harper and Row, 1949.

8485. Roosevelt, Eleanor R. *This Is My Story.* New York: Harper and Row, 1937.

8486. Roosevelt, Eleanor R. *Tomorrow Is Now.* New York: Harper and Row, 1963.

8487. Roosevelt, Eleanor R. "White House Speaks." *Ladies' Home Journal* 57 (June 1940): 21, 121-124.

8488. Roosevelt, Elliott, and James Brough. *Mother R.: Eleanor Roosevelt's Untold Story.* New York: Putnam, 1977.

8489. Steinberg, Alfred. *Mrs. R.: The Life of Eleanor Roosevelt.* New York: Putnam, 1958.

8490. Torres, Louis. *Eleanor Roosevelt National Historic Site.* Denver, CO: Denver Service Center, Mid-Atlantic, North-Atlantic Team, Branch of Historic Preservation, National Park Service, United States Department of the Interior, 1980.

8491. Watrous, Hilda R. *In League with Eleanor.* New York: Foundation for Citizen Education, 1984.

8492. Whitemen, Marjorie M. "Mrs. Franklin D. Roosevelt and the Human Rights Commission." *American Journal of International Law* 62 (October 1968): 918-921.

8493. Whitney, Sharon. *Eleanor Roosevelt*. New York: Franklin Watts, 1982.

8494. Winfield, Betty H. "Mrs. Roosevelt's Press Conference Association: The First Lady Shines a Light." *Journalism History* 8 (Summer 1981): 54-55, 63-70.

8495. Youngs, J. William T. *Eleanor Roosevelt*. Boston: Little, Brown, 1985.

Public Career

8496. Bellush, Bernard. "Apprenticeship for the Presidency: Franklin D. Roosevelt as Governor of New York." Ph.D. dissertation, Columbia University, 1951.

8497. Bellush, Bernard. *Franklin D. Roosevelt as Governor of New York*. New York: Columbia University Press, 1955.

8498. Braden, Waldo W., and Earnest Brandenburg. "The Early Speaking of Franklin D. Roosevelt." *FDR Collector* 3 (May 1951): 3-23.

8499. Carlson, Earland I. "Franklin D. Roosevelt's Fight for the Presidential Nomination, 1928-1932." Ph.D. dissertation, University of Illinois, 1955.

8500. Carlson, Earland I. "Franklin D. Roosevelt's Post-Mortem of the 1928 Election." *American Journal of Political Science* 8 (August 1964): 298-308.

8501. Chambers, Clarke A. "FDR, Pragmatist-Idealist: An Essay in Historiography." *Pacific Northwest Quarterly* 52 (April 1961): 50-55.

8502. Coady, Joseph W. "Franklin D. Roosevelt's Early Washington Years (1913-1920)." Ph.D. dissertation, St. John's University, 1968.

8503. Gravlee, Grady J. "A Rhetorical Study of Franklin Delano Roosevelt's 1920 Campaign." Ph.D. dissertation, Louisiana State University, Agricultural and Mechanical College, 1963.

8504. Kybal, Vlastimil. "Senator Franklin D. Roosevelt, 1910-1913." *FDR Collector* 4 (November 1952): 3-29.

8505. Lindley, Ernest K. *Franklin D. Roosevelt, A Career in Progressive Democracy*. New York: Blue Ribbon Books, 1931.

8506. Neumann, William L. "Franklin D. Roosevelt and Japan 1913-1933." *Pacific Historical Review* 22 (May 1953): 143-153.

8507. Paton, William A. "Mistral's Opinion of Roosevelt." *Outlook* 126 (October 27, 1920): 369-371.

8508. Pennington, Paul J. "A Rhetorical Study of the Gubernatorial Speaking on Franklin D. Roosevelt." Ph.D. dissertation, Louisiana State University, Agricultural and Mechanical College, 1957.

8509. Perkins, Frances. "Franklin Roosevelt's Apprenticeship." *New Republic* 132 (April 25, 1955): 19-21.

8510. Rollins, Alfred B., Jr. "The Political Education of Franklin Roosevelt: His Career in New York Politics, 1909-1928." Ph.D. dissertation, Harvard University, 1953.

8511. Rollins, Alfred B., Jr. "Young Franklin D. Roosevelt as the Farmer's Friend." *New York History* 43 (April 1962): 186-198.

8512. Rollins, Alfred B., Jr. "Young Franklin Roosevelt and the Moral Crusaders." *New York History* 37 (January 1956): 3-16.

8513. Schlesinger, Arthur M., Jr. *The Crisis of the Old Order, 1919-1933*. Boston: Houghton Mifflin, 1957.

8514. Slichter, Gertrude A. "Franklin D. Roosevelt and the Farm Problem, 1929-1932." *Mississippi Valley Historical Review* 43 (September 1956): 238-258.

8515. Slichter, Gertrude A. "Franklin D.

Roosevelt's Farm Policy as Governor of New York State, 1928-1932." *Agricultural History* 33 (October 1959): 238-258.

8516. Tugwell, Rexford G. "The Preparation of a President." *Western Political Quarterly* 1 (June 1948): 131-153.

8517. Zavin, Howard S. "Forward to the Land: Franklin D. Roosevelt and the City, 1882-1933." Ph.D. dissertation, New York University, 1972.

Presidential Years

General

8518. Adams, David K. "Hoover and Roosevelt." *British Association for American Studies Bulletin* 1 (September 1960): 72-78.

8519. Adams, David K. "Roosevelt and Kennedy." *British Association for American Studies Bulletin* 1 (December 1960): 29-39.

8520. Adams, Frederick B. "Mr. Roosevelt Continues, As President and Author." *Bibliographical Society of America Papers* 37 (1943): 223-232.

8521. Allen, Hugh A. *Roosevelt and the Will of God*. New York: Lifetime Editions, 1950.

8522. Allen, Robert S., and Drew Pearson. "How the President Works." *Harper's Magazine* 173 (June 1936): 1-14.

8523. Allen, Robert S., and Drew Pearson. "Men around the President." *Harper's Magazine* 168 (February 1934): 267-277.

8524. Appleby, Paul H. "Roosevelt's Third-Term Decision." *American Political Science Review* 46 (September 1952): 754-765.

8525. Barron, Gloria J. "A Study in Presidential Leadership: Franklin D. Roosevelt in the Pre-war Years, 1939-1941." Ph.D. dissertation, Tufts University, 1971.

8526. Basso, Hamilton. "That Man in the White House: Partial Evaluation of Roosevelt's Career." *New Republic* 103 (July 22, 1940): 106-108.

8527. Beard, Charles A. "Roosevelt's Place in History." *Events* 3 (February 1938): 81-86.

8528. Bellush, Bernard. "An Interpretation of Franklin D. Roosevelt." In *Essays in American Historiography: Papers Presented in Honor of Allan Nevins*, edited by Donald H. Sheehan and Harold C. Syrett, 287-309. New York: Columbia University Press, 1960.

8529. Bellush, Bernard, and Jewel Bellush. "A Radical Response to the Roosevelt Presidency: The Communist Party (1933-1945)." *Presidential Studies Quarterly* 10 (Autumn 1980): 645-661.

8530. Benson, Thomas W. "Inaugurating Peace: Franklin D. Roosevelt's Last Speech." *Speech Monographs* 36 (June 1969): 138-147.

8531. Berlin, Isaiah. "President Franklin Delano Roosevelt." *Political Quarterly* 26 (December 1955): 336-344.

8532. Berlin, Isaiah. "Roosevelt through Foreign Eyes." *Atlantic Monthly* 196 (July 1955): 67-72.

8533. Beschloss, Michael R. *Kennedy and Roosevelt: The Uneasy Alliance*. New York: Norton, 1980.

8534. Bhana, Surendra. "An Attempt by the Roosevelt Administration to 'Reinforce' Self-Government in Puerto Rico: The Elective Governor Bill of 1943." *Revista Interamericana Review* 2 (Winter 1973): 559-573.

8535. Biddle, Francis. *In Brief Authority*. Garden City, NY: Doubleday, 1962.

8536. Bishop, James A. *FDR's Last Year, April 1944-1945*. New York: Morrow, 1974.

8537. Blum, John M. *The Progressive Presidents: Roosevelt, Wilson, Roosevelt, Johnson*. New York: Norton, 1980.

8538. Blum, John M. *Roosevelt and Morgenthau*. Boston: Houghton Mifflin, 1972.

8539. Blum, John M. "That Kind of a Liberal: Franklin D. Roosevelt after Twenty-five Years." *Yale Review* 60 (October 1970): 14-23.

8540. Braden, Waldo W. "Franklin D. Roosevelt Visits Louisiana." *Louisiana History* 8 (Autumn 1967): 379-383.

8541. Braden, Waldo W., and Earnest Brandenburg. "Roosevelt's Fireside Chats." *Speech Monographs* 22 (November 1955): 290-302.

8542. Brandenburg, Earnest, and Waldo W. Braden. "Franklin Delano Roosevelt." *History and Criticism of American Public Address* 3 (1955): 458-530.

8543. Bratzel, John F., and Leslie B. Rout. "FDR and the 'Secret Map.'" *Wilson Quarterly* 9 (January 1985): 167-173.

8544. Brockway, A. Fenner. *Will Roosevelt Succeed? A Study of Fascist Tendencies in America*. London: Routledge, 1934.

8545. Brogan, Denis W. *The Era of Franklin D. Roosevelt: A Chronicle of the New Deal and the Global War*. New Haven, CT: Yale University Press, 1950.

8546. Brown, Wilson. "Aide to Four Presidents." *American Heritage* 6 (February 1955): 66-96.

8547. Burke, Waldemar. "The Roosevelt Administrations." *Current History* 39 (October 1960): 220-224.

8548. Burns, James M. "F. D. R.: The Last Journey." *American Heritage* 21 (August 1970): 8-11, 78-85.

8549. Burns, James M. "FDR: The Untold Story of His Last Year." *Saturday Review of Literature* 53 (April 11, 1970): 12-15, 39.

8550. Butow, R. J. C. "The FDR Tapes." *American Heritage* 33 (February 1982): 8-24.

8551. Cameron, Turner C., Jr. "The Political Philosophy of Franklin Delano Roosevelt." Ph.D. dissertation, Princeton University, 1940.

8552. Clapper, Raymond. "Cuff-Links Clubs." *Review of Reviews* 91 (April 1935): 47-50, 69.

8553. Clapper, Raymond. "Third Term for Roosevelt?" *Current History* 50 (August 1939): 13-16.

8554. Conkin, Paul K. *FDR and the Origins of the Welfare State*. New York: Crowell, 1967.

8555. Connor, Robert D. W. "FDR Visits the National Archives." *American Archivist* 12 (October 1949): 323-332.

8556. Crane, Milton, ed. *The Roosevelt Era*. New York: Boni and Gaer, 1947.

8557. Cronin, Thomas E., and William R. Hochman. "Franklin D. Roosevelt and the American Presidency." *Presidential Studies Quarterly* 15 (Spring 1985): 277-286.

8558. Culbert, David. "'Croak' Carter: Radio's Voice of Doom." *Pennsylvania Magazine of History and Biography* 97 (July 1973): 287-317.

8559. Daniels, Jonathan. *White House Witness: 1942-1945*. Garden City, NJ: Doubleday, 1975.

8560. Daniels, Jonathan, ed. *The Complete Presidential Press Conferences of Franklin Delano Roosevelt*. 12 vols. New York: De Capo Press, 1972.

8561. Davis, Kenneth S. "Incident in Miami." *American Heritage* 32 (December 1980): 86-95.

8562. Democratic Party National Committee, 1932-1936. *The Case against Franklin D. Roosevelt.* Washington, DC: Record Publishing Co., 1936.

8563. Denny, George V., Jr., ed. "What's Your Opinion? Should Roosevelt Run for a Third Term? Symposium." *Current History* 50 (September 1939): 45-49.

8564. Divine, Robert A. "Franklin D. Roosevelt and Collective Security, 1933." *Mississippi Valley Historical Review* 48 (1968): 42-59.

8565. Donahoe, Bernard F. *Private Plans and Public Dangers: The Story of FDR's Third Nomination.* Notre Dame, IN: University of Notre Dame Press, 1965.

8566. Dorsett, Lyle W. *Franklin D. Roosevelt and the City Bosses.* Port Washington, NY: Kennikat Press, 1977.

8567. Dorwart, Jeffery M. "The Roosevelt-Astor Espionage Ring." *New York History* 62 (July 1981): 307-322.

8568. Downs, Olin. *Franklin Roosevelt at Hyde Park: Documented Drawings and Test.* New York: American Artists Group, 1949.

8569. Dunn, James W. "Presidential Franklin D. Roosevelt and the United States Army, 1933-1940." Ph.D. dissertation, University of Hawaii, 1977.

8570. Eiselen, Malcolm R. "The Roosevelts and the Third Term Tradition: A Study in Political Parallels." *Social Science* 16 (January 1940): 27-34.

8571. Elletson, D. H. *Roosevelt and Wilson.* New York: International Publications Service, 1965.

8572. Farley, James A. *Behind the Ballots: The Personal History of a Politician.* New York: Harcourt, Brace, 1938.

8573. Farley, James A. *Jim Farley's Story: The Roosevelt Years.* New York: McGraw-Hill, 1948.

8574. Feis, Herbert. "When Roosevelt Died." *Virginia Quarterly Review* 46 (Autumn 1970): 576-589.

8575. Finch, Edward R. "Franklin Delano Roosevelt, The Twenty-third Lawyer-President." *United States Law Review* 67 (March 1933): 138-142.

8576. Fine, Robert S. "Roosevelt's Radio Chatting: Its Development and Impact during the Great Depression." Ph.D. dissertation, New York University, 1977.

8577. Flynn, Edward J. *You're the Boss.* New York: Viking Press, 1947.

8578. Flynn, George Q. "Franklin D. Roosevelt and American Catholicism, 1932-1936." Ph.D. dissertation, Louisiana State University, Agricultural and Mechanical College, 1966.

8579. Flynn, John T. *Country Squire in the White House.* Garden City, NY: Doubleday, 1940.

8580. Flynn, John T. "Mr. Hopkins and Mr. Roosevelt." *Yale Review* 28 (June 1939): 667-679.

8581. Flynn, John T. *The Roosevelt Myth.* Rev. ed. New York: Devin-Adair, 1956.

8582. Frankfurter, Felix. "The Memorial to F. D. R.: What the President Wanted." *Atlantic Monthly* 207 (March 1961): 39-40.

8583. Frankfurter, Felix. "Remarks at the Graveside of Franklin D. Roosevelt, Hyde Park, Memorial Day." *Centennial Review* 9 (Spring 1965): 156-159.

8584. Frisch, Morton J. "Roosevelt on Peace and Freedom." *Journal of Politics* 29 (August 1967): 585-596.

8585. Frisch, Morton J. "Roosevelt the Conservator: A Rejoinder to Hofstadter."

Journal of Politics 25 (May 1963): 361-372.

8586. Galbraith, John K. "FDR: A Practical Magician." *American Heritage* 34 (February 1983): 90-93.

8587. Gallagher, Hugh G. *FDR's Splendid Deception.* New York: Dodd, Mead, 1985.

8588. Garraty, John A. *Right-Hand Man: The Life of George W. Perkins.* New York: Harper and Row, 1960.

8589. Genizi, Haim. "James McDonald and the Roosevelt Administration." In *Bar-Ilan Studies in History,* edited by Pinhas Artzi, 285-306. Ramat-Gan, Israel: Bar-Ilan University Press, 1978.

8590. George, Elsie L. "The Woman Appointees of the Roosevelt and Truman Administrations: A Study of Their Impact and Effectiveness." Ph.D. dissertation, American University, 1972.

8591. Giusti, James R. "FDR's Historic Voyage." *All Hands* 784 (May 1982): 28-31.

8592. Goldman, Eliot. "Justice William O. Douglas: The 1944 Vice Presidential Nomination and His Relationship with Roosevelt, A Historical Perspective." *Presidential Studies Quarterly* 12 (Summer 1982): 377-385.

8593. Green, Thomas L. "Black Cabinet Members in the Franklin Delano Roosevelt Administration." Ph.D. dissertation, University of Colorado, 1981.

8594. Greer, Thomas H. *What Roosevelt Thought: The Social and Political Ideas of Franklin D. Roosevelt.* East Lansing: Michigan State University Press, 1958.

8595. Guerrant, Edward O. *Herbert Hoover: Franklin Roosevelt: Comparisons and Contrasts.* Cleveland, OH: Allen, 1960.

8596. Guffey, Joseph F. *Roosevelt Again!* Philadelphia: Franklin, 1940.

8597. "Hail to the Chief — The Fourth Term Begins." *Democratic Digest* 22 (February 1945): 7-10.

8598. Hale, William H. "Was There a Man Named Roosevelt?" *New Republic* 120 (January 3, 1949): 22-26.

8599. Hallett, George H., Jr. "Conversation with F. D. R.: President Favored P. R., Electoral College Reform." *National Municipal Review* 34 (June 1945): 304-305.

8600. Hallgren, Mauritz A. *The Gay Reformer: Profits before Plenty under Franklin D. Roosevelt.* New York: Knopf, 1935.

8601. Harrelson, Elmer H. "Roosevelt and the United States Army, 1937-1940: A Study in Challenge-Response." Ph.D. dissertation, University of New Mexico, 1971.

8602. Hassett, William D. *Off The Record with FDR, 1942-1945.* New Brunswick, NJ: Rutgers University Press, 1958.

8603. Hassett, William D. "The President Was My Boss." *Saturday Evening Post* 229 (October 10, 17, 24, 31, November 7, 14, 21, 28, 1953): 19-21, 22-23, 32-33, 38-39, 30, 30, 36, 38-39.

8604. Herder, John H. "A Human Relations Study of Roosevelt and Mussolini: A Comparative Study of the Principles and Practices of Democratic Conference Leadership as Represented by Franklin Roosevelt and of Autocratic Conference Leadership as Represented by Benito Mussolini." Ph.D. dissertation, New York University, 1954.

8605. High, Stanley. *Roosevelt — And Then?* New York: Harper and Row, 1937.

8606. Hofstadter, Richard. "Franklin D. Roosevelt: The Patrician as Opportunist." In his *The American Political Tradition and the Men Who Made It,* 311-347. New York: Knopf, 1948.

8607. Holli, Melvin G., and C. David

Tompkins. "Roosevelt vs. Newett: The Politics of Libel." *Michigan History* 47 (December 1963): 338-356.

8608. "Hotel Delivery: Friendly Fireside Chats Swell Presidential Mail to All-Time Peak." *Literary Digest* 123 (March 6, 1936): 6-7.

8609. Hoyt, Morgan H. "Roosevelt Enters Politics." *FDR Collector* 1 (May 1949): 3-9.

8610. Hughes, Emmet J. "American Presidents and the Style with Which They Shaped the Success or Failure of Their Policies: Part One of a Two-Part Article — From Washington to the Dawn of the Franklin D. Roosevelt Era." *Smithsonian* 2 (March 1972): 28-36.

8611. Ickes, Harold L. "Why I Want Roosevelt for a Third Term." *Look* 3 (June 20, 1939): 6-9.

8612. "If People Can Take It the President Can." *Life* 2 (February 1, 1937): 11-15.

8613. Ingram, Marvin L. "Franklin D. Roosevelt's Exercise of the Veto Power." Ed.D. dissertation, New York University, 1947.

8614. Jacoby, Robert L. *Calendar of the Speeches and Other Published Statements of Franklin D. Roosevelt, 1910-1920.* Hyde Park, NY: Franklin D. Roosevelt Library, 1952.

8615. Jeffries, John W. *Testing the Roosevelt Coalition: Connecticut Society and Politics in the Era of World War II.* Knoxville: University of Tennessee Press, 1979.

8616. Jenkins, Starr. "American Statesmen as Men of Letters: Franklin, Adams, Jefferson, John Quincy Adams, Lincoln, Theodore Roosevelt, and Wilson Considered as Writers." Ph.D. dissertation, University of New Mexico, 1972.

8617. Johannsen, Dorothea E. "Reactions to the Death of President Roosevelt." *Journal of Abnormal and Social Psychology* 41 (April 1946): 218-222.

8618. Johnson, Gerald W. "FDR: A Political Portrait." *Atlantic Monthly* 199 (March 1957): 69-72.

8619. Johnson, Lyndon B. "In Commemoration of the 82nd Anniversary of the Birth of Franklin Delano Roosevelt." *Centennial Review* 9 (Spring 1965): 153-155.

8620. Johnson, Walter. *The American President and the Art of Communication, An Inaugural Lecture Delivered before the University of Oxford on 13 May 1958.* Oxford: Clarendon Press, 1958.

8621. Jones, Alfred H. "Roosevelt and Lincoln: The Political Uses of a Literary Image." Ph.D. dissertation, Yale University, 1968.

8622. Jones, Alfred H. *Roosevelt's Image Brokers: Poets, Playwrights, and the Use of the Lincoln Symbol.* Port Washington, NY: Kennikat Press, 1974.

8623. Judson, Harry P. "Roosevelt and the Third Term." *Independent* 72 (March 28, 1912): 653-655.

8624. Kanawada, Leo V. *Franklin D. Roosevelt's Diplomacy and American Catholics, Italians, and Jews.* Ann Arbor: UMI Research Press, 1982.

8625. Keyerleber, Karl. "Roosevelt and the Fourth Term." *Current History* 7 (September 1944): 172-177.

8626. Kiernan, Reginald H. *President Roosevelt.* London: G. G. Harrap, 1948.

8627. Kilpatrick, Carroll, ed. *Roosevelt and Daniels: A Friendship in Politics.* Chapel Hill: University of North Carolina Press, 1952.

8628. Kingdon, Frank. *Architects of the Republic: George Washington, Thomas Jefferson, Abraham Lincoln, Franklin D.*

Roosevelt. New York: Alliance Publishing Co., 1947.

8629. Klehr, Harvey. "The Stranger Case of Roosevelt's Secret Agent." *Encounter* 59 (December 1982): 84-91.

8630. Klingbeil, Kurt A. "FDR and American Religious Leaders: A Study of President Franklin D. Roosevelt and His Relationship to Selected American Religious Leaders." Ph.D. dissertation, New York University, 1972.

8631. Kluckhohn, Frank L. "When F. D. R. Makes a Decision." *New York Times Magazine* 91 (November 2, 1941): 5, 23.

8632. Knowles, Archibald C. *Franklin Delano Roosevelt, The Great Liberal*. Burlington, NJ: Enterprise Publishing Co., 1936.

8633. Knox, Paul. "White House Reception." *Reader's Digest* 28 (May 1936): 48-50.

8634. Ladd, Everett C., Jr., and Charles D. Hadley. *Transformations of the American Party System: Political Coalitions from the New Deal to the 1970's*. New York: Norton, 1975.

8635. Larson, Bethene W. "Franklin D. Roosevelt's Visit to Sidney during the Drought of 1936." *Nebraska History* 65 (Spring 1984): 1-14.

8636. "*Life* Goes to Inauguration: Ceremony Is Simple But High Jinks around It Are Gay and Expensive." *Life* 18 (February 5, 1945): 108-110, 113.

8637. Loebs, Bruce D. "A Study of Franklin D. Roosevelt's Rhetorical Strategies in Pursuing His Prewar Goals in 1940 and 1941." Ph.D. dissertation, University of Oregon, 1968.

8638. Looker, Earle. *The American Way: Franklin Roosevelt in Action*. New York: John Day, 1933.

8639. McAvoy, Thomas. "Roosevelt: A Modern Jefferson." *Review of Politics* 7 (July 1945): 270-279.

8640. McCoy, Donald R. "Trends in Viewing Herbert Hoover, Franklin D. Roosevelt, Harry S. Truman, and Dwight D. Eisenhower." *Midwest Quarterly* 20 (Winter 1979): 117-136.

8641. McElvaine, Robert S. "Roosevelt and Reagan." *Christian Century* 99 (May 12, 1982): 556-558.

8642. McIntire, Ross T., and George Creel. *White House Physician*. New York: Putnam, 1946.

8643. McKown, Robin. *Roosevelt's America*. New York: Grosset and Dunlap, 1962.

8644. Malone, Dumas. "Mr. Jefferson to Mr. Roosevelt: An Imaginary Letter." *Virginia Quarterly Review* 19 (Spring 1943): 161-177.

8645. Martin, Oliver. "Inaugurating a President." *Transmitter* 25 (February 1937): 1-6.

8646. Milkis, Sidney M. "Franklin D. Roosevelt and the Transcendence of Partisan Politics." *Political Science Quarterly* 100 (Autumn 1985): 479-504.

8647. Miller, Delbert C. "How Our Community Heard about the Death of President Roosevelt: A Research Note on Mass Communication." *American Sociological Review* 10 (October 1945): 691-694.

8648. Millis, Walter. "Roosevelt in Retrospect." *Virginia Quarterly Review* 21 (July 1945): 321-330.

8649. Moley, Raymond. *After Seven Years*. New York: Harper and Row, 1939.

8650. Monblatt, Bruce L. "Colonel Robert R. McCormick, the *Chicago Tribune*, and Franklin D. Roosevelt, 1932-1941." Master's thesis, American University, 1964.

8651. Nesbitt, Victoria H. K. *White House Diary.* Garden City, NY: Doubleday, 1948.

8652. Neumann, Robert G. "Leadership: Franklin Roosevelt, Truman, Eisenhower, and Today." *Presidential Studies Quarterly* 10 (Winter 1980): 10-19.

8653. Neustadt, Richard E. "Approaches to Staffing the Presidency: Notes on FDR and JFK." *American Political Science Review* 57 (December 1963): 855-863.

8654. Nevins, Allan. *The Place of Franklin D. Roosevelt in History.* New York: Humanities Press, 1965.

8655. Nevins, Allan. "The Place of Franklin D. Roosevelt in History." *American Heritage* 17 (June 1966): 12-15, 101-104.

8656. Nicholas, Herbert G. "Roosevelt and Public Opinion." *Fortnightly* 163 (May 1945): 303-308.

8657. Nixon, Edgar B., ed. *Franklin D. Roosevelt and Conservation, 1911-1945.* 2 vols. Hyde Park, NY: Franklin D. Roosevelt Library, 1957.

8658. Niznik, Monica L. "Thomas G. Corcoran, The Public Service of Franklin Roosevelt's 'Tommy the Cork.'" Ph.D. dissertation, University of Notre Dame, 1981.

8659. Notaro, Carmen A. "Franklin D. Roosevelt and the American Communists: Peacetime Relations, 1932-1941." Ph.D. dissertation, State University of New York, Buffalo, 1969.

8660. Oliver, Robert T. "The Speech That Established Roosevelt's Reputation." *Quarterly Journal of Speech* 31 (October 1945): 274-282.

8661. Orlansky, Harold. "Reactions to the Death of President Roosevelt." *Journal of Social Psychology* 26 (November 1947): 235-266.

8662. Parker, Maude. "New Social Deal." *Saturday Evening Post* 206 (April 28, 1934): 10-11, 97-98.

8663. Patterson, James T. "F. D. R. and the Democratic Triumph." *Current History* 47 (October 1964): 216-220.

8664. Pearson, Drew, and Robert S. Allen. "How the President Works." *Harper's Magazine* 173 (June 1936): 1-14.

8665. Perkins, Dexter. *The New Age of Franklin Roosevelt, 1932-1945.* Chicago: University of Chicago Press, 1957.

8666. Peterson, Merrill D. "Bowers, Roosevelt, and the New Jefferson." *Virginia Quarterly Review* 34 (Autumn 1958): 530-543.

8667. Phillips, Cabell. *From the Crash to the Blitz.* New York: Macmillan, 1969.

8668. Polenberg, Richard. "Historians and the Liberal Presidency: Recent Appraisals of Roosevelt and Truman." *South Atlantic Quarterly* 75 (Winter 1976): 20-35.

8669. Polenberg, Richard. *Reorganizing Roosevelt's Government.* Cambridge, MA: Harvard University Press, 1966.

8670. Polenberg, Richard. "Roosevelt, Carter, and Executive Reorganization: Lessons of the 1930's." *Presidential Studies Quarterly* 9 (Winter 1979): 35-46.

8671. "Presidency: Its Tradition Is Leadership in Freedom: Will Franklin Roosevelt Preserve That Tradition?" *Fortune* 25 (January 1942): 36-41.

8672. "President Roosevelt Answers a Call to Run for a Third Term." *Life* 9 (July 29, 1940): 15-19.

8673. Ragland, James F. "Franklin D. Roosevelt and Public Opinion, 1933-1940." Ph.D. dissertation, Stanford University, 1954.

8674. Range, Willard. *Franklin D. Roo-*

sevelt's World Order. Athens: University of Georgia Press, 1959.

8675. Reilly, Michael F. *I Was Roosevelt's Shadow.* London: W. Foulsham and Co., 1946.

8676. Reilly, Michael F. *Reilly of the White House.* New York: Simon and Schuster, 1947.

8677. Robinson, Edgar E. *The Roosevelt Leadership, 1933-1945.* Philadelphia: Lippincott, 1955.

8678. Robinson, George C. "Veto Record of Franklin D. Roosevelt." *American Political Science Review* 36 (February 1942): 75-78.

8679. Rollins, Alfred B., Jr. *Franklin D. Roosevelt and the Age of Action.* New York: Dell, 1960.

8680. Rollins, Alfred B., Jr. *Roosevelt and Howe.* New York: Knopf, 1962.

8681. Roosevelt, James. "Staffing My Father's Presidency: A Personal Reminiscence." *Presidential Studies Quarterly* 12 (Winter 1982): 48-49.

8682. "Roosevelt's Men." *Life* 18 (April 23, 1945): 73-81.

8683. Rosenman, Samuel I. "What Makes a President." *Ladies' Home Journal* 69 (May 1952): 40-41.

8684. Rosenman, Samuel I. *Working with Roosevelt.* New York: Harper and Row, 1952.

8685. Ross, Leland M. *This Democratic Roosevelt.* New York: Dutton, 1932.

8686. Rossiter, Clinton L. "Political Philosophy of F. D. Roosevelt: A Challenge to Scholarship." *Review of Politics* 11 (January 1949): 84-90.

8687. Rosten, Leo C. "President Roosevelt and the Washington Correspondents." *Public Opinion Quarterly* 1 (January 1937): 36-52.

8688. Rothchild, Donald S. "F. D. R.: Leader in a Time of Drift." *Colby Library Quarterly* 55 (September 1960): 143-150.

8689. Rotunda, Ronald D. "The 'Liberal' Label: Roosevelt's Capture of a Symbol." *Public Policy* 17 (1968): 377-408.

8690. Ruskowski, Casimer W. *Is Roosevelt an Andrew Jackson?* Boston: Bruce Humphries, 1939.

8691. Ryan, Halford R. "Roosevelt's First Inaugural: A Study of Technique." *Quarterly Journal of Speech* 65 (April 1979): 137-149.

8692. Ryan, Halford R. "Roosevelt's Fourth Inaugural Address." *Quarterly Journal of Speech* 67 (May 1981): 157-166.

8693. Sanford, Fillmore H. "Public Orientation to Roosevelt." *Public Opinion Quarterly* 15 (Summer 1951): 189-216.

8694. Sargent, James E. "FDR, Foreign Policy, and the Domestic First Perspective, 1933-1936: An Appraisal." *Peace and Change* 3 (Spring 1975): 24-29.

8695. Schiffman, Joseph. "Observations of Roosevelt's Literary Style." *Quarterly Journal of Speech* 35 (April 1949): 222-226.

8696. Schlesinger, Arthur M., Jr. "Roosevelt and His Detractors." *Harper's Magazine* 200 (June 1950): 62-68.

8697. Schmidt, William T., ed. "Letters to Their President: Mississippians to Franklin D. Roosevelt, 1932-1933." *Journal of Mississippi History* 40 (August 1978): 231-252.

8698. Shappee, Nathan D. "Zangara's Attempted Assassination of Franklin D. Roosevelt." *Florida Historical Quarterly* 37 (October 1958): 101-110.

8699. Sharon, John H. "The Fireside Chat." *FDR Collector* 1 (November 1949): 3-20.

8700. Sheffer, Martin S. "The Attorney General and Presidential Power: Robert H. Jackson, Franklin Roosevelt, and the Prerogative Presidency." *Presidential Studies Quarterly* 12 (Winter 1982): 54-65.

8701. Sherwood, Robert E. *Roosevelt and Hopkins: An Intimate History*. Rev. ed. New York: Grosset and Dunlap, 1950.

8702. Shipler, Guy E. "Franklin Roosevelt and Religion." *Churchman* 169 (May 1, 1955): 10-11.

8703. Showan, Daniel P. "The Hoover-Roosevelt Relationship during the Interregnum." *Lock Haven Bulletin* 1 (1961): 24-50.

8704. Sirevag, Torbjorn. "Franklin D. Roosevelt and the Use of History." *Americana Norwegica* 2 (1968): 299-342.

8705. Skau, George H. "Franklin D. Roosevelt and the Expansion of Presidential Power." *Current History* 66 (June 1974): 246-248, 274-275.

8706. Smith, A. Merriman. *Thank You, Mr. President: A White House Notebook*. New York: Harper and Row, 1946.

8707. Smith, Helena H. "President Never Rings Twice: The White House in Action." *Delineator* 126 (May 1935): 4-5, 73.

8708. Soapes, Thomas F. "The Fragility of the Roosevelt Coalition: The Case of Missouri." *Missouri Historical Review* 72 (October 1977): 38-58.

8709. Steele, Richard W. "The Pulse of the People: Franklin D. Roosevelt and the Gauging of American Public Opinion." *Journal of Contemporary History* 9 (October 1974): 195-216.

8710. Stephanson, Anders. "The CPUSA Conception of the Rooseveltian State, 1933-1939." *Radical History Review* 24 (Fall 1980): 160-176.

8711. Sterba, Richard. "Report on Some Emotional Reactions to President Roosevelt's Death." *Psychoanalytic Review* 33 (October 1946): 393-398.

8712. Stiles, Lela. *The Man behind Roosevelt: The Story of Louis McHenry Howe*. Cleveland, OH: World Publishing, 1954.

8713. Sussman, Leila A. *Dear FDR: A Study of Political Letter-Writing*. Totowa, NJ: Bedminster Press, 1963.

8714. Sussman, Leila A. "FDR and the White House Mail." *Public Opinion Quarterly* 20 (Spring 1956): 5-16.

8715. Syrett, John. "Roosevelt vs. Farley: The New York Gubernatorial Election of 1942." *New York History* 56 (January 1975): 51-81.

8716. Thompson, Kenneth W., ed. *The Roosevelt Presidency: Four Intimate Perspectives of Franklin Delano Roosevelt*. Lanham, MD: University Press of America, 1983.

8717. Thornton, Harrison J. "The Two Roosevelts at Chautauqua." *New York History* 28 (January 1947): 33-65.

8718. "To Growl Warnings: Cartoonists on FDR." *Library of Congress Information Bulletin* 40 (December 1981): 457-458.

8719. Tugwell, Rexford G. *The Art of Politics, As Practiced by Three Great Americans: Franklin D. Roosevelt, Luis M. Marin, and Fiorello H. La Guardia*. Garden City, NY: Doubleday, 1958.

8720. Tugwell, Rexford G. "The Compromising Roosevelt." *Western Political Quarterly* 6 (June 1953): 320-341.

8721. Tugwell, Rexford G. "The Fallow Years of Franklin D. Roosevelt." *Ethics* 66 (January 1956): 98-116.

8722. Tugwell, Rexford G. "Franklin D. Roosevelt on the Verge of the Presidency." *Antioch Review* 16 (March 1956): 46-79.

8723. Tugwell, Rexford G. "The Protagonists: Roosevelt and Hoover." *Antioch Review* 13 (December 1953): 419-442.

8724. Tugwell, Rexford G. "Roosevelt and Howe." *Antioch Review* 14 (September 1954): 367-373.

8725. Tugwell, Rexford G. "Roosevelt and the Bonus Marchers of 1932." *Political Science Quarterly* 87 (Summer 1972): 363-376.

8726. Tugwell, Rexford G. "Transition: Hoover to Roosevelt 1932-1933." *Centennial Review* 9 (Spring 1965): 160-191.

8727. Tugwell, Rexford G. "The Two Great Roosevelts." *Western Political Quarterly* 5 (March 1952): 84-93.

8728. Ulig, Frank, and William R. Mathews. "Franklin Delano Roosevelt: A Disciple of Mahan." *U.S. Naval Institute Proceedings* 79 (May 1953): 561-562.

8729. Van Patten, Paul L. "B. O. B. and F. D. R.: A Stage in the Growth of the Institutional Presidency." Ph.D. dissertation, University of Notre Dame, 1983.

8730. Wann, Andrew J. "Franklin D. Roosevelt and the Administrative Organization of the Executive Branch." Ph.D. dissertation, University of Missouri, 1961.

8731. Wann, Andrew J. "Franklin D. Roosevelt and the Bureau of the Budget." *University of Missouri Business and Government Review* 9 (March/April 1968): 32-41.

8732. Wann, Andrew J. *The President as Chief Administrator: A Study of Franklin D. Roosevelt*. Washington, DC: Public Affairs Press, 1968.

8733. Watson, Richard L., Jr. "Franklin D. Roosevelt in Historical Writing, 1950-1957." *South Atlantic Quarterly* 57 (Winter 1958): 104-126.

8734. Welles, Sumner. "Two Roosevelt Decisions: One Debit, One Credit." *Foreign Affairs* 29 (January 1951): 182-204.

8735. Wharton, Don, ed. *The Roosevelt Omnibus*. New York: Knopf, 1934.

8736. White, Graham J. *Franklin Delano Roosevelt and the Press*. Chicago: University of Chicago Press, 1979.

8737. Whitehurst, Ben. *Dear Mr. President*. New York: Dutton, 1937.

8738. Williams, Dorothy Q. "The Treatment of the Second Roosevelt Administration in Three Popular Magazines." Ph.D. dissertation, University of Chicago, 1947.

8739. Willoughby, William R. "The Roosevelt Campobello International Park Commission." *Dalhousie Review* 54 (Summer 1974): 289-297.

8740. Wilson, John F. "An Analysis of the Criticism of Selected Speeches by Franklin D. Roosevelt." Ph.D. dissertation, University of Wisconsin, 1955.

8741. Winfield, Betty H. "F. D. R.'s Pictorial Image, Rules and Boundaries." *Journalism History* 5 (Winter 1978-1979): 110-114.

8742. Winfield, Betty H. "Franklin D. Roosevelt's Efforts to Influence the News during His First Press Conferences." *Presidential Studies Quarterly* 11 (Spring 1981): 189-199.

8743. Wolf, T. Phillip. "Bronson Cutting and Franklin Roosevelt: Factors in Presidential Endorsement." *New Mexico Historical Review* 52 (October 1977): 317-334.

8744. Wolfskill, George, and John A. Hudson. *All but the People: Franklin D. Roosevelt and His Critics, 1933-1939*. New York: Macmillan, 1969.

8745. Woods, John A. *Roosevelt and Modern America*. New York: Macmillan, 1960.

Congress

8746. Clifford, J. Garry. "A Note on the Break between Senator Nye and President Roosevelt in 1939." *North Dakota History* 49 (Summer 1982): 14-17.

8747. Cobb, James C. "The Big Boy Has Scared the Lard out of Them." *Research Studies* 43 (1975): 123-125.

8748. Crowell, Laura. "The Building of the 'Four Freedoms' Speech." *Speech Monographs* 22 (November 1955): 266-283.

8749. Fagin, Vernon A. "Franklin D. Roosevelt, Liberalism in the Democratic Party, and the 1938 Congressional Elections: The Urge to Purge." Ph.D. dissertation, University of California, Los Angeles, 1979.

8750. Grant, Philip A., Jr. "Roosevelt, the Congress, and the United Nations." *Presidential Studies Quarterly* 13 (Spring 1983): 279-285.

8751. Hall, Alvin L. "Politics and Patronage: Virginia's Senators and the Roosevelt Purges of 1938." *Virginia Magazine of History and Biography* 82 (July 1974): 331-350.

8752. Harrison, Richard A. "The Runciman Visit to Washington in January 1937." *Canadian Journal of History* 19 (August 1984): 217-239.

8753. Hopper, John E. "The Purge: Franklin D. Roosevelt and the 1938 Democratic Nominations." Ph.D. dissertation, University of Chicago, 1967.

8754. Lindley, Ernest K. "A Review of President Roosevelt and Congress." *Literary Digest* 117 (June 2, 1934): 7, 42.

8755. Mooney, Booth. *Roosevelt and Rayburn: A Political Partnership*. Philadelphia: Lippincott, 1971.

8756. O'Reilly, Kenneth. "The Roosevelt Administration and Legislative-Executive Conflict: The FBI vs. the Dies Committee." *Congress and the Presidency* 10 (Spring 1983): 79-93.

8757. Polenberg, Richard. "Franklin Roosevelt and the Purge of John O'Connor." *New York History* 49 (July 1968): 306-326.

8758. Price, Charles M., and Joseph Boskin. "Roosevelt 'Purge': A Reappraisal." *Journal of Politics* 28 (August 1966): 660-670.

8759. Snowiss, Sylvia. "Presidential Leadership of Congress: An Analysis of Roosevelt's First Hundred Days." *Publius* 1 (1971): 59-60.

8760. Swain, Martha H. "The Lion and the Fox: The Relationship of President Franklin D. Roosevelt and Senator Pat Harrison." *Journal of Mississippi History* 38 (November 1976): 333-359.

8761. Wheeler, Burton K. "My Years with Roosevelt." In *As We Saw the Thirties: Essays on the Social and Political Movements of a Decade,* edited by Rita Simon, 190-215. Urbana: University of Illinois Press, 1967.

8762. Zebroski, Shirley. "Franklin D. Roosevelt and the 77th Congress: Domestic Issues." Ph.D. dissertation, Ohio University, 1983.

Domestic Policy

8763. Adams, John C. "Franklin D. Roosevelt's Gold Policies in a Farm Sector Strategy, 1933." Ph.D. dissertation, Indiana University, 1976.

8764. Alderson, William T., ed. "Taft, Roosevelt, and the U.S. Steel Case: A Letter of Jacob McGavock Dickinson." *Tennessee Historical Quarterly* 18 (September 1959): 266-272.

8765. Alexander, Albert. "The President and the Investigator: Roosevelt and Dies." *Antioch Review* 15 (March 1955): 106-117.

8766. Allen, Dan C. "Franklin D. Roosevelt and the Development of an American Occupation Policy in Europe." Ph.D. dissertation, Ohio State University, 1976.

8767. Armstrong, William M. "Franklin D. Roosevelt's Economic Thought." *American Journal of Economics and Sociology* 17 (April 1958): 329-331.

8768. Bolles, Blair. "Our Uneconomic Royalist: High Cost of Dr. Roosevelt." *American Mercury* 43 (March 1938): 265-269.

8769. Cross, Whitney R. "Ideas in Politics: The Conservation Policies of the Two Roosevelts." *Journal of the History of Ideas* 14 (June 1953): 421-438.

8770. Fine, Sidney. "President Roosevelt and the Automobile Code." *Mississippi Valley Historical Review* 45 (June 1958): 23-50.

8771. Freidel, Frank B. *F. D. R. and the South*. Baton Rouge: Louisiana State University Press, 1965.

8772. Frisch, Morton J. "Franklin D. Roosevelt and the Problem of Democratic Liberty." *Ethics* 72 (April 1962): 180-192.

8773. Ickes, Harold L. "My Twelve Years with F. D. R." *Saturday Evening Post* 220 (June 5, 12, 19, 26, 1948): 15-17, 34-35, 30-31, 36-37; 221 (July 3, 10, 17, 24, 1948): 30-31, 32-33, 28, 28.

8774. Ickes, Harold L. *The Secret Diary of Harold L. Ickes*. 3 vols. New York: Simon and Schuster, 1953-1955.

8775. Kirby, John B. *Black Americans in the Roosevelt Era: Liberalism and Race*. Knoxville: University of Tennessee Press, 1980.

8776. Kirkendall, Richard S. "Franklin D. Roosevelt and the Service Intellectual." *Journal of American History* 49 (December 1962): 456-471.

8777. Kirkendall, Richard S. *Social Scientists and Farm Politics in the Age of Roosevelt*. Columbia: University of Missouri Press, 1966.

8778. Kleiler, Frank M. "The World War II Battles of Montgomery Ward." *Chicago History* 5 (1976): 19-27.

8779. Kyvig, David E. "Raskob, Roosevelt, and Repeal." *Historian* 37 (May 1975): 469-487.

8780. Leiter, William M. "The Presidency and Non-Federal Government: FDR and the Promotion of State Legislative Action." *Presidential Studies Quarterly* 9 (Spring 1979): 101-121.

8781. Leuchtenburg, William E. "Roosevelt, Norris, and the 'Seven Little TVA's.'" *Journal of Politics* 14 (August 1952): 418-441.

8782. Linder, Leo J. "The Right to Economic Security: A Study of the Development of the Roosevelt Social Security Work and Relief Program." *National Lawyer's Guild Practitioner* 39 (Spring 1982): 33-58.

8783. Lowitt, Richard. "Present at the Creation: George W. Norris, Franklin D. Roosevelt, and the TVA Enabling Act." *East Tennessee Historical Society's Publications* 48 (1976): 116-126.

8784. Lowrie, Walter E. "Roosevelt and the Passamequoddy Bay Tidal Project." *Historian* 31 (November 1968): 64-89.

8785. McFarland, Charles K. "Coalition of Convenience: The Roosevelt-Lewis Courtship, 1933-1941." Ph.D. dissertation, University of Arizona, 1965.

8786. Merrill, Jeffrey. "Planning for New Health Human-Power." *Social Policy* 6 (November/December 1975): 36-43.

8787. Moley, Raymond. "FDR-JFK: A Brain Truster Compares Two Presidents, Two Programs." *Newsweek* 57 (April 17, 1961): 32-34, 37.

8788. Nichols, Jeannette P. "Roosevelt's Monetary Diplomacy in 1933." *American Historical Review* 56 (January 1951): 295-317.

8789. O'Conner, James F. T. *The Banking Crisis and Recovery under the Roosevelt Administration.* Chicago: Callaghan, 1938.

8790. O'Reilly, Kenneth. "A New Deal for the FBI: The Roosevelt Administration, Crime Control, and National Security." *Journal of American History* 69 (December 1982): 638-658.

8791. Ostrower, Gary B. "The American Decision to Join the International Labor Organization." *Labor History* 16 (Fall 1975): 495-504.

8792. Owen, Anna L. *Conservation under FDR.* New York: Praeger, 1983.

8793. Polenberg, Richard. "Franklin D. Roosevelt and the Reorganization Controversy: 1936-1939." Ph.D. dissertation, Columbia University, 1964.

8794. Polenberg, Richard. "Franklin Roosevelt and Civil Liberties: The Case of the Dies Committee." *Historian* 30 (Autumn 1968): 165-178.

8795. Pusateri, C. Joseph. "FDR, Huey Long, and the Politics of Radio Regulation." *Journal of Broadcasting* 21 (Winter 1977): 85-95.

8796. Pusateri, C. Joseph. "A Study in Misunderstanding: Franklin D. Roosevelt and the Business Community." *Social Studies* 60 (October 1969): 204-211.

8797. Ragland, James F. "Merchandisers of the First Amendment: Freedom and Responsibility of the Press in the Age of Roosevelt, 1933-1940." *Georgia Review* 16 (Winter 1962): 366-391.

8798. Ramsay, Marion L. *Pyramids of Power: The Story of Roosevelt, Insull, and the Utility Wars.* Indianapolis, IN: Bobbs-Merrill, 1937.

8799. Rosen, Elliot A. *Hoover, Roosevelt, and the Brains Trust: From Depression to New Deal.* New York: Columbia University Press, 1977.

8800. Rosen, Elliot A. "Roosevelt and the Brains Trust: An Historiographical Overview." *Political Science Quarterly* 87 (December 1972): 531-557.

8801. Ross, B. Joyce. "Mary McLeod Bethune and the National Youth Administration: A Case Study of Power Relationships in the Black Cabinet of Franklin D. Roosevelt." *Journal of Negro History* 60 (January 1975): 1-28.

8802. Ross, Earle D. "Roosevelt and Agriculture." *Mississippi Valley Historical Review* 14 (December 1927): 287-310.

8803. Rozwenc, Edwin C. *Roosevelt, Wilson, and the Trusts.* Boston: Heath, 1950.

8804. Saalberg, John J. "Roosevelt, Fechner, and the CCC — A Study in Executive Leadership." Ph.D. dissertation, Cornell University, 1962.

8805. Salmond, John A. "Aubrey Williams Remembers: A Note on Franklin D. Roosevelt's Attitude toward Negro Rights." *Alabama Review* 25 (January 1972): 62-77.

8806. Sternsher, Bernard. "The Stimson Doctrine: F. D. R. versus Moley and Tugwell." *Pacific Historical Review* 31 (August 1962): 281-290.

8807. Sternsher, Bernard. "Tugwell's Appraisal of F. D. R." *Western Political Quarterly* 15 (March 1962): 67-79.

8808. Sutton, Anthony C. *Wall Street and FDR.* New Rochelle, NY: Arlington House, 1975.

8809. Trani, Eugene P. "Conflict of Compromise: Harold L. Ickes and Franklin D. Roosevelt." *North Dakota Quarterly* 36 (Winter 1968): 20-29.

8810. Venkataramani, M. S. "Norman Thomas, Arkansas Sharecroppers, and the Roosevelt Agricultural Policies, 1933-1937." *Arkansas Historical Quarterly* 24 (Spring 1965): 3-28.

8811. Wallfisch, M. Charles. "Franklin D. Roosevelt and Equal Educational Opportunity." *High School Journal* 66 (October/November 1982): 51-56.

8812. Weiss, Nancy J. *Farewell to the Party of Lincoln: Black Politics in the Age of FDR*. Princeton, NJ: Princeton University Press, 1983.

8813. White, Leonard D. "Franklin D. Roosevelt and the Public Service." *Public Personnel Review* 6 (July 1945): 139-146.

8814. Wicker, Elmus R. "Roosevelt's 1933 Monetary Experiment." *Journal of American History* 57 (March 1971): 864-879.

8815. Woods, James R. "The Legend and the Legacy of Franklin D. Roosevelt and the Civilian Conservation Corps (CCC)." D.S.S. dissertation, Syracuse University, 1964.

Elections

8816. Blayney, Michael S. "Honor among Gentlemen: Herbert Pell, Franklin Roosevelt, and the Campaign of 1936." *Rhode Island History* 39 (August 1980): 94-102.

8817. Cowperthwaite, L. LeRoy. "A Criticism of the Speaking of Franklin D. Roosevelt in the Presidential Campaign of 1932." *Speech Monographs* 18 (August 1951): 190-191.

8818. Crowell, Laura. "An Analysis of Audience Persuasion in the Major Addresses of Franklin D. Roosevelt in the Presidential Campaign of 1936." Ph.D. dissertation, University of Iowa, 1949.

8819. Crowell, Laura. "Franklin D. Roosevelt's Audience Persuasion in the 1936 Campaign." *Speech Monographs* 17 (March 1950): 48-64.

8820. Ficken, Robert E. "Political Leadership in War-Time: Franklin D. Roosevelt and the Elections of 1942." *Mid-America* 57 (January 1975): 20-37.

8821. Gertz, Elmer. "Roosevelt and Stevenson: Their First Presidential Campaigns." *FDR Collector* 5 (May 1953): 18-27.

8822. Gosnell, Harold F. *Champion Campaigner: Franklin D. Roosevelt*. New York: Macmillan, 1952.

8823. Gravlee, Grady J. "Franklin D. Roosevelt's Speech Preparation during His First National Campaign." *Speech Monographs* 31 (November 1964): 437-460.

8824. Guilfoyle, James H. *On the Trail of the Forgotten Man: A Journal of the Roosevelt Presidential Campaign*. Boston: Peabody Master Printers, 1933.

8825. Hope, Ben W. "The Rhetoric of Defense: A Study of the Tactics and Techniques of Refutation in President Franklin D. Roosevelt's Speeches in His Three Campaigns for Reelection." Ph.D. dissertation, Ohio State University, 1960.

8826. Jakoubek, Robert E. "A Jeffersonian's Dissent: John W. Davis and the Campaign of 1936." *West Virginia History* 35 (January 1974): 145-153.

8827. Jensen, Richard. "Cities Reelect Roosevelt: Ethnicity, Religion, and Class in 1940." *Ethnicity* 8 (June 1981): 189-195.

8828. McKay, S. S. "O'Daniel, Roosevelt, and the Texas Republican Counties: A Comparison of the O'Daniel with the Anti-Roosevelt Votes in 1940 and 1944."

Southwestern Social Science Quarterly 26 (June 1945): 1-21.

8829. Miller, Vivian I. "The 1932 Campaign: The Beginning of the New Deal." Ph.D. dissertation, Indiana University, 1970.

8830. Misse, Fred B. "Franklin Roosevelt and the Polish Vote in 1944." *Midwest Quarterly* 21 (Spring 1980): 317-332.

8831. Moscow, Warren. *Roosevelt and Willkie*. Englewood Cliffs, NJ: Prentice-Hall, 1968.

8832. Norton, Laurence. "A Symbol Analysis of Roosevelt and Dewey Speeches in the 1944 Presidential Campaign." Ph.D. dissertation, University of Wisconsin, 1950.

8833. Olson, Lester C. "Portraits in Praise of a People: A Rhetorical Analysis of Norman Rockwell's Icons in the Franklin D. Roosevelt's 'Four Freedoms' Campaign." *Quarterly Journal of Speech* 69 (February 1983): 15-24.

8834. Oulahan, Richard. *The Man Who. . . : The Story of the 1932 National Convention*. New York: Dial, 1971.

8835. Parmet, Herbert S., and Marie B. Hecht. *Never Again: A President Runs for a Third Term*. New York: Macmillan, 1968.

8836. Partin, John W. "Roosevelt, Byrnes, and the 1944 Vice Presidential Nomination." *Historian* 42 (November 1979): 85-100.

8837. Patenaude, Lionel V. "The Garner Vote Switch to Roosevelt: 1932 Democratic Convention." *Southwestern Historical Quarterly* 79 (October 1975): 189-204.

8838. Posner, Russell. "California's Role in the Nomination of Franklin D. Roosevelt." *California Historical Society Quarterly* 39 (June 1960): 121-139.

8839. Ray, Robert F. "An Evaluation of the Public Speaking of Franklin D. Roosevelt and Thomas E. Dewey in the Presidential Campaign of 1944." Ph.D. dissertation, State University of Iowa, 1947.

8840. Redding, W. Charles. "Methodological Study of 'Rhetorical Postulates' Applied to a Content Analysis of the 1944 Campaign Speeches of Dewey and Roosevelt." Ph.D. dissertation, University of Southern California, 1956.

8841. Robinson, Edgar E. *They Voted for Roosevelt: The Presidential Vote, 1932-1944*. Stanford, CA: Stanford University Press, 1947.

8842. Robinson, Rex E. "Persuasion in the Speeches of the Presidential Campaign of 1940." Ph.D. dissertation, University of Wisconsin, 1947.

8843. Ross, Hugh. "Roosevelt's Third-term Nomination." *Mid-America* 44 (April 1962): 80-94.

8844. Ross, Hugh. "The Third-Term Campaign of 1940." Ph.D. dissertation, Stanford University, 1960.

8845. Sadler, Charles. " 'Political Dynamite': The Chicago Polonia and President Roosevelt in 1944." *Illinois State Historical Society Journal* 71 (May 1978): 119-132.

8846. Schnell, J. Christopher. "Missouri Progressives and the Nomination of F. D. R." *Missouri Historical Review* 68 (April 1974): 269-279.

8847. Spencer, Thomas T. "FDR's Forgotten Friend: Henry H. McPike and the 1932 Democratic Presidential Nomination." *California History* 63 (Summer 1984): 194-199.

8848. Spencer, Thomas T. "Labor Is with Roosevelt: The Pennsylvania Labor Non-Partisan League and the Election of 1936." *Pennsylvania History* 46 (January 1979): 3-16.

8849. Spencer, Thomas T. "The Roosevelt All-Party Agricultural Committee and the 1936 Election." *Annals of Iowa* (Summer 1979): 44-57.

8850. Tugwell, Rexford G. "Must We Draft Roosevelt?" *New Republic* 102 (May 13, 1940): 630-633.

8851. Tugwell, Rexford G. "The Progressive Orthodoxy of Franklin D. Roosevelt." *Ethics* 64 (October 1953): 1-21.

8852. Warburg, James. *Hell Bent for Election*. Garden City, NY: Doubleday, 1935.

Foreign Affairs

8853. Accinelli, Robert D. "The Roosevelt Administration and the World Court Defeat, 1935." *Historian* 40 (May 1978): 463-478.

8854. Adler, Selig. "Franklin D. Roosevelt Foreign Policy: An Assessment." *International Review of History and Political Science* 15 (May 1978): 1-17.

8855. Adler, Selig. "United States Policy on Palestine in the FDR Era." *American Jewish Historical Quarterly* 62 (September 1972): 11-29.

8856. Bader, Ernest B. "Some Aspects of American Public Reaction to Franklin D. Roosevelt's Japanese Policy, 1933-1941." Ph.D. dissertation, University of Nebraska, 1957.

8857. Barron, Gloria J. *Leadership in Crisis: FDR and the Path to Intervention*. Port Washington, NY: Kennikat Press, 1973.

8858. Beard, Charles A. "Neutrality: Shall We Have Revision? President's Policy, and the People's." *New Republic* 97 (January 18, 1939): 307-308.

8859. Bennett, Edward M. "Franklin D. Roosevelt and Russian-American Relations, 1933-1939." Ph.D. dissertation, University of Illinois, 1961.

8860. Bishop, Donald G. *The Roosevelt-Litvinov Agreements*. Syracuse, NY: Syracuse University Press, 1965.

8861. Brandenburg, Earnest. "An Analysis and Criticism of Franklin D. Roosevelt's Speeches on International Affairs Delivered between September 3, 1939 and December 7, 1941." Ph.D. dissertation, State University of Iowa, 1953.

8862. Brandenburg, Earnest. "Franklin D. Roosevelt's International Speeches, 1939-1941." *Speech Monographs* 16 (August 1949): 21-41.

8863. Brandenburg, Earnest. "The Preparation of Franklin D. Roosevelt's Speeches." *Quarterly Journal of Speech* 35 (April 1949): 214-221.

8864. Bryniarski, Joan L. "Against the Tide: Senate Opposition to the Internationalist Foreign Policy of Presidents Franklin D. Roosevelt and Harry S. Truman, 1943-1949." Ph.D. dissertation, University of Maryland, 1972.

8865. Bryson, Thomas A. "Roosevelt's Quarantine Speech, the Georgia Press, and the Borg Thesis: A Note." *Australian Journal of Political History* 21 (August 1975): 95-98.

8866. Burke, Robert L. "Franklin D. Roosevelt and the Far East: 1913-1941." Ph.D. dissertation, Michigan State University, 1969.

8867. Chowdhry, Carol. "Dusk of Empire: Roosevelt and Asian Colonialism, 1941-1945." Ph.D. dissertation, University of Virginia, 1973.

8868. Clauss, Errol M. "The Roosevelt Administration and Manchukuo, 1933-1941." *Historian* 32 (August 1970): 595-611.

8869. Cole, Wayne S. *Roosevelt and the*

Isolationists. Lincoln: University of Nebraska Press, 1983.

8870. Crocker, George N. *Roosevelt's Road to Russia.* Chicago: Regnery, 1959.

8871. Crossman, Richard H. "Did F. D. R. Escape Wilson's Failure? Idealism vs. Power Politics in American Foreign Policy." *Commentary* 8 (November 1949): 418-423.

8872. Dallek, Robert. *Franklin D. Roosevelt and American Foreign Policy, 1932-1945.* New York: Oxford University Press, 1979.

8873. Dallek, Robert. "Franklin D. Roosevelt as World Leader: A Review Article." *American Historical Review* 76 (December 1971): 1503-1513.

8874. Dallek, Robert. "Roosevelt's Ambassador: The Public Career of William E. Dodd." Ph.D. dissertation, Columbia University, 1964.

8875. Donovan, John C. "Congressional Isolationists and the Roosevelt Foreign Policy." *World Politics* 3 (April 1951): 299-316.

8876. Dulles, Foster R., and Gerald Ridinger. "The Anti-Colonial Policies of Franklin D. Roosevelt." *Political Science Quarterly* 70 (March 1955): 1-18.

8877. Eyre, James K. *The Roosevelt-MacArthur Conflict.* Chambersburg, PA: Craft Press, 1950.

8878. Fagan, George V. "Franklin D. Roosevelt and Naval Limitation." *U.S. Naval Institute Proceedings* 81 (April 1955): 411-418.

8879. Flynn, George Q. "Franklin D. Roosevelt and the Vatican: The Myron Taylor Appointment." *Catholic Historical Review* 58 (July 1972): 171-194.

8880. Flynn, George Q. *Roosevelt and Romanism: Catholics and American Diplomacy, 1937-1945.* Westport, CT: Greenwood Press, 1976.

8881. Fohlen, Claude. "The Foreign Policy of F. D. Roosevelt: Some Reflections." *Amerikastudien/American Studies* (West Germany) 21 (1976): 109-118.

8882. Gellman, Irwin F. *Roosevelt and Batista: Good Neighbor Diplomacy in Cuba: 1933-1945.* Albuquerque: University of New Mexico Press, 1973.

8883. Guerrant, Edward O. *Roosevelt's Good Neighbor Policy.* Albuquerque: University of New Mexico Press, 1950.

8884. Habibuddin, Syed M. "Franklin D. Roosevelt's Anti-Colonial Policy towards Asia: Its Implications for India, Indo-China, and Indonesia (1941-45)." *Journal of Indian History* 53 (December 1975): 497-522.

8885. Haight, John M., Jr. "FDR's 'Big Stick.'" *U.S. Naval Institute Proceedings* 106 (July 1980): 68-73.

8886. Haines, Gerald K. "The Roosevelt Administration Interprets the Monroe Doctrine." *Australian Journal of Politics and History* 24 (December 1978): 322-345.

8887. Haines, Gerald K. "Under the Eagle's Wing: The Franklin Roosevelt Administration Forges an American Hemisphere." *Diplomatic History* 1 (Fall 1977): 373-388.

8888. Halperin, Samuel, and Irvin Oder. "United States in Search of a Policy: Franklin D. Roosevelt and Palestine." *Review of Politics* 24 (July 1962): 320-341.

8889. Hammersmith, Jack L. "Franklin Roosevelt, the Polish Question, and the Election of 1944." *Mid-America* 59 (January 1977): 5-17.

8890. Harrison, Richard A. "A Presidential Demarche: Franklin D. Roosevelt's Personal Diplomacy and Great Britain,

1936-37." *Diplomatic History* 5 (Summer 1981): 245-273.

8891. Heinrichs, Waldo H. "Roosevelt and Truman: The Presidential Perspective." In *Uncertain Years: Chinese-American Relations, 1947-1950,* edited by Dorothy Borg and Waldo Heinrichs, 3-12. New York: Columbia University Press, 1980.

8892. Hess, Gary R. "Franklin Roosevelt and Indochina." *Journal of American History* 59 (September 1972): 353-367.

8893. Iakovlev, N. N. "F. Roosevelt: Proponent of Collaboration with the Soviet Union." *Soviet Studies in History* 2 (Spring 1974): 3-29.

8894. Izek, Hersch. "Roosevelt and the Polish Question, 1941-1945." Ph.D. dissertation, University of Minnesota, 1980.

8895. Jablon, Howard. "Cordell Hull, the State Department, and the Foreign Policy of the First Roosevelt Administration, 1933-1936." Ph.D. dissertation, Rutgers University, 1967.

8896. Kahn, Gilbert N. "Presidential Passivity on a Nonsalient Issue: President Franklin D. Roosevelt and the 1935 World Court Fight." *Diplomatic History* 4 (Spring 1980): 137-159.

8897. Kanawada, Leo V. "The Ethnic Factor in American Diplomacy during the Presidency of Franklin D. Roosevelt: 1933-1939." Ph.D. dissertation, St. John's University, 1980.

8898. Keating, John S. "Mission to Mecca: A Postscript." *U.S. Naval Institute Proceedings* 104 (April 1978): 74-77.

8899. Kennedy, Thomas C. "Beard vs. F. D. R. on National Defense and Rearmament." *Mid-America* 50 (January 1968): 22-41.

8900. Kimball, Warren F., and Bruce Bartlett. "Roosevelt and Prewar Commitments to Churchill: The Tyler Kent Affair." *Diplomatic History* 5 (Autumn 1981): 291-311.

8901. LaFeber, Walter F. "Roosevelt, Churchill, and Indochina: 1942-1945." *American Historical Review* 80 (December 1975): 1277-1295.

8902. Lash, Joseph P. *Roosevelt and Churchill, 1939-1941: The Partnership That Saved the West.* New York: Norton, 1976.

8903. Lazalier, James H. "Surrogate Diplomacy: Franklin D. Roosevelt's Personal Envoys, 1941-1945." Ph.D. dissertation, University of Oklahoma, 1973.

8904. Lindley, Christopher. "Franklin D. Roosevelt and the Politics of Isolationism, 1932-1936." Ph.D. dissertation, Cornell University, 1963.

8905. McNeal, Robert H. "Roosevelt through Stalin's Spectacles." *International Journal* 18 (Spring 1963): 194-206.

8906. Maddox, Robert J. "Roosevelt and Stalin: The Final Days." *Continuity* 6 (Spring 1983): 113-122.

8907. Mannering, Lynne M. "A Venture into Internationalism: Roosevelt and the Refugee Crisis of 1938." Master's thesis, North Texas State University, 1978.

8908. Mathews, John M. "Roosevelt's Latin-American Policy." *American Political Science Review* 29 (October 1935): 805-820.

8909. Matson, William L. "William Lyon Mackenzie King and Franklin Delano Roosevelt: Their Effect on Canadian-American Relations, 1935-1939." Ph.D. dissertation, University of Maine, 1973.

8910. Messer, Robert L. *The End of an Alliance: James F. Byrnes, Roosevelt, Truman, and the Origins of the Cold War.* Chapel Hill: University of North Carolina Press, 1982.

8911. Miller, James E. "The Politics of

Relief: The Roosevelt Administration and the Reconstruction of Italy, 1943-1944." *Prologue* 13 (Autumn 1981): 193-208.

8912. Mitchell, Wayne S. "The Roosevelt Administration, Anti-Imperialism, and the Grand Alliance." Master's thesis, American University, 1969.

8913. Neumann, William L. *After Victory: Churchill, Roosevelt, Stalin, and the Making of Peace*. New York: Harper and Row, 1967.

8914. Neumann, William L. "Franklin Delano Roosevelt: A Disciple of Admiral Mahan." *U.S. Naval Institute Proceedings* 78 (July 1952): 713-719.

8915. Nixon, Edgar B. *Franklin D. Roosevelt and Foreign Affairs*. 3 vols. Cambridge, MA: Harvard University Press, 1970.

8916. Parzen, Herbert. "The Roosevelt Palestine Policy, 1943-1945: An Exercise in Dual Diplomacy." *American Jewish Archives* 26 (April 1974): 31-65.

8917. Patterson, James T. "Eating Humble Pie: A Note on Roosevelt, Congress, and Neutrality Revision in 1939." *Historian* 31 (May 1969): 407-414.

8918. Peterson, Barbara B. "FDR's 'Quarterbacking' of U.S. Naval Policy in the Pacific, 1933-1939." *Pacific Historian* 17 (1973): 61-72; (1973): 60-73.

8919. Peterson, Hans J. "The Post-War German View of Franklin Delano Roosevelt." Ph.D. dissertation, University of Denver, 1966.

8920. Pogue, Forrest C. "The Big Three and the United Nations." In *The Meaning of Yalta: Big Three Diplomacy and the New Balance of Power*, edited by John L. Snell, 167-187. Baton Rouge: Louisiana State University Press, 1956.

8921. Range, Willard. "Franklin D. Roosevelt's Theory of International Relations." Ph.D. dissertation, University of North Carolina, 1958.

8922. Ray, Deborah W. "The Fakoradi Route: Roosevelt's Prewar Venture beyond the Western Hemisphere." *Journal of American History* 62 (September 1975): 340-358.

8923. Reynolds, David. "FDR on the British: A Postscript." *Massachusetts Historical Society Proceedings* 90 (1978): 106-110.

8924. Reynolds, David. "FDR's Foreign Policy and the British Royal Visit to the U.S.A., 1939." *Historian* 45 (August 1983): 461-472.

8925. Reynolds, David. "Roosevelt, the British Left, and the Appointment of John G. Winant as United States Ambassador to Britain in 1941." *International History Review* 4 (August 1982): 393-413.

8926. Sbrega, John J. "The Anticolonial Policies of Franklin D. Roosevelt: A Reappraisal." *Political Science Quarterly* 101 (1986): 65-84.

8927. Schlesinger, Arthur M., Jr. "A Comment of Roosevelt and His Foreign Policy Critics." *Political Science Quarterly* 94 (Spring 1979): 33-36.

8928. Smith, M. J. J. "F. D. R. and the Brussels Conference, 1937." *Michigan Academician* 14 (Fall 1981): 109-122.

8929. Steele, Richard W. "Franklin D. Roosevelt and His Foreign Policy Critics." *Political Science Quarterly* 94 (Spring 1979): 15-32.

8930. Tansill, Charles C. *Back Door to War: The Roosevelt Foreign Policy, 1933-1941*. Chicago: Regnery, 1952.

8931. Traina, Richard P. *American Diplomacy and the Spanish Civil War*. Bloomington: Indiana University Press, 1968.

8932. "Under the Eagle's Wing: The Franklin Roosevelt Administration Forges an American Hemisphere." *Diplomatic History* 1 (Fall 1977): 373-388.

8933. Van Deusen, Robert C. "Good Neighbor Idealism in the Roosevelt Era." Master's thesis, American University, 1961.

8934. Wallace, William V. "Roosevelt and British Appeasement, 1938." *Bulletin of the British Association for American Studies* 5 (December 1962): 4-30.

8935. Warner, Geoffrey. "From Teheran to Yalta: Reflections on F. D. R.'s Foreign Policy." *International Affairs* 43 (July 1967): 530-536.

8936. Watt, Donald C. "Roosevelt and Chamberlain: Two Appeasers." *International Journal* 28 (Spring 1973): 185-204.

8937. Weinrich, William A. "Business and Foreign Affairs: The Roosevelt Defense Program, 1937-1941." Ph.D. dissertation, University of Oklahoma, 1971.

8938. Wells, Edward F. "FDR and the Marines." *Fortitudine* 11 (Autumn/Winter 1981-1982): 18-19.

8939. Whitehead, Donald F. "The Making of Foreign Policy during President Roosevelt's First Term, 1933-1937." Ph.D. dissertation, University of Chicago, 1952.

8940. Woods, Randall B. "Hull and Argentina: Wilsonian Diplomacy in the Age of Roosevelt." *Journal of Interamerican Studies and World Affairs* 16 (August 1974): 350-371.

8941. Woods, Randall B. *The Roosevelt Foreign Policy Establishment and the 'Good Neighbor': The United States and Argentina, 1941-1945.* Lawrence: Regents Press of Kansas, 1980.

8942. Woytak, Richard A. "Roosevelt's Early Foreign Policy Reflected in Polish Diplomatic Dispatches from Washington (1932-1933)." *Polish Review* 21 (1976): 217-224.

8943. Young, Lowell T. "Franklin D. Roosevelt and America's Islets: Acquisition of Territory in the Caribbean and in the Pacific." *Historian* 35 (February 1943): 205-220.

8944. Young, Lowell T. "Franklin D. Roosevelt and Imperialism." Ph.D. dissertation, University of Virginia, 1970.

8945. Young, Lowell T. "Franklin D. Roosevelt and the Expansion of the Monroe Doctrine." *North Dakota Quarterly* 42 (Winter 1974): 23-32.

Judicial

8946. Baker, Leonard. *Back to Back, The Duel between F. D. R. and the Supreme Court.* New York: Macmillan, 1967.

8947. Barnes, William R., and Arthur W. Littlefield, eds. *The Supreme Court Issue and the Constitutions.* New York: Barnes and Noble, 1937.

8948. Bowman, Eileen M. "Walter Lippman's Reaction to Franklin D. Roosevelt's 1937 Court-Packing Plan." Master's thesis, Michigan State University, 1978.

8949. Canon, Alfred O. "Mr. Justice Rutledge and the Roosevelt Court." *Vanderbilt Law Review* 10 (February 1957): 167-192.

8950. Cathcart, Arthur M. "The Supreme Court and the New Deal." *Southern California Law Review* 9 (June 1936): 315-333.

8951. Cope, Alfred H., and Fred Krinsky, eds. *Franklin D. Roosevelt and the Supreme Court.* Rev ed. Boston: Heath, 1969.

8952. Crouch, Barry A. "Dennis Chavez and Roosevelt's 'Court Packing' Plan." *New Mexico Historical Review* 42 (October 1967): 261-280.

8953. Dause, Charles A. "An Analysis of the 1937 Public Debate over Franklin D.

Roosevelt's Court Reform Proposal." Ph.D. dissertation, Wayne State University, 1969.

8954. Dilliard, Irving. "Mr. Roosevelt and the Supreme Court: The Observations of a Citizen." *Survey Graphic* 26 (February 1937): 93-96.

8955. Duram, James C. "Supreme Court Packing and the New Deal: The View from Southwestern Michigan." *Michigan History* 52 (Spring 1968): 13-27.

8956. Eriksson, Erik M. *The Supreme Court and the New Deal, A Study of Recent Constitutional Interpretation.* Los Angeles: Lymanhouse, 1941.

8957. Galloway, Russell W., Jr. "The Roosevelt Court: The Liberals Conquer (1937-1941) and Divide (1941-1946)." *Santa Clara Law Review* 23 (Spring 1983): 491-542.

8958. Ganoe, John T. "The Roosevelt Court and the Commerce Clause." *Oregon Law Review* 24 (February 1945): 71-147.

8959. Gardner, Robert W. "Roosevelt and Supreme Court Expansion." *Connecticut Review* 3 (October 1969): 58-68.

8960. Gressley, Gene M. "Joseph C. O'Mahoney, FDR, and the Supreme Court." *Pacific Historical Review* 40 (May 1971): 183-202.

8961. Jaffe, Louis L. "Professors and Judges as Advisors to Government: Reflections on the Roosevelt-Frankfurter Relationship." *Harvard Law Review* 83 (December 1969): 366-376.

8962. Leuchtenburg, William E. "Franklin D. Roosevelt's Supreme Court 'Packing' Plan." In *Essays on the New Deal,* edited by Harold M. Hollingsworth and William F. Holmes, 69-115. Austin: University of Texas Press, 1969.

8963. Leuchtenburg, William E. "The Origins of Franklin D. Roosevelt's 'Court-Packing' Plan." *Supreme Court Review* (1966): 347-400.

8964. Lichty, Joanne D. "The Roosevelt Court-Packing Plan: The Role of Farm and Labor Groups." Master's thesis, American University, 1969.

8965. Lowitt, Richard. "Only God Can Change the Supreme Court." *Capitol Studies* 5 (Spring 1977): 9-24.

8966. McLain, J. Dudley, Jr. "Supreme Court Controversies of Presidents Roosevelt and Nixon: A Consideration of the Political Nature of the Presidential Power of Judicial Appointment." *Georgia State Bar Journal* 8 (November 1971): 145-179.

8967. Mason, Alpheus T. "Harlan Fiske Stone and FDR's Court Plan." *Yale Law Journal* 61 (July 1952): 791-817.

8968. Mason, Alpheus T. "Politics and the Supreme Court: President Roosevelt's Proposal." *University of Pennsylvania Law Review* 85 (May 1937): 659-677.

8969. Morrison, Rodney J. "Franklin D. Roosevelt and the Supreme Court: An Example of the Use of Probability Theory in Political History." *History and Theory* 16 (1977): 137-146.

8970. Nagy, Edward C. "Franklin D. Roosevelt, the Senate, and the Supreme Court Fight of 1937: A Critical Turning Point for the New Deal." Master's thesis, Stephen F. Austin State University, 1977.

8971. Niedziela, Theresa A. "Franklin D. Roosevelt and the Supreme Court." *Presidential Studies Quarterly* 6 (Fall 1976): 51-57.

8972. Oddo, Gilbert L. "Justice Douglas and the Roosevelt Court." Ph.D. dissertation, Georgetown University, 1952.

8973. Patenaude, Lionel V. "Garner, Sumners, and Connally: The Defeat of the Roosevelt Court Bill in 1937." *Southwestern Historical Quarterly* 74 (July 1970): 36-51.

8974. Phelps, Bernard F. "A Rhetorical Analysis of the 1937 Addresses of Franklin D. Roosevelt in Support of Court Reform." Ph.D. dissertation, Ohio State University, 1957.

8975. Pritchett, C. Herman. *The Roosevelt Court: A Study in Judicial Politics and Values, 1937-1947.* New York: Quadrangle Books, 1948.

8976. Pritchett, C. Herman. "The Roosevelt Court: Votes and Values." *American Political Science Review* 42 (February 1948): 53-67.

8977. Pusey, Merlo J. "F. D. R. vs. the Supreme Court." *American Heritage* 9 (April 1958): 24-27, 105-107.

8978. Saylor, J. R. "Court Packing Prior to FDR." *Baylor Law Review* 20 (Spring 1968): 147-165.

8979. Scanlan, Alfred L. "The Roosevelt Court Becomes the Truman Court." *Notre Dame Lawyer* 26 (Winter 1951): 214-267.

8980. Sirevag, Torbjorn. "Rooseveltian Ideas and the 1937 Court Fight: A Neglected Factor." *Historian* 33 (August 1971): 578-595.

8981. Smith, Charles W., Jr. "President Roosevelt's Attitude toward the Courts." *Kentucky Law Journal* 31 (May 1943): 301-315.

8982. Tugwell, Rexford G. "Roosevelt and Frankfurter: An Essay Review." *Political Science Quarterly* 85 (March 1970): 99-170.

New Deal

8983. Albertson, Dean. *Roosevelt's Farmer, Claude R. Wickard in the New Deal.* New York: Columbia University Press, 1961.

8984. Allen, William R. "Irving Fisher, F. D. R., and the Great Depression." *History of Political Economy* 9 (Winter 1977): 560-587.

8985. Auerbach, Jerold S. "New Deal, Old Deal, or Raw Deal: Some Thoughts on New Left Historiography." *Journal of Southern History* 35 (February 1969): 18-30.

8986. Bellush, Jewel. "Old and New Left Reappraisals of the New Deal and Roosevelt's Presidency." *Presidential Studies Quarterly* 9 (Summer 1979): 243-265.

8987. Bernstein, Barton J., ed. *Towards a New Past: Dissenting Essays in American History.* New York: Random House, 1968.

8988. Billington, Monroe. "The Alabama Clergy and the New Deal." *Alabama Review* 32 (July 1979): 214-225.

8989. Billington, Monroe. "Roosevelt, the New Deal, and the Clergy." *Mid-America* 54 (January 1972): 20-33.

8990. Billington, Monroe, and Cal Clark. "The Episcopal Clergy and the New Deal: Clerical Response to Franklin D. Roosevelt's Letter of Inquiry, September 1935." *Historical Magazine of the Protestant Episcopal Church* 52 (September 1983): 293-305.

8991. Boles, John B. "Franklin D. Roosevelt and the New Deal." *Social Humanities Review* 4 (Spring 1970): 163-177.

8992. Braeman, John. "The Historian as Activist: Charles A. Beard and the New Deal." *South Atlantic Quarterly* 79 (Autumn 1980): 364-374.

8993. Braeman, John. "The Making of the Roosevelt Coalition: Some Reconsiderations." *Canadian Review of American Studies* 11 (Autumn 1980): 233-253.

8994. Bremer, William W. "Along the 'American Way': The New Deal's Work Relief Programs for the Unemployed." *Journal of American History* 62 (December 1975): 636-652.

8995. Carter, John F. *The New Dealers: By the Unofficial Observer.* New York: Simon and Schuster, 1934.

8996. Cohen, Jacob. "Schlesinger and the New Deal." *Dissent* 8 (Autumn 1961): 461-472.

8997. Cohen, Wilbur J. "FDR and the New Deal: A Personal Reminiscence." *Milwaukee History* 6 (Autumn 1983): 70-82.

8998. Collins, Robert M. "Positive Business Responses to the New Deal: The Roots of the Committee for Economic Development, 1933-1942." *Business History Review* 52 (Autumn 1978): 369-391.

8999. Conkin, Paul K. *The New Deal.* 2d ed. New York: Crowell, 1975.

9000. Curlee, Joan E. "Some Aspects of the New Deal: The Pre-1936 Writings of Six of Roosevelt's Advisers." Ph.D. dissertation, Vanderbilt University, 1957.

9001. Dawson, Nelson L. "Louis D. Brandeis, Felix Frankfurter, and Franklin D. Roosevelt: The Origins of a New Deal Relationship." *American Jewish History* 68 (September 1978): 32-42.

9002. Dawson, Nelson L. *Louis D. Brandeis, Felix Frankfurter, and the New Deal.* Hamden, CT: Archon Books, 1980.

9003. Degler, Carl N., ed. *The New Deal.* Chicago: Quadrangle Books, 1970.

9004. Dizikes, John. *Britain, Roosevelt, and the New Deal: British Opinion, 1932-1938.* New York: Garland, 1979.

9005. Dorsett, Lyle W. "Frank Hague, Franklin Roosevelt, and the Politics of the New Deal." *New Jersey History* 94 (Spring 1976): 23-35.

9006. Droze, Wilmon, H. "The New Deal's Shelterbelt Project, 1934-1942." In *Essays on the New Deal,* edited by Harold M. Hollingsworth and William F. Holmes, 23-48. Austin: University of Texas Press, 1969.

9007. Einaudi, Mario. *The Roosevelt Revolution.* New York: Harcourt, Brace, 1959.

9008. Ekirch, Arthur A. *Ideologies and Utopias: The Impact of the New Deal on American Thought.* Chicago: Quadrangle Books, 1969.

9009. Ellingwood, Albert R. "The New Deal and the Constitution." *Illinois Law Review* 28 (February 1934): 729-751.

9010. Eulau, Heinz. "Neither Ideology nor Utopia: The New Deal in Retrospect." *Antioch Review* 19 (Winter 1959-1960): 523-537.

9011. Feder, Donald. "Benito and Franklin." *Reason* 14 (1982): 29-32.

9012. Freidel, Frank B., ed. *The New Deal and the American People.* Englewood Cliffs, NJ: Prentice-Hall, 1964.

9013. Frisch, Morton J. *Franklin D. Roosevelt: The Contribution of the New Deal to American Political Thought and Practice.* New York: Twayne, 1975.

9014. Fusfeld, Daniel R. *The Economic Thought of Franklin D. Roosevelt and the Origins of the New Deal.* New York: Columbia University Press, 1956.

9015. Fusfeld, Daniel R. "Roots of the New Deal: The Economic Thought of Franklin D. Roosevelt to 1932." Ph.D. dissertation, Columbia University, 1953.

9016. Galbraith, John K. "On the Economics of F. D. R.: What a President Ought to Know." *Commentary* 22 (August 1956): 172-175.

9017. Gardner, Lloyd C. *Economic Aspects of New Deal Diplomacy.* Madison: University of Wisconsin Press, 1964.

9018. Goll, Eugene W. "Frank R. Kent's Opposition to Franklin D. Roosevelt and the New Deal." *Maryland Historical Magazine* 63 (June 1968): 158-171.

9019. Graham, Otis L. "Historians and the New Deals: 1944-1960." *Social Studies* 54 (April 1963): 133-140.

9020. Graham, Otis L., ed. *The New Deal: The Critical Issues*. Boston: Little, Brown, 1971.

9021. Hamby, Alonzo L., ed. *The New Deal*. New York: Weybright, 1969.

9022. Hand, Samuel B. "Al Smith, Franklin D. Roosevelt, and the New Deal: Some Comments on Perspective." *Historian* 27 (May 1965): 366-381.

9023. Hankin, C. A. "The Supreme Court and the New Deal." *Editorial Research Reports* 2 (1935): 413-428.

9024. Hawley, Ellis W. *The New Deal and the Problem of Monopoly, 1933-1939: A Study in Economic Ambivalence*. Princeton, NJ: Princeton University Press, 1966.

9025. Hevener, John W. "A New Deal for Harlan: The Roosevelt Labor Policies in a Kentucky Coal Field, 1931-1939." Ph.D. dissertation, Ohio State University, 1971.

9026. Humphrey, Hubert H. *Political Philosophy of the New Deal*. Baton Rouge: Louisiana State University Press, 1970.

9027. Hurd, Charles. *When the New Deal Was Young and Gay*. New York: Hawthorne, 1965.

9028. Jacob, Charles E. *Leadership in the New Deal*. Englewood Cliffs, NJ: Prentice-Hall, 1967.

9029. Jacobson, J. Mark. "Inherent Executive Power of Removal: A Reexamination in the Light of the New Deal." *New Jersey Law Review* 1 (January 1935): 32-64.

9030. Jones, Byrd L. "A Plan for Planning in the New Deal." *Social Science Quarterly* 50 (December 1969): 525-534.

9031. Jones, Gene D. "The Origin of the Alliance between the New Deal and the Chicago Machine." *Illinois State Historical Society Journal* 67 (June 1974): 253-274.

9032. Karl, Barry D. *Executive Reorganization and Reform in the New Deal, The Genesis of Administrative Management, 1900-1939*. Cambridge, MA: Harvard University Press, 1963.

9033. Kelly, Lawrence C. "Choosing the New Deal Indian Commissioner: Ickes vs. Collier." *New Mexico Historical Review* 49 (October 1974): 269-284.

9034. Kirkendall, Richard S. "The New Deal as Watershed: The Recent Literature." *Journal of American History* 54 (March 1968): 839-852.

9035. Kirkendall, Richard S., ed. *The New Deal: The Historical Debate*. New York: Wiley, 1973.

9036. Koeniger, A. Cash. "The New Deal and the States: Roosevelt versus the Byrd Organization in Virginia." *Journal of American History* 68 (March 1982): 876-896.

9037. Lapomarda, Vincent A. "A New Deal Democrat in Boston: Maurice J. Tobin and the Policies of Franklin D. Roosevelt." *Essex Institute of Historical Collections* 108 (April 1972): 135-152.

9038. Lawrence, David. *Beyond the New Deal*. New York: McGraw-Hill, 1934.

9039. Lee, Bradford A. "The New Deal Reconsidered." *Wilson Quarterly* 6 (Spring 1982): 62-76.

9040. Leff, Mark H. "Taxing the 'Forgotten Man': The Politics of Social Security Finance in the New Deal." *Journal of American History* 70 (September 1983): 359-381.

9041. Leiter, William M. "The Presidency and Non-Federal Government: The

Benefactor-Aversion Hypothesis, The Case of Public Assistance Policies in the New Deal and Nixon Administrations." *Presidential Studies Quarterly* 11 (Spring 1981): 280-288.

9042. Lepawsky, Albert. "The Planning Apparatus: A Vignette of the New Deal." *Journal of the American Institute of Planners* 42 (January 1976): 16-32.

9043. Leuchtenburg, William E. *Franklin D. Roosevelt and the New Deal, 1932-1940.* New York: Harper and Row, 1963.

9044. Leuchtenburg, William E. "The Legacy of FDR." *Wilson Quarterly* 6 (Spring 1982): 77-93.

9045. Leuchtenburg, William E. "The New Deal and the Analogue of War." In *Change and Continuity in Twentieth-Century America,* edited by John Braeman, Robert H. Bremner, and Everett Walters, 81-143. Columbus: Ohio State University Press, 1964.

9046. Leuchtenburg, William E., ed. *The New Deal: A Documentary History.* Columbia: University of South Carolina Press, 1968.

9047. Lindley, Ernest K. *The Roosevelt Revolution, First Phase.* New York: Viking Press, 1933.

9048. Louchheim, Katie, ed. *The Making of the New Deal: The Insiders Speak.* Cambridge, MA: Harvard University Press, 1983.

9049. McFarland, Charles K. *Roosevelt, Lewis, and the New Deal, 1933-1940.* Fort Worth: Texas Christian University Press, 1970.

9050. McKinzie, Richard D. *The New Deal for Artists.* Princeton, NJ: Princeton University Press, 1973.

9051. Major, John, ed. *The New Deal.* New York: Barnes and Nobles, 1967.

9052. Mencken, Henry L. "Constitution for the New Deal." *American Mercury* 41 (June 1937): 129-136.

9053. Michelson, Charles. *The Ghost Talks.* New York: Putnam, 1944.

9054. Mitchell, Broadus. *Depression Decade, From New Era through New Deal, 1929-1941.* New York: Rinehart, 1947.

9055. Moley, Raymond. *The First New Deal.* New York: Harcourt, Brace, 1966.

9056. Moley, Raymond, Rexford G. Tugwell, and Ernest K. Lindley. "Symposium: Early Days of the New Deal." In *The Thirties: A Reconsideration in the Light of the American Political Tradition,* edited by Morton J. Frisch and Martin Diamond, 124-143. Dekalb: Northern Illinois University Press, 1968.

9057. Moore, James R. "Sources of New Deal Economic Policy: The International Dimension." *Journal of American History* 61 (December 1974): 728-744.

9058. Moore, Jamie W. "New Deal Diplomacy: Paradigms and Models." *Peace and Change* 3 (Spring 1975): 30-42.

9059. Nash, Gerald D. "Franklin D. Roosevelt and Labor: The World War I Origins of the Early New Deal Policy." *Labor History* 1 (Winter 1960): 39-52.

9060. Nevins, Allan. *The New Deal and World Affairs: A Chronicle of International Affairs, 1933-1945.* New Haven, CT: Yale University Press, 1950.

9061. Patterson, James T. "The New Deal and the States." *American Historical Review* 73 (October 1967): 70-84.

9062. Patterson, James T. *The New Deal and the States: Federalism in Transition.* Princeton, NJ: Princeton University Press, 1969.

9063. Rankin, Robert S. "Presidency under the New Deal." *South Atlantic Quarterly* 33 (April 1934): 152-164.

9064. Rauch, Basil. *The History of the*

New Deal, 1933-1938. New York: Putnam, 1944.

9065. Robinson, George W. "Right of Roosevelt: Negativism and the New Deal, 1933-1937." Ph.D. dissertation, University of Wisconsin, 1956.

9066. Romasco, Albert U. *The Politics of Recovery: Roosevelt's New Deal.* New York: Oxford University Press, 1983.

9067. Rosen, Elliot A. "Intranationalism vs. Internationalism: The Interregnum Struggle for the Sanctity of the New Deal." *Political Science Quarterly* 81 (June 1966): 274-297.

9068. Sargent, James E. "FDR and Lewis W. Douglas: Budget Balancing and the Early New Deal." *Prologue* 6 (Spring 1974): 33-43.

9069. Sargent, James E. "Oral History, Franklin D. Roosevelt and the New Deal: Some Recollections of Adolf A. Berle, Jr., Lewis W. Douglas, and Raymond Moley." *Oral History Review* 1 (1973): 92-110.

9070. Sargent, James E. *Roosevelt and the Hundred Days: Struggle for the Early New Deal.* New York: Garland, 1981.

9071. Sargent, James E. "Roosevelt's Economy Act: Fiscal Conservatism and the Early New Deal." *Congressional Studies* 7 (Winter 1980): 33-51.

9072. Schnell, J. Christopher. "New Deal Scandals: E. Y. Mitchell and F. D. R.'s Commerce Department." *Missouri Historical Review* 69 (July 1975): 357-375.

9073. Schoenherr, Steven E. "Selling the New Deal: Stephen T. Early's Role as Press Secretary to Franklin D. Roosevelt." Ph.D. dissertation, University of Delaware, 1976.

9074. Seligman, Lester G., and Elmer E. Cornwell, Jr. *New Deal Mosaic: Roosevelt Confers with His National Emergency Council, 1933-1936.* Eugene: University of Oregon Books, 1965.

9075. Sellers, Steven A. "The Editorial Reaction of Texas Daily Newspapers to Franklin Delano Roosevelt and the New Deal, 1932-1938." Master's thesis, North Texas State University, 1977.

9076. Sirevag, Torbjorn. "The New Deal of War." *American Studies in Scandinavia* (Norway) 7 (1975): 81-99.

9077. Sternsher, Bernard. "Assessing Roosevelt and the New Deal: The Short Run and the Long Run." In *The New Deal: Viewed from Fifty Years,* edited by Lawrence E. Gelfand and Robert J. Neymeyer, 91-106. Iowa City: Center for the Study of the Recent History of the United States, 1983.

9078. Sternsher, Bernard. *Rexford G. Tugwell and the New Deal.* New Brunswick, NJ: Rutgers University Press, 1964.

9079. Strauss, David. "The Roosevelt Revolution: French Observers and the New Deal." *American Studies* 14 (Autumn 1973): 25-42.

9080. Tugwell, Rexford G. "The New Deal: The Available Instruments of Governmental Power." *Western Political Quarterly* 2 (December 1949): 545-580.

9081. Tugwell, Rexford G. *Roosevelt's Revolution: The First Year, A Personal Perspective.* New York: Macmillan, 1977.

9082. Walter, John C. "Exploding a Myth: F. D. R. and the Politics of U.S. Naval Expansion during the New Deal." *Shipmate* 41 (October 1978): 15-18.

9083. Wilson, William H. "The Two New Deals: A Valid Concept?" *Historian* 28 (February 1966): 268-288.

9084. Winfield, Betty H. "The New Deal Publicity Operation: Foundation for the Modern Presidency." *Journalism Quarterly* 61 (Spring 1984): 40-48.

9085. Wolfskill, George. "The New Deal Critics: Did They Miss the Point?" In *Essays on the New Deal,* edited by Harold

M. Hollingworth and William F. Holmes, 49-68. Austin: University of Texas Press, 1969.

9086. Wright, Esmond. "How Relevant Is the New Deal?" *Encounter* 58-59 (June/July 1983): 92-99.

9087. Wright, Esmond. "The Roosevelt Revolution of 1933-1938." *History Today* 12 (December 1962): 821-832.

9088. Zinn, Howard, ed. *New Deal Thought*. Indianapolis, IN: Bobbs-Merrill, 1966.

World War II

9089. Abbazia, Patrick. *Mr. Roosevelt's Navy: The Private War of the U.S. Atlantic Fleet, 1939-1942*. Annapolis, MD: Naval Institute Press, 1975.

9090. Adler, Selig. "Franklin D. Roosevelt and Zionism: The Wartime Record." *Judaism* 21 (Summer 1972): 265-276.

9091. Bailey, Thomas A., and Paul B. Ryan. *Hitler vs. Roosevelt: The Undeclared Naval War*. New York: Macmillan, 1979.

9092. Baker, Leonard. *Roosevelt and Pearl Harbor*. New York: Macmillan, 1970.

9093. Beard, Charles A. *President Roosevelt and the Coming of the War, 1941: A Study in Appearances and Realities*. New Haven, CT: Yale University Press, 1948.

9094. Benedict, Blaine D. "Roosevelt and Poland, 1943-1945: Decision-Making as a Choice among Value-Goals." Ph.D. dissertation, University of Pennsylvania, 1977.

9095. Berlin, Isaiah. "Mr. Churchill and F. D. R." *Cornhill Magazine* 164 (Winter 1949): 219-240.

9096. Bernstein, Barton J. "Roosevelt, Truman, and the Atomic Bomb, 1941-1945: A Reinterpretation." *Political Science Quarterly* 90 (Spring 1975): 23-69.

9097. Bernstein, Barton J. "The Uneasy Alliance: Roosevelt, Churchill, and the Atomic Bomb, 1940-1945." *Western Political Quarterly* 29 (June 1976): 202-230.

9098. Blum, Albert. "Roosevelt, the M-Day Plans, and the Military-Industrial Complex." *Military Affairs* 36 (April 1972): 44-45.

9099. Borg, Dorothy. "Notes on Roosevelt's 'Quarantine' Speech." *Political Science Quarterly* 72 (September 1957): 405-433.

9100. Brambilla, Marius G., Jr. "Despair and Hope: The Wartime Foreign Policy of FDR." Ph.D. dissertation, American University, 1970.

9101. Butow, R. J. C. "Backdoor Diplomacy in the Pacific: The Proposal for a Konoye-Roosevelt Meeting, 1941." *Journal of American History* 59 (June 1972): 48-72.

9102. Catton, Bruce. *The War Lords of Washington*. New York: Harcourt, Brace, 1948.

9103. Dallek, Robert. "Allied Leadership in the Second World War: Roosevelt." *Survey* 21 (1975): 1-42.

9104. Dallek, Robert. *The Roosevelt Diplomacy and World War II*. New York: Holt, Rinehart and Winston, 1970.

9105. DeCola, Thomas G. "Roosevelt and Mussolini: The Critical Years, 1938-1941." Ph.D. dissertation, Kent State University, 1967.

9106. Divine, Robert A. *Roosevelt and World War II*. 2d ed. Baltimore, MD: Penguin, 1972.

9107. Eagles, Charles W. "Two 'Double V's': Jonathan Daniels, FDR, and Race Relations during World War II." *North

Carolina Historical Review 59 (July 1982): 252-270.

9108. Emerson, William. "Franklin Roosevelt as Commander in Chief in World War II." *Military Affairs* 22 (Winter 1958): 181-207.

9109. Esthus, Raymond A. "President Roosevelt's Commitment to Britain to Intervene in a Pacific War." *Mississippi Valley Historical Review* 50 (June 1963): 28-38.

9110. Fehrenbach, T. R. *F. D. R.'s Undeclared War, 1939 to 1941.* New York: McKay, 1967.

9111. Feingold, Henry L. "Courage First and Intelligence Second: The American Jewish Secular Elite, Roosevelt, and the Failure to Rescue." *American Jewish History* 72 (June 1983): 424-460.

9112. Feingold, Henry L. *The Politics of Rescue: The Roosevelt Administration and the Holocaust, 1938-1945.* New Brunswick, NJ: Rutgers University Press, 1970.

9113. Feingold, Henry L. "Roosevelt and the Holocaust: Reflections on New Deal Humanitarianism." *Judaism* 18 (Summer 1969): 259-276.

9114. Feis, Herbert. *Churchill, Roosevelt, Stalin: The War They Waged and the Peace They Sought.* Princeton, NJ: Princeton University Press, 1957.

9115. Fenno, Richard F., Jr. *The Yalta Conference.* 2d ed. Lexington, MA: Heath, 1972.

9116. Fish, Hamilton. *Tragic Deception: FDR and America's Involvement in W.W. II.* Old Greenwich, CT: Devin-Adair, 1983.

9117. Franklin, Mitchell. "War Power of the President: An Historical Justification of Mr. Roosevelt's Message of September 7, 1942." *Tulane Law Review* 17 (November 1942): 217-253.

9118. Freeley, Austin J. "A Comparison and Analysis of the Factors of Rhetorical Invention in Selected Wartime Speeches of Franklin Delano Roosevelt and Winston Spencer Churchill." Ph.D. dissertation, Northwestern University, 1955.

9119. Gross, Richard E. "Why Study about F. D. R. and Hitler?" *Social Education* 47 (October 1983): 372-373.

9120. Guedalla, Philip. "Roosevelt, Churchill, and Hitler: Do They Lead or Are They Led?" *New York Times Magazine* 90 (April 20, 1941): 3, 31.

9121. Haight, John M., Jr. "France and the Aftermath of Roosevelt's 'Quarantine Speech.'" *World Politics* 14 (January 1962): 283-306.

9122. Haight, John M., Jr. "Franklin D. Roosevelt and a Naval Quarantine of Japan." *Pacific Historical Review* 40 (May 1971): 203-226.

9123. Haight, John M., Jr. "Roosevelt and the Aftermath of the 'Quarantine Speech.'" *Review of Politics* 24 (April 1962): 233-259.

9124. Jacobs, Travis B. "Roosevelt's 'Quarantine Speech.'" *Historian* 24 (August 1962): 483-502.

9125. Jones, Manfred. "Roosevelt, Churchill, and America's Entrance into World War II." In *Proceedings of the Conference on War and Diplomacy*, edited by David H. White, 81-87. Charleston, SC: Citadel Press, 1976.

9126. Kahn, Herman. "World War II and Its Background: Research Materials at the Franklin D. Roosevelt Library and Policies Concerning Their Use." *American Archivist* 17 (April 1954): 149-162.

9127. Kimball, Warren F. "Churchill and Roosevelt: The Personal Equation." *Prologue* 6 (Fall 1974): 169-182.

9128. Kimball, Warren F., ed. *Franklin D. Roosevelt and the World Crisis, 1937-1945.* Lexington, MA: Heath, 1973.

9129. Kimball, Warren F. "The Mythical Yalta Myth." *Society for the History of American Foreign Relations Newsletter* 13 (1982): 21-23.

9130. Kinsella, William E., Jr. "Franklin D. Roosevelt and the Necessity of War." Ph.D. dissertation, Georgetown University, 1974.

9131. Kinsella, William E., Jr. *Leadership in Isolation: FDR and the Origins of the Second World War.* Cambridge, MA: Schenkman, 1978.

9132. Leahy, William D. *I Was There: The Personal Story of the Chief of Staff to Presidents Roosevelt and Truman.* New York: McGraw-Hill, 1950.

9133. LeBeau, John J. "Civilian Military-Political Leadership in Wartime: Roosevelt, the Military, and the Second Front Decisions." Ph.D. dissertation, University of Massachusetts, 1978.

9134. Leutze, James R. "If Britain Should Fall: Roosevelt and Churchill and British-American Naval Relations: 1938-1940." Ph.D. dissertation, Duke University, 1970.

9135. Leutze, James R. "The Secret of the Churchill-Roosevelt Correspondence September 1939-May 1940." *Journal of Contemporary History* 10 (July 1975): 465-491.

9136. Lewis, John M. "Franklin D. Roosevelt and United States Strategy in World War II." Ph.D. dissertation, Cornell University, 1979.

9137. Lowenthal, Mark M. "Roosevelt and the Coming of the War: The Search for United States Policy 1937-1942." *Journal of Contemporary History* 16 (July 1981): 413-440.

9138. McFarland, Keith D. *Harry H. Woodring: A Political Biography of FDR's Controversial Secretary of War.* Lawrence: University Press of Kansas, 1975.

9139. Matloff, Maurice. "Franklin Delano Roosevelt as War Leader." In *Total War and Cold War: Problems in Civilian Control of the Military*, edited by Harry L. Coles, 42-65. Columbus: Ohio State University Press, 1962.

9140. Matloff, Maurice. "Was the Invasion of Southern France a Blunder?" *U.S. Naval Institute Proceedings* 84 (July 1958): 35-45.

9141. Matz, Eliahu. "Political Actions vs. Personal Relations." *Midstream* 27 (April 1981): 41-48.

9142. Matzozky, Eliyho. "An Episode: Roosevelt and the Mass Killing." *Midstream* 26 (August/September 1980): 17-19.

9143. Morison, Samuel E. "Did Roosevelt Start the War? History through a Beard." *Atlantic Monthly* 182 (August 1948): 91-97.

9144. Morton, Henry C. *Atlantic Meeting.* New York: Dodd, Mead, 1943.

9145. Neumann, William L. "Roosevelt's Foreign Policy Decisions, 1940-1945." *Modern Age* 19 (Summer 1975): 272-284.

9146. O'Connor, Raymond G. *Diplomacy for Victory: FDR and Unconditional Surrender.* New York: Norton, 1971.

9147. O'Leary, Paul M. "Wartime Rationing and Governmental Organization." *American Political Science Review* 39 (December 1945): 1089-1109.

9148. Price, Don K. "Notes from the War Memoirs." *Public Administration Review* 10 (Summer 1950): 197-207.

9149. Rauch, Basil. *Roosevelt, From Munich to Pearl Harbor: A Study in the Creation of a Foreign Policy.* New York: Creative Age Press, 1950.

9150. Riste, Olav. "Free Ports in North Norway: A Contribution to the Study of FDR's Wartime Policy towards the

USSR." *Journal of Contemporary History* 5 (1970): 77-95.

9151. Riste, Olav. "An Idea and a Myth: Roosevelt's Free Ports Scheme for North Norway." In *Americana Norvegica*, Vol. 4, edited by Brita Seyersted, 379-397. Oslo: Universitets Forlaget, 1973.

9152. Sainsbury, Keith. *The Turning Point: Roosevelt, Stalin, Churchill, and Chiang-Kai-Shek, 1943: The Moscow, Cairo, and Teheran Conferences*. London: Oxford University Press, 1985.

9153. Smith, Gaddis. *American Diplomacy during the Second World War, 1941-1945*. New York: Wiley, 1965.

9154. Snell, John L. *The Meaning of Yalta: Big Three Diplomacy and the New Balance of Power*. Baton Rouge: Louisiana State University Press, 1956.

9155. Sontag, Raymond J. "Reflections of the Yalta Papers." *Foreign Affairs* 33 (July 1985): 615-623.

9156. Stalin, Joseph. *Stalin's Correspondence with Churchill, Attlee, Roosevelt, and Truman, 1941-1945*. New York: Dutton, 1958.

9157. Steele, Richard W. *The First Offensive, 1942: Roosevelt, Marshall, and the Making of American Strategy*. Bloomington: Indiana University Press, 1973.

9158. Steele, Richard W. "The Great Debate: Roosevelt, the Media, and the Coming of the War, 1940-1941." *Journal of American History* 71 (June 1984): 69-92.

9159. Steele, Richard W. "News of the 'Good War': World War II News Management." *Journalism Quarterly* 62 (Winter 1985): 707-716.

9160. Stelzner, Hermann G. " 'War Message,' December 8, 1941: An Approach to Language." *Speech Monographs* 33 (November 1966): 419-437.

9161. Stettinius, Edward R., Jr. *Roosevelt and the Russians: The Yalta Conference*. Garden City, NY: Doubleday, 1949.

9162. Strange, Russell P. "The Atlantic and Arcadia Conferences: The First Two Wartime Meetings of Roosevelt and Churchill." Master's thesis, University of Maryland, 1953.

9163. Strange, Russell P. "Atlantic Conference — The First Roosevelt-Churchill Meeting." *U.S. Naval Institute Proceedings* 79 (April 1953): 388-397.

9164. Theoharis, Athan G. "Roosevelt and Truman of Yalta: The Origins of the Cold War." *Political Science Quarterly* 87 (June 1972): 210-241.

9165. Toskova, Vitka. "The Policy of the United States towards the Axis Satellites (1943-1944)." *Bulgarian Historical Review* 7 (1979): 3-26.

9166. Towne, Ralph L., Jr. "Roosevelt and the Coming of the World War II: An Analysis of the War Issues Treated by Franklin D. Roosevelt in Selected Speeches, October 5, 1937 to December 7, 1941." Ph.D. dissertation, Michigan State University, 1961.

9167. Van Everen, Brooks. "Franklin D. Roosevelt and the German Problem: 1914-1945." Ph.D. dissertation, University of Colorado, 1970.

9168. Viorst, Milton. *Hostile Allies: FDR and Charles De Gaulle*. New York: Macmillan, 1965.

9169. Waller, George M. *Pearl Harbor: Roosevelt and the Coming of the War*. Boston: Heath, 1953.

9170. Walter, John C. "Congressman Carl Vinson and Franklin D. Roosevelt: Naval Preparedness and the Coming of World War II, 1932-1940." *Georgia History Quarterly* 64 (Autumn 1980): 294-305.

9171. Wilson, Theodore A. *The First Summit: Roosevelt and Churchill at Pla-*

centia Bay, 1941. Boston: Houghton Mifflin, 1969.

9172. Winnacker, Rudolph A. "Yalta — Another Munich?" *Virginia Quarterly Review* 24 (Autumn 1948): 521-537.

9173. Wohlstetter, Roberta. "Cuba and Pearl Harbor: Hindsight and Foresight." *Foreign Affairs* 43 (July 1965): 691-707.

Writings

9180. Roosevelt, Franklin D. *Ah That er' of Years Ago."* FDR Collector* 2 (May 1950): 3-25.

9175. Crowell, Laura. "The Franklin Field Address." *FDR Collector* 4 (May 1952): 3-13.

9176. Crowell, Laura. "Word Changes Introduced *Ad Libitum* in Five Speeches by Franklin Delano Roosevelt." *Speech Monographs* 25 (November 1958): 231-242.

9177. Drexel, Constance. "Unpublished Letters of FDR to His French Governess." *Parents Magazine* 26 (September 1951): 30-31.

9178. Kimball, Warren F., ed. *Churchill and Roosevelt: The Complete Correspondence.* Princeton, NJ: Princeton University Press, 1984.

9179. Rauch, Basil, ed. *Franklin D. Roosevelt: Selected Speeches, Messages, Press Conferences, and Letters.* New York: Holt, 1957.

9180. Roosevelt, Franklin D. *Ah That Voice: The Fireside Chats of Franklin Delano Roosevelt.* Compiled by Kenneth D. Yeilding and Paul H. Carlson. Odessa, TX: John Ben Sheppard, Jr., Library of the Presidents, Presidential Museum, 1974.

9181. Roosevelt, Franklin D. *As FDR Said: A Treasury of His Speeches, Conversations, and Writings.* Edited by Frank Kingdom. New York: Duell, Sloan and Pearce, 1950.

9182. Roosevelt, Franklin D. "Call to Duty: I Had Not Planned to Run Again." *Vital Speeches* 6 (August 1, 1940): 610-613.

9183. Roosevelt, Franklin D. *Complete Presidential Press Conferences of Franklin D. Roosevelt, 1933-1945.* 12 vols. New York: Da Capo Press, 1972.

9184. Roosevelt, Franklin D. *F. D. R., Columnist: The Uncollected Columns of Franklin D. Roosevelt.* Edited by Donald S. Carmichael. Chicago: Pellegrine and Cudahy, 1947.

9185. Roosevelt, Franklin D. *F. D. R.: His Personal Letters, 1905-1945.* 4 vols. Edited by Elliot Roosevelt and Joseph P. Lash. New York: Duell, Sloan and Pearce, 1947-1950.

9186. Roosevelt, Franklin D. *For the President — Personal and Secret: Correspondence between Franklin D. Roosevelt and William C. Bullitt.* Edited by Orville H. Bullitt. Boston: Houghton Mifflin, 1972.

9187. Roosevelt, Franklin D. *Franklin D. Roosevelt and Foreign Affairs, January 1937 — August 1939.* 16 vols. Edited by Donald B. Schewe. New York: Garland, 1979-1980.

9188. Roosevelt, Franklin D. *Franklin D. Roosevelt's Own Story, Told in His Own Words from His Private and Public Papers as Selected by Donald Day.* Boston: Little, Brown, 1951.

9189. Roosevelt, Franklin D. *Government — Not Politics.* New York: Covici-Friede, 1932.

9190. Roosevelt, Franklin D. *The Happy Warrior, Alfred E. Smith: A Study of a Public Servant.* Boston: Houghton Mifflin, 1928.

9191. Roosevelt, Franklin D. " 'I've Got This Thing Simplified.' " By Marquis W. Childs. *American Heritage* 8 (April 1961): 38-39, 91-93.

9192. Roosevelt, Franklin D. *Looking Forward.* New York: John Day, 1933.

9193. Roosevelt, Franklin D. *Memorable Quotations of Franklin D. Roosevelt.* Edited by E. Taylor Parks and Lois F. Parks. New York: Crowell, 1965.

9194. Roosevelt, Franklin D. *Nothing to Fear, The Selected Addresses of Franklin Delano Roosevelt, 1932-1945.* Edited by B. D. Zevin. Boston: Houghton Mifflin, 1946.

9195. Roosevelt, Franklin D. *On Our Way.* New York: Day, 1934.

9196. Roosevelt, Franklin D. *The Public Papers and Addresses of Franklin D. Roosevelt, With a Special Introduction and Explanatory Notes by President Roosevelt.* 13 vols. Compiled by Samuel I. Rosenman. New York: Russell and Russell, 1969.

9197. Roosevelt, Franklin D. *Public Papers of Franklin D. Roosevelt, Forty-eighth Governor of the State of New York, Second Term, 1932.* Albany, NY: J. B. Lyon, 1939.

9198. Roosevelt, Franklin D. *Rendezvous with Destiny: Addresses and Opinions of Franklin Delano Roosevelt.* Edited by J. B. S. Hardman. New York: Dryden Press, 1944.

9199. Roosevelt, Franklin D. "Reorganization of the Federal Government Administration: Increasing the Powers of the President?" *Vital Speeches* 3 (February 1, 1937): 249-251.

9200. Roosevelt, Franklin D. *Roosevelt and Churchill: Their Secret Wartime Correspondence.* Edited by Frances L. Lowenheim, Harold D. Langley, and Manfred Jones. New York: Saturday Review Press, 1975.

9201. Roosevelt, Franklin D. *Roosevelt and Frankfurter: Their Correspondence, 1928-1945.* Boston: Little, Brown, 1968.

9202. Roosevelt, Franklin D. *The Roosevelt Reader: Selected Speeches, Messages, Press Conferences, and Letters of Franklin D. Roosevelt.* Edited by Basil Rauch. New York: Rinehart, 1957.

9203. Roosevelt, Franklin D. "The Shooting Has Started: Navy Day Address, October 27, 1941." *Vital Speeches* 8 (November 15, 1941): 66-68.

9204. Roosevelt, Franklin D. "Sinking of the Robin Moor: Message to Congress, June 20, 1941." *Vital Speeches* 7 (July 1, 1941): 546.

9205. Roosevelt, Franklin D. *The Sunny Side of FDR.* Edited by M. S. Venkataramani. Athens: Ohio University Press, 1973.

9206. Roosevelt, Franklin D. *Wartime Correspondence between President Roosevelt and Pope Pius XII.* Edited by Myron C. Taylor. New York: Macmillan, 1947.

9207. Roosevelt, Franklin D. *The Wit and Wisdom of Franklin D. Roosevelt.* Edited by Maxwell Meyersohn. Boston: Beacon Press, 1950.

9208. Roosevelt, Franklin D., ed. *Records of Crum Elbow Precinct, Dutchess County, NY, 1738-1761, Together with Records of Charlotte Precinct, 1762-1785, Records of Clinton Precinct, 1786-1788, and Records of the Town of Clinton, 1789-1799.* Poughkeepsie, NY: Dutchess County Historical Society, 1940.

9209. Roosevelt, Franklin D., ed. *Records of the Town of Hyde Park, Dutchess County.* Hyde Park, NY: Dutchesss County Historical Society, 1928.

9210. Rosenau, James N., ed. *The Roosevelt Treasury.* Garden City, NY: Doubleday, 1951.

Harry S Truman

Biographies

9211. Byrnes, James F. *All in One Lifetime*. New York: Harper and Row, 1958.

9212. Clemens, Cyril. *The Man from Missouri, A Biography of Harry S. Truman*. Webster Groves, MO: International Mark Twain Society, 1945.

9213. Collins, David R. *Harry S. Truman: People's President*. Easton, MD: Garrard, 1975.

9214. Crane, John M. *The Pictorial Biography of Harry S. Truman, Thirty-second President of the United States*. Philadelphia: Curtis, 1948.

9215. Daniels, Jonathan. *The Man of Independence*. Philadelphia: Lippincott, 1950.

9216. Dayton, Eldorour. *Give 'Em Hell Harry: An Informal Biography of the Terrible-Tempered Mr. T*. New York: Devin-Adair, 1956.

9217. Eaton, Richard O., and LaValle Hart. *Meet Harry S. Truman*. Washington, DC: Dumbarton House, 1945.

9218. Faber, Doris. *Harry Truman*. New York: Abelard-Schuman, 1973.

9219. Ferrell, Robert H. *Truman, A Centenary Remembrance*. New York: Viking Press, 1984.

9220. Gies, Joseph. *Harry S. Truman, A Pictorial Biography*. Garden City, NY: Doubleday, 1968.

9221. Gosnell, Harold F. *Truman's Crises: A Political Biography of Harry S. Truman*. Westport, CT: Greenwood Press, 1980.

9222. Hayman, LeRoy. *Harry S. Truman: A Biography*. New York: Crowell, 1969.

9223. Hedley, John H. *Harry S. Truman, The "Little" Man from Missouri*. Woodbury, NY: Barron's, 1979.

9224. Helm, William P. *Harry Truman, A Political Biography*. New York: Duell, Sloan and Pearce, 1947.

9225. Hersey, John. "Profiles: Harry S. Truman." *New Yorker* 27 (April 7, 1951): 42-46, 48-56.

9226. Hersey, John. "Profiles: Mr. President, II: Ten O'Clock Meeting." *New Yorker* 27 (April 14, 1951): 38-55.

9227. Hersey, John. "Profiles: Mr. President, III: Forty-eight Hours." *New Yorker* 27 (April 21, 1951): 36-40, 42, 46, 48, 51, 52-53, 54-57.

9228. Hersey, John. "Profiles: Mr. President, IV: Ghosts in the White House." *New Yorker* 27 (April 28, 1951): 36-38, 40, 42-50, 53-55.

9229. Hersey, John. "Profiles: Mr. President, V: A Weighing of Words." *New Yorker* 27 (May 5, 1951): 36-53.

9230. Jenkins, Roy. *Truman.* New York: Harper and Row, 1986.

9231. Kelton, Nancy. *Harry Four Eyes.* Thousand Oaks, CA: Raintree Publishers, 1977.

9232. Kish, Francis B. "Citizen-Soldier: Harry S. Truman, 1884-1972." *Military Review* 53 (February 1973): 30-44.

9233. Lerner, Max. "Harry S. Truman: A Miniature Portrait." In his *Actions and Passions*, 219-224. New York: Simon and Schuster, 1949.

9234. McNaughton, Frank, and Walter Hehmeyer. *Harry Truman, President.* New York: McGraw-Hill, 1948.

9235. McNaughton, Frank, and Walter Hehmeyer. *This Man Truman.* New York: Whittlesey House, 1945.

9236. Martin, Ralph G. *President from Missouri: Harry S. Truman.* New York: Messner, 1964.

9237. Melton, David. *Harry S. Truman: The Man Who Walked with Giants.* Independence, MO: Independence Press, 1980.

9238. Miller, Merle. *Plain Speaking: An Oral Biography of Harry S. Truman.* New York: Berkley, 1974.

9239. Mollman, John P. *Harry S. Truman: A Biography.* New York: Monarch Press, 1966.

9240. Robbins, Charles. *Last of His Kind: An Informal Portrait of Harry S. Truman.* New York: Morrow, 1979.

9241. Schauffler, Edward R. *Harry Truman, Son of the Soil.* Kansas City, KS: Schauffler Publishing Co., 1947.

9242. Sheldon, Ted, ed. *Harry S. Truman: The Man from Missouri.* Kansas City, MO: Hallmark, 1970.

9243. Steinberg, Alfred. *The Man from Missouri: The Life and Times of Harry S. Truman.* New York: Putnam, 1962.

9244. Thomson, David S. *A Pictorial Biography: HST.* New York: Grosset and Dunlap, 1973.

9245. Truman, Margaret. *Harry S Truman.* New York: Pocket Books, 1972.

9246. U.S. Congress. House. *Memorial Services in the Congress of the United States and Tributes in Eulogy of Harry S. Truman.* 93d Cong., 1st sess., 1973. Washington, DC: U.S. Government Printing Office, 1973.

9247. Wolfson, Victor. *The Man Who Cared: A Life of Harry S. Truman.* New York: Farrar, Straus, 1966.

Private Life

9248. Acheson, Dean G. " 'Dear Boss': Unpublished Letters from Dean Acheson to Ex-President Harry Truman." *American Heritage* 31 (February/March 1980): 44-48.

9249. Arthur, Robert A. "Harry Truman Chuckles Dryly." *Esquire* 76 (September 1971): 136-139.

9250. Arthur, Robert A. "The Wit and Sass of Harry S. Truman." *Esquire* 76 (August 1971): 62-67.

9251. Clemens, Cyril. *Mark Twain and Harry S. Truman.* Webster Groves, MO: International Mark Twain Society, 1950.

9252. Gallu, Samuel. *"Give 'Em Hell Harry": Reminiscences.* New York: Viking Press, 1975.

9253. Giglio, James N., and Greg G. Thielen. *Truman in Cartoon and Caricature.* Ames: Iowa State University Press, 1984.

9254. Goodman, Mark, ed. *Give 'Em Hell, Harry!* New York: Award Books, 1974.

9255. *Harry S. Truman: Mini Play.* Stockton, CA: Stevens and Shea, 1977.

9256. Helicher, Karl. "The Education of Harry S. Truman." *Presidential Studies Quarterly* 14 (Fall 1984): 581-582.

9257. Kempton, Greta. "Painting the Truman Family." *Missouri Historical Review* 67 (April 1973): 335-349.

9258. Kirkendall, Richard S. "Harry S. Truman: A Missouri Farmer in the Golden Age." *Agricultural History* 48 (October 1974): 467-483.

9259. Kornitzer, Bela. *American Fathers and Sons.* New York: Hermitage House, 1952.

9260. Robbins, Jhan. *Bess and Harry: An American Love Story.* New York: Putnam, 1980.

9261. Truman, Margaret. *Souvenir, Margaret Truman's Own Story.* New York: McGraw-Hill, 1956.

9262. Van Patten, James J. "Harry S. Truman — Educator." *Educational Forum* 34 (March 1970): 379-381.

Public Career

9263. Coffin, Tristram. *Missouri Compromise.* Boston: Little, Brown, 1947.

9264. Crenshaw, James T. "Harry S. Truman: A Study of the Missouri Democratic Senatorial Primary Races of 1934 and 1940." Ph.D. dissertation, Vanderbilt University, 1976.

9265. Fink, Gary M., and James W. Hilty. "Prologue: The Senate Voting Record of Harry S. Truman." *Journal of Interdisciplinary History* 4 (Autumn 1973): 207-235.

9266. Grant, Philip A., Jr. "The Election of Harry S. Truman to the United States Senate." *Missouri Historical Society Bulletin* 36 (January 1980): 103-109.

9267. Harris, Edward A. "Harry S. Truman." In *Public Men in and out of Office,* edited by John T. Salter, 322-343. Chapel Hill: University of North Carolina Press, 1946.

9268. Kirkendall, Richard S. "Truman and the Pendergast Machine: A Comment." *American Studies* 7 (Fall 1966): 36-39.

9269. McClure, Arthur F., and Donna Costigan. "The Truman Vice Presidency: Constructive Apprenticeship or Brief Interlude?" *Missouri Historical Review* 65 (April 1971): 318-341.

9270. Maher, M. Patrick Ellen. "The Role of the Chairman of a Congressional Investigating Committee: A Case Study of the Special Committee of the Senate to Investigate the National Defense Program, 1941-1948." Ph.D. dissertation, St. Louis University, 1962.

9271. Mason, Frank. *Truman and the Pendergasts.* Evanston, IL: Regency, 1964.

9272. Miller, Richard L. "Harry S. Truman, Cannoneer." *Army* 34 (May 1984): 49-53.

9273. Milligan, Maurice. *The Inside Story of the Pendergast Machine by the Man Who Smashed It.* New York: Scribner's, 1948.

9274. Mitchell, Franklin D. "Who Is Judge Truman? The Truman-for-Governor Movement of 1931." *American Studies* 7 (Fall 1966): 3-15.

9275. Mitchell, Franklin D., Lyle W. Dorsett, Gene Schmidtlein, and Richard S. Kirkendall. "Truman and the Pendergast Machine." *Midcontinent American Studies Journal* 7 (Fall 1966): 3-39.

9276. Powell, Eugene J. *Tom's Boy Harry: The First Complete, Authentic Story of Harry Truman's Connection with the Pendergast Machine.* Jefferson City, MO: Hawthorn, 1948.

9277. Reddig, William M. *Tom's Town: Kansas City and the Pendergast Legend.* Philadelphia: Lippincott, 1947.

9278. Rhodes, Richard. "Harry's Last Hurrah." *Harper's* 240 (January 1970): 48-58.

9279. Roper, William L. "With Harry Truman in World War I." *National Guard* 36 (July 1982): 25-30.

9280. Schmidtlein, Gene. "Harry S. Truman and the Pendergast Machine." *American Studies* 7 (Fall 1966): 28-35.

9281. Schmidtlein, Gene. "Truman, The Senator." Ph.D. dissertation, University of Missouri, 1962.

9282. Schmidtlein, Gene. "Truman's First Senatorial Election." *Missouri Historical Review* 57 (January 1963): 128-155.

9283. Tammens, William D. "Harry S. Truman's Courthouse Years: The Missouri Proving Ground for a Future U.S. President." *Gateway Heritage* 4 (Spring 1984): 22-29.

Presidential Years

General

9284. Abels, Jules. *Out of the Jaws of Victory.* New York: Holt, 1959.

9285. Abels, Jules. *The Truman Scandals.* Chicago: Regnery, 1956.

9286. Acheson, Dean G. "The Truman Years." *Foreign Service Journal* 42 (August 1965): 22-24.

9287. Albjerg, Victor L. "Truman and Eisenhower: Their Administrations and Campaigns." *Current History* 47 (October 1964): 221-228.

9288. Allen, Robert S., and William V. Shannon. *The Truman Merry-Go-Round.* New York: Vanguard Press, 1950.

9289. Atkinson, David N., and Dale A. Neuman. "Toward a Cost Theory of Judicial Alignments: The Case of the Truman Bloc." *Midwest Journal of Political Science* 13 (May 1969): 271-283.

9290. Berger, Henry W. "Bipartisanship, Senator Taft, and the Truman Administration." *Political Science Quarterly* 90 (Summer 1975): 221-237.

9291. Bernstein, Barton J. *Politics and Policy of the Truman Administration.* Chicago: Quadrangle Books, 1970.

9292. Bernstein, Barton J. "The Presidency under Truman." *Yale Political Review* 4 (Fall 1964): 8-9, 24.

9293. Bernstein, Barton J. "Truman, the Eightieth Congress, and the Transformation of Political Culture." *Capitol Studies* 2 (Spring 1973): 65-75.

9294. Bernstein, Barton J. "Truman's Record." *Progressive Magazine* 30 (October 1966): 46-48.

9295. Bernstein, Barton J., and Allen J. Matusow, eds. *The Truman Administration: A Documentary History.* New York: Harper and Row, 1966.

9296. Braden, George D. "Mr. Justice Minton and the Truman Bloc." *Indiana Law Journal* 26 (Winter 1951): 153-168.

9297. Brown, John M. "The Trumans Leave the White House." *Saturday Review* 36 (February 7, 1953): 9-11, 47-49.

9298. Brown, Wilson. "Aide to Four Presidents." *American Heritage* 6 (February 1955): 66-96.

9299. Cady, Darrel R. "The Truman Administration's Reconversion Policies, 1945-1947." Ph.D. dissertation, University of Kansas, 1974.

9300. Christenson, Reo M. "Carter and

Truman: A Reappraisal of Both." *Presidential Studies Quarterly* 13 (Spring 1983): 313-323.

9301. Clubb, Oliver E. *The Witness and I.* New York: Columbia University Press, 1974.

9302. Cochran, Bert. *Harry Truman and the Crisis Presidency.* Freeport, NY: Funk and Wagnalls, 1973.

9303. Cornwell, Elmer E., Jr. "The Truman Presidency." In *The Truman Period as a Research Field*, edited by Richard S. Kirkendall, 213-255. Columbia: University of Missouri Press, 1967.

9304. Daniels, Jonathan. "Mr. President." *Holiday* 7 (February 1950): 52-61, 114, 116.

9305. Davis, Elmer. "Harry S. Truman and the Verdict of History." *Reporter* 3 (February 1953): 17-22.

9306. Donovan, Robert J. *Conflict and Crisis: Presidency of Harry S. Truman: 1945-1948.* New York: Norton, 1979.

9307. Donovan, Robert J. *Tumultuous Years: The Presidency of Harry S. Truman, 1949-1953.* New York: Norton, 1982.

9308. Druks, Herbert, ed. *From Truman through Johnson: A Documentary History, Truman and Eisenhower.* Vol. 1. New York: Robert Speller, 1971.

9309. Dunar, Andrew J. *The Truman Scandals and the Politics of Morality.* Columbia: University of Missouri Press, 1984.

9310. Farrar, Ronald. "Harry Truman and the Press: A View from Inside." *Journalism History* 8 (Summer 1981): 56-62.

9311. Farrar, Ronald. *Reluctant Servant: The Story of Charles G. Ross.* Columbia: University of Missouri Press, 1969.

9312. Ferrell, Robert H. *Harry S. Truman and the Modern American Presidency.* Boston: Little, Brown, 1983.

9313. Ferrell, Robert H., ed. "A Visitor to the White House, 1947: The Diary of Vic H. Housholder." *Missouri Historical Review* 78 (April 1984): 311-336.

9314. Fischer, John. "Mr. Truman's Politburo." *Harper's Magazine* 202 (June 1951): 29-36.

9315. Fowler, Robert H. " 'The Truman Presidency' Reviewed: It Doesn't Take a Genius to Be a 'Great' President." *American History Illustrated* 1 (August 1966): 41-43.

9316. Garson, Robert. "The Alienation of the South: A Crisis for Harry S. Truman and the Democratic Party, 1945-1948." *Missouri Historical Review* 64 (July 1970): 448-471.

9317. George, Elsie L. "The Women Appointees of the Roosevelt and Truman Administrations: A Study of Their Impact and Effectiveness." Ph.D. dissertation, American University, 1972.

9318. Giglio, James N. "Harry S. Truman and the Multifarious Ex-Presidency." *Presidential Studies Quarterly* 12 (Spring 1982): 239-255.

9319. Grayson, A. G. "North Carolina and Harry Truman, 1944-1948." *Journal of American Studies* 9 (December 1975): 283-300.

9320. Griffith, Robert. "Truman and the Historians: The Reconstruction of Postwar American History." *Wisconsin Magazine of History* 59 (Autumn 1975): 20-50.

9321. Gustafson, Merlin. "The Church, the State, and the Military in the Truman Administration." *Rocky Mountain Social Science Journal* 2 (October 1966): 2-10.

9322. Gustafson, Merlin. "Religion and Politics in the Truman Administration." *Rocky Mountain Social Science Journal* 6 (October 1966): 125-134.

9323. Hamby, Alonzo L. "The Clash of Perspectives and the Need for New Syntheses." In *The Truman Period as a Research Field*, edited by Richard S. Kirkendall, 113-148. Columbia: University of Missouri Press, 1974.

9324. Hamby, Alonzo L. "Harry S. Truman and American Liberalism, 1945-1948." Ph.D. dissertation, University of Missouri, 1965.

9325. Hamby, Alonzo L. "The Liberals, Truman, and FDR as Symbol and Myth." *Journal of American History* 56 (March 1970): 859-867.

9326. "Harry Truman: His Career, Achievements, Views." *Congressional Quarterly Weekly Report* 30 (December 16, 1972): 3164-3167.

9327. Hartmann, Susan M. *Truman and the 80th Congress*. Columbia: University of Missouri Press, 1971.

9328. Hasting, Ann C. "Intraparty Struggle: Harry S. Truman, 1945-1948." Ph.D. dissertation, St. Louis University, 1972.

9329. Haynes, Richard F. *The Awesome Power: Harry S. Truman as the Commander in Chief*. Baton Rouge: Louisiana State University Press, 1973.

9330. Hechler, Ken. *Working with Truman: A Personal Memoir of the White House Years*. New York: Putnam, 1982.

9331. Heller, Francis H. *The Truman White House: The Administration of the Presidency 1945-1953*. Lawrence: Regents Press of Kansas, 1980.

9332. Henry, David R. "Decision-Making in the Truman Administration." Ph.D. dissertation, Indiana University, 1976.

9333. Hersey, John. *Aspects of the Presidency: Truman and Ford in Office*. New Haven, CT: Ticknor and Fields, 1980.

9334. Hopkins, John E. "An Investigation of the Speech and Statement Preparation Process during the Presidential Administration of Harry S. Truman, 1945-1953." Ph.D. dissertation, Ohio University, 1970.

9335. Huthmacher, J. Joseph, ed. *The Truman Years: The Reconstruction of Postwar America*. Hinsdale, IL: Dryden Press, 1973.

9336. Jarman, Rufus. "Washington's Worst Politician." *Saturday Evening Post* 221 (July 24, 1948): 20-21, 62-65.

9337. Johnson, Walter. *The American President and the Art of Communication: An Inaugural Lecture Delivered before the University of Oxford on 13 May 1958*. Oxford: Clarendon Press, 1958.

9338. Kelly, Frank K. "H. S. Truman: An Uncommon Common Man." *Center Magazine* 6 (March/April 1973): 60-63.

9339. Kirkendall, Richard S. "Harry Truman." In *America's Eleven Greatest Presidents*, edited by Morton Borden, 225-288. Chicago: Rand McNally, 1971.

9340. Kirkendall, Richard S. "Truman's Path to Power." *Social Science* 43 (April 1968): 67-73.

9341. Kirkendall, Richard S., ed. *The Truman Period as a Research Field, A Reappraisal, 1972*. Columbia: University of Missouri Press, 1974.

9342. Knebel, Fletcher. "The Inside Story of the Ike-Truman Feud." *Look* 19 (September 6, 1955): 21-25.

9343. Koenig, Louis W., ed. *The Truman Administration: Its Principles and Practice*. New York: New York University Press, 1956.

9344. Kulka, Giora. "Congressional Opposition to President Truman." Ph.D. dissertation, Harvard University, 1972.

9345. Leahy, William D. *I Was There: The Personal Story of the Chief of Staff to*

Presidents Roosevelt and Truman. New York: McGraw-Hill, 1950.

9346. Lee, R. Alton. "Truman-80th Congress Struggle over Tax Policy." *Historian* 33 (November 1970): 68-82.

9347. Lehman, Milton. "They're Fixing Up Over at the Trumans'." *Collier's* 126 (October 28, 1950): 36-37, 61, 63.

9348. Leuchtenburg, William E. "The Legacy of FDR." *Wilson Quarterly* 6 (Spring 1982): 77-93.

9349. Leuchtenburg, William E. "Truman Was a Hell of a President — Give 'Em Harry." *New Republic* 190 (May 21, 1984): 19-23.

9350. Lorenz, Alfred L., Jr. "Truman and the Press Conference." *Journalism Quarterly* 43 (Winter 1966): 671-679.

9351. Lorenz, Lawrence. "Truman and the Broadcaster." *Journal of Broadcasting* 13 (Winter 1968-1969): 17-22.

9352. Lukacs, John. *1945 Year Zero.* Garden City, NY: Doubleday, 1978.

9353. McCoy, Donald R. "Harry S. Truman: Personality, Politics, and Presidency." *Presidential Studies Quarterly* 12 (Spring 1982): 216-225.

9354. McCoy, Donald R. *The Presidency of Harry S. Truman.* Lawrence: University Press of Kansas, 1984.

9355. McCoy, Donald R. "Trends in Viewing Herbert Hoover, Franklin D. Roosevelt, Harry S. Truman, and Dwight D. Eisenhower." *Midwest Quarterly* 20 (Winter 1977): 117-136.

9356. Maddox, Robert J. "Harry S. Truman's Early Months in the White House." *American History Illustrated* 7 (November 1972): 12-22.

9357. Markel, Lester. "After Four Years: Portrait of Harry Truman." *New York Times Magazine* 98 (April 10, 1949): 7-9, 56-59.

9358. Merrill, John. "How *Time* Stereotyped Three U.S. Presidents." *Journalism Quarterly* 42 (Autumn 1965): 563-570.

9359. Miller, Merle. "Few Lessons in History from Harry Truman." *Esquire* 81 (January 1974): 53-62.

9360. "Mr. Truman's White House." *Fortune* 45 (February 1952): 74-79, 190, 192, 194, 196, 199.

9361. Mitchell, Franklin D. "An Act of Presidential Indiscretion: Harry S. Truman, Congressman McDonough, and the Marine Corps Incident of 1950." *Presidential Studies Quarterly* 11 (Fall 1981): 565-575.

9362. Morgan, H. Wayne. "History and the Presidency: Harry S. Truman." *Phylon 19* (Summer 1958): 162-170.

9363. Morrissey, Charles T. "Truman and the Presidency — Records and Oral Recollections." *American Archivist* 28 (January 1965): 53-61.

9364. Murray, Randall L. "Harry S. Truman and Press Opinion, 1945-1953." Ph.D. dissertation, University of Minnesota, 1973.

9365. Neumann, Robert G. "Leadership: Franklin Roosevelt, Truman, Eisenhower, and Today." *Presidential Studies Quarterly* 10 (Winter 1980): 10-19.

9366. Nigro, Felix A. "Pauley Case." *Southwestern Social Science Quarterly* 40 (March 1960): 341-349.

9367. O'Donnell, James F. " 'I, Harry S. Truman, Do Solemnly Swear...': How Millions Heard and Saw the Inauguration through the Magic of Radio and Television, Aided by Telephone Equipment and Know-How." *Transmitter* 37 (March/April 1949): 4-10.

9368. Parker, Daniel F. "The Political and Social Views of Harry S. Truman." Ph.D. dissertation, University of Pennsylvania, 1951.

9369. Pemberton, William E. *Bureaucratic Politics: Executive Reorganization during the Truman Administration.* Columbia: University of Missouri Press, 1979.

9370. Phillips, Cabell. "Johnson Has the Kind of Troubles Truman Had." *New York Times Magazine* 117 (October 22, 1967): 34-35, 110, 112, 114, 116, 119-120, 122.

9371. Phillips, Cabell. *The Truman Presidency: The History of a Triumphant Succession.* New York: Macmillan, 1966.

9372. Poen, Monte M. *Harry S. Truman versus the Medical Lobby: The Genesis of Medicare.* Columbia: University of Missouri Press, 1979.

9373. Polenberg, Richard. "Historians and the Liberal Presidency: Recent Appraisals of Roosevelt and Truman." *South Atlantic Quarterly* 75 (Winter 1976): 20-35.

9374. Pollard, James E. "President Truman and the Press." *Journalism Quarterly* 28 (Fall 1951): 457-468.

9375. Pollard, James E. "Truman and the Press: Final Phase, 1951-53." *Journalism Quarterly* 30 (Summer 1953): 273-286.

9376. Pritchard, Robert L. "Southern Politics and the Truman Administration: Georgia as a Test Case." Ph.D. dissertation, University of California, Los Angeles, 1970.

9377. Republican Party National Committee. *The Truman Chronology: A Day-by-Day Record of the Presidency of Harry S. Truman.* Washington, DC: Research Division, Republican National Committee, 1948.

9378. Riddle, Donald H. *The Truman Committee: A Study in Congressional Responsibility.* New Brunswick, NJ: Rutgers University Press, 1964.

9379. Rogge, Edward A. "The Speechmaking of Harry S. Truman." Ph.D. dissertation, University of Missouri, 1958.

9380. Rosenfield, L. W. "A Case Study in Speech Criticism: The Nixon-Truman Analog." *Speech Monographs* 35 (November 1968): 435-450.

9381. Rudoni, Dorothy J. *Harry S Truman: A Study in Presidential Perspective.* Ph.D. dissertation, Southern Illinois University, 1968.

9382. Schoenebaum, Eleanora W., ed. *The Truman Years.* New York: Facts on File, 1978.

9383. Shalett, Sidney M. "Dinner with the President." *American Magazine* 145 (February 1948): 34-35, 129-134.

9384. Sitkoff, Harvard. "Years of the Locust: Interpretations of Truman's Presidency since 1965." In *The Truman Period as a Research Field,* edited by Richard S. Kirkendall, 75-112. Columbia: University of Missouri Press, 1974.

9385. Smith, Geoffrey S. "'Harry, We Hardly Know You': Revisionism, Politics, and Diplomacy, 1945-1954." *American Political Science Review* 70 (June 1976): 560-582.

9386. Smith, Kathy B. "Harry Truman: Man of His Times." *Presidential Studies Quarterly* 13 (Winter 1983): 70-80.

9387. Stokes, Thomas L. "Harry Truman, Politician Extraordinary." *New York Times Magazine* 99 (May 7, 1950): 13, 52-54.

9388. Stone, Isidor F. *Truman Era.* New York: Monthly Review Press, 1953.

9389. Street, Kenneth W. "Harry S. Truman: His Role as Legislative Leader." Ph.D. dissertation, University of Texas, 1963.

9390. Theoharis, Athan G. "Attorney General Tom Clark, Internal Security, and the Truman Administration." *New*

University Thought 6 (1968): 16-22.

9391. Theoharis, Athan G. "The Escalation of the Loyalty Program." In *Politics and Policies of the Truman Administration*, edited by Barton J. Bernstein, 242-268. Chicago: Quadrangle Books, 1970.

9392. Theoharis, Athan G. "Ignoring History: HST, the Revisionists, and the Press." *Chicago Journalism Review* 6 (March 1973): 14-15.

9393. Theoharis, Athan G. "The Rhetoric of Politics: Foreign Policy, Internal Security, and Domestic Politics in the Truman Era, 1945-1950." In *Politics and Policies of the Truman Administration*, edited by Barton J. Bernstein, 196-241. Chicago: Quadrangle Books, 1970.

9394. Theoharis, Athan G. *Seeds of Repression: Harry S Truman and the Origins of McCarthyism*. Chicago: Quadrangle Books, 1971.

9395. Theoharis, Athan G. "The Truman Administration and the Decline of Civil Liberties: The FBI's Success in Securing Authorization for a Preventive Detention." *Journal of American History* 64 (March 1978): 1010-1030.

9396. Theoharis, Athan G. "The Truman Presidency: Trial and Error." *Wisconsin Magazine of History* 55 (Autumn 1971): 49-58.

9397. Theoharis, Athan G., ed. *The Truman Presidency: The Origins of the Imperial Presidency and the National Security State*. Standfordville, NY: Earl M. Coleman, 1979.

9398. Thompson, Francis H. *The Frustration of Politics: Truman, Congress, and the Loyalty Issue*. Rutherford, NY: Fairleigh Dickinson University Press, 1979.

9399. Thompson, Francis H. "Truman and Congress: The Issue of Loyalty, 1946-1952." Ph.D. dissertation, Texas Tech University, 1970.

9400. Thompson, Kenneth W., ed. *The Truman Presidency: Intimate Perspectives*. Lanham, MD: University Press of America, 1984.

9401. "Truman Sworn-in in the White House: He Becomes 33rd President." *Life* 18 (April 23, 1945): 28-29.

9402. Underhill, Robert. *The Truman Persuasion*. Ames: Iowa State University Press, 1981.

9403. Underwood, James E. "Studying Individual Presidents: Truman, Eisenhower, Kennedy, and Carter." *Congress and the Presidency* 11 (Spring 1984): 93-104.

9404. Wagnon, William O., Jr. "John Roy Steelman: Native Son to Presidential Advisor." *Arkansas Historical Quarterly* 27 (Autumn 1968): 205-225.

9405. Waltrip, John R. *Public Power during the Truman Administration*. New York: Arno, 1979.

9406. White, William S. *The Responsibles: Truman, Taft, Eisenhower, JFK, Johnson*. New York: Harper and Row, 1972.

9407. Wills, Garry. "I'm Not Wild about Harry." *Esquire* 85 (1976): 90-95.

9408. Williams, Herbert L. "I Was Truman's Ghost." *Presidential Studies Quarterly* 12 (Spring 1982): 256-259.

9409. Williams, Herbert L. "Truman and the Press (April 23, 1945-January 20, 1953)." Ph.D. dissertation, University of Missouri, 1954.

9410. Williams, Robert J. "Harry S. Truman and the American Presidency." *Journal of American Studies* 13 (December 1979): 393-408.

9411. Willson, Roger E. "The Truman Committee." Ph.D. dissertation, Harvard University, 1966.

9412. Yang, Matthew Y. "The Truman

Committee." Ph.D. dissertation, Harvard University, 1948.

9413. Zornow, William F. *America at Mid-Century: The Truman Administration, The Eisenhower Administration.* Cleveland, OH: Allen Press, 1959.

9414. Zuckert, Eugene M. "Power of High Office Did Not Change Him." *Officer* 60 (May 1984): 32-35.

Atomic Bomb

9415. Bernstein, Barton J. "Roosevelt, Truman, and the Atomic Bomb, 1941-1945: A Reinterpretation." *Political Science Quarterly* 90 (Spring 1975): 23-69.

9416. Fogelman, Edwin, ed. *Hiroshima: The Decision to Use the A-Bomb.* New York: Scribner's, 1964.

9417. Giovannitti, Len, and Fred Freed. *The Decision to Drop the Bomb.* New York: Coward-McCann, 1965.

9418. Hikins, James W. "The Rhetoric of 'Unconditional Surrender' and the Decision to Drop the Atomic Bomb." *Quarterly Journal of Speech* 69 (November 1983): 379-400.

9419. Loebs, Bruce D. "Nagasaki: The Decision and the Mistake." *Rendezvous* 7 (Spring 1972): 53-69.

9420. Messer, Robert L. "New Evidence on Truman's Decision." *Bulletin of the Atomic Scientists* 41 (August 1985): 50-56.

9421. Morton, Louis. "The Decision to Use the Atomic Bomb." In *Command Decisions,* edited by Kent R. Greenfield, 388-410. New York: Harcourt, Brace, 1959.

9422. Schilling, Warner R. "The H-Bomb Decision: How to Decide without Actually Choosing." *Political Science Quarterly* 76 (March 1961): 24-45.

9423. Schoenberger, Walter S. *Decision of Destiny.* Athens: Ohio University Press, 1969.

9424. Sherwin, Martin J. "The Atomic Bomb as History: An Essay Review." *Wisconsin Magazine of History* 53 (Winter 1969): 128-134.

9425. Sherwin, Martin J. *A World Destroyed: The Atomic Bomb and the Grand Alliance.* New York: Knopf, 1975.

9426. Snowman, Daniel. "President Truman's Decision to Drop the First Atomic Bomb." *Political Studies* 14 (October 1966): 364-373.

9427. Stimson, Henry L. "The Decision to Use the Atomic Bomb." *Harper's* 194 (February 1947): 97-107.

9428. York, Herbert F. *The Advisors: Oppenheimer, Teller, and the Superbomb.* San Francisco: Freeman, 1976.

Domestic Policy

9429. Atwell, Cynthia M. "Harry S. Truman and His Presidential Administration as an Influence on Music in the United States, 1945-1952." D.M.A. dissertation, University of Missouri, 1979.

9430. Berman, William C. *The Politics of Civil Rights in the Truman Administration.* Columbus: Ohio State University Press, 1970.

9431. Bernstein, Barton J. "The Ambiguous Legacy: The Truman Administration and Civil Rights." In his *Politics and Policies of the Truman Administration,* 269-314. Chicago: Quadrangle Books, 1970.

9432. Bernstein, Barton J. "Charting a Course between Inflation and Depression: Secretary of the Treasury Fred Vinson and the Truman Administration's Tax Bill." *Kentucky Historical Society Register* 66 (January 1968): 53-64.

9433. Bernstein, Barton J. "Reluctance and Resistance: Wilson Wyatt and Veterans' Housing in the Truman Administration." *Kentucky Historical Society Register* 65 (January 1967): 47-66.

9434. Bernstein, Barton J. "The Truman Administration and Its Reconversion Wage Policy." *Labor History* 6 (Fall 1965): 214-231.

9435. Bernstein, Barton J. "The Truman Administration and the Politics of Inflation." Ph.D. dissertation, Harvard University, 1963.

9436. Bernstein, Barton J. "The Truman Administration and the Steel Strike of 1946." *Journal of American History* 52 (March 1966): 791-803.

9437. Billington, Monroe. "Civil Rights, President Truman, and the South." *Journal of Negro History* 58 (April 1973): 127-139.

9438. Billington, Monroe. "Freedom to Serve: The President's Committee on Equality and Treatment and Opportunity in the Armed Forces, 1949-1950." *Journal of Negro History* 51 (October 1966): 262-274.

9439. Branyan, Robert L. "Antimonopoly Activities during the Truman Administration." Ph.D. dissertation, University of Oklahoma, 1961.

9440. Caute, David. *The Great Fear: The Anti-Communist Purge under Truman and Eisenhower.* New York: Simon and Schuster, 1978.

9441. Davies, Richard O. *Housing Reform during the Truman Administration.* Columbia: University of Missouri Press, 1966.

9442. Davies, Richard O. "Social Welfare Policies." In *The Truman Period as a Research Field*, edited by Richard S. Kirkendall, 191-200. Columbia: University of Missouri Press, 1967.

9443. Davies, Richard O. "The Truman Housing Program." Ph.D. dissertation, University of Missouri, 1963.

9444. DeLuna, Phyllis R. "Public versus Private Power during the Truman Administration: A Study of Fair Deal Liberalism." Ph.D. dissertation, University of Alberta, 1974.

9445. Edwards, Robert V. *Truman's Inheritance.* Caldwell, ID: Caxton, 1952.

9446. Farrelly, David G. "Searches and Seizures during the Truman Era." *Southern California Law Review* 25 (December 1951): 1-13.

9447. Fisher, Donald C. "An Analytical Study of Harry S. Truman's Concept of Free Speech during the McCarthy Era." Master's thesis, Murray State University, 1973.

9448. Gross, Bertram M., and John P. Lewis. "The President's Economic Staff during the Truman Administration." *American Political Science Review* 48 (March 1954): 114-130.

9449. Grothaus, Larry. "Kansas City Blacks, Harry Truman, and the Pendergast Machine." *Missouri Historical Review* 69 (October 1974): 65-82.

9450. Hah, Chong-do, and Robert M. Lindquist. "The 1952 Steel Seizure Revisited: A Systematic Study in Presidential Decision Making." *Administrative Science Quarterly* 20 (December 1975): 587-604.

9451. Hamby, Alonzo L. *Beyond the New Deal: Harry S. Truman and American Liberalism.* New York: Columbia University Press, 1973.

9452. Hamby, Alonzo L. "The Vital Center, the Fair Deal, and the Quest for a Liberal Political Economy." *American Historical Review* 77 (June 1972): 653-678.

9453. Hamby, Alonzo L., ed. *Harry S.*

Truman and the New Deal. Boston: Heath, 1974.

9454. Harper, Alan D. *The Politics of Loyalty: The White House and the Communist Issue, 1946-1952.* Westport, CT: Greenwood Press, 1969.

9455. Heller, Francis H., ed. *Economics and the Truman Administration.* Lawrence: Regents Press of Kansas, 1981.

9456. Herren, Robert S. "Wage-Price Policy during the Truman Administration: A Postwar Problem and the Search for Its Solution." Ph.D. dissertation, Duke University, 1975.

9457. Kathka, David A. "The Bureau of Reclamation in the Truman Administration: Personnel, Politics, and Policy." Ph.D. dissertation, University of Missouri, 1976.

9458. Kauper, Paul G. "The Steel Seizure Case: Congress, the President, and the Supreme Court." *Michigan Law Review* 51 (December 1952): 141-182.

9459. Kirstein, Peter N. "Agribusiness, Labor, and the Wetbacks: Truman's Commission on Migratory Labor." *Historian* 40 (August 1978): 650-667.

9460. Kuter, Laurence S. "Truman's Secret Management of the Airlines." *Aerospace Historian* 24 (Autumn 1977): 181-183.

9461. Lammie, Wayne D. "Unemployment in the Truman Administration: Political, Economic, and Social Aspects." Ph.D. dissertation, Ohio State University, 1973.

9462. Lea, L. B. "The Steel Case: Presidential Seizure of Private Industry." *Northwestern University Law Review* 47 (July/August 1952): 289-313.

9463. Lee, R. Alton. "Harry S. Truman and the Taft-Hartley Act." Ph.D. dissertation, University of Oklahoma, 1962.

9464. Lee, R. Alton. *Truman and Taft-Hartley: A Question of Mandate.* Lexington: University of Kentucky Press, 1966.

9465. McCann, Maurice J. "The Truman Administration and Education." Ph.D. dissertation, Southern Illinois University, 1976.

9466. McClure, Arthur F. "The Truman Administration and Labor Relations, 1945-1948." Ph.D. dissertation, University of Kansas, 1965.

9467. McClure, Arthur F. *The Truman Administration and the Problems of Post-War Labor: 1945-1948.* Rutherford, NJ: Fairleigh Dickinson University Press, 1969.

9468. McConnell, Grant. *The President Seizes the Steel Mills.* University: University of Alabama Press, 1960.

9469. McConnell, Grant. *The Steel Seizure of 1952.* Syracuse, NY: Inter-University Case Program, 1960.

9470. McCoy, Donald R., and Richard T. Ruetten. *Quest and Response: Minority Rights and the Truman Administration.* Lawrence: University Press of Kansas, 1973.

9471. Mann, Seymour Z. "Policy Formulation in the Executive Branch: The Taft-Hartley Experience." *Western Political Quarterly* 13 (September 1960): 597-608.

9472. Marcus, Maeva. *Truman and the Steel Seizure Case: Limits of Presidential Power.* New York: Columbia University Press, 1977.

9473. Martin, Don T. "The Public Statements of Presidents Truman and Eisenhower on Federal Aid to Education." Ph.D. dissertation, Ohio State University, 1970.

9474. Matusow, Allen J. *Farm Policies and Politics in the Truman Years.* New York: Atheneum, 1970.

9475. Mrozek, Donald J. "The Truman Administration and the Enlistment of the Aviation Industry in Postwar Defense." *Business History Review* 48 (Spring 1974): 73-94.

9476. Neustadt, Richard E. "Congress and the Fair Deal: A Legislative Balance Sheet." *Public Policy* 5 (1954): 351-381.

9477. Olson, John M. C., Jr. "An Analysis of Fiscal Policy during the Truman Administration (1945-1953)." Ph.D dissertation, University of Southern California, 1966.

9478. Peterson, Gale E. *President Harry S. Truman and the Independent Regulatory Commissions, 1945-1952.* New York: Garland, 1985.

9479. Pfeiffer, Edward J. "The President and Domestic Public Policy: A Study of Harry S. Truman." Ph.D. dissertation, Claremont Graduate School, 1982.

9480. Piccilo, Peter E. "The Role of the Budget Bureau in Truman's Domestic Legislative Program: An Examination of Atomic Energy Control, Military Unification, Housing, and Civil Rights." Ph.D. dissertation, State University of New York, Binghamton, 1974.

9481. Poen, Monte M. "The Truman Administration and National Health Insurance." Ph.D. dissertation, University of Missouri, 1967.

9482. Ramsey, John W. "The Director of the Bureau of the Budget as a Presidential Aide: 1921-1952, With Emphasis on the Truman Years." Ph.D. dissertation, University of Missouri, 1967.

9483. Richardson, Elmo R. *Dams, Parks, and Politics: Resource Development and Preservation in the Truman-Eisenhower Era.* Lexington: University Press of Kentucky, 1973.

9484. Ruetten, Richard T., and Donald R. McCoy. *Quest and Response: Minority Rights in the Truman Administration.* Lawrence: University Press of Kansas, 1973.

9485. Salant, Walter S. "Some Intellectual Contributions of the Truman Council of Economic Advisers to Policy-Making." *History of Political Economy* 5 (Spring 1973): 36-49.

9486. Stebbins, Phillip. "Truman and the Seizure of Steel: A Failure in Communication." *Historian* 34 (November 1971): 1-21.

9487. Taylor, Harry S. "Truman's Point Four Program: Educational Considerations." Ph.D. dissertation, University of Missouri, 1982.

9488. Truman Library. Institute for National and International Affairs. *Conference of Scholars on the Truman Administration and Civil Rights, April 5-6, 1968.* Independence, MO: The Author, 1968.

9489. Vaughan, Philip H. "The City and the American Creed: A Liberal Awakening during the Early Truman Period, 1946-48." *Phylon* 34 (March 1973): 51-62.

9490. Vaughan, Philip H. "President Truman's Committee on Civil Rights: The Urban Implications." *Missouri Historical Review* 66 (April 1972): 413-430.

9491. Vaughan, Philip H. "The Truman Administration's Fair Deal for Black America." *Missouri Historical Review* 70 (April 1976): 291-305.

9492. Vaughan, Philip H. *The Truman Administration's Legacy for Black America.* Reseda, CA: Mojave Books, 1976.

9493. Vaughan, Philip H. "Urban Aspects of Civil Rights and the Early Truman Administration, 1946-1948." Ph.D. dissertation, University of Oklahoma, 1971.

9494. Vietor, Richard H. K. "The Synthetic Liquid Fuels Program: Energy Politics in the Truman Era." *Business History Review* 54 (Spring 1980): 1-34.

9495. Wagnon, William O., Jr. "The Politics of Economic Growth: The Truman Administration and the 1949 Recession." Ph.D. dissertation, University of Missouri, 1970.

9496. Weaver, Samuel H. "The Truman Administration and Federal Aid to Education." Ph.D. dissertation, American University, 1972.

9497. Wilson, Donald E. "The History of President Truman's Air Policy Commission and Its Influence on Air Policy 1947-1949." Ph.D. dissertation, University of Denver, 1978.

9498. Wright, Peter M. "Wyoming and the O.P.A.: The Postwar Politics of Decontrol." *Annals of Wyoming* 52 (Spring 1980): 25-33.

Elections

9499. Brembeck, Cole S. "Harry Truman at the Whistle Stops." *Quarterly Journal of Speech* 38 (February 1952): 42-50.

9500. Brembeck, Cole S. "The Persuasive Speaking of Truman and Dewey in the 1948 Presidential Campaign." Ph.D. dissertation, University of Wisconsin, 1951.

9501. Carroll, Raymond L. "1948 Truman Campaign: The Threshold of the Modern Era." *Journal of Broadcasting* 24 (Spring 1980): 173-187.

9502. Chrisman, James R. "The Rhetoric of the Presidential Campaign of 1948: A Content Analysis of Selected Addresses of Harry S Truman and Thomas E. Dewey." Ph.D. dissertation, Oklahoma State University, 1974.

9503. Hazel, Harry C., Jr. "Harry Truman: Practical Persuader." *Today's Speech* 22 (Spring 1974): 25-31.

9504. Heed, Thomas J. "Prelude to Whistlestop: Harry S. Truman, The Apprentice Campaigner." Ed.D. dissertation, Columbia University, 1975.

9505. Lubell, Samuel. "Who Really Elected Truman?" *Saturday Evening Post* 221 (January 22, 1949): 15-17, 54-64.

9506. Ross, Irwin. *The Loneliest Campaign: The Truman Victory of 1948*. New York: New American Library, 1968.

9507. Shaver, Mark D. "Harry S. Truman: An Examination and Evaluation of His Use of Ethical Appeal in Selected Speeches from the 1948 Presidential Campaign." Master's thesis, North Texas State University, 1975.

9508. Sitkoff, Harvard. "Harry Truman and the Election of 1948: The Coming of Age of Civil Rights in American Politics." *Journal of Southern History* 37 (November 1971): 597-616.

9509. Stacy, Bill W. "The Campaign Speaking of Harry S. Truman in the 1948 Presidential Election." Ph.D. dissertation, Southern Illinois University, 1968.

9510. Wallace, Lew. "The Truman-Dewey Upset." *American History Illustrated* 11 (October 1976): 20-30.

Foreign Affairs

9511. Bhana, Surendra. "The Development of Puerto Rican Autonomy under the Truman Administration, 1945-1952." Ph.D. dissertation, University of Kansas, 1971.

9512. Bhana, Surendra. "Puerto Rico and the Truman Administration, 1945-47: Self-Government 'Little by Little.'" *Prologue* 5 (Fall 1973): 155-165.

9513. Bryniarski, Joan L. "Against the Tide: Senate Opposition to the Internationalist Foreign Policy of Presidents

Franklin D. Roosevelt and Harry S Truman, 1943-1949." Ph.D. dissertation, University of Maryland, 1972.

9514. Bullard, Anthony R. "Harry S. Truman and the Separation of Powers in Foreign Affairs." Ph.D. dissertation, Columbia University, 1972.

9515. Carlton, John T. "Truman Championed Strong Reserve Forces." *Air Force Times* 44 (May 21, 1984): 14.

9516. Carr, Albert H. Z. *Truman, Stalin, and Peace.* Garden City, NY: Doubleday, 1950.

9517. Cary, Otis. "The Sparing of Kyoto: Mr. Stimson's 'Pet City.'" *Japan Quarterly* 22 (October/December 1975): 337-347.

9518. Clifford, J. Garry. "President Truman and the Peter the Great's Will." *Diplomatic History* 4 (Fall 1980): 371-385.

9519. Cunningham, Frank D. "Harry S. Truman and Universal Military Training, 1945." *Historian* 46 (May 1984): 397-415.

9520. Dallek, Robert. "The Truman Era." In *America-East Asian Relations: A Survey,* edited by Ernest R. May and James C. Thomson, Jr., 356-375. Cambridge, MA: Harvard University Press, 1972.

9521. Deaton, Dorsey M. "The Protestant Crisis: Truman's Vatican Ambassador Controversy of 1951." Ph.D. dissertation, Emory University, 1970.

9522. Druks, Herbert. "Dealing with the Russians: The Truman Experience." *East Europe* 20 (August 1971): 2-8.

9523. Druks, Herbert. *Harry S. Truman and the Russians: 1945-1953.* New York: Speller and Sons, 1967.

9524. Feaver, John H. "The Truman Administration and China, 1945-1950: The Policy of Restrained Intervention." Ph.D. dissertation, University of Oklahoma, 1980.

9525. Ferrell, Robert H. "Truman Foreign Policy: A Traditional View." In *The Truman Period as a Research Field: A Reappraisal,* edited by Richard S. Kirkendall, 11-45. Columbia: University of Missouri Press, 1974.

9526. Ferrell, Robert H., ed. "Truman at Potsdam." *American Heritage* 31 (June/July 1980): 36-47.

9527. Freidell, Theodore D. "Truman's Point Four: Legislative Enactment and Development in Latin America." Ph.D. dissertation, University of Missouri, 1965.

9528. Fuller, Daniel J., and Michael T. Ruddy. "Myths in Progress: Harry Truman and *Meeting at Potsdam.*" *American Studies* 18 (Fall 1977): 99-106.

9529. Gaddis, John L. "Harry S. Truman and the Origins of Containment." In *Makers of American Diplomacy: From Benjamin Franklin to Henry Kissinger,* edited by Frank J. Merli and Theodore A. Wilson, 493-522. New York: Scribner's, 1974.

9530. Gardner, Lloyd C. "Truman Era Foreign Policy: Recent Historical Trends." In *The Truman Period as a Research Field: A Reappraisal,* edited by Richard S. Kirkendall, 47-74. Columbia: University of Missouri Press, 1974.

9531. Garfield, Gene J. "The Genesis of Involvement: The Truman Decision to Assist the French in Indochina." Ph.D. dissertation, Southern Illinois University, 1972.

9532. Glinka-Janczewski, George H. "American Policy toward Poland under the Truman Administration, 1945-1952." Ph.D. dissertation, Georgetown University, 1966.

9533. Gottlieb, Amy Z. "Refugee Immigration: The Truman Directive." *Prologue* 13 (Spring 1981): 4-17.

9534. Graebner, Norman A. "Global Containment: The Truman Years." *Current History* 57 (August 1969): 77-83, 115-116.

9535. Graebner, Norman A. "The Truman Administration and the Cold War." *Current History* 35 (October 1958): 223-228.

9536. "Harry Truman: Foreign Policy Master Builder." *Economist* 291 (April 28, 1984): 41-43.

9537. Heim, Keith M. "Hope without Power: Truman and the Russians, 1945." Ph.D. dissertation, University of North Carolina, 1973.

9538. Heinrichs, Waldo H. "Roosevelt and Truman: The Presidential Perspective." In *Uncertain Years: Chinese-American Relations, 1947-50*, edited by Dorothy Borg and Waldo Heinrichs, 3-12. New York: Columbia University Press, 1980.

9539. Hensley, Carl W. "Harry S. Truman: Fundamental Americanism in Foreign Policy Speechmaking, 1945-1946." *Southern Speech Communication Journal* 40 (Winter 1975): 180-190.

9540. Herring, George C. "The Truman Administration and the Restoration of French Sovereignty in Indochina." *Diplomatic History* 1 (Spring 1977): 97-117.

9541. Hoffecker, Carol E. "President Truman's Explanation of His Foreign Policy to the American People." Ph.D. dissertation, Harvard University, 1967.

9542. Kelley, John L. "An Insurgent in the Truman Cabinet: Henry A. Wallace's Effort to Redirect Foreign Policy." *Missouri Historical Review* 77 (October 1982): 64-93.

9543. Koenig, Louis W. "Foreign Aid to Spain and Yugoslavia: Harry Truman Does His Duty." In *The Uses of Power*, edited by Alan F. Westin, 73-116. New York: Harcourt, Brace and World, 1962.

9544. Koenig, Louis W., ed. "Truman's Global Leadership." *Current History* 39 (October 1960): 225-229.

9545. Kolinsky, M. "The Efforts of the Truman Administration to Resolve the Arab-Israeli Conflict." *Middle Eastern Studies* 20 (January 1984): 81-94.

9546. Lichtheim, George. "Europe's Democracy and American Imperialism: Despite Truman's Election the Fear Persists." *Commentary* 7 (January 1949): 1-7.

9547. McLellan, David S., and John W. Reuss. "Foreign and Military Policies." In *The Truman Period as a Research Field*, edited by Richard S. Kirkendall, 15-85. Columbia: University of Missouri Press, 1967.

9548. May, Ernest R. *The Truman Administration and China, 1945-1949*. Philadelphia: Lippincott, 1975.

9549. Messer, Robert L. *The End of an Alliance: James F. Brynes, Roosevelt, Truman, and the Origins of the Cold War*. Chapel Hill: University of North Carolina Press, 1982.

9550. Miscamble, Wilson D. "Anthony Eden and the Truman-Molotov Conversations, April 1945." *Diplomatic History* 2 (Spring 1978): 167-180.

9551. Miscamble, Wilson D. "The Evaluation of an Internationalist: Harry S. Truman and American Foreign Policy." *Australian Journal of Politics and History* 23 (August 1977): 268-283.

9552. Miscamble, Wilson D. "Harry S. Truman, the Berlin Blockade, and the 1948 Election." *Presidential Studies Quarterly* 10 (Summer 1980): 306-316.

9553. Misse, Fred B. "Truman, Berlin, and the 1948 Election." *Missouri Historical Review* 76 (January 1982): 164-173.

9554. Miyasato, Seagen. "The Truman Administration and Indochina: Case Studies in Decision Making." *Japanese Journal of American Studies* 1 (1981): 119-150.

9555. Mrozek, Donald J. "Progressive Dissenter: Herbert Hoover's Opposition to Truman's Overseas Military Policy." *Annals of Iowa* 43 (Spring 1976): 275-291.

9556. Nagorski, Zygmunt. "The Potsdam Conference: Two Viewpoints." *Polish Review* 6 (Winter/Spring 1961): 107-116.

9557. Noer, Thomas J. "Truman, Eisenhower, and South Africa: The 'Middle Road' and Apartheid." *Journal of Ethnic Studies* 11 (Spring 1983): 75-104.

9558. O'Connor, Raymond G. "Truman: New Powers in Foreign Policy." *Australian Journal of Politics and History* 25 (1979): 319-326.

9559. Paterson, Thomas G. *Cold War Critics: Alternatives to American Policy in the Truman Years.* Chicago: Quadrangle Books, 1971.

9560. Paterson, Thomas G. "Presidential Foreign Policy, Public Opinion, and Congress: The Truman Years." *Diplomatic History* 3 (Winter 1979): 1-18.

9561. Paterson, Thomas G. "The Quest for Peace and Prosperity: International Trade, Communism, and the Marshall Plan." In *Politics and Policies of the Truman Administration*, edited by Barton J. Bernstein, 78-112. Chicago: Quadrangle Books, 1970.

9562. Peterson, Frank R. "Harry S. Truman and His Critics: The 1948 Progressives and the Origins of the Cold War." In *Essays on Radicalism in Contemporary America*, edited by Leon B. Blair, 32-62. Austin: University of Texas Press, 1972.

9563. Postbrief, Sam. "Departure from Incrementalism in U.S. Strategic Planning: The Origins of NSC-68." *Naval War College Review* 33 (March/April 1980): 34-57.

9564. Purifoy, Lewis M. *Harry Truman's China Policy: McCarthyism and the Diplomacy of Hysteria, 1947-1951.* New York: New Viewpoints, 1976.

9565. Quade, Quentin L. "A Second Dimension of Leadership: The Truman Administration in Foreign Policy." Ph.D. dissertation, University of Notre Dame, 1965.

9566. Quade, Quentin L. "Truman Administration and the Separation of Powers: The Case of the Marshall Plan." *Review of Politics* 27 (January 1965): 58-77.

9567. Robinson, Edgar E., et al. *Powers of the President in Foreign Affairs, 1945-1965: Harry S. Truman, Dwight D. Eisenhower, John F. Kennedy, Lyndon B. Johnson.* San Francisco: Commonwealth Club of California, 1966.

9568. Rosenberg, J. Philipp. "The Belief System of Harry S. Truman and Its Effect on Foreign Policy Decision-Making during His Administration." *Presidential Studies Quarterly* 12 (Spring 1982): 226-238.

9569. Rosenberg, J. Philipp. "The Cheshire Ultimatum: Truman's Message to Stalin in the 1946 Azerbaijan Crisis." *Journal of Politics* 41 (August 1979): 933-940.

9570. Sand, Gregory W. "Clifford and Truman: A Study in Foreign Policy and National Security, 1945-1949." Ph.D. dissertation, St. Louis University, 1973.

9571. Sander, Alfred D. "Truman and the National Security Council: 1945-1947." *Journal of American History* 59 (September 1972): 369-388.

9572. Schmidt, Terry P. "An Image Analysis of International Politics: Harry S. Truman and the Soviet Union, 1945-1947." Ph.D. dissertation, University of Denver, 1977.

9573. Secrest, Donald E. "American Policy toward Neutralism during the Truman and Eisenhower Administrations." Ph.D. dissertation, University of Michigan, 1967.

9574. Siegel, Howard B. "Strengths and Limitations of Informal Resources for Presidential Influence on Foreign Policy Legislation: The Truman Years." Ph.D. dissertation, Brown University, 1978.

9575. Sorenson, Dale. "The Language of a Cold Warrior: A Content Analysis of Harry Truman's Public Statements." *Social Science History* 3 (Winter 1979): 171-186.

9576. Stalin, Joseph. *Stalin's Correspondence with Churchill, Attlee, Roosevelt, and Truman, 1941-1945*. New York: Dutton, 1958.

9577. Theoharis, Athan G. "Roosevelt and Truman on Yalta: The Origins of the Cold War." *Political Science Quarterly* 87 (June 1972): 210-241.

9578. Thorpe, James A. "Truman's Ultimatum to Stalin on the 1946 Azerbaijan Crisis: The Making of a Myth." *Journal of Politics* 40 (February 1978): 188-195.

9579. Tozer, Warren W. "Last Bridge to China: The Shanghai Power Company, the Truman Administration, and the Chinese Communists." *Diplomatic History* 1 (Winter 1977): 64-78.

9580. Walton, Richard J. *Henry Wallace, Harry Truman, and the Cold War*. New York: Viking Press, 1976.

Korean War

9581. Cho, Soon-sung. "United States Policy toward Korean Reunification during the Truman Administration." *Journal of Asiatic Studies* 13 (1970): 79-90.

9582. Cushman, Donald P. "A Comparative Study of President Truman's and President Nixon's Justification for Committing Troops to Combat in Korea and Cambodia." Ph.D. dissertation, University of Wisconsin, 1974.

9583. Donovan, Robert J. *Nemesis: Truman and Johnson in the Coils of War in Asia*. New York: St. Martin's Press, 1984.

9584. Hedley, John H. "The Truman Administration and the 'Loss' of China: A Study of Public Attitudes and the President's Policies from the Marshall Mission to the Attack on Korea." Ph.D. dissertation, University of Missouri, 1964.

9585. Henderson, Thomas G. "Editorial Reaction of Selected Major Indiana Daily Newspapers to a National Controversy — The Truman, MacArthur Conflict." Ed.D. dissertation, Ball State University, 1977.

9586. Karp, Walter. "Truman vs. MacArthur." *American Heritage* 35 (April/May 1984): 84-95.

9587. Kirkendall, Richard S. *Harry S Truman, Korea, and the Imperial Presidency*. Saint Charles, MO: Forum Press, 1975.

9588. Kirkendall, Richard S. "Harry S Truman: The Decision to Intervene." In *American Diplomacy in the Twentieth Century*, edited by Warren F. Kimball, 1-14. St. Louis, MO: Forum Press, 1980.

9589. Kwak, Tae-Hwan. "U.S.-Soviet Relations: Truman's Containment Policy Revisited." *Korea and World Affairs* 4 (Winter 1980): 607-622.

9590. Lo, Clarence Y. H. "The Truman Administration's Military Budgets during the Korean War." Ph.D. dissertation, University of California, Berkeley, 1978.

9591. Lofgren, Charles A. "Mr. Truman's War: A Debate and Its Aftermath." *Review of Politics* 31 (April 1969): 223-241.

9592. Lowitt, Richard, ed. *The Truman-MacArthur Controversy*. Chicago: Rand McNally, 1967.

9593. Matray, James I. "America's Reluctant Crusade: Truman's Commitment to Combat Troops in the Korean War." *Historian* 42 (May 1980): 437-455.

9594. Matray, James I. "Captive of the Cold War: The Decision to Divide Korea at the 38th Parallel." *Pacific Historical Review* 50 (May 1981): 145-168.

9595. Matray, James I. "Truman's Plan for Victory: National Self-Determination and the Thirty-eighth Parallel Decision in Korea." *Journal of American History* 62 (September 1979): 314-333.

9596. Rovere, Richard H., and Arthur M. Schlesinger, Jr. *The General and the President and the Future of American Foreign Policy.* New York: Farrar, 1952.

9597. Ryan, Halford R. "Harry S Truman: A Misdirected Defense for MacArthur's Dismissal." *Presidential Studies Quarterly* 11 (Fall 1981): 576-582.

9598. Seltzer, Robert V. "The Truman-Johnson Analog: A Study of Presidential Rhetoric in Limited War." Ph.D. dissertation, Wayne State University, 1976.

9599. Snyder, Richard C., and Glenn D. Paige. "The United States Decision to Resist Aggression in Korea." *Presidential Studies Quarterly* 3 (December 1958): 341-378.

9600. Spanier, John. *The Truman-MacArthur Controversy and the Korean War.* 2d ed. New York: Norton, 1965.

9601. Thompson, Mark E. "The Truman-MacArthur Controversy: A Bibliographical Essay." *Studies in History and Society* 5 (Spring 1974): 66-73.

9602. Twedt, Michael S. "The War Rhetoric of Harry S. Truman during the Korean Conflict." Ph.D. dissertation, University of Kansas, 1969.

9603. Wiltz, John E. "Truman and MacArthur: The Wake Island Meeting." *Military Affairs* 42 (December 1978): 169-176.

Middle East

9604. Abramson, Arthur C. "The Formulation of American Foreign Policy towards the Middle East during the Truman Administration, 1945-1948." Ph.D. dissertation, University of California, 1981.

9605. Bickerton, Ian J. "President Truman's Recognition of Israel." *American Jewish Historical Quarterly* 58 (December 1968): 170-240.

9606. Bickerton, Ian J. "President Truman's Recognition of Israel: Two Views." *American Jewish Archives* 33 (April 1981): 141-152.

9607. Cohen, Michael J. "Truman and Palestine, 1945-1948: Revisionism, Politics, and Diplomacy." *Modern Judaism* 2 (February 1982): 1-22.

9608. Cohen, Michael J. "Truman and the State Department: The Palestine Trusteeship Proposal, March, 1948." *Jewish Social Studies* 43 (Spring 1981): 165-187.

9609. Ganin, Zvi. *Truman, American Jewry, and Israel, 1945-1948.* New York: Holmes and Meier, 1979.

9610. Haron, Miriam J. "Palestine and the Anglo-American Connection." *Modern Judaism* 2 (May 1982): 199-211.

9611. Jacobson, Edward. "Two Presidents and a Haberdasher —1948." *American Jewish Archives* 20 (April 1968): 3-15.

9612. Klieman, Aaron S. "President Truman and the Recognition of Israel in 1948." Ph.D. dissertation, Columbia University, 1964.

9613. Kolinsky, M. "The Efforts of the Truman Administration to Resolve the Arab-Israeli Conflict." *Middle Eastern Studies* 20 (January 1984): 81-94.

9614. Parzen, Herbert. "President Truman and the Palestine Quandry: His Initial Experience, April-December, 1945."

Jewish Social Studies 35 (January 1973): 42-72.

9615. Rosenberg, J. Philipp. "Berlin and Israel 1948: Foreign Policy Decision-Making during the Truman Administration." Ph.D. dissertation, University of Illinois, 1977.

9616. Sheres, Richard S. "Dissent over Palestine: President Truman and His Advisors." Master's thesis, American University, 1977.

9617. Slonim, Shlomo. "The 1948 American Embargo on Arms to Palestine." *Political Science Quarterly* 94 (Fall 1979): 495-514.

9618. Slonim, Shlomo. "President Truman, the State Department, and the Palestine Question." *Wiener Library Bulletin* 34 (1981): 15-29.

9619. Snetsinger, John G. "Truman and the Creation of Israel." Ph.D. dissertation, Stanford University, 1970.

9620. Snetsinger, John G. *Truman, the Jewish Vote, and the Creation of Israel.* Stanford, CA: Hoover Institute Press, 1974.

9621. Weinstein, Allen, and Moshe Ma'oz. *Truman and the American Commitment to Israel: A Thirtieth Anniversary Conference.* Jerusalem: Harry S. Truman Research Institute for the Advancement of Peace, Hebrew University, 1981.

Truman Doctrine

9622. Borchard, Edwin M. "Intervention: The Truman Doctrine and the Marshall Plan." *American Journal of International Law* 41 (October 1947): 885-888.

9623. Buckley, Gary J. "The Truman Doctrine and Public Opinion: An Application of a Conceptual Framework of James N. Rosenau." Ph.D. dissertation, University of Denver, 1973.

9624. Freeland, Richard M. *The Truman Doctrine and the Origins of McCarthyism: Foreign Policy, Domestic Politics, and Internal Security, 1946-1948.* New York: Knopf, 1972.

9625. Gaddis, John L. "Reconsiderations: Was the Truman Doctrine a Real Turning Point?" *Foreign Affairs* 52 (January 1974): 386-402.

9626. Graber, Doris A. "The Truman and Eisenhower Doctrines in the Light of the Doctrine of Non-Intervention." *Political Science Quarterly* 73 (September 1958): 321-334.

9627. Heinlein, David L. "The Truman Doctrine: A Chief Executive in Search of the Presidency." Ph.D. dissertation, Johns Hopkins University, 1975.

9628. Iselin, John J. "The Truman Doctrine: A Study in the Relationship between Crisis and Foreign Policy-Making." Ph.D. dissertation, Harvard University, 1965.

9629. Iselin, John J. "The Truman Doctrine: Its Passage through Congress and the Aftermath." *Foreign Service Journal* 44 (May 1967): 19-22.

9630. Kaiser, Robert G. "The Truman Doctrine: How It All Began." *Foreign Service Journal* 44 (May 1967): 17-18.

9631. Kernell, Samuel. "The Truman Doctrine Speech: A Case Study of the Dynamics of Presidential Leadership." *Social Science History* 1 (Fall 1976): 20-45.

9632. Knight, Jonathan. "American International Guarantees for the Straits: Prelude to the Truman Doctrine." *Middle Eastern Studies* 13 (May 1977): 241-250.

9633. Koenig, Louis W. "The Truman Doctrine and NATO." *Current History* 57 (July 1969): 18-23, 53.

9634. Kousoulas, D. George. "Truman Doctrine and the Stalin-Tito Rift: A Reappraisal." *South Atlantic Quarterly* 72 (Summer 1973): 427-439.

9635. Lehman, Ronald F. "Vandenberg, Taft, and Truman: Principle and Politics in the Announcement of the Truman Doctrine." Ph.D. dissertation, Claremont Graduate School, 1975.

9636. Lun, Ngoh G. "Truman and Containment: The Rationale and Application of the Truman Doctrine." *Journal of the History Society* (Singapore) 2 (1978): 63-68.

9637. McFadyen, Barbara D. *The Truman Doctrine: Its Origin and Evolution.* Boulder: University of Colorado Press, 1965.

9638. Ryan, Henry B., Jr. "The American Intellectual Tradition Reflected in the Truman Doctrine." *American Scholar* 42 (Spring 1973): 294-307.

9639. Satterthwaite, Joseph C. "The Truman Doctrine: Turkey." *Annals of the American Academy of Political and Social Science* 401 (May 1972): 74-84.

9640. Warner, Geoffrey. "The Truman Doctrine and the Marshall Plan." *International Affairs* 50 (January 1974): 82-92.

9641. Weiner, Bernard. "The Truman Doctrine: Background and Presentation." Ph.D. dissertation, Claremont Graduate School, 1967.

9642. Wittner, Lawrence S. "The Truman Doctrine and the Defense of Freedom." *Diplomatic History* 4 (Spring 1980): 161-187.

9643. Xydis, Stephen G. "The Truman Doctrine in Perspective." *Balkan Studies* 8 (1967): 239-262.

Writings

9644. Ferrell, Robert H. "The Private Papers of Harry S. Truman." *Society for Historians of American Foreign Relations Newsletter* 11 (1980): 1-7.

9645. Ferrell, Robert H., ed. *Dear Bess: The Letters from Harry Truman to Bess Truman, 1910-1959.* New York: Norton, 1983.

9646. Ferrell, Robert H., ed. *Off the Record: The Private Papers of Harry S. Truman.* New York: Harper and Row, 1978.

9647. Heller, Francis H. "The Writing of the Truman Memoirs." *Presidential Studies Quarterly* 13 (Winter 1983): 81-84.

9648. Mark, Eduard. "'Today Has Been a Historical One': Harry S Truman's Diary of the Potsdam Conference." *Diplomatic History* 43 (Summer 1980): 317-326.

9649. Poen, Monte M., ed. *Strictly Personal and Confidential: The Letters Harry Truman Never Mailed.* Boston: Little, Brown, 1982.

9650. Rogers, Benjamin. "'Dear Mr. President': The Hoover-Truman Correspondence." *Palimpsest* 55 (September/October 1974): 152-158.

9651. Schnapper, Morris B., ed. *The Truman Program: Addresses and Messages.* Washington, DC: Public Affairs Press, 1949.

9652. Settel, Trudy S. *The Quotable Harry S. Truman.* Anderson, SC: Drake House, 1967.

9653. Truman, Harry S. *The Autobiography of Harry S Truman*, edited by Robert H. Ferrell. Boulder: Colorado Associated University Press, 1980.

9654. Truman, Harry S. "The First Atomic Bombing at Hiroshima." In *The Impact of Air Power: National Security and World Politics*, edited by Eugene E. Emme, et al., 83-85. Princeton, NJ: Van Nostrand, 1959.

9655. Truman, Harry S. *Freedom and Equality, Addresses.* Edited by David S. Horton. Columbia: University of Missouri Press, 1960.

9656. Truman, Harry S. *Good Old Harry: The Wit and Wisdom of Harry S Truman.* Compiled by George S. Caldwell. New York: Hawthorn, 1966.

9657. Truman, Harry S. *Letters Home.* Edited by Monte M. Poen. New York: Putnam, 1983.

9658. Truman, Harry S. *The Man from Missouri: The Memorable Words of the Thirty-third President.* Edited by Ted Sheldon. Kansas City, MO: Hallmark, 1970.

9659. Truman, Harry S. *Memoirs.* 2 vols. Garden City, NY: Doubleday, 1955-1956.

9660. Truman, Harry S. *Mr. Citizen.* New York: Bernard Geis Associates, 1960.

9661. Truman, Harry S. *Mr. President: The First Publication from the Personal Diaries of Harry S Truman, 32nd President of the U.S.A.* Edited by William Hillman. New York: Farrar, Straus and Young, 1952.

9662. Truman, Harry S. "The Most Mistreated of Presidents." *North Carolina Historical Review* 36 (April 1955): 197-204.

9663. Truman, Harry S. "My View of the Presidency." *Look* 11 (November 1958): 25-31.

9664. Truman, Harry S. "Presidential Powers: Address, May 8, 1954." *Vital Speeches* 20 (June 1, 1954): 487-489.

9665. Truman, Harry S. *Truman Speaks.* New York: Columbia University Press, 1960.

9666. Truman, Harry S. *The Truman Wit.* Edited by Alex J. Goldman. New York: Citadel Press, 1966.

9667. Truman, Harry S. *The Truman Years: The Words and Times of Harry S. Truman.* Edited by Robert L. Palley. Waukesha, WI: Country Beautiful, 1976.

9668. Truman, Harry S. *The Words of Harry Truman.* Edited by Robert J. Donovan. New York: Newmarket Press, 1984.

9669. Truman, Margaret, ed. *Letters from Father: The Truman Family's Personal Correspondence.* New York: Pinnacle Books, 1982.

Dwight D. Eisenhower

Biographies

9670. Ambrose, Stephen E. *Eisenhower: President and Elder Statesman, 1952-1969.* New York: Simon and Schuster, 1984.

9671. Ambrose, Stephen E. *Eisenhower, Soldier, General of the Army, President-Elect.* New York: Simon and Schuster, 1983.

9672. Ambrose, Stephen E. *Ike: Abilene to Berlin.* New York: Harper and Row, 1973.

9673. American Heritage Magazine and United Press International. *Eisenhower, American Hero: The Historical Record of His Life.* New York: American Heritage Publishing Co., 1969.

9674. Army Times. *The Challenge and the Triumph: The Story of Dwight D. Eisenhower.* New York: Putnam, 1966.

9675. Beckhard, Arthur J. *The Story of Dwight D. Eisenhower.* New York: Grosset and Dunlap, 1956.

9676. Blumenson, Martin. *Eisenhower.* New York: Ballantine Books, 1972.

9677. Childs, Marquis W. *Eisenhower: Captive Hero: A Critical Study of the General and the President.* New York: Harcourt Brace, 1958.

9678. Cook, Blanche W. *The Declassified Eisenhower: A Divided Legacy.* Garden City, NY: Doubleday, 1981.

9679. Cutler, Robert. *No Time for Rest.* Boston: Little, Brown, 1966.

9680. Davis, Kenneth S. *Soldiers of Democracy: A Biography of Dwight Eisenhower.* Garden City, NY: Doubleday, 1952.

9681. Donovan, Robert J. *Eisenhower: The Inside Story.* New York: Harper and Row, 1956.

9682. Field, Rudolph. *Ike, Man of the Hour.* New York: Universal, 1952.

9683. Field, Rudolph. *Mister American: Dwight David Eisenhower, An Evaluation.* New York: R. Field, 1952.

9684. Friedman, Irving I. *Meet General Ike.* New York: Virson, 1948.

9685. Gunther, John. *Eisenhower, The Man and the Symbol.* New York: Harper and Row, 1951.

9686. Hatch, Alden. *General Ike, A Biography of Dwight D. Eisenhower.* Rev. ed. New York: Holt, 1952.

9687. Hicks, Wilson, ed. *This Is Ike: The Picture Story of the Man.* New York: Holt, 1952.

9688. Jameson, Henry B. *They Still Call Him Ike.* New York: Vantage Press, 1972.

9689. Johnson, George. *Eisenhower: The*

Life and Times of a Great General, President, and Statesman. Derby, CT: Monarch Press, 1962.

9690. LaFay, Howard. " '. . . And I've Always Loved My Country' — The Eisenhower Story." *National Geographic Magazine* 136 (July 1969): 1-39.

9691. Larson, Arthur. *Eisenhower: The President Nobody Knew.* New York: Scribner's, 1968.

9692. Lee, R. Alton. *Dwight D. Eisenhower: Soldier and Statesman.* Chicago, IL: Nelson-Hall, 1981.

9693. Longgood, William F. *Ike, A Pictorial Biography.* New York: Time-Life Books, 1969.

9694. Lovelace, Delos W. *Ike Eisenhower: Statesman and Soldier of Peace.* New York: Harper and Row, 1969.

9695. Lyon, Peter. *Eisenhower: Portrait of the Hero.* Boston: Little, Brown, 1974.

9696. McCann, Kevin. *Man from Abilene.* Garden City, NY: Doubleday, 1952.

9697. McKeogh, Michael J., and Richard Lockridge. *Sgt. Mickey and General Ike.* New York: Putnam, 1946.

9698. Miller, Francis T. *Eisenhower.* Philadelphia: Winston, 1944.

9699. Morgan, Kay S. *Past Forgetting: My Love Affair with Dwight D. Eisenhower.* New York: Simon and Schuster, 1976.

9700. Morin, Relman. *Dwight D. Eisenhower: A Gauge of Greatness.* New York: Simon and Schuster, 1969.

9701. Neal, Steve. *The Eisenhowers.* Lawrence: University Press of Kansas, 1984.

9702. Neal, Steve. *The Eisenhowers: Reluctant Dynasty.* Garden City, NY: Doubleday, 1978.

9703. Nixon, Richard M. "Dwight D. Eisenhower, 1890-1969." *American County Government* 34 (March 1969): 24-26.

9704. Pinkley, Virgil, and James F. Scheer. *Eisenhower Declassified.* Old Tappan, NJ: Revell, 1979.

9705. Pusey, Merlo J. *Eisenhower: The President.* New York: Macmillan, 1956.

9706. Ramsey, Don, ed. *Ike: A Great American.* Kansas City, MO: Hallmark, 1972.

9707. Reeder, Russell P. *Dwight David Eisenhower, Fighter for Peace.* Champaign, IL: Garrard, 1968.

9708. Russell, Don. *Invincible Ike: The Inspiring Life Story of Dwight D. Eisenhower.* Chicago: Successful Living Publications, 1952.

9709. Sherman, Diane F. *The Boy from Abilene: The Story of Dwight D. Eisenhower.* Philadelphia: Westminster Press, 1968.

9710. Slater, Ellis D. *The Ike I Knew.* s.l.: Ellis D. Slater Trust, 1980.

9711. Smith, A. Merriman. *Meet Mister Eisenhower.* New York: Harper and Row, 1955.

9712. Snyder, Marty, and Glenn Kittler. *My Friend Ike.* New York: Fell, 1956.

9713. Steinberg, Alfred. *Dwight David Eisenhower.* New York: Putnam, 1968.

9714. Taylor, Maxwell D. *The Uncertain Trumpet.* New York: Harper and Row, 1960.

9715. U.S. Congress. House. *Memorial Services in the Congress of the United States and Tributes in Eulogy of Dwight David Eisenhower.* Washington, DC: U.S. Government Printing Office, 1970.

9716. Whitney, David C. *The Picture Life of Dwight D. Eisenhower.* New York: Franklin Watts, 1968.

9717. Wykes, Alan. *The Biography of*

General Dwight D. Eisenhower. New York: Galley Press, 1982.

Private Life

9718. Bearss, Edwin C. *Eisenhower National Historic Site.* Washington, DC: Office of History and Historic Architecture, National Park Service, 1970.

9719. Brandon, Dorothy B. *Mamie Doud Eisenhower: A Portrait of a First Lady.* New York: Scribner's, 1954.

9720. Cohen, Stan. *The Eisenhowers, Gettysburg's First Family.* Charleston, WV: Pictorial Histories Publishing Co., 1983.

9721. David, Lester, and Irene David. *Ike and Mamie, The Story of the General and His Lady.* New York: Putnam, 1981.

9722. Gustafson, Merlin. "President Eisenhower's Hobby." *Presidential Studies Quarterly* 13 (Winter 1983): 98-100.

9723. Hatch, Alden. *Red Carpet for Mamie.* New York: Holt, 1954.

9724. Homan, Delmar C. "Dwight Eisenhower and William Shakespeare." *Heritage Kansas* 9 (Spring 1976): 13-17.

9725. Kornitzer, Bela. *The Great American Heritage: The Story of the Five Eisenhower Brothers.* New York: Farrar, Strauss and Giroux, 1955.

9726. McCarty, Nancy. "With Ike at Gettysburg." *Airman* 16 (June 1972): 40-42.

9727. O'Donnell, Francis J. "Ike's Other Presidency." *Humanities* 2 (October 1981): 4-5.

9728. Sageser, A. Bower. "Dwight D. Eisenhower: First Citizen of Kansas." *Kansas Quarterly* 2 (Summer 1970): 118-125.

9729. Summersby, Kathleen M. *Eisenhower Was My Boss.* New York: Prentice-Hall, 1948.

9730. Rhodes, Richard. "Ike: Artist in Iron." *Harper's* 241 (July 1970): 70-77.

Public Career

9731. Ambrose, Stephen E. *Eisenhower and Berlin, 1945: The Decision to Halt at the Elbe.* New York: Norton, 1967.

9732. Ambrose, Stephen E. "Eisenhower and the Intelligence Community in World War II." *Journal of Contemporary History* 16 (January 1981): 153-166.

9733. Ambrose, Stephen E. "Eisenhower, the Intelligence Community, and the D-Day Invasion." *Wisconsin Magazine of History* 64 (Summer 1981): 261-277.

9734. Ambrose, Stephen E. "Eisenhower's Greatest Decision." *American History Illustrated* 4 (May 1969): 4-11.

9735. Ambrose, Stephen E. "Fateful Friendship." *American Heritage* 20 (April 1969): 40-41, 97-103.

9736. Ambrose, Stephen E. "How Ike Was Chosen." *American History Illustrated* 3 (November 1968): 20-25, 27-30.

9737. Ambrose, Stephen E. *The Supreme Commander: The War Years of General Dwight D. Eisenhower.* Garden City, NJ: Doubleday, 1970.

9738. Barclay, C. N. "Dwight David Eisenhower, 1890-1969: A Tribute to the Supreme Allied Commander, 1942-45." *Army Quarterly and Defense Journal* (Great Britain) 98 (1969): 136-140.

9739. Blumenson, Martin. "Ike and His Indispensable Lieutenants." *Army* 30 (June 1980): 50-60.

9740. Butcher, Harry C. *My Three Years with Eisenhower: The Personal Diary of Captain Harry C. Butcher, USNR, Naval*

Aide to General Eisenhower, 1942 to 1945. New York: Simon and Schuster, 1946.

9741. Coffman, Edward M. "My Room Mate Is Dwight Eisenhower." *American Heritage* 24 (April 1973): 102-103.

9742. Cooling, Benjamin F. "Dwight D. Eisenhower at the Army War College, 1927-1928." *Parameters* 5 (1975): 26-36.

9743. DeWeerd, Harvey A. "General Eisenhower." *American Mercury* 61 (July 1945): 16-25.

9744. Eisenhower, David. *Eisenhower at War: 1943-1945.* New York: Random House, 1986.

9745. Emerich, Duncan. "The Poet and the General: Carl Sandburg Meets General Eisenhower." *Saturday Review* 31 (March 20, 1948): 9-11, 45-46.

9746. Evans, Medford. "General Patton: Why They Didn't Let George Do It." *American Opinion* 18 (September 1975): 11-18, 89, 91, 93-94.

9747. Fowler, John G., Jr. "Command Decision." *Military Review* 59 (June 1979): 2-6.

9748. Funk, Arthur L. "Churchill, Eisenhower, and the French Resistance." *Military Affairs* 45 (February 1981): 29-33.

9749. Funk, Arthur L. "Eisenhower, Giraud, and the Command of 'TORCH.'" *Military Affairs* 35 (October 1971): 103-108.

9750. Godfrey, Gordon. "Dwight David Eisenhower." *Contemporary Review* 214 (April 1969): 177-178.

9751. Hansen, Laurence J. *What It Was Like Flying for 'Ike.'* Largo, FL: Aero-Medical Consultants, 1983.

9752. Holden, Jack. "He Flew with Eisenhower in the Best Circles." *Soldiers* 26 (December 1971): 53-54.

9753. Holmes, Julius C. "Eisenhower's African Gamble." *Collier's* 117 (January 12, 1946): 14-15; (January 19, 1946): 27-30.

9754. Hunter, T. M. "Foch and Eisenhower: A Study in Allied Supreme Command." *Army Quarterly and Defense Journal* 87 (1963): 33-52.

9755. Jacobs, Travis B. "Dwight D. Eisenhower's Presidency of Columbia University." *Presidential Studies Quarterly* 15 (Summer 1985): 555-560.

9756. Morton, Louis. "The Philippine Army, 1935-39: Eisenhower's Memorandum to Quezon." *Military Affairs* 12 (Summer 1948): 103-107.

9757. Pogue, Forrest C. "Why Eisenhower's Forces Stopped at the Elbe." *World Politics* 4 (April 1952): 356-368.

9758. Rourke, John T. "Marshall, Eisenhower, and the Military Mind." *Military Review* 61 (February 1981): 26-32.

9759. Rovere, Richard H. "Eisenhower over the Shoulder." *American Scholar* 31 (Spring 1962): 176-180.

9760. Sixsmith, Eric K. G. *Eisenhower as Military Commander.* New York: Stein and Day, 1983.

9761. Smith, Walter B. *Eisenhower's Six Great Decisions: Europe, 1944-1945.* New York: Longmans, Green, 1956.

9762. Weigley, Russell F. *Eisenhower's Lieutenants: The Campaign of France and Germany, 1944-1945.* Bloomington: Indiana University Press, 1981.

Presidential Years

General

9763. Adams, Sherman. *First-Hand Report: The Story of the Eisenhower Admin-*

istration. New York: Harper and Row, 1961.

9764. Albertson, Dean, ed. *Eisenhower as President.* New York: Hill and Wang, 1963.

9765. Albjerg, Victor L. "Truman and Eisenhower: Their Administrations and Campaigns." *Current History* 47 (October 1964): 221-228.

9766. Alexander, Charles C. *Holding the Line: The Eisenhower Era, 1952-1961.* Bloomington: Indiana University Press, 1975.

9767. Anderson, Wayne W. "President Eisenhower's White House Staff: Its Organization and Operation." Ph.D. dissertation, Georgetown University, 1974.

9768. Archer, Jules. *Battlefield President: Dwight D. Eisenhower.* New York: Messner, 1967.

9769. Benson, Ezra T. *Cross Fire: The Eight Years with Eisenhower.* Garden City, NY: Doubleday, 1962.

9770. Bosha, Francis J. "William Faulkner and the Eisenhower Administration." *Journal of Mississippi History* 42 (February 1980): 49-54.

9771. Bragg, William, Jr. *Eisenhower the President: Crucial Days: 1951-1960.* Englewood Cliffs, NJ: Prentice-Hall, 1981.

9772. Branyan, Robert L. "Eisenhower the Politician." *American Chronicle* 1 (January 1972): 43-47.

9773. Branyan, Robert L., and Lawrence H. Larsen. *The Eisenhower Administration, 1953-1961: A Documentary History.* 2 vols. New York: Random House, 1971.

9774. Brown, John M. *Through These Men: Some Aspects of Our Passing History.* New York: Harper and Row, 1956.

9775. Buchanan, Wiley. *Red Carpet at the White House.* New York: Dutton, 1964.

9776. Buckley, William F. "The Tranquil World of Dwight D. Eisenhower." *National Review* 5 (January 18, 1958): 57-59.

9777. Cecile, Robert E. "Crisis Decision-Making in the Eisenhower and Kennedy Administrations: The Application of an Analytical Scheme." Ph.D. dissertation, University of Oklahoma, 1965.

9778. Cotter, Cornelius P. "Eisenhower as Party Leader." *Political Science Quarterly* 98 (Summer 1983): 255-283.

9779. Crable, Richard E. "Ike — Identification, Argument, and Paradoxical Appeal." *Quarterly Journal of Speech* 63 (April 1977): 188-195.

9780. Davidson, Robert H. "While Millions Watched and Listened, A President Took Office." *Transmitter* 41 (March/April 1953): 2-4, 65-66.

9781. DeSantis, Vincent P. "Eisenhower Revisionism." *Review of Politics* 38 (April 1976): 190-207.

9782. Druks, Herbert, ed. *From Truman through Johnson: A Documentary History.* Vol. 1, *Truman and Eisenhower.* New York: Robert Speller, 1971.

9783. Egleton, Clive. *The Eisenhower Deception.* New York: Atheneum, 1981.

9784. Ekirch, Arthur A. "Eisenhower and Kennedy: The Rhetoric and the Reality." *Midwest Quarterly* 17 (Spring 1976): 279-290.

9785. Erskine, Helen W. "Dick and Pat Nixon — The Team on Ike's Team." *Collier's* 134 (July 9, 1954): 32-37.

9786. Ewald, William B., Jr. *Eisenhower the President: Crucial Days, 1951-1960.* Englewood Cliffs, NJ: Prentice-Hall, 1981.

9787. Fairbanks, James D. "Religious Dimensions of Presidential Leadership: The Case of Dwight Eisenhower." *Presi-*

dential Studies Quarterly 12 (Spring 1982): 260-267.

9788. Farnsworth, David. "The Eisenhower Presidency Gets New Higher Rating." *Wichita State University Alumni Report* 2 (September/October 1980): 12-14.

9789. Ferrell, Robert H., ed. *The Diary of James C. Haggerty: Eisenhower in Mid-Course — 1954-1955.* Bloomington: Indiana University Press, 1983.

9790. Freidel, Frank B. "Thirty-fourth President, 1953-1961." *National Geographic Magazine* 129 (January 1966): 90-99.

9791. Frier, David A. *Conflict of Interest in the Eisenhower Administration.* Ames: Iowa State University Press, 1969.

9792. Geelhoed, E. Bruce. "Executive at the Pentagon: Re-examining the Role of Charles E. Wilson in the Eisenhower Administration." *Military Affairs* 44 (February 1980): 1-7.

9793. Goldman, Sheldon. "Characteristics of Eisenhower and Kennedy: Appointees to the Lower Federal Courts." *Western Political Quarterly* 18 (December 1965): 755-762.

9794. Graebner, Norman A. "Eisenhower's Popular Leadership." *Current History* 39 (October 1960): 230-236, 244.

9795. Greenstein, Fred I. "Eisenhower as an Activist President: A Look at New Evidence." *Political Science Quarterly* 94 (Winter 1979-1980): 575-599.

9796. Greenstein, Fred I. *The Hidden-Hand Presidency: Eisenhower as Leader.* New York: Basic Books, 1982.

9797. Griffith, Robert. "Dwight D. Eisenhower and the Corporate Commonwealth." *American Historical Review* 87 (February 1982): 87-122.

9798. Griffith, Robert. "Why They Like Ike." *Review of American History* 7 (December 1979): 577-583.

9799. Halperin, Morton H. "The Gaither Committee and the Policy Process." *World Politics* 13 (April 1961): 360-384.

9800. Handlin, Oscar. "The Eisenhower Administration: A Self Portrait." *Atlantic Monthly* 212 (November 1963): 67-72.

9801. Flannelly, Margaret E. "An Analysis of the Role of the White House Staff in the Administrations of President Dwight D. Eisenhower and President John F. Kennedy." Ph.D. dissertation, University of Notre Dame, 1969.

9802. Harlow, Bryce. "Text of Address at Nashville Symposium, 21 October 1973." *Center House Bulletin* 4 (Winter 1974): 7-9.

9803. Harris, Seymour E. *The Economics of the Political Parties: With Special Attention to Presidents Eisenhower and Kennedy.* New York: Macmillan, 1962.

9804. Heeney, A. D. P. "Washington under Two Presidents: 1953-57: 1959-62." *International Journal* 22 (Summer 1967): 500-511.

9805. Hobbs, Edward H. "The President and Administration — Eisenhower." *Public Administration Review* 18 (Fall 1958): 306-313.

9806. Hoxie, R. Gordon. "Eisenhower and Presidential Leadership." *Presidential Studies Quarterly* 13 (Fall 1983): 589-612.

9807. Hyman, Herbert H., and Paul B. Sheatsley. "The Political Appeal of President Eisenhower." *Political Opinion Quarterly* 17 (Winter 1953-1954): 443-460.

9808. Hyman, Sidney. "The Cabinet's Job as Eisenhower Sees It." *New York Times Magazine* 107 (July 20, 1958): 7, 38-41.

9809. Hyman, Sidney. "Eisenhower Glow

Is Fading Away." *Reporter* 17 (September 19, 1957): 11-15.

9810. Hyman, Sidney. "Eisenhower's Presidency: The Known and the Foreseeable." *Reporter* 14 (March 22, 1956): 13-17.

9811. "It Couldn't Have Happened Anyplace Else in the World." *Life* 34 (February 2, 1953): 14-22.

9812. Jeffries, Ona G. *In and Out of the White House, From Washington to the Eisenhowers: An Intimate Glimpse into the Social and Domestic Aspects of the Presidential Life.* New York: Wilfred Funk, 1960.

9813. Joes, Anthony J. "Eisenhower Revisionism: The Tide Comes In." *Presidential Studies Quarterly* 15 (Summer 1985): 561-571.

9814. Johnson, Miles B. *The Government Secrecy Controversy: A Dispute Involving the Government and the Press in the Eisenhower, Kennedy, and Johnson Administrations.* New York: Vantage Press, 1967.

9815. Johnson, Walter. *The American President and the Art of Communication: An Inaugural Lecture Delivered before the University of Oxford on 13 May 1958.* Oxford: Clarendon Press, 1958.

9816. Kempton, Murray. "Epistles from the Eisenhower Age." *Commentary* 35 (March 1963): 232-238.

9817. Kempton, Murray. "The Underestimation of Dwight D. Eisenhower." *Esquire* 68 (September 1967): 108-109, 156.

9818. Knebel, Fletcher. "The Inside Story of the Ike-Truman Feud." *Look* 19 (September 6, 1955): 21-25.

9819. Langbein, F. W. "Teamwork Played Its Part in Good Communications for the Inauguration of a President." *Transmitter* 45 (March/April 1957): 2-5.

9820. Leo, J. "Dwight David Eisenhower: Ranking an Ex-President." *Commonweal* 90 (April 11, 1969): 95-96.

9821. McAuliffe, Mary S. "Commentary: Eisenhower, The President." *Journal of American History* 68 (December 1981): 625-632.

9822. McCoy, Donald R. "Trends in Viewing Herbert Hoover, Franklin D. Roosevelt, Harry S. Truman, and Dwight D. Eisenhower." *Midwest Quarterly* 20 (Winter 1979): 117-136.

9823. McInerney, Thomas J. "Eisenhower Governance and the Power to Command: A Perspective on Presidential Leadership." *Presidential Studies Quarterly* 11 (Spring 1981): 262-270.

9824. MacIsaac, David. "Eisenhower: A Reputation in Transition." *Air University Review* 33 (September/October 1982): 86-99.

9825. MacMillan, Harold. *Pointing the Way: 1959-61.* London: Macmillan, 1972.

9826. MacMillan, Harold. *Riding the Storm: 1956-59.* London: Macmillan, 1971.

9827. Marshall, Charles B. "Eisenhower's Second Term." *New Republic* 153 (November 6, 1965): 25-27.

9828. Merrill, John. "How 'Time' Stereotyped Three U.S. Presidents." *Journalism Quarterly* 42 (Autumn 1965): 563-570.

9829. Morrow, Everett F. *Black Man in the White House: A Diary of the Eisenhower Years by the Administrative Officer for Special Projects, The White House, 1955-60.* New York: Coward-McCann, 1963.

9830. Murphy, Charles J. V. "The Eisenhower Shift." *Fortune* 53 (January 1956): 82-87, 206-208.

9831. Murphy, Charles J. V. "Eisenhower's White House." *Fortune* 48 (July 1953): 75-77, 176, 178, 180-186.

9832. Nadich, Judah. *Eisenhower and the Jews*. New York: Twayne, 1953.

9833. National Cartoonists Society. *President Eisenhower's Cartoon Book, By 95 of America's Leading Cartoonists*. New York: Fell, 1956.

9834. Neumann, Robert G. "Leadership: Franklin Roosevelt, Truman, Eisenhower, and Today." *Presidential Studies Quarterly* 10 (Winter 1980): 10-19.

9835. Niebuhr, Reinhold. "The Eisenhower Era." *New Leader* 43 (October 3, 1960): 3-4.

9836. Parmet, Herbert S. *Eisenhower and the American Crusades*. New York: Macmillan, 1972.

9837. Pear, R. H. "The American Presidency under Eisenhower." *Political Quarterly* 28 (January 1957): 5-12.

9838. Pendergrass, Bonnie B. *Public Power, Politics, and Technology in the Eisenhower and Kennedy Years: The Hanford Dual-Purpose Reactor Controversy, 1956-1962*. New York: Arno, 1979.

9839. Pollard, James E. "Eisenhower and the Press: The Final Phase." *Journalism Quarterly* 38 (Spring 1961): 181-186.

9840. Pollard, James E. "Eisenhower and the Press: The First Two Years." *Journalism Quarterly* 32 (Summer 1955): 285-300.

9841. Prothro, James W. "Verbal Shifts in the American Presidency: A Content Analysis." *American Political Science Review* 50 (September 1956): 726-750.

9842. Reichard, Gary W. "Eisenhower and the Bricker Amendment." *Prologue* 6 (Summer 1974): 88-99.

9843. Reichard, Gary W. "Eisenhower as President: The Changing View." *South Atlantic Quarterly* 77 (Summer 1978): 265-281.

9844. Reichard, Gary W. *The Reaffirmation of Republicanism: Eisenhower and the Eighty-third Congress*. Knoxville: University of Tennessee Press, 1975.

9845. Richardson, Elmo. *The Presidency of Dwight D. Eisenhower*. Lawrence: Regents Press of Kansas, 1979.

9846. Rovere, Richard H. "Eisenhower and the New President." *Harper's* 220 (May 1960): 31-35.

9847. Rovere, Richard H. *The Eisenhower Years: Affairs of State*. New York: Farrar, Straus and Cudahy, 1956.

9848. Rosamond, Robert. *Crusade for Peace: Eisenhower's Presidential Legacy with the Program for Action*. Lexington, MA: Lexington Books, 1962.

9849. Ryan, Halford R. "A Rhetorical Analysis of General Eisenhower's Public Speaking from 1945 to 1951." Ph.D. dissertation, University of Illinois, 1972.

9850. Sandler, Shmuel. "Reconciling Domestic and International Politics: The Eisenhower and the Nixon Presidencies." Ph.D. dissertation, Johns Hopkins University, 1977.

9851. Sellen, Robert W., and Paul S. Holbo. *The Eisenhower Era*. Hinsdale, IL: Dryden Press, 1974.

9852. Shannon, William V. "Eisenhower as President: A Critical Appraisal of the Record." *Commentary* 26 (November 1958): 390-398.

9853. Smith, A. Merriman. *A President's Odyssey*. New York: Harper and Row, 1961.

9854. Strauss, Lewis L. *Men and Decisions*. Garden City, NY: Doubleday, 1962.

9855. Strum, Harvey. "Eisenhower's Solar Energy Policy." *Public Historian* 6 (Spring 1984): 37-50.

9856. Sweet, Kenneth F. "The Eisenhower Administration in Crisis Decision-Making." Ph.D. dissertation, Indiana University, 1975.

9857. Taylor, Robert L. "A Week inside the White House." *Collier's* 133 (February 19, 1954): 23-27; (March 5, 1954): 30-37.

9858. Thompson, Kenneth W., ed. *The Eisenhower Presidency: Eleven Intimate Perspectives of Dwight D. Eisenhower.* Lanham, MD: University Press of America, 1984.

9859. Underwood, James E. "Studying Individual Presidents: Truman, Eisenhower, Kennedy, and Carter." *Congress and the Presidency* 11 (Spring 1984): 93-104.

9860. Varney, Harold L. "Earl Warren: Ike's Worst Appointment." *American Mercury* 87 (August 1958): 5-13.

9861. Weaver, James D. "The Commander in Chief, Civilian Supremacy, Command and Control: Civil-Military Relations in the Eisenhower Presidency." Ph.D. dissertation, New York University, 1972.

9862. Welch, Robert H.W. *The Politician.* Belmont, MA: Belmont, 1964.

9863. White, William S. *The Responsibles: Truman, Taft, Eisenhower, JFK, Johnson.* New York: Harper and Row, 1972.

9864. Williams, Cleveland A. "Senate Confirmation: The Eisenhower Years." Ph.D. dissertation, Southern Illinois University, 1962.

9865. Wright, Robert. "Eisenhower's Fifties." *Antioch Review* 38 (Summer 1980): 277-290.

9866. Zand, Dale E. "Fred I. Greenstein: The Hidden-Hand Presidency: Eisenhower as Leader." *Journal of Applied Behavioral Science* 21 (1985): 237-246.

9867. Zornow, William F. *America at Mid-Century: The Truman Administration, The Eisenhower Administration.* Cleveland, OH: Allen Press, 1959.

Domestic Policy

9868. Anderson, John W. *Eisenhower, Brownell, and the Congress: The Tangled Origins of the Civil Rights Bill of 1956-1957.* University: University of Alabama Press, 1964.

9869. Bartley, N.V. "Looking Back at Little Rock." *Arkansas Historical Quarterly* 25 (Summer 1966): 101-116.

9870. Branyan, Robert L. "McCarthy and Eisenhower." *Continuum* 6 (Autumn 1968): 353-360.

9871. Brown, Stuart G. "Eisenhower and Stevenson in the McCarthy Era: A Study in Leadership." *Ethics* 69 (July 1955): 233-254.

9872. Burk, Robert F. *The Eisenhower Administration and Black Civil Rights.* Knoxville: University of Tennessee Press, 1984.

9873. Caute, David. *The Great Fear: The Anti-Communist Purge under Truman and Eisenhower.* New York: Simon and Schuster, 1978.

9874. Davis, Clint. "Ike the Conservationist." *American Forests* 75 (June 1969): 28-29, 42-44.

9875. Duram, James C. "'A Good Growl': The Eisenhower Cabinet's January 16, 1959 Discussion of Federal Aid to Education." *Presidential Studies Quarterly* 8 (Fall 1978): 434-444.

9876. Duram, James C. *A Moderate among Extremists: Dwight D. Eisenhower and the School Desegregation Crisis.* Chicago: Nelson-Hall, 1981.

9877. Green, Harold P. "The Oppenheimer Case: A Study in the Abuse of Law."

Bulletin of the Atomic Scientists 33 (September 1977): 12-16, 56-61.

9878. Hauge, Gabriel. "Economics of Eisenhower Dynamic Conservatism." *Commercial and Financial Chronicle* 182 (October 27, 1955): 1749, 1776-1777.

9879. Henry, Patrick. "And I Don't Care What It Is: The Tradition-History of a Civil Religion Proof-Text." *American Academy of Religion Journal* 49 (March 1981): 35-49.

9880. Holmans, A. E. "The Eisenhower Administration and the Recession, 1953-1955." *Oxford Economic Papers* 10 (February 1958): 34-54.

9881. Hyman, Sidney. "Science: The President's New Power." *Saturday Review* 40 (February 2, 1957): 40-44.

9882. Jeong, Dong-Kuen. "A Fiscal Policy Decision Model for the United States Economy: A Revealed Preference Inquiry into the Optimal Policy Solution during the First Year of the Eisenhower Administration." Ph.D. dissertation, Wayne State University, 1974.

9883. Kenski, Henry C. "The Impact of Unemployment on Presidential Popularity from Eisenhower to Nixon." *Presidential Studies Quarterly* 7 (Spring/Summer 1977): 114-126.

9884. Killian, James R., Jr. *Sputnik, Scientists, and Eisenhower: A Memoir of the First Special Assistant to the President for Science and Technology*. Cambridge, MA: MIT Press, 1977.

9885. Kistiakowsky, George B. *A Scientist at the White House: The Private Diary of President Eisenhower's Special Assistant for Science and Technology*. Cambridge, MA: Harvard University Press, 1976.

9886. Kovaleff, Theodore P. "The Antitrust Record of the Eisenhower Administration." *Antitrust Bulletin* 21 (Winter 1976): 586-610.

9887. Kovaleff, Theodore P. *Business and Government during the Eisenhower Administration: A Study of the Antitrust Policy of the Antitrust Division of the Justice Department*. Athens: Ohio University Press, 1980.

9888. Kovaleff, Theodore P. "Divorce American Style: The Dupont-General Motors Case." *Delaware History* 18 (Spring/Summer 1978): 28-42.

9889. Lambert, C. Roger. "Drought, Texas Cattlemen, and Eisenhower." *Journal of the West* 16 (January 1977): 66-70.

9890. McAuliffe, Mary S. "Dwight D. Eisenhower and Wolf Ladejinsky: The Politics of the Declining Red Scare, 1954-55." *Prologue* 14 (Fall 1982): 108-127.

9891. Martin, Don T. "The Public Statements of President Truman and Eisenhower on Federal Aid to Education." Ph.D. dissertation, Ohio State University, 1970.

9892. Mayer, Michael S. "Eisenhower's Conditional Crusade: The Eisenhower Administration and Civil Rights, 1953-1957." Ph.D. dissertation, Princeton University, 1984.

9893. Mitchell, James. "Government and Labor in the Eisenhower Administration." *Current History* 37 (September 1959): 129-132, 145.

9894. Mollan, Robert W. "Congressional Policy-Making during the Eisenhower Administration Regarding Internal Security: A Description and Evaluation." Ph.D. dissertation, University of Minnesota, 1967.

9895. Murphy, Charles J. V. "The Budget and Eisenhower." *Fortune* 56 (July 1957): 96-99, 228-230.

9896. Nieburg, H. L. "The Eisenhower AEC and Congress: A Study in Executive-Legislative Relations." *American Journal of Political Science* 6 (May 1962): 115-148.

9897. Peterson, Trudy H. "The Agricultural Trade Policy of the Eisenhower Administration." Ph.D. dissertation, University of Iowa, 1975.

9898. Rappaport, Percy. "The Bureau of the Budget: A View from the Inside." *Journal of Accountancy* 101 (March 1956): 31-37.

9899. Richardson, Elmo R. *Dams, Parks, and Politics: Resource Development and Preservation in the Truman-Eisenhower Era.* Lexington: University Press of Kentucky, 1973.

9900. Rochester, Stuart I. *Takeoff at Mid-Century: Federal Civil Aviation Policy in the Eisenhower Years, 1953-1961.* Washington, DC: Federal Aviation Administration, 1976.

9901. Rowe, Richard B. "The Eisenhower Administration and the Recession of 1957-58." Ph.D. dissertation, University of California, Santa Barbara, 1976.

9902. Saulnier, Raymond J. "The Eisenhower Economic Policies: Policies That Succeeded in Ending Inflation, 1956-61." *Presidential Studies Quarterly* 4 (Summer/Fall 1974): 28-34.

9903. Schapsmeier, Edward L., and Frederick H. Schapsmeier. "Eisenhower and Ezra Taft Benson: Farm Policy in the 1950s." *Agricultural History* 44 (October 1970): 369-378.

9904. Scher, Seymour. "Regulatory Agency Control through Appointment: The Case of the Eisenhower Administration and the NLRB." *Journal of Politics* 23 (November 1961): 667-688.

9905. Schlundt, Ronald A. "Civil Rights Policies in the Eisenhower Years." Ph.D. dissertation, Rice University, 1973.

9906. Strum, Harvey. "Eisenhower's Solar Energy Policy." *Public Historian* 6 (Spring 1984): 37-50.

9907. Sundquist, James L. *Politics and Policy: The Eisenhower, Kennedy, and Johnson Years.* Washington, DC: Brookings Institution, 1968.

9908. Tiffany, David M. "Agricultural Policy-Making in the Eisenhower Administration." Ph.D. dissertation, State University of New York, Binghamton, 1974.

9909. Van Dusen, George. "Politics of 'Partnership': The Eisenhower Administration and Conservation, 1952-60." Ph.D. dissertation, Loyola University, 1973.

9910. Von Furstenberg, George M., and James M. Boughton. "Stabilization Goals and the Appropriateness of Fiscal Policy during the Eisenhower and Kennedy-Johnson Administrations." *Public Finance Quarterly* 1 (January 1973): 5-28.

9911. Walsh, John. "The Eisenhower Era: Transition Years for Science." *Science* 164 (April 4, 1969): 50-53.

9912. Yarnell, Allen L. "Eisenhower and McCarthy: An Appraisal of Presidential Strategy." *Presidential Studies Quarterly* 10 (Winter 1980): 90-98.

9913. Zingale, Donald P. " 'Ike' Revisited on Sport and National Fitness." *Research Quarterly* 48 (March 1977): 12-18.

Elections

9914. Ackerman, Donald H., Jr. "The Write-in Vote for Dwight Eisenhower in the Spring, 1952, Minnesota Primary: Minnesota Politics in the Grass-Root Level." Ph.D. dissertation, Syracuse University, 1954.

9915. Barkin, Steve M. "Eisenhower's Television Planning Board: An Unwritten Chapter in the History of Political Broadcasting." *Journal of Broadcasting* 27 (Fall 1983): 319-331.

9916. Bauer, Otto F. "A Study of the Political Debate between Dwight D. Eisenhower and Adlai E. Stevenson in the Presidential Campaign of 1956." Ph.D. dissertation, Northwestern University, 1959.

9917. Bowman, Georgia B. "A Study of the Reporting by 27 Metropolitan Newspapers of Selected Speeches of Adlai Stevenson and Dwight Eisenhower in the 1952 Presidential Campaign." Ph.D. dissertation, University of Iowa, 1957.

9918. Childs, Marquis W. "Why Ike Said No." *Collier's* 122 (August 28, 1948): 14-15, 76-77.

9919. Clevenger, Theodore, Jr., and Eugene Knepprath. "A Quantitative Analysis of Logical and Emotional Content in Selected Campaign Addresses of Eisenhower and Stevenson." *Western Speech* 30 (Summer 1966): 144-150.

9920. Dailey, Joseph M. "The Eisenhower-Nixon Campaign Organization of 1952." Ph.D. dissertation, University of Illinois, 1975.

9921. Dishman, Robert B. "The Eisenhower Pre-Convention Campaign in New Hampshire, 1952." *New England Quarterly* 26 (March 1953): 3-26.

9922. Eulau, Heinz. *Class and Party in the Eisenhower Years: Class Roles and Perspectives in the 1952 and 1956 Elections.* Glencoe, IL: Free Press, 1962.

9923. Freeley, Austin J. "Ethos, Eisenhower, and the 1956 Campaign." *Central States Speech Journal* 9 (Spring 1958): 24-26.

9924. Grant, Philip A., Jr. "The 1952 Minnesota Republican Primary and the Eisenhower Candidacy." *Presidential Studies Quarterly* 9 (Summer 1979): 311-315.

9925. Griese, Noel L. "Rosser Reeves and the 1952 Eisenhower TV Spot Blitz." *Journal of Advertising* 4 (1975): 34-38.

9926. Hollitz, John E. "Eisenhower and the Admen: The Television 'Spot' Campaign of 1952." *Wisconsin Magazine of History* 66 (Autumn 1982): 25-39.

9927. Knepprath, Hubert E. "The Elements of Persuasion in the National Broadcast Speeches of Eisenhower and Stevenson during the 1956 Presidential Campaign." Ph.D. dissertation, University of Wisconsin, 1962.

9928. Lewis, Mort R. "Lincoln, Stevenson, and Yours Truly." *Manuscripts* 27 (Fall 1975): 280-284.

9929. McMillan, Edward L. "Texas and the Eisenhower Campaigns." Ph.D. dissertation, Texas Technological University, 1960.

9930. Ratcliffe, S. K. "General Eisenhower's Triumph." *Contemporary Review* 82 (December 1952): 321-326.

9931. Reid, Ronald F., and N. B. Beck. "The Campaign Speaking of Dwight D. Eisenhower." *Speaker* 35 (January 1953): 11-12, 17.

9932. Rucker, Bryce W. "A Study of Associated Press, International News Service, and United Press Reports of Attendance and Reactions of Crowds at Appearances of Eisenhower, Stevenson, Nixon, and Kefauver in the 1956 Presidential Campaign." Ph.D. dissertation, University of Missouri, 1959.

9933. Sillars, Malcolm O. "An Analysis of Intervention in the 1952 Presidential Campaign Addresses of Dwight D. Eisenhower and Adlai E. Stevenson." Ph.D. dissertation, University of Iowa, 1955.

9934. Tobin, Richard L. "An Eisenhower Aide Looks Back: Nominating a President." *Saturday Review* 3 (February 7, 1976): 25-27.

Foreign Affairs

9935. Ambrose, Stephen E., and Richard

H. Immerman. *Ike's Spies: Eisenhower and the Espionage Establishment*. Garden City, NY: Doubleday, 1981.

9936. Andrews, John D. "Eisenhower and Middle Eastern Foreign Policy: A Rhetoric of Consensus." Ph.D. dissertation, Northwestern University, 1978.

9937. Bacchus, Wilfred A. "The Relationship between Combat and Peace Negotiations: Fighting while Talking in Korea, 1951-1953." *Orbis* 17 (Summer 1973): 545-574.

9938. Baum, Keith W. "Treating the Allies Properly: The Eisenhower Administration, NATO, and the Multilateral Force." *Presidential Studies Quarterly* 13 (Winter 1983): 85-97.

9939. Bernstein, Barton J. "Foreign Policy in the Eisenhower Administration." *Foreign Service Journal* 50 (May 1973): 17-20.

9940. Biadasz, Frances E. "Defense Reorganization during the Eisenhower Administrations." Ph.D. dissertation, Georgetown University, 1961.

9941. Billings-Yun, Melanie S. "Decision against War: Eisenhower and Dien Bien Phu, 1954." Ph.D. dissertation, Harvard University, 1982.

9942. Browne, Bernard G. "The Foreign Policy of the Democratic Party during the Eisenhower Administration." Ph.D. dissertation, University of Notre Dame, 1968.

9943. Brune, Lester H. "The Eisenhower Administration and Defense Policy." *Armed Forces and Society* 6 (Spring 1980): 511-516.

9944. Capitanchik, David B. *The Eisenhower Presidency and American Foreign Policy*. London: Routledge and Kegan Paul, 1969.

9945. Converse, Philip E., and Georges Dupeux. "DeGaulle and Eisenhower: Public Image of the Victorious General." In *Elections and the Political Order,* edited by Angus Campbell and Philip E. Converse, et al., 292-345. New York: Wiley, 1966.

9946. Cooke, Alistair. "Eisenhower's Virtues." *Listener* 81 (April 3, 1969): 452-453.

9947. Cottrell, Alvin J. "The Eisenhower Era in Asia." *Current History* 57 (August 1969): 84-87, 117-118.

9948. DeConde, Alexander. "Dwight D. Eisenhower: Reluctant Use of Power." In *Powers of the President in Foreign Affairs,* edited by Edgar E. Robinson, 79-132. San Francisco: Commonwealth Club of America, 1966.

9949. DeNovo, John A. "The Eisenhower Doctrine." In *Encyclopedia of American Foreign Policy,* edited by Alexander DeConde, 292-301. New York: Scribner's, 1978.

9950. DiBacco, Thomas V. "American Business and Foreign Aid: The Eisenhower Years." *Business History Review* 41 (Spring 1967): 21-35.

9951. DiBacco, Thomas V. "Return to Dollar Diplomacy? American Business Reaction to the Eisenhower Foreign Aid Program, 1953-1961." Ph.D. dissertation, American University, 1965.

9952. Divine, Robert A. *Eisenhower and the Cold War*. New York: Oxford University Press, 1981.

9953. Divine, Robert A. "Eisenhower, Dulles, and the Nuclear Test Ban Issue — Memorandum of a White House Conference, 24 March 1958." *Diplomatic History* 2 (Summer 1978): 321-330.

9954. Domer, Thomas. "Sport in Cold War America, 1953-1963: The Diplomatic and Political Use of Sport in the Eisenhower and Kennedy Administrations."

Ph.D. dissertation, Marquette University, 1976.

9955. Ealy, Lawrence O. "Eisenhower and the Panamanian Questions." In his *Yanqui Politics and the Isthmian Canal*, 109-119. University Park: Pennsylvania State University Press, 1971.

9956. Eberly, Susan K. "The Eisenhower Doctrine: A Study of United States Middle-East Policy in the Years 1957-58." Master's thesis, American University, 1965.

9957. Genco, Stephen J. "The Eisenhower Doctrine: Deterrence in the Middle East, 1957-1958." In *Deterrence in American Foreign Policy: Theory and Practice*, edited by Alexander George and Richard Smoke, 309-362. New York: Columbia University Press, 1974.

9958. Graber, Doris A. "The Truman and Eisenhower Doctrines in the Light of the Doctrine of Non-Intervention." *Political Science Quarterly* 73 (September 1958): 321-334.

9959. Gray, Colin S. "The Defense Policies of the Eisenhower Administrations, 1953-1961." Ph.D. dissertation, Oxford University, 1970.

9960. Gray, Colin S. " 'Gap' Prediction and America's Defense: Arms Race Behavior in the Eisenhower Years." *Orbis* 16 (Spring 1972): 257-274.

9961. Haight, David. "The Papers of C. D. Jackson: A Glimpse at President Eisenhower's Psychological Warfare Expert." *Manuscripts* 28 (Winter 1976): 27-37.

9962. Herring, George C., and Richard H. Immerman. "Eisenhower, Dulles, and Dienbienphu: 'The Day We Didn't Go to War' Revisited." *Journal of American History* 71 (September 1984): 343-363.

9963. Howard, Harry N. "The Regional Pacts and the Eisenhower Doctrine." *Annals of the American Academy of Political and Social Science* 401 (May 1972): 85-94.

9964. Hoxie, R. Gordon. "Presidential Leadership and American Foreign Policy: Some Reflections on the Taiwan Issue, With Particular Considerations on Alexander Hamilton, Dwight Eisenhower, and Jimmy Carter." *Presidential Studies Quarterly* 9 (Spring 1979): 131-143.

9965. Huston, James A. "The Eisenhower Era." *Current History* 57 (July 1969): 24-30, 53.

9966. Immerman, Richard H. *The CIA in Guatemala: The Politics of Intervention.* Austin: University of Texas Press, 1982.

9967. Immerman, Richard H. "Eisenhower and Dulles: Who Made the Decisions?" *Political Psychology* 1 (Autumn 1979): 3-20.

9968. Kaufman, Burton I. *Trade and Aid: Eisenhower's Foreign Economic Policy.* Baltimore, MD: Johns Hopkins University Press, 1982.

9969. Kinnard, Douglas. *President Eisenhower and Strategy Management: A Study in Defense Politics.* Lexington: University Press of Kentucky, 1977.

9970. Kinnard, Douglas. "President Eisenhower and the Defense Budget." *Journal of Politics* 39 (August 1977): 596-623.

9971. Kinnard, Douglas. "Strategic Innovation and the Eisenhower Administration: A Study of the Interaction of Substance and Process in Defense Politics." Ph.D. dissertation, Princeton University, 1973.

9972. LaFeber, Walter F. "Arias, Remon, and Eisenhower." In his *The Panama Canal: The Crisis in Historical Perspective*, 90-131. New York: Oxford University Press, 1978.

9973. Lewis, Craig. "Eisenhower Takes Strong Stand to Defend Military Budget Policy." *Aviation Week and Space Technology* 72 (February 22, 1960): 33-34.

9974. Litfin, A. Duane. "Eisenhower on the Military-Industrial Complex: Critique of a Rhetorical Strategy." *Central States Speech Journal* 25 (Fall 1974): 198-209.

9975. McClelland, Charles A. "Decisional Opportunity and Political Controversy: The Quemoy Case." *Journal of Conflict Resolution* 6 (September 1962): 201-213.

9976. Mayers, David. "Eisenhower's Containment Policy and the Major Communist Powers, 1953-56." *International History Review* 5 (February 1983): 59-83.

9977. Mensonides, Louis J. "United States Foreign Policy: Germany 1945-1959, With Emphasis on the Eisenhower Administration." Ph.D. dissertation, University of Kentucky, 1964.

9978. Millis, Walter. "Military Problems of the New Administration." *Foreign Affairs* 31 (January 1953): 215-224.

9979. Moran, Charles R. "The Hemispheric Bank Issue in the Latin American Policy of the Eisenhower Administration." Ph.D. dissertation, University of Missouri, 1971.

9980. Morgenthau, Hans J. "What the President and Mr. Dulles Don't Know." *New Republic* 135 (December 17, 1956): 14-18.

9981. Murphy, Robert D. "The Soldier and the Diplomat." *Foreign Service Journal* 29 (May 1952): 17-19, 49-50.

9982. Nelson, Anna K. "The 'Top of Policy Hill': President Eisenhower and the National Security Council." *Diplomatic History* 7 (Fall 1983): 307-326.

9983. Noer, Thomas J. "Truman, Eisenhower, and South Africa: The 'Middle Road' and Apartheid." *Journal of Ethnic Studies* 11 (Spring 1983): 75-104.

9984. Plischke, Elmer. "The Eisenhower-Krushchev Visits: Diplomacy at the Summit." *Maryland Magazine* 30 (September/October 1959): 6-9.

9985. Plischke, Elmer. "Eisenhower's Correspondence Diplomacy with the Kremlin: Case Study in Summit Diplomatics." *Journal of Politics* 30 (February 1968): 137-159.

9986. Quester, George H. "Was Eisenhower a Genius?" *International Security* 4 (Fall 1979): 159-179.

9987. Reichard, Gary W. "Divisions and Dissent: Democrats and Foreign Policy, 1952-1956." *Political Science Quarterly* 93 (Spring 1978): 51-72.

9988. Rice, Andrew E. "Building a Constituency for the Foreign Aid Program: The Record of the Eisenhower Years." Ph.D. dissertation, Syracuse University, 1963.

9989. Rifai, Abdul H. "The Eisenhower Administration and the Defense of the Arab Middle East." Ph.D. dissertation, American University, 1966.

9990. Robinson, Edgar E., et al. *Powers of the President in Foreign Affairs, 1945-1965: Harry S Truman, Dwight D. Eisenhower, John F. Kennedy, Lyndon B. Johnson.* San Francisco: Commonwealth Club of California, 1966.

9991. Rostow, Walt W. *Eisenhower, Kennedy, and Foreign Aid.* Austin: University of Texas Press, 1984.

9992. Rostow, Walt W. *Open Skies: Eisenhower's Proposal of July 21, 1955.* Arlington: University of Texas Press, 1983.

9993. Rushkoff, Bennett C. "Eisenhower, Dulles, and the Quemoy-Matsu Crisis, 1954-1955." *Political Science Quarterly* 96 (Fall 1981): 465-480.

9994. Salami, George R. "The Eisenhower Doctrine: A Study in Alliance Politics." Ph.D. dissertation, Catholic University of America, 1974.

9995. Saunders, Richard M. "Military Force in the Foreign Policy of the Eisenhower Presidency." *Political Science Quarterly* 100 (May 1984): 138-143.

9996. Saunders, Richard M. "The 1954 Indochina Crisis." *Military Review* 58 (April 1978): 68-78.

9997. Scribner, Charles R. "The Eisenhower and Johnson Administrations' Decision-Making on Vietnamese Intervention: A Study of Contrasts." Ph.D. dissertation, University of California, Santa Barbara, 1980.

9998. Secrest, Donald E. "American Policy toward Neutralism during the Truman and Eisenhower Administrations." Ph.D. dissertation, University of Michigan, 1967.

9999. Sigler, Wayne. "The American Response to the Communist Challenge, 1945-1963." *Towson State Journal of International Affairs* 3 (1969): 143-158.

10000. Soapes, Thomas F. "A Cold Warrior Seeks Peace: Eisenhower's Strategy for Nuclear Disarmament." *Diplomatic History* 4 (Winter 1980): 57-71.

10001. Straight, Michael. "How Ike Reached the Russians at Geneva." *New Republic* 133 (August 1, 1955): 7-11.

10002. Takamatsu, Motoyuki. "Eisenhower-Dulles Confrontation in the First Taiwan Crisis, 1954-55." *Asian Quarterly* (Japan) 10 (April/June 1978): 1-32.

10003. Toner, James H. "Exceptional War, Exceptional Peace: The 1953 Cease-Fire in Korea." *Military Review* 56 (July 1976): 3-13.

10004. Wise, David, and Thomas B. Ross. *The U-2 Affair.* New York: Random House, 1962.

10005. Wolf, John B. "An Interpretation of the Eisenhower Doctrine: Lebanon 1958." Ph.D. dissertation, American University, 1968.

10006. Yizhar, Michael. "The Eisenhower Doctrine: A Case Study of American Foreign Policy Formulation and Implementation." Ph.D. dissertation, New School of Social Research, 1969.

10007. Yizhar, Michael. "The Formulation of the United States Middle East Resolution (1957)." *Wiener Library Bulletin* 26 (1972-1973): 2-7.

10008. Yizhar, Michael. "Israel and the Eisenhower Doctrine." *Wiener Library Bulletin* 28 (1975): 58-64.

10009. York, Herbert F. "Eisenhower's Other Warning." *Physics Today* 30 (January 1977): 9-11.

Writings

10010. Ambrose, Stephen E. "Interviewing Ike." *American History Illustrated* 5 (October 1970): 10-15.

10011. Cooke, Alistair. "Recollections of Churchill in Wartime — General Eisenhower Talks to Alistair Cooke." *Listener* 80 (July 18, 1968): 74-78.

10012. Eisenhower, Dwight D. *At Ease: Stories I Tell to Friends.* Garden City, NY: Doubleday, 1967.

10013. Eisenhower, Dwight D. *Crusade in Europe.* Garden City, NY: Doubleday, 1948.

10014. Eisenhower, Dwight D. *Eisenhower Speaks: Dwight D. Eisenhower in His Messages and Speeches.* Edited by Rudolph L. Treuenfels. New York: Farrar, Straus, 1948.

10015. Eisenhower, Dwight D. "Eisenhower vs. Congress: Letter with Memorandum Prepared by Attorney General Brownell." *U.S. News & World Report* 36 (May 28, 1954): 105-109.

10016. Eisenhower, Dwight D. *General Dwight D. Eisenhower: Remarks at Freedoms Foundation at Valley Forge, 1948-1969.* Edited by Edward Salt. Valley

Forge, PA: Freedoms Foundation, 1969.

10017. Eisenhower, Dwight D. *Ike's Letters to a Friend, 1941-1958.* Edited by Robert W. Griffith. Lawrence: University Press of Kansas, 1984.

10018. Eisenhower, Dwight D. *In Review: Pictures I've Kept: A Concise Pictorial Autobiography.* Garden City, NY: Doubleday, 1969.

10019. Eisenhower, Dwight D. *Letters to Mamie.* Garden City, NY: Doubleday, 1978.

10020. Eisenhower, Dwight D. *Mandate for Change: The White House Years, 1953-56.* Garden City, NY: Doubleday, 1963.

10021. Eisenhower, Dwight D. "Mr. Eisenhower's Review of His Presidency." *Current Notes on International Affairs* (Australia) 32 (1961): 40-51.

10022. Eisenhower, Dwight D. *The Papers of Dwight David Eisenhower: The War Years.* 9 vols. Edited by Alfred D. Chandler and Louis Galambos. Baltimore, MD: Johns Hopkins University Press, 1970-1984.

10023. Eisenhower, Dwight D. *Peace with Justice: Selected Addresses of Dwight D. Eisenhower.* New York: Columbia University Press, 1961.

10024. Eisenhower, Dwight D. *The Quotable Dwight D. Eisenhower.* Edited by Elsie Gallagher. Anderson, SC: Drake House, 1967.

10025. Eisenhower, Dwight D. *Selected Speeches of Dwight David Eisenhower, 34th President of the United States.* Washington, DC: U.S. Government Printing Office, 1970.

10026. Eisenhower, Dwight D. "Some Thoughts on the Presidency." *Reader's Digest* 93 (November 1968): 49-55.

10027. Eisenhower, Dwight D. *Waging Peace, 1956-1961: The White House Years.* Garden City, NY: Doubleday, 1965.

10028. Eisenhower, Dwight D. *What Eisenhower Thinks.* Edited by Allan Taylor. Rev. ed. New York: Crowell, 1953.

10029. Ferrell, Robert H., ed. *The Eisenhower Diaries.* New York: Norton, 1981.

10030. Hobbs, Joseph P. *Dear General: Eisenhower's Wartime Letters to Marshall.* Baltimore, MD: Johns Hopkins Press, 1971.

John F. Kennedy

Biographies

10031. Bilainkin, George. "Contemporary Profile — President Kennedy — 1940 and 1961." *Contemporary Review* 199 (November 1961): 113-119, 141.

10032. Blair, Joan, and Clay Blair, Jr. *The Search for J. F. K.* New York: Berkley, 1976.

10033. Bradlee, Benjamin C. *Conversations with Kennedy.* New York: Norton, 1975.

10034. Bradlee, Benjamin C. *That Special Grace.* New York: Lippincott, 1964.

10035. Burner, David. *The Torch Is Passed: The Kennedy Brothers and American Liberalism.* New York: Atheneum, 1984.

10036. Burns, James M. *John Kennedy: A Political Profile.* New York: Harcourt, Brace, 1960.

10037. Carr, William H. A. *JFK: A Complete Biography, 1917-1963.* New York: Lancer, 1964.

10038. Carr, William H. A. *JFK: An Informal Biography.* New York: Lancer, 1962.

10039. Cutler, John H. *Honey Fritz: Three Steps to the White House.* Indianapolis, IN: Bobbs-Merrill, 1962.

10040. Dickerson, Nancy, and Robert Drew. *Being with John F. Kennedy.* Los Angeles: Direct Cinema, 1983.

10041. Dollen, Charles. *John F. Kennedy, American.* Boston: St. Paul Editions, 1965.

10042. Fay, Paul B. *The Pleasure of His Company.* New York: Harper and Row, 1966.

10043. Flavius, Brother. *In Virtue's Cause: A Story of John F. Kennedy.* Notre Dame, IN: Dujarie Press, 1967.

10044. Gadney, Reg. *Kennedy.* New York: Holt, Rinehart and Winston, 1983.

10045. Hanff, Helene. *John F. Kennedy: Young Man of Destiny.* Garden City, NY: Doubleday, 1965.

10046. Kelly, Regina Z. *John F. Kennedy.* Chicago: Follett, 1969.

10047. Lasky, Victor. *JFK: The Man and the Myth.* New York: Macmillan, 1963.

10048. Lasky, Victor. *John F. Kennedy: What's behind the Image?* Washington, DC: Free World Press, 1960.

10049. Levine, Israel E. *Young Man in the White House: John Fitzgerald Kennedy.* New York: Messner, 1964.

10050. Lincoln, Evelyn. *My Twelve Years with John F. Kennedy.* New York: McKay, 1965.

10051. Longford, Frank P. *Kennedy.*

London: Weidenfeld and Nicholson, 1976.

10052. Lowe, Jacques. *Kennedy: A Time Remembered*. Topsfield, MA: Merrimack, 1983.

10053. Lowe, Jacques. *Portrait: The Emergence of John F. Kennedy*. New York: McGraw-Hill, 1961.

10054. Lyons, Louis M. "The Legend of John Kennedy." *Massachusetts Review* 5 (Winter 1964): 209-212.

10055. Manchester, William R. *One Brief Shining Moment: Remembering Kennedy*. Boston: Little, Brown, 1983.

10056. Manchester, William R. *Portrait of a President: John F. Kennedy in Profile*. Boston: Little, Brown, 1967.

10057. Markmann, Charles L., and Mark Sherwin. *John F. Kennedy: A Sense of Purpose*. New York: St. Martin's Press, 1961.

10058. Menendez, Albert J. *John F. Kennedy: Catholic and Humanist*. Buffalo, NY: Prometheus, 1979.

10059. Meyers, Joan S., ed. *John Fitzgerald Kennedy . . . As We Remember Him*. New York: Macmillan, 1965.

10060. Miller, Alice P., comp. *A Kennedy Chronology*. New York: Birthdate Research, 1968.

10061. O'Donnell, Kenneth P., and David F. Powers. *Johnny, We Hardly Knew Ye: Memories of John Fitzgerald Kennedy*. Boston: Little, Brown, 1972.

10062. Parmet, Herbert S. *Jack: The Struggles of John F. Kennedy*. New York: Dial, 1980.

10063. Parmet, Herbert S. *JFK: The Presidency of John F. Kennedy*. New York: Dial, 1983.

10064. Rosenberg, Hyman S. *Short Biography of President John F. Kennedy*. Newark, NJ: Alpco, 1963.

10065. Salinger, Pierre. *With Kennedy*. Garden City, NY: Doubleday, 1966.

10066. Sammis, Edward R. *John Fitzgerald Kennedy, Youngest President*. New York: Scholastic Book Services, 1961.

10067. Saunders, Frank, and James Southwood. *Torn Lace Curtains*. New York: Holt, Rinehart and Winston, 1982.

10068. Schneidman, J. Lee. *John F. Kennedy*. Boston: G. K. Hall, 1974.

10069. Schwab, Peter, and J. Lee Sheidman. *John F. Kennedy*. New York: Twayne, 1974.

10070. Shapp, Martha. *The Picture Life of John Fitzgerald Kennedy*. New York: Franklin Watt, 1966.

10071. Sorensen, Theodore C. *Kennedy*. New York: Harper and Row, 1965.

10072. Stewart, Charles J., and Bruce Kendall, eds. *A Man Named John F. Kennedy: Sermons on His Assassination*. Glen Rock, NJ: Paulist Press, 1964.

10073. Stuart, Friend. *Of Kennedys and Kings*. San Marcos, CA: Dominion, 1971.

10074. Webb, Robert. *The Living JFK*. New York: Grossett and Dunlap, 1964.

10075. Wicker, Tom. *Kennedy without Tears: The Man beneath the Myth*. New York: Morrow, 1964.

Private Life

10076. Associated Press. *Triumph and Tragedy: The Story of the Kennedys*. New York: Morrow, 1968.

10077. Barnes, Clare. *John F. Kennedy: Scrimshaw Collector*. Boston: Little, Brown, 1964.

10078. Bissell, Richard. "Carefree Harvard Days of Three Presidents." *McCall's* 90 (October 1962): 89-91.

10079. Bouvier, Jacqueline, and Lee Bouvier. *One Special Summer.* New York: Delacorte Press, 1974.

10080. Brant, Irving. *The Books of James Madison, With Some Comments on the Readings of FDR and JFK: An Address Delivered during the Celebration of the 25th Anniversary of the Tracy W. McGregor Library, 1929-1964.* Charlottesville: University of Virginia, 1965.

10081. Brennan, John F. *The Evolution of Everyman: Ancestral Lineage of John F. Kennedy.* Dundalk, Ireland: Dundalgan Press, 1968.

10082. Christopherson, Edmund. *'Westward I Go Free': The Story of J. F. K. in Montana.* Missoula, MT: Earthquake Press, 1964.

10083. Clinch, Nancy G. *The Kennedy Neurosis: A Psychological Portrait of an American Dynasty.* New York: Grossett and Dunlap, 1973.

10084. Collier, Peter, and David Horowitz. *The Kennedys: An American Drama.* New York: Summit Books, 1984.

10085. Dallas, Rita, and Jeanira Ratcliffe. *The Kennedy Case.* New York: Putnam, 1973.

10086. Damore, Leo. *The Cape Cod Years of John Fitzgerald Kennedy.* Englewood Cliffs, NJ: Prentice-Hall, 1967.

10087. Daniel, Lois, ed. *The World of the Kennedy Women.* Kansas City, MO: Hallmark, 1973.

10088. Davis, John H. *The Bouviers: Portrait of an American Family.* New York: Farrar, 1969.

10089. Davis, John H. *The Kennedys: Dynasty and Disaster, 1848-1984.* New York: McGraw-Hill, 1984.

10090. Dinneen, Joseph F. *The Kennedy Family.* Boston: Little, Brown, 1959.

10091. Dunleavy, Stephen, and Peter Brennan. *Those Wild, Wild Kennedy Boys!* New York: Pinnacle Books, 1976.

10092. Exner, Judith. *My Story.* New York: Grove Press, 1977.

10093. Frishauer, Willi. *Jacki.* London: Joseph, 1976.

10094. Gallagher, Mary B. *My Life with Jacqueline Kennedy.* Edited by Frances S. Leighton. New York: McKay, 1969.

10095. Hall, Gordon, and Ann Pinchot. *Jacqueline Kennedy: A Biography.* New York: Fell, 1964.

10096. Herndon, Booton. *The Humor of JFK.* Greenwich, CT: Fawcett, 1964.

10097. Hirsch, Phil, and Edward Hymoff, eds. *The Kennedy Courage.* New York: Pyramid, 1965.

10098. Kelley, Kitty. *Jackie Oh!* Secaucus, NJ: Lyle Stuart, 1978.

10099. Kennedy, Rose F. *Times to Remember.* Garden City, NY: Doubleday, 1974.

10100. Knebel, Fletcher. "What You Don't Know about Kennedy: The Human Side of Our Next President." *Look* 25 (January 17, 1961): 80-82, 84, 86.

10101. Koskoff, David E. *Joseph P. Kennedy: A Life and Times.* Englewood Cliffs, NJ: Prentice-Hall, 1974.

10102. Larrabee, Harold A. "New England Family: The Kennedys." *New England Quarterly* 42 (September 1969): 436-445.

10103. Look. *JFK Memorial Book: New Color Pictures of His Family, A Color Visit to His Ireland, Pages from a Family Album, The Unknown JFK.* New York: Look, 1964.

10104. McCarthy, Joseph W. *The Remarkable Kennedys.* New York: Dial, 1960.

10105. McEvoy, Kevin, comp. *Two Ken-*

nedys. Glen Rock, NJ: Paulist Press, 1969.

10106. McTaggart, Lynne. *Kathleen Kennedy, Her Life and Times.* New York: Dial, 1983.

10107. Marvin, Richard. *The Kennedy Curse.* New York: Belmont, 1969.

10108. Plimpton, George. "Newport Notes: The Kennedys and Other Salts." *Harper's Magazine* 226 (March 1968): 39-74.

10109. Reston, James. *Sketches in the Sand.* New York: Knopf, 1967.

10110. Rhea, Mini. *I Was Jacqueline Kennedy's Dressmaker.* New York: Fleet, 1962.

10111. Roddy, Joseph. "Irish Origins of a President." *Look* 25 (March 14, 1961): 17-25.

10112. Salisbury, Harrison. *The Kennedys: A New York Times Profile.* New York: Arno, 1980.

10113. Schlesinger, Arthur M., Jr. *Robert Kennedy and His Times.* Boston: Houghton Mifflin, 1978.

10114. Sciacca, Tony. *Kennedy and His Women.* New York: Manor Books, 1976.

10115. Shaw, Mark. *The John F. Kennedys: A Family Album.* New York: Farrar, 1964.

10116. Shepard, Tazewell T. *John F. Kennedy: Man of the Sea.* New York: Morrow, 1965.

10117. Shulman, Irving. *"Jackie": The Exploitation of a First Lady.* New York: Trident, 1970.

10118. Sidey, Hugh. "The President's Voracious Reading Habits." *Life* 50 (March 17, 1961): 55-56, 59-60.

10119. Stafford, Jean. *A Mother in History.* New York: Bantam Books, 1966.

10120. Steiner, Paul. *175 Little-Known Facts about JFK.* New York: Citadel Press, 1964.

10121. Thayer, Mary V. *Jacqueline Bouvier Kennedy.* Garden City, NY: Doubleday, 1961.

10122. Van Gelder, Lawrence. *The Untold Story: Why the Kennedys Lost the Book Battle.* New York: Award Books, 1967.

10123. Vidal, Gore. "The Holy Family." *Esquire* 67 (April 1967): 99-102.

10124. Walker, Gerald, and Donald A. Allen. "Jack Kennedy at Harvard." *Coronet* 50 (May 1961): 82-95.

10125. Wayne, Stephen J., Cheryl Beil, and Jay Falk. "Public Perceptions about Ted Kennedy and the Presidency." *Presidential Studies Quarterly* 12 (Winter 1982): 84-90.

10126. Whalen, Richard J. *The Founding Father: The Story of Joseph P. Kennedy and the Family He Raised to Power.* New York: New American Library, 1964.

10127. Wofford, Harris. *Of Kennedys and Kings.* New York: Farrar, Straus and Giroux, 1980.

10128. Wolff, Perry S. *A Tour of the White House with Mrs. John F. Kennedy.* Garden City, NY: Doubleday, 1962.

10129. Wolin, Howard E. "Grandiosity and Violence in the Kennedy Family." *Psychohistory Review* 8 (Winter 1979): 27-37.

Public Career

10130. Adams, David K. "Roosevelt and Kennedy." *British Association for American Studies Bulletin* 1 (December 1960): 29-39.

10131. Alsop, Stewart. "The Battle of

Wisconsin: Kennedy vs. Humphrey." *Saturday Evening Post* 232 (April 2, 1960): 19-21, 93-94.

10132. Alsop, Stewart. "Kennedy's Magic Formula." *Saturday Evening Post* 233 (August 13, 1960): 26-27, 58-60.

10133. Altschuler, Bruce E. "Kennedy Decides to Run: 1968." *Presidential Studies Quarterly* 10 (Summer 1980): 348-352.

10134. Bowles, Chester. "The Foreign Policy of Senator Kennedy." *America* 104 (October 15, 1960): 69-73.

10135. Burns, James M. "Kennedy's Liberalism." *Progressive Magazine* 24 (October 1970): 18-21.

10136. Cater, Douglass. "The Cool Eye of John F. Kennedy." *Reporter* 21 (December 10, 1959): 27-32.

10137. Cater, Douglass. "A Tide in the Affairs of John F. Kennedy." *Reporter* 23 (August 4, 1960): 16-18.

10138. Chamberlain, John. "The Chameleon Image of John F. Kennedy." *National Review* 8 (April 23, 1960): 261-263.

10139. Coffin, Tristram. "John Kennedy: Young Man in a Hurry." *Progressive Magazine* 23 (December 1959): 10-18.

10140. Donovan, Robert J. *PT 109: John F. Kennedy in World War II.* New York: McGraw-Hill, 1961.

10141. Gray, Charles H. "A Scale Analysis of the Voting Records of Senators Kennedy, Johnson, and Goldwater, 1957-1960." *American Political Science Review* 59 (September 1965): 615.

10142. Healy, Paul F. "The Senate's Gay Young Bachelor." *Saturday Evening Post* 225 (June 13, 1953): 26-27, 123-124, 126-127, 129.

10143. Hersey, John. "Survival: Lieut. J. F. Kennedy, A PT Skipper in the Solomons." *New Yorker* 20 (June 17, 1944): 31-34, 37-38, 40, 42-43.

10144. "A Kennedy Runs for Congress: The Boston-Bred Scion of a Former Ambassador Is a Fighting-Irish Conservative." *Look* 10 (June 11, 1946): 32, 34-36.

10145. "Kennedy's Biography, Voting Record, Stands on Issues." *Congressional Quarterly Weekly Report* 18 (May 13, 1960): 843-852.

10146. "Kennedy's Biography, Voting Record, Stands on Issues." *Congressional Quarterly Weekly Report* 18 (July 22, 1960): 1275-1282.

10147. Land, Guy. "John F. Kennedy's Southern Strategy, 1956-1960." *North Carolina Historical Review* 56 (January 1979): 41-63.

10148. Louchheim, Katie. *By the Political Sea.* Garden City, NY: Doubleday, 1970.

10149. Mallan, John P. "Massachusetts, Liberal and Corrupt." *New Republic* 127 (October 13, 1952): 10-12.

10150. Nurse, Ronald J. "America Must Not Sleep: The Development of John F. Kennedy's Foreign Policy Attitudes, 1947-1960." Ph.D. dissertation, Michigan State University, 1971.

10151. Sanghvi, Ramesh. *John F. Kennedy: A Political Biography.* Bombay: Perennial Press, 1961.

10152. Sheerin, John B. "Senator Kennedy Vetoes Aid to Catholic Education." *Catholic World* 189 (April 1959): 4-7.

10153. Tregaskis, Richard W. *John F. Kennedy and PT-109.* New York: Random House, 1962.

10154. Tregaskis, Richard W. *John F. Kennedy: War Hero.* New York: Dell, 1962.

10155. Turner, Russell. "Senator Kennedy, The Perfect Politician." *American Mercury* 84 (March 1957): 33-40.

10156. "We Agree, Mr. Kennedy." *Life* 33 (August 25, 1952): 22.

10157. Whipple, Chandler. *Lt. John F. Kennedy — Expendable!* New York: Universal, 1962.

10158. Wyden, Peter, and Samuel Shaffer. "This Is John Fitzgerald Kennedy." *Newsweek* 51 (June 23, 1958): 29-30, 33-34.

Presidential Years

General

10159. Adler, William, ed. *Kids' Letters to President Kennedy.* New York: Morrow, 1962.

10160. Agronsky, Martin, et al. *Let Us Begin: The First 100 Days of the Kennedy Administration.* New York: Simon and Schuster, 1961.

10161. Allees, Arnold E. *Tulips, Tears, Traumas, and Turmoil in the Kennedy Era.* New York: Theo Gaus' Sons, 1969.

10162. Alsop, Stewart. "How's Kennedy Doing?" *Saturday Evening Post* 234 (September 16, 1961): 44-45, 101, 103-104, 106.

10163. Alsop, Stewart. "Kennedy's Grand Strategy." *Saturday Evening Post* 235 (March 31, 1962): 11-17.

10164. Bagdikian, Ben H. "JFK to LBJ: Paradoxes of Change." *Columbia Journalism Review* 2 (Winter 1964): 32-36.

10165. Bailey, Thomas A. "Johnson and Kennedy: The Two Thousand Days." *New York Times Magazine* 116 (November 6, 1966): 30-31, 134-135, 137, 139-140; (November 27, 1966): 159-160; (December 4, 1966): 22.

10166. Balfour, Nancy. "A Difficult Start for President Kennedy." *World Today* 17 (October 1961): 419-424.

10167. Balfour, Nancy. "President Kennedy Takes Over." *World Today* 17 (March 1961): 102-110.

10168. Ballot, Paul, ed. *The Thousand Days: John Fitzgerald Kennedy as President.* New York: Citadel Press, 1964.

10169. Barcella, Ernest L. "New Man in the White House." *Today's Health* 39 (February 1961): 22-27, 73-78.

10170. Barlow, Jeffrey G. "President John F. Kennedy and His Joint Chiefs of Staff." Ph.D. dissertation, University of South Carolina, 1981.

10171. Berendt, J. "Ten Years Later: A Look at the Record: What the School Books Are Teaching Our Kids about JFK." *Esquire* 80 (November 1973): 140-143.

10172. Berthold, Carol A. "The Image and Character of President John F. Kennedy: A Rhetorical-Critical Approach." Ph.D. dissertation, Northwestern University, 1975.

10173. Bishop, James A. *A Day in the Life of President Kennedy.* New York: Bantam Books, 1964.

10174. Bloncourt, Pauline. *An Old and a Young Leader: Winston Churchill and John Kennedy.* London: Faber, 1970.

10175. Brinkley, Alan. "Kennedy in Retrospect." *New England Social Studies Bulletin* 41 (Winter 1983-1984): 7-15.

10176. Brogan, Denis W. "The Catholic Politician." *Atlantic Monthly* 210 (August 1962): 83-89.

10177. Bundy, McGeorge. "The History-Maker." *Massachusetts Historical Society Proceedings* 90 (1978): 75-88.

10178. Burns, James M. "The Four Kennedys of the First Year." *New York Times Magazine* 111 (January 14, 1962): 9, 70, 72.

10179. Burns, James M. "Kennedy's

First Year." *Nation* 194 (January 6, 1962): 14-15.

10180. Burns, James M. "A New Size-up of the President: Interview." *U.S. News & World Report* 51 (December 4, 1961): 44-46, 49.

10181. Cahn, Robert. "Dear Mr. President." *Saturday Evening Post* 234 (July 29, 1961): 26-27, 47-48.

10182. Carleton, William G. "The Cult of Personality Comes to the White House." *Harper's Magazine* 223 (December 1961): 63-68.

10183. Carleton, William G. "Kennedy in History: An Early Appraisal." *Antioch Review* 24 (Fall 1964): 277-299.

10184. Carter, Richard. "What Women Really Think of the Kennedys." *Good Housekeeping* 156 (June 1963): 73-75, 176, 178-179, 182.

10185. Cater, Douglass. "The Kennedy Look in the Arts." *Horizon* 4 (September 1961): 4-17.

10186. Childs, Marquis W. "Bobby and the President." *Good Housekeeping* 154 (May 1962): 80-81, 162, 164, 167, 169.

10187. Cipes, Robert M. "The Wiretap War: Kennedy, Johnson, and the FBI." *New Republic* 155 (December 24, 1966): 16-22.

10188. Cleveland, Harlan. *Great Power and Great Diversity: The Perceptions and Policies of President Kennedy*. Washington, DC: U.S. Department of State, 1964.

10189. Cochran, Charles L. "The Recognition of States and Governments by President John F. Kennedy: An Analysis." Ph.D. dissertation, Tufts University, 1969.

10190. Collins, Frederic W. "The Mind of John F. Kennedy." *New Republic* 144 (May 8, 1961): 15-20.

10191. Comstock, Jim. *Pa and Ma and Mister Kennedy*. Richwood, WV: Appalachian Press, 1965.

10192. Congressional Quarterly. *President Kennedy's Program*. Washington, DC: Congressional Quarterly, 1961.

10193. Cooke, Alistair. "Too Many Kennedys? The Public Face of JFK." *Show* 3 (April 1963): 69-73.

10194. Cousins, Norman. "The Legacy of John F. Kennedy." *Saturday Review* 46 (December 7, 1963): 21-27.

10195. Craig, G. M. "Eisenhower and Kennedy." *International Journal* 21 (Winter 1965-1966): 110-114.

10196. Craig, G. M. "Kennedy's First Year." *International Journal* 17 (Winter 1961-1962): 7-16.

10197. Crane, Philip M. *The Democrat's Dilemma*. New York: Regnery, 1964.

10198. Crown, James T. "President Kennedy — As the World Knew Him." *Coronet* 29 (January 1964): 18-25.

10199. Crown, James T., and George P. Penty. *Kennedy in Power*. New York: Ballantine Books, 1961.

10200. Davidson, Bill. *President Kennedy Selects Six Brave Presidents*. New York: Harper and Row, 1962.

10201. Decter, Midge. "Kennedyism." *Commentary* 49 (January 1970): 19-27.

10202. Degler, Carl N. "Johnson and Kennedy: The Public View." *Reviews in American History* 5 (March 1977): 130-136.

10203. "The Democratic President-Elect John Fitzgerald Kennedy." *Newsweek* 56 (November 14, 1960): 1-15.

10204. Diamond, Sigmund. "On the Road to Camelot." *Labor History* 21 (Spring 1980): 279-290.

10205. Donald, Aida D., ed. *John F. Kennedy and the New Frontier. New York: Hill and Wang, 1966.

10206. Druks, Herbert, ed. *From Truman through Johnson: A Documentary History.* Vol. 2, *Kennedy and Johnson.* New York: Robert Speller, 1971.

10207. Eagle, Hazel. "After a Roman Kind." *Spectator* 209 (October 5, 1961): 478-479.

10208. Ecroyd, Donald H. "Recording the President." *Quarterly Journal of Speech* 48 (October 1962): 336-340.

10209. Ekirch, Arthur A. "Eisenhower and Kennedy: The Rhetoric and the Reality." *Midwest Quarterly* 17 (Spring 1976): 279-290.

10210. Erskine, Hazel G. "The Polls: Kennedy as President." *Public Opinion Quarterly* 28 (Summer 1964): 334-342.

10211. Evans, M. Stanton, Allan H. Ryskind, and William Schultz. *The Fringe on Top: Political Wildlife along the New Frontier.* New York: American Features, 1963.

10212. Evening Star, Washington, DC. *The New Frontiersmen: Profiles of the Men around Kennedy.* Washington, DC: Public Affairs Press, 1961.

10213. Fagan, Myron C. *The Kennedy Boys and Our Invisible Government.* Hollywood, CA: Cinema Educational Guild, 1962.

10214. Fagan, Myron C. *Why Kennedy Must Be Impeached!* Hollywood, CA: Cinema Educational Guild, 1962.

10215. Fairlie, Henry. *The Kennedy Promise: Politics of Expectation.* Garden City, NY: Doubleday, 1973.

10216. Faith, Samuel J. *See Jack Run.* Newark, NJ: Deanebra, 1963.

10217. Fanta, J. Julius. *Sailing with President Kennedy: The White House Yachtsman.* New York: Sea Lore, 1968.

10218. Fedler, Fred, Ron Smith, and Mike Meeske. "*Time* and *Newsweek* Favor John F. Kennedy, Criticize Robert and Edward Kennedy." *Journalism Quarterly* 60 (Autumn 1983): 489-496.

10219. Felkins, Patricia K. "Perceptions of J. F. K.: Image and Myth." Ph.D. dissertation, University of Missouri, 1975.

10220. Fischer, John. "The Kennedy Era, Stage Two: A Forecast." *Harper's Magazine* 224 (February 1962): 14, 16, 21-22, 24.

10221. Fitzgerald, Gordon. *A Catholic Rebels.* Dallas, TX: Teacher Publishing Co., 1962.

10222. Fitzsimons, Louise. *The Kennedy Doctrine.* New York: Random House, 1972.

10223. Fixler, Philip E., Jr. "A Content Analysis of American Presidential Rhetoric: An Exploratory Study of Misrepresentative and Deceptive Language in the Major Communications of Presidents Kennedy, Johnson, and Nixon." Ph.D. dissertation, University of Southern California, Los Angeles, 1979.

10224. Flannelly, Margaret E. "An Analysis of the Role of the White House Staff in the Administrations of President Dwight D. Eisenhower and President John F. Kennedy." Ph.D. dissertation, University of Notre Dame, 1969.

10225. Freidel, Frank B. "Thirty-sixth President, 1963." *National Geographic Magazine* 129 (January 1966): 110-119.

10226. Freidin, Seymour, and George Bailey. *The Experts.* New York: Macmillan, 1968.

10227. Fritchey, Clayton. "White House Style-Makers: L. B. Johnson vs. J. F. Kennedy." *Harper's Magazine* 232 (April 1966): 47-49.

10228. Frolick, S. J. *Once There Was a President.* New York: Black Star, 1980.

10229. Fuchs, Lawrence H. *John F. Kennedy and American Catholicism.* New York: Meredith, 1967.

10230. Garrison, Jim. *A Heritage of Stone.* New York: Putnam, 1970.

10231. Gass, Oscar. "The New Frontier Fulfilled." *Commentary* 32 (December 1961): 461-473.

10232. Gass, Oscar. "Political Economy and the New Administration." *Commentary* 31 (September 1961): 277-287.

10233. Golden, James L. "John F. Kennedy and the 'Ghosts.'" *Quarterly Journal of Speech* 52 (December 1966): 348-357.

10234. Goldman, Sheldon. "Characteristics of Eisenhower and Kennedy: Appointees to the Lower Federal Courts." *Western Political Quarterly* 18 (December 1965): 755-762.

10235. Green, Joseph, Jr. "The Public Image of President Kennedy." *Catholic World* 193 (May 1961): 106-112.

10236. Gromyko, Anatolii A. *Through Russian Eyes: President Kennedy's 1036 Days.* Washington, DC: International Library, 1973.

10237. Grossman, Richard L., ed. *Let Us Begin: The First 100 Days of the Kennedy Administration.* New York: Simon and Schuster, 1961.

10238. Hahn, Dan F. "Ask Not What a Youngster Can Do for You: Kennedy's Inaugural Address." *Presidential Studies Quarterly* 12 (Fall 1982): 610-614.

10239. Halberstam, David. *The Best and the Brightest.* New York: Random House, 1972.

10240. Hamilton, Charles. *The Robot That Helped to Make a President: A Reconnaissance into the Mysteries of John F. Kennedy's Signature.* New York: The Author, 1965.

10241. Hansen, Erik A. "President John F. Kennedy's Declaration of Independence: A Study in the Presidential Rhetoric." *American Studies in Scandinavia* 13 (1981): 111-127.

10242. Hanson, Galen A. *A Summons for All Seasons: An Interpretive Study of President John F. Kennedy's Commencement Address at American University, June 10, 1963.* Detroit, MI: Harlo Press, 1966.

10243. Harris, Louis. *The Anguish of Change.* New York: Norton, 1973.

10244. Harris, Seymour E. *The Economics of the Political Parties: With Special Attention to Presidents Eisenhower and Kennedy.* New York: Macmillan, 1962.

10245. Hart, John. "Staffing the Presidency: Kennedy and the Office of Congressional Relations." *Presidential Studies Quarterly* 13 (Winter 1983): 101-110.

10246. Hartke, Vance, and John M. Redding. *Inside the New Frontier.* New York: McFadden, 1962.

10247. Healy, Paul F. "There Goes the President! An Inside View of His Intricate Planning Which Assures Mr. Kennedy's Safety on His Whirlwind Trips." *Saturday Evening Post* 235 (January 20, 1962): 80-83.

10248. Heath, Jim F. *Decade of Disillusionment: The Kennedy-Johnson Years.* Bloomington: Indiana University Press, 1975.

10249. Helde, Thomas T. "The Kennedy-Johnson Years." *Current History* 57 (July 1969): 31-35.

10250. Heller, Deane, and David Heller. *The Kennedy Cabinet: America's Men of Destiny.* Derby, CT: Monarch Press, 1961.

10251. Herter, Christian A. "U.S. Aims in the Kennedy Round." *Atlantic Community Quarterly* 2 (Summer 1964): 240-246.

10252. Hirsch, Phil, ed. *The Kennedy War Heroes.* New York: Pyramid, 1960.

10253. Hoyt, Robert G. "Opinion Worth Noting." *America* 104 (November 5, 1960): 171-175.

10254. Huberman, Leo, and Paul M. Sweezey. "The Kennedy-Johnson Boom." In *America in the '60s: Cultural Authorities in Transition*, edited by Ronald Lora, 131-143. New York: Wiley, 1974.

10255. Hudson, H. P. "PR in the Kennedy White House." *Public Relations Quarterly* 28 (Witner 1983): 5-8.

10256. Hyman, Sidney. "Inside the Kennedy 'Kitchen Cabinet.'" *New York Times Magazine* 5 (March 1961): 27, 86, 88-89.

10257. Hyman, Sidney. "The Testing of Kennedy." *New Republic* 45 (October 2, 1961): 11-14.

10258. "Impressions of the New President." *Blackwood's Magazine* 289 (June 1961): 481-488.

10259. Ions, Edmund S. *The Politics of John F. Kennedy*. New York: Barnes and Noble, 1967.

10260. Janeway, Michael. "LBJ and the Kennedys." *Atlantic Monthly* 229 (February 1972): 48-58.

10261. Jeffries, John W. "The 'Quest for National Purpose' of 1960." *American Quarterly* 30 (Fall 1978): 451-470.

10262. Jenkins, John H. *Neither the Fanatics nor the Faint-Hearted: The Tour Leading to the President's Death and Two Speeches He Could Not Give*. Austin, TX: Pemberton Press, 1963.

10263. Kaleb, George. "Kennedy as Statesman." *Commentary* 44 (June 1966): 54-60.

10264. Kazin, Alfred. "The President and Other Intellectuals." *American Scholar* 30 (Fall 1961): 498-516.

10265. Keefe, Robert. "On Cowboys and Collectives: The Kennedy-Nixon Generation." *Massachusetts Review* 21 (Fall 1980): 551-560.

10266. Kemper, Deane A. "'Your Generous Invitation': Events Preceding the Appearance of John F. Kennedy before the Greater Houston Ministerial Association." *Houston Review* 3 (Fall 1981): 288-307.

10267. "Kennedy's First Eighteen Months, The Record: With Chart." *U.S. News & World Report* 53 (July 23, 1962): 39-43.

10268. "Kennedy's View of Presidency: A Leader Must Lead." *Business Week* (March 17, 1962): 25-27.

10269. Kerwin, Jerome G. *Politics, Government, Catholics*. New York: Paulist Press, 1961.

10270. Kluckhohn, Frank L. *America Listen! The Kennedy Administration and the Washington Scene — A Revealing Report on Power, Politics, and Current Chaos in Our Federal Government*. Derby, CT: Monarch Press, 1962.

10271. Knebel, Fletcher. "Kennedy and His Pals." *Look* 25 (April 25, 1961): 117-118, 120, 123-125.

10272. Knebel, Fletcher. "Kennedy's Decisions: How He Reaches Them." *Look* 25 (June 20, 1961): 27-29.

10273. Koch, Thilo. *Fighters for a New World*. New York: Putnam, 1969.

10274. Kondracke, Morton. "Kennedy the President." *New Republic* 179 (September 23, 1978): 12-14.

10275. Kraft, Joseph. "The Kennedy Era, State Two." *Harper's Magazine* 224 (February 1962): 29-36.

10276. Kraft, Joseph. "Kennedy's Working Staff." *Harper's Magazine* 225 (December 1962): 29-36.

10277. Kraft, Joseph. "Washington Insight, Kennedy and the Intellectuals."

Harper's Magazine 227 (November 1963): 112, 114-117.

10278. Krock, Arthur. "Impression of Johnson, the Kennedys, and Today's Government." *U.S. News & World Report* 61 (December 19, 1966): 44-49.

10279. LaFeber, Walter F. "Kennedy, Johnson, and the Revisionists." *Foreign Service Journal* 50 (May 1973): 31-33, 39.

10280. Lane, Thomas A. *The Leadership of President Kennedy.* Caldwell, ID: Caxton, 1964.

10281. Latham, Earl. *John F. Kennedy and Presidential Power.* Lexington, MA: Heath, 1972.

10282. Lecht, Leonard A. *Goals, Priorities, and Dollars, The Next Decade.* New York: Free Press, 1966.

10283. Lemke, William E. "The Political Thought of John F. Kennedy: To the Inaugural Address." Ph.D. dissertation, University of Maine, 1973.

10284. Lenrow, Adele L. "A Toulmin Analysis of the Argumentation Patterns in Selected Speeches of Joseph Kennedy, John Kennedy, Robert Kennedy, and Edward Kennedy." Ed.D. dissertation, Columbia University, 1971.

10285. Lerner, Daniel. "Europe's Image of Kennedy: Europeans Imbue the New U.S. President with Their Own Hopes, Desires, and Aspirations." *New Leader* 43 (December 5, 1960): 3-6.

10286. Lessard, Suzannah. "A New Look at John Kennedy." *Washington Monthly* 3 (October 1971): 8-18.

10287. Leuchtenburg, William E. "John F. Kennedy, Twenty Years Later." *American Heritage* 35 (December 1983): 50-59.

10288. Leuchtenburg, William E. "The Legacy of FDR." *Wilson Quarterly* 6 (Spring 1982): 77-93.

10289. Leuchtenburg, William E. "President Kennedy and the End of the Postwar World." *American Review* 4 (Winter 1963): 18-29.

10290. Lewis, Ted. "Kennedy: Profile of a Technician: With Editorial Comment, 'What's He Up To?' " *Nation* 196 (February 2, 1963): 81-82, 92-94.

10291. Lincoln, Anne H. *The Kennedy White House Parties.* New York: Viking Press, 1967.

10292. Lincoln, Evelyn. *Kennedy and Johnson.* New York: Holt, Rinehart and Winston, 1968.

10293. Lippmann, Walter. "Kennedy at Mid-Term." *Newsweek* 61 (January 21, 1963): 24-26, 29.

10294. Logan, Andy. "JFK: The Stained Glass Image." *American Heritage* 18 (August 1967): 4-7.

10295. Lord, Donald C. *John F. Kennedy: The Politics of Confrontation and Conciliation.* Woodbury, NY: Barron's, 1975.

10296. McGarvey, Patrick J. *CIA: The Myth and the Madness.* New York: Saturday Review Press, 1972.

10297. MacMillan, Harold. *At the End of the Day: 1961-63.* London: Macmillan, 1973.

10298. McQuain, Thomas J., Jr. *An Analysis of the Inaugural Address of John F. Kennedy.* Parson, WV: McClain, 1977.

10299. Maddox, Robert J. "Kennedy as President: A 10-Year Perspective." *American History Illustrated* 8 (November 1973: 4-8, 46-60.

10300. Martin, Ralph G. *A Hero for Our Times: An Intimate Story of the Kennedy Years.* New York: Macmillan, 1983.

10301. Massey, Robert J. "The First Hundred Days of the New Frontier." *U.S. Naval Institute Proceedings* 87 (August 1961): 27-33.

10302. Matusow, Allen J. "John F. Kennedy and the Intellectuals." *Wilson Quarterly* 7 (Autumn 1983): 140-153.

10303. Mayhew, Aubrey. *The World's Tribute to JFK in Medallic Art.* New York: Morrow, 1966.

10304. "The Meaning of the Life and Death of John F. Kennedy." *Current* 45 (January 1964): 6-42.

10305. *A Memory of John F. Kennedy.* Dublin: Wood Printing Works, n.d.

10306. Merrill, John. "How *Time* Stereotyped Three U.S. Presidents." *Journalism Quarterly* 42 (Autumn 1965): 563-570.

10307. Meyer, Karl E. "The Men around Kennedy." *Progressive Magazine* 24 (September 1960): 18-20.

10308. Meyer, Karl E. *The New America: Politics and Society in the Age of the Smooth Deal.* New York: Basic Books, 1961.

10309. Miroff, Bruce. *Pragmatic Illusions: The Presidential Politics of John F. Kennedy.* New York: McKay, 1976.

10310. "Mr. Kennedy Takes the Stage." *Round Table* 51 (March 1961): 154-159.

10311. Moley, Raymond. "FDR-JFK: A Brain Truster Compares Two Presidents, Two Programs." *Newsweek* 57 (April 17, 1961): 32-34, 37.

10312. Mongar, Thomas M. "Personality and Decision-Making: John F. Kennedy in Four Crisis Decisions." *Canadian Journal of Political Science* 2 (July 1969): 200-225.

10313. Morgenthau, Hans J. "The Trouble with Kennedy." *Commentary* 33 (January 1962): 51-55.

10314. Morrow, Robert. *Betrayal.* Chicago: Regnery, 1976.

10315. Murphy, Charles J. V. "Now the President Will Decide on His Own." *Life* 52 (February 16, 1962): 70-72, 74, 76, 79-81.

10316. National Broadcasting System. *Memo to JFK from N. B. C. News.* New York: Putnam, 1961.

10317. Navasky, Victor S. *Kennedy Justice.* New York: Atheneum, 1971.

10318. Neustadt, Richard E. "Approaches to Staffing the Presidency: Notes on FDR and JFK." *American Political Science Review* 57 (December 1963): 855-863.

10319. Neustadt, Richard E. "Kennedy in the Presidency: A Premature Appraisal." *Political Science Quarterly* 79 (September 1964): 321-334.

10320. Nevins, Allan, ed. *The Burden and the Glory: The Hopes and Purposes of President Kennedy's Second and Third Years in Office as Revealed in His Public Statements and Addresses.* New York: Harper and Row, 1964.

10321. "A New Hand, A New Voice, A New Verve." *Life* 50 (January 27, 1961): 16-30.

10322. New York Times. *The Kennedy Years.* New York: Viking Press, 1964.

10323. Newman, James R. "Testing: What Does Kennedy Mean?" *New Republic* 146 (March 26, 1962): 11-13.

10324. "News Under Kennedy: Reporting in the First Year." *Columbia Journalism Review* 1 (Spring 1962): 11-20.

10325. O'Brien, Lawrence F. *No Final Victories: A Life in Politics from John F. Kennedy to Watergate.* Garden City, NY: Doubleday, 1974.

10326. O'Donnell, Kenneth P. "LBJ and the Kennedys." *Life* 69 (August 7, 1970): 44-56.

10327. Opotowsky, Stan. *The Kennedy Government.* New York: Dutton, 1961.

10328. Osborne, Leonard L. "Rhetorical Patterns in President Kennedy's Major Speeches: A Case Study." *Presidential Studies Quarterly* 10 (Summer 1980): 332-335.

10329. Ouh, Yoon B. "An Analysis of the Kennedy Administration's 1961 Proposal for a New Economic Aid Policy and Aid Organization." D.P.A. dissertation, New York University, 1966.

10330. Paper, Lewis J. *The Promise and the Performance: The Leadership of John F. Kennedy.* New York: Crown, 1975.

10331. Parmet, Herbert S. "JFK: Twenty Years Later." *New England Social Studies Bulletin* 41 (Winter 1983-1984): 16-25.

10332. Pendergrass, Bonnie B. *Public Power, Politics, and Technology in the Eisenhower and Kennedy Years: Hanford Dual-Purpose Reactor Controversy, 1956-1962.* New York: Arno, 1979.

10333. "Peril and Opportunity: President Kennedy's Call to Action." *Round Table* 51 (March 1961): 111-114.

10334. Pike, James A. *A Roman Catholic in the White House.* Garden City, NY: Doubleday, 1960.

10335. Ploughman, Piers. "The Potboiler Reconsidered: A Comment on 'JFK through Russian Eyes.'" *Political Science Quarterly* 90 (Spring 1975): 127-130.

10336. Polsby, Nelson W. "JFK through Russian Eyes." *Political Science Quarterly* 90 (Spring 1975): 117-126.

10337. Reginald, R., and Jeffrey M. Elliot. *If J. F. K. Had Lived: A Political Scenario.* San Bernadino, CA: Borgo Press, 1982.

10338. Republican Party National Committee. *The Kennedy Log: A Daily Chronology of the Presidency of John F. Kennedy, January 20-December 31, 1961.* Washington, DC: Republican National Committee, 1962.

10339. Riemer, Neal. "Kennedy's Grand Democratic Design." *Review of Politics* 27 (January 1965): 3-16.

10340. Rigdon, William M. *White House Sailor.* Garden City, NY: Doubleday, 1962.

10341. Roche, John P. "The Limits of Kennedy's Liberalism." *New Leader* 45 (October 1, 1962): 8-11.

10342. Rollins, Alfred B., Jr. *The Oral History Project of the John Fitzgerald Kennedy Library: Report to the Harvard University Committee.* Cambridge, MA: Harvard University Press, 1965.

10343. Rosenberg, Bruce A. "Kennedy in Camelot: The Arthurian Legend in America." *Western Folklore* 35 (January 1976): 52-59.

10344. Rovere, Richard H. "Letter from Washington." *New Yorker* 36 (November 19, 1960): 203-210.

10345. Russell, G. Darrell, Jr. *Lincoln and Kennedy: Looked at Kindly Together.* New York: Carlton Press, 1973.

10346. "Salinger's Book Tells TV Tales: Debates Won Presidency, JFK Believed." *Broadcasting* 71 (September 12, 1966): 67-68.

10347. Schlesinger, Arthur M., Jr. *A Thousand Days: John F. Kennedy in the White House.* Boston: Houghton Mifflin, 1965.

10348. Schnapper, Morris B. *New Frontiers of the Kennedy Administration: Texts of the Task Force Reports Prepared for the President.* Washington, DC: Public Affairs Press, 1961.

10349. Seligman, Ben B. "Tariffs, the Kennedy Administration, and American Politics." *Commentary* 33 (March 1962): 185-196.

10350. Shaffer, William R. "A Discriminant Function Analysis of Position-Taking: Carter vs. Kennedy." *Presidential Studies Quarterly* 10 (Summer 1980): 451-468.

10351. Shannon, William V. "The Kennedy Administration: The Early Months." *American Scholar* 30 (Fall 1961): 481-488.

10352. Sheerin, John B. "How Fair Are Kennedy's Critics?" *Catholic World* 190 (March 1960): 333-335.

10353. Sidey, Hugh. *John F. Kennedy, President: A Reporter's Inside Story.* New York: Atheneum, 1963.

10354. Smith, Gary D. "The Pulse of Presidential Popularity: Kennedy in Crisis." Ph.D. dissertation, University of California, Los Angeles, 1978.

10355. Smith, Malcolm E. *Kennedy's 13 Great Mistakes in the White House.* New York: National Forum of America, 1968.

10356. Soloveytchik, George. "American Impressions." *Contemporary Review* 200 (July 1961): 350-354.

10357. Soloveytchik, George. "Washington Today." *Contemporary Review* 202 (September 1962): 113-118.

10358. Sorensen, Theodore C. *The Kennedy Legacy.* New York: Macmillan, 1969.

10359. Speel, Charles J., II. "Theological Concepts of Magistracy: A Study of Constantinus [sic], Henry VIII, and John F. Kennedy." *Church History* 32 (June 1963): 130-149.

10360. Spragens, William C. "Kennedy Era Speechwriting, Public Relations, and Public Opinion." *Presidential Studies Quarterly* 14 (Winter 1984): 78-86.

10361. Stern, James. "The Kennedy Policy: A Favorable View." *Industrial Relations* 3 (February 1964): 21-32.

10362. Stoughton, Cecil, Chester V. Clifton, and Hugh Sidey. *The Memories — JFK, 1961-1963 — of Cecil Stoughton, The President's Photographer, and Major General Chester V. Clifton, The President's Military Aide.* New York: Norton, 1973.

10363. Stuart, Roger W. *The Thought Brigade: America's Influential Ghosts-in-Government.* New York: Obolensky, 1963.

10364. Tanzer, Lester, ed. *The Kennedy Circle.* Washington: Luce, 1961.

10365. Taylor, Maxwell D. *Responsibility and Response.* New York: Harper and Row, 1967.

10366. Thomison, Dennis. "Trouble in Camelot: An Early Skirmish of Kennedy's New Frontier." *Journal of Library History, Philosophy, and Comparative Librarianship* 13 (Spring 1978): 148-156.

10367. Thompson, Nelson. *The Dark Side of Camelot.* Chicago: Playboy Press, 1976.

10368. Tillett, Paul, ed. *The Political Vocation.* New York: Basic Books, 1965.

10369. Toscano, Vincent L. "Since Dallas: Images of John F. Kennedy in Popular and Scholarly Literature, 1963-1973." Ph.D. dissertation, State University of New York, 1975.

10370. "Towards a Second Term: Mr. Kennedy's Record and Prospects." *Round Table* 53 (September 1963): 353-357.

10371. Travell, Janet. *Office Hours: Day and Night.* New York: World Publishing, 1968.

10372. Tully, Andrew. *CIA: The Inside Story.* New York: Morrow, 1962.

10373. Underwood, James E. "Studying Individual Presidents: Truman, Eisenhower, Kennedy, and Carter." *Congress and the Presidency* 11 (Spring 1984): 93-104.

10374. U.S. Congress. Senate. *Memorial Addresses in the Congress of the United States and Tributes in Eulogy of John Fitzgerald Kennedy.* 88th Cong., 2d sess.,

1964. Washington, DC: U.S. Government Printing Office, 1964.

10375. Wamble, Thelma. *Look Over My Shoulder: Letters about President John F. Kennedy to John Allen Gould, Grandson of John Fitzherbert Miller.* New York: Vantage Press, 1969.

10376. Weisl, Edwin L. "Look Inside the Johnson-Kennedy Contest." *U.S. News & World Report* 64 (April 8, 1968): 48-50.

10377. White, William S. "How to Put Kennedy Back in the Senate." *Harper's Magazine* 223 (December 1961): 84-86.

10378. White, William S. *The Responsibles: Truman, Taft, Eisenhower, JFK, Johnson.* New York: Harper and Row, 1972.

10379. Wicker, Tom. *JFK and LBJ: The Influence of Personality upon Politics.* New York: Morrow, 1968.

10380. Wicker, Tom. "Kennedy as Public Speakah." *New York Times Magazine* 111 (February 25, 1962): 14, 70-71.

10381. Wicker, Tom. "Total Political Animal." *New York Times Magazine* 111 (April 15, 1962): 26, 128-130.

10382. Wicklein, John. "John Kennedy and the Catholic Issue: 1960-1964." In *Religion and Contemporary Society*, edited by Harold Stahmer, 215-253. New York: Macmillan, 1963.

10383. Wiesner, Jerome B. "John F. Kennedy: A Remembrance." *Science* 142 (November 29, 1963): 1147-1150.

10384. Wills, Garry. *The Kennedy Imprisonment: A Meditation on Power.* Boston: Little, Brown, 1982.

10385. Wimer, Kurt. "Can Kennedy Succeed Where Wilson Failed?" *Contemporary Review* 202 (November 1962): 223-229.

10386. Wolfarth, Donald D. "John F. Kennedy in the Tradition of Inaugural Speeches." *Quarterly Journal of Speech* 47 (April 1961): 124-132.

10387. Wolfe, James S. "The Kennedy Myth: American Civil Religion in the Sixties." Ph.D. dissertation, Graduate Theological Union, 1975.

10388. Wright, Jack, Jr. "A Comparison of the Projected Image of John F. Kennedy in the Mass Media with the Held-Image of a Sample of College Students." Ph.D. dissertation, Louisiana State University, Agricultural and Mechanical College, 1969.

Assassination

10389. Alpert, Augusta. "A Brief Communication on Children's Reactions to the Assassination of the President." *Psychoanalytic Study of the Child* 19 (1964): 313-320.

10390. Associated Press. *The Torch Is Passed: The Associated Press Story of the Death of a President.* New York: Parallax Publishing Co., 1967.

10391. Attwood, William. "Twenty Years after Dallas." *Virginia Quarterly Review* 59 (Autumn 1983): 557-563.

10392. Back, Kurt W., and Judith Saravay. "From Bright Ideas to Social Research: Studies of the Kennedy Assassination." *Public Opinion Quarterly* 31 (Summer 1967): 253-264.

10393. Bagdikian, Ben H. "The Assassin." *Saturday Evening Post* 236 (December 14, 1963): 22-27.

10394. Baker, Dean C. *The Assassination of President Kennedy: A Study of the Press Coverage.* Ann Arbor: Department of Journalism, University of Michigan, 1965.

10395. Banta, Thomas J. "The Kennedy Assassination: Early Thoughts and Emotions." *Public Opinion Quarterly* 28 (Summer 1964): 216-224.

10396. Baskerville, Donald A. "Assassination of President John F. Kennedy: Moves to Re-open the Investigation: A Selected List of References." *Library of Congress Information Bulletin* 35 (December 3, 1976): 752-757.

10397. Berkeley, Edmund C., ed. "The Assassination of President John F. Kennedy ... Report No. 2." *Computers and Automation* 19 (July 1970): 29-36.

10398. Berkeley, Edmund C., ed. "Patterns of Political Assassination: How Many Coincidences Make a Plot?" *Computers and Automation* 19 (September 1970): 39-48.

10399. Berkeley, Edmund C. "Political Assassinations in the United States...." *Computers and People* 24 (March 1975): 3.

10400. Bethell, Thomas N. "Earl Warren: On the Mob's Payroll?" *Washington Monthly* 8 (March 1976): 35-46.

10401. Bickley, Eugene H. "Memories of the JFK Funeral." *Soldiers* 29 (November 1974): 48-51.

10402. Biller, Owen A. "Suicide Related to the Assassination of President J. F. Kennedy." *Suicide and Life Threatening Behavior* 7 (Spring 1977): 40-44.

10403. Bishop, James A. *The Day Kennedy Was Shot.* New York: Funk and Wagnalls, 1968.

10404. Blakey, G. Robert, and Richard N. Billings. *The Plot to Kill the President.* New York: Time Books, 1981.

10405. Bloomgarden, Henry S. *The Gun: A 'Biography' of the Gun That Killed John F. Kennedy.* New York: Grossman, 1975.

10406. Bonner, Judith W. *Investigation of a Homicide: The Murder of John F. Kennedy.* Anderson, SC: Drake House, 1969.

10407. Buchanan, Thomas A. *Who Killed Kennedy?* New York: Putnam, 1964.

10408. Condon, Richard. " 'Manchurian Candidate' in Dallas." *Nation* 197 (December 28, 1963): 449-451.

10409. Cottrell, John. *Anatomy of Assassination.* London: Muller, 1966.

10410. Cottrell, John. *Assassination! The World Stood Still.* London: New English Library, 1964.

10411. Crotty, William J., ed. *Assassination and the Political Order.* New York: Harper and Row, 1971.

10412. Curry, Jesse. *JFK: Assassination File.* Dallas: American Poster and Printing Co., 1969.

10413. Cushman, Robert F. "Why the Warren Commission?" *New York University Law Review* 40 (May 1965): 477-503.

10414. Denson, R. B., comp. *Destiny in Dallas: Assassin and Assassin's Assassin.* Dallas, TX: Dexco Corporation, 1964.

10415. Donoghue, Mary A. *Assassination: Murder in Politics.* Chatsworth, CA: Major Books, 1975.

10416. Dunning, John L. "The Kennedy Assassination as Viewed by Communist Media." *Journalism Quarterly* 41 (Spring 1964): 163-169.

10417. Epstein, Edward J. *Inquest: The Warren Commission and the Establishment of Truth.* New York: Viking Press, 1966.

10418. Epstein, Edward J. *Legend: The Secret World of Lee Harvey Oswald.* New York: McGraw-Hill, 1978.

10419. Ferrari, Alfred J. "Kennedy Assassinations and Political Detours (A Possibly Romantic Posthumous Speculation)." *Minority of One* 10 (1968): 7-9.

10420. *Four Dark Days in History: November 22, 23, 24, 25, 1963: A Photo His-*

tory of President Kennedy's Assassination. Los Angeles: Special Publications, 1963.

10421. Fox, Sylvan. *The Unanswered Questions about President Kennedy's Assassination.* New York: Award Books, 1965.

10422. Freese, Paul L. "The Warren Commission and the Fourth Shot: A Reflection on the Fundamentals of Forensic Fact-Finding." *New York University Law Review* 40 (May 1965): 424-465.

10423. Gay, Donovan L., ed. *The Assassination of President John F. Kennedy: The Warren Commission Report and Subsequent Interest.* Washington, DC: Library of Congress, 1975.

10424. Gertz, Elmer, and Wayne B. Giampietro. "The Trial of 'State Cases' — A Postscript on the Jack Ruby Trial." *DePaul Law Review* 16 (Spring/Summer 1967): 285-308.

10425. Goldberg, Jeffrey. "Waiting for Justice: The JFK Case Is Not Closed." *Inquiry Magazine* 3 (January 7 and 21, 1980): 15-19.

10426. Goldman, Alex J. *John Fitzgerald Kennedy: The World Remembers.* New York: Fleet, 1968.

10427. Goodhart, Arthur L. "Three Famous Legal Hoaxes: The Tichborne Case, The Dreyfus Affair, The Alleged Conspiracy to Assassinate President Kennedy." *Association of the Bar of the City of New York Record* 22 (June 1967): 415-437.

10428. Goodhart, Arthur L. "The Warren Commission from the Procedural Standpoint." *New York University Law Review* 40 (May 1965): 404-423.

10429. Greenberg, Bradley S. "Diffusion of News of the Kennedy Assassination." *Public Opinion Quarterly* 28 (Summer 1964): 225-232.

10430. Greenberg, Bradley S., and Edwin B. Parker. *The Kennedy Assassination and the American Public: Social Communication in Crisis.* Stanford, CA: Stanford University Press, 1965.

10431. Henderson, Bruce, and Sam Summerlin. *1:33 In Memoriam: John F. Kennedy.* New York: Cowles Educational Corporation, 1968.

10432. Joesten, Joachim. *Oswald: Assassin or Fall Guy?* New York: Marzani and Munsell, 1964.

10433. Johnson, James P. "The Assassination in Dallas: A Search for Meaning." *Journal of Psychohistory* 7 (Summer 1979): 105-121.

10434. Johnson, Marion M., comp. *Preliminary Inventory of the Records of the President's Commission of the Assassination of President Kennedy.* Washington, DC: National Archives and Records Service, General Services Administration, 1970.

10435. Katz, Joseph. "President Kennedy's Assassination." *Psychoanalytic Review* 51 (Winter 1964-1965): 121-124.

10436. Katz, Joseph. "President Kennedy's Assassination: Freudian Comments." *Journal of Individual Psychology* 23 (May 1967): 20-23.

10437. Knight, Janet, M., ed. *Three Assassinations: The Deaths of John and Robert Kennedy and Martin Luther King.* New York: Facts on File, 1971.

10438. Kurtz, Michael L. "The Assassination of John F. Kennedy: A Historical Perspective." *Historian* 45 (November 1982): 1-19.

10439. Kurtz, Michael L. "Lee Harvey Oswald in New Orleans: A Reappraisal." *Louisiana History* 21 (Winter 1980): 7-22.

10440. Lane, Mark. *Rush to Judgment: A Critique of the Warren Commission's Inquiry into the Murders of President John*

F. Kennedy, Officer J. D. Tippit, and Lee Harvey Oswald. New York: Holt, Rinehart and Winston, 1966.

10441. Lattimer, John K. *Lincoln and Kennedy: Medical and Ballistic Comparisons of Their Assassinations.* New York: Harcourt, Brace, Jovanovich, 1980.

10442. Lattimer, John K., Edward B. Schlesinger, and H. Houston Merritt. "President Kennedy's Spine Hit by First Bullet." *Bulletin of the New York Academy of Medicine* 53 (April 1977): 280-291.

10443. Lattimer, John K., Gary Lattimer, and Jon Lattimer. "Could Oswald Have Shot President Kennedy? Further Ballistic Studies." *Bulletin of the New York Academy of Medicine* 48 (April 1972): 513-524.

10444. Lewis, Richard W. *The Scavengers and Critics of the Warren Report.* New York: Delacourt Press, 1967.

10445. Lifton, David S. *Best Evidence: Disguise and Deception in the Assassination of John F. Kennedy.* New York: Macmillan, 1980.

10446. Lifton, David S., comp. *Document Addendum to the Warren Report.* El Segundo, CA: Sightext Publications, 1968.

10447. McConnell, Brian. *Assassination.* London: Leslie Frewin, 1969.

10448. McDonald, Hugh C. *Appointment in Dallas: The Final Solution to the Assassination of JFK.* New York: McDonald, 1975.

10449. McKinley, James. *Assassination in America.* New York: Harper and Row, 1977.

10450. McMillan, Priscilla. *Marina and Lee.* New York: Harper and Row, 1977.

10451. Manchester, William R. *The Death of a President: November 20-November 25, 1963.* New York: Harper and Row, 1967.

10452. Marina, William. "Shooting down the Conspiracy Theory." *Reason* 11 (1979): 18-24.

10453. Matthews, James P., et al. *The Complete Kennedy Saga.* Los Angeles: Associated Professional Services, 1963.

10454. Mayo, John B. *Bulletin from Dallas: The President Is Dead: The Story of John F. Kennedy's Assassination as Covered by Radio and TV.* Hicksville, NY: Exposition Press, 1967.

10455. Meagher, Sylvia. *Accessories after the Fact: The Warren Commission, the Authorities, and the Report.* Indianapolis, IN: Bobbs-Merrill, 1967.

10456. Meagher, Sylvia. *Subject Index to the Warren Report and Hearings and Exhibits.* New York: Scarecrow Press, 1966.

10457. Model, F. Peter, and Robert J. Groden. *JFK: The Case for Conspiracy.* New York: Manor Books, 1976.

10458. Morin, Relman. *Assassination.* New York: Signet, 1968.

10459. National Broadcasting Company. *There Was a President.* New York: Random House, 1966.

10460. Newman, Albert H. *The Assassination of John F. Kennedy: The Reasons Why.* New York: Potter, 1970.

10461. Oglesby, Carl. *The Yankee and Cowboy War: Conspiracies from Dallas to Watergate.* Mission, KS: Sheed Andrews and McMeel, 1976.

10462. O'Toole, George. *The Assassination Tapes: An Electronic Probe into the Murder of John F. Kennedy and the Dallas Coverup.* New York: Penthouse, 1975.

10463. Payne, Darwin. *The Press Corps and the Kennedy Assassination.* Lexington, KY: Association for Education in Journalism, 1970.

10464. Phelan, James R. "The Assassination That Will Not Die: Critics of the

Warren Report Have Produced No Hard New Evidence, But Their Irresponsible Polemics and Absurd Theories Have Left the Public More Dubious Than Ever." *New York Times Magazine* 125 (November 23, 1975): 25-26, 109-111, 120-123, 126, 132.

10465. Roberts, Charles W. *The Truth about the Assassination.* New York: Grossett and Dunlap, 1967.

10466. Roffman, Howard. *Presumed Guilty: Lee Harvey Oswald in the Assassination of President Kennedy.* Rutherford, NJ: Fairleigh Dickinson University Press, 1975.

10467. Rogers, Warren. "The Persecution." *Look* 33 (August 26, 1969): 53-56.

10468. Salandria, Vincent J. "The Assassination of President JFK: A Model for Explanation." *Computers and Automation* 20 (December 1971): 32-40.

10469. Sauvage, Leo. *The Oswald Affair: An Examination of the Contradictions and Omissions of the Warren Report.* Cleveland, OH: World Publishing, 1966.

10470. Scobey, Alfredda. "Lawyers' Notes on the Warren Commission Report." *American Bar Association Journal* 51 (January 1965): 39-43.

10471. Scott, Peter D., Paul L. Hoch, and Russell Stetter. *The Assassinations: Dallas and Beyond.* New York: Random House, 1976.

10472. Sheatsley, Paul B., and Jacob Feldman. "The Assassination of President Kennedy: A Preliminary Report on Public Reactions and Behavior." *Political Opinion Quarterly* 28 (Summer 1964): 189-215.

10473. Sherwood, John J. "Authoritarianism, Moral Realism, and President Kennedy's Death." *British Journal of Social and Clinical Psychology* 5 (December 1966): 264-269.

10474. Sparrow, John. *After the Assassination: A Positive Appraisal of the Warren Report.* New York: Chilmark, 1967.

10475. Stetler, Russell. "Can Congress Crack the Kennedy Assassination?" *Inquiry Magazine* 15 (March 6, 1978): 11-15.

10476. "Symposium on the Warren Commission Report." *New York Law Review* 40 (May 1965): 404-524.

10477. Tamney, Joseph B. "A Study of Involvement: Reactions to the Death of President Kennedy." *Sociologus* 19 (1969): 66-78.

10478. Thompson, Josiah. *Six Seconds in Dallas: A Micro-Study of the Kennedy Assassination.* New York: Random House, 1968.

10479. Tomkins, Silvan S. "Reactions to the Assassination of President Kennedy." In *Affect, Cognition, and Personality,* edited by Silvan S. Tomkins and Carroll E. Izard, 172-197. London: Tavistock Publications, 1966.

10480. United Press International. *Four Days: The Historical Record of the Death of President Kennedy.* New York: American Heritage Publishing Co., 1964.

10481. U.S. President's Commission on the Assassination of President Kennedy. *Investigation of the Assassination of President John F. Kennedy.* 26 vols. Washington, DC: U.S. Government Printing Office, 1964.

10482. U.S. President's Commission on the Assassination of President Kennedy. *The Witnesses.* Selected and edited from the Warren Commission's Hearings by the *New York Times.* New York: McGraw-Hill, 1965.

10483. Van Bemmelen, J. M. "Did Lee Harvey Oswald Act without Help?" *New York University Law Review* 40 (May 1965): 466-476.

10484. Walker, John H. "We Can Prevent Presidential Assassinations." *Look* 28 (February 11, 1964): 124-126.

10485. Webb, Lucas. *The Attempted Assassination of John F. Kennedy.* San Bernadino, CA: Borgo Press, 1976.

10486. Wecht, Cyril H. "The Medical Evidence in the Assassination of President John F. Kennedy." *Forensic Science* 12 (May 1964): 105-128.

10487. Wecht, Cyril H. "Pathologists' View of JFK Autopsy: An Unsolved Case." *Modern Medicine* 41 (November 27, 1972): 28-32.

10488. Wecht, Cyril H. "Why Is the Rockefeller Commission So Singlemindedly about a Lone Assassin in the Kennedy Case?" *Journal of Legal Medicine* 3 (July/August 1975): 22-25.

10489. Weisberg, Harold. *Post Mortem: JFK Assassination Cover-up Smashed!* Frederick, MD: The Author, 1975.

10490. Weisberg, Harold. *Whitewash: The Report on the Warren Report.* Hyattstown, MD: The Author, 1966.

10491. Whalen, Richard J. "The Kennedy Assassination." *Saturday Evening Post* 240 (January 14, 1967): 19-25.

10492. White, Stephen. *Should We Now Believe the Warren Report?* New York: Macmillan, 1968.

10493. Wise, Dan, and Marietta M. Maxfield. *The Day Kennedy Died.* San Antonio: Naylor Co., 1964.

10494. Wise, David. "Secret Evidence on the Kennedy Assassination." *Saturday Evening Post* 241 (April 6, 1968): 70-73.

10495. Wolfenstein, Martha, and Gilbert Kliman, eds. *Children and the Death of a President: Multi-Disciplinary Studies.* Garden City, NY: Doubleday, 1965.

10496. Yarmey, A. Daniel, and Maurice P. Bull. "Where Were You When President Kennedy Was Assassinated?" *Bulletin of the Psychonomic Society* 11 (February 1978): 133-135.

Congress

10497. Bolling, Richard. *Power in the House: A History of the Leadership of the House of Representatives.* New York: Dutton, 1968.

10498. Burke, Vincent, and Frank Eleazer. "How Kennedy Gets What He Wants ... Methods to Sway Congress in the Future." *Nation's Business* 49 (September 1961): 96-102.

10499. Dameron, Kenneth, Jr. "President Kennedy and Congress, Process and Politics." Ph.D. dissertation, Harvard University, 1975.

10500. Fox, Douglas M., and Charles H. Clapp. "The House Rules Committee and the Programs of the Kennedy and Johnson Administrations." *American Journal of Political Science* 14 (November 1970): 667-672.

10501. Fuller, Helen. "Kennedy's First Congress." *New Republic* 147 (October 27, 1962): 12-14.

10502. Hyman, Sidney. "The President and Congress." *Progressive Magazine* 25 (December 1961): 17-20.

10503. "Kennedy Boxscore: Congress Approves 5 Percent of President's Requests." *Congressional Quarterly Weekly Report* 21 (August 2, 1963): 1358-1369.

10504. Kilpatrick, Carroll. "The Kennedy Style and Congress." *Virginia Quarterly Review* 39 (Winter 1963): 1-11.

10505. Lewis, Eleanor G. "The House Committee on Rules and the Legislative Program of the Kennedy and Johnson Administrations." *Capital Studies* 6 (Fall 1978): 27-38.

10506. Lewis, Ted. "Congress versus Kennedy." *Nation* 195 (July 14, 1962): 4-6.

10507. Lewis, Ted. "Kennedy's Legislative Strategy." *Nation* 192 (March 25, 1961): 247-249.

10508. McCarthy, Joe. "One Election JFK Can't Win." *Look* 26 (November 6, 1962): 23-27.

10509. MacNeil, Neil. "The House Confronts Mr. Kennedy." *Fortune* 65 (January 1962): 70-73, 166, 171-172, 174.

10510. Mansfield, Michael J. *Summary of the Three-Year Kennedy Record, and Digest of Major Accomplishments of the Eighty-seventh and the Eighty-eighth Congress, 1961-1963.* Washington, DC: U.S. Government Printing Office, 1964.

10511. Margolis, Howard. "Bombers and the Constitution: Can Congress Order Kennedy to Develop a Weapon?" *Science* 135 (March 16, 1962): 906-907.

10512. Renka, Russell D. "Bargaining with Legislative Whales in the Kennedy and Johnson Administrations." *Legislative Studies Quarterly* 6 (February 1981): 161-162.

10513. Renka, Russell D. "Kennedy, Johnson, and the Congress: Serial Gaming in Legislative Policy Coalitions." Ph.D. dissertation, University of Texas, 1979.

10514. Renka, Russell D. "Presidential Lobbying of Congress: Coalition Building in the Kennedy-Johnson Years." Ph.D. dissertation, University of Texas, 1979.

10515. Ripley, Randall B. *Kennedy and Congress.* Morristown, NJ: General Learning Press, 1972.

10516. "Veto Power and *Kennedy v. Sampson:* Burning a Hole in the President's Pocket." *Northwestern University Law Review* 69 (September/October 1974): 587-625.

10517. "What They Say about JFK: Congressmen Tell What's on Their Minds." *U.S. News & World Report* 53 (July 30, 1962): 31-34.

10518. White, William S. "The Kennedy Era, Stage Two: The Coming Battle with Congress." *Harper's Magazine* 224 (February 1962): 96-97, 102.

10519. "Why Congress Balks at Kennedy." *U.S. News & World Report* 52 (April 2, 1962): 33-35.

10520. "Why Kennedy's Program Is in Trouble with Congress: Interview, M. Mansfield." *U.S. News & World Report* 53 (September 17, 1962): 62-69.

10521. Williams, Robert J., and David A. Kershaw. "Kennedy and Congress: The Struggle for the New Frontier." *Political Studies* 27 (September 1979): 390-404.

Cuba

10522. Abel, Elie. *The Missile Crisis.* New York: Lippincott, 1966.

10523. Abel, Elie. *The Missiles of October: The Story of the Cuban Missile Crisis 1962.* London: MacGibbon and Kee, 1969.

10524. Allison, Graham T. *The Essence of Decision: Explaining the Cuban Missile Crisis.* Boston: Little, Brown, 1971.

10525. Backer, Jack E. "The 'Prestige Press' and News Management in the Cuban Crisis." *Journalism Quarterly* 41 (Spring 1964): 264-265.

10526. Bernstein, Barton J. "Coverage and Commitment: The Missiles of October." *Foreign Service Journal* 52 (December 1975): 9-11.

10527. Bernstein, Barton J. "The Cuban Missile Crisis." In *Reflections on the Cold War: A Quarter Century of American Foreign Policy,* edited by Lynn H. Miller and

Ronald W. Pruessen, 130-133. Philadelphia: Temple University Press, 1974.

10528. Bernstein, Barton J. "The Cuban Missile Crisis: Trading the Jupiters in Turkey?" *Political Science Quarterly* 95 (Spring 1980): 97-125.

10529. Branch, Taylor, and George Crile III. "The Kennedy Vendetta." *Harper's Magazine* 251 (August 1975): 49-53, 63.

10530. Cecile, Robert E. "Crisis Decision-Making in the Eisenhower and Kennedy Administrations: The Application of an Analytical Scheme." Ph.D. dissertation, University of Oklahoma, 1965.

10531. Chayes, Abram. *The Cuban Missile Crisis: International Crises and the Role of Law*. New York: Oxford University Press, 1974.

10532. Crane, Robert D. "The Cuban Missile Crisis: A Strategic Analysis of American and Soviet Policy." *Orbis* 6 (Winter 1963): 528-563.

10533. Dewart, Leslie. "The Cuban Missile Crisis Revisited." *Studies on the Left* 5 (Spring 1965): 15-37.

10534. Dinerstein, Herbert S. *The Making of a Missile Crisis: October 1962*. Baltimore, MD: Johns Hopkins University Press, 1976.

10535. Divine, Robert A., ed. *The Cuban Missile Crisis*. New York: Quadrangle Books, 1971.

10536. Fallows, James. "Crazies by the Tail: Bay of Pigs, Diem, and Liddy." *Washington Monthly* 6 (September 1974): 50-58.

10537. Hafner, Donald L. "Bureaucratic Politics and 'Those Frigging Missiles': JFK, Cuba, and U.S. Missiles in Turkey." *Orbis* 21 (Summer 1977): 307-333.

10538. Holsti, Ole R. "Time, Alternatives, and Communication: The 1914 and Cuban Missile Crises." In *International Crises: Insights from Behavioral Research*, edited by Charles F. Hermann, 58-80. New York: Free Press, 1972.

10539. Johnson, Haynes. *The Bay of Pigs: The Invasion of Cuba by Brigade 2506*. London: Hutchinson, 1964.

10540. Kahan, Jerome H., and Anne K. Long. "The Cuban Missile Crisis: A Study of Its Strategic Context." *Political Science Quarterly* 87 (December 1972): 564-590.

10541. Kennedy, Robert F. *Thirteen Days: A Memoir of the Cuban Missile Crisis*. New York: Norton, 1971.

10542. Larson, David L., ed. *The Cuban Crisis of 1962, Selected Documents and Chronology*. Boston: Houghton Mifflin, 1963.

10543. Mailer, Norman. "The Big Bite: On Kennedy and Existential Politics: On Kennedy and the Bay of Pigs: On Jackie Kennedy." *Esquire* 60 (November 1963): 26, 28, 30, 32.

10544. Merchant, Jerrold J. "Kennedy-Khrushchev Strategies of Persuasion during the Cuban Missile Crises." Ph.D. dissertation, University of Southern California, 1971.

10545. Meyer, Karl E., and Tad Szulc, eds. *The Cuban Invasion: The Chronicle of a Disaster*. New York: Praeger, 1962.

10546. Nathan, James A. "The Missile Crisis: His Finest Hour Now." *World Politics* 27 (January 1975): 256-281.

10547. Schulz, Donald E. "Kennedy and the Cuban Connection." *Foreign Policy* 26 (Spring 1977): 121-139.

10548. Selesnick, Herbert L. "The Diffusion of Crisis Information: A Computer Simulation of Soviet Mass Media Exposure during the Cuban Missile Crisis and the Aftermath of President Kennedy's Assassination." Ph.D. dissertation, University of Massachusetts, 1970.

10549. Steel, Ronald. "The Kennedys and the Missile Crisis." In *Readings in American Foreign Policy*, edited by Morton Halperin and Arnold Kanter, 202-210. Boston: Little, Brown, 1973.

Domestic Affairs

10550. Anderson, Clinton. *Outsider in the Senate*. New York: World Publishing, 1970.

10551. Ball, Desmond. *Politics and Force Levels: The Strategic Missile Program of the Kennedy Administration*. Berkeley: University of California Press, 1980.

10552. Berkowitz, Edward D. "Politics of Mental Retardation during the Kennedy Administration." *Social Science Quarterly* 61 (June 1980): 128-143.

10553. Blough, Roger M. "My Side of the Steel Price Story, As Told to Eleanor Harris." *Look* 27 (January 29, 1963): 19-23.

10554. Booker, Simeon. "What Negroes Can Expect from Kennedy." *Ebony* 16 (January 1961): 33-36, 38.

10555. Bradley, Pearl G. "A Criticism of the Modes of Persuasion Found in Selected Civil Rights Addresses of John F. Kennedy, 1962-1963." Ph.D. dissertation, Ohio State University, 1967.

10556. Brauer, Carl M. *John F. Kennedy and the Second Reconstruction*. New York: Columbia University Press, 1978.

10557. Brauer, Carl M. "The Kennedy Administration and Civil Rights." Ph.D. dissertation, Harvard University, 1973.

10558. Brauer, Carl M. "Kennedy, Johnson, and the War on Poverty." *Journal of American History* 69 (June 1981): 98-119.

10559. Domer, Thomas. "Sport in Cold War America, 1953-1963: The Diplomatic and Political Use of Sport in the Eisenhower and Kennedy Administrations." Ph.D. dissertation, Marquette University, 1976.

10560. Eliot, George F. *Reserve Forces and the Kennedy Strategy*. Harrisburg, PA: Stackpole, 1962.

10561. Farrington, John P. "A Study of New Deal Thought in the Kennedy and Johnson Administrations." Ph.D. dissertation, University of Colorado, 1975.

10562. Fritchey, Clayton. "A Tale of One City and Two Men: Foreign Policies of Kennedy and Johnson." *Harper's Magazine* 233 (December 1966): 108-113.

10563. Gershenson, Alvin H. *Kennedy and Big Business*. Beverly Hills, CA: Book Company of America, 1964.

10564. Gilbert, Robert E. "John F. Kennedy and Civil Rights for Black Americans." *Presidential Studies Quarterly* 12 (Summer 1982): 386-399.

10565. Godden, Richard, and Richard Maidment. "Anger, Language, and Politics: John F. Kennedy and the Steel Crisis." *Presidential Studies Quarterly* 10 (Summer 1980): 317-331.

10566. Golden, Harry L. *Mr. Kennedy and the Negroes*. Cleveland, OH: World Publishing, 1964.

10567. Hadwiger, Don F., and Ross B. Talbot. *Pressures and Protests: The Kennedy Farm Program and the Wheat Referendum of 1963*. San Francisco: Chandler, 1965.

10568. Harris, Seymour E. *The Economics of the Kennedy Years and a Look Ahead*. New York: Harper and Row, 1964.

10569. Harrison, Cynthia E. "A 'New Frontier' for Women: The Public Policy of the Kennedy Administration." *Journal of America History* 67 (December 1980): 630-646.

10570. Hart, John. "Kennedy, Congress,

and Civil Rights." *Journal of American Studies* 13 (August 1979): 165-178.

10571. Harvey, James C. *Civil Rights during the Kennedy Administration.* Jackson: University Press of Mississippi, 1971.

10572. Heath, Jim F. *John F. Kennedy and the Business Community.* Chicago: University of Chicago Press, 1969.

10573. Holder, Calvin B. "Racism toward Black African Diplomats during the Kennedy Administration." *Journal of Black Studies* 14 (September 1983): 31-48.

10574. "Kennedy Seeks Modest Regulatory Reforms." *Public Utilities Fortnightly* 67 (May 1961): 677-678.

10575. Knopp, Daniel L. *Scouting the War on Poverty: Social Reform Politics in the Kennedy Administration.* Lexington, MA: Lexington Books, 1971.

10576. Lawson, Steven F. " 'I Got It from the *New York Times*': Lyndon Johnson and the Kennedy Civil Rights Program." *Journal of Negro History* 67 (Summer 1982): 159-172.

10577. Lemon, Richard. *The Troubled American.* New York: Simon and Schuster, 1969.

10578. Lomax, Louis E. "The Kennedys Move in on Dixie." *Harper's Magazine* 224 (May 1962): 27-33.

10579. Lord, Donald C. "JFK and Civil Rights." *Presidential Studies Quarterly* 8 (Spring 1978): 151-163.

10580. Lowther, Kevin, and C. Payne Lucas. *Keeping Kennedy's Promise: The Peace Corps — Unmet Hope of the New Frontier.* Boulder, CO: Westview Press, 1978.

10581. McConnell, Grant. *Steel and the Presidency, 1962.* New York: Norton, 1963.

10582. Madow, Pauline, ed. *The Peace Corps.* New York: H. W. Wilson, 1964.

10583. Mills, Bert. "President Kennedy, 'Lobbyist for the Consumer.' " *Sales Management* 86 (January 20, 1961): 33-37.

10584. Moynihan, Daniel P. "The Democrats, Kennedy, and the Murder of Dr. King." *Commentary* 45 (May 1968): 15-29.

10585. Nossiter, Bernard D. *The Mythmakers: An Essay on Power and Wealth.* Boston: Houghton Mifflin, 1964.

10586. O'Hara, William T., ed. *John F. Kennedy on Education.* New York: Columbia University Teacher's College Press, 1966.

10587. Ostman, Ronald E., and William A. Babcock. "Three Major U.S. Newspapers' Content and President Kennedy's Press Conference Statements Regarding Space Exploration and Technology." *Presidential Studies Quarterly* 13 (Winter 1983): 111-120.

10588. Price, Hugh D. "The Congress: Race, Religion, and the Rules Committee: The Kennedy Aid-to-Education Bills." In *The Uses of Power: Cases in American Politics,* edited by Alan F. Westin, 1-71. New York: Harcourt, Brace and World, 1962.

10589. Price, Hugh D. "Schools, Scholarships, and Congressmen, The Kennedy Aid-to-Education Program." In *The Centers of Power, Three Cases in American National Government,* edited by Allan F. Westin, 53-106. New York: Harcourt, Brace and World, 1964.

10590. Riccards, Michael P. "Rare Counsel: Kennedy, Johnson, and the Civil Rights Bill of 1963." *Presidential Studies Quarterly* 11 (Summer 1981): 395-398.

10591. Rossant, M. J. "The Economic Education of John F. Kennedy." *Reporter* 28 (February 14, 1963): 22-25.

10592. Rovere, Richard H. "The Kennedy Tax Proposals." *New Yorker* 38 (August 25, 1962): 101-107.

10593. Rowen, Hobart. *The Free Enterprisers: Kennedy, Johnson, and the Business Establishment.* New York: Putnam, 1964.

10594. Rukeyser, Merryle S. *The Kennedy Recession: A Complete Study of the Causes of Our Stagnating Economy and Our Loss of World-Wide Prestige.* Derby, CT: Monarch Press, 1963.

10595. Shank, Alan. *Presidential Policy Leadership: Kennedy and Social Welfare.* Lanham, MD: University Press of America, 1980.

10596. Sullivan, Donald F. "The Civil Rights Programs of the Kennedy Administration: A Political Analysis." Ph.D. dissertation, University of Oklahoma, 1965.

10597. Sundquist, James L. *Politics and Policy: The Eisenhower, Kennedy, and Johnson Years.* Washington, DC: Brookings Institution, 1968.

10598. Von Furstenberg, George M., and James M. Boughton. "Stabilizing Goals and the Appropriateness of Fiscal Policy during the Eisenhower and Kennedy-Johnson Administrations." *Public Finance Quarterly* 1 (January 1973): 5-28.

10599. Warner, David C., ed. *Toward New Human Rights: The Social Policies of the Kennedy and Johnson Administrations.* Austin: LBJ School of Public Affairs, University of Texas, 1977.

10600. "When Kennedy Meets Businessmen." *U.S. News & World Report* 53 (July 30, 1962): 35.

Elections

10601. Barrow, Lionel C. "Factors Related to Attention to the First Kennedy-Nixon Debate." *Journal of Broadcasting* 5 (Summer 1961): 229-238.

10602. Blanshard, Paul. *God and Man in Washington.* Boston: Beacon Press, 1960.

10603. Bradford, Richard H. "John F. Kennedy and the 1960 Presidential Primary in West Virginia." *South Atlantic Monthly* 75 (Spring 1976): 161-172.

10604. Burns, James M. "John F. Kennedy: Candidate on the Eve: Liberalism without Tears." *New Republic* 143 (October 31, 1960): 14-16.

10605. Crews, James M., Jr. "J. F. K. and the Mountaineers: John F. Kennedy's Rhetoric in the 1960 West Virginia Presidential Primary." Ph.D. dissertation, Florida State University, 1980.

10606. "Debate Score: Kennedy Up, Nixon Down, Sindlerger Study Shows Switch in Sentiment toward Candidates." *Broadcasting* 59 (November 7, 1960): 27-29.

10607. Felknor, Bruce. *Dirty Politics.* New York: Norton, 1966.

10608. Fischer, John. "Editor's Easy Chair: The Choice." *Harper's Magazine* 221 (October 1960): 14, 16, 19-20.

10609. Flinn, Thomas A. "How Mr. Nixon Took Ohio: A Short Reply to Senator Kennedy's Question." *Western Political Quarterly* 15 (June 1962): 274-279.

10610. Fuchs, Lawrence H. "A Catholic as President?" *America* 99 (September 13, 1958): 620-623.

10611. Fuchs, Lawrence H. "The Senator and the Lady." *American Heritage* 25 (October 1974): 57-61, 81-83.

10612. Fuller, Helen. *Year of Trial: Kennedy's Crucial Decisions.* New York: Harcourt, Brace, 1962.

10613. Goldman, Eric F. "The 1947 Kennedy-Nixon 'TubeCity' Debate." *Saturday Review* 4 (October 16, 1976): 12-13.

10614. "Great Debate Rightly Named: Nixon, Kennedy Set a Precedent That

Will Be Hard to Abandon." *Broadcasting* 59 (October 3, 1960): 88-91.

10615. Harrison, Selig S. "Kennedy as President." *New Republic* 142 (June 27, 1960): 9-15.

10616. Hudson, W. Gail. "The Role of Humor in John F. Kennedy's 1960 Presidential Campaign." Ph.D. dissertation, Southern Illinois University, 1979.

10617. Katz, Elihu, and Jacob J. Feldman. "The Kennedy-Nixon Debates: A Survey of Surveys." In *Public Opinion and Politics*, edited by William J. Crotty, 409-431. New York: Holt, Rinehart and Winston, 1970.

10618. Katz, Elihu, and Jacob J. Feldman. "Who Won the Kennedy-Nixon Debates?" In *Speech Communication*, edited by Howard Martin and Kenneth Andersen, 297-311. Boston: Allyn and Bacon, 1968.

10619. Kaufer, David S. "The Ironist and Hypocrite as Presidential Symbols: A Nixon-Kennedy Analog." *Communication Quarterly* 27 (Fall 1979): 20-26.

10620. Kemper, Deane A. "John F. Kennedy before the Greater Houston Ministerial Association, September 12, 1960: The Religious Issue." Ph.D. dissertation, Michigan State University, 1968.

10621. "The Kennedys: A Family Political Machine." *Look* 24 (July 19, 1960): 43-46.

10622. Levin, Murray B. *Kennedy Campaigning*. Boston: Beacon Press, 1966.

10623. Lisle, Teddy D. "The Canonical Impediment: John F. Kennedy and the Religious Issue during the 1960 Presidential Campaign." Ph.D. dissertation, University of Kentucky, 1982.

10624. Martin, Ralph G., and Ed Plaut. *Front Runner, Dark Horse*. Garden City, NY: Doubleday, 1960.

10625. Maurois, Andre. *From the New Freedom to the New Frontier*. New York: McKay, 1963.

10626. Miller, Helen. "A Catholic for President?" *New Republic* 137 (November 18, 1957): 10-13; (November 25, 1957): 10-13; (December 2, 1957): 10-12.

10627. Mullen, James J. "Newspaper Advertising in the Kennedy-Nixon Campaign." *Journalism Quarterly* 40 (Winter 1963): 3-11.

10628. Phillips, Cabell. "How to Be a Presidential Candidate." *New York Times Magazine* 107 (July 13, 1958): 11, 52, 54.

10629. Polisky, Jerome B. "The Kennedy-Nixon Debates: A Study in Political Persuasion." Ph.D. dissertation, University of Wisconsin, 1965.

10630. Powell, James G. "An Analytical and Comparative Study of the Persuasion of Kennedy and Nixon in the 1960 Campaign." Ph.D. dissertation, University of Wisconsin, 1963.

10631. Powell, James G. "Reactions to John F. Kennedy's Delivery Skills during the 1960 Campaign." *Western Speech* 32 (Winter 1968): 59-68.

10632. Rosenthal, Paul I. "Ethos in the Presidential Campaign of 1960: A Study of the Basic Persuasive Process of the Kennedy-Nixon Debates." Ph.D. dissertation, University of California, Los Angeles, 1963.

10633. Samovar, Larry A. "Ambiguity and Unequivocation in the Kennedy-Nixon Television Debates." *Quarterly Journal of Speech* 48 (October 1962): 277-274.

10634. Samovar, Larry A. "Ambiguity and Unequivocation in the Kennedy-Nixon Television Debates: A Rhetorical Analysis." *Western Speech* 29 (Fall 1965): 211-218.

10635. Sather, Lawrence A. "Biography

as Rhetorical Criticism: An Analysis of John F. Kennedy's 1960 Presidential Campaign by Selected Biographers." Ph.D. dissertation, Washington State University, 1974.

10636. Schlesinger, Arthur M., Jr. *Kennedy or Nixon: Does It Make Any Difference?* New York: Macmillan, 1960.

10637. Sherman, Roger N. "An Objective Analysis of Language Choice in the First Nixon-Kennedy Debate." Ph.D. dissertation, University of Michigan, 1965.

10638. Silvestri, Vito N. "John F. Kennedy: His Speaking in the Wisconsin and West Virginia Primaries 1960." Ph.D. dissertation, Indiana University, 1966.

10639. Sink, George T. "John F. Kennedy's Road to the White House." Master's thesis, Western Michigan University, 1970.

10640. Smith, William D. "Alfred E. Smith and John F. Kennedy: The Religious Issue during the Presidential Campaigns of 1928 and 1960." Ph.D. dissertation, Southern Illinois University, 1964.

10641. Vanocur, Sander. "Humphrey vs. Kennedy: High Stakes in Wisconsin." *Reporter* 22 (March 17, 1960): 28-30.

10642. Wolfe, James S. "The Religious Issue Revisited: Presbyterian Responses to Kennedy's Presidential Campaign." *Journal of Presbyterian History* 59 (Spring 1979): 1-18.

Foreign Affairs

10643. Alsop, Joseph. "The Most Important Decision in U.S. History, and How the President Is Facing It." *Saturday Review* 44 (August 5, 1961): 7-9, 27-28.

10644. Aron, Raymond. "DeGaulle and Kennedy: The Nuclear Debate." *Atlantic Monthly* 210 (August 1962): 33-38.

10645. Attwood, William. "A Preview of Kennedy's Foreign Policy." *Look* 25 (January 31, 1961): 27-29.

10646. Bagnall, Joseph A. *President John F. Kennedy, A Grand and Global Alliance: The Summons to World Peace through World Law.* Minneapolis, MN: Burgess, 1968.

10647. Barbarash, Ernest E., comp. *John F. Kennedy on Israel, Zionism, and Jewish Issues.* New York: Herzl, 1965.

10648. Beck, Kent M. "The Kennedy Image: Politics, Camelot, and Vietnam." *Wisconsin Magazine of History* 58 (Autumn 1974): 45-55.

10649. Biglow, Frank W. "The Alliance for Progress, the OAS, and the Kennedy Administration: A Decision-Making Study of United States Foreign Policy Objectives in Latin America, 1960-1963." Ph.D. dissertation, University of California, Berkeley, 1972.

10650. Bowles, Chester. "Foreign Policy under President Kennedy." *Progressive Magazine* 26 (April 1962): 10-13.

10651. Brandon, Donald. "Kennedy's Record in Foreign Affairs." *Catholic World* 195 (July 1962): 219-227.

10652. Bundy, McGeorge. "The Presidency and Peace." *Foreign Affairs* 42 (April 1964): 353-366.

10653. Bunnell, Frederick P. "The Kennedy Initiatives in Indonesia, 1962-1963." Ph.D. dissertation, Cornell University, 1969.

10654. Catudal, Honore M. *Kennedy and the Berlin Wall Crisis.* Ardsley-on-Hudson, NY: Transnational Publishers, 1980.

10655. Chai, Jae H. "Presidential Control of the Foreign Policy Bureaucracy: The Kennedy Case." *Presidential Studies Quarterly* 8 (Fall 1978): 391-403.

10656. Colombo, Claudius M. "Chinese

Communist Perceptions of the Foreign Policy of John F. Kennedy, 1961-1963." Ph.D. dissertation, New York University, 1982.

10657. Costigliola, Frank. "The Failed Design: Kennedy, De Gaulle, and the Struggle for Europe." *Diplomatic History* 8 (Summer 1984): 227-252.

10658. Cousins, Norman. *The Improbable Triumvirate: John F. Kennedy — Pope John — Nikita Khrushchev.* New York: Norton, 1972.

10659. Coyle, Beth F. "The Requirements of National Security Policy as Conceived by the Kennedy Administration." Master's thesis, American University, 1968.

10660. Craig, G. M. "John Fitzgerald Kennedy." *International Journal* 19 (Winter 1963-1964): 1-6.

10661. "The Crisis in Foreign Affairs." *American Federationist* 67 (November 1960): 7-11.

10662. Curtis, Thomas B., and John R. Vastine. *The Kennedy Round and the Future of American Trade.* New York: Praeger, 1972.

10663. Draper, Theodore. "Vietnam: From Kennedy to Johnson." In *Twentieth Century America,* edited by Barton J. Bernstein and Allen J. Matusow, 477-499. New York: Harcourt, Brace, 1969.

10664. Drischler, Alvin P. "The Sources of the American Hegemonic Strategy: A Comparison of Foreign Policies under Presidents Nixon and Kennedy." Ph.D. dissertation, Princeton University, 1973.

10665. Eckhardt, William, and Ralph K. White. "A Test of the Mirror-Image Hypothesis: Kennedy and Khrushchev." *Journal of Conflict Resolution* 11 (September 1967): 325-332.

10666. Etzioni, Amitai. "JFK's Russian Experiment." *Psychology Today* 3 (December 1969): 42-45, 62-63.

10667. Etzioni, Amitai. "The Kennedy Experiment." *Western Political Quarterly* 20 (June 1967): 361-380.

10668. Evans, John W. *Kennedy Round in American Trade Policy: The Twilight of the GATT?* Cambridge, MA: Harvard University Press, 1971.

10669. Firestone, Bernard J. "Presidents and Detente: A Case Study of John F. Kennedy and the Soviet Union, 1963." Ph.D. dissertation, City University of New York, 1979.

10670. Firestone, Bernard J. *The Quest for Nuclear Stability: John F. Kennedy and the Soviet Union.* Westport, CT: Greenwood Press, 1982.

10671. "For a Year's Foreign Policy: 'A' for JFK." *Life* 52 (April 13, 1962): 4.

10672. Galloway, John, ed. *The Kennedys and Vietnam.* New York: Facts on File, 1971.

10673. Gazit, Mordechai. *President Kennedy's Policy toward the Arab States and Israel: Analysis and Documents.* Tel Aviv: Shiloah Center for Middle Eastern and African Studies, Tel Aviv University, 1982.

10674. Ghent, Jocelyn. "Did He Fall or Was He Pushed? The Kennedy Administration and the Collapse of the Diefenbaker Government." *International History Review* 1 (1979): 246-270.

10675. Harrington, Joseph F. "Romanian-American Relations during the Kennedy Administration." *East European Quarterly* 18 (June 1984): 215-236.

10676. Hartley, Anthony. "John Kennedy's Foreign Policy." *Foreign Policy* 14 (Fall 1971): 77-87.

10677. Heeney, A. D. P. "Washington under Two Presidents: 1955-57: 1959-

62." *International Journal* 22 (Summer 1967): 500-511.

10678. Hennessy, Maurice N. *I'll Come Back in the Springtime: John F. Kennedy and the Irish.* New York: Ives Washington, 1966.

10679. Hill, Kenneth L. "President Kennedy and the Neutralization of Laos." *Review of Politics* 31 (July 1969): 353-369.

10680. Hilsman, Roger. *To Move a Nation: The Politics of Foreign Policy in the Administration of John F. Kennedy.* Garden City, NY: Doubleday, 1967.

10681. Hurley, Robert M. "President John F. Kennedy and Vietnam, 1961-1963." Ph.D. dissertation, University of Hawaii, 1970.

10682. Kalb, Madeleine, and Marvin Kalb. "How Mr. Kennedy Looks to the Russians." *Report* 23 (December 8, 1960): 33-34, 51-52.

10683. Kern, Montague. "The Presidency and the Press: John F. Kennedy's Foreign Policy Crises and the Politics of Newspaper Coverage." Ph.D. dissertation, Johns Hopkins University, 1980.

10684. Kraft, Joseph. *The Grand Design: From Common Market to Atlantic Partnership.* New York: Harper and Row, 1962.

10685. Kuter, Laurence S. "JFK and LBJ Consider Aerospace Defense." *Aerospace Historian* 25 (Spring 1978): 1-4.

10686. Leacock, Ruth. "JFK, Business, and Brazil." *Hispanic American Historical Review* 59 (November 1979): 636-673.

10687. McSherry, James E. *Khrushchev and Kennedy in Retrospect.* Arlington, VA: Open Door Press, 1972.

10688. Mahajani, Usha. "Kennedy and the Strategy of Aid: The Clay Report and After." *Western Political Quarterly* 18 (September 1965): 656-668.

10689. Mahajani, Usha. "President Kennedy and United States Policy in Laos, 1961-1963." *Journal of Southeast Asian Studies* 2 (Spring 1971): 87-99.

10690. Maher, Theodore J. "The Kennedy and Johnson Responses to Latin-American Coups d'Etat." *World Affairs* 131 (October/November/December 1968): 184-197.

10691. Mahoney, Richard D. *J. F. K. Ordeal in Africa.* New York: Oxford University Press, 1983.

10692. Mahoney, Richard D. "The Kennedy Policy in the Congo, 1961-1963." Ph.D. dissertation, Johns Hopkins University, 1980.

10693. Marshall, Robert A., ed. *Kennedy and Africa.* New York: Pyramid, 1967.

10694. Muravchik, Joshua. "Kennedy's Foreign Policy: What the Record Shows." *Commentary* 68 (December 1979): 31-43.

10695. Nixon, Richard M. "Cuba, Castro, and John F. Kennedy: Some Reflections on U.S. Foreign Policy." *Reader's Digest* 85 (November 1964): 283-300.

10696. Noer, Thomas J. "The New Frontier and African Neutralism: Kennedy, Nkrumah, On the Volta River Project." *Diplomatic History* 8 (Winter 1984): 61-80.

10697. Norwood, Bernard. "The Kennedy Round: A Try at Linear Trade Negotiations." *Journal of Law and Economics* 12 (October 1969): 297-319.

10698. Nunnerly, David. *President Kennedy and Britain.* New York: St. Martin's Press, 1972.

10699. Nurse, Ronald J. "Critic of Colonialism: JFK and Algerian Independence." *Historian* 39 (February 1977): 307-326.

10700. Orr, David W. "Innovation and Foreign Policy: The Kennedy Years, 1961-

1963." Ph.D. dissertation, University of Pennsylvania, 1973.

10701. Paranjoti, Violet. *President John F. Kennedy: Creative Statesmanship in the Field of Foreign Affairs.* New York: Carlton Press, 1965.

10702. Paterson, Thomas G. "Bearing the Burden: A Critical Look at JFK's Foreign Policy." *Virginia Quarterly Review* 54 (Spring 1978): 193-212.

10703. Patrick, Richard. "Presidential Leadership in Foreign Affairs Reexamined: Kennedy and Laos without Radical Revisionism." *World Affairs* 140 (Winter 1978): 245-258.

10704. Pelz, Stephen E. "John F. Kennedy's 1961 Vietnam War Decisions." *Journal of Strategic Studies* 4 (December 1981): 356-385.

10705. Pelz, Stephen E. " 'When Do I Have Time to Think?' John F. Kennedy, Roger Hilsman, and the Laotian Crisis of 1962." *Diplomatic History* 3 (Spring 1979): 215-229.

10706. Peretz, Don. "The United States, the Arabs, and Israel: Peace Efforts of Kennedy, Johnson, and Nixon." *Annals of the American Academy of Political and Social Sciences* 401 (May 1972): 116-125.

10707. Preeg, Ernest H. *Traders and Diplomats: An Analysis of the Kennedy Round of Negotiations under the General Agreement on Tariffs and Trade.* Washington, DC: Brookings Institution, 1970.

10708. Robinson, Edgar E., et al. *Powers of the President in Foreign Affairs, 1945-1965: Harry S. Truman, Dwight D. Eisenhower, John F. Kennedy, Lyndon B. Johnson.* San Francisco: Commonwealth Club of California, 1966.

10709. Rose, Richard. *People and Politics: Observations across the Atlantic.* New York: Basic Books, 1970.

10710. Rostow, Walt W. *Eisenhower, Kennedy, and Foreign Affairs.* Austin: University of Texas Press, 1984.

10711. Rostow, Walt W. "The 'New Look' in U.S. World Policy: Advice President Kennedy Is Getting." *U.S. News & World Report* 50 (February 13, 1961): 75-81.

10712. Rust, William J., et al. *Kennedy in Vietnam: American Vietnam Policy, 1960-1963.* New York: Scribner's, 1985.

10713. Seaborg, Glenn T., and Benjamin S. Loeb. *Kennedy, Khrushchev, and the Test Ban.* Berkeley: University of California Press, 1981.

10714. Sheerin, John B. "President Kennedy's Foreign Policy." *Catholic World* 192 (February 1961): 260-263.

10715. Singh, Ram, and M. K. Haldar, eds. *Kennedy through Indian Eyes.* New York: International Publishing Services, 1964.

10716. Smith, Jeane E. "Kennedy and Defense: The Formative Years." *Queen's Quarterly* 74 (Winter 1967): 627-647.

10717. Snell, David. "America's New President Deals with the Tough Guys of Europe, De Gaulle and Khrushchev." *Life* 50 (June 9, 1961): 42-49.

10718. Stuart, Douglas, and Harvey Starr. "The 'Inherent Bad Faith Model' Reconsidered: Dulles, Kennedy, and Kissinger." *Political Psychology* 3 (Fall/Winter 1981-1982): 1-33.

10719. Toole, Morton E. "The Kennedy Corollary to the Monroe Doctrine." Master's thesis, American University, 1966.

10720. Van Cleve, John V. "The Latin American Policy of President Kennedy: A Reexamination: Case Peru." *Inter-American Economic Affairs* 30 (Spring 1977): 29-44.

10721. Walton, Richard J. *Cold War and*

Counterrevolution: The Foreign Policy of John F. Kennedy. Baltimore, MA: Penguin, 1972.

10722. Weidner, Edward W. *Prelude to Reorganization: The Kennedy Foreign Aid Message of 1961*. Syracuse, NY: Inter-University Case Program, 1969.

10723. Whiteside, Henry O. "Kennedy and the Kremlin: Soviet-American Relations, 1961-1963." Ed.D. dissertation, Stanford University, 1968.

10724. Wood Printing Works. *A Memory of John Fitzgerald Kennedy: Visit to Ireland 26th-29th June, 1963*. Dublin: Wood Printing Works, 1963.

10725. Wrone, James G. "Effective Rates of Protection in the United States: An Analysis of the Kennedy Round Tariff Reductions." Ph.D. dissertation, University of Illinois, 1970.

10726. Wszelaki, Jan H., ed. *John F. Kennedy and Poland: Selections of Documents, 1948-1963*. New York: Polish Institute of Arts and Sciences in America, 1964.

Press

10727. Bingham, Worth, and Ward S. Just. "President and the Press." *Reporter* 26 (April 12, 1962): 18-23.

10728. Boehm, Randolph, and R. Dale Grinder, comps. *A Guide to Appointment Book of President Kennedy (1961-1963) and President Kennedy and the Press (1961-1963)*. Edited by Paul Kesaris. Frederick, MD: University Publications of America, 1982.

10729. Cater, Douglass. "Mr. Kennedy's Open Door Policy." *Reporter* 24 (April 27, 1961): 33-35.

10730. Chase, Harold W., and Allen H. Lerman, eds. *Kennedy and the Press: The News Conferences*. New York: Crowell, 1965.

10731. Johnson, George W. *Kennedy Presidential Press Conferences*. Vol. 1. Crugers, NY: E. M. Coleman Enterprises, 1978.

10732. Johnson, Miles B. *Government Secrecy Controversy: A Dispute Involving the Government and the Press in the Eisenhower, Kennedy, and Johnson Administrations*. New York: Vantage Press, 1967.

10733. Kessel, John H. "Mr. Kennedy and the Manufacture of News." *Parliamentary Affairs* 16 (Summer 1963): 293-301.

10734. Knebel, Fletcher. "Kennedy vs. the Press." *Look* 26 (August 28, 1962): 17-21.

10735. Krock, Arthur. "Mr. Kennedy's Management of the News." *Fortune* 67 (March 1963): 82, 201-202.

10736. Kyes, Elizabeth A. "President Kennedy's Press Conferences as 'Shapers' of the News." Ph.D. dissertation, University of Iowa, 1968.

10737. Ostman, Ronald E., William Babcock, and J. Cecilia Fallert. "Relation of Questions and Answers in Kennedy's Press Conferences." *Journalism Quarterly* 58 (Winter 1981): 575-581.

10738. Pollard, James E. "The Kennedy Administration and the Press." *Journalism Quarterly* 41 (Winter 1964): 3-14.

10739. Sanders, Luther W. "A Content Analysis of President Kennedy's First Six Press Conferences." *Journalism Quarterly* 42 (Winter 1965): 114-115.

10740. Sharp, Harry W., Jr. "The Kennedy News Conference." Ph.D. dissertation, Purdue University, 1967.

10741. White, William S. "Kennedy's Seven Rules for Handling the Press." *Harper's Magazine* 222 (April 1961): 92-97.

Writings

10742. Adler, William, ed. *The Complete Kennedy Wit*. New York: Citadel Press, 1967.

10743. Adler, William, ed. *John F. Kennedy and the Young People of America*. New York: McKay, 1965.

10744. Adler, William, ed. *The Kennedy Wit*. New York: Citadel Press, 1964.

10745. Adler, William, ed. *More Kennedy Wit*. New York: Bantam Books, 1965.

10746. David, Jay, ed. *The Kennedy Reader*. Indianapolis, IN: Bobbs-Merrill, 1967.

10747. Gardner, Gerald C., ed. *The Quotable Mr. Kennedy*. New York: Abelard-Schuman, 1962.

10748. Gardner, Gerald C., ed. *The Shining Moments: The Words and Moods of John F. Kennedy*. New York: Pocket Books, 1964.

10749. Goldman, Alex J., ed. *The Quotable Kennedy*. New York: Citadel Press, 1965.

10750. Kennedy, John F. " 'An Address to the United Nations, September 25, 1961.' " In *The United States and the United Nations*, edited by Franz B. Gross, 277-288. Norman: University of Oklahoma Press, 1964.

10751. Kennedy, John F. "Algerian Crisis: A New Phase?" *America* 98 (October 5, 1957): 15-17.

10752. Kennedy, John F. "America's Stake in Vietnam: Address, June 1, 1956." *Vital Speeches* 22 (August 1, 1956): 617-619.

10753. Kennedy, John F. "Challenge of Political Courage." *New York Times Magazine* 105 (December 18, 1955): 13, 32, 34, 36.

10754. Kennedy, John F. "Congressional Lobbies: A Chronic Problem Re-examined." *Georgetown Law Journal* 45 (Summer 1957): 535-567.

10755. Kennedy, John F. "The Crisis in Foreign Affairs." *American Federationist* 67 (November 1960): 7-11.

10756. Kennedy, John F. "A Democrat Looks at Foreign Policy." *Foreign Affairs* 36 (October 1957): 44-59.

10757. Kennedy, John F. *Every Citizen Holds Office*. Washington, DC: Citizenship Committee, National Education Association, 1964.

10758. Kennedy, John F. "Fate of the Nation." *National Education Journal* 47 (January 1958): 10-11.

10759. Kennedy, John F. *The First Book Edition of John F. Kennedy's Inaugural Address*. New York: Franklin Watts, 1965.

10760. Kennedy, John F. "Floor Beneath Wages Is Gone." *New Republic* 128 (July 20, 1953): 14-15.

10761. Kennedy, John F. *Good Fences Make Good Neighbors Convocation (Address), October 8, 1957, the University of New Brunswick*. Fredericton: University of New Brunswick Press, 1960.

10762. Kennedy, John F. "Great Day in American History." *Collier's* 136 (November 25, 1955): 40-43, 46.

10763. Kennedy, John F. "If India Fails." *Progressive Magazine* 22 (January 1958): 8-11.

10764. Kennedy, John F. *A John F. Kennedy Memorial Miniature*. New York: Random House, 1966.

10765. Kennedy, John F. *John F. Kennedy Speaks: The Texts of Eleven Major Speeches by the Late President Together with a Selection of Photographs*. Manila, Philippines: Regional Service Center, 1964.

10766. Kennedy, John F. *John Fitzgerald Kennedy: A Compilation of Statements and Speeches Made during His Service in the United States Senate and House of Representatives.* Washington, DC: U.S. Government Printing Office, 1964.

10767. Kennedy, John F. *Joint Radio-Television Broadcasts, 1960.* New York: CBS News, 1960.

10768. Kennedy, John F. "Kennedy and Humphrey Answer Five Key Questions." *New Leader* 43 (March 28, 1960): 3-7.

10769. Kennedy, John F. *Kennedy and the Press.* New York: Crowell, 1965.

10770. Kennedy, John F. *The Kennedy Presidential Press Conferences.* New York: E. M. Coleman Enterprises, 1978.

10771. Kennedy, John F. "Labor Racketeers and Political Pressure." *Look* 23 (May 12, 1959): 17-21.

10772. Kennedy, John F. "The Lesson of Cuba." *Department of State Bulletin* 44 (May 8, 1961): 659-661.

10773. Kennedy, John F. *Let the Lady Hold up Her Head: Reflections on American Immigration Policy.* New York: American Jewish Committee, 1957.

10774. Kennedy, John F. *A Nation of Immigrants.* Rev. ed. New York: Harper and Row, 1964.

10775. Kennedy, John F. "New England and the South." *Atlantic Monthly* 193 (January 1954): 32-36.

10776. Kennedy, John F. "New Frontier: An Exclusive Interview: Interrogator, Patrick Donaghy." *Catholic World* 192 (November 1960): 80-86.

10777. Kennedy, John F. "President Kennedy on History." *American Heritage* 15 (February 1964): 2-6.

10778. Kennedy, John F. *President Kennedy Speaks.* Washington, DC: United States Information Agency, 1961.

10779. Kennedy, John F. "President's Message on the Regulatory Agencies." *Public Utilities Fortnightly* 67 (May 1961): 693-702.

10780. Kennedy, John F. "Profession of Politics: Address, June 3, 1957." *Vital Speeches* 23 (August 15, 1957): 657-659.

10781. Kennedy, John F. *Profiles in Courage.* New York: Harper and Row, 1956.

10782. Kennedy, John F. "Ross of Kansas: The Man Who Saved a President." *Harper's* 211 (December 1955): 40-44.

10783. Kennedy, John F. *Sam Houston and the Senate.* Austin, TX: Pemberton Press, 1970.

10784. Kennedy, John F. *A Selection of Speeches and Statements on the United Nations by President John F. Kennedy.* New York: American Association for the United Nations, 1963.

10785. Kennedy, John F. "Shame of the States." *New York Times Magazine* 107 (May 18, 1958): 12, 37-38, 40.

10786. Kennedy, John F. "Social Security: Constructive If Not Bold." *New Republic* 130 (February 8, 1954): 14-15.

10787. Kennedy, John F. "Special Message on Conflicts of Interest, Submitted to Congress, April 27, 1961." In *The Political Vocation,* edited by Paul Tillett, 443-453. New York: Basic Books, 1965.

10788. Kennedy, John F. *The Strategy for Peace.* Edited by Alan Nevins. New York: Harper and Brothers, 1960.

10789. Kennedy, John F. "Take the Academics out of Politics." *Saturday Evening Post* 228 (June 2, 1956): 36-37, 46, 49-50.

10790. Kennedy, John F. "To Keep the Lobbyist within Bounds." *New York Times Magazine* 105 (February 19, 1956): 11, 40, 42, 44, 47.

10791. Kennedy, John F. *To Turn the*

Tide: A Selection from President Kennedy's Public Statements from His Election through the 1961 Adjournment of Congress, Setting Forth the Goals of His First Legislative Year. Edited by John W. Gardner. New York: Harper and Row, 1962.

10792. Kennedy, John F. "War in Indochina." *Vital Speeches* 20 (May 1, 1954): 418-424.

10793. Kennedy, John F. "What Should the U.S. Do in Indochina?" *Foreign Policy Bulletin* 33 (May 15, 1954): 4-6.

10794. Kennedy, John F. "What's Wrong with Social Security?" *American Magazine* 156 (October 1953): 19, 109-112.

10795. Kennedy, John F. "When the Executive Fails to Lead." *Reporter* 19 (September 18, 1958): 14-17.

10796. Kennedy, John F. *Why England Slept.* New York: Funk, 1940.

10797. Kennedy, John F. *Words to Remember.* Kansas City, MO: Hallmark, 1967.

10798. Kennedy, John F., Lyndon B. Johnson, Hubert H. Humphrey, and Thomas H. Kuchel. *Moral Crisis: The Case for Civil Rights.* Minnesota, MN: Gilbert Publishing Co., 1964.

10799. Kennedy, John F., ed. *As We Remember Joe.* Cambridge, MA: University Press, 1945.

10800. Kennedy, John F., et al. *Creative America.* New York: Ridge Press, 1964.

10801. Klein, Arthur L., ed. *Spoken Art Treasury of John F. Kennedy Addresses.* New Rochelle, NY: Spoken Arts, 1972.

10802. Lewis, Edward, and Richard Rhodes. *John F. Kennedy: Words to Remember.* New York: Hallmark, 1967.

10803. Meyersohn, Maxwell, comp. *Memorable Quotations of John F. Kennedy.* New York: Crowell, 1965.

10804. Peacock Press. *A Kennedy Keepsake — John F. Kennedy, 1917-1963.* Berkeley, CA: Peacock Press, 1964.

10805. Pedersen, Wesley, and Bernard Quint, eds. *Legacy of a President: The Memorable Words of John Fitzgerald Kennedy.* Washington, DC: U.S. Information Agency, 1964.

10806. Schneider, Nicholas A., comp. *Religious Views of John F. Kennedy in His Own Words.* St. Louis, MO: B. Herder, 1965.

10807. Schneider, Nicholas A., and Nathalie S. Rockhill, comps. *John F. Kennedy Talks to Young People.* New York: Hawthorn, 1968.

10808. Schwarz, Urs, ed. *John F. Kennedy, 1917-1963.* London: Hamlyn, 1964.

10809. Settel, Trudy S., ed. *The Faith of JFK.* New York: Dutton, 1965.

10810. Settel, Trudy S., ed. *The Wisdom of JFK.* New York: Dutton, 1965.

10811. Wood, James P. *The Life and Words of John F. Kennedy.* Elm Grove, WI: Country Beautiful Foundation, 1964.

Lyndon B. Johnson

Biographies

10812. Auchincloss, Kenneth. "Lyndon B. Johnson, 1908-1973." *Newsweek* 85 (February 5, 1973): 31-36.

10813. Bard, Bernard. *LBJ: The Picture Story of Lyndon Baines Johnson.* New York: Lion Press, 1966.

10814. Cater, Douglass. "Hard-Won Destiny of Lyndon Johnson." *Reporter* 29 (December 19, 1963): 17-19.

10815. Cormier, Frank. *LBJ: The Way He Was.* Garden City, NY: Doubleday, 1977.

10816. Elliott, Bruce. *The Johnson Story.* New York: Macfadden-Bartell, 1964.

10817. Evans, Rowland, Jr., and Robert D. Novak. *Lyndon B. Johnson: The Exercise of Power: A Political Biography.* New York: Signet Books, 1968.

10818. Frantz, Joe B. *LBJ: Images of a Vibrant Life.* Austin, TX: Friends of the LBJ Library, 1973.

10819. Frantz, Joe B. "Opening a Curtain: The Metamorphosis of Lyndon B. Johnson." *Journal of Southern History* 45 (February 1979): 3-26.

10820. Frantz, Joe B., comp. *37 Years of Public Service: The Honorable Lyndon B. Johnson.* Austin, TX: Shoal Creek Publishers, 1974.

10821. Goldman, Eric F. *The Tragedy of Lyndon Johnson: A Historian's Interpretation.* New York: Knopf, 1969.

10822. Halberstam, David. "Lyndon." *Esquire* 78 (August 1972): 73-88.

10823. Harwood, Richard, and Haynes Johnson. *Lyndon: A Washington Post Pictorial Biography.* New York: Praeger, 1973.

10824. Kearns, Doris. "The Art of Biography: The Power and Pathos of LBJ." *New Republic* 180 (March 3, 1979): 27-29.

10825. Kearns, Doris. *Lyndon Johnson and the American Dream.* New York: Harper and Row, 1976.

10826. Kearns, Doris. "Who Was Lyndon Baines Johnson? Part I: The Man Who Would Be Loved." *Atlantic Monthly* 237 (May 1976): 33-50.

10827. Kearns, Doris. "Who Was Lyndon Baines Johnson? Part II: The Great Society, The Bitter End." *Atlantic Monthly* 237 (June 1976): 65-90.

10828. King, Larry L. "My Hero: LBJ." *Harper's Magazine* 233 (October 1966): 51-61.

10829. Kluckhohn, Frank L. *The Inside on LBJ.* Derby, CT: Monarch Books, 1964.

10830. "Lyndon Johnson: 1908-1973."

Time 101 (February 5, 1973): 29-33.

10831. Miller, Merle. *Lyndon Johnson: An Oral Biography*. New York: Putnam, 1980.

10832. Mooney, Booth. *LBJ: An Irreverent Chronicle*. New York: Crowell, 1976.

10833. Mooney, Booth. *The Lyndon Johnson Story*. Rev. ed. New York: Farrar, Straus and Cudahy, 1964.

10834. Newlon, Clarke. *L. B. J.: The Man from Johnson City*. New York: Dodd, Mead, 1964.

10835. Olds, Helen. *Lyndon Baines Johnson*. New York: Putnam, 1965.

10836. Podell, Jack, ed. *The Johnson Story*. New York: Macfadden-Bartell, 1964.

10837. Provence, Harry. *Lyndon B. Johnson: A Biography*. New York: Fleet, 1964.

10838. Reedy, George E. *Lyndon B. Johnson: A Memoir*. Kansas City, MO: Andrews and McMeel, 1982.

10839. Rulon, Philip R. *The Compassionate Samaritan: The Life of Lyndon Baines Johnson*. Chicago: Nelson-Hall, 1981.

10840. Singer, Kurt, and Jane Sherrod. *Lyndon Baines Johnson, Man of Reason*. Minneapolis, MN: T. S. Denison, 1964.

10841. Steinberg, Alfred. *Sam Johnson's Boy: A Close-up of the President from Texas*. New York: Macmillan, 1968.

10842. Valenti, Jack. *A Very Human President*. New York: Norton, 1975.

10843. Wheeler, Keith, and William Lambert. "The Man Who Is the President." *Life* 57 (August 14, 1964): 25-73; (August 21, 1964): 62-72.

10844. White, William S. *The Professional: Lyndon B. Johnson*. Boston: Houghton Mifflin, 1964.

10845. Whitney, David C. *Let's Find Out about Lyndon Baines Johnson*. New York: Franklin Watts, 1967.

10846. Williams, T. Harry. "Lyndon Johnson and the Art of Biography." *Among Friends of LBJ* (July 15, 1978): 4-5.

10847. Zeiger, Henry A. *Lyndon B. Johnson: Man and President*. New York: Popular Library, 1963.

Private Life

10848. Adler, William, ed. *The Johnson Humor*. New York: Simon and Schuster, 1965.

10849. Bearss, Edwin C. *Lyndon B. Johnson National Historic Site*. Washington, DC: U.S. National Park Service, 1971.

10850. Benson, Judith, ed. "Remembering LBJ." *Texas Monthly* 4 (January 1976): 86-88.

10851. Carpenter, Liz. *Ruffles and Flourishes: The Warm and Tender Story of a Simple Girl Who Found Adventure in the White House*. Garden City, NY: Doubleday, 1970.

10852. Casoni, Jennifer. *Sincerely, Lyndon: The Handwriting of Lyndon Baines Johnson*. Rockville Center, NY: University Autograph, 1984.

10853. Clemens, Cyril. *Mark Twain and Lyndon B. Johnson*. Kirkwood, MO: Mark Twain Journal, 1967.

10854. Dugger, Ronnie. "LBJ: The Hill Country Roots." *Texas Observer* 9 (May 7, 1982): 1, 4-8.

10855. Fallows, James. "Bill Moyers: His Heart Belongs to Daddy." *Washington Monthly* 6 (July 1974): 37-50.

10856. Fredericks, Janet P. "The Educational Views of Lyndon Baines Johnson

Prior to His Presidency." Ph.D. dissertation, Loyola University, 1982.

10857. Gorden, William L., and Robert Bunker. "The Sentimental Side of Mr. Johnson." *Southern Speech Communication Journal* 32 (Autumn 1966): 58-66.

10858. Janos, Leo. "Last Days of LBJ." *Reader's Digest* 103 (September 1973): 191-194.

10859. Janos, Leo. "The Last Days of the President: LBJ in Retirement." *Atlantic Monthly* 232 (July 1973): 35-41.

10860. Johnson, Claudia A. T. "The LBJ Nobody Knew: A Conversation With Lady Bird Johnson." *U.S. News & World Report* 75 (December 24, 1973): 34-38.

10861. Johnson, Claudia A. T. *A White House Diary.* New York: Holt, 1970.

10862. Johnson, Sam H. *My Brother Lyndon.* Chicago: Cowles, 1970.

10863. King, Larry L. "Bringing up Lyndon." *Texas Monthly* 4 (January 1976): 78-85, 107-109.

10864. King, Larry L. "An Epitaph for LBJ." *Harper's Magazine* 236 (April 1968): 14-22.

10865. King, Larry L. "My Hero, LBJ." *Harper's Magazine* 233 (October 1966): 51-61.

10866. Klaw, Barbara. "Lady Bird Johnson Remembers." *American Heritage* 32 (December 1980): 4-17.

10867. Kopkind, Andrew. "LBJ: The Last Roundup." *Ramparts Magazine* 11 (April 1973): 10-12.

10868. Kowert, Art. "LBJ's Boyhood among the German-Americans in Texas." *American-German Review* 34 (August/September 1968): 2-6.

10869. Leighton, Francis S., ed. *The Johnson Wit.* New York: Citadel Press, 1965.

10870. Leighton, Francis S., and Helen P. Baldwin. *They Call Her Lady Bird.* New York: Macfadden-Bartell, 1964.

10871. Long, Stuart. "A Texan Remembers Lyndon." *Nation* 199 (October 19, 1964): 235-239.

10872. McKinney, R. Kay. *LBJ: His Home and Heritage.* San Angelo, TX: Anchor, 1964.

10873. Maguire, Jack R. *A President's Country: A Guide to the LBJ Country of Texas.* Austin, TX: Shoal Creek Publishers, 1973.

10874. Miller, Merle. "Lyndon's Last Years." *New York Times Magazine* 129 (August 3, 1980): 26-29, 40, 44-47.

10875. Montgomery, Ruth. *Mrs. LBJ: An Intimate Portrait of the First Lady.* New York: Holt, Rinehart and Winson, 1964.

10876. Pollack, Jack. "Heart Attack Saved His Life." *Today's Health* 36 (October 1958): 17-19.

10877. Pool, William, Emmie Craddock, and David E. Conrad. *Lyndon Baines Johnson: The Formative Years.* San Marcos: Southwest Texas State College Press, 1965.

10878. Porterfield, Bill. "Farewell to LBJ: A Hill Country Valediction." *Texas Monthly* 1 (May 1973): 37-43.

10879. Porterfield, Bill. *LBJ Country.* Garden City, NY: Doubleday, 1965.

10880. Riley, Philip. "Lyndon B. Johnson: The Long, Tall Texan." *Southwestern Journal of Social Education* 12 (Fall/Winter 1981): 9-12.

10881. Roche, Bruce. "LBJ as a Student Editor." *Quill* 38 (February 1964): 18-19.

10882. Rulon, Philip R. "The Education of Lyndon Baines Johnson." *Presidential Studies Quarterly* 12 (Summer 1982): 400-406.

10883. Schmertz, Mildred F. "In Praise of a Monument to Lyndon B. Johnson." *Architectural Record* 150 (November 1971): 113-120.

10884. Smith, Marie. *The President's Lady.* New York: Random House, 1964.

10885. Thompson, Pat. *Lady Bird's Man.* Los Angeles: Holloway House, 1964.

10886. White, J. Roy. *The Restoration of the Birthplace of President Lyndon B. Johnson.* Austin, TX: n.p., 1965.

10887. Wicker, Tom. "LBJ down on the Farm." *Esquire* 62 (October 1964): 90-93.

Public Career

10888. Alsop, Stewart. "Lyndon Johnson: How Does He Do It?" *Saturday Evening Post* 231 (January 24, 1959): 13-14.

10889. Bagdikian, Ben H. "The New Lyndon Johnson." *Saturday Evening Post* 235 (February 24, 1962): 93-97.

10890. Baker, Leonard. *The Johnson Eclipse: A President's Vice Presidency.* New York: Macmillan, 1966.

10891. Burns, Mary H. "Theoretical Aspects and Applications of Leadership: The Senate Years of Lyndon B. Johnson." Master's thesis, University of Texas, 1971.

10892. Caidin, Martin, and Edward Hymoff. *The Mission.* Philadelphia: Lippincott, 1964.

10893. Caro, Robert A. "The Years of Lyndon Johnson: Longlea." *Atlantic Monthly* 250 (November 1982): 146-154.

10894. Caro, Robert A. "The Years of Lyndon Johnson: Lyndon and Mister Sam." *Atlantic Monthly* 248 (November 1981): 41-63.

10895. Caro, Robert A. "The Years of Lyndon Johnson: The First Campaign." *Atlantic Monthly* 249 (April 1982): 34-42, 75-89.

10896. Caro, Robert A. "The Years of Lyndon Johnson: The Path to Power." *Atlantic Monthly* 248 (October 1981): 38-75.

10897. Caro, Robert A. *The Years of Lyndon Johnson: The Path to Power.* New York: Knopf, 1982.

10898. Caro, Robert A. "The Years of Lyndon Johnson: The Power of Money." *Atlantic Monthly* 250 (October 1982): 50-84.

10899. Cater, Douglass. "Coming to Terms with Lyndon." *Reporter* 22 (July 7, 1960): 16-18.

10900. Cater, Douglass. "Lyndon Johnson, Rising Democratic Star." *Reporter* 8 (January 20, 1953): 34-37.

10901. Cater, Douglass. "Trouble in Lyndon Johnson's Back Yard." *Reporter* 13 (December 1, 1955): 31-35.

10902. Cooper, Jacqueline. "Lyndon Johnson and Civil Rights: The Senate Years." Master's thesis, University of Texas, 1975.

10903. Crawford, Kenneth. "LBJ: Who's That?" *Newsweek* 61 (February 11, 1963): 39.

10904. Davidson, Bill. "Texas Political Powerhouse ... Lyndon Johnson." *Look* 23 (August 4, 1959): 38-46.

10905. Deason, Willard. "On LBJ: An Interview at the American Kennel Club, April 21, 1976." *Purebred Dogs American Kennel Gazette* 88 (September 1976): 28-40.

10906. Dugger, Ronnie. *The Politician: The Life and Times of Lyndon Johnson: The Drive for Power, From the Frontier to Master of the Senate.* New York: Norton, 1982.

10907. Dyer, Stanford P. "Lyndon B.

Johnson and the Politics of Civil Rights, 1935-1960: The Art of Moderate Leadership." Ph.D. dissertation, Texas Agricultural and Mechanical University, 1978.

10908. Dyer, Stanford P., and Merrell A. Knighten. "Discrimination after Death: Lyndon Johnson and Felix Longoria." *Southern Studies* 17 (Winter 1978): 411-426.

10909. Gray, Charles H. "A Scale Analysis of the Voting Records of Senators Kennedy, Johnson, and Goldwater, 1957-1960." *American Political Science Review* 59 (September 1965): 615.

10910. Haley, James E. *A Texan Looks at Lyndon: A Study in Illegitimate Power.* Canyon, TX: Palo Duro Press, 1964.

10911. Hall, Robert N. "Lyndon B. Johnson's Speaking in the 1941 Senate Campaign." *Southern Speech Journal* 30 (Autumn 1964): 15-23.

10912. Hall, Robert N. "Lyndon Johnson's Speech Preparation." *Quarterly Journal of Speech* 51 (April 1965): 168-176.

10913. Hall, Robert N. "A Rhetorical Analysis of Selected Speeches of Senator Lyndon B. Johnson, 1955-1961." Ph.D. dissertation, University of Michigan, 1963.

10914. Harrison, Selig S. "Lyndon Johnson's World." *New Republic* 142 (June 13, 1960): 15-23.

10915. Hendrix, Jerry A. "A Comparative Analysis of Selected Public Addresses by Allan Shivers and Lyndon B. Johnson in the Texas Pre-Convention Campaign of 1956." Master's thesis, University of Oklahoma, 1957.

10916. Huitt, Ralph K. "Democratic Party Leadership in the Senate." *American Political Science Review* 55 (June 1961): 333-344.

10917. Humphreys, Milton E. "LBJ — Senate Majority Leader." Master's thesis, East Texas State University, 1969.

10918. Healy, Paul F. "Frantic Gentleman from Texas." *Saturday Evening Post* 223 (May 19, 1951): 34-36.

10919. Janeway, Eliot. "Johnson of the Watchdog Committee." *New York Times Magazine* 101 (June 17, 1951): 13-15.

10920. Janeway, Michael C. "Lyndon Johnson and the Rise of Conservatism in Texas." Honor's thesis, Harvard University, 1962.

10921. Janeway, Sharon K. "Making of a Senator from Texas — 1948." Master's thesis, Southwest Texas State University, 1970.

10922. "Johnson Biography, Record in Congress, Leadership Reviewed." *Congressional Quarterly Weekly Report* 18 (June 24, 1960): 1090-1099.

10923. "Johnson Biography, Record in Congress, Leadership Reviewed." *Congressional Quarterly Weekly Report* 18 (July 22, 1980): 1286-1295.

10924. "Johnson Biography, Record in Congress, Leadership, Role as Vice-President." *Congressional Quarterly Weekly Report* 22 (September 11, 1964): 2057-2068.

10925. "Johnson Biography, Record in Congress, Leadership, Role as Vice-President." *Congressional Quarterly Weekly Report* 21 (November 29, 1963): 2069-2096.

10926. Johnson, Carolyn M. "A Southern Response to Civil Rights: Lyndon Baines Johnson and Civil Rights Legislation 1956-1960." Master's thesis, University of Houston, 1975.

10927. Just, Ward S. "What Ever Happened to Lyndon Johnson?" *Reporter* 28 (January 17, 1963): 27-31.

10928. Kahl, Mary. *Ballot Box 13: How*

Lyndon Johnson Won His 1948 Senate Race by 87 Contested Votes. Jefferson, NC: McFarland, 1983.

10929. Knebel, Fletcher. "Boston-Austin Axis." *Look* 26 (January 2, 1962): 70-71.

10930. Knippa, Edwin W. "The Early Political Life of Lyndon B. Johnson, 1931-1937." Master's thesis, Southwest Texas State University, 1967.

10931. Lucier, Jim. "Johnson and the Dead Men Who Voted." *American Opinion* 7 (April 1964): 1-9.

10932. McMahon, Patrick. "Knowland and Johnson in '56?" *American Mercury* 79 (October 1954): 39-44.

10933. "Majority Leader's Career, Policies Examined." *Congressional Quarterly Weekly Report* 14 (May 25, 1956): 597-599.

10934. Neuberger, Richard. "Making a Scapegoat of Lyndon Johnson." *New Republic* 133 (July 4, 1955): 9-10.

10935. Partin, James W. "The Texas Senatorial Election of 1941." Master's thesis, Texas Technological College, 1941.

10936. Payne, Alvin N. "A Study of the Persuasive Efforts of Lyndon Baines Johnson in the Southern States in the Presidential Campaign of 1960." Master's thesis, Albilene Christian College, 1968.

10937. Potter, Philip. "How LBJ Got the Nomination for Vice President in 1960." *Reporter* 30 (June 18, 1964): 16-20.

10938. Riccards, Michael P. "Rare Counsel: Kennedy, Johnson, and the Civil Rights Bill of 1963." *Presidential Studies Quarterly* 11 (Summer 1981): 395-398.

10939. Roell, Craig H. "Image and Power: Lyndon B. Johnson and the 1957 Civil Rights Act." Master's thesis, University of Texas, 1980.

10940. Rovere, Richard H. "Letter from Washington: LBJ's Credibility Gap and Public Opinion." *New Yorker* 43 (September 23, 1967): 157-160, 164-168.

10941. Shaffer, Samuel. "Senator Lyndon Johnson ... The Texan Who Is Jolting Washington." *Newsweek* 49 (July 27, 1955): 24-26.

10942. Soloveytchik, George. "Contemporary Profile: Vice-President Lyndon B. Johnson." *Contemporary Review* 203 (May 1963): 223-229.

10943. Stewart, John G. "Two Strategies of Leadership: Johnson and Mansfield." In *Congressional Behavior,* edited by Nelson W. Polsby, 61-92. New York: Random House, 1971.

10944. Sullivan, Austin P., Jr. "Lyndon Johnson and the Senate Majority Leadership." Honor's thesis, Princeton University, 1964.

10945. Welch, June R. *The Texas Senator.* Dallas, TX: GLA Press, 1978.

10946. White, William S. "Two Texans Who Will Run Congress." *New York Times Magazine* 106 (December 30, 1956): 5, 17, 20.

10947. White, William S. "Who Is Lyndon Johnson?" *Harper's Magazine* 216 (March 1958): 53-58.

10948. Wicker, Tom. "Bostonian vs. the Texan." *New York Times Magazine* 110 (October 23, 1960): 19, 114-116.

10949. Wicker, Tom. "LBJ in Search of His New Frontier." *New York Times Magazine* 110 (March 19, 1961): 29, 123-124.

10950. Williams, David. "The Legend of Lyndon Johnson." *Progressive Magazine* 21 (April 1957): 20-21.

10951. Yankelovich, Daniel. "U.S. Voter's Image of Ideal President." *Life* 48 (March 21, 1960): 135.

Presidential Years

General

10952. Alsop, Stewart. "Johnson Takes Over: The Untold Story." *Saturday Evening Post* 237 (February 15, 1964): 17-22.

10953. Amrine, Michael. *This Awesome Challenge: The Hundred Days of Lyndon Johnson.* New York: Putnam, 1964.

10954. Anderson, James E. "Presidential Management of the Bureaucracy and the Johnson Presidency: A Preliminary Exploration." *Congress and the Presidency* 11 (Autumn 1985): 137-164.

10955. Bagdikian, Ben H. "The Era of Johnson Normalcy." *Columbia Journalism Review* 3 (Winter 1965): 10-13.

10956. Bagdikian, Ben H. "Inner Inner Circle around Johnson." *New York Times Magazine* 114 (February 28, 1965): 21, 78, 80, 82, 84.

10957. Bagdikian, Ben H. "JFK to LBJ: Paradoxes of Change." *Columbia Journalism Review* 2 (Winter 1964): 32-36.

10958. Bagdikian, Ben H. "Press Agent — But Still President." *Columbia Journalism Review* 4 (Summer 1965): 10-13.

10959. Bailey, Thomas A. "Johnson and Kennedy: The Two Thousand Days." *New York Times Magazine* 116 (November 6, 1966): 30-1, 134-135, 137, 139-140; (November 27, 1966): 159-160; (December 4, 1966): 22.

10960. Baker, James T. "Lyndon Johnson: America's Oedipus?" *Southern Humanities Review* 8 (Spring 1974): 127-139.

10961. Balfour, Nancy. "President Johnson at Mid-Term." *World Today* 23 (January/December 1967): 216-222.

10962. Banks, Michael. "President Johnson in a Changing World." *British Survey* 26 (1964): 1-12.

10963. Baskin, Darryl B. "The President, the Congress, and the Goldwater Majority." *International Review of History and Political Science* 5 (February 1968): 13-19.

10964. Bell, Jack. *The Johnson Treatment: How Lyndon B. Johnson Took Over the Presidency and Made It His Own.* New York: Harper and Row, 1965.

10965. Bendiner, Robert. *Obstacle Course on Capitol Hill.* New York: McGraw-Hill, 1964.

10966. Berman, Larry. "Johnson and the White House Staff." In *Exploring the Johnson Years*, edited by Robert A. Divine, 187-213. Austin: University of Texas Press, 1981.

10967. Bickel, Alexander M. "Voting the Court Up or Down: Fortas, Johnson, and the Senate." *New Republic* 159 (September 28, 1968): 21-23.

10968. Bishop, James A. *A Day in the Life of President Johnson.* New York: Random House, 1967.

10969. Blum, John M. *The Progressive Presidents: Roosevelt, Wilson, Roosevelt, Johnson.* New York: Norton, 1980.

10970. Boller, Paul F., Jr. "LBJ and the Art of Quotations." *Social Work Review* 51 (Winter 1966): 1-8.

10971. Bornet, Vaughn D. *Presidency of Lyndon B. Johnson.* Lawrence: University Press of Kentucky, 1983.

10972. Borst, Philip W. "President Johnson and the 89th Congress: A Functional Analysis of a System under Stress." Ph.D. dissertation, Claremont Graduate School, 1968.

10973. Brandon, Henry. "White House in Transition: L. B. Johnson's Mystifying Image." *Saturday Review* 49 (June 11, 1966): 10.

10974. Branyan, Robert L., and Lee R. Alton. "Lyndon B. Johnson and the Art of the Possible." *Southwestern Social Science Quarterly* 45 (December 1964): 213-225.

10975. Brinegard, Lou. "A Rhetorical Analysis of the Speaking of Lyndon Baines Johnson." Master's thesis, Baylor University, 1972.

10976. Brinkley, David. "Leading from Strength: LBJ in Action." *Atlantic Monthly* 215 (February 1965): 49-54.

10977. Broder, David S. "The Fallacy of LBJ's Consensus." *Washington Monthly* 3 (December 1971): 7-13.

10978. Brody, Richard A., and Benjamin I. Page. "The Impact of Events on Presidential Popularity: The Johnson and Nixon Administrations." In *Perspectives on the Presidency*, edited by Aaron B. Wildavsky, 136-147. Boston: Little, Brown, 1975.

10979. Brogan, Denis W. "LBJ and the American Intellectuals." *Encounter* 32 (June 1969): 68-77.

10980. Burns, James M. "The Legacy of the 1000 Days." *New York Times Magazine* 113 (December 1, 1963): 21, 118, 120.

10981. Califano, Joseph A., Jr. *A Presidential Nation*. New York: Norton, 1975.

10982. Carson, Gerald. "The Speech That Toppled a President." *American Heritage* 15 (August 1964): 108-111.

10983. Cerny, P. G. "The Mismatched President: LBJ and the USA." *Government and Opposition* 6 (Spring 1971): 253-262.

10984. Chamberlain, John. "Which Way with LBJ?" *National Review* 15 (December 17, 1963): 525-527.

10985. Chase, Harold W. "The Johnson Administration — Judicial Appointments — 1963-1966." *Minnesota Law Review* 52 (1968): 965-999.

10986. Chase, James S. "The Vantage Point." *Arkansas Historical Quarterly* 31 (Winter 1972): 386-388.

10987. Chi, Keon S. "Creative Federalism: A Study of Intergovernmental Relations under the Johnson Administration." Ph.D. dissertation, Claremont Graduate School, 1970.

10988. Christian, George. *The President Steps Down: A Personal Memoir of the Transfer of Power*. New York: Macmillan, 1970.

10989. Cipes, Robert M. "The Wiretap War: Kennedy, Johnson, and the FBI." *New Republic* 155 (December 24, 1966): 16-22.

10990. Claya, Marlene J. "An Analysis of the Seven Major Speeches Delivered by President Lyndon Johnson in the First Sixty Days of His Administration." Master's thesis, Wayne State University, 1964.

10991. Condray, Suzanne E. "Ghostwriting of Select Speeches of Lyndon B. Johnson." Master's thesis, Colorado State University, 1977.

10992. Condray, Suzanne E. "Speechwriting in Rhetorical Criticism: An Extension of Theory as Applied to the Johnson Administration." Ph.D. dissertation, Louisiana State University, Agricultural and Mechanical College, 1980.

10993. Conkin, Paul K. "The Johnson Years: An Essay Review." *Wisconsin Magazine of History* 56 (Autumn 1972): 59-64.

10994. Connelly, Fred M., Jr. "A Rhetorical Analysis of Selected Speeches of Lyndon Baines Johnson on the War in Vietnam." Ph.D. dissertation, Ohio State University, 1967.

10995. Cooke, Alistair. "LBJ." In his *Talk about America*, 90-96. New York: Knopf, 1969.

10996. Craig, G. M. "President Johnson's Victory." *International Journal* 20 (Winter 1964-1965): 79-80.

10997. Cunliffe, Marcus, and Andrew Hacker. "Presidential Politics, 1968." *Commentary* 45 (February 1968): 27-39.

10998. Davie, Michael. "A British Editor's Size-up of President Johnson." *U.S. News & World Report* 61 (August 29, 1966): 40-46.

10999. Davie, Michael. *Lyndon B. Johnson: A Foreign Observer's Viewpoint*. 2d ed. New York: Ballantine Books, 1966.

11000. Davis, Eric L. "Building Coalitions in Congress: Legislative Liaison in the Johnson White House." Ph.D. dissertation, Stanford University, 1978.

11001. Deakin, James. "The Dark Side of LBJ." *Esquire* 68 (August 1967): 45-48, 134-135.

11002. Deakin, James. "How Johnson Sees the World." *War/Peace Report* 7 (January 1967): 3-6.

11003. Deakin, James. *Lyndon Johnson's Credibility Gap*. Washington, DC: Public Affairs Press, 1968.

11004. Degler, Carl N. "Johnson and Kennedy: The Public View." *Reviews in American History* 5 (March 1977): 130-136.

11005. Delson, Jane. "Ethos or 'Image' in Contemporary Political Persuasion with Particular Reference to Lyndon B. Johnson, 1964." Ph.D. dissertation, University of California, Los Angeles, 1967.

11006. Divine, Robert A. "Assessing Lyndon Johnson." *Wilson Quarterly* 6 (Summer 1982): 142-150.

11007. Druks, Herbert, ed. *From Truman through Johnson: A Documentary History*. Vol. 2, *Kennedy and Johnson*. New York: Robert Speller, 1971.

11008. Elzy, Martin I. "Illinois Viewed from the Johnson White House." *Illinois State Historical Society Journal* 74 (Spring 1981): 3-16.

11009. Fairlie, Henry. "Johnson and the Intellectuals." *Commentary* 40 (October 1965): 49-55.

11010. Fallows, James. "Crazies by the Tail: Bay of Pigs, Diem, and Liddy." *Washington Monthly* 6 (September 1974): 50-58.

11011. Fisher, Linda L. "The Presidency and Implementation: A Case Study of the Johnson Administration." Ph.D. dissertation, George Washington University, 1982.

11012. Fixler, Philip E., Jr. "A Content Analysis of American Presidential Rhetoric: An Exploratory Study of Misrepresentative and Deceptive Language in the Major Communications of Presidents Kennedy, Johnson, and Nixon." Ph.D. dissertation, University of Southern California, 1979.

11013. "Flying High and Fast: Lyndon Johnson Is a Changed Man Today." *Business Week* 1809 (May 2, 1964): 21-24.

11014. "43 Top Aides Have Served President Johnson since 1963." *Congressional Quarterly Weekly Report* 26 (October 18, 1968): 2879-2881.

11015. Fowler, Robert H. "AHI Readers Appraise LBJ." *American History Illustrated* 3 (May 1968): 19.

11016. Frady, Marshall. "Cooling Off with LBJ." *Harper's Magazine* 238 (June 1969): 65-72.

11017. Frankel, Max. "Why the Gap between L. B. J. and the Nation: Failure to Communicate." *New York Times Magazine* 126 (January 7, 1968): 37-48.

11018. Frantz, Joe B. "Why Lyndon?" *Western Historical Quarterly* 11 (January 1980): 5-15.

11019. Fritchey, Clayton. "White House

Style-Makers: L. B. Johnson vs. J. F. Kennedy." *Harper's Magazine* 232 (April 1966): 47-49.

11020. Furlow, Barbara. "Portrait of Two Presidents: Nixon and Johnson." *U.S. News & World Report* 67 (July 28, 1969): 52-54.

11021. Galbraith, John K. *The Case for Lyndon Johnson*. Washington, DC: Democratic National Committee, 1964.

11022. Gallois, Pierre. "America's Getting Tough — And It's All to Our Good." *Realities* 180 (November 1965): 33-37.

11023. Gantt, Fred. *The Chief Executive in Texas*. Austin: University of Texas Press, 1964.

11024. Geyelin, Philip. *Lyndon B. Johnson and the World*. New York: Praeger, 1966.

11025. Gimlin, Hoyt. "Credibility Gaps and the Presidency." *Editorial Research Reports* 1 (February 7, 1968): 83-100.

11026. Goetcheus, Vernon M. "Presidential Party Leadership: Relations between President Johnson and House Democrats in the 89th Congress." Ph.D. dissertation, University of Wisconsin, 1967.

11027. Goldman, Eric F. "The White House and the Intellectuals." *Harper's Magazine* 238 (January 1969): 31-45.

11028. Goldman, Sheldon. "Johnson and Nixon Appointees to the Lower Federal Courts: Some Socio-Political Perspectives." *Journal of Politics* 34 (August 1972): 934-942.

11029. Graff, Henry F. "Lyndon B. Johnson: Frustrated Achiever." In *Power and the Presidency,* edited by Philip C. Dolce and George H. Skau, 153-163. New York: Scribner's, 1976.

11030. Graff, Henry F. *The Tuesday Cabinet: Deliberation and Decision on Peace and War under Lyndon B. Johnson.* Englewood Cliffs, NJ: Prentice-Hall, 1970.

11031. "Great Society Bows In: Inauguration of Lyndon B. Johnson Sets Tone of Integration for Nation." *Ebony* 20 (April 1965): 66-68, 70, 72-73.

11032. Greenberg, Daniel S. "LBJ at Princeton: Some Words about Intellectuals and Government." *Science* 152 (May 27, 1966): 1223-1225.

11033. Greenfield, Meg. "LBJ and the Democrats." *Reporter* 34 (June 2, 1966): 8-13.

11034. Greenstein, Fred I. "Popular Images of the President." *American Journal of Psychiatry* 122 (November 1965): 523-529.

11035. Griffin, Robert P. "89th Congress in Perspective: What LBJ Wants, LBJ Gets: Address, November 15, 1965." *Vital Speeches* 32 (December 15, 1965): 140-143.

11036. Guy, William L. "Thoughts on a White House Dinner, January, 1967." *North Dakota History* 36 (Spring 1969): 189-195.

11037. Halberstam, David. *The Best and the Brightest*. New York: Random House, 1972.

11038. Hamilton, Dagmar S. "Johnson's Cabinet Appointments." *Discovery* 4 (December 1979): 12-15.

11039. Harrison, Selig S. "World of Lyndon Johnson." *New Republic* 149 (December 7, 1963): 13-14.

11040. Hart, Roderick P. "Language of the Presidency." *Discovery* 5 (Spring 1981): 4-7.

11041. Haveles, Harry P., Jr. "The Power to Persuade: Presidential Leadership in Congress: Lyndon Johnson and the 89th and 90th Congresses." Honor's thesis, Harvard College, 1976.

11042. Heath, Jim F. *Decade of Disillusionment: The Kennedy-Johnson Years.* Bloomington: Indiana University Press, 1975.

11043. Heinlein, J.C. "The Johnson Staff and National Security Policy." In *Essays on Modern Politics and History,* edited by Han-Kyo Kim, 206-225. Athens: Ohio University Press, 1969.

11044. Helde, Thomas T. "The Kennedy-Johnson Years." *Current History* 57 (July 1969): 31-35.

11045. Heleniak, Roman. "Lyndon Johnson in New Orleans." *Louisiana History* 21 (Summer 1980): 263-275.

11046. Heren, Louis. *No Hail, No Farewell.* New York: Harper and Row, 1970.

11047. Horowitz, Irving L. "Lyndon Baines Johnson and the Rise of Presidential Militarism." *Social Science Quarterly* 53 (September 1972): 395-402.

11048. Huberman, Leo, and Paul M. Sweezey. "The Kennedy-Johnson Boom." In *America in the 1960's: Cultural Authorities in Transition,* edited by Ronald Lora, 131-143. New York: Wiley, 1974.

11049. Huitt, Ralph K. "Lyndon B. Johnson and Senate Leadership." In *The Presidency and the Congress: A Shifting Balance of Power?,* edited by William S. Livingston, 253-264. Austin: Lyndon B. Johnson School of Public Affairs, University of Texas, 1979.

11050. Humphrey, David C. "Tuesday Lunch at the Johnson White House: A Preliminary Assessment." *Diplomatic History* 8 (Winter 1984): 81-101.

11051. Janeway, Michael. "LBJ and the Kennedys." *Atlantic Monthly* 229 (February 1972): 48-58.

11052. Joesten, Joachim. *The Dark Side of Lyndon Baines Johnson.* London: Dawnay, 1968.

11053. Johnson, Ellis A. "On the Proclamation of President Johnson, 23 November 1963." *Social Studies* 55 (April 1964): 127-129.

11054. "Johnson's Stands and Votes on Key Issues." *Congressional Quarterly Weekly Report* 22 (September 11, 1964): 2069-2090.

11055. Kahn, Roger. "The Revolt against LBJ." *Saturday Evening Post* 241 (February 10, 1968): 17-21.

11056. Kearns, Doris. "Angels of Vision." In *Telling Lives,* edited by Marc Pachter, 90-103. Washington, DC: New Republic Books, 1979.

11057. Kearns, Doris. "Lyndon Johnson's Political Personality." *Political Science Quarterly* 91 (Autumn 1976): 385-409.

11058. King, Larry L. "LBJ through Watergate — Colored Glasses." *New Times* 3 (August 23, 1974): 14-16, 20-23.

11059. Kluckhohn, Frank L. *Lyndon's Legacy: A Candid Look at the President's Policy-Makers.* New York: Devin-Adair, 1964.

11060. Knebel, Fletcher. "After the Shots: The Ordeal of Lyndon Johnson." *Look* 28 (March 10, 1964): 26-28, 30, 33.

11061. Koenig, Louis W. "LBJ's Place in History: A Professional View." *U.S. News & World Report* 65 (December 2, 1968): 52-62.

11062. Kraft, Joseph. "Johnson's Talent Hunt." *Harper's Magazine* 230 (March 1965): 40-46.

11063. Kraft, Joseph. "Presidential Politics in LBJ Style." *Harper's Magazine* 228 (March 1964): 113-116.

11064. Krock, Arthur. "Impression of Johnson, the Kennedy's, and Today's Government." *U.S. News & World Report* 61 (December 19, 1966): 44-49.

11065. Ladd, Bruce. *Crisis in Credibility.* New York: New American Library, 1968.

11066. LaFeber, Walter F. "Kennedy, Johnson, and the Revisionists." *Foreign Service Journal* 50 (May 1973): 31-33, 39.

11067. Lapham, Louis H. "Who Is Lyndon Johnson?" *Saturday Evening Post* 238 (September 11, 1965): 21-25, 65-67, 70-72.

11068. Levitt, Theodore. "The Johnson Treatment." *Harvard Business Review* 45 (January/February 1967): 114-118.

11069. Lichtenstein, Nelson, ed. *The Johnson Years.* New York: Facts on File, 1976.

11070. "A Look at the Inner Workings of the White House: Interview with Bill D. Moyers, Top Aide to the President." *U.S. News & World Report* 60 (June 13, 1966): 78-85.

11071. Lowi, Theodore J. "One Dimensional President: Lyndon Johnson's *Vantage Point.*" *Social Science Quarterly* 53 (September 1972): 409-416.

11072. "Lyndon B. Johnson: A Presidency Tempered in Congress." *Congressional Quarterly Weekly Report* 31 (January 27, 1973): 124-129.

11073. "The Lyndon Johnson Touch." *Round Table* 54 (June 1964): 255-261.

11074. McCroskey, James C., and Samuel V. O. Prichard. "Selective Exposure and Lyndon B. Johnson's 1966 'State of the Union' Address." *Journal of Broadcasting* 2 (Autumn 1967): 331-337.

11075. McPherson, Harry. "Beyond Words: Writing for the President." *Atlantic Monthly* 229 (April 1972): 39-45.

11076. McPherson, Harry. *A Political Education: A Journal of Life with Senators, Generals, Cabinet Members, and Presidents.* Boston: Little, Brown, 1972.

11077. McWilliams, Wilson C. "Lyndon Johnson and the Politics of Mass Society." In *Leadership in America: Consensus, Corruption, and Charisma*, edited by Peter D. Bathory, 177-192. New York: Longman, 1978.

11078. Magrath, C. Peter. "Lyndon Johnson and the Paradox of the Presidency: Concerning President as Nonpartisan Leader." *Yale Review* 54 (June 1965): 481-493.

11079. Martin, Harold H. "The Johnson Touch." *Saturday Evening Post* 237 (October 31, 1964): 21-27.

11080. Massaro, John. "LBJ and the Fortas Nomination for Chief Justice." *Political Science Quarterly* 97 (Winter 1982-1983): 603-621.

11081. Merenda, Peter F., Torab Bassiri, Reza Shapurian, and Walter V. Clarke. "Iranian Perceptions of the Reza Shah, Presidents Nixon and Johnson, and the Ideal Self." *Perceptual and Motor Skills* 33 (October 1971): 428-430.

11082. Meyer, Karl E. "Lyndon B. Johnson: Opportunity for Greatness." *Progressive Magazine* 28 (January 1964): 16-19.

11083. Miller, Merle. "The Longest Weekend." *Texas Monthly* 8 (September 1980): 142-147.

11084. Morgenthau, Hans J. "Truth and Power: The Intellectuals and the Johnson Administration." *New Republic* 155 (November 26, 1966): 8-14; 155 (December 24, 1966): 35-36.

11085. Nelson, Bryce. "Communication Gap: LBJ's Monologue with the Intellectuals." *Science* 157 (July 14, 1967): 173-176.

11086. Nelson, Bryce. "Exit Goldman, Enter Roche: Can LBJ and Intellectuals Be Friends?" *Science* 153 (September 23, 1966): 1505-1507.

11087. Nelson, Bryce. "LBJ's 'Great Congress': Rubber Stamp or Creativity?" *Science* 154 (November 4, 1966): 620-622.

11088. Neustadt, Richard E. "How LBJ Is Doing His Job: Interview Analyzing Use of Presidential Power." *U.S. News & World Report* 57 (August 3, 1964): 34-37.

11089. Odegard, Peter H. *The Johnson Administration*. New York: Harper and Row, 1964.

11090. O'Donnell, Kenneth P. "LBJ and the Kennedys." *Life* 69 (August 7, 1970): 44-56.

11091. Patton, John H. "An End and a Beginning: Lyndon B. Johnson's Decisive Speech of March 31, 1968." *Today's Speech* 21 (Summer 1973): 33-41.

11092. Phelps, Waldo, and Andrea Beck. "Lyndon Johnson's Address at the U.C.L.A. Charter Day Ceremony." *Western Speech* 29 (Summer 1965): 162-171.

11093. Phillips, Cabell. "Johnson Has the Kind of Troubles Truman Had." *New York Times Magazine* 117 (October 22, 1967): 34-35, 110, 112, 114, 116, 119-120, 122.

11094. Picque, Nicholas D. "Lyndon Johnson and the 89th Congress." *Christianity and Crisis* 25 (September 20, 1965): 184-187.

11095. "Political Troubles Ahead for LBJ." *U.S. News & World Report* 63 (September 25, 1967): 46-50.

11096. Polsby, Nelson W. "A Note on the President's Modest Proposal." *Public Administration Review* 26 (September 1966): 156-159.

11097. Potter, Philip. "Johnson: The First Hundred Days." *New Republic* 30 (March 7, 1964): 6-8.

11098. "President Dumping: W. H. Taft and L. B. Johnson, Americus." *New Republic* 157 (October 28, 1967): 11-13.

11099. Redford, Emmette S., and Marlan Blissett. *Organizing the Executive Branch: The Johnson Presidency*. Chicago: University of Chicago Press, 1981.

11100. Redford, Emmette S., and Richard T. McCulley. *White House Operations: The Johnson Presidency*. Austin: University of Texas Press, 1986.

11101. Reinert, A. "Why Jack Valenti Still Sleeps Soundly." *Texas Monthly* 2 (July 1974): 68-73.

11102. Renka, Russell D. "Bargaining with Legislative Whales in the Kennedy and Johnson Administrations." *Legislative Studies Quarterly* 6 (February 1981): 161-162.

11103. Renka, Russell D. "Kennedy, Johnson, and the Congress: Serial Gaming in Legislative Policy Coalitions." Ph.D. dissertation, University of Texas, 1979.

11104. Renka, Russell D. "Presidential Lobbying of Congress: Coalition Building in the Kennedy-Johnson Years." Ph.D. dissertation, University of Texas, 1979.

11105. Roberts, Charles W. "LBJ, Three Years after Dallas." *Virginia Journal of Education* 60 (December 1966): 9-12.

11106. Roberts, Charles W. *L. B. J.'s Inner Circle*. New York: Delacorte Press, 1965.

11107. Roberts, Charles W. "LBJ's View of the LBJ Years." *Newsweek* 78 (November 1, 1971): 22-26.

11108. Roberts, Charles W. "The Press Views LBJ: Fearsome Antagonist." *Nation* 203 (October 24, 1966): 406-411.

11109. Roche, John P. *Sentenced to Life*. New York: Macmillan, 1974.

11110. Roche, John P. "Will the Kennedy Legacy Prevail?" *Current* 52 (October 1964): 11-13.

11111. Rogers, Warren. "The Truth

about LBJ's Credibility." *Look* 31 (May 2, 1967): 70-72.

11112. Rosenblum, Sig, and Charles Antin, eds. *LBJ Lampooned: Cartoon Criticism of Lyndon B. Johnson.* New York: Cobble Hill Press, 1968.

11113. Rostow, Eugene V. "LBJ Reconsidered." *Esquire* 75 (April 1971): 118-119.

11114. Schlesinger, Arthur M., Jr. "What Kind of President Will Johnson Make Now?" *U.S. News & World Report* 57 (November 16, 1964): 53-55.

11115. Schott, Richard L., and Dagmar S. Hamilton. *People, Positions, and Power: The Political Appointments of Lyndon Johnson.* Chicago: University of Chicago Press, 1983.

11116. Shannon, William V. "The President and the Intellectuals." *Commonweal* 79 (December 27, 1963): 385-387.

11117. Sherrill, Robert G. *The Accidental President.* New York: Grossman, 1967.

11118. Sherrill, Robert G. "Cold Eye on Johnson." *Nation* 202 (January 3, 1966): 4-7.

11119. Sherrill, Robert G. "Looking Back at Johnson." *Nation* 208 (January 13, 1969): 42-45.

11120. Sherrill, Robert G. "Politics on the King's Ranch." *New York Times Magazine* 115 (June 5, 1966): 43, 103-108.

11121. Sidey, Hugh. "Measure of a Man." *Life* 59 (December 3, 1965): 53-58.

11122. Sidey, Hugh. *A Very Personal Presidency: Lyndon Johnson in the White House.* New York: Atheneum, 1968.

11123. Smith, Nancy K. "Presidential Task Force Operation during the Johnson Administration." *Presidential Studies Quarterly* 15 (Spring 1985): 320-329.

11124. Smith, Robert W. "The 'Second' Inaugural Address of Lyndon Baines Johnson: A Definitive Text." *Speech Monograph* 34 (March 1967): 102-108.

11125. Soloveytchik, George. "President Johnson's Problems." *Contemporary Review* 209 (September 1966): 120-126.

11126. Spragens, William C. "The Myth of the Johnson 'Credibility Gap.'" *Presidential Studies Quarterly* 10 (Fall 1980): 629-635.

11127. Steele, John L. "Political Virtuoso Gathers Forces to Take on the Job." *Life* 55 (December 13, 1963): 32-35.

11128. Steinbeck, John. *A President — Not a Candidate.* Washington, DC: Democratic National Committee, 1964.

11129. Stern, Laurence. "Lyndon Johnson Today." *Progressive Magazine* 29 (September 1965): 13-15.

11130. Stewart, John G. "The Testing of Lyndon B. Johnson." *Christianity and Crisis* 24 (March 2, 1964): 23-26.

11131. Stolley, Richard B. "L. B. J. Reaches Out (Ouch!) to Rally His Consensus." *Life* 61 (September 2, 1966): 12-21.

11132. Sundquist, James L. *Politics and Policy: The Eisenhower, Kennedy, and Johnson Years.* Washington, DC: Brookings Institution, 1986.

11133. Swanson, Donald R. "The Use of Logical Proof in the Speeches of Lyndon Baines Johnson as Shown by an Analysis of Eight Selected Speeches Delivered between the Dates of December 17, 1963, and January 4, 1965." Master's thesis, University of Montana, 1965.

11134. Taylor, Blaine. "An Exclusive Interview with William Lukash M.D., Personal Physician to the President of the United States." *Maryland State Medical Journal* 26 (November 1977): 35-41.

11135. Thomas, Norman C., and Harold

L. Wolman. "Policy Formulation in the Institutionalized Presidency: Johnson Task Forces." In *Presidential Advisory System*, edited by Thomas E. Cronin and Sanford Greenberg, 124-143. New York: Harper and Row, 1969.

11136. Thompson, Edward W. "The Johnson Power Techniques: A Study in the Power Techniques Used by Lyndon Johnson as Explained by His Contemporary Biographers." Master's thesis, Prairie View Agriculture and Mechanical College, 1972.

11137. Tyler, Gus. "Johnson and the Intellectuals: Duel in the ADA." *Midstream* 13 (August/September 1967): 35-45.

11138. U.S. Congress. Senate. *Tributes to the President and Mrs. Lyndon Baines Johnson in the Congress of the United States.* 91st Cong., 1st sess., 1969. Washington, DC: U.S. Government Printing Office, 1969.

11139. Warner, David C., ed. *Toward New Human Rights: The Social Policies of the Kennedy and Johnson Administrations.* Austin: LBJ School of Public Affairs, University of Texas, 1977.

11140. Warner, Richard R. "The Concept of Creative Federalism in the Johnson Administration." Ph.D. dissertation, American University, 1970.

11141. Warner, Robert M. "The Anatomy of a Speech: Lyndon Johnson's Great Society Address." *Michigan Historical Collections Bulletin* 28 (December 1978): 1-15.

11142. Watson, W. Marvin. "The White House at Work: A Mystery Explained." *U.S. News & World Report* 60 (February 7, 1966): 36-37.

11143. Ways, Max. "Intellectuals and the Presidency." *Fortune* 75 (April 1967): 146-149.

11144. Wechsler, James A. "Lyndon Johnson on the Eve." *Progressive Magazine* 28 (September 1964): 10-12.

11145. Weintal, Edward, and Charles Bartlett. *Facing the Brink.* New York: Scribner's, 1967.

11146. Weisl, Edwin L. "Look Inside the Johnson-Kennedy Contest." *U.S. News & World Report* 64 (April 8, 1968): 48-50.

11147. Welsh, David. "Building Lyndon Johnson." *Ramparts Magazine* 6 (January 1969): 104-114.

11148. "What's Happened to the LBJ Image?" *U.S. News & World Report* 60 (January 17, 1966): 39-41.

11149. White, William S. "Democrats' Board of Directors." *New York Times Magazine* 104 (July 10, 1955): 10-11.

11150. White, William S. *The Responsibles: Truman, Taft, Eisenhower, JFK, Johnson.* New York: Harper and Row, 1972.

11151. Wicker, Tom. "Bill Moyers: Johnson's Good Angel." *Harper's Magazine* 231 (October 1965): 41-49.

11152. Wicker, Tom. "It Is the People Who Face the Test, They Will Determine Whether the New President Can Overcome Stanpattism in Congress." *New York Times Magazine* 108 (December 1963): 19, 115-117.

11153. Wicker, Tom. *JFK and LBJ: The Influence of Personality upon Politics.* New York: Morrow, 1968.

11154. Wicker, Tom. "Johnson's Men: Valuable Hunks of Humanity." *New York Times Magazine* 113 (May 3, 1964): 11, 104-107.

11155. Wicker, Tom. "Lyndon Johnson Is Ten Feet Tall." *New York Times Magazine* 114 (May 23, 1965): 23, 88-89, 91-92.

11156. Wicker, Tom. "One Year of

LBJ." *New Republic* 153 (November 13, 1965): 13-22.

11157. Williams, James M. *The Constitutional Basis for the Impeachment of Lyndon B. Johnson.* Minneapolis, MN: Citizens for Governmental Restraint, 1968.

11158. Williams, T. Harry. "Huey, Lyndon, and Southern Radicalism." *Journal of American History* 60 (September 1973): 267-293.

11159. Wise, David. "Twilight of a President." *New York Times Magazine* 118 (November 3, 1968): 27-29, 122, 124, 126, 128-131.

11160. Wolfenstein, E. Victor. "The Two Wars of Lyndon Johnson." *Politics and Society* 4 (1974): 357-396.

11161. Yager, Thomas C. *Presidents, Prime Ministers, and Premiers: President Lyndon B. Johnson.* Los Angeles: American Institute, 1969.

Domestic Policy

11162. Alexander, Joseph. "Presidential Intervention: The Crisis in Collective Bargaining." *Mississippi Valley Journal of Business and Economics* 2 (Spring 1967): 23-37.

11163. Anderson, James E. "The Management of Wage-Price Policies in the Johnson and Carter Administrations." *Policy Studies Journal* 12 (June 1984): 733-746.

11164. Anderson, James E., and Jared E. Hazleton. *Managing Macroeconomic Policy: The Johnson Presidency.* Austin: University of Texas Press, 1986.

11165. Beck, Susan A. "The Limits of Presidential Activism: Lyndon Johnson and the Implementation of the Community Action Program." Ph.D. dissertation, Columbia University, 1985.

11166. Bennett, Lerone. "What Negroes Can Expect from President Lyndon Johnson." *Ebony* 19 (January 1964): 81-84.

11167. Billington, Monroe. "Lyndon B. Johnson and Blacks: The Early Years." *Journal of Negro History* 62 (January 1977): 26-42.

11168. Brauer, Carl M. "Kennedy, Johnson, and the War on Poverty." *Journal of American History* 69 (June 1981): 98-119.

11169. Burkart, Joan M. "Selected Education Legislation of the Lyndon Baines Johnson Administration and Implications for School Health Education." Ph.D. dissertation, University of Texas, 1973.

11170. Carroll, James D. "The Implications of President Johnson's Memoranda of September 13 and 14, 1965: For the Funding of Academic Research by Federal Agencies: A Study of Federal-University Research Policies." Ph.D. dissertation, Syracuse University, 1967.

11171. Cavaioli, Frank J. *President Lyndon B. Johnson and the Immigration Law of 1965.* Farmingdale: State University of New York Press, 1976.

11172. Cochrane, James L. "Economists and Presidential Decision Making: The Johnson Years." *Presidential Studies Quarterly* 8 (Winter 1978): 32-35.

11173. Cochrane, James L. "Energy Policy in the Johnson Administration: Logical Order versus Economic Pluralism." In *Energy Policy in Perspective,* edited by Craufurd D. Goodwin, 337-394. Washington, DC: Brookings Institution, 1981.

11174. Coor, Lattie F. "LBJ Revisited." *Washington University Magazine* 43 (Spring 1973): 22-26.

11175. Crevilli, John P. "The Final Act of the Greatest Conservation President." *Prologue* 12 (Winter 1980-1981): 172-191.

11176. Davis, Larry L. "An Examination

of the Development and Implementation of the ESEA of 1965 during the Johnson Administration." Ph.D. dissertation, Ball State University, 1980.

11177. Donovan, John C. *The Politics of Poverty.* New York: Pegasus, 1970.

11178. Eckstein, Otto. "The Unmistakable Brand of LBJ: The Fiscal '65 Budget." *Challenge* 12 (April 1964): 4-7.

11179. Emme, Eugene M. "Presidents and Space." In *Between Sputnik and the Shuttle: New Perspectives on American Astronautics,* edited by Frederick C. Durant III, 5-138. San Diego, CA: Unvelt, 1981.

11180. "Equal Time Applicable to LBJ News Sessions: That's FCC Vote." *Broadcasting* 67 (October 5, 1964): 45-46.

11181. Ezell, Macel D. "Two Sides of Lyndon Johnson's Commitment to Education." *University College Quarterly* 25 (January 1980): 20-29.

11182. Farrington, John P. "A Study of New Deal Thought in the Kennedy and Johnson Administrations." Ph.D. dissertation, University of Colorado, 1975.

11183. Fox, Douglas M., and Charles H. Clapp. "The House Rules Committee and the Programs of the Kennedy and Johnson Administrations." *American Journal of Political Science* 14 (November 1970): 667-672.

11184. Fuertsch, David F. "Lyndon B. Johnson and Civil Rights: The Rhetorical Development of a Political Realist." Ph.D. dissertation, University of Texas, 1974.

11185. Greenberg, Daniel S. "LBJ Directive: He Says Spread the Research Money." *Science* 151 (September 24, 1965): 1483-1485.

11186. Gutierrez, Arturo. "Analysis and Comparison of the Lyndon Baines Johnson Education Papers and Headstart Research." Ph.D. dissertation, University of Texas, 1972.

11187. Halperin, Morton H. "The Decision to Deploy the ABM: Bureaucratic and Domestic Politics in the Johnson Administration." *World Politics* 25 (October 1972): 62-95.

11188. Harvey, James C. *Black Civil Rights during the Johnson Administration.* Jackson: University Press of Mississippi, 1973.

11189. Hawkinson, Robert E. "Presidential Program Formulation in Education: Lyndon Johnson and the 89th Congress." Ph.D. dissertation, University of Chicago, 1977.

11190. Henderson, William L., and David L. Smith. "Johnson Economic Policies." *MSU Business Topics* 14 (Winter 1966): 37-46.

11191. James, Jo Anne. "Lyndon Johnson and the Black American." Master's thesis, Texas Agricultural and Industrial University, 1971.

11192. Jencks, Christopher. "Johnson vs. Poverty." *New Republic* 150 (March 28, 1964): 15-18.

11193. "Johnson, Goldwater Records Diverge on Civil Rights." *Congressional Quarterly Weekly Report* 22 (August 7, 1965): 1691-1698.

11194. "Johnson Stress on Military Space Seen." *Aviation Week and Space Technology* 79 (December 2, 1963): 26-28.

11195. Kearney, Philip. "The 1964 Presidential Task Force on Education and the ESEA of 1965." Ph.D. dissertation, University of Chicago, 1967.

11196. King, Ronald F. "The President and Fiscal Policy in 1966: The Year Taxes Were Not Raised." *Polity* 17 (Summer 1985): 685-714.

11197. Lander, Louise, ed. *War on Pover-*

ty. New York: Facts on File, 1967.

11198. Langer, Elinor. "LBJ at NIH: President Offers Kind Words for Basic Research." *Science* 158 (July 28, 1967): 403-405.

11199. Langer, Elinor. "Scientists and Engineers for LBJ: A War and Three Years Later." *Science* 158 (September 28, 1967): 1533-1536.

11200. Lawson, Simpson F. "Washington and the White House: What Have They Done for Us Lately?" *Washingtonian* 9 (November 1973): 101-104.

11201. Lawson, Steven F. "I Got It from the *New York Times*: Lyndon Johnson and the Kennedy Civil Rights Program." *Journal of Negro History* 67 (Summer 1982): 159-172.

11202. Lawson, Steven F., and Mark I. Gelfand. "Consensus and Civil Rights: Lyndon B. Johnson and the Black Franchise." *Prologue* 8 (Summer 1976): 65-76.

11203. Leuchtenburg, William E. "The Legacy of FDR." *Wilson Quarterly* 6 (Spring 1982): 77-93.

11204. Lewis, Eleanor G. "The House Committee on Rules and the Legislative Program of the Kennedy and Johnson Administrations." *Capital Studies* 6 (Fall 1978): 27-38.

11205. McCoy, Charla D. "The Education President: Lyndon Baines Johnson's Public Statements on Instruction and the Teaching Profession." Ph.D. dissertation, University of Texas, 1975.

11206. Meyers, Harold B. "L. B. J.'s Romance with Business." *Fortune* 70 (September 1964): 130-133, 222, 226, 230.

11207. Miroff, Bruce. "Presidential Leverage over Social Movements: The Johnson White House and Civil Rights." *Journal of Politics* 43 (February 1981): 2-23.

11208. Morrow, Rosemary. "Lyndon B. Johnson on Education." *Southwestern Journal of Social Education* 12 (Autumn/Winter 1981): 34-41.

11209. Moynihan, Daniel P. *Maximum Feasible Misunderstanding: Community Action in the War on Poverty*. New York: Free Press, 1969.

11210. Moynihan, Daniel P. "Presidency and the Negro: The Movement Lost." *Commentary* 43 (February 1967): 31-45.

11211. Mullen, Avis A. "A Historical Analysis of Lyndon Baines Johnson's Contributions to Minority Groups: Emphasis on Speeches and the Elementary and Secondary Education Act, 1965." Ph.D. dissertation, University of Texas, 1976.

11212. Murray, Agnes L. "President Lyndon B. Johnson's Appointments to the Regulatory Commissions." Master's thesis, University of Texas, 1970.

11213. Pyle, Christopher, and Richard Morgan. "Johnson's Civil Rights Shake-up." *New Leader* 48 (October 11, 1965): 3-6.

11214. Redard, Thomas E. "The Politics of Beautification in the Johnson Administration." Master's thesis, University of Texas, 1976.

11215. Reedy, George. "The True Dawn of Civil Rights." *Washington Monthly* 14 (May 1983): 46-51.

11216. Rosen, Gerald R. "Johnson and the Businessmen." *Dun's Review* 85 (May 1965): 40-43.

11217. Roucek, Joseph S. "The Politics of President Johnson's 'War on Poverty.'" *Il Politico* 31 (1966): 293-320.

11218. Rowen, Hobart. *The Free Enterprisers: Kennedy, Johnson, and the Business Establishment*. New York: Putnam, 1964.

11219. Rustin, Bayard, and Tom Kahn. "Johnson So Far, II: Civil Rights." *Com-*

mentary 39 (June 1965): 43-46.

11220. Sanders, Charles L. "LBJ and Civil Rights." *Ebony* 29 (March 1974): 154-158.

11221. Schreiber, Flora R. "LBJ's Feel for Science." *Science Digest* 57 (April 1965): 9-11.

11222. Scruggs, Donald L. "Lyndon Baines Johnson and the National Advisory Commission on Civil Disorders (The Kerner Commission): A Study of Johnson Domestic Policy-Making System." Ph.D. dissertation, University of Oklahoma, 1980.

11223. Sherrill, Robert G. "LBJ and the Oil Men: Five Lessons in Black Power." *Ramparts Magazine* 5 (January 1967): 35-40.

11224. Slevin, Joseph R. "Washington Desk: LBJ's Legislative Achievements." *Dun's Review* 86 (November 1965): 5-6.

11225. Stanley, James D. "A Study of USOE, With Special Emphasis on the Lyndon B. Johnson Presidency." Ph.D. dissertation, North Texas State University, 1976.

11226. Sullivan, Samuel L. "President Lyndon Baines Johnson and the Common School, 1963-1969." Ed.D. dissertation, Oklahoma State University, 1973.

11227. Tevis, Martha. "Lyndon Johnson and Education for All the People." *Educational Studies* 12 (Winter 1981-1982): 395-402.

11228. Thomas, Norman C. "Policy Formulation for Education: The Johnson Administration." In *The Presidency in Contemporary Context*, edited by Norman C. Thomas, 318-330. New York: Dodd, Mead, 1975.

11229. Van Patten, James J. "Lyndon Baines Johnson: Education's Friend." *School and Community* 59 (September 1972): 4-5.

11230. Von Furstenberg, George M., and James M. Boughton. "Stabilization Goals and the Appropriateness of Fiscal Policy during the Eisenhower and Kennedy-Johnson Administrations." *Public Finance Quarterly* 1 (January 1973): 5-28.

11231. Warren, Earl. "Lyndon B. Johnson and Civil Rights." *Texas Law Review* 51 (January 1973): 196-206.

11232. Wason, James R. "Labor-Management under the Johnson Administration." *Current History* 49 (August 1965): 65-70, 116.

11233. Ways, Max. "The Two Lyndon Johnsons and the U.S. of 1964." *Fortune* 69 (January 1964): 80-83.

11234. Weaver, Robert C. "Eleanor and L. B. J. and Black America." *Crisis* 79 (1972): 186-193.

11235. Wilson, George C. "Johnson Maps Strong Aerospace Efforts." *Aviation Week and Space Technology* 82 (February 1, 1965): 16-18.

11236. Wolfson, Elaine M. "The President and the Poor: The Interface of Fiscal and Social Policy Making during the Johnson Presidency." Ph.D. dissertation, New York University, 1977.

11237. Wright, Bette L. "Selected Health Legislation of the Lyndon Baines Johnson Administration, 1964-1968, and Its Implications for Secondary School Health Education." Ed.D. dissertation, University of Texas, 1976.

11238. Zarefsky, David H. *President Johnson's War on Poverty: Rhetoric and History.* University: University of Alabama Press, 1985.

11239. Zarefsky, David H. "President Johnson's War on Poverty: The Rhetoric of Three 'Establishment' Movements." *Communication Monographs* 44 (November 1977): 352-373.

11240. Zarefsky, David H. "Subordinating the Civil Rights Issue: Lyndon Johnson in 1964." *Southern Speech Communication Journal* 48 (Winter 1983): 103-118.

Elections

11241. Alsop, Stewart. "Can Anyone Beat LBJ?" *Saturday Evening Post* 240 (June 3, 1967): 27-31.

11242. Bean, Louis H., and Roscoe Drummond. "LBJ and the Elections: Trouble Ahead." *Look* 30 (October 4, 1966): 89-90.

11243. Brand, H. "Why Vote for Lyndon Johnson?" *Dissent* 11 (Autumn 1964): 385-388.

11244. Brooks, William D. "A Field Study of the Johnson and Goldwater Campaign Speeches in Pittsburgh." *Southern Speech Journal* 32 (Summer 1967): 273-281.

11245. Brooks, William D. "A Study of the Relationships of Selected Factors to Changes in Voting Attitudes of Audiences Listening to Political Speeches of President Johnson and Senator Goldwater." Ph.D. dissertation, Ohio University, 1964.

11246. Bryant, Peter S. "The Rhetoric of Lyndon B. Johnson in the 1964 Presidential Campaign." Master's thesis, University of Iowa, 1967.

11247. Connelly, Fred M., Jr. "Some Questions Concerning Lyndon Johnson's Rhetoric in the 1964 Presidential Campaign." *Southern Speech Journal* 37 (Autumn 1971): 11-20.

11248. Davidson, Bill. "Lyndon Johnson ... Can a Southerner Be Elected President?" *Look* 23 (August 18, 1959): 63-64.

11249. Emery, Edwin. "Press Support for Johnson and Goldwater." *Journalism Quarterly* 41 (Autumn 1964): 485-488.

11250. Faltermayer, Edmund K. "What Business Wants from Lyndon Johnson." *Fortune* 71 (February 1965): 122-125.

11251. Goldberg, Philip A., and Milton J. Stark. "Johnson or Goldwater? Some Personality and Attitude Correlates of Political Choice." *Psychological Reports* 17 (1965): 627-631.

11252. Harding, H. F. "Democratic Nominee: Lyndon B. Johnson." *Quarterly Journal of Speech* 50 (December 1964): 409-414.

11253. Mullen, James J. "Newspaper Advertising in the Johnson-Goldwater Campaign." *Journalism Quarterly* 45 (Summer 1968): 219-225.

11254. Roche, John P. "A Professor Votes for Mr. Johnson." *Catholic Mind* 63 (December 1965): 10-17.

11255. Rovere, Richard H. "The Campaign: Johnson." *New Yorker* 40 (October 17, 1964): 217-226.

Foreign Affairs

11256. "Adenauer Talks about Johnson: Exclusive Interview with Former Chancellor of West Germany." *U.S. News & World Report* 55 (December 16, 1963): 44-47.

11257. Cerny, P. G. "The Fall of Two Presidents and Extraparliamentary Opposition: France and the United States in 1968." *Government and Opposition* 5 (Summer 1970): 287-306.

11258. Cregier, Don M. "The World of LBJ: The President's Style in Foreign Policy." *Christian Century* 83 (July 6, 1966): 859-861.

11259. Ealy, Lawrence O. "President Johnson Fails to End the Panama Problem." In his *Yanqui Politics and the Isthmian Canal,* 120-137. University Park: Pennsylvania State University Press, 1971.

11260. Franck, Thomas M., and Edward Weisband. *The Johnson-Brezhnev Doctrines: Verbal Behavior Analysis of Super Power Confrontations.* New York: Center for International Studies, New York University, 1970.

11261. Fritchey, Clayton. "A Tale of One City and Two Men: Foreign Policies of Kennedy and Johnson." *Harper's Magazine* 233 (December 1966): 108-113.

11262. Gelb, Leslie H. "The Pentagon Papers and the Vantage Point." *Foreign Policy* 6 (Spring 1972): 25-41.

11263. Haley, P. Edward. "Comparative Intervention: Mexico in 1914 and the Dominican Republic in 1965." *Australian Journal of Politics and History* 20 (April 1974): 32-44.

11264. Hoopes, Townsend. *The Limits of Intervention: An Inside Account of How the Johnson Policy of Intervention Was Reversed.* Rev. ed. College Park: University of Maryland Press, 1973.

11265. Kuter, Laurence S. "JFK and LBJ Consider Aerospace Defense." *Aerospace Historian* 25 (Spring 1978): 1-4.

11266. "Lyndon Johnson and Prime Minister Inonu." *Middle East Journal* 20 (Summer 1976): 386-393.

11267. Maher, Theodore J. "The Kennedy and Johnson Responses to Latin-American Coups d'Etat." *World Affairs* 131 (October/November/December 1968): 184-197.

11268. Morgenthau, Hans J. "Globalism, Johnson's Moral Crusade." *New Republic* 153 (July 3, 1965): 19-22.

11269. Peretz, Don. "The United States, the Arabs, and Israel: Peace Efforts of Kennedy, Johnson, and Nixon." *Annals of the American Academy of Political and Social Sciences* 410 (May 1972): 116-125.

11270. Plischke, Elmer. "The President's Inner Foreign Policy Team." *Review of Politics* 30 (July 1968): 292-307.

11271. Robinson, Edgar E., et al. *Powers of the President in Foreign Affairs, 1945-1965: Harry S. Truman, Dwight D. Eisenhower, John F. Kennedy, Lyndon B. Johnson.* San Francisco: Commonwealth Club of California, 1966.

11272. Rogers, Jimmie N. "An Investigation of Senator J. William Fulbright's Attitudes toward President Lyndon B. Johnson as Demonstrated in Selected Foreign Policy Addresses: An Evaluative Assertion Analysis." Ph.D. dissertation, Florida State University, 1972.

11273. Roseman, Alvin. "Foreign Aid under Lyndon Johnson." *Current History* 50 (June 1966): 335-341.

11274. Rudolph, Lloyd I., et al. *The Regional Imperative: U.S. Foreign Policy towards South Asian States under Presidents Johnson and Nixon.* Atlantic Highlands, NJ: Humanities Press, 1980.

11275. Sellen, Robert W. "Old Assumptions versus New Realities: Lyndon Johnson and Foreign Policy." *International Journal* 28 (Spring 1973): 204-229.

11276. Stanley, James G. "United States' Foreign Policy vis-a-vis Western Europe during the Johnson Administration: A Change in Priorities?" Ph.D. dissertation, American University, 1976.

11277. Weintraub, Sidney, ed. *Economic Coercion and U.S. Foreign Policy Implications of Case Studies from the Johnson Administration.* Boulder, CO: Westview Press, 1982.

11278. Weisband, Edward, and Thomas M. Franck. "The Brezhnev-Johnson Two-World Doctrine." In *Beyond Conflict and Containment,* edited by Milton J. Rosenberg, 247-275. New Brunswick, NJ: Transaction Books, 1972.

Great Society

11279. Bailey, Sidney K. "Co-ordinating the Great Society." *Reporter* 43 (May 24, 1966): 39-41.

11280. Burns, James M., ed. *To Heal and to Build: The Programs of President Lyndon B. Johnson.* New York: McGraw-Hill, 1968.

11281. Gettleman, Marvin E., and David Mermelstein, eds. *The Great Society Reader: The Failure of American Liberalism.* New York: Random House, 1967.

11282. Ginsberg, Eli, and Robert M. Solow, eds. *The Great Society: Lessons for the Future.* New York: Basic Books, 1974.

11283. Gross, Bertram M. *A Great Society?* New York: Basic Books, 1968.

11284. Lekachman, Robert. "Death of a Slogan — The Great Society, 1967." *Commentary* 43 (January 1967): 56-61.

11285. Lekachman, Robert. "The Great Society." *Commentary* 39 (June 1965): 37-42.

11286. Lekachman, Robert. "Johnson So Far, I: The Great Society." *Commentary* 39 (June 1965): 37-42.

11287. Leuchtenburg, William E. "The Genesis of the Great Society." *Reporter* 34 (April 21, 1966): 36-39.

11288. Levitan, Sar A., and Robert Taggart. "The Great Society Did Succeed." *Political Science Quarterly* 91 (Winter 1976-1977): 601-618.

11289. McNaught, Kenneth. "American Progressives and the Great Society." *Journal of American History* 53 (December 1966): 504-520.

11290. Roucek, Joseph S. "The Slow-Down of President Johnson's 'Great Society' Programme." *Contemporary Review* 211 (December 1967): 296-304.

11291. Thomas, Norman C. "President Johnson's Great Society." *Christian Century* 93 (March 9, 1966): 300-303.

11292. Toll, William. "Policy under the Great Society: Reflections on the Sources of Policy and of Violence." *Journal of Human Relations* 18 (1970): 849-874.

Press

11293. Cooper, Stephen L. "A Rhetorical Assessment of Lyndon Johnson's Presidential Press Conferences." Ph.D. dissertation, Louisiana State University, Agricultural and Mechanical College, 1972.

11294. Cormier, Frank. "Johnson and the Press." *Saturday Review* 49 (September 10, 1966): 70-72.

11295. Cornwell, Elmer E., Jr. "The Johnson Press Relations Style." *Journalism Quarterly* 43 (Spring 1966): 3-9.

11296. Culbert, David. "Johnson and the Media." In *Exploring the Johnson Years*, edited by Robert A. Divine, 214-248. Austin: University of Texas Press, 1981.

11297. Deakin, James. "I've Got a Secret: President Johnson and the Press." *New Republic* 152 (January 30, 1965): 13-15.

11298. Goodwin, Doris K., ed. *The Johnson Presidential Press Conferences.* 2 vols. New York: E. M. Coleman Enterprises, 1978.

11299. Hayllar, Ben. *The Image of Lyndon Baines Johnson: The Journalist's Role in the Making of a Public Image.* Dubuque, IA: Kendall-Hunt, 1972.

11300. Johnson, George W., ed. *Johnson Presidential Press Conference.* 2 vols. St. Paul, MN: E. M. Coleman Enterprises, 1978.

11301. Johnson, Miles B. *The Government Secrecy Controversy: A Dispute Involving the Government and the Press in the Eisenhower, Kennedy, and Johnson*

Administrations. New York: Vantage Press, 1967.

11302. "Johnson's Inauguration: Broadcaster's Field Day." *Broadcasting* 68 (January 25, 1965): 72-73.

11303. Latimer, Harry D. "The Press Secretaries of Lyndon Johnson." Ph.D. dissertation, Brown University, 1973.

11304. Pardue, Eugenia. "The President and the Press: A Case Study of Lyndon Johnson and the Washington Press Corps." Master's thesis, Texas Christian University, 1969.

11305. Purvis, H. Hoyt, ed. *The Presidency and the Press*. Austin: Lyndon B. Johnson School of Public Affairs, University of Texas, 1976.

11306. Rivers, Caryl. "LBJ's Strongly Personal Press Shop Irks Reporters." *Editor & Publisher* 97 (December 5, 1964): 9-10.

11307. Stolley, Richard B. "Widening No Man's Land: President vs. the Press." *Life* 58 (May 7, 1965): 34-39.

11308. Stone, Philip, and Richard A. Brody. "Modeling Opinion Responsiveness to Daily News: The Public and Lyndon Johnson, 1965-1968." *Social Science Information* 9 (February 1970): 95-122.

11309. Turner, Kathleen J. "Press Influence on Presidential Rhetoric: Lyndon Johnson at Johns Hopkins University, April 7, 1965." *Central States Speech Journal* 33 (Autumn 1982): 425-436.

11310. "Will LBJ Change Style of News Parley?" *Editor & Publisher* 98 (January 23, 1965): 12-13.

11311. "World's Biggest TV Studio: Broadcasters Ready to Give Record-Breaking Coverage to Inauguration of President Johnson." *Broadcasting* 68 (January 18, 1965): 78-79.

Vietnam

11312. Ball, George W. "Top Secret: The Prophecy the President Rejected." *Atlantic Monthly* 230 (July 1972): 36-49.

11313. Bradley, George L. "A Critical Analysis of Lyndon Johnson's 'Peace' Rhetoric, 1963-1969." Ph.D. dissertation, University of Kansas, 1974.

11314. Bunge, Walter, et al. "Johnson's Information Strategy for Vietnam: An Evaluation." *Journalism Quarterly* 45 (Autumn 1968): 419-425.

11315. Casey, Francis M. "The Vietnam Policy of President Lyndon Baines Johnson in Response to the Theory of the Protracted Conflict as Applied in the Politics of Indochina: A Case Study of Threat Perception and Assessment in the Crisis Management Process of a Pluralistic Society." Ph.D. dissertation, Claremont Graduate School, 1976.

11316. Cherwitz, Richard A. "Lyndon Johnson and the 'Crisis' of Tonkin Bay: A President's Justification of War." *Western Journal of Speech Communication* 42 (Spring 1978): 93-104.

11317. Cherwitz, Richard A. "The Rhetoric of the Gulf of Tonkin: A Study of the Crisis Speaking of President Lyndon B. Johnson." Ph.D. dissertation, University of Iowa, 1978.

11318. Cochrane, James L. "The Johnson Administration: Moral Suasion Goes to War." In *Exhortation and Controls: The Search for a Wage-Price Policy 1945-1971*, edited by Craufurd D. Goodwin, 193-293. Washington, DC: Brookings Institution, 1975.

11319. Donovan, Robert J. *Nemesis: Truman and Johnson in the Coils of War in Asia*. New York: St. Martin's Press, 1984.

11320. Draper, Theodore. "Vietnam: From Kennedy to Johnson." In *Twentieth*

Century America, edited by Barton J. Bernstein and Allen J. Matusow, 477-499. New York: Harcourt, Brace, 1969.

11321. Dudman, Richard. "The 'Eyes Only' Committee for Lyndon's War." *Nation* 227 (December 23, 1978): 695-697.

11322. Ellsberg, Daniel. "The Quagmire Myth and the Stalemate Machine." *Public Policy* 19 (Spring 1971): 217-274.

11323. Goulden, Joseph C. *Truth Is the First Casualty: The Gulf of Tonkin Affair, Illusion and Reality.* Chicago: Rand McNally, 1969.

11324. Goulding, Phil G. *Confirm or Deny: Informing the People on National Security.* New York: Harper and Row, 1970.

11325. Graff, Henry F. "Decision in Vietnam: How Johnson Makes Foreign Policy." *New York Times Magazine* 114 (July 4, 1965): 4-7, 16-20.

11326. Grice, George L. " 'We Are a People of Peace, But . . .': A Rhetorical Study of President Lyndon B. Johnson's Statements on United States Military Involvement in Vietnam." Ph.D. dissertation, University of Texas, 1976.

11327. Harrington, Michael. "Johnson Budget and Vietnam." *Dissent* 14 (March/April 1967): 133-135.

11328. Hayes, James T. "Lyndon Baines Johnson's Public Defense of the Vietnam War, 1964-1969: The Evolution of a Rhetorical Position." Ph.D. dissertation, University of Wisconsin, 1975.

11329. Johnson, Gerald W. "The Superfluity of LBJ." *American Scholar* 37 (Spring 1968): 221-226.

11330. King, Larry L. "Machismo in the White House: LBJ and Vietnam." *American Heritage* 27 (August 1976): 8-13, 98-101.

11331. Lipset, Seymour M. "The President, the Polls, and Vietnam." *Trans-Action* 3 (September/October 1966): 19-24.

11332. Logue, Cal M., and John H. Patton. "From Ambiguity to Dogma: The Rhetorical Symbols of Lyndon B. Johnson on Vietnam." *Southern Speech Communication Journal* 47 (Spring 1982): 310-329.

11333. Miller, Lawrence W., and Lee Sigelman. "Is the Audience the Message? A Note on LBJ's Vietnam Statements." *Public Opinion Quarterly* 42 (Spring 1978): 71-80.

11334. Morgenthau, Hans J. "Johnson's Dilemma: The Alternatives Now in Vietnam." *New Republic* 154 (May 28, 1966): 12-16.

11335. Moyers, Bill D. "Bill Moyers Talks about the War and LBJ: An Interview." *Atlantic Monthly* 222 (July 1968): 29-37.

11336. Moyers, Bill D. "One Thing We Learned." *Foreign Affairs* 46 (July 1968): 657-664.

11337. Mutnick, Jeffrey. "American Intervention in Vietnam: The Public Image Presented by Lyndon Baines Johnson." Ph.D. dissertation, Indiana University, 1977.

11338. Partney, Gerald D., Jr. "Lyndon Johnson's Speaking on the Vietnam War: Argumentative Appeals and Rhetorical Strategies." Ph.D. dissertation, University of Iowa, 1975.

11339. Pearson, Drew. "Ghosts That Haunted LBJ: His Decision to Withdraw." *Look* 32 (July 23, 1968): 25-29.

11340. Quill, J. Michael. *Lyndon Johnson and the Southern Military Tradition.* Washington, DC: University Press of America, 1977.

11341. Schandler Herbert Y. *The Unmaking of a President: Lyndon Johnson and Vietnam.* Princeton, NJ: Princeton University Press, 1977.

11342. Scribner, Charles R. "The Eisenhower and Johnson Administration's Decision Making on Vietnamese Intervention: A Study of Contrasts." Ph.D. dissertation, University of California, Santa Barbara, 1980.

11343. Seisler, J. M. "The Press and Decisions: LBJ and Vietnam." Ph.D. dissertation, University of London, 1975.

11344. Seltzer, Robert V. "The Truman-Johnson Analog: A Study of Presidential Rhetoric in Limited War." Ph.D. dissertation, Wayne State University, 1976.

11345. Sigelman, Lee. "The Commander in Chief and the Public: Mass Response to Johnson's March 31, 1968 Bombing Halt Speech." *Journal of Political and Military Sociology* 8 (Spring 1980): 1-14.

11346. Sigelman, Lee. "Rallying to the President's Support: A Reappraisal of the Evidence." *Polity* 11 (Summer 1979): 542-561.

11347. Sigelman, Lee, and Lawrence W. Miller. "Understanding Presidential Rhetoric: Vietnam Statements of Lyndon Johnson." *Communication Research* 5 (January 1978): 25-56.

11348. Sigford, Rolf N. "The Rhetoric of the Vietnam War: Presidents Johnson and Nixon." Ph.D. dissertation, University of Minnesota, 1973.

11349. Smith, F. Michael. "Rhetorical Implications of Aggression Thesis in the Johnson Administration's Vietnam Argumentation." *Central States Speech Journal* 23 (Winter 1972): 217-224.

11350. Starner, Frances L. "Halfway with LBJ?" *Far Eastern Economic Review* 50 (November 11, 1965): 297-299.

11351. Stoler, Mark A. "Aiken, Mansfield, and the Tonkin Gulf Crisis: Notes from the Congressional Leadership Meeting at the White House, August 4, 1964." *Vermont History* 50 (Spring 1982): 80-94.

11352. Swomley, John M., Jr. "Peace Negotiations and President Johnson." *Minority of One* 10 (1968): 10-12.

11353. Turner, Kathleen J. "The Effect of Presidential-Press Interaction on Lyndon B. Johnson's Vietnam War Rhetoric." Ph.D. dissertation, Purdue University, 1978.

11354. Van, Thu. "A Vietnamese Letter to President Johnson." *Michigan Quarterly Review* 6 (Spring 1967): 75-84.

11355. Vogelgesang, Sandra L. *The Long Dark Night of the Soul: Intellectual Left vs. Johnson's Vietnam Policy, 1964-1968.* New York: Harper and Row, 1974.

11356. Westerfield, H. Bradford. "What Use Are Three Versions of the Pentagon Papers?" *American Political Science Review* 69 (June 1975): 685-696.

11357. Wicker, Tom. "The Wrong Rubicon: LBJ and the War." *Atlantic Monthly* 221 (May 1968): 65-84.

11358. Workman, Randall G. "Lyndon B. Johnson and Vietnam: The Rhetorical Influence of Presidential Power." Ph.D. dissertation, Indiana University, 1978.

Writings

11359. Brayman, Harold. *The President Speaks off the Record.* Princeton, NJ: Dow Jones, 1976.

11360. Cannon, James. "An Interview with LBJ." *Newsweek* 66 (August 2, 1965): 20-25.

11361. Johnson, Lyndon B. *The Choices We Face.* New York: Bantam Books, 1969.

11362. Johnson, Lyndon B. *The Johnson Presidential Press Conferences.* New York: E. M. Coleman Enterprises, 1978.

11363. Johnson, Lyndon B. "My Heart Attack Taught Me How to Live." *American Magazine* 162 (July 1956): 15-17.

11364. Johnson, Lyndon B. *My Hope for America.* New York: Random House, 1964.

11365. Johnson, Lyndon B. *No Retreat from Tomorrow, President Lyndon B. Johnson's Messages to the Ninetieth Congress.* Garden City, NY: Doubleday, 1967.

11366. Johnson, Lyndon B. *The Promise of New Asia.* Washington, DC: U.S. Government Printing Office, 1966.

11367. Johnson, Lyndon B. *The Quotable Lyndon B. Johnson.* Edited by Sarah H. Hayes. New York: Grosset and Dunlap, 1968.

11368. Johnson, Lyndon B. "The Roosevelt Legacy: Facing the Realities of Our Time." *Department of State Bulletin* 55 (September 12, 1966): 371-372.

11369. Johnson, Lyndon B. *A Time for Action: A Selection from the Speeches and Writings of Lyndon B. Johnson, 1953-1964.* New York: Atheneum, 1964.

11370. Johnson, Lyndon B. *This America.* New York: Random House, 1966.

11371. Johnson, Lyndon B. *To Heal and to Build: The Programs of President Lyndon B. Johnson.* Edited by James M. Burns. New York: McGraw-Hill, 1968.

11372. Johnson, Lyndon B. *The Vantage Point: Perspectives of the Presidency, 1963-1969.* New York: Holt, Rinehart and Winston, 1971.

11373. Kesaris, Paul, ed. *A Guide to Daily Diary of President Johnson (1963-1969).* Frederick: MD: University Publications of America, 1980.

11374. Rulon, Philip R., ed. *Letters from the Hill Country: The Correspondence between Rebekah and Lyndon Baines Johnson.* Austin, TX: Thorp Springs Press, 1983.

11375. Shepherd, Jack, and Christopher W. Wren. *Quotations from Chairman LBJ.* New York: Simon and Schuster, 1968.

Richard Nixon

Biographies

11376. Abrahamsen, David. *Nixon vs. Nixon: An Emotional Tragedy.* New York: Farrar, Straus and Grioux, 1977.

11377. Allen, Gary. *Richard Nixon: The Man behind the Mask.* Belmont, MA: Western Islands, 1971.

11378. Alsop, Stewart. *Nixon and Rockefeller: A Double Portrait.* Garden City, NY: Doubleday, 1960.

11379. Andrews, Phillip. *This Man Nixon: The Life Story of California Senator Richard M. Nixon (Born 1913), Republican Candidate for Vice President of the United States, His Rise to Fame, His Prosecution of the Hiss Case, His Nomination.* Philadelphia: Winston, 1952.

11380. Brodie, Fawn M. *Richard Nixon: The Shaping of His Character.* Cambridge, MA: Harvard University Press, 1983.

11381. Campbell, Ann R. *The Picture Life of Richard Milhous Nixon.* New York: Franklin Watts, 1969.

11382. Cavan, Sherri. *20th Century Gothic: America's Nixon.* San Francisco: Wigan Pier Press, 1979.

11383. Chesen, Eli S. *President Nixon's Psychiatric Profile: A Psychodynamic-Genetic Interpretation.* New York: P. H. Wyden, 1973.

11384. Costello, William. *The Facts about Nixon: The Unauthorized Biography of Richard M. Nixon: The Formative Years: 1913-1959.* New York: Viking Press, 1960.

11385. DeHart, Frank. *Traumatic Nixon.* Washington, DC: n.p., 1979.

11386. DeToledano, Ralph. *Nixon.* Rev. ed. New York: Duell, Sloan and Pearce, 1960.

11387. DeToledano, Ralph. *One Man Alone: Richard M. Nixon.* New York: Funk and Wagnalls, 1969.

11388. Eisenhower, Julie N., comp. *Eye on Nixon: A Photographic Study of the President and the Man.* New York: Hawthorn, 1972.

11389. Ferlinghetti, Lawrence. *Tyrannius Nix?* New York: New Directions, 1969.

11390. Hart, Roderick P. "Absolutism and Situation: Prolegomena to a Rhetorical Biography of Richard M. Nixon." *Communication Monographs* 43 (August 1976): 204-228.

11391. Hess, Stephen, and Earl Mazo. *Nixon: A Political Portrait.* New York: Harper and Row, 1968.

11392. Hoffman, Paul. *The New Nixon.* New York: Tower Publications, 1970.

11393. Hoyt, Edwin P. *The Nixons: An*

American Family. New York: Random House, 1972.

11394. Hughes, Arthur J. *Richard M. Nixon.* New York: Dodd, Mead, 1972.

11395. Johnson, George. *Richard Nixon: An Intimate and Revealing Portrait of One of America's Key Political Figures.* Derby, CT: Monarch Press, 1961.

11396. Keogh, James. *This Is Nixon.* New York: Putnam, 1956.

11397. Klein, Herbert G. *Making It Perfectly Clear.* Garden City, NY: Doubleday, 1980.

11398. Kornitzer, Bela. *The Real Nixon: An Intimate Biography.* New York: Rand McNally, 1960.

11399. Lasky, Victor. *Richard Nixon.* New York: Putnam, 1984.

11400. Longford, Frank P. *Nixon, A Study in Extremes of Fortune.* London: Weidenfeld and Nicolson, 1980.

11401. Mankiewicz, Frank. *Perfectly Clear: Nixon from Whittier to Watergate.* New York: Praeger, 1975.

11402. Mazo, Earl. *Richard Nixon: A Political and Personal Portrait.* Rev. ed. New York: Avon, 1960.

11403. Mazo, Earl, and Stephen Hess. *Nixon, A Political Portrait.* New York: Harper and Row, 1968.

11404. Schulte, Renee K., ed. *The Young Nixon: An Oral Inquiry.* Fullerton: Oral History Program, California State University, 1978.

11405. Voorhis, Horace J. *The Strange Case of Richard Milhous Nixon.* New York: Popular Library, 1972.

Private Life

11406. Anderson, Walt. "Self-Actualization of Richard M. Nixon." *Journal of Humanistic Psychology* 15 (Winter 1975): 27-35.

11407. Anson, Robert S. *Exile: The Unquiet Oblivion of Richard M. Nixon.* New York: Simon and Schuster, 1984.

11408. Bell, Raymond M. *The Ancestry of Richard Milhous Nixon.* Washington, PA: n.p., 1971.

11409. Brashear, Ernest. "Who Is Richard Nixon?" *New Republic* 127 (September 1, 1952): 9-12; (September 8, 1952): 9-11.

11410. Brown, Steven R. "Richard Nixon and the Public Conscience: The Struggle for Authenticity." *Journal of Psychohistory* 6 (Summer 1978): 93-111.

11411. Brown, Thomas M. "The Exile: One Year of San Clemente." *New York Times Magazine* 124 (August 3, 1975): 8-9, 28-29, 33.

11412. Cameron, Juan. "Richard Nixon's Very Personal White House." *Fortune* 82 (July 1970): 57-59.

11413. David, Lester. *The Lonely Lady of San Clemente: The Story of Pat Nixon.* New York: Crowell, 1978.

11414. Diamond, Edwin. "Psychojournalism: Nixon on the Couch." *Columbia Journal Review* 12 (March/April 1974): 7-11.

11415. Higgins, George. *The Friends of Richard Nixon.* Boston: Little, Brown, 1975.

11416. Jackson, Donald. "The Young Nixon." *Life* 69 (November 6, 1970): 54-66.

11417. Johnson, James P. "Nixon and the Psychohistorians: A Review Essay." *Psychohistory Review* 7 (1979): 38-42.

11418. Kilpatrick, Carroll. "Leonard Garment Is Bright, Musical, A Known New York Liberal, and a Man Close to Richard Nixon." *Washington Post* 184 (June 7, 1970): 17, 27-33.

11419. Marvick, Elizabeth W. "Psychohistory and Richard M. Nixon." *Psychology Today* 6 (July 1972): 77-80.

11420. Mazlish, Bruce. *In Search of Nixon: A Psychological Inquiry.* Baltimore, MD: Penguin, 1972.

11421. Mazlish, Bruce. "Toward a Psychohistorical Inquiry: The 'Real' Richard Nixon." *Journal of Interdisciplinary History* 1 (Autumn 1970): 49-105.

11422. Mazon, Mauricio. "Young Richard Nixon: A Study in Political Precocity." *Historian* 41 (November 1978): 21-40.

11423. Muller, Rene J. "The Fictional Richard Nixon." *Nation* 219 (July 6, 1974): 6-11.

11424. Nixon, Patricia R. "I Say He's a Wonderful Guy." *Saturday Evening Post* 225 (September 6, 1952): 17-19.

11425. Nuechterlein, James A. "Richard Nixon's Character and Fate." *Queen's Quarterly* 86 (Spring 1979): 16-25.

11426. Renshon, Stanley A. "Psychological Analysis and Presidential Personality: The Case of Richard Nixon." *History of Childhood Quarterly* 2 (Winter 1975): 415-450.

11427. Rogin, Michael, and John Lottier. "The Inner History of Richard Milhous Nixon." *Trans-Action* 9 (November/December 1971): 19-28.

11428. Seelye, John. "The Measure of His Company: Richard M. Nixon in Amber." *Virginia Quarterly Review* 53 (Autumn 1977): 585-606.

11429. "Some Tax Questions Raised by President Nixon's Real Estate Transactions." *Journal of Real Estate Taxation* 1 (Spring 1974): 259-263.

11430. Stepanek, Robert H. "The Nixon 'Special.'" *American Aviation Historical Society Journal* 26 (1981): 30-33.

11431. Woodstone, Arthur. *Nixon's Head.* New York: St. Martin's Press, 1972.

Public Career

11432. Arnold, William A. *Back When It All Began: The Early Nixon Years: Being Some Reminiscences of President Nixon's Early Political Career by His First Administrative Assistant and His Press Secretary.* New York: Vantage Press, 1975.

11433. Bullock, Paul. "'Rabbits and Radicals': Richard Nixon's 1946 Campaign against Jerry Voorhis." *Southern California Quarterly* 55 (Fall 1973): 319-359.

11434. Carter, John F. *Republicans on the Potomac: The New Republicans in Action.* New York: McBride, 1953.

11435. Coughlan, Robert. "Success Story of a Vice President." *Life* 35 (December 14, 1953): 146-148.

11436. Dailey, Joseph M. "The Eisenhower-Nixon Campaign Organization of 1952." Ph.D. dissertation, University of Illinois, 1975.

11437. Erskine, Helen W. "Dick and Pat Nixon — The Team on Ike's Team." *Collier's* 134 (July 9, 1954): 32-37.

11438. Flaningam, Carl D. "Complementary Images: The Off-Year Election Campaigns of Richard Nixon in 1954 and Spiro Agnew in 1970." Ph.D. dissertation, Purdue University, 1973.

11439. Frost, David. *"I Gave Them a Sword": Behind the Scenes of the Nixon Interviews.* New York: Morrow, 1978.

11440. Griffin, Clifford S. "The Magic of Richard Nixon." *Reviews in American History* 10 (June 1982): 269-274.

11441. Harris, Mark. *Mark the Glove*

Boy: Or, The Last Days of Richard Nixon. New York: Macmillan, 1964.

11442. Healy, Paul F. "Busiest Vice-President We Ever Had." *Saturday Evening Post* 226 (September 19, 1953): 22-23.

11443. Hiss, Alger. *In the Court of Public Opinion.* New York: Harper and Row, 1957.

11444. Hyman, Sidney. "Between Throttlebottom and Jefferson." *New York Times Magazine* 103 (March 28, 1954): 12, 59-60, 62, 64.

11445. Kissel, Bernard C. "Richard M. Nixon: Definition of an Image." *Quarterly Journal of Speech* 46 (December 1960): 357-361.

11446. Kleinau, Marvin D. "The Role of Rhetoric in the Political Resurrection of Richard M. Nixon: 1963-1968." Ph.D. dissertation, Southern Illinois University, 1978.

11447. Malcolm, Donald F. "The Man Who Wants Second Place." *New Republic* 135 (July 30, 1956): 13-14.

11448. "Nixon, Herter Compared on House Key Votes." *Congressional Quarterly Weekly Report* 14 (August 17, 1956): 1022-1025.

11449. "Nixon's Key Votes in House and Senate, 1947-52." *Congressional Quarterly Weekly Report* 26 (August 16, 1968): 2163-2165.

11450. "Nixon's Participation in Decisions Examined." *Congressional Quarterly Weekly Report* 18 (September 16, 1960): 1577-1580.

11451. Reuben, William A. *The Honorable Mr. Nixon.* 2d ed. New York: Action Books, 1958.

11452. "Review of Nixon's Life, Voting Record, Stands on Issues." *Congressional Quarterly Weekly Report* 18 (August 12, 1960): 1394-1398.

11453. Roper, William L. "Nixon's Man to See." *Nation* 181 (July 2, 1955): 4-7.

11454. Rowse, Arthur E. *Slanted News: A Case Study of the Nixon and Stevenson Fund Stories.* Westport, CT: Greenwood Press, 1973.

11455. Scobie, Ingrid W. "Helen Gahagan Douglas and Her 1950 Senate Race with Richard M. Nixon." *Southern California Quarterly* 58 (Spring 1976): 113-126.

11456. "What's Wrong with the Way We Pick Our Presidents?" *U.S. News & World Report* 97 (July 23, 1984): 28-30.

11457. Wills, Garry. "The Hiss Connection through Nixon's Life." *New York Times Magazine* 123 (August 25, 1974): 8-9, 40, 42, 44, 46.

11458. Wills, Garry. *Nixon Agonistes: The Crisis of the Self-Made Man.* Boston: Houghton Mifflin, 1970.

11459. Wilson, Richard L. "Is Nixon Fit to Be President?" *Look* 17 (February 24, 1953): 33-42.

11460. Witcover, Jules. *The Resurrection of Richard Nixon.* New York: Putnam, 1970.

Presidential Years

General

11461. Aberbach, Joel D., and Bert A. Rockman. "Clashing Beliefs within the Executive Branch: The Nixon Administration Bureaucracy." *American Political Science Review* 70 (June 1976): 456-468.

11462. Alsop, Stewart. "Nixon and the Square Majority: Is the Fox a Lion?" *Atlantic Monthly* 229 (February 1972): 41-47.

11463. Atkins, Ollie. *The White House*

Years: Triumph and Tragedy. Chicago: Playboy Press, 1977.

11464. Balfour, Nancy. "President Nixon's Second Term." *World Today* (Great Britain) 29 (March 1973): 98-107.

11465. Barber, James D. "President Nixon and Richard Nixon: Character Trap." *Psychology Today* 8 (October 1974): 113-118.

11466. Barfield, Claude E. "Nixon Reorganization Raises Questions about Role of Science in Federal Policy-Making." *National Journal* 5 (March 24, 1973): 405-415.

11467. Baudhuim, E. Scott. "From Campaign to Watergate: Nixon's Communication Image." *Western Speech* 38 (Summer 1974): 182-189.

11468. Bhagwati, Jagdish. "The United States in the Nixon Era: The End of Innocence." *Daedalus* 101 (Fall 1972): 25-48.

11469. Blackstock, Paul W. "The Intelligence Community under the Nixon Administration." *Armed Forces and Society* 1 (Winter 1975): 321-350.

11470. Bonafede, Dom. "Agencies Resist Nixon Directive to Cut Back Spending on Public Relations." *National Journal* 3 (July 24, 1971): 1551-1556.

11471. Bonafede, Dom. "Bureaucracy, Congress, Interests See Threat in Nixon Reorganization Plan." *National Journal* 3 (May 8, 1971): 977-986.

11472. Bonafede, Dom. "Charles W. Colson, President's Liaison with Outside World." *National Journal* 2 (August 8, 1970): 1689-1694.

11473. Bonafede, Dom. "New Task Forces Seek Ideas for President's 1970 Program." *National Journal* 1 (November 1, 1969): 2-3, 6.

11474. Bonafede, Dom. "Nixon Personnel Staff Works to Restructure Federal Policies." *National Journal* 3 (December 11, 1971): 2440-2448.

11475. Bonafede, Dom. "Nixon's First-Year Appointments Reveal Pattern of His Administration." *National Journal* 2 (January 24, 1970): 182-192.

11476. Bonafede, Dom. "Nixon's Troubles Being Enhanced Role for Cabinet, Better Working Relationships." *National Journal* 5 (October 6, 1973): 1472-1478.

11477. Bonafede, Dom. "President Nixon's Executive Reorganization Plans Prompt Praise and Criticism." *National Journal* 5 (March 10, 1973): 329-344.

11478. Bonafede, Dom. "President Still Seeks to Restore Staff Efficiency, Morale." *National Journal* 6 (January 5, 1974): 1-6.

11479. Bonafede, Dom. "Speechwriters Play Strategic Role in Conveying, Shaping Nixon's Policies." *National Journal* 4 (February 19, 1972): 311-320.

11480. Bonafede, Dom, and L. Allin. "President's News Digest Is a Potpourri in Two Daily Doses." *National Journal* 6 (January 1974): 131-136.

11481. Bonafede, Dom, and Jonathan Cottin. "Nixon, In Reorganization Plan, Seeks Tighter Rein on Bureaucracy." *National Journal* 2 (March 21, 1970): 620-626.

11482. Bonafede, Dom, and Andrew J. Glass. "Nixon Deals Cautiously with Hostile Congress." *National Journal* 2 (June 27, 1970): 1353-1366.

11483. Bowler, Marion K. *The Nixon Guaranteed Income Proposal: Substance and Process in Policy Change.* Cambridge, MA: Ballinger, 1974.

11484. Brandon, Henry. "The Balance of Mutual Weakness: Nixon's Voyage into the World of the 1970s." *Atlantic Monthly* 231 (January 1973): 35-42.

11485. Brandon, Henry. *The Retreat of American Power.* Garden City, NY: Doubleday, 1973.

11486. Brody, Richard A., and Benjamin I. Page. "The Impact of Events on Presidential Popularity: The Johnson and Nixon Administrations." In *Perspectives on the Presidency,* edited by Aaron B. Wildavsky, 136-147. Boston: Little, Brown, 1975.

11487. Brummett, Barry. "Presidential Substance: The Address of August 15, 1973." *Western Speech Communication* 39 (Fall 1975): 249-259.

11488. Buchanan, Patrick J. *A New Majority: President Nixon at Mid-Passage.* Philadelphia: Girard Bank, 1973.

11489. Chace, James. "Five-Power World of Richard Nixon." *New York Times Magazine* 121 (February 20, 1972): 14-15, 47-47.

11490. Chadwin, M. L. "Nixon's Expropriation Policy Seeks to Soothe Angry Congress." *National Journal* 4 (January 22, 1972): 148-156.

11491. Chapel, William G. "Speechwriting in the Nixon Administration." *Journal of Communication* 26 (Spring 1976): 65-72.

11492. Church, Russell T. "President Richard M. Nixon's Crisis Rhetoric, 1969-1972." Ph.D. dissertation, Temple University, 1977.

11493. Cole, Richard L., and David A. Caputo. "Presidential Control of the Senior Civil Service: Assessing the Strategies of the Nixon Years." *American Political Science Review* 73 (June 1979): 399-413.

11494. Collins, Robert M. "Richard M. Nixon: The Psychic, Political, and Moral Uses of Sport." *Journal of Sport History* 10 (Summer 1983): 77-84.

11495. Congressional Quarterly. *Nixon: The Years of His Presidency.* Washington, DC: Congressional Quarterly, 1970.

11496. Craig, G. M. "The Campaign, Nixon, and American Atlantic Policy." *International Journal* 24 (Spring 1969): 302-309.

11497. Curtis, Alan M. "Political Speechwriting ('Ghostwriting') in the Nixon Administration, 1968-1972: Implications for Rhetorical Criticism." Ph.D. dissertation, University of Southern California, 1973.

11498. Dean, John W., III. *Blind Ambition: The White House Years.* New York: Simon and Schuster, 1976.

11499. Dean, John W., III. "*Playboy* Interview: John Dean." *Playboy* 22 (January 1975): 65-66, 68-80.

11500. Destler, Irving M. "The Nixon System, A Further Look." *Foreign Service Journal* 51 (February 1974): 9-15, 28-29.

11501. Drury, Allen. *Courage and Hesitation: Notes and Photographs of the Nixon Administration.* Garden City, NY: Doubleday, 1971.

11502. Dworkin, Ronald. "The Jurisprudence of Richard Nixon." *New York Review of Books* 18 (May 4, 1972): 27-35.

11503. Ehrlichman, John. *Witness to Power: The Nixon Years.* New York: Simon and Schuster, 1982.

11504. Einhorn, Jessica P. "The Effect of Bureaucratic Politics on the Expropriation Policy of the Nixon Administration: Two Case Studies, 1969-1972." Ph.D. dissertation, Princeton University, 1974.

11505. Eisenhower, David, and Julie Eisenhower. "Interview with David and Julie Eisenhower." *U.S. News & World Report* 75 (October 8, 1973): 34-40.

11506. Ettlinger, Catherine. "Nixon's Head Hunter: Jerry Jones Claims the White House Fills Its Vacancies Rapidly."

Government Executive 6 (January 1974): 50-53.

11507. Etzioni, Amitai, and Peggy Anderson. "Willing Hands for What?" *Washington Monthly* 1 (June 1969): 44-51.

11508. Evans, Rowland, Jr., and Robert D. Novak. *Nixon in the White House: The Frustration of Power.* New York: Vintage, 1971.

11509. "The Fairness Problem Reexamined: Has the Press Done a Job on Nixon?" *Columbia Law Review* 12 (January/February 1974): 50-58.

11510. Fallows, James. "Crazies by the Tail: Bay of Pigs, Diem, and Liddy." *Washington Monthly* 6 (September 1974): 50-58.

11511. Felknor, Bruce. *Dirty Politics.* New York: Norton, 1966.

11512. Fixler, Philip, Jr. "A Content Analysis of American Presidential Rhetoric: An Exploratory Study of Misrepresentative and Deceptive Language in the Major Communications of Presidents Kennedy, Johnson, and Nixon." Ph.D. dissertation, University of Southern California, 1979.

11513. Fox, Douglas M., ed. "A Mini-Symposium: President Nixon's Proposals for Executive Reorganization." *Public Administration Review* 34 (September/October 1974): 487-495.

11514. Furlow, Barbara. "Portrait of Two Presidents: Nixon and Johnson." *U.S. News & World Report* 67 (July 28, 1969): 52-54.

11515. Gartner, Alan, Colin Green, and Frank Riessman. *What Nixon Is Doing to Us.* New York: Harper and Row, 1973.

11516. Gibson, James W., and Patricia K. Felkins. "A Nixon Lexicon." *Western Speech* 38 (Summer 1974): 190-198.

11517. Ginger, Ann F. "The Nixon-Burger Court and What to Do about It." *National Lawyer's Guild Practitioner* 33 (Fall 1976): 143-151.

11518. Glass, Andrew J. "Congress Weighs Novel Procedures to Overturn Nixon Impoundment Policy." *National Journal* 5 (February 17, 1973): 236-242.

11519. Goldbloom, Maurice J. "Nixon So Far." *Commentary* 49 (March 1970): 29-38.

11520. Goldman, Sheldon. "Johnson and Nixon Appointees to the Lower Federal Courts: Some Socio-Political Perspectives." *Journal of Politics* 34 (August 1972): 934-942.

11521. Goldwater, Barry M. "Barry Goldwater Speaks His Mind on Richard Nixon." *U.S. News & World Report* 76 (February 1974): 38-42.

11522. Gonchar, Ruth M., and Dan F. Hahn. "Richard Nixon and Presidential Mythology." *Journal of Applied Communications Research* 1 (Winter/Spring 1973): 25-48.

11523. Gottschall, Jon S. "The Nixon Appointments to the United States Courts of Appeals: The Impact of the Law and Order Issue on the Rights of the Accused." Ph.D. dissertation, University of Massachusetts, 1976.

11524. Guerra, David M. "Network Television News Policy and the Nixon Administration: A Comparison." Ph.D. dissertation, New York University, 1974.

11525. Haight, Timothy R., and Richard A. Brody. "Mass Media and Presidential Popularity: Presidential Broadcasting and News in the Nixon Administration." *Communication Research* 4 (January 1977): 41-60.

11526. Haldeman, Harry R. *The Ends of Power.* New York: New York Times Books, 1978.

11527. Hall, Gus. *Lame Duck in Turbu-*

lent Waters: The Next Four Years of Nixon. New York: New Outlook, 1972.

11528. Hallett, Douglas. "A Low-Level Memoir of the Nixon White House." *New York Times Magazine* 124 (October 20, 1974): 39-42, 52, 56-63, 67, 70.

11529. Hartley, Anthony. "The Nixon Regime." *Encounter* 32 (March 1969): 20-24.

11530. Henderson, Charles P. *The Nixon Theology.* New York: Harper and Row, 1972.

11531. Henderson, John T. "Leadership Personality and War: The Cases of Richard Nixon and Anthony Eden." *Political Science* (New Zealand) 28 (December 1976): 141-164.

11532. Henkin, Louis. "Executive Privilege: Mr. Nixon Loses But the Presidency Largely Prevails." *UCLA Law Review* 22 (October 1974): 40-46.

11533. Hentoff, Nat. "Librarians and the First Amendment after Nixon." *Wilson Library Bulletin* 48 (May 1974): 742-747.

11534. Herbers, John. "The Other Presidency." *New York Times Magazine* 113 (March 3, 1974): 16-17, 30, 32, 34, 36, 38, 41.

11535. Hersh, Seymour M. *The Price of Power: Kissinger in the Nixon White House.* New York: Summit Books, 1983.

11536. Hess, Allen K., and Dan Grossett. "Nixon and the Media: A Study of Non-Immediacy in Newspaper Editorials as Reflective of Geographical Attitude Differences." *Psychological Reports* 34 (June 1974): 1055-1058.

11537. "A History of Nixon's Relations with Congress, 1969-73." *Congressional Quarterly Weekly Report* 31 (September 15, 1973): 2428-2429.

11538. "How Nixon Handles World's Biggest Job: Interview with H. R. Haldeman, Assistant to the President." *U.S. News & World Report* 69 (September 14, 1970): 56-62.

11539. "How Nixon's White House Works." *Time Magazine* (June 8, 1970): 15-20.

11540. Howard, A. E. Dick. "Mr. Justice Powell and the Emerging Nixon Majority." *Michigan Law Review* 70 (January 1972): 445-468.

11541. "John Connally: Mr. Nixon's No. 2 Man?" *Newsweek* 78 (August 9, 1971): 16-20.

11542. "Judicial Interpretation of the Nixon Presidency." *Cumberland Law Review* 6 (Spring 1975): 213-242.

11543. Kaufman, K. A. "New Cabinet Is Cast from Nixon Mold." *Iron Age* 203 (January 2, 1969): 94-97.

11544. Kauper, Paul G. "Judicial Review and 'Strict Construction' of the Constitution: President Nixon and the Supreme Court of the United States." *Zeitschrift fur auslaandisches offentliches Recht und Volkerrecht* 30 (December 1970): 631-645.

11545. Kenski, Henry C. "The Impact of Unemployment on Presidential Popularity from Eisenhower to Nixon." *Presidential Studies Quarterly* 7 (Spring/Summer 1977): 114-126.

11546. Keogh, James. *President Nixon and the Press.* New York: Funk and Wagnalls, 1972.

11547. Khan, Rais A. "The Nixon Administration — Problems and Prospects." *Pakistan Horizon* 22 (1969): 3-21.

11548. King, Andrew A., and Floyd D. Anderson. "Nixon, Agnew, and the 'Silent Majority': A Case Study in the Rhetoric of Polarization." *Western Speech* 35 (Fall 1971): 243-255.

11549. Kisteneff, Alexis P. "The New Federalism of Richard Nixon as Counter-

Revolution to the American Liberal State: A Study in Political Theory and Public Policy." Ph.D. dissertation, Brown University, 1977.

11550. Koenig, Louis W. "Recipe for Presidency's Destruction." *George Washington Law Review* 43 (January 1975): 376-379.

11551. Laing, Robert B., and Robert L. Stevenson. "Public Opinion Trends in the Last Days of the Nixon Administration." *Journalism Quarterly* 53 (Summer 1976): 294-302.

11552. Lashner, Marilyn A. *The Chilling Effect in TV News: Intimidation by the Nixon White House*. New York: Praeger, 1984.

11553. Leiter, William M. "The Presidency and Non-Federal Government: The Benefactor-Aversion Hypothesis, The Case of Public Resistance Policies in the New Deal and Nixon Administrations." *Presidential Studies Quarterly* 11 (Spring 1981): 280-288.

11554. Lessard, Suzannah. "Nixon and His Own Staff: The View from Their Own Mirror." *Washington Monthly* 4 (May 1972): 53-59.

11555. Lichtenstein, Nelson, and Eleanora W. Schoenebaum, eds. *Political Profiles: The Nixon/Ford Years*. New York: Facts on File, 1979.

11556. Lieberman, Carl. "President Nixon and Reorganization of the Executive Branch." *International Review of History and Political Science* 9 (November 1972): 16-27.

11557. Luce, David R. "Polishing up the Language of a Sedition Statute: The Smith Act, Nixon's 'Smith Act,' and the 'Smith Act' in the McCellan-Hruska Criminal Code Bill." *Loyola University of Los Angeles Law Review* 9 (March 1976): 303-322.

11558. Lukas, J. Anthony. *Nightmare: The Underside of the Nixon Years*. New York: Viking Press, 1976.

11559. Lurie, Ranan R. *Nixon Rated Cartoons*. Rev. ed. New York: Quadrangle Books, 1974.

11560. McCullar, Francis M., and William A. Howell. "No, Sir, Mr. President." *United States Army Aviation Digest* 19 (August 1973): 2-3.

11561. McKenzie, Richard B., and Bruce Yandle. "The Logic of 'Irrational' Politics: Nixon's Reelection Committee." *Public Finance Quarterly* 8 (January 1980): 39-55.

11562. McLain, J. Dudley, Jr. "Supreme Court Controversies of Presidents Roosevelt and Nixon: A Consideration of the Political Nature of the Presidential Power of Judicial Appointment." *Georgia State Bar Journal* 8 (November 1971): 145-179.

11563. Malone, Dumas. "Executive Privilege: Jefferson and Burr and Ehrlichman." *New York Review of Books* 21 (July 18, 1974): 36-40.

11564. Manning, Clarence A. "The Position of President Nixon." *Ukrainian Quarterly* 25 (Summer 1969): 165-173.

11565. Marcell, David W. "Poor Richard: Nixon and the Problem of Innocence." In *American Character and Culture in a Changing World: Some Twentieth-Century Perspectives*, edited by John A. Hague, 325-337. Westport, CT: Greenwood Press, 1979.

11566. Martin, David L. "Presidential Attitudes toward the Bureaucracy: The White House Tapes." *Bureaucrat* 4 (July 1975): 223-224.

11567. Marvell, Charles. *In Defense of Nixon: A Study in Political Psychology and Political Pathology*. Albuquerque, NM: American Classical Call Press, 1976.

11568. Meehan, Mary. "Nixon's Flying

Fuhrerbunker." *Washington Monthly* 6 (April 1974): 22-28.

11569. Merenda, Peter F., Torab Bassiri, Reza Shapurian, and Walter V. Clarke. "Iranian Perceptions of the Reza Shah, Presidents Nixon and Johnson, and the Ideal Self." *Perceptual and Motor Skills* 33 (October 1971): 428-430.

11570. Millen, William. *Nixonia: Fact, Fable, Fantasy.* New York: Exposition Press, 1970.

11571. Moe, Ronald C. "Senate Confirmation of Executive Appointments: The Nixon Era." *Academy of Political Science Proceedings* 32 (1975): 141-152.

11572. Mollenhoff, Clark R. *Game Plan for Disaster: An Ombudsman's Report on the Nixon Years.* New York: Norton, 1976.

11573. Morgenthau, Hans J. "The Aborted Nixon Revolution." *New Republic* 169 (August 11, 1973): 17-19.

11574. Murphy, Timothy F. "The Politics of Anticommunism: Its Utilization in the Careers of Richard Nixon and Joseph McCarthy." Master's thesis, Florida Atlantic University, 1972.

11575. Neruda, Pablo. *Incitement to Nixonicide.* Houston, TX: Quixote, 1979.

11576. New York Times. *The End of a Presidency.* New York: Bantam Books, 1973.

11577. Nihart, Brooke. "New Staff System after One Year." *Armed Forces Journal* 107 (April 4, 1970): 25-29.

11578. "Nixon: A Four-Year Record of Pluses and Minuses." *Congressional Quarterly Weekly Report* 30 (August 26, 1972): 2121-2140.

11579. "The Nixon Administration and the News Media." *Congressional Quarterly Weekly Report* 30 (January 1, 1973): 3-7.

11580. "Nixon Cabinet." *Congressional Quarterly Weekly Report* 30 (December 2, 1972): 3075-3083.

11581. *Nixon: The Fifth Year of His Presidency.* Washington, DC: Congressional Quarterly, 1974.

11582. *Nixon: The First Year of His Presidency.* Washington, DC: Congressional Quarterly, 1970.

11583. *Nixon: The Fourth Year of His Presidency.* Washington, DC: Congressional Quarterly, 1973.

11584. *Nixon: The Second Year of His Presidency.* Washington, DC: Congressional Quarterly, 1971.

11585. *Nixon: The Third Year of His Presidency.* Washington, DC: Congressional Quarterly, 1972.

11586. "*Nixon v. Fitzgerald:* A Justifiable Separation of Powers Argument for Absolute Presidential Civil Damages Immunity?" *Iowa Law Review* 68 (March 1983): 557-584.

11587. "*Nixon v. Fitzgerald:* Presidential Immunity as a Constitutional Imperative." *Catholic University Law Review* 32 (Spring 1983): 759-785.

11588. "The Nixon Years." *Washington Post* 97 (August 9, 1974): 1-24.

11589. "Nixon's Inner Circle of Businessmen." *Business Week* (July 31, 1971): 52-56.

11590. "Nixon's Private Circle." *U.S. News & World Report* 74 (May 1973): 23-25.

11591. O'Brien, Robert W., and Elizabeth Jones. *The Night Nixon Spoke.* Los Alamitos, CA: Hwong Publications, 1976.

11592. "On Nixon Appointments to the Executive Office of the President and the Various Executive Departments." *Congressional Quarterly Weekly Report* 27 (January 31, 1969): 191-196.

11593. Orenstein, Aviva A. "Presidential Immunity from Civil Liability: *Nixon v. Fitzgerald.*" *Cornell Law Review* 68 (January 1983): 236-256.

11594. Osborne, John. *The Fifth Year of the Nixon Watch.* New York: Liveright, 1974.

11595. Osborne, John. *The First Two Years of the Nixon Watch.* New York: Liveright, 1971.

11596. Osborne, John. *The Fourth Year of the Nixon Watch.* New York: Liveright, 1973.

11597. Osborne, John. *The Last Nixon Watch.* Washington, DC: New Republic, 1975.

11598. Osborne, John. *The Nixon Watch.* New York: Liveright, 1970.

11599. Osborne, John. "Nixon's Command Staff." *New Republic* 160 (February 15, 1969): 15-17.

11600. Osborne, John. *The Second Year of the Nixon Watch.* New York: Liveright, 1971.

11601. Osborne, John. "Summing up of a Nixon-Watcher." *New Republic* 159 (October 26, 1968): 15-17.

11602. Osborne, John. *The Third Year of the Nixon Watch.* New York: Liveright, 1972.

11603. Osgood, Robert E., Robert W. Tucker, Francis E. Rourke, Herbert S. Dinerstein, Laurence W. Martin, David P. Calleo, Benjamin M. Rowland, and George Liska. *Retreat from Empire? The First Nixon Administration.* Baltimore, MD: Johns Hopkins University Press, 1973.

11604. Peebles, Thomas H. "Mr. Justice Frankfurter and the Nixon Court: Some Reflections on Contemporary Judicial Conservatism." *American University Law Review* 24 (Fall 1974): 1-90.

11605. Pellicciotti, Joseph M. "*Nixon v. Fitzgerald:* Presidential Immunity." *Res Gestae* 26 (November 1982): 222-225.

11606. Peters, Charles. "The Prince and His Courtiers: At the White House, the Kremlin, and the Reichschancellery." *Washington Monthly* 4 (February 1973): 30-39.

11607. Peters, Mike. *The Nixon Chronicles.* Dayton, OH: Lorenz Press, 1976.

11608. Pomper, Gerald M. "Nixon and the End of Presidential Politics." *Society* 10 (March/April 1973): 14-16.

11609. Porter, William E. *Assault on the Media: The Nixon Years.* Ann Arbor: University of Michigan Press, 1975.

11610. "President Nixon's Proposal on the Insanity Defense." *Journal of Psychiatry and Law* 1 (Fall 1973): 297-334.

11611. "The Public Record of Richard M. Nixon." *Congressional Quarterly Weekly Report* 25 (June 23, 1967): 1081-1091.

11612. "The Public Record of Richard M. Nixon." *Congressional Quarterly Weekly Report* 26 (August 16, 1968): 2145-2163.

11613. Quint, Peter E. "Separation of Powers under Nixon: Reflections on Constitutional Liberties and the Rule of Law." *Duke Law Journal* (February 1981): 1-70.

11614. Raven, Bertram H. "Nixon Group." *Journal of Social Issues* 30 (1974): 297-320.

11615. Reeves, Richard. "Nixon's Men Are Smart But No Swingers." *New York Times Magazine* 118 (September 29, 1968): 28-29, 127-132.

11616. Reichley, A. James. "Conservative Roots of the Nixon, Ford, and Reagan Administrations." *Political Science Quarterly* 96 (Winter 1981-1982): 537-550.

11617. Reichley, A. James. *Conservatives*

in an Age of Change: The Nixon and Ford Administrations. Washington, DC: Brookings Institution, 1981.

11618. "Rhetoric Meets Reality." *Life* 66 (January 31, 1969): 18-31.

11619. Rhodes, Edwin S. "From Burr to Nixon." *Federal Bar Journal* 35 (Summer/Fall 1976): 218-227.

11620. "Richard M. Nixon: End of a Remarkable Career." *Congressional Quarterly Weekly Report* 32 (August 10, 1974): 2083-2126.

11621. Roberts, Dick. "Who Rules Nixon?" *International Socialist Review* 34 (November 1973): 6-13.

11622. Robitscher, Jonas. "Stigmatization and Stonewalling: The Ordeal of Martha Mitchell." *Journal of Psychohistory* 6 (Winter 1979): 393-408.

11623. Rogin, Michael. "The King's Two Bodies: Abraham Lincoln, Richard Nixon, and Presidential Self-Sacrifice." *Massachusetts Review* 20 (Autumn 1979): 553-573.

11624. Rosenberg, Leonard B. "Luck of Design: The Fall of Richard M. Nixon." *Politico* (Italy) 40 (December 1975): 706-709.

11625. Roth, Philip. *Our Gang (Starring Tricky and His Friends)*. New York: Random House, 1971.

11626. Sandler, Samuel. "Reconciling Domestic and International Politics: The Eisenhower and the Nixon Presidencies." Ph.D. dissertation, Johns Hopkins University, 1977.

11627. Saxon, Thomas J., Jr. "The Evolution of the National Security System under President Nixon." Ph.D. dissertation, University of Maryland, 1971.

11628. Scheer, Robert. *America after Nixon*. New York: McGraw-Hill, 1974.

11629. Schoenebaum, Eleanora W., ed. *Profiles of an Era: The Nixon/Ford Years*. New York: Harcourt, Brace, Jovanovich, 1979.

11630. Schwartz, Bernard. "Bad Presidents Make Hard Law: Richard M. Nixon in the Supreme Court." *Rutgers Law Review* 31 (May 1978): 22-40.

11631. Semple, Robert B. "The Middle American Who Edits Ideas for Nixon." *New York Times Magazine* 119 (April 12, 1970): 32-33, 60, 62, 64, 67, 69-70, 72, 74.

11632. Semple, Robert B. "Richard M. Nixon: A Tentative Evaluation." In *Power and the Presidency*, edited by Philip C. Dolce and George H. Skau, 164-174. New York: Scribner's, 1976.

11633. Seymour, Whitney N., Jr. *United States Attorney, An Inside View of 'Justice' in America under the Nixon Administration*. New York: Morrow, 1975.

11634. Simon, James F. *In His Own Image: The Supreme Court in Richard Nixon's America*. New York: McKay, 1973.

11635. Smith, Franklin B. *Assassination of President Nixon*. Rutland, VT: Academy Books, 1976.

11636. Smith, Lincoln. "President Nixon's Regulatory Appointments." *Public Utilities Fortnightly* 88 (December 9, 1971): 34-39.

11637. Spalding, Henry D. *The Nixon Nobody Knows*. Middle Village, NY: Jonathan David, 1972.

11638. Spear, Joseph C. "The President and the Press: A Critical Analysis of the Nixon Administration's Policy toward the News Media." Master's thesis, American University, 1973.

11639. Sprague, R. E. "Nixon, Ford, and the Political Assassinations and Attempted Assassinations." *Presidential Studies Quarterly* 10 (Summer 1980): 336-347.

11640. Stewart, Maxwell S. "Nixon's

New Federalism." *Current History* 61 (November 1971): 279-283, 307.

11641. Strachan, Jill P. "Richard Nixon: Representative Religious American." Ph.D. dissertation, Syracuse University, 1981.

11642. Strong, Frank R. "President, Congress, Judiciary: One Is More Equal Than the Others." *American Bar Association Journal* 60 (September 1974): 1050-1052.

11643. Tetter, Dwight L., Jr. "Kicking Nixon Around Once More." *Reviews in American History* 4 (December 1976): 607-613.

11644. Ulmer, S. Sidney, and John A. Stookey. "Nixon's Legacy to the Supreme Court: A Statistical Analysis of Judicial Behavior." *Florida State University Law Review* 3 (Summer 1975): 331-347.

11645. U.S. Congress. House. Committee on the Judiciary. *White House Staff and President Nixon's Campaign Organizations*. Washington, DC: U.S. Government Printing Office, 1974.

11646. U.S. General Accounting Office. *Protection of the President at Key Biscayne and San Clemente (with Information on Protection of Past Presidents)*. Washington, DC: General Accounting Office, 1973.

11647. Vale, Vivian. "The Collaborative Chaos of Federal Administration." *Government and Opposition* 8 (Spring 1973): 177-194.

11648. Vale, Vivian. "The Obligation to Spend: Presidential Impoundment of Congressional Appropriations." *Political Studies* 25 (December 1977): 508-522.

11649. Van Alstyne, William W. "President Nixon: Toughing It Out with the Law." *American Bar Association Journal* 59 (December 1973): 1398-1402.

11650. Van Der Linden, Frank. *Nixon's Quest for Peace*. Washington, DC: Luce, 1972.

11651. Vidal, Gore. *An Evening with Richard Nixon*. New York: Random House, 1972.

11652. Viorst, Milton. "Nixon of the O.P.A." *New York Times Magazine* 121 (October 3, 1971): 70, 72, 74, 76.

11653. Viorst, Milton. "William Rogers Thinks Like Richard Nixon." *New York Times Magazine* 121 (February 27, 1972): 12-13, 30-38.

11654. Washington Post. *The Fall of a President*. New York: Delacorte Press, 1974.

11655. Whitfield, Stephen J. "Richard Nixon as a Comic Figure." *American Quarterly* 37 (Spring 1985): 114-132.

11656. Wildavsky, Aaron B. "Richard Nixon, President of the United States." *Trans-Action* 5 (October 1968): 8-15.

11657. Wills, Garry. "Richard Nixon's Seventh Crisis." *New York Times Magazine* 122 (July 8, 1973): 7, 21, 24-25, 27-28.

11658. Wilson, Gerald L. "Strategy of Explanation: Richard M. Nixon's August 8, 1974, Resignation Address." *Communication Quarterly* 24 (Summer 1976): 14-20.

11659. Wise, David. "The Defending of the President." *New York Times Magazine* 123 (May 26, 1974): 10-11, 57, 60-62, 64-66.

11660. Zill, Anne B. "Twelve Columnists Look at Richard Nixon after a Year." Master's thesis, American University, 1970.

Domestic Policy

11661. Alexander, Jim R. "Congress and the Nixon Welfare Reform Proposals: A Study in the Formation of Public Policy." Ph.D. dissertation, American University, 1974.

11662. "Association Board of Governors Faults President Nixon for Flouting Laws and Courts and Urges a New Special Prosecutor." *American Bar Association Journal* 59 (December 1973): 1389-1392.

11663. Banfield, Edward C., Nathan Glazer, Michael Harrington, Tom Kahn, Christopher Lasch, Robert Lekachman, Bayard Rustin, Gus Tyler, and George F. Will. "Nixon, the Great Society, and the Future of Social Policy: A Symposium." *Commentary* 55 (May 1973): 31-61.

11664. Barber, Rims, and Joseph J. Huttie, Jr. "Nixonian Economics: Another View." *New South* 28 (Spring 1973): 72-78.

11665. Berman, Bruce J. "Richard Nixon and the New Corporate State." *Queen's Quarterly* 80 (Autumn 1973): 425-433.

11666. Biggs, Ernest E. "The Educational Policies of Richard M. Nixon." Ed.D. dissertation, Auburn University, 1973.

11667. Bonafede, Dom. "Ehrlichman Acts as a Policy Broker in Nixon's Formalized Domestic Council." *National Journal* 3 (June 12, 1971): 1235-1244.

11668. Brandow, G. E. "A Discussion of the 1973 Economic Report of the President: The Food Price Problem." *American Journal of Agricultural Economics* 55 (August 1973): 385-390.

11669. Burby, John F. "President's Budget Requests Seek to Reshape Domestic Government." *National Journal* 5 (February 3, 1973): 139-145.

11670. Burby, John F., and Harry Lenhart, Jr. "Nixon's Change in Game Plan Reflects Confidence in CEA, McCracken." *National Journal* 3 (August 21, 1971): 1743-1753.

11671. Burke, Vee J., and Vincent Burke. *Nixon's Good Deed: Welfare Reform and Supplemental Security Income.* New York: Columbia University Press, 1974.

11672. Busch, D. Carolyn, and Lee E. Hartman, Jr. "Jefferson and Hackney: Charting the Direction of the Nixon Court." *Public Welfare* 31 (Spring 1973): 55-63.

11673. Cottin, Jonathan. "Ash Council, Governors Fault Nixon's Intergovernmental Relations Office." *National Journal* 3 (January 23, 1971): 182-185.

11674. Davidson, Lawrence S. "The Macroeconomic Impact of the Nixon Wage and Price Controls: A General Equilibrium Approach." *Journal of Macroeconomics* 5 (Fall 1983): 399-420.

11675. Davidson, Lawrence S. "The Nixon Wage and Price Controls: A Theoretical and Empirical Analysis." Ph.D. dissertation, University of North Carolina, 1977.

11676. Doctors, Samuel I., and Anne S. Huff. *Minority Enterprise and the President's Council.* Cambridge, MA: Ballinger, 1973.

11677. Doctors, Samuel I., and Harvey A. Juris. "Management and Technical Assistance for Minority Enterprise: Some Guidelines for Design and Implementation of the President's Program." *Urban Affairs Quarterly* 7 (June 1972): 473-487.

11678. Drischler, Alvin P. "General-Purpose Forces in the Nixon Budgets." *Survival* 15 (May/June 1973): 119-123.

11679. English, H. Edward. "Nixon's Economic Opportunities." *International Journal* 24 (Spring 1969): 310-326.

11680. Epstein, Edward J. "The Krogh File — The Politics of 'Law and Order.'" *Public Interest* 39 (Spring 1975): 99-124.

11681. Forbes, Jack D. *Native Americans and Nixon: Presidential Politics and Minority Self-Determination, 1969-1972.* Los Angeles: American Indian Studies Center, UCLA, 1981.

11682. Fowlkes, Frank V. "Connally Revitalizes Treasury, Assumes Stewardship of Nixon's New Economic Policy." *National Journal* 3 (October 2, 1971): 1988-1997.

11683. Fry, Bobby J. "Nixon's Program of Wage and Price Controls." Master's thesis, North Texas State University, 1974.

11684. Gammill, Patrick D. "The Evolution of Spectator Sports and the Emergence of the Garrison State: The Nixon Sports Campaign." Ph.D. dissertation, University of Texas, 1982.

11685. Gass, Oscar. "The Nixon Economy." *Worldview* 16 (July 1973): 7-14.

11686. Glass, Andrew J. "Democratic Challenge to Nixon Budget Bogs Down over Lack of Alternative Proposals." *National Journal* 5 (April 14, 1973): 527-534.

11687. Grossack, Irvin M., and Michel Fratianni. "President Nixon's New Economic Policies." *Indiana Business Review* 46 (August/September 1971): 1-16.

11688. Hogue, W. Dickerson. "International Implications of President Nixon's Blockbuster Economic Changes." *Indiana Business Review* 46 (August/September 1971): 20-24.

11689. Iglehart, John K. "Governors Lose Enthusiasm for Nixon's Revenue-Sharing Programs." *National Journal* 5 (June 30, 1973): 935-943.

11690. Iglehart, John K., William Lilley III, and Timothy B. Clark. "Budget Strains Alliance between Nixon and State-Local Officials." *National Journal* 5 (February 17, 1973): 215-225.

11691. Iglehart, John K., Judith Robinson, Andrea F. Schoenfeld, and Ed Willingham. "HEW's Agency Heads Gain Power as Nixon Philosophy Brings Turmoil and Change." *National Journal* 2 (September 19, 1970): 2036-2051.

11692. Lekachman, Robert. "The New American Tories: A Critique of Nixon's Welfare Program." *Dissent* 16 (November/December 1969): 471-476.

11693. Lekachman, Robert. "Nixon's Program." *Commentary* 47 (June 1969): 67-72.

11694. McGee, Gale W. "A Constitutional Crisis." *Freedom at Issue* 4 (1973): 7-8, 21-23.

11695. Miller, Roger L., and Raburn M. Williams. *The New Economics of Richard Nixon: Freezes, Floats, and Fiscal Policy.* New York: Harper's Magazine Press, 1972.

11696. Minks, Merle E. "President Nixon's Energy Message and Petroleum Industry Lawyer." *Natural Resources Lawyer* 6 (Fall 1973): 513-536.

11697. Mitchell, Clarence. "Moods and Changes: The Civil Rights Record of the Nixon Administration." *Notre Dame Lawyer* 49 (October 1973): 63-77.

11698. Morrison, Rodney J. *Expectations and Inflation: Nixon, Politics, and Economics.* Lexington, MA: Lexington Books, 1973.

11699. Morton, Rogers C. B. "The Nixon Administration Energy Policy." *Annals of the American Academy of Political and Social Science* 410 (November 1973): 65-74.

11700. Moynihan, Daniel P. *The Politics of a Guaranteed Income: The Nixon Administration and the Family Assistance Plan.* New York: Vintage Books, 1973.

11701. Mullaney, Thomas R. "A Populist in the Nixon Cabinet." *New York Affairs* 2 (Summer 1975): 50-59.

11702. Nathan, Richard P. *The Plot That Failed: Nixon and the Administrative Presidency.* New York: Wiley, 1975.

11703. Nelson, Bryce. "Nixon Forms Advisory Panels on Science, Space, Health." *Science* 162 (December 13, 1968): 1255.

11704. Niskanen, William, and Robert Berry. "The 1973 Economic Report of the President." *Journal of Money, Credit and Banking* 5 (May 1973): 693-703.

11705. Ott, David. *Nixon, McGovern, and the Federal Budget*. Washington, DC: American Enterprise Institute for Public Policy Research, 1972.

11706. Panetta, Leon E., and Peter Gall. *Bring Us Together: The Nixon Team and the Civil Rights Retreat*. Philadelphia: Lippincott, 1971.

11707. Phillips, H. H. "President Nixon's Energy Message and Electric Generating Industry Lawyer." *Natural Resources Lawyer* 6 (Fall 1973): 537-542.

11708. "President Nixon Approves Legislation Creating a National Legal Services Corporation." *American Bar Association Journal* 60 (September 1974): 1045-1049.

11709. Randall, Ronald. "Presidential Power versus Bureaucratic Intransigence: The Influence of the Nixon Administration on Welfare Policy." *American Political Science Review* 73 (September 1979): 795-810.

11710. Silk, Leonard S. *Nixonomics*. New York: Praeger, 1973.

11711. Sobel, Lester A., ed. *Inflation and the Nixon Administration*. 2 vols. New York: Facts on File, 1974-1975.

11712. Stauffer, Robert F. "President Nixon's Energy Message and Coal Industry Lawyer." *Natural Resources Lawyer* 6 (Fall 1973): 543-552.

11713. Taylor, William W. "Unintended Consequences of the Nixon Welfare Plan." *Social Work* 15 (October 1970): 15-22.

11714. Thompson, Frank, Jr., and Daniel H. Pollitt. "Congressional Control of Judicial Remedies: President Nixon's Proposed Moratorium on 'Busing' Orders." *North Carolina Law Review* 50 (June 1972): 809-841.

11715. Wilhite, Allen W. "Wage-Price Controls and the Labor Market's Response: The Nixon Controls of 1972." Ph.D. dissertation, University of Illinois, 1981.

11716. Will, George F. "Nixon, the Great Society, and the Future of Social Policy: Comments." *Commentary* 55 (May 1973): 31-61.

Elections

11717. American Institute for Political Communication. *The 1972 Presidential Campaign, Nixon Administration, Mass Media Relationship: A Book Based on a Comprehensive Study of the Communications Performance and Practices of the Administration in Power and of Major Newspaper and Broadcast Organizations before, during, and Immediately after the 1972 General Election Contest*. Washington, DC: The Institute, 1974.

11718. Balfour, Nancy. "Nixon's the One for America?" *World Today* 24 (November 1968): 467-475.

11719. Barrow, Lionel C. "Factors Related to Attention to the First Kennedy-Nixon Debate." *Journal of Broadcasting* 5 (Summer 1961): 229-238.

11720. Bonafede, Dom. "Nixon Models Campaign Organization after His Successful Version of 1968." *National Journal* 3 (September 11, 1971): 1876-1884.

11721. Cathcart, Robert S., and Edward A. Schwarz. "The New Nixon or Poor Richard?" *North American Review* 253 (September/October 1968): 8-12.

11722. "Debate Score: Kennedy Up, Nixon Down: Sindlinger Study Shows Switch in Sentiment toward Candidates." *Broadcasting* 59 (November 7, 1960): 27-29.

11723. Fischer, John. "Editor's Easy Chair: The Choice." *Harper's Magazine* 221 (October 1960): 14, 16, 19-20.

11724. Flinn, Thomas A. "How Mr. Nixon Took Ohio: A Short Reply to Senator Kennedy's Question." *Western Political Quarterly* 15 (June 1962): 274-279.

11725. Friel, Charlotte. "The Influence of Television in the Political Career of Richard M. Nixon, 1946-1962." Ph.D. dissertation, New York University, 1968.

11726. Goldman, Eric F. "The 1947 Kennedy-Nixon 'TubeCity' Debate." *Saturday Review* 4 (October 16, 1976): 12-13.

11727. "Great Debate Rightly Named: Nixon-Kennedy Set a Precedent That Will Be Hard to Abandon." *Broadcasting* 59 (October 3, 1960): 88-91.

11728. Greene, Bob. *Running: A Nixon-McGovern Campaign Journal.* Chicago: Regnery, 1973.

11729. Gruyters, Hans. *Nixon-McGovern?* Utrecht: Het Spectrum, 1972.

11730. Hatfield, Mark O. "Richard Nixon for President." *Christianity and Crisis* 28 (July 22, 1968): 165-166.

11731. Hofstetter, C. Richard, and Cliff Zukin. "TV Network News and Advertising in the Nixon and McGovern Campaigns." *Journalism Quarterly* 56 (Spring 1979): 106-115, 152.

11732. Honomichl, Jack J. "Nixon's Swing Vote Concept Offers Lesson to Marketers." *Advertising Age* 42 (December 13, 1971): 45-46.

11733. Howe, Russell W., and Sarah H. Trott. "The Truth at Last: How Nixon Beat Humphrey." *Washington Monthly* 8 (December 1976): 50-53.

11734. Katz, Elihu, and Jacob J. Feldman. "The Kennedy-Nixon Debates: A Survey of Surveys." In *Public Opinion and Politics*, edited by William J. Crotty, 409-431. New York: Holt, Rinehart and Winston, 1970.

11735. Katz, Elihu, and Jacob J. Feldman. "Who Won the Kennedy-Nixon Debates?" In *Speech Communication*, edited by Howard Martin and Kenneth Andersen, 297-311. Boston: Allyn and Bacon, 1968.

11736. Kaufer, David S. "The Ironist and Hypocrite as Presidential Symbols: A Nixon-Kennedy Analog." *Communication Quarterly* 27 (Fall 1979): 20-26.

11737. Keefe, Robert. "On Cowboys and Collectives: The Kennedy-Nixon Generation." *Massachusetts Review* 21 (Fall 1980): 551-560.

11738. Kissel, Bernard C. "A Rhetorical Study of Selected Speeches Delivered by Vice-President Richard M. Nixon during the Convention and Presidential Campaign of 1956." Ph.D. dissertation, University of Michigan, 1959.

11739. Lilley, William, III. "Nixon Inroads among Democratic Mayors Weaken Party's Old Coalition." *National Journal* 4 (July 15, 1972): 1143-1150.

11740. Locke, Larry W. "A Study of Richard M. Nixon's Public 1968 Campaign Promises and Their Fulfillment during His First Term in Office." Ph.D. dissertation, Kent State University, 1978.

11741. Lurie, Leonard. *The Running of Richard Nixon.* New York: Coward, McCann and Geoghegan, 1972.

11742. McGinniss, Joe. *The Selling of the President, 1968.* New York: Trident Press, 1969.

11743. McGuckin, Henry E., Jr. "A Value Analysis of Richard Nixon's 1952 Campaign-Fund Speech." *Southern*

Speech Journal 33 (Summer 1968): 259-269.

11744. Mullen, James J. "Newspaper Advertising in the Kennedy-Nixon Campaign." *Journalism Quarterly* 40 (Winter 1963): 3-11.

11745. Murphy, Reg, and Hal Gulliver. *The Southern Strategy.* New York: Scribner's, 1971.

11746. "Nixon: Not-So-Dark Horse." *Forbes* 92 (November 1, 1963): 11-12.

11747. Pearl, Arthur. *Landslide: The How and Why of Nixon's Victory.* Secaucus, NJ: Citadel Press, 1973.

11748. Polisky, Jerome B. "The Kennedy-Nixon Debates: A Study in Political Persuasion." Ph.D. dissertation, University of Wisconsin, 1965.

11749. Polsby, Nelson W. *The Citizen's Choice: Humphrey or Nixon.* Washington, DC: Public Affairs Press, 1968.

11750. Powell, James G. "An Analytical and Comparative Study of the Persuasion of Kennedy and Nixon in the 1960 Campaign." Ph.D. dissertation, University of Wisconsin, 1963.

11751. Real, Michael R. "Popular Culture, Media Propaganda, and the 1972 'CREEP Campaign.'" *Journal of Popular Culture* 8 (Winter 1974): 644-652.

11752. Rosenfield, L. W. "A Case Study in Speech Criticism: The Nixon-Truman Analog." *Speech Monographs* 35 (November 1968): 435-450.

11753. Rosenthal, Paul I. "Ethos in the Presidential Campaign of 1960: A Study of the Basic Persuasion Process of the Kennedy-Nixon Debates." Ph.D. dissertation, University of California, Los Angeles, 1963.

11754. Samovar, Larry A. "Ambiguity and Unequivocation in the Kennedy-Nixon Television Debates." *Quarterly Journal of Speech* 48 (October 1962): 274-277.

11755. Samovar, Larry A. "Ambiguity and Unequivocation in the Kennedy-Nixon Television Debates: A Rhetorical Analysis." *Western Speech* 29 (Fall 1965): 211-218.

11756. Schlesinger, Arthur M., Jr. *Kennedy or Nixon: Does It Make Any Difference?* New York: Macmillan, 1960.

11757. Shelly, Walter L. "Political Profiles of the Nixon, Humphrey, and Wallace Voters in the Texas Panhandle, 1968: A Study in Voting Behavior." Ph.D. dissertation, Texas Tech University, 1972.

11758. Sherman, Roger N. "An Objective Analysis of Language Choice in the First Nixon-Kennedy Debate." Ph.D. dissertation, University of Michigan, 1965.

11759. Smith, Craig R. "Richard Nixon's 1968 Acceptance Speech as a Model of Dual Audience Adaptation." *Today's Speech* 19 (Fall 1971): 15-22.

11760. Stephenson, William. "Operational Study of an Occasional Paper on the Kennedy-Nixon Television Debates." *Psychological Record* 14 (October 1964): 475-488.

11761. Thomas, David A. "A Qualitative Content Analysis of Richard M. Nixon's Treatment of Selected Issues in His Presidential Campaign Oratory in the 1960 and 1968 Elections." Ph.D. dissertation, Michigan State University, 1973.

11762. Trent, Judith S. "An Examination and Comparison of the Rhetorical Style of Richard Milhous Nixon in the Presidential Campaigns of 1960 and 1968: A Content Analysis." Ph.D. dissertation, University of Michigan, 1970.

11763. Vose, Clement E. "Nixon Project." *Political Science* 16 (Summer 1983): 512-521.

11764. Whalen, Joan C. "The Identification of Journal 'Topoi' in the 1960 Presidential Campaign Speeches of Vice-President Richard M. Nixon." Master's thesis, California State University, Fullerton, 1976.

11765. Wills, Garry. "Nixon Convention." *National Review* 20 (August 17, 1968): 845-850.

11766. Wills, Garry. "Nixon's Dog." *Esquire* 72 (August 1969): 40, 43, 48, 52, 91-95.

11767. Wilson, Graham K., and Philip M. Williams. "Mr. Nixon's Triumph." *Parliamentary Affairs* 26 (Spring 1973): 186-200.

11768. Wimberley, Ronald C. "Civil Religion and the Choice for President Nixon in '72." *Social Forces* 59 (September 1980): 44-61.

11769. Zukin, Clifford, and C. Richard Hofstetter. *Campaign Attributes Reflected in Nixon and McGovern Advertisements: A Propagandistic Baseline.* Columbus: Polimetrics Laboratory, Department of Political Science, Ohio State University, 1974.

Foreign Affairs

11770. Anthony, William H. "Public Diplomacy and the Nixon Doctrine, Reaction by Foreign and American Media and the U.S. Information Agency's Role." Ph.D. dissertation, George Washington University, 1976.

11771. Aron, Raymond. "Richard Nixon and the Future of American Foreign Policy." *Daedalus* 101 (Fall 1972): 1-24.

11772. Bacus, Karen P. "The Rhetoric of the Press: Newspaper Treatment of Richard Nixon's Major Statements on Vietnam, 1969-1970." Ph.D. dissertation, University of Kansas, 1974.

11773. Bender, Lynn D. "U.S.-Cuban Policy under the Nixon Administration: Subtle Modifications." *Revista Interamericana* 2 (Fall 1972): 330-341.

11774. Berger, Roland. "China's Policy and the Nixon Visit." *Journal of Contemporary Asia* 2 (1972): 3-16.

11775. Binning, William C. "The Nixon Foreign Aid Policy for Latin America." *Inter-American Economic Affairs* 25 (Summer 1971): 31-45.

11776. Brenner, Michael. "Problem of Innovation and Nixon-Kissinger Foreign Policy." *International Studies Quarterly* 17 (September 1973): 255-294.

11777. Brzezinski, Zbigniew. "The Deceptive Structure of Peace." *Foreign Policy* 14 (Spring 1974): 35-55.

11778. Brzezinski, Zbigniew. "Half Past Nixon." *Foreign Policy* 3 (Summer 1971): 3-21.

11779. Butwell, Richard. "The Nixon Doctrine in Southeast Asia." *Current History* 61 (December 1971): 321-326.

11780. Caldwell, Dan. "American-Soviet Detente and the Nixon-Kissinger Grand Design and Grand Strategy." Ph.D. dissertation, Stanford University, 1978.

11781. Cohen, Akiba A., Hilde T. Himmelwe, and Haviva S. Bar. "Effects on Contact on Evaluation: Reactions of the Israeli Public to President Nixon's Visit to Israel, June 1974." *Communication Research* 2 (April 1975): 163-172.

11782. Cohen, Samuel T. "Whatever Happened to the Nixon Doctrine?" *Policy Review* 26 (Fall 1983): 88-92.

11783. Cushman, Donald P. "A Comparative Study of President Truman's and President Nixon's Justification for Committing Troops to Combat in Korea and Cambodia." Ph.D. dissertation, University of Wisconsin, 1974.

11784. Drischler, Alvin P. "The Sources

of the American Hegemonic Strategy: A Comparison of Foreign Places under Presidents Nixon and Kennedy." Ph.D. dissertation, Princeton University, 1973.

11785. Fitzgerald, Frances. *Fire in the Lake*. Boston: Little, Brown, 1972.

11786. Gardner, Lloyd C., ed. *The Great Nixon Turnaround: America's New Foreign Policy in the Post-Liberal Era (How a Cold Warrior Climbed Clean Out of His Skin)*. New York: New Viewpoints, 1973.

11787. Garrett, Stephen A. "Nixonian Foreign Policy: A New Balance of Power or a Revived Concert?" *Polity* 8 (Spring 1976): 389-421.

11788. Geyelin, Philip. "Impeachment and Foreign Policy." *Foreign Policy* 15 (Summer 1974): 183-190.

11789. Ghanayem, Ishaq I. "The Nixon-Kissinger Middle East Strategy, 1969-1974." Ph.D. dissertation, University of California, Santa Barbara, 1980.

11790. Girling, John L. S. "Nixon's Algeria — Doctrine and Disengagement in Indochina." *Pacific Affairs* 44 (Winter 1971-1972): 527-544.

11791. Glass, Andrew J. "Nixon Gives Israel Massive Aid But Reaps No Jewish Political Harvest." *National Journal* 4 (January 8, 1972): 57-72.

11792. Gregg, Richard B., and Gerald A. Hauser. "Richard Nixon's April 30, 1970 Address on Cambodia: The 'Ceremony' of Confrontation." *Speech Monographs* 40 (August 1973): 167-181.

11793. Hahn, Walter F. "The Nixon Doctrine: Design and Dilemmas." *Orbis* 16 (Summer 1972): 361-376.

11794. Halperin, Morton H. "America and Asia: The Impact of Nixon's China Policy." *Foreign Service Journal* 49 (August 1972): 12-19, 28.

11795. Henderson, John T. "The United States and Her Allies." *Round Table* 239 (July 1970): 231-234.

11796. Herr, Donald F. "Presidential Influence and Bureaucratic Politics: Nixon's Policy toward Cuba." Ph.D. dissertation, Yale University, 1978.

11797. Hubbell, John G. "President Nixon, Cambodia, and New Chances for Peace." *Reader's Digest* 97 (July 1970): 54-63.

11798. Jensen, Daniel D. "Nixon's Trip to China, 1972: Three Views." Ph.D. dissertation, Illinois State University, 1982.

11799. Jones, Alan M., Jr., ed. *United States Foreign Policy in a Changing World: The Nixon Administration, 1969-1973*. New York: McKay, 1973.

11800. Kaltefleiter, Werner. "Europe and the Nixon Doctrine: A German Point of View." *Atlantic Community Quarterly* 11 (Winter 1973-1974): 456-469.

11801. Kaplan, Lawrence S. "NATO and the Nixon Doctrine Ten Years Later." *Orbis* 24 (Spring 1980): 149-164.

11802. Kerr, Malcolm H. "Nixon's Second Term: Policy Prospects in the Middle East." *Journal of Palestine Studies* 2 (Spring 1973): 14-29.

11803. Kintner, William R. *The Impact of President Nixon's Visit to Peking on International Politics*. Philadelphia: Foreign Policy Research Institute, 1972.

11804. Kohl, Wilfred L. "The Nixon-Kissinger Foreign Policy System and the U.S.-European Relations: Patterns of Policy Making." *World Politics* 28 (October 1976): 1-43.

11805. Kolodziej, Edward A. "Congress and Foreign Policy: The Nixon Years." *Academy of Political Science Proceedings* 32 (1975): 167-179.

11806. Kolodziej, Edward A. "Foreign

Policy and the Politics of Interdependence: The Nixon Presidency." *Polity* 9 (Winter 1976): 121-173.

11807. Laird, Melvin R., Gale W. McGee, Robert P. Griffin, and Thomas C. Schelling. *The Nixon Doctrine*. Washington, DC: American Enterprise Institute for Public Policy Research, 1972.

11808. Lee, Jung H. "The Impact of the Nixon Doctrine on South Korea: A Critical Analysis of U.S.-South Korean Relations, 1969-1976." Ph.D. dissertation, Catholic University of America, 1980.

11809. Levin, N. Gordon. "Nixon, the Senate, and the War." *Commentary* 50 (November 1970): 69-84.

11810. Lewis, Flora. "The Nixon Doctrine." *Atlantic Monthly* 226 (November 1970): 6-19.

11811. Litwak, Robert S. *Detente and the Nixon Doctrine: American Foreign Policy and the Pursuit of Stability, 1969-1976*. New York: Cambridge University Press, 1984.

11812. Maxey, David R. "How Nixon Decided to Invade Cambodia." *Look* 34 (August 11, 1970): 22-28.

11813. Medick, Monika. "The Nixon New Economic Policy: Economic and Security Interests in U.S.-European Relations." *Amerikastudien/American Studies* (West Germany) 23 (1978): 73-89.

11814. Murphy, William F. "Rhetorical Processes and Patterns in the Nixon Addresses on Vietnam and Related News Coverage." Ph.D. dissertation, University of Pittsburgh, 1979.

11815. Newman, Robert P. "Under the Veneer: Nixon's Vietnam Speech of November 3, 1969." *Quarterly Journal of Speech* 56 (April 1970): 168-178.

11816. Nicholas, Herbert G. "The Nixon Line." In *The Year Book of World Affairs*, edited by George W. Keeton, 15-25. New York: Praeger, 1971.

11817. Overholt, William H. "President Nixon's Trip to China and Its Consequences." *Asian Survey* 13 (July 1973): 707-721.

11818. Owens, Dennis J. "The Establishment of a Doctrine: Executive Privilege after *U.S. v. Nixon*." *Texas Southern University Law Review* 4 (1976): 22-49.

11819. Papp, Daniel S. "Nixon, Brezhnev, Ford, and Watergate: The Effects of Domestic Crisis on Soviet American Relations." *Georgia Political Science Association Journal* 4 (Spring 1976): 3-20.

11820. Peretz, Don. "The United States, the Arabs, and Israel: Peace Efforts of Kennedy, Johnson, and Nixon." *Annals of the American Academy of Political and Social Science* 401 (May 1972): 116-125.

11821. Pipes, Richard. "America, Russia, and Europe in the Light of the Nixon Doctrine." *Survey* 19 (Summer 1973): 30-40.

11822. "President Nixon's China Initiative: Conference Report." *Orbis* 15 (Winter 1972): 1206-1219.

11823. Price, Morris. "The Nixon Years (1969-1974): Duplicity in United States Policies toward Southern Africa." Ph.D. dissertation, St. John's University, 1977.

11824. Price, Raymond. *With Nixon*. New York: Viking Press, 1977.

11825. Rather, Dan, and Gary P. Gates. *The Palace Guard*. New York: Harper and Row, 1974.

11826. Ravenal, Earl C. "The Nixon Doctrine and Our Asian Commitments." *Foreign Affairs* 49 (January 1971): 201-217.

11827. Ravenal, Earl C. "Nixon's Challenge to Carter: No More Mr. Nice Guy."

Foreign Policy 29 (Winter 1977-1978): 27-42.

11828. Rennagel, William C. "Organization Responsiveness to the President: The Military Response to the Nixon Doctrine." Ph.D. dissertation, Ohio State University, 1977.

11829. Roberts, Chalmers M. "Foreign Policy under a Paralyzed Presidency." *Foreign Affairs* 52 (July 1974): 677-689.

11830. Rosenberger, Leif R. "The Evolution of the Nixon-Kissinger Policy toward the Soviet Union: An Analysis of the Cold War Legacy and the Ambivalent Pursuit of Detente." Ph.D. dissertation, Claremont Graduate School, 1980.

11831. Rudolph, Lloyd I., et al. *The Regional Imperative: U.S. Foreign Policy towards South Asian States under Presidents Johnson and Nixon*. Atlantic Highlands, NJ: Humanities Press, 1980.

11832. Safford, Jeffrey J. "The Nixon-Castro Meeting of 19 April 1959." *Diplomatic History* 4 (Fall 1980): 425-431.

11833. Scoville, Herbert, Jr. "Flexible Madness?" *Foreign Policy* 14 (Spring 1974): 164-177.

11834. Shawcross, William. *Sideshow: Kissinger, Nixon, and the Destruction of Cambodia*. New York: Simon and Schuster, 1979.

11835. "Showdown on War — Congress vs. Nixon." *U.S. News & World Report* 68 (May 25, 1970): 35.

11836. Sigford, Rolf N. "The Rhetoric of the Vietnam War: Presidents Johnson and Nixon." Ph.D. dissertation, University of Minnesota, 1973.

11837. Sloan, John W. "Three Views of Latin America: President Nixon, Governor Rockefeller, and the Latin American Consensus of Vina del Mar." *Orbis* 14 (Winter 1971): 934-950.

11838. Sorley, Lewis. *Arms Transfers under Nixon: A Policy Analysis*. Lexington: University of Kentucky Press, 1983.

11839. Sorley, Lewis. "Conventional Arms Transfers and the Nixon Administration: A Policy Analysis." Ph.D. dissertation, Johns Hopkins University, 1979.

11840. Summers, Laura. "Cambodia: Model of the Nixon Doctrine." *Current History* 65 (December 1973): 252-256, 276.

11841. Szulc, Tad. *The Illusion of Peace: Foreign Policy in the Nixon-Kissinger Years*. New York: Viking Press, 1978.

11842. Tsou, Tang. "Statesmanship and Scholarship." *World Politics* 26 (April 1974): 428-451.

11843. Vogt, Erich. *The Role of Berlin and the Four-Power Negotiations in the Foreign Policy Press of the Nixon Administration*. Berlin: Freie Universitaet Berlin, 1980.

11844. Whitney, David C. *The Week That Changed the World: President Richard M. Nixon's Historic Visit to Communist China, February 21-28, 1972*. Chicago: J. G. Ferguson, 1972.

11845. Wilcox, Francis O. "President Nixon, the Congress, and Foreign Policy." *Michigan Quarterly Review* 9 (Winter 1970): 37-43.

11846. Wildavsky, Aaron B. "Was Nixon Tough? Dilemmas of American Statecraft." *Society* 16 (November/December 1978): 25-35.

11847. Wilson, Richard, ed. *The President's Trip to China: A Pictorial Record of the Historic Journey to the People's Republic of China with Text by Members of the American Press Corps*. New York: Bantam Books, 1972.

11848. Wu, Fu-Mei Chiu. "The China Policy of Richard M. Nixon from Confrontation to Negotiation." Ph.D. dissertation, University of Utah, 1976.

Watergate

11849. American Civil Liberties Union. *Why President Nixon Should Be Impeached.* Washington, DC: Public Affairs Press, 1974.

11850. Anderson, Patrick. "The President's Accuser." *New York Times Magazine* 122 (July 8, 1973): 8-9, 16-20.

11851. Apple, R. W. "Haldeman the Fierce, Haldeman the Faithful, Haldeman the Fallen." *New York Times Magazine* 122 (May 6, 1973): 38-39, 103-107.

11852. Barber, James D. "The Nixon Brush with Tyranny." *Political Science Quarterly* 92 (Winter 1977-1978): 581-605.

11853. Benoit, William L. "Richard M. Nixon's Rhetorical Strategies in His Public Statements on Watergate." *Southern Speech Communication Journal* 47 (Winter 1982): 192-211.

11854. Bonafede, Dom. "Nixon Legal Defense Increases Office Costs, Staff." *National Journal* 6 (June 1974): 976-977.

11855. Boudin, Leonard B. "Presidential Pardons of James R. Hoffa and Richard M. Nixon: Have the Limitations on the Pardon Power Been Exceeded?" *University of Colorado Law Review* 48 (Fall 1976): 1-39.

11856. Boyd, Richard W., and David J. Hadley. "Presidential and Congressional Response to Political Crisis — Nixon, Congress, and Watergate." *Congress and the Presidency* 10 (Autumn 1983): 195-217.

11857. Bramwell, Dana G. *The Tragedy of King Richard: Shakespearean Watergate.* Salina, KS: Survey Publishing Co., 1974.

11858. Buckley, William F. "Reflections on the Resignation." *National Review* 26 (August 30, 1974): 954.

11859. Conyers, John, Jr. "Why Nixon Should Be Impeached." *Black Scholar* 6 (October 1974): 2-8.

11860. Dennis, Jack. "Who Supports the Presidency?" *Society* 13 (April 1976): 48-53.

11861. Destephen, Daniel E. "Tactics in Conflict: A Study of Tactic Usage in the Controversy over the Impeachment of President Richard M. Nixon." Ph.D. dissertation, University of Utah, 1977.

11862. Diamond, Edwin. "Tapeshock: The Nixon Transcripts." *Columbia Journalism Review* 13 (July 1974): 5-9.

11863. Dobrovir, William A., Joseph D. Gebhardt, Samuel J. Buffone, and Andra N. Oakes. *The Offenses of Richard M. Nixon: A Guide to His Impeachable Offenses.* New York: Quadrangle Books, 1974.

11864. Drew, Elizabeth. *Washington Journal, The Events of 1973-1974.* New York: Random House, 1974.

11865. Drew, Elizabeth. "Washington: The Nixon Court." *Atlantic Monthly* 230 (November 1972): 6-10.

11866. Eiland, Millard F. "Journalistic Criticism of Richard Nixon's Watergate Speaking of 1973." Ph.D. dissertation, Louisiana State University, Agricultural and Mechanical College, 1974.

11867. Eilberg, Joshua. "Investigation by the Committee on the Judiciary of the House of Representatives into the Charges of Impeachable Conduct against Richard M. Nixon." *Temple Law Quarterly* 48 (Winter 1975): 204-240.

11868. Finch, Gerald B. "Impeachments and the Dynamics of Public Opinion: A Comment on 'Guilty, Yes: Impeachment,

No.'" *Political Science Quarterly* 89 (June 1974): 301-304.

11869. Flatto, Elie. "The Impeachment of Richard M. Nixon." *Contemporary Review* 226 (March 1975): 146-148.

11870. Freidman, Leon, ed. *United States v. Nixon: The President before the Supreme Court.* New York: Chelsea House, 1974.

11871. Fry, Brian R., and John S. Stolarek. "The Nixon Impeachment Vote: A Speculative Analysis." *Presidential Studies Quarterly* 11 (Summer 1981): 387-394.

11872. Glass, Andrew J. "Watergate Diminishes Nixon's Leverage, Forces Series of Legislative Compromises." *National Journal* 5 (July 21, 1973): 1049-1056.

11873. Greenstein, Fred I. "A President Is Forced to Resign: Watergate, White House Organization, and Nixon's Personality." In *America in the Seventies: Problems, Policies, and Politics,* edited by Allan P. Sindler, 50-101. Boston: Little, Brown, 1977.

11874. Gunther, Gerald. "Judicial Hegemony and Legislative Autonomy: The Nixon Case and the Impeachment Process." *UCLA Law Review* 22 (October 1974): 30-39.

11875. Hager, L. Michael. "Constitution, the Court, and the Cover-up: Reflections on *U.S. vs. Nixon.*" *Oklahoma Law Review* 29 (Summer 1976): 591-606.

11876. Hamilton, James W. "Some Reflections on Richard Nixon in the Light of His Resignation and Farewell Speeches." *Journal of Psychohistory* 4 (Spring 1977): 491-511.

11877. Harrell, Jackson, B. L. Ware, and Wil A. Linkugel. "Failure of Apology in American Politics: Nixon on Watergate." *Speech Monographs* 42 (November 1975): 245-261.

11878. Hartnett, Robert C. "Press Comment on the 'Nixon Case.'" *America* 88 (October 11, 1952): 40-41.

11879. Howard, David M. "Nixon's Watergate: Man's Depravity." *Christianity Today* 21 (June 3, 1977): 12-14.

11880. Hughes, Emmet J. "A White House Taped." *New York Times Magazine* 123 (June 9, 1974): 17, 65-73.

11881. Hurwitz, Leon, Barbara Green, and Hans E. Segal. "International Press Reactions to the Resignation and Pardon of Richard M. Nixon: A Content Analysis of Four Elite Newspapers." *Comparative Politics* 9 (October 1976): 107-123.

11882. Jaworski, Leon. "Case against the President." *Criminal Law Bulletin* 13 (July/August 1977): 253-265.

11883. Katula, Richard A. "Apology of Richard M. Nixon." *Today's Speech* 23 (Fall 1975): 1-5.

11884. Kurland, Philip B. "*United States v. Nixon:* Who Killed Cock Robin?" *UCLA Law Review* 22 (October 1974): 68-75.

11885. Kutner, Luis. "Legal Note on the Nixon Pardon: Equal Justice vis-a-vis Due Process." *Akron Law Review* 9 (Fall 1975): 243-256.

11886. Kutner, Luis. "Nixon v. Cox: Due Process of Executive Authority." *St. John's Law Review* 48 (March 1974): 441-460.

11887. Levy, Leonard W. *Against the Law: The Nixon Court and Criminal Justice.* New York: Harper and Row, 1974.

11888. Lurie, Leonard. *The Impeachment of Richard Nixon.* Berkeley, CA: Berkeley Medallion Book Co., 1973.

11889. Macgill, Hugh C. "The Nixon Pardon: Limits on the Benign Prerogative." *Connecticut Law Review* 7 (Fall 1974): 56-92.

11890. McKibbin, Michael K. "On Executive Clemency: The Pardon of Richard

M. Nixon." *Pepperdine Law Review* 2 (1975): 353-382.

11891. Mankiewicz, Frank. *U.S. v. Richard M. Nixon: The Final Crisis.* New York: Quadrangle Books, 1975.

11892. Meagher, Eileen M. "The Public Hearings on the House Judiciary Committee on the Impeachment of Nixon: An Act of National Ritual." Ph.D. dissertation, Rensselaer Polytechnic Institute, 1979.

11893. Mudd, Samuel, and Alan Pohlman. "Sensitivity of Image Profile and Clarity Measures to Change: Nixon through Watergate." *Journal of Applied Psychology* 61 (April 1976): 223-228.

11894. New York Times. *The Watergate Hearings.* New York: Bantam Books, 1973.

11895. O'Brien, Francis W. "Dissenting Opinions of *Nixon v. Sirica:* An Argument for Executive Privilege in the White House Tapes Controversy." *Southwestern Law Journal* 28 (Spring 1974): 373-390.

11896. Overland, Doris. "The Great Watergate Conspiracy: A TV Blitzkrieg?" *Contemporary Review* 233 (July 1978): 29-32.

11897. Rodgers, Harrell R., Jr., and Edward B. Lewis. "Student Attitudes toward Mr. Nixon: The Consequences of Negative Attitudes toward a President for Political System Support." *American Politics Quarterly* 3 (October 1975): 423-436.

11898. Rosenberg, Harold. "Thugs Adrift." *Partisan Review* 40 (1973): 341-348.

11899. Rothenberg, Alan B. "Why Nixon Taped Himself." *Psychoanalytic Review* 62 (Summer 1975): 201-223.

11900. Safire, William. *Before the Fall: An Inside View of the Pre-Watergate White House.* Garden City, NY: Doubleday, 1975.

11901. Safire, William. "Last Days in the Bunker." *New York Times Magazine* 123 (August 18, 1974): 6, 40, 42, 44, 52-54.

11902. Schleifer, Richard. "On Behalf of Richard M. Nixon: The Copyrightability of the Nixon Presidential Watergate Tapes." *Copyright Law Symposium* 26 (1981): 53-94.

11903. Shannon, William V. *They Could Not Trust the King: Nixon, Watergate, and the American People.* New York: Collier Books, 1974.

11904. Sherrill, Robert G. "Zealots for Nixon: Gaudy Night at the Watergate." *Nation* 215 (September 25, 1972): 230-234.

11905. Sirica, John J. *To Set the Record Straight: The Break-In, the Tapes, the Conspirators, the Pardon.* New York: Norton, 1979.

11906. Stathis, Stephen W. "Nixon, Watergate, and American Foreign Policy." *Presidential Studies Quarterly* 13 (Winter 1983): 129-147.

11907. Sussman, Barry. *The Great Coverup: Nixon and the Scandal of Watergate.* New York: New American Library, 1974.

11908. Thatcher, C. Marshall. "*United States v. Nixon:* What Price Unanimity?" *Ohio Northern University Law Review* 2 (1974): 303-317.

11909. Tillinghast, Diana S. "Information Seeking on Watergate and President Nixon's Resignation and Attitudes toward Nixon and the Mass Media." Ph.D. dissertation, Michigan State University, 1976.

11910. U.S. Congress. House. Committee on the Judiciary. *Impeachment of Richard M. Nixon, President of the United States: The Final Report of the Committee on the Judiciary, House of Representatives, Peter*

W. Rodino, Jr., Chairman. New York: Viking Press, 1975.

11911. U.S. Congress. House. Committee on the Judiciary. *Pardon of Richard M. Nixon and Related Matters: Hearings before the Subcommittee on Criminal Justice.* 93d Cong., 2d sess., 1974. Washington, DC: U.S. Government Printing Office, 1975.

11912. Vartabedian, Robert A. "A Case Study in Contemporary Apologia: The Self-Defense Rhetoric of Richard Nixon." Ph.D. dissertation, University of Oklahoma, 1981.

11913. Wainer, Howard. "Predicting the Outcome of the Senate Trial of Richard M. Nixon." *Behavioral Science* 19 (November 1974): 404-406.

11914. Washington Post. *The Presidential Transcripts.* New York: Delacorte Press, 1974.

11915. Waters, Craig. "The Agony of Egil Krogh." *Washingtonian* 9 (May 1974): 60-67.

11916. Whitcover, Jules. "The Two Hats of Herbert Klein." *Columbia Journalism Review* 9 (Spring 1971): 26-30.

11917. White, Larry D. "Nixon's Push on the Marshmallow: Reorganization and Watergate, 1968-1974." *Rendezvous* 8 (Winter 1973-1974): 21-38.

11918. White, Theodore H. *Breach of Faith: The Fall of Richard Nixon.* New York: Atheneum, 1975.

11919. *The White House Transcripts: The Full Text of the Submission of Recorded Presidential Conversations to the Committee on the Judiciary of the House of Representatives by President Richard M. Nixon.* New York: Bantam Books, 1974.

11920. Zeisel, Hans. "Can You Hear Me, Mr. President?" *Canadian Dimension* 9 (1973): 27-37.

Writings

11921. Hall, Perry D., ed. *The Quotable Mr. Nixon.* Anderson, SC: Drake House, 1967.

11922. Horowitz, Irving L. "When the President Does It: What the Tapes Reveal: Opinion of Presidential Powers Expressed in Nixon-Frost Interviews." *Nation* 224 (June 18, 1977): 751-754.

11923. Morehead, Joe. "Into the Hopper: Tennis Elbow of the Soul: The Public Papers of Richard Nixon, 1973-1974." *Serials Librarian* 1 (Spring 1977): 207-214.

11924. Nixon, Richard M. "Asia after Vietnam." *Foreign Affairs* 46 (October 1967): 111-125.

11925. Nixon, Richard M. *The Challenges We Face.* New York: McGraw-Hill, 1960.

11926. Nixon, Richard M. *The Clearest Choice.* Washington: n.p., 1972.

11927. Nixon, Richard M. *A Conversation with the President.* Washington, DC: U.S. Government Printing Office, 1970.

11928. Nixon, Richard M. "Cuba, Castro, and John F. Kennedy: Some Reflections on U.S. Foreign Policy." *Reader's Digest* 85 (November 1984): 283-300.

11929. Nixon, Richard M. *Education for the 1970's: Renewal and Reform: Messages to the Congress.* Washington, DC: U.S. Government Printing Office, 1970.

11930. Nixon, Richard M. *Leaders.* New York: Warner, 1982.

11931. Nixon, Richard M. "Nature of the Presidency: Address, September 19, 1968." *Vital Speeches* 35 (October 15, 1968): 6-8.

11932. Nixon, Richard M. "Nixon Presidential Press Conferences." *Journal of American Studies* 13 (August 1979): 280.

11933. Nixon, Richard M. *The Nixon Presidential Press Conferences.* New York: E. M. Coleman Enterprises, 1978.

11934. Nixon, Richard M. *No More Vietnams.* New York: Arbor House, 1985.

11935. Nixon, Richard M. "President Nixon Delineates Authority of American Ambassadors." *Department of State Bulletin* 62 (January 1970): 30-31.

11936. Nixon, Richard M. "President Nixon's State of the Union Message." *Current History* 66 (March 1974): 131-132.

11937. Nixon, Richard M. "President Nixon's Veto of War Power Measure Overridden by the Congress." *Department of State Bulletin* 69 (November 26, 1973): 662-664.

11938. Nixon, Richard M. "The President's Message to Congress on Equal Educational Opportunity." *Current History* 62 (June 1972): 305, 311.

11939. Nixon, Richard M. *The Real War.* New York: Warner, 1980.

11940. Nixon, Richard M. *RN: The Memoirs of Richard Nixon.* New York: Grosset and Dunlap, 1978.

11941. Nixon, Richard M. *Setting the Course: The First Year.* New York: Funk and Wagnalls, 1970.

11942. Nixon, Richard M. *Six Crises: With New Preface.* New York: Pocket Books, 1968.

11943. Nixon, Richard M. *United States Foreign Policy for the 1970's: Building for Peace: A Report by President Richard Nixon to the Congress, February 25, 1971.* New York: Harper and Row, 1971.

11944. Nixon, Richard M. "United States Foreign Policy for the 70's: Shaping a Durable Peace." *Africa Today* 20 (Spring 1973): 3-10.

11945. Nixon, Richard M. *The Young Nixon: An Oral Inquiry.* Edited by Renee K. Schule. Fullerton: Richard M. Nixon Project, Oral History Program, California State University, 1978.

11946. Westin, Alan F., and John Shattuck. "The Second Deposing of Richard Nixon." *Civil Liberties Review* 3 (June/July 1976): 8-23, 84-96.

Gerald R. Ford

Biographies

11947. Aaron, Jan. *Gerald R. Ford, President of Destiny*. New York: Fleet, 1975.

11948. LeRoy, Dave. *Gerald Ford: Untold Story*. Arlington, VA: R. W. Beatty, 1974.

11949. MacDougall, Malcolm D. *We Almost Made It*. New York: Crown, 1977.

11950. Mollenhoff, Clark R. *The Man Who Pardoned Nixon*. New York: St. Martin's Press, 1976.

11951. Vestal, Bud. *Jerry Ford, Up Close: An Investigative Biography*. New York: Coward, McCann and Geoghegan, 1974.

11952. Watson, Christopher, ed. *Gerald R. Ford: Our 38th President*. New York: Mayfair Publications, 1974.

Private Life

11953. Baker, James T. "To the Former Miss Betty Bloomer of Grand Rapids: A Very Human First Lady." *Christian Century* 93 (October 13, 1976): 863-865.

11954. Bennett, Ralph K. "What Sort of Man Is Gerald Ford?" *Reader's Digest* 104 (March 1974): 73-78.

11955. Block, Jean L. "Betty Ford Nobody Knows." *Good Housekeeping* 178 (May 1974): 88-89.

11956. Cassiday, Bruce B. *Betty Ford: Woman of Courage*. Waterbury, CT: Dale Books, 1978.

11957. Collins, Paul. *Gerald R. Ford: A Man in Perspective: As Portrayed in the Gerald R. Ford Mural by Paul Collins*. Grand Rapids, MI: Eerdmans, 1976.

11958. Farrell, Robert E. "What Kind of Man Is Gerald Ford?" *Business Week* (August 3, 1974): 6.

11959. Feinman, Jeffrey. *Betty Ford*. New York: Universal Award House, 1976.

11960. Ford, Betty, and Chris Chase. *The Times of My Life*. New York: Harper and Row, 1978.

11961. Fremont-Smith, E. "Reporting (gasp!) What Betty Ford Said." *Columbia Journalism Review* 14 (November 1975): 15-16.

Public Career

11962. Carter, Luther J. "President Ford: Maine Street to Pennsylvania Avenue." *Science* 185 (August 30, 1974): 764-766.

11963. "Congressman Ford." *New Yorker* 12 (November 1973): 40-43.

11964. Graham, Donald. "The Vice Presidency: From Cigar Store Indian to Crown Prince." *Washington Monthly* 6 (April 1974): 41-44.

11965. Jones, Charles O. *Minority Party Leadership in Congress*. Boston: Little, Brown, 1970.

11966. Moley, Raymond. "Ford for Vice President?" *Newsweek* 56 (July 11, 1960): 96.

11967. Natoli, Marie D. "The Vice Presidency: Gerald Ford as Healer?" *Presidential Studies Quarterly* 10 (Fall 1980): 662-664.

11968. Ralph Nader Congress Project. *Gerald R. Ford: Republican Congressman from Michigan*. Washington, DC: Grossman Publishers, 1972.

Presidential Years

11969. American Enterprise Institute for Public Policy Research. *A Discussion with Gerald R. Ford: The American Presidency*. Washington, DC: The Institute, 1977.

11970. Auletta, Ken. *The Streets Were Paved with Gold*. New York: Random House, 1980.

11971. Balz, Daniel J. "Ford Continues to Refine Legislative Proposals for Message." *National Journal* 7 (January 17, 1975): 39-46.

11972. Banker, Stephen R. "Homogeneous Coverage Analysis: A Case Study of Ford's Press Conferences." Master's thesis, Indiana University, 1982.

11973. Barber, James D. "Ford: Will He Turn Tough?" *U.S. News & World Report* 2 (September 1974): 22-26.

11974. Baroody, William J., Jr. "Gerald R. Ford and the New Politics." *Presidential Studies Quarterly* 7 (Spring/Summer 1977): 91-95.

11975. Bell, D. Bruce, and Beverly W. Bell. "Desertion and Antiwar Protest: Findings from the Ford Clemency Program." *Armed Forces and Society* 3 (Spring 1977): 433-443.

11976. Bitzer, Lloyd, and Theodore Reuter. *Carter vs. Ford: The Counterfeit Debates of Nineteen Seventy-six*. Madison: University of Wisconsin Press, 1980.

11977. Bonafede, Dom. "Ford Administration Promises Reformation Restoration." *National Journal* 6 (August 17, 1974): 1217-1222.

11978. Bonafede, Dom. "Ford and Staff Tend to Business . . . and Wait." *National Journal* 6 (August 10, 1974): 1179-1190.

11979. Bonafede, Dom. "Ford Begins Moves to Reshape His Administration." *National Journal* 6 (December 7, 1974): 1825-1830.

11980. Bonafede, Dom. "Ford Leaves Office Structure Intact." *National Journal* 7 (June 28, 1975): 974.

11981. Bonafede, Dom. "Ford Reverses Trend in Strengthening Cabinet Role." *National Journal* 7 (May 3, 1975): 652-656.

11982. Bonafede, Dom. "Ford's First 100 Days Find Skepticism Replacing Euphoria." *National Journal* 6 (November 6, 1974): 1711-1714.

11983. Bonafede, Dom. "Ford's Lobbyists Expect Democrats to Revise Tactics." *National Journal* 7 (June 1975): 923-927.

11984. Bonafede, Dom. "Presidential Staff Continues Growth under Ford." *National Journal* 7 (August 2, 1975): 1110-1111.

11985. Bonafede, Dom. "Rockefeller's Role Fails to Match Ford Promise." *National Journal* 7 (August 23, 1975): 1191.

11986. Bonafede, Dom. "Speech Writers Shun Flourishes in Moulding Ford's Image." *National Journal* 7 (January 25, 1975): 123-127.

11987. Bonafede, Dom. "Staff Is Organized to Ensure Accessibility to Ford." *National Journal* 6 (December 28, 1974): 1954-1958.

11988. Bresler, Robert J. "Agenda for a New Conservative President." *Intellect* 103 (November 1974): 99, 134.

11989. Cameron, Juan. "The Management Problem in Ford's White House." *Fortune* 92 (July 1975): 74-81, 176.

11990. Cameron, Juan. "Suppose There's a President Ford in Your Future." *Fortune* 89 (March 1974): 103.

11991. Carlile, Donald E. "The *Mayaguez* Incident — Crisis Management." *Military Review* 56 (October 1976): 3-14.

11992. Casserly, John J. *The Ford White House: The Diary of a Speechwriter.* Boulder: Colorado Associated University Press, 1977.

11993. Chaffee, Steven H., and Sun Yuel Choe. "Time of Decision and Media Use during the Ford-Carter Campaign." *Public Opinion Quarterly* 44 (Spring 1980): 53-69.

11994. Chamberlain, John. "Ford's Hundred Days." *National Review* 27 (March 28, 1975): 329-332.

11995. Collier, Peter. "Ford and the Media: CBS Declares a Honeymoon." *Ramparts* 13 (October 1974): 45-50.

11996. Cook, Philip S. "Ford Gets the Twice-Over." *Newsweek* 82 (November 12, 1973): 41-42.

11997. Congressional Quarterly. *Presidency, 1975.* Washington, DC: Congressional Quarterly, 1976.

11998. Congressional Quarterly. *Presidency, 1974.* Washington, DC: Congressional Quarterly, 1975.

11999. Congressional Quarterly. *Presidency, 1976.* Washington, DC: Congressional Quarterly, 1977.

12000. Congressional Quarterly. *President Ford: The Man and His Record.* Washington, DC: Congressional Quarterly, 1974.

12001. Corrigan, Richard. "Ford Position Strengthened by Lack of Consensus in Congress." *National Journal* 7 (June 7, 1975): 837-841.

12002. Crewdson, Prudence. "Ford Presses Deregulation as Alternative to Proposed Consumer Advocacy Agency." *Congressional Quarterly Weekly Report* 38 (May 10, 1975): 988-989.

12003. Cronin, Thomas E. "An Agenda for Ford." *Commonweal* 100 (September 6, 1974): 472-475.

12004. Crouse, Janice S. "The Carter-Ford Campaign Debates, 1976: The Images and Issues in Political Persuasion." Ph.D. dissertation, State University of New York, Buffalo, 1979.

12005. Diamond, Edwin. "The Ford and Carter Commercials They Didn't Dare Run." *More* 6 (December 1976): 12-17.

12006. Dobriansky, Lev E. "The Unforgettable Ford Gaffe." *Ukrainian Quarterly* 33 (Winter 1977): 366-377.

12007. Duncan, Rodger D. "The Rhetoric of Rebuttal: A Critical Study of the 'Identification' Strategies Employed by Democratic Congressional Leaders in Response to Nationally Televised Economic Addresses by President Gerald R. Ford." Ph.D. dissertation, Purdue University, 1976.

12008. Evans, Rowland, Jr., and Robert D. Novak. "Jerry Ford: The Eisenhower of the Seventies?" *Atlantic Monthly* 234 (August 1974): 25-32.

12009. Falk, Richard A. "President Gerald Ford, CIA Covert Operations, and the Status of International Law." *American Journal of International Law* 69 (April 1975): 354-358.

12010. Farrell, Robert E. "What Kind of Man Is Gerald Ford?" *Business Week* (August 3, 1974): 6.

12011. Feigenbaum, Edward D. "Staffing, Organization, and Decision Making in the Ford and Carter White Houses." *Presidential Studies Quarterly* 10 (Summer 1980): 364-377.

12012. Ferretti, Fred. *The Year the Big Apple Went Bust.* New York: Putnam, 1976.

12013. Feuerwerger, Marvin C. "The Ford Administration and Israel: Early Signals." *Midstream* 20 (December 1974): 13-19.

12014. Feuerwerger, Marvin C. "Ford and Israel." *Midstream* 21 (October 1975): 30-36.

12015. "Ford and Carter and Energy." *Public Utilities Fortnightly* 98 (October 21, 1976): 14-16.

12016. "Ford's Economic Team: A Firm with One Client." *Congressional Quarterly Weekly Report* 32 (November 23, 1974): 3173-3179.

12017. Frank, Richard S. "Ford Economic Aides Seek to Solve Export Policy Dispute." *National Journal* 7 (April 26, 1975): 609-611.

12018. Fuller, Cheryl E. S. "A Weaverian Study of President Ford's Efforts to Sell His Energy Package." Master's thesis, North Texas State University, 1975.

12019. "Gerald Ford: A New Conservative President." *Congressional Quarterly Weekly Report* 32 (August 10, 1974): 2077-2082.

12020. "Gerald R. Ford: Close Scrutiny before Confirmation." *Congressional Quarterly Weekly Report* 31 (October 20, 1973): 2759-2772.

12021. Gribben, William J. "The 'Aspect' of Argument in the Ford-Carter Debates of 1976." Master's thesis, University of West Florida, 1981.

12022. Hahn, Dan F. "Corrupt Rhetoric: President Ford and the *Mayaguez* Affair." *Communication Quarterly* 28 (Spring 1980): 38-43.

12023. Haider, Donald H. "Presidential Management Initiatives: A Ford Legacy to Executive Management Improvement." *Public Administration Review* 39 (May/June 1979): 248-259.

12024. Hamm, Michael J. "The *Pueblo* and *Mayaguez* Incidents: A Study of Flexible Response and Decision Making." *Asian Survey* 17 (June 1977): 545-555.

12025. Hartmann, Robert T. "How Ford Runs the White House: Interview with President's Three Top Advisors." *U.S. News & World Report* 23 (September 23, 1974): 28-33.

12026. Hartmann, Robert T. *Palace Politics: An Inside Account of the Ford Years.* New York: McGraw-Hill, 1980.

12027. Havemann, Joel. "Ford Endorses 172 Goals of 'Management by Objective' Plan." *National Journal* 6 (October 26, 1974): 1597-1605.

12028. Head, Simon. "Things Come Right for Mr. Ford." *New Statesman* 90 (July 18, 1975): 73.

12029. Hersey, John. *Aspects of the Presidency: Truman and Ford in Office.* New Haven, CT: Ticknor and Fields, 1980.

12030. Hersey, John. *The President: A Minute-by-Minute Account of a Week in the Life of Gerald Ford.* New York: Knopf, 1975.

12031. Hodgson, James D. "President Ford's New Economic Program." *Pacific*

Community 6 (January 1975): 314-319.

12032. "How President Ford Views the System." *Fortune* 91 (April 1975): 80-81.

12033. Howell, David, Margaret-Mary Howell, and Robert Kronman. *Gentlemanly Attitudes: Jerry Ford and the Campaign of '76.* Washington, DC: HKJV Publications, 1980.

12034. Hoxie, R. Gordon. "Staffing the Ford and Carter Presidencies." *Presidential Studies Quarterly* 10 (Summer 1980): 378-401.

12035. Kerbel, Matthew R. "Against the Odds: Media Access in the Administration of President Gerald Ford." *Presidential Studies Quarterly* 16 (Winter 1986): 76-91.

12036. Kincade, William H. "U.S. Civil Defense Decision Making: The Ford and Carter Administrations." Ph.D. dissertation, American University, 1980.

12037. Klipper, Leslie A. "An Analysis of Personality Characteristics in the 1976 General Election Television Commercials of Carter and Ford." Master's thesis, Indiana University, 1980.

12038. Kolodney, David. "Gerald Ford: Understudy for Defeat." *Ramparts* 13 (October 1974): 8-13.

12039. Laird, Melvin R. "America's New Leadership: The President I Know." *Reader's Digest* 105 (November 1974): 97-104.

12040. Lang, Gladys E., and Kurt Lang. "Immediate and Delayed Responses to a Carter-Ford Debate: Assessing Public Opinion." *Public Opinion Quarterly* 42 (Fall 1978): 322-341.

12041. Lellouche, Pierre. "Breaking the Rules without Quite Stopping the Bomb: European Views." *International Organization* 35 (Winter 1981): 39-58.

12042. Lichtenstein, Nelson, and Eleanora W. Schoenebaum, eds. *Political Profiles: The Nixon/Ford Years.* New York: Facts on File, 1979.

12043. Lipset, Seymour M. "Is Ford Another Truman?" *New Society* 37 (August 1976): 443-444.

12044. Mashek, John. "A Day in the Life of the President: Minute-by-Minute Report from inside the White House." *U.S. News & World Report* 78 (February 24, 1975): 12-19.

12045. Massaro, John. "Fortacast — Dark Clouds over President Ford's Forthcoming Supreme Court Nominations." *Federal Bar Journal* 34 (Fall 1975): 257-278.

12046. Melusky, Joseph A. "An Electoral College Fable: How the Carter-Ford Election Might Have Made Ronald Reagan President in 1976." *Presidential Studies Quarterly* 11 (Summer 1981): 384-386.

12047. Mitchell, Clarence. "Mr. Ford and Civil Rights: A Mixed Record." *Crisis* 81 (January 1974): 7-11.

12048. Morrow, Gary R. "Changes in Perceptions of Ford and Carter Following First Presidential Debate." *Perceptual and Motor Skills* 45 (October 1977): 423-429.

12049. Mulder, Ronald D. "The Political Effects of the Carter-Ford Debate: An Experimental Analysis." *Sociological Focus* 11 (January 1978): 33-45.

12050. Nakamura, Robert T. "Impressions of Ford and Reagan." *Political Science Quarterly* 92 (Winter 1977-1978): 647-654.

12051. Oneal, Dennis J. "The Treatment of James Earl Carter and Gerald R. Ford during the 1976 Election Campaign by Television Network Commentators Eric Sevareid and Howard K. Smith: An Evaluative Assertion Analysis." Ph.D. dissertation, University of Southern Mississippi, 1979.

12052. Osborne, John. *White House Watch: The Ford Years.* Washington, DC: New Republic, 1977.

12053. Papp, Daniel S. "Nixon, Brezhnev, and Watergate: The Effect of a Domestic Crisis on Soviet American Relations." *Georgia Political Science Association Journal* 4 (Spring 1976): 3-20.

12054. "Public Record of Gerald R. Ford." *Congressional Quarterly Weekly Report* 31 (October 20, 1973): 2759-2771.

12055. Reichley, A. James. "Conservative Roots of the Nixon, Ford, and Reagan Administrations." *Political Science Quarterly* 96 (Winter 1981-1982): 537-550.

12056. Reichley, A. James. *Conservatives in an Age of Change: The Nixon and Ford Administrations.* Washington, DC: Brookings Institution, 1981.

12057. Reeves, Richard. *A Ford, Not a Lincoln.* New York: Harcourt, Brace, Jovanovich, 1975.

12058. Rose, Douglas D. "Citizen Uses of the Ford-Carter Debates." *Journal of Politics* 41 (February 1979): 214-221.

12059. Saulnier, Raymond J. "The President's Economic Report: A Critique." *Journal of Portfolio Management* 2 (Summer 1976): 57-58.

12060. Schoenebaum, Eleanora, W., ed. *Profiles of an Era: The Nixon/Ford Years.* New York: Harcourt, Brace, Jovanovich, 1979.

12061. "Science: The Doors to the White House Reopen." *Congressional Quarterly Weekly Report* 32 (October 12, 1974): 2834-2840.

12062. Shannon, William V. "Is Gerald Ford Really Necessary?" *Worldview* 17 (July 1974): 13-18.

12063. Sidey, Hugh. *Portrait of a President.* New York: Harper and Row, 1975.

12064. Slater, William T. "The White House Press Corps during the Ford Administration." Ph.D. dissertation, Stanford University, 1978.

12065. Sloan, John W. "The Ford Presidency: A Conservative Approach to Economic Management." *Presidential Studies Quarterly* 14 (Fall 1984): 526-537.

12066. Smith, Raymond G. "The Carter-Ford Debates: Some Perceptions from Academe." *Central States Speech Journal* 28 (Winter 1977): 250-257.

12067. Sobel, Lester A., ed. *Presidential Succession: Ford, Rockefeller, and the 25th Amendment.* New York: Facts on File, 1975.

12068. Sprague, R. E. "Nixon, Ford, and the Political Assassination and Attempted Assassinations." *Presidential Studies Quarterly* 10 (Summer 1980): 336-347.

12069. Stelzner, Hermann G. "Ford's War on Inflation: A Metaphor That Did Not Cross." *Communication Monographs* 44 (November 1977): 284-297.

12070. Swanson, Linda L., and David L. Swanson. "The Agenda-Setting Function of the Ford-Carter Debate." *Communication Monographs* 45 (November 1978): 347-353.

12071. Swanson, Roger F. "The Ford Interlude and the U.S.-Canadian Relationship." *American Review of Canadian Studies* 8 (Spring 1978): 3-17.

12072. terHorst, Jerald F. *Gerald Ford and the Future of the Presidency.* New York: Third Press, 1975.

12073. U.S. Congress. House. *Tributes to Honorable Gerald R. Ford, President of the United States, To Commemorate Him for His Years of Service to the Nation, February 1, 1977: Delivered in the House of Representatives of the United States.* 95th Cong., 1st sess., 1977. Washington, DC: U.S. Government Printing Office, 1977.

12074. U.S. Congress. Senate. Committee on Rules and Administration. *Nomination of Gerald R. Ford to be Vice President of the United States.* Hearings. 93d Cong., 1st sess., 1973. Washington, DC: U.S. Government Printing Office, 1973.

12075. U.S. Library of Congress. Congressional Research Service. *Analysis of the Philosophy of Voting Record of Gerald R. Ford, Nominee for Vice President of the United States.* Washington, DC: Congressional Research Service, 1973.

12076. U.S. President. *The Ford Presidency.* Washington, DC: U.S. Government Printing Office, 1976.

12077. U.S. White House. Office of Communications. *The Ford Presidency: A Portrait of the First Two Years.* Edited by Stefan A. Halper, et al. Washington, DC: U.S. Government Printing Office, 1976.

12078. Wayne, Stephen J. "Running the White House: The Ford Experience." *Presidential Studies Quarterly* 7 (Spring/Summer 1977): 95-101.

12079. Wellemeyer, Marilyn. "President Ford's Hard Choices on Energy." *Fortune* 91 (January 1975): 74-77.

12080. "What's Wrong with the Way We Pick Our Presidents?" *U.S. News & World Report* 97 (July 23, 1984): 28-30.

12081. Wides, Jeffrey W. "Perceived Economic Competency and the Ford/Carter Election." *Public Opinion Quarterly* 43 (Winter 1979): 535-543.

12082. Wills, Garry. "He's Not So Dumb." *New York Review of Books* 22 (October 16, 1975): 18-22, 24-26.

12083. Witherspoon, Patricia A. D. "The Rhetoric of Gerald R. Ford: A Multidimensional Analysis of Presidential Communication." Ph.D. dissertation, University of Texas, 1977.

12084. Wrong, Dennis H. "Auguries for 1976 — Will Ford Make It?" *Dissent* 23 (Winter 1976): 6-9.

12085. Zutz, Robert. "The Recapture of the S.S. *Mayaguez:* Failure of the Consultation Clause of the War Powers Resolution." *New York University Journal of International Law and Politics* 8 (Winter 1976): 457-478.

Writings

12086. Ford, Gerald R. *A Conversation with Gerald R. Ford: Thoughts on Economics and Politics in the 1980's.* Washington, DC: American Enterprise Institute for Public Policy Research, 1980.

12087. Ford, Gerald R. *A Discussion with Gerald R. Ford: The American Presidency.* Washington, DC: American Enterprise Institute for Public Policy Research, 1977.

12088. Ford, Gerald R. "Exercise and Sports." *Journal of Health, Physical Education and Recreation* 45 (April 1974): 10-11.

12089. Ford, Gerald R. "Fiftieth Anniversary of the Foreign Service." *Department of State Bulletin* 71 (July 22, 1974): 145-147.

12090. Ford, Gerald R. "Impeachment: A Mace for the Federal Judiciary." *Notre Dame Lawyer* 46 (Summer 1971): 669-677.

12091. Ford, Gerald R. "Lessons from the Presidency." *Christianity Today* 21 (July 29, 1977): 18-19.

12092. Ford, Gerald R. "On the Threshold of the White House." *Atlantic Monthly* 234 (July 1974): 63-65.

12093. Ford, Gerald R. "The Rule of Law: Equal Justice for All." *Vital Speeches* 40 (December 15, 1973): 1975-1979.

12094. Ford, Gerald R. *Selected Speeches*

by Gerald R. Ford. Edited by Michael V. Doyle. Arlington, VA: R. W. Beatty, 1973.

12095. Ford, Gerald R. *Seminar in Economic Policy with Gerald R. Ford.* Washington, DC: American Enterprise Institute for Public Policy Research, 1978.

12096. Ford, Gerald R. *A Time To Heal: The Autobiography of Gerald R. Ford.* New York: Harper and Row, 1979.

12097. Ford, Gerald R. "Viewpoint: Seizing the Opportunity." *Regulation* 2 (January/February 1978): 15-17.

12098. Ford, Gerald R. *A Vision for America.* Northridge, CA: Lord John Press, 1980.

12099. Ford, Gerald R. *The War Powers Resolution: Striking a Balance between the Executive and Legislative Branches.* Washington, DC: American Enterprise Institute for Public Policy Research, 1977.

12100. Ford, Gerald R. "What Can Save the G.O.P.?" *Fortune* 71 (January 1965): 140-141, 230-231.

12101. Ford, Gerald R., and John R. Stiles. *Portrait of the Assassin.* New York: Simon and Schuster, 1965.

12102. Winter-Berger, Robert N. *The Gerald Ford Letters.* Secaucus, NJ: Lyle Stuart, 1974.

Jimmy Carter

Biographies

12103. Allen, Frederick. *Jimmy Carter, A Photobiography.* Houston: EFP Publishing, 1976.

12104. Allen, Gary. *Jimmy Carter — Jimmy Carter.* Seal Beach, CA: Seventy-Six Press, 1976.

12105. Callahan, Dorothy M. *Jimmy, The Story of the Young Jimmy Carter.* Garden City, NY: Doubleday, 1979.

12106. Collins, Tom. *The Search for Jimmy Carter.* Waco, TX: Word Books, 1976.

12107. DeHart, Frank. *America's Jimmy Carter.* Washington, DC: F. DeHart, 1979.

12108. Hyatt, Richard. *The Carters of Plains.* Huntsville, AL: Altrode Publishers, 1977.

12109. Klein, Ernst. *Jimmy Carter.* Stockholm: Pan/Norstedt, 1977.

12110. Kucharsky, David. *The Man from Plains: The Mind and Spirit of Jimmy Carter.* New York: Harper and Row, 1976.

12111. Lasky, Victor. *Jimmy Carter: The Man and the Myth.* New York: Marek, 1979.

12112. Mercer, Charles E. *Jimmy Carter.* New York: Putnam, 1977.

12113. Meyer, Peter. *James Earl Carter: The Man and the Myth.* Kansas City, MO: Sheed, Andrews and McMeel, 1978.

12114. Miller, William L. *Yankee from Georgia: The Emergence of Jimmy Carter.* New York: Times Books, 1978.

12115. Mollenhoff, Clark R. *The President Who Failed: Carter Out of Control.* New York: Macmillan, 1980.

12116. Norton, Howard, and Bob Slosser. *The Miracle of Jimmy Carter.* Plainfield, NJ: Logos International, 1976.

12117. Poynter, Margaret. *The Jimmy Carter Story.* New York: Messner, 1978.

12118. Thomas, Sunny. *Jimmy Carter: From Peanuts to Presidency.* Cornwall, Ontario: Vesta Publications, 1978.

12119. Walker, Barbara J. *The Picture Life of Jimmy Carter.* New York: Franklin Watts, 1977.

Private Life

12120. Adler, William, ed. *The Wit and Wisdom of Jimmy Carter.* Secaucus, NJ: Citadel Press, 1977.

12121. Aldrich, Nelson W. "President's New Clothes." *Nation* 227 (November 25, 1978): 574-577.

12122. Beisel, David R. "Toward a Psychohistory of Jimmy Carter." *Journal of Psychohistory* 5 (Fall 1977): 151-173.

12123. Carter, Rosalynn. *First Lady from Plains.* Thorndike, ME: Thorndike Press, 1984.

12124. Darvick, Herman. "The Many Signatures of Jimmy Carter." *Manuscripts* 34 (Winter 1982): 61-67.

12125. DeMause, Lloyd. "Jimmy Carter and American Fantasy." *Journal of Psychohistory* 5 (Fall 1977): 151-173.

12126. DeMause, Lloyd, and Henry Ebel, eds. *Jimmy Carter and American Fantasy: Psychohistorical Explorations.* New York: Two Continents, 1977.

12127. Ebel, Henry. "But What Kind of Baby Is Jimmy Carter?" *Journal of Psychohistory* 5 (Fall 1977): 259-269.

12128. Elovitz, Paul H. "Three Days in Plains." *Journal of Psychohistory* 5 (Fall 1977): 175-199.

12129. Gaver, Jessyca R. *The Faith of Jimmy Carter.* New York: Manor Books, 1977.

12130. Hall, Gordon L. *Rosalynn Carter, Her Life Story.* New York: Fell, 1979.

12131. Hefley, James, and Marti Hefley. *The Church That Produced a President.* New York: Wyden Books, 1977.

12132. Holifield, E. Brooks. "Three Strands of Jimmy Carter's Religion." *New Republic* 174 (June 5, 1976): 15-17.

12133. Klenbort, Marcia. *The Road To Plains: A Guide to Plains and Nearby Places of Interest in Southwest Georgia.* Atlanta: Avery Press, 1977.

12134. Langford, Edna, and Linda Maddox. *Rosalynn: Friend and First Lady.* Old Tappan, NJ: Revell, 1980.

12135. Mazlish, Bruce, and Edwin Diamond. *Jimmy Carter: A Character Portrait.* New York: Simon and Schuster, 1979.

12136. Michaelson, Wes. "Piety and Ambition of Jimmy Carter." *Sojourners* 5 (October 1976): 15-18.

12137. Neyland, James. *The Carter Family Scrapbook: An Intimate Closeup of America's First Family.* New York: Grosset and Dunlap, 1977.

12138. Nielsen, Niels C., Jr. *The Religion of President Carter.* Nashville: T. Nelson, 1977.

12139. Norton, Howard. *Rosalynn.* Plainfield, NJ: Logos, 1977.

12140. Pippert, Wesley G. "Does Carter's Christianity Count?: Moral Leadership Is Essential." *Christianity Today* 23 (November 3, 1978): 15-21.

12141. Ratcliff, Carter. "The American Artist from Loner to Lobbyist." *Art in America* 65 (March/April 1977): 10-12.

12142. Scheer, Robert, and Barry Golson. "Jimmy Carter: A Candid Conversation." *Playboy* 23 (November 1976): 63-86.

12143. Solomon, Martha. "Jimmy Carter and *Playboy:* A Sociolinguistic Perspective on Style." *Quarterly Journal of Speech* 64 (April 1978): 173-192.

12144. Stanford, Phil. "Most Remarkable Piece of Fiction Jimmy Carter Ever Read." *Columbia Journalism Review* 15 (July 1976): 13-17.

12145. Wooten, James T. *Dasher: The Roots and the Rising of Jimmy Carter.* New York: Summit Books, 1978.

Public Career

12146. Bowden, Elizabeth G. "The Gubernatorial Administration of Jimmy Carter." Master's thesis, University of Georgia, 1980.

12147. Chapman, Stephen. "Governor vs. Governor: Reagan's and Carter's Performances." *Atlantic* 246 (October 1980): 6-16.

12148. Fink, Gary M. *Prelude to the Presidency: The Political Character and Legislative Leadership-Style of Governor Jimmy Carter.* Westport, CT: Greenwood Press, 1980.

Presidential Years

General

12149. Abernathy, M. Glenn, Dilys M. Hill, and Phil Williams, eds. *The Carter Years: The President and Policy Making.* New York: St. Martin's Press, 1984.

12150. Adams, Bruce, and Kathryn Kavanagh-Baran. *Promise and Performance: Carter Builds a New Administration.* Lexington, MA: Lexington Books, 1979.

12151. Adler, William, ed. *Kids' Letters to President Carter.* New York: Grosset and Dunlap, 1978.

12152. Baker, James T. *A Southern Baptist in the White House.* Philadelphia: Westminster Press, 1977.

12153. Baker, Ross K. "The Outlook for the Carter Administration." In *The Election of 1976: Reports and Interpretations*, edited by Gerald Pomper, 115-162. New York: McKay, 1977.

12154. Balz, Daniel J. "Carter's Honeymoon on the Hill: How Long Can It Last?" *National Journal* 8 (November 13, 1976): 1618-1623.

12155. Bonafede, Dom. "At the White House, You Can't Tell the Players without a Scorecard." *National Journal* 11 (October 6, 1979): 1641-1643.

12156. Bonafede, Dom. "Carter and Congress: It Seems That 'If Something Can Go Wrong It Will.' " *National Journal* 9 (November 12, 1977): 1756-1761.

12157. Bonafede, Dom. "Carter's Relationship with Congress: Making a Mountain Out of a 'Moorehill.' " *National Journal* 9 (March 26, 1977): 456-463.

12158. Bonafede, Dom. "Charles Kirbo — The President's One-Man 'Kitchen Cabinet.' " *National Journal* 10 (July 22, 1978): 1152-1156.

12159. Bonafede, Dom. *The Presidency: The Carter White House and Post-Watergate Presidency.* Washington, DC: Government Research Corporation, 1977.

12160. Brower, Brock. "Bureaucrats Redux." *Harper's* 254 (March 1977): 25-26.

12161. Brummett, Barry. "Towards a Theory of Silence as a Political Strategy." *Quarterly Journal of Speech* 66 (October 1980): 289-303.

12162. Burch, Philip H., Jr. *The New Deal to the Carter Administration.* New York: Holmes and Meier, 1980.

12163. Butterfield, D. Anthony, and Gary N. Powell. "Convergent Validity in Student's Perceptions of Jimmy Carter, Ted Kennedy, and the Ideal President." *Perceptual and Motor Skills* 52 (February 1981): 51-56.

12164. Caddell, Patrick H. "Trapped in a Downward Spiral." *Public Opinion* 2 (October/November 1979): 2-7.

12165. Campbell, Colin. *Managing the Presidency: Carter, Reagan, and the Search for Executive Harmony.* Pittsburgh, PA: University of Pittsburgh Press, 1986.

12166. "Carter's Multimedia Presidency." *Broadcasting* 92 (March 14, 1977): 25-26.

12167. Chomsky, Noam. "The Carter Administration: Myth and Reality." *Australian Quarterly* 50 (March 1978): 8-36.

12168. Christenson, Reo M. "Carter and Truman: A Reappraisal of Both." *Presidential Studies Quarterly* 13 (Spring 1983): 313-323.

12169. Clark, Timothy B. "Putting It to the Bureaucrats." *National Journal* 11 (May 26, 1979): 873.

12170. Cockburn, Alexander. "Jimmy Carter's Perfumed Garden." *New Statesman* 92 (July 16, 1976): 67-68.

12171. Cohen, Richard E. "The Carter-Congress Rift: Who's Really to Blame?" *National Journal* 10 (April 22, 1978): 630-632.

12172. Congressional Quarterly. *Presidency, 1977*. Washington, DC: Congressional Quarterly, 1978.

12173. Congressional Quarterly. *President Carter*. Washington, DC: Congressional Quarterly, 1977.

12174. Congressional Quarterly. *President Carter, 1980*. Edited by Margaret Thompson. Washington, DC: Congressional Quarterly, 1981.

12175. Congressional Quarterly. *President Carter, 1978*. Edited by John L. Moore. Washington, DC: Congressional Quarterly, 1979.

12176. Congressional Quarterly. *President Carter, 1979*. Edited by John L. Moore. Washington, DC: Congressional Quarterly, 1980.

12177. Dempsey, John R. "Carter Reorganization: A Midterm Appraisal." *Public Administration Review* 39 (January/February 1979): 74-77.

12178. DeSantis, Vincent P. "Jimmy Carter and His Presidency." *World Review* 19 (October 1980): 37-54.

12179. Deutsch, Richard. "Carter's Congressional Rift." *Africa Report* 23 (November 1978): 46-49.

12180. Elshtain, Jean B. "Presidential Language: The Love Song of J. Carter." *Nation* 230 (April 26, 1980): 481, 497-500.

12181. Erickson, Keith V. "Jimmy Carter: The Rhetoric of Private and Civic Piety." *Western Journal of Speech Communication* 44 (Summer 1980): 235-251.

12182. Etheredge, Lloyd S. "Perspective and Evidence in Understanding Jimmy Carter." *Psychohistory Review* 6 (Spring 1978): 53-59.

12183. Feigenbaum, Edward D. "Staffing, Organization, and Decision Making in the Ford and Carter White Houses." *Presidential Studies Quarterly* 10 (Summer 1980): 364-377.

12184. Fischer, Raymond L. "Jimmy Carter, Gerald Rafshoon, and Operation Recovery." *USA Today* 107 (May 1979): 14-16.

12185. Fleisher, Richard, and Jon R. Bond. "Assessing Presidential Support in the House: Lessons from Reagan and Carter." *Journal of Political Science* 45 (August 1983): 745-758.

12186. Flowers, Ronald B. "President Jimmy Carter, Evangelicalism, Church-State Relations, and Civil Religion." *Journal of Church and State* 25 (Winter 1983): 113-132.

12187. Gardner, Gerald C. *Who's in Charge Here? 1980*. New York: Bantam Books, 1979.

12188. Gelineau, Elaine P., and Peter F. Merenda. "Students' Perceptions of Jimmy Carter, Ted Kennedy, and the Ideal President." *Perceptual and Motor Skills* 51 (August 1980): 147-155.

12189. Gergen, David. "Will Carter Put out the Fire? An Ambiguous Beginning." *Regulation* 1 (September/October 1977): 21-26.

12190. Gottschall, Jon S. "Carter Judicial Appointments — The Influence of Affirmative-Action and Merit Selection in Voting on the United States Courts of Appeals." *Judicature* 67 (October 1983): 164-173.

12191. Graebner, Norman A. "From Carter to Reagan: An Uneasy Transition." *Australian Journal of Politics and History* 27 (1981): 304-329.

12192. Griffin, Daniel L. "The Political Philosophy of Jimmy Carter." Master's thesis, Pacific Lutheran University, 1977.

12193. Hahn, Dan F. "The Rhetoric of Jimmy Carter, 1976-1980." *Presidential Studies Quarterly* 14 (Spring 1984): 265-288.

12194. Hahn, Dan F., and J. Justin Gustainis. "Anatomy of an Enigma: Jimmy Carter's 1980 State of the Union Address." *Communication Quarterly* 33 (Winter 1985): 43-49.

12195. Harberger, Arnold C. "In Defense of Carter: A Personal Overview." *National Tax Journal* 22 (March 1969): 164-177.

12196. Hargrove, Erwin C. "The Uses and Limits of Skill in Presidential Leadership: The Case of Jimmy Carter." *Policy Studies Journal* 13 (December 1985): 287-294.

12197. Harrington, Michael. "Mr. Carter's Arena: America and the World." *Social Policy* 7 (January/February 1977): 4-7.

12198. Hess, Stephen. "Portrait of a President." *Wilson Quarterly* 1 (Winter 1977): 38-48.

12199. Howell, Leon. "Waiting for Carter." *Christianity and Crisis* 37 (February 7, 1977): 13-15.

12200. Hoxie, R. Gordon. "Staffing the Ford and Carter Presidencies." *Presidential Studies Quarterly* 10 (Summer 1980): 378-401.

12201. Huddleston, Mark W. "The Carter Civil Service Reforms: Some Implications for Political Theory and Public Administration." *Political Science Quarterly* 96 (Winter 1981-1982): 607-621.

12202. Hughes, Arthur J. "Amazin' Jimmy and a Mighty Fortress Was Our Teddy: Theodore Roosevelt and Jimmy Carter." *Presidential Studies Quarterly* 9 (Winter 1979): 80-82.

12203. Hughes, Emmet J. "Presidency vs. Jimmy Carter." *Fortune* 98 (December 4, 1978): 50-64.

12204. Isaacs, Harold. *Jimmy Carter's Peanut Brigade*. Edited by Doris M. Isaacs. Dallas, TX: Taylor Publishing Co., 1977.

12205. Isbeu, Florence. "Carter's Civil Libertarians: Potomac Fever." *Civil Liberties Review* 4 (July/August 1977): 55-58.

12206. Jasinowski, Jerry J. "The First Two Years of the Carter Administration: An Appraisal." *Presidential Studies Quarterly* 9 (Winter 1979): 11-15.

12207. Johnson, Haynes B. *In the Absence of Power: Governing America*. New York: Viking Press, 1980.

12208. Jones, Charles O. "Keeping Faith and Losing Congress: The Carter Experience in Washington." *Presidential Studies Quarterly* 14 (Summer 1984): 437-445.

12209. Jones, Rochelle, and Peter Woll. "Carter vs. the Bureaucrats: The Interest Vested in Chaos." *Nation* 224 (April 2, 1977): 402-404.

12210. Jordan, Hamilton. *Crisis: The Last Year of the Carter Presidency*. New York: Putnam, 1982.

12211. Kadis, Phillip M. "Jimmy Carter: A Big Grin for Culture." *Art News* 76 (May 1977): 50-54.

12212. Kessel, John H. "The Structure of the Carter White House." *American Jour-*

nal of Political Science 27 (August 1983): 431-463.

12213. Kirkwood, Ron B. "Carter, Reagan, and the Quest for Leadership." *Policy Studies Review* 4 (November 1984): 360-364.

12214. Lanouette, William J. "Carter's Science Adviser Doing Part of His Job Well: Frank Press, Unlike Science Advisers in Previous Administrations, Automatically Plays an Important Role Because Science Is Important to This President." *National Journal* 11 (January 6, 1979): 14-19.

12215. Laqueur, Walter. "The World and President Carter." *Commentary* 65 (February 1978): 56-63.

12216. Lazarus, Simon, and Harry Huge. "Looking Forward to President Carter." *New Republic* 174 (June 5, 1976): 11-14.

12217. Leapman, M. "American Mood, 1979: President Carter's First 30 Months Prove a Disappointment." *Round Table* (October 1979): 343-346.

12218. Lee, David D. "The Politics of Less: The Trials of Herbert Hoover and Jimmy Carter." *Presidential Studies Quarterly* 13 (Spring 1983): 305-312.

12219. Lemann, Nicholas. "Why Carter Fails: Taking the Politics Out of Government." *Washington Monthly* 10 (September 1978): 12-23.

12220. Lens, Sidney. "Jimmy Carter and the New Reality." *Christian Century* 94 (January 5-12, 1977): 10-14.

12221. Leubsdorf, Carl P. "Winging It with Jimmy." *Columbia Journalism Review* 17 (July 1978): 42-43.

12222. Light, Larry. "The Hill Takes a Dim View of the Carter Cabinet Purge." *Congressional Quarterly Weekly Report* 37 (July 21, 1979): 1431-1432.

12223. Lipset, Seymour M. "Presidential Greatness in the Age of Carter." *American Spectator* 11 (June/July 1978): 7-10.

12224. Locander, Robert. "Carter and the Press: The First Two Years." *Presidential Studies Quarterly* 10 (Winter 1980): 106-119.

12225. Lynch, Edward J. "The White House Family Feud." *Policy Review* 13 (Summer 1980): 109-128.

12226. Maddox, Robert L. *Preacher at the White House.* Nashville, TN: Broadman Press, 1984.

12227. "Managing the News, White House Style: Press Releases, Private Briefings, an Army of Publicists — All Are Part of President Carter's Drive to Improve His Public Standing." *U.S. News & World Report* 85 (September 4, 1978): 17-19.

12228. Marshall, Eliot. "Efficiency Expert: Carter's Plan to Shake up the Bureaucracy." *New Republic* 175 (August 21, 1976): 15-17.

12229. Martin, Martha A. "Ideologues, Ideographs, and 'The Best Men': From Carter to Reagan." *Southern Speech Communication Journal* 49 (Fall 1983): 12-25.

12230. Merrill, F. T. "How Carter Stopped Playing Politics and Started Having Trouble with Congress." *Washington Monthly* 9 (July/August 1977): 28-30.

12231. Milakovich, Michael E. "Bureaucratic Politics in a Year of Transition." *Midwest Review of Public Administration* 11 (June 1977): 157-159.

12232. Miles, Rufus E., Jr. "Considerations for a President Bent on Reorganization." *Public Administration Review* 37 (March/April 1977): 155-162.

12233. Moe, Ronald C. *The Carter Reorganization Effort: A Review and Assessment.* Washington, DC: Congressional Research Service, 1980.

12234. Morris, Roger. "Carter's Cabinet:

The Who's Who Treatment." *Columbia Journalism Review* 15 (March/April 1977): 34-35.

12235. Morrow, Lance. "Who Is Jimmy Carter?" *Horizon* 21 (February 1978): 60-65.

12236. Mullen, William F. "Perceptions of Carter's Legislative Successes and Failures: Views from the Hill and the Liaison Staff." *Presidential Studies Quarterly* 12 (Fall 1982): 522-533.

12237. Neuhaus, Richard J. "Carter Presidency and Real Watershed." *Worldview* 19 (September 1976): 28-30.

12238. Neumann, Robert G. "Leadership: Franklin Roosevelt, Truman, Eisenhower, and Today." *Presidential Studies Quarterly* 10 (Winter 1980): 10-19.

12239. Orr, C. Jack. "Reporters Confront the President: Sustaining a Counterpoised Situation." *Quarterly Journal of Speech* 66 (February 1980): 17-32.

12240. Osborne, John. "Carter in Transit." *New Republic* 175 (December 11, 1976): 12-14.

12241. Paletz, David L., and Robert M. Entman. "Presidents, Power, and the Press." *Presidential Studies Quarterly* 10 (Summer 1980): 416-426.

12242. Patton, John H. "A Government as Good as Its People: Jimmy Carter and the Restoration of Transcendence to Politics." *Quarterly Journal of Speech* 63 (October 1977): 249-257.

12243. Peters, Charles. "Why Jimmy Carter Doesn't Hire Jimmy Carters." *Washington Monthly* 8 (February 1977): 12-15.

12244. Petras, James. "President Carter and the New Morality." *Monthly Review* 29 (April 1977): 42-50.

12245. Pfiffner, James P. "The Carter-Reagan Transition: Hitting the Ground Running." *Presidential Studies Quarterly* 13 (Fall 1983): 623-645.

12246. Polenberg, Richard. "Roosevelt, Carter, and Executive Reorganization: Lessons of the 1930's." *Presidential Studies Quarterly* 9 (Winter 1979): 35-46.

12247. Powell, Jody. *The Other Side of the Story.* New York: Morrow, 1984.

12248. "President Carter's Attack on Lawyers, President Spann's Response, and Chief Justice Burger's Remarks." *American Bar Association Journal* 64 (June 1978): 840.

12249. "President Carter's Notre Dame Address." *Review of Politics* 39 (July 1977): 291-297.

12250. "Public Affairs and Populism: A Day with the Carter Administration Public Affairs Team." *Public Relations Journal* 33 (July 1977): 26-27.

12251. Quint, Peter E. "The Separation of Powers under Carter." *Texas Law Review* 62 (February 1984): 785-891.

12252. Randolph, Eleanor. "The 'Whip-His-Ass' Story, Or The Gang That Couldn't Leak Straight." *Washington Monthly* 11 (September 1979): 50-51.

12253. Reeves, Richard. *Convention, Jimmy Carter for President in '76.* New York: Harcourt, 1977.

12254. Reilly, Ann M. "Can Carter Cut Costly Rules?" *Dun's Review* 112 (September 1978): 88-92.

12255. Rockman, Bert A. "Carter's Troubles." *Society* 17 (July/August 1980): 34-40.

12256. Rosati, Jerel A. "The Carter Administration's Image of the International System: The Development and Application of a Belief System Framework." Ph.D. dissertation, American University, 1982.

12257. Rosen, Gerald R. "Coal: Carter

and Congress Hold the Key." *Dun's Review* 109 (February 1977): 56-60.

12258. Schweigler, Gebhard. "Carter Dilemma: Strengths and Weaknesses of the American President." *Europa-Archiv* 34 (January 25, 1979): 53-62.

12259. Schweigler, Gebhard. "Carter's Dilemmas: Presidential Power and Its Limits." *World Today* 35 (February 1979): 46-55.

12260. Shaffer, William R. "A Discriminant Function Analysis of Position Taking: Carter vs. Kennedy." *Presidential Studies Quarterly* 10 (Summer 1980): 451-468.

12261. Shaull, Richard. "Shoring Up: President Carter as Baptist Leader." *Sojourners* 7 (January 1978): 12-14.

12262. Sheaffer, Robert. "President Carter's UFO Is Identified as Planet Venus." *Humanist* 37 (July/August 1977): 46-47.

12263. Shogan, Robert. *Promises to Keep: Carter's First 100 Days.* New York: Crowell, 1977.

12264. Shoup, Laurence H. *The Carter Presidency and Beyond: Power and Politics in the 1980's.* Palo Alto: Ramparts Press, 1980.

12265. Sicherman, Harvey. "Crossroads of a Presidency." *Orbis* 22 (Fall 1978): 499-502.

12266. Sklar, Holly. "Trilateralism and the Right: Crisis and Continuity in Policy from Carter to Reagan." *Radical Religion* 5 (1981): 22-36.

12267. "State of the Union Address by the President of the United States." *Atlantic Community Quarterly* 18 (Spring 1980): 3-11.

12268. Stewart, David W. "Cooperative Extension, the Carter Administration, and the 95th Congress: An Empirical Model of the Politics of Appropriation." Ph.D. dissertation, University of Wisconsin, 1979.

12269. Sundquist, James L. "Jimmy Carter as Public Administrator: An Appraisal at Mid-Term." *Public Administrative Review* 39 (January/February 1979): 3-11.

12270. Tays, Dwight L. "The Carter Doctrine." Ph.D. dissertation, University of Mississippi, 1982.

12271. Thomas, Norman C. "The Carter Administration Memoirs: A Review Essay." *Western Political Quarterly* 39 (June 1986): 348-361.

12272. Towell, Pat. "House Easily Sustains Carter Weapons Veto." *Congressional Quarterly Weekly Report* 36 (September 9, 1978): 2415-2417.

12273. Underwood, James E. "Studying Individual Presidents: Truman, Eisenhower, Kennedy, and Carter." *Congress and the Presidency* 11 (Spring 1984): 93-104.

12274. Vukadinovic, Radovan. "Carter's Team at the Halfway Mark." *Atlantic Community Quarterly* 17 (Summer 1979): 221-226.

12275. Wall, James M. "Great Expectations: Carter's Challenge." *Christian Century* 93 (November 17, 1976): 998-999.

12276. Weaver, Suzanne. "From Candidate to President." *Public Interest* 50 (Winter 1978): 161-167.

12277. Williams, John A. "The Carter Administration: Three Accounts." *Air University Review* 35 (March/April 1984): 103-107.

Domestic Policy

12278. Anderson, Bernard E. "The Carter Economics: A Symposium." *Journal of Post Keynesian Economics* 1 (Fall 1978): 31-33.

12279. Anderson, James E. "The Management of Wage-Price Policies in the Johnson and Carter Administrations."

Policy Studies Journal 12 (June 1984): 733-746.

12280. Anderson, Martin. "Why Carter's Welfare Reform Plan Failed." *Policy Review* 5 (Summer 1978): 37-39.

12281. Armstrong, Barbara. "The New President in the White House: New Priority for Mental Health." *Hospital and Community Psychiatry* 28 (March 1977): 198-202.

12282. Bartlett, Bruce R. "Killing the Messenger: The Carter Administration and the Facts about Oil and Gas." *Washington Monthly* 10 (April 1978): 57-60.

12283. Bell, James F., and Arthur E. Wilmarth. "The Interstate Banking Controversy — President Carter McFadden Act Report." *Banking Law Journal* 99 (September 1982): 722-744.

12284. Bosworth, Barry P. "The Carter Administration's Anti-Inflation Program." *Academy of Political Science Proceedings* 33 (1979): 12-19.

12285. Break, George F. "Integrating Corporate and Personal Income Taxes: The Carter Commission Proposals." *Law and Contemporary Problems* 34 (Autumn 1969): 726-735.

12286. Brozen, Yale. "Why Carter's Game Plan Won't Work." *Reason* 8 (1977): 14-18.

12287. Cameron, Juan. "Where Does the President Stand on Nuclear Energy?" *Fortune* 97 (June 1978): 99.

12288. "Carter, Reagan Outline Attitudes on Regulation of Broadcasting." *Broadcasting* 98 (June 9, 1980): 67-68.

12289. "Carter Unveils Energy Agency Blueprint." *Oil and Gas Journal* 75 (March 7, 1977): 64-66.

12290. Churchill, Mae. "Carter's Born-Again War on Crime." *Social Policy* 9 (November/December 1978): 40-45.

12291. Clarke, Thomas H. "President Carter and Business Community." *Business Horizons* 20 (February 1977): 15-19.

12292. Conn, Joseph. "Carter, Reagan, Anderson, and Church-State Issues." *Humanist* 40 (November/December 1980): 22-23.

12293. Dewald, William G., and Maurice Marchon. "Macroeconomic Goals and Prospects of the Carter Administration." *Ohio State University Bulletin of Business Research* 53 (November 1978): 1-8.

12294. "Ford and Carter and Energy." *Public Utilities Fortnightly* 98 (October 21, 1976): 14-16.

12295. Fragomen, Austin T., Jr. "President Carter's Amnesty and Sanctions Proposal." *International Migration Review* 11 (Winter 1977): 524-532.

12296. Gottschalk, Peter T. "Principles of Tax Transfer Integration and Carter's Welfare-Reform Proposal." *Journal of Human Resources* 13 (Summer 1978): 332-348.

12297. Greenspan, Alan, Alfred E. Kahn, Marvin H. Kosters, and Rudolph Oswald. "On Carter's Anti-Inflation Policy." *Regulation* 3 (January/February 1979): 17-30.

12298. Groves, Harold M. "Taxing the Family Unit: The Carter Commission's Proposals and U.S. Practice." *National Tax Journal* 22 (March 1969): 109-120.

12299. Hahn, Dan F. "Flailing the Profligate: Carter's Energy Sermon of 1979." *Presidential Studies Quarterly* 10 (Fall 1980): 583-587.

12300. Hammond, Michael E. "Carter Lifts His Sights." *Financial World* 148 (December 15, 1979): 16-20.

12301. Hastedt, Glenn P. "Military Reorganization, Civil-Military Relations, and the Carter Presidency." *Bureaucrat* 9 (Summer 1980): 23-30.

12302. Hausner, V. A. "Urban and Regional Policy in the United States: The Approach of the Carter Administration." *Regional Studies* 17 (October 1983): 366-369.

12303. Heebner, A. Gilbert. "The Carter Economics: A Symposium." *Journal of Post Keynesian Economics* 1 (Fall 1978): 33-36.

12304. Higgs, Robert. "Carter's Wage-Price Guidelines: A Review of the First Year." *Policy Review* 11 (Winter 1980): 97-113.

12305. Houstoun, L. O., Jr. "The Carter Urban Policy a Year Later." *Antioch Review* 37 (Spring 1979): 134-147.

12306. Iglehart, John K. "Carter Administration's Health Budget: Charting New Priorities with Limited Dollars." *Milbank Memorial Fund Quarterly* 56 (Winter 1978): 51-77.

12307. Isaacson, W. J. "President Carter's Anti-Inflation Program: Solution or Illusion?" *Employee Relations Law Journal* 4 (1979) 469-470.

12308. Kantowicz, Edward R. "The Limits of Incrementalism: Carter's Efforts at Tax Reform." *Journal of Policy Analysis and Management* 4 (Winter 1985): 217-233.

12309. Kincade, William H. "U.S. Civil Defense Decision Making: The Ford and Carter Administrations." Ph.D. dissertation, American University, 1980.

12310. King, Joan H. "Establishing the U.S. Department of Education during the Carter Administration, 1978-1979." Ph.D. dissertation, Claremont Graduate School, 1980.

12311. Lamb, Charles M. "Equal Employment Opportunity and the Carter Administration." *Policy Studies Journal* 8 (Winter 1979): 377-383.

12312. Lefevre, Stephen R. "Trials of Termination: President Carter and the Breeder Reactor Program." *Presidential Studies Quarterly* 15 (Spring 1985): 330-342.

12313. Lekachman, Robert. "The Carter Economics: A Symposium." *Journal of Post-Keynesian Economics* 1 (Fall 1978): 39-42.

12314. Lekachman, Robert. "Carter's Energy Plan: Grade It 'C' for Effort." *Christian Century* 37 (May 16, 1977): 98-100.

12315. Levy, Michael E. "Fiscal Policy: The First Nine Months under the Carter Administration." *Business Economics* 13 (January 1978): 73-78.

12316. Lewis, Nancy. "The Carter Record." *Change* 8 (October 1976): 22-25, 64.

12317. Light, Alfred R. "The Carter Administration's National Energy Plan: Pressure Groups and Organizational Politics in the Congress." *Policy Studies Journal* 7 (Autumn 1978): 68-75.

12318. Litvack, Sanford M. "The Ebb and Flow of Antitrust Enforcement: The Reagan and Carter Administrations." *Brigham Young University Law Review* (Fall 1982): 849-856.

12319. Lorne, S. M. "Attorney-Client Relationships after Carter and Johnson." *Journal of Comparative Corporate Law and Securities Regulation* 3 (July 1981): 151-167.

12320. Lynn, Barry W. "Mr. Carter's Pardon-Amnesty: Selective Redemption." *Christianity and Crisis* 37 (November 7, 1977): 37-42.

12321. Lynn, Laurence E., Jr. *The President as Policy Maker: Jimmy Carter and Welfare Reform.* Philadelphia: Temple University Press, 1981.

12322. McAllister, Eugene. "An Analysis of Carter's Wage Insurance Plan." *Policy Review* 8 (Spring 1979): 103-104.

12323. MacDowell, Francesca J. "President Carter Announces Water Policy Initiatives." *Natural Resources Journal* 19 (January 1979): 191-196.

12324. Mancke, Richard B. "The American Response: 'On the Job Training'?" *Orbis* 23 (Winter 1980): 785-801.

12325. Mazzoni, Tim L. "Jimmy Carter, Education President." *Phi Delta Kappan* 58 (March 1977): 547-549.

12326. Mead, Walter J. "Economic Appraisal of President Carter's Energy Program." *Science* 197 (July 22, 1977): 340-345.

12327. Metzger, H. Peter. "Environmental Activists Capture Washington." *Reason* 11 (1979): 25-29, 32.

12328. Mieszkowski, Peter. "Carter on the Taxation of International Income Flows." *National Tax Journal* 22 (March 1969): 97-108.

12329. Minsky, Hyman P. "The Carter Economics: A Symposium." *Journal of Post-Keynesian Economics* 1 (Fall 1978): 42-45.

12330. Myers, Robert J. "Okun's Law and the Carter Social Security Proposals." *Journal of Risk and Insurance* 45 (June 1978): 335-339.

12331. Nickel, Herman "Carter's Cactus Flower at HUD." *Fortune* 98 (November 6, 1978): 110-113.

12332. Ortner, Robert. "The Carter Economics: A Symposium." *Journal of Post-Keynesian Economics* 1 (Fall 1978): 26-30.

12333. Parker, Alan. "Western Energy after Carter." *Lloyds Bank Review* 127 (January 1978): 28-43.

12334. Parker, Frank L. "Thermal Pollution Consequences of the Implementation of the President's Energy Message on Increased Coal Utilization." *Environmental Health Perspectives* 33 (December 1979): 303-314.

12335. Pechman, Joseph A., and Benjamin A. Obner. "Simulation of the Carter Commission Tax Proposals for the United States." *National Tax Journal* 22 (March 1969): 2-23.

12336. Pelham, Ann. "Congress Balks at Some Carter Plans." *Congressional Quarterly Weekly Report* 37 (August 4, 1979): 1580-1581.

12337. Rutledge, John, and Jeffrey Speakes. "Carter vs. Reagan: How Their Policies Would Affect Prices, Economy." *Commodities* 9 (October 1980): 27-31.

12338. Saddler, Hugh. "Fraser, Carter, and the Uranium Market." *Intervention* 9 (October 1977): 30-42.

12339. St. John, Jeffrey. *Jimmy Carter's Betrayal of the South.* Ottawa, IL: Green Hill Publishers, 1976.

12340. Saulnier, Raymond J. "The President's Economic Report: A Critique." *Journal of Portfolio Management* 4 (Summer 1978): 45-46.

12341. Saulnier, Raymond J. "The President's Economic Report: A Critique." *Journal of Portfolio Management* 5 (Summer 1979): 11-12.

12342. Saulnier, Raymond J. "The President's Economic Report: A Critique." *Journal of Portfolio Management* 6 (Summer 1980): 37-39.

12343. Scheele, Paul E. "President Carter and the Water Projects: A Case Study in Presidential and Congressional Decision-Making." *Presidential Studies Quarterly* 8 (Fall 1978): 348-364.

12344. Shattuck, John H. F. "You Can't Depend on It: The Carter Administration and Civil Liberties." *Civil Liberties Review* 4 (January/February 1978): 10-27.

12345. Sheele, Paul E. "President Carter

and the Water Projects." *Presidential Studies Quarterly* 8 (Fall 1978): 348-364.

12346. Singer, James W. "Carter in 1980 — Not Ideal, But Maybe Labor's Best Hope." *National Journal* 11 (July 28, 1979): 1252-1255.

12347. Slitor, Richard E. "The Carter Proposals on Capital Gains: Economic Effects and Policy Implications for the United States." *National Tax Journal* 22 (March 1969): 66-78.

12348. Smith, H. Shelton. "Black Power and Jimmy Carter." *Christianity and Crisis* 36 (September 20, 1976): 205-206.

12349. Stanfield, Rochelle L. "The Development of President Carter's Urban Policy: One Small Step for Federalism." *Publius* 8 (Winter 1978): 39-53.

12350. Stephens, David. "President Carter, the Congress, and NEA: Creating the Department of Education." *Political Science Quarterly* 98 (Winter 1983-1984): 641-663.

12351. Stone, Chuck. "Black Political Power in the Carter Era." *Black Scholar* 8 (January/February 1977): 6-15.

12352. Stone, Chuck. "Black Scholar Debate — Jordan-Carter Exchange — Carter's Paternalistic Racism and Inept Presidency." *Black Scholar* 9 (March 1978): 39-41.

12353. Sudol, Ronald A. "The Rhetoric of Strategic Retreat: Carter and the Panama Canal Debate." *Quarterly Journal of Speech* 65 (December 1979): 379-391.

12354. Sylves, Richard T. "Carter's Nuclear Licensing Reform versus Three Mile Island." *Publius* 10 (Winter 1980): 69-79.

12355. Thomas, Dan B., and Larry Baas. "Presidential Identification and Mass Public Compliance with Official Policy: The Case of the Carter Energy Program." *Policy Studies Journal* 10 (March 1982): 448-465.

12356. Thurow, Lester C. "The Carter Economics: A Symposium." *Journal of Post Keynesian Economics* 1 (Fall 1978): 23-26.

12357. Tobin, James. "The Carter Economics: A Symposium." *Journal of Post-Keynesian Economics* 1 (Fall 1978): 19-23.

12358. Ulmer, Melville J. "The Carter Economics: A Symposium." *Journal of Post Keynesian Economics* 1 (Fall 1978): 37-39.

12359. Watters, Pat. "Probing Jimmy Carter's Civil Liberties Record." *Civil Liberties Review* 3 (August/September 1976): 7-22.

12360. Weintraub, Sidney. "The Carter Economic Council's Thalidomide TIP." *Journal of Post-Keynesian Economics* 3 (Spring 1981): 459-462.

12361. Witt, Peter Von. "U.S. International Energy Policy and President Carter's National Energy Program." *Europa-Archiv* 32 (1977): 586-594.

12362. Wolman, Harold, and Astrid E. Merget. "The Presidency and Policy Formulation: President Carter and the Urban Policy." *Presidential Studies Quarterly* 10 (Summer 1980): 402-415.

12363. Wright, L. Hart. "Carter's Projected 'Zero-based' Review of the Internal Revenue Code: Is Our Tax Code to Be 'Born Again'?" *Michigan Law Review* 75 (April/May 1977): 1286-1317.

Elections

12364. Alexander, John F. "Did We Blow It?: The Evangelical Right Mobilized for Reagan, But Carter Wasn't Good Enough for the Left: Were We Crazy?" *Other Side* 113 (February 1981): 10-15.

12365. Baas, Larry, and Dan B. Thomas. "Dissonance and Perception during a

Presidential Campaign: Pre-Election and Post-Election Findings from the Carter-Ford Contest." *Journal of Social Psychology* 112 (December 1980): 305-306.

12366. Beniger, James R. "The Legacy of Carter and Reagan: Political Reality Overtakes the Myth of Presidential Primaries." *Intellect* 105 (February 1977): 234-237.

12367. Bitzer, Lloyd, and Theodore Reuter. *Carter vs. Ford: The Counterfeit Debates of Nineteen Seventy-six*. Madison: University of Wisconsin Press, 1980.

12368. Bremner, John E. "The Winning Candidate." *Washington Monthly* 8 (May 1976): 58-61.

12369. Brenner, Michael. "Proliferation Watch: Carter's Bungled Promise." *Foreign Policy* 36 (Fall 1979): 89-101.

12370. "Carter-Reagan Debate: Bringing It All Together for Campaign '80." *Broadcasting* 99 (November 3, 1980): 23-24.

12371. Chaffee, Steven H., and Sun Yuel Choe. "Time of Decision and Media Use during the Ford-Carter Campaign." *Public Opinion Quarterly* 44 (Spring 1980): 53-69.

12372. Crouse, Janice S. "The Carter-Ford Campaign Debates, 1976: The Images and Issues in Political Persuasion." Ph.D. dissertation, State University of New York, Buffalo, 1979.

12373. Davis, Eric L. "Legislative Liaison in the Carter Administration." *Political Science Quarterly* 94 (Summer 1979): 287-301.

12374. Devlin, L. Patrick. "Reagan's and Carter's Ad Men Review the 1980 Television Campaigns." *Communication Quarterly* 30 (Winter 1982): 3-12.

12375. Diamond, Edwin. "The Ford and Carter Commercials They Didn't Dare Run." *More* 6 (December 1976): 12-17.

12376. Douglass, Bruce. "Gamble of Carter's Piety." *Christianity and Crisis* 36 (October 4, 1976): 220-224.

12377. Ferriter, Tom, John McDermott, and James Flansbury. "Jimmy Carter: Kennedy or Kefauver?" *Washington Monthly* 7 (February 1976): 17-20.

12378. Gelineau, Elaine P., and Peter F. Merenda. "Students' Pre-Election Perceptions of Jimmy Carter and Ronald Reagan." *Perception and Motor Skills* 52 (April 1981): 491-498.

12379. Germond, Jack, and Jules Witcover. *Blue Smoke and Mirrors: How Reagan Won and Why Carter Lost the Election of 1980*. New York: Viking Press, 1981.

12380. Glad, Betty. *Jimmy Carter: In Search of the Great White House*. New York: Norton, 1980.

12381. Godden, Jean H. *Carter: The Will to Win*. Cincinnati, OH: Mosaic Press, 1980.

12382. Gribben, William J. "The 'Aspect' of Argument in the Ford-Carter Debates of 1976." Master's thesis, University of West Florida, 1981.

12383. Hahn, Dan F. "One's Reborn Every Minute: Carter's Religious Appeal in 1976." *Communication Quarterly* 28 (Summer 1980): 56-62.

12384. Hartman, John J. "Carter and the Utopian Group-Fantasy." *Journal of Psychohistory* 5 (Fall 1977): 239-258.

12385. Havic, John J., and Florence Heffron. "Iowa Caucuses: Carter's Early Campaign for the Presidential Nomination." *Midwest Quarterly* 20 (Autumn 1978): 32-48.

12386. Hill, Dilys M., and Phil Williams. "The Carter Legacy, Mondale, and the Democratic Party." *World Today* 40 (October 1984): 413-419.

12387. Himmelfarb, Milton. "Carter and the Jews." *Commentary* 62 (August 1976): 45-48.

12388. Johnstone, Christopher L. "Electing Ourselves in 1976: Jimmy Carter and the American Faith." *Western Journal of Speech Communication* 42 (Fall 1978): 241-249.

12389. Klipper, Leslie A. "An Analysis of Personality Characteristics in the 1976 General Election Television Commercials of Carter and Ford." Master's thesis, Indiana University, 1980.

12390. Lang, Gladys E., and Kurt Lang. "Immediate and Delayed Responses to a Carter-Ford Debate: Assessing Public Opinion." *Public Opinion Quarterly* 42 (Fall 1978): 322-341.

12391. Lee, David D. "The South and the American Mainstream: The Election of Jimmy Carter." *Georgia Historical Quarterly* 61 (Spring 1977): 7-12.

12392. Light, Larry. "Voting Support for Carter Remained Low during 1978 for Democratic President." *Congressional Quarterly Weekly Report* 36 (December 9, 1978): 3407-3413.

12393. Linden, Louis. "Carter for President." *Nation* 231 (July 12, 1980): 34.

12394. Lott, Davis N. *Jimmy Carter and How He Won: A Pictorial Documentary*. Los Angeles: Peterson, 1976.

12395. Maloney, Gary D., and Terry F. Buss. "Information, Interest, and Attitude Change: Carter and the 1976 Post-Convention Campaign." *Central States Speech Journal* 31 (Spring 1980): 63-73.

12396. Melusky, Joseph A. "An Electoral College Fable: How the Carter-Ford Election Might Have Made Ronald Reagan President in 1976." *Presidential Studies Quarterly* 11 (Summer 1981): 384-386.

12397. Morrow, Gary R. "Changes in Perception of Ford and Carter Following First Presidential Debate." *Perceptual and Motor Skills* 45 (October 1977): 423-429.

12398. Mulder, Ronald D. "The Political Effects of the Carter-Ford Debate: An Experimental Analysis." *Sociological Focus* 11 (January 1978): 33-45.

12399. Oneal, Dennis J. "The Treatment of James Earl Carter and Gerald R. Ford during the 1976 Election Campaign by Television Network Commentators Eric Sevareid and Howard K. Smith: An Evaluative Assertion Analysis." Ph.D. dissertation, University of Southern Mississippi, 1979.

12400. Peirce, Neal R., and Jerry Hagstrom. "The Voters Send Carter a Message: Time for a Change to Reagan." *National Journal* 12 (November 8, 1980): 1876-1878.

12401. Peters, Charles. "Concerns about Carter and His Chief Courtier." *Washington Monthly* 8 (December 1976): 2-8.

12402. Rarick, David L., Mary B. Duncan, David G. Lee, and Laurinda W. Porter. "The Carter Persona: An Empirical Analysis of the Rhetorical Visions of Campaign '76." *Quarterly Journal of Speech* 63 (October 1977): 258-273.

12403. Richmond, Michael E. M. "Carter and the Jews." *Christian Century* 93 (October 27, 1976): 926-928.

12404. Riemer, Yosef, and Robert H. Binstock. "Campaigning for the Senior Vote: A Case Study of Carter's 1976 Campaign." *Gerontologist* 18 (December 1978): 517-524.

12405. Rose, Douglas D. "Citizen Uses of the Ford-Carter Debates." *Journal of Politics* 41 (February 1979): 214-221.

12406. Sarasohn, Judy. "Carter Voting Support Holds Steady in Congress Despite Plunge in Polls: Slight Drop from 1978." *Congressional Quarterly Weekly Report* 38 (January 12, 1980): 91-97.

12407. Schram, Martin. *Running for President 1976: The Carter Campaign.* New York: Stein and Day, 1977.

12408. Shapiro, Walter. "The Intractables." *Washington Monthly* 8 (May 1976): 12-18.

12409. Shapiro, Walter. "Triumph and the Trivia: Inside the Carter Headquarters in Pennsylvania." *Washington Monthly* 8 (July/August 1976): 31-39.

12410. Sigelman, Lee, and Carol K. Sigelman. "Judgements of the Carter-Reagan Debate: The Eyes of the Beholders." *Public Opinion Quarterly* 48 (Fall 1984): 624-628.

12411. Smith, Raymond G. "The Carter-Ford Debates: Some Perceptions from Academe." *Central States Speech Journal* 28 (Winter 1977): 250-257.

12412. Spalding, Phinizy. "Georgia and the Election of Jimmy Carter." *Georgia Historical Quarterly* 61 (Spring 1977): 13-22.

12413. Stroud, Kandy. *How Jimmy Won: The Victory Campaign from Plains to the White House.* New York: Morrow, 1977.

12414. Swanson, Linda L., and David L. Swanson. "The Agenda-Setting Function of the Ford-Carter Debate." *Communication Monographs* 45 (November 1978): 347-353.

12415. Szanton, Peter. "Questions of Power, Matters of Right." *Round Table* 267 (July 1977): 207-214.

12416. Tiemens, Robert K., Susan A. Hellweg, Philip Kipper, and Steven L. Phillips. "An Integrative Verbal and Visual Analysis of the Carter-Reagan Debate." *Communication Quarterly* 33 (Winter 1985): 34-42.

12417. "What's Wrong with the Way We Pick Our Presidents?" *U.S. News & World Report* 97 (July 23, 1984): 28-30.

12418. Wheeler, Leslie. *Jimmy Who? An Examination of Presidential Candidate Jimmy Carter: The Man, His Career, His Stands on the Issues.* Woodbury, NY: Barron's, 1976.

12419. Wides, Jeffrey W. "Perceived Economic Competency and the Ford-Carter Election." *Public Opinion Quarterly* 43 (Winter 1979): 535-543.

12420. Witcover, Jules. "Iowa: How Carter Won the First Battle." *Washington Monthly* 9 (July/August 1977): 68-75.

12421. Witcover, Jules. *Marathon: The Pursuit of the Presidency 1972-1976.* New York: New American Library, 1978.

12422. Wolin, Howard E. "Carter at the Center." *Center Magazine* 10 (January/February 1977): 49-58.

Foreign Affairs

12423. Adelman, Kenneth L. "The Runner Stumbles: Carter's Foreign Policy in the Year One." *Policy Review* 3 (Winter 1978): 89-116.

12424. Allen, H. C. "Quiet Strength: American Foreign Policy under President Carter." *Round Table* (April 1977): 146-152.

12425. Ank, Le Thi. "Open Letter to President Carter about Indochina Refugees." *Worldview* 22 (May 1979): 11-12.

12426. Aronson, Shlomo. "Carter and the Middle East: An Early Report Card." *Jerusalem Quarterly* 3 (Summer 1977): 31-43.

12427. Baker, Ross K. "Carter on Apartheid." *Worldview* 20 (May 1977): 4-7.

12428. Ball, Nicole, and Milton Leitenberg. "The Foreign Arms Sales of the Carter Administration." *Bulletin of the Atomic Scientists* 35 (February 1979): 31-36.

12429. Ball, Nicole, and Milton Leitenberg. "The Foreign Arms Sales Policy of the Carter Administration." *Alternatives* 4 (March 1979): 527-556.

12430. Barnum, John W. "Carter Administration Stumbles at Bermuda: Setback for U.S. International Aviation Policy." *Regulation* 2 (January/February 1978): 18-30.

12431. Beard, Robin. "The Carter Administration's Salt II Proposals." *Journal of Social and Political Studies* 2 (Fall 1977): 143-154.

12432. Bell, Coral. "From Carter to Reagan." *Foreign Affairs* 63 (1985): 490-510.

12433. Bell, Coral. "Virtue Unrewarded: Carter's Foreign Policy at Mid-Term." *International Affairs* 54 (October 1978): 559-572.

12434. Ben-Zvi, Abraham. "The Carter Presidency and the Palestinian Question." *Wiener Library Bulletin* 33 (1980): 55-65.

12435. Bishop, Joseph W., Jr. "Carter's Last Capitulation." *Commentary* 71 (March 1981): 32-35.

12436. Coffey, Joseph I. "SALT under the Carter Administration." *Naval War College Review* 31 (Winter 1979): 6-29.

12437. Cohen, Marc J. "Food for Development: The Carter Administration and United States Food Aid to Southeast Asia." Ph.D. dissertation, University of Wisconsin, 1983.

12438. Collins, Larry. "Prospects of Foreign Policy under Carter's Administration." *International Perspectives* (Canada) (May/June 1977): 25-30.

12439. Council on Religion and International Affairs. "CRIA's First Moral Audit: The Carter Years." *Worldview* 24 (February 1981): 27-30.

12440. Dugard, John. "Silence Is Not Golden." *Foreign Policy* 46 (Spring 1982): 37-48.

12441. Dunn, Keith A. "Detente and Deterrence: From Kissinger to Carter." *Parameters* 7 (1977): 46-55.

12442. Edwards, John. "Carter Looks Asia's Best Bet." *Far Eastern Economic Review* 110 (October 24, 1980): 17.

12443. Fagen, Richard R. "The Carter Administration and Latin America: Business as Usual?" *Foreign Affairs* 57 (1979): 652-669.

12444. Feldman, Elliot J., and Lily G. Feldman. "The Special Relationship between Canada and the United States." *Jerusalem Journal of International Relations* 4 (1980): 56-85.

12445. Fishlow, Albert. "Flying Down to Rio: Perspectives on U.S.-Brazil Relations." *Foreign Affairs* 57 (Winter 1978-1979): 387-405.

12446. Franko, Lawrence G. "Carter Administration's Clash with European Economic Interests." *Atlantic Community Quarterly* 16 (Winter 1978-1979): 440-451.

12447. Freedman, Robert O. "The Soviet Image of the Carter Administration's Policy toward the USSR from the Inauguration to the Invasion of Afghanistan: A Preliminary Analysis." *Korea and World Affairs* 4 (Summer 1980): 229-267.

12448. Gershman, Carl. "Andrew Young Affair." *Commentary* 68 (November 1979): 25-33.

12449. Girling, John L. S. "Carter's Foreign Policy: Realism or Ideology?" *World Today* 33 (November 1977): 417-424.

12450. "*Goldwater v. Carter:* The Supreme Court Dismissed the Complaint of Twenty-six Congressmen Challenging the Authority of President Carter to Unilaterally Terminate the Mutual Defense Treaty with Taiwan." *Brooklyn Journal of International Law* 7 (Winter 1981): 111-133.

12451. Hammond, Michael E. "Carter Defense Budget: A Frigate Navy and Its Implications." *Financial World* 147 (March 1, 1978): 20-25.

12452. Han, Yung-Chul. "The Carter Administration's Policy toward East Asia: With Focus on Korea." *American Studies International* 18 (Autumn 1979): 35-48.

12453. Hoffmann, Stanley. "Foreign Policy Transition: Requiem." *Foreign Policy* 42 (Spring 1981): 3-26.

12454. Hoffmann, Stanley. "Muscle and Brains." *Foreign Policy* 37 (Winter 1979-1980): 3-27.

12455. Hoffmann, Stanley. "Old Wine, Old Bottles: American Foreign Policy and the Politics of Nostalgia." *Millennium* 9 (Autumn 1980): 91-107.

12456. Hoxie, R. Gordon. "Presidential Leadership and American Foreign Policy: Some Reflections on the Taiwan Issue, With Particular Considerations on Alexander Hamilton, Dwight Eisenhower, and Jimmy Carter." *Presidential Studies Quarterly* 9 (Spring 1979): 131-143.

12457. Hughes, Thomas L. "Carter and the Management of Contradictions." *Foreign Policy* 31 (Summer 1978): 34-55.

12458. Hulett, Louisa S. "Carter, Salt II, Detente II." *Australian Journal of Politics and History* 28 (1982): 190-200.

12459. "Iranian Hostage Agreement Cases: The Evolving Presidential Claims Settlement Power." *Southwestern Law Journal* 35 (February 1982): 1055-1077.

12460. Johansen, Robert C. *Jimmy Carter's National Security Policy: A World Order Critique.* New York: World Policy Institute, 1980.

12461. Johnston, Whittle. "The New Diplomacy of President Carter." *Australian Journal of Politics and History* 24 (August 1978): 159-173.

12462. "Joint Communique of United States and Soviet Union Given in Vienna on June 18, 1979 after Meeting of President Carter with President Brezhnev." *Revista de Politica Internacional* (July/August 1979): 232-238.

12463. Joyce, James A. "Was Carter Trapped over the ILO?" *Contemporary Review* 232 (March 1978): 129-133.

12464. Korb, Lawrence J. "The Arms Control Implications of the Carter Defense Budget." *Naval War College Review* 31 (Fall 1978): 3-16.

12465. Lacqueur, Walter. "World and President Carter." *Commentary* 65 (February 1978): 56-63.

12466. LaFeber, Walter F. "From Confusion to Cold War: The Memoirs of the Carter Administration." *Diplomatic History* 8 (Winter 1984): 1-12.

12467. LaFeber, Walter F. "Torrijos, Kissinger, and Carter." In his *The Panama Canal: The Crisis in Historical Perspective.* New York: Oxford University Press, 1978.

12468. Lange, Peter, and Maurizio Vannicelli. "Carter in the Italian Maze." *Foreign Policy* 33 (Winter 1978-1979): 161-173.

12469. Lanouette, William J. "Who's Setting Foreign Policy — Carter or Congress?" *National Journal* 10 (July 15, 1978): 1116-1123.

12470. Ledeen, Michael. "Carter's Foreign Policy." *Presence Liberale: Quarterly Review of Politics, Economy and Culture* 1 (November 1980): 64-72.

12471. Lellouche, Pierre. "Breaking the Rules without Quite Stopping the Bomb: European Views." *International Organization* 35 (Winter 1981): 39-58.

12472. "Letter of President Carter Concerning the Neutron Bomb." *Politishche*

Studien 28 (September/October 1977): 535-536.

12473. Levine, Steven I. "China Policy during Carter's Year One." *Asian Survey* 18 (May 1978): 437-447.

12474. Lipset, Seymour M., and William Schneider. "Carter vs. Israel: What the Polls Reveal." *Commentary* 64 (November 1977): 21-29.

12475. Lissakers, Karin. "Money and Manipulation." *Foreign Policy* 44 (Fall 1981): 107-126.

12476. Lockwood, Edgar. "The Future of the Carter Policy toward Southern Africa." *Issue* 7 (Winter 1977): 11-16.

12477. Lowenthal, Abraham F. "Latin America: A Not-So Special Relationship." *Foreign Policy* 32 (Fall 1978): 107-126.

12478. McGeehan, Robert. "Carter's Crises: Iran, Afghanistan, and Presidential Politics." *World Today* 36 (May 1980): 163-171.

12479. McLain, Glenn A. "South Korea: Carter's Dilemma." *Contemporary Review* 232 (June 1978): 300-305.

12480. Martin, Serge G. "The President's Power to Terminate Treaties: The Unanswered Question of Goldwater." *Journal of International Law and Economics* 14 (Winter 1980): 301-319.

12481. Martin de la Escalera, Carmen. "President Carter's Visit to Mexico." *Revista de Politica Internacional* 162 (March/April 1979): 158-160.

12482. Miller, Linda B. "Carter and the Palestinians." *Jerusalem Quarterly* 11 (Spring 1979): 21-35.

12483. Morris, Roger. "Thomson, Moyers, and Ball: Prophets without Office." *Washington Monthly* 9 (June 1977): 45-51.

12484. Musil, Robert K. "Carter as Commander in Chief: The Rising Cost of Defense Policies." *Christian Century* 95 (May 3, 1978): 466-469.

12485. Obadele, Imari A. "Open Letter to United States President Jimmy Carter from RNA President Imari Abubakari." *Black Scholar* 10 (October 1978): 53-67.

12486. Olson, William C. "World from Both Ends of Pennsylvania Avenue: President Carter's Foreign Policy Problems." *Round Table* 272 (October 1978): 333-339.

12487. Pastor, Robert. "Continuity and Change in United States Foreign Policy — Carter and Reagan on El Salvador." *Journal of Policy Analysis and Management* 3 (Winter 1984): 175-190.

12488. Pearson, Frederic S., J. Marvin Reynolds, and Keith E. Meyer. "The Carter Foreign Policy and the Use of International Organization: The Limits of Policy Innovation." *World Affairs* 142 (Fall 1979): 75-97.

12489. "President Carter's Attempt to Halt Travel to Iran and the Constitutional Right to Travel." *Syracuse Journal of International Law and Commerce* 9 (Spring 1982): 115-136.

12490. Ram, Susan. "Intervention in Nicaragua — Carter and Now Reagan Find the Options Limited." *Economic and Political Weekly* 18 (November 19, 1983): 1977-1982.

12491. Reich, Bernard. "United States Middle East Policy in the Carter and Reagan Administrations." *Australian Outlook* 38 (August 1984): 72-80.

12492. Reich, Michael. "Why Carter Can't Reduce Military Spending." *Monthly Review* 29 (June 1977): 53-58.

12493. Robinson, Clarence A., Jr. "Carter Defense Plans Concern Congress." *Aviation Week and Space Technology* 108 (March 20, 1978): 20-23.

12494. Rodman, Peter W. "The Hostage

Crisis: How Not to Negotiate." *Washington Quarterly* 4 (Summer 1981): 9-24.

12495. Rostow, Eugene V. "The Giant Still Sleeps." *Orbis* 24 (Summer 1980): 311-321.

12496. Rudnick, David. "Winding Road of Good Intentions: Consideration of President Carter's Foreign Policies." *Round Table* 268 (October 1977): 345-350.

12497. Sale, Richard T. "Carter and Iran: From Idealism to Disaster." *Washington Quarterly* 3 (Autumn 1980): 75-87.

12498. Sapin, Burton M. "Isn't It Time for a Modest Presidency in Foreign Affairs? Reflections on the Carter Performance." *Presidential Studies Quarterly* 10 (Winter 1980): 19-28.

12499. Sarkesian, Sam C. *Defense Policy and the Presidency: Carter's First Years.* Boulder, CO: Westview Press, 1979.

12500. Schemmer, Benjamin F. "Presidential Courage — And the April 1980 Iranian Rescue Mission." *Armed Forces Journal International* 118 (May 1981): 60-62.

12501. Schultz, Louis P. "*Goldwater v. Carter:* The Separation of Powers and the Problem of Executive Prerogative." *Presidential Studies Quarterly* 12 (Winter 1982): 34-41.

12502. Schweigler, Gebhard. "Carter's Detente Policy: Change or Continuity?" *World Today* 34 (March 1978): 81-89.

12503. Shepherd, George W., Jr. "The Struggle to a New Southern African Policy: The Carter Task." *Journal of Southern African Affairs* 2 (January 1977): 99-120.

12504. Shichor, David, and Donald R. Ranish. "President Carter's Vietnam Amnesty: An Analysis of a Public Policy Decision." *Presidential Studies Quarterly* 10 (Summer 1980): 443-450.

12505. Smith, Gaddis. "Ideals under Siege: Carter's Foreign Policy." *Yale Review* 73 (Spring 1984): 354-366.

12506. Smith, Gaddis. *Morality, Reason, and Power: American Diplomacy in the Carter Years.* New York: Hill and Wang, 1985.

12507. Smith, Joseph B. "What Carter Didn't Know about Mexico and Why He Didn't Know It." *Washington Monthly* 11 (June 1979): 42-47.

12508. Smith, Michael. "From the 'Year of Europe' to a Year of Carter: Continuing Patterns and Problems in Euro-American Relations." *Journal of Common Market Studies* 17 (September 1978): 26-44.

12509. Sonnenfeldt, Helmut. "Russia, America, and Detente." *Foreign Affairs* 56 (January 1978): 275-294.

12510. Spiegel, Steven L. "Camp David Diplomacy." *Center Magazine* 12 (May/June 1979): 12-31.

12511. Szulc, Tad. "Springtime for Carter." *Foreign Policy* 27 (Summer 1977): 178-191.

12512. Thornton, Thomas P. "American Interest in India under Carter and Reagan." *SAIS Review* 5 (Winter/Spring 1985): 179-190.

12513. Thornton, Thomas P. "Between the Stools — United States Policy towards Pakistan during the Carter Administration." *Asian Survey* 22 (October 1982): 959-977.

12514. Tillinghast, David R. "The Carter Commission Report and International Investment Transactions: Integration and Ambiguous Intentions." *National Tax Journal* 22 (March 1969): 79-96.

12515. "Transfer of the Panama Canal by Treaty without House Approval: *Edwards v. Carter.*" *Harvard Law Review* 92 (December 1978): 524-535.

12516. Tucker, Robert W. "Middle East:

Carterism without Carter?" *Commentary* 72 (September 1981): 27-36.

12517. "Unilateral Presidential Treaty Termination Power by Default: An Analysis of *Goldwater v. Carter* (Mem. 100 S Ct. 533)." *Texas International Law Journal* 15 (Spring 1980): 317-378.

12518. Urban, George. "A Long Conversation with Dr. Zbigniew Brzezinski: 'The Perils of Foreign Policy.'" *Encounter* 56 (May 1981): 12-30.

12519. Vargashidalgo, Rafael V. "United States and Latin America under President Carter." *Revista de Politica Internacional* 155 (January/February 1978): 7-43.

12520. Wachman, Alan M. "Carter's Constitutional Conundrum: An Examination of the President's Unilateral Termination of a Treaty." *Fletcher Forum* 8 (Summer 1984): 427-457.

12521. Watt, Donald C. "Return to Americanism: Foreign Policy of President Carter." *Political Quarterly* 48 (October/December 1977): 429-439.

12522. Weber, Arnold R. "How to Make Presidential Policy: Tale of Two Camp David Meetings." *Dun's Review* 114 (October 1979): 10.

12523. Weinstein, Allen. "Press and Foreign Policy: Freedom of Information and Carter Foreign Policy: Act One." *Washington Quarterly* 2 (Spring 1979): 39-43.

12524. Williams, Jonathan D. "Defense Policy — The Carter-Reagan Record." *Washington Quarterly* 6 (Autumn 1983): 77-92.

12525. Woodard, Kim. "The Second Transition: America in Asia under Carter." *SAIS Review* 25 (Winter 1981): 129-148.

12526. Yakovee, Rehavie U. "Arms for Oil — Oil for Arms: An Analysis of President Carter's 1978 Planes 'Package Deal' Sale to Egypt, Israel, and Saudi Arabia." Ph.D. dissertation, Claremont Graduate School, 1983.

Human Rights

12527. Altenberg, Les, and Robert Cathcart. "Jimmy Carter on Human Rights — A Thematic Analysis." *Central States Speech Journal* 33 (Fall 1982): 446-457.

12528. Balthazar, Louis. "President Carter and Human Rights: The Contradiction of American Policy." *International Perspectives* (May/August 1979): 22-24.

12529. Bloomfield, Lincoln P. "From Ideology to Program to Policy — Tracking the Carter Human Rights Policy." *Journal of Policy Analysis and Management* 2 (Fall 1982): 1-12.

12530. Cohen, Roberta. "Human Rights Diplomacy — The Carter Administration and the Southern Cone." *Human Rights Quarterly* 4 (Spring 1982): 212-242.

12531. Helicher, Karl. "The Response of the Soviet Government and Press to Carter's Human Rights Policies." *Presidential Studies Quarterly* 13 (Spring 1983): 296-305.

12532. Horton, Scott, and Randy Sellier. "The Utility of Presidential Certifications of Compliance with United States Human-Rights Policy — The Case of El Salvador." *Wisconsin Law Review* (1982): 825-861.

12533. Howell, John M. "The Carter Human Rights Policy as Applied to the Soviet Union." *Presidential Studies Quarterly* 13 (Spring 1983): 286-295.

12534. Kirkpatrick, Jeane J. "Establishing a Viable Human Rights Policy." *World Affairs* 143 (Spring 1981): 323-334.

12535. LeFever, Ernest W., ed. *Morality and Foreign Policy: A Symposium on Pres-*

ident Carter's Stance. Washington, DC: Ethics and Public Policy Center, 1977.

12536. Loescher, G. D. "Carter's Human Rights Policy and the 95th Congress." *World Today* 35 (April 1979): 149-159.

12537. Loescher, G. D. "U.S. Human Rights Policy and International Financial Institutions." *World Today* 33 (December 1977): 453-463.

12538. Molineu, Harold. "Carter and Human Rights: Administrative Impact of a Symbolic Policy." *Policy Studies Journal* 8 (Summer 1980): 879-884.

12539. Mower, A. Glenn, Jr. *The United States, the United Nations, and Human Rights: The Eleanor Roosevelt and Jimmy Carter Eras.* Westport, CT: Greenwood Press, 1979.

12540. Muravchik, Joshua. *The Uncertain Crusade: Jimmy Carter and the Dilemmas of Human Rights Policy.* Lanham, MD: Hamilton Press, 1986.

12541. Ogburn, Robert W. "Implementing the Carter Human Rights Policy in South Korea: Historic Milieu." *Towson State Journal of International Affairs* 14 (1980): 75-91.

12542. O'Leary, James P. "On Grading the President's Human Rights Performance." *Journal of Intergroup Relations* 7 (September 1979): 26-29.

12543. Petro, Nicolai N. *The Predicament of Human Rights: The Carter and Reagan Policies.* Lanham, MD: University Press of America, 1983.

12544. Salzberg, John P. "The Human Rights Program in Congress: Some Policy Implications from the 1977 Hearings." *International Studies Notes* 4 (Winter 1977): 1-5.

12545. Schlesinger, Arthur M., Jr. "Human Rights and the American Tradition." *Foreign Affairs* 57 (1979): 503-526.

12546. Schneider, Mark L. "Human Rights Policy under the Carter Administration." *Law and Contemporary Problems* 43 (Spring 1979): 261-267.

12547. Tsai, Wei-ping. "Morality and Diplomacy — President Carter's Foreign Policy Orientation." *Issues and Studies* 13 (April 1977): 1-11.

12548. Tyson, Brady. "Preserving, Protecting, and Promoting Human Rights: A Viewpoint from an Official in the Carter Administration." *Engage/Social Action Forum* 9 (July/August 1981): 34-38.

12549. Warshawsky, Howard. "The Department of State and Human Rights Policy: A Case Study of the Human Rights Bureau." *World Affairs* 142 (Winter 1980): 188-215.

Writings

12550. Carter, Jimmy. *The Blood of Abraham.* Boston: Houghton Mifflin, 1985.

12551. Carter, Jimmy. *A Government as Good as Its People.* New York: Simon and Schuster, 1977.

12552. Carter, Jimmy. *Keeping Faith: Memories of a President.* New York: Bantam Books, 1982.

12553. Carter, Jimmy. *I'll Never Lie to You: Jimmy Carter in His Own Words.* Compiled by Robert L. Turner. New York: Ballantine Books, 1976.

12554. Carter, Jimmy. "My Personal Faith in God: Former President Tells How Christian Faith Shaped Presidency and How Presidency Tested His Faith." *Christianity Today* 27 (March 4, 1983): 15-21.

12555. Carter, Jimmy. "My Views on the Environment." *EPA Journal* 3 (January 1977): 6-7.

12556. Carter, Jimmy. *Negotiation: The Alternative to Hostility.* Macon, GA: Merer University Press, 1984.

12557. Carter, Jimmy. "President Carter Message on Libraries and Information." *Library Journal* 105 (November 1980): 2278-2279.

12558. Carter, Jimmy. *Presidential Campaign 1976.* Washington, DC: U.S. Government Printing Office, 1976.

12559. Carter, Jimmy. *The Spiritual Journal of Jimmy Carter, In His Own Words.* Compiled by Wesley G. Pippert. New York: Macmillan, 1978.

12560. Carter, Jimmy. *Why Not the Best?* Nashville, TN: Broadman Press, 1975.

12561. Carter, Jimmy, Ronald Reagan, and John Anderson. "The Candidates Answer: Carter, Reagan, and Anderson Give Their Views on Law-Related Issues." *American Bar Association Journal* 66 (October 1980): 1208-1215.

Ronald Reagan

Biographies

12562. Anderson, Janice. *Ronald Reagan.* New York: Exeter Books, 1982.

12563. Boyarsky, Bill. *Ronald Reagan: His Life and Rise to the Presidency.* New York: Random House, 1981.

12564. Cannon, Lou. *Reagan.* New York: Putnam, 1982.

12565. Edwards, Lee. *Ronald Reagan, A Political Biography.* Rev. ed. Houston, TX: Nordland Publishing International, 1981.

12566. Fox, Mary V. *Mister President: The Story of Ronald Reagan.* Hillside, NY: Enslow Publications, 1982.

12567. Frank, Alan. *Screen Greats: Ronald Reagan.* New York: Bookthrift, 1982.

12568. Hannaford, Peter. *The Reagans, A Personal Portrait.* New York: Coward, McCann and Geoghegan, 1981.

12569. Lawson, Don. *The Picture Life of Ronald Reagan.* New York: Franklin Watts, 1981.

12570. Rasmussen, Della M., and Phyllis Colonna. *Power of Determination: Featuring the Story of Ronald Reagan.* Antioch, CA: Power Tales, Eagle Systems International, 1981.

12571. Slosser, Bob. *Reagan Inside Out.* Waco, TX: Word Books, 1984.

12572. Smith, Hedrick, Adam Clymer, Leonard Silk, Robert Lindsey, and Richard Burt. *Reagan: The Man, The President.* New York: Macmillan, 1980.

12573. Trimble, Vance H. *Reagan: The Man from Main Street.* Cincinatti, OH: Mosaic Press, 1980.

Private Life

12574. Adler, William, ed. *The Reagan Wit.* Naperville, IL: Caroline House, 1981.

12575. Bonafede, Dom. "The Reagans Bring New Ambience to the Washington Social Scene." *National Journal* 23 (June 6, 1981): 1021-1024.

12576. Elwood, Roger. *Nancy Reagan: A Special Kind of Love.* New York: Pocket Books, 1976.

12577. Leamer, Laurence. *Make-Believe: The Story of Nancy and Ronald Reagan.* New York: Harper and Row, 1983.

12578. Lucchese, Sam, and Tad Mizwa. "The President and His Boots." *Western Outfitter* 12 (April 1981): 44-48.

12579. McClelland, Doug. *Hollywood on Ronald Reagan: Friends and Enemies Discuss Our President, The Actor.* London: Faber and Faber, 1983.

12580. Thomas, J. Mark. "Reagan in the

State of Nature." *Christianity and Crisis* 44 (September 17, 1984): 321-325.

12581. Thomas, Tony. *The Films of Ronald Reagan.* Secaucus, NJ: Citadel Press, 1982.

12582. Trudeau, Gary B. *In Search of Reagan's Brain.* New York: Holt, Rinehart and Winston, 1981.

12583. Reagan, Nancy. *Nancy.* New York: Berkley, 1981.

12584. Shapiro, Walter. "A Century of Progress: Madeleine Lee, Meet Nancy Reagan." *Washington Monthly* 13 (March 1981): 47-49.

12585. White, Patricia M. *The Invincible Irish: Ronald Wilson Reagan, Irish Ancestry and Immigration to America.* Santa Barbara, CA: Portola Press, 1981.

Public Career

12586. Biggart, Nicole W. "The Administrations of Governors Ronald Reagan and Jerry Brown." Ph.D. dissertation, University of California, Berkeley, 1981.

12587. Boyarsky, Bill. *The Rise of Ronald Reagan.* New York: Random House, 1968.

12588. Brown, Edmund G. *Reagan and Reality: The Two Californias.* New York: Praeger, 1970.

12589. Cannon, Lou. "The Reagan Years: An Evaluation of the Governor Californians Won't Soon Forget." *California Journal* 5 (November 1974): 360-366.

12590. Chapman, Stephen. "Governor vs. Governor: Reagan's and Carter's Performances." *Atlantic* 246 (October 1980): 6-16.

12591. Culver, John H. "Governors and Judicial Appointments in California." *State Government* 54 (1981): 130-134.

12592. Drayton, William B. "A Comparative Study of the Warren, Knight, Brown, and Reagan Administrations." Master's thesis, California State University, Fullerton, 1967.

12593. Hamilton, Gary G., and Nicole W. Biggart. *Governor Reagan, Governor Brown: A Sociology of Executive Power.* New York: Columbia University Press, 1984.

12594. Joe, Barbara E. "Reagan's Welfare Fraud." *Washington Monthly* 12 (October 1980): 34-36.

12595. Leipold, L. Edmond. *Ronald Reagan: Governor and Statesman.* Minneapolis, MN: T. S. Denison, 1968.

12596. Leuchtenburg, William E. "Reagan, Ronald's Liberal Past." *New Republic* 188 (November 20, 1983): 18.

12597. Oliver, Ronald E. "California Administrative Reorganization through the Reagan Administration." Ph.D. dissertation, Claremont Graduate School, 1980.

12598. Rickenbacker, William F. "Case for Ronald Reagan." *Christianity and Crisis* 28 (July 22, 1968): 166-168.

12599. Ritter, Kurt W. "Ronald Reagan and 'The Speech': The Rhetoric of Public Relations Politics." *Western Speech* 32 (Winter 1968): 50-58.

12600. Rose, Ernest D., and Douglas Fuchs. "Reagan vs. Brown: A TV Image Playback." *Journal of Broadcasting* 12 (Summer 1968): 247-260.

12601. Smith, Martin. "Lessons from the California Experience." *Change* 12 (September 1980): 32-39.

12602. Stang, Alan. "Matter of Ronald Reagan and Henry Kissinger." *American Opinion* 23 (June 1980): 47-54.

12603. Steffgen, Kent H. *Here's the Rest of Him.* Reno, NV: Forsight Books, 1968.

Presidential Years

12604. Adams, William C. "Recent Fables about Ronald Reagan." *Public Opinion* 7 (October/November 1984): 6-9.

12605. Adler, William, ed. *Kids' Letters to President Reagan.* New York: Evans, 1982.

12606. "Agreement on Reagan Library Reached by Meese and Stanford." *Library Journal* 109 (March 15, 1984): 526-527.

12607. Allen, Richard V., and William L. Armstrong. "What Conservatives Think of Ronald Reagan?" *Policy Review* 27 (Winter 1984): 12-19.

12608. American Bar Association. "The Reagan Presidency: How Well Lawyers Fare." *American Bar Association Journal* 67 (January 1981): 21-23.

12609. Arieff, Irwin B. "Reagan Courts Legislators in Visit to Hill." *Congressional Quarterly Weekly Report* 38 (November 22, 1980): 3393-3394.

12610. Arieff, Irwin B. "Senator Paul Laxalt: Reagan's Man on the Hill." *Congressional Quarterly Weekly Report* 38 (November 22, 1980): 3396-3398.

12611. Bamford, James. "How I Got the NSA Files . . . How Reagan Tried to Get Them Back." *Nation* 235 (November 6, 1982): 466-468.

12612. Bantz, Charles R., Sandra G. Petronio, and David L. Rarick. "News Diffusion after the Reagan Shooting." *Quarterly Journal of Speech* 69 (August 1983): 317-327.

12613. Barnes, Fred. "The Republican Party after Reagan: Jack and George." *New Republic* 186 (April 28, 1982): 20-23.

12614. Barrett, Laurence I. *Gambling with History: Reagan in the White House.* Garden City, NY: Doubleday, 1983.

12615. Beer, Samuel H. "Ronald Reagan: New Deal Conservative?" *Society* 20 (January/February 1983): 40-44.

12616. Biggart, Nicole W. "The Administration: Deaver Destructs, Reagan Rearranges." *Economist* 295 (April 20, 1985): 24-25.

12617. Biggart, Nicole W. "Management Style as Strategic Interaction: The Case of Ronald Reagan." *Journal of Applied Behavioral Science* 17 (July/September 1981): 291-308.

12618. Blumenthal, Sidney. "Reagan the Unassailable." *New Republic* 189 (September 12, 1983): 11-16.

12619. Bonafede, Dom. "From a 'Revolution' to a 'Stumble'—The Press Assesses the First 100 Days." *National Journal* 13 (May 16, 1981): 879-882.

12620. Bonafede, Dom. "Reagan and His Kitchen Cabinet Are Bound by Friendship and Ideology." *National Journal* 13 (April 11, 1981): 605-609.

12621. Borland, Jay, and Malcolm Vance. *The Ronald Reagan Hollywood Quiz Book.* New York: Bookthrift, 1981.

12622. Bormann, Ernest G. "Fantasy Theme Analysis of the Television Coverage of the Hostage Release and the Reagan Inaugural." *Quarterly Journal of Speech* 68 (May 1982): 133-145.

12623. Bradley, Bert B. "Jefferson and Reagan: The Rhetoric of Two Inaugurals." *Southern Speech Communication Journal* 48 (Winter 1983): 119-136.

12624. Brownstein, Ronald. "With or without Supreme Court Changes, Reagan Will Reshape the Federal Bench." *National Journal* 16 (December 8, 1984): 2338-2341.

12625. Brownstein, Ronald, and Nina Easton. *Reagan's Ruling Class: Portraits of the President's Top 100 Officials.* Washington, DC: Presidential Accountability Group, 1983.

12626. Burnham, Walter D. "The Ascendancy of the Right — Why Are Reagan and Thatcher Strong in Times of Recession?" *Dissent* 30 (Fall 1983): 434-441.

12627. Caldwell, Margaret. "President Reagan's Report Card." *New Republic* 189 (November 1983): 8-12.

12628. Campbell, Colin. *Managing the Presidency: Carter, Reagan, and the Search for Executive Harmony.* Pittsburgh, PA: University of Pittsburgh Press, 1986.

12629. Campbell, John C. "The Reagan Plan and the Western Alliance." *Atlantic Community Quarterly* 21 (Spring 1983): 71-85.

12630. Carter, Lief H. "Judicial Review of the Reagan Revolution." *Judicature* 65 (May 1982): 458-469.

12631. Ceaser, James W. "As Good as Their Words: Reagan's Rhetoric." *Public Opinion* 7 (June/July 1984): 10-12.

12632. Chester, Edward W. "Shadow or Substance? Critiquing Reagan's Inaugural Address." *Presidential Studies Quarterly* 11 (Spring 1981): 172-176.

12633. Clark, Charles S. "Reagan Parsimonious in Use of Pardon Power." *Congressional Quarterly Weekly Report* 42 (November 3, 1984): 2878-2880.

12634. Clark, Joseph. "A President Who Keeps His Promises." *Dissent* (Spring 1981): 135-136.

12635. Cline, Ray S. *The CIA under Reagan, Bush, and Casey: The Evolution of the Agency from Roosevelt to Reagan.* Washington, DC: Acropolis Books, 1981.

12636. Coaldrake, Peter. "Ronald Reagan and 'Cabinet Government': How Far a Collegial Approach." *Politics* 16 (November 1981): 276-283.

12637. Cohen, Richard E. "Deadlock on Capitol Hill: Despite His Wage Victory, President Reagan Will Need Congress's Cooperation to Carry Out His Program." *National Journal* 16 (November 10, 1984): 2134-2139.

12638. Cohodas, Nadine. "Presidential Support Study Shows Reagan Rating Fell 10 Percentage Points in 1982." *Congressional Quarterly Weekly Report* 41 (January 15, 1983): 94-97.

12639. Cohodas, Nadine. "Reagan Slow in Appointing Women, Blacks, Hispanics to Federal Judiciary Seats." *Congressional Quarterly Weekly Report* 39 (December 26, 1981): 2559-2561.

12640. Cohodas, Nadine. "Reagan's Judicial Selections Draw Differing Assessments." *Congressional Quarterly Weekly Report* 41 (January 15, 1983): 83-84.

12641. Congressional Quarterly. *President Reagan.* Washington, DC: Congressional Quarterly, 1981.

12642. Congressional Quarterly. "Reagan Proposes a New Federalism." *Congressional Quarterly Weekly Report* 40 (January 30, 1982): 147-154.

12643. Congressional Quarterly. *Reagan: The Next Four Years.* Washington, DC: Congressional Quarterly, 1985.

12644. Congressional Quarterly. *Reagan's First Year.* Washington, DC: Congressional Quarterly, 1982.

12645. Congressional Quarterly. "Voting Record of '81 Shows the Romance and Fidelity of Reagan Honeymoon on Hill." *Congressional Quarterly Weekly Report* 40 (January 2, 1982): 18-24.

12646. Crespi, Irving. "Does the Public Approve of Ronald Reagan?" *Public Opinion* 4 (October/November 1981): 20, 41.

12647. Dallek, Robert. *Ronald Reagan:*

The Politics of Symbolism. Cambridge, MA: Harvard University Press, 1984.

12648. "The Decision Makers." *National Journal* 13 (September 19, 1981): 1677-1688.

12649. DeMause, Lloyd. *Reagan's America.* New York: Creative Roots, 1984.

12650. Destler, Irving M. "Reagan and Congress — Lessons of 1981." *Washington Quarterly* 5 (Spring 1982): 3-15.

12651. Donovan, Hedley. "Reagan's First 200 Days." *Fortune* 21 (September 1981): 62-72.

12652. Donovan, Hedley. "A Vacuum in Leadership." *Fortune* 105 (March 22, 1982): 86-90.

12653. Dugger, Ronnie. "Ronald Reagan and the Imperial Presidency." *Nation* 231 (November 1, 1980): 430-436.

12654. Dye, Thomas R. *Who's Running America? — The Reagan Years.* 3d ed. Englewood Cliffs, NJ: Prentice-Hall, 1983.

12655. Easterbrook, Gregg. "The Republican Soul." *Washington Monthly* 13 (July/August 1981): 13-24.

12656. Edelman, Toby S. "Reagan's Attempt to Control the Federal Administrative Process Is Unconstitutional." *Clearinghouse Review* 15 (December 1981): 646-648.

12657. Ehlke, Richard C., and Harold C. Relyea. "The Reagan Administration Order on Security Classification — A Critical Assessment." *Federal Bar News and Journal* 30 (February 1983): 91-97.

12658. Etheredge, Lloyd S. "President Reagan's Counseling." *Political Psychology* 5 (December 1984): 737-740.

12659. Etzioni, Amitai. "A Management Computer for the President." *Technology Review* 86 (January 1983): 38-45.

12660. Evans, M. Stanton. *The Reason for Reagan.* La Jolla, CA: La Jolla Rancho Press, 1968.

12661. Evans, Rowland, Jr., and Robert D. Novak. *The Reagan Revolution.* New York: Dutton, 1981.

12662. Fairbanks, James D. "Reagan, Religion, and the New Right." *Midwest Quarterly* 23 (Spring 1982): 327-345.

12663. Felton, John. "Congress, Reagan Seek 'War Powers' Accord." *Congressional Quarterly Weekly Report* 41 (September 17, 1983): 1923-1925.

12664. Fisher, Walter R. "Romantic Democracy, Ronald Reagan, and Presidential Heroes." *Western Journal of Speech Communication* 46 (Summer 1982): 299-310.

12665. Fleisher, Richard, and Jon R. Bond. "Assessing Presidential Support in the House: Lessons from Reagan and Carter." *Journal of Political Science* 45 (August 1983): 745-758.

12666. Flick, Rachel. "What Do Women Want? — The 3 Reasons for Ronald Reagan Gender Gap." *Policy Review* 27 (Winter 1984): 80-82.

12667. Fowler, W. Gary. "Judicial Selection under Reagan and Carter — A Comparison of their Initial Recommendation Procedures." *Judicature* 67 (January 1984): 265-283.

12668. Fritz, Sara. "The 9-to-5 Presidency: Is It Working?" *U.S. News & World Report* 90 (March 23, 1981): 27-30.

12669. Fritz, Sara. "Reagan's Big Three." *U.S. News & World Report* 91 (November 2, 1982): 28-31.

12670. Gantz, Walter. "The Diffusion of News about the Attempted Reagan Assassination." *Journal of Communication* 33 (Winter 1983): 56-66.

12671. Gartner, Alan, Colin Greer, and Frank Riessman. *Beyond Reagan: Alter-*

natives for the '80's. New York: Harper and Row, 1984.

12672. Gladstone, Leslie. *Presidential Appointments of Women during the Reagan Administration.* Washington, DC: Congressional Research Service, 1984.

12673. Glaros, Roberta, and Bruce Miroff. "Watching Ronald Reagan: Viewer's Reactions to the President on Television." *Congress and the Presidency* 10 (Spring 1983): 25-46.

12674. Goldman, Sheldon. "Reagan Judicial Appointments at Mid-Term — Shaping the Bench in His Own Image." *Judicature* 66 (March 1983): 334-347.

12675. Goodman, James A. "Reagan's Rule of Law, 2: A Politician Called Smith." *Nation* 234 (April 10, 1982): 429-431.

12676. Goodman, John L. *Public Opinion during the Reagan Administration: National Issues, Private Concerns.* Washington, DC: Urban Institute Press, 1984.

12677. Gould, A., and R. Sacks. "Why the Inconsistencies — Behind Reagan Dense Pack Plan." *Nation* 235 (1982): 295-296.

12678. Graebner, Norman A. "From Carter to Reagan: An Uneasy Transition." *Australian Journal of Politics and History* 27 (1981): 304-329.

12679. Green, Mark. "The President (Mis) Speaks: There He Goes Again." *Nation* 234 (March 6, 1982): 273-274.

12680. Green, Mark, and Gail McColl. *There He Goes Again, Ronald Reagan's Reign of Error.* New York: Pantheon, 1983.

12681. Greenstein, Fred I. *The Reagan Presidency: An Early Assessment.* Baltimore, MD: Johns Hopkins University Press, 1983.

12682. Greenstein, Fred I., and Robert Wright. "Reagan ... Another Ike?" *Public Opinion* 3 (December/January 1981): 51-55.

12683. Gregen, David R. "Following the Leaders: How Ronald Reagan and Margaret Thatcher Have Changed Public Opinion." *Public Opinion* 18 (June/July 1985): 16-19.

12684. Hertzberg, Arthur. "Reagan and the Jews." *New York Review of Books* 32 (1985): 11-14.

12685. Hobbs, Charles D. *Ronald Reagan's Call to Action: Realistic Democracy.* Chicago: Nelson-Hall, 1976.

12686. Hooley, John. "The Reagan Presidency: A First Testing." *Antioch Review* 39 (Fall 1981): 488-500.

12687. Horowitz, Irving L. "Social Science and the Reagan Administration." *Journal of Policy Analysis and Management* 1 (Fall 1981): 125-129.

12688. Howell, Leon. "Revamping the Image of America: At the Nation's PR Agency, Reaganism Reigns." *Christianity and Crisis* 43 (October 31, 1983): 407-409.

12689. Hunter, Allen. "In the Wings: New Right Organization and Ideology." *Radical America* 15 (Spring 1981): 113-138.

12690. Iannaccone, Laurence. "The Reagan Presidency." *Journal of Learning Disabilities* 14 (February 1981): 55-59.

12691. Inbau, Fred E. "Over-Reaction — The Mischief of *Miranda v. Arizona.*" *Journal of Criminal Law and Criminology* 73 (Summer 1982): 797-810.

12692. "Into Reaganland." *Dissent* 28 (Spring 1981): 135-163.

12693. Jahnke, Art, and Gerald Peary. "Death in the Nursery — Reagan Save-the-Babe Rule." *Nation* 237 (July 1983): 41-42.

12694. Janeway, Eliot. "Who Runs Reagan?" *Investors Chronicle* 61 (July 30, 1982): 252-253.

12695. Johnson, R. W. "One Up to Reagan." *New Society* 66 (October 5, 1983): 28.

12696. Judis, John. "Can Reagan Keep the Promise of Liberalism?" *Progressive Magazine* 45 (January 1981): 22-27.

12697. Judis, John. "The Contradictory Conservatism of Reagan Hero — The 2 Faces of Chambers, Whittaker." *New Republic* 190 (April 16, 1984): 25.

12698. Kaufman, Irving R. "An Open Letter to President Reagan on Judge Picking." *American Bar Association Journal* 67 (April 1981): 443-444.

12699. Kegley, Charles W., Jr., and Eugene R. Wittkopf. "The Reagan Administration's World View." *Orbis* 26 (Spring 1982): 223-244.

12700. Keller, Bill. "Presidential Support." *Congressional Quarterly Weekly Report* 40 (January 2, 1982): 18-24.

12701. Keller, Bill. "Ronald Reagan's Inner Circle Combines 'California Mafia' with Nixon and Ford Alumni." *Congressional Quarterly Weekly Report* 38 (October 4, 1980): 2913-2922.

12702. Kessel, John H. "The Structures of the Reagan White House." *American Journal of Political Science* 28 (May 1984): 231-258.

12703. Kidder, Rushworth M. "The United States Presidency: Reflections on Ronald Reagan." *Round Table* (January 1981): 40-48.

12704. Kinsley, Michael. "Reagan-Bashing Is Fun, But a Trap Awaits — Liberals and Deficits." *New Republic* 189 (December 31, 1983): 15-17.

12705. Kirkwood, Ron B. "Carter, Reagan, and the Quest for Leadership." *Policy Studies Review* 4 (November 1984): 360-364.

12706. Kirschten, Dick. "After a Year, The Reagan White House May Be Beginning to Feel the Strain." *National Journal* 14 (January 23, 1982): 140-144.

12707. Kirschten, Dick. "In Reagan's White House, It's Gergen Who's Taken Control of Communications." *National Journal* 13 (July 25, 1981): 1329-1331.

12708. Kirschten, Dick. "Reagan and the Federal Machine." *National Journal* 13 (January 17, 1981): 88-93.

12709. Kirschten, Dick. "Reagan Sends a Message — In Spite of the Bullet: He's Still in Charge." *National Journal* 13 (April 4, 1981): 562-563.

12710. Kirschten, Dick. "Reagan Sings of Cabinet Government, and Anderson Leads the Chorus: As the President's Assistant for Policy Development." *National Journal* 13 (May 9, 1981): 824-827.

12711. Kirschten, Dick. "The Reagan Team Comes to Washington, Ready to Get Off to a Running Start: Where Jimmy Carter Kept His Transition and Campaign Staffs Separate, The Leaders of Ronald Reagan's Well-Organized Staff Were Part of the Campaign." *National Journal* 12 (November 15, 1980): 1924-1926.

12712. Kirschten, Dick. "Reagan's Battle Plan." *National Journal* 13 (February 21, 1981): 300, 302-303.

12713. Kirschten, Dick. "Reagan's Cabinet Councils May Have Less Influence Than Meets the Eye." *National Journal* 13 (July 11, 1981): 1242-1247.

12714. Kirschten, Dick. "Reagan's Political Chief Rollins: We Will Help Our Friends First." *National Journal* 14 (June 12, 1982): 1054-1057.

12715. Kirschten, Dick. "Reagan's Revolution." *National Journal* 13 (August 29, 1981): 1532-1536.

12716. Kirschten, Dick. "Under Reagan, Power Resides with Those Who Station Themselves at His Door: The President May Rely on His Cabinet as a Platform for Political Ideology, But the Real Power in the Administration Lies with the Pragmatists on the White House Staff." *National Journal* 16 (February 25, 1984): 361-364.

12717. Kirschten, Dick. "With Reagan Coming in at Quarterback, White House Ready to Field New Team: The Arrival of Treasury Secretary Donald T. Regan at the White House as Chief of Staff Is Likely to Mean Many Changes in the Top Echelons of the President's Staff." *National Journal* 17 (January 19, 1985): 148-151.

12718. Ladd, Everett C., Jr. "Does Reagan Have a Problem with Women?" *Public Opinion* 4 (December/January 1981-1982): 48-49.

12719. Ladd, Everett C., Jr. "Reagan Ratings: The Story the Media Missed." *Public Opinion* 8 (June/July 1985): 20-22.

12720. Landau, Jack C. "President Reagan and the Press: Dark Days Ahead for the First Amendment as the Administration Coordinates Political Forces to Censor and Restrict a Broad Range of News about Government." *News Media and the Law* 6 (February/March 1982): 4-5.

12721. Landau, Yehezkel. "The President and the Prophets: Balancing Biblical Warnings and Promises." *Sojourners* 13 (June/July 1984): 13, 24-25.

12722. Lanouette, William J. "Reagan in the White House: Don't Look for Change Overnight." *National Journal* 12 (November 8, 1980): 1872-1875.

12723. Lanouette, William J. "Reagan Non-Policy." *Bulletin of the Atomic Scientists* 38 (August/September 1982): 32-33.

12724. Leathers, Charles G. "Thatcher-Reagan Conservatism and Schumpeter's Prognosis for Capitalism." *Review of Social Economy* 42 (April 1984): 16-31.

12725. Lewis, David A. *Can Reagan Beat the Zero Curse?* Harrison, AK: New Leaf Press, 1984.

12726. Lewis, Joseph. *What Makes Reagan Run? A Political Profile.* New York: McGraw-Hill, 1968.

12727. McCurdy, Howard E. "Crowding and Behavior in the White House." *Psychology Today* 15 (April 1981): 21-25.

12728. McElvaine, Robert S. "Roosevelt and Reagan." *Christian Century* 99 (May 12, 1982): 556-558.

12729. McGlothlin, Don C. *Star to Guide Us.* Wheeling, IL: Presidential Publishers, 1982.

12730. McQuaid, John. "A Docudrama Starring Reagan — B-Movie." *New Republic* 189 (September 5, 1983): 9-10.

12731. Mansfield, Harvey C. "The American Congressional Election — Reagan's Recalcitrant Economy." *Government and Opposition* 18 (Spring 1983): 144-156.

12732. Martin, Howard H. "President Reagan's Return to Radio." *Journalism Quarterly* 61 (Winter 1984): 817-821.

12733. Martin, Martha A. "Idealogues, Ideographs, and 'The Best Men': From Carter to Reagan." *Southern Speech Communication Journal* 49 (Fall 1983): 12-25.

12734. Mates, Leo. "Reagan at Mid-Term." *Contemporary Review* 242 (April 1983): 169-172.

12735. Mathews, Christopher J. "From GE Theater to the Desk in the Oval Office — Your Host, Ronald Reagan." *New Republic* 190 (March 26, 1984): 15-18.

12736. Mathias, Charles M., Jr. "The War Powers Resolution: Resolving the

Dilemma." *SAIS Review* 5 (Winter/Spring 1985): 43-50.

12737. Millar, William R. "Ronald Reagan and an American Monomyth or the Lone Ranger Rides Again." *American Baptist Quarterly* 2 (March 1983): 32-42.

12738. Nakamura, Robert T. "Impressions of Ford and Reagan." *Political Science Quarterly* 92 (Winter 1977-1978): 647-654.

12739. Nathan, Richard P. "The Untold Story of Reagan's 'New Federalism.'" *Public Interest* 77 (Fall 1984): 96-105.

12740. Newfarmer, Richard. "A Look at Reagan's Revolution in Development Policy." *Challenge* 26 (September/October 1983): 34-43.

12741. Newland, Chester A. "A Midterm Appraisal — The Reagan Presidency — Limited Government and Political Administration." *Public Administration Review* 43 (January/February 1983): 1-21.

12742. "9 Hours inside the Oval Office: Exclusive Eyewitness Report on the President at Work, Minute by Minute." *U.S. News & World Report* 91 (July 6, 1981): 14-20.

12743. Olson, David M. "Success and Content in Presidential Roll Calls: The First Three Years of the Reagan Administration." *Presidential Studies Quarterly* 15 (Summer 1985): 602-610.

12744. "One of Their Own in the White House." *Broadcasting* 100 (January 26, 1981): 23-24.

12745. Ornstein, Norman J. *President and Congress: Assessing Reagan's First Year*. Washington, DC: American Enterprise Institute for Public Policy Research, 1982.

12746. Ornstein, Norman J. "Reagan's Coming Collision with Congress." *Fortune* 105 (February 8, 1982): 78-80, 82.

12747. Owens, Patrick. "The Making of Reagan: The President from GE." *Nation* 232 (January 31, 1981): 106-109.

12748. Palmer, John L., ed. *Perspectives on the Reagan Years*. Washington, DC: Urban Institute Press, 1986.

12749. Palmer, John L., and Isabel V. Sawhill, eds. *The Reagan Record*. Scranton, PA: Ballinger, 1984.

12750. Petro, Nicolai N. *The Predicament of Human Rights: The Carter and Reagan Policies*. Lanham, MD: University Press of America, 1983.

12751. Pfiffner, James P. "The Carter-Reagan Transition: Hitting the Ground Running." *Presidential Studies Quarterly* 13 (Fall 1983): 623-645.

12752. Pierard, Richard V. "Mending the Fence: Reagan and the Evangelicals." *Reformed Journal* 33 (June 1983): 18-21.

12753. Pierard, Richard V. "Reagan and the Evangelicals: The Making of a Love Affair." *Christian Century* 100 (December 21-28, 1983): 1182-1185.

12754. Pillemer, David B. "Flashbulb Memories of the Assassination Attempt on Reagan." *Cognition* 16 (February 1984): 63-80.

12755. Piven, Frances F., and Richard A. Cloward. "Reagan Sows the Wind: The New Age of Protest." *Nation* 234 (April 7, 1982): 447.

12756. "President Reagan." *New Republic* 181 (December 1, 1979): 3.

12757. Pressman, Steven. "Reagan and Congress: President's Leadership Style and Split in GOP Ranks Are Key to Second Term Success." *Congressional Quarterly Weekly Report* 42 (October 27, 1984): 2781-2786.

12758. Quirk, Paul J. "What Must a President Know?" *Society* 20 (January/February 1983): 52-62.

12759. "Rating Reagan to Date: Opinion Roundup." *Public Opinion* 4 (August/September 1981): 38.

12760. Reagan, Michael D. "The Reagan 'Mandate,' Public Law and the Ethics of Policy Change." *Congress and the Presidency* 12 (Autumn 1985): 153-164.

12761. "Reagan Chooses a Mainstream Cabinet." *National Journal* 12 (December 20, 1980): 2174-2179.

12762. "Reagan Is Hit in His Television Debut." *Broadcasting* 100 (February 16, 1981): 75-76.

12763. "Reagan Library Debate Generates More Heat." *Library Journal* 109 (January 1984): 12-13.

12764. "Reagan Support Fades in Key Votes of 1982." *Congressional Quarterly Weekly Report* 41 (January 15, 1983): 117-131.

12765. "Reagan's Executive Agency Lobbyists." *Congressional Quarterly Weekly Report* 39 (December 5, 1981): 2387-2392.

12766. "Reagan's Legislative Liaison Team Profiled." *Congressional Quarterly Weekly Report* 39 (May 2, 1981): 747-751.

12767. Reichley, A. James. "Conservative Roots of the Nixon, Ford, and Reagan Administrations." *Political Science Quarterly* 96 (Winter 1981-1982): 537-550.

12768. Robinson, Clarence A., Jr. "Reagan Team Asks Capabilities, Priorities of Services." *Aviation* 113 (December 8, 1980): 9, 16-21.

12769. Robinson, Clarence A., Jr. "Reagan to Accelerate Acquisition: Transition Team Rancor Causes Concern." *Aviation Week and Space Technology* 113 (November 24, 1980): 16-18.

12770. Robinson, Michael J., and Margaret Sheehan. "Brief Encounters with the Fourth Kind: Reagan's Press Honeymoon." *Public Opinion* 3 (December/January 1981): 56-59.

12771. "Ronald Reagan's Early Marks." *Public Opinion* 4 (December/January 1981-1982): 22-23.

12772. Roper, Burns. "Presidential Popularity: Do People Like the Actor or His Actions?" *Public Opinion* 6 (October/November 1983): 42-44.

12773. Rothschild, Emma. "The Costs of Reaganism." *New York Review of Books* 31 (March 15, 1984): 14-17.

12774. Rowe, Jonathan, and Paul Glastris. "The Official 1984 Reagan Scorecard." *Washington Monthly* 15 (July/August 1984): 30-38.

12775. Russell, Leon W. "The Pendleton/Reagan Regime." *Journal of Intergroup Relations* 11 (Spring 1983): 13-15.

12776. Saasta, Timothy. "Strings on Employee Giving — The Charities of Reagan's Choice." *Nation* 237 (August 1983): 146-147.

12777. Samuelson, Robert J., Christopher Madison, and Michael R. Gordon. "Memo to: President-Elect Ronald Reagan." *National Journal* 47 (November 22, 1980): 1968-1979.

12778. Sarasohn, Judy, and Laura B. Weiss. "Secret Service Praised for Quick Action: Agency Seeks Better Intelligence Links." *Congressional Quarterly Weekly Report* 39 (April 4, 1981): 586.

12779. Scheele, Henry Z. "Ronald Reagan's 1980 Acceptance Address: A Focus on American Values." *Western Journal of Speech Communication* 48 (Winter 1984): 51-61.

12780. Schneider, Jerrold E. "The Reagan Presidency and the Reagan Experiment." *Congress and the Presidency* 11 (Spring 1984): 105-114.

12781. Schwartz, Herman. "Reagan's Rule of Law 1: A Department Called Justice." *Nation* 234 (April 10, 1982): 415.

12782. Schwartz, Herman. "Tops in Taps — Reagan's Bullish on Bugging." *Nation* 236 (June 4, 1983): 697-699.

12783. Schweigler, Gebhard. "The Reagan Presidency: A New Beginning." *Europa-Archiv* 36 (May 10, 1981): 271-280.

12784. Scofield, Edward. *Reagan, "B" Actor, "B" President?* Santa Monica, CA: Dennis-Landman, 1983.

12785. Shaw, Peter. "John Hinckley: A Face in the Crowd." *Commentary* 72 (September 1981): 65-67.

12786. Sheeder, Dave. "The President's Day — Air Force's Best Helped Make It Special." *Airman* 25 (March 1981): 20-27.

12787. Sheldon, Courtney R. "How Reagan Rates with Congress." *U.S. News & World Report* 91 (October 12, 1981): 27-29.

12788. Sherry, Paul H. "Is There Life after Reagan?" *Christianity and Crisis* 42 (June 21, 1982): 189-193.

12789. Siegel, Frederick F. *Troubled Journey: From Pearl Harbor to Ronald Reagan.* New York: Hill and Wang, 1984.

12790. Sinclair, Barbara. "Agenda Control and Policy Success: Ronald Reagan and the 97th House." *Legislative Studies Quarterly* 10 (August 1985): 291-314.

12791. Singer, James W. "Changing of the Guard: Reagan's Chance to Remold the Senior Bureaucracy." *National Journal* 12 (November 29, 1980): 2028-2031.

12792. Smith, Curt. "Waltzing into the White House." *Saturday Evening Post* 253 (January/February 1981): 58-63.

12793. Spring, Beth. "Rating Reagan: How Has His Presidency Altered the Political Landscape?" *Christianity Today* 27 (October 7, 1983): 44-50.

12794. Steinfels, Peter. "Christianity and Democracy: Baptizing Reaganism." *Christianity and Crisis* 42 (March 29, 1982): 80-85.

12795. Stix, Daniel L., and Robert H. Rock. "The Reagan Presidency: Implications for Human-Resource Management." *Personnel Journal* 60 (February 1981): 100.

12796. Thompson, Elaine V. "Reagan and the 97th Congress or Just How Long Is Pennsylvania Avenue?" *Australian Journal of Politics and History* 28 (1982): 56-67.

12797. Thompson, Elaine V. "Ronald Reagan — A Watching Brief." *Australian Quarterly* 54 (Winter 1982): 136-146.

12798. Thornton, Jeannye, and Ronald A. Taylor. "Reagan's War on Red Tape Draws Blood." *U.S. News & World Report* 92 (January 18, 1982): 62-63.

12799. Tirman, John. "Reagan's Nuke Plan, Life Support System for a Terminal Patient." *Nation* 234 (January 23, 1982): 72-75.

12800. Valis, Wayne H., ed. *The Future under President Reagan.* Westport, CT: Arlington House, 1981.

12801. Van Der Linden, Frank. *The Real Reagan: What He Believes, What He Has Accomplished, What We Can Expect from Him.* New York: Morrow, 1981.

12802. Van Til, William. "Alternative Reagans." *Phi Delta Kappan* 62 (February 1981): 450-451.

12803. Voigt, Tracy. *Critique of the Reagan Administration: First Year, 1981.* Los Angeles, CA: Tracy Voigt, 1982.

12804. Wall, James M. "Mr. Reagan

Speaks Only to 'Believers.'" *Christian Century* 100 (March 23-30, 1980): 259.

12805. Wehr, Elizabeth. "Numerous Factors Favoring Good Relationship between Reagan and New Congress." *Congressional Quarterly Weekly Report* 39 (January 24, 1981): 172-175.

12806. Wehr, Elizabeth. "Reagan Shooting Tests Cabinet Government." *Congressional Quarterly Weekly Report* 39 (April 4, 1981): 579-581.

12807. Weisman, Steven R. "Test of the Man and the Presidency." *New York Times Magazine* (April 26, 1981): 51-56, 76-84.

12808. Witt, Elder. "Reagan Renews Campaign for Supreme Court Blessing of Administration Policies." *Congressional Quarterly Weekly Report* 41 (September 24, 1983): 1991-1995.

12809. Wolfe, Alan. "Beyond Reagan." *Working Papers Magazine* 8 (November/December 1981): 38-41.

12810. Wolfe, Alan. "How Reagan Uses Truth: Ignorance as Public Policy." *Nation* 234 (April 3, 1982): 385.

12811. Wolin, Sheldon S. "Reagan Country." *New York Review of Books* 27 (December 18, 1980): 9-12.

12812. Woodward, Gary C. "Reagan as Roosevelt: The Elasticity of Pseudo-Populist Appeals." *Central States Speech Journal* 34 (Spring 1983): 44-58.

12813. Yackle, Larry W. "The Reagan Administration's Habeas-Corpus Proposals." *Iowa Law Review* 68 (May 1983): 609-666.

12814. Zuckert, Catherine H. "Reagan and That Unnamed Frenchman (De Tocqueville): On the Rationale for the New (Old) Federalism." *Review of Politics* 45 (July 1983): 421-442.

Budget

12815. Adams, Gordon. "Reagan Defense Budget — Congress Begins the Debate." *Bulletin of the Atomic Scientists* 39 (April 1983): 25-27.

12816. Anderson, J. R. "Bankrupting America: The Impact of President Reagan's Military Budget." *International Journal of Health Services* 11 (1981): 623-629.

12817. Burke, John P. "Does Presidential Influence Count?: Explaining Variation in the Reagan Budget Cycles, 1981-1983." *Policy Studies Journal* 12 (June 1984): 719-732.

12818. Clark, Timothy B. "Reagan's Budget: Economic, Political Gambles." *National Journal* 14 (February 13, 1982): 268-285.

12819. Cowan, Wayne H., ed. "Understanding Reagan's Budget." *Christianity and Crisis* 41 (April 13, 1981): 100-109.

12820. Danziger, Sheldon, and Robert Haveman. "The Reagan Budget: A Sharp Break with the Past." *Challenge* 24 (May/June 1981): 5-13.

12821. "Financing Reagan's Deficit." *Economic and Political Weekly* 19 (February 25, 1984): 335-336.

12822. Gist, John R. "The Reagan Budget: A Significant Departure from the Past." *PS* 14 (Fall 1981): 738-746.

12823. Green, Bill. "Reagan Defense Budget — Mortgaging Our Future." *Bulletin of the Atomic Scientists* 39 (April 1983): 28-29.

12824. Griffiths, David R. "Weinberger Alerts Reagan on Future Funding Needs." *Aviation Week and Space Technology* 114 (June 22, 1981): 26-28.

12825. Hertzberg, Hazel W. "The Indian Country, The Budget Is Very Bad News

— Reaganomics on the Reservation." *New Republic* 187 (November 22, 1982): 15-18.

12826. Lekachman, Robert. "Subsidizing Reaganism — Why Liberals Should Hate the Deficit." *Nation* 238 (February 1984): 209.

12827. LeLoup, Lance T. "After the Blitz: Reagan and the U.S. Budget Process." *Legislative Studies Quarterly* 7 (August 1982): 321-340.

12828. Levitt, Jane. "Federal Health Policy and the Reagan Budget Cuts." *Policy Perspectives* 3 (1983): 217-236.

12829. Moynihan, Daniel P. "The Biggest Spender of Them All — Reagan Bankrupt Budget." *New Republic* 189 (December 31, 1983): 18-21.

12830. Pennev, Rudolph G. "The Fiscal Strategy of the Reagan Administration." *Aussenwirtschaft* 37 (December 1982): 417-426.

12831. Peters, Jean, et al. "The Reagan Budget: Redistribution of Power and Responsibilities, Five Perspectives." *PS* 14 (Fall 1981): 731-766.

12832. "Reagan Plans Big Cuts in DOE Budget." *Oil and Gas Journal* 79 (February 23, 1981): 52-54.

12833. "Reagan Reaffirms Tax Plans." *Tax Notes* 11 (September 15, 1980): 548-549.

12834. "Reagan's Energy Budget Draws Bipartisan Opposition." *Public Utilities Fortnightly* 109 (March 8, 1982): 56-58.

12835. Shultz, Paul T., and Howard J. Golden. "Effects of President Reagan Tax Law Revision." *Employee Relations Law Journal* 7 (Winter 1982): 507-510.

12836. Stockman, David A. *The Triumph of Politics: Why the Reagan Revolution Failed*. New York: Harper and Row, 1986.

Domestic Policy

12837. Beman, Lewis. "Reaganizing the Inner Cities." *Fortune* 104 (December 1981): 98.

12838. Bovard, James. "Fast Times at the Arts Endowment — Still Speeding under the Reagan Administration." *Policy Review* 29 (Summer 1984): 89-90.

12839. Brakel, Samuel J. "Legal Services for the Poor in the Reagan Years." *American Bar Association Journal* 68 (July 1982): 820-822.

12840. Braverman, Miriam. "From Adam Smith to Ronald Reagan: Public Libraries as a Public Good." *Library Journal* 107 (February 1982): 397-401.

12841. Bromberg, M. D. "National Health Policies under the Reagan Administration and the New Congress." *American Journal of Hospital Pharmacy* 38 (1981): 315-320.

12842. Brown, Eric S. "Will President Reagan's Energy Policy Lead Households to Conserve?" *Energy Journal* 3 (January 1982): 85-89.

12843. Brown, Lawrence D. "Health Policy in the Reagan Administration: A Critical Appraisal." *Bulletin of the New York Academy of Medicine* 59 (January/February 1983): 31-40.

12844. Brownfeld, Allan C., and J. A. Parker. "The Reagan Administration and Civil Rights: A Confused and Confusing Record." *Lincoln Review* 3 (Summer 1983): 3-21.

12845. "Carter, Reagan Outline Attitudes on Regulation of Broadcasting." *Broadcasting* 98 (June 9, 1980): 67-68.

12846. Clark, David L., and Mary A. Amiot. "The Impact of the Reagan Administration on Federal Election Policy." *Phi Delta Kappan* 63 (December 1981): 258-262.

12847. Clark, Susan E. "Neighborhood Policy Options: The Reagan Agenda." *Journal of the American Planning Association* 50 (Autumn 1984): 493-501.

12848. Cohen, Neal M. "The Reagan Administration's Urban-Policy." *Town Planning Review* 54 (July 1983): 304-315.

12849. Cohen, Toby. "Reagan RX for Health Costs — Voodoo Medical Economics." *Nation* (March 1983): 335-336.

12850. Conaway, James. "Looking at Reagan." *Atlantic Monthly* 246 (October 1980): 32-45.

12851. Cornelius, Wayne A. "The Reagan Administration's Proposals for a New United States Immigration Policy: An Assessment of Potential Effects." *International Migration Review* 15 (Winter 1981): 769-778.

12852. Coser, Lewis. "Reagan and the Welfare State: Thoughts out of Season." *Dissent* 29 (Winter 1982): 9-12.

12853. Crandall, Robert W. "Has Reagan Dropped the Ball?" *Regulation* 5 (September/October 1981): 15-18.

12854. Days, Drew S. "Turning Back the Clock — The Reagan Administration and Civil Rights." *Harvard Civil Rights-Civil Liberties Law Review* 19 (Summer 1984): 309-347.

12855. "Deregulation: A Fast Start for the Reagan Strategy." *Business Week* (March 9, 1981): 62-67.

12856. Drew, Elizabeth. "1980: Reagan." *New Yorker* 29 (September 1980): 106-108, 125.

12857. Dugger, Ronnie. *On Reagan: The Man and His Presidency*. New York: McGraw-Hill, 1983.

12858. Eads, George C., and Michael Fix. *The Reagan Regulatory Strategy: An Assessment*. Washington, DC: Urban Institute Press, 1984.

12859. Eads, George C., and Michael Fix. *Relief or Reform?: Reagan's Regulatory Dilemma*. Washington, DC: Urban Institute Press, 1984.

12860. Edgar, David. "Reagan's Hidden Agenda: Racism and the New American Right." *Race and Class* 22 (Winter 1981): 221-238.

12861. Ehrenreich, Barbara, and David Nasaw. "Reagan's War on Children: Kids as Consumers and Commodities." *Nation* 236 (May 14, 1983): 597-599.

12862. Emling, Diane C. "The Reagan Scheme as Welfare-Reform." *Public Welfare* 41 (Spring 1983): 22-26.

12863. Finegold, Kenneth, and Richard M. Valelly. "Fattening the Fat Cats — Reagan Picks a Farm Program." *Nation* 236 (February 5, 1983): 140-141.

12864. Finn, Chester E. "Affirmative Action under Reagan." *Commentary* 73 (April 1982): 17-28.

12865. Florance, Valerie. "The Reagan Administration and Health Information — A Summary of Trends." *Government Publications Review* 11 (January/February 1984): 71-74.

12866. Freedman, Tracy, and David Weir. "Reagan's War on Children: Polluting the Most Vulnerable." *Nation* 236 (November 19, 1983): 600-604.

12867. Galbraith, John K. "A Policy Divided against Itself Cannot Stand: The Market and Reagan." *New Republic* 185 (September 23, 1981): 15-18.

12868. Geimer, William S. "Legal-Services for the Poor after the Reagan Years." *American Bar Association Journal* 68 (October 1982): 1262-1263.

12869. Gerberg, Mort. *Your Unofficial Guide to Reaganworld*. New York: Putnam, 1982.

12870. Goff, David H., and Linda D.

Goff. "Regulation of Television Advertising to Children: The Policy Dispute in Its Second Decade." *Southern Speech Communication Journal* 48 (Fall 1982): 38-50.

12871. Guzzardi, Walter. "Reagan's Reluctant Deregulations." *Fortune* 105 (March 8, 1982): 34-40.

12872. "Has Reagan Served Business Well?" *U.S. News & World Report* 93 (December 6, 1982): 39-41.

12873. Hill, Charles E. "Energy Problems Facing the Poor — Federal Aid under the Reagan Administration and the Challenges Facing Advocates." *Clearinghouse Review* (July 1982): 219-231.

12874. Hiller, David. "Immigration Policies of the Reagan Administration." *University of Pittsburgh Law Review* 44 (Winter 1983): 495-505.

12875. Holden, Constance. "The Reagan Years: Environmentalists Tremble." *Science* 210 (November 28, 1980): 988-989.

12876. Ippolito, Dennis S. "The Reagan Initiatives." In his *Hidden Spending: The Politics of Federal Credit Programs*, 106-129. Chapel Hill: University of North Carolina Press, 1984.

12877. Kaiser, Robert G. "Your Host of Hosts." *New York Review of Books* 31 (June 28, 1984): 38-41.

12878. Kaplan, George R. "Some Cranky Fulminations on Reagan and Education." *Phi Delta Kappan* 63 (May 1982): 592-595.

12879. Katz, James E. "United States Energy Policy — Impact of the Reagan Administration." *Energy Policy* 12 (June 1984): 135-145.

12880. Keefe, David E. "Governor Reagan, Welfare Reform, and AFDC Fertility." *Social Service Review* 57 (June 1983): 234-253.

12881. Keigher, Sharon M. "Reagan's New Federalism and the 1971 California Medi-Cal Reforms." *Urban and Social Change Review* 16 (Summer 1983): 3-8.

12882. Kemble, Penn. "How Reagan NLRB Is Subverting Industrial Democracy — The New Anti-Union Crusade." *New Republic* 189 (September 19-26, 1983): 18-20.

12883. Kirschten, Dick. "Putting the Social Issues on Hold: Can Reagan Get Away with It?" *National Journal* 13 (October 10, 1981): 1810-1815.

12884. Kraft, Michael E. "Political Constraints on Development of Alternative Energy Sources: Lessons from the Reagan Administration." *Policy Studies Journal* 13 (December 1984): 319-330.

12885. Kraft, Michael E., and Norman J. Vig. "Environmental Policy in the Reagan Presidency." *Political Science Quarterly* 99 (Fall 1984): 415-439.

12886. Lash, Jonathan, Katherine Gillman, and David Sheridan. *A Season of Spoils: The Reagan Administration's Attack on the Environment*. New York: Pantheon Books, 1984.

12887. Lekachman, Robert. "Reagan Joy and Misery Index." *New Society* 68 (May 3, 1984): 175-177.

12888. Litvack, Sanford M. "The Ebb and Flow of Antitrust Enforcement: The Reagan and Carter Administrations." *Brigham Young University Law Review* (Fall 1982): 849-856.

12889. Loeb, Paul R. *Hope in Hard Times: America's Peace Movement and the Reagan Era*. Lexington, MA: Lexington Books, 1986.

12890. Lovell, C. H. "Intergovernmental Deregulation — Readings from the First Reagan Years." *Environment and Planning: Government and Policy* 1 (July 1983): 273-284.

12891. McClelland, Barney F. "The Shadow of Life: What It Means to Be Poor and Forgotten in Reagan's America." *Otherside* 148 (January 1984): 22-24.

12892. McClaughry, John. "Ronald Reagan's Vision of a Human Scale Future." *Futurist* 15 (December 1981): 30-31.

12893. McCormick, Joseph P., II. "A Look at the Reagan Administration's Proposed Housing Cuts." *Urban League Review* 5 (Summer 1981): 68-74.

12894. Martin, Keith D. "The Urban Crisis, Continued: Reagan's Program, and an Alternative." *Christianity and Crisis* 42 (November 29, 1982): 374-379.

12895. Merry, Robert W. "The Social Security Hot Potato — Could Ronald Reagan Have Handled It Better?" *Policy Review* 28 (Spring 1984): 64-68.

12896. Michaelson, Michael G. "Reagan Administration Health Legislation — The Emergence of a Hidden Agenda." *Harvard Journal on Legislation* 20 (Summer 1983): 575-599.

12897. Miller, Richard B. "Conversations with the Reagan Regulators." *Bankers Magazine* 165 (March/April 1982): 34-49.

12898. Miller, William H. "Plea for Help from Reagan's Deregulators." *Industry Week* 209 (June 1981): 58-62.

12899. Moldea, Dan E. "Reagan and the Teamsters — More Than Just Good Friends." *Nation* 236 (June 11, 1983): 732-734.

12900. Nathan, Richard P., and Fred C. Doolittle. *The Consequences of Cuts: The Effects of the Reagan Domestic Program on State and Local Government.* Princeton, NJ: Urban and Regional Research Center, Princeton University, 1984.

12901. Navarro, V. "Selected Myths Guiding the Reagan Administration's Health Policies." *International Journal of Health Services* 14 (1984): 321-328.

12902. Neier, Aryeh. "Civil Liberties after Reagan — Don't Count on the Courts." *Nation* 238 (June 9, 1984): 700-702.

12903. Novak, Michael. "The Rich, the Poor, and the Reagan Administration." *Commentary* 76 (August 1983): 27-31.

12904. O'Banion, Kerry. "Reagan's Energy Program: A Time for Conservation." *Nation* 232 (January 1981): 16-20.

12905. Peirce, Neal R. "Reagan to Nation's Governors — The Federal Aid Cupboard Is Bare." *National Journal* 48 (November 28, 1981): 2109-2113.

12906. Piven, Frances F., and Richard A. Cloward. *New Class War: Reagan's Attacks on the Welfare State and Its Consequences.* New York: Pantheon Books, 1982.

12907. "President Reagan and the Legal Services Corporation." *Creighton Law Review* 15 (1981-1982): 711-732.

12908. "Reading Reagan." *Economist* 286 (March 26, 1983): 19-22.

12909. "The Reagan Administration and the Future of the Electric Utility Industry." *Public Utilities Fortnightly* 110 (August 5, 1982): 44-47.

12910. "Reagan Administration Anti-Crime Agenda." *Contemporary Drug Problems* 9 (Winter 1980): 475-492.

12911. "Reagan Commitment to Environment Fulfilled in EPA's '81 Success." *EPA Journal* 8 (January/February 1982): 10-11.

12912. "Reagan Shooting Aftermath." *Congressional Quarterly Weekly Report* 39 (April 4, 1981): 579-587.

12913. "Reagan's Plan for the Nation." *Public Utilities Fortnightly* 109 (March 4, 1982): 45-47.

12914. "Reagan's Pressure Points." *New Republic* 189 (August 29, 1983): 5-6.

12915. Reilly, Ann M. "What Business Wants from Reagan." *Dun's Review* 117 (March 1981): 46-49, 52-53.

12916. Reza, Ali M. "The Impact of President Reagan's Sudden Decontrol of Petroleum Prices on Petroleum Consumption." *Energy Journal* 2 (July 1981): 129-133.

12917. Rosenberg, Sam. "Reagan Social Policy and Labour Force Restructuring." *Cambridge Journal of Economics* 7 (June 1983): 179-196.

12918. Schlechty, David L. "Export Control Policy and Licensing Program of the Reagan Administration — New Focus — New Direction." *Federal Bar News and Journal* 29 (1982): 33-37.

12919. Schwartz, Herman. "Let 'Em Freeze in the Dark — Reagan Uncaps Natural Gas." *Nation* 236 (March 19, 1983): 330-332.

12920. Smith, Bruce L. R., and James D. Carroll. "Reagan and the New Deal: Repeal or Replay." *PS* 14 (Fall 1981): 758-766.

12921. Smith, V. Kerry, ed. *Environmental Policy under Reagan's Executive Order: The Role of Benefit-Cost Analysis.* Chapel Hill: University of North Carolina Press, 1984.

12922. Stricker, Frank. "Causes of the Great Depression, Or What Reagan Doesn't Know about the 1920's." *Economic Forum* 14 (Winter 1983-1984): 41-58.

12923. Udall, Morris K. "Introduction to Volume 10." *Ecology Law Quarterly* 10 (Winter 1982): 1-3.

12924. Vig, Norman J., and Michael E. Kraft. *Environmental Policy in the 1980s: Reagan's New Agenda.* Washington, DC: Congressional Quarterly, 1984.

12925. Weidenbaum, Murray L. "Regulatory Reform — A Report Card for the Reagan Administration." *California Management Review* 26 (Fall 1983): 8-24.

12926. Whitney, Kevin. "Capitalizing on a Congressional Void: Executive Order No. 12291." *American University Law Review* 31 (Spring 1982): 613-650.

12927. Williamson, Richard S. "Commentary — The Reagan Administration's Position on Antitrust Liability of Municipalities." *Catholic University Law Review* 32 (Winter 1983): 371-378.

12928. Wing, Kenneth R. "The Impact of Reagan Era Politics on the Federal Medicaid Program." *Catholic University Law Review* 33 (Fall 1983): 1-93.

12929. Winslow, Art. "Reagan Indian Policy — Speaking with Forked Tongue." *Nation* 236 (February 12, 1983): 177-179.

Elections

12930. Alexander, John F. "Did We Blow It?: The Evangelical Right Mobilized for Reagan, But Carter Wasn't Good Enough for the Left: Were We Crazy?" *Otherside* 113 (February 1981): 10-15.

12931. Allen, Gary. "Republican Convention and Ronald Reagan." *American Opinion* 23 (September 1980): 1-6, 93-110.

12932. Alter, Jonathan. "Rooting for Reagan." *Washington Monthly* 12 (January 1981): 12-17.

12933. Beniger, James R. "The Legacy of Carter and Reagan: Political Reality Overtakes the Myth of Presidential Primaries." *Intellect* 105 (February 1977): 234-237..

12934. Bolce, Louis. "The Role of Gender in Recent Presidential Elections: Reagan and the Reverse Gender Gap." *Presiden-*

tial Studies Quarterly 15 (Spring 1985): 372-385.

12935. Brudney, Jeffrey L., and Gary W. Copeland. "Evangelicals as a Political Force: Reagan and the 1980 Religious Vote." *Social Science Quarterly* 65 (December 1984): 1072-1079.

12936. "Carter-Reagan Debate: Bringing It All Together for Campaign '80." *Broadcasting* 99 (November 1980): 23-24.

12937. Chapman, Stu. "Reagan Plays Leading Man in Bid for Votes of Physicians." *Legal Aspects of Medical Practice* 8 (July 1980): 14-19.

12938. Collins, Lora S. "Clues to a Reagan Presidency." *Across the Board* 17 (October 1980): 15-21.

12939. Conn, Joseph. "Carter, Reagan, Anderson, and Church-State Issues." *Humanist* 40 (November/December 1980): 22-23.

12940. Devine, Donald J. *Reagan Electionomics: How Reagan Ambushed the Pollsters.* Ottawa, IL: Green Hill Publishers, 1983.

12941. Devlin, L. Patrick. "Reagan's and Carter's Ad Men Review the 1980 Television Campaigns." *Communication Quarterly* 30 (Winter 1982): 3-12.

12942. Douglas, James. "Was Reagan's Victory a Watershed in American Politics?" *Political Quarterly* 52 (April/June 1981): 171-183.

12943. "Evangelicals Support Reagan's Re-Election, But Only Narrowly." *Christianity Today* 27 (November 11, 1983): 74-75.

12944. Gelineau, Elaine P., and Peter F. Merenda. "Student's Pre-Election Perceptions of Jimmy Carter and Ronald Reagan." *Perception and Motor Skills* 52 (April 1981): 491-498.

12945. Germond, Jack, and Jules Witcover. *Blue Smoke and Mirrors: How Reagan Won and Why Carter Lost the Election of 1980.* New York: Viking, 1981.

12946. Greenberg, Jack. "The Blacks, Reaganism, and 1984." *Dissent* 30 (Fall 1983): 414-416.

12947. Hibbs, Douglas A., Jr. "President Reagan's Mandate from the 1980 Elections: A Shift to the Right?" *American Politics Quarterly* 10 (October 1982): 387-420.

12948. Ingold, Beth A. J., and Theodore O. Windt, Jr. "Trying to 'Stay the Course': President Reagan's Rhetoric during the 1982 Election." *Presidential Studies Quarterly* 14 (Winter 1984): 84-97.

12949. Johnson, Stephen D., and Joseph B. Tamney. "The Christian Right and the 1980 Presidential Election." *Journal for the Scientific Study of Religion* 21 (June 1982): 123-131.

12950. Johnston, Ron J. "It Was Geography That Saw Reagan Home." *Geographical Magazine* 53 (January 1981): 285-286.

12951. Krasner, Michael. "Reagan's Manipulated Mandate." *Social Policy* 11 (March/April 1981): 26-28.

12952. Lindsey, Robert. "What the Record Says about Reagan." *New York Times Magazine* 129 (June 29, 1980): 12-20.

12953. Marable, Manning. "Reaganism, Racism, and Reaction: Black Political Realignment in the 1980's." *Black Scholar* 13 (Fall 1982): 2-13.

12954. Melusky, Joseph A. "An Electoral College Fable: How the Carter-Ford Election Might Have Made Ronald Reagan President in 1976." *Presidential Studies Quarterly* 11 (Summer 1981): 384-386.

12955. Reilly, Ann M., and Miriam Rozen. "Reagan Woos the Interest Groups."

Dun's Business Month 122 (October 1983): 70-77.

12956. Rogers, Joel. "Beating Reagan — The Politics of Voter Registration." *Nation* 239 (July 21-28, 1984): 33, 45-51.

12957. Rothenberg, Irene F. "Chicanos, the Panama Canal Issues, and the Reagan Campaign: Reflections from 1976 and Projections for 1980:" *Journal of Ethnic Studies* 7 (Winter 1980): 37-49.

12958. Rowland, Robert C., and Roger A. Payne. "The Context-Embeddedness of Political Discourse: A Re-evaluation of Reagan's Rhetoric in the 1982 Midterm Election Campaign." *Presidential Studies Quarterly* 14 (Fall 1984): 500-511.

12959. Rutledge, John, and Jeffrey Speakes. "Carter vs. Reagan: How Their Policies Would Affect Prices, Economy." *Commodities* 9 (October 1980): 27-31.

12960. Sigelman, Lee, and Carol K. Sigelman. "Judgements of the Carter-Reagan Debate: The Eyes of the Beholders." *Public Opinion Quarterly* 48 (Fall 1984): 624-628.

12961. Stacks, John F., Jack Germond, and Jules Witcover. "How the Democrats Gave Us Reagan: The Ten Key Moments of the 1980 Campaign." *Washington Monthly* 13 (February 1982): 8-20.

12962. Tiemens, Robert K. "An Integrative Verbal and Visual Analysis of the Carter-Reagan Debate." *Communication Quarterly* 33 (Winter 1985): 34-42.

12963. Tuchman, Mitch. "Ladies and Gentlemen, The Next President of the United States." *Film Comment* 16 (July/August 1980): 49-58.

12964. Wead, Doug, and Bill Wead. *Reagan, In Pursuit of the Presidency, 1980.* Plainfield, NJ: Haven Books, 1980.

12965. White, F. Clifton, and William J. Gill. *Why Reagan Won: A Narrative History of the Conservative Movement 1964-1981.* Chicago: Regnery, 1981.

12966. Williamson, Richard S. "1980: The Reagan Campaign — Harbinger of a Revitalized Federalism." *Publius* 11 (Summer 1981): 147-153.

12967. Wilson, James Q. "Reagan and the Republican Revival." *Commentary* 70 (October 1980): 25-32.

Foreign Affairs

12968. Alter, Jonathan. "Reagan's Dr. Strangelove." *Washington Monthly* 13 (June 1981): 10-17.

12969. Anderson, William D., and Sterling J. Kernek. "How 'Realistic' Is Reagan's Diplomacy?" *Political Science Quarterly* 100 (Fall 1985): 389-410.

12970. Arnott, Teresa, and Joel Kreiger. "Thatcher and Reagan: State Theory and the 'Hyper-Capitalist' Regime." *New Political Science* 8 (Spring 1982): 9-37.

12971. Aruri, Naseer H., and Fouad M. Moughrabi. "The Reagan Middle East Initiative." *Journal of Palestine Studies* 12 (Winter 1983): 10-30.

12972. Aruri, Naseer H., Fouad M. Moughrabi, and Joe Stork. *Reagan and the Middle East.* Belmont, MA: Association of Arab-American University Graduates, 1983.

12973. Auw, David C. L. "Commitment, Policy Legacy, and Policy Options — The United States ROC Relations under Reagan." *Issues and Studies* 18 (March 26, 1982): 8-27.

12974. Bell, Coral. "From Carter to Reagan." *Foreign Affairs* 63 (1985): 490-510.

12975. Bennett, Roy. "Reagan's Foreign Policy: New Dangers." *Social Policy* 13 (Summer 1982): 17-24.

12976. Ben-Zvi, Abraham. *The Reagan Presidency and the Palestinian Predicament.* Tel Aviv: Center for Strategic Studies, Tel Aviv University, 1982.

12977. Beres, Louis R. "Nation without a Soul, Policy without a Purpose." *Chitty's Law Journal* 29 (January 1981): 1-12.

12978. Bialer, Seweryn, and Joan Afferica. "Reagan and Russia." *Foreign Affairs* 61 (Winter 1982-1983): 249-271.

12979. Bonior, David E. "Reagan and Central America." *SAIS Review* 25 (1981): 3-11.

12980. Burns, William J. "The Reagan Administration and the Philippines." *World Today* 38 (March 1982): 97-104.

12981. Caldwell, Lawrence T., and Robert Legvold. "Reagan through Soviet Eyes." *Foreign Policy* 52 (Fall 1983): 3-21.

12982. Coker, Christopher. "Reagan and Africa." *World Today* 38 (April 1982): 123-130.

12983. Connell-Smith, Gordon. "The Crisis in Central America — Reagan Options." *World Today* 39 (October 1983): 385-392.

12984. Crewe, Ivor. "Britain Evaluates Ronald Reagan." *Public Opinion* 7 (October/November 1984): 46-49.

12985. Davies, Derek, and Nayan Chanda. "The View from the White House." *Far Eastern Economic Review* 124 (May 17, 1984): 30-32.

12986. Davis, Vincent. "Early Reagan Security Policy in a Comparative Perspective: Some Tentative Observations." *International Studies Notes* 8 (Spring 1981) 1-6.

12987. "The Deadly Connection: Reagan and the Middle East." *MERIP Reports* 14 (November/December 1984): 3-34.

12988. Destler, Irving M., and Eric R. Alterman. "Congress and Reagan's Foreign Policy." *Washington Quarterly* 7 (Winter 1984): 91-101.

12989. Doran, Charles F. "Canada and the Reagan Administration: Left Hand, Right Hand." *International Journal* 36 (Winter 1980-1981): 236-240.

12990. Dudney, Robert S. "Is There a Game Plan? Critics Blame Feuding and Inexperience inside the Reagan Administration for Confusion in Foreign Policy." *U.S. News & World Report* 96 (April 30, 1984): 26-29.

12991. Echeverri-Gent, Elisavinda. "Central America — Fruits of the 'Reagan Solution.'" *Economic and Political Weekly* 19 (February 11, 1984): 241-242.

12992. Fatton, Robert. "The Reagan Foreign Policy toward South Africa: The Ideology of the New Cold War." *African Studies Review* 27 (March 1984): 57-82.

12993. Felton, John. "Reagan Military Moves Test Hill Foreign Policy Powers: Central America, Northern Africa." *Congressional Quarterly Weekly Report* 41 (August 13, 1983): 1665-1667.

12994. Finger, Seymour M. "The Reagan-Kirkpatrick Policies and the United Nations." *Foreign Affairs* 62 (Winter 1984): 436-457.

12995. Gelb, Leslie H., and Anthony Lake. "Four More Years: Diplomacy Restored?" *Foreign Affairs* 63 (1985): 465-489.

12996. Gerjuoy, Edward. "Embargo on Ideas — The Reagan Isolationism." *Bulletin of the Atomic Scientists* 38 (November 1982): 31-37.

12997. Girling, John L. S. "Reagan and the Third World." *World Today* 37 (November 1981): 407-413.

12998. Glad, Betty. "Black-and-White Thinking: Ronald Reagan's Approach to

Foreign Policy." *Political Psychology* 4 (March 1983): 33-76.

12999. Gordon, Michael R. "Who Is the Real Reagan behind U.S. Soviet Policy?" *National Journal* 16 (September 15, 1984): 1704-1713.

13000. Grunwald, Henry. "Foreign Policy under Reagan II." *Foreign Affairs* 63 (Winter 1984-1985): 219-239.

13001. Haig, Alexander M. *Caveat: Realism, Reagan, and Foreign Policy.* New York: Macmillan, 1984.

13002. Hale, David. "Reagan versus Thatcher." *Policy Review* 19 (Winter 1982): 91-109.

13003. Harrison, Michael M. "Reagan's World." *Foreign Policy* (Summer 1981): 3-16.

13004. Hazleton, William A. "Questions That Will Not Die — Human Rights Concerns and the Reagan Foreign Policy." *Co-Existence* 21 (1984): 37-49.

13005. Hocking, Brian, and Michael Smith. "Reagan, Congress, and Foreign Policy: A Troubled Partnership." *World Today* 40 (May 1984): 188-198.

13006. Hughes, Thomas L. "Up from Reaganism." *Foreign Policy* 41 (Fall 1981): 3-32.

13007. Inoue, Shigenobu. "Reagan's Asia-Pacific Policy." *Issues and Studies* 17 (September 1981): 27-34.

13008. Kirkpatrick, Jeane J. *The Reagan Phenomenon — and Other Speeches on Foreign Policy.* Washington, DC: American Enterprise Institute for Public Policy Research, 1983.

13009. Knight, Andrew. "Ronald Reagan's Watershed Year?" *Foreign Affairs* 61 (1982): 511-540.

13010. Kolko, Gabriel. "Crises to the Right of United States ... Reagan in Search of a Global Policy." *Nation* 235 (October 30, 1982): 430-432.

13011. Kolko, Gabriel. "Next Phase of the Reagan Administration's Foreign Policy — The Search for a General Strategy." *Journal of Contemporary Asia* 12 (1982): 324-330.

13012. Krauthammer, Charles. "What's Good for General Motors: The Reagan Foreign Policy." *Policy Review* 20 (Spring 1982): 140-146.

13013. Kreczko, Alan J. "Support Reagan Initiative." *Foreign Policy* 9 (Winter 1982-1983): 140-153.

13014. Kuniholm, Bruce R. "What the Saudis Really Want: A Primer for the Reagan Administration." *Orbis* 25 (Spring 1981): 107-121.

13015. LaFeber, Walter F. "The Reagan Administration and Revolutions in Central America." *Political Science Quarterly* 99 (Spring 1984): 1-26.

13016. Laqueur, Walter. "Reagan and the Russians." *Commentary* 73 (January 1982): 19-26.

13017. Larson, David L. "The Reagan Administration and the Law of the Sea." *Ocean Development and International Law Journal* 11 (Summer/Fall 1982): 297-320.

13018. Larson, Deborah W. "The Open Door for Reagan." *SAIS Review* 4 (Summer/Fall 1984): 13-24.

13019. Lawrence, Robert. "Reagan's Africa Arsenal." *Southern Africa* 13 (November/December 1980): 19-21.

13020. Lenczowski, J. "Foreign Policy for Reaganauts." *Policy Review* 18 (Fall 1981): 77-95.

13021. Leng, Russell J. "Reagan and the Russians: Crisis Bargaining Beliefs and the Historical Record." *American Political Science Review* 78 (June 1984): 338-355.

13022. Liebenow, J. Gus. "American Policy in Africa: The Reagan Years." *Current History* 82 (March 1983): 97-101, 133-136.

13023. Manning, Robert A. "China-Reagan Chance Hit." *Foreign Policy* 54 (Spring 1984): 83-101.

13024. Miller, Linda B. "Reagan's Foreign Policy: Old Wine, Old Bottles." *World Today* 37 (March 1981): 88-92.

13025. Munton, Don. "Reagan, Canada, and the Common Environment." *International Perspectives* (May/June 1982): 3-6.

13026. Naylor, R. T. "Reaganism and the Future of the International Payments System." *Third World Quarterly* 4 (October 1982): 655-676.

13027. Nye, Joseph S., Jr. "U.S. Power and Reagan Policy." *Orbis* 26 (Summer 1982): 391-411.

13028. Pastor, Robert. "Continuity and Range in United States Foreign Policy — Carter and Reagan on El Salvador." *Journal of Policy Analysis and Management* 3 (Winter 1984): 190.

13029. Pattakos, Alex N., and Kenneth I. Palmer. "Downeast But Not Down Under — Maine Responds to the Reagan Challenge." *Publius* 13 (Spring 1983): 39-49.

13030. Percy, Charles H. "The Partisan Gap." *Foreign Policy* 45 (Winter 1981-1982): 3-15.

13031. Perlmutter, Amos. "Reagan's Middle East Policy: A Year-One Assessment." *Orbis* 26 (Spring 1982): 26-29.

13032. Peterzell, Jay. *Reagan's Secret Wars*. Washington, DC: Center for National Security Studies, 1984.

13033. Podhoretz, Norman. "The Reagan Road to Detente." *Foreign Affairs* 63 (1985): 447-464.

13034. Quandt, William B. "Reagan's Lebanon Policy: Trial and Error." *Middle East Journal* 38 (Spring 1984): 237-254.

13035. Ram, Susan. "Intervention in Nicaragua — Carter and Now Reagan Find the Options Limited." *Economic and Political Weekly* 18 (November 19, 1983): 1977-1982.

13036. Ravenhill J., and D. Rothchild. "Reagan African Policy — A New Unilateralism." *International Journal* 38 (January 1983): 107-127.

13037. "Reagan's Visit Enhances Mutual Understanding." *Beijing Review* 27 (May 7, 1984): 6-8.

13038. Record, Jeffrey. "Jousting with Unreality — Reagan Military Strategy." *International Security* 8 (Winter 1984): 3-18.

13039. Reich, Bernard. "United States Middle East Policy in the Carter and Reagan Administrations." *Australian Outlook* 38 (August 1984): 72-80.

13040. Reisman, W. Michael. "Critical Defense Zones and International Law: The Reagan Codicil." *American Journal of International Law* 76 (July 1982): 589-591.

13041. Richelson, Jeffrey. "PD-59, NSDD-13, and the Reagan Strategic Modernization Program." *Journal of Strategic Studies* 6 (1983): 125-146.

13042. Rielly, John E. "American Opinion — Continuity, Not Reaganism." *Foreign Policy* 51 (Spring 1983): 86-104.

13043. Ross, David F. "Ronald Reagan: Missionary to the Caribbean." *Witness* 66 (September 1983): 4-7.

13044. Rubner, Michael. "The Reagan Administration, the 1973 War Powers Resolution, and the Invasion of Grenada." *Political Science Quarterly* 100 (Winter 1985-1986): 627-648.

13045. Schlesinger, Stephen. "Behind the

Honduran Buildup — Reagan Secret War on Nicaragua." *Nation* 236 (January 1983): 9-11.

13046. Sen, S. Sudhir. "Reagan Policy in Central America." *Economic and Political Weekly* 18 (June 4, 1983): 1003-1004.

13047. Serfaty, Simon. "Waiting for Reagan." *SAIS Review* 25 (1981): 23-32.

13048. Sherrill, Robert G. "The Acid Rain War — Reagan Inc. Dumps on Canada." *Nation* 235 (September 4, 1982): 173-174.

13049. Shigenobu, I. "Reagan's Asia Pacific Policy." *Issues and Studies* 17 (September 1981): 27-34.

13050. Simes, Dimitri K. "Soviet Perspectives on the Reagan Administration." *Atlantic Community Quarterly* 21 (Summer 1983): 132-139.

13051. Swearingen, Rodger. "Reagan and Russia: The New Course." *Korea and World Affairs* 6 (Summer 1982): 292-311.

13052. Szulc, Tad. "Dateline Washington: The Vicar Vanquished." *Foreign Policy* 43 (Summer 1981): 173-186.

13053. Talbott, Strobe. *The Russians and Reagan.* New York: Vintage, 1984.

13054. Tate, Dale, and Andy Plattner. "Tumultuous Debate: House Ratifies Saving Plan in Stunning Reagan Victory." *Congressional Quarterly Weekly Report* 39 (June 27, 1981): 1127-1129.

13055. Thomas, Dan B., and Lee Sigelman. "Presidential Identification and Policy Leadership: Experimental Evidence on the Reagan Case." *Policy Studies Journal* 12 (June 1984): 663-676.

13056. Thornton, Thomas P. "American Interest in India under Carter and Reagan." *SAIS Review* 5 (Winter/Spring 1985): 179-190.

13057. Toba, Reijiro. "Asean Favors Reagan's Hard Line Foreign Policy." *Asia Pacific Community* (Winter 1981): 55-68.

13058. Tucker, Robert W. "Foreign Policy: Thoughts on a Second Reagan Administration." *SAIS Review* 5 (Winter/Spring 1985): 1-10.

13059. Unterberger, Betty M. "Behind Reagan's Secret Order — Burying the Diplomatic Record." *Nation* 234 (May 8, 1982): 555-557.

13060. Whelan, Joseph G. "Soviet-American Relations in the Reagan Administration — A Prophecy Fulfilled." *Issues and Studies* 20 (January 1984): 76-97.

13061. Whittle, Richard. "Reagan Foreign Policy Requests Challenged." *Congressional Quarterly Weekly Report* 39 (April 18, 1981): 685-688.

13062. Williams, Jonathan D. "Defense Policy — The Carter-Reagan Record." *Washington Quarterly* 6 (Autumn 1983): 77-92.

13063. Wipfler, William L. "Reagan Policy in Central America: U.S. Opts for Militarism over Human Rights." *Witness* 64 (May 1981): 10-13.

13064. Wright, Claudia. "Shadow on Sand: Strategy and Deception in Reagan's Policy towards the Arabs." *Journal of Palestine Studies* 11 (Spring 1982): 3-36.

13065. Wright, Gerald C., Jr. "Canada and the Reagan Administration: Anxious Days Are Here Again." *International Journal* 36 (Winter 1980-1981): 228-236.

13066. Yaniv, Avner, and Robert J. Lieber. "Reagan and the Middle East." *Washington Quarterly* 6 (Autumn 1983): 125-137.

13067. Yee, Herbert S. "Reagan Global Strategy — A Chinese View." *Asia Pacific Community* 27 (Summer 1983): 92-107.

13068. Yeh, Po-t'ang. "An Analysis of Reagan Visit to Mainland China." *Issues and Studies* 20 (July 1984): 70-80.

Nuclear Weapons

13069. Beres, Louis R. "Reagan Nuclear Strategy." *Center Magazine* 15 (November/December 1982): 17-26.

13070. Clarke, Duncan L. "Arms Control and Foreign Policy under Reagan." *Bulletin of the Atomic Scientists* 37 (November 1981): 12-19.

13071. Cocburn, Alexander, and James Ridgeway. "The Freeze Movement versus Reagan." *New Left Review* 137 (January/February 1983): 5-21.

13072. Cross, Frank B., and Cyril V. Smith. "The Reagan Administration's Nonproliferation Non-Policy." *Catholic University Law Review* 33 (Spring 1984): 633-665.

13073. Drell, Sidney D., Philip J. Farley, and David Holloway. "Preserving the ABM Treaty: A Critique of the Reagan Strategic Defense Initiative." *International Security* 9 (Fall 1984): 51-91.

13074. Drell, Sidney D., Philip J. Farley, and David Holloway. *The Reagan Strategic Defense Initiative: A Technical, Political, and Arms Control Assessment.* Hagerstown, MD: Ballinger Publishing Company, 1985.

13075. Eichner, Alfred S. "Reagan's Doubtful Game Plan." *Challenge* 24 (May/June 1981): 19-27.

13076. Gansler, Jacques S. "Can the Defense Industry Respond to the Reagan Initiatives?" *International Security* 6 (Spring 1982): 102-121.

13077. Garfinkle, Adam M. "The Nuclear Freeze and the Presidential Politics of 1984." *Contemporary Review* 244 (June 1984): 287-291.

13078. Jasani, Bhupendra. "The Reagan Star War Syndrome and Militarization of Outer Space." *Bulletin of Peace Proposals* 14 (1983): 243-245.

13079. Jastrow, Robert. "Reagan vs. the Scientists — Why the President Is Right about Missile Defense." *Commentary* 77 (January 1984): 23-32.

13080. Keyworth, George A. *President Reagan's New Defense Initiative: A Road to Stability.* Stanford, CA: Hoover Institution Press, 1984.

13081. Korb, Lawrence J., and Linda P. Brady. "Rearming America: The Reagan Administration Defense Program." *International Security* 9 (Winter 1984-1985): 3-18.

13082. Luck, Edward C. "The Reagan Administration's Nuclear Strategy." *Current History* 82 (May 1983): 193-196, 232-233.

13083. Nichols, Teresa A., and Barbara H. Bink. "Special Report: The Reagan Administration, Congress, and Nuclear Power." *Public Utilities Fortnightly* 110 (November 11, 1982): 38-42.

13084. Posen, Barry R., and Stephen Van Enera. "Defense Policy and the Reagan Administration: Departure from Containment." *International Security* 8 (Summer 1983): 3-45.

13085. Robinson, Clarence A., Jr. "Reagan Details Defense Boost." *Aviation Week and Space Technology* 113 (November 10, 1980): 14-16.

13086. Scheer, Robert. *With Enough Shovels: Reagan, Bush, and Nuclear War.* New York: Random House, 1982.

13087. Smith, Fritz. "Conservative Think Tanks and Reagan Defense Policy." *Towson State Journal of International Affairs* 19 (Fall 1984): 35-46.

13088. Talbott, Strobe. *Deadly Gambits: The Reagan Administration and the Stalemate in Nuclear Arms Control.* New York: Vintage, 1985.

13089. Winnick, Andrew. "Rapid Deployment and Nuclear War — Reagan's

New Military Strategies." *Socialist Review* 14 (January/February 1984): 10-30.

Reaganomics

13090. Ackerman, Frank. *Reaganomics: Rhetoric vs. Reality*. Boston: South End Press, 1982.

13091. Barber, Gerard, Seymour Slavin, and Susan Barnett. "Impact of Reagan Economics on Social Services in the Private Sector." *Urban and Social Change Review* 16 (Winter 1983): 27-32.

13092. Bartlett, Bruce R. "The Conservative Critics of Reaganomics." *Intercollegiate Review* 18 (Fall/Winter 1982): 39-47.

13093. Barlett, Bruce R. *Reaganomics: Supply Side Economics in Action*. Westport, CT: Arlington House, 1981.

13094. Bergsten, C. Fred. "The Costs of Reaganomics." *Foreign Policy* 44 (Fall 1981): 24-36.

13095. Bonafede, Dom. "Reagan's Economic Advisers Share Task of Shaping and Explaining Reaganomics." *National Journal* 14 (February 6, 1982): 245-248.

13096. Bronfenbrenner, Martin. "Notes on Reaganomics." *Lecture Notes in Economics and Mathematical Systems* 210 (1983): 64-77.

13097. Brown, Lorenzo. "Reaganomics: The Reagan Economic Proposals and Their Implications for Black America." *Crisis* 88 (April 1981): 138-145.

13098. Buchanan, James M. "The Political Ambiguity of Reagan Economics: Marginal Adjustment or Structural Shift?" *Journal of Monetary Economics* 3 (November 1982): 287-296.

13099. Carnoy, Martin, Derek Shearer, and Russell Rumberger. *A New Social Contract: The Economy and Government after Reagan*. New York: Harper and Row, 1983.

13100. Collum, Danny. "Assault on the Poor: The Reagan Administration's Economic Policies." *Sojourners* 10 (July 1981): 12-16.

13101. Danziger, Sheldon, et al. "Reviewing Reagan's Economic Program." *Challenge* 26 (January/February 1984): 42-50.

13102. Dugger, William M. "An Institutionalist Critique of President Reagan's Economic Program." *Journal of Economic Issues* 16 (September 1982): 791-814.

13103. Easton, Nina. *Reagan's Squeeze on Small Business: How the Administration Plan Will Increase Economic Concentration*. Washington, DC: Learning Research Project, 1982.

13104. Enright, S. M. "Effect of Reaganomics on the United States Health Care System." *American Journal of Hospital Pharmacy* 39 (1982): 1169-1175.

13105. Fisher, Anne B. "What's Left of Reaganomics?" *Fortune* 109 (February 20, 1984): 42-46.

13106. Garten, Jeffrey E. "On Automatic Pilot." *World Policy Journal* 1 (Spring 1984): 483-494.

13107. Graham, Daniel O. "High Frontier: The Next Four Years." *Journal of Social, Political and Economic Studies* 9 (Winter 1984): 405-411.

13108. Gregg, Gail, and Dale Tate. "United They Stand: Reagan Economic Officials Put Differences behind Them." *Congressional Quarterly Weekly Report* 39 (February 7, 1981): 259-261.

13109. Hale, David. "Rescuing Reaganomics." *Policy Review* 20 (Spring 1982): 57-69.

13110. Harriss, C. Lowell. "Successes and Failures of President Reagan's Economic

Policies." *Presidential Studies Quarterly* 14 (Fall 1984): 519-525.

13111. Hulten, Charles R., and Isabel V. Sawhill, eds. *The Legacy of Reaganomics: Prospects for Long-term Growth.* Washington, DC: Urban Institute Press, 1984.

13112. Jensen, Rita H., ed. "Reaganomics: Supply-Side or Blind-Side?" *Church and Society* 73 (January/February 1983): 10-83.

13113. Kaufman, Henry. "Reaganomics: Why Isn't Wall Street Convinced?" *Challenge* 24 (September/October 1981): 43-48.

13114. Kimzey, Bruce W. *Reaganomics.* St. Paul, MN: West Publishing Co., 1983.

13115. Kirschten, Dick. "Reaganomics Puts Business on the Spot." *National Journal* 13 (December 19, 1981): 2229-2232.

13116. Klein, Philip A. "Reagan's Economic Policies: An Institutional Assessment." *Journal of Economic Issues* 17 (June 1983): 463-474.

13117. Leonard, Mary. "Reaganomics and K-12 Education, Some Responses from the Private Sector." *Phi Delta Kappan* 63 (May 1982): 600-602.

13118. McNamar, R. T. "President Reagan's Economic Program." *Presidential Studies Quarterly* 11 (Summer 1981): 324-329.

13119. Manvel, Allen D. "Observations on a Presidential Image." *Tax Notes* 16 (August 23, 1982): 774-776.

13120. Marshall, Ray. "Comments of the Institutional View of Reaganomics." *Journal of Economic Issues* 17 (June 1983): 503-506.

13121. Nau, Henry R. "Where Reaganomics Works." *Foreign Policy* 57 (Winter 1984-1985): 14-37.

13122. Nyren, Karl. "Hooper and Reaganomics." *Library Journal* 107 (April 1, 1982): 684-685.

13123. Petr, Jerry L. "Economic Evolution and Economic Policy: Is Reaganomics a Sustainable Force?" *Journal of Economic Issues* 16 (December 1982): 1005-1012.

13124. Power, Marilyn. "Falling through the 'Safety Net': Women, Economic Crisis, and Reaganomics." *Feminist Studies* 10 (Spring 1984): 31-58.

13125. "President Reagan's Economic Program." *Fortune* 102 (December 1, 1980): 9-10.

13126. "President Reagan's Plan." *Current History* 82 (January 1983): 33.

13127. Redenius, Charles. "The Supply-Side Alternative: Reagan and Thatcher's Economic Policies." *Journal of Social, Political and Economic Studies* 8 (Summer 1983): 189-209.

13128. Reich, Robert B. "How the Rage for Supply-Side Riches Is Impoverishing Our Politics: Beyond Reaganomics." *New Republic* 185 (November 18, 1981): 19.

13129. Reich, Robert B., and Felix G. Rohatyn. "Coping with Reagan's Economic Legacy." *World Policy Journal* 2 (Fall 1984): 1-32.

13130. Rousseas, Stephen. *The Political Economy of Reaganomics: A Critique.* Armonc, NY: M. E. Sharpe, 1982.

13131. Saulnier, Raymond J. "The President's Economic Report: A Critique." *Journal of Portfolio Management* 8 (Summer 1982): 50.

13132. Saulnier, Raymond J. "The President's Economic Report: A Critique" *Journal of Portfolio Management* 9 (Summer 1983): 58-59.

13133. Schneider, William. "Reaganomics Is the President's Weak Spot — Running on Empty." *New Republic* 190 (March 5, 1984): 12-15.

13134. Sillin, John O., Steven Herod, and Robert W. Shaw, Jr. "Reagan Economics and Electric Utilities: Will Rate Actions Limit Benefits?" *Public Utilities Fortnightly* 110 (August 5, 1982): 15-21.

13135. Simmons, Althea T. L. "Civil Rights and Reaganomics." *Crisis* 91 (April 1984): 8-10.

13136. Sprinkel, Beryl W. "Reaganomics Is Working." *Challenge* 25 (July/August 1982): 51-53.

13137. Stone, Charles F., and Isabel V. Sawhil. *Economic Policy in the Reagan Years*. Washington, DC: Urban Institute Press, 1984.

13138. Stubblebine, William C., and Thomas D. Willett, eds. *Reaganomics: A Midterm Report*. San Francisco: ICS Press, 1983.

13139. Thurow, Lester C. "Reaganomics." *Aussenwirtschaft* 37 (December 1982): 407-415.

13140. Tobin, James. "The 1982 Economic Report of the President: The Annual Report of the Council of Economic Advisers: Comment." *Journal of Monetary Economics* 3 (November 1982): 297-308.

13141. U.S. President. *America's New Beginning: A Program for Economic Recovery*. Washington, DC: The White House, Office of the Press Secretary, 1981.

13142. Weintraub, Sidney, and Marvin Goodstein, eds. *Reaganomics in the Stagflation Economy*. Philadelphia: University of Pennsylvania Press, 1983.

13143. Willingham, Alex. "The Themes and Policies of Reaganomics." *Urban League Review* 8 (Summer 1984): 19-26.

13144. Wilson, George W. "Where Reaganomics Succeeded, Where It Failed, and Why." *Business Horizons* 27 (July/August 1984): 2-8.

13145. Zinam, Oleg. "A Note on Reaganomics." *Atlantic Economic Journal* 4 (December 1982): 98.

Writings

13146. Arca, Emil, and Gregory J. Pamel. *The Triumph of the American Spirit: The Presidential Speeches of Ronald Reagan*. Detroit, MI: National Reproductions Corporation, 1985.

13147. Reagan, Ronald. *Creative Society: Some Comments on Problems Facing America*. 2d ed. Old Greenwich, CT: Devin-Adair, 1981.

13148. Reagan, Ronald. "President Imposes Economic Sanctions on the U.S.S.R. and Poland." *Business America* 5 (January 1982): 3-4.

13149. Reagan, Ronald. *Sincerely, Ronald Reagan*. Edited by Helene Von Damm. New York: Berkley, 1980.

13150. Reagan, Ronald. *Where's the Rest of Me? The Autobiography of Ronald Reagan*. New York: Karz Publishers, 1981.

Author Index

Aaron, Daniel, 6645
Aaron, Jan, 11947
Abbatt, William, 4037
Abbazia, Patrick, 9089
Abbott, Abbott A., 3464
Abbott, John S. C., 1, 3465, 5576
Abbott, Lawrence F., 1061, 1440, 4559, 6335, 6425, 6426, 6646, 7986
Abbott, Lyman, 4272-4274, 4459, 6071, 6525, 6647, 7012
Abbott, Martin, 4786
Abel, Elie, 10522, 10523
Abels, Jules, 7968, 9284, 9285
Aberbach, Joel D., 11461
Abernathy, John R., 6336, 6427
Abernathy, M. Glenn, 12149
Abernethy, Arthur T., 2
Abernethy, Thomas P., 2008, 2829, 3225, 5414
Abrahamsen, David, 11376
Abramowitz, Mildred W., 8460
Abrams, Richard M., 6648, 7013, 7014, 7263, 7363, 7987
Abrams, Rochonne, 1170
Abramson, Arthur C., 9604
Accinelli, Robert D., 7523, 7878, 8185, 8853
Acheson, Dean G., 9248, 9286
Ackerman, Donald H., Jr., 9914
Ackerman, Frank, 13090
Adair, Douglass, 869, 968, 2318, 2369, 1171, 1405, 1881, 2203
Adam, G. Mercer, 5248
Adams, Abigail S., 870-873
Adams, Bruce, 12150
Adams, Charles F., 848, 874, 1026, 2614, 2657, 5084, 6109
Adams, Charles J., 7936
Adams, David K., 8107, 8518, 8519, 10130
Adams, Dickinson W., 1613, 2286
Adams, Francis A., 6649
Adams, Franklin P., 7364
Adams, Frederick B., 8520
Adams, Gordon, 12815

Adams, Henry, 875, 2453, 2454, 2209-2211, 2667
Adams, Herbert B., 1366
Adams, Hewitt D., 1686
Adams, James T., 849, 1062, 1882, 2204
Adams, John, 1027-1053, 2205, 2206
Adams, John C., 8763
Adams, John Q., 2668-2708
Adams, Mary P., 2012, 2097
Adams, Randolph G., 3, 416, 1063
Adams, Samuel H., 7813
Adams, Sherman, 9763
Adams, W. Howard, 1172, 1335
Adams, William C., 12604
Adcock, Louis H., 1655
Adelman, Kenneth L., 12423
Adler, Selig, 6271, 7524, 8854, 8855, 9090
Adler, William, 10159, 10742-10745, 10848, 12120, 12151, 12574, 12605
Afferica, Joan, 12978
Agar, Herbert, 3466
Agresto, John, 2370
Agronsky, Martin, 10160
Ahl, Frances N., 2931
Aikman, Lonnelle, 4
Akeley, Carl E., 6428
Akers, Charles W., 876
Albert, Alphaeus H., 417
Albertson, Dean, 8983, 9764
Albjerg, Marguerite H., 5464
Albjerg, Victor L., 2932, 8186, 9287, 9765
Alden, John R., 5
Alderfer, Harold F., 7814
Alderman, Edwin A., 1064, 2336, 2525, 7129, 7130
Alderson, William T., 5510, 8764
Aldrich, Charles, 5085
Aldrich, Nelson W., 12121
Aldridge, Derek A., 4787
Alexander, Albert, 8765
Alexander, Charles C., 9766
Alexander, Edward P., 1173
Alexander, Holmes, 620, 3055
Alexander, Jim R., 11661

641

Alexander, John F., 12364, 12930
Alexander, Joseph, 11162
Alfonso, Oscar M., 6650, 6827
Alger, Horatio, Jr., 4428
Alington, Argentine F., 8322
Allan, Alfred K., 1336
Allees, Arnold E., 10161
Allen, Dan C., 8766
Allen, David G., 2709
Allen, Donald A., 10124
Allen, Eric R., 4461
Allen, Frederick, 12103
Allen, Gary, 11377, 12104, 12931
Allen, H. C., 12424
Allen, Hugh A., 8521
Allen, James S., 3774
Allen, Milford E., 2098
Allen, Richard V., 12607
Allen, Robert S., 8522, 8523, 8664, 9288
Allen, Walter, 5577
Allen, William R., 8984
Allin, L., 11480
Allison, Andrew M., 1174
Allison, Graham T., 10524
Allison, Hildreth M., 7015
Allison, John M., 877, 1175
Alpert, Augusta, 10389
Alson, E. Bowles, 7131
Alsop, Joseph, 8323, 8324, 10643
Alsop, Stewart, 10131, 10132, 10162, 10163, 10888, 10952, 11241, 11378, 11462
Altenberg, Les, 12527
Alter, Jonathan, 12932, 12968
Alter, N. B., 621
Alterman, Eric R., 12988
Altherr, Thomas L., 6429
Alton, Lee R., 10974
Altschuler, Bruce E., 10133
Alvord, Clarence W., 1808, 1883
Ambler, Charles H., 514
Ambrose, Stephen E., 4462, 6121, 9670-9672, 9731-9737, 9935, 10010
Ambrosious, Lloyd E., 7264, 7663, 7664
American Bar Association, 12608
American Civil Liberties Union, 11849
American Enterprise Institute for Public Policy Research, 11969
American Heritage Magazine, 9673
American Institute for Political Communication, 11717
American Philosophical Society, 2013
Ames, Marilyn C., 3807
Amiot, Mary A., 12846
Ammon, Harry, 1988, 1997, 2417, 2526, 2539, 2540
Amos, James, 6337
Amrine, Michael, 10953
Ander, Oscar F., 3885

Anderson, Adrian, 7365
Anderson, Bernard E., 12278
Anderson, Clinton, 10550
Anderson, David D., 3467, 7132
Anderson, Dice R., 1989
Anderson, Donald F., 7016, 7017
Anderson, Dwight G., 3468
Anderson, Fenwick, 7869
Anderson, Floyd D., 11548
Anderson, J. R., 12816
Anderson, James E., 10954, 11163, 11164, 12279
Anderson, James W., 4613, 7442
Anderson, Janice, 12562
Anderson, John, 9868, 12561
Anderson, Judith I., 6966
Anderson, Judith L., 1687
Anderson, Ken, 4941
Anderson, Levere, 3660
Anderson, Louise K., 3362
Anderson, Marcus, 3886
Anderson, Martin, 12280
Anderson, Patricia A., 6
Anderson, Patrick, 11850
Anderson, Peggy, 11507
Anderson, Ray M., 678
Anderson, Richard D., 4333
Anderson, Robert G., 6338
Anderson, Walt, 11406
Anderson, Wayne W., 9767
Anderson, William D., 12969
Anderson, William G., 984, 985
Andrews, Avery D., 6526
Andrews, Byron, 6329
Andrews, Helen R., 5086
Andrews, John D., 9936
Andrews, Mary R. S., 5054
Andrews, Phillip, 11379
Andrews, Rena M., 5465
Andrews, Stuart, 1441, 1844
Andrews, William L., 679
Angel, Edward, 2541
Angle, Paul M., 3661, 3662, 3775-3782, 3864, 4039, 4191, 4334, 4429, 4463, 4614, 4615, 5250-5252
Ank, Le Thi, 12425
Annin, Robert E., 7133
Anson, Robert S., 11407
Anthony, Katharine S., 2337
Anthony, William H., 11770
Anti, Charles, 11112
Apple, R. W., 11851
Appleby, Joyce, 911, 986, 1522
Appleby, Paul H., 8524
Appleman, Roy E., 3808, 5253
Arca, Emil, 13146
Archer, Jules, 7134, 9768
Archer, Mary U., 7265
Archer, William, 7184

Author Index

Arieff, Irwin B., 12609, 12610
Aring, Charles D., 878, 2207
Armitage, Charles H., Jr., 6110
Armour, Rollin S., 4788
Armstrong, Barbara, 12281
Armstrong, Walter P., 2338
Armstrong, William H., 3799
Armstrong, William L., 12607
Armstrong, William M., 8767
Army Times, 9674
Arnett, Alex M., 7692
Arnett, Ethel S., 2339
Arnold, Isaac N., 3469, 3470, 5180
Arnold, Malcolm H., 1442
Arnold, Matthew, 5578
Arnold, Peri E., 8108, 8109
Arnold, Samuel B., 4789
Arnold, Thurman, 6430
Arnold, William A., 11432
Arnott, Teresa, 12970
Aron, Raymond, 10644, 11771
Aronson, Shlomo, 12426
Aronson, Sidney H., 987, 2014, 2933
Arrowood, Charles F., 1367
Arthur, Robert A., 9249, 9250
Arthur, Samuel J., 4376
Aruri, Naseer H., 12971, 12972
Asbell, Bernard, 8325, 8326, 8392
Asberry, Robert L., 2455
Asbury, Herbert, 7969
Ashby, John H., 3070
Ashe, Samuel A., 418, 4464, 4560
Asher, Cash, 7815
Ashford, Gerald, 2831
Ashton, J. Hubley, 3931
Ashworth, John, 1884
Ashworth, Mary W., 691
Associated Press, 10076, 10390
Athearn, Clarence R., 7185
Atkins, Ollie, 11463
Atkinson, David N., 9289
Atkinson, Eleanor, 3663, 3664, 4430
Attwood, William, 10391, 10645
Atwell, Cynthia M., 9429
Atwell, Priscilla A., 1523
Atwood, Harry, 5109
Aubere, Jewell H., 4192
Auble, John L., 4104
Auchampaugh, Philip G., 3382, 3391-3392, 3416-3419
Auchincloss, Kenneth, 10812
Auer, John J., 4465
Auerbach, Jerold S., 7366, 8985
Auerbach, Joseph S., 6651
Aulaire, Ingri M., 7
Auletta, Ken, 11970
Auw, David C. L., 12973
Avary, Myrta L., 5254

Avery, Laurence G., 7367
Avery, Sheldon B., 7266
Axson, Stockton, 7267
Ayres, Philip W., 680, 4193

Baas, Larry, 12355, 12365
Babcock, Bernie, 3665
Babcock, William, 10587, 10737
Baber, Adin, 5255
Bacchus, Wilfred A., 9937
Bachelder, Louise, 3666
Bacheller, Irving, 8, 4431
Back, Kurt W., 10392
Backer, Jack E., 10525
Bacon, Charles R., 7448
Bacote, Clarence A., 6272
Bacus, Karen P., 11772
Badeau, Adam, 5579, 5690
Bader, Ernest B., 8856
Baer, Emily A., 5256
Baetzhold, Howard G., 5895
Bagby, Wesley M., 7449, 7870
Bagdikian, Ben H., 10164, 10393, 10889, 10955-10958
Bagnall, Joseph A., 10646
Bailey, Bernadine F., 3471
Bailey, Consuelo N., 6043
Bailey, George, 10226
Bailey, Howard, 3340
Bailey, John W., Jr., 6273
Bailey, Kenneth M., 7186
Bailey, Louis J., 3932
Bailey, Sidney K., 11279
Bailey, Thomas A., 2208, 6652, 6828, 7268, 7665, 7666, 9091, 10165, 10959
Bailyn, Bernard, 1688
Bain, George C., 6122
Bains, Rae, 3472
Baird, Hiram K., 419
Bakeless, John, 4942
Baker, Dean C., 10394
Baker, George W., Jr., 6218, 7525-7532
Baker, Gordon E., 2209
Baker, James T., 10960, 11953, 12152
Baker, Leonard, 8946, 9092, 10890
Baker, Ray S., 7018, 7135, 7187
Baker, Richard C., 6653
Baker, Ross K., 12153, 12427
Baker, William S., 9, 10, 420, 421, 554, 622
Balch, Stephen H., 7368
Balch, William R., 5580
Baldridge, H. A., 555
Baldwin, Elbert F., 7369
Baldwin, Helen P., 10870
Baldwin, James, 3473
Baldwin, Joseph G., 1065, 2934
Bale, Florence G., 5658
Balfour, Nancy, 10166, 10167, 10961, 11464, 11718

Ball, Desmond, 10551
Ball, George W., 11312
Ball, Nicole, 12428, 12429
Ballard, Colin R., 4943
Ballard, Rene N., 7019
Ballot, Paul, 10168
Balthazar, Louis, 12528
Balz, Daniel J., 11971, 12154
Bamford, James, 12611
Bancroft, Aaron, 11, 12
Bancroft, George, 3097, 4377
Bancroft, T. B., 4194
Banes, Ruth A., 850, 1066
Banfield, Edward C., 11663
Banker, Stephen R., 11972
Banks, Charles E., 6339
Banks, Michael, 10962
Banning, Lance, 1845, 1885, 2319, 2371, 2372
Banninga, Jerald L., 2615-2617
Banta, Thomas J., 10395
Bantz, Charles R., 12612
Bar, Haviva S., 11781
Barany, George, 7533
Barbarash, Ernest E., 10647
Barbee, David R., 2935, 3179, 4466
Barber, Gerard, 13091
Barber, James D., 5467, 7988, 8187, 11465, 11852, 11973
Barber, Rims, 11664
Barber, William J., 8188
Barcella, Ernest L., 10169
Barck, Dorothy C., 422, 423
Barclay, C. N., 9738
Bard, Bernard, 10813
Bardolph, Richard, 5141
Barfield, Claude E., 11466
Baringer, William E., 4432, 4467, 4659, 4660
Barker, Charles E., 7020
Barker, E. Eugene, 424
Barker, Eugene C., 2936
Barker, Harry E., 4433
Barker, Wharton, 5980
Barkin, Steve M., 9915
Barlett, Bruce R., 13093
Barlow, Jeffrey G., 10170
Barnard, George G., 3474
Barnard, Harry, 5791, 5792
Barnes, Clare, 10077
Barnes, Fred, 12613
Barnes, Harry E., 7136, 7188
Barnes, Howard A., 2099
Barnes, Lemuel C., 327
Barnes, William H., 5581
Barnes, William R., 8947
Barnett, Susan, 13091
Barnhart, John D., 3162
Barnum, Augustine, 6072
Barnum, John W., 12430

Barnwell, Robert W., 3475
Baron, Sherry, 1656
Baron, Stephan M., 2618
Barondess, Benjamin, 3420, 3421, 5257
Baroody, William J., Jr., 11974
Barre, W. L., 3332
Barrett, Frank W. Z., 4790
Barrett, Joseph H., 5258, 5259
Barrett, Laurence I., 12614
Barrett, Marvin, 1067
Barrett, Wayne, 251
Barringer, William E., 4550
Barron, Gloria J., 8525, 8857
Barrow, Lionel C., 10601, 11719
Barsness, John A., 6527
Bartlett, Bruce R., 8900, 12282, 13092
Bartlett, Charles, 11145
Bartlett, David V., 3358, 3476
Bartlett, David W., 4468
Bartlett, Linda, 1714
Bartlett, Truman H., 3667
Bartley, N. V., 9869
Barton, Bruce, 7937, 7970
Barton, George, 556, 5741, 7189
Barton, Robert, 3668, 3768
Barton, William E., 537, 3477, 3669-3672, 3809-3814, 3887, 4040, 4041, 4074, 4195, 4275, 4378, 4434, 4435, 4469, 4661, 4791, 5055
Barzilay, Rhea, 5270
Barzun, Jacques, 4042
Baskerville, Donald A., 10396
Baskin, Darryl B., 912, 2373, 10963
Basler, Roy P., 3478, 3673, 3888, 4043, 4044, 4379, 4470, 5142, 5181, 5260, 5261
Bassett, John S., 2712, 2832, 2937, 3071, 3209, 3226, 5838
Bassett, Margaret B., 3815
Bassiri, Torab, 11081
Basso, Hamilton, 8327, 8526
Bateman, Herman E., 8393
Bates, David H., 4944, 4945
Bates, Finis L., 4792
Bates, Jack W., 2619
Bates, Richard O., 5920
Batman, Richard D., 8110
Baudhuim, E. Scott, 11467
Bauer, Charles J., 3674, 3816, 4616
Bauer, K. Jack, 3236
Bauer, Otto F., 9916
Baugh, Albert C., 1068
Baum, Dale, 6123
Baum, Keith W., 9938
Baumann, Roland M., 1886
Baumgardner, James L., 4662, 5468
Baur, John E., 5839
Baxter, Maurice G., 4663
Bayard, Charles J., 6654
Baylen, Joseph O., 3407, 7021

Bayless, R. W., 5469
Bayne, Julia T., 3817
Beach, James C., 6340
Beale, Howard K., 5470, 6431, 6829
Beall, John N., 4793
Bean, Louis H., 11242
Bear, James A., Jr., 1688-1690
Beard, Charles A., 1069, 1176, 1809, 1810, 7269, 8527, 8858, 9093
Beard, Robin, 12431
Beardslee, Clark S., 4075
Bearss, Edwin C., 8079, 9718, 10849
Beasley, Maurine, 8461, 8462
Beattie, Donald W., 623
Beatty, Albert R., 425, 765
Beatty, Bess, 5840
Beatty, James P., 2131
Beck, Andrea, 11092
Beck, James M., 13, 557, 558
Beck, Kent M., 10648
Beck, N. B., 9931
Beck, Susan A., 11165
Becker, Carl, 1524
Becker, J. W., 4794
Beckhard, Arthur J., 9675
Beckner, Lucien, 4076
Bedini, Silvio A., 1657
Beelen, George D., 7879, 7880
Beer, Samuel H., 12615
Beers, Henry A., 6528
Beeton, Beverly, 5841
Behl, William A., 6655, 6656
Beil, Cheryl, 10125
Beisel, David R., 12122
Beiswanger, William, 1313
Bell, Beverly W., 11975
Bell, Carl I., 3359
Bell, Coral, 12432, 12433, 12974
Bell, D. Bruce, 11975
Bell, Herbert C. F., 7270
Bell, Jack, 10964
Bell, James F., 12283
Bell, John L., Jr., 5471
Bell, Raymond M., 11408
Bell, Rudolph M., 2456
Bell, Samuel R., 6657
Bell, Sidney, 7534, 7535
Bellamy, Francis, 155
Bellot, Hugh H., 1689, 7137
Bellush, Bernard, 8496, 8497, 8528, 8529
Bellush, Jewel, 8529, 8986
Beloff, Max, 1406, 1811, 2320
Belohlavek, John M., 2938-2940
Beman, Lewis, 12837
Bemis, Samuel F., 681, 682, 1070, 2580, 2620, 2658-2660
Bender, Lynn D., 11773
Bender, Robert J., 7370

Bendiner, Robert, 10965
Benedict, Blaine D., 9094
Benedict, Michael L., 5472, 5473
Beniger, James R., 12366, 12933
Benjamin, R. M., 4561
Benjamin, Thomas, 3237
Bennett, Edward M., 8859
Bennett, H. Omer, 1614
Bennett, Hiram R., 4879
Bennett, Hugh H., 1292
Bennett, John W., 6658
Bennett, Lerone, 1407, 11166
Bennett, Ralph K., 11954
Bennett, Roy, 12975
Benoit, William L., 11853
Benson, C. Randolph, 1177, 2210
Benson, Ezra T., 9769
Benson, Godfrey R., 4196
Benson, Judith, 10850
Benson, Lee, 2833
Benson, Thomas W., 8530
Bent, Silas, 3300
Bentley, Hubert B., 5415, 5474
Benton, Joel, 6124
Ben-Zvi, Abraham, 12434, 12976
Berendt, J., 10171
Berens, John F., 361
Beres, Louis R., 12977, 13069
Berge, William H., 6659
Bergen, A., 4562
Berger, Henry W., 9290
Berger, Jason, 8463
Berger, Raoul, 2177
Berger, Roland, 11774
Bergeron, Paul H., 988, 2941, 2942, 3238
Bergquist, Harold E., Jr., 2621
Bergsten, C. Fred, 13094
Beringause, Arthur F., 6660
Berkeley, Dorothy S., 2542
Berkeley, Edmund C., 2542, 10397-10399
Berkhofer, Robert F., 1690
Berkley, Henry J., 426
Berkowitz, Edward D., 8189, 10552
Berlin, Isaiah, 8531, 8532, 9095
Berman, Bruce J., 11665
Berman, Eleanor D., 1337, 1443
Berman, Larry, 10966
Berman, William C., 9430
Bernard, John, 2015
Bernard, Kenneth A., 4380, 4946, 4947, 5110, 5182
Bernstein, Barton J., 8987, 9096, 9097, 9291-9295, 9415, 9431-9436, 9939, 10526-10528
Bernstein, Samuel, 1846
Berry, Mildred F., 5262, 5263
Berry, Robert, 11704
Berthold, Carol A., 10172
Berwanger, Eugene R., 5436
Beschloss, Michael R., 8533

Best, Gary D., 7478, 8080, 8111-8116
Bestor, Arthur E., 2211, 4045
Bethell, Thomas N., 10400
Betts, Edwin M., 1491, 1492, 2412-2414
Beveridge, Albert J., 3479, 4197
Beveridge, John W., 5183
Bezanson, Walter E., 4617
Bezayiff, David, 913
Bhagwati, Jagdish, 11468
Bhana, Surendra, 8534, 9511, 9512
Biadasz, Frances E., 9940
Bialer, Seweryn, 12978
Biancolli, Louis, 1338
Bias, Randolph, 1887
Bickel, Alexander M., 7022, 10967
Bickerton, Ian J., 9605, 9606
Bickley, Eugene H., 10401
Biddle, Francis, 8535
Bigelow, John, 1178
Biggart, Nicole W., 12586, 12593, 12616, 12617
Biggs, Ernest E., 11666
Biglow, Frank W., 10649
Bilainkin, George, 10031
Bill, Alfred H., 3239
Biller, Owen A., 10402
Billias, George A., 624
Billings, Richard N., 10404
Billings-Yun, Melanie S., 9941
Billington, Monroe, 7450, 8988-8990, 9437, 9438, 11167
Billington, Ray A., 3210, 3341
Binder, Frederick M., 914, 2332-2334, 2834
Binger, Carl, 1071, 1072
Bingham, Worth, 10727
Bink, Barbara H., 13083
Binney, Charles C., 6125
Binney, Horace, 683
Binning, William C., 11775
Binns, Henry B., 3481, 3482
Binsse, Harry L., 428
Binstock, Robert H., 12404
Birge, William S., 156
Bishirjian, Richard J., 7271
Bishop, Donald G., 8860
Bishop, H. O., 3135
Bishop, James A., 4795, 8536, 10173, 10403, 10968
Bishop, Joseph B., 6878
Bishop, Joseph W., Jr., 12435
Bissell, Richard, 6432, 8394, 10078
Bissell, Wilson S., 6111
Bissett, Clark P., 3483
Bitzer, Lloyd, 11976, 12367
Black, Chauncey F., 6112
Black, Harold G., 7603
Black, Ruby A., 8464
Blackburn, Joyce, 6341
Blacknall, Oscar W., 4471
Blackorby, Edward C., 6661

Blackstock, Paul W., 11469
Blaine, James G., 5921, 5981, 6232
Blair, Albert L., 1888
Blair, Clay, Jr., 10032
Blair, Francis G., 5264
Blair, Harry C., 3675
Blair, Joan, 10032
Blair, John L., 7971, 7989, 7990
Blair, Montgomery, 3072
Blake, May B., 3098
Blake, Nelson M., 6126, 6830
Blake, W. B., 427
Blakey, G. Robert, 10404
Blakey, George T., 6529
Blanchard, Sherman, 7834
Bland, Raymond L., 8176
Blanshard, Paul, 10602
Blanton, Wyndham B., 157
Blau, Joseph L., 2835
Blayney, Michael S., 8816
Blazsik, Gloria E., 6831
Blegen, Theodore C., 3889
Blinderman, Charles S., 1073
Blissett, Marlan, 11099
Bliven, Bruce, 1179
Block, Jean L., 11955
Block, Robert H., 7536, 7537
Blodgett, Geoffrey, 6127
Bloncourt, Pauline, 10174
Bloom, Robert L., 3890, 5056, 5143
Bloom, Sol, 684
Bloomfield, Lincoln P., 12529
Bloomgarden, Henry S., 10405
Blough, Roger M., 10553
Blue, Merle D., 3891
Blum, Albert, 9098
Blum, Herman, 3892
Blum, John M., 6530, 6662, 6879, 7190, 7272, 7371, 7372, 8537-8539, 10969
Blumenson, Martin, 9676, 9739
Blumenthal, Henry, 7479
Blumenthal, Sidney, 12618
Blunk, S. M., 4335
Blynn, William C., 5842
Boas, Norman F., 3363
Boatmon, Ellis G., 7816
Bobbe, Dorothie D., 879, 2581
Bober, Robert A., 7191
Bobr-Tylingo, Stanislaw, 3408
Boehm, Dwight, 1691
Boehm, Randolph, 10728
Boemeke, Manfred F., 7480
Bolce, Louis, 12934
Boles, John B., 989, 8991
Boller, Paul F., Jr., 328, 685, 1180, 4046, 10970
Bolles, Blair, 8768
Bolling, John R., 7604
Bolling, Richard, 10497

Bollinger, James W., 4664
Bolt, Robert, 6128, 7023
Bolton, Theodore, 428
Bomberger, C. M., 158
Bonafede, Dom, 11470-11482, 11667, 11720, 11854, 11977-11987, 12155-12159, 12575, 12619, 12620, 13095
Bonaparte, Charles J., 6663
Bond, Beverly W., Jr., 2543, 3136, 3150
Bond, Jon R., 12185, 12665
Bone, Beverly, 4796
Bonior, David E., 12979
Bonn, Franklyn G., Jr., 1889, 2374
Bonner, James C., 2837
Bonner, Judith W., 10406
Booker, Simeon, 10554
Boorstin, Daniel J., 1074
Boosel, Harry X., 3933
Booth, Edward T., 1181, 3137
Boothe, Leon E., 7605, 7606
Borchard, Edwin M., 9622
Bordon, Morton, 14
Borg, Dorothy, 9099
Borglum, Gutzon, 3676
Borit, Gabor S., 4168, 4472-4475, 4665, 4880, 5265, 5266
Borland, Jay, 12621
Bormann, Ernest G., 12622
Bornet, Vaughn D., 8067, 10971
Borst, Philip W., 10972
Borst, William A., 4476
Bosha, Francis J., 9770
Boskin, Joseph, 8758
Bosworth, Barry P., 12284
Bottorff, William K., 1075, 1076
Boucher, Jonathan, 559
Boudin, Leonard B., 11855
Boughton, James M., 9910, 10598, 11230
Bourgin, Frank P., 1749
Bourke, Paul F., 2375
Bourne, Miriam A., 252
Boutell, Lewis H., 1444
Boutwell, George S., 5691, 5742
Bouvier, Jacqueline, 10079
Bouvier, Lee, 10079
Bovard, James, 12838
Bowden, Elizabeth G., 12146
Bowen, Catherine D., 915
Bowen, Clarence W., 363, 686
Bowen, David W., 5437, 5438
Bowen, Henry C., 4198
Bowers, Claude G., 1077, 1182, 1183, 1692, 1693, 2090-2093, 2100, 2178, 2335-2337, 2836, 2943, 3240, 5399, 7273
Bowers, John H., 3484
Bowler, Marion K., 11483
Bowles, Chester, 10134, 10650
Bowling, Kenneth R., 687, 1184

Bowman, Albert H., 1847
Bowman, Eileen M., 8948
Bowman, Georgia B., 9917
Bowman, Isaiah, 1694
Box, Pelham H., 7373
Boyarsky, Bill, 12563, 12587
Boyd, James P., 5582, 6073
Boyd, Julian P., 1185, 1186, 1445, 1695, 1696, 1812, 1848, 2016, 2179, 2180, 2215
Boyd, Richard W., 11856
Boyd, Thomas M., 560
Boykin, Edward, 2216
Brabson, Fay W., 5400
Bracken, Dorothy K., 4006
Braden, George D., 9296
Braden, Waldo W., 4477, 8395, 8498, 8540-8542
Bradford, Gamaliel, 3818, 6074, 6433, 6664, 7274, 7275, 7972
Bradford, M. E., 3893, 4105
Bradford, Richard H., 10603
Bradlee, Benjamin C., 10033, 10034
Bradley, Bert B., 2017, 12623
Bradley, George L., 11313
Bradley, Jared W., 2457, 2101
Bradley, Pearl G., 10555
Bradley, Vernon S., 7451
Bradshaw, Herbert C., 3175
Brady, Cyrus T., 2713
Brady, Linda P., 13081
Braeman, John, 7138, 8992, 8993
Bragdon, Henry W., 7192
Bragg, William, Jr., 9771
Brainerd, Lawrence, 7835
Brakel, Samuel J., 12839
Bramantip, Bocardo, 3894
Brambilla, Marius G., Jr., 9100
Bramwell, Dana G., 11857
Branch, Taylor, 10529
Brand, H., 11243
Brand, Katherine E., 7193, 7727
Brandeis, Erich, 8328
Brandenburg, Earnest, 8395, 8498, 8541, 8542, 8861-8863
Brandes, Joseph, 8117, 8118
Brandon, Donald, 10651
Brandon, Dorothy B., 9719
Brandon, Henry, 10973, 11484, 11485
Brandow, G. E., 11668
Brandt, Harvey, 8396
Brandt, Keith, 4436, 4666
Branscombe, Arthur, 253
Branson, Roy, 2376
Brant, Irving, 1064-1067, 1120-1128, 1201-1204, 2340, 8397, 10080
Branton, Harriet K., 2593
Branyan, Robert L., 9439, 9772, 9773, 9870, 10974
Brasch, Frederick E., 1658
Brashear, Ernest, 11409

Brasington, George F., Jr., 2838, 2944
Bratzel, John F., 8543
Brauer, Carl M., 10556-10558, 11168
Braverman, Miriam, 12840
Brayman, Harold, 11359
Break, George F., 12285
Breen, Timothy H., 916
Breiseth, Christopher N., 4618, 4619
Brembeck, Cole S., 9499, 9500
Bremer, William W., 8994
Bremner, John E., 12368
Brennan, John F., 10081
Brennan, Peter, 10091
Brenner, Michael, 11776, 12369
Brenner, Walter C., 4797
Brent, Robert A., 1187, 1615, 2018, 2770, 2839
Bresler, Robert J., 11988
Brewer, Paul W., 2019
Brewster, Eugene V., 7276
Briceland, Alan V., 2102
Bridges, David L., 1078
Bridges, Roger D., 4948, 5267, 5475
Bridgman, Richard, 1293
Brigham, Clarence S., 7938
Brigham, Johnson, 1616
Brinegard, Lou, 10975
Brinkley, Alan, 10175
Brinkley, David, 10976
Brisbin, James S., 5743, 5922-5924, 6034
Bristol, F. M., 6254
Bristow, Joseph L., 6274
Britton, Nan, 7836
Brockett, Linus P., 5268, 5583
Brockway, A. Fenner, 8544
Broder, David S., 10977
Brodie, Bernard, 7139
Brodie, Fawn M., 1279-1281, 1408, 1409, 11380
Brody, Richard A., 10978, 11308, 11486, 11525
Brogan, Denis W., 1188, 3485, 8545, 10176, 10979
Bromberg, M. D., 12841
Bromfield, Louis, 1525
Bronfenbrenner, Martin, 13096
Brooke, Walter E., 766
Brooks, Chester L., 6434
Brooks, Elbridge S., 5584
Brooks, Eugene C., 7374
Brooks, Joan L., 2103
Brooks, Noah, 3486, 4199, 4200, 4437, 4667, 4668, 4949, 4950, 5184
Brooks, Phillip C., 917
Brooks, Sydney, 6531
Brooks, William D., 11244, 11245
Brooks, William E., 5585, 7194
Brough, James, 8368, 8450, 8488
Broun, Heywood, 1189
Browder, Earl, 1183, 1952
Brower, Brock, 12160
Brown, B. Bolton, 1493

Brown, Charles R., 3487
Brown, Clarence A., 4047
Brown, Claude T., 7939
Brown, Edmund G., 12588
Brown, Edward A., 2020
Brown, Elizabeth G., 1428
Brown, Emma E., 5586, 5925
Brown, Eric S., 12842
Brown, Everett S., 688, 2556
Brown, Glenn, 2217, 6435
Brown, Harriet G., 6342
Brown, Harry J., 5954, 5982
Brown, J. Hay, 3422
Brown, John E., 7375
Brown, John M., 9297, 9774
Brown, L. H., 7940
Brown, Lawrence D., 12843
Brown, Lorenzo, 13097
Brown, Lytle, 5692
Brown, Norman D., 2945
Brown, Ralph A., 990
Brown, Ralph H., 2218
Brown, Richard H., 2840, 2841, 3073
Brown, Roger L., 2462
Brown, Roland W., 1659
Brown, Sharon, 1697, 1698
Brown, Steven R., 11410
Brown, Stuart G., 1082, 1894, 9871
Brown, Thomas M., 11411
Brown, Walter F., Jr., 991
Brown, Wenzell, 3367, 5843
Brown, William G., 2714, 6436
Brown, William H., 1813
Brown, William M., 159
Brown, Wilson, 7991, 8190, 8546, 9298
Browne, Bernard G., 9942
Browne, Charles A., 1294, 1660, 1661
Browne, Edythe H., 1190
Browne, Francis F., 3488
Browne, Ray B., 3934
Browne, Robert H., 4478
Brownfeld, Allan C., 12844
Brownlow, Louis, 7481
Brownlow, Paul C., 5439
Brownstein, Ronald, 12624, 12625
Brozen, Yale, 12286
Bruce, H. Addington, 2104
Bruce, Philip A., 2021
Bruce, Robert V., 4951
Brudney, Jeffrey L., 12935
Bruenn, Howard G., 8398
Brumbaugh, Martin G., 6343
Brumgardt, John R., 4881, 4952
Brummett, Barry, 11487, 12161
Brune, Lester H., 9943
Bruns, Roger, 2946
Brush, Edward H., 6255
Bryan, George S., 3895

Bryan, Martin, 7026
Bryan, Mina R., 1699
Bryan, William A., 429
Bryan, William J., 1526, 7125, 7452
Bryant, Blanche B., 7920
Bryant, Peter S., 11246
Bryce, James, 2022
Bryner, Byron L., 4336
Bryniarski, Joan L., 8864, 9513
Bryson, Lyman, 4669
Bryson, Thomas A., 5659, 7538, 8865
Brzezinski, Zbigniew, 11777, 11778
Buchanan, James, 3457-3460, 13098
Buchanan, Patrick J., 11488
Buchanan, Russell, 6532
Buchanan, Thomas A., 10407
Buchanan, Wiley, 9775
Buck, Solon J., 4337
Buckingham, John E., 4798
Buckley, Gary J., 9623
Buckley, William F., 9776, 11858
Buckmaster, Henrietta, 5693
Buehrig, Edward H., 7539, 7540, 7607
Buell, Augustus C., 2715
Buffington, Joseph, 329, 330
Buffone, Samuel J., 11863
Bugg, James L., Jr., 2842
Buice, David, 4670
Bulfinch, Thomas, 1191
Bull, Maurice P., 10496
Bulla, Charles D., 15
Bullard, Anthony R., 9514
Bullard, F. Lauriston, 3677, 3678, 3819, 3820, 3935, 4106, 4671-4673, 5111, 5965
Bullitt, William C., 7140, 7150
Bullock, Alonzo M., 3489
Bullock, Helen C. D., 1192, 1339, 2219
Bullock, Paul, 11433
Bumgardner, Edward, 5440
Bumstead, Samuel A., 1193
Bundy, Jonas M., 5926
Bundy, McGeorge, 10177, 10652
Bunge, Walter, 11314
Bunker, Robert, 10857
Bunnell, Frederick P., 10653
Burby, John F., 11669, 11670
Burch, Philip H., Jr., 12162
Burdick, Frank, 7541
Burger, Warren E., 2181
Burgess, John W., 5844
Burgin, William G., 6533
Burk, Robert F., 9872
Burkart, Joan M., 11169
Burke, Edmund J., 2138
Burke, John E., 2843
Burke, John P., 12817
Burke, Pauline W., 2771
Burke, Robert L., 8866

Burke, Vee J., 11671
Burke, Vincent, 10498, 11671
Burke, W. J., 362
Burke, Waldemar, 8547
Burkett, Elmer J., 6534
Burkman, Thomas W., 7608
Burleigh, Anne H., 851
Burner, David, 7453, 8039, 10035
Burnet, Whittier, 625
Burnette, Ollen L., 5983, 6050, 6129
Burnham, J. H., 4479
Burnham, Walter D., 12626
Burns, Edward M., 2325, 2386, 2463
Burns, James M., 8329, 8330, 8548, 8549, 10036, 10135, 10178-10180, 10604, 10980, 11280
Burns, Mary H., 10891
Burns, Richard D., 7609
Burns, William J., 12980
Burr, Frank A., 5587
Burr, Nelson R., 4480
Burr, Samuel J., 3121
Burroughs, John, 6437-6439
Burt, Jesse, 3211, 4674
Burt, Richard, 12572
Burt, Silas W., 4048
Burton, Alma H., 5588
Burton, David H., 6344, 6440, 6665, 6666, 6832-6835, 6984, 7024, 7376
Burton, Harold H., 2464
Busch, D. Carolyn, 11672
Busch, Noel F., 626, 6345
Busey, Samuel C., 2023
Bush, Alfred L., 1194
Bush-Brown, Albert, 8399
Buss, Terry F., 12395
Butcher, Harry C., 9740
Butler, Joseph G., Jr., 254
Butler, Lorine L., 880
Butler, William A., 3056
Butow, R. J. C., 8550, 9101
Butt, Archibald W., 6667, 6668, 7025
Butterfield, D. Anthony, 12163
Butterfield, Lyman H., 881, 882, 1054, 1055, 1195, 1953, 1954, 2220, 2221, 2594
Butterfield, Roger, 8331
Butturff, Dorothy D., 8465
Butwell, Richard, 11779
Byrnes, James F., 9211

Cabell, Nathaniel F., 2222
Cable, Mary, 1494
Cabral, Peter C., 2772
Caddell, Patrick H., 12164
Cadenhead, Ivie, 6346, 6669
Cadman, S. Parkes, 3936
Cadwallader, Sylvanus, 5694
Cady, Darrel R., 9299
Caemmerer, Hans P., 255

Cahn, Edmond N., 2341
Cahn, Robert, 10181
Caidin, Martin, 10892
Cain, Marvin R., 2844, 3183, 4953, 5112, 5185
Caldwell, Charles, 16
Caldwell, Dan, 11780
Caldwell, Joshua W., 2773
Caldwell, Lawrence T., 12981
Caldwell, Lynton K., 1429, 1895
Caldwell, Margaret, 12627
Caldwell, Mary F., 2774, 2775
Caldwell, Robert G., 5927
Calhoun, Frederick S., 7542
Califano, Joseph A., Jr., 10981
Calkins, Carlos G., 992
Callahan, Dorothy M., 12105
Callahan, North, 17
Callanan, Harold J., 2622
Callcott, Wilfred H., 3241
Calleo, David P., 11603
Calver, William L., 430
Cameron, Juan, 11412, 11989, 11990, 12287
Cameron, Turner C., Jr., 8551
Cammerer, H. Paul, 561
Camp, Norma C., 331
Campbell, Ann R., 11381
Campbell, Charles S., Jr., 6836
Campbell, Colin, 12165, 12628
Campbell, Helen M., 689, 2024, 2465, 4675, 5744
Campbell, Janet, 562
Campbell, John A., Jr., 3423
Campbell, John C., 12629
Campbell, John P., 6670, 7027
Campbell, John T., 5896
Campbell, Mrs. A., 2776
Campbell, Willard S., 4077
Campbell-Copeland, Thomas, 6075, 6212
Canby, Courtlandt, 4954
Cane, Guy, 6671
Canfield, Cass, 627, 918, 1955
Canfield, Frederick A., 2777
Canfield, Leon H., 7377
Cannon, James, 11360
Cannon, Jouett T., 3821
Cannon, Lou, 12564, 12589
Canon, Alfred O., 8949
Capitanchik, David B., 9944
Cappon, Lester J., 767
Capps, Donald, 4078
Caputo, David A., 11493
Carabelli, Angelina J., 4676
Cardiff, Ira D., 4079
Cardinale, Gary W., 4677
Cardoso, J. J., 186
Cardwell, Guy A., 2139
Carey, Alma P., 1368
Carey, George W., 2387
Carey, John P., 1369

Carey, Paul M., 2140
Carleton, William G., 3074, 3896, 7195, 7277, 8119, 10182, 10183
Carlile, Donald E., 11991
Carlson, Earland I., 8499, 8500
Carlson, Robert E., 3424
Carlton, John T., 9515
Carlton, Mabel M., 1083
Carman, Harry J., 4678
Carman, Travers D., 6672
Carmen, Ira H., 8191
Carmichael, Donald S., 8400, 9174
Carmichael, Orton H., 5057
Carmon, Harry J., 3342
Carnegie, Dale B., 3490
Carnoy, Martin, 13099
Caro, Robert A., 10893-10898
Carpenter, C. C., 4338
Carpenter, Ernest C., 7921
Carpenter, Francis B., 4679
Carpenter, John A., 5589, 5590
Carpenter, Liz, 10851
Carpenter, Richard V., 5113
Carr, Albert H. Z., 9516
Carr, Clark E., 4882, 5058, 5059
Carr, James A., 993
Carr, William H. A., 10037, 10038
Carriere, Joseph M., 1849, 2223
Carrington, Henry B., 18
Carroll, Bishop J., 364
Carroll, Eber M., 2661
Carroll, James D., 11170, 12920
Carroll, John A., 690, 691
Carroll, Raymond L., 9501
Carroll, Warren H., 919
Carruthers, Olive, 3679
Carsley, Mark K., 2141
Carson, Gerald, 10982
Carson, Hampton L., 692
Carson, Herbert L., 5060
Carson, Steven L., 4481
Carter, Clarence E., 3151
Carter, Hodding, 5745
Carter, Jimmy, 12550-12561
Carter, John, 7992
Carter, John F., 8995, 11434
Carter, Lief H., 12630
Carter, Luther J., 11962
Carter, Orrin N., 4620
Carter, Purvis M., 7543
Carter, Richard, 10184
Carter, Rosalynn, 12123
Carwardine, Richard, 3157
Cary, Barbara, 3491
Cary, Otis, 9517
Casdorph, Paul D., 6535
Case, Carleton B., 6441
Casey, Francis M., 11315

Cash, Kenneth P., 3897
Cashdollar, Charles D., 5476
Caskey, W. M., 5441, 5442
Casoni, Jennifer, 10852
Casserly, John J., 11992
Cassiday, Bruce B., 11956
Castel, Albert, 5416, 5417, 5477
Castelot, Andre, 160
Catchings, Benjamin S., 2224
Cater, Douglass, 10136, 10137, 10185, 10729, 10814, 10899-10901
Cathcart, Arthur M., 8950
Cathcart, Robert, 11721, 12527
Cathey, James H., 4107
Catlin, George B., 515
Catton, Bruce, 4680, 4955-4957, 5695-5698, 5746, 9102
Catton, William, 4957
Catudal, Honore M., 10654
Caute, David, 9440, 9873
Cauthen, Irby B., Jr., 1370
Cavaioli, Frank J., 11171
Cavan, Sherri, 11382
Cavanagh, Catherine F., 365, 1084
Cavanagh, John W., 693
Cavanah, Frances E., 4438
Cave, Alfred A., 2845
Caverno, Charles, 3783
Ceaser, James W., 12631
Cecile, Robert E., 9777, 10530
Cerny, P. G., 10983, 11257
Chace, James, 11489
Chadsey, Charles E., 5478
Chadwin, M. L., 11490
Chaffee, Steven H., 11993, 12371
Chafin, Eugene W., 3680
Chai, Jae H., 10655
Chalmers, David M., 6673, 7973
Chamberlain, Alexander F., 1527
Chamberlain, Eugene T., 6113
Chamberlain, Ivory, 3333
Chamberlain, John, 10138, 10984, 11994
Chamberlin, Everett, 5747
Chambers, Clarke A., 8501
Chambers, William N., 2947
Chambrum, Charles A., 4958
Chan, Loren B., 7610
Chanda, Nayan, 12985
Chandler, Albert, 3938
Chandler, Josephine C., 4439
Chandler, Julian A. C., 1371, 1372
Chandler, Lester V., 7482
Chandler, Robert J., 4681, 4682
Chandler, Walter, 3242
Chandler, William E., 6044
Chang, Richard T., 5660
Channing, Edward, 2025
Chapel, William G., 11491

Chapin, Benjamin, 4381
Chapin, Henry D., 6442
Chapin, Walter T., 5479
Chapman, Ervin S., 4959
Chapman, Francis, 4563
Chapman, John J., 4049
Chapman, Stephen, 12147, 12590
Chapman, Stu, 12937
Chapple, Joseph M., 5661, 6256, 7378, 7817, 7818
Charbonneau, Louis H., 4564
Charles, Joseph, 920, 1896
Charnwood, Godfrey R. B., 3492, 3681, 3939, 3940, 4201, 6347
Chase, Chris, 11960
Chase, Enoch A., 161
Chase, Harold W., 10730, 10985
Chase, James S., 2846, 10986
Chase, Lucien B., 3243
Chase, Salmon P., 4960
Chaudhuri, Joyotpaul, 1528, 1529
Chavez, Leo E., 8120
Chay, Jongsuk, 7028
Chayes, Abram, 10531
Cheatham, Edgar, 1495
Cheatham, Patricia, 1495
Cherwitz, Richard A., 11316, 11317
Chesen, Eli S., 11383
Chessman, G. Wallace, 6536-6539
Chester, Edward W., 12632
Chesterton, G. K., 19
Chetlain, Augustus L., 5591
Chi, Keon S., 10987
Chianese, Mary L., 1530
Chiang, C. Y. Jesse, 1197
Chicago Historical Society, 3941
Chidsey, Donald B., 1897, 2716, 3168
Childs, Catherine M., 628
Childs, George W., 5592
Childs, Marquis W., 9677, 9918, 10186
Chinard, Gilbert, 366, 852, 1085, 1446, 1731-1734, 2105, 2425-2427
Chipperfield, Burnett M., 3682
Chittenden, Lucius E., 4683, 4684
Chitwood, Oliver P., 3180
Cho, Soon-sung, 9581
Choate, Joseph H., 3493, 4382
Choe, Sun Yuel, 11993, 12371
Chomsky, Noam, 12167
Chowdhry, Carol, 8867
Chrisman, Herring, 4202
Chrisman, James R., 9502
Christensen, Lois E., 563
Christenson, Reo M., 9300, 12168
Christian, George, 10988
Christopherson, Edmund, 10082
Chroust, Anton-Hermann, 2948, 5187
Chu, James C. Y., 4482
Chuinard, E. G., 1198

Church, Russell T., 11492
Church, William C., 5748
Churchill, Allen, 8401
Churchill, Mae, 12290
Cimprich, John, 5443
Ciolli, Antoinette, 1662
Cipes, Robert M., 10187, 10989
Civitello, Maryann, 7667
Clapp, Charles H., 10500, 11183
Clapper, Raymond, 8552, 8553
Clarfield, Gerard H., 694, 994
Clark, Allen C., 2342, 4685, 4686
Clark, Anna, 2949
Clark, Austin H., 1663
Clark, Bayard S., 4799
Clark, Bennett C., 2582
Clark, Blanche H., 5418
Clark, Cal, 8990
Clark, Charles H., 7029
Clark, Charles S., 12633
Clark, David L., 12846
Clark, George P., 906
Clark, Graves G., 1086
Clark, Jonathan, 20
Clark, Joseph, 12634
Clark, Kenneth B., 1447
Clark, Leon P., 4081, 4082
Clark, Mary K., 4883
Clark, Philip, 21, 3494
Clark, Susan E., 12847
Clark, Thomas A., 22
Clark, Thomas D., 2778
Clark, Timothy B., 12169, 12818
Clark, Truman R., 7030
Clark, William B., 629
Clarke, Asia, 4800
Clarke, Charles F., 6348
Clarke, Duncan L., 13070
Clarke, John P., 6540
Clarke, Thomas H., 12291
Clarke, Walter V., 11081, 11569
Claudy, Carl H., 306
Clauss, Errol M., 8868
Claussen, E. Neal, 3409
Claya, Marlene J., 10990
Cleaves, Freeman, 3122
Cleland, Hugh, 516
Clemens, Cyril, 7993, 9212, 9251, 10853
Clemens, J. R., 162
Clemens, William M., 6349
Clements, Kendrick A., 7645, 7646, 8121, 8122
Clendenen, Clarence C., 5845
Cleveland, Grover, 6189-6202
Cleveland, Harlan, 10188
Clevenger, Theodore, Jr., 9919
Clifford, J. Garry, 8746, 9518
Clifton, Chester V., 10362
Clinch, Nancy G., 10083

Cline, Ray S., 12635
Cloud, Archibald J., 163
Cloward, Richard A., 12755, 12906
Clubb, Oliver E., 9301
Clymer, Adam, 12572
Coady, Joseph W., 8502
Coaldrake, Peter, 12636
Cobb, James C., 8747
Cobb, Joseph B., 1087
Cobb, William T., 6443
Cobbett, William, 2717
Coblentz, Catherine C., 164
Cocburn, Alexander, 13071
Cochran, Bert, 9302
Cochran, Charles L., 10189
Cochrane, Elizabeth, 5804
Cochrane, James L., 11172, 11173, 11318
Cockburn, Alexander, 12170
Coe, Edward B., 23
Coffey, Joseph I., 12436
Coffin, Charles C., 3495, 5928, 6035
Coffin, Tristram, 9263, 10139
Coffman, Edward M., 9741
Coggeshall, E. W., 4801
Coggins, James C., 3823
Cohalan, Daniel F., 2779
Cohen, Akiba A., 11781
Cohen, I. Bernard, 1664
Cohen, Jacob, 8996
Cohen, Julius H., 6674
Cohen, Marc J., 12437
Cohen, Michael J., 9607, 9608
Cohen, Morris L., 1430
Cohen, Neal M., 12848
Cohen, Richard E., 12171, 12637
Cohen, Roberta, 12530
Cohen, Samuel T., 11782
Cohen, Stan, 9720
Cohen, Toby, 12849
Cohen, Wilbur J., 8997
Cohen, William, 2142
Cohodas, Nadine, 12638-12640
Coit, Margaret L., 883, 2718
Coker, Christopher, 12982
Colbourn, H. Trevor, 1199, 1535, 2388
Colburn, Harvey, 4203
Colby, Bainbridge, 7379
Cole, Adelaide M., 256, 884
Cole, Arthur C., 4687, 4884, 5114
Cole, Charles C., 2026
Cole, Cornelius C., 4204
Cole, Donald B., 3099
Cole, Richard L., 11493
Cole, Terrence, 5846
Cole, Wayne S., 8869
Coleman, Charles H., 4339, 4885
Coleman, Christopher B., 517, 3898
Coleman, Elizabeth T., 3176

Coleman, John, 2143
Coles, Harry L., 1700
Coletta, Paolo E., 6130, 6275-6277, 6675, 6837, 7031, 7032, 7454, 7693
Colket, Meredith B., Jr., 518
Collier, Bonnie B., 5269
Collier, Peter, 10084, 11995
Collin, Richard H., 6676-6678, 6838
Collins, David R., 9213
Collins, Frederic W., 10190
Collins, Herbert R., 2595
Collins, J. Richard, 623
Collins, Larry, 12438
Collins, Lora S., 12938
Collins, Paul, 11957
Collins, Robert M., 8998, 11494
Collins, Tom, 12106
Collum, Danny, 13100
Colombo, Claudius M., 10656
Colonna, Phyllis, 12570
Colquhoun, Archibald R., 6350
Colver, Anne, 3496
Colyar, Arthur S., 2719
Cometti, Elizabeth, 1200, 1701
Commager, Henry S., 1201, 1536, 1702
Comstock, Helen, 1202
Comstock, Jim, 10191
Conant, Alban J., 4205
Conant, James B., 1373, 1374
Conaway, James, 12850
Condict, Alden S., 5270, 8402
Condict, Lewis, 2708
Condie, Thomas, 24, 25
Condon, Richard, 10408
Condray, Suzanne E., 10991, 10992
Cone, Leon W., Jr., 3075
Conger, Arthur L., 4961, 5593, 5699
Congressional Quarterly, 10192, 11495, 11997-12000, 12172-12176, 12641-12645
Conkin, Paul K., 8554, 8999, 10993
Conkling, Clinton L., 4886
Conkwright, P. J., 1483
Conn, Joseph, 12292, 12939
Connally, Ernest A., 5419
Connell-Smith, Gordon, 12983
Connelly, Fred M., Jr., 10994, 11247
Connery, Thomas B., 5984
Conniff, James, 2389, 2390
Connor, Robert D. W., 8555
Conrad, David E., 6679, 10877
Conrow, Wilford S., 437
Converse, Julius O., 5929
Converse, Philip E., 9945
Conwell, Russell H., 3942, 5793, 5930-5932
Conyers, John, Jr., 11859
Cook, Blanche W., 7544, 9678
Cook, Claude R., 8041
Cook, K. DeLynn, 1174

Cook, Philip S., 11996
Cook, Richard A., 2950
Cook, Roy B., 519
Cook, Theodore A., 2106, 2466
Cooke, Alistair, 9946, 10011, 10193, 10995
Cooke, J. W., 2228
Cooke, Jacob E., 995, 2027, 2028
Cooke, John E., 1088, 1203, 1814
Cookinham, Henry J., 5594, 5933
Coolidge, Archibald C., 1703
Coolidge, Calvin, 165, 8029-8037
Coolidge, Grace A., 7941-7943
Coolidge, Harold J., 1204
Coolidge, Louis A., 5595
Coolidge, Richard B., 166
Coolidge, Ruth D., 166
Cooling, Benjamin F., 9742
Coombs, Lovell, 5596
Cooney, Charles F., 307, 4802
Cooper, Homer H., 4483
Cooper, Jacqueline, 10902
Cooper, John M., Jr., 6680, 6681, 7196, 7545-7547, 7694
Cooper, Joseph, 2029
Cooper, Stephen L., 11293
Coor, Lattie F., 11174
Cope, Alfred H., 8951
Cope, Frank D., 4962
Copeland, Gary W., 12935
Coppee, Henry, 5700
Corbett, Elizabeth, 5662
Corbin, John, 257, 695, 696, 2107, 7278
Corckell, William, 5597
Cordingley, Nora E., 6880
Coren, Robert W., 7837
Corey, Albert B., 8403
Corey, Herbert, 8040
Corgan, Michael T., 6682
Corlett, William S., Jr., 4108
Cormier, Frank, 10815, 11294
Cornelius, Wayne A., 12851
Corning, A. Elwood, 167, 6234
Cornwell, Elmer E., Jr., 7380, 7995, 9074, 9303, 11295
Corrigan, Richard, 12001
Corry, John, 26, 27
Corson, Oscar T., 4109, 4110, 5271, 5663-5665, 5701, 6683
Cortada, James W., 4383
Corwin, Edward S., 2343, 2344, 2189, 7381
Coser, Lewis, 12852
Cosmas, Graham A., 6787
Costanzo, Joseph F., 1617
Costello, Frank B., 2467
Costello, William, 11384
Costigan, Donna, 9269
Costigliola, Frank, 10657
Cotter, Cornelius P., 9778

Cottin, Jonathan, 11481, 11673
Cottman, George S., 4340
Cottom, Robert I., Jr., 5966
Cotton, Edward H., 6352, 6353, 6973
Cottrell, Alvin J., 9947
Cottrell, John, 10409, 10410
Cottrill, Dale E., 7819, 7881
Coughlan, Robert, 11435
Coulcomb, Charles A., 28
Coulter, E. Merton, 5749, 7033
Coulter, John, 4688, 5985, 6278
Council on Religion and International Affairs, 12439
Count, Susan J., 4689
Cournos, Helen S. N., 921
Cournos, John, 921
Coursey, W. S., 6279
Courtenay, Calista, 3497
Cousins, Norman, 10194, 10658
Cowan, Wayne H., 12819
Cowen, Benjamin R., 4206
Cowley, Robert, 8192
Cowperthwaite, L. LeRoy, 8404, 8817
Cox, Earnest S., 5188
Cox, Henry C., 4384
Cox, Isaac J., 2108, 2544
Cox, James M., 1089
Cox, John H., 5420, 5480, 5750
Cox, LaWanda C., 5189, 5420, 5480, 5750
Cox, R. Merritt, 1704
Cox, Stephen D., 1448
Coyle, Beth F., 10659
Coyle, David C., 6684
Crable, Richard E., 9779
Crackel, Theodore J., 2030, 2031
Craddock, Emmie, 10877
Crady, Wilson, 3683
Crafts, William A., 5598
Cragan, Thomas M., 1295
Craig, G. M., 10195, 10196, 10660, 10996, 11496
Craig, Hardin, 7197, 7728
Cramer, John H., 4963
Cranch, William, 853
Crandall, Robert W., 12853
Crane, Fergus, 1705
Crane, James L., 5666
Crane, John M., 9214
Crane, Milton, 8556
Crane, Philip M., 10197
Crane, Robert D., 10532
Crane, William D., 5401
Cranston, Ruth, 7141
Crapol, Edward P., 2623
Craven, Avery O., 3041
Craven, Bruce, 2720, 2780, 2781
Cravens, Francis, 3498
Crawford, Charlotte, 7034
Crawford, Kenneth, 10903

Crawford, Nelson A., 1618
Creel, George, 5751, 7279, 7695, 8642
Creelman, James, 4083, 4084, 6685
Cregier, Don M., 11258
Crenshaw, Frank S., 1314
Crenshaw, James T., 9264
Crespi, Irving, 12646
Cress, Larry D., 996
Cresson, William P., 2518
Crevilli, John P., 11175
Crew, C. C., 3499
Crewdson, Prudence, 12002
Crewe, Ivor, 12984
Crews, James M., Jr., 10605
Crews, Kenneth D., 7455
Crile, George, III, 10529
Cripe, Helen L., 1340, 1341
Crissey, Elwell, 4690
Croce, Lewis H., 4691, 4692
Crocker, George N., 8870
Crocker, Lionel, 4621
Crockett, David, 3057
Crofts, Daniel W., 4693, 4887
Croll, P. C., 3500
Cromer, Lord, 3684
Cronin, Thomas E., 8557, 12003
Cronon, E. David, 7142, 7280
Crook, William H., 4207, 4803, 5847
Crosby, Earl W., 7483
Crosby, Franklin, 3501
Cross, Frank B., 13072
Cross, Nelson, 5599
Cross, Whitney R., 6686, 8769
Cross, Wilbur, 6131
Crosskey, William W., 2391
Crossman, Richard H., 8871
Crosson, David, 6687
Crotty, William J., 10411
Crouch, Barry A., 8952
Crouse, Janice S., 12004, 12372
Crowell, Laura, 8405, 8748, 8818, 8819, 9175, 9176
Crowley, John W., 6881
Crown, James T., 10198, 10199
Crowther, Samuel, 8193
Croy, Homer, 3943, 3944
Crume, John B., 5752
Cubberly, Frederick, 2782
Cuff, Robert D., 7281, 7484, 7485, 7696, 8123, 8124
Culbert, David, 8558, 11296
Cullen, Charles T., 2229
Cullen, Joseph P., 308, 2951
Culver, John H., 12591
Culyer, John Y., 4804
Cummin, Hazel E., 431
Cuneo, Sherman A., 7820
Cunliffe, Marcus, 432, 433, 1706, 2468, 4484, 6688, 10997

Cunningham, Frank D., 9519
Cunningham, J. O., 3685
Cunningham, John L., 3686
Cunningham, Noble E., Jr., 1898, 1899, 2232-2234
Curlee, Joan E., 9000
Curran, George A., 7382
Curran, John W., 4805-4807
Current, Richard N., 3502, 3824, 4111, 4485, 4694, 4695, 4964, 4965, 8194
Currey, J. Seymour, 4341
Currie, George E., 4808
Currie, Stephen, 3307
Curry, Earl R., 8195
Curry, George W., 7668
Curry, Jesse, 10412
Curry, Patricia E., 2469
Curry, Roy W., 7548, 7549
Curti, Merle, 7282
Curtis, Alan M., 11497
Curtis, George H., 7550
Curtis, George T., 3383
Curtis, James C., 2847, 2952, 3100-3102
Curtis, Natalie, 6444, 6445
Curtis, Thomas B., 10662
Curtis, Thomas E., 1090
Curtis, William E., 3503
Cushing, Caleb, 3123, 3124
Cushing, Otho, 6354
Cushman, Donald P., 9582, 11783
Cushman, Esther C., 5272
Cushman, Robert F., 10413
Custis, George W., 29, 258
Cuthbert, Norma B., 4696
Cutler, John H., 10039
Cutler, Robert, 9679
Cutright, Paul R., 2035, 6355, 6356, 6446

Dabney, Virginius, 1375, 1410, 1496, 7198
Dabney, William M., 1990
Daggett, Athern P., 7993
Dahl, Curtis, 2953, 4697
Dahlinger, Charles W., 4888
Daiker, Virginia, 1707
Dailey, Joseph M., 9920, 11436
Dailey, Wallace F., 6882
Dall, Curtos B., 8332
Dallas, Rita, 10085
Dallek, Robert, 8872-8874, 9103, 9104, 9520, 12647
Dalton, Brian J., 7383
Dalton, David C., 1376
Dalton, Kathleen M., 6447, 6448
Dameron, Kenneth, Jr., 10499
Damiani, Brian P., 6280
Damore, Leo, 10086
Dana, Charles A., 4698, 5600
Danelski, David J., 6985
Dangerfield, George, 2470, 2519, 2557

Daniel, Frederick S., 1206
Daniel, John W., 367, 2230, 6281
Daniel, Lois, 10087
Daniel, Marjorie L., 7199
Daniel, Robert L., 7200
Daniels, Jonathan, 1900, 2211, 4045, 7143, 7283, 8406, 8559, 8560, 9215, 9304
Daniels, Josephus, 7144, 7384, 7697
Daniels, Winthrop M., 7145
Danielson, Elena S., 8275
Danziger, Sheldon, 12820, 13101
Dargo, George, 2036
Darling, Jay N., 8042
Darvick, Herman, 12124
Dauer, Manning J., 564, 854, 922, 923, 1708
Daugherty, Harry M., 7821
Daugherty, James, 2144, 3504
Daughters of the American Revolution, Indiana, 3138
D'Aulaire, Ingri M., 3505
Dause, Charles A., 8953
Davenport, Frederick M., 6541, 6542, 6689, 7456
David, Beverly R., 5805
David, Irene, 9721
David, Jay, 10746
David, Lester, 9721, 11413
David, Michael, 4486
Davidson, Bill, 368, 2624, 4385, 5481, 6048, 6690, 10200, 10904, 11248
Davidson, John W., 7385, 7386
Davidson, Lawrence S., 11674, 11675
Davidson, Robert H., 8196, 9780
Davie, Michael, 10998, 10999
Davies, Derek, 12985
Davies, Richard O., 9441-9443
Davis, Allen F., 6543
Davis, Andrew M., 2783, 2784
Davis, Betty E., 1497
Davis, Burke, 630, 2721
Davis, Burnet V., 4112
Davis, Clint, 9874
Davis, Cullum, 3687
Davis, David B., 2145, 2146
Davis, Edwin, 332, 4342
Davis, Elmer, 9305
Davis, Eric L., 11000, 12373
Davis, Glenn, 6449, 6544
Davis, Harold E., 5934
Davis, Harvey O., 3688
Davis, J. M., 1393
Davis, John H., 10088, 10089
Davis, John M., 4208, 4889
Davis, John W., 520, 1431
Davis, Joseph, 8043
Davis, Kenneth S., 8333, 8334, 8407, 8466, 8561, 9680
Davis, Larry L., 11176
Davis, Norman H., 7611

Davis, Oscar K., 6235, 6691, 6967
Davis, Richard, 1207, 1208, 1377, 1449, 1537
Davis, Robert R., Jr., 1209, 3425, 3426
Davis, Thomas J., 1091
Davis, Vincent, 12986
Davison, Kenneth E., 5848-5854, 5897, 5898
Dawbarn, Charles, 6692
Dawes, Charles G., 5986, 6282, 7944
Dawes, Henry L., 5987
Dawidoff, Robert, 2147
Dawson, Moses, 3058, 3139
Dawson, Nelson L., 9001, 9002
Day, Berry, 5667
Day, David S., 8197
Day, Donald, 7729
Dayer, Roberta A., 7698
Days, Drew S., 12854
Dayton, Eldorour, 9216
Deakin, James, 11001-11003, 11297
DeAlba, Pedro, 2231
DeAlvarez, Leo P., 5061
Dean, Elizabeth L., 2345
Dean, John W., III, 11498, 11499
Deane, Hugh, 8125
Dearing, Mary R., 5482
Dearmonst, Nelson S., 2182
Deason, Willard, 10905
Deaton, Dorsey M., 9521
DeBarthe, Joseph, 7838
Decatur, Stephen, 168
Decker, Joe F., 6839
DeCola, Thomas G., 9105
DeConde, Alexander, 697, 698, 1850, 8126, 8198, 9948
Decter, Midge, 10201
Defalco, Anthony A., 1538
Degler, Carl N., 3343, 8044, 9003, 10202, 11004
DeHart, Frank, 11385, 12107
DeJouvenel, Bertrand, 7146
DeLaBedoyere, Michael, 369
Delahay, Mark W., 3506
Delaplaine, Edward S., 5115
DeLeon, Daniel, 2392, 1539
D'Elia, Donald J., 1540
Dell, Christopher, 4699, 5166
DelPapa, Eugene M., 8199
Delson, Jane, 11005
DeLuna, Phyllis R., 9444
Delzell, Earl B., 2785
Demarest, William H., 333
DeMause, Lloyd, 12125, 12126, 12649
Deming, Henry C., 5601
Democratic Party National Committee, 8562
DeMotte, William H., 4809
Dempsey, John R., 12177
Denison, Charles W., 5602
Dennett, Tyler, 6840, 6841
Dennis, Frank L., 4622

Dennis, Jack, 11860
Denny, George V., Jr., 8563
DeNovo, John A., 9949
Densford, John P., 1378
Denson, R. B., 10414
Dent, Thomas, 4209
Depew, Chauncey M., 6357
DePuy, Henry F., 3042
DeRosier, Arthur H., Jr., 2954
DeSantis, Vincent P., 5855, 5856, 5988, 6051, 6132, 6219, 9781, 12178
Desmond, Alice, 259
Destephen, Daniel E., 11861
Destler, Irving M., 11500, 12650, 12988
DeTerra, Helmut, 1541, 2346
Dethloff, Henry C., 1901
DeToledano, Ralph, 11386, 11387
Detweiler, Philip F., 1815
Detweiler, Susan, 434
Deutsch, Eberhard P., 2786
Deutsch, Richard, 12179
Devine, Donald J., 12940
Devine, Francis E., 924
Devlin, L. Patrick, 7551, 12374, 12941
Devol, Edward, 1851
DeVoto, Bernard, 3244
DeVries, George, Jr., 6693
Dewald, William G., 12293
Dewart, Leslie, 10533
DeWeerd, Harvey A., 7699, 9743
Dewey, Donald O., 1136-1138, 2347
Dewey, Frank L., 1210, 1432, 1433, 1709
Dewey, John, 1902, 6358
DeWitt, Cornelius H., 1903
DeWitt, David M., 4810, 5483, 5484
DeWitt, Howard A., 7552, 7882
DeWitt, John H., Jr., 2787, 5421
Dexter, Walter F., 8081
DeYoung, Harry R., 7730
Diamond, Edwin, 11414, 11862, 12005, 12135, 12375
Diamond, Martin, 3507
Diamond, Sigmund, 2232, 10204
Diamond, William, 7486
DiBacco, Thomas V., 9950, 9951
Dibner, Bern, 8082
Dickerson, Nancy, 10040
Dickson, Charles E., 2520, 2545
Dickson, Edward A., 4487
Dickson, Thomas H., 7201
Didier, Eugene L., 1434, 2788
Dieck, Herman, 6076
Dietze, Gottfried, 2396
Diggins, John P., 2148
Dilliard, Irving, 5116, 8954
Dimock, Marshall E., 7387, 7487
Dinerstein, Herbert S., 10534, 11603
Dinneen, Joseph F., 10090

Dinnerstein, Leonard, 3184
D'Innocenzo, Michael, 5163
Dishman, Robert B., 9921
Dittenhoefer, Abram J., 4890
Divine, Robert A., 8564, 9106, 9952, 9953, 10535, 11006
Dix, John P., 1904
Dixon, Lawrence W., 2183
Dixon, Thomas, 7821
Dizikes, John, 9004
Doane, Franklin C., 8045
Doane, Gilbert H., 6045
Dobriansky, Lev E., 12006
Dobrovir, William A., 11863
Dobson, Wayne W., 5485
Doctors, Samuel I., 11676, 11677
Dodd, William E., 1710, 1852, 2789, 2790, 4488, 4700, 4966, 4967, 7202, 7284-7286
Dodge, Daniel K., 3508, 3945
Dodge, Grenville M., 4210, 5669, 5753
Doenecke, Justus D., 5989, 6052
Doherty, Herbert J., Jr., 2848, 2849
Dollen, Charles, 10041
Dolliver, Jonathan, 7035
Domer, Thomas, 5486, 9954, 10559
Donahoe, Bernard F., 8565
Donald, Aida D., 1145, 10205
Donald, David, 3509, 3825, 4565, 4701, 5487, 5488, 5732
Donaldson, Thomas, 1092
Donder, George A., 4566
Dondero, George A., 3689
Donnelly, Marian C., 1315
Donoghue, Mary A., 10415
Donovan, Frank, 1816, 2397, 5190
Donovan, Hedley, 12651, 12652
Donovan, Herbert D. A., 3076
Donovan, John C., 8875, 11177
Donovan, Michael J., 6450
Donovan, Robert J., 9306, 9307, 9583, 9681, 10140, 11319
Donovan, Theresa A., 3368
Doolittle, Fred C., 12900
Doran, Charles F., 12989
Dorfman, Joseph, 997, 1542, 1905
Dorris, Jonathan T., 4702, 4703, 4968, 5489
Dorris, Mary C., 2791
Dorroh, David L., 7036
Dorsett, Lyle W., 8566, 9005, 9275
Dorsey, John M., 1211
Dorsey, Marian V., 435
Dorsheimer, William, 6114
Dorwart, Jeffery M., 8567
Dos Passos, John, 1093, 2037, 2326
Doster, William E., 4969
Doswell, Sallie J., 1512
Doty, Margaret De F., 370
Doughty, Francis W., 2792

Douglas, George W., 6359
Douglas, James, 12942
Douglas, Paul H., 4623
Douglas, William O., 5191
Douglass, Bruce, 12376
Douglass, Elisha P., 1906
Douglass, William B., 169
Douty, Esther, 2038
Dowd, Morgan D., 4113
Dowdey, Clifford, 3899
Dowding, Nancy E., 3690
Dowe, Charles E., 699
Downes, Randolph C., 2039, 2955, 7822, 7839-7841, 7866, 7871, 7872
Downey, Matthew T., 6133
Downey, William G., Jr., 2625
Downing, Jack, 2722
Downs, Olin, 8568
Doyle, Burton T., 5935, 6036
Dozer, Donald M., 5062, 6213
Drake, Douglas C., 8127
Drakeman, Donald L., 2471
Draper, Andrew S., 3510, 5274, 5670
Draper, Theodore, 2398, 10663, 11320
Drayton, William B., 12592
Dreher, Ernest O., 5192
Drell, Sidney D., 13073, 13074
Dressler, Thomas H. B., 8200
Drew, Elizabeth, 11864, 11865, 12856
Drew, Robert, 10040
Drexel, Constance, 9177
Dreher, Frederick E., 6451
Drinker, Frederick E., 6451
Drinkwater, John, 4489, 5193
Drischler, Alvin P., 10664, 11678, 11784
Drouin, Edmond G., 1619, 2399
Droze, Wilmon H., 9006
Druks, Herbert, 9308, 9522, 9523, 9782, 10206, 11007
Drummond, Roscoe, 11242
Drury, Allen, 11501
DuBois, William E. B., 5167, 5490, 5754, 5857, 6283
Dubovitskii, G. A., 3103
Duckett, Kenneth W., 7842
Dudden, Arthur P., 7287
Dudman, Richard, 11321
Dudney, Robert S., 12990
Duff, John B., 7669
Duff, John J., 4567
Duffy, Herbert S., 6968
Dugard, John, 12440
Dugger, Ronnie, 10854, 10906, 12653, 12857
Dugger, William M., 13102
Duke, Richard T. W., Jr., 1212
Dulebohn, George R., 6134
Dulles, Foster R., 8876
Dumbauld, Edward, 1213, 1214, 1817, 1911-1913, 2184, 2185, 2233

Dumond, Dwight L., 3427, 7288
Dunar, Andrew J., 9309
Dunbar, Leslie W., 2472
Duncan, Mary B., 12402
Duncan, Rodger D., 12007
Dunlap, John R., 1907, 2850, 4114
Dunlap, Lloyd A., 5144, 5194
Dunleavy, Stephen, 10091
Dunn, James W., 8569
Dunn, Keith A., 12441
Dunn, Robert L., 6969
Dunn, Waldo H., 127
Dunne, Edward F., 3691
Dunne, Gerald T., 5755
Dunning, John L., 10416
Dunning, William A., 5422, 5423, 5491, 5756
Dupeux, Georges, 9945
Dupuy, Trevor N., 4970
Duram, James C., 8955, 9875, 9876
Durden, Robert F., 6135, 7147
Durham, Harriet F., 3826
Durishin, John F., 4971
Duroselle, Jean-Baptiste, 7576
Dutcher, George M., 565
DuVal, Miles P., Jr., 6842
Duyckinck, Evert A., 2040
Dwight, H. G., 1215
Dwight, Theodore, 1094
Dworkin, Ronald, 11502
Dye, John S., 5603
Dye, Thomas R., 12654
Dyer, Brainerd, 3294, 3318
Dyer, Oliver, 2723
Dyer, Stanford P., 10907, 10908
Dyer, Thomas G., 6546, 6547

Eads, George C., 12858, 12859
Eagle, Hazel, 10207
Eagles, Charles W., 9107
Ealy, Lawrence O., 9955, 11259
Early, Ruth H., 1216
East, Ernest E., 5275
East, Robert A., 855, 2583
Easterbrook, Gregg, 12655
Eastman, Fred, 1095
Easton, Nina, 12625, 13103
Eaton, Clement, 1435, 1908, 2851
Eaton, Doris A., 7488
Eaton, Dorman, 5858
Eaton, Dorothy S., 768
Eaton, Edward B., 4152
Eaton, John, 4211, 5757
Eaton, John H., 2724-2727, 2752
Eaton, Richard O., 9217
Eaton, Vincent L., 3946
Eaton, William D., 7289
Ebel, Henry, 12126, 12127
Eberle, Louise, 6452

Eberly, Susan K., 9956
Echeverri-Gent, Elisavinda, 12991
Eckenrode, Hamilton J., 5794
Eckert, Edward K., 5702
Eckhardt, William, 10665
Eckley, Wilton, 8046
Eckstein, Otto, 11178
Ecroyd, Donald H., 10208
Edelman, Toby S., 12656
Edgar, David, 12860
Edmonds, Franklin S., 5604
Edmunds, George F., 5899
Edson, Susan A., 5924
Edward, C., 1665
Edwards, Elisha J., 4085
Edwards, Everett E., 1296, 1297
Edwards, George B., 7126
Edwards, Herbert J., 4050
Edwards, John, 8201, 12442
Edwards, Lee, 12565
Edwards, Mike W., 1714
Edwards, Richard E., 8202
Edwards, Robert V., 9445
Egan, Clifford, 1096
Egan, Maurice F., 6548
Egleton, Clive, 9783
Egloff, Franklin R., 6360
Ehlke, Richard C., 12657
Ehrenreich, Barbara, 12861
Ehrlichman, John, 11503
Ehrmann, Bess V., 3693, 4704
Ehrmann, Max, 4343
Eichner, Alfred S., 13075
Eiland, Millard F., 11866
Eilberg, Joshua, 11867
Einaudi, Mario, 9007
Einhorn, Jessica P., 11504
Einhorn, Lois J., 2400
Einstein, Lewis, 6361
Eiselen, Malcolm R., 7457, 8570
Eisen, Gustavus A., 436, 437
Eisendrath, Joseph L., Jr., 3784, 5063, 5276
Eisenhower, David, 9744, 11505
Eisenhower, Dwight D., 10012-10028
Eisenhower, Julie N., 11388, 11505
Eisenschiml, Otto, 4811-4813
Eitler, Anita T., 6694
Ekirch, Arthur A., 6645, 9008, 9784, 10209
Elazar, Daniel J., 4115
Eleazer, Frank, 10498
Elias, Edith, 3511
Eliasberg, W. G., 8408
Eliot, Charles W., 566, 7148
Eliot, Christopher R., 5195
Eliot, George F., 10560
Ellesin, Dorothy E., 438
Elletson, D. H., 7388, 8571
Ellett, Katherine T., 3169

Ellingwood, Albert R., 9009
Elliot, Jeffrey M., 10337
Elliott, Bruce, 10816
Elliott, Margaret R. A., 7203
Ellis, Edward S., 1097, 1217, 6236, 6261, 6284, 6362
Ellis, Ivan C., 567
Ellis, Richard E., 2186
Ellsberg, Daniel, 11322
Ellsworth, Clayton S., 6695
Ellsworth, Edward W., 4490
Ellsworth, John W., 925
Elmore, Harry, 4705
Elovitz, Paul H., 12128
Elshtain, Jean B., 12180
Elson, Henry W., 6309
Elwood, Roger, 12576
Ely, James W., Jr., 2793, 2794
Elzy, Martin I., 11008
Emerich, Duncan, 9745
Emerson, Edwin, 8047
Emerson, William, 9108
Emery, Edwin, 11249
Emery, Noemi, 30
Emling, Diane C., 12862
Emme, Eugene M., 11179
Emmons, William, 3059
Emsley, Bert, 5064
Endy, Melvin B., Jr., 4276
Enera, Stephen Van, 13084
Engel, Bernard F., 4814
Engelman, Rose C., 568
England, George A., 170
English, H. Edward, 11679
Enright, S. M., 13104
Ensor, Allison R., 3947
Entman, Robert M., 12241
Epstein, Edward J., 10417, 10418, 11680
Erickson, Gary L., 4277
Erickson, Keith V., 12181
Ericson, Eston E., 4568
Erikkson, Erik H., 7290
Eriksson, Erik M., 2596, 2795, 2956-2958, 3338, 8956
Ershkowitz, Herbert, 2975
Erskine, Hazel G., 10210
Erskine, Helen W., 9785, 11437
Esterow, Milton, 439
Esthus, Raymond A., 6843, 6844, 7037, 9109
Etheredge, Lloyd S., 12182, 12658
Ettlinger, Catherine, 11506
Etzioni, Amitai, 10666, 10667, 11507, 12659
Eubanks, Seaford W., 1450
Eulau, Heinz, 9010, 9922
Eulenberg, Herbert, 309
Evans, Edith R., 1715
Evans, John W., 10668
Evans, Joseph F., 4344

Evans, M. Stanton, 10211, 12660
Evans, Medford, 9746
Evans, Nelson W., 521, 522
Evans, Rowland, Jr., 10817, 11508, 12008, 12661
Evans, Sam T., 3827
Evans, William A., 3828
Evans, William B., 926
Evening Star, Washington, DC, 10212
Everett, Edward, 31, 2597
Everett, Edwin M., 171
Everett, Robert B., 3245
Everman, Henry E., 8128
Ewald, William B., Jr., 9786
Ewing, Elbert W. R., 5900
Ewing, Thomas, 3185
Exner, Judith, 10092
Eyre, James K., 8877
Ezell, John S., 7291
Ezell, Macel D., 11181

Faber, Doris, 8467, 9218
Fabian, Bernhard, 1543
Fabian, Monroe H., 3140
Fabricant, Noah D., 8409-8411
Fagan, George V., 8878
Fagan, Myron C., 10213, 10214
Fagen, Richard R., 12443
Fagin, Vernon A., 8749
Fairbanks, Avard T., 3694
Fairbanks, James D., 9787, 12662
Faircloth, Ronald W., 2959
Fairfield, Louis W., 334
Fairlie, Henry, 10215, 11009
Faith, Samuel J., 10216
Falk, Gerhard, 7996
Falk, Jay, 10125
Falk, Richard A., 12009
Falkner, Leonard, 998
Fallert, J. Cecilia, 10737
Fallows, James, 10536, 10855, 11010, 11510
Fallows, Samuel, 6237
Faltermayer, Edmund K., 11250
Fancher, Betsy, 8412
Fanta, J. Julius, 10217
Farber, Joseph C., 1098, 1104
Farley, Foster M., 3428
Farley, James A., 8572, 8573
Farley, Philip J., 13073, 13074
Farmer, Frances, 7731
Farnell, Robert S., 569, 927, 1544, 2401
Farnell, Stewart, 1013
Farnen, Russell F., Jr., 5703
Farnsworth, David, 9788
Farnum, George R., 2626, 2627, 5704, 5795, 6214
Farrand, Max, 570, 2348
Farrar, Broadus F., 6453
Farrar, Ronald, 9310, 9311
Farrell, Brian, 2796

Farrell, Nancy, 700
Farrell, Robert E., 11958
Farrelly, David G., 9446
Farrington, Harry W., 32, 4491, 6697
Farrington, John P., 10561, 11182
Farrison, W. Edward, 1411
Farriss, Charles S., 33, 4492, 6698
Fatton, Robert, 12992
Faulkner, Harold U., 6136
Fausold, Martin L., 8203-8205
Faust, A. B., 2598
Faust, Richard H., 2797
Fawcett, Waldon, 6699-6701
Fay, Bernard, 34, 8335
Fay, Paul B., 10042
Feaver, John H., 9524
Feder, Donald, 9011
Fedler, Fred, 10218
Fehrenbach, T. R., 9110
Fehrenbacher, Don E., 4116, 4493-4496, 4624, 4625, 4706, 4707, 5117, 5118, 5168, 5196, 5277, 5278
Feigenbaum, Edward D., 12011, 12183
Feinberg, Barbara S., 8336
Feingold, Henry L., 9111-9113
Feinman, Jeffrey, 11959
Feis, Herbert, 8574, 9114
Feis, Ruth S., 5967
Feldberg, Michael, 2960
Feldman, Elliot J., 12444
Feldman, Jacob J., 10472, 10617, 10618, 11734, 11735
Feldman, Lily G., 12444
Felkins, Patricia K., 10219, 11516
Felknor, Bruce, 10607, 11511
Feller, Daniel, 2961
Feller, John Q., Jr., 6702
Fellman, Michael, 2852
Felton, John, 12663, 12993
Fendall, Lonny W., 6845
Fenno, Richard F., Jr., 7974, 9115
Fenton, Charles, 6549
Ferdon, Nona S., 8413
Ferguson, Charles W., 6550
Ferguson, Duncan, 4569
Ferguson, Eugene S., 2042
Ferguson, Henry N., 1498
Ferguson, Robert A., 1545
Ferguson, William J., 4815, 4816
Ferlege, Herbert R., 6883
Ferling, John E., 928
Ferlinghetti, Lawrence, 11389
Ferrari, Alfred J., 10419
Ferrell, Robert H., 7389, 7700, 7997, 8206, 9219, 9312, 9313, 9525, 9526, 9644-9646, 9789, 10029
Ferretti, Fred, 12012
Ferris, George T., 6077
Ferriter, Tom, 12377

Fesler, James W., 8129
Fesperman, Francis I., 1219
Fess, Simeon D., 372, 373, 7998
Feuerlicht, Roberta, 6363
Feuerwerger, Marvin C., 12013, 12014
Ficken, Robert E., 7883, 8820
Field, Rudolph, 9682, 9683
Fielding, Mantle, 441, 442, 479
Fields, Joseph E., 260
Fifield, Russell H., 7553
Fillmore, Millard, 3352-3355, 4497
Finch, Edward R., 8575
Finch, Gerald B., 11868
Findley, Paul, 4551, 5279
Fine, Robert S., 8576
Fine, Sidney, 6285, 8770
Finegold, Kenneth, 12863
Finger, Charles J., 6364
Finger, Seymour M., 12994
Fink, Gary M., 9265, 12148
Finkelnburg, G. A., 1436
Finn, Chester E., 12864
Fiore, Jordan D., 4345
Firestone, Bernard J., 10669, 10670
Fischer, David H., 929, 1909
Fischer, John, 9314, 10220, 10608, 11723
Fischer, Leroy H., 4212, 4708, 4891, 4892
Fischer, Raymond L., 12184
Fischer, Robert, 6703, 7038
Fish, Carl R., 35, 2962, 4278, 4709
Fish, Daniel, 4626
Fish, Hamilton, 631, 8337, 9116
Fish, Peter G., 6986
Fisher, Aileen L., 3829
Fisher, Anne B., 13105
Fisher, Donald C., 9447
Fisher, Everett, 5990
Fisher, George P., 1546
Fisher, Linda L., 11011
Fisher, Louis, 6137
Fisher, Marvin, 1547
Fisher, N., 571
Fisher, Walter R., 12664
Fishlow, Albert, 12445
Fishwick, Marshall W., 1099
Fiske, Daniel W., 4817
Fitzgerald, Frances, 11785
Fitzgerald, Gordon, 10221
Fitzgerrell, James J., 4279
FitzPatrick, Benedict, 443
Fitzpatrick, John C., 36, 172, 173, 261, 335, 702, 770
Fitzsimons, Louise, 10222
Fix, Michael, 12858, 12859
Fixler, Philip E., Jr., 10223, 11012, 11512
Flagg, Norman G., 3695
Flanagan, Vincent, 37
Flaningam, Carl D., 11438

Flannelly, Margaret E., 9801, 10224
Flansbury, James, 12377
Flatto, Elie, 11869
Flavius, Brother, 10043
Fleckles, Elliot, 4280
Fleischman, Richard K., 5197
Fleisher, Richard, 12185, 12665
Fleming, Denna F., 7612
Fleming, Thomas J., 38, 771, 1100, 1499, 1716, 3948
Flemings, Corinne K., 6704
Fleser, Arthur F., 7975-7977
Flexner, James T., 39-43, 632
Flick, Alexander C., 572
Flick, Rachel, 12666
Flinn, Thomas A., 10609, 11724
Florance, Valerie, 12865
Floto, Igwa, 7670
Flower, B. O., 1956
Flowers, Ronald B., 12186
Floyd, Mildred D., 2109
Flynn, Edward J., 8577
Flynn, George Q., 8578, 8879, 8880
Flynn, John T., 8579-8581
Fogelman, Edwin, 9416
Fohlen, Claude, 8881
Foley, Hamilton, 7613
Foley, John P., 1220, 1221
Foley, William E., 2149
Folliard, Edward T., 7390
Foner, Eric, 4086, 5492
Foote, Henry W., 1620, 1621
Forbes, Jack D., 11681
Ford, Betty, 11960
Ford, Gerald R., 12086-12101
Ford, Henry J., 573, 6138, 7149
Ford, John, 6551
Ford, Paul L., 44-46, 1101, 1451, 1853, 2234
Ford, Susan, 885, 1342
Ford, Worthington C., 47, 174, 1102, 1602, 1717, 1991, 2628-2630, 5280
Forgie, George B., 4087
Forman, Samuel E., 2235
Forman, Sidney, 2043
Fornoff, Charles W., 2402
Forrest, W. M., 1622
Forsythe, Robert S., 2853
Fortenbaugh, Robert, 336
Fosdick, Raymond B., 7204
Foster, Bertram G., 3696
Foster, Franklin P., 1910
Foster, G. Allen, 5493
Foster, Genevieve, 48, 3512, 6365
Foster, Herbert D., 3319
Foster, Lillian, 5402
Foulke, William D., 6705
Fowler, John G., Jr., 9747
Fowler, Robert H., 9315, 11015

Fowler, Samuel, 1548
Fowler, W. Gary, 12667
Fowler, Wilton B., 7554
Fowlkes, Frank V., 11682
Fox, Dixon R., 374, 633
Fox, Douglas M., 10500, 11183, 11513
Fox, Edward J., 4117
Fox, Mary V., 12566
Fox, Sylvan, 10421
Fox-Genovese, Elizabeth, 2798
Frady, Marshall, 11016
Fraenkel, Ernest, 7576
Fragomen, Austin T., Jr., 12295
Francesconi, Robert A., 7732
Franck, Thomas M., 11260, 11278
Franck, Timothy D., 5859
Frank, Alan, 12567
Frank, Glenn, 7843
Frank, John P., 4570, 5119
Frank, Richard S., 12017
Frankel, Max, 11017
Frankfurter, Felix, 8582, 8583
Frankie, Richard J., 7489
Franklin, Francis, 1911
Franklin, John H., 4118, 4119, 5198
Franklin, Mitchell, 2110, 2111, 9117
Franko, Lawrence G., 12446
Franks, Kenny A., 6454
Frantz, Joe B., 10818-10820, 11018
Frary, Ihna T., 1316
Fraser, Hugh R., 2963, 3186
Frassanito, William A., 5705
Fratianni, Michel, 11687
Frazier, Carl, 4346
Fredericks, Janet P., 10856
Fredman, Lionel E., 999, 2473
Fredrickson, George M., 4498, 5199
Freed, Fred, 9417
Freedman, Robert O., 12447
Freedman, Tracy, 12866
Freeland, Richard M., 9624
Freeley, Austin J., 9118, 9923
Freeman, Andrew A., 4347
Freeman, Douglas S., 49, 50, 539
Freese, Paul L., 10422
Freidel, Frank B., 2044, 2964, 6286, 6287, 8338, 8414-8416, 8771, 9012, 9790, 10225
Freidell, Theodore D., 9527
Freidin, Seymour, 10226
Freidman, Leon, 11870
Fremont-Smith, E., 11961
French, Charles W., 3513
Freshly, Dwight L., 5424
Freud, Sigmund, 7140, 7150
Fried, Albert, 1912, 5281
Friedlander, Robert A., 6846
Friedman, Irving I., 9684
Friel, Charlotte, 11725

Friend, Henry C., 3697
Frier, David A., 9791
Frierson, William L., 5494
Fries, Sylvia D., 4710
Frisch, Morton J., 4120, 8584, 8585, 8772, 9013
Frishauer, Willi, 10093
Fritchey, Clayton, 10227, 10562, 11019, 11261
Fritchman, Stephen H., 1103
Fritz, Sara, 12668, 12669
Frolick, S. J., 10228
Frost, David, 11439
Frost, John, 51, 52, 2728, 2729, 3295, 3296
Frost, Lawrence A., 5605
Frothingham, Thomas G., 703
Fry, Bobby J., 11683
Fry, Brian R., 11871
Fry, Joseph A., 704, 6288
Fry, Joseph R., 3297
Fry, Norman E., 5860
Fry, Richard T., 6847
Fuchs, Douglas, 12600
Fuchs, Lawrence H., 10229, 10610, 10611
Fuertsch, David F., 11184
Fuess, Claude M., 7922, 7923, 7945
Fujita, Fumiko, 3246, 3429
Fuller, Cheryl E. S., 12018
Fuller, Corydon E., 6018
Fuller, Daniel J., 9528
Fuller, Helen, 10501, 10612
Fuller, John D. P., 3247
Fuller, John F. C., 5706, 5707
Fuller, Melville W., 1913
Funk, A. B., 4088
Funk, Arthur L., 9748, 9749
Furlow, Barbara, 11020, 11514
Fusfeld, Daniel R., 9014, 9015

Gabelle, James, 401
Gable, John A., 6552, 6553, 6706
Gabriel, Ralph H., 1549
Gaddis, John L., 9529, 9625
Gadney, Reg, 10044
Gaffey, Margaret Y., 7170
Gahn, Bessie W., 262
Gaines, Anne-Rosewell J., 7555
Gaines, William H., Jr., 7205, 7206, 7391
Galbraith, John K., 8586, 9016, 11021, 12867
Galbreath, C. B., 375, 523, 2150, 5671, 7823, 7844
Gall, Peter, 11706
Gallagher, Hugh G., 8417, 8418, 8587
Gallagher, Mary B., 10094
Gallardo, Florence, 3830
Gallois, Pierre, 11022
Galloway, John, 10672
Galloway, Linda B., 2799
Galloway, Russell W., Jr., 8957
Gallu, Samuel, 9252
Gammans, Harold W., 3950

Gammill, Patrick D., 11684
Ganin, Zvi, 9609
Ganoe, John T., 8958
Gansler, Jacques S., 13076
Ganter, Herbert L., 1379, 1550
Gantt, Fred, 11023
Gantz, Walter, 12670
Garbett, Arthur S., 1343
Garcia, George F., 8130, 8207
Gardner, Gerald C., 10747, 10748, 12187
Gardner, Joseph L., 2236, 6455
Gardner, Lloyd C., 9017, 9530, 11786
Gardner, Robert W., 8959
Garfield, Gene J., 9531
Garfield, Harry A., 7207
Garfield, James A., 6019-6032
Garfield, James R., 6707
Garfinkle, Adam M., 13077
Garland, Claude M., 444
Garland, Hamlin, 5606, 5607, 6456, 6457
Garner, James W., 7392
Garner, Wayne L., 3698
Garraghan, Gilbert J., 376
Garrard, Daniel, 3152
Garraty, John A., 6366, 6458, 7151, 7208, 7209, 8588
Garrett, Stephen A., 11787
Garrett, Wendell D., 886, 1104, 1222
Garrison, Curtis W., 5861, 5880
Garrison, Elisha E., 6708, 6709, 7490
Garrison, Frank W., 1551
Garrison, Jim, 10230
Garson, Robert, 9316
Garten, Jeffrey E., 13106
Gartner, Alan, 11515, 12671
Garvey, Daniel E., 8131
Gass, Oscar, 10231, 10232, 11685
Gatell, Frank O., 3077
Gates, Arnold F., 3699, 3900, 4818
Gates, Gary P., 11825
Gatewood, Willard B., Jr., 6710-6717, 7096, 7292, 7293, 7491
Gaus, John M., 8208
Gauss, Charles E., 1344
Gaver, Jessyca R., 12129
Gawthrop, Louis C., 7492
Gay, Donovan L., 10423
Gay, James T., 3141, 6703
Gay, Sydney H., 2327
Gazit, Mordechai, 10673
Geary, James W., 5282
Gebhardt, Joseph D., 11863
Geddes, Donald, 8339
Geelhoed, E. Bruce, 9792
Geer, Emily A., 5807-5811
Geimer, William S., 12868
Gelb, Leslie H., 11262, 12995
Gelders, Ruth B., 1345

Gelfand, Lawrence E., 7556, 8048
Gelfand, Mark I., 11202
Gelineau, Elaine P., 12188, 12378, 12944
Gellman, Irwin F., 8882
Genco, Stephen J., 9957
Genizi, Haim, 8589
Genung, John F., 4499
George, Alexander L., 7152, 7210, 7212, 7294, 7340
George, Elsie L., 8590, 9317
George, Joseph, Jr., 5145-5147, 5283
George, Juliette L., 7152, 7210-7212, 7340
George, Marian M., 705, 3514
Georgiady, Nicholas P., 1105
Gerard, James W., 7557
Gerberg, Mort, 12869
Gergen, David, 12189
Gerjuoy, Edward, 12996
German, James C., Jr., 6718, 7039
Germond, Jack, 12379, 12945, 12961
Gernon, Blaine B., 3831, 4348, 4711
Gerry, Margarita S., 2800, 4213, 5495
Gershenson, Alvin H., 10563
Gershman, Carl, 12448
Gerson, Louis L., 7558
Gerson, Noel B., 2349, 5496
Gertz, Elmer, 8821, 10424
Gervasi, Frank, 8132
Gerwig, George W., 53
Gettleman, Marvin E., 11281
Geyelin, Philip, 11024, 11788
Ghanayem, Ishaq I., 11789
Ghent, Jocelyn, 10674
Ghent, W. J., 4121
Gholson, Sam C., 5812
Giampietro, Wayne B., 10424
Gibbs, George, 707, 1000
Gibbs, William E., 5862
Gibson, Hugh, 8083, 8311, 8312
Gibson, James W., 11516
Gibson, Scott L., 6554
Gibson, William M., 6555
Giddens, Paul H., 4819
Gienapp, William E., 5284
Gies, Joseph, 8340, 9220
Giglio, James N., 8133, 9253, 9318
Gilbert, C. E., 4972
Gilbert, Clinton W., 7999
Gilbert, Robert E., 10564
Gilder, Joseph B., 6556
Gilder, Richard W., 4712, 4713, 6078, 6079
Gilderhus, Mark T., 7559, 7647, 7648
Gilfond, Duff, 7924
Gill, William J., 12965
Gillam, Victor, 6289
Gillespie, Veronica M., 6557
Gillett, William, 5758
Gilley, B. H., 3248

Gillis, James A., 6139
Gillman, Katherine, 12886
Gilman, Bradley, 6558
Gilman, Daniel C., 2521, 2522
Gilmore, James R., 4973, 5936
Gilmore, William J., 7213
Gilpin, Henry D., 1106
Gimlin, Hoyt, 11025
Ginger, Ann F., 11517
Ginsberg, Eli, 11282
Ginzl, David J., 8209-8212
Giovannitti, Len, 9417
Gipson, Lawrence H., 5497
Girling, John L. S., 11790, 12449, 12997
Gist, John R., 12822
Gittleman, Edwin, 1818
Giusti, James R., 8591
Glad, Betty, 12380, 12998
Glad, Paul W., 6290, 7978
Gladstone, Kerana, 7946
Gladstone, Leslie, 12672
Glaros, Roberta, 12673
Glaser, David P., 7649
Glass, Andrew J., 11482, 11518, 11686, 11791, 11872
Glastris, Paul, 12774
Glazer, Nathan, 11663
Glazier, Kenneth M., 7295
Gleason, D. H. L., 4820
Gleason, Gene, 887
Glenn, James A., 7824
Glick, Wendell, 2631
Glinka-Janczewski, George H., 9532
Gloneck, James F., 4893, 5444
Glover, Richard, 2474
Glover, Waldo F., 4714
Godden, Jean H., 12381
Godden, Richard, 10565
Godfrey, Gordon, 9750
Goebel, Dorothy B., 3125
Goetcheus, Vernon M., 11026
Goetsch, Charles C., 6559
Goff, David H., 12870
Goff, Frederick R., 1223
Goff, John S., 6053
Goff, Linda D., 12870
Goff, Reda C., 2801
Goldberg, Jeffrey, 10425
Goldberg, M. Hirsh, 2965
Goldberg, Philip A., 11251
Goldberg, Richard T., 8419
Goldberg, Stephen H., 1854
Goldbloom, Maurice J., 11519
Golden, Harry L., 10566
Golden, Howard J., 12835
Golden, James L., 10233
Goldhurst, Richard, 5608
Goldman, Alex J., 10426, 10749

Goldman, Eliot, 8592
Goldman, Emma, 6291
Goldman, Eric F., 7701, 10613, 10821, 11027, 11726
Goldman, Sheldon, 9793, 10234, 11028, 11520, 12674
Goldsmith, B. H., 6459
Goldsmith, Marcus A., 4388
Goldwater, Barry M., 11521
Goll, Eugene W., 9018
Golladay, V. Dennis, 1224
Golson, Barry, 12142
Gonchar, Ruth M., 11522
Gonya, Gary J., 5863
Gooch, Robert K., 1718, 2045
Good, Douglas, 4715
Good, H. G., 772, 2584
Goode, Cecil E., 525
Goodell, Stephen, 7560
Goodfellow, Donald M., 2599
Goodfellow, Guy F., 8000
Goodhart, Arthur L., 4571, 10427, 10428
Goodman, Florence J., 5065
Goodman, James A., 12675
Goodman, James F., 4281
Goodman, John L., 12676
Goodman, Mark, 9254
Goodman, Nathan G., 1107
Goodpasture, Albert V., 3212
Goodrich, Frederick E., 6115
Goodspeed, Edgar J., 1623
Goodstein, Marvin, 13142
Goodwin, Doris K., 11298
Goodwin, Maud W., 2350
Goodwin, Paul G., 6719
Goodwin, Philo A., 2730
Gorden, William L., 10857
Gordon, Armistead C., 3170
Gordon, Charles U., 6257
Gordon, Donald C., 6720
Gordon, Leonard, 4716
Gordon, Michael R., 12777, 12999
Gordy, Wilbur F., 3515
Gore, John R., 4440
Gores, Stan, 6560
Gosnell, Harold F., 6561, 8822, 9221
Goss, Dwight, 4717
Gotlieb, Howard B., 3187
Gott, Joseph W., 634
Gottlieb, Amy Z., 9533
Gottlieb, Kevin C., 7214
Gottschalk, Peter T., 12296
Gottschall, Jon S., 11523, 12190
Gould, A., 12677
Gould, Elizabeth P., 888
Gould, Jean, 8420
Gould, Levi S., 4214
Gould, Lewis L., 6292, 6293, 6562, 7040

Gould, William D., 1624
Goulden, Joseph C., 11323
Goulding, Phil G., 11324
Govan, Thomas P., 1914, 2966, 2967
Gow, Douglas P., 6848
Graber, Doris A., 9626, 9958
Grabill, Joseph L., 7561
Graebner, Norman A., 3249-3251, 4122, 4123, 4718, 9534, 9535, 9794, 12191, 12678
Graf, LeRoy P., 5445, 5569
Graff, Henry F., 1108, 11029, 11030, 11325
Graff, Polly A. C., 1819
Graff, Steward, 6460
Gragg, Larry, 2968
Graham, Daniel O., 13107
Graham, Donald, 11964
Graham, Otis L., 8341, 9019, 9020
Graham, Pearl M., 1412
Graham, Sally H., 7493
Grampp, William D., 1552
Granato, Leonard A., 1603
Grant, Frederick D., 5672, 5673
Grant, Jesse R., 5609, 5674, 5675
Grant, Philip A., Jr., 7702, 8750, 9266, 9924
Grant, Ulysses S., 177, 3701, 5778-5787
Grant, Ulysses S., III, 5610
Grantham, Dewey W., Jr., 6367, 6461, 6721
Grattan, C. Hartley, 7671
Gravlee, Grady J., 8503, 8823
Gray, Arthur, 263
Gray, Charles H., 10141, 10909
Gray, Colin S., 9959, 9960
Gray, Francis C., 1225
Gray, Giles W., 1719
Gray, William C., 3516
Grayson, A. G., 9319
Grayson, Benson L., 3344
Grayson, Cary T., 7215
Greeley, Horace, 4215, 4389
Greely, Arthur W., 1666
Green, Barbara, 11881
Green, Bill, 12823
Green, Cleveland M., 7494
Green, Colin, 11515, 12671
Green, Fletcher M., 2969, 4894
Green, Francis M., 5937
Green, Harold P., 9877
Green, Horace, 5611, 7925, 7947, 7948, 8001
Green, James A., 3126
Green, John W., 2802
Green, Joseph, Jr., 10235
Green, Mark, 12679, 12680
Green, Thomas L., 8593
Greenberg, Bradley S., 10429, 10430
Greenberg, Daniel S., 11032, 11185
Greenberg, Jack, 12946
Greene, Bob, 11728
Greene, Francis V., 4974

Greene, John C., 1667, 1668
Greene, L. LeRoy, 377
Greene, Peter, 3702
Greenfield, Meg, 11033
Greenspan, Alan, 11034
Greenstein, Fred I., 9795, 9796, 11034, 11873, 12297, 12681
Greenwood, Isaac J., 445
Greer, Thomas H., 8594
Gregen, David R., 12683
Gregg, Gail, 13108
Gregg, Richard B., 11792
Gressley, Gene M., 8960
Greve, Charles T., 6974
Grey, Lennox, 889
Gribben, William J., 12021, 12382
Gribbin, William, 930
Grice, George L., 11326
Gridley, Eleanor, 3517
Grieb, Kenneth J., 7884, 7885
Grierson, Francis, 4282, 4500
Griese, Noel L., 9925
Griffin, Appleton P. C., 446
Griffin, Clifford S., 11440
Griffin, Daniel L., 12192
Griffin, Martin I. J., 337
Griffin, Robert P., 11035, 11807
Griffin, Solomon B., 7216
Griffis, William E., 3334
Griffith, Albert H., 3703, 3951
Griffith, Robert, 9320, 9797, 9798
Griffith, William, 6722
Griffiths, David R., 12824
Grim, Marvin P., 1302
Grimes, Gail, 3187
Grimsley, Elizabeth T., 3832
Grinde, R. Dale, 10728
Grinnell, Frank W., 931
Griswald, Ralph E., 1329
Griswold, A. Whitney, 1298, 1720, 1915, 1916
Griswold, Rufus W., 178
Grob, Gerald N., 3901
Groden, Robert J., 10457
Gromyko, Anatolii A., 10236
Gronet, Richard W., 2558
Gross, Anthony, 5285
Gross, Bertram M., 9448, 11283
Gross, Edwin K., 7845
Gross, K. Frederick, 179
Gross, Richard E., 9119
Grossack, Irvin M., 11687
Grossett, Dan, 11536
Grossman, Richard L., 10237
Grosvenor, Charles H., 6238
Grothaus, Larry, 9449
Grout, Josiah, 4390
Grover, Leonard, 4051
Groves, Harold M., 12298

Gruber, Michael, 3518
Grunwald, Henry, 13000
Gruyters, Hans, 11729
Guedalla, Philip, 378, 9120
Guernsey, A. H., 1413
Guerra, David M., 11524
Guerrant, Edward O., 8049, 8595, 8883
Guerrero, Linda D., 932
Guffey, Joseph F., 8596
Guilfoyle, James H., 8824
Guinness, Desmond, 1317, 1318
Gulliver, Hal, 11745
Gummere, Richard M., 890
Gunderson, Robert G., 3704, 4572, 4719, 5087
Gunn, John W., 5286
Gunther, Gerald, 11874
Gunther, John, 8342, 8421, 9685
Gurley, James L., 1625
Gurley, Phineas D., 4821
Gurney, Clare, 8422
Gurney, Gene, 8422
Gustafson, Merlin, 8213, 9321, 9322, 9722
Gustafson, Milton O., 2559
Gustainis, J. Justin, 12194
Guth, James L., 8134
Guthrie, Blaine A., Jr., 2560
Gutierrez, Arturo, 11186
Gutman, Richard J. S., 3952
Guy, William L., 11036
Guzzardi, Walter, 12871
Guzzetta, Charles, 1721

Habberton, John, 54
Haber, Paul, 8423
Habibuddin, Syed M., 6723, 6724, 8884
Hackensmith, C. W., 3833
Hacker, Andrew, 10997
Hacker, Jeffrey H., 8343
Hackett, Charles W., 2662
Hadden, John, 635
Hadley, Charles D., 8634
Hadley, David J., 11856
Hadwiger, Don F., 10567
Haerdter, Robert, 3705
Hafner, Donald L., 10537
Hagan, Horace H., 2403
Hagan, William T., 6563
Hagedorn, Hermann, 6368, 6369, 6462-6465, 6725
Hagen, Olaf T., 6466
Hager, L. Michael, 11875
Hager, Paul A., 5425
Hagstrom, Jerry, 12400
Hah, Chong-do, 9450
Hahn, Dan F., 5088, 10238, 11522, 12022, 12193, 12194, 12299, 12383
Hahn, Harlan, 7041
Hahn, Walter F., 11793
Haider, Donald H., 12023

Haig, Alexander M., 13001
Haight, David, 9961
Haight, John M., Jr., 8885, 9121-9123
Haight, Timothy R., 11525
Haines, Charles G., 1917
Haines, Gerald K., 8886, 8887
Halasz, Nicholas, 8344
Halberstam, David, 10239, 10822, 11037
Halbert, Sherrill, 5120, 5121
Halda, M. K., 10715
Haldeman, Harry R., 11526
Hale, Annie R., 6370
Hale, David, 13002, 13109
Hale, Edward E., 55, 1109, 3115
Hale, William B., 6726, 7153-7155, 7393
Hale, William H., 8598
Halevy, Daniel, 7156
Haley, James E., 10910
Haley, John W., 180
Haley, P. Edward, 7042, 7650, 11263
Halford, E. W., 3158
Hall, Abraham O., 5089
Hall, Alvin L., 8751
Hall, Clifton R., 5446
Hall, Edward H., 2527
Hall, Gordon L., 1414, 10095, 12130
Hall, Gus, 11527
Hall, J. Leslie, 1626
Hall, James, 3127
Hall, Kermit L., 2970
Hall, Perry D., 11921
Hall, Richard, 1553
Hall, Robert N., 10911-10913
Hall, Tom G., Jr., 7495, 7496, 8135
Hall, William, 5760
Hallam, John S., 447
Hallett, Douglas, 11528
Hallett, George H., Jr., 8599
Hallgren, Mauritz A., 8600
Halperin, Bernard S., 5498
Halperin, Morton H., 9799, 11187, 11794
Halperin, Samuel, 8888
Halsey, Robert H., 2046
Halstead, Albert, 6727
Halstead, Murat, 3430, 4895, 6239, 6371
Halsted, James A., 8424
Hambrecht, George P., 3706, 4391
Hamby, Alonzo L., 9021, 9323-9325, 9451-9453
Hamill, John, 8050
Hamilton, Alexander, 1001
Hamilton, Charles, 4153, 4896, 10240
Hamilton, Dagmar S., 11038, 11115
Hamilton, David E., 8214
Hamilton, Gary G., 12593
Hamilton, Holman, 3298, 3308, 3311, 3312, 3320, 3321, 3953, 4501, 4720
Hamilton, James A., 3078
Hamilton, James W., 11876

Hamilton, Joseph G. de Roulhac, 891, 1426-1428, 1554, 1627, 1722, 2237, 4502, 4503
Hamilton, Mary A., 3519
Hamilton, Stanislaus M., 574
Hamlett, J. Arthur, 5200
Hamm, Michael J., 12024
Hammersmith, Jack L., 8889
Hammett, Hugh B., 6140
Hammond, Bray, 2971, 2972
Hammond, Michael E., 12300, 12451
Hamowy, Ronald, 1820
Hampton, Vernon B., 8084
Han, Yung-Chul, 12452
Hanaford, Phebe A., 3520
Hanby, Alice L. H., 4721
Hanchett, William, 2187, 4822-4824
Hancock, Harold B., 708
Hancock, Morris H., 56
Hancock, Sibyl, 6372
Hand, Samuel B., 9022
Handford, Thomas, 6116, 6373
Handler, Edward, 892, 933
Handlin, Lilian, 3521
Handlin, Oscar, 3521, 9800
Handy, Edward S. C., 7497
Haney, James E., 6728
Hanff, Helene, 10045
Hankin, C. A., 9023
Hankins, John E., 4050
Hanna, William F., III., 4349, 4350, 4975, 5148
Hannaford, Peter, 12568
Hannah, Mary E., 5287
Hannon, Stuart L., 4216
Hans, Nicholas, 1957
Hansen, Erik A., 10241
Hansen, Laurence J., 9751
Hanson, Galen A., 10242
Hapgood, Norman, 57, 709, 3522, 4504
Haraszti, Zoltan, 448, 449, 773, 774, 856, 1628
Harbaugh, William H., 6374, 7703
Harberger, Arnold C., 12195
Harbison, Winfred A., 4722, 4897
Harbord, James G., 6564
Harbrecht, Rosemary, 1346
Hard, William, 8051, 8215
Harding, H. F., 11252
Harding, Warren G., 7913-7915
Hardison, Edwin T., 5447
Hardy, O., 5709
Hareven, Tamara K., 8468
Hargrove, Erwin C., 6729, 12196
Harkness, David J., 4052-4054
Harlan, Edgar R., 3707, 5288
Harlow, Alvin F., 6375
Harlow, Bryce, 9802
Harmon, Joseph, 5968
Harney, Gilbert, 6215
Haron, Miriam J., 9610

Harper, Alan D., 9454
Harper, Ellahue A., 4573
Harper, George M., 7733
Harper, Robert S., 4976, 5149
Harrell, Jackson, 11877
Harrelson, Elmer H., 8601
Harrington, Joseph F., 10675
Harrington, Michael, 11327, 11663, 12197
Harris, Alfred G., 5201-5204
Harris, Carlton D., 338
Harris, Edward A., 9267
Harris, Estelle, 264
Harris, H. Wilson, 7157, 7394
Harris, Louis, 10243
Harris, Mark, 11441
Harris, Mary M., 4217
Harris, Ramon, 1229
Harris, Ray B., 7846, 7847
Harris, Seymour E., 9803, 10244, 10568
Harris, Sheldon H., 4898
Harris, William C., 5864
Harrison, Benjamin, 6227-6232, 7562
Harrison, Cynthia E., 10569
Harrison, James A., 58
Harrison, James T., 5426
Harrison, Joseph H., Jr., 3079
Harrison, Lowell H., 2047, 2238, 3188, 4825, 4977, 5205
Harrison, Mary L., 1230
Harrison, Michael M., 13003
Harrison, Richard A., 8752, 8890
Harrison, Selig S., 10615, 10914, 11039
Harrison, William H., 3163-3166
Harriss, C. Lowell, 13110
Harrity, Richard, 8345, 8469
Harrold, Frances L., 1555, 1992
Hart, Albert B., 59-62, 265, 710, 6883
Hart, Andrew D., 1380
Hart, Charles H., 450-453, 1110
Hart, Franklin W., 5206
Hart, Hugh, 3523
Hart, James, 2048, 8085
Hart, John, 10245, 10570
Hart, LaValle, 9217
Hart, Roderick P., 11040, 11390
Hartje, Robert, 5761
Hartke, Vance, 10246
Hartley, Anthony, 10676, 11529
Hartman, Daniel W., 1556
Hartman, John J., 12384
Hartman, Lee E., Jr., 11672
Hartmann, Robert T., 12025, 12026
Hartmann, Susan M., 9327
Hartnett, Robert C., 11878
Hartwell, Alena, 7825
Harvard University Library, 6884
Harvey, A. R., 7158
Harvey, Alexander M., 1821, 1918

Harvey, Cordelia A. P., 4154
Harvey, George, 6081, 7458-7460, 7949, 8002
Harvey, James C., 10571, 11188
Harwell, Richard B., 4505
Harwood, Richard, 10823
Harwood-Staderman, Richard, 194
Hash, Ronald J., 2151
Haskins, Caryl P., 1500
Haskins, Ralph W., 5427, 5448
Hassett, William D., 8602, 8603
Hastedt, Glenn P., 12301
Hasting, Ann C., 9328
Hatch, Alden, 7217, 8346, 9686, 9723
Hatfield, Mark O., 5991, 11730
Hattaway, Herman, 4978
Hauer, Stanley R., 1452
Hauge, Gabriel, 9878
Hauptman, Laurence M., 6566
Hauser, Gerald A., 11792
Hauser, Robert E., 7886, 7887
Hausner, V. A., 12302
Haveles, Harry P., Jr., 11041
Haveman, Robert, 12820
Havemann, Joel, 12027
Haverlin, Carl, 4979
Havic, John J., 12385
Havig, Alan, 6730
Havlik, Robert J., 4506
Hawkins, Seth C., 5969
Hawkinson, Robert E., 11189
Hawley, Ellis W., 8136-8138, 9024
Haworth, Paul L., 310, 526, 1415, 1453, 5901, 5902
Haws, Willard, 5449
Hawthorne, Nathaniel, 3360
Hay, John, 3584, 4980
Hay, Logan, 5122
Hay, Robert P., 379, 893, 1723, 2528, 2803, 2804, 2854
Hay, Thomas R., 4981
Hayden, Jay G., 6467
Hayden, Sidney, 339
Hayes, Frederic H., 1002
Hayes, James T., 11328
Hayes, John L., 5292
Hayes, Melvin L., 4899
Hayes, Merwyn A., 5499
Hayes, Rutherford B., 5913-5917
Hayes, Walter S., Jr., 5813
Hayes, Webb C., 5865
Haygood, William C., 6567
Hayllar, Ben, 11299
Hayman, LeRoy, 9222
Haynes, Richard F., 9329
Hays, James, Jr., 181
Hays, Willard, 5428
Hazel, Harry C., Jr., 9503
Hazelton, Gerry W., 4900

Hazen, Charles D., 1855
Hazlet, Raymond L., 8425
Hazleton, Jared E., 11164
Hazleton, William A., 13004
Hazlitt, William, 182
Head, Simon, 12028
Headley, Joel T., 63, 636, 2731, 5612, 5613, 5710
Headley, Phineas C., 5614-5616
Heald, Edward T., 6240
Healey, Robert M., 1629
Healy, David, 7563
Healy, Laurin H., 6731
Healy, Paul F., 10142, 10247, 10918, 11442
Heath, Jim F., 10248, 10572, 11042
Heathcote, Charles W., 5066, 5150
Heatwole, C. J., 1319
Hechler, Ken, 9330
Hechler, Kenneth W., 7043
Hecht, Marie B., 2585, 8835
Heckman, Richard A., 4627-4632, 5151
Heckscher, August, 7296, 7395, 7734
Hedges, Brown, 1630
Hedges, Job E., 6468
Hedley, John H., 9223, 9584
Heebner, A. Gilbert, 12303
Heed, Thomas J., 9504
Heeney, A. D. P., 9804, 10677
Heffron, Florence, 12385
Heffron, Paul T., 6732
Hefley, James, 12131
Hefley, Marti, 12131
Hehmeyer, Walter, 9234, 9235
Heim, Keith M., 9537
Hein, David, 3524, 4124, 4283, 4284
Heinlein, David L., 9627
Heinlein, J. C., 11043
Heinrichs, Waldo H., 8891, 9538
Heiskell, Samuel G., 2732
Helde, Thomas T., 10249, 11044
Helderman, Leonard C., 183
Heleniak, Roman, 11045
Helicher, Karl, 6469, 8426, 9256, 12531
Hellegers, John F., 2855
Hellenbrand, Harold, 1381, 1454
Heller, David, 10250
Heller, Deane, 10250
Heller, Edmund, 6961
Heller, Francis H., 9331, 9455, 9647
Hellerman, Leon, 3252
Hellman, C. Doris, 2049
Hellman, George S., 775
Hellweg, Susan A., 12416
Helm, Katherine, 3834
Helm, William P., 9224
Helms, Dorcas K., 2050
Hemminger, Art, 4826
Hemphill, James C., 7396
Hemphill, W. Edwin, 575, 2112

Hench, Atcheson L., 1455
Henderson, Archibald, 711
Henderson, Bruce, 10431
Henderson, Charles P., 11530
Henderson, Daniel M., 6376, 6470
Henderson, F. P., 8427
Henderson, John C., 1382
Henderson, John T., 11531, 11795
Henderson, Paul V. N., 7651
Henderson, Thomas G., 9585
Henderson, William L., 11190
Hendrick, Burton J., 4982
Hendricks, Gordon, 5814
Hendrickson, Embert J., 6849
Hendrickson, John P., 8276
Hendrickson, Walter B., 1231
Hendrix, Jerry A., 2051, 7397, 10915
Henkels, Stan V., 184, 1232, 2239
Henkin, Louis, 11532
Henley, Leonard, 64
Henline, Ruth, 1456
Henneman, John B., 1457
Hennessy, Maurice N., 10678
Hennessy, Michael E., 7926
Hennighausen, Louis P., 3835
Henrich, Joseph G., 2052
Henriot, Peter J., 7297
Henry, Anne H., 5289
Henry, Charles E., 6032
Henry, David R., 9332
Henry, Milton L., Jr., 4983
Henry, Patrick, 9879
Hensel, William U., 3394-3397, 6082
Hensley, Carl W., 9539
Hentoff, Nat, 11533
Herbers, John, 11534
Herbert, Hilary A., 6141
Herbert, Leila, 311
Herbert, William C., 2973
Herbert Hoover Presidential Library, 8086, 8277
Herd, Elmer D., Jr., 2733
Herder, John H., 8604
Heren, Louis, 11046
Herndon, Booton, 10096
Herndon, William H., 3525, 3526, 4574
Herod, Steven, 13134
Herold, Charles J., 7735
Herold, David E., 4827
Herr, Donald F., 11796
Herren, Robert S., 9456
Herrick, Cheesman A., 3800, 3902
Herring, George C., 9540, 9962
Herring, Pendleton, 7298, 7299
Herriott, Frank I., 4575, 4901, 5290
Hersey, John, 9225-9229, 9333, 10143, 12029, 12030
Hersh, Seymour M., 11535
Herter, Christian A., 10251

Hertz, Emanuel, 3527, 4218, 4285, 4576-4578, 4984
Hertzberg, Arthur, 12684
Hertzberg, Hazel W., 12825
Herzberg, Max J., 1458
Heslep, Robert D., 1383, 1384, 1557
Hess, Allen K., 11536
Hess, Earl, 4985
Hess, Gary R., 8892
Hess, Stephen, 7044, 11391, 11403, 12198
Hesseltine, William B., 4723-4726, 4902, 4986, 5169, 5762
Heuring, A. J., 5152
Heusser, Albert H., 7218
Hevener, John W., 9025
Heysinger, I. W., 4987
Hibbs, Douglas A., Jr., 12947
Hickerson, Frank R., 5815
Hickey, Donald R., 2053, 2805
Hickey, James T., 3836-3839, 3954-3956
Hickman, George H., 3213
Hickok, Lorena A., 8470
Hicks, Frederick C., 6987
Hicks, Wilson, 9687
Hiebert, Ray E., 8347
Hiebert, Roselyn, 8347
Higgins, George, 11415
Higgins, Lucy P., 3840
Higginson, Thomas W., 2054
Higgs, Robert, 12304
High, Stanley, 8605
Hikins, James W., 9418
Hill, C. William, 1558
Hill, Charles E., 12873
Hill, Charles P., 8348
Hill, Dilys M., 12149, 12386
Hill, Frederick T., 65, 540, 541, 3903, 4579, 4633, 5207, 5617, 5903
Hill, Harry W., 8139
Hill, Howard C., 6850
Hill, Isaac, 2734
Hill, John W., 3528, 4286, 4287, 4507
Hill, Kenneth L., 10679
Hill, Larry D., 7652, 7653
Hiller, David, 12874
Hillis, Newell D., 380, 4288
Hillman, Franklin P., 3410
Hilsman, Roger, 10680
Hilty, James W., 9265
Himmelfarb, Milton, 12387
Himmelwe, Hilde T., 11781
Hinckley, Ted C., 5992, 6220, 7654
Hindman, E. James, 7045
Hines, Mary E., 1559
Hinsdale, Burke A., 5952
Hinshaw, David, 8052
Hinton, Wayne K., 3345
Hirsch, Phil, 10097, 10252

Hirschfield, Robert S., 4727
Hirshson, Stanley P., 6216
Hirst, David, 7300
Hirst, Francis W., 2240
Hiss, Alger, 11443
Hitchcock, Margaret R., 1233
Hixon, Ada H., 527
Hobbs, Charles D., 12685
Hobbs, Edward H., 9805
Hobbs, Joseph P., 10030
Hobbs, Richard G., 5618
Hobby, Laura A., 185
Hobson, Charles F., 2404
Hobson, Jonathan T., 3957
Hoch, Paul L., 10471
Hochfield, Sylvia, 454
Hochman, Steven H., 1563
Hochman, William R., 8557
Hocking, Brian, 13005
Hodder, Frank H., 3322
Hodges, George, 542
Hodgin, Fred B., 7631
Hodgson, James D., 12031
Hoehling, Mary D., 2663
Hoes, Ingrid W., 2529
Hoeveler, J. David, Jr., 1560
Hoff-Wilson, Joan, 8053, 8140, 8141, 8471
Hoffecker, Carol E., 9541
Hoffman, Frederick J., 7979
Hoffman, John, 2241
Hoffman, Paul, 11392
Hoffman, William S., 2856, 2974
Hoffmann, Stanley, 12453-12455
Hoffs, Joshua A., 7159
Hofstadter, Richard, 1561, 1919, 1920, 2857, 6733, 6734, 8606
Hofstetter, C. Richard, 11731, 11769
Hogue, W. Dickerson, 11688
Hohner, Robert A., 7398
Holbo, Paul S., 6294, 9851
Holbrook, Francis X., 6861
Holcombe, Arthur N., 576
Holden, Constance, 12875
Holden, Jack, 9752
Holden, Raymond, 4728
Holder, Calvin B., 10573
Holder, Jean S., 1003
Holifield, E. Brooks, 12132
Holland, Corabelle A., 266, 1234
Holland, Josiah G., 3529
Holland, William M., 3060
Holli, Melvin G., 8607
Holliday, Carl, 1822, 3708, 4289
Hollingsworth, J. Rogers, 6142
Hollis, Christopher, 1111
Hollister, Howard C., 6988
Hollitz, John E., 9926
Holloway, David, 13073, 13074

Holm, James N., 5970
Holman, Tom, 5099
Holmans, A. E., 9880
Holmes, Frederick L., 4351
Holmes, Julius C., 9753
Holmes, Mabel D., 66
Holsti, Ole R., 10538
Holt, William S., 7399
Holzer, Harold, 455, 456, 3709, 3710, 3958, 3997, 4155-4168, 4729, 4903-4905, 5208
Homan, Delmar C., 9724
Honeywell, Roy J., 1385, 1386, 2055
Honomichl, Jack J., 11732
Hooes, Rose G., 2530
Hoogenboom, Ari, 2806, 2975
Hoogenboom, Olive, 2806
Hooker, Helene M., 6568
Hooley, John, 12686
Hoopes, Townsend, 11264
Hoover, Herbert, 8278-8313, 8321
Hoover, Lou H., 8313
Hoover Presidential Library Association, 8315
Hope, Ben W., 8825
Hope, Eva, 3530, 5993
Hopkins, John E., 9334
Hopper, John E., 8753
Hoppin, Charles A., 267-271, 543
Horgan, Paul, 3531, 3532, 3959
Horn, James J., 3253
Horn, Stanley F., 2807, 3043
Horner, Harlan H., 3533, 4290, 4508, 5153
Hornig, Edgar A., 7046
Horowitz, David, 10084
Horowitz, Irving L., 11047, 11922, 12687
Horowitz, Murray M., 4906, 4988
Horsman, Reginald, 2152
Horton, Rushmore G., 3461
Horton, Scott, 12532
Hosford, Hester E., 7160, 7301, 7400
Hoskins, Janina W., 2113
Hoslett, Schuyler D., 2114
Hosterman, Arthur D., 5938
Hostetter, Ida L. K., 3411
Hostick, King V., 4509
Houdek, John T., 5866, 5994
Houghton, William M., 1724
Hourihan, William J., 6735
House, Albert V., Jr., 3534, 4291, 5867
House, Edward M., 7219, 7672
House, Roy T., 6377
Houser, Martin L., 3801, 3802
Houston, David F., 7401
Houston, Michael, 7402
Houstoun, L. O., Jr., 12305
Howard, A. E. Dick, 11540
Howard, David M., 11879
Howard, Eleanor V., 6472
Howard, Harry N., 9963

Howard, James Q., 3711, 5796
Howard, John R., 577, 1958, 5291
Howard, Oliver O., 3313, 4219, 4220, 5619
Howard, Seymour, 1347
Howard, Thomas W., 5500
Howard, Victor B., 5209
Howard, Vincent W., 7403
Howe, Beverly W., 3960
Howe, George F., 6054, 6055
Howe, Herbert B., 776
Howe, John R., Jr., 934, 935
Howe, Russell W., 11733
Howell, David, 12033
Howell, Edward B., 6473
Howell, John M., 12533
Howell, Leon, 12199, 12688
Howell, Margaret-Mary, 12033
Howell, Wilbur S., 1112
Howell, William A., 11560
Howells, William D., 3535, 5292, 5797, 5917
Howes, Raymond, 457
Howland, Edward, 5620
Howland, Glenn C., 4730
Howland, Harold J., 6569
Hoxie, R. Gordon, 8087, 8217, 9806, 9964, 12034, 12200, 12456
Hoyt, Edwin P., 3171, 3299, 3361, 3384, 6241, 6474, 11393
Hoyt, Morgan H., 8609
Hoyt, Robert G., 10253
Hruska, Thomas J., Jr., 7302
Hubard, William J., 458
Hubbard, Elbert, 67, 1235, 3712
Hubbard, George U., 4292
Hubbard, Paul G., Jr., 4907
Hubbell, Jay B., 1459, 5090
Hubbell, John G., 11797
Hubbell, John T., 3431
Huberman, Leo, 10254, 11048
Hubert, James H., 5210
Huddleston, Mark W., 12201
Hudson, H. P., 10255
Hudson, J. Paul, 459
Hudson, John A., 8744
Hudson, Manley O., 7614
Hudson, W. Gail, 10616
Huegli, Jon M., 1921
Huff, Anne S., 11676
Huge, Harry, 12216
Hugh-Jones, Edward M., 7303
Hughes, Arthur J., 6736, 11394, 12202
Hughes, Charles E., 2352
Hughes, David F., 5501
Hughes, Emmet J., 8610, 11880, 12203
Hughes, Paul F., 3785
Hughes, Rupert, 68
Hughes, Thomas L., 12457, 13006
Hugins, Roland, 6143

Hugins, Walter E., 2976
Huitt, Ralph K., 10916, 11049
Hulbert, Archer B., 186, 187, 272, 382
Hulbert, Mary A., 7220
Hulett, Louisa S., 12458
Hulten, Charles R., 13111
Hummel, Jeffrey R., 2977
Humphrey, David C., 11050
Humphrey, Grace, 4392
Humphrey, Hubert H., 9026, 10798
Humphreys, Milton E., 10917
Hunt, Eugenia, 4221
Hunt, Gaillard, 1004, 2328, 2405, 2475, 2056, 5502
Hunt, Katharine C., 2353
Hunt, Samuel F., 5293
Hunt, Thomas C., 1376
Hunt-Jones, Conover, 2354
Hunter, Allen, 12689
Hunter, T. M., 9754
Huntley, William B., 1631
Hurd, Charles, 9027
Hurley, Robert M., 10681
Hurt, James, 3904
Hurvitz, Haggai, 7498, 8142
Hurwitz, Howard L., 6570
Hurwitz, Leon, 11881
Hurwitz, Michael R., 4828
Hussey, Lyman A., Jr., 6851
Huston, James A., 9965
Hutchins, Cortelle, 69, 189, 273
Hutchins, Frank, 69, 188, 189, 273, 1113
Hutchinson, J. R., 3844
Hutchinson, Paul, 70
Huth, Richard A., 5868
Huthmacher, J. Joseph, 7564, 8218, 9335
Hutson, James H., 936-938
Huttie, Joseph J., Jr., 11664
Hutton, Amy, 3398
Hutton, Ann H., 637
Hyatt, Richard, 12108
Hyde, Arthur M., 8075
Hyman, Harold M., 3760, 4731, 4829, 5123, 5211, 5503, 5711
Hyman, Herbert H., 9807
Hyman, Sidney, 9808-9810, 9881, 10256, 10257, 10502, 11444
Hymoff, Edward, 10097, 10892

Iacuzzi, Alfred, 857
Iakovlev, N. N., 8893
Iannaccone, Laurence, 12690
Ickes, Harold L., 6378, 8611, 8773, 8774
Iglehart, Ferdinand C., 6379
Iglehart, John E., 5294
Iglehart, John K., 11689-11691, 12306
Ignasias, C. Dennis, 7888
Ikard, Robert W., 3221
Illick, Joseph E., 2600

Illinois State Historical Society, 3961
Immerman, Richard H., 9935, 9962, 9966, 9967
Inbau, Fred E., 12691
Ingersoll, David E., 2406
Ingersoll, Robert G., 3536
Ingold, Beth A. J., 12948
Ingram, Marvin L., 8613
Inoue, Shigenobu, 13007
Ions, Edmund S., 10259
Ippolito, Dennis S., 12876
Irelan, John R., 3061
Ireton, Robert E., 2188
Irving, Washington, 71-74
Irwin, Frank, 2242
Irwin, Ramon L., 3254
Irwin, William H., 8054
Isaacs, A. Joakim, 5712
Isaacs, Harold, 12204
Isaacson, W. J., 12307
Isbeu, Florence, 12205
Iselin, John J., 9628, 9629
Isely, Bliss, 544
Isham, Norman M., 1320
Israel, John, 1562, 1563
Ives, Mabel L., 638
Izek, Hersch, 8894

Jablon, Howard, 8895
Jackson, Andrew, 3044-3051
Jackson, Carlton L., 2858, 2978
Jackson, Donald, 274, 639, 1237, 2057, 11416
Jackson, Mrs. F. Nevill, 460
Jackson, H. LeRoy, 3713
Jackson, Isaac R., 3129-3131
Jackson, Joseph, 578
Jackson, Samuel T., 4293
Jacob, Charles E., 9028
Jacobs, David, 7615
Jacobs, Henry, 5067
Jacobs, Travis B., 9124, 9755
Jacobs, Victor, 1238
Jacobs, William J., 8472
Jacobson, Edward, 9611
Jacobson, J. Mark, 9029
Jacoby, Robert L., 8614
Jaffa, Harry V., 4634, 4635
Jaffe, Louis L., 8961
Jager, Ronald, 6144
Jahnke, Art, 12693
Jahoda, Gloria, 2058
Jakoubek, Robert E., 8826
James, D. D., 4636
James, Edith, 7221, 7704
James, Felix, 5553
James, Jeannie H., 3841
James, Jo Anne, 11191
James, Marquis, 1959, 2735-2737
Jameson, Henry B., 9688

Janeway, Eliot, 10919, 12694
Janeway, Michael, 10260, 10920, 11051
Janeway, Sharon K., 10921
Janny, W. A., 5091
Janos, Leo, 10858, 10859
Jansky, Cyril M., Jr., 8143
Jarman, Rufus, 9336
Jasani, Bhupendra, 13078
Jasinowski, Jerry J., 12206
Jastrow, Robert, 13079
Jaworski, Leon, 11882
Jayne, William, 3537
Jefferson, Henry, 4352
Jefferson, Isaac, 2153
Jefferson, Thomas, 2443-2486
Jeffreys-Jones, Rhodri, 6295
Jeffries, Ana G., 6975
Jeffries, John W., 8615, 10261
Jeffries, Ona G., 9812
Jencks, Christopher, 11192
Jenkins, Charles F., 579
Jenkins, John H., 10262
Jenkins, John S., 2738-2740, 3214
Jenkins, Roy, 9230
Jenkins, Starr, 939, 1460, 2632, 4055, 7565, 8616
Jenkinson, Isaac, 2059
Jenks, Anton S., 7848
Jennings, A. H., 4393
Jennings, David H., 7616, 7849, 7889
Jennings, Janet, 3538
Jennison, Keith W., 3714
Jensen, Billie B., 7499, 7566
Jensen, Daniel D., 11798
Jensen, Richard, 6262, 6571, 8827
Jensen, Rita H., 13112
Jeong, Dong-Kuen, 9882
Jerome, C., 3385
Jillson, Calvin C., 2407
Jillson, Willard R., 528-530, 4169, 5154
Joe, Barbara E., 12594
Joes, Anthony J., 9813
Joesten, Joachim, 10432, 11052
Johannesen, Richard L., 2633
Johannsen, Dorothea E., 8617
Johannsen, Robert W., 3905, 4637, 4638
Johansen, Bruce E., 2154
Johansen, Robert C., 12460
Johns, Jane M., 4222, 4908
Johnson, Albert W., 75
Johnson, Allen, 1994, 2189, 3255
Johnson, Alvin P., 8428
Johnson, Andrew, 5570-5573
Johnson, Arthur M., 6737, 6738
Johnson, Bradley T., 76
Johnson, Byron B., 4223
Johnson, Carolyn M., 10926
Johnson, Cary, Jr., 1725
Johnson, Claudia A. T., 10860, 10861

Johnson, Donald, 7705
Johnson, Ellis A., 5155, 11053
Johnson, Evans C., 7850
Johnson, George, 9689, 11395
Johnson, George B., 4294
Johnson, George W., 10731, 11300
Johnson, Gerald W., 312, 2741, 7161, 7304, 7305, 8618, 11329
Johnson, Glenn A., 8144
Johnson, Haynes, 10539, 10823, 12207
Johnson, James P., 7500, 8088, 8219, 8220, 10433, 11417
Johnson, Judge, 5798
Johnson, Kenneth R., 3432
Johnson, Luciana, 1922
Johnson, Ludwell H., 4989, 4990, 5212, 5213
Johnson, Lyndon B., 8619, 10798, 11361-11372
Johnson, Marion M., 10434
Johnson, Miles B., 9814, 10732, 11301
Johnson, Monroe, 2531, 2532, 5124
Johnson, Peggy A., 1633
Johnson, R. W., 12695
Johnson, Richard R., 777
Johnson, Roger T., 8003
Johnson, Sam H., 10862
Johnson, Stephen D., 12949
Johnson, Theodore R., 7306
Johnson, Walter, 8620, 9337, 9815
Johnson, William R., 8145
Johnson, Willis F., 2634, 7826
Johnston, Elizabeth B., 77, 461
Johnston, Ron J., 12950
Johnston, Thomas T., 7927
Johnston, Whittle, 12461
Johnston, William D., 6380
Johnstone, Christopher L., 12388
Johnstone, Robert M., Jr., 2060
Johnstone, William J., 340, 341, 4295, 4296
Joline, Adrian H., 3067
Jones, Alan M., Jr., 11799
Jones, Alfred H., 8621, 8622
Jones, Anna C., 1726
Jones, Archer, 4978
Jones, Byrd L., 9030
Jones, Charles O., 11965, 12208
Jones, Dallas L., 7501
Jones, E. Alfred, 462
Jones, Edgar D., 1634, 4125, 4297
Jones, Elizabeth, 11591
Jones, Evan R., 4732, 5713
Jones, Frank H., 5676
Jones, Gene D., 9031
Jones, Henry C., 3803
Jones, Howard, 1461, 3104
Jones, James F., Jr., 1564
Jones, James S., 5403, 5504
Jones, Jenkin L., 4298
Jones, Maldwyn A., 2601

Jones, Manfred, 9125
Jones, Paul W., 1604
Jones, Robert F., 78, 712
Jones, Rochelle, 12209
Jones, Terry L., 5714
Jordan, Daniel P., 1995
Jordan, David S., 6475
Jordan, Harriet P., 4639
Jordan, Hamilton, 12210
Jordan, Winthrop D., 2155
Jordau, Philip D., 4126
Josephson, Emanuel M., 8429
Josephson, Matthew, 6145, 6739
Joshi, Manoj K., 4991
Joslin, Theodore G., 8055
Joyce, James A., 12463
Joynt, Robert H., 4992
Judge, Joseph, 1501
Judis, John, 12696, 12697
Judson, Clara I., 1727, 2742, 3539, 6381
Judson, Harry P., 8623
Juergens, George, 6740
Juris, Harvey A., 11677
Jusserand, Jean A., 580, 3540, 6476
Just, Ward S., 10727, 10927

Kadis, Phillip M., 12211
Kagle, Steven E., 858
Kahan, Jerome H., 10540
Kahl, Mary, 10928
Kahn, Alfred E., 11034
Kahn, David M., 5677
Kahn, Gilbert N., 8896
Kahn, Herman, 9126
Kahn, Roger, 11055
Kahn, Tom, 11219, 11663
Kaine, John L., 4441
Kaiser, P. H., 4353
Kaiser, Robert G., 9630, 12877
Kalb, Madeleine, 10682
Kalb, Marvin, 10682
Kaleb, George, 10263
Kallen, Horace M., 1348, 1502
Kaltefleiter, Werner, 11800
Kanawada, Leo V., 8624, 8897
Kane, Richard D., 7890, 8004
Kansas State Historical Society, 5295
Kantowicz, Edward R., 12308
Kaplan, George R., 12878
Kaplan, Lawrence S., 2056-2060, 2476, 11801
Karl, Barry D., 8221, 9032
Karlsrud, Robert A., 8146
Karp, Walter, 9586
Karsner, David, 2743
Kates, Herbert, 8
Kathka, David A., 9457
Katterjohn, Monte, 8430
Katula, Richard A., 11883

Katz, Elihu, 10617, 10618, 11734, 11735
Katz, James E., 12879
Katz, Joseph, 10435, 10436
Katz, Milton, 7307
Katz, Stanley N., 1960
Kaufer, David S., 10619, 11736
Kauffman, Erie, 191
Kauffman, Mike, 4830
Kaufman, Burton I., 713, 7308, 7567, 7706, 9968
Kaufman, Henry, 13113
Kaufman, Irving R., 12698
Kaufman, K. A., 11543
Kauper, Paul G., 9458, 11544
Kavanagh-Baran, Kathryn, 12150
Kaye, Jacqueline, 2635
Kazin, Alfred, 10264
Kean, Robert G. H., 1996
Kearney, James R., 8431
Kearney, Philip, 11195
Kearns, Doris, 10824-10827, 11056, 11057
Keast, Lewis, 192
Keating, John S., 8898
Keckley, Elizabeth H., 4224
Keefe, David E., 12880
Keefe, Robert, 10265, 11737
Keeler, Lucy E., 5816-5818
Keen, William W., 6146
Kegley, Charles W., Jr., 12699
Kehl, James A., 6221
Kehoe, Loretta, 8222
Keigher, Sharon M., 12881
Keiser, David S., 3842
Keith, Charles P., 6210
Keller, Bill, 12700, 12701
Keller, Morton, 6382
Keller, William F., 1728
Kelley, Darwin, 1961, 4993
Kelley, John L., 9542
Kelley, Kitty, 10098
Kelley, Robert, 6147
Kelley, William D., 3541
Kellogg, Vernon, 8056, 8089
Kelly, Florence F., 7309
Kelly, Frank K., 7461, 9338
Kelly, John J., Jr., 940
Kelly, Lawrence C., 9033
Kelly, Regina Z., 895, 10046
Kelsey, Harry, 5100
Kelton, Nancy, 9231
Kemble, Penn, 12882
Kemper, Deane A., 10266, 10620
Kempf, Edward J., 4089, 4127
Kempton, Greta, 9257
Kempton, Murray, 9816, 9817
Kendal, Bruce, 10072
Kendrick, Benjamin B., 6296
Kendrick, Jack E., 7404
Kennan, George F., 7707

Kennedy, John F., 10750-10800
Kennedy, Patrick J., 2408
Kennedy, Robert F., 10541
Kennedy, Rose F., 10099
Kennedy, Thomas C., 8899
Kenner, Sumner, 193
Kenski, Henry C., 9883, 11545
Keogh, James, 11396, 11546
Keppler, Joseph, 6148
Kerbel, Matthew R., 12035
Kern, Jean B., 7462
Kern, Montague, 10683
Kernek, Sterling J., 7568, 12969
Kernell, Samuel, 9631
Kerney, James, 7222, 7310-7312
Kerr, K. Austin, 7502
Kerr, Laura, 2602
Kerr, Malcolm H., 11802
Kersey, Vierling, 163
Kershaw, David A., 10521
Kerwin, Jerome G., 10269
Kerwood, John, 3962, 5763, 5995
Kesaris, Paul, 11373
Kesilman, Sylvan H., 3190
Kessel, John H., 10733, 12212, 12702
Kessler, Sanford, 1632
Ketcham, Henry, 3542
Ketcham, Ralph L., 941, 1220-1222, 1565, 1729, 1962, 2329, 2330, 2355, 2356, 2409, 2410, 2495, 2636
Ketchen, John C., 5953
Ketchum, Richard M., 79
Kettell, Thomas P., 3433
Keyerleber, Karl, 8625
Keys, Thomas B., 4394, 4831
Keyworth, George A., 13080
Khan, Rais A., 11547
Kharas, Theodore, 3543
Kichorowsky, Theodosia, 4832
Kidd, T. W. S., 4909
Kidder, Rushworth M., 12703
Kielbowicz, Richard B., 2979
Kiell, Norman, 6477
Kiernan, Reginald H., 8626
Kilar, Jeremy W., 5505, 5506
Killen, Linda R., 7569
Killian, James R., Jr., 9884
Kilmartin, Thomas W., 7950
Kilpatrick, Carroll, 8627, 10504, 11418
Kim, Donggill, 4395
Kim, Won M., 6852
Kimball, Marie G., 1314-1316, 1349, 1416, 1417, 1440-1444, 1703-1706, 1730, 2061, 2288
Kimball, S. Fiske, 1245, 1246, 1350, 1351, 1507, 1521-1526, 2062
Kimball, Warren F., 8900, 9127-9129, 9178
Kimmel, Stanley P., 3963
Kimzey, Bruce W., 13114

Kincade, William H., 12036, 12309
Kincaid, Robert L., 3804, 4396, 4397, 4994, 5296
Kindig, Everett W., II., 2980
King, Andrew A., 11548
King, Charles, 5621
King, Grace, 313
King, Horatio C., 3434, 6258
King, Irving H., 714
King, Jeffrey S., 5101, 5102
King, Joan H., 12310
King, Judson, 6741
King, Larry L., 10828, 10863-10865, 11058, 11330
King, Pendleton, 6117
King, Robert P., 3964
King, Ronald F., 11196
King, Willard L., 4580, 4733, 4910
Kingdon, Frank, 715, 1823, 2156, 3544, 8628
Kingery, Hugh M., 80
Kingston, John, 81
Kinnaird, Clark, 82, 8349
Kinnaird, Virginia, 3843
Kinnard, Douglas, 9969-9971
Kinsella, William E., Jr., 9130, 9131
Kinsley, Michael, 12704
Kinsolving, Arthur B., 1635
Kintner, William R., 11803
Kipper, Philip, 12416
Kirby, John B., 8775
Kirk, Harris E., 7223
Kirk, Russell A., 1636
Kirkendall, Richard S., 8776, 8777, 9034, 9035, 9258, 9268, 9275, 9339-9341, 9587, 9588
Kirkland, Carolina M., 83
Kirkland, Frederic R., 1963
Kirkpatrick, Jeane J., 12534, 13008
Kirkwood, Ron B., 12213, 12705
Kirschten, Dick, 12706-12717, 12883, 13115
Kirstein, Peter N., 9459
Kirwan, Kent A., 7313
Kish, Francis B., 9232
Kissel, Bernard C., 11445, 11738
Kisteneff, Alexis P., 11549
Kistiakowsky, George B., 9885
Kitchens, Joseph, 6572
Kite, Elizabeth S., 640
Kittler, Glenn, 9712
Kittredge, George L., 463
Klaber, John J., 464
Klapthor, Margaret B., 465, 1824, 2357
Klaw, Barbara, 10866
Kleber, Louis C., 3191
Kleeman, Rita, 8432
Klehr, Harvey, 8629
Kleiler, Frank M., 8778
Klein, Arthur L., 10801
Klein, Ernst, 12109
Klein, Frederic S., 3401, 3436
Klein, Herbert G., 11397

Klein, Philip A., 13116
Klein, Philip S., 3386, 3399, 3400, 3402, 3435, 3437, 3438
Klein, Rose S., 716
Kleinau, Marvin D., 11446
Klement, Frank, 3366, 3965
Klenbort, Marcia, 12133
Klenner, Hermann, 1566
Kleppner, Paul, 4911
Kless, Margaret E., 6149
Klieman, Aaron S., 9612
Klima, Gilbert, 10495
Kline, Sherman J., 2603
Klingbeil, Kurt A., 8630
Klingberg, Frank J., 2859, 2981
Klingberg, Frank W., 3439
Klingelhofer, Herbert E., 2604
Klipper, Leslie A., 12037, 12389
Kloman, William, 1964
Kluckhohn, Frank L., 8631, 10270, 10829, 11059
Knapp, Frank A., Jr., 2637
Knapp, Sally E., 8473
Knebel, Fletcher, 9342, 9818, 10100, 10271, 10272, 10734, 10929, 11060
Knee, Stuart E., 6742
Knepprath, Eugene, 9919
Knepprath, Hubert E., 9927
Knight, Andrew, 13009
Knight, Franklin, 466
Knight, George M., 194
Knight, Janet M., 10437
Knight, Jonathan, 9632
Knight, Lucian L., 7617
Knighten, Merrell A., 10908
Knippa, Edwin W., 10930
Knock, Thomas J., 7314, 7503, 7618
Knoles, George H., 1637, 1731, 6150
Knollenberg, Bernhard, 84, 641, 642, 942, 943
Knopp, Daniel L., 10575
Knott, Alexander W., 7570
Knowles, Archibald C., 8632
Knowles, Robert E., 3906
Knowlton, Daniel C., 383
Knox, Dudley W., 643, 644
Knox, J. H. Mason, Jr., 195
Knox, John, 8057
Knox, Katherine M., 467, 468
Knox, Paul, 8633
Knox, Thomas W., 6217
Knudson, Jerry W., 1418, 2063, 2064, 2190
Koch, Adrienne, 944, 945, 1005, 1117, 1154-1160, 1767-1769, 1997, 2165-2168
Koch, Thilo, 10273
Kocher, Douglas J., 6056
Koenig, Louis W., 2065, 3068, 9343, 9543, 9544, 9633, 11061, 11550
Koeniger, A. Cash, 9036
Koerselman, Gary H., 8147, 8148

Kohl, Wilfred L., 11804
Kohler, Max J., 2289
Kohlsaat, Herman H., 5715
Kohn, Richard H., 717
Kolinsky, M., 9545, 9613
Kolko, Gabriel, 13010, 13011
Kolodney, David, 12038
Kolodziej, Edward A., 11805, 11806
Kolpas, Norman, 3545
Komroff, Manuel, 3546
Kondracke, Morton, 10274
Kooker, Arthur R., 4128
Koontz, Louis K., 275
Kopkind, Andrew, 10867
Korb, Lawrence J., 12464, 13081
Kornhauser, Samuel J., 7047
Kornitzer, Bela, 9259, 9725, 11398
Koskoff, David E., 10101
Kosters, Marvin H., 11034
Kottman, Richard N., 8223-8226
Koudelka, Janet, 6014
Kousoulas, D. George, 9634
Kovaleff, Theodore P., 9886-9888
Kowert, Art, 10868
Kozlowski, Wladyslaw M., 581
Kraft, Barbara S., 6573
Kraft, Joseph, 10275-10277, 10684, 11062, 11063
Kraft, Michael E., 12884, 12885, 12924
Kramer, Eugene, 1006
Krancik, John, 1352
Krans, Horatio S., 4398
Kranz, Henry B., 5297
Krasner, Michael, 12951
Krauthammer, Charles, 13012
Krebs, Frank J., 5869
Kreczko, Alan J., 13013
Kreiger, Joel, 12970
Kremm, Thomas W., 4912, 6151
Krinsk, Fred, 8951
Krislov, Samuel, 2191
Krock, Arthur, 1419, 10278, 10735, 11064
Krog, Carl E., 8149
Kronman, Robert, 12033
Krout, John A., 582
Krueger, David W., 3192
Krug, Mark M., 4640, 5214
Kubicek, Earl C., 3966, 4299, 5125
Kucharsky, David, 12110
Kuchel, Thomas H., 10798
Kuenzli, Esther W., 1247
Kuhns, William T., 6259
Kukla, Jon, 1420, 1496
Kulka, Giora, 9344
Kull, Irving S., 5788
Kullnick, Max, 6574
Kundson, Jerry W., 2066
Kunhardt, Dorothy M., 3547, 4833
Kunhardt, Philip B., Jr., 4833, 5068

Kuniholm, Bruce R., 13014
Kunkel, Mable, 3548
Kuper, Theodore F., 1118, 1248, 1732
Kupfer, Barbara S., 2982
Kurland, Gerald, 999, 7827
Kurland, Philip B., 11884
Kurtz, Henry I., 5507
Kurtz, Michael L., 10438, 10439
Kurtz, Stephen G., 946, 1007, 1008
Kuter, Laurence S., 9460, 10685, 11265
Kutler, Stanley I., 6989-6992
Kutner, Luis, 6731, 11885, 11886
Kwak, Tae-Hwan, 9589
Kybal, Vlastimil, 8504
Kyes, Elizabeth A., 10736
Kyle, Otto R., 4354
Kyvig, David E., 8779

Lacqueur, Walter, 12465
Lacy, Alexander B., 2067
Ladd, Bruce, 11065
Ladd, Everett C., Jr., 8634, 12718, 12719
Ladenson, Alex, 1353
Ladies' Hermitage Association, 2808
Lael, Richard L., 7571
LaFay, Howard, 9690
Lafayette, Marquis, 2290, 2291
LaFeber, Walter F., 2710, 6152-6154, 8901, 9972, 10279, 11066, 12466, 12467, 13015
LaFevre, Benjamin, 6083
LaForte, Robert S., 6885
Laidley, W. S., 196
Laing, Alexander, 1733
Laing, Robert B., 11551
Laird, Melvin R., 11807, 12039
Lake, Anthony, 12995
Lake, Harry F., 4641
Lamb, Charles M., 12311
Lamb, Martha J. R. N., 384, 718
Lambert, C. Roger, 8227, 8228, 9889
Lambert, Oscar D., 3193
Lambert, William, 10843
Lamberton, James M., 342
Lambeth, William A., 1327
Lamers, Claude C., 1570
Lammie, Wayne D., 9461
Lamon, Ward H., 4225, 4399
Lancaster, Dabney S., 1387
Land, Guy, 10147
Landau, Jack C., 12720
Landau, Yehezkel, 12721
Lander, Louise, 11197
Landi, Alexander R., 2418
Landin, Harold W., 1861
Landis, C. I., 469
Landis, Frederick, 4581
Lane, Ann M., 2157
Lane, Lawrence, 1571

Lane, Mark, 10440
Lane, Rose W., 8058
Lane, Thomas A., 10280
Lane, W. B., 6203
Lang, Gladys E., 12040, 12390
Lang, H. Jack, 4056
Lang, Jane, 7504
Lang, Kurt, 12040, 12390
Lang, Lincoln A., 6478
Lang, Louis J., 8005
Langbein, F. W., 9819
Langdon, William C., 4995
Lange, Peter, 12468
Langer, Elinor, 11198, 11199
Langer, William L., 7315
Langford, Edna, 12134
Lanier, John J., 343
Lanis, Edward S., 4834
Lanouette, William J., 12214, 12469, 12722, 12723
Lansden, John M., 4226
Lansing, Robert, 7673, 7674
Lape, Fred, 1009
Lapham, Louis H., 11067
Lapomarda, Vincent A., 9037
Lapsley, Arthur B., 5298
Laqueur, Walter, 12215, 13016
Largent, Robert J., 3256
Larke, Julian K., 5622, 5716
Larned, Josephus N., 385, 3715, 4090
Larrabee, Harold A., 10102
Larsen, Lawrence H., 9773
Larsen, Peter, 6853
Larson, Arthur, 9691
Larson, Bethene W., 8635
Larson, David L., 10542, 13017
Larson, Deborah W., 13018
Larson, Martin A., 1119, 1249
Larson, Robert W., 6743, 7048
Lasch, Christopher, 11663
Lash, Jonathan, 12886
Lash, Joseph P., 8350, 8474-8476, 8902
Lashner, Marilyn A., 11552
Laska, Vera, 1056
Laski, Harold J., 7316
Lasky, Joseph, 8351
Lasky, Victor, 10047, 10048, 11399, 12111
Latane, John H., 7224, 7225
Latcham, John S., 6260
Latham, Earl, 7317, 10281
Lathem, Edward C., 7928
Lathrop, Barnes F., 2561
Lathrop, Mary F., 1734
Lathrop, Stanley E., 3786
Latimer, Harry D., 11303
Latner, Richard B., 2860, 2983-2986
Latrobe, Benjamin, 314
Lattimer, Gary, 10443
Lattimer, John K., 4835, 10441-10443

Lattimer, Jon, 10441
Laugel, Antoine A., 4227
Laughlin, Clara E., 4836
Laughlin, J. Laurence, 6479
Laukhuff, Perry, 7406
Lavender, David, 3323
Lawing, Hugh A., 5429
Lawrence, David, 7162, 7407, 7463, 9038
Lawrence, Henry W., 197, 719, 3907
Lawrence, Robert, 13019
Lawson, Don, 12569
Lawson, Elizabeth, 4913
Lawson, McEwan, 3549
Lawson, Simpson F., 11200
Lawson, Steven F., 10576, 11201, 11202
Lazalier, James H., 8903
Lazarus, Simon, 12216
Lea, James H., 3844
Lea, L. B., 9462
Leacock, Ruth, 10686
Leacock, Stephen B., 5215
Leahy, William D., 9132, 9345
Leamer, Laurence, 12577
Leapman, M., 12217
Lear, Tobias, 583
Learned, Henry B., 3257
Learned, Marion D., 3716
Leary, John J., Jr., 6480
Leary, William J., Jr., 7464
Lease, Martin H., Jr., 7049
Leathers, Charles G., 12724
LeBeau, John J., 9133
Lebow, Richard N., 7572
Lebowich, Joseph, 5717
Lebowitz, Michael A., 2861
Lecht, Leonard A., 10282
Lecky, William, 2419
Ledeen, Michael, 12470
Leduc, Gilbert F., 584
Lee, Bradford A., 9039
Lee, David D., 8150, 8229, 12218, 12391
Lee, David G., 12402
Lee, Gordon C., 1388
Lee, Henry, 2987
Lee, Jung H., 11808
Lee, R. Alton, 9346, 9463, 9464, 9692
Leech, Margaret, 5954, 6297
LeFever, Ernest W., 12535
Lefevre, Stephen R., 12312
Leff, Mark H., 9040
Leff, Michael C., 4515, 5299
Lefroy, A. H. F., 7050
Legvold, Robert, 12981
Lehman, Milton, 9347
Lehman, Ronald F., 9635
Lehmann-Hartleben, Karl, 1120, 1250
Leibiger, Stuart, 4510
Leighton, Francis S., 10869, 10870

Leighton, Isabel, 7980
Leiner, Frederick C., 6854
Leipold, L. Edmond, 12595
Leitenberg, Milton, 12428, 12429
Leiter, B. Kelly, 5718, 5764
Leiter, William M., 8780, 9041, 11553
Leitman, Spencer L., 5719
Lekachman, Robert, 11284-11286, 11663, 11692, 11693, 12313, 12314, 12826, 12887
Leland, Charles G., 5216
Lellouche, Pierre, 12041, 12471
LeLoup, Lance T., 12827
Lemann, Nicholas, 12219
Lemke, William E., 10283
Lemmon, Walter M., 4300
Lemon, Richard, 10577
Lenczowski, J., 13020
L'Enfant, Pierre C., 720
Leng, Russell J., 13021
Lenhart, Harry, Jr., 11670
Lenrow, Adele L., 10284
Lens, Sidney, 12220
Lentin, Antony, 7675
Lentz, John J., 1235
Leo, J., 9820
Leonard, Mary, 13117
Lepawsky, Albert, 9042
Lepore, Herbert P., 7505
Lerche, Charles O., Jr., 2068
Lerman, Allen H., 10730
Lerman, Louis, 1251
Lerner, Daniel, 10285
Lerner, Max, 9233
LeRoy, Dave, 11948
LeRoy, James A., 7051
Lerski, George J., 8151
Lessard, Suzannah, 10286, 11554
Leubsdorf, Carl P., 12221
Leuchtenburg, William E., 8352, 8781, 8962, 8963, 9043-9046, 9348, 9349, 10287-10289, 11203, 11287, 12596
Leupp, Francis E., 6383, 6575, 6744, 6745
Leutze, James R., 9134, 9135
Levin, David, 1825
Levin, Murray B., 10622
Levin, N. Gordon, 7619, 11809
Levine, Carol, 6746
Levine, Israel E., 10049
Levine, Steven I., 12473
Levitan, Sar A., 11288
Levitsky, Ihor, 1462
Levitt, Jane, 12828
Levitt, Theodore, 11068
Levy, Aaron, 4511
Levy, Leonard W., 2158, 11887
Levy, Michael E., 12315
Levy, Richard, 2069
Levy, T. Aaron, 3550

Lewellyn, Robert, 1998
Lewis, Alfred H., 1826, 2744, 2745, 2988
Lewis, Anthony M., 1969, 1970, 1999
Lewis, Craig, 9973
Lewis, David A., 12725
Lewis, Edward, 10802
Lewis, Edward B., 11897
Lewis, Edward S., 3142
Lewis, Eleanor G., 10505, 11204
Lewis, Fielding O., 198
Lewis, Flora, 11810
Lewis, Gene D., 5300
Lewis, H. H. Walker, 5508
Lewis, Jan, 1572
Lewis, John M., 9136
Lewis, John P., 9448
Lewis, Joseph, 3717, 5217, 12726
Lewis, Lloyd, 3551, 4996, 5170, 5623
Lewis, Mary E., 2638
Lewis, McMillan, 7226
Lewis, Montgomery, 3908
Lewis, Mort R., 4057, 9928
Lewis, Nancy, 12316
Lewis, Richard W., 10444
Lewis, Ted, 10290, 10506, 10507
Lewis, Theodore B., 4355
Lewis, Thompson H., 386
Lewis, Walker, 5904
Lewis, William D., 6384
Li, Tien-yi, 7573
Libby, Orin G., 721
Lichtenstein, Gaston, 199, 1971
Lichtenstein, Nelson, 11069, 11555, 12042
Lichtheim, George, 9546
Lichty, Joanne D., 8964
Liebenow, J. Gus, 13022
Lieber, Robert J., 13066
Lieberman, Carl, 722, 11556
Lifton, David S., 10445, 10446
Liggett, Walter W., 8059
Light, Alfred R., 12317
Light, Larry, 12222, 12392
Lightman, Marjorie, 8471
Lightner, David, 5126
Lilienthal, David E., 3718
Lilley, William, III, 11691, 11739
Lincoln, A., 6576, 6886, 6887
Lincoln, Abraham, 5301-5359
Lincoln, Anne H., 10291
Lincoln, Evelyn, 10050, 10292
Lincoln, Mary T., 3845-3847
Lincoln, Natalie S., 470, 471
Lincoln, Robert T., 3848
Lincoln, Waldo, 3849
Lincoln-Douglas Society, 4642
Lincoln Group of Chicago, 4228
Lincoln Memorial University. Abraham Lincoln Library and Museum, 3968

Linden, Louis, 12393
Linder, Leo J., 8782
Linder, Usher F., 4401
Lindley, Christopher, 8904
Lindley, Ernest K., 8353, 8505, 8754, 9047, 9056
Lindley, Thomas F., Jr., 1573
Lindquist, Robert M., 9450
Lindsey, David, 2746, 4998, 5218, 5996, 6057, 6298
Lindsey, Edward, 7620
Lindsey, Richard A., 3969
Lindsey, Robert, 12572, 12952
Lindstrom, Ralph G., 4301
Lingelbach, Anna L., 1736
Lingley, Charles R., 6155
Link, Arthur S., 7163-7167, 7227, 7318-7322, 7408-7413, 7442, 7465, 7466, 7574-7576, 7621, 7708, 7981
Linkugel, Wil A., 4734, 11877
Linn, William, 1121
Lint, Gregg L., 947
Linthicum, Richard, 7736
Lionberger, I. H., 2809
Lippincott, Horace M., 200
Lippman, Theo, 8433
Lippmann, Walter, 7323, 10293
Lipset, Seymour M., 11331, 12043, 12223, 12474
Lipsky, George A., 2639
Lisio, Donald J., 8230, 8231
Lisitzky, Genevieve H., 1122
Liska, George, 11603
Lisle, Teddy D., 10623
Lissakers, Karin, 12475
Literary Society of Washington, 5997
Litfin, A. Duane, 9974
Little, David, 1574, 2192
Little, John E., 948
Little, Shelby M., 85
Little, Thomas, 6888
Littlefiel, Arthur W., 8947
Litvack, Sanford M., 12318, 12888
Litwak, Robert S., 11811
Liu, Zuochang, 1575
Lively, Bruce R., 201
Livermore, Seward W., 7577, 7709, 7710
Llewellyn, Robert, 1508
Lloyd, Craig, 8232
Lloyd, John A., 4356
Lo, Clarence Y. H., 9590
Locander, Robert, 12224
Lochner, Louis P., 8152
Locke, Charles E., 4302
Locke, David R., 5450
Locke, Larry W., 11740
Lockridge, Richard, 9697
Lockridge, Ross F., 3553, 6211
Lockwood, Charles, 8006
Lockwood, Edgar, 12476
Lockwood, Theodore D., 5219

Author Index 679

Lodge, Henry C., 86, 2420, 4129, 6385, 6747, 6748, 6889, 6962, 7414
Loeb, Benjamin S., 10713
Loeb, Paul R., 12889
Loebs, Bruce D., 8637, 9419
Loescher, Burt G., 645
Loescher, G. D., 12536, 12537
Lofgren, Charles A., 9591
Logan, Andy, 10294
Logue, Cal M., 11332
Lohof, Bruce A., 8153, 8154, 8316
Lokensgard, Hjalmar O., 1389
Lokke, Carl L., 1737
Lomask, Milton, 5509
Lomax, Louis E., 10578
Lombard, M. E., 723
Lonergan, Thomas S., 4130
Long, Anne K., 10540
Long, Charles C., 202
Long, Everett L., 2070
Long, John D., 3554
Long, Joseph C., 5127
Long, Orie W., 1354
Long, Stuart, 10871
Longacre, Edward G., 4357, 4735
Longaker, Richard P., 2989-2991, 7415
Longford, Frank, 3555, 10051, 11400
Longgood, William F., 9693
Longworth, Alice R., 6481, 6482
Looker, Earle, 6386, 6483, 6577, 8638
Loos, Rita E., 6749
Lorant, Stefan, 2071, 3556, 4170, 4171, 6387, 8354
Lord, Donald C., 10295, 10579
Lord, Frank B., 7416, 7417
Lorentz, Pare, 8434
Lorenz, Alfred L., Jr., 4914, 9350
Lorenz, Lawrence, 9351
Lorne, S. M., 12319
Lossing, Benson J., 87, 780, 5939
Loth, David G., 7168, 7622
Lott, Davis N., 12394
Lottier, John, 11427
Lotts, Velma C., 1738
Louchheim, Katie, 9048, 10148
Louisiana State Museum, New Orleans, 3324
Louthan, Henry T., 3971
Loux, Martha D., 3972
Lovat-Fraser, J. A., 2562, 2992
Lovelace, Delos W., 9694
Lovell, C. H., 12890
Low, A. Maurice, 7169
Lowden, Lucy, 4915
Lowe, Gabriel L., 2862
Lowe, Jacques, 10052, 10053
Lowenthal, Abraham F., 12477
Lowenthal, Mark M., 9137
Lowerre, Nan K. J., 7891
Lowi, Theodore J., 11071

Lowitt, Richard, 8155, 8783, 8965, 9592
Lowitz, Sadyebeth, 3557
Lowrie, Walter E., 8784
Lowry, Edward G., 6750, 7052, 8233
Lowther, Kevin, 10580
Lubell, Samuel, 9505
Lucas, C. Payne, 10580
Lucas, Frederic A., 1669
Lucas, Stephen E., 6578
Lucchese, Sam, 12578
Luce, David R., 11557
Lucey, Lawrence, 6579
Lucier, Jim, 10931
Luck, Edward C., 13082
Lucke, Jessie, 2293
Ludwig, Emil, 3558, 3720, 8355
Luebke, Frederick C., 1638, 4916
Lufkin, Richard F., 3787, 3788
Lukacs, John, 9352
Lukas, J. Anthony, 11558
Lukonic, Joseph L., 1576
Lun, Ngoh G., 9636
Lunardini, Christine, 7503, 7506
Lurie, Leonard, 11741, 11888
Lurie, Ranan R., 11559
Luther, Frederic N., 1299
Luthin, Reinhard H., 3342, 3559, 4678, 4917, 5128
Luttrell, Clifton B., 1577
Lutz, Donald S., 2421
Lycan, Gilbert L., 949
Lydon, James G., 1639
Lykes, Richard W., 3909
Lyman, Jane L., 2159
Lyman, T. P. H., 1123
Lynch, Denis T., 3062, 6084
Lynch, Edward J., 12225
Lynch, William O., 1578, 3325, 4644
Lynd, Staughton, 1972
Lynn, Barry W., 12320
Lynn, Kenneth S., 1827
Lynn, Laurence E., Jr., 12321
Lyon, Peter, 9695
Lyons, Eugene, 8060-8062
Lyons, Louis M., 8007, 10054

Mabee, Charles, 1640
McAdie, Alexander, 1252
McAdoo, Eleanor R., 7170
McAdoo, William G., 7228
McAfee, Hoyt, 8435
McAllister, Eugene, 12322
Macartney, Clarence E., 4303, 4999, 5720
McAuliffe, Mary S., 9821, 9890
McAvoy, Thomas, 8639
McBee, Silas, 7053
McBride, Robert M., 2993
McBride, Robert W., 4229
McBrien, D. D., 2072

McCabe, James D., 5678, 5765, 5940, 5941, 6037
McCaleb, Walter F., 6388
McCamant, Wallace S., 88, 89
McCann, Alfred W., 90
McCann, Kevin, 9696
McCann, Maurice J., 9465
McCarthy, Charles H., 203, 5171, 5172
McCarthy, G. Michael, 6156, 6299, 8156, 8157
McCarthy, Joe, 10508
McCarthy, Joseph W., 10104
McCarthy, Richard J., 2115
McCarty, Burke, 4837
McCarty, Nancy, 9726
MacChesney, Nathan W., 3560
McClary, Ben H., 3973
McClaughry, John, 12892
McClellan, George B., 6085
McClelland, Barney F., 12891
McClelland, Charles A., 9975
McClelland, Clarence P., 4918
McClelland, Doug, 12579
McClelland, Stewart W., 3974
McClintock, E. C., 1443
McClure, Alexander K., 3561, 4058, 4131, 5000, 6242
McClure, Arthur F., 9269, 9466, 9467
McClure, James B., 5624, 5942
McClure, Stanley W., 3975
McClure, William E., 724
McColl, Gail, 12680
McColley, Robert, 1923
McComas, Joseph P., 344
McComb, Walter J., 6751, 7054
McCombs, William F., 7467
McConnell, Brian, 10447
McConnell, Grant, 9468, 9469, 10581
McCorison, J. L., Jr., 3976
MacCorkle, Stuart A., 2193
McCormac, Eugene I., 3215
McCormick, Joseph P., II, 12893
McCormick, Richard P., 2863, 2994
McCormick, Robert R., 5721
McCormick, Thomas, 6300, 7324
McCorvey, Thomas C., 1579
McCoy, Charla D., 11205
McCoy, Charles A., 3216, 3258
McCoy, Donald R., 8008, 8234, 8640, 9353-9355, 9470, 9484, 9822
McCoy, Drew R., 1165-1167, 1580, 1739
McCoy, Samuel, 859, 8009
McCracken, George E., 3069
McCrary, J. Peyton, 5173, 5174
McCrary, Royce C., Jr., 2995
McCroskey, James C., 11074
McCullar, Francis M., 11560
McCulley, Richard T., 11100
McCullough, David, 6484, 6810
McCurdy, Howard E., 12727

McCusker, John J., 8436
McCutcheon, John T., 6580
McDermott, John, 12377
MacDonald, Carlos F., 6301
McDonald, Forrest, 725, 2073
McDonald, Hugh C., 10448
McDonald, Timothy G., 6302, 7711
MacDonald, William, 2864
McDonough, James L., 5510
McDonough, John, 4736
MacDougall, Malcolm D., 11949
MacDowell, Francesca J., 12323
Mace, William H., 646, 3562
McElhiney, Thomas, 3063
McElroy, Robert M., 6086
McElvaine, Robert S., 8641, 12728
McEvoy, Kevin, 10105
McFadden, L. E., 3805
McFadyen, Barbara D., 9637
McFarland, Charles K., 7507, 8785, 9049
McFarland, Keith D., 9138
McFarlane, Ian D., 3387
McFaul, John M., 2865
McFeely, William S., 4737, 5625
McGarvey, Patrick J., 10296
McGee, Dorothy H., 8063
McGee, Gale W., 11694, 11807
McGeehan, Robert, 12478
McGhee, James E., 5722
Macgill, Hugh C., 11889
McGinniss, Joe, 11742
McGinty, Brian, 5156
McGlothlin, Don C., 12729
McGlynn, Frank, 4402
McGrane, Reginald C., 3105
McGrath, Dennis R., 2425
McGrath, Paul C., 1862
McGregor, Thomas B., 3850
McGroarty, William B., 387
McGuckin, Henry E., Jr., 11743
McGuire, Edward C., 345
McHale, Francis, 6970
McHargue, Daniel S., 7055
McIlwaine, Henry R., 2294
McInerney, Thomas J., 9823
McIntire, Ross T., 8642
McIntyre, Duncan T., 5220
MacIsaac, David, 9824
McKay, Ernest A., 4738
Mackay, Kenneth C., 7982
McKay, S. S., 8828
McKee, Delber L., 6855
McKee, John H., 7951
McKeldin, Theodore, 204
McKenna, George, 1740
Mackenzie, Compton, 8356
McKenzie, Richard B., 11561
Mackenzie, William L., 3064

McKeogh, Michael J., 9697
McKibbin, Michael K., 11890
McKim, Katherine J., 647
McKinley, James, 10449
McKinley, Silas B., 3300, 7171
McKinley, William, 6330-6333
McKinney, R. Kay, 10872
Mackinnon, William P., 3440, 3441
McKinstry, Levi C., 5955
McKinzie, Richard D., 9050
McKitrick, Eric L., 5404, 5511
McKown, Paul, 7508
McKown, Robin, 8643
Mackoy, Harry B., 6976
McLain, Glenn A., 12479
McLain, J. Dudley, Jr., 8966, 11562
McLaughlin, Andrew C., 2480, 2711, 5129
McLaughlin, Robert, 726, 3563
MacLaury, Judson, 6058
McLean, Hulda H., 8090
MacLean, William J., 2640, 2641
MacLeish, Archibald, 1253
McLellan, David S., 9547
McLemore, R. A., 2116
MacLeod, Julia H., 2074
McLoughlin, William G., 2160
MacMahon, Arthur W., 7418, 7419
McMahon, Edward, 2866, 5130
McMahon, Patrick, 10932
McMains, Howard F., 7056
McMaster, John B., 727, 5626
McMillan, Edward L., 9929
MacMillan, Harold, 9825, 9826, 10297
McMillan, Priscilla, 10450
McMurray, Richard, 5001
McMurry, Donald L., 6222
McMurtrie, Douglas C., 4304
McMurtry, R. Gerald, 3403, 3679, 3910, 3977-3979, 4054, 4059, 4358
McNamar, R. T., 13118
McNaught, Kenneth, 11289
McNaughton, Frank, 9234, 9235
McNaul, Willard C., 2161
McNeal, Robert H., 8905
McNeil, Floyd A., 5131
MacNeil, Neil, 10509
McNeill, Sarah B., 2996
Macoll, John D., 2642, 2643
McPherson, Elizabeth G., 3080
McPherson, Harry, 11075, 11076
McPherson, James M., 5766, 5870
McPike, H. G., 3721
McQuaid, John, 12730
McQuaid, Kim, 8189
McQuain, Thomas J., Jr., 10298
MacRae, D. A., 7325
McRae, Sherwin, 472
McSeveney, Samuel T., 6157

McSherry, James E., 10687
McSpadden, J. Walker, 6389
McTaggart, Lynne, 10106
McWilliams, Tennant S., 6303
McWilliams, Wilson C., 11077
Maddox, Linda, 12134
Maddox, Robert J., 6581, 7712, 7713, 7983, 8906, 9356, 10299
Maddox, Robert L., 12226
Madison, Charles A., 7623
Madison, Christopher, 12777
Madison, Dolley, 2358
Madison, James, 1239-1257
Madison, Lucy F., 91, 3564
Madow, Pauline, 10582
Magnuson, Roger P., 1641
Magrath, C. Peter, 11078
Maguire, Jack R., 10873
Mahajani, Usha, 10688, 10689
Maher, M. Patrick Ellen, 9270
Maher, Theodore J., 10690, 11267
Mahoney, Joseph F., 7420
Mahoney, Richard D., 10691, 10692
Mahoney, Tom, 8437
Maidment, Richard, 10565
Mailer, Norman, 10543
Majeske, Penelope K., 5512
Major, John, 9051
Malcolm, Donald F., 11447
Malcolm, James, 2867
Malin, James C., 6582
Mallam, William D., 4513, 5723
Mallan, John P., 6583, 10149
Malone, Dumas, 1254, 1324-1329, 1390, 1391, 1421, 1828, 1941-1944, 2000, 2162, 2194, 2275-2279, 2295, 4514, 8644, 11563
Malone, James H., 5513
Malone, Thomas J., 1829, 3980
Maloney, Gary D., 12395
Maltby, Charles, 3566
Mamatey, Victor S., 7714
Manchester, William R., 10055, 10056, 10451
Mancke, Richard B., 12324
Manijak, William, 7676
Mankiewicz, Frank, 11401, 11891
Mann, Seymour Z., 9471
Mannering, Lynne M., 8907
Manners, William, 6584, 6993
Manning, Clarence A., 11564
Manning, Robert A., 13023
Manning, Seaton W., 3369
Manning, Warren H., 1327
Mannix, Richard, 2117
Mansfield, Edward D., 5627
Mansfield, Harvey C., 1130, 2296, 12731
Mansfield, Luther S., 3309
Mansfield, Michael J., 10510
Mantell, Martin E., 5514, 5767

Mantripp, J. C., 3722
Manvel, Allen D., 13119
Ma'oz, Moshe, 9621
Marable, Manning, 12953
Marcell, David W., 11565
Marchman, Watt P., 5799, 5820-5823, 5831, 5832, 5865, 5871, 5872
Marchon, Maurice, 12293
Marcus, Maeva, 9472
Margolis, Howard, 10511
Margulies, Herbert F., 6585, 7873, 8010, 8158
Marina, William, 10452
Marion, David E., 7326
Mark, Eduard, 9648
Markam, Lois, 6390
Markel, Lester, 9357
Markens, Isaac, 4305, 4739, 4740
Markmann, Charles L., 10057
Markowitz, Arthur A., 728
Markowitz, Arthur M., 4838
Marks, Frederick W., 6856, 6857
Marmor, Michael, 7340
Marr, William L., 5221
Marraro, Howard R., 2497-2500
Marsh, Philip M., 1745, 1746, 1805-1809, 1863, 1924, 2546
Marsh, Richard D., 3259
Marsh, William J., Jr., 8235
Marshall, Charles B., 9827
Marshall, Edward C., 5628
Marshall, Eliot, 12228
Marshall, John, 648, 2195
Marshall, Lynn L., 2997, 5451
Marshall, Ray, 13120
Marshall, Robert A., 10693
Marszalek, John F., Jr., 4741, 6158
Martin de la Escalera, Carmen, 12481
Martin, Dan M., 2644
Martin, David A., 2998
Martin, David L., 5132, 11566
Martin, Don T., 9473, 9891
Martin, Dorothy V., 7851
Martin, Edwin T., 1581, 1870-1872
Martin, Harold H., 11079
Martin, Howard H., 12732
Martin, James M., 3851
Martin, John S., 1463
Martin, Keith D., 12894
Martin, Laurence W., 7677, 11603
Martin, Lawrence, 7327
Martin, Martha A., 12229, 12733
Martin, Oliver, 8645
Martin, Patricia M., 3567
Martin, Ralph G., 8345, 8469, 9236, 10300, 10624
Martin, Serge G., 12480
Martin, William, 7715, 8236
Marvell, Charles, 11567
Marvick, Elizabeth W., 11419

Marvin, Richard, 10107
Marx, Rudolf, 8438
Marx, Rudolph, 205
Mashek, John, 12044
Maslowski, Peter, 5175, 5515
Mason, Alpheus T., 6994-6998, 8967, 8968
Mason, Frank, 9271
Mason, Julian, 7716
Masonic Trowel, Springfield, IL., 4230
Massachusetts Historical Society, 950
Massaro, John, 11080, 12045
Massey, Mary E., 3852
Massey, Robert J., 10301
Masters, Edgar L., 3568, 6087
Mates, Leo, 12734
Mathews, Christopher J., 12735
Mathews, John M., 8908
Mathews, William R., 8728
Mathias, Charles M., Jr., 12736
Matloff, Maurice, 9139, 9140
Matray, James I., 9593-9595
Matson, William L., 8909
Matsuda, Takeshi, 7578
Matteson, David M., 585
Matthews, Albert, 388-394, 473, 586
Matthews, Brander, 6586, 6587
Matthews, James P., 10453
Matthews, Richard K., 1131
Matthewson, Timothy M., 729
Mattison, Ray H., 6434, 6466, 6485, 6588
Mattson, Robert L., 6589
Matusow, Allen J., 9295, 9474, 10302
Matz, Eliahu, 9141
Matzozky, Eliyho, 9142
Maurer, M., 649
Maurice, Frederick, 5002
Maurois, Andre, 10625
Maxey, David R., 11812
Maxfield, M. Richard, 1174
Maxfield, Marietta M., 10493
Maxwell, William Q., 4742
May, Ernest R., 2563, 9548
May, James T., 5829
Mayer, Arno J., 7579
Mayer, Frederick, 1925, 2163
Mayer, Michael S., 9892
Mayers, David, 9976
Mayhew, Aubrey, 10303
Maynard, Douglas, 4919
Maynard, Nettie C., 4306
Mayo, Barbara, 1255
Mayo, Bernard, 587, 1422, 1747, 1973, 1974
Mayo, Edward L., 2868
Mayo, John B., 10454
Mayo, Katherine, 650
Mayo, Lawrence S., 2645
Mayor, A. Hyatt, 1355
Mazlish, Bruce, 11420, 11421, 12135

Mazo, Earl, 11391, 11402, 11403
Mazon, Mauricio, 11422
Mazuza, George, 8205
Mazyck, Walter H., 588
Mazzoni, Tim L., 12325
Mead, Edwin D., 474, 730, 1864
Mead, Franklin B., 3981
Mead, Sidney E., 2426
Mead, Walter J., 12326
Meade, Robert D., 5003
Meadowcroft, Enid, 92, 3569
Meagher, Eileen M., 11892
Meagher, Sylvia, 10455, 10456
Meaney, Neville K., 7328
Means, Gaston B., 7852
Meany, Edmond S., 93, 3982
Mearns, David C., 1748, 2211, 3570, 3911, 3983, 4045, 4403, 5361
Mecklenburg, George, 3984
Medick, Monika, 11813
Medlin, Dorothy, 1464
Mee, Charles L., Jr., 7828
Meehan, Mary, 11568
Meerse, David E., 3412, 3442-3444
Meese, William A., 3723
Meeske, Mike, 10218
Mehlinger, Howard D., 1256
Mehta, M. J., 1642
Meier, Hugo A., 1673
Meisen, Adolf F., 2001
Mellen, George F., 2810
Mellon, James, 4172
Melton, David, 9237
Melusky, Joseph A., 12046, 12396, 12954
Mencken, Henry L., 7892, 9052
Mendelson, Wallace, 2196
Menendez, Albert J., 10058
Mensonides, Louis J., 9977
Mercer, Charles E., 12112
Merchant, Jerrold J., 10544
Meredith, H. L., 7952
Meredith, John R., 8237
Meredith, Roy, 4173, 4174
Meredith, Wyndham R., 475
Merenda, Peter F., 11081, 11569, 12188, 12378, 12944
Merget, Astrid E., 12362
Merk, Frederick, 3194, 3260
Merk, Lois B., 3260
Mermelstei, David, 11281
Merriam, Arthur L., 3985
Merriam, C. Hart, 6486
Merriam, Charles E., 1582, 1749, 1926, 3571, 6752, 7329
Merriam, Eve, 8357
Merriam, George E., 781
Merrill, Boynton, 1423
Merrill, F. T., 12230

Merrill, Horace S., 6159
Merrill, Jeffrey, 8786
Merrill, John, 9358, 9828, 10306
Merrill, Milton R., 6753
Merritt, Dixon, 8011
Merritt, H. Houston, 10442
Merritt, Richard L., 7468
Merry, Robert W., 12895
Mervin, David, 7421
Merwin, Henry C., 1132
Meschutt, David, 896, 1257, 1750
Meserve, Frederick H., 4175
Messer, Robert L., 8910, 9420, 9549
Metcalf, Evan B., 8159
Metcalf, Henry H., 3370
Metzger, H. Peter, 12327
Meyer, Donald H., 1927
Meyer, Howard N., 5629
Meyer, Karl E., 10307, 10308, 10545, 11082
Meyer, Keith E., 12488
Meyer, Peter, 12113
Meyers, Harold B., 11206
Meyers, Joan S., 10059
Meyers, Marvin, 2427, 2428, 2869, 2870
Meyers, Robert C. V., 6391
Meyersohn, Maxwell, 10803
Michael, Charles D., 6392
Michaelson, Michael G., 12896
Michaelson, Wes, 12136
Michel, Dorothy, 5070
Michelson, Charles, 9053
Middleton, Thomas J., 5516
Midgley, Louis, 1751
Miers, Earl S., 3789, 5724, 5725
Mieszkowski, Peter, 12328
Milakovich, Michael E., 12231
Milburn, John G., 6088
Miles, Edwin A., 897, 2871, 2872, 3261
Miles, Mary L., 3790
Miles, Rufus E., Jr., 12232
Miley, Cora, 3106, 3195, 3262
Milkis, Sidney M., 8646
Millar, William R., 12737
Millen, William, 11570
Miller, Alice P., 10060
Miller, August C., Jr., 1300
Miller, C. L., 3413
Miller, Charles R., 6263
Miller, Clara G., 7853
Miller, David H., 7678
Miller, Delbert C., 8647
Miller, Douglas T., 2873
Miller, Francis T., 3572, 9698
Miller, Helen, 315, 10626
Miller, James E., 8911
Miller, James M., 6393
Miller, John C., 2164
Miller, Joseph M., 5998

Miller, Justin, 5133
Miller, Lawrence W., 11333, 11347
Miller, Linda B., 12482, 13024
Miller, M. Sammy, 7509
Miller, Marion M., 3724, 4060
Miller, Merle, 9238, 9359, 10831, 10874, 11083
Miller, Nathan, 6487, 8358, 8439
Miller, Randall, 651
Miller, Raymond C., 6590
Miller, Richard B., 12897
Miller, Richard G., 2999
Miller, Richard L., 9272
Miller, Roger L., 11695
Miller, Sue F., 1509
Miller, Vivian I., 8829
Miller, Walter L., 8064
Miller, William D., 652
Miller, William H., 12898
Miller, William L., 5092, 12114
Milligan, Maurice, 9273
Milliken, R. C. V., 206
Millis, Walter, 6304, 8648, 9978
Mills, Bert, 10583
Milner, Duncan C., 3725
Milton, George F., 5004, 5405, 5430, 5517
Mims, Edwin, 7422
Minger, Ralph E., 4132, 7057-7062
Minks, Merle E., 11696
Minnigerode, Meade, 276, 1258
Minor, Charles L., 3573
Minor, Wilma F., 3726
Minsky, Hyman P., 12329
Mintz, Max M., 589, 1830, 3081
Mirkin, Harris G., 1975
Miroff, Bruce, 1010, 10309, 11207, 12673
Miscamble, William G., 5452
Miscamble, Wilson D., 9550-9552
Misse, Fred B., 8830, 9553
Missouri Historical Society, 4839
Mitchell, Broadus, 207, 951, 1928, 9054
Mitchell, Clarence, 11697, 12047
Mitchell, David, 7624
Mitchell, Franklin D., 9274, 9275, 9361
Mitchell, Henry, 1301
Mitchell, James, 476, 9893
Mitchell, S. Weir, 545
Mitchell, Stewart, 5999
Mitchell, Wayne S., 8912
Mitchell, William D., 731
Mitchell, Wilmot B., 3727
Mitgang, Herbert, 3574, 4404, 5157
Miyasato, Seagen, 9554
Mizwa, Tad, 12578
Model, F. Peter, 10457
Moe, Ronald C., 8160, 8161, 11571, 12233
Moffat, Alexander D., 1465
Mohrmann, Gerald P., 4515, 5299
Moldea, Dan E., 12899

Moley, Raymond, 8649, 8787, 9055, 9056, 10311, 11966
Molineu, Harold, 12538
Mollan, Robert W., 9894
Mollenhoff, Clark R., 11572, 11950, 12115
Mollman, John P., 9239
Monaghan, Jay, 4061, 4645, 4743, 4744, 4920
Monahon, Clifford P., 732
Monblatt, Bruce L., 8650
Mondadori, Arnoldo, 95
Mongar, Thomas M., 10312
Monroe, James, 2573-2578
Monroe, Sarah, 590
Montaque, Mary L., 591
Montgomery, Harry E., 4584
Montgomery, Henry, 1466, 1467, 1510, 3132, 3301
Montgomery, Mabel, 8359
Montgomery, Ruth, 10875
Moody, Frank K., 8440
Moody, Robert E., 2874, 3082
Mooney, Booth, 7172, 8755, 10832, 10833
Mooney, Chase C., 5453
Mooney, Christopher F., 7717
Moore, A. Georgory, 6858
Moore, Charles, 208, 277-281, 316, 546, 592, 653, 4062, 5071
Moore, Dorothy L., 5905
Moore, Glover, 2564, 2565
Moore, Guy W., 4840
Moore, J. Preston, 5005
Moore, James R., 7679, 9057
Moore, Jamie W., 9058
Moore, John H., 1754
Moore, Joseph H., 6591
Moore, Powell, 3227-3229
Moore, R. Walton, 209, 477
Moore, Virginia, 2331, 2360
Moore, William G., 5518
Moores, Charles W., 3575, 4585, 4586
Moos, Malcolm, 7984
Moran, Charles R., 9979
Moran, Philip R., 7854
Morehead, Joe, 11923
Morgan, Arthur E., 4442
Morgan, Edmund S., 96, 97, 593, 952, 1831, 1832
Morgan, George, 2523
Morgan, H. Wayne, 2646, 5873, 6243, 6264-6267, 6305, 9362
Morgan, James, 2080, 4443, 6394
Morgan, John H., 478, 479
Morgan, Kay S., 9699
Morgan, Richard, 11213
Morgan, Robert J., 1976, 2429, 2430, 3196, 3197
Morgan, Ted, 8360
Morgan, William G., 1011, 2647, 2875
Morgenthau, Hans J., 9980, 10313, 11084, 11268, 11334, 11573
Morin, Relman, 9700, 10458

Morison, Elting E., 6755, 6890-6892
Morison, Samuel E., 547, 1392, 9143
Morlando, Anne, 5088
Morrel, Martha M., 3217
Morris, Charles, 6082, 6242, 6395, 6396
Morris, Edmund, 6592, 6593, 6756, 6810
Morris, Griffith, 210
Morris, James R., 4841
Morris, Jeffrey B., 7063
Morris, Mabel, 2165
Morris, Richard B., 594, 3000
Morris, Robert L., 5176, 5519
Morris, Roger, 12234, 12483
Morris, Roland S., 1437
Morris, Sylvia J., 6488
Morris, Walter J., 2605, 2606
Morrison, Howard, 465
Morrison, J. E., 6203
Morrison, Katherine L., 2607
Morrison, Rodney J., 8969, 11698
Morrissey, Charles T., 9363
Morrow, Everett F., 9829
Morrow, Gary R., 12048, 12397
Morrow, Honore M. W., 3853
Morrow, L. C., 1393
Morrow, Lance, 12235
Morrow, Robert, 10314
Morrow, Rosemary, 11208
Morrow, William W., 395
Morse, Anson D., 1012
Morse, John T., Jr., 860, 1133, 2586, 3576, 3728
Morton, Henry C., 9144
Morton, Jennie C., 480
Morton, Louis, 9421, 9756
Morton, Rogers C. B., 11699
Mosby, John S., 5726
Moscow, Henry, 1134
Moscow, Warren, 8831
Moses, Belle, 317, 8361
Moses, Elbert R., 3577
Moses, John, 6131
Mosher, O. W., Jr., 7229
Mosley, James D., 211
Moss, Frank, 7330
Mothner, Ira, 7625
Mott, David C., 2811
Mott, Francis J., 481
Mott, Frank H., 6089
Mott, Frank L., 1610
Mott, Royden J., 1643
Motter, Thomas H. V., 7331
Moughrabi, Fouad M., 12971, 12972
Moulton, Gary E., 5103
Mowbray, Jay H., 6451, 6594
Mower, A. Glenn, Jr., 12539
Mowry, Duane, 3729
Mowry, George E., 3388, 6595, 6596, 6757
Moyers, Bill D., 11335, 11336

Moynihan, Daniel P., 7510, 7580, 10584, 11209, 11210, 11700, 12829
Mrozek, Donald J., 8162, 9475, 9555
Mudd, Richard, 4842
Mudd, Samuel, 11893
Muessig, Raymond H., 8163
Mugleston, William F., 3001
Mugridge, Donald H., 898
Muir, Dorothy T., 654
Mulder, Gerhard E., 4133
Mulder, John M., 7230-7232
Mulder, Ronald D., 12049, 12398
Mullaney, Thomas R., 11701
Mullen, Arthur F., 1833
Mullen, Avis A., 11211
Mullen, James J., 10627, 11253, 11744
Mullen, William F., 12236
Muller, H. N., 2118
Muller, Rene J., 11423
Mullins, William H., 8238
Mumford, Lewis, 1755
Mumford, Mary E., 3578
Mumper, James A., 2081
Munn, Charles A., 482
Munro, William B., 2876
Munson, Lyman E., 2082, 4745
Munton, Don, 13025
Munves, James, 1834
Murakata, Akiko, 6597
Muravchik, Joshua, 10694, 12540
Murillo-Jimenez, Hugo, 7581
Murphy, Charles J. V., 9830, 9831, 9895, 10315
Murphy, Dan, 1135
Murphy, Eloise C., 6598
Murphy, James P., 3730
Murphy, James W., 7916
Murphy, Mable A., 548
Murphy, Reg, 11745
Murphy, Richard, 6893
Murphy, Robert D., 9981
Murphy, Timothy F., 11574
Murphy, Walter F., 6999, 7000
Murphy, William F., 11814
Murphy, William J., Jr., 953
Murr, J. Edward, 4359
Murray, Agnes L., 11212
Murray, Anne W., 3107, 3153, 3326
Murray, Randall L., 9364
Murray, Richard K., 7893
Murray, Robert K., 7511, 7855, 7894-7897, 8012
Mushkat, Jerome, 5520
Musil, Robert K., 12484
Muskie, Stephen O., 8441
Musmanno, Michael A., 4746
Mussey, Virginia T. H., 483
Musso, Louis, III, 6397
Musto, David F., 899, 2608
Mutch, Verna E., 3987

Mutersbaugh, Bert M., 1611
Mutnick, Jeffrey, 11337
Muzzey, David S., 212, 1136, 1583
Myers, Albert C., 549
Myers, Elisabeth P., 2747, 5800, 6971
Myers, James E., 4307
Myers, Robert J., 12330
Myers, William S., 7233, 8239, 8240

Nadal, Ehrman S., 4231, 4232
Nadich, Judah, 9832
Nadler, Solomon, 2533
Nagel, Paul, 861, 2587
Nagorski, Zygmunt, 9556
Nagy, Edward C., 8970
Nakamura, Robert T., 12050, 12738
Nance, Joseph H., 3108
Nasaw, David, 12861
Nash, George H., 8065, 8091
Nash, Gerald D., 8164, 8362, 9059
Nash, Howard P., Jr., 5521
Nash, J. V., 346
Nash, Roderick, 1137
Nason, Elias, 5768
Nathan, James A., 10546
Nathan, Meyer J., 6599
Nathan, Richard P., 11702, 12739, 12900
National Broadcasting Company (NBC), 10459
National Broadcasting System, 10316
National Cartoonists Society, 9833
Natoli, Marie D., 11967
Nau, Henry R., 13121
Navarro, V., 12901
Navasky, Victor S., 10317
Naylor, R. T., 13026
Neal, Nevin E., 7507
Neal, Steve, 9701, 9702
Needham, David C., 7064
Needham, Henry B., 6489
Neeley, Mary A., 6160
Neely, Mark E., Jr., 3912, 3988, 3989, 4134, 4168, 4516, 4747, 5006, 5222
Neier, Aryeh, 12902
Neil, Henry, 6244
Neill, Edward D., 4748
Nelsen, Clair E., 8092, 8165
Nelson, Anna K., 3263, 3264, 9982
Nelson, Anson, 3222
Nelson, Bryce, 11085-11087, 11703
Nelson, Fanny, 3222
Nelson, Gerry, 6490
Nelson, Henry L., 6090, 6758
Nelson, Paul D., 5223
Nelson, Virginia A., 1977
Nelson, William, 98
Neruda, Pablo, 11575
Nesbitt, Victoria H. K., 8651
Ness, Gary C., 7065, 7066

Nettels, Curtis P., 595, 5454
Neu, Charles E., 6859, 6860, 7332
Neuberger, Richard, 10934
Neufeld, Maurice F., 2877
Neuhaus, Richard J., 12237
Neuman, Dale A., 9289
Neumann, Robert G., 8652, 9365, 9834, 12238
Neumann, William L., 8506, 8913, 8914, 9145
Neustadt, Richard E., 8653, 9476, 10318, 10319, 11088
Nevin, David J., 5943, 6038
Nevins, Allan, 3287, 3445, 3579, 3580, 4135, 4517, 4646, 5072, 5364, 5769, 6091, 6101, 7173, 7856, 8654, 8655, 9060, 10320
Newbold, Catherine, 5224
Newfarmer, Richard, 12740
Newhall, Beaumont, 2609
Newkirk, Garrett, 3990
Newland, Chester A., 12741
Newlon, Clarke, 10834
Newman, Albert H., 10460
Newman, Francis W., 4749
Newman, James R., 10323
Newman, Leonard, 4921
Newman, Ralph G., 3854, 3991, 4843, 5365
Newman, Robert P., 11815
Newton, Joseph F., 1644, 3581, 3582, 4405
Newton, Walter H., 8240
New York Public Library, 396
New York Public Library, Syracuse, 6512
New York Times, 10322, 11576, 11894
Ney, Virgil, 655
Neyland, James, 12137
Nicholas, Herbert G., 7333, 7576, 8656, 11816
Nichols, Alice, 3446
Nichols, David A., 5104-5106
Nichols, Edward J., 3315
Nichols, Frederick D., 1328, 1329
Nichols, Hugh L., 5679
Nichols, Jeannette P., 5874, 6306, 8788
Nichols, Roy F., 3364, 3371, 3447, 4518
Nichols, Teresa A., 13083
Nickel, Herman, 12331
Nickell, Franklin D., 5727
Nicolay, Helen, 3002, 4091, 4233, 4234, 4750, 5366
Nicolay, John G., 1511, 3583, 3584
Niebuhr, Reinhold, 9835
Nieburg, H. L., 9896
Niedziela, Theresa A., 8971
Nielsen, Niels C., Jr., 12138
Nieman, Donald G., 5522
Nigro, Felix A., 3083, 9366
Nigro, Louis J., 7582
Nihart, Brooke, 11577
Nikol, John, 6861
Niles, Blair, 282
Nisenson, Samuel, 8363
Niskanen, William, 11704

Niven, John, 3109
Nixon, Edgar B., 8657, 8915
Nixon, Patricia R., 11424
Nixon, Richard M., 9703, 10695, 11924-11945
Niznik, Monica L., 8658
Nobel, Charles, 7334
Noble, George B., 7680
Noble, Ransom E., Jr., 7335, 7336
Nock, Albert J., 1138
Noer, Thomas J., 9557, 9983, 10696
Noggle, Burl, 7737, 7898
Nolan, Carolyn G., 1356
Nolan, James B., 596
Nolan, Jeannette C., 2748, 3585
Noland, Nancy, 1259
Noonan, John T., Jr., 2197, 2566, 2648
Nordham, George W., 99, 100, 213, 283, 397, 484
Norris, James D., 7874
Norris, O. O., 5367
Norris, Walter B., 214
North, Gene, 6977
North, Ira L., 5971
North, Sterling, 3586
Northrop, F. S. C., 1674
Northrop, Henry D., 6204
Northrup, Jack, 4519, 4520
Norton, Aloysius A., 6398
Norton, Anthony B., 3160
Norton, Charles B., 6161
Norton, Eliot, 3732
Norton, Howard, 12116, 12139
Norton, John N., 347
Norton, Laurence, 8832
Norton, Paul F., 1756, 2083
Norwood, Bernard, 10697
Norwood, Irving C., 6759
Nossiter, Bernard D., 10585
Notaro, Carmen A., 5368, 5406, 8659
Notter, Harley, 7583
Novak, Michael, 12903
Novak, Robert D., 10817, 11508, 12008, 12661
Nuechterlein, James A., 11425
Nuesse, George C., 348
Nunnerly, David, 10698
Nurse, Ronald J., 10150, 10699
Nye, Joseph S., Jr., 13027
Nye, Russell B., 3003, 7067
Nyren, Karl, 13122

Oakes, Andra N., 11863
Oakleaf, Joseph B., 3733, 4922
Oates, Stephen B., 3587, 3588, 3913, 4444, 4751, 5007, 5225, 5226
Obadele, Imari A., 12485
O'Banion, Kerry, 12904
Oberholtzer, Ellis P., 3589
Obner, Benjamin A., 12335
O'Boyle, James, 101

O'Brian, John, 3346
O'Brien, Dennis J., 7584
O'Brien, Francis W., 7681, 8241, 11895
O'Brien, James J., 8093
O'Brien, Lawrence F., 10325
O'Brien, Matthew C., 656
O'Brien, Michael J., 215, 6492
O'Brien, Patrick G., 8242
O'Brien, Robert L., 6102, 6162
O'Brien, Robert W., 11591
O'Connell, Margaret J., 3992
O'Conner, James F. T., 8789
O'Connor, Edmund, 8364
O'Connor, Raymond G., 9146, 9558
O'Connor, Richard, 8013
Oddo, Gilbert L., 8972
Odegard, Peter H., 11089
Odell, Samuel W., 5728
Oder, Broeck N., 5523
Oder, Irvin, 8888
O'Donnell, Francis J., 9727
O'Donnell, James F., 9367
O'Donnell, Kenneth P., 10061, 10326, 11090
Oedel, Howard T., 5008
Offner, John L., 6307
O'Gara, Gordon C., 6760
Ogburn, Floyd, Jr., 1468
Ogburn, Robert W., 12541
Ogden, James M., 4587
Ogg, Frederic A., 3004, 5630, 6493
Ogilvie, John S., 5944, 6245
Oglesby, Carl, 10461
O'Grady, Joseph P., 7626, 7682
O'Hara, William T., 10586
Okie, Howard S., 5729
Olcott, Charles S., 6246
Oldham, G. Ashton, 349
Oldroyd, Osborn H., 3993, 4844, 4923, 6308
Olds, Helen, 10835
Oldys, Henry, 5369
O'Leary, James P., 12542
O'Leary, Paul M., 9147
Oliver, Andrew, 862, 2588
Oliver, David L., 4752
Oliver, John W., 1675
Oliver, Robert T., 8660
Oliver, Ronald E., 12597
Olsen, Otto H., 5009
Olson, David M., 12743
Olson, James S., 8094, 8166, 8167, 8243, 8244
Olson, John M. C., Jr., 9477
Olson, Julius E., 4360
Olson, Keith W., 7423
Olson, Lester C., 8833
Olson, William C., 6862, 12486
Oneal, Dennis J., 12051, 12399
O'Neal, William B., 1330
O'Neill, Scannell, 350

Onstott, R. J., 5370
Opotowsky, Stan, 10327
O'Reilly, Kenneth, 8245, 8756, 8790
Orenstein, Aviva A., 11593
Orfield, Lester B., 8168
Orlansky, Harold, 8661
Ornstein, Norman J., 12745, 12746
Orr, C. Jack, 12239
Orr, David W., 10700
Ortiz-Garcia, Angel L., 5524
Ortner, Robert, 12332
Orton, Vrest, 8014
Ortquist, Richard T., 8246
Osborn, George C., 7234-7238, 7512, 7738
Osborn, Henry F., 1676, 1677, 6494
Osborn, Robert W., 1978
Osborne, Duffield, 6495
Osborne, John, 11594-11602, 12052, 12240
Osborne, Leonard L., 10328
Osborne, Thomas J., 6163
Osgood, Ernest S., 1757
Osgood, Robert E., 7627, 11603
Ostendorf, Lloyd, 3855, 3958, 3994-3997, 4153, 4167, 4177-4179, 4845, 5010
Ostman, Ronald E., 10587, 10737
Ostrander, Gilman M., 1357
Ostrower, Gary B., 8791
O'Sullivan, John, 8442
Oswald, Rudolph, 12682
O'Toole, George, 10462
Ott, David, 11705
Ouh, Yoon B., 10329
Oulahan, Richard, 8834
Overholt, William H., 11817
Overland, Doris, 11896
Owen, Anna L., 8792
Owen, G. Frederick, 4309, 4310
Owens, Dennis J., 11818
Owens, John W., 7899
Owens, Patrick, 2649, 12747
Owens, Robert L., 3448
Owsley, Clifford D., 5073
Owsley, Harriet C., 3052

Packard, J. F., 5680
Packard, Roy D., 3590, 4552
Pad, Dennis N., 5824
Padover, Saul K., 216, 1139, 1758, 1835, 7628
Page, Benjamin I., 10978, 11486
Page, Elwin L., 597, 3372, 4361, 4521
Page, Rosewell, 1836
Page, Thomas N., 318
Paget, R. L., 6334
Paige, Glenn D., 9599
Paletz, David L., 12241
Palm, Charles G., 8275, 8317
Palmer, John L., 12748, 12749
Palmer, John M., 733, 5011, 5012, 7718

Palmer, Kenneth I., 13029
Palmer, Lillian R., 284
Palmer, Loomis T., 5631
Palmer, Robert R., 1929, 1979
Palmer, Upton S., 5875
Paltsits, Victor H., 734
Paludan, Phillip S., 4522
Pamel, Gregory J., 13146
Pancake, John S., 1930, 2481
Panetta, Leon E., 11706
Pape, T., 217, 485-487
Paper, Lewis J., 10330
Papp, Daniel S., 11819, 12053
Paradise, Frank I., 3591
Paranjoti, Violet, 10701
Pardue, Eugenia, 11304
Pargellis, Stanley, 4136
Parish, P. J., 5013
Park, Clyde W., 5632
Park, Joseph H., 5158
Park, Julian, 3347
Parker, Alan, 12333
Parker, Alton B., 6600
Parker, Daniel F., 9368
Parker, Edwin B., 10430
Parker, Frank L., 12334
Parker, George F., 6092, 6093, 6103, 6104, 6118-6120, 6164-6171
Parker, J. A., 12844
Parker, Malcolm E., 7683
Parker, Maude, 8662
Parker, Owen W., 6000
Parker, Theodore, 1140
Parker, William, 2302
Parker, Wyman W., 5825, 5918
Parkes, Henry B., 1931
Parkman, Francis, 3265
Parks, Edd W., 1358, 1584
Parks, Gordon E., 3084
Parks, Joseph H., 5455
Parks, Warren B., 2878
Parks, William, 1585
Parmet, Herbert S., 8835, 9836, 10062, 10063, 10331
Parrington, Vernon L., 1932
Parris, Troy C., 7655
Parry, Judge, 3734
Parsons, Edward B., 6863, 7719
Parsons, Elsie W., 7068
Parsons, Eugene, 102, 103
Parsons, Frank, 5371
Parsons, Lewis B., 4846
Parsons, Lynn H., 2610, 2650, 2651
Parsons, R. C., 3005, 4847
Partin, James W., 10935
Partin, John W., 8836
Partin, Robert, 104
Partney, Gerald D., Jr., 11338

Parton, James, 1141, 1260, 1933, 2002, 2084, 2749, 2750
Partridge, Bellamy, 8443
Parzen, Herbert, 8916, 9614
Pastor, Robert, 12487, 13028
Patenaude, Lionel V., 8837, 8973
Paterson, Thomas G., 9559-9561, 10702
Paton, William A., 4235, 8507
Patrick, Richard, 10703
Pattakos, Alex N., 13029
Patterson, Archibald W., 7239
Patterson, C. Perry, 1438, 1586, 1837, 2198, 2482
Patterson, David S., 7585
Patterson, James T., 8663, 8917, 9061, 9062
Patterson, Raymond A., 7069
Patterson, Robert F., 4406
Patton, James W., 5525
Patton, John H., 11091, 11332, 12242
Patton, John S., 1394, 1512, 1678
Paul, Cedar, 3592
Paul, Eden, 3592
Paulding, James K., 105, 2361
Paullin, Charles O., 285, 2664, 4063, 4553, 4753
Paulmier, Hilah, 5372
Payne, Alma J., 5801
Payne, Alvin N., 10936
Payne, Darwin, 10463
Payne, Frank O., 488, 3998, 3999, 6496, 6497
Payne, Roger A., 12958
Payne, Thomas, 6172
Peacock Press, 10804
Peale, Rembrandt, 489
Pear, R. H., 9837
Pearl, Arthur, 11747
Pearson, Charles W., 598, 5373
Pearson, Drew, 8522, 8523, 8664, 11339
Pearson, Edmund L., 6399
Pearson, Frederic S., 12488
Pearson, Samuel C., 900, 1645
Peary, Gerald, 12693
Peary, Robert E., 6761
Pease, Theodore C., 4754
Pechman, Joseph A., 12335
Peck, Harry T., 6094, 6762
Peckham, Charles A., 6268
Peckham, Howard H., 3133, 3144
Peden, William H., 1261, 1359, 1759, 1760
Pedersen, Wesley, 10805
Peebles, Thomas H., 11604
Peek, George A., Jr., 1057
Peffer, E. Louise, 6763
Peirce, Clyde R., 6864
Peirce, Neal R., 12400, 12905
Peirce, William F., 4848
Peixotto, Irma M., 782
Pelham, Ann, 12336
Pellicciotti, Joseph M., 11605
Pelz, Stephen E., 10704, 10705

Pemberton, William E., 9369
Pendergrass, Bonnie B., 9838, 10332
Pendleton, Lawson A., 3404
Pennel, Orrin H., 4311
Pennev, Rudolph G., 12830
Penniman, James H., 319, 735
Penniman, Josiah H., 4312
Pennington, Paul J., 8508
Pennoyer, Sylvester, 2483
Pennypacker, Isaac R., 736, 3915, 5227
Penty, George P., 10199
Percy, Charles H., 13030
Perdue, M. Kathleen, 5526
Peretz, Don, 10706, 11269, 11820
Perkins, Dexter, 2567, 2665, 8665
Perkins, Frances, 8365, 8509
Perkins, Frederic B., 4755
Perkins, Hazlehurst B., 1492
Perkins, Norman C., 6173
Perling, Joseph J., 3177
Perlmutter, Amos, 13031
Perman, Michael, 5527
Perry, Armstrong, 286
Perry, Bliss, 7240
Perry, Frances M., 6309, 6400
Perry, James R., 4064
Perry, Lewis, 3006
Peskin, Allan, 5945-5947, 5972, 5973, 6001-6007
Pessen, Edward, 2879-2886
Peters, Charles, 11606, 12243, 12401
Peters, Jean, 12831
Peters, Madison C., 4313
Peters, Mike, 11607
Petersen, Arnold, 1142
Petersen, William F., 4647
Peterson, Barbara B., 8918
Peterson, Frank R., 9562
Peterson, Fred, 4849
Peterson, Gale E., 9478
Peterson, Gary L., 4648
Peterson, Gloria, 4000
Peterson, Hans J., 8919
Peterson, Martin S., 1302
Peterson, Merrill D., 954, 955, 1262, 1343-1345, 1469, 1470, 1961-1964, 1980, 1981, 2085, 8666
Peterson, Raymond G., Jr., 218
Peterson, Trudy H., 9897
Peterzell, Jay, 13032
Petr, Jerry L., 13123
Petras, James, 12244
Petro, Nicolai N., 12543, 12750
Petronio, Sandra G., 12612
Pettengill, Samuel B., 1146
Petz, Weldon, 5014
Pew, William A., 737
Pfeiffer, Edward J., 9479
Pfiffner, James P., 12245, 12751

Phau, Donald, 1765
Phayre, Ignatius, 7900
Phelan, James R., 10464
Phelan, Mary K., 5093
Phelps, Bernard F., 8974
Phelps, Charles A., 5633
Phelps, Glenn A., 738
Phelps, Waldo, 11092
Phelps, William L., 4137
Phifer, Gregg, 5374, 5528-5534, 7629
Philbrick, Thomas, 1471
Philip, Kenneth, 8247
Philips, Edith, 1766
Philips, Edward H., 1263
Phillips, Cabell, 8667, 9370, 9371, 10628, 11093
Phillips, Charles, 106, 398, 3736, 4065
Phillips, Daniel T., 4092
Phillips, David G., 6764
Phillips, Edward H., 6765
Phillips, H. H., 11707
Phillips, Harry I., 7929
Phillips, Isaac N., 3593, 3594, 4236
Phillips, Josephine, 4407
Phillips, Kim T., 2887
Phillips, P. Lee, 531
Phillips, Steven L., 12416
Piccard, Paul J., 7469
Piccilo, Peter E., 9480
Pickell, John, 550
Pickens, Buford, 1331
Pickett, Mrs. George, 4237
Pickett, William P., 5228
Picknell, John, 551
Picque, Nicholas D., 11094
Pier, Arthur S., 287
Pierard, Richard V., 1982, 12752, 12753
Pierce, Michael D., 5535
Pierson, Hamilton W., 1513
Pike, James A., 10334
Pillemer, David B., 12754
Pillsbury, Albert E., 5229
Pinchbeck, Raymond, 2484
Pinchot, Ann, 10095
Pinchot, Gifford, 6498, 7070
Pinkett, Harold T., 6766
Pinkley, Virgil, 9704
Pipes, Richard, 11821
Pippert, Wesley G., 12140
Pisney, Raymond F., 7337, 7338, 7630
Pitkin, Thomas M., 5731
Pitkin, William A., 6601, 7071
Pitzer, Donald E., 7917
Piven, Frances F., 12755, 12906
Pixton, John E., Jr., 6310
Planck, Gary R., 4238, 4850, 4851, 5230
Plattner, Andy, 13054
Plaut, Ed, 10624
Pleasants, Samuel A., 1395

Plesur, Milton, 5876
Pletcher, David M., 3266, 6008, 6059
Plimpton, George, 10108
Plischke, Elmer, 9984, 9985, 11270
Ploughman, Piers, 10335
Plous, Harold J., 3007
Plumer, William, 1767
Plummer, Mark A., 4093, 4649
Podell, Jack, 10836
Podhoretz, Norman, 13033
Poen, Monte M., 9372, 9481, 9649
Pogue, Forrest C., 8920, 9757
Pohlman, Alan, 11893
Poland, Charles P., Jr., 5134
Pole, Jack R., 1934
Polenberg, Richard, 8668-8670, 8757, 8793, 8794, 9373, 12246
Polisky, Jerome B., 10629, 11748
Polk, James K., 3288-3292
Polk, John F., 3267
Polk, Sarah C., 3223
Pollack, Jack, 10876
Pollard, Cheryl C., 8457
Pollard, James E., 9374, 9375, 9839, 9840, 10738
Pollard, Josephine, 107, 5634
Pollenberg, Richard, 7956
Polley, Robert L., 8095
Pollin, Burton R., 6499
Pollitt, Daniel H., 11714
Pollock, Fred E., 6865
Polsby, Nelson W., 10336, 11096, 11749
Pomeroy, Earl S., 5135, 7339
Pomper, Gerald M., 11608
Pool, William, 10877
Poole, Susan D., 6060
Poore, Benjamin P., 5635
Pope, T., 288
Porter, Daniel R., 5833
Porter, Frank G., 399
Porter, Horace, 5770
Porter, J. M., 1013
Porter, Laurinda W., 12402
Porter, Robert P., 6247
Porter, William E., 11609
Porterfield, Bill, 10878, 10879
Posen, Barry R., 13084
Posner, Russell, 8838
Post, Jerrold M., 7340
Post, Regis H., 6767, 6768
Postbrief, Sam, 9563
Potter, David M., 3916, 4924, 8444
Potter, Jeffrey, 8445
Potter, John M., 4756, 4852
Potter, Philip, 10937, 11097
Potts, Louis W., 7857
Pound, Ezra, 901, 2303
Powell, Burt E., 1865
Powell, C. Frank, 3302

Powell, E. P., 599, 1014, 1264, 1646, 1935
Powell, Eugene J., 9276
Powell, Gary N., 12163
Powell, J. H., 219
Powell, James G., 10630, 10631, 11750
Powell, Jody, 12247
Powell, Lyman P., 7631
Power, John C., 3595
Power, Marilyn, 13124
Powers, David F., 10061
Poynter, Margaret, 12117
Prager, Annabelle, 1494
Pratt, Fletcher, 4757
Pratt, Harry E., 3596, 3597, 3737-3740, 3791, 4180, 4362, 4588
Pratt, Julius W., 2547, 3268
Pratt, Lowell C., 6500
Pratt, Silas G., 4002
Preeg, Ernest H., 10707
Prentice, Royal A., 6602
Prescott, F. C., 1472
Prescott, Frederick, 1936
Pressly, Thomas J., 3449, 3917, 4138
Pressman, Steven, 12757
Prestage, Jewel L., 8169
Preston, Howard W., 600
Preston, John H., 220
Prestor, Howard W., 783
Preu, James A., 7341
Price, Charles M., 8758
Price, Don K., 9148
Price, Glenn W., 3270
Price, Hugh D., 10588, 10589
Price, John W., 1647
Price, Kate H., 601
Price, Morris, 11823
Price, Raymond, 11824
Price, Ruth P., 5877
Price, W. W., 6311
Price, William J., 1439
Prichard, Samuel V. O., 11074
Prince, Carl E., 2087
Pringle, Henry F., 6401, 6603, 6972
Pritchard, Robert L., 9376
Pritchett, C. Herman, 8975, 8976
Pritchett, Henry S., 6312
Procter, Addison G., 5375
Prothro, James W., 9841
Provence, Harry, 10837
Provine, W. A., 784
Prucha, Francis P., 2813, 2888
Pruessen, Ronald W., 7342
Prufer, Julius F., 2003
Prussing, Eugene E., 221-223
Pryor, Helen B., 8096, 8097
Pryor, John C., 2004
Pukl, Joseph M., Jr., 3230-3232
Pullar, Walter S., 5015

Pulley, Judith, 1265, 1866
Purcell, Richard J., 1396, 3373
Purdy, Virginia C., 2814
Purifoy, Lewis M., 9564
Purvis, H. Hoyt, 11305
Purvis, Thomas L., 3918
Pusateri, C. Joseph, 8795, 8796
Pusey, Merlo J., 8977, 9705
Putnam, Carleton, 6402, 6501
Putnam, Charles, 6403
Putnam, George H., 3598, 4925, 5016
Putnam, Samuel, 1867
Putnam, Tarrant, 490
Pyle, Christopher, 11213
Pyne, John M., 7513

Quade, Quentin L., 9565, 9566
Quandt, William B., 13034
Quarles, Benjamin, 5231
Quarles, Joseph V., 3741
Quester, George H., 9986
Quill, J. Michael, 11340
Quin, Bernard, 10805
Quincy, Josiah, 2589
Quinlan, John, 6770
Quinn, James H., 4589
Quinn, Patrick F., 1303
Quinn, Thomas B., 6771
Quinn, Yancey M., Jr., 2815
Quint, Howard H., 7997
Quint, Peter E., 11613, 12251
Quirk, Paul J., 12758
Quirk, Robert E., 7586
Quitt, Martin H., 2816

Rabinowitz, Howard, 400
Rable, George C., 5456, 5536
Rachal, William M. E., 2431, 2535
Radcliffe, Richard, 2568
Radosh, Ronald, 7587
Radziwill, Catherine, 602, 6866
Rae, John B., 8318
Raffo, Peter, 7632
Ragan, Allen E., 7001, 7002
Ragland, James F., 8673, 8797
Rahskopf, Horace G., 2652
Rakestraw, Lawrence, 6772
Rakosnik, Eugene, 6061
Ralph Nader Congress Project, 11968
Ram, Susan, 12490, 13035
Ramage, Burr J., 5537
Ramsay, David, 108
Ramsay, Marion L., 8798
Ramsey, Don, 9706
Ramsey, John W., 9482
Ranck, Edwin C., 6604
Ranck, James B., 3405
Randall, David A., 1838

Author Index

Randall, E. O., 603, 1868
Randall, Henry S., 1147
Randall, James G., 740, 1768, 3599, 3600-3602, 4003, 4139, 4758, 4759, 5017-5019, 5136, 5732, 7588, 7684
Randall, Robert L., 4094, 4408
Randall, Ronald, 7073, 11709
Randall, Ruth P., 3856-3859
Randolph, Eleanor, 12252
Randolph, Howard S. F., 491
Randolph, Sarah N., 1424
Raney, McKendree L., 4239
Range, Willard, 8674, 8921
Ranish, Donald R., 12504
Rank, Vernon E., 3085
Rankin, David C., 4926
Rankin, Frank C., 4004
Rankin, Henry B., 3603, 4005, 4095, 4240
Rankin, Mrs. Mckee, 4853
Rankin, Robert S., 8249, 9063
Ranlett, F. J., 6502
Ransom, Frederick D., 5834
Ransom, William L., 4590
Rantoul, Robert S., 4241
Rappaport, Armin, 2569
Rappaport, Percy, 9898
Rarick, David L., 12402, 12612
Raringer, William E., 4927
Rasmussen, Della M., 3604, 12570
Ratcliff, Carter, 12141
Ratcliffe, Jeanira, 10085
Ratcliffe, S. K., 9930
Rather, Dan, 11825
Ratner, Sidney, 5772
Rauch, Basil, 9064, 9149, 9179
Raven, Bertram H., 11614
Ravenal, Earl C., 11826, 11827
Ravenhill J., 13036
Rawley, James A., 4140, 4523, 5020
Ray, Deborah W., 8922
Ray, P. Orman, 3381
Ray, Robert F., 8839
Rayback, Joseph G., 3065, 3086-3089, 3271
Rayback, Robert J., 3335, 3336
Raymond, Henry J., 3605, 4760, 4761
Rayner, Kenneth, 5407
Read, Allen W., 2817
Read, Harry D., 7289
Read, Harry, 4854
Reagan, Michael D., 12760
Reagan, Nancy, 12583
Reagan, Ronald, 12561, 13147-13150
Real, Michael R., 11751
Record, Jeffrey, 13038
Redard, Thomas E., 11214
Reddig, William M., 9277
Redding, John M., 10246
Redding, W. Charles, 8840

Redenius, Charles, 13127
Redfield, William C., 7429
Redford, Emmette S., 11099, 11100
Redway, Maurine W., 4006
Ree, Dale, 8317
Reece, Brazilla C., 5408
Reed, Anna C., 109
Reed, Marvin E., Jr., 6605
Reeder, Russell P., 9707
Reedy, George, 10838, 11215
Reep, Thomas P., 4363
Rees, George L., 6773
Reese, Lee F., 5538
Reeves, Earl, 8066
Reeves, Jesse S., 3198, 3272
Reeves, Richard, 11615, 12057, 12253
Reeves, Thomas C., 6039, 6046, 6047, 6049, 6062-6066
Reginald, R., 10337
Reich, Bernard, 12491, 13039
Reich, Michael, 12492
Reich, Robert B., 13128, 13129
Reichard, Gary W., 7902, 9842-9844, 9987
Reichley, A. James, 11616, 11617, 12055, 12056, 12767
Reichley, Nancy, 7953
Reid, Edith G., 7174
Reid, J. A., 6010
Reid, John, 956, 2752
Reid, R. A., 6010
Reid, Ronald F., 5074, 7343, 9931
Reid, Whitelaw, 1266, 3606, 4409
Reiff, Philip, 7685
Reilly, Ann M., 12254, 12915, 12955
Reilly, Michael F., 8675, 8676
Reilly, Tom, 4650, 4928
Reinert, A., 11101
Reinertson, John, 7589
Reingold, Nathan, 2653
Reinhardt, John F., 1587
Reisman, W. Michael, 13040
Reisner, Christian F., 6503
Reissman, Frank, 11515
Relyea, Harold C., 12657
Remey, Oliver E., 6606
Remini, Robert V., 2753-2756, 2818, 2889, 3009-3011, 3090-3092, 3110
Renka, Russell D., 10512-10514, 11102-11104
Rennagel, William C., 11828
Renne, Louis O., 4364
Rennick, Percival G., 3742
Renshon, Stanley A., 11426
Reps, John W., 1267
Republican party. National Committee, 5636, 9377, 10338
Republican party. New Hampshire, 3012
Reston, James, 10109
Reter, Ronald F., 6774, 6867

Reuben, William A., 11451
Reuss, John W., 9547
Reuter, Frank T., 741, 7074
Reuter, Theodore, 11976, 12367
Revill, Janie, 2819
Reyerson, Richard A., 957
Reynolds, Beatrix, 401
Reynolds, David, 8923-8925
Reynolds, J. Marvin, 12488
Reza, Ali M., 12916
Rezneck, Samuel, 3111
Reznikoff, Phillip, 224
Rhea, Mini, 10110
Rhoads, William B., 8446-8448
Rhodes, Benjamin D., 8250
Rhodes, Edwin S., 11619
Rhodes, James A., 3860
Rhodes, James F., 5878, 6313, 6775
Rhodes, Richard, 9278, 9730, 10802
Rhodes, Thomas L., 1514
Ricard, Serge, 6404, 6607
Riccards, Michael P., 10590, 10938
Rice, Allen T., 4243
Rice, Andrew E., 9988
Rice, Charles D., 2149
Rice, H. LaMarr, 5232
Rice, Howard C., Jr., 1195, 1268, 1269, 1679, 1769, 1869
Rice, Philip A., II, 1870
Rice, William G., 6175
Richards, John T., 3607, 4591, 5376
Richards, Leonard L., 958, 2890
Richardson, Albert D., 5637
Richardson, E. P., 1270, 1271
Richardson, Elmo R., 7075, 9483, 9845, 9899
Richardson, Guy, 5377
Richardson, James D., 1148
Richardson, Joe M., 6067
Richardson, Lyon N., 5879, 5880
Richardson, William D., 2166
Richardson, William H., 659, 660
Richelson, Jeffrey, 13041
Riches, William T. M., 4762, 5457
Richman, Michael, 4007
Richmond, Michael E. M., 12403
Rickenbacker, William F., 12598
Riddle, Albert G., 6040
Riddle, Donald H., 9378
Riddle, Donald W., 4554-4556
Riddleberger, Patrick W., 5539
Rideing, William H., 110
Ridgeway, James, 13071
Ridinger, Gerald, 8876
Ridley, Maurice R., 3608
Ridout, Edith M., 661
Ridpath, John C., 5948
Rielly, John E., 13042
Riemer, Neal, 2332, 2432, 2433, 2434, 10339

Riemer, Yosef, 12404
Riessman, Frank, 12671
Rietveld, Ronald D., 4855, 5233
Rifai, Abdul H., 9989
Rigdon, William M., 10340
Riis, Jacob A., 6504
Riley, I. Woodbridge, 2005
Riley, Philip, 10880
Rinaldi, Nicholas, 320
Rindlaub, M., 4244, 4245
Ringenberg, William C., 5956
Ringwalt, John L., 5638
Rinn, Fauneil J., 8251
Ripel, Barbara D., 959
Ripley, Randall B., 10515
Rippy, J. Fred, 6868
Risjord, Norman K., 2119, 2548
Riste, Olav, 9150, 9151
Ritcheson, Charles R., 1871, 1872
Ritter, Halsted L., 225
Ritter, Kurt W., 12599
Ritze, C. C., 3861
Rivers, Caryl, 11306
Rives, William C., 2333
Rivoire, Mario, 111
Ro, Kwang H., 6869
Roady, Elston, 7471
Robbins, Charles, 9240
Robbins, Jan C., 1612
Robbins, Jessie M., 226
Robbins, Jhan, 9260
Robbins, Peggy, 2820, 4314
Robbins, William G., 8252
Roberson, Samuel A., 1304
Roberts, Allen E. G., 351
Roberts, Chalmers M., 11829
Roberts, Charles W., 10465, 11105-11108
Roberts, Derrell, 7344
Roberts, Dick, 11621
Roberts, George C., 7472
Roberts, Gerald F., 6505
Roberts, John G., 2304
Roberts, Kenneth L., 7954
Roberts, Octavia, 4365
Robertson, Archie, 6608
Robertson, Deane, 4856
Robertson, James O., 4008
Robertson, John B., 4763
Robertson, Pearl L., 6176-6178
Robertson, Peggy, 4856
Robins, Elizabeth, 1272
Robinson, A. H., 5075
Robinson, Clarence A., Jr., 12493, 12768, 12769, 13085
Robinson, Corinne R., 6405
Robinson, Dan M., 5458
Robinson, Edgar E., 8067, 8677, 8841, 9567, 9990, 10708, 11271

Author Index

Robinson, Elwyn B., 6609
Robinson, Fred N., 492
Robinson, George C., 8678
Robinson, George W., 9065
Robinson, Judith, 11691
Robinson, Lloyd, 5906
Robinson, Luther E., 4066, 4315
Robinson, Michael J., 12770
Robinson, Rex E., 8842
Robitscher, Jonas, 11622
Roche, Bruce, 10881
Roche, John P., 10341, 11109, 11110, 11254
Rochefort, David A., 6776
Rochester, Stuart I., 9900
Rock, Robert H., 12795
Rockhill, Nathalie S., 10807
Rockman, Bert A., 11461, 12255
Roddy, Joseph, 10111
Roderick, Lee, 4020
Rodesch, Jerrold C., 960, 2654
Rodgers, Harrell R., Jr., 11897
Rodman, Peter W., 12494
Roe, Edward T., 6248
Roebuck, James R., Jr., 7076
Roell, Craig H., 10939
Roelofs, H. Mark, 5076
Roffman, Howard, 10466
Rofinot, Henry L., 7903, 8017
Rogers, Agnes, 3609
Rogers, Benjamin, 8253, 9650
Rogers, Cameron, 7930
Rogers, Jimmie N., 11272
Rogers, Joel, 12956
Rogers, Joseph M., 5907
Rogers, Kate B., 4009
Rogers, Lindsay, 7430
Rogers, Robert, Jr., 1937
Rogers, Warren, 10467, 11111
Rogers, William W., 6786
Rogge, Edward A., 9379
Rogin, Michael, 3013, 4764, 7345, 11427, 11623
Rogow, Arnold A., 2435
Rohatyn, Felix G., 13129
Rohrs, Richard C., 3014
Roll, Charles, 4929
Rollins, Alfred B., Jr., 8449, 8510-8512, 8679, 8680, 10342
Romano, Louis G., 1105
Romasco, Albert U., 8254, 9066
Roosevelt, Eleanor R., 8366, 8477-8487
Roosevelt, Elliott, 8367, 8368, 8450, 8488
Roosevelt, Franklin D., 9180-9209
Roosevelt, Hall, 8451
Roosevelt, James, 8369, 8452, 8453, 8681
Roosevelt, Nicholas, 6406, 6407
Roosevelt, Sara D., 8370
Roosevelt, Theodore, 6889, 6894-6962
Roosevelt, Thomas A., 6870

Root, Elihu, 4010, 6408
Roper, Burns, 12772
Roper, Donald M., 3093
Roper, R. C., 4316
Roper, William L., 9279, 11453
Rosamond, Robert, 9848
Rosati, Jerel A., 12256
Roscoe, Theodore, 4857
Rose, Douglas D., 12058, 12405
Rose, Ernest D., 12600
Rose, Galen L., 6011
Rose, Richard, 10709
Rose, Uriah M., 4410
Roseman, Alvin, 11273
Rosen, Elliot A., 8255, 8799, 8800, 9067
Rosen, Gerald R., 11216, 12257
Rosen, Philip T., 8242
Rosenau, James N., 9210
Rosenberg, Bruce A., 10343
Rosenberg, Emily S., 7590
Rosenberg, Harold, 11898
Rosenberg, Hyman S., 10064
Rosenberg, J. Philipp, 9568, 9569, 9615
Rosenberg, Leonard B., 11624
Rosenberg, Sam, 12917
Rosenberger, Francis C., 2088
Rosenberger, Leif R., 11830
Rosenberry, Cecil R., 6012
Rosenblum, Marcus, 8372
Rosenblum, Sig, 11112
Rosenfield, L. W., 9380, 11752
Rosenman, Samuel I., 8683, 8684
Rosenthal, Herbert H., 6612
Rosenthal, Paul I., 10632, 11753
Rosewater, Victor, 5908
Roske, Ralph J., 4592, 5540, 5541
Rosmond, James A., 6778
Ross, B. Joyce, 8801
Ross, David F., 13043
Ross, Dorothy, 7241
Ross, Earle D., 4524, 6179, 8802
Ross, Edmund G., 5542
Ross, Hugh, 8843, 8844
Ross, Irwin, 9506
Ross, Ishbel, 3862, 5681, 6979, 7242, 7955
Ross, Leland M., 8685
Ross, Michael, 1770, 2436
Ross, Riley R., 4411
Ross, Rodney A., 3863
Ross, Thomas B., 10004
Rossant, M. J., 10591
Rossiter, Clinton L., 961, 962, 1771, 2437, 8686
Rosten, Leo C., 8687
Rostow, Eugene V., 11113, 12495
Rostow, Walt W., 9991, 9992, 10710, 10711
Roth, Lawrence V., 5021
Roth, Philip, 11625
Rothchild, D., 13036

Rothchild, Donald S., 8688
Rothenberg, Alan B., 11899
Rothenberg, Irene F., 12957
Rothschild, Alonzo, 3610, 4445
Rothschild, Emma, 12773
Rothschild, Richard, 1772
Rothwell, C. F., 8319
Rotunda, Ronald D., 8689
Roucek, Joseph S., 11217, 11290
Rourke, Francis E., 11603
Rourke, John T., 9758
Rousseas, Stephen, 13130
Rout, Leslie B., 8543
Rovere, Richard H., 9596, 9759, 9846, 9847, 10344, 10592, 10940, 11255
Rowe, Jonathan, 12774
Rowe, Joseph M., Jr., 7077
Rowe, Richard B., 9901
Rowen, Hobart, 10593, 11218
Rowland, Benjamin M., 11603
Rowland, Eron O., 2891
Rowland, John A., 6779
Rowland, Robert C., 12958
Rowse, Arthur E., 11454
Royall, Margaret S., 5543
Royner, B. L., 1149
Royster, Charles, 2006
Roz, Firmin, 112, 8371
Rozen, Miriam, 12955
Rozett, John M., 3015
Rozwenc, Edwin C., 2892, 2893, 7514, 8803
Rubinger, Naphtali J., 4317
Rubner, Michael, 13044
Ruck, William S., 1332
Rucker, Bryce W., 9932
Ruddy, Michael T., 9528
Rudnick, David, 12496
Rudolph, Lloyd I., 11274, 11831
Rudolph, Norman, 227
Rudoni, Dorothy J., 9381
Ruetten, Richard T., 9470, 9484
Ruiz, Ramon E., 4525
Rukeyser, Merryle S., 10594
Rulon, Philip R., 10839, 10882, 11374
Rumberger, Russell, 13099
Runfola, Ross T., 8170
Runk, Edward J., 493
Rush, Richard, 289
Rushford, Jerry B., 5957
Rushkoff, Bennett C., 9993
Ruskowski, Casimer W., 8690
Russ, William A., Jr., 3450, 5022, 8256
Russel, Robert R., 3348, 3374
Russell, Ada, 113
Russell, Don, 9708
Russell, Francis, 7829, 7858-7860, 7918, 8018
Russell, G. Darrell, Jr., 3611, 10345
Russell, Henry B., 6249

Russell, J. F. S., 5544
Russell, Leon W., 12775
Russell, Phillips, 1588
Russell, Robert, 5459
Russell, Robert G., 5545
Russell, Thomas H., 6409, 7830
Russell, William E., 1938
Russo, David J., 3016
Rust, William J., 10712
Rustin, Bayard, 11219, 11663
Rutland, Robert A., 1939, 2362, 2438, 2486
Rutledge, Archibald, 4412, 5023, 5024
Rutledge, John, 12337, 12959
Ryan, Daniel J., 4366
Ryan, Halford R., 8691, 8692, 9597, 9849
Ryan, Henry B., Jr., 9638
Ryan, Joseph F., 4765
Ryan, Paul B., 9091
Ryerson, Edward, 963, 7431
Ryskind, Allan H., 10211

Saalberg, John J., 8804
Saasta, Timothy, 12776
Sabine, William, 228
Sabki, Hisham, 7686
Sacks, R., 12677
Saddler, Hugh, 12338
Sadler, Charles, 8845
Sadler, David F., 6780
Sadler, Elizabeth H., 1515
Sadler, Julius T., Jr., 1318
Safford, Jeffrey J., 7591, 7721, 11832
Safire, William, 11900, 11901
Sageser, A. Bower, 9728
Sainsbury, Keith, 9152
Saint, Percy, 1940
St. John, Jeffrey, 12339
Salami, George R., 9994
Salandria, Vincent J., 10468
Salant, Walter S., 9485
Sale, Richard T., 12497
Salinger, Pierre, 10065
Salisbury, Harrison, 10112
Salmond, John A., 8805
Saltman, Helen S., 964, 965
Salzberg, John P., 12544
Sammis, Edward R., 10066
Samovar, Larry A., 10633, 10634, 11754, 11755
Samuels, Ernest, 4526
Samuelson, Robert J., 12777
Sanchez-Torrento, Eugenio, 3612
Sand, Gregory W., 9570
Sand, Norbert, 1397
Sandburg, Carl, 3613, 3864, 4011, 4012, 4067, 4175, 4446, 5025, 5026
Sander, Alfred D., 9571
Sanders, Charles L., 11220
Sanders, Frederick K., 966

Sanders, Luther W., 10739
Sanders, Neill F., 4766-4768
Sandler, S. Gerald, 1648
Sandler, Samuel, 9850, 11626
Sandos, James A., 7656
Sanford, Charles B., 1473
Sanford, Charles L., 1360
Sanford, Fillmore H., 8693
Sanghvi, Ramesh, 10151
Santrey, Laurence, 114, 1150
Sapin, Burton M., 12498
Sarasohn, Judy, 12406, 12778
Saravay, Judith, 10392
Sargent, George H., 229
Sargent, James E., 8694, 9068-9071
Sarkesian, Sam C., 12499
Sather, Lawrence A., 10635
Satterthwaite, Joseph C., 9639
Satz, Ronald N., 2894, 2895
Saulnier, Raymond J., 9902, 12059, 12340-12342, 13131, 13132
Saunders, Frances W., 230, 7243, 7244, 7346
Saunders, Frank, 10067
Saunders, Richard M., 9995, 9996
Sauvage, Leo, 10469
Savage, Hugh, 8171
Savage, John, 3605, 5409
Sawhil, Isabel V., 12749, 13111, 13137
Sawitzky, William, 494
Sawyer, Joseph D., 115
Sawyer, Robert W., 5958
Sawyer, Roland D., 7931
Saxon, Thomas J., Jr., 11627
Saylor, J. R., 8978
Sbrega, John J., 8926
Scandrett, Richard M., 7956
Scanlan, Alfred L., 8979
Scanlon, James E., 2120
Scarry, Robert J., 3337
Schachner, Nathan, 1273, 1773
Schacht, John N., 8098, 8099
Schaedler, Louis C., 2363
Schafer, Joseph, 116
Schaff, David S., 1839
Schambra, William, 4413
Schandler, Herbert Y., 11341
Schapsmeier, Edward L., 1941, 4651, 6613, 7904, 9903
Schapsmeier, Frederick H., 1941, 4651, 6613, 7904, 9903
Schauffler, Edward R., 9241
Schauffler, Robert H., 5378, 5379
Scheele, Henry Z., 12779
Scheele, Paul E., 12343
Scheer, James F., 9704
Scheer, Robert, 11628, 12142, 13086
Scheiber, Harry N., 3017, 7432, 7504, 7515, 7722
Scheiber, Jane L., 7722

Scheick, William J., 1474
Scheinberg, Stephen J., 6781, 6782
Scheiner, Seth N., 6783
Scheips, Paul J., 3451
Schelin, Robert C., 3349
Schelling, Thomas C., 11807
Schemmer, Benjamin F., 12500
Scher, Seymour, 9904
Schick, Joseph S., 1475
Schiffman, Joseph, 8695
Schilling, Warner R., 9422
Schimpf, Sheila O., 5159
Schlechty, David L., 12918
Schlegel, Marvin W., 5177
Schleifer, Richard, 11902
Schlesinger, Arthur M., Jr., 2757, 8373, 8374, 8454, 8513, 8696, 8927, 9596, 10113, 10347, 10636, 11114, 11756, 12545
Schlesinger, Arthur M., Sr., 321, 5027
Schlesinger, Edward B., 10442
Schlesinger, Stephen, 13045
Schlundt, Ronald A., 9905
Schlup, Leonard, 3233, 6180-6182, 7003, 7097
Schluter, Herman, 5234
Schmertz, Mildred F., 10883
Schmickle, William E., 7633
Schmidt, Ferdinand, 117
Schmidt, Patricia B., 6614
Schmidt, Terry P., 9572
Schmidt, William T., 8697
Schmidtlein, Gene, 9275, 9280-9282
Schmucker, Samuel M., 118, 1151
Schnapper, Morris B., 9651, 10348
Schneider, Herbert W., 1589
Schneider, Jerrold E., 12780
Schneider, Mark L., 12546
Schneider, Nicholas A., 10806, 10807
Schneider, William, 12474, 13133
Schneidman, J. Lee, 10068
Schnell, J. Christopher., 8846, 9072
Schoch, Henry A., 6784
Schoenberger, Walter S., 9423
Schoenebaum, Eleanora W., 9382, 11555, 11629, 12042, 12060
Schoenfeld, Andrea F., 11691
Schoenherr, Steven E., 9073
Schofield, Kent M., 8172, 8173
Scholes, Marie V., 7078, 7657
Scholes, Walter V., 7078, 7657
Schoonover, Thomas, 5546, 5547
Schoor, Gene, 8375
Schortemeier, Frederick E., 7919
Schott, Richard L., 11115
Schouler, James, 1152, 3792, 5548, 5549, 5574
Schram, Martin, 12407
Schreiber, Flora R., 11221
Schroeder, John F., 119, 231
Schroeder, John H., 3273, 3274

Schruben, Francis W., 7861
Schullery, Paul, 6785
Schulte, Renee K., 11404
Schultz, Harold S., 2334, 2439, 4141
Schultz, Louis P., 7079, 7080, 12501
Schultz, William, 10211
Schulz, Constance B., 902, 967, 1649, 1650
Schulz, Donald E., 10547
Schurz, Carl, 3614, 3743
Schuyler, Montgomery, 4013, 4068
Schuyler, Robert L., 3275
Schutz, John A., 968
Schwab, Peter, 10069
Schwabe, Klaus, 7634
Schwartz, Barry, 742
Schwartz, Bernard, 2305, 2516, 11630
Schwartz, Donald R., 7516
Schwartz, Edward, 1691
Schwartz, Herman, 12781, 12782, 12919
Schwarz, Edward A., 11721
Schwarz, Jordan A., 8257, 8258
Schwarz, Urs, 10808
Schweigler, Gebhard, 12258, 12259, 12502, 12783
Schweikart, Larry, 5235
Schwengel, Frederic D., 5028
Sciacca, Tony, 10114
Scobey, Alfredda, 10470
Scobie, Ingrid W., 11455
Scofield, Edward, 12784
Scott, George T., 5826
Scott, Henry E., 7245
Scott, James B., 2440, 4414, 6871, 7905
Scott, Milton R., 4415, 5380
Scott, Peter D., 10471
Scott, W., 743
Scott, Winfield, 3452
Scovel, James M., 4014, 4246, 5431
Scoville, Herbert, Jr., 11833
Scoville, Samuel, Jr., 3744, 4247
Scribner, Charles R., 9997, 11342
Scripps, John L., 3615, 4930
Scruggs, Donald L., 11222
Scruggs, J. H., Jr., 1942
Scudder, Horace E., 120
Seaborg, Glenn T., 10713
Seager, Robert, 3173
Searcher, Victor, 4015, 4416, 5094
Sears, Louis M., 121, 744, 745, 1873, 1943, 2121, 7246
Seasongood, Murray, 746
Seaver, William J., 3793
Secrest, Donald E., 9573, 9998
Sedgwick, Paul J., 4858
See, Anna P., 7957
Seelye, Elizabeth, 122
Seelye, John, 11428
Sefton, James E., 5550, 5551
Segal, Charles M., 4931

Segal, Hans E., 11881
Seifert, Shirley, 5733
Seisler, J. M., 11343
Seitz, Don C., 290, 4016, 4527
Selby, John E., 969
Selby, Paul, 5381, 5382
Selesnick, Herbert L., 10548
Seligman, Ben B., 10349
Seligman, Lester G., 9074
Sellen, Robert W., 6615, 6616, 7592, 9851, 11275
Sellers, Charles G., Jr., 2758, 2821, 2822, 2896, 3018, 3218, 3234, 3235, 3276, 3453
Sellers, Horace W., 2306
Sellers, Steven A., 9075
Sellier, Randy, 12532
Seltzer, Alan L., 7347
Seltzer, Louis B., 7081
Seltzer, Robert V., 9598, 11344
Semonche, John E., 6964
Semple, Robert B., 11631, 11632
Sen, S. Sudhir, 13046
Sensabaugh, George F., 1651
Serfaty, Simon, 13047
Serpell, Jean K., 1874
Sessions, Tommie G., 7658
Sestanovich, Stephen, 1875
Settel, Trudy S., 9652, 10809, 10810
Severa, Joan, 6567
Severn, John K., 6786
Severn, William, 3219, 5410
Sewall, William W., 6410, 6411
Seward, William H., 2590, 4248
Sewell, Richard H., 4528
Seymour, Charles, 7175, 7348, 7672, 7687, 7723
Seymour, Whitney N., Jr., 11633
Shachtman, Tom, 7176
Shackelford, George G., 1361, 1425
Shaffe, Arthur H., 7874
Shaffer, Dallas S., 4769
Shaffer, Samuel, 10158, 10941
Shaffer, William R., 10350, 12260
Shalett, Sidney, 8369, 9383
Shalhope, Robert E., 1944, 2897
Shane, M., 7473
Shank, Alan, 10595
Shanks, Alexander G., 7433
Shannon, David A., 7247, 7248
Shannon, Frederick F., 7249
Shannon, Joseph B., 2167
Shannon, William V., 9288, 9852, 10351, 11116, 11903, 12062
Shapiro, Walter, 12408, 12409, 12584
Shapley, Harlow, 1590
Shapp, Martha, 10070
Shappee, Nathan D., 8698
Shapurian, Reza, 11081, 11569
Sharkey, Robert P., 5460
Sharon, John H., 8699

Sharp, Alfred, 3616
Sharp, Harry W., Jr., 10740
Sharp, James R., 3019
Shattuck, John, 11946, 12344
Shaull, Richard, 12261
Shaver, Mark D., 9507
Shaw, Albert, 3617, 6412
Shaw, Archer H., 5383
Shaw, Elton R., 232, 3745, 4859
Shaw, George W., 4249
Shaw, James, 3746
Shaw, John, 5949
Shaw, Lord, 4593
Shaw, Mark, 10115
Shaw, Peter, 863, 970, 12785
Shaw, Robert W., Jr., 13134
Shawcross, William, 11834
Shawen, Lena B., 8455
Shawen, Neil M., 1398
Shea, John D. G., 4017
Sheaffer, Robert, 12262
Shearer, Derek, 13099
Sheatsley, Paul B., 9807, 10472
Sheeder, Dave, 12786
Sheehan, Bernard W., 1591, 1775, 2168, 2169
Sheehan, Margaret, 12770
Sheehan, Vincent, 1945
Sheele, Paul E., 12345
Sheerin, John B., 10152, 10352, 10714
Sheffer, Martin S., 7875, 8700
Sheidman, J. Lee, 10069
Sheldon, Courtney R., 12787
Sheldon, Ted, 9242
Shelley, Fred, 3199, 6069
Shelly, Walter L., 11757
Shelton, William H., 495
Shepard, Edward M., 3066
Shepard, Tazewell T., 10116
Shepardson, Donald E., 6872
Shepherd, George W., Jr., 12503
Shepherd, Henry E., 1476
Shepherd, Jack, 864, 2591, 11375
Sheppard, Robert D., 3747, 4096
Sheres, Richard S., 9616
Sheridan, David, 12886
Sherlock, Richard K., 4142
Sherman, Diane F., 9709
Sherman, E. David, 1274
Sherman, Frederic F., 496, 497
Sherman, Richard B., 6314, 7906
Sherman, Roger N., 10637, 11758
Sherman, Stewart P., 1776
Sherman, Stuart P., 6617
Sherrill, Robert G., 11117-11120, 11223, 11904, 13048
Sherrod, Jane, 10840
Sherry, Paul H., 12788
Sherwin, Mark, 10057

Sherwin, Martin J., 9424, 9425
Sherwood, A., 4417
Sherwood, John, 3919, 10473
Sherwood, Robert E., 8701
Shichor, David, 12504
Shideler, James H., 8174
Shigenobu, I., 13049
Shimakawa, Masashi, 2170
Shipler, Guy E., 8702
Shippen, Rebecca L., 2089
Shirley, Ralph, 3618
Shively, Frances C., 604
Shofner, Jerrell H., 5552
Shogan, Robert, 12263
Shonting, Donald A., 1477
Shook, Chester R., 3748
Shore, Miles F., 6618
Shores, Venila L., 5881
Shorey, Paul, 7177
Short, Howard E., 5959
Short, Isaac M., 4318, 4447
Shotwell, James T., 7349
Shoup, Laurence H., 12264
Showalter, William J., 532
Showan, Daniel P., 8259, 8703
Showerman, Grant, 7350
Shrady, George F., 5682, 5683
Shreve, L. G., 662
Shriver, Phillip R., 7098, 8100
Shulim, Joseph I., 1876
Shulimson, Jack, 6787
Shulman, Irving, 10117
Shultz, Paul T., 12835
Shurr, Georgia H., 1877
Shuster, George N., 3619
Shutes, Milton H., 3620, 3749, 4097
Sicherman, Harvey, 12265
Sidey, Hugh, 10118, 10353, 10362, 11121, 11122, 12063
Siebeneck, Henry K., 3200
Siebert, Wilbur H., 605
Siegel, Frederick F., 12789
Siegel, Howard B., 9574
Sievers, Harry J., 6205-6208
Sifton, Paul G., 785, 2307, 2364, 2517, 2579
Sigelman, Carol K., 12410, 12960
Sigelman, Lee, 11333, 11345-11347, 12410, 12960, 13055
Sigelschiffer, Saul, 4652
Sigford, Rolf N., 11348, 11836
Sigler, Wayne, 9999
Silbey, Joel H., 3020, 3277
Silk, Leonard, 11710, 12572
Sill, Leonora, 8456
Sillars, Malcolm O., 9933
Sillin, John O., 13134
Silva, Ruth C., 8068
Silver, David M., 5137

Silver, Thomas B., 7958-7960
Silverman, Eliane L., 6788, 6789
Silverman, Jason H., 5236
Silvestri, Vito N., 10638
Simes, Dimitri K., 13050
Simmons, Althea T. L., 13135
Simmons, William K., 5789
Simon, Donald E., 4932
Simon, James F., 11634
Simon, John Y., 5553, 5684, 5734, 5790
Simon, Paul, 4529
Simpson, Lloyd D., 1777
Simpson, Stephen, 747, 1153
Sinclair, Andrew, 7831
Sinclair, Barbara, 12790
Sinclair, Robert, 5639
Sindlinger, Edmond S., 533
Singer, James W., 12346, 12791
Singer, Kurt, 10840
Singh, Ram, 10715
Singletary, Michael W., 2898
Singletary, Otis A., 3278
Singleton, Marvin K., 2441
Sink, George T., 10639
Sinkler, George, 5882, 6223
Sioussat, St. George L., 3414, 5554
Sipe, Chester H., 322
Sirevag, Torbjorn, 8704, 8980, 9076
Sirica, John J., 11905
Sisson, Daniel, 1015
Sisson, Edward O., 5237
Sitkoff, Harvard, 9384, 9508
Sixsmith, Eric K. G., 9760
Sizer, Rosanne, 8260
Skaggs, David C., 663
Skallerup, Harry R., 1478
Skau, George H., 7434, 8705
Skeen, C. Edward, 1778, 1779, 2442, 2549
Skinner, Charles R., 6315
Skinner, R. P., 6619
Sklar, Holly, 12266
Sklar, Kathryn K., 3865
Skousen, W. Cleon, 1174
Slater, Ellis D., 9710
Slater, William T., 12064
Slavin, Seymour, 13091
Slemp, Campbell B., 8038
Slevin, Joseph R., 11224
Slichter, Gertrude A., 8514, 8515
Slitor, Richard E., 12347
Sloan, John W., 11837, 12065
Sloane, William M., 606
Slonim, Shlomo, 9617, 9618
Slosser, Bob, 12116, 12571
Slosson, Preston W., 7862, 7961
Slotnick, Elliot E., 7004
Smalley, E. V., 5960
Smelser, Marshall, 748, 749, 971

Smeno, Kenneth, 6620
Smiley, David L., 4530
Smith, A. Merriman, 8706, 9711, 9853
Smith, Abbot, 2335, 2487
Smith, Beverly, 8019
Smith, Brian L., 6790
Smith, Bruce L. R., 12920
Smith, Carlton B., 2550
Smith, Charles W., Jr., 8981
Smith, Craig R., 11759
Smith, Culver H., 2899
Smith, Curt, 12792
Smith, Cyril V., 13072
Smith, D. C., 4531
Smith, Daniel M., 7435, 7635
Smith, David E., 1680
Smith, David L., 11190
Smith, Doris N., 1399
Smith, Dwight L., 3621
Smith, Edward G., 6413
Smith, Elbert B., 2900, 3454
Smith, F. Dumont, 402, 607
Smith, F. Michael, 11349
Smith, Franklin B., 11635
Smith, Frederic C., 6791
Smith, Fritz, 13087
Smith, Gaddis, 9153, 12505, 12506
Smith, Gary D., 10354
Smith, Gene, 5555, 5735, 7436, 8069
Smith, Geoffrey S., 9385
Smith, George W., 4367
Smith, Grace P., 4019
Smith, Graeme M., 2823
Smith, Guy-Harold, 534, 535
Smith, H. Shelton, 12348
Smith, Harold C., 291
Smith, Harvey G., 3866
Smith, Hedrick, 12572
Smith, Helen B., 904
Smith, Helena H., 8707
Smith, James M., 123, 1016, 1017
Smith, Jeane E., 10716
Smith, John D., 3622
Smith, John S., 7517
Smith, Joseph B., 12507
Smith, Justin H., 3279
Smith, Kathy B., 9386
Smith, Lincoln, 11636
Smith, Loren E., 2443
Smith, M. J. J., 8928
Smith, Malcolm E., 10355
Smith, Margaret B., 403
Smith, Marie, 10884
Smith, Martin, 12601
Smith, Merritt R., 664
Smith, Michael, 12508, 13005
Smith, Nancy K., 11123
Smith, Nicholas, 5640

Smith, Page, 865, 1154
Smith, Raymond G., 12066, 12411
Smith, Richard N., 8070
Smith, Richard W., 3094
Smith, Robert H., 2091
Smith, Robert T., 6869
Smith, Robert W., 11124
Smith, Ron, 10218
Smith, Ronald A., 6510
Smith, Russell M., 5575
Smith, Samuel G., 3750
Smith, Theodore C., 5974, 6033
Smith, Thomas A., 5835, 5961
Smith, Thomas E. V., 750
Smith, Thomas V., 1592, 3920, 4143, 4319
Smith, V. Kerry, 12921
Smith, Walter B., 9761
Smith, William D., 10640
Smith, William E., 3021
Smith, William H., 6792
Smith, William L., 1018, 2092
Smithline, Arnold, 1652
Smoot, Joseph G., 2611
Smucker, Isaac, 751
Smylie, James H., 752
Smyser, George H., 3867
Smyth, Clifford, 124, 866, 1946, 2759, 5238, 5641, 6183, 6793, 7636
Smyth, Mary W., 498
Smyth, William H., 5802
Smythe, Donald, 6573
Snell, David, 10717
Snell, John L., 9154
Snelling, William J., 2760
Snetsinger, John G., 9619, 9620
Snider, Denton J., 3623
Snow, Jane E., 6250
Snow, Marshall S., 4250
Snowiss, Sylvia, 8759
Snowman, Daniel, 9426
Snyder, Charles M., 3356, 3357
Snyder, J. Richard, 8020, 8261
Snyder, Marty, 9712
Snyder, Richard C., 9599
Soapes, Thomas F., 8708, 10000
Sobel, Lester A., 11711, 12067
Sobel, Robert, 8262
Sognnaes, Reodar F., 499
Solo, Robert M., 11282
Solomon, Martha, 12143
Soloveytchik, George, 10356, 10357, 10942, 11125
Solvick, Stanley D., 7005, 7006, 7082-7084
Somit, Albert, 2901-2903, 3022-3024
Somkin, Fred, 5095
Sondermann, Fred A., 7724
Sonnenfeldt, Helmut, 12509
Sontag, Raymond J., 9155
Sorensen, Theodore C., 10071, 10358
Sorenson, Dale, 9575
Sorley, Lewis, 11838, 11839
Soule, Harris W., 7962
Souryal, Safwat S., 3025
Southwood, James, 10067
Sowerby, E. Millicent, 1275, 1276
Sowle, Patrick, 5029
Spackman, S. G. F., 8376
Spalding, Henry D., 11637
Spalding, Phinizy, 12412
Spanier, John, 9600
Sparks, Edwin E., 4653
Sparks, Jared, 125, 608
Sparrow, John, 10474
Spaulding, Oliver L., Jr., 233
Speakes, Jeffrey, 12337, 12959
Speakman, Frederick B., 4320
Spear, Joseph C., 11638
Spears, Zarel C., 3751
Spector, Robert M., 5138
Speel, Charles J., II, 10359
Speer, Emory, 5030, 5642
Spencer, Ivor D., 4933
Spencer, Omar C., 4594
Spencer, Thomas E., 1400
Spencer, Thomas T., 8847-8849
Spender, Harold, 323
Spengler, Joseph J., 972, 1593, 2444
Spetter, Allen B., 6224
Spiegel, Steven L., 12510
Spielman, William C., 6251
Spiro, Jeffery H., 1878
Spitzka, Edward A., 6301
Spivak, Burton, 2322-2324
Spivey, Herman E., 1277
Spragens, William C., 10360, 11126
Sprague, Dean, 5239
Sprague, Lynn T., 2824
Sprague, R. E., 11639, 12068
Sprague, Stuart S., 2093
Sprague, Ver Lynn, 3868
Sprague, Waldo C., 905, 2612
Spratt, John S., 1681
Spring, Agnes W., 6794
Spring, Beth, 12793
Spring, Samuel, 7007
Sprinkel, Beryl W., 13136
Sproat, John G., 5556, 5883
Spurlin, Charles, 3316
Squires, J. Duane, 3869, 4770, 4771
Stacks, John F., 12961
Stacy, Bill W., 9509
Stafford, Jean, 10119
Stagg, John C., 1231-1233
Stagner, Stephen, 6795
Stahl, Rose M., 7085
Stalin, Joseph, 9156, 9576
Stampp, Kenneth M., 5031, 5557, 5558

Stanfield, Rochelle L., 12349
Stanford, Phil, 12144
Stang, Alan, 12602
Stanley, James D., 11225
Stanley, James G., 11276
Stanley-Brown, Joseph, 5962
Stansfield, F. W. H., 5643
Stanton, Robert B., 4251
Stapleton, Joseph G., 6873
Stapley, Mildred, 1333
Stark, Bruce, 2904
Stark, Milton J., 11251
Starkey, Larry, 4860
Starner, Frances L., 11350
Starr, Harvey, 10718
Starr, John, 7867
Starr, John W., 3624, 3752, 4321
Starr, Michael E., 5975
Startt, James D., 7688-7690
Stathis, Stephen W., 2570, 3201, 4020, 11906
Stauffer, Robert F., 11712
Stead, John P., 1947
Stearns, Charles, 3303
Stearns, Clifford B., 753
Stebbins, Phillip, 4772, 9486
Steel, Anthony, 2551
Steel, Ronald, 10549
Steele, John L., 11127
Steele, Richard W., 8709, 8929, 9157-9159
Steele, Robert V. P., 5411
Steele, Thomas J., 609
Steers, Edward, Jr., 4861
Stefansson, Vilhjalmur, 6621
Steffens, Lincoln, 6796
Steffgen, Kent H., 12603
Stegeman, Janet, 610
Stegeman, John, 610
Stein, Harry H., 6797
Stein, Max, 5384
Stein, Nathaniel E., 611, 754
Steinbeck, John, 11128
Steinberg, Alfred, 7178, 8071, 8489, 9243, 9713, 10841
Steiner, Bernard C., 2905
Steiner, Paul, 10120
Steinfels, Peter, 12794
Stelzner, Hermann G., 9160, 12069
Stenberg, Richard R., 2655, 2906-2909, 3026, 3027, 3280, 3415
Stepanek, Robert H., 11430
Stephanson, Anders, 8710
Stephens, David, 12350
Stephenson, Nathaniel W., 126, 127, 3281, 3753, 4773
Stephenson, William, 11760
Ster, Gerald E., 5281
Sterba, Richard, 8711
Sterling, Adaline W., 234

Sterling, Peter R., 1780
Stern, Clarence A., 6316, 6317
Stern, James, 10361
Stern, Laurence, 11129
Stern, Madeleine B., 5963
Stern, Norton B., 5773
Stern, Philip V. D., 4021, 4368, 4418, 4862
Sternberg, Richard R., 1278
Sternsher, Bernard, 8806, 8807, 9077, 9078
Sternstein, Jerome L., 5909
Stetler, Russell, 10475
Stetson, Charles W., 235
Stetter, Russell, 10471
Stettinius, Edward R., Jr., 9161
Stevens, Alice B., 5685
Stevens, Charles M., 4448
Stevens, H. Beresford, 3870
Stevens, Harry R., 2910
Stevens, Lucia A., 5160
Stevens, Maud L., 612
Stevens, Michael E., 2171
Stevens, Sylvester K., 3921, 5077
Stevens, Walter B., 4252, 5686
Stevenson, Adlai E., 1781, 6184, 6318
Stevenson, Augusta, 552, 2761, 5687
Stevenson, Charles S., 4774
Stevenson, Robert L., 11551
Stewart, Charles J., 4654, 4863, 10072
Stewart, David M., 7907, 8021
Stewart, David W., 12268
Stewart, Donald H., 906
Stewart, Gideon T., 2592
Stewart, John G., 10943, 11130
Stewart, Judd, 4595
Stewart, Kate M., 6511, 7099
Stewart, Maxwell S., 11640
Stewart, Peter C., 2842
Stewart, Robert A., 1782
Stewart, Thomas D., 4022
Stewart, William J., 8457
Stickley, Julia W., 2825
Stidger, William L., 8458
Stiles, John R., 12101
Stiles, Lela, 8712
Stillman, Richard J., II, 7351
Stillson, Albert C., 6798
Stilwell, Lewis D., 5884
Stimmel, Smith, 4253
Stimson, Henry L., 9427
Stinchcombe, William C., 1019
Stirk, S. D., 2613
Stix, Daniel L., 12795
Stockbridge, Frank P., 7474
Stockman, David A., 12836
Stockton, Frank R., 1516
Stoddard, William O., 128, 867, 1983, 2491, 2571, 2666, 3028, 3112, 3134, 3202, 3220, 3327, 3350, 3375, 3455, 3625-3627, 3754, 4254, 5032, 5161,

5559, 5644, 5885, 6013, 6041, 6095
Stokes, Thomas L., 9387
Stolarek, John S., 11871
Stolba, K. Marie, 1362
Stoler, Mark A., 11351
Stolley, Richard B., 11131, 11307
Stone, Charles F., 13137
Stone, Chuck, 12351, 12352
Stone, Gene, 1155
Stone, Irving, 3580, 3871
Stone, Isidor F., 9388
Stone, Philip, 11308
Stone, Ralph A., 7637, 7638
Stookey, John A., 11644
Storch, Neil T., 973
Storer, Malcolm, 500
Storey, Helen A., 1517
Storey, Moorfield, 4864
Stork, Joe, 12972
Stoughton, Cecil, 10362
Stout, Ralph, 6799
Stowe, William M., 2172
Strachan, Jill P., 11641
Stradling, James M., 5033
Straight, Michael, 10001
Strange, Russell P., 9162, 9163
Stratton, David H., 7437, 8175
Stratton, Maud, 8101
Straus, Oscar S., 6185, 6319, 6800, 7086
Strauss, David, 9079
Strauss, Lewis L., 9854
Street, Charles M., 4775
Street, Julian L., 6414
Street, Kenneth W., 9389
Stricker, Frank, 12922
Strickler, Joe, 5385
Strong, Frank R., 11642
Stroud, Kandy, 12413
Strozier, Charles B., 3628, 3687, 5386
Strum, Harvey, 9855, 9906
Strunsky, Rose, 3629, 4144
Strunsky, Simeon, 6622
Stryker, Lloyd P., 5412
Stuart, Douglas, 10718
Stuart, Friend, 10073
Stuart, Reginald C., 2325-2328, 2492
Stuart, Roger W., 10363
Stubblebine, William C., 13138
Stubbs, Roy S., 4596
Stults, Taylor, 6801
Stutler, Boyd B., 4532
Styron, Arthur, 2524
Sudol, Ronald A., 12353
Sullivan, Austin P., Jr., 10944
Sullivan, Donald F., 10596
Sullivan, John L., 2911-2913
Sullivan, Mark, 1783, 7863, 8022
Sullivan, Samuel L., 11226

Sullivan, William A., 2914
Sullivan, Wilson, 3095, 8377
Summerlin, Sam, 10431
Summers, Laura, 11840
Summersby, Kathleen M., 9729
Summy, Ralph, 1784
Sumner, Charles, 4145
Sumner, Guy L., 3630, 4069, 4419
Sumner, William G., 2762, 3029
Sumpter, Arthur, 3304, 3305
Sundquist, James L., 9907, 10597, 11132, 12269
Suppiger, Joseph E., 3631, 3632, 3922, 4023, 4024, 4322, 5107
Surface, Frank M., 8176
Surface, George T., 1682
Suro, Dario, 1334
Susma, Warren I., 7564, 8218
Sussman, Barry, 11907
Sussman, Leila A., 8713, 8714
Sutter, Richard L., 974
Sutton, Anthony C., 8808
Sutton, Robert P., 1948
Sutton, Walter A., 7593
Swain, Martha H., 8760
Swancara, Frank, 1653, 2493
Swaney, Homer H., 5935, 6036
Swanson, David L., 12070, 12414
Swanson, Donald R., 11133
Swanson, Linda L., 12070, 12414
Swanson, Roger F., 12071
Swearingen, Rodger, 13051
Sweeney, Martin A., 4099
Sweet, Kenneth F., 9856
Sweet, Rachel A., 7594
Sweet, W. W., 4865
Sweetman, Jack, 7659
Sweezey, Paul M., 10254, 11048
Swift, Clarence F., 4420
Swift, Donald C., 5886, 5887
Swift, John L., 5645
Swift, Lester L., 3923
Swiggett, Howard, 129
Swindler, William F., 3203
Swing, David, 5976
Swint, Henry L., 5827
Swisher, Jacob A., 5774, 8102
Swomley, John M., Jr., 11352
Sydnor, William, 352
Syle, Bertrand C., 130, 4098
Sylves, Richard T., 12354
Symmes, John C., 3145
Symonds, Craig L., 5034
Syrett, Harold C., 2915
Syrett, John, 8715
Szanton, Peter, 12415
Szasz, Paul C., 1785
Szulc, Tad, 10545, 11841, 12511, 13052

Taft, Charles P., 6980
Taft, Helen H., 6981
Taft, Robert, Jr., 6982
Taft, William H., 7100-7126
Tagg, James D., 755
Taggart, Robert, 7250, 11288
Taggert, Hugh T., 1020
Takamatsu, Motoyuki, 10002
Talbot, Ross B., 10567
Talbott, Strobe, 13053, 13088
Tammens, William D., 9283
Tamney, Joseph B., 10477, 12949
Tanner, Douglas W., 2129
Tansill, Charles C., 8930
Tanzer, Lester, 10364
Tappan, George L., 5560
Tarbell, Ida M., 3633, 3755, 3756, 3924, 4255, 4256, 4449, 6320
Tarr, Joel A., 6802
Tarshis, Rebecca, 3675
Tarter, Brent, 6513, 8263
Tate, Dale, 13054, 13108
Tatsch, Jacob H., 353
Tatum, Lawrie, 5775
Tauber, Gisela, 1156
Tausek, Joseph, 5078
Taussig, Frank W., 5387
Taylor, Blaine, 11134
Taylor, Cornelia J., 1157
Taylor, Edward M., 131
Taylor, George R., 3030
Taylor, Hannis, 4655
Taylor, Harry S., 9487
Taylor, James H., 7251
Taylor, John M., 5035, 5950, 5977
Taylor, Lloyd C., 3365, 3406
Taylor, Malcolm, 354
Taylor, Maurice P., 5162
Taylor, Maxwell D., 9714, 10365
Taylor, Rhea A., 3925
Taylor, Robert J., 975
Taylor, Robert L., 9857
Taylor, Ronald A., 12798
Taylor, William W., 11713
Taylor, Zachary, 3329-3331
Tays, Dwight L., 12270
Tays, George, 3282
Teagle, Rhoda, 7963
Teague, Michael, 6482
Tebbel, John W., 536
Tegeder, Vincent G., 4776
Teichmann, Howard, 6514
Teillard, Dorothy L., 3926
Teitelbaum, Louis M., 7660
Temin, Peter, 2916
Temkin, Owsei, 6014
Temple, Oliver P., 5461
Temple, Wayne C., 3757-3759, 3794, 3841, 3872, 3873, 3927, 4025, 4257, 4533, 4534, 4557, 4597, 5736
Tenney, Craig D., 5036
Teplin, Joseph, 6803
TerHorst, Jerald F., 3128, 12072
Tetter, Dwight L., Jr., 11643
Tevis, Martha, 11227
Thacker, May, 7864
Thane, Elswyth, 2365
Thatcher, C. Marshall, 11908
Thayer, Mary V., 10121
Thayer, William M., 132, 3634, 3635, 4777, 5646, 5951
Thayer, William R., 133, 6415, 8378
Theisen, Lee S., 3283
Thelen, David P., 5888
Theodore, Terry C., 5037, 5038, 5737
Theodore Roosevelt Centennial Commission, 6416
Theoharis, Athan G., 9164, 9390-9397, 9577
Thielen, Greg G., 9253
Thistlethwaite, Mark E., 501
Thomas, Addison C., 6804
Thomas, Benjamin P., 3636-3638, 3760, 4070, 4146, 4369, 4421, 4450, 4535, 4778
Thomas, Charles M., 2308
Thomas, Charles S., 2199
Thomas, Dan B., 12355, 12365, 13055
Thomas, David A., 11761
Thomas, Elbert D., 1158
Thomas, Harrison C., 6186
Thomas, Henry, 8379
Thomas, J. Mark, 12580
Thomas, Katherine E., 2366
Thomas, Norman C., 11135, 11228, 11291, 12271
Thomas, Robert C., 3031
Thomas, Sunny, 12118
Thomas, Tony, 12581
Thomas, W. G. M., 4422
Thomison, Dennis, 10366
Thompson, Arthur W., 2917
Thompson, Bram, 7438
Thompson, Charles M., 4026, 4100
Thompson, Charles W., 6626
Thompson, D. P., 1279
Thompson, David D., 3639
Thompson, Edward W., 11136
Thompson, Elaine V., 12796, 12797
Thompson, Francis H., 9398, 9399
Thompson, Frank, Jr., 11714
Thompson, George L., 553
Thompson, Harry C., 976
Thompson, Jack M., 5978
Thompson, Josiah, 10478
Thompson, Kenneth W., 8716, 9400, 9858
Thompson, Mark E., 9601
Thompson, Nelson, 10367
Thompson, Pat, 10885
Thompson, Ray, 404

Author Index

Thompson, Seymour D., 3032, 4656
Thompson, William B., 6805
Thompson, Wilma, 1364
Thomson, Alfred R., 292
Thomson, David S., 9244
Thornton, Harrison J., 6806, 6807, 8717
Thornton, Jeannye, 12798
Thornton, Thomas P., 12512, 12513, 13056
Thornton, William W., 1159, 1160
Thorpe, Francis N., 977, 1984, 2309
Thorpe, James A., 9578
Thorpe, Russell W., 502, 1280
Thorsen, Niels A., 7518
Thorsmar, Thora, 134
Thorup, Oscar A., 1281
Throne, Mildred, 6321, 8103
Thurber, James, 3284
Thurow, Glen E., 4108, 4323
Thurow, Lester C., 12356, 13139
Thweatt, John H., 3293
Thwing, Eugene, 6417
Tiemens, Robert K., 12416, 12962
Tiffany, David M., 9908
Tiffany, Otis H., 5635
Tilberg, Frederick, 5079, 5080
Tillett, Paul, 10368
Tilley, John S., 3640
Tillinghast, David R., 12514
Tillinghast, Diana S., 11909
Tilly, Bette B., 2918
Tilton, Clint C., 5039
Timmons, Clarence P., 7865
Tindall, William, 6015
Tinsley, James A., 6808
Tirman, John, 12799
Toba, Reijiro, 13057
Tobin, James, 12357, 13140
Tobin, Richard L., 9934
Todd, Charles S., 3146
Todd, Helen, 5647
Todd, Terry E., 1402
Tokuda, Sumiko, 4423
Toll, William, 11292
Tomkins, Silvan S., 10479
Tompkins, C. David, 8607
Toner, James H., 10003
Toner, Joseph M., 236
Toole, Morton E., 10719
Torodash, Martin, 7595, 7596
Torres, Louis, 8490
Toscano, Vincent L., 10369
Toskova, Vitka, 9165
Totten, John R., 7964
Tourtellot, Arthur B., 7739
Towell, Pat, 12272
Towne, Charles H., 6418
Towne, Ralph L., Jr., 9166
Towner, Ausburn, 756

Townsend, George W., 6252
Townsend, Samuel C., 5828
Townsend, Virginia F., 135
Townsend, William H., 3761, 3874, 4598-4607, 4657, 5240
Tozer, Warren W., 9579
Tracey, Kathleen H., 8320
Trachtenberg, Alexander, 1786
Tracy, Gilbert A., 5388
Tracy, John E., 5561
Train, Arthur C., 8072
Traina, Richard P., 8931
Trainor, M. Rosaleen, 1787
Trani, Eugene P., 7597, 7725, 7832, 7908, 8809
Trask, David F., 7598, 7639, 7640, 7726
Trattner, Walter I., 6627
Travell, Janet, 10371
Travis, Paul D., 7087
Treadway, Sandra G., 136
Treadway, William E., 3762
Trefousse, Hans L., 5040, 5178, 5179, 5562-5566
Tregaskis, Richard W., 10153, 10154
Tregle, Joseph G., 2919
Trent, Judith S., 11762
Trent, William P., 613, 1161, 1788
Trenton Times, 405
Trescot, William H., 757, 1021
Tribble, Edwin, 7252
Trickey, Katharine S., 3224
Trimble, Vance H., 12573
Triplett, Frank, 6096
Trott, Sarah H., 11733
Trotter, Reginald G., 614
Trow, Clifford W., 7641, 7661, 7662
Trudeau, Gary B., 12582
True, Katharine M., 1282
True, Marshall, 5041
True, Rodney H., 1683
Trueblood, David E., 3641
Truesdell, Winfred P., 4181
Truett, Randle B., 4867
Truman, Benjamin C., 5502
Truman, Harry S., 9653-9668
Truman, Margaret, 9245, 9261, 9669
Truman Library, Institute for National and International Affairs, 9488
Trumble, Alfred, 6016
Trump, Fred, 3875
Tsai, Wei-ping, 12547
Tsou, Tang, 11842
Tuchman, Barbara W., 6628, 6810, 7253
Tuchman, Mitch, 12963
Tucker, David, 1479
Tucker, Edward L., 3033
Tucker, Frank H., 7352
Tucker, George, 1163
Tucker, Glenn, 4258, 4324
Tucker, Ray T., 8265

Tucker, Robert W., 11603, 12516, 13058
Tuckerman, Frederick, 503
Tuckerman, Henry T., 504
Tugwell, Rexford G., 6097, 6809, 8266-8268, 8380-8382, 8516, 8719-8727, 8850, 8851, 8982, 9056, 9080, 9081
Tully, Andrew, 2494, 10372
Tully, Grace G., 8383
Tumulty, Joseph P., 7254
Tupper, Frederick, 6629
Turner, Arlin, 4259
Turner, Harriot S., 5432
Turner, Henry A., 7353-7355, 7439
Turner, James W., 4370
Turner, John J., Jr., 5163
Turner, Junius T., 293
Turner, Justin G., 3876, 4027
Turner, Kathleen J., 11309, 11353
Turner, Kathryn, 1022
Turner, Lynn W., 1789, 2572
Turner, Russell, 10155
Turner, Thomas R., 4868-4871
Twedt, Michael S., 9602
Tweton, D. Jerome, 6811-6813
Tyler, Gus, 11137, 11663
Tyler, John, 3204-3207, 6253
Tyler, Lyon G., 1790, 3181, 3208, 3763, 3877, 3928
Tyler, Moses C., 1840, 4260
Tyrner-Tyrnauer, A. R., 5042
Tyson, Brady, 12548
Tyson, Carl N., 8023

Udall, Morris K., 12923
Ulig, Frank, 8728
Ulmer, Melville J., 12358
Ulmer, S. Sidney, 2445, 11644
Ulrich, Bartow A., 5139
Umbreit, Kenneth B., 7008
Unck, Dunkam, 6068
Underhill, Robert, 9402
Underwood, James E., 9403, 9859, 10373, 12273
Unger, Frederic W., 6516
Union College, 6042
United Press International, 9673, 10480
U.S. Commission on Organization of the Executive Branch of the Government, 8178
U.S. Congress. House, 9246, 9715, 12073
U.S. Congress. House. Committee on the Judiciary, 11645, 11910, 11911
U.S. Congress. Senate, 10374, 11138
U.S. Congress. Senate. Committee on Rules and Administration, 12074
U.S. Constitution Sesquicentennial Commission, 758
U.S. Department of State, 759
U.S. General Accounting Office, 11646
U.S. George Washington Bicentennial Commission, 237, 406
U.S. Library of Congress. Congressional Research Service, 12075
U.S. Library of Congress. Manuscript Division, 665, 6070
U.S. National Park Service, 5433
U.S. President, 12076, 13141
U.S. President's Commission on the Assassination of President Kennedy, 10481, 10482
U.S. War Department, 7128
U.S. White House. Office of Communications, 12077
Unterberger, Betty M., 13059
Upham, Charles W., 137
Upton, Richard F., 3376
Urban, George, 12518
Urofsky, Melvin I., 7519, 7520
Urquidi, Donald, 7609
Utley, Francis L., 4424
Utley, George B., 6965
Utley, Robert M., 5738

Vale, Vivian, 11647, 11648
Valelly, Richard M., 12863
Valenti, Jack, 10842
Valentine, John, 8459
Valis, Wayne H., 12800
Vallandigham, E. N., 666
Valliere, Kenneth L., 3034
Van, Thu, 11354
Van Alstyne, Richard W., 3351, 6322
Van Alstyne, William W., 11649
Van Bemmelen, J. M., 10483
Van Buren, Martin, 3116-3119
Vance, Malcolm, 12621
Van Cleve, John V., 10720
Van Dalen, D. B., 4779
Vanderbilt, Paul, 4182
Van Der Linden, Frank, 2094, 11650, 12801
Vanderoef, John S., 2446
Van Deusen, Glyndon G., 2921, 2922, 3035
Van Deusen, Robert C., 8933
Vandiver, Frank E., 5043
Van Doren, Mark A., 4028
Van Dusen, George, 9909
Van Dyke, Henry, 138
Van Dyke, Paul, 139, 140
Van Everen, Brooks, 9167
Van Gelder, Lawrence, 10122
Van Hoesen, Henry B., 4536
Van Horn, James, 3285
Van Loon, Hendrik W., 1164, 1165
Van Meter, Robert H., Jr., 8179
Van Natter, Francis M., 4451
Vannest, Charles G., 4452
Vannicelli, Maurizio, 12468
Vanocur, Sander, 10641
Van Orden, William H., 5648
Van Patten, James J., 9262, 11229

Author Index

Van Patten, Paul L., 8729
Van Pelt, Charles E., 1427
Van Sickle, Clifton E., 5829
Van Til, William, 12802
Varg, Paul A., 6874
Vargashidalgo, Rafael V., 12519
Varin, Rene L., 407
Varney, Harold L., 9860
Vartabedian, Robert A., 11912
Vastine, John R., 10662
Vaughan, Harold C., 1023, 5910
Vaughan, Olive, 4183
Vaughan, Philip H., 9489-9493
Vaught, Edgar S., 615
Vazzano, Frank P., 5889
Veach, Rebecca M., 3687
Venkataramani, M. S., 6814, 8384, 8810
Verner, Coolie, 1680-1683, 1791
Vernon, A. W., 5688
Vernon, Merle, 355
Vestal, Bud, 11951
Vestal, Samuel C., 667
Vevier, Charles, 6875, 6876
Veysey, Laurence R., 7255
Vickers, James E., 4872
Victor, Orville J., 3642
Vidal, Gore, 10123, 11651
Viele, Egbert L., 4371
Viereck, George S., 6419, 7256
Vietor, Richard H. K., 9494
Vig, Norman J., 12885, 12924
Vile, Jonas, 2302
Villard, Henry, 3795
Vinson, John W., 4261
Viola, Herman J., 3317, 5108
Viorst, Milton, 9168, 11652, 11653
Virginia. Governor, 2310
Virginia. University, 2312
Virginia. University. Library, 2311
Vivian, James F., 7088, 7599
Vlaun, Joan G., 8269
Vogelgesang, Sandra L., 11355
Vogt, Daniel C., 8270
Vogt, Erich, 11843
Vogt, Per, 8385
Voigt, Tracy, 12803
Volk, Leanard W., 4029
Volwiler, Albert T., 6225, 6517
Von Abele, Rudolph, 978
Von Furstenberg, George M., 9910, 10598, 11230
Voorhees, Daniel W., 2313
Voorhis, Horace J., 11405
Vose, Clement E., 11763
Vose, Reuben, 5389
Voss, Frederick, 8386
Vossler, Otto, 1985
Vrooman, Frank B., 6420
Vukadinovic, Radovan, 12274

Wachman, Alan M., 12520
Wade, Mary H., 3643, 6815, 8104
Wagenknecht, Edward C., 4071, 6421
Wagner, Bill, 8105
Wagner, William J., 8106
Wagnon, William O., Jr., 9404, 9495
Wagoner, Jean B., 294
Wagoner, Jennings, Jr., 1403
Wagstaff, Thomas, 5434
Wainer, Howard, 11913
Waite, Edward F., 1792
Wakefield, Sherman D., 3764, 4934
Waksmudski, John, 6269, 6323, 6324
Waldo, Samuel P., 979, 1986, 2552-2554, 2763, 2764
Waldron, Webb, 5044
Walker, Albert H., 7089
Walker, Alexander, 2923
Walker, Arda S., 2826-2828, 2924
Walker, Barbara J., 12119
Walker, Don D., 6518, 7090
Walker, Gerald, 10124
Walker, Jenny G., 408
Walker, John H., 10484
Walker, Kenneth R., 3147, 7009, 7866
Walker, Mary M., 2447
Walker, Turnley, 8387
Wall, Bernhardt, 3796
Wall, Charles C., 141, 238
Wall, James M., 12275, 12804
Wallace, D. D., 2130
Wallace, Edward S., 3377
Wallace, Lew, 6209, 9510
Wallace, M. G., 1518
Wallace, Sarah A., 3036, 3178
Wallace, William V., 8934
Waller, George M., 9169
Wallfisch, M. Charles, 8811
Wallis, G. B., 5097
Walsh, Correa M., 980
Walsh, John, 9911
Walsh, Robert, 2765
Walsh, William S., 5164
Walter, James, 505
Walter, John C., 9082, 9170
Walters, Helen B., 4425
Waltmann, Henry G., 5776
Walton, Brian G., 3286, 3328
Walton, Clyde C., 4537
Walton, Craig, 1594
Walton, Richard J., 9580, 10721
Waltrip, John R., 9405
Walworth, Arthur C., 7179
Wamble, Thelma, 10375
Wanamaker, John, 3765
Wanamaker, Reuben M., 3644
Wande, Meghan R., 8341
Wann, Andrew J., 7440, 8730-8732

Author Index 707

Warburg, James, 8852
Ward, Geoffrey C., 3687, 8388
Ward, James E., 1305
Ward, John W., 2925
Warde, William F., 1793, 4147
Ware, B. L., 11877
Warner, David C., 10599, 11139
Warner, Geoffrey, 8935, 9640
Warner, Hoyt L., 7010
Warner, Lee H., 3378, 3379
Warner, Richard R., 11140
Warner, Robert M., 6630, 11141
Warren, Charles, 981, 1024, 1794, 2095, 2201
Warren, Earl, 7011, 11231
Warren, Harris G., 8073
Warren, Louis A., 3645, 3878-3884, 4030, 4101, 4184, 4325, 4372, 4426, 4453, 4454, 4538, 5080, 5241
Warren, Raymond, 3766, 4326, 4455
Warren, Sidney, 7876
Warshawsky, Howard, 12549
Washburn, Charles G., 6631-6633
Washburn, Mabel T. R., 761, 6983
Washburn, Robert M., 7932
Washington, George, 786-847
Washington, John E., 4262
Washington, S. H. Lee, 295, 296
Washington, W. Lanier, 506, 507, 616, 617
Washington Benevolent Society, 410
Washington Post, 11654, 11914
Wason, James R., 2926, 11232
Wasson, Woodrow W., 5964
Waterman, Julian S., 2202
Waters, Craig, 11915
Waters, Henry F. G., 299
Watrous, Hilda R., 8491
Watson, Christopher, 11952
Watson, Francis J. B., 1795
Watson, Harry L., 2927
Watson, Richard L., Jr., 6634, 6816, 7356, 8074, 8733
Watson, Ross, 1283
Watson, Stuart L., 4456
Watson, Thomas E., 1166, 2766, 2767
Watson, W. Marvin, 11142
Watt, Donald C., 8936, 12521
Watters, Pat, 12359
Watterson, Henry, 3767, 5911, 6817
Watts, R. A., 4873
Wayland, John W., 241, 1484, 1595, 1684
Wayne, Stephen J., 10125, 12078
Ways, Max, 11143, 11233
Wead, Bill, 12964
Wead, Doug, 12964
Weaver, Bettie W., 1284
Weaver, Bill L., 5567, 5890
Weaver, David B., 2595
Weaver, James D., 9861

Weaver, Neal, 1306
Weaver, Robert C., 11234
Weaver, Samuel H., 9496
Weaver, Suzanne, 12276
Webb, Lucas, 10485
Webb, Robert, 10074
Webb, Ross A., 5891
Weber, Arnold R., 12522
Weber, Paul J., 2448
Webster, Daniel, 982, 1796
Webster, Homer J., 3154
Webster, Sidney, 3380
Wechsler, James A., 11144
Wecht, Cyril H., 10486-10488
Wecter, Dixon, 1797
Weed, Thurlow, 3339
Weeks, Eugene M., 7965
Weems, Mason L., 142-144
Wehr, Elizabeth, 12805, 12806
Weichmann, Louis J., 4874
Weidenbaum, Murray L., 12925
Weidner, Edward W., 10722
Weigand, Wayne A., 7091
Weigley, Russell F., 9762
Weik, J. William, 3526
Weik, Jesse W., 3525, 3646, 4263, 4264, 4539, 4875, 5081
Weinberg, Albert K., 762, 6325
Weinberger, Bernhard W., 242
Weiner, Bernard, 9641
Weingast, David E., 8389
Weinrich, William A., 8937
Weinstein, Allen, 9621, 12523
Weinstein, Edwin A., 7257, 7258, 7340, 7441, 7442
Weintal, Edward, 11145
Weintraub, Sidney, 11277, 12360, 13142
Weir, David, 12866
Weisband, Edward, 11260, 11278
Weisberg, Harold, 10489, 10490
Weisenburger, Francis P., 3768, 6270, 7357
Weisl, Edwin L., 10376, 11146
Weisman, Steven R., 12807
Weiss, Harry B., 670, 1596
Weiss, Laura B., 12778
Weiss, Nancy J., 8812
Weissman, Benjamin M., 8180, 8271
Weissman, Philip, 4876
Welch, June R., 10945
Welch, Robert H. W., 9862
Weld, Horatio H., 145
Wellemeyer, Marilyn, 12079
Welles, Albert, 300
Welles, Edward O., Jr., 243
Welles, Gideon, 4780, 4781
Welles, Sumner, 8734
Welling, Richard, 6519
Welliver, Judson C., 7985
Wells, Edward F., 8938

Wells, Ruth M., 5462
Wells, Samuel F., Jr., 7600
Wells, Wells, 7259
Welsh, David, 11147
Went, G. Stanley V., 6635
Werner, Morris R., 7867
Werstein, Irving, 5045
Wert, Jeffry, 2928, 6818
Wertenbaker, Thomas J., 1285
Wescott, John W., 7740
Wessel, Thomas R., 6819, 7092
Wessen, Ernest J., 5098
Wesser, Robert F., 6820
West, Andrew F., 6105
West, Elisabeth H., 3120
West, Henry L., 6326, 6327
West, Richard S., Jr., 5046, 5047, 5830
Westerfield, H. Bradford, 11356
Westermeier, Clifford P., 6636
Westin, Alan F., 11946
Westwood, Howard C., 4782, 5048, 5049, 5739
Wetmore, Alexander, 4185
Wettstein, A. Arnold, 2314
Wettstein, Carl T., 4327
Weyant, Robert G., 1597
Weymouth, Lally, 1167
Whalen, Joan C., 11764
Whalen, Richard J., 10126, 10491
Wham, Benjamin, 1841
Wham, George D., 3806
Wharton, Anne H., 301
Wharton, Don, 8735
Whatley, George C., 3037
Whealen, John J., 3054
Whealon, John F., 1798
Wheare, Kenneth C., 3647
Wheelan, Fairfax H., 6520
Wheeler, Burton K., 8761
Wheeler, Daniel E., 3648
Wheeler, Everett P., 6098
Wheeler, Keith, 10843
Wheeler, Leslie, 12418
Whelan, Joseph G., 13060
Whelen, Henry, Jr., 509
Whelpley, James D., 6637, 8025
Whipple, Chandler, 10157
Whipple, Wayne, 146-148, 244, 3769, 3770, 4265, 4266, 4457, 6422, 8390
Whitaker, W. Richard, 7877, 7909, 7910
Whitcomb, Paul S., 4148, 5082
Whitcover, Jules, 11916
White, Andrew D., 2173
White, Charles T., 4031, 4328, 4458
White, Elliott, 5242
White, F. Clifton, 12965
White, George E., 6638
White, Graham J., 8736
White, Horace, 3797
White, J. Roy, 10886
White, Larry D., 11917
White, Leonard D., 1949, 2096, 3038, 6821, 8813
White, Lucia, 1598
White, Morton G., 1598
White, Patricia M., 12585
White, Ralph K., 10665
White, Stephen, 10492
White, Theodore H., 11918
White, William A., 6521, 7180, 7933, 7934
White, William S., 9406, 9863, 10377, 10378, 10518, 10741, 10844, 10946, 10947, 11149, 11150
Whitehead, Donald F., 8939
Whitehead, John M., 4103
Whitehurst, Alto L., 3096
Whitehurst, Ben, 8737
Whiteley, Emily S., 671, 672
Whitemen, Marjorie M., 8492
Whiteside, Henry O., 10723
Whitfield, Stephen J., 11655
Whitford, Kathryn, 4072
Whiting, Edward E., 7935, 8026
Whiting, Margaret A., 1685
Whiting, William F., 7966
Whitlock, Brand, 3649
Whitner, Robert L., 5777
Whitney, David C., 9716, 10845, 11844
Whitney, Henry C., 3650, 4608
Whitney, Janet P., 907
Whitney, Kevin, 12926
Whitney, Sharon, 8493
Whitridge, Arnold, 2367
Whittemore, Frances D., 510
Whittle, Richard, 13061
Whittlesey, Walter L., 245
Whitty, J. H., 1286
Whytlaw, Mary G., 7093
Wibberly, Leonard P. O., 1168
Wick, Wendy C., 511
Wickard, Claude R., 1307
Wicker, Elmus R., 8814
Wicker, Tom, 10075, 10379-10381, 10887, 10948, 10949, 11151-11156, 11357
Wicklein, John, 10382
Wicks, Elliot K., 1654
Wickser, Philip J., 6106
Wides, Jeffrey W., 12081, 12419
Wiebe, Robert H., 6822
Wiegand, Wayne A., 6640
Wiesner, Jerome B., 10383
Wiest, Walter E., 4149
Wight, Pocahontas W., 5794
Wilbur, Henry W., 5243
Wilbur, Marguerite K., 1169
Wilbur, Ray L., 8075
Wilbur, William H., 149
Wilcox, Francis O., 11845

Author Index

Wildavsky, Aaron B., 11656, 11846
Wilensky, Norman M., 7094
Wiley, Bell I., 3651, 4427
Wiley, Earl W., 3652, 4373, 4540-4543
Wilgus, A. Curtis, 5165
Wilhelm, Donald G., 6522
Wilhite, Allen W., 11715
Wilkin, Jacob W., 5649
Wilkins, Robert P., 6641, 7475
Will, George F., 11663, 11716
Willard, Samuel, 868
Willet, Thomas D., 13138
Willett, Edward, 5650
William, C. L., 7260
William, Phil, 12149
Williams, Charles R., 5803
Williams, Cleveland A., 9864
Williams, David, 10950
Williams, Dorothy Q., 8738
Williams, Edward K., 1485
Williams, Francis H., 3653
Williams, Gary L., 4544
Williams, Harry, 5463
Williams, Henry L., 5390
Williams, Herbert L., 9408, 9409
Williams, J. R., 7868, 8272
Williams, Jack K., 6642, 7443
Williams, James M., 11157
Williams, Jesse L., 6099, 6107
Williams, John A., 6226
Williams, John Allen, 12277
Williams, John H. H., 7181
Williams, John S., 1799
Williams, Jonathan D., 12524, 13062
Williams, Kenneth P., 5050
Williams, Kenneth R., 1599
Williams, Morley J., 1308
Williams, Phil, 12386
Williams, Philip M., 11767
Williams, Raburn M., 11695
Williams, Robert J., 9410, 10521
Williams, T. Harry, 1519, 4545, 5051, 5052, 5740, 5836, 10846, 11158
Williams, Talcott, 4073, 7642
Williams, Wayne C., 3654
Williams, William A., 6328
Williamson, Hugh P., 983
Williamson, Mary L., 150, 151
Williamson, Richard S., 12927, 12966
Willingham, Alex, 13143
Willingham, Ed, 11691
Willis, Edward F., 8181
Willis, John, 6643
Willoughby, William R., 8739
Wills, Garry, 246, 618, 619, 763, 1842, 5892, 9407, 10384, 11457, 11458, 11657, 11765, 11766, 12082
Wills, John W., 5391

Willson, Roger E., 9411
Wilmarth, Arthur E., 12283
Wilmerding, Lucius, Jr., 2536, 2555, 4186
Wilson, Carol, 8321
Wilson, David L., 5790, 7832
Wilson, Donald E., 9497
Wilson, Douglas L., 1287, 1309
Wilson, Edith B. G., 7261
Wilson, Francis G., 1800
Wilson, George C., 11235
Wilson, George W., 13144
Wilson, Gerald L., 11658
Wilson, Graham K., 11767
Wilson, Hazel, 324
Wilson, James G., 302, 4267, 4268, 5083, 5651, 5652
Wilson, James H., 5653
Wilson, James Q., 12967
Wilson, John F., 7911, 8740
Wilson, John R. M., 8273, 8274
Wilson, Major L., 2929, 3113, 3114, 4546
Wilson, Milburn L., 1510-1512
Wilson, Richard, 11459, 11847
Wilson, Robert E., 3156
Wilson, Robert L., 6523
Wilson, Rufus R., 4187, 4188, 4269, 4270, 5140, 5244
Wilson, Samuel M., 247, 248
Wilson, Theodore A., 9171
Wilson, Theodore R., 7262
Wilson, William H., 9083
Wilson, Woodrow, 7741-7812
Wilstach, Paul, 325, 908, 1058, 1288, 1289, 1520, 1521, 1801, 2315, 2316
Wiltse, Charles M., 1600, 1879, 1950, 1951, 2656
Wiltshire, Susan F., 2174
Wiltz, John E., 9603
Wimberley, Ronald C., 11768
Wimer, Charles A., 6017
Wimer, Kurt, 7444, 7477, 7643, 7644, 7912, 10385
Wimer, Sarah, 7912
Windley, Lathan A., 249, 2175
Windt, Theodore O., Jr., 12948
Wineberger, James A., 326
Winfield, Betty H., 8494, 8741, 8742, 9084
Wing, Kenneth R., 12928
Winkler, E. T., 5919
Winkler, John K., 7182
Winn, Ralph B., 5392
Winnacker, Rudolph A., 9172
Winnick, Andrew, 13089
Winslow, Art, 12929
Winston, Alexander, 1290
Winston, Robert W., 5413
Winter-Berger, Robert N., 12102
Winters, Donald L., 8182
Winthrop, Robert C., 152
Wipfler, William L., 13063

Wirt, William, 909, 1802
Wise, Dan, 10493
Wise, David, 10004, 10494, 11159, 11659
Wise, Henry A., 3182
Wise, James W., 1803
Wise, Jennings C., 7359
Wise, John S., 413
Wish, Harvey, 1987
Wister, Owen, 153, 5654, 6423, 6644, 6877
Witcover, Jules, 11460, 12379, 12420, 12421, 12945, 12961
Withers, Henry, 5245
Witherspoon, Patricia A. D., 12083
Withey, Lynne, 910
Witt, Elder, 12808
Witt, Peter Von, 12361
Wittke, Carl F., 1804, 5893
Wittkopf, Eugene R., 12699
Wittner, Lawrence S., 9642
Wofford, Harris, 10127
Wohlstetter, Roberta, 9173
Wold, Ann M., 8391
Woldman, Albert A., 3929, 4609, 4610, 4783
Wolf, George D., 4547
Wolf, Hazel C., 4725, 4726
Wolf, John B., 10005
Wolf, T. Phillip, 8743
Wolf, William J., 4329, 4330
Wolfarth, Donald D., 10386
Wolfe, Alan, 12809, 12810
Wolfe, Harold, 8076
Wolfe, J. W., 4032
Wolfe, James S., 10387, 10642
Wolfe, Maxine G., 2537
Wolfe, Richard J., 4033
Wolfe, Udolpho, 2538
Wolfenstein, E. Victor, 11160
Wolfenstein, Martha, 10495
Wolff, Christopher, 7445
Wolff, Perry S., 10128
Wolff, Philippe, 1486
Wolfskill, George, 8744, 9085
Wolfson, Elaine M., 11236
Wolfson, Victor, 9247
Wolgemuth, Kathleen L., 7521, 7522
Wolin, Howard E., 10129, 12422
Wolin, Sheldon S., 12811
Wolkins, George G., 512
Woll, Peter, 12209
Wolman, Harold, 11135, 12362
Wood, Clarence A., 3148
Wood, Clement, 7833, 8077
Wood, Frederick S., 6424
Wood, G. S., 1805
Wood, Harry, 4034
Wood, James P., 10811
Wood, John, 1025
Wood, Leonora W., 3655

Wood Printing Works, 10724
Woodall, Charles L., 4331
Woodard, Kim, 12525
Woodburn, James A., 2449
Woodburn, Robert O., 1404
Woodfin, Maude H., 1487, 2007
Woodhouse, Edward S., 7360
Woodrow Wilson Centennial Celebration Commission, 7361
Woods, James R., 8815
Woods, John A., 8745
Woods, Randall B., 6823, 7601, 8940, 8941
Woods, Robert A., 7967
Woodson, C. G., 414
Woodstone, Arthur, 11431
Woodward, C. Vann, 5568, 5894
Woodward, Gary C., 12812
Woodward, Isaiah A., 673, 3456, 4784
Woodward, William E., 154, 5655
Woody, Robert H., 3656
Woolery, William K., 1880
Wooten, James T., 12145
Workman, Charles H., 4035
Workman, Randall G., 11358
Workmaster, Wallace F., 6108
Works, John D., 6824
Worner, William F., 303, 304, 2930, 3389, 3390, 3462, 3463
Woytak, Richard A., 8942
Wren, Christopher W., 11375
Wright, Allen H., 4611
Wright, Anna M. R., 3771
Wright, Annie F. F., 4878
Wright, Bette L., 11237
Wright, Carrie D., 3772
Wright, Claudia, 13064
Wright, Elliot, 2450
Wright, Esmond, 674, 1059, 1806, 2368, 7602, 9086, 9087
Wright, Frances F., 2768
Wright, Gerald C., Jr., 13065
Wright, Jack, Jr., 10388
Wright, James C., 4332
Wright, John S., 5246
Wright, L. Hart, 12363
Wright, Louis B., 1365
Wright, Marcia, 5393, 6233
Wright, Marcus J., 5656
Wright, Peter M., 9498
Wright, Robert, 9865
Wright-Davis, Mary, 5394
Wriston, Henry M., 764
Wrone, David R., 4150, 4151
Wrone, James G., 10725
Wrong, Dennis H., 12084
Wrong, George M., 675
Wroth, L. Kinvin, 1060
Wszelaki, Jan H., 10726

Wu, Fu-Mei Chiu, 11848
Wyatt, Euphemia V. R., 358
Wyatt, Joseph R., III, 5912
Wyatt-Brown, Bertram, 5979
Wyden, Peter, 10158
Wykes, Alan, 9717
Wylie, Theodore W. J., 359
Wyllie, John C., 2317
Wyman, Charles L., 676
Wyman, William I., 1291
Wynne, Patricia H., 4935

Xydis, Stephen G., 9643

Yackle, Larry W., 12813
Yager, Thomas C., 11161
Yakovee, Rehavie U., 12526
Yandle, Bruce, 11561
Yang, Matthew Y., 9412
Yaniv, Avner, 13066
Yankelovich, Daniel, 10951
Yarborough, Ralph W., 4548
Yarbrough, Edward, 2769
Yarmey, A. Daniel, 10496
Yarnell, Allen L., 9912
Yates, John H., 360
Yates, Richard, 5657
Yee, Herbert S., 13067
Yeh, Po-t'ang, 13068
Yizhar, Michael, 10006-10008
Yoder, Edwin M., 513, 1601, 1807
York, Herbert F., 9428, 10009
Young, George B., 6187
Young, James H., 5053
Young, John R., 5689
Young, John W., 2451
Young, Lowell T., 8943-8945
Young, Mary E., 3039

Young, Norwood, 677
Young, Rowland L., 415
Young, Stanley P., 3174
Younger, Edward, 7362
Youngs, J. William T., 8495
Yzenbaard, John H., 3149, 4549, 5395

Zahm, J. A., 6524
Zaitseva, N. D., 2176, 3040
Zall, Paul M., 5396
Zand, Dale E., 9866
Zane, Charles S., 4271
Zane, John M., 4612
Zarefsky, David H., 11238-11240
Zavin, Howard S., 8517
Zebroski, Shirley, 8762
Zeiger, Henry A., 10847
Zeisel, Hans, 11920
Zieger, Robert H., 8028, 8078, 8183, 8184
Ziglar, William L., 6825
Zill, Anne B., 11660
Zilversmit, Arthur, 3773
Zimmern, Alfred E., 7446
Zinam, Oleg, 13145
Zingale, Donald P., 9913
Zinn, Howard, 9088
Zinsmeister, Robert, Jr., 3798, 4036, 5397, 5398
Zivojinovic, Dragan R., 7691
Zobe, Hiller B., 1060
Zoellner, Robert H., 5247
Zornow, William F., 3930, 4785, 4936-4940, 6188, 9413, 9867
Zuckert, Catherine H., 12814
Zuckert, Eugene M., 9414
Zukin, Clifford, 11731, 11769
Zunder, Theodore A., 250
Zutz, Robert, 12085
Zvesper, John, 2452

Subject Index

ABM. *See* Antiballistic Missile
Abolitionism, and Lincoln, 5186
Abraham Lincoln Library and Museum, 3968, 4023
Abubakari, Imari, 12485
Account book, of Washington, 782
Acheson, Dean, 9248
Acid rain, 13048
Adams, Abigail, 862, 870-873, 876, 879, 883, 884, 904, 910, 1027, 1037, 1056, 1265, 2205
Adams, Brooks, 2607, 2653, 6583, 6645, 6660
Adams, Dickinson W., 2286
Adams, Henry, 2085, 2607, 2653, 2673, 2904, 6507
Adams, John, 641, 651, 707, 848-1060
   biographies, 848-868
   presidential years, 984-1025
   private life, 869-910
   public career, 911-983
   writings, 1026-1060
Adams, John Quincy, 2580-2711
   biographies, 2580-2592
   presidential years, 2657-2666
   private life, 2593-2613
   public career, 2614-2656
   writings, 2667-2711
Adams, Josephine T., 8629
Adams, Louisa, 2591, 2602
Adams, Samuel, 627, 918, 1955, 7837
Adams-Clay bargain, 2561
Adams-Onis Treaty of 1819, 917
Ade, George, 7056
Adenauer, Konrad, 11257
Advertising, on television, 12870
Advice and consent, 6774
AEC. *See* Atlantic Energy Commission
AFDC. *See* Aid to Families with Dependent Children
Affirmative Action, 12864
Afghanistan, 12447, 12478
AFL. *See* American Federation of Labor
Africa
   and Eisenhower, 9753
   and Grant, 5689
   and Kennedy, 10691-10693, 10696
   northern, 12993
   and Reagan, 12982, 13019, 13022, 13036
   and Theodore Roosevelt, 6428, 6474, 6516, 6845, 6895, 6896, 6961
   southern, 11823, 12476, 12503
Africans, and John Q. Adams, 2566, 2648, 2672
Afro-Americans, and Theodore Roosevelt, 6728
Agenda setting, 12414
Agnew, Spiro, 11438, 11548
Agriculture, 1492-1512, 4524, 5557, 6811, 8802
   activities, 310
   policy, 7903, 8017, 8141, 8810, 9908
   price, 7496
   trade policy, 9897
Aid, foreign
   and Eisenhower, 9950, 9951, 9988, 9991
   and Kennedy, 10722
   and Lyndon Johnson, 11775
   and Nixon, 11775
Aid to Families with Dependent Children (AFDC), and Reagan, 12880
Aides-de-camp, of Washington, 672
Aiken, George, 11351
Air Policy Commission, 9497
Airlines, 9460
Alabama, 6160, 7404, 8988
Alaska, 6652
Albany, NY, 5670, 6536, 8511
Albany Regency, 3077, 3090
Albemarle County, VA, 2574
Aldrich, Nelson, 6778
Alexandria, VA, 352, 365
Alfred (ship), 8436
Alger, Horatio, 4008
Algeria, 11790
   crisis, 10751
   independence, 10699
Alien and Sedition Acts, 748
Aliens, 12295
Alleghany Mountains, 839, 3984

Subject Index

Alliance for Progress, 10649
Allis-Chalmers Corporation, 10204
Ambassadors, 6830, 11935
Amendments
    First, 2441, 2471, 2493, 11533, 12720
    Fourteenth, 5120
    Ninth, 215
    Twenty-fifth, 12067
American Child Health Association, 8133
American Federation of Labor (AFL), and Hoover, 8142
American Institute of Architects, 6769
American Liberty League, 8826
American Philosophical Society, 1532, 2013
American University, 10242
Americans for Democratic Action, 9325
Ames, Fisher, 2670
Amherst College, 7936, 7947, 7950
Amidon, Charles, 6620
Amnesty, 4682, 4702, 5489, 12295, 12320, 12504
Anarchy, 6237, 6285
Ancestry
    of Kennedy, 10081
    of Lincoln, 3809, 3810, 3819, 3842, 3844, 4959
    of Nixon, 11408
    of Reagan, 12585
    of Theodore Roosevelt, 6431, 6492
    of Taft, 6985
    of Van Buren, 3069
    of Washington, 265, 266, 288, 298, 299, 302, 322
Anderson, Chandler, 7562
Anderson, James W., 7212
Anderson, John, 6227, 12292, 12561, 12939
Anderson, Richard H., 5044
Anderson, Martin, 12710
Anderson, Maxwell, 7367
Anderson, Robert, 5037
Andrew Johnson National Monument, 5429, 5433
Angell, James B., 7811
Anglophobia, 2124, 3104
Animals
    and Theodore Roosevelt, 6961
    and Washington, 164
Annapolis
    Jefferson in, 1715
    Washington in, 555, 661
Anthracite crisis, 8028
Antiballistic Missile
    and Lyndon Johnson, 11187
    and Reagan, 13073
Anti-Imperialism, and Franklin D. Roosevelt, 8912
Anti-Masonic party, 3167, 3338, 3349
Antitrust, 6822, 7101, 9886, 9887, 12318
    enforcement, 12888
    liability, 12927
Apartheid, 9557, 9983, 12427
Appalachia, 4456
Appeasement, 7516, 7675

Appointments, regulatory, 11636
Appomattox, 5579
Appropriations, 6026, 11648
Arabs, 10706, 11269, 11820, 13064
    and Israeli conflict, 9545, 9613
    states, 10673
Arbitration Treaties of 1911, 6670, 7027
Arcadia Conference, 9162
Architecture
    and Franklin D. Roosevelt, 8447, 8448
    and Jefferson, 1514-1534
Argentina, 7601, 8940, 8941
Aristocracy, and Jefferson, 1570
Arizona, 4034
Arkansas, 2098, 6710, 8227, 8810
Arlington, VA, Washington in, 161
Armed forces, 8273
Armenia, 7538, 7875
Arms, 12526
    control, 12464, 13070, 13074, 13088
    limitation talks, 6854
    nuclear, 13069-13089
    race, 9960
    sales, 12428
    transfers, 11838, 11839
Armstrong, Duff, 4569, 4604
Armstrong, John, 2442, 2549
Army
    and Adams, 953
    Continental, 626, 655, 661, 665, 673, 804
    and Garfield, 6030
    and Grant, 5639, 5643
    and Jackson, 2727, 2730, 2763, 2805
    and Jefferson, 2031, 2057
    and Andrew Johnson, 5503
    and Lincoln, 4955, 5033, 5041
    of the Potomac, 4981
    Reserve, 10560
    and Franklin D. Roosevelt, 8569, 8601
    and Theodore Roosevelt, 6564
    War College, 9742
Arnold, Isaac N., 4242
Aroostook War, 3104
Art, Washington in, 513
Arthur, Chester A., 6034-6070
    biographies, 6034-6042
    presidential years, 6050-6058
    private life, 6043-6047
    public career, 6048, 6049
    writings, 6069, 6070
Arthur, Malvina, 6046
Arts, 236, 1335, 1337, 1348, 1355, 8446, 10185
    endowment, 12838
    and Franklin D. Roosevelt, 6604
Asgill, Charles, 650
Ash Council, 11673
Asia, 11826
    and Carter, 12442, 12525

colonialism, 8867
East, 7076
and Eisenhower, 9947
Grant visits, 5689
and Lyndon Johnson, 11366
and Nixon, 11794, 11924
Pacific policy, 13007, 13049
and Franklin D. Roosevelt, 8884
and Theodore Roosevelt, 6841
South, 11274, 11831
Southeast, 11779, 12427
and war, 11319
Asquith, Herbert, 4705
Assassination, 6606, 10389-10496, 12068, 12670, 12754
  of Garfield, 5932, 5935, 5942, 5995, 6000, 6002, 6011, 6012, 6015, 6036
  attempt on Jackson, 2946, 2978, 3014
  of Lincoln, 4786-4878
  of McKinley, 6244, 6285, 6291, 6301, 6314, 6315
  attempt on Theodore Roosevelt, 6560
Associated Press, 9932, 10390
Athens, GA, Taft's visit to, 7033
Atlantic Alliance, 12455
Atlantic Conference, 9162, 9163
Atomic Energy Commission, 9896
Attlee, Clement R., 9156, 9576
Attorney general, 5112, 5119, 6694, 8700, 9390, 10015, 10317
Attorney-client relationships, 12319
Atwood, Elbridge, 5398
Australia, 4825
Austria-Hungary, 7683
Authority, presidential, 5889
Autographs, of Washington, 783
Automobile code, 8770
Autopsy, of Kennedy, 10487
Avery, Waightstill, 1435
Aviation industry, 9475, 9900, 12430
  commercial, 8150
Axis satellites, 9165
Ayers, E. A., 9310
Azerbaijan Crisis, 9569, 9578

Bache, Benjamin F., 755
Bache, Richard, 732
Bacon, Edmund, 1513
Badlands, 6464, 6490
Baker, Edward D., 3675, 3692, 4487
Baker, James A., 12669, 12713
Baker, Ray S., 6782, 7173
Bakshian, Aram, 11491
Balance of power, 1858, 1870, 7607, 8920, 9154
Baldwin, Simon E., 6559
Balfour Declaration, 7524, 7572
Ballinger-Pinchot controversy, 7085
Baltimore, 2388
  Hayes visit to, 5817

and Lincoln, 4466, 4893, 5444
plot, 4696
and Washington, 364
and Wilson, 7454
Bancroft, George, 5466
Banister, Marion, 8590, 9317
Bank bill, and Washington, 687
Bank war, 2966, 3007, 3009, 3017
Bank of England, 221
Bank of the U. S., 221, 2993
Banking
  under Hoover, 8217, 8244, 8270, 8789
  interstate, 12283
  under Jackson, 2973, 2977, 2997, 2998
  Jefferson on, 1577
Baptist, 12261
  Carter a, 12152
  and the Lincoln assassination, 4788
Bargaining, collective, 11162
Barlow, Joel, 250
Barnard, George G., 3839
Barney, Hiram, 5364
Barrett, Oliver R., 4011
Bartlett, Truman H., 3743
Bassett, John S., 3292
Bates, Edward, 4226, 5112, 5119
Batista, Fulgencio, 8882
Battle of the Bulge, 9738, 9761
Battle of Kaserine Pass, 9738
Battle of Monterey, 3316
Battle of Okee-chobee, 3314
Battle of Olustee, 5001
Bay of Pigs, 10312, 10536, 10539, 10543, 11010, 11510
Baylor, George, 628
Beale, General, 5779
Beall, John Y., 4739
Beard, Charles A., 8899, 8992
Beckley, John, 2058
Bed, history of Lincoln, 3994
Bedell, Grace, 3709
Beecher, Charles E., 4247
Beliot, WI, Lincoln in, 3786
Belknap, Jeremy, 2645
Bellarmine, Robert, 1798, 1839
Belmont, MI, campaign, 5722, 5734
Benjamin, Eugene, 7673
Bennett, James G., 5163
Bennett, Richard B., 8226
Benson, Ezra T., 9903
Benton, Thomas H., 6926, 6952
Berger, Warren, 2469, 12248
Berle, Adolf A., 9069
Berlin
  blockade, 9552
  crisis, 10654, 10687
  and Eisenhower, 9672, 9731
  and Israel, 9615

Subject Index

and Nixon, 11843
and Truman, 9553
Bermuda, and Carter, 12430
Berrien, John M., 2967
Bethune, Mary M., 8801
Beveridge, Albert J., 3619, 3671
Beverly, MA, and New England fleet, 623
Bible
   and John Q. Adams, 2689
   and Jefferson, 1219, 1462, 1623, 1640, 2262
   and Lincoln, 4300, 4303
Bicameral system, 980
Bicentennial, and Washington, 372, 375, 383, 414, 449
Biddle, Alexander, 1044
Biddle, James, 583
Biddle, Nicholas, 979, 1986, 2966, 2971, 2972, 3030
Bigelow, William S., 6597
Bigotry, in politics, 1649
Bill of Rights, 2136
Billiard table, and John Adams, 897
Billings, Hammat, 5633
Bingham, Benjamin F., 6508
Bipartisanship, and Truman administration, 9290
Birds
   and Franklin D. Roosevelt, 8456
   and Theodore Roosevelt, 6446
Birth
   of Garfield, 5934
   of Grant, 5663
   of Jackson, 2733
   of Lincoln, 4410
   of Franklin D. Roosevelt, 8619
   of Theodore Roosevelt, 6416
   of Washington, 199, 303, 388
Birthplace
   of John Adams, 905
   of John Q. Adams, 2612
   of Arthur, 6044, 6045, 6047
   of Cleveland, 6100
   of Coolidge, 8006
   of Jackson, 2781, 2819
   of Jefferson, 1245
   of Lyndon Johnson, 10886
   of Lincoln, 3808, 4000
   of Washington, 268, 270, 285, 286, 424, 459
   of Wilson, 7205
Bissell, William H., 5284
Bixby, Lydia A., 3669, 3677
Bixby, William K., 5686
Black, Chauncey F., 3534
Black, Hugo, 5504
Black, Jeremiah S., 3431
Black Hawk War, 3707, 3730
Blacks, 7064, 7488
   and John Adams, 914, 2132
   and Coolidge, 8004
   and Eisenhower, 9872

and Garfield, 6027, 6029
and Grant, 5754
and Harding, 7890, 7906
and Hayes, 5840
and Hoover, 8207, 8210
and Jackson, 2834
and Jefferson, 1407, 2134
and Andrew Johnson, 5437, 5438, 5443, 5490, 5498, 5539, 5548
and Lyndon Johnson, 11166, 11167, 11188, 11191, 11202, 11210, 11223
and Kennedy, 10554, 10564, 10566
and Lincoln, 5181, 5183, 5185, 5188, 5189, 5191, 5196, 5197, 5210, 5228, 5231
and McKinley, 6272, 6783
and Madison, 2504
power of, 12348, 12351
and Reagan, 12639, 12946, 12953, 13097
and Reconstruction, 5857
and Franklin D. Roosevelt, 8593, 8775, 8801, 8812
and Theodore Roosevelt, 6825
and Taft, 7018
and Truman, 9449, 9489, 9491, 9492
and Washington, 588
and Wilson, 7494, 7504, 7522, 7722
Blackstone's Commentaries, 2202
Blades, Franklin, 4189
Blaine, James G., 3141, 5871, 5897, 5972, 6121, 6163, 6224, 6232
Blair, Francis P., 2806, 2900
Blair, James G., 1709
Blair, Montgomery, 5040
Blair House, 9261
Bliss, W. W., 6000
Bloomington, IL, and Lincoln, 4362, 4934, 5275
Bly, Nellie, 5804
Bodyguards, of Lincoln, 4213
Bogota, William H. Harrison in, 3156
Bookplates
   by Henry Adams, 2673
   of John Adams, 874
Books
   and John Q. Adams, 2606, 2673
   and Garfield, 5963
   and Jefferson, 1223, 1353, 1359, 1363
   and Lincoln, 4040, 4056, 4069, 4605
   and Franklin D. Roosevelt, 8406, 8459
   in White House Library, 8264
Booth, John W., 4792, 4800, 4815, 4822, 4824, 4836, 4839, 4853, 4860, 4876
Boston
   and Andrew Jackson, 2879
   police strike in, 8018
   and the Revolution, 1955
Boston Athenaeum
   John Q. Adams collection in, 2673
   Washington collection in, 446

Boston Massacre trials, 956
Boston Patriot, 1031
Boston Public Library, Washington materials in, 448, 449, 773, 774
Botany, and Jefferson, 1683
Boucher, Jonathan, 559
Bourbon democracy, 6135
    leader, 6159
Boutwell, George S., 5486
Bouvier, Jacqueline, 10079, 10088
Bowdoin, James, 152
Bowers, Claude G., 8666
Boyd, Ben, 4856
Boyd, Julian P., 1688
Boyhood
    of Grant, 5663, 5676
    of Hoover, 8102
    of Washington, 540, 543, 546
Braddock Campaign, 653
Bradley, Omar N., 9739
Brady, James S., 12707
Brady, Mathew B., 3686, 4173
Brains Trust, 8255, 8799, 8800
Brandeis, Louis D., 7520, 7524, 9001, 9002
Brazil, 12445
    and Kennedy, 10686
    Theodore Roosevelt in, 6954
Brazoria County, TX, 3189
Breckinridge, John, 2047, 2238
Brecknock trial, 4568
Breedlove, James W., 3044
Brezhnev, Leonid I., 11260, 11278, 11819, 12053, 12462
Bricker Amendment, 9842
Bright, John, 7769
Bristow, Benjamin H., 5891, 5897, 7087
Britton, Nan, 7838
Broadcast
    political, 9915
    regulations, 8131, 8143, 8144, 12845
Brodie, Fawn, 1096
Brooklyn, and 1860 election, 4932
Brooks, Noah, 3846, 4667, 4949, 5156
Brooks, Phillips, 4799
Brow, Brockden, 2026
Brown, Charles B., 1760
Brown, Edmund G., 12591, 12592
Brown, Jerry, 12586, 12591, 12593, 12600
Brown, John, 3456, 3997, 4532, 5007
Brown University Library, and Lincoln letters, 5328
Browne, William G., 5812
Brownell, Herbert, 9868, 10015
Browning, Orville H., 4242, 4663, 4754
Brownlow, Parson, 5427
Brownlow, William G., 5452
Brownsville affair, 6808
Brussels Conference, 1737, 8928

Bryan, William J., 5919, 6130, 6142, 6275, 6290, 6318, 6675, 7125, 7454, 7599, 7693, 12967
Bryan-Chamorro Treaty, 7529
Bryant, William C., 1277
Bryce, James, 7749
Brzezinski, Zbigniew, 12518
Buchanan, James, 3382-3463
    biographies, 3382-3390
    Douglas feud, 3412
    presidential years, 3416-3456
    private life, 3391-3406
    public career, 3407-3415
    writings, 3457-3463
Budget
    Bureau of the, 8731, 9471, 9480, 9482, 9898
    and Eisenhower, 9895
    and Lyndon Johnson, 11178, 11327
    and Nixon, 11669, 11678, 11686, 11690, 11705
    and Reagan, 12815-12836
    and Franklin D. Roosevelt, 9068
Buena Vista, 3296
Buffalo, NY, 6110, 6120, 6197
Bulgaria, 9165
Bull, John, 3268
Bull Moose, 6535, 6552
Bullitt, William C., 7290, 9186
Bundy, McGeorge, 10233
Bunker Hill Monument, 982, 1796
Bureau of Corporations, 6737
Bureau of Pension, 6222
Bureau of Reclamation, 9457
Bureau of the Budget, 8731, 9471, 9482, 9898
Bureaucracy
    and Carter, 12160, 12169, 12209, 12228, 12231
    and Hoover, 8108, 8189
    and Lyndon Johnson, 10954
    and Nixon, 11461, 11471, 11481, 11566
    and Reagan, 12791
Burger, Warren, 7004, 11517
Burgess, John W., 6659
Burial, of Lincoln, 3985
Burke, Edmund, 924, 3370, 3381, 7297
Burleson, Albert S., 7365, 7705
Burn, John W., 4189
Burnet, Gilbert, 1472
Burns, Arthur, 12016
Burns, John, 5066
Burr, Aaron, 1900, 2008, 2050, 2059, 2080, 2177, 2194, 11563, 11619
Burroughs, John, 6453, 8104
Burt, Silas, 6066, 6190
Burton, OH, 5929
Bush, George, 12635
Bushnell, Horace, 2099
Business
    activities, 218
    and Carter, 12291
    civilization, 6583

and Cleveland, 6152, 6170
community, 8796
culture, 7978
and Eisenhower, 9887, 9950
interests, 7562
and Lyndon Johnson, 11206, 11216, 11218, 11250
and Kennedy, 10563, 10572, 10600, 10686
and McKinley, 6303
man, 225, 272
and Nixon, 11589
and Reagan, 12872, 13115
and Franklin D. Roosevelt, 8937, 8998
and Theodore Roosevelt, 6749
small, 13103
and Wilson, 7484, 7485, 7519
Busing, 11714
Busts
  of Jefferson, 1196
  of Theodore Roosevelt, 6452
  of Washington, 435, 462, 464, 475
Butcher, Harry C., 9740
Butler, Anthony, 2906
Butler, Benjamin F., 3310, 4906, 5723, 6123
Butt, Archie, 6623, 6667, 6668
Buttre, J. C., 3867
Byrd, Harry F., 8751, 9036
Byrd, William, 1487
Byrnes, James F., 8836, 8910, 9549

Cabell, Joseph C., 2222
Cabinet
  under Buchanan, 3416, 3423
  under Carter, 12222, 12234
  under Cleveland, 6141
  under Eisenhower, 9808
  under Ford, 11981
  government, 7750, 7753
  under Harding, 7897, 7899, 7904
  under Benjamin Harrison, 6226
  under Hoover, 8170
  under Jackson, 2837, 2952, 2995, 3026
  under Lyndon Johnson, 11030, 11038
  under Kennedy, 10250, 10256
  kitchen, 2984, 2991, 12158, 12620
  under Lincoln, 3961, 4693, 4698, 4737, 4750, 4960
  under Nixon, 11476, 11543, 11701
  under Polk, 3257
  under Reagan, 12636, 12710, 12713, 12761, 12806
  under Franklin D. Roosevelt, 8593, 8722, 8801
  under Theodore Roosevelt, 6663
  under Truman, 9542
  under Wilson, 7396, 7401, 7423, 7429
Cabrera, Luis, 7645
Cabrera, Manuel E., 7531
Cairo Conference, 9152

Caldwallader, Sylvanus, 5694
Calhoun, John C., 912, 1523, 1558, 1788, 2174, 2373, 2447, 2746, 2944, 3027
California
  Alien Land Law Controversy, 7505
  and Lincoln, 4682
  Mafia, 12701
  Medi-Cal reform, 12881
  and Reagan, 12588, 12597, 12601
  and Republican party, 8110
  and Franklin D. Roosevelt, 8838
  and Theodore Roosevelt, 6500
  and Wilson, 7456, 7457
Calvinism, and Wilson, 7594
Call, Richard K., 3047
Callender, James, 1102, 1410, 1426, 1717
Cambodia, 9582, 11783, 11792, 11797, 11812, 11834, 11840
Cambridge, MA, 2682
Camelot, 10204, 10343, 10366, 10367, 10648
Camp David meetings, 12510, 12522
Campaign
  ad men, 9926, 12941
  Arthur, 6062, 6063
  Carter, 12365, 12371, 12385, 12395, 12399, 12402, 12404, 12413, 12558
  Cleveland, 6075
  Eisenhower, 9765, 9919-9921, 9923, 9926, 9927, 9929, 9931-9933
  Ford, 11993, 12033
  Grant, 5770
  Harding, 7872
  Benjamin Harrison, 6213, 6226
  Hayes, 5719
  Hoover, 8119, 8156, 8172, 8173
  Lyndon Johnson, 10895, 10911, 10915, 10936, 11244, 11246, 11247, 11253
  Kennedy, 10616, 10623, 10630-10632, 10635, 10642
  Lincoln, 4540, 4627, 4629, 4630, 4632, 4637, 4654, 4879-4940, 5316
  McKinley, 6310
  Nixon, 11433, 11436, 11467, 11720, 11728, 11731, 11738, 11740, 11743, 11744, 11750, 11761
  Polk, 3230-3232
  Reagan, 12941, 12957, 12961, 12966
  Franklin D. Roosevelt, 8503, 8816-8819, 8823-8826, 8829, 8832, 8840, 8842
  Theodore Roosevelt, 6539, 6620, 6631, 6672, 6716
  Taft, 7026, 7056
  Taylor, 3326
  Truman, 9287, 9501, 9502, 9506, 9507, 9509
  Washington, 754
  Wilson, 7465
Campbell, Charles, 2153
Campobello, 8441, 11368

Canada, 12071
  Anglo relations, 6851
  and Carter, 12444
  and Hoover, 8225, 8226
  and Jefferson, 2118
  and Reagan, 12989, 13025, 13048, 13065
  and Franklin D. Roosevelt, 8909
  and Taft, 7087
Canisius, Theodore, 5290
Cannon, Joseph G., 4192
Cannonism, 7006
Cape Fear Valley, 958
Caperton, William B., 7563
Capitalism, 719, 2857, 8218
Capitol, 307, 464, 561, 1707, 1756, 1758
  Virginia, 2352
Cardozo, Benjamin N., 2197, 8191
Caribbean, 6850, 7525, 7543, 8943, 13043
Carman, Travers D., 6545
Carnegie, Andrew, 4008
Carpenter, Francis B., 4164
Carpenter, Liz, 10851
Carranza, Venustiano, 7645, 7647, 7648, 7653, 7662
Carroll, John, 989
Carter, Boake, 8558
Carter, 'Croak,' 8558
Carter, Dennis C., 3941
Carter, Jimmy, 12103-12561
  biographies, 12103-12119
  domestic policy, 12278-12363
  elections, 12364-12422
  Ford debate, 11976, 12004, 12040, 12049, 12066, 12367, 12372, 12390, 12398, 12411
  foreign affairs, 12423-12526
  as governor, 12147
  human rights, 12527-12549
  presidential years, 12149-12529
  private life, 12120-12145
  public career, 12146-12148
  and Reagan debate, 12370, 12410, 12416, 12936, 12962
  writings, 12550-12561
Carter, Lillian, 12128
Carter, Rosalyn, 12123, 12130, 12134, 12139
Carter Doctrine, 12270
Cartoons
  and Eisenhower, 9833
  and Hayes, 5853
  and Jackson, 2911
  and Lyndon Johnson, 11112
  and Lincoln, 3617, 4187
  and Nixon, 11559
  and Franklin D. Roosevelt, 8718
  and Theodore Roosevelt, 6412, 6580
  and Truman, 9253
Cary, Archibald, 2292
Casey, William, 12635

Cass, Lewis, 2832
Castro, Cipriano, 6849, 6863
Castro, Fidel, 10695, 11832, 11928
Caterino, Enrico, 1035
Catholic Herald, 5147
Catholicism
  ceremonies in White House, 2825
  and Kennedy, 10058, 10221, 2486, 10269, 10382, 10602, 10610, 10626
  and Lincoln, 4275, 4278
  and Franklin D. Roosevelt, 8578, 8678, 8880
  and Theodore Roosevelt, 6826
  and Washington, 327
  and Wilson, 7766
Catron, John, 3420
Cattlemen, and Eisenhower, 9889
CCC. *See* Civilian Conservation Corps
Centennial
  Garfield, 5934, 5990
  Grant, 5665, 5671
  Hayes, 5835
  Lincoln, 3940, 4400
  of Lincoln's admission to the bar, 4609
  Washington, 362, 384, 411
  Wilson, 7341
Central America, and Reagan, 12979, 12983, 12991, 12993, 13015, 13046, 13063
Central Intelligence Agency (CIA), 9966, 10296, 10372, 12009, 12635
Central Presbyterian Church, Washington, DC, 7251
Cerrachi, Giuseppe, 1196
Chamberlain, Austen, 8936
Chamberlain, George E., 7266
Champaign County, IL, 4611
Chandler, Zachariah, 5040
Charities, of Reagan, 12776
Charleston, 601, 5008
  Convention, 5459
  riot, 4941
Charnwood, Lord, 3728
Chase, Salmon P., 4371, 4668, 4689, 4936, 4960, 5001, 5501, 5526, 5755, 5965
Chase, William M., 5812, 5823
Chatham, William E., 7809
Chautauqua, 5859, 6807, 8717
Chavez, Dennis, 8952
Checker's speech, 9380, 11516, 11766
Chemistry, and Jefferson, 1294, 1661
Chesapeake-Leopard Crisis, 2630
Cheshire Ultimatum, 9569
Chiang-Kai-Shek, 9152
Chicago
  Bar Association, 5376
  Historical Society, 3289, 5375
  and Lincoln, 3831, 4275, 4341, 4348, 4933
  mayor, 4494
  and New Deal, 9031

720 Subject Index

press and Arthur, 6056
and Franklin D. Roosevelt, 8845
Chicago Times, 5036
Chicago Tribune, 5764, 8650
Chickamauga, 5974
Chickasaw Indians, 2778
Children
  Reagan's war on, 12861, 12866
  and Theodore Roosevelt, 6460, 6506, 6951
China, 1563, 12973
  and Buchanan, 3428
  and Carter, 12473
  and McKinley, 6300
  and Nixon, 11774, 11794, 11798, 11803, 11817, 11822, 11844, 11847, 11848
  and Opium War with Great Britain, 2669
  and Reagan, 13007, 13023, 13068
  and Franklin D. Roosevelt, 8891
  and Theodore Roosevelt, 6855, 6858, 6874, 6876
  and Truman, 8891, 9524, 9548, 9564, 9579, 9584
  and Wilson, 7573, 7578, 7594, 7597
Chinard, Gilbert, 869
Chinaware, of Washington, 434
Chiniquy, Charles P., 5283
Christianity, and Reagan, 12794
Christmas, and Washington, 172, 227, 637
Church, and Truman administration, 9321
Church-state issues, 2469, 12292, 12939
Churchill, Winston, 8900-8902, 8913, 9095, 9097, 9118, 9120, 9125, 9127, 9135, 9144, 9152, 9156, 9162, 9163, 9171, 9178, 9200, 9576, 9748, 10011, 10174
CIA. *See* Central Intelligence Agency
Cincinnati
  Astronomical Society, 2697
  Lincoln's speech in, 5300
  Taft in, 6976
Cinema, Lincoln's image in, 3952
Civil damages immunity, 11586
Civil defense, 12036, 12309
Civil disobedience, and Jefferson, 1975
Civil liability, 11593
Civil libertarians, 12205
Civil Rights, 10576, 10579, 10798, 10907
  Act, 10939
  Act of 1957, 11215
  Act of 1964, 11045
  Bill of 1963, 10590, 10938
  and Eisenhower, 9868, 9872, 9892, 9905
  and Ford, 12047
  and Lyndon Johnson, 10902, 10926, 11184, 11188, 11193, 11202, 11207, 11213, 11215, 11219, 11220, 11231, 11240
  and Kennedy, 10555, 10557, 10564, 10570, 10596
  and Nixon, 11697, 11706
  and Reagan, 12844, 12854, 13135
  and Truman, 9430, 9431, 9437, 9480, 9488, 9493, 9508
Civil service, 987, 2014, 2933, 2956, 11493, 12169, 12201
  reform, 5858, 5868, 5880, 6190, 6705
  Reform Act, 12205
Civil War, 3449, 4222, 4701, 4941-5053, 5460, 5732
  and freedmen, 5757
  and Garfield, 6030
  generals in, 5050, 5051, 5615, 5702, 5706, 5707, 5720
  and Grant, 5702, 5724
  Kansas problem, 3445
  in Kentucky, 5240
  and McKinley, 6330
  Northern seditionists, 5004
  origin of, 3438
  and slavery, 5243
  stage production, 5037, 5737
  and Tennessee, 5461
Civilian Conservation Corps (CCC), 8804, 8815
Claiborne, W. C. C., 2101, 2457
Clark, Allen C., 6508
Clark, Edward T., 7971
Clark, Tom, 9390
Clark, William, 2035
Clarkson, James S., 6216, 6687, 6782
Classics, 885, 1342, 1365, 5958
Clay, Cassius M., 4530
Clay, Henry, 1011, 1065, 2907, 2934, 3192, 3233, 3989, 4125, 5864, 6333
Clay Report, 10688
Clayton Act, 9886
Clayton-Bulwer Treaty, 3351
Clemenceau, Georges, 7663, 7673
Clemency, 4703, 11975
Clemons, Samuel L., 8104
Clergy, 2399, 1619, 8988-8990
Cleveland, Grover, 6071-6202
  biographies, 6071-6099
  presidential years, 6121-6188
  private life, 6100-6108
  public career, 6109-6120
  writings, 6189-6202
Clifton, Chester V., 10362
Clinton, DeWitt, 2533
Clinton, George, 811
Coal, 7500, 9025, 11712
  Strike of 1914, 7499
  utilization, 12334
Coalitions, political, 8634
Coast Guard, 714
Coat of Arms, Washington's, 485, 487
Cobb, Frank, 7366, 7383
Coffee, John, 2832
Coffin, William G., 4180, 5099
Coinage, 6714, 6963
Colburn, Edward A., 4203

Colby, Bainbridge, 7635
Cold War
  Carter, 12466
  Eisenhower, 9952
  Nixon, 10721, 11830
  Reagan, 12992
  Franklin D. Roosevelt, 8910
  sport in the, 9954
  Truman, 9164, 9535, 9549, 9559, 9562, 9577, 9580, 9594
Coleman, Ann, 3400
Coleridge, Samuel, 2040
Coles County, Lincoln in, 4339
Colfax, Schuyler, 5583, 5637, 5743
College of William and Mary, 1371, 1372
Collier, John, 9033
Collins, Paul, 11957
Colonel Harland Sanders Center for Lincoln Studies, 4036
Colonialism, 10699
Colonization, black, 5236, 5247
Colorado
  and Cleveland, 6156
  coal strike, 7480
  and Andrew Johnson, 5436
  and McKinley, 6299
  and Theodore Roosevelt, 6654, 6794
Colson, Charles W., 11472
Colt, LeBaron Bradford, 7097
Columbia, 3166
Columbia Broadcasting Corporation, 10492, 11995
Columbia University, 9755
Columbian Institute, 853
Commander in Chief
  Carter, 12484
  Eisenhower, 9861
  Garfield, 5639
  Lyndon Johnson, 11345
  Lincoln, 4970, 4974, 4987
  McKinley, 6279
  Madison, 2458, 2468, 9108
  Truman, 9329
  Washington, 12, 27, 648, 651, 661, 665, 673, 703, 735, 804
Commerce, 704, 1295, 2123
  Clause, 8958
  Department, 8117, 9072
  and Jefferson, 1764
  power, 6991
  secretary of, 8118, 8136, 8144, 8170
Commissions, regulatory, 8177, 11212
Committee on Civil Rights, 9490
Committee on the Conduct of the War, 5463
Committee to Re-elect the President (CREEP), 11751
Common Market, 10684
Communism, 8529, 8659, 9561, 10204
  anti, 11574

purge, 9440, 9873
Community Action Program, 11165
Compromise of 1850, 3320, 3322, 3348
Confederacy, 4702, 4968, 5157, 5489
Confederation, 680
  Congress, 2545
Congress. *See also* House of Representatives; Senate
  aid to education, 10588
  and Buchanan, 3423
  and busing, 11714
  and Carter, 12156, 12157, 12171, 12208, 12230, 12257, 12268, 12317, 12336, 12350, 12406, 12469
  Continental, 642
  and Eisenhower, 9844, 9868, 9894, 9896
  and Ford, 11965
  and Garfield, 5982, 6019
  and Hayes, 5889
  and Hoover, 8222, 8257, 8258
  Investigating Committee, 9270
  and Jackson, 16
  and Jefferson, 1314, 2067, 2070, 2193
  and Andrew Johnson, 5478, 5485, 5521
  and Lyndon Johnson, 10946, 10972, 11000, 11026, 11035, 11041, 11094, 11103, 11189
  Joint Committee on the Conduct of the War, 5048
  and Kennedy, 10498, 10499, 10501-10504, 10506, 10510, 10511, 10515, 10518-10521
  and Lincoln, 4551-4556, 4708, 4731, 4752, 4763, 5022
  Lobbies, 10754
  McKinley in, 6264
  Majority leader, 10933
  members of, 7404, 7536
  Minority party leadership, 11965
  and Nixon, 11471, 11518, 11537, 11642, 11661, 11805, 11835, 11845, 11856
  and Reagan, 12637, 12650, 12663, 12745, 12746, 12757, 12787, 12796, 12805, 12988, 13005
  and Franklin D. Roosevelt, 8749, 8750, 8754, 8759, 8762
  Rules Committee, 10588
  Southern members, 7363
  and treaties, 6774
  and Truman, 9293, 9327, 9346, 9378, 9398, 9399, 9560, 9629
  and Tyler, 3203
  voting behavior in, 2456, 3277
  and Wilson, 7709, 7710, 7720
Conkling, Roscoe, 5881, 5984, 5987
Connally, John, 11541, 11682
Connally, Tom, 8973
Connecticut
  and Franklin D. Roosevelt, 8615
  and Washington, 565
Connor, David, 3267
Conrad, Robert T., 3297

722 Subject Index

Consensus of Vina del Mar, 11837
Conservation, 8149
  Ballinger-Pinchot controversy, 7085
  and Eisenhower, 9874, 9909
  energy, and Reagan, 12904
  and Hoover, 8121
  and Jefferson, 1292
  and Franklin D. Roosevelt, 8657, 8792
  and Theodore Roosevelt, 6355, 6661, 6684, 6686, 6706, 6772, 6785
  and Taft, 7070, 7075
Conservatism
  and Lincoln, 4513
  in Texas, 10920
Conspiracy trial, against Lincoln, 4805-4807, 4820, 4827, 4828, 4831, 4840, 4858, 4861, 4866, 4871, 4873
Constitution, 1033, 7079, 7107, 7445, 7793, 8947, 8956, 9009, 10511, 11544, 11694, 11875
  and John Adams, 916, 931, 981, 1013
  crisis of 1867/1868, 5482
  and Fillmore, 3334
  and Jackson, 2931
  and Jefferson, 1586, 1810, 1813, 1828, 1830, 1833, 1837, 1918, 1975
  Lincoln's view of, 4109, 4115, 5061, 5109, 5118, 5123
  and Madison, 2325, 2347, 2377, 2378, 2395, 2397, 2404, 2431, 2432, 2439, 2449, 2499
  and New York Historical Society, 2683
  and Polk, 3256
  power, 5550
  Taft's view, 7080
  and Washington, 558, 576, 582, 585, 607, 615, 724, 738, 753
Constitutional Convention, 2449
Consuls
  English, and Lincoln, 4766-4768
  Jefferson and, 1865
  origin of, 973
Consumer Advocacy Agency, 12002
Containment
  Eisenhower and, 9976
  Reagan and, 13084
  Franklin D. Roosevelt and, 9529
  Truman and, 9534, 9636
Continental Light Dragoons, 645
Convention, nominating
  Democratic, 6188, 8837
  and Lincoln, 4539, 4900, 5375
  of 1912, 7452
  Republican, 5176, 5519, 12931
Cookbook, of Jefferson, 1242
Cooke, Alistair, 10011
Cooke, Jacob E., 1184
Cooke, John E., 656
Coolidge, Calvin, 7920-8038
  biographies, 7920-7935
  as governor, 7970
  presidential years, 7986-8028
  private life, 7936-7967
  public career, 7968-7985
  writings, 8029-8038
Coolidge, Grace, 7943, 7955
Coolidge, Thomas J., 1326
Cooper, Thomas, 1017
Cooper Union, 4515, 4734, 4925, 5299
Copeland, Charles, 8404
Copperfield, David, 8088
Copperheads, and Lincoln, 4733, 5145, 5146
Corbett, Boston, 4223
Corbin, John, 176
Corcoran, Thomas G., 8658
Corcoran Gallery of Art, 437
Corneau and Diller Drug Store, 3954
Corruption, 3442
Cortot, Jean P., 431
Corwin, Edward S., 7233
Corwin, Thomas, 4465
Cost-benefit analysis, 12921
Costa Rica, 7532, 7581
Cosway, Maria, 1192, 1195, 1200, 1416, 1420, 1427
Council at Vincennes, 3143
Council of Economic Advisers, 9485, 11670, 13140
Country Beautiful, 8095
County Life Commission, 6695
Coups d'etat, 10690, 11267
Court
  of Appeals, 11523, 12190
  bureaucracy, 6999
  Federal, 9793, 10234, 11028, 11520
  and Jefferson, 2178, 2186, 2193
  and Lincoln, 5111
  packing plan, 8948, 8952, 8955, 8962-8964, 8967
  Pennsylvania, 2185
  reform, 7112, 8953, 8974
  of St. James, 3368
  of Versailles, 1866
  Washington's attitude toward, 209
Courtship
  of Lincoln, 3856
  of Washington, 278
Cowles, Anna R., 6920
Cox, James M., 7869
Cox, Minnie M., 6715
Coxe, Tench, 2027, 2028
Cranch, Mary, 873
Crawford, William, 833
Credibility gap, and Lyndon Johnson, 10940, 11003, 11025, 11111, 11126, 11160
Credit Mobilier Company, 6028
CREEP. *See* Committee to Re-elect the President
Crevecoeur, Michel, 1598
Crime, 6947, 11680, 12290
  control, 8790

Crittenden Compromise, 4784
Croly, George W., 7271
Crook, William H., 4213, 5497, 5847
Cuba, 7060, 7527, 8019, 8882, 9173, 10539, 10695, 10772, 11773, 11796, 11928
Cuban Crisis of 1898, 6303, 6312
Cuban Missile Crisis, 10312, 10522-10549, 10687
Cunningham, William, 1030
Curley, James M., 8824
Currency, 6306
Currey, Benjamin, 3034
Curtis, Daniel P., 256
Curtis, Eleanor P., 274
Curtis, Elizabeth P., 279
Curtis, George W., 5880
Curtis, John P., 275, 279, 776
Curtis, Martha, 263, 275
Curtis, Parke, 161
Cushing, Charles, 1040
Cushman, W. H. W., 3758
Custis, Nelly, 316
Custom House, 5858
Czolgosz, Leon F., 6301

Dairy industry, 8134
Dallas, George M., 3368
Dams
  Eisenhower and, 9899
  Truman and, 9483
D'angers, David, 464
Daniels, Jonathan, 9107
Daniels, Joseph, 8627
Darrell, William, 1016
Darwin, Charles, 4417
Daugherty, Harry M., 7871
Davies, Samuel, 361
Davis, A. D., 12128
Davis, David, 4226, 4910, 5340
Davis, Jefferson, 613, 1788, 3381, 4918, 4972, 4989, 4998, 5043, 5045, 5052
Davis, John W., 8826
Dawes, Charles, 5986, 6310
Dawson, Moses, 3054
Day, Gavin, 10252
Dayton, Elias, 777
Dean, John, 11850
Death
  John Adams, 2610
  Garfield, 5932, 5942, 5998, 6017
  William H. Harrison, 3142, 3144, 3147
  Jefferson, 893
  Kennedy, 10262, 10390, 10473, 10477, 10480, 10495
  Lincoln, 4791, 4812, 4814, 4816, 4817
  Monroe, 2528, 2535
  Franklin D. Roosevelt, 8398, 8408, 8429, 8430, 8617, 8647, 8661
  Wilson, 7276

Deaver, Michael, 12616, 12669
DeBrehan, Madame, 1244
Decatur, IL, Lincoln in, 4354
Decimalization, 2049
Declaration of Independence, 591, 1092, 2008-2043, 4145, 4470
DeCorny, Madame, 1244
Defense, 753, 2074, 5031, 6426, 9475, 9960, 10716, 12453, 12493, 13040, 13085
  aerospace, 10685
  budget, 9970, 12451, 12464, 12815, 12823
  industry, 13076
  initiative, 13080
  missile, 13079
  policy, 694, 9943, 9959, 12499, 12524, 13062, 13084, 13087
  politics, 9969, 9971
  program, 8937, 13081
  reorganization, 9940
DeGaulle, Charles, 9168, 9945, 10644, 10657, 10717
Delaware, and Washington, 708
DeMiranda, Francisco, 749
Democracy
  and Cleveland, 6130
  and Jackson, 2754, 2759, 2829, 2833, 2835, 2839, 2840, 2845, 2850, 2851, 2864, 2872, 2873, 2893, 2896, 2943, 2963, 2980
  and Jefferson, 1811, 1881, 1892, 1893, 1903, 1904, 1906, 1907, 1910, 1915, 1926, 1931, 1942, 1943, 2145-2148, 1950, 1951
  and Lincoln, 4114, 4128, 4143, 4148, 4635
  and Reagan, 12794
  and Theodore Roosevelt, 6723
  and Taft, 7018
  and Wilson, 7603, 7623, 7636
Democratic party
  Carter and, 12386
  Cleveland and, 6159
  Eisenhower and, 9942
  history of, 6112
  Polk and, 3286
  Franklin D. Roosevelt and, 8749
  Truman and, 9316
  Van Buren and, 3075, 3084, 3092, 3103
  Wilson and, 7466
Denny, Harmar, 3167
Depew, Chauncey M., 6779
Depression, 9054
  agricultural, 8147
  causes of, 12922
  and Congress, 8258
  and Hoover, 8069, 8073, 8098, 8206, 8262, 8269
  and Franklin D. Roosevelt, 8984
  unemployment and, 8246
DePriest Incident, 8197
Deregulation, 12002, 12871, 12898
  intergovernmental, 12890

Des Moines, IO, Grant's speech in, 5775
Desegregation, 9876
Desk, of Hayes, 5846
DeStoeckl, Edouard, 4421
Detente, 11780, 11830, 12441, 12458, 12502, 12509, 13033
DeTesse, Madame, 1244
Dewey, John, 1384, 1400, 1538, 1793, 4147
Dewey, Thomas E., 8832, 8839, 8840, 9500, 9502, 9510
Dewson, Mary W., 8590, 9317
Diamond, Martin, 4413
Diaz, Porfirio, 7034
Dick, Charles, 6779
Dickerman, Marion, 8407
Dickinson, Anna E., 5053
Dickinson, Donald M., 6128
Dickinson, Jacob M., 8764
Dickinson, John, 943
Dies, Martin, 8765, 8794
Dies Committee, 8756, 8794
Dinsmoor, Silas, 2918
Diplomacy
  John Adams and, 917, 937, 957, 1023, 11770, 12461, 12506, 12969, 12995
  Arthur and, 6050
  Cleveland and, 6129, 6187
  economic, 8117
  Eisenhower and, 9985
  Fillmore and, 3351
  Garfield and, 5983
  Harding and, 7879, 7880, 7882
  Hayes and, 5862
  Hoover and, 8181, 8206
  Jackson and, 2938
  Jefferson and, 2116, 2122
  Lincoln and, 4743
  maritime, 7721
  Polk and, 3264, 3266, 3272
  Franklin D. Roosevelt and, 8880, 8890, 8897, 8920, 8940, 9146, 9153, 9154
  Theodore Roosevelt and, 6837, 6838, 6856, 6857, 6876, 7031
  Taft and, 7059, 7076
  Truman and, 9607
  Washington and, 680, 697, 757, 1021
  Wilson and, 7534, 7535, 7545, 7553, 7564, 7576, 7579, 7582, 7591, 7598, 7600, 7633, 7635, 7640, 7679, 7683, 7704, 7714
Disability
  presidential, 7435
  and Franklin D. Roosevelt, 8419
Disarmament
  nuclear, 10000
  and Wilson, 7609
Disciples of Christ, 5957
Discrimination, commercial, 2424
District Emancipation Act, 5202, 5203

District of Columbia, and Lincoln, 5111, 5201-5204
Dix, Dorothea, 3357
Doctors, of Lincoln, 3620
Dodd, William E., 8874
Dodge, Cleveland H., 7200, 7561
Dodsley's Annual Register, 214
Dole, W. P., 5103
Dollar diplomacy, 7078, 7578, 7590, 9951
Domestic Council, 11667
Domestic policy, 7508, 8762-8815, 9429-9498
Dominican Republic, 7885, 11263
  diplomacy, 8195
Donaldson, Thomas, 5871
Donelson, Andrew J., 3290
Donelson, Emily, 2771
Dos Passos, John, 5072
Douglas, Helen G., 11455
Douglas, Lewis W., 9068, 9069
Douglas, Stephen A., 5183, 5315, 5316
Douglas, William O., 8592, 8972
Douglass, Frederick, 4618
Downing, Samuel R., 5150
Drama, Lincoln in, 4052
Drawings
  of Jefferson, 1270, 1271
  of Lincoln, 4187
  of Washington, 494
Dred Scott decision, 3417, 5122
  justices, 3420
Dreyfus Affair, 10427
Drought, and Hoover, 8192, 8214, 8227
Dry Sundays, and Theodore Roosevelt, 6818
Duane, James, 812
Dublin, 7013, 7015
DuBois, W. E. B., 7295
Dueling, 2660
Dufief, Nicholas G., 1766
Dulles, John F., 7342, 9953, 9962, 9967, 9980, 9993, 10002, 10718
Dummer, Henry E., 5250
Dupont Corporation, 9888
Dutchess County, NY, and Franklin D. Roosevelt, 8440, 9208, 9209

Early, Stephen T., 8552, 9073
Eaton, John H., 2796, 2862
Eaton, Margaret, 2796
Eaton, Peggy, 2935, 2953
Economic Report of the President, 11668, 12059, 12340-12342, 13131, 13132, 13140
Economics
  development, 8998
  management of, and Ford, 12065
  philosophy of, and Jefferson, 1542
  planning, and Harding cabinet, 8170
  policy, 8188, 8266, 9057, 11190
  political, 1739, 2422, 2424, 2444, 2622
  recovery in, and Hoover, 8202

supply-side, 13093, 13112, 13127, 13128
Truman administration and, 9495
Economists, and Lyndon Johnson, 11172
Ecuador, and Wilson, 7590
Eden, Anthony, 9550, 11531
Edison, Thomas A., 7275
Education
   and John Adams, 2679
   aid to Catholic, 10152
   Department of, 11225, 12310, 12350
   and Eisenhower, 9875, 9891
   equal opportunity, 8811, 11938
   of Garfield, 5964
   Head Start program in, 11186
   higher, 1369, 7489
   and Hoover, 8163
   and Jefferson, 1566-1604, 1629
   and Kennedy, 10586, 10588, 10589
   and Lincoln, 4490
   of Lincoln, 3799-3806
   and Lyndon Johnson, 10882, 11169, 11181, 11185, 11189, 11205, 11208, 11227, 11229
   and Nixon, 11666
   and Reagan, 12878
   of Franklin D. Roosevelt, 8414, 8426
   and Truman, 9262, 9465, 9473, 9487, 9496
   and Washington, 165, 192
   of Wilson, 7230
Edwards, George B., 7126
Edwards, Helen D., 3955
Edwards v. Carter, 12515
Egypt
   and Carter, 12510, 12526
   nationalism, 6832
Egypt, IL, 4367
Ehrlichman, John, 2194, 11563, 11667
Eisen, Gustavus A., 436
Eisenhower, David, 11505
Eisenhower, Dwight D., 9670-10030
   biographies, 9670-9717
   domestic policy, 9868-9913
   elections, 9914-9934
   foreign affairs, 9935-10009
   presidential years, 9763-10009
   private life, 9718-9730
   public career, 9731-9762
   writings, 10010-10030
Eisenhower, Julie, 11505
Eisenhower, Mamie, 9719, 9721, 9723, 10019
Eisenhower Doctrine, 9949, 9956, 9957, 9959, 9963, 9965, 9994, 10005, 10006, 10008
El Salvador
   and Reagan, 12487, 12532, 13028
   and Wilson, 7530
Elbe, 9731, 9757
Elder, Samuel S., 4257
Elections
   Carter, 12037, 12051, 12081, 12153, 12379, 12419
   Cleveland, 6121, 6128, 6151, 6163, 6175
   Eisenhower, 9922
   Ford, 12037, 12051, 12081, 12153, 12419
   Garfield, 5992
   Grant, 5766
   Hayes, 5898, 5902
   Andrew Johnson, 5523, 5545
   Lincoln, 5163
   McKinley, 6273
   1941 Texas senatorial, 10935
   Reagan, 12379, 12846, 12944, 12945, 12947, 12948, 12958
   Franklin D. Roosevelt, 8500, 8820, 8848, 8889
   Theodore Roosevelt, 6582, 6595, 6599, 6627
   Truman, 9266, 9282, 9552, 9553
   Wilson, 7455, 7464
Elective governor bill of 1943, 8534
Electoral college, 4109, 12046, 12396, 12954
   reform, 2394, 8599
   vote, 2572, 2664
Electoral Commission, 5900
Electric utilities industry, 11707, 12909, 13134
Elementary and Secondary Education Act, 1765, 11211
Elkins, Stephen B., 6226
Ellicott, Andrew, 2277
Ellsberg, Daniel, 11917
Ely, Ezra S., 2953
Emancipation, 5221, 5243
   in Kentucky, 5205
   Proclamation, 5190, 5194, 5198, 5214
   Statute, 5195
Embargo
   on arms, 9617
   and Jefferson, 2103, 2114, 2117, 2118, 2321-2323
   and Madison, 2492
Emerson, Ralph W., 566, 1400
Employment, equal opportunity, 12311
Energy
   atomic, 9480
   Carter and, 12282, 12294, 12299, 12314, 12317, 12326, 12333, 12334, 12355, 12361
   Ford and, 12015, 12018, 12079
   Nixon and, 11707, 11712
   nuclear, 12287, 12312
   Reagan and, 11173, 11699, 12832, 12834, 12842, 12873, 12879, 12904, 12919, 13083
   solar, 9855, 9906
   sources, Reagan, 12884
   Truman administration, 9494
Engineer
   Hoover as, 8063, 8065
   for Lyndon Johnson, 11199
   Washington as, 169, 177, 202
Engravings
   of Cleveland, 6096

of Lincoln, 4161
Enlightenment, 618, 945, 1469, 1536, 1589, 2416
Entomology, economics, and Jefferson, 1596
Environment, 12555, 12875, 12886, 12911, 13025
   activists, 12327
   policy, 12885, 12921, 12924
Equal rights, 5211, 5522
Equality, 2143, 2148, 2167, 5191, 5199, 5235
Erie, PA, Lincoln in, 5086
Espionage, 9935
Ethnicity, and Franklin D. Roosevelt election, 8827
Etiquette, Jeffersonian, 1209
Eucharistic Congress, 4275
Europe, 933, 1769, 2328, 5689, 8766, 10657, 11800, 11804, 11813, 11821, 12508
   Central, 7533
   East Central, 7714
   socialism, 7589
Euthanasia, 4142
Evangelicals, 3157, 12186, 12752, 12753, 12935, 12943
Everett, Alexander H., 2688, 2711
Everett, Charles, 2574
Everett, Edward, 5074
Ewing, James S., 4189
Executive branch, 11592
   power, 1565
   reorganization, 8168, 8670, 9032, 9368, 11477, 11513, 11556, 12246
Executive privilege, 2194, 11532, 11563, 11895, 12501
Exeter, NH, Lincoln in, 3785
Export policy, 12017, 12918
Extradition, 996

Fair Deal, 9444, 9452, 9476, 9491
Fairbanks, Charles W., 6792
Fairbanks, Newton H., 7871
Fairfax, Sally, 251, 257, 283, 287
Fairfield, VT, 6044
Fall, Albert B., 7661, 7662, 8175
Family
   of Carter, 12137
   of Hayes, 5811
   of Jefferson, 1605-1639
   of Lincoln, 3807-3884, 3961
   of McKinley, 6235
   of Washington, 251-304
Family Assistance Plan, 11700
Faneuil Hall, 2597
Far East, 6831, 6859, 7548, 7553, 7578, 8866
Farley, Jim, 8573
Farm
   crisis, 8147
   leaders, 8155
   policy, 8204, 8515, 9474, 9903
   politics, 8777
   problem, 8514
   program, 10567, 12863
   of Washington, 170, 253
Farmer
   Jefferson as, 1302, 1312
   and Franklin D. Roosevelt, 8964
   Truman as, 9258
   Washington as, 175, 218
Father. *See also* Family
   of Grant, 5667
   of Lincoln, 3882
Faubus, Governor, 9869
Faulkner, William, 9770
Fay, James, 8757
FBI. *See* Federal Bureau of Investigation
FCC. *See* Federal Communications Commission
Fechner, Robert, 8804
Federal Bureau of Investigation (FBI), 2190, 3169, 8245, 8756, 8790, 9395, 10187, 10989
Federal Communications Commission (FCC), 11180
Federal Convention, 570, 575, 2391, 2407, 2435, 2437, 2440, 2506, 2510
Federal Employer's Liabilities Act, 6559
Federal Farm Board Project, 8174
Federal Hall, 760
Federal Reserve Law, 6709, 7490
Federal Trade Commission, 12870
   credit programs, 12876
Federalism, 722, 1008, 2667, 9062, 11140, 11549, 11640, 12349, 12642, 12739, 12814, 12881, 12966
Federalist Papers, 2369, 2375, 2389, 2398, 2410, 2430, 2502
Federalist party, 922, 1909
Federalists, 854, 958, 1891, 1923, 2087, 2412
Fell, Jesse W., 5150, 5329
Ferguson, Adam, 2376
Fernandina Unionists, 5552
Fillmore, Millard, 3332-3357
   biographies, 3332-3337
   presidential years, 3340-3351
   private life, 3338
   public career, 3339
   writings, 3352-3357
Films
   Ronald Reagan, 12581
   Theodore Roosevelt in, 6557
Fingerprint, of Lincoln, 3944
Finley, John, 6080
Fireside chats, 8541, 8608, 8699, 9180
Fiscal policy, 2091, 9477, 9910, 10598, 11196, 11230, 11236, 11695, 12315
   conservatism, 9071
   strategy, 12830
Fish, Hamilton, 5769
Fisher, Irving, 8984
Fitness, national, 9913
Fitzgerald, John, 2854

Flag (US), 487
Fleming, Arthur S., 9875
Florida
   and Arthur, 6067
   and Hayes/Tilden contest, 5900
   and Hoover, 8212
   and Jackson, 2726, 2917, 2949
   and Lincoln, 4788, 5001
   and Theodore Roosevelt, 6786
Floyd, John B., 3419
Foch, Ferdinand, 9754
Fogg, George G., 5323
Food
   Administration, 8134
   crisis during World War II, 7496
   price problem under Nixon, 11668
   relief, and Hoover, 8120, 8228
Foraker, Joseph B., 6296, 6808
Forbush, Gabrielle, 8370
Ford, Betty, 11953, 11955, 11956, 11959-11961
Ford, Gerald R., 11947-12102
   biographies, 11947-11952
   Carter debate, 12021, 12048, 12058, 12070, 12382, 12397, 12405, 12414
   presidential years, 11969-12085
   private life, 11953-11961
   public career, 11962-11968
   writings, 12086-12102
Ford, Henry, 7275
Ford, Paul L., 2308
Ford, Worthington C., 840
Ford's Theatre, 4797, 4826, 4867
Foreign affairs. *See also* Foreign policy
   John Adams, 948
   Carter, 12423-12549
   Eisenhower, 9935-10009
   Harding, 7888, 7891
   Jefferson, 2101
   Lyndon Johnson, 11256-11278
   Kennedy, 10643-10726, 10755
   Lincoln, 4743
   McKinley, 6294
   Madison, 2457
   Nixon, 11770-11848
   Reagan, 12968-13068
   Franklin D. Roosevelt, 8853-8945
   Truman, 9511-9580
   Wilson, 7523-7602
Foreign policy, 949, 2115. *See also* Foreign affairs
   John Adams, 1041, 2650, 2658
   Arthur, 6059
   Buchanan, 3429
   Cleveland, 6134
   economic, 8118
   Garfield, 5981, 6008
   Harding, 7882, 7905
   Hoover, 8206, 8239, 8269
   Jackson, 2940

   Jefferson, 1847, 1854, 1856, 1859, 1880, 2124
   Kennedy, 10134, 10150, 10562, 10756
   Madison, 2424
   Nixon, 11906, 11928, 11943, 11944
   Polk, 3246, 3255
   Franklin D. Roosevelt, 8463, 8694, 9145, 9149
   Theodore Roosevelt, 6867
   Taft, 7061
   Truman, 9393, 9628
   Washington, 682, 741, 764, 994
   Wilson, 7633, 7703, 7785, 7786
Foreign Service, 7577, 12089
Forest reserve, 6156, 6299, 6679, 6772
Fort Harrison, 3314
Fort Lesley McNair, 4830
Fort Meigs, 3159
Fort Snelling, 3330
Fort Stevens, 4353
Fort Sumter, 5013, 5023, 5044
Fort Trumbull, 5269
Fortas, Abe, 10967, 11080
Founding fathers, 1645, 1966, 2416
Four Freedoms Campaign, 8748, 8833
Fourteen Points, of Wilson, 7614, 7685
France, 366, 580, 11257
   and John Adams, 985, 995, 1042
   Alliance, 698
   fleet, 2474
   and Jackson, 3031
   and Jefferson, 1258, 1857, 1862, 1874
   Jefferson in, 1213, 1855, 1860, 1867, 1929
   and Monroe, 2543
   naturalists, 1456
   public opinion, 7680
   resistance in, 9748
   Revolution, 744, 745, 1853, 1861, 1866, 1877, 2044-2046
   and Franklin D. Roosevelt, 9121, 9140
   security, 7664
Frankfurter, Felix, 6771, 8961, 8982, 9001, 9002, 9201, 11604
Franklin, Benjamin, 152, 566, 577, 627, 730, 918, 926, 939, 973, 1360, 1598, 1864, 1954, 1955, 1957, 1959, 1962, 1963, 2154, 2632, 4055, 5291, 7565, 8616
Fraser, Malcomb, 12338
Frazer, Oliver, 480
Free Soil Movement, 3096
Freedmen
   and Andrew Johnson, 5553
   and Lincoln, 5757
Freedmen's Bureau, 5522
Freedom, 1523
   academic, 2209
   of conscience, 327
   of information, 12523
   and Jefferson, 1730, 1731, 1809, 2138, 2163, 2167

Subject Index

and Lincoln, 5068, 5226, 5232, 5239, 5245
Freedoms Foundation, 10016
Freemason, 159, 342, 353, 2686
Fremont, John C., 3282, 5040, 5284
Fremont, OH, 5816
Fremont, OH, Hayes memorial in, 5806
Freeport, IL, Lincoln statue in, 3949
   Lincoln/Douglas debate in, 4625, 4642, 4656
Freneau, 1603, 1805-1807, 1924, 2546
Freud, Sigmund, 7159, 7290
Frost, Robert, 10759
Fulbright, J. William, 11272
Fuller, Richard, 4466
Funeral
   of Coolidge, 7940
   of William H. Harrison, 3142
   of Kennedy, 10401
   of Lincoln, 3979, 4794, 4821, 4843, 4865
   oration, on Washington, 396
Furniture fund, Monroe, 2536

Gag rule, 2687
Gage, Lyman, 6295
Gaither Committee, 9799
Galena, IL, 5658, 5666, 5715
Galesburg, IL, Lincoln at, 4344
Gallatin, Albert, 2063, 2066, 2091, 2117
Galt, Edith B., 7252, 7783
Gamble, Robert, 2292
Gardiner, Julia, 3187, 3208
Gardner, Philip B., 305
Garfield, James A., 5920-6033
   biographies, 5920-5951
   presidential years, 5980-6017
   private life, 5952-5964
   public career, 5965-5979
   writings, 6018-6033
Garfield, Moolie, 5967
Garland, Augustus H., 6180
Garment, Leonard, 11418
Garner, John N., 8837, 8973
Garrison, William L., 5219
Gates, Horatio, 589
Geary, John W., 3381
Gender gap, and Reagan, 12666, 12934
Genealogy, of Hoover family, 8090
General Agreement on Tariffs and Trade, 10707
General Motors, 9888
Generals
   Eisenhower, 9671, 9684, 9686, 9737
   Washington, 647, 663, 676
Genet, Edmund C., 1258, 1603
Genuga County Teachers' Institute, 5929
Geographer
   Jefferson as, 1666, 1682
   Washington as, 532
George III, 627, 918, 1871, 1872, 1955
George, Walter F., 8747

Georges, Comte de Buffon, 1665
Georgetown, MD, 824
Georgia
   black officeholders in, 6272
   and Carter, 12412
   and Harding, 7886
   and Hoover, 8211
   and Jackson, 2948, 2959, 2974
   Plains, 12133
   presidential visits to, 5749
   and Franklin D. Roosevelt, 3433, 8865
   and Truman, 9376
Gergen, David R., 12707
German-Americans, 10688
Germantown, Washington in, 404, 579
Germany, 11256
   and Eisenhower, 9977
   and Hoover, 8152
   Jefferson in, 1213
   and the League of Nations, 7634
   and Wilson, 7675, 7724
Gerry, Elbridge, 1006
Gerry, Margarita S., 5847
Gettysburg Address, 3747, 5054-5083, 5257
Ghent, negotiation of, 2680
Ghostwriting
   for Andrew Johnson, 5420
   for Lyndon Johnson, 10991
   for Nixon, 11497
Gifts, to Lincoln, 4729
Gill, John, 818
Gilmer, Francis W., 2248
Gilmer, Thomas W., 3457
Gilmore, John A., 4693
Girardin, Louis H., 1766
Giraud, Henri, 9749
Gladstone, William E., 7776
Glass, Carter, 8751
Glass, Francis, 80, 98
Glasscoch, William E., 6535
Gnosticism, of Lincoln, 4105
Gold policy, of Franklin D. Roosevelt, 8763
Goldwater, Barry, 10141, 10909, 10963, 11193, 11244, 11245, 11249, 11251, 11253, 11521, 12480
Goldwater v. Carter, 12501, 12517
Gollaher, Austin, 4440
Good Neighbor Policy, 8195, 8882, 8933, 8941
Goodpaster, Andrew, 9952
Goodwin, Richard R., 10233
Gore, Thomas P., 7087, 7450
Gore-McLemore Resolution, 7711
Gospel Hill, 7205, 7206
Gould, John A., 10375
Government, local, 1711
Governors
   and Federal aid, 12905
   and Lincoln, 4986

Subject Index

and states' rights, 4725
Grandchildren, of Jefferson, 1407, 1409
Grant, Jesse, 5666
Grant, Julia D., 5681, 5684
Grant, Sam, 5623
Grant, Ulysses S., 5576-5790
   biographies, 5576-5657
   presidential years, 5741-5777
   private life, 5658-5689
   public career, 5690-5740
   writings, 5778-5790
Grant Monument, 5677
Grayson, William, 628
Great Britain, 1283, 2114, 2122, 4766, 7554, 9134
   during American Revolution, 680
   and Kennedy, 10698
   liberals, 7677
   Lincoln in, 3960
   and Opium War, 2669
   prime ministers, 11161
   and Reagan, 12984
   and Franklin D. Roosevelt, 6865, 8890, 8934, 9004, 9109
   and Theodore Roosevelt, 6833
Great Society, 10827, 11261, 11279-11292, 11663, 11715
Greeley, Horace, 3533, 4215, 4389, 5144, 5153, 5155, 5766
Green County, IL, voting behavior, 3015
Green River, Lincoln's land on, 3821
Greenspan, Alan, 12016
Greenville, TN, Andrew Johnson's homestead in, 5419
Grenada, 13044
Grey, Edward, 7657
Grigsby, Melvin, 6589, 6639
Grocer, Lincoln as, 3668
Groton, Franklin D. Roosevelt at, 8405, 8414, 8445
Grouseland, 3138
Guatemala, 7531, 9966
Guiteau, Charles J., 6002, 6016
Gurowski, Adam, 4891, 4892

Haas, Philip, 2609
Habeas corpus, 5124, 5132, 12813
Haggerty, James C., 9789
Hague, Frank, 9005
Haiti, 7563
   revolution, 729
   slave revolt, 2053
Haldeman, H. R., 11538, 11851
Hale, Edward E., 8104
Hallet, Etienne S., 2277
Halstead, Jenny, 5872
Halstead, Murat, 3430, 4895, 4902
Hamilton, Alexander, 797, 951, 1065, 2371, 2401, 2467, 2509, 2934, 12456
   on John Adams, 1001

and the Constitution, 1828, 1841
and foreign policy, 949, 1847, 1856, 9964
and Jefferson, 941, 1882, 1883, 1887, 1890, 1897, 1900, 1924, 1925, 1928, 1930, 1941, 1949, 2112-2114, 2133-2136, 2204
and Washington, 207, 567, 568, 594, 749
and Wilson, 7326
Hamlet, and Lincoln, 4049
Hamlin, Hannibal, 5258, 5292, 5389
Hampton Roads Peace Conference, 5049
Hancock, John, 1987, 2626
Handwriting, of Lincoln, 4043
Hanford Dual-Purpose Reactor Controversy, 10332
Hanks, Nancy, 3712, 3811
Hanna, Mark, 6270
Hapsburg Monarch, 7691
Hardin County, KY, 4358
Harding, William G., 7813-7919
   biographies, 7813-7833
   presidential years, 7878-7912
   private life, 7834-7868
   public career, 7869-7877
   writings, 7913-7919
Harlan, John M., 9025
Harper, George M., 7233
Harper's Ferry, 3456
   armory, 664
Harris, George W., 3973
Harris, Thomas E., 3972
Harrison, Benjamin, 3135, 6203-6233
   biographies, 6203-6209
   presidential years, 6218-6226
   private life, 6210, 6211
   public career, 6212-6217
   writings, 6227-6233
Harrison, James T., 5426
Harrison, Pat, 8760
Harrison, Reging B., 5426
Harrison, Robert H., 628
Harrison, William Henry, 3121-3167
   biographies, 3121-3134
   as governor, 3155
   presidential years, 3157-3161
   private life, 3135-3149
   public career, 3150-3156
   writings, 3162-3167
Hart, Albert B., 176
Harvard University, 586, 2682, 2684
   Kennedy at, 10124
   presidents at, 10078
   Franklin D. Roosevelt at, 8404, 8414, 8415
   Theodore Roosevelt at, 6479, 6519, 6520
   Theodore Roosevelt collection at, 6882, 6888
   Theodore Roosevelt symposium at, 6810
Hawaii, 6139, 6140, 6218
Hawley-Smoot Tariff, 8261
Hawthorne, Nathaniel, 3378, 3379, 4063
Hay, John, 4536, 4980, 5029, 6801

730 Subject Index

Hay, Milton, 4242
Hayes, Lucy W., 5807-5810, 5819
Hayes, Rutherford B., 5791-5919
   biographies, 5791-5803
   election, 5895-5912
   as governor, 5833, 5834, 5835
   presidential years, 5837-5912
   private life, 5804-5830
   public career, 5831-5836
   writings, 5913-5919
Hayes, Samuel J., 3046
Hayes-Conkling controversy, 5881
Hayes Memorial Library and Museum, 5806, 5818
Hayes-Tilden contest, 5896, 5899, 5900, 5902-5904, 5906, 5908-5912
Haywood trial, 6781
Head Start, 11186
Health, 8393, 11169, 11703, 12306
   assistance, 10493
   care system, 13104
   costs, 12849
   education, 11237
   information, 12865
   insurance, 9481
   of Lyndon Johnson, 10876, 11363
   legislation, 11237, 12896
   of Lincoln, 3620
   mental, 10552, 12281
   policy, 12828, 12841, 12843, 12901
   of Polk, 3221
   public, 2046
   of Franklin D. Roosevelt, 8411, 8438
   of Theodore Roosevelt, 6477
   of Washington, 157, 195, 205
   of Wilson, 7211
Health, Education and Welfare Department, 11691
Hearst Tournament of Orators, 2388
Heirlooms, of Washington, 161, 443, 471
Helvetius, 1597
Hemings, Sally, 1406, 1408, 1410, 1412, 1418, 1426, 1496
Hendricks, Thomas A., 6083, 6096, 6112, 6113, 6116
Hennock, Frieda B., 8590, 9317
Henry, Charles E., 6032
Henry, Charles H., 7874
Henry, Patrick, 587, 1435, 1973, 1974, 2239, 2400, 2441
Henry VIII, 253, 10359
Herline, Edward, 4164
Hermitage, 2774, 2791, 2807, 2808
Herndon, William H., 3825, 4093, 4304, 4565, 4574, 5397
Herrick, Myron T., 7098
Herter, Christian, 11448
Hesler, Alexander, 4185
HEW. *See* Health, Education and Welfare Department

Hewitt, Abram S., 6133
Heyward, Thomas, 601
Hiller, Joseph, 451
Hilsman, Roger, 10705
Hinckley, John, 12785
Hinsdale, Burke A., 6022
Hiram College, 5952, 5975, 6022
Hiroshima, 9416, 9654
Hiss, Alger, 11379, 11451, 11942
Historiography, 1689, 2897, 4493, 6404, 7347, 7849, 8501, 8985
Hitchcock, Ethan A., 5041
Hitler, Adolf, 9091, 9119, 9120
Ho Chi Minh, 1566
Hobart, Garret A., 6249, 6329
Hobby, 9722
Hockaday, John M., 3440
Hodgenville, KY, 4030
Hodgson, P. A., 9741
Hoffa, James R., 11855
Hofstadter, Richard, 8585
Holmes, Oliver W., 2197
Holocaust, 9112, 9113
Homestead
   bill, 5554
   law, 5516
Honduras, 7526, 13045
Hoover, Herbert, 8039-8321
   biographies, 8039-8078
   presidential years, 8185-8274
   private life, 8079-8106
   public career, 8107-8184
   writings, 8275-8321
Hoover, Lou Henry, 8096, 8097
Hoover-Bennett meeting, 8226
Hoover Commission, 8129, 8132, 8160, 8161, 8168, 8169, 8177, 8178, 8208
Hoover Doctrine, 8194
Hoover Library, 8314
Hopi-land, 6445
Hopkins, Harry L., 8098, 8580
Houdon, Jean A., 447, 472, 477, 619
House, Colonel, 7152, 7212, 7219, 7256, 7566, 7589, 7670
House, Edward M., 7539
House of Burgesses, 592
House of Morgan, 6822
House of Representatives, 2029. *See also* Congress
   Committee on the Judiciary of the, 11867, 11910, 11919
   Committee on Un-American Activities, 8765
   Divided Speech, 4495, 4507
   on the impeachment of Nixon, 11892
   rules, 1813
   Rules Committee, 10500, 10505, 11183, 11204
Housholder, Vic H., 9313
Housing, 9433, 9443, 9480
   cuts, 12893

Housing and Urban Development, 12331
Houston Ministerial Association, 10266, 10620
Houston, Sam, 2909, 4782, 10783
Houzeau, Jean-Charles, 4926
Hovey, Alvin P., 4985
Howard, William A., 5905
Howe, Louis M., 8552, 8680, 8712, 8724
Howells, William D., 5801, 5917, 6555
Hubbard, Elbert, 3712
HUD. *See* Housing and Urban Development
Huddy, Joshua, 650
Huerta, Victoriano, 7651, 7654, 7657
Hughes, Charles E., 6986, 7456, 7457
Hulbert, Mary, 7244
Hull, Cordell, 7601, 8895, 8940
Hull, William, 2141
Human-resource management, 12795
Human rights, 588, 1566, 6594, 10599, 12235, 12527-12549, 12809, 13004, 13063
Human Rights Commission, 8492
Humanitarianism, 9113
Humboldt, Alexander von, 1541
Hume, David, 1577, 1594, 2369, 2376, 2398
Humor, 2348, 3698, 3769, 4484, 5286, 5287, 6441, 10096, 10616
Humphrey, Hubert, 10131, 10641, 10768, 10798, 11733, 11749, 11757
Hungary, 9165
Hunt, Gaillard, 759
Hunting
  and Theodore Roosevelt, 6429, 6511, 6524, 6912, 6919, 6957
  and Washington, 206
Huntington Library, 3048
Hurley, Edward, 7591
Hutchings, Andrew J., 2787
Hutchins, Thomas, 2241
Hyde Park, 8366, 8422, 8450, 8456, 8568, 8583, 9209
Hyman, Harold, 5212

Ickes, Harold L., 8774, 8809, 9033
Illinois, 4365, 11008
  General Assembly, Lincoln speech in, 5279
  General Education Convention, 4490
  and Grant, 5718, 5736
  and Andrew Johnson, 5523
  legislature, 4529
  and Lincoln, 4472, 4490, 4509, 4733, 5266
  Lincoln in, 4447, 4469
  River, 2241
  and Theodore Roosevelt, 6802
  State House, 4534
  tax, 5266
Illinois Daily Journal, 5305
Illness
  of Lincoln, 4089
  of Franklin D. Roosevelt, 8398, 8410
  of Washington, 198
  of Wilson, 7258
ILO. *See* International Labor Organization
Immigrants, 10774
  vote for Lincoln, 4911
Immigration, 7123
  Law of 1965, 11171
  policy, 10773, 12851, 12874
Immunity, presidential, 11587, 11593
Impeachment, 11868, 12090
  and the army, 5711
  of Jackson, 3005, 5469, 5472, 5473, 5475, 5483, 5486, 5494, 5501, 5502, 5504, 5506-5508, 5510, 5520, 5525-5527, 5536, 5542, 5546, 5551, 5555, 5561, 5563-5565, 5568, 5570, 5573
  and Nixon, 11788, 11849, 11859, 11861, 11863, 11867, 11871, 11874, 11888
Imperial presidency, 12653
Imperialism, 6328, 6835, 6838, 9546
  and Cleveland, 6150
  and Franklin D. Roosevelt, 8944
Impersonators, of Lincoln, 3952
Impoundment, 11518, 11648
Inauguration
  of Buchanan, 3432, 3435
  buttons, 417, 430
  of Cleveland, 6122, 6174
  of Coolidge, 8014
  of Eisenhower, 9819
  of Fillmore, 3347
  of Garfield, 5942, 5986, 6009
  of Grant, 5763, 5771
  of Harding, 7901
  of William H. Harrison, 3161
  of Hayes, 5865
  of Hoover, 8196
  of Jackson, 3008
  of Jefferson, 2023, 2069, 2086
  of Lyndon Johnson, 11031, 11124, 11302, 11311
  address of Kennedy, 10238, 10283, 10298, 10386
  of Lincoln, 5071, 5084-5098, 5257
  of Madison, 2485
  of Reagan, 12622, 12623, 12632
  of Franklin D. Roosevelt, 8597, 8612, 8636, 8691, 8692, 8722
  of Theodore Roosevelt, 6699, 6744
  of Truman, 9367
  of Washington, 679, 684, 686, 688, 699, 706, 718, 723, 727, 732, 739, 750, 751, 756, 760, 761, 795
  of Wilson, 7364, 7378
Income
  guaranteed, 11483, 11700
  Supplemental Security, 11671
India, 8479, 8884, 10715, 10762, 12512, 13056
Indian
  Affairs, Superintendent of, 5099

Subject Index

commissioner, 9033
policy, 12929
reservations, 6571
Rights Association, 6563
Indiana
and William H. Harrison, 3154
and Jackson, 2778, 2816
and Lincoln, 4929
Lincoln in, 4340, 4359, 4444, 4451, 4452, 4454, 4587
and Truman, 9585
volunteers, and Taylor, 3317
and Wilson, 7472
Indianola Affair, 6715
Indians
and John Adams, 2651
Cherokees, 2157, 2160, 2176, 3034, 3040
Chickasaw, 2778
Choctow, 2954
and Grant, 5775, 5776, 5777
and William H. Harrison, 3130
and Hayes, 5842, 5850
and Hoover, 8247, 8252
Iroquois, 549
and Jackson, 2824, 2888, 2894, 2895, 2950, 2974, 3006, 3013, 3039
and Jefferson, 1591, 2133, 2141, 2149, 2152, 2154, 2165, 2168, 2170, 2171
and Lincoln, 5099-5108
of Mississippi Territory, 2797
plains, 5101
and Reagan, 12825
and Theodore Roosevelt, 6444
Seminoles, 2726, 2928
and Tecumseh, 3139, 3143
Yakima Reservation, 5777
Individualism, and Hoover, 8081, 8115, 8200, 8238
Indochina
and Carter, 12425
and Eisenhower, 9996
and Kennedy, 10792, 10793
and Nixon, 11790
and Franklin D. Roosevelt, 8884, 8892, 8901
and Truman, 9531, 9540, 9554
Indonesia
and Kennedy, 10653
and Franklin D. Roosevelt, 8884
Industrial Conference, First, 7498
Industrial Conference, Second, 7478
Industry, 221, 9462
conflict in, 8142
Inflation, 9432, 9435, 9902, 11711, 12069
anti, 12284, 12297, 12307
Information Agency, 11770
Ingersoll, Robert G., 5387
Ingham, Samuel D., 2995
Inonu, Ismet, 11266
Intelligence community, 9732, 9733, 11469

Intergovernmental relations, 10987
Office, 11673
International Labor Organization, 8791, 12463
International News Service, 9932
International payments system, 13026
Internationalism, 6277, 8907, 9067
Internationalist, 8864
Interposition, 1729, 2409, 2636
Interventionism, 7703
Intranationalism, 9067
Inventor
Lincoln as, 3735
Washington as, 181, 186, 236
Iowa
and Carter, 12420
caucuses, 12385
and Lincoln, 3707, 4901
and McKinley, 6321
and Theodore Roosevelt in, 6791
territory, 2811
and Wilson, 7462
Iran, 11081, 12478, 12489, 12497
hostage crisis, 12459
rescue mission, 12500
Ireland, 2676
and John Adams, 2635
and Kennedy, 10305
and Washington, 215
Irish-Americans, and Wilson, 7682
Irvine, William, 834
Isolationism, 7694, 8869, 8875, 8904
Israel
and Carter, 12474, 12510, 12526
and Eisenhower, 10008
and Ford, 12013, 12014
and Lyndon Johnson, 11269
and Kennedy, 10647, 10673, 10706
and Nixon, 11781, 11791, 11820
and Reagan, 13031
and Theodore Roosevelt, 6873
and Truman, 9605, 9606, 9609, 9612, 9615, 9619-9621
Italy
and Carter, 12468
and Jefferson, 1213, 1248, 1361
Renaissance, 1447
and Franklin D. Roosevelt, 8911
and Wilson, 7555, 7568, 7582

Jackson, Andrew, 2712-3054
biographies, 2712-2769
as governor, 2848
presidential years, 2931-3040
private life, 2770-2828
public career, 2829-2929
writings, 3041-3054
Jackson, Charles D., 9961
Jackson, Rachel D., 2775, 2820, 2823

Subject Index   733

Jackson, Robert H., 8700
Jackson, Sheldon, 6220
Jacquess, James F., 4324, 4328
James, Barber, 6260
Janny, W. A., 5091
Janson, John, 693
Japan
　and American crises, 6870
　Grant in, 5660
　Kyoto, 9517
　and Lincoln, 4423
　and Reagan, 13007
　and Franklin D. Roosevelt, 8506, 8856, 9122
　and Theodore Roosevelt, 6828, 6840, 6844, 6860
　and Taft, 7059, 7068
Jay, John, 1848
Jay Treaty, 698
Jefferson, Maria, 1421
Jefferson, Mary, 1284
Jefferson, Polly, 1421
Jefferson, Randolph, 2276
Jefferson, Thomas, 1261-2517
　agriculture, 1492-1512
　architecture, 1513-1534
　arts, 1535-1565
　biographies, 1261-1369
　Declaration of Independence, 2008-2043
　diplomat, 2044-2080
　education, 1566-1604
　family, 1605-1627
　foreign affairs, 2297-2330
　as governor, 1971, 2001
　human rights, 2331-2376
　judicial, 2377-2402
　law, 1628-1639
　literature, 1640-1687
　Monticello, 1688-1721
　party politics, 2081-2151
　philosophy, 1722-1801
　presidential years, 2208-2402
　press, 1802-1812
　private life, 1370-1885
　public career, 1886-2207
　religion, 1813-1854
　Revolution, 2152-2187
　science, 1855-1885
　Virginia politics, 2188-2207
　writings, 2403-2517
Jefferson Monument, 1754, 1759
Jefferson National Expansion Memorial, 1697, 1698
Jesuits, 1843
Jews
　and Carter, 12387, 12403
　and Eisenhower, 9832
　and Grant, 5712, 5717
　and Jefferson, 2289
　and Lincoln, 4305, 4307, 4317, 5210

　and Franklin D. Roosevelt, 8624, 9142
　and Theodore Roosevelt, 6801
　and Truman, 9609
John Fitzgerald Kennedy Library, 10342
Johns Hopkins University, 7807, 11309
Johnson, Andrew, 5399-5575
　biographies, 5399-5413
　as governor, 5441-5443, 5446, 5474
　presidential years, 5464-5568
　private life, 5414-5434
　public career, 5434-5463
　writings, 5569-5575
Johnson, Cave, 3291
Johnson, Hiram, 6576, 6886, 6887, 7505, 7552, 7882
Johnson, Lady Bird, 10866, 10870, 10875, 10884, 10885
Johnson, Ludwell, 5211
Johnson, Lyndon B., 10812-11375
　biographies, 10812-10847
　domestic policy, 11162-11240
　elections, 11241-11255
　foreign affairs, 11256-11278
　Great Society, 11279-11292
　presidential years, 10952-11358
　press, 11293-11311
　private life, 10848-10887
　public career, 10888-10951
　retirement, 10859
　Vietnam, 11312-11358
　writings, 11359-11375
Johnson, Robert U., 3701
Johnson, Sam, 10841
Johnson City, TX, 10834
Johnston, John D., 3807
Joint Chiefs of Staff, 10170
Jonas, Abraham, 4931
Jones, Annie M., 12128
Jones, Jerry, 11506
Jones, John P., 979
Joshua Fry S., 4994
Juarez, Benito, 4716
Judge
　Andrew Jackson as, 2782, 2793
　Washington as, 209
Judges, 3032, 8961
Judiciary, 1738, 2183, 2187, 2190, 2199, 2970, 2989, 6724, 7103, 11642
　Act of 1789, 3413
　alignments, 9289
　appointments, 8966, 10985, 11562, 12190, 12674
　behavior, 11644
　conservatism, 11604
　exactness, 6989
　hegemony, 11874
　review, 2181, 2191, 2196, 2198, 2463, 2477, 2482, 11544, 12630
　seats, 12639

734 Subject Index

selection, 12640, 12667
supremacy, 5117
unanimity, 6990
Jurisprudence, 1429
Justice of the Peace, Washington as, 179
Justice
   civil, 7112
   criminal, 6554, 11887
   Department of, 6702, 6819, 7092, 10317
   social, 6579
Justin Pierre, Count de Rieux, 2282

Kailan Mines Swindle, 8125
Kalamazoo, MI, Lincoln's address in, 5217
Kansas, 3445, 3446, 4734, 9728, 10782
   Nebraska Act, 5275
   Nebraska bill, 3374
Kansas City, MO, 6940, 9449
Kansas City Star, 6799
Kasson, John A., 5368
Kautz, August V., 4802
Keep Commission, 6766
Kefauver, Estes, 9932, 12377
Kendall, Amos, 2997
Kennedy, Edward, 10091, 10125, 10218, 10284, 12163, 12188
Kennedy, Jacqueline, 10093-10095, 10098, 10110, 10117, 10121
Kennedy, John F., 10031-10811
   assassination, 10389-10496
   biographies, 10031-10075
   Congress, 10497-10521
   Cuba, 10522-10549
   domestic affairs, 10550-10600
   elections, 10601-10642
   family, 10084, 10089, 10090, 10102, 10104, 10108, 10112, 10115, 10122, 10129, 10178
   foreign affairs, 10643-10726
   Nixon debate, 10601, 10606, 10613, 10614, 10617, 10618, 10629, 10632, 10634, 11726, 11734, 11735, 11748, 11753, 11755, 11760
   presidential years, 10159-10741
   press, 10727-10741
   private life, 10076-10129
   public career, 10130-10158
   writings, 10742-10811
Kennedy, Joseph, Jr., 10252, 10799
Kennedy, Joseph P., 10101, 10126, 10284
Kennedy, Kathleen, 10106
Kennedy, Robert, 10091, 10113, 10186, 10218, 10284, 10317, 10437
Kennedy v. Sampson, 10516
Kent, Frank R., 9018
Kent, Tyler G., 9135
Kentucky, 529
   and Buchanan, 3403
   and Garfield, 6024
   and Hayes, 5890

and Jefferson, 2093
and Andrew Johnson, 5567
and Lincoln, 3979, 4372, 4444, 4455, 4544, 4599, 4752, 5154, 5209, 5240, 5451
and Monroe, 2545
presidents from, 3321
and Franklin D. Roosevelt, 9025
and Washington, 247, 248
Kenyon College, 5821, 5830
Kern, John W., 7472
Kerner Commission, 11222
Key, David M., 5867
Key Biscayne, FL, Nixon in, 11646
Khartum, 6895
Khrushchev, Nikita, 9984, 10659, 10665, 10687, 10713, 10717, 11942
Kinealy, James, 4856
King, Martin Luther, 10437, 10584
King, Rufus, 749
King, William Lyon M., 8909
Kings College, 776
Kingston, NY, Washington in, 240
Kirbo, Charles, 12158
Kirby, Ephraim, 2102
Kirkpatrick, Jeane, 12994
Kissinger, Henry, 10718, 11535, 11776, 11780, 11787, 11789, 11804, 11830, 11834, 11841, 12441, 12467, 12602
Kitchin, Claude, 7692
Klein, Herbert, 11916
Knight, Goodwin, 12592
Know Nothing Movement, 3349, 4898
Knox, Chase, 6694
Konoye, Prince Fuminaro, 9101
Korea, 9937, 11783, 12452
   intervention, 6869
   policy, of Theodore Roosevelt, 6852
   South, 11808, 12479, 12541
   War, 9581-9603
Kosciuszko, Thaddeus, 581, 1173
Krogh, Egil, 11680, 11915
Kuchel, Thomas H., 10798
Kuper, Theodore F., 1499

Labor, 4991, 9466, 9467, 12917
   and Carter, 12346
   commissioner of, 6058
   and Hoover, 8146, 8184
   and Jackson, 2877, 2879, 2881, 2883, 2914, 2926
   and Andrew Johnson, 5458
   and Lincoln, 4121, 4459, 5234
   and McKinley, 6323
   management, 11232
   migratory, 9459
   racketeers, 10771
   and Franklin D. Roosevelt, 8449, 8848, 8964, 9059
   and Theodore Roosevelt, 6570

Subject Index

and Taft, 6995
and Truman, 9459
and Washington, 174
and Wilson, 7480, 7501, 7517
Ladejinsky, Wolf, 9890
Lafayette, Marquis de, 69, 160, 366, 602, 1495, 2290, 2699
La Follette, Robert M., 6585
La Guardia, Fiorello, 6729, 8719
Lambert, William H., 5354
Lamon, Ward H., 5039
Lancaster, PA, and Washington, 303, 304
Land
   grants, 521, 530, 3707
   policy, 6763, 8201
   speculator, Washington as, 527
Landscape Garden Movement, and Jefferson, 1304
Lane, Franklin K., 7423
Lane, Harriet, 3406, 3411
Lansing, MI, 7662
Lansing, Robert, 7435, 7533, 7693
Laos, 10679, 10689, 10703, 10705
Latin America
   and Carter, 12443, 12477, 12519
   and Cleveland, 6154
   and Eisenhower, 9979
   and Harding, 7884
   and Hoover, 8198
   and Lyndon Johnson, 11267
   and Kennedy, 10649, 10690, 10720
   and Nixon, 11775, 11837
   and Franklin D. Roosevelt, 8908
   and Truman, 9527
   and Wilson, 7560
Latrobe, Benjamin, 314, 1707, 1756, 2277, 2357
Lauchheimer Controversy, 7091
Laugel, Antoine A., 4227
Law
   administrative, 2048
   Common, 1616
   Constitutional, 1163, 1712, 2464, 4113
   international, 12009, 13040
   martial, 2657
   and Monroe, 2537
   of nations, 1873, 1879
   and order issue, 11523
   public, 12760
   of the sea, 13017
   slave, 5204
   Thomas, 279
   and Washington, 100
Law Enforcement Assistance Administration, 12290
Lawrence, John, 8400
Lawyer
   Buchanan, 3395
   Cleveland as, 6106, 6111
   education of, 1428
   Garfield as, 5968

Andrew Jackson as, 2788, 2794, 2809, 2812
Jefferson as, 1431, 1634-1639
Lincoln as, 3607, 4558-4612, 4620, 5265
McKinley as, 6247, 6263
Madison as, 2344
Franklin D. Roosevelt, 8575
Van Buren as, 3056
Wilson as, 7235
Lawyers, 12248
   and Washington, 209
Laxalt, Paul, 12610
Leadership
   political, 1010, 3025, 6127, 6177, 6178, 6267, 7419
   presidential, 2079, 6294, 7403, 7995, 8525, 8759, 9631, 9806, 9823, 10595, 11041, 12456
League of Nations, 616, 7122, 7468, 7603-7644, 7732, 7912
Leahy, William D., 9132
Leale, Charles A., 4854
Lear, Tobias, 168, 583, 814
Leavenworth KS, Lincoln in, 5295
Lebanon, 10005, 13034
Leclerc expedition, 1737
Lee, Harry, 2006
Lee, Henry, 604
Lee, Madeleine, 12584
Lee, Richard H., 969
Lee, Robert E., 4966, 5027, 5037, 5617, 5642, 5707, 5728, 5735, 7795
Legal Services
   Corporation, 11708, 12907
   for the poor, 12839, 12868
Legal tender case, 5755
Legare, Hugh S., 3183
Legislation
   autonomy, 11874
   and executive conflict, 8756
   leader, 7418
   liaison, 11000, 12766
   and Lincoln, 4537
   policy coalition, 10513, 11103
Leighton, Isabelle, 8370
Lemen, James, 2161
L'Enfant, Pierre C., 2277
Lenin, Vladimir, 1772, 7275
Lenroot, Irvine L., 7873, 8158
Letters, to Carter, 12151
Leutze-Stellwagen mask, of Washington, 437
Levy, Jefferson M., 1494
Levy, Uriah P., 1494, 1498
Lewis, Fielding, 817
Lewis, John L., 8098, 8785, 9049
Lewis, Joseph J., 5150
Lewis, Mary, 2825
Lewis, Meriwether, 1170, 1678, 2035, 2057
Lewis, Nelly C., 316
Lewis, Robert, 773

Subject Index

Lewisson, Walter U., 448
Lexington, KY, and Lincoln, 3874
Liberalism, 1400
  and black Americans, 8775
  and Jackson, 3007
  Jeffersonian, 1908, 2831
  and Kennedy, 10035, 10135, 10341, 10604
  and Lincoln, 4142
  and Reagan, 12696
  and Truman, 9324, 9444, 9451
  and Wilson, 7303
Liberties, civil, 1997, 2135, 2158, 2417, 3003, 5110, 5114, 5128, 6723, 7515, 8794, 9395, 12359, 12902
Liberty, 1124, 1169, 2156, 2228, 8772
Liberty Hall, 183
Librarian, Jefferson as, 1063
Librarians, and First Amendment, 11533
Libraries
  and Carter, 12557
  public, 12840
Library
  of Congress, 1735, 2301, 2411, 2515, 2517
  of Garfield, 5963
  of Jefferson, 1261, 1275, 1287
  Reagan, 12606, 12763
  of Washington, 190
Liddy, E. Gordon, 10536, 11010, 11510
Lincoln, Abraham, 3464-5398
  assassination, 4786-4878
  biographies, 3464-3656
  campaigns, 4879-4940
  chronologies, 3774-3798
  and Civil War, 4941-5053
  Douglas debates, 4613-4657
  education of, 3799-3806
  family of, 3807-3884
  and Gettysburg Address, 5054-5083
  inauguration of, 5084-5098
  and Indians, 5099-5108
  and judiciary, 5109-5140
  as lawyer, 4558-4612
  legend, 3885-3930
  life-mask of, 3996, 4005, 4029
  Lincolniana, 3931-4036
  liquor and, 3725, 3761, 4016
  literature, 4037-4073
  lithographs of, 4161
  as member of Congress, 4550-4557
  personality, 4074-4103
  philosophy, 4104-4151
  portraits and prints, 4152-4188
  presidential years, 4658-5247
  and the press, 5141-5165
  private life, 3657-4458
  public career of, 4459-4657
  recollections of, 4189-4271
  and Reconstruction, 5166-5179
  religion of, 4272-4332
  Shields duel, 3721
  and slavery, 5180-5247
  and Thornton debate, 4483, 4531
  travels of, 4333-4373
  tributes to, 4374-4427
  writings, 5248-5398
  youth of, 4428-4458
Lincoln, Abraham, Sr., 3878
Lincoln, Mary T., 3815, 3825, 3845-3847, 3852, 3853, 3855, 3859, 3860, 3862-3865, 3868, 3871-3873, 3876, 4221, 4616
Lincoln, Mordecai, 3821
Lincoln, Robert T., 3836, 3838, 3839, 3854
Lincoln, Sarah B., 3822, 3883
Lincoln, Tad, 3816, 3817, 3820
Lincoln, Thomas, 3822
Lincoln County, KY, 3821
Lincoln Group
  of Boston, 4380
  of Chicago, 4228
Lincoln Memorial, 5264
Lincoln Memorial Tablet, 3967
Lincoln Memorial University, 3947, 3953, 3974, 3978, 4024, 4025, 4033, 5014
Lincoln Monument, 3985
Lincolniana, 3931-4036, 4166, 5267, 5284
Link, Arthur S., 7212, 7328, 7523
Lippman, Walter, 8948
Literary Society of Washington, 5997
Literature
  and Jefferson, 1640-1687
  and Lincoln, 4037-4073
  Washington in, 429, 474
Little Rock, AK, 9869
Liu Tho-Ch'ang, 1562
Livingston, Edward, 2830
Lloyd George, David, 6729, 7516, 7673, 7675
Lloyd, William A., 4942
Lobbying, presidential, 10514, 11104
Lobbyists, 10790, 11983
Locke, John, 1528, 1529, 1587, 1632, 1648
Lodge, George C., 6881
Lodge, Henry C., 6962, 7038, 7414, 7571, 7662, 7732
Logan, Stephen T., 4606
London Punch, 5164
London Times, 5165
Long, Huey, 8795, 11158
Long Island, NY, Washington in, 792
Longlea estate, 10893
Longoria, Felix, 10908
Longworth, Alice R., 6481, 6482, 6514
Longworth, Nicholas, 6972
Los Angeles, CA, 5773, 5839
Louisiana
  government bill of 1804, 2120
  and Grant, 5714

and Jefferson, 2098, 2110
and Lincoln, 5173, 5174
and Polk, 3248
Purchase, 2104, 2109, 2112, 2130
and Franklin D. Roosevelt, 8540
and Taylor, 3324
Love
　of Lincoln, 3664, 3731, 3772, 5278
　of Washington, 222
Love affairs
　of Jefferson, 1203
　of Lincoln, 3726, 3745
　of Franklin D. Roosevelt, 8454
　of Washington, 232
　of Wilson, 7238
Lovingood, Sut, 3973
Lowitz, Anson, 3557
Lowitz, Sadyebeth, 3557
Loyalty, 9399, 9454
　issue, 9398
　program, 9391
Lukash, William, 11134
Lutherans, 837, 4277
Lyceum, Franklin, 2704
Lyndon, Sam R., 10894
Lyons, James, 3199

McAdoo, 7402, 7502, 8838
MacArthur, Douglas, 7058, 8877, 9585, 9586, 9592, 9596, 9597, 9600, 9601, 9603
McCarthy, Joseph R., 9869-9871, 9912, 11574
McCarthyism, 9394, 9447, 9564, 9624
McCellan-Hruska criminal code bill, 11557
McClellan, George B., 4907, 5702, 5740
McCollum decision, 2493
McCormick, Robert R., 8650
McCracken, Paul, 11670
McCumber, Porter, Jr., 7003
McDonald, James, 8589
McDonough, Gordon L., 9361
McDowell, Ephraim, 3221
McFadden Act Report, 12283
McGlynn, Frank, 4103
McGovern, George, 11705, 11728, 11729, 11731, 11767, 11769
　as governor, 6614
McHenry, James, 989
Machiavelli, 2406, 2451
McIntyre, Marvin H., 8552
Mackenzie, William L., 8909
McKinley, William, 6234-6334
　biographies, 6234-6253
　as governor, 6266, 6269
　presidential years, 6271-6328
　private life, 6254-6260
　public career, 6261-6270
　writings, 6329-6334
McLellan, Charles W., 5272

MacMorrogh, Dermot, 2676
McNamara, Robert, 10560
McNary, Charles L., 8003
McNeil, Hermon A., 4583
Macon County, IL, and Lincoln, 4342
McPike, Henry H., 8847
Macroeconomic policy, 11164
MacVeagh, Franklin, 7015
　goals, 12293
　management, 8159
Madison, Dolley, 1107-1110, 2331, 2337, 2339, 2342, 2345, 2349, 2350, 2353, 2357, 2358, 2360
Madison, James, 1061-1260
　biographies, 1061-1078
　presidential years, 1196-1237
　private life, 1079-1111
　public career, 1112-1195
　writings, 1238-1260
Magna Carta, 1977
Magraw, W. M. F., 3440
Mahan, Alfred T., 6659, 6671, 6682, 8728, 8914
Mail, presidential, 8608
　of Lincoln, 4778
Maine
　Canada boundary, 3104
　and Reagan, 13029
Malone, Dumas, 1762
Malthus, Thomas R., 1580, 2422
Management
　administrative, 9032
　crisis, 11315, 11991
　by objective, 12027
Manchukuo, 8868
Mandell, Edward, 7152
Mansfield, Michael, 10520, 10943, 11351
Manship, Paul, 3981
Mao Tse-Tung, 1947
Map maker, Washington as, 531
Marbury, 2181
Marbury vs. Madison, 2464, 2480, 2483
Marcy, William L., 3267
Marin, Luis M., 8719
Marine Corps, 8938, 9361. *See also* Military
Marriage
　of John Adams, 883
　of Lincoln, 3858
　of Washington, 263, 278
Marshall, George C., 9157, 9758, 10030
Marshall, John, 1022, 2177, 2179, 2189, 2195, 2200, 2201
Marshall, Thomas R., 7375
Marshall Plan, 9325, 9561, 9566, 9584, 9622, 9640
Marx, Karl, 1525, 2392
Maryland
　ancestry of Monroe, 2532
　and Washington, 549
　and Wilson, 7451
Maryland Institute for the Promotion of the Me-

chanic Arts, 3206
Mason
 McKinley as, 6258
 Washington as, 158, 337, 339, 343, 348, 351, 841
Mason, Andrew J., 2795
Masonic Institution, 2691
Masonry, Lincoln and, 4230
Mass media, 991, 9158, 10388, 11296, 11525, 11536, 11638, 11770, 11909, 12719
 access, 12035
 propaganda, 11751
Massachusetts
 and John Q. Adams, 2597
 and Cleveland, 6123
 and Coolidge, 8033
 Historical Society, 2669, 2696
 and Kennedy, 10149
 Lincoln in, 4350, 4352, 4975
 Senate, 2685
Master, Edgar L., 3662
Mathematics, and Jefferson, 1680
Mather, Cotton, 1825
Matson Slave Case, 5220
Mayaguez incident, 11991, 12022, 12024, 12085
Mayflower (yacht), 7991
Maynard, Lizzre G., 3955
Mayors, and Nixon, 11739
Mazzei, Philip, 2497-2500
Medals, 473, 500, 4032
Mediation Movement, 7585
Medicaid, 12928
Medical lobby, and Truman, 9372
Medicare, 9372
Medicine, Jefferson influence on, 1681
Medora, ND, and Theodore Roosevelt, 6471
Meese, Edwin, 12606, 12669
Melville, Herman, 2166, 3309
Memphis, TN, and Andrew Johnson, 5455
Mencken, H. L., 7984
Mendel, Edward, 5395
Meredith, James, 10312
Metallurgy, collection of Hoover, 8318
Methodists, and Lincoln, 4328
Mexico, 3305
 and John Q. Adams, 2637
 annexation of, 2637, 3266
 business interests in, 7562
 Carter and, 12481, 12507
 Harding and, 7879, 7880, 7888, 7908
 William H. Harrison and, 3151
 and the Hayes administration, 5862
 intervention of, 11263
 Andrew Johnson and, 5546, 5547
 and Monroe, 2544
 and Pierce, 3379
 and Polk, 3247, 3252, 3256
 Revolution, 7645-7662
 Southern Railroad, 5709

Taft and, 7042
War, 3236, 3237, 3250, 3263, 3264, 3266, 3270, 3273, 3274, 3278-3281, 3295, 3303, 3305, 3324, 3329, 4474, 4516, 4525
Meyer, George, 6640
Miami, FL, 8561
Michigan
 and the depression, 8246
 and Jackson, 2970, 5435, 5505
Middle East
 and Carter, 12426, 12491, 12516
 and Eisenhower, 9936, 9956, 9957, 9965, 9989, 10007
 and Nixon, 11789, 11802
 and Reagan, 12971, 12972, 12987, 13031, 13039, 13066
 and Truman, 9604-9621
 and Wilson, 7686
Mifflin, Thomas, 628
Mikado, 7068
Milburn, John G., 6080
Military, 11047
 budget, 9590, 9973, 12816
 and Carter, 12301, 12492
 and civil relations, 5017, 12301
 and Eisenhower, 9861, 9978
 career of Grant, 5620, 5622, 5626, 5699
 and William H. Harrison, 3139, 3143, 3146, 3152
 and Hoover, 8162, 8274
 industrial complex, 9098, 9974, 10009
 and Jackson, 2805, 3331
 and Jefferson, 2012, 2043
 and Lincoln, 4978
 and Monroe, 2550
 and Reagan, 12993, 13038, 13089
 and Franklin D. Roosevelt, 9133
 and Theodore Roosevelt, 6798
 and Truman, 9321, 9480, 9519, 9547, 9555
 and Washington, 56, 178, 649, 667
Millar, John, 2376
Millennialism, 4149
Miller, Anson S., 4260
Miller, John C., 2147
Miller, John F., 10375
Milligan case, 4993
Mills, Clark, 3996
Mills life-mask of Lincoln, 3996
Milton, John, 1651
Milwaukee, WI, Lincoln in, 5360
Miniatures
 of Lincoln, 3997
 of Madison, 2515
 of Washington, 478, 512
Mining, and Hoover, 8318
Minnesota
 and Eisenhower, 9914, 9924
 and Lincoln, 4337

and Taylor, 3311
Minstral, Lew D., 6716
Minton, Sherman, 9296
Miranda v. Arizona, 12691
Missionaries, 2905, 7597
Mississippi
 flood of 1927, 8154
 freedmen of, 5757
 and Hoover, 8210, 8270
 Jacksonian democracy in, 2872
 and Andrew Johnson, 5426
 River, 2241, 8101
 and Franklin D. Roosevelt, 8697
 territory, 2797, 2891
Missouri
 Compromise, 2556, 5380
 controversy, 2564
 crisis, 2841
 River, 2241
 and Franklin D. Roosevelt, 8708, 8846
 and Truman, 9264
Mistral, Frederick, 8507
Mitchell, E. Y., 9072
Mitchell, James T., 476
Mitchell, Martha, 11622
Mobile, AL, Wilson in, 7344
Mohawk Valley, Washington in, 621
Moley, Raymond, 8806, 9069
Moltke, Helmuth von, 606
Mondale, Walter, 12386
Monetary policy
 diplomacy, 8788
 experiment, 8814
 reform, 7482
Money
 and Jefferson, 1577
 and Lincoln, 3755
 and Reconstruction, 5460
 and Washington, 99
Monopoly
 and Franklin D. Roosevelt, 9024
 and Theodore Roosevelt, 6673
Monroe, James, 2518-2579
 biographies, 2518-2524
 presidential years, 2556-2572
 private life, 2525-2538
 public career, 2539-2555
 writings, 2573-2579
Monroe Doctrine, 2106, 2466, 2559, 2562, 2563, 2623, 2625, 2628, 2629, 3260, 6868, 7123, 7648, 8886, 8945, 10719
Monroe House, 2527
Monroe Tavern, 590
Monroe-Pinckney Treaty, 2129, 2551
Montalto Observatory, 1315
Montana, Theodore Roosevelt in, 6473
Montesquieu, Baron de, 1564, 2704
Montgomery, AL, 6160

Monticello, 1083, 1181, 1255, 1305, 1325, 1688-1721
 art gallery for, 1347
 furnishings, 1488, 1503, 1504, 1506, 1517
 gardens, 1308, 1313, 1491, 1492, 1500, 1502
Montpelier, 2395
Moody, William H., 6732
Moore, Sarah, 590
Moore, W. G., 5518
Morality
 and foreign policy, 7580
 and the founding fathers, 2416
 and Jefferson, 1613, 1966
 and Lincoln, 5233
 public, 4118, 4119
 and Theodore Roosevelt, 6856
Morellet, Andre, 1464
Morey, H. L., 5992
Morgan, Edwin D., 4523, 5087
Morgan, J. P., 7698
Morgan, Kay S., 9699
Morgan, Richard P., 4189
Morgenthau, Henry, 8538
Mormons, 4292, 5235
Moroccan crises, 6853
Morris, Edmund, 6618
Morris, Gouverneur, 1830, 6913
Morris, Laura H., 6713
Morris, Roger, 427
Morton, Levi P., 6215
Mosby's Rangers, 5726
Moscow Conference, 9152
Mount McGregor, 5579
Mount Vernon, 280, 305-326, 408, 799
Moyers, Bill, 10855, 11070, 11151, 11335, 12483
Mudd, Samuel A., 4845, 4851
Mugwumps, 6123
Mulberry Grove, 610
Mullaly, John, 5146
Muncie, IN, and Reagan, 12949
Municipalities, and Reagan, 12927
Murry, Alexander, 979, 1986
Museum of Natural History in Paris, 1679
Music
 of Civil War, 4947
 and Jefferson, 1336, 1356, 1362, 1364, 1539-1541, 1543-1545
 and Theodore Roosevelt, 6444
 and Truman, 9429
 of Washington's time, 237
Musick, Sam, 3674
Mussolini, Benito, 7275, 8604, 9105
Myers, Alonzo, 5230

Nagasaki, 9419
Napoleon, 1852, 1858, 1859, 1876, 2474, 5042
Narayan, Jayaprakash, 1784
Nashville, TN, and Andrew Jackson, 2815

Nasser, Gamel A., 3025
National Advisory Commission on Civil Disorders, 11222
National Archives, 3024, 8555
National Association of Evangelicals, 12804
National Broadcasting Corporation, 10459
National Broadcasting System, 10316
National Conference on Youth Fitness, 9913
National Credit Corporation, 8166
National Emergency Council, 9074
National Gazette, 1604, 1605, 1609
National Guard, 10560
National Institutes of Health, 11198
National Labor Relations Board, 9471, 9904, 12882
National Progressive Republican League, 6585
National security, 8790, 9397, 9570, 10659, 11043, 11324, 11627, 12460
National Security Agency, 12611
National Security Council, 9571, 9982
National Union Movement, 5434
National Youth Administration, 8460, 8801
Nationalism, 719, 2323, 1536, 2557, 4140, 4986, 6793, 7671
NATO. *See* North Atlantic Treaty Organization
Naturalist
   Jefferson as a, 1299
   Theodore Roosevelt as a, 6341, 6356, 6429, 6486, 6494, 6511, 6524
Nature, and John Q. Adams, 892
Nature of man, 2355, 2400
Navy, 2052, 2074, 4753, 5046, 5047, 6735, 6738, 6760, 6798, 6861, 7563, 9089. *See also* Military
   and John Q. Adams, 984, 985, 992
   and the American Revolution, 979, 1986
   Chiriqui station sites, 3451
   expansion, during the New Deal, 9082
   founding of the, 971
   limitation, and Franklin D. Roosevelt, 8878
   New England fleet, 623
   operations of, 6928
   policy, 8918
   preparedness, 9170
   and Washington, 201, 629, 643, 644
NBC. *See* National Broadcasting Corporation
Nebraska, and McKinley, 6273
Negotiation of Ghent, 2680
Neighborhood policy, 12847
Neill, Edward D., 4748
Nelson, Samuel, 3203
Nemours, Pierre Samuel du Pont de, 2295
Nephews, of Jefferson, 1423
Netherlands, 950
   and John Q. Adams, 936
Neutrality
   and Eisenhower, 9998
   and Jefferson, 1878
   and Franklin D. Roosevelt, 8858, 8917
   and Theodore Roosevelt, 6532
   and Truman, 9573
   and Washington, 690
   and Wilson, 7540, 7575
Nevada
   and Hoover, 8244
   and Lincoln, 4671
   Wilson in, 7610
New Almaden Mine, 3749
New Deal, 8545, 8955, 8985, 8986, 8991, 8997, 8999, 9000, 9003, 9012-9015, 9017, 9020, 9021, 9027, 9030, 9034, 9035, 9038, 9039, 9043, 9045, 9048, 9050-9052, 9055, 9057, 9058, 9065-9067, 9070, 9071, 9076, 9077, 9079, 9083, 9084, 9086, 9088
   and Alabama clergy, 8988
   and Britain, 9004
   and the budget, 9068
   and the Chicago machine, 9031
   and the clergy, 8989
   and the Constitution, 9009
   and governmental power, 9080
   and Frank Hague, 9005
   and historians, 9019
   history of the, 9046, 9064
   and Hoover, 8128
   and Jefferson, 1741
   and Frank R. Kent, 9018
   and labor policies, 9025
   leadership in the, 9028
   and monopoly, 9024
   and the National Emergency Council, 9074
   political philosophy of, 9026
   and the presidency, 9063
   reform and the, 9032
   Shelterbelt Project, 9006
   and Al Smith, 9022
   and social security, 9040
   and the states, 9036, 9061, 9062
   and the Supreme Court, 9023
   and Texas newspapers, 9075
   and Truman, 9453
   and the unemployed, 8994
   and World affairs, 9060
New Frontier, 10205, 10211, 10212, 10231, 10246, 10301, 10348, 10366, 10521, 10569, 10625, 10696, 10776, 10949, 11261
New Hampshire
   Eisenhower campaign in, 9921
   and Lincoln, 4361, 4915
   Washington in, 597
New Jersey
   legislature, 7353
   and Washington campaign, 660
   and Wilson, 7301, 7321, 7335, 7476
New Kent, VA, and Washington's marriage, 263
New Left, 7264
New Mexico, 6743, 7048
   volunteers, 6636

New Orleans, LA
  and Jackson, 2815, 2919, 2923
  Lyndon Johnson in, 11045
  and Lee H. Oswald, 10439
  Port of, 2093
New Right, 12662, 12689, 12706, 12860
New Salem, IL, and Lincoln, 4363, 4434, 4450, 4535
New York City
  Board of Police Commissioners, 6554
  fiscal crisis, 11970, 12012
  and Lincoln, 4765
  mayor, 4481
  and Washington, 583, 669, 750, 812
  Washington Centennial in, 362
New York Herald, 5323
New York Historical Society, 423, 2683
New York state, 572, 3076, 3098, 6566
  civil service reforms, 5858
  and Fillmore, 3349
  and Andrew Johnson, 5464
  Lincoln in, 4347
  and Franklin D. Roosevelt, 8496, 8510, 8715
  and Theodore Roosevelt, 6570, 6820
  and Van Buren, 3086
  and Washington, 811
New York Times, 4849, 10576, 11201
New York University, 7119
Newark, NJ, 4887
Newburyport, MA, and John Q. Adams, 2698
Newcomb, Simon, 6014
Newport, NH, and Pierce papers, 3381
Newport, RI
  and Kennedy, 10108
  and Washington, 612
Newspapers
  advertising, 10627, 11253, 11744
  daily, 9075
  and Eisenhower, 9917
  and Gettysburg Address, 5074
  and Grant, 5718
  and Jackson, 2957, 2979
  and Lyndon Johnson, 5540
  and Kennedy coverage, 10683
  and Kennedy press conferences, 10587
  and Nixon, 11536, 11772, 11881
  and Truman, 9585
Newsweek, 10281
Niagara, Lincoln at, 4333
Nicaragua, 7021, 7529, 8013, 12490, 13035, 13045
Nicholas, John, 564, 1224, 1708
Nichols, Martha Ann P., 440
Nicholson, A. O. P., 2818
Nicolay, John G., 4233, 4234
NIH. *See* National Institutes of Health
Niles, Hezekiah, 1055
Nixon, Pat, 9785, 11413, 11437
Nixon, Richard, 11376-11946
  biographies, 11376-11946
  domestic policy, 11661-11716
  elections, 11717-11769
  foreign affairs, 11770-11848
  Frost interviews, 11922
  Kennedy debate, 10619, 10637, 11727, 11758
  presidential years, 11461-11920
  private life, 11406-11431
  public career, 11432-11460
  resignation, 11876, 11881, 11909
  Watergate, 11849-11920
  writings, 11921-11946
Nixon Doctrine, 11770, 11779, 11782, 11793, 11801, 11808, 11810, 11811, 11821, 11828, 11840
Nixon v. Cox, 11886
Nixon v. Fitzgerald, 11593
Nixon v. Sirica, 11895
Nixonia, 11570
Nkrumah, Kwame, 10696
Nobel Peace Prize, 6553
Non-Partisan League, 7088
Nonproliferation, 13072
Norfolk, VA, and Lincoln, 4992
Normalcy, 7845, 7896, 7903, 7911, 8012, 8017
Norris, George W., 8781, 8783
North Atlantic Treaty Organization, 9633, 9938, 11801
North Carolina
  and Jackson, 2856, 2927
  and Jefferson, 1971
  and Lincoln, 3823, 5141
  and Polk, 3269
  and Truman, 9319
  and Van Buren, 3080
North Dakota, 6454
  Badlands, 6434, 6485
  and peace issue, 7475
  Theodore Roosevelt in, 6517
Norway, and World War II, 9150, 9151
Notre Dame, Carter address at, 12249
NSA. *See* National Security Agency
Nullification, 1729, 2409, 2636, 2860, 3018
Numismatics, 3964
Nye, James W., 8746

OAS. *See* Organization of American States
"Oberon" (poem), 2598
O'Connor, John, 8757
O'Daniel, 8828
O'Donnell, Freeman, 10252
Office of Congressional Relations, 10245
Office-seeking
  and John Adams administration, 1004
  and Jefferson administration, 2056
Ogdensburg Agreement, 6865
Oglesby, Richard J., 4093, 4222, 5249, 5397
Ohio, 5834

chief justices from, 7009
and Hayes, 5887
Indians in, 3163
and Jackson, 2980
Jackson party in, 2910
and Lincoln, 3768, 4366, 5316
Michigan boundary dispute, 2955
National Guard, 6268
and Nixon, 10609
presidents, 5860
progressivism in, 7010
reform in, 5979
River, 375, 534, 535, 2241
State University, 5813
and Taft, 7073
and Washington, 514, 516, 518, 519, 521, 523, 533, 603, 792, 805
Oil, 7898, 12282, 12526
crisis, 7584
pollution control, 8127
Oklahoma, Theodore Roosevelt visits, 6790
O'Mahoney, Joseph C., 8960
O'Meehan, Thomas, 463, 492
O'Neale, Peggy, 2935
Onstott, R. J., 5370
Opdyke, George, 4481
Open Door policy, 6855, 6874, 6875, 10729
Operation Overlord, 9736, 9738
Operation Recovery, 12184
Opium War, 2669
Oppenheimer, J. Robert, 9428, 9877
Orange County, NY, Washington in, 634
Ordinance of 1690, 1784, 1868
Oregon, 3265
Compromise of 1846, 3275
and foreign policy, 3246
and Hayes-Tilden controversy, 5908
and Mexican War, 3266
and Polk, 3251
Organization of American States, 10649
Orlando, Vittorio E., 7673
Orphan, Hoover as, 8219, 8220
Osborn, Chase S., 6630
Ossian, Jefferson and, 1446, 1455
Oswald, Lee H., 10393, 10408, 10418, 10432, 10439-10440, 10443, 10450, 10458, 10466, 10469, 10483
Otis, Harrison G., 2626, 2685
Overton, John, 2802, 2862, 3043
Owen, Robert, 1580, 2422
Owens, Mary, 3679

Pacificism, of Jefferson, 1554
Page, Thomas N., 7555
Paine, Thomas, 2671
Paintings, of Lincoln, 4163, 4165, 4186
Pakistan, during Carter administration, 12513
Palaeontology, 1659, 1669, 1676, 1677

Palestine, 9608, 9610, 9614, 9616-9618
and Carter, 12434, 12482
and Reagan, 12976
and Franklin D. Roosevelt administration, 8855, 8888, 8916
and Truman, 9607
and Wilson, 7524, 7572
Palo Alto, Battle of, 3296, 3314
Pan American Conference, Fifth, 7599
Pan American policy, 7559, 7570
Panama, 7057, 7528, 11259
Congress, 2662
and Eisenhower, 9955
libel cases, 6864
revolution, 6846, 6861
Panama Canal, 6842, 6916, 7057, 9972
and Carter, 12235, 12352, 12515
and Reagan, 12957
tolls, 7536
Panic of 1837, 3105
Panic of 1907, 6943
Paquet, A. C., 3933
Pardon, 5489
by Carter, 12320, 12633
of Confederates, 4702
by Ford, 11950
by Lincoln, 4672, 4686
of Nixon, 11855, 11881, 11885, 11890, 11905, 11911
Parents, of Lincoln, 3850, 3880, 3881
Paris
Jefferson in, 1214, 1240, 1269, 1290
Monroe in, 2541
Peace Conference, 7663, 7672
Parks, 9483
Parks, Samuel C., 4212
Parrington, Vernon L., 1561
Parsons, Theophilus, 2692
Passamequoddy Bay Tidal Project, 8784
Patowmack Company, 520
Patriotism, 6647
of Lincoln, 4130, 4448
of Washington, 466
Patronage
and Buchanan, 3443, 3444
and Garfield, 6032
and Hoover, 8209, 8211, 8212
and Jackson, 2964
and Jefferson, 2019
and Andrew Johnson, 5468
and Lincoln, 4509, 4662, 4709, 4776, 5186
and McKinley, 6274
and Polk, 3249
and Franklin D. Roosevelt, 8751
and Taft, 7041
Patton, George S., 9735, 9739, 9746
Paul, Alice, 7495
Pauley, Edwin W., 9366

Subject Index

Payne-Aldrich tariff, 7083
Peabody, Elizabeth, 4259
Peabody, Endicott, 8405
Peace
   Conference of 1919, 7670, 7673
   Corps, 10580, 10582
   issue in 1914 election, 7475
   and Lyndon Johnson, 11352
   and Lincoln, 5018
   and McKinley, 6276
   and Nixon, 11820
   in Reagan era, 12889
   and Truman, 9516, 9561
   and Wilson, 7465, 7626
   World, 7611, 7615
Peale, Charles W., 428, 494, 2306
Peale, James, 428
Peale, Rembrandt, 428, 489
Peale, Willson, 428
Pearl Harbor, 9092, 9149, 9169, 9173
Peck, Mrs., 7220
Pell, Herbert, 8816
Pendergast machine, 9268, 9271, 9273, 9275-9277, 9280, 9449
Pendleton, George H., 4463
Penn Gazette, 706
Pennell Club of Philadelphia, 4378
Pennsylvania
   and Carter campaign, 12409
   and Coolidge, 8028
   and Jackson, 2855, 2887
   and Jefferson, 1713, 2185
   Labor Non-Partisan League, 8848
Pentagon Papers, 11356
Peoria, IL, Lincoln in, 4336, 4615, 5305
Pericles, 5065
Perkins, George W., 8588
Peru, and Kennedy administration, 10720
Peterson, Fred, 4849
Petition, right of, 2706
Petroleum
   decontrol, 12916
   industry, 11696
   prices, 12916
Phelps, Richard H., 4946
Philadelphia
   John Adams in, 957
   Hayes in, 5835
   and Andrew Johnson, 5476
   Lincoln and, 4355, 4539
   Washington in, 578
Philippines
   Army, 9756
   and McKinley, 6276
   and Reagan, 12980
   and Taft, 7051, 7058, 7065, 7074, 7128
   and Theodore Roosevelt, 6650, 6827
   and Wilson, 7549

Philologist, Theodore Roosevelt as, 1467, 1476
Photograph, of Lincoln, 3855, 4153, 4171, 4175, 4178, 4179, 4180, 4182, 4185
Physicians, vote for Reagan, 12937
Physiocrats, and Jefferson, 1551, 1553
Pickering, Timothy, 1263, 2053, 2685
Pierce, Franklin, 3358-3381
   biographies, 3358-3361
   presidential years, 3367-3380
   private life, 3362-3365
   public career, 3366
   writings, 3381
Pierce, Jane M., 3363
Piety, 371, 12136, 12181, 12376
Pigeon Creek Baptist Church, 3798
Pinchot, Gifford, 6885, 8028
Pinckney, Charles C., 989
Pinckney, Mrs. Charles C., 316
Pinckney Plan, 2445
Pine Knot, 6439, 6513
Pinkerton, Allen, 4834, 4996
Pinkerton records, 4696
Pirates, 2074, 4682
   barbary pirates, 993, 2074
   Malaysian, 2938
Pitcher, John, 4721
Pitman, Benn, 4819, 4827
Pittsburgh, PA
   Lyndon Johnson in, 11244
   Lincoln in, 4888
Plains, GA, 12108, 12123, 12128, 12133
Platt, Thomas C., 6551, 6561
Playboy
   Carter interview, 12143
   John Dean interview, 11499
Ploughjogger letters, 964, 965
Plummer, William, 2572
Poe, Edgar A., 1475
Poe Cottage, and Theodore Roosevelt, 6499
Poetry
   and Jefferson, 1484
   of Lincoln, 4054, 4064
   and Franklin D. Roosevelt, 8622
   and Theodore Roosevelt, 6418
Poindexter, George, 2871
Point Four Program, 9487, 9527
Poland
   Buchanan in, 3408
   and Hoover, 8151
   Jefferson and, 2113
   Kennedy and, 10726
   Franklin D. Roosevelt and, 8889, 9094
   and Truman, 9532
   and Wilson, 7558, 7676
Police, 4850
   commissioner, Theodore Roosevelt as, 6526
   and Lincoln, 4735
   state, 2180

744 Subject Index

strike, 8001, 8018
Policy
   formulation, 9471, 9485, 11228, 12362, 12710
   leadership, 13055
   success, 12790
Political parties, 746
   alignment of, 2545
   battles in, 2836
   conflict in, 3015
   government of, 1940
   leadership in, 2479, 2934, 7471, 7513, 9778, 11026
   loyalty in, 3016
   struggle within, 9328
   system of, 920, 1896, 1919, 2618, 2656, 2863, 2927, 8634
Polk, James K., 3209-3293
   biographies, 3209-3220
   presidential years, 3236-3286
   private life, 3221-3224
   public career, 3225-3235
   writings, 3287-3293
Polk, Sarah C., 3222-3224
Polk-Stockton Intrigue, 3270
Polls
   and Carter, 12474
   and Lyndon Johnson, 11331
   and Kennedy, 10210
   and Reagan, 12940
Pollution, thermal, 12334
Poor, and Reagan administration, 12839, 12868, 12873, 12891, 12903, 13100
Pope, John, 4322
Pope John, 10658
Pope Pius XII, 9206
Popes Creek Plantation, 136
Popularity, presidential, 9883, 11545, 12772
   of Kennedy, 10345
   of Nixon, 11486, 11525
Pork-Packing Agreement, 8123
Portland, OR, Wilson in, 7641
Portraits, 4173, 4176, 4181, 4184, 4188
   of John Q. Adams, 2588
   of Cleveland, 6096
   of Benjamin Harrison, 6204
   of Jefferson, 1110, 1202, 1246, 1268, 1280
   of Lincoln, 3617, 3743, 4152, 4169, 4905
   of McKinley, 6249, 6308
   of Wilson, 7346
Ports, free, 9150, 9151
Portsmouth Peace Conference, 6866
Post, Regis H., 7030
Potsdam, 9526, 9528, 9556, 9648
Poverty, 1721, 11177, 11192
Powell, Lewis F., 11540
Power, presidential, 6293, 8705, 8966, 11088, 12259
Prebie, Edward, 979, 1986

Presbyterians, 1638, 3396, 6147
President's Assistant for Policy Development, 12710
President's Committee on Equality and Treatment and Opportunity in the Armed Forces, 9438
President's Council on Youth Fitness, 9913
Presidential Claims Settlement Power, 12459
Press
   and John Q. Adams, 991
   and Arthur, 6056
   and Carter, 11638, 11878, 12064, 12224, 12227, 12241, 12523
   and Coolidge, 7990, 8007
   coverage of Cuban crisis, 10525
   and Eisenhower, 9814, 9839, 9840
   and Harding, 7877, 7910
   and Hoover, 8092, 8251
   and Jackson, 2973
   and Jefferson, 1603, 1610, 1612, 2020, 2064, 2190
   and Andrew Johnson, 5464, 5532
   and Lyndon Johnson, 11108, 11293-11311
   and Kennedy, 10394, 10463, 10727-10741
   and Lincoln, 4187, 4650, 5141-5165
   and Polk, 3238, 3248
   and Reagan, 12619, 12770
   and Franklin D. Roosevelt, 8736, 8797, 8865
   and Theodore Roosevelt, 6740
   secretary, 9073, 11303
   and Truman, 9310, 9364, 9374, 9375, 9392, 9409
   and Wilson, 7403, 7470, 7649, 7689
Press, Frank, 12214
Press conferences
   of Coolidge, 7997
   of Ford, 11972
   and Lyndon Johnson, 11293, 11298, 11300
   and Kennedy, 10587, 10731, 10736, 10737, 10739
   of Nixon, 11932, 11933
   of Eleanor Roosevelt, 8461, 8462
   of Franklin D. Roosevelt, 8560, 8742, 9183
   and Truman, 9350
   of Wilson, 7380
Pressure groups, 7676, 12317
Primaries, 7470, 9264, 10638, 12366, 12933
   and Eisenhower, 9914, 9924
   and Kennedy, 10603, 10605
Princeton University
   Cleveland at, 6104, 6105
   Lyndon Johnson at, 11032
   Wilson at, 7197, 7208, 7214, 7218, 7233
Prints
   and Lincoln, 4156-4160, 4162, 4164, 4168
   and Washington, 455, 456
Professors, and Franklin D. Roosevelt, 8961
Progressive Era, 7094, 7412
Progressive Movement, 6569, 6596, 6614, 6734, 7010, 7084, 7321, 7335, 7443, 7465, 7981, 7982
Progressive party, 6568

Subject Index

Prohibition, 4031, 5861
Propaganda, 2899, 2958, 7582, 7714, 7888
Property, private, 7120
Protestant crusade, 3341
Providence Conference, 4726
Psychobiography, 1156, 7213
Psychohistory, 11417, 11419, 11421, 12122, 12126
Psychojournalism, 11414
Public Land Commission, 6812
Public opinion, 8673
   and Carter, 12390
   and Harding, 7888
   and Lyndon Johnson, 10940
   and Kennedy, 10241, 10360
   and Lincoln, 4868, 4870, 4871
   and Nixon, 11443, 11551, 11868
   and Reagan, 12676, 12683
   and Franklin D. Roosevelt, 8656, 8709
   and Theodore Roosevelt, 6801
   and Truman, 9560, 9623
   and Wilson, 7538
Public relations, 10360, 11470
   management, 8232
Pueblo incident, 12024
Puerto Rico, 8534, 9512
   appropriation crisis and, 7030
   autonomy, 9511
   Unionist party of, 7030
Puritan ethic, 941, 1962
Putnam, James, 887
Pyramid Park, and Theodore Roosevelt, 6466

Quakerism, of Lincoln, 4294
Quarantine speech, 8865, 9099, 9121, 9123, 9124
Queen Victoria, 5846
Quemoy case, 9975, 9993
Quesnay de Beaurepaire, 2304
Quezon y Molina, Manuel, 9756
Quincy, MA, and John Q. Adams, 1032, 2612

Race relations
   and John Q. Adams, 2641
   and Benjamin Harrison, 6223
   and Hoover, 8130, 8156, 8157, 8197, 8211
   and Jefferson, 2148
   and Lincoln, 5200, 5223
   and Franklin D. Roosevelt, 8775
   and Theodore Roosevelt, 6547, 6947
   and Wilson, 7479
   during World War II, 9107
Racism, 2155, 10573, 12352, 12953
Radicalism, 1710, 11158
Radicals, 4545, 4776, 5405, 5498, 5562
Radio
   and Coolidge, 7989
   and 'Croak' Carter, 8558
   and Harding, 7909
   and Kennedy assassination, 10454

Reagan on, 12732
   regulation, 8795
   and Franklin D. Roosevelt, 8541, 8576, 8608, 8699, 9180
Rafinesque, Constantine S., 2212
Rafshoon, Gerald, 12184
Railroads, 3624, 6673, 7502, 7590
   workers on, 6324
Raisuli, Ahmed ibn-Muhammed, 6628
Ramsey, Betty, 262
Ranch life, of Theodore Roosevelt, 6454, 6478, 6485, 6490, 6517, 6937
Randolph, Edmund, 628
Randolph, John, of Roanoke, 1065, 2934
Randolph, Thomas J., 1788, 2939
Randolph Macon College, 3204
Raskob, John J., 8779
Rationalism, 1549
Rauch, Basil, 9083
Rawlins, John A., 5704
Rayburn, Sam, 7435, 8755
Raymond, Henry J., 5029
Reading, PA, and Washington, 596
Reagan, Nancy, 12583, 12584
Reagan, Ronald, 12562-13150
   biographies, 12562-12573
   budget, 12815-12836
   domestic policy, 12837-12929
   elections, 12930-12967
   foreign affairs, 12968-13068
   as governor, 12147, 12589, 12595
   nuclear weapons, 13069-13089
   presidential years, 12604-13145
   private life, 12574-12585
   public career, 12586-12603
   Reaganomics, 13090-13145
   writings, 13146-13150
Recession, 9495, 9880, 9901, 12286
Reconstruction, 5166-5179, 5226, 5480, 5556, 5558, 5745, 5750, 5756, 5758
   Act, 5524
   and blacks, 5490, 5539, 5754, 5857
   and Congress, 5521
   economic state of, 5460
   Finance Corporation, 8164, 8167, 8244, 8270
   and Grant, 5748, 5767
   and Andrew Johnson, 5436, 5470, 5471, 5476, 5478, 5497, 5511, 5512, 5533
   politics of, 5487, 5514
   and Republican convention, 5519
   in Texas, 5479
Red Cross, 8227, 8228
Reed, James A., 4304
Reed, Joseph, 628
Reed, William B., 3428
Reeder, Benjamin F., 196
Reeves, Owen T., 4189
Reeves, Rosser, 9925

Subject Index

Reform, administrative, 3023
Regan, Donald T., 12717
Regulation
   agencies, and Kennedy, 10779
   agency control, 9904
   of grain futures, 8145
   of railroads, 6673
   and Reagan, 12853, 12858, 12859, 12897, 12926
   reform, 10574, 12925
   of television, 12288, 12870
Regulatory Commissions, independent, 9478
Reid, Helen R., 9934
Reid, Whitelaw, 6204, 6212, 6217
Reilly, Michael F., 8676
Religion
   and John Q. Adams, 2701
   and aid to education, 10588
   Carter and, 12132, 12138
   civil, 7271, 9879, 10387, 11768, 12186
   and equality, 2448
   of the founding fathers, 900
   of Garfield, 5959, 5964
   and Hoover, 8213
   and Jackson, 2828
   and Jefferson, 1473, 1813-1854, 2192
   and Kennedy, 10623, 10640, 10642
   liberty, 2405, 3376
   and Lincoln, 4108, 4272-4332, 4959
   Madison and, 2356, 2450, 2451, 2471
   and 1928 election, 8068
   and Reagan, 12662
   and Franklin D. Roosevelt, 8630, 8827
   and Theodore Roosevelt, 6515, 8702
   and Taft, 7023
   and Truman, 9322
   and Washington, 327-360
   and Wilson, 7230
Remington, Frederic, 6638
Reorganization, 11481, 12232, 12233
   Executive, 8168, 8670, 9032, 9369, 11477, 11513, 12246
Republican Convention of 1920, 7847
Republican party, 1922, 1937, 4722, 4888, 5214, 6219, 6751, 6820, 7054, 7886, 7887, 8110, 8207, 12613
Republicanism, 1881, 1921, 2868
   and John Q. Adams, 911
   and Jefferson, 1927, 1944
   and McKinley, 6317
   of Madison, 2412, 2425, 2434
   and Tyler, 3190
Republicans, 1894, 1899
   and Hayes administration, 5887
   and Hoover, 8210-8212
   Jeffersonian, 1898, 2486
   and Lincoln, 4687
   and Theodore Roosevelt, 6711
Revill, Janie, 2819

Revolution, 4522
   and John Q. Adams, 915, 919, 925, 930, 937, 975, 999
   and Samuel Adams, 918
   and Jefferson, 1539, 2152-2187
   and Madison, 2370, 2427
   medical affairs during, 668
   and Monroe, 2530
   and naval heroes, 979
   and Washington, 41, 129, 156, 466, 608, 620-677
Reza Shah, 11081, 11569
RFC. *See* Reconstruction Finance Corporation
Rhea letter hoax, 2908
Rhetoric
   of Carter, 12193
   of Ford, 12083
   of Jefferson, 1443, 1463
   of Lincoln, 4543, 5261
   of Nixon, 11762
Rhode Island
   and Lincoln, 4349
   and Washington, 180, 600
Rice, John H., 1208
Rice Institute, 7267
Richards, A. C., 4850
Richmond Enquirer, 1611
Richmond, VA, Monroe in, 2535
Rights, minority
   and Lyndon Johnson, 11211
   and Nixon, 11676, 11677, 11681
   and Truman, 9470, 9484
Riots, in Jacksonian era, 2960
Ritchie, Thomas, 1611
Robbins, H. M., 6197
Robbins, Jonathan, 996
Robert Hudson Tannahill Research Library, 816
Roberts, Clifford, 9934
Robertson, Archibald, 490
Robin Moor, 9204
Robinson, George F., 3933
Robinson, Jeremy, 2558
Robinson, William, 9934
Rockefeller, Nelson, 11378, 11837, 11985, 12067
Rockefeller Commission, 10488
Rockhill, William W., 6874
Rockville, MD, Lincoln in, 4373
Rockwell, Norman, 8833
Rodin, Peter W., Jr., 11910
Rogers, Will, 7952, 8023
Rogers, William, 11653
Rogin, Michael P., 2798
Rollins, Edward J., 12714
Romania, 9165
Roosevelt, Edith K., 6488
Roosevelt, Eleanor, 8350, 8431, 8460-8495, 12539
Roosevelt, Franklin D., 8322-9210
   biographies, 8322-8391
   Congress, 8476-8762

Subject Index 747

domestic policy, 8763-8815
elections, 8816-8852
foreign affairs, 8853-8945
as governor of New York, 8496, 8497, 8515
judicial, 8946-8982
New Deal, 8983-9088
poliomyelitis, 8392, 8409, 8411, 8420
presidential years, 8518-9173
private life, 8392-8495
public career, 8496-8517
Eleanor Roosevelt, 8460-8495
World War II, 9089-9173
writings, 9174-9210
Roosevelt, James, 8416
Roosevelt, Kermit, 6925
Roosevelt, Mrs. James, 8370
Roosevelt, Sara D., 8432
Roosevelt, Theodore, 6335-6965
biographies, 6335-6424
foreign affairs, 6827-6877
as governor, 6538, 6566
presidential years, 6645-6877
private life, 6425-6524
public career, 6525-6644
writings, 6878-6965
Roosevelt Campobello International Park Commission, 8739
Roosevelt Corollary, 6848, 6868
Roosevelt Court, 8972
Roosevelt Purges of 1938, 8751
Roosevelt-Litvinov Agreements, 8860
Roosevelt-Stewart Alliance, 6654
Root, Elihu, 4414, 7550
Root, Robert K., 7233
Rosecrans, William S., 5977
Rosenau, James N., 9623
Ross, Charles G., 9311
Ross, Edmund G., 5440
Ross, John, 5103
Rough Riders, 6581, 6589, 6602, 6639, 6942
Rousseau, Jean J., 2390, 2704
Ruby, Jack, 10424
Rule of law, 4113, 4522, 4759
Runciman, Walter, 8752
Rush, Benjamin, 881, 968, 1044, 1540, 1953
Russo-Japanese War, 6841, 6859, 6863
Rutherford, Lucy M., 8454
Rutledge, Ann, 3665, 3699, 3726, 3742, 4393
Rutledge, Wiley B., 8949

Sagamore Hill, 6460, 6463
Sailor, Kennedy as a, 10340
St. Clair, Arthur, 2039
Saint-Gaudens, Augustus, 6714, 6963
St. Lawrence Seaway Treaty of 1932, 8223
St. Louis, MO, Grant in, 5686
St. Paul's Chapel, 344
St. Peter's Church, 263

Salem, IL, Lincoln in, 3879, 4369
Salem, MA, Washington in, 571
Salinger, Pierre, 10346
SALT, 12436
SALT II, 12431, 12458
San Clemente, CA, Nixon in, 11411, 11413, 11646
Sandburg, Carl, 3690, 3739, 9745
Sandusky, OH, Hayes in, 5832
Sangamon, IL, Lincoln in, 4364
Santa Anna, 3241
Santo Domingo, 5752, 7593
Sargent, John S., 7346
Sargent, Nathan, 5369
Satire
  in Jacksonian era, 2911
  of John Adams, 965
Saudi Arabia, 12526, 13014, 13031
Saum, Lewis, 3524
Savage, Edward, 441
Sawyer, Frederick, 4855
Scandals
  Jefferson, 1405, 1410, 1496
  Truman, 9285, 9309
  Washington, 173
  Williamsburg, 1709
Scheffer, Arnold, 2291
Schlesinger, Arthur, Jr., 8996, 10233
Schoolmaster
  Arthur as, 6049
  of Lincoln, 4453
Schumpeter, Joseph, 12724
Schurz, Carl, 4394, 5893
Science
  adviser, 12214
  and Eisenhower administration, 9881, 9884, 9885
  and Jefferson, 1306, 1855-1885
  and Lyndon Johnson administration, 11199, 11221
  and Nixon administration, 11466, 11703
  and Wilson administration, 7269
Scott, Winfield, 2731, 3104, 3267, 3305, 3306
Scottish Enlightenment, 1820, 2376
Scrimshaw collector, Kennedy as, 10077
Scripps, John L., 4328, 4930
Sculpture
  of Lincoln, 3958, 3998
  of Madison, 2351
  of Theodore Roosevelt, 6496, 6497
  of Washington, 510
Sea power, 1002, 6671
Searches and seizures, 9446
Seattle, WA
  Harding in, 7883
  and Hoover, 8238
Secession, 2634, 3427, 3431, 4924, 4962, 5024, 5456
Secrecy
  and age of Jefferson, 2182
  and Eisenhower administration, 9814

748 Subject Index

and Lyndon Johnson administration, 11301
and Kennedy administration, 10732
Secret Service, and Reagan, 12778
Security, 2030
   classification, 12657
   collective, 7627, 8564
   interests, 11813
   internal, 9390, 9393, 9624, 9894
   leaks, 3263
Sedition, 1016, 1017, 11557
Segregation, 7506, 7521, 7890, 8004
Seidman, L. William, 12016
Selby, England, and Washington, 297
Selective Service, 7789
Seminole Indians, 2928
   War, 2726
Senate, 1555
   and Cleveland, 6137
   confirmation, 9864, 11571
   Foreign Relations Committee, 5983, 6050, 6129, 7437, 7613
   and Hoover, 8171
   Andrew Johnson in the, 5545
   and Lyndon Johnson, 10891, 10906, 10916, 10967
   Kennedy in the, 10134
   leadership, 3320, 11049
   and Lincoln, 4885
   majority leader, 10917, 10944
   Nixon, 11809, 11913
   and Franklin D. Roosevelt, 8751, 8970
   and Theodore Roosevelt, 6774
   Special Committee to Investigate the National Defense Program, 9270
   and Truman, 9513
   voting, 9265
   and Wilson, 7538
   and the World Court, 8010
Separation of church and state, 1625, 1641, 1643, 2385, 2426, 2493, 7074
Separation of powers, 996, 1961, 9514, 9566, 11586, 11613, 12251, 12501
Sevareid, Eric, 12051, 12399
Sewall, Bill, 6411
Sewall, Jonathan, 1043
Seward, William H., 4508, 4781, 5013
Seward-Fillmore feud, 3342
Seymour, Charles, 7219
Shakers, 3376
Shakespeare, William, 4059, 9724
Shanghai Power Company, 9579
Shannon, Joseph B., 2167
Shantung question, 7553
Shaples, James, 467
Shaw, Bernard, 7201
Sheffield Scientific School, 7104
Shelby, Isaac, 2778
Shelbyville, IL, Lincoln in, 4531

Sherman Act, 9886
Sherman Antitrust Act, 7039
Sherman, John, 5475, 5874
Sherman, William T., 4210, 4674, 5710, 5740, 5753
Shields, James, 3969
Shivers, Allan, 10915
Short, William, 1232, 1417, 1425, 2259, 2336
Siberia, 7712, 7713
Sickles, Daniel E., 5909
Sidney, NB, Franklin D. Roosevelt in, 8635
Silent majority, 11548
Silesia, 2613, 2690
Simon, John Y., 5782
Simon, William E., 12016
Simpson, Gilbert, 525
Simpson, Matthew, 4328, 4865
Sinclair, John, 796, 815
Slataper, Felician, 3845
Slater Fund for Negro Education, 5916
Slavery, 2161, 2619, 5224
   John Adams view of, 935
   and John Q. Adams, 2617
   and Buchanan, 3404
   and Jackson, 2804, 3003
   and Jacksonianism, 2841, 2890
   and Jefferson, 1418, 2131, 2140, 2142, 2345-2348, 2150, 2151, 2159, 2164, 2372-2375
   and Lincoln, 4711, 5180-5247
   at Monticello, 2153
   and Polk, 3259
   in Tennessee, 5453
   trade in, 3425, 3426
   and Van Buren, 3094
   and Washington, 249, 588
Sleeping sentinel, 4683, 4686, 4714
Small, William, 1379
Smith, Adam, 2376, 12840
Smith, Alfred E., 2876, 8156, 8157, 9022, 9190, 10640
Smith, Hilda W., 8590, 9317
Smith, Howard K., 12051, 12399
Smith, Joseph, 1751
Smith, Justin H., 4525
Smith, Mrs. Samuel H., 403
Smith, Robert, 2481
Smith, Samuel, 2481
Smith, Walter G., 5659
Smith Act, 11557
Smoot, Reed, 6753
Smoot-Hawley Tariff, 8224
Smuts, Jan, 7668
Social choice theory, 2425
Social compact theory, 1546
Social Darwinism, 6835
Social science, 12687
   research, 8221
Social security, 8782, 9040, 10786, 10794, 12330, 12895

Social services, 13091
Social workers, 6627
Socialism, 6673
  European, 7589
Society of the Cincinnati of the State of Virginia, 475, 788
Socrates, 1772
Solomons, Adolphus S., 4407
Somers, W. H., 4611
Sommers, S., 810
Songs, 463, 492, 498, 3959
  Lincoln liked, 4318
Sons
  of Lincoln, 3826, 3857
  of Theodore Roosevelt, 6426
Sorenson, Theodore, 10233
South, the, 711
  Arthur and, 6051
  Carter and, 12339, 12391
  Fillmore and, 3343
  Garfield and, 5988
  Harding and, 7887
  Benjamin Harrison and, 6219
  Hayes and, 5869
  Hoover and, 8209
  Andrew Johnson and, 5454, 5535
  Lincoln and, 3599, 4502, 4505
  New England and, 10775
  Franklin D. Roosevelt and, 8771
  Theodore Roosevelt and, 6603, 6721
  Taft and, 7036, 7053, 7064
  Truman and, 9316, 9437
South Africa, 9557, 9983, 12440, 12992
South America, 2100, 8139
South Carolina, 2733, 3431, 5471, 6711
Sovereignty, 7057
Soviet Union
  and John Q. Adams, 2620, 2646
  American relations with, 10723, 11819, 12053, 13060
  and Carter, 12462, 12531, 12533
  fleet, 4774
  and Garfield, 5992
  and Hoover, 8180, 8271
  and Kennedy, 10669, 10670, 10682
  Kremlin in, 9985, 10723
  and Lincoln, 4783
  mass media, 10548
  and Nixon, 11821, 11830
  and Reagan, 12978, 12981, 12999, 13016, 13021, 13050, 13053
  and Franklin D. Roosevelt, 8859, 8870, 8893, 9161
  and Theodore Roosevelt, 6866
  St. Petersburg, 2675, 3407
  Taft in, 7062
  and Truman, 9522, 9523, 9537, 9572, 9589
  and Wilson, 7569, 7587, 7712, 7713, 7725

  and World War II, 9150
Space, programs, 10493, 10587, 11179, 11194, 11703
Spain, 438, 657, 2101, 2457, 3052
  Civil War, 8931
  law, 2110, 2831
Spanish-American War, 6287, 6288, 6302, 6307
Spann, Gloria C., 12128
Spargo, John, 7587
Sparks, Jared, 767
Special assistant for science and technology, 9885
Special assistant to the president for science and technology, 9884
Speech, freedom of, 1694, 9447
Speeches, 5466, 7397
  Checkers, 9380, 11516, 11766
  graduation, 5918
  of Lyndon Johnson, 10992
  of Kennedy, 10242, 10360
  of Lincoln, 4541, 4542, 5257, 8508
  of Nixon, 11479, 11491, 11497, 11759
  Quarantine, 8865, 9099, 9121, 9123, 9124
  Reagan acceptance, 12779
  of Truman, 9379, 9539
  Washington farewell, 683, 704, 713, 728, 734, 763, 825
Spencer County, IN, Lincoln and, 4335
Spiegel Grove, OH, 5818, 5828
  Hayes in, 5816
Spiritualism, and Lincoln, 4279, 4306, 4314
Spoils system, 2964, 3001, 3440, 5858, 5886
Sport
  and the Eisenhower administration, 9913, 9954
  and the Ford administration, 12088
  and the Kennedy administration, 10559
  and the Nixon administration, 11494, 11684
  and the Theodore Roosevelt administration, 6510
Sportsmen
  Theodore Roosevelt as, 6409
  Washington as, 802
Springfield, IL, 3836, 3879, 4334, 4370, 4619, 4927, 4928, 5350
Sputnik, 9884
Square Deal, 6805, 6955, 7082
Stael, Mme. de, 2288
Staff
  of Carter, 12183, 12200
  of Ford, 11984, 12011, 12034
  of Kennedy, 10245, 10318
  of Nixon, 11478, 11554, 11577
  of Reagan, 12711, 12716, 12717
  of Franklin D. Roosevelt, 8653, 8681
  Truman's economic, 9448
Stalin, Joseph, 8905, 8906, 8913, 9114, 9152, 9516, 9569, 9576, 9578, 9634
Stamp collector, Franklin D. Roosevelt as, 8437, 8455
Stanford University, Reagan library at, 12606

750 Subject Index

Stanton, Edwin, 4371, 4732, 4751, 4757, 4796, 4864, 5503, 5512, 5615, 5711, 5713
Stanton, Elizabeth C., 3865
Stanton, Robert L., 3621
Star, Marion, 7840
Star Wars, 13078
State
  laws, 2404
  legislative, 8780
  rights, 3018, 4986
State Department, 5224, 7667, 8895, 9608, 9618
  Secretary of, 1851, 1863, 2381, 2547, 3414
State Historical Society of Wisconsin, 6567
State House (Annapolis), 661
State of the Union address, 11936, 12194, 12267
Statues, Lincoln, 3949, 3961, 3970, 3981, 3987, 4007, 4010
Steel, 7519, 10581
  corporation, 6943
  crisis, 10565
  mills, 9468
  price, 10553
  seizure, 9450, 9458, 9462, 9468, 9469, 9472, 9486, 10302
  strike, 9436
Steelman, John R., 9404
Steffens, Lincoln, 6797
Stepchildren, of Jefferson, 1419
Stephens, Alexander H., 3701, 5254
Stepmother, of Lincoln, 3883
Stern, Alfred W., 3919
Stevenson, Adlai E. (1835-1914), 8821, 9871, 9916, 9917, 9919, 9927, 9928, 9932, 9933
Stevenson, Adlai E. (1900-1965), 5287, 6075, 6082, 6092, 6181
Stevenson, Andrew, 2614
Stewart, Judd, 5323
Stimson, Henry L., 9517
Stimson Doctrine, 8194, 8806
Stockmen's Association, 6588
Stockton, Robert F., 3270, 3280
Stoddard, William O., 3754, 4254, 5161
Stone, Harlan F., 8967
Storey, George H., 4176, 4864
Stoughton, Cecil, 10362
Stowe, Harriet B., 3865
Strategic Defense Initiative, 13073, 13074
Strategic Missile Program, 10551
Strauss, Lewis, 9896
Strong, Josiah, 6659
Struck, Russell J., 2660
Stuart, Gilbert, 442, 453, 454, 496, 503, 1257
Stuart, James E. B., 5864
Style, presidential, 5467. 7988, 8187
Suffrage, 6029
Suicide, related to Kennedy assassination, 10402
Sulgrave Manor, 217, 291, 295, 296
Sullivan, John, 1665

Sully, Thomas, 1202
Summers, Hatton, 8973
Summersby, Kathleen M., 9729
Sumner, Charles, 4864, 4977
Sumners, Hatton, 8973
Supreme Court, 2672, 5513, 7004, 7106, 7121, 7124
  appointments, 7000, 7907, 8021
  and Arthur, 7101
  and Carter, 12450
  and Garfield, 5969
  and Grant, 5772
  and Hoover, 8241, 8249, 8946
  and Jackson, 2948
  and Jefferson, 2188, 2192, 2201
  justice, 6985
  justices, 3421
  and Lincoln, 5113, 5116, 5122
  and Nixon, 11544, 11562, 11604, 11630, 11634, 11644, 11865
  nominations, 6144, 12045
  and Reagan, 12624
  and Franklin D. Roosevelt, 8947, 8950, 8951, 8954, 8956-8960, 8965, 8966, 8968, 8969, 8970, 8971, 8975, 8977, 9023
  and Chief Justice Taft, 6974, 6980, 6992, 6995, 6996, 6998-7002, 7007, 7009, 7011
  Taft appointments to, 7055
  and Truman, 9458
  in Washington era, 731
Surratt, John H., 4871
Surratt, Mary E., 4840
Surveyor, Washington as, 531
Swain, James B., 5029
Swartwout, Samuel, 3042
Swesshelm, Jane Grey, 3965
Switzerland, 10001
Swords, and Washington, 425
Symmes, John C., 3145

Taft, Bryan, 7046
Taft, Helen, 6975
Taft, Lorado, 3970
Taft, Robert A., 9290
Taft, William H., 6966-7129
  biographies, 6966-6972
  presidential years, 7012-7095
  private life, 6973-6983
  public career, 6984-7011
  writings, 7096-7129
Taft Arbitration Treaties, 7038
Taft-Hartley Act, 9325, 9463, 9464, 9471
Taft-Katsura Agreement, 7028, 7037
Taiwan
  and Carter, 12450, 12456, 12501, 12520
  and Eisenhower, 9964
  1954/1955 crisis, 10002
  and Reagan, 12973
Taney, Roger, 2997, 5115, 5124

Tang Shao-Yi Mission, 6831
Tariff
  John Q. Adams and, 2643
  Commission, 8020
  Henry Clay and, 6333
  of 1832, 2999
  Kennedy and, 10349, 10725
  Lincoln and, 4665, 5387
  McKinley and, 6305, 6316
  Theodore Roosevelt and, 6653, 6778
  Van Buren and, 3110
  Washington and, 694
  Wilson and, 7595, 7596
Taxation, 7803, 12335
  bill, 9432
  and Carter, 12298
  code, 12363
  excise, 1886
  income, 12285
  of international income, 12328
  law revision, 12835
  and Lincoln, 4472
  plans, 12833
  policy, 9346
  reform, 12308
  transfer, 12296
Taylor, John, 1558
Taylor, Myron, 8879
Taylor, Zachary, 3294-3331
  biographies, 3294-3306
  presidential years, 3318-3328
  private life, 3307-3309
  public career, 3310-3317
  writings, 3329-3331
Teamsters, 12899
Teapot Dome, 7867, 7893, 7898, 8175
Technology
  and Eisenhower, 9838
  and Jefferson, 1673, 2229
  and the Kennedy administration, 10332, 10587
  and Lincoln, 4506
Tecumseh, 3139, 3143
Teeth, of Washington, 499
Teheran Conference, 9152
Television
  advertising, 12870
  commentators, 12051, 12399
  Ford/Carter commercials, 12037, 12375, 12389
  Kennedy assassination on, 10454
  Nixon and, 11524, 11552, 11725
  Planning Board, 9915
  Reagan and, 12673, 12762, 12941
  regulation of, 12288, 12870
  Truman and, 9367
Teller, Edward, 9428
Temple Hill, NY, Washington at, 167, 633
Ten million acre bill, 3369
Tennessee
  and John Q. Adams, 988
  and Harding, 7902
  and Hoover, 8156, 8157
  and Jackson, 2732, 2793, 2941, 2942
  and Andrew Johnson, 5401, 5414, 5425, 5427, 5443, 5446, 5447, 5452, 5453, 5461, 5462, 5474, 5515, 5525
  and Lincoln, 4662, 5175
  and Polk, 3225, 3227, 3229, 3238, 3245
  State Penitentiary, 5415
  and Washington, 248
Tennessee Valley Authority, 6741, 8781
  Enabling Act, 8783
Tenure of Office
  Act, 6158
  Fourth term, 8597, 8625
  Third term, 2045, 5741, 5742, 5760, 8022, 8027, 8524, 8553, 8563, 8565, 8570, 8611, 8623, 8672, 8835, 8843, 8844
Terre Haute, IN, Lincoln and, 4343
Terrell, Robert H., 7509
Terrorism, 6823
Texas, 2831, 10873
  and annexation, 3266
  conservatism in, 10920
  and Eisenhower, 9889, 9929
  Jackson and, 2906, 2909, 2996
  and the Mexican War, 3281
  1956 campaign, 10915
  1941 senatorial election, 10935
  1967 election in, 11757
  Polk and, 3233
  Reconstruction in, 5479
  Revolution, 2936
  Franklin D. Roosevelt and, 8828, 9075
  Theodore Roosevelt and, 6562, 6765
  Taft in, 6977, 7040
Thatcher, Margaret, 12626, 12683, 12724, 12970, 13002, 13127
Theater
  and Lincoln, 4051
  and Washington, 46
Theology, and Jefferson, 1625
Think tanks, 13087
Thomas, John T., 3822
Thomas, Norman, 8810
Thomas Jefferson Memorial Foundation, 1489, 1494, 1498
Thomson, Will, 5091
Thomson-Urrutia Treaty, 7571
Thornton, Anthony, 4531
Thornton, William, 2217, 2277
Three Mile Island, 12354
Thurman, Allen G., 6073, 6076
Tichborne Case, 10427
Ticknor, George, 1354
Tilghman, Tench, 662
Time, 9358, 10218, 10306

Tinoco, 7581
Tippit, J. D., 10440
Tito, 9634
Tobin, Maurice J., 9037
Tocqueville, Alexis de, 2166, 3093, 12894
Todd, Mary, 3830, 3833, 3834, 3874
Todd, Robert S., 3837
Tolstoy, Leo, 1462
Tomb
   of Lincoln, 3961, 3962
   of Washington, 307, 326, 481
Tombs, Robert, 1788
Tongass National Forest, 6679
Torrey, Jay L., 6589, 6639
Townsend, George A., 4787
Tracy W. McGregor Library, 2340, 8397, 10080
Trade, 9968, 10662, 10668
   Expansion Act, 10241
   foreign, 7567, 7706
   international, 9561, 10668
Transcripts, presidential, 11914
Treason
   and Lincoln, 4939
   and Pierce, 3366
Treasury, secretary of, 1000, 9432
Treaties
   Mutual Defense, 12450, 12501, 12520
   power to terminate, 12480, 12517, 12520
Treaty of Paris, 6275
Treaty of San Ildefonso, 2097
Treaty of Versailles, 7468, 7895
Tremont Temple, Lincoln at, 3792
Trent Affair, 4510
Trenton, NJ, Washington in, 405
Trilateralism, 12266
Trist, Nicholas P., 2018, 2770
Trotter, William M., 7506
Trudeau, Pierre E., 12071, 12444
Truman, Bess, 9645
Truman, Harry S., 9211-9669
   atomic bomb, 9415-9428
   biographies, 9211-9247
   domestic policy, 9429-9498
   elections, 9499-9510
   foreign affairs, 9511-9580
   Korean War, 9581-9603
   Middle East, 9604-9621
   presidential years, 9284-9643
   private life, 9248-9262
   public career, 9263-9283
   Truman Doctrine, 9622-9643
   writings, 9644-9669
Truman, Margaret, 9261
Truman Committee, 9378, 9411, 9412
Truman Doctrine, 9622-9643
Truman-Molotov conversations, 9550
Trumbull, John, 495, 889, 1270, 1271
Trumbull, Lyman, 4592, 4640, 5284

Trust, Nicholas P., 1255
Trusts, 7514, 7520, 8803
Tugwell, Rexford G., 8776, 8806, 8807, 9078
Tumulty, Joe, 7371
Turkey, 7572, 9639, 10528, 10537
Turner, Frederick, 6742
Turpie-Foraker Amendment, 6294
Twain, Mark, 3947, 5578, 5895, 6555, 9251, 10853
Twiggs, David E., 3306
Tyler, John, 3168-3208
   biographies, 3168-3174
   presidential years, 3183-3203
   private life, 3175-3178
   public career, 3179-3182
   writings, 3204-3208
Tyler, Julia G., 3173, 3178
Tyler, Priscilla C., 3176
Tyler, Robert, 3176
Tyler Kent Affair, 8900

U-2 affair, 10004
Underwood, John C., 4977
Underwood, Oscar W., 7850
Underwood Act, 7595
Underwood Tariff, 7403, 7541
Unemployment, 8246, 8994, 9461, 9883
Union, anti-crusade, 12882
United Mine Workers, 8785
United Nations, 10003, 10750, 10784, 12539, 12994
United Press, 9932
U.S. attorney, 11633
U.S. Military Telegraph Corporation, 4944
U.S. Sanitary Commission, 4742
U.S. Steel, 6718, 6943, 8764
U.S. v. Nixon, 11818, 11875, 11884, 11891, 11908
U.S.S. *Maryland*, 8139
Universities, with Washington's name, 457
University of Illinois, 4995
University of Missouri, 1759
University of Oxford, 9337, 9815
University of Pennsylvania, 200
University of Virginia, 1317, 1330, 1366, 1375, 1380, 1394, 1398, 1401, 1402, 1563, 2022, 2222, 3205
   medical instruction at, 1380
Upham, Charles, 2693
Uranium market, 12338
Urbana, IL, Lincoln statue in, 3970
Urban policy, 9489, 9490, 9493, 12302, 12305, 12349, 12362, 12848, 12894
Utah
   and Buchanan, 3440, 3441
   and Taft, 7090
Utilitarianism, 2649
Utopia, 9008, 9010

Valenti, Jack, 11101
Vallandighan, Clement L., 5036

Valley Forge, Washington at, 626
Van Buren, Martin, 3055-3120
  biographies, 3055-3066
  presidential years, 3097-3114
  private life, 3067-3069
  public career, 3070-3096
  writings, 3115-3120
Van Dyke, Paul, 6080
Van Winkle, Peter G., 5469, 5500
Vance, Cyrus, 1851
Vance, Mariah, 3994
Vandenberg, Arthur H., 9635
Vatican, 7691, 8879, 9521
Vaughan, Harry H., 9336
Venezuela
  and Cleveland, 6126, 6152, 6153, 6167
  and Theodore Roosevelt, 6849
Vera Cruz, 3267, 3306, 7586, 7659
Vermont
  and Arthur, 6049
  and Coolidge, 8014
  and Lincoln, 4714, 4730
Vernon, Edward, 408
Versailles, 7468, 7663-7691, 7895
Veto
  of Carter, 12272
  pension, 6176
  of Reconstruction Act, 5524
  of Franklin D. Roosevelt, 8613, 8678
Vice President
  Ford as, 11964, 11966, 11967, 12074
  Andrew Johnson as, 5484
  Lyndon Johnson as, 10890, 10937, 10942
  Lincoln's vote for, 4539
  Nixon as, 11435, 11442, 11738
  Truman as, 9269
  Tyler as, 3181
  Henry Wilson as, 5768
Vicksburg, MS, 5708, 5725
Vidal, Gore, 3897
Vietnam War
  Dien Bien Phu, 9941, 9962, 10536
  and Eisenhower, 9997
  and Lyndon Johnson, 10994, 11125, 11160, 11312-11358
  and Kennedy, 10648, 10663, 10672, 10681, 10704, 10712, 10752
  news coverage of, 11814
  and Nixon, 11772, 11814, 11815, 11836, 11924
  Tonkin Bay, 11316, 11351
Villa, Pancho, 7656, 7660
Vincennes, IN, Lincoln in, 5152
Vinson, Carl, 9170
Vinson, Fred, 9432
Virginia
  and John Q. Adams, 2614
  campaigns, 5705
  Cavaliers, 656
  colonial, 2441
  Constitution, 969, 1989, 1991
  General Court of, 2274
  and Jefferson, 1207, 1404, 1449, 1537, 2192-2195, 2198-2203, 2005
  Jeffersonian Republicans in, 1988
  and Monroe, 2524, 2529, 2535, 2539
  and New Deal, 9036
  and Theodore Roosevelt, 6513, 6527
  senators, 8751
  and Washington, 84, 320
  and Wilson, 7391
Virginia Berkley Memorial Collection, 426
Volta River Project, 10696
Voluntarism, during Hoover era, 8124, 8133, 8166
Von Humboldt, Alexander, 2346
Voorhis, Jerry, 11433
Vossler, Otto, 1979
Voting behavior
  in the age of Jackson, 3015, 3020
  in 1968 Texas election, 11757
Voting record
  of Ford, 12075
  of Lyndon Johnson, 10909
  of Kennedy, 10141, 10145, 10146
  of Reagan, 12645

Wabash River, 2241
Wade, Ben, 5563
Wadsworth, James S., 5211-5213
Wage and price policies, 11163, 12279
  controls, 11674, 11675, 11683, 11715, 12304
  insurance plan, 12322
  treaty, 9456
  and Truman administration, 9434
Wakefield, birthplace of Washington, 255, 270, 271, 286, 424
Wales, Jefferson memorial in, 1234
Walker, Robert, 6266, 7963
Walker-McKinley Fund, 6266
Wallace, George, 11757
Wallace, Henry A., 8098, 8836, 9542, 9580
Wallace, Henry C., 7904
Walsh, Thomas J., 8175
War, 730, 928, 2325-2328
  on Crime, 12298
  debts, 825
  Department, 4824, 4945
  of 1812, 2459, 2461, 2462, 2476, 2486, 2487, 2490, 2738, 2891, 3150, 6929
  on Poverty, 10558, 10575, 11160, 11168, 11197, 11209, 11238, 11239
  powers, 2111, 4971, 11937, 12085, 12099, 12663, 12736, 13044
  protests, 11975
  Refugee Board, 9141

754 Subject Index

Room, 6701
secretary of, 2442, 3760, 4757, 7128, 9138
Ward, Montgomery, 8778
Warm Springs, GA, 8387, 8412, 8427, 8433, 8448
Warren, Earl, 9860, 10400, 12592
Warren, James, 1052
Warren, Louis A., 3622
Warton in Lonsdale, 266, 292
Washington, Booker T., 6721, 6786
Washington, George, 1-847, 7759
  biographies, 1-154
  family, 251-304
  Mount Vernon, 305-326
  presidential years, 678-764
  private life, 155-553
  public career, 554-677
  religion, 327-360
  Revolution, 620-677
  tributes, 361-415
  Washingtoniana, 416-513
  the West, 514-536
  writings, 765-847
  youth, 537-553
Washington, Lawrence, 253, 408
Washington, Martha, 256, 259, 284, 294, 301, 315, 505
Washington, William, 506, 507, 628
Washington and Lee University, 183
Washington Conference of 1921-1922, 8179
Washington Monument, 432, 435, 459
Washington Society, 403
Washingtoniana, 416-513
Watergate, 10461, 11058, 11401, 11467, 11819, 11849-11920, 12053
  hearings, 11894
  tapes, 11566, 11895, 11902, 11905, 11919
Waterhouse, Benjamin, 1048, 2046, 2599
Watson, Tom, 6546
Wealth, of Washington, 218
Weapons, 10511, 12272
  atomic bomb, 9096, 9097, 9415-9428, 9654
  B-1 bomber, 12235
  neutron bomb, 12472
  nuclear, 13069-13089
Webb, Samuel, 628
Weber, Max, 7281, 7345
Webster, Daniel, 577, 888, 1958, 2945, 3319, 4137, 4485, 5291, 10762
Wedding
  of Theodore Roosevelt, 6472
  of Washington, 290
Weed, Thurlow, 5029
Weights and measures, 2049, 2702
Weik, Jesse W., 4197, 4258
Weinberger, Casper, 11669, 12824
Weinstein, Edwin A., 7210, 7212
Welfare
  policy, 9442, 11709

  programs, 8189, 11692
  and Reagan, 12594
  reform, 11661, 11671, 11713, 12280, 12321, 12862, 12880
  state, 8554, 12852, 12906
Welles, Charles R., 4736, 5317
Wentworth, John, 4494
Wertenbaker, Thomas J., 176
Wesley, John, 7770
West Point, 183
  founding of, 2030
West Virginia
  Kennedy and, 10603, 10605, 10638
  Lincoln and, 4769, 4770
Whalon, Johathan, 4027
Wheat
  prices, 7495, 8135
  referendum, 10567
Wheatland, Buchanan's home, 3401
Wheatly, Phillis, 609
Wheeler, Burton, K., 8761
Wheeler, William A., 5797
Whig party, 2863, 4473
  and John Q. Adams, 2644
  and William H. Harrison, 3157, 3197
  in Jacksonian era, 2922
  and Lincoln, 4509
  and Seward-Fillmore feud, 3342
  in Tennessee, 3225
Whiskey Rebellion, 678, 717
White, Edward D., 7007, 7063
White, Harry D., 9380
White, Horace, 4482
White, Judge, 2802
White, William A., 6885, 7872
White House
  Conference on Families, 12225
  Congressional Liaison Office, 9802
  Coolidge in the, 7941, 7942
  furnishings, 1505, 2353
  Hayes in the, 5854
  library, 8264
  Dolley Madison in the, 2357
  mail, 8714
  offices, 6769
  physician, 8642
  press relations, 8265
  recipes, 2366
  restoration, 6435
  staff, 10244, 10966
White Mountains, Grant in the, 5685
Whitehall, 7698
Whitehead, John M., 4103
Whitman, Walt, 4041, 4047
Wickard, Claude R., 8983
Wieland, Christopher M., 2598
Wilde, Richard H., 3033
Wilkie, John, 6295

Wilkinson, James, 2108
Willard, Charles D., 6922
Willey, Waitman T., 5469
William II, 6640, 6872
Williams, Aubrey, 8805
Williams, John S., 7875
Williams, William, 481
Williamsburg, VA, 1390, 1709, 3199
Willkie, Wendell, 8831
Wills
  of presidents, 2595
  of Washington, 223, 822
Wills, Garry, 1820, 1827
Wilmot Proviso, 3286
Wilson, Charles E., 9792
Wilson, Edith B., 7176, 7217, 7221
Wilson, Ellen A., 7243, 7790
Wilson, Henry, 4738, 5581, 5633, 5768
Wilson, James, 6666
Wilson, Joseph R., 7234
Wilson, M. L., 8776
Wilson, Woodrow, 7129-7812
  biographies, 7129-7183
  campaigns, 7447-7477
  domestic policy, 7478-7522
  foreign affairs, 7523-7602
  as governor, 7300, 7312
  League of Nations, 7603-7644
  Mexican Revolution, 7645-7662
  presidential years, 7363-7726
  private life, 7184-7262
  public career, 7263-7362
  Versailles, 7663-7691
  World War I, 7692-7726
  writings, 7727-7812
Wilson Doctrine, 7620
Wilson-McCook Scheme, 7324
Winant, John G., 8925
Wing, Henry E., 4256
Winthrop, John, 931
Wirt, William, 2239, 2844
Wisconsin
  Kennedy in, 10638, 10641
  and Lincoln, 4154, 4360, 4724
  State Fair, 5360
  and Wilson, 7455
Wise, Henry A., 3456
Wister, Owen, 6423, 6518, 6638, 7716
Wit
  of Carter, 12120
  of Lyndon Johnson, 10869
  of Kennedy, 10742, 10744, 10745
  of Lincoln, 3666, 5355, 5384
  of Franklin D. Roosevelt, 9207
  of Truman, 9250, 9656
  of Wilson, 7736
Witherspoon, John, 591
Wolcott, Oliver, 1000

Women
  appointees, 8590, 9317
  and the Hayes administration, 5841
  and the Kennedy administration, 10569
  Kennedy's opinion of, 10184
  and the Lincoln administration, 5181
  and the Reagan administration, 12639, 12718, 13124
  and Theodore Roosevelt, 6789
  suffrage, 7493, 7503, 7507
Wood, Leonard, 6545, 6589, 8104
Woodbury, Levi, 2975
Woodford, Stewart L., 6245
Woodring, Harry H., 9138
Woodrow, Harriet A., 7238
Wool, John E., 3306, 3310
Woolley, Melling, 3052
Worcester, MA, John Q. Adams in, 887
Working Men's Movement, 2885, 2976
Workman, Charles H., 4035
Works Progress Administration, 8786
World Court, 7124, 7550, 7878, 8010, 8185, 8853, 8896
World War I, 7692-7726
  food crisis in, 7496
  and Hoover-Wallace controversy, 8182
  prisoners of war, 8181
  and Theodore Roosevelt, 6573, 6615, 6839
  and Russia, 10001
  submarine policy, 7711
  Truman and, 9279
World War II, 9089-9173, 9732
  Atlantic Fleet, 9089
  censorship and, 7705
  D-Day invasion, 9733
  mobilization of blacks in, 7722
  Normandy invasion, 9734, 9761
  Polish question, 8894
  political leadership, 8820
  TORCH command, 9749
  unconditional surrender, 9418
Worth, William S., 3306, 3310
Worthington, Thomas, 3162
Wright, Hendrick B., 3409
Wright, Joseph, 462, 491
Wright, Patience, 462
Writ of habeas corpus, 5121
Wyatt, Wilson, 9433
Wyoming, and the OPA, 9498

XYZ Affair, 1006, 1019, 1023

Yale University, Taft address at, 7104
Yalta, 8920, 8935, 9115, 9129, 9154, 9155, 9161, 9164, 9172, 9577
Yancey, William L., 5424
Yankee Club, 391
Yates, Abraham, 2435

756 *Subject Index*

Yates, Richard, 4519, 4520
Yellowstone National Park, 6064, 6785
Yorkshire, England, and Washington, 486
Young, Andrew, 12448

Yugoslavia, 8113, 9543

Zangara, Giuseppe, 8561, 8698
Zionism, 7524, 9090, 10647

REF E 176.1 .M27 1987